2395

STRUCTURE AND MEANING

STRUCTURE
AND
MEANING:
AN
INTRODUCTION
TO
LITERATURE

SECOND EDITION

ANTHONY DUBÉ

J. KARL FRANSON
University of Maine at Farmington

JAMES W. PARINS
University of Arkansas at Little Rock

RUSSELL E. MURPHY
University of Arkansas at Little Rock

HOUGHTON MIFFLIN COMPANY *Boston*

Dallas   Geneva, Illinois   Hopewell, New Jersey   Palo Alto   London

Printed in the U.S.A.
Library of Congress Catalog Card Number: 82-83173
ISBN: 0-395-32570-6

Acknowledgments

Cover photograph: Eliot Porter, "Foxtail Grass." Lake City, Colorado. August 1957. Dye-transfer photograph. The Metropolitan Museum of Art, Gift of Eliot Porter in honor of David H. McAlpin, 1979.

Part opening art: "Autumn Weeds," a wood engraving by Charles Joslin.

Albee, Edward. *The Sandbox* reprinted by permission of Coward, McCann & Geoghegan, Inc. from *The Sandbox* by Edward Albee. Copyright © 1960 by Edward Albee. CAUTION: *The Sandbox* is the sole property of the author and is fully protected by copyright. It may not be acted either by professionals or amateurs without written consent. Public readings, radio and television broadcasts are likewise forbidden. All enquiries concerning these rights should be addressed to: The William Morris Agency, 1350 Avenue of the Americas, New York, N.Y. 10019. Allen, Paula Gunn. "Hoop Dancer" from *Four Indian Poets,* edited by John R. Milton, Dakota Press, Vermillion, S.D., 1974, by permission of the author. Allen, Samuel (Paul Vesey). "In My Father's House" reprinted by permission of the author, Samuel Allen. alta. "The Vow" from *Letters to Women,* Shameless Hussy Press, 1969, reprinted by permission of the author. Amini, Johari. "Identity" from *Images in Black* reprinted by permission of the author. Anderson, Sherwood. "I Want to Know Why" from *The Triumph of the Egg* reprinted by permission of Harold Ober Associates Incorporated. Copyright © 1921 by B. W. Heubsch. Renewed 1948 by Eleanor Copenhaver Anderson. Auden, W. H. "Musée des Beaux Arts" copyright 1940 and renewed 1968 by W. H. Auden. Reprinted from *W. H. Auden: Collected Poems,* by W. H. Auden, edited by Edward Mendelson, by permission of Random House, Inc., and Faber & Faber Ltd. Baldwin, James. "Sonny's Blues" from *Going to Meet the Man* © 1948, 1951, 1957, 1958, 1960, 1965 by James Baldwin. Permission granted by the Dial Press. Baraka, Imamu Amiri (LeRoi Jones). "A Poem for Black Hearts" from *Black Magic Poetry 1961-1967* reprinted by permission of Ronald Hobbs Literary Agency. "In Memory of Radio" and "Preface to a Twenty Volume Suicide Note" from *Preface to a Twenty Volume Suicide Note* by LeRoi Jones. Copyright © 1961 by LeRoi Jones. Reprinted by permission of Corinth Books. Barth, John. From "Lost in the Funhouse," copyright © 1967 by The Atlantic Monthly Company from the book *Lost in the Funhouse* by John Barth. Reprinted by permission of Doubleday & Company, Inc. Borges, Jorge Luis. "The Shape of the Sword" from *Labyrinths.* Copyright © 1964 by New Directions Publishing Corporation. Reprinted by permission of New Directions. Bradbury, Ray. "There Will Come Soft Rains" copyright © 1950 by Ray Bradbury, copyright renewed 1978. Reprinted by permission of the Harold Matson Company, Inc. Brecht, Bertolt. *The Caucasian Chalk Circle,* tr. Eric Bentley and Maja Apelman, Grove Press, 1966, reprinted by permission of University of Minnesota Press. Brooks, Gwendolyn. From *The World of Gwendolyn Brooks* by Gwendolyn Brooks: "kitchenette building" (page 465) copyright 1944 by Gwendolyn Brooks Blakely. "The Chicago Picasso" (page 595) copyright © 1968 by Gwendolyn Brooks Blakely. "We Real Cool: The Pool Players. Seven at the Golden Shovel" (page 577) copyright © 1959 by Gwendolyn Brooks Blakely. Reprinted by permission of Harper & Row, Publishers, Inc. Carver, Raymond. "Photograph of My Father in His Twenty-Second Year" from *At Night the Salmon Move.* Capra Press. Copyright © 1976. Used by permission of the author. Chayefsky, Paddy. *Marty* copyright © 1955 by Paddy Chayefsky. Reprinted by permission of Simon & Schuster, a Division of Gulf & Western Corporation. Chekhov, Anton. *The Cherry Orchard* from *Chekhov: The Major Plays,* translated by Ann Dunnigan. Copyright © 1964 by Ann Dunnigan. Reprinted by arrangement with The New American Library, Inc., New York, N.Y. Cruz, Victor Hernandez. "Today is a day of great joy" from *Snaps,* by Victor Hernandez Cruz. Copyright © 1969 by Victor Hernandez

Acknowledgments continue on page 1345.

CONTENTS

5. Style ... *182*

6. Other Stories to Read ... *217*

7. The Longer Story ... *373*

POETRY

Introduction ... *435*

14. The Scheme of Meaning ... 559

15. Other Poems to Read ... 585

DRAMA

EVALUATING LITERATURE

PREFACE

The purpose of *Structure and Meaning* is to provide a comprehensive introductory study of fiction, poetry, and drama for the beginning student of literature.

The table of contents for this second edition has been thoroughly revised and expanded. The anthology now includes thirty-five stories, a novella, over two hundred and fifty poems, and a dozen plays. More than half of these works are new to this edition. Representing both classic and contemporary works, selections were carefully chosen for their enduring literary excellence, their wide range and variety of style and theme, their proven appeal to students, and their ability to evoke challenging responses to the human experience.

The pedagogical design of *Structure and Meaning* is intended to help students achieve a greater understanding and appreciation of these works of literature. In this edition, new exercises and writing topics have been added throughout each chapter. A new chapter entitled "Making Judgments About Literature" is included, and considerations on evaluating literature have been incorporated into the discussion of each genre. Some new critical essays have been added to the chapter "Writing About Literature" to stimulate discussion and to provide students with guidance in their own writing. The glossary has been expanded and clarified to reinforce understanding of literary terms discussed in this text.

Unchanged in this edition are the clear, concise explanations that precede selections; the consistent, step-by-step approach to the discussion of each genre; and the continuing emphasis on structure — the way good authors choose, order, and express their meanings. In addition, we have again tried to produce a volume flexible enough in its organization to allow for varying instructional styles and student needs. The instructor may systematically explore the elements of each genre; focus on a topical or thematic approach; selectively assign exercises and topics for writing as desired; or assign readings exclusively for pleasure. Whatever approach is taken, our aim is to provide students with the tools for unlocking the rich storehouse of experience that fiction, poetry, and drama can offer.

We wish to thank the following individuals for their helpful suggestions in revising this text: Keith Beyer, Northwest Community College, Wyoming; Mary Jane Burns, Johnson County Community College, Kansas; Viralene J. Coleman, University of Arkansas, Pine Bluff; Michael Flachmann, California State University, Bakersfield; Marie M. Garrett, Patrick Henry Community College, Virginia; Elizabeth Keyser, Westridge School for Girls, California; Thomas McCall, University of North Carolina, Wilmington; Albert Parra, Central Florida Community College; Janet M. Schwarzkopf, Western Kentucky University; David Vaughn, Wesley College, Delaware; and Robert Vetrick, Lakeland Community College, Ohio.

STRUCTURE
AND
MEANING

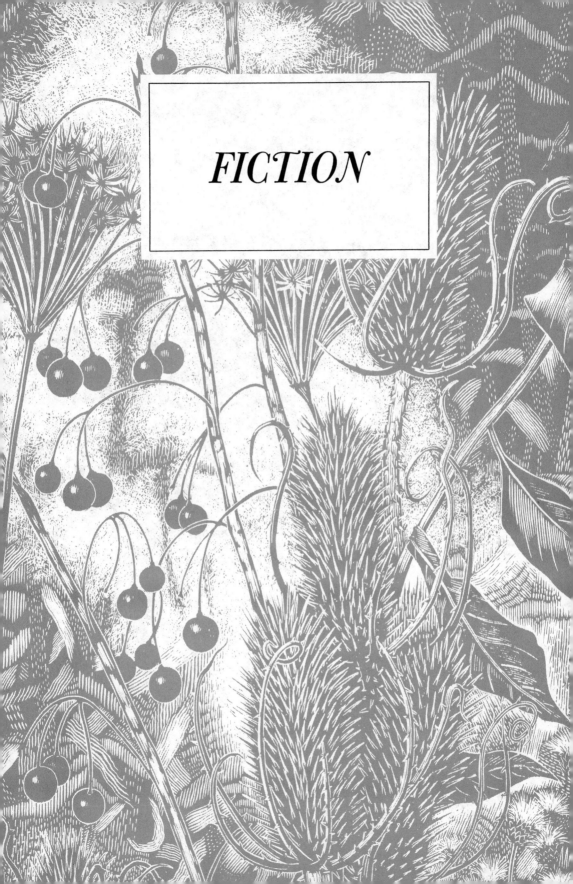

FICTION

What is fiction?

Fiction emerges from a writer's imagination. Fiction embraces the present, the past, and the future, and proffers values to hold on to as well as dreams to reach for. At its best, it makes us look at life from a new perspective. On library shelves everywhere sit thousands of faces of fiction — a vast diversity of shapes, character, and charm. Somewhere in the crowd is a type likely to catch each eye and engage each fancy.

A work of fiction is an imaginative narrative written in prose. Believable *characters,* convincing *dialogue,* and an interesting *plot* are among the essential ingredients of fiction. Because fiction writers share their thoughts with us through words, the writer's *style* — the words that the writer chooses and how he or she puts them together — is critical to our understanding of the craft of a given work and of its effect on us.

Like any work of art, fiction offers us a unique experience. A story is like a trip. It takes us from one place to another, delights us with scenes, characters, and events, and returns us newly equipped for a more enriched existence. Like music, painting, drama or poetry, a story exists, at least in part, to give us pleasure.

The ways in which we derive enjoyment from reading fiction are countless. For some readers, a story or a novel is primarily a temporary escape from reality. They enjoy a suspenseful plot and eagerly follow the adventures of fascinating or mysterious people, rushing through the narrative to find out what happens or, in the case of murder mysteries, "whodunit."

Serious fiction may attract readers with these very same ingredients. In addition, however, it can delight us with the aesthetic pleasures that come from discovering the artistic skills of many writers: how they structure their diction and syntax to make us think and feel in ways we had scarcely imagined before; how they fashion character; how they manage their selection, arrangement, and emphasis of details to make the human experience they wish to share with us comprehensible. We can value serious fiction not only for the enjoyment it gives but also for the understanding it communicates.

A story offers us a vicarious experience, a way out of reality, a means of escape. As we read a story, we seem to slip away quietly from the fixed, dull routines and pressures of daily living. As the author transports us to a distant place and acquaints us with new people, we lose ourselves and become involved immediately in the events of the story and the conflicts of others.

A story can also tender companionship and solace. Reading a story prevents us from being alone with our depression or feelings of inadequacy. We do not need to be companionless when we are confused, disillusioned, or unable to solve difficult problems. Instead, we can stroll through pages of fiction and find someone who has faced the problems we face and felt the emotions we feel. This company can be both comforting and enlightening.

A story permits some insight into human behavior. Many stories penetrate the lives of characters with whom we can identify. These stories also explore situations, problems, and concerns that we can appreciate. Often this experience holds meaning for us; it may tell us who we are and what we are about. In serious fiction, we rarely observe a character in conflict without coming away with insight into some aspect of human nature or of life.

The experience of reading fiction, then, is dynamic. It can change us emotionally and intellectually. As we ponder and evaluate what we are reading, we establish new relationships, expand our views, deepen our convictions, and discover new approaches or solutions to life's complexities. Through a story such as Stephen Crane's "The Open Boat," we may learn that suffering can make men brothers. Shirley Jackson's "The Lottery" may drive home to us the frightening truth that superstition can unleash cruelty and violence in otherwise decent people. Our concept of love may gain another dimension when we accompany a poor old woman on an arduous journey in Eudora Welty's "A Worn Path."

As we read a work of literature, at some point we develop a sense of its quality. In the case of fiction, we may decide that the story it tells is "great," "good," or just "so-so," and thus we begin to evaluate. Often our initial response is subjective, based largely on personal tastes and prejudices. Such a reaction is natural; after all, we must start somewhere. No doubt many professional critics first come to an assessment of an author's work by way of preference and bias. But sheer curiosity might get the better of us and make us ask: *Why?* Why is this story so enjoyable or moving, and that one not quite satisfying? To find out, we need to probe the elements of fiction and study its techniques. We need to examine the parts so that we might gain a fuller understanding and appreciation of the whole.

Though we may make valuable judgments that take into account a writer's history and personality or the acclaim he or she receives from established critics and scholars, here we will stress the work itself: how it is made and what it means. We will also be trying to help develop a set of criteria — standards of judgment — that will encourage informed exchanges and reasoned opinions about a given work of fiction.

In carefully reading the fiction of almost any well-known writer, however original the story or brilliant the portrayal of the leading character, we may discover some weaknesses. Perhaps the author introduces the conflict rather late, or has a penchant for long descriptive passages. More important than finding fault, however, is determining what the author is trying to do and identifying and assessing the techniques he or she uses to make the whole effective. If we are to arrive at any conclusion about quality or the lack of it, we must examine many parts of a story. Furthermore, we must recognize that each part does not function alone but works to serve the whole.

Throughout the chapters that follow, you will be given ample opportunity to evaluate the quality of fiction. As an aid to analysis, a discussion of one aspect of fiction and evaluative questions precede each group of stories. Each story in the first five chapters is followed by exercises and essay topics, as well as a selected bibliography. Chapters 6 and 7 also contain assignments.

In dealing with fiction, this book concentrates on the short story, although it also offers you an opportunity to sample a short novel, Joseph Conrad's *Heart of Darkness*, which has a chapter all to itself. Because of the length of short stories, their authors do not have as much room to work in as do novelists.

Consequently, the short story is usually much more restricted in scope than is the novel, in terms both of characters and of situations. The short story may focus on a single character or even on a single episode. Indeed, in contrast to most novels, it may illuminate only one aspect of a situation or of a character's personality rather than attempt a full development of either. But no matter how long or short a work of fiction is, conflict is essential to it. And conflict is revealed by plot.

1. PLOT

Simply stated, plot is the story line or action line or conflict line of a story. It is what *happens* in fiction, the arrangement of interrelated acts or incidents that force characters to reveal their traits.

A simple summary of a conventional plot can be made in one sentence: Boy and girl meet (situation); boy and girl lose each other (complication); boy and girl reclaim their love (resolution). A conventional plot can be illustrated by a diagram. The *introduction* sets the stage for the action that will follow; the *point of attack* initiates the action, showing the main character in conflict with self, others, nature's forces, or social forces; the *complications* make the problem more difficult to solve; the *climax* presents the opposing forces at the apex of their struggle; the *resolution* settles the outcome of the conflict; and the *conclusion* terminates the action.

We can achieve a more detailed description of a plot by using an eight-point analysis and explaining each point in greater detail. Although this somewhat formal analysis has been used for so many years that it has become classic, it is applicable to most of the stories in this anthology, even the most modern. Of course, the eight points can be varied and rearranged.

Protagonist — the chief character
Prize — the protagonist's goal, objective, or purpose
Obstacle — the opposing force or forces
Point of attack — the introduction of the problem (the conflict)
Complications — temporary hindrances
Climax — the point of highest emotional intensity
Resolution — the solving of the problem
Theme — the main point of the story

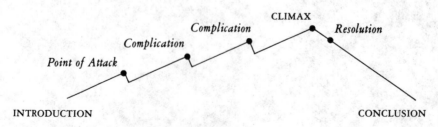

Conventional Plot Structure

6

What happens in fiction happens to characters, and the main character, the one in whose fortunes we are usually most interested, is called the **protagonist.** Man or woman, child or adult, that character generally controls or forces most of the important action. One of many such characters is Leo Finkle in Bernard Malamud's "The Magic Barrel." In his quest for love, he encounters many difficulties, and we follow his struggle to the end of the story. We are interested. Almost instantly we observe every move he makes; we want to know what will happen to him. We might be pained, happy, disappointed, touched by his sensitivity, or angered by his stupidity. Often his desires, thoughts, speeches, and actions become ours.

If we sympathize with the protagonist, we cheer as we might if a baseball pitcher were on the verge of completing a no-hit game. We want the protagonist to solve the problem, achieve the goal — in short, to win. How can we fail to sympathize with Elisa in John Steinbeck's story "The Chrysanthemums" (Chapter 2) — a lovely young woman whose environment and situation have robbed her of feminine warmth and the kind of love that is obviously missing in her life? If, on the other hand, we do not sympathize with the protagonist, we may be eager for him or her to get a deserved comeuppance. In Edith Wharton's "Roman Fever," for instance, we are repelled by Mrs. Slade's cruelty to Mrs. Ansley, and we hope that she will suffer for it. Of course, we may have mixed feelings about, and sometimes sheer pity for, the main character. But generally speaking, the protagonist engages our emotions in some fashion and makes us care about *what* happens and *why* it happens. On the other hand, if we are totally indifferent to the protagonist, we probably will not care what happens and may not want to read on.

All protagonists want something. What they seek or move toward, sometimes unconsciously, is the **prize** or goal. The prize is so important to the protagonist that he or she will contend against strong opposition, even kill, to achieve it. Mr. Martin tries to outwit a coworker in James Thurber's story "The Catbird Seat," while in Sherwood Anderson's "I Want to Know Why" (Chapter 3), a boy inquires into the matter of ugliness in the world. In some fiction the prize may be instantly clear to the reader; in other narratives it may become evident only at the conclusion of the story.

To be sure, a story does not take shape until **conflict** erupts, or until there is opposition to the desires of the protagonist. Conflict creates a story. It produces an obligatory clash between opposing forces.

Ordinarily, the protagonist fights against another character or group of characters, known as **antagonists.** For example, the protagonist may be a girl from the wrong side of the tracks who tries to prove herself to the wealthy parents of the boy she loves. Sometimes the central character contends against the forces of nature, society, or fate; a man and his companions fight for survival as they row a small boat in a churning sea. Or the main character struggles against some aspect of himself or herself: a man grapples to control a raging temper, which has already caused him to lose his job and his self-respect and now threatens to incite him to commit murder. Although we identify conflict chiefly as external or internal, physical or mental, it generally involves a combination of some or all of these aspects.

For conflict to exist, someone or something opposes the protagonist in the pursuit of the goal. This force (another character, especially the antagonist;

society; the environment; fate; or some aspect of the self), intent on defeating the main character, is the **obstacle.**

More often than not, the forces in conflict clash in an incident that occurs early in the story — the earlier the better, from the point of view of the reader, for who will read far into a story or novel that shows no semblance of conflict? As soon as the reader has identified the protagonist, recognized the prize, and met the obstacle, the interest aroused by conflict has been created. This incident or initial complication that introduces the conflict is called the **point of attack.**

In F. Scott Fitzgerald's "Babylon Revisited" (Chapter 3), the conflict is introduced when Charlie Wales asks Marion Peters for custody of his daughter; in Stephen Crane's "The Open Boat" (Chapter 4), conflict begins with the men's struggle to conquer the stormy seas and reach shore safely. Usually at this point in the story the reader asks, "Will the protagonist gain the prize?" This all-important question, which the reader asks several times as the plot develops and moves through complications toward the climax, will not be answered until the resolution.

Whereas the obstacle remains in opposition to the protagonist throughout the action, only to be removed (if it is removed at all), at the point of resolution, a **complication** normally subdues the protagonist or impedes progress toward the goal temporarily. In Crane's story, when the chief characters, who are trying to make it to shore (prize — survival) despite the antagonistic forces of nature (obstacle — sea or fate), suddenly find their food and water supplies exhausted, that discovery sets them back only for a while and therefore serves as a complication. Although their struggle has been made more difficult, nothing much has really changed. Survival is still possible, and the battle continues.

Once the conflict has advanced through a series of complications, it reaches the point of highest emotional intensity — the **climax.** Purposely, the action has moved toward this crucial scene in which the opposing forces confront each other. At this point tension is high. For the protagonist and the antagonist, the forces in conflict, it is the moment of truth. Here the reader asks for the last time the question he or she posed at the point of attack and at various moments of crisis in the story: "Will the protagonist gain the prize?" When the boy in James Joyce's "Araby" (Chapter 4) finally arrives at the bazaar, we may ask, "Will he gain the fulfillment he seeks?" Near the conclusion of "The Open Boat," as the four weary men swim toward shore, we may ask, "Will they make it?"

Once these questions have been answered, we have the **resolution,** or dénouement, which presents the outcome of the conflict. Occasionally the author offers no clear-cut resolution, but the writer usually solves the problem in some fashion. The protagonist wins or loses. He *does* make it to shore safely, or he drowns; the young woman from the bottom rung of the socioeconomic ladder *does* prove herself a worthy bride-to-be, or she does not; the raging man *does* suddenly come to grips with his problem, or he kills his best friend.

As the resolution settles a conflict or an argument, it may also shed light on the central meaning of the story — its thesis or premise, which we shall call its **theme.** By means of the theme, the writer communicates to us a truth or a principle about the human condition. Though we may discuss an author's theme fully in an essay, we should be able to sum it up in a brief statement for the sake of review. For example, "Suffering makes men brothers" may express one of the major themes of "The Open Boat," while "A man may be pushed so far that he feels the need to retaliate" may point to the main theme of "The Catbird Seat."

Note how a theme can change depending on different resolutions: If the four men in their dinghy all survive their contest with the high seas, the author may be saying that we can conquer the forces of nature. If the men all drown, then the writer must be saying that we cannot defeat nature. If only one man out of four survives, then the author may be saying that our chances of survival against nature's forces are only slight. And if the only man surviving happens to be the strongest of the group, the author may be saying that only the fittest survive, whereas if the one surviving is the weakest, then the author may be telling us that people have little to say about what happens to them and are controlled by fate. (For further details about theme, see Chapter 4.)

Of course, not every resolution brings a clear victory or defeat to the protagonist, nor does each necessarily elucidate meaning. Some stories are complex, dealing with spiritual, psychological, or symbolic manifestations; and the more complex the story is, the more involuted its theme is likely to be.

After the resolution, what remains moves swiftly to the **conclusion** — the end of the story. Even these last few sentences often carry certain importance, for they may tie up loose ends or clarify meaning. Some stories offer a surprise ending, a final climax. The French writer Guy de Maupassant specialized in such stories, and you will find one of them, "The Necklace," at the end of this chapter.

In addition to the elements of plot we have already examined, several characteristics deserve the attention of the discriminating reader and are valuable to the student who seeks a better understanding and appreciation of the structure of plot.

A plot develops **chronologically** if the events unfold in precisely the order in which they occurred, or **retrospectively** (in a flashback) if the action shifts to something that happened earlier, as in William Faulkner's "A Rose for Emily." Modern writers rarely narrate the action in a strictly chronological manner; instead, they combine both techniques. Furthermore, writers use the **summary method** or the **dramatic (scenic) method** to reveal some actions. An action revealed by summary usually covers long periods of time, and the summary reads like a historical report. On the other hand, the action presented by the dramatic method generally focuses on more significant matter, enlarges its details, and heightens its effects with dialogue. In such a story — for instance, Carson McCullers's "A Tree, a Rock, a Cloud" (Chapter 3) — readers feel that what is happening is happening *now,* and they are seeing it all.

Stories also contain another kind of action that prepares us for a plunge into the tensions of the conflict: **exposition.** Generally exposition furnishes background information, introduces characters, and establishes setting. The information may be presented in a block at the beginning of a story or spread piecemeal throughout the story as needed.

Setting, which refers to time and place and all that time and place imply, is sometimes established in the early pages of a story. But when setting assumes a larger role than mere physical description, it is prominent throughout the story. Among its several key functions, setting may set tone, mood, or atmosphere, shape conflict, reveal character, or contribute to the emotional, metaphorical, and overall significance of a story. Crane's vivid description of the sea in "The Open Boat" is so necessary to the action that the setting becomes, in essence, another character, the antagonist to the men in the dinghy; Eudora Welty's path, including all its barriers, not only shapes the physical conflict in "A Worn Path" but casts light upon the social conflict in the story.

Another important element of a story is **foreshadowing,** which the writer achieves by a particular speech, action, or symbol. To foreshadow is to hint at and prepare for a more important future action; for example, the death of a small bird may suggest the death of an important character. Foreshadowing serves any number of diverse functions, such as explaining motivation, heightening suspense, or insuring credibility. Consider the following incident:

> Alone in his dimly lit study, a man sits at his desk, fidgeting. From a drawer he takes out a gun and verifies that it is loaded. Suddenly, without warning, another man enters the room. As the visitor approaches, the man at the desk quickly shoves the gun into his coat pocket. The visitor, we learn, is a business partner, unhappy over recent business failures. An argument erupts and the man at the desk pulls out his revolver and fires repeatedly into the body of his associate.

In this scene the presence of the gun before the entrance of the second character establishes the mood, creates suspense, and makes the killing plausible.

Closely connected to foreshadowing is the element that creates the curiosity or anxiety we feel as we read on, disturbed and excited about what will happen next. This is called **suspense.** But what makes a story credible to us is **plausibility.** This may be defined as the quality that makes us accept an action as true or makes us believe that it could happen.

The four stories that follow are particularly good examples of the varied ways in which writers can create suspense out of fairly simple ingredients, and achieve plausibility even for an unlikely event. They also provide an excellent lesson in **artistic unity,** for the process of arranging events into a sequence, selecting details, and developing a story that communicates something is not an accident. On the contrary, every element in a story interacts with every other element to serve a precise purpose. Nothing is irrelevant or wasted. The author develops each part logically and makes it work with every other part to achieve the desired effects.

Questions Evaluating Plot

1. Can you summarize the story? What are its chief points?

2. Is the plot coherent? Are there any elements that do not fit in well?

3. Who is the protagonist? What is the prize? The conflict?

4. What or who opposes the protagonist? Who wins? Who loses?

5. Is there a clear-cut resolution?

6. Does the story achieve suspense? How?

7. If there is a surprise ending, is it made believable by what has gone before?

8. How important is the setting?

9. How are special features such as irony or symbolism effective?

10. How do the various elements work to achieve unity, meaning, and effect?

James Thurber (1894–1961)

The Catbird Seat

Mr. Martin bought the pack of Camels on Monday night in the most crowded cigar store on Broadway. It was theatre time and seven or eight men were buying cigarettes. The clerk didn't even glance at Mr. Martin, who put the pack in his overcoat pocket and went out. If any of the staff at F & S had seen him buy the cigarettes, they would have been astonished, for it was generally known that Mr. Martin did not smoke, and never had. No one saw him.

It was just a week to the day since Mr. Martin had decided to rub out Mrs. Ulgine Barrows. The term "rub out" pleased him because it suggested nothing more than the correction of an error — in this case an error of Mr. Fitweiler. Mr. Martin had spent each night of the past week working out his plan and examining it. As he walked home now he went over it again. For the hundredth time he resented the element of imprecision, the margin of guesswork that entered into the business. The project as he had worked it out was casual and bold, the risks were considerable. Something might go wrong anywhere along the line. And therein lay the cunning of his scheme. No one would ever see in it the cautious, painstaking hand of Erwin Martin, head of the filing department at F & S, of whom Mr. Fitweiler had once said, "Man is fallible but Martin isn't." No one would see his hand, that is, unless it were caught in the act.

Sitting in his apartment, drinking a glass of milk, Mr. Martin reviewed his case against Mrs. Ulgine Barrows, as he had every night for seven nights. He began at the beginning. Her quacking voice and braying laugh had first profaned the halls of F & S on March 7, 1941 (Mr. Martin had a head for dates). Old Roberts, the personnel chief, had introduced her as the newly appointed special adviser to the president of the firm, Mr. Fitweiler. The woman had appalled Mr. Martin instantly, but he hadn't shown it. He had given her his dry hand, a look of studious concentration, and a faint smile. "Well," she had said, looking at the papers on his desk, "are you lifting the oxcart out of the ditch?" As Mr. Martin recalled that moment, over his milk, he squirmed slightly. He must keep his mind on her crimes as a special adviser, not on her peccadillos as a personality. This he found difficult to do, in spite of entering an objection and sustaining it. The faults of the woman as a woman kept chattering on in his mind like an unruly witness. She had, for almost two years now, baited him. In the halls, in the elevator, even in his own office, into which she romped now and then like a circus horse, she was constantly shouting these silly questions at him. "Are you lifting the oxcart out of the ditch? Are you tearing up the pea patch? Are you hollering down the rain barrel? Are you scraping around the bottom of the pickle barrel? Are you sitting in the catbird seat?"

It was Joey Hart, one of Mr. Martin's two assistants, who had explained what the gibberish meant. "She must be a Dodger fan," he had said. "Red Barber announces the Dodger games over the radio and he uses those expressions — picked 'em up down South." Joey had gone on to explain one or two. "Tearing up the pea patch" meant going on a rampage; "sitting in the catbird seat" meant sitting pretty, like a batter with three balls and no strikes on him. Mr. Martin dismissed all this with an effort. It had been annoying, it had driven him near to distraction, but he was too solid a man to be moved to murder by anything so childish. It was fortunate, he reflected as he passed on to the important charges against Mrs. Barrows, that he had stood up under it so well. He had maintained always an outward appearance of polite tolerance. "Why, I even believe you like the woman," Miss Paird, his other assistant, had once said to him. He had simply smiled.

A gavel rapped in Mr. Martin's mind and the case proper was resumed. Mrs. Ulgine Barrows stood charged with willful, blatant, and persistent attempts to destroy the efficiency and system of F & S. It was competent, material, and relevant to review her advent and rise to power. Mr. Martin had got the story from Miss Paird, who seemed always able to find things out. According to her, Mrs. Barrows had met Mr. Fitweiler at a party, where she had rescued him from the embraces of a powerfully built drunken man who had mistaken the president of F & S for a famous retired Middle Western football coach. She had led him to a sofa and somehow worked upon him a monstrous magic. The aging gentleman had jumped to the conclusion there and then that this was a woman of singular attainments, equipped to bring out the best in him and in the firm. A week later he had introduced her into F & S as his special adviser. On that day confusion got its foot in the door. After Miss Tyson, Mr. Brundage, and Mr. Bartlett had been fired and Mr. Munson had taken his hat and stalked out, mailing in his resignation later, old Roberts had been emboldened to speak to Mr. Fitweiler. He mentioned that Mr. Munson's department had been "a little disrupted" and hadn't they perhaps better resume the old system there? Mr. Fitweiler had said certainly not. He had the greatest faith in Mrs. Barrows' ideas. "They require a little seasoning, a little seasoning, is all," he had added. Mr. Roberts had given it up. Mr. Martin reviewed in detail all the changes wrought by Mrs. Barrows. She had begun chipping at the cornices of the firm's edifice and now she was swinging at the foundation stones with a pickaxe.

Mr. Martin came now, in his summing up, to the afternoon of Monday, November 2, 1942 — just one week ago. On that day, at 3 P.M., Mrs. Barrows had bounced into his office. "Boo!" she had yelled. "Are you scraping around the bottom of the pickle barrel?" Mr. Martin had looked at her from under his green eyeshade, saying nothing. She had begun to wander about the office, taking it in with her great, popping eyes. "Do you really need *all* these filing cabinets?" she had demanded suddenly. Mr. Martin's heart had jumped. "Each of these files," he had said, keeping his voice even, "plays an indispensable part in the system of F & S." She had brayed at him, "Well, don't tear up the pea patch!" and gone to the door. From there she had bawled, "But you sure have got a lot of fine scrap in here!" Mr. Martin could no longer doubt that the finger was on his beloved department. Her pickaxe was on the upswing, poised for the first blow. It had not come yet; he had received no blue memo from the enchanted Mr. Fitweiler bearing nonsensical instructions deriving from the obscene woman. But there was no doubt in Mr. Martin's mind that one would be forthcoming. He must act quickly. Already a precious week had gone by. Mr. Martin stood up in his living room, still holding his milk glass. "Gentlemen of the jury," he said to himself, "I demand the death penalty for this horrible person."

The next day Mr. Martin followed his routine, as usual. He polished his glasses more often and once sharpened an already sharp pencil, but not even Miss Paird noticed. Only once did he catch sight of his victim; she swept past him in the hall with a patronizing "Hi!" At five-thirty he walked home, as usual, and had a glass of milk, as usual. He had never drunk anything stronger in his life — unless you could count ginger ale. The late Sam Schlosser, the S of F & S, had praised Mr. Martin at a staff meeting several years before for his temperate habits. "Our most efficient worker neither drinks nor smokes," he had said. "The results speak for themselves." Mr. Fitweiler had sat by, nodding approval.

Mr. Martin was still thinking about that red-letter day as he walked over to the Schrafft's on Fifth Avenue near Forty-sixth Street. He got there, as he always did, at eight o'clock. He finished his dinner and the financial page of the *Sun* at a quarter to nine, as he always did. It was his custom after dinner to take a walk. This time he walked down Fifth Avenue at a casual pace. His gloved hands felt moist and warm, his forehead cold. He transferred the Camels from his overcoat to a jacket pocket. He wondered, as he did so, if they did not represent an unnecessary note of strain. Mrs. Barrows smoked only Luckies. It was his idea to puff a few puffs on a Camel (after the rubbing-out), stub it out in the ashtray holding her lipstick-stained Luckies, and thus drag a small red herring across the trail. Perhaps it was not a good idea. It would take time. He might even choke, too loudly.

Mr. Martin had never seen the house on West Twelfth Street where Mrs. Barrows lived, but he had a clear enough picture of it. Fortunately, she had bragged to everybody about her ducky first-floor apartment in the perfectly darling three-story red-brick. There would be no doorman or other attendants; just the tenants of the second and third floors. As he walked along, Mr. Martin realized that he would get there before nine-thirty. He had considered walking north on Fifth Avenue from Schrafft's to a point from which it would take him until ten o'clock to reach the house. At that hour people were less likely to be coming in or going out. But the procedure would have made an awkward loop in the straight thread of his casualness, and he had abandoned it. It was impossible to figure when people would be entering or leaving the house, anyway. There was a great risk at any hour. If he ran into anybody, he would simply have to place the rubbing-out of Ulgine Barrows in the inactive file forever. The same thing would hold true if there were someone in her apartment. In that case he would just say that he had been passing by, recognized her charming house, and thought to drop in.

It was eighteen minutes after nine when Mr. Martin turned into Twelfth Street. A man passed him, and a man and a woman, talking. There was no one within fifty paces when he came to the house, halfway down the block. He was up the steps and in the small vestibule in no time, pressing the bell under the card that said "Mrs. Ulgine Barrows." When the clicking in the lock started, he jumped forward against the door. He got inside fast, closing the door behind him. A bulb in a lantern hung from the hall ceiling on a chain seemed to give a monstrously bright light. There was nobody on the stair, which went up ahead of him along the left wall. A door opened down the hall in the wall on the right. He went toward it swiftly, on tiptoe.

"Well, for God's sake, look who's here!" bawled Mrs. Barrows, and her braying laugh rang out like the report of a shotgun. He rushed past her like a football tackle, bumping her. "Hey, quit shoving!" she said, closing the door behind them. They were in her living room, which seemed to Mr. Martin to be lighted by a hundred lamps. "What's after you?" she said. "You're as jumpy as a goat." He found he was unable to speak. His heart was wheezing in his throat. "I — yes," he finally brought out. She was jabbering and laughing as she started to help him off with his coat. "No, no," he said. "I'll put it here." He took it off and put it on a chair near the door. "Your hat and gloves, too," she said. "You're in a lady's house." He put his hat on top of the coat. Mrs. Barrows seemed larger than he had thought. He kept his gloves on. "I was passing by," he said. "I recognized — is there anyone here?" She laughed louder than ever. "No," she said, "we're all alone. You're as white as a sheet, you funny man. Whatever *has* come over you? I'll mix you a toddy." She started toward a door across the room. "Scotch-and-soda be all right? But say, you don't drink, do you?" She turned and gave him her amused look. Mr. Martin pulled himself together. "Scotch-and-soda will be all right," he heard himself say. He could hear her laughing in the kitchen.

Mr. Martin looked quickly around the living room for the weapon. He had counted on finding one there. There were andirons and a poker and something in a corner that looked like an Indian club. None of them would do. It couldn't be that way. He began to pace around. He came to a desk. On it lay a metal paper knife with an ornate handle. Would it be sharp enough? He reached for it and knocked over a small brass jar. Stamps spilled out of it and it fell to the floor with a clatter. "Hey," Mrs. Barrows yelled from the kitchen, "are you tearing up the pea patch?" Mr. Martin gave a strange laugh. Picking up the knife, he tried its point against his left wrist. It was blunt. It wouldn't do.

When Mrs. Barrows reappeared, carrying two high-balls, Mr. Martin, standing there with his gloves on, became acutely conscious of the fantasy he had wrought. Cigarettes in his pocket, a drink prepared for him — it was all too grossly improbable. It was more than that; it was impossible. Somewhere in the back of his mind a vague idea stirred, sprouted. "For heaven's sake, take off those gloves," said Mrs. Barrows. "I always wear them in the house," said Mr. Martin. The idea began to bloom, strange and wonderful. She put the glasses on a coffee table in front of a sofa and sat on the sofa. "Come over here, you odd little man," she said. Mr. Martin went over and sat beside her. It was difficult getting a cigarette out of the pack of Camels, but he managed it. She held a match for him, laughing. "Well," she said, handing him his drink, "this is perfectly marvellous. You with a drink and a cigarette."

Mr. Martin puffed, not too awkwardly, and took a gulp of the highball. "I drink and smoke all the time," he said. He clinked his glass against hers. "Here's nuts to that old windbag, Fitweiler," he said, and gulped again. The stuff tasted awful, but he made no grimace. "Really, Mr. Martin," she said, her voice and posture changing, "you are insulting our employer." Mrs. Barrows was now all special adviser to the president. "I am preparing a bomb," said Mr. Martin, "which will blow the old goat higher than hell." He had only had a little of the drink, which was not strong. It couldn't be that. "Do you take dope or something?" Mrs. Barrows asked coldly. "Heroin," said Mr. Martin. "I'll be coked to the gills when I bump that old buzzard off." "Mr. Martin!" she shouted, getting to her feet. "That will be all of that. You must go at once." Mr. Martin took another swallow of his drink. He tapped his cigarette out in the ashtray and put the pack of Camels on the coffee table. Then he got up. She stood glaring at him. He walked over and put on his hat and coat. "Not a word about this," he said, and laid an index finger against his lips. All Mrs. Barrows could bring out was "Really!" Mr. Martin put his hand on the doorknob. "I'm sitting in the catbird seat," he said. He stuck his tongue out at her and left. Nobody saw him go.

Mr. Martin got to his apartment, walking, well before eleven. No one saw him go in. He had two glasses of milk after brushing his teeth, and he felt elated. It wasn't tipsiness, because he hadn't been tipsy. Anyway, the walk had worn off all effects of the whiskey. He got in bed and read a magazine for a while. He was asleep before midnight.

Mr. Martin got to the office at eight-thirty the next morning, as usual. At a quarter to nine, Ulgine Barrows, who had never before arrived at work before ten, swept into his office. "I'm reporting to Mr. Fitweiler now!" she shouted. "If he turns you over to the police, it's no more than you deserve!" Mr. Martin gave her a look of shocked surprise. "I beg your pardon?" he said. Mrs. Barrows snorted and bounced out of the room, leaving Miss Paird and Joey Hart staring after her. "What's the matter with that old devil now?" asked Miss Paird. "I have no idea," said Mr. Martin, resuming his work. The other two looked at him and then at each other. Miss Paird got up and went out. She walked slowly past the closed door of Mr. Fitweiler's office. Mrs. Barrows was yelling inside, but she was not braying. Miss Paird could not hear what the woman was saying. She went back to her desk.

Forty-five minutes later, Mrs. Barrows left the president's office and went into her own, shutting the door. It wasn't until half an hour later that Mr. Fitweiler sent for Mr. Martin. The head of the filing department, neat, quiet, attentive, stood in front of the old man's desk. Mr. Fitweiler was pale and nervous. He took his glasses off and twiddled them. He made a small, bruffing sound in his throat. "Martin," he said, "you have been with us more than twenty years." "Twenty-two, sir," said Mr. Martin. "In that time," pursued the president, "your work and your — uh — manner have been exemplary." "I trust so, sir," said Mr. Martin. "I have understood, Martin," said Mr. Fitweiler, "that you have never taken a drink or smoked." "That is correct, sir," said Mr. Martin. "Ah, yes." Mr. Fitweiler polished his glasses. "You may describe what you did after leaving the office yesterday, Martin," he said. Mr. Martin allowed less than a second for his bewildered pause. "Certainly, sir," he said. "I walked home. Then I went to Schrafft's for dinner. Afterward I walked home again. I went to bed early, sir, and read a magazine for a while. I was asleep before eleven." "Ah, yes," said Mr. Fitweiler again. He was silent for a moment, searching for the proper words to say to the head of the filing department. "Mrs. Barrows," he said finally, "Mrs. Barrows has worked hard, Martin, very hard. It grieves me to report that she has suffered a severe breakdown. It has taken the form of a persecution complex accompanied by distressing hallucinations." "I am very sorry, sir," said Mr. Martin. "Mrs. Barrows is under the delusion," continued Mr. Fitweiler, "that you visited her last evening and behaved yourself in an — uh — unseemly manner." He raised his hand to silence Mr. Martin's little pained outcry. "It is the nature of these psychological diseases," Mr. Fitweiler said, "to fix upon the least likely and most innocent party as the — uh — source of persecution. These matters are not for the lay mind to grasp, Martin. I've just had my psychiatrist, Dr. Fitch, on the phone. He would not, of course, commit himself, but he made enough generalizations to substantiate my suspicions. I suggested to Mrs. Barrows, when she had completed her — uh — story to me this morning, that she visit Dr. Fitch, for I suspected a condition at once. She flew, I regret to say, into a rage, and demanded — uh — requested that I call you on the carpet. You may not know, Martin, but Mrs. Barrows had planned a reorganization of your department — subject to my approval, of course, subject to my approval. This brought you, rather than anyone else, to her mind — but again that is a phenomenon for Dr. Fitch and not for us. So, Martin, I am afraid Mrs. Barrows' usefulness here is at an end." "I am dreadfully sorry, sir," said Mr. Martin.

It was at this point that the door to the office blew open with the suddenness of a gas-main explosion and Mrs. Barrows catapulted through it. "Is the little rat denying it?" she screamed. "He can't get away with that!" Mr. Martin got up and moved discretely to a point beside Mr. Fitweiler's chair. "You drank and smoked at my apartment," she bawled at Mr. Martin, "and you know it! You called Mr. Fitweiler an old windbag and said you were going to blow him up when you got coked to the gills on your heroin!" She stopped yelling to catch her breath and a new glint came into her popping eyes. "If you weren't such a drab, ordinary little man," she said, "I think you'd planned it all. Sticking your tongue out, saying you were sitting in the catbird seat, because you thought no one would believe me when I told it! My God, it's really too perfect!" She brayed loudly and hysterically, and the fury was on her again. She glared at Mr. Fitweiler. "Can't you see how he has tricked us, you old fool? Can't you see his little game?" But Mr. Fitweiler had been surreptitiously pressing all the buttons under the top of his desk and employees of F & S began pouring into the room. "Stockton," said Mr. Fitweiler, "you and Fishbein will take Mrs. Barrows to her home. Mrs. Powell, you will go with them." Stockton, who had played a little football in high school, blocked Mrs. Barrows as she made for Mr. Martin. It took him and Fishbein together to force her out of the door into the hall, crowded with stenographers and office boys. She was still screaming imprecations at Mr. Martin, tangled and contradictory imprecations. The hubbub finally died out down the corridor.

"I regret that this has happened," said Mr. Fitweiler. "I shall ask you to dismiss it from your mind, Martin." "Yes, sir," said Mr. Martin, anticipating his chief's "That will be all" by moving to the door. "I will dismiss it." He went out and shut the door, and his step was light and quick in the hall. When he entered his department he had slowed down to his customary gait, and he walked quietly across the room to the W20 file, wearing a look of studious concentration.

Exercises

1. List several of the more important incidents or actions that constitute the plot.

2. Who is the protagonist? Cite specific reasons for your choice. Identify the prize.

3. Who is the antagonist? Describe the conflict. Is the struggle primarily internal or external?

4. At what point in the story is the conflict clearly introduced or positively known to the reader?

5. Point out a complication or two, and explain why each is a complication.

6. Identify the climactic scene in the story. Explain why it is the climax.

7. Does the protagonist achieve the goal or not? Precisely where in the story do you find the resolution?

8. Underneath the comic surface, what serious point does the author make?

Topics for Writing

1. Do you find the plot of this story plausible? In an essay, discuss and evaluate some of the means Thurber uses to make the sequence and interrelation of events credible.

2. Write a narrative dealing with the experience of someone who is pushed around to the point of retaliation.

3. Write a plot summary.

Selected Bibliography James Thurber

Brady, C. A. "What Thurber Saw." *Commonweal,* 75 (December 8, 1961), 274–276.
Brandon, Henry. "Everybody Is Getting Very Serious: A Conversation with James Thurber." *New Republic,* 144 (May 15, 1961), 18.
Cooke, Alistair, ed. "James Thurber in Conversation with Alistair Cooke." *Atlantic Monthly,* 197 (August 1956), 36–40.
Cowley, Malcolm. "Salute to Thurber." *Saturday Review,* 44 (November 25, 1960), 14–18, 63–64.
Downing, Francis. "Thurber." *Commonweal,* 41 (March 9, 1945), 518–519.
Elias, Robert H. "James Thurber: The Primitive, the Innocent, and the Individual." *American Scholar,* 27 (Summer 1958), 355–363.
Hasley, Louis. "James Thurber: Artist in Humor." *South Atlantic Quarterly,* 73 (1974), 506–507.
Holmes, Charles S. "James Thurber and the Art of Fantasy." *Yale Review,* 55 (October 1965), 17–33.
Morsberger, Robert E. *James Thurber.* New York: Twayne, 1964.

Bernard Malamud (1914–)

The Magic Barrel

Not long ago there lived in uptown New York, in a small, almost meager room, though crowded with books, Leo Finkle, a rabbinical student in the Yeshivah University. Finkle, after six years of study, was to be ordained in June and had been advised by an acquaintance that he might find it easier to win himself a congregation if he were married. Since he had no present prospects of marriage, after two tormented days of turning it over in his mind, he called in Pinye Salzman, a marriage broker whose two-line advertisement he had read in the *Forward*.

The matchmaker appeared one night out of the dark fourth-floor hallway of the graystone rooming house where Finkle lived, grasping a black, strapped portfolio that had been worn thin with use. Salzman, who had been long in the business, was of slight but dignified build, wearing an old hat, and an overcoat too short and tight for him. He smelled frankly of fish, which he loved to eat, and although he was missing a few teeth, his presence was not displeasing, because of an amiable manner curiously contrasted with mournful eyes. His voice, his lips, his wisp of beard, his bony fingers were animated, but give him a moment of repose and his mild blue eyes revealed a depth of sadness, a characteristic that put Leo a little at ease although the situation, for him, was inherently tense.

He at once informed Salzman why he had asked him to come, explaining that his home was in Cleveland, and that but for his parents, who had married comparatively late in life, he was alone in the world. He had for six years devoted himself almost entirely to his studies, as a result of which, understandably, he had found himself without time for a social life and the company of young women. Therefore he thought it the better part of trial and error — of embarrassing fumbling — to call in an experienced person to advise him on these matters. He remarked in passing that the function of the marriage broker was ancient and honorable, highly approved in the Jewish community, because it made practical the necessary without hindering joy. Moreover, his own parents had been brought together by a matchmaker. They had made, if not a financially profitable marriage — since neither had possessed any worldly goods to speak of — at least a successful one in the sense of their everlasting devotion to each other. Salzman listened in embarrassed surprise, sensing a sort of apology. Later, however, he experienced a glow of pride in his work, an emotion that had left him years ago, and he heartily approved of Finkle.

The two went to their business. Leo had led Salzman to the only clear place in the room, a table near a window that overlooked the lamp-lit city. He seated himself at the matchmaker's side but facing him, attempting by an act of will to suppress the unpleasant tickle in his throat. Salzman eagerly unstrapped his portfolio and removed a loose rubber band from a thin packet of much-handled cards. As he flipped through them, a gesture and sound that physically hurt Leo, the student pretended not to see and gazed steadfastly out the window. Although it was still February, winter was on its last legs, signs of which he had for the first time in years begun to notice. He now observed the round white moon, moving high in the sky through a cloud menagerie, and watched with half-open mouth as it penetrated a huge hen, and dropped out of her like an egg laying itself. Salzman, though pretending through eyeglasses he had just slipped on to be engaged in scanning the writing on the cards, stole occasional glances at the young man's distinguished face, noting with pleasure the long, severe scholar's nose, brown eyes heavy with learning, sensitive yet ascetic lips, and a certain, almost hollow quality of the dark cheeks. He gazed around at shelves upon shelves of books and let out a soft, contented sigh.

When Leo's eyes fell upon the cards, he counted six spread out in Salzman's hand.

"So few?" he asked in disappointment.

"You wouldn't believe me how much cards I got in my office," Salzman replied. "The drawers are already filled to the top, so I keep them now in a barrel, but is every girl good for a new rabbi?"

Leo blushed at this, regretting all he had revealed of himself in a curriculum vitae he had sent to Salzman. He had thought it best to acquaint him with his strict standards and specifications, but in having done so, felt he had told the marriage broker more than was absolutely necessary.

He hesitantly inquired, "Do you keep photographs of your clients on file?"

"First comes family, amount of dowry, also what kind promises," Salzman replied, unbuttoning his tight coat and settling himself in the chair. "After comes pictures, rabbi."

"Call me Mr. Finkle. I'm not yet a rabbi."

Salzman said he would, but instead called him doctor, which he changed to rabbi when Leo was not listening too attentively.

Salzman adjusted his horn-rimmed spectacles, gently cleared his throat and read in an eager voice the contents of the top card:

"Sophie P. Twenty four year. Widow one year. No children. Educated high school and two years college. Father promises eight thousand dollars. Has wonderful wholesale business. Also real estate. On the mother's side comes teachers, also one actor. Well known on Second Avenue."

Leo gazed up in surprise. "Did you say a widow?"

"A widow don't mean spoiled, rabbi. She lived with her husband maybe four months. He was a sick boy she made a mistake to marry him."

"Marrying a widow has never entered my mind."

"This is because you have no experience. A widow, especially if she is young and healthy like this girl, is a wonderful person to marry. She will be thankful to you the rest of her life. Believe me, if I was looking now for a bride, I would marry a widow."

Leo reflected, then shook his head.

Salzman hunched his shoulders in an almost imperceptible gesture of disappointment. He placed the card down on the wooden table and began to read another:

"Lily H. High school teacher. Regular. Not a substitute. Has savings and new Dodge car. Lived in Paris one year. Father is successful dentist thirty-five years. Interested in professional man. Well Americanized family. Wonderful opportunity.

"I knew her personally," said Salzman. "I wish you could see this girl. She is a doll. Also very intelligent. All day you could talk to her about books and theyater and what not. She also knows current events."

"I don't believe you mentioned her age?"

"Her age?" Salzman said, raising his brows. "Her age is thirty-two years."

Leo said after a while, "I'm afraid that seems a little too old."

Salzman let out a laugh. "So how old are you, rabbi?"

"Twenty-seven."

"So what is the difference, tell me, between twenty-seven and thirty-two? My own wife is seven years older than me. So what did I suffer? — Nothing. If Rothschild's a daughter wants to marry you, would you say on account her age, no?"

"Yes," Leo said dryly.

Salzman shook off the no in the yes. "Five years don't mean a thing. I give you my word that when you will live with her for one week you will forget her age. What does it mean five years — that she lived more and knows more than somebody who is younger? On this girl, God bless her, years are not wasted. Each one that it comes makes better the bargain."

"What subject does she teach in high school?"

"Languages. If you heard the way she speaks French, you will think it is music. I am in the business twenty-five years, and I recommend her with my whole heart. Believe me, I know what I'm talking, rabbi."

"What's on the next card?" Leo said abruptly.

Salzman reluctantly turned up the third card:

"Ruth K. Nineteen years. Honor student. Father offers thirteen thousand cash to the right bridegroom. He is a medical doctor. Stomach specialist with marvelous practice. Brother in law owns own garment business. Particular people."

Salzman looked as if he had read his trump card.

"Did you say nineteen?" Leo asked with interest.

"On the dot."

"Is she attractive?" He blushed. "Pretty?"

Salzman kissed his finger tips. "A little doll. On this I give you my word. Let me call the father tonight and you will see what means pretty."

But Leo was troubled. "You're sure she's that young?"

"This I am positive. The father will show you the birth certificate."

"Are you positive there isn't something wrong with her?" Leo insisted.

"Who says there is wrong?"

"I don't understand why an American girl her age should go to a marriage broker."

A smile spread over Salzman's face.

"So for the same reason you went, she comes."

Leo flushed. "I am pressed for time."

Salzman, realizing he had been tactless, quickly explained. "The father came, not her. He wants she should have the best, so he looks around himself. When we will locate the right boy he will introduce him and encourage. This makes a better marriage than if a young girl without experience takes for herself. I don't have to tell you this."

"But don't you think this young girl believes in love?"

Leo spoke uneasily.

Salzman was about to gaffaw but caught himself and said soberly, "Love comes with the right person, not before."

Leo parted dry lips but did not speak. Noticing that Salzman had snatched a glance at the next card, he cleverly asked, "How is her health?"

"Perfect," Salzman said, breathing with difficulty. "Of course, she is a little lame on her right foot from an auto accident that it happened to her when she was twelve years, but nobody notices on account she is so brilliant and also beautiful."

Leo got up heavily and went to the window. He felt curiously bitter and upbraided himself for having called in the marriage broker. Finally, he shook his head.

"Why not?" Salzman persisted, the pitch of his voice rising.

"Because I detest stomach specialists."

"So what do you care what is his business? After you marry her do you need him? Who says he must come every Friday night in your house?"

Ashamed of the way the talk was going, Leo dismissed Salzman, who went home with heavy, melancholy eyes.

Though he had felt only relief at the marriage broker's departure, Leo was in low spirits the next day. He explained it as arising from Salzman's failure to produce a suitable bride for him. He did not care for his type of clientele. But when Leo found himself hesitating whether to seek out another matchmaker, one more polished than Pinye, he wondered if it could be — his protestations to the contrary, and although he honored his father and mother — that he did not, in essence, care for the matchmaking institution? This thought he quickly put out of mind yet found himself still upset. All day he ran around in the woods — missed an important appointment, forgot to give out his laundry, walked out of a Broadway cafeteria without paying and had to run back with the ticket in his hand; had even not recognized his landlady in the street when she passed with a friend and courteously called out, "A good evening to you, Doctor Finkle." By nightfall, however, he had regained sufficient calm to sink his nose into a book and there found peace from his thoughts.

Almost at once there came a knock on the door. Before Leo could say enter, Salzman, commercial cupid, was standing in the room. His face was gray and meager, his expression hungry, and he looked as if he would expire on his feet. Yet the marriage broker managed, by some trick of the muscles, to display a broad smile.

"So good evening. I am invited?"

Leo nodded, disturbed to see him again, yet unwilling to ask the man to leave.

Beaming still, Salzman laid his portfolio on the table. "Rabbi, I got for you tonight good news."

"I've asked you not to call me rabbi. I'm still a student."

"Your worries are finished. I have for you a first-class bride."

"Leave me in peace concerning this subject." Leo pretended lack of interest.

"The world will dance at your wedding."

"Please, Mr. Salzman, no more."

"But first must come back my strength," Salzman said weakly. He fumbled with the portfolio straps and took out of the leather case an oily paper bag, from which he extracted a hard, seeded roll and a small, smoked white fish. With a quick motion of his hand he stripped the fish out of its skin and began ravenously to chew. "All day in a rush," he muttered.

Leo watched him eat.

"A sliced tomato you have maybe?" Salzman hesitantly inquired.

"No."

The marriage broker shut his eyes and ate. When he had finished he carefully cleaned up the crumbs and rolled up the remains of the fish, in the paper bag. His spectacled eyes roamed the room until he discovered, amid some piles of books, a one-burner gas stove. Lifting his hat he humbly asked, "A glass of tea you got, rabbi?"

Conscience-stricken, Leo rose and brewed the tea. He served it with a chunk of lemon and two cubes of lump sugar, delighting Salzman.

After he had drunk his tea, Salzman's strength and good spirits were restored.

"So tell me, rabbi," he said amiably, "you considered some more the three clients I mentioned yesterday?"

"There was no need to consider."

"Why not?"

"None of them suits me."

"What then suits you?"

Leo let it pass because he could give only a confused answer.

Without waiting for a reply, Salzman asked, "You remember this girl I talked to you — the high school teacher?"

"Age thirty-two?"

But surprisingly, Salzman's face lit in a smile. "Age twenty-nine."

Leo shot him a look. "Reduced from thirty-two?"

"A mistake," Salzman avowed. "I talked today with the dentist. He took me to his safety deposit box and showed me the birth certificate. She was twenty-nine years last August. They made her a party in the mountains where she went for her vacation. When her father spoke to me the first time I forgot to write the age and I told you thirty-two, but now I remember this was a different client, a widow."

"The same one you told me about? I thought she was twenty-four?"

"A different. Am I responsible that the world is filled with widows?"

"No, but I'm not interested in them, nor for that matter, in school teachers."

Salzman pulled his clasped hands to his breast. Looking at the ceiling he devoutly exclaimed, "Yiddishe kinder, what can I say to somebody that he is not interested in high school teachers? So what then you are interested?"

Leo flushed but controlled himself.

"In what else will you be interested," Salzman went on, "if you not interested in this fine girl that she speaks four languages and has personally in the bank ten thousand dollars? Also her father guarantees further twelve thousand. Also she has a new car, wonderful clothes, talks on all subjects, and she will give you a first-class home and children. How near do we come in our life to paradise?"

"If she's so wonderful, why wasn't she married ten years ago?"

"Why?" said Salzman with a heavy laugh. " — Why? Because she is *partikiler*. This is why. She wants the *best*."

Leo was silent, amused at how he had entangled himself. But Salzman had aroused his interest in Lily H., and he began seriously to consider calling on her. When the marriage broker observed how intently Leo's mind was at work on the facts he had supplied, he felt certain they would soon come to an agreement.

Late Saturday afternoon, conscious of Salzman, Leo Finkle walked with Lily Hirschorn along Riverside Drive. He walked briskly and erectly, wearing with distinction the black fedora he had that morning taken with trepidation out of the dusty hat box on his closet shelf, and the heavy black Saturday coat he had thoroughly whisked clean. Leo also owned a walking stick, a present from a distant relative, but quickly put temptation aside and did not use it. Lily, petite and not unpretty, had on something signifying the approach of spring. She was au courant, animatedly, with all sorts of subjects, and he weighed her words and found her surprisingly sound — score another for Salzman, whom he uneasily sensed to be somewhere around, hiding perhaps high in a tree along the street, flashing the lady signals with a pocket mirror; or perhaps a cloven-hoofed Pan, piping nuptial ditties as he danced his invisible way before them, strewing wild buds on the walk and purple grapes in their path, symbolizing fruit of a union, though there was of course still none.

Lily startled Leo by remarking, "I was thinking of Mr. Salzman, a curious figure, wouldn't you say?"

Not certain what to answer, he nodded.

She bravely went on, blushing, "I for one am grateful for his introducing us. Aren't you?"

He courteously replied, "I am."

"I mean," she said with a little laugh — and it was all in good taste, or at least gave the effect of being not in bad — "do you mind that we came together so?"

He was not displeased with her honesty, recognizing that she meant to set the relationship aright, and understanding that it took a certain amount of experience in life, and courage, to want to do it quite that way. One had to have some sort of past to make that kind of beginning.

He said that he did not mind. Salzman's function was traditional and honorable — valuable for what it might achieve, which, he pointed out, was frequently nothing.

Lily agreed with a sigh. They walked on for a while and she said after a long silence, again with a nervous laugh, "Would you mind if I asked you something a little bit personal? Frankly, I find the subject fascinating." Although Leo shrugged, she went on half embarrassedly, "How was it that you came to your calling? I mean was it a sudden passionate inspiration?"

Leo, after a time, slowly replied, "I was always interested in the Law."

"You saw revealed in it the presence of the Highest?"

He nodded and changed the subject. "I understand that you spent a little time in Paris, Miss Hirschorn?"

"Oh, did Mr. Salzman tell you, Rabbi Finkle?" Leo winced but she went on, "It was ages ago and almost forgotten. I remember I had to return for my sister's wedding."

And Lily would not be put off. "When," she asked in a trembly voice, "did you become enamored of God?"

He stared at her. Then it came to him that she was talking not about Leo Finkle, but of a total stranger, some mystical figure, perhaps even passionate prophet that Salzman had dreamed up for her — no relation to the living or dead. Leo trembled with rage and weakness. The trickster had obviously sold her a bill of goods, just as he had him, who'd expected to become acquainted with a young lady of twenty-nine, only to behold, the moment he laid eyes upon her strained and anxious face, a woman past thirty-five and aging rapidly. Only his self control had kept him this long in her presence.

"I am not," he said gravely, "a talented religious person," and in seeking words to go on, found himself possessed by shame and fear. "I think," he said in a strained manner, "that I came to God not because I loved Him, but because I did not."

This confession he spoke harshly because its unexpectedness shook him.

Lily wilted. Leo saw a profusion of loaves of bread go flying like ducks high over his head, not unlike the winged loaves by which he had counted himself to sleep last night. Mercifully, then, it snowed, which he would not put past Salzman's machinations.

He was infuriated with the marriage broker and swore he would throw him out of the room the minute he reappeared. But Salzman did not come that night, and when Leo's anger had subsided, an unaccountable despair grew in its place. At first he thought this was caused by his disappointment in Lily, but before long it became evident that he had involved himself with Salzman without a true knowledge of his own intent. He gradually realized — with an emptiness that seized him with six hands — that he had called in the broker to find him a bride because he was incapable of doing it himself. This terrifying insight he had derived as a result of his meeting and conversation with Lily Hirschorn. Her probing questions had somehow irritated him into revealing — to himself more than her — the true nature of his relationship to God, and from that it had come upon him, with shocking force, that apart from his parents, he had never loved anyone. Or perhaps it went the other way, that he did not love God so well as he might, because he had not loved man. It seemed to Leo that his whole life stood starkly revealed and he saw himself for the first time as he truly was — unloved and loveless. This bitter but somehow not fully unexpected revelation brought him to a point of panic, controlled only by extraordinary effort. He covered his face with his hands and cried.

The week that followed was the worst of his life. He did not eat and lost weight. His beard darkened and grew ragged. He stopped attending seminars and almost never opened a book. He seriously considered leaving the Yeshivah,[1] although he was deeply troubled at the thought of the loss of all his years of study — saw them like pages torn from a book, strewn over the city — and at the devastating effect of this decision upon his parents. But he had lived without knowledge of himself, and never in the Five Books[2] and all the Commentaries — mea culpa[3] — had the truth been revealed to him. He did not know where to turn, and in all this desolating loneliness there was no *to whom,* although he often thought of Lily but not once could bring himself to go downstairs and make the call. He became touchy and irritable, especially with his landlady, who asked him all manner of personal questions; on the other hand, sensing his own disagreeableness, he waylaid her on the stairs and apologized abjectly, until mortified, she ran from him. Out of this, however, he drew the consolation that he was a Jew and that a Jew suffered. But gradually, as the long and terrible week drew to a close, he regained his composure and some idea of purpose in life: to go on as planned. Although he was imperfect, the ideal was not. As for his quest of a bride, the thought of continuing afflicted him with anxiety and heartburn, yet perhaps with this new knowledge of himself he would be more successful than in the past. Perhaps love would now come to him and a bride to that love. And for this sanctified seeking who needed a Salzman?

1. Yeshivah: Seminary.
2. Five Books: Song of Solomon, Ruth, Lamentations, Ecclesiastes, and Esther, books of the Old Testament.
3. Mea culpa: Latin for "my fault."

The marriage broker, a skeleton with haunted eyes, returned that very night. He looked, withal, the picture of frustrated expectancy — as if he had steadfastly waited the week at Miss Lily Hirschorn's side for a telephone call that never came.

Casually coughing, Salzman came immediately to the point: "So how did you like her?"

Leo's anger rose and he could not refrain from chiding the matchmaker: "Why did you lie to me, Salzman?"

Salzman's pale face went dead white, the world had snowed on him.

"Did you not state that she was twenty-nine?" Leo insisted.

"I give you my word — "

"She was thirty-five, if a day. *At least* thirty-five."

"Of this don't be too sure. Her father told me — "

"Never mind. The worst of it was that you lied to her."

"How did I lie to her, tell me?"

"You told her things about me that weren't true. You made me out to be more, consequently less than I am. She had in mind a totally different person, a sort of semi-mystical Wonder Rabbi."

"All I said, you was a religious man."

"I can imagine."

Salzman sighed. "This is my weakness that I have," he confessed. "My wife says to me I shouldn't be a salesman, but when I have two fine people that they would be wonderful to be married, I am so happy that I talk too much." He smiled wanly. "This is why Salzman is a poor man."

Leo's anger left him. "Well, Salzman, I'm afraid that's all."

The marriage broker fastened hungry eyes on him.

"You don't want any more a bride?"

"I do," said Leo, "but I have decided to seek her in a different way. I am no longer interested in an arranged marriage. To be frank, I now admit the necessity of premarital love. That is, I want to be in love with the one I marry."

"Love?" said Salzman, astounded. After a moment he remarked, "For us, our love is our life, not for the ladies. In the ghetto they — "

"I know, I know," said Leo. "I've thought of it often. Love, I have said to myself, should be a by-product of living and worship rather than its own end. Yet for myself I find it necessary to establish the level of my need and fulfill it."

Salzman shrugged but answered, "Listen, rabbi, if you want love, this I can find for you also. I have such beautiful clients that you will love them the minute your eyes will see them."

Leo smiled unhappily. "I'm afraid you don't understand."

But Salzman hastily unstrapped his portfolio and withdrew a manila packet from it.

"Pictures," he said, quickly laying the envelope on the table.

Leo called after him to take the pictures away, but as if on the wings of the wind, Salzman had disappeared.

March came. Leo had returned to his regular routine. Although he felt not quite himself yet — lacked energy — he was making plans for a more active social life. Of course it would cost something, but he was an expert in cutting corners; and when there were no corners left he would make circles rounder. All the while Salzman's pictures had lain on the table, gathering dust.

Occasionally as Leo sat studying, or enjoying a cup of tea, his eyes fell on the manila envelope, but he never opened it.

The days went by and no social life to speak of developed with a member of the opposite sex — it was difficult, given the circumstances of his situation. One morning Leo toiled up the stairs to his room and stared out the window at the city. Although the day was bright his view of it was dark. For some time he watched the people in the street below hurrying along and then turned with a heavy heart to his little room. On the table was the packet. With a sudden relentless gesture he tore it open. For a half-hour he stood by the table in a state of excitement, examining the photographs of the ladies Salzman had included. Finally, with a deep sigh he put them down. There were six, of varying degrees of attractiveness, but look at them long enough and they all became Lily Hirschorn: all past their prime, all starved behind bright smiles, not a true personality in the lot. Life, despite their frantic yoohooings, had passed them by; they were pictures in a briefcase that stank of fish. After a while, however, as Leo attempted to return the photographs into the envelope, he found in it another, a snapshot of the type taken by a machine for a quarter. He gazed at it a moment and let out a cry.

Her face deeply moved him. Why, he could at first not say. It gave him the impression of youth — spring flowers, yet age — a sense of having been used to the bone, wasted; this came from the eyes, which were hauntingly familiar, yet absolutely strange. He had a vivid impression that he had met her before, but try as he might he could not place her although he could almost recall her name, as if he had read it in her own handwriting. No, this couldn't be; he would have remembered her. It was not, he affirmed, that she had an extraordinary beauty — no, though her face was attractive enough; it was that *something* about her moved him. Feature for feature, even some of the ladies of the photographs could do better; but she leaped forth to his heart — had *lived,* or wanted to — more than just wanted, perhaps regretted how she had lived — had somehow deeply suffered: it could be seen in the depths of those reluctant eyes, and from the way the light enclosed and shone from her, and within her, opening realms of possibility: this was her own. Her he desired. His head ached and eyes narrowed with the intensity of his gazing, then as if an obscure fog had blown up in his mind, he experienced fear of her and was aware that he had received an impression, somehow, of evil. He shuddered, saying softly, it is thus with us all. Leo brewed some tea in a small pot and sat sipping it without sugar, to calm himself. But before he had finished drinking, again with excitement he examined the face and found it good: good for Leo Finkle. Only such a one could understand him and help him seek whatever he was seeking. She might, perhaps, love him. How she had happened to be among the discards in Salzman's barrel he could never guess, but he knew he must urgently go find her.

Leo rushed downstairs, grabbed up the Bronx telephone book, and searched for Salzman's home address. He was not listed, nor was his office. Neither was he in the Manhattan book. But Leo remembered having written down the address on a slip of paper after he had read Salzman's advertisement in the "personals" column of the *Forward.* He ran up to his room and tore through his papers, without luck. It was exasperating. Just when he needed the matchmaker he was nowhere to be found. Fortunately Leo remembered to look in his wallet. There on a card he found his name written and a Bronx address. No phone number was listed, the reason — Leo now recalled — he had originally communicated with Salzman by letter. He got on his coat, put a hat on over his skull cap and hurried to the subway station. All the way to the far end of the Bronx he sat on the edge of his seat. He was more than once tempted to take out the picture and see if the girl's face was as he remembered it, but he refrained, allowing the snapshot to remain in his inside coat pocket, content to have her so close. When the train pulled into the station he was waiting at the door and bolted out. He quickly located the street Salzman had advertised.

The building he sought was less than a block from the subway, but it was not an office building, nor even a loft, nor a store in which one could rent office space. It was a very old tenement house. Leo found Salzman's name in pencil on a soiled tag under the bell and climbed three dark flights to his apartment. When he knocked, the door was opened by a thin, asthmatic, gray-haired woman, in felt slippers.

"Yes?" she said, expecting nothing. She listened without listening. He could have sworn he had seen her, too, before but knew it was an illusion.

"Salzman — does he live here? Pinye Salzman," he said, "the matchmaker?"

She stared at him a long moment. "Of course."

He felt embarrassed. "Is he in?"

"No." Her mouth, though left open, offered nothing more.

"The matter is urgent. Can you tell me where his office is?"

"In the air." She pointed upward.

"You mean he has no office?" Leo asked.

"In his socks."

He peered into the apartment. It was sunless and dingy, one large room divided by a half-open curtain, beyond which he could see a sagging metal bed. The near side of the room was crowded with rickety chairs, old bureaus, a three-legged table, racks of cooking utensils, and all the apparatus of a kitchen. But there was no sign of Salzman or his magic barrel, probably also a figment of the imagination. An odor of frying fish made Leo weak to the knees.

"Where is he?" he insisted. "I've got to see your husband."

At length she answered, "So who knows where he is? Every time he thinks a new thought he runs to a different place. Go home, he will find you."

"Tell him Leo Finkle."

She gave no sign she had heard.

He walked downstairs, depressed.

But Salzman, breathless, stood waiting at his door.

Leo was astounded and overjoyed. "How did you get here before me?"

"I rushed."

"Come inside."

They entered. Leo fixed tea, and a sardine sandwich for Salzman. As they were drinking he reached behind him for the packet of pictures and handed them to the marriage broker.

Salzman put down his glass and said expectantly, "You found somebody you like?"

"Not among these."

The marriage broker turned away.

"Here is the one I want," Leo held forth the snapshot.

Salzman slipped on his glasses and took the picture into his trembling hand. He turned ghastly and let out a groan.

"What's the matter?" cried Leo.

"Excuse me. Was an accident this picture. She isn't for you."

Salzman frantically shoved the manila packet into his portfolio. He thrust the snapshot into his pocket and fled down the stairs.

Leo, after momentary paralysis, gave chase and cornered the marriage broker in the vestibule. The landlady made hysterical outcries but neither of them listened.

"Give me back the picture, Salzman."

"No." The pain in his eyes was terrible.

"Tell me who she is then."

"This I can't tell you. Excuse me."

He made to depart, but Leo, forgetting himself, seized the matchmaker by his tight coat and shook him frenziedly.

"Please," sighed Salzman. *"Please."*

Leo ashamedly let him go. "Tell me who she is," he begged. "It's very important for me to know."

"She is not for you. She is a wild one — wild, without shame. This is not a bride for a rabbi."

"What do you mean wild?"

"Like an animal. Like a dog. For her to be poor was a sin. This is why to me she is dead now."

"In God's name, what do you mean?"

"Her I can't introduce to you," Salzman cried.

"Why are you so excited?"

"Why," he asks," Salzman said, bursting into tears. "This is my baby, my Stella, she should burn in hell."

Leo hurried up to bed and hid under the covers. Under the covers he thought his life through. Although he soon fell asleep he could not sleep her out of his mind. He woke, beating his breast. Though he prayed to be rid of her, his prayers went unanswered. Through days of torment he endlessly struggled not to love her; fearing success, he escaped it. He then concluded to convert her to goodness, himself to God. The idea alternately nauseated and exalted him.

He perhaps did not know that he had come to a final decision until he encountered Salzman in a Broadway cafeteria. He was sitting alone at a rear table, sucking the bony remains of a fish. The marriage broker appeared haggard, and transparent to the point of vanishing.

Salzman looked up at first without recognizing him. Leo had grown a pointed beard and his eyes were weighted with wisdom.

"Salzman," he said, "love has at last come to my heart."

"Who can love from a picture?" mocked the marriage broker.

"It is not impossible."

"If you can love her, then you can love anybody. Let me show you some new clients that they just sent me their photographs. One is a little doll."

"Just her I want," Leo murmured.

"Don't be a fool, doctor. Don't bother with her."

"Put me in touch with her, Salzman," Leo said humbly. "Perhaps I can be of service."

Salzman had stopped eating and Leo understood with emotion that it was now arranged.

Leaving the cafeteria, he was, however, afflicted by a tormenting suspicion that Salzman had planned it all to happen this way.

Leo was informed by letter that she would meet him on a certain corner, and she was there one spring night, waiting under a street lamp. He appeared, carrying a small bouquet of violets and rosebuds. Stella stood by the lamp post, smoking. She wore white with red shoes, which fitted his expectations, although in a troubled moment he had imagined the dress red, and only the shoes white. She waited uneasily and shyly. From afar he saw that her eyes — clearly her father's — were filled with desperate innocence. He pictured, in her, his own redemption. Violins and lit candles revolved in the sky. Leo ran forward with flowers outthrust.

Around the corner, Salzman, leaning against a wall, chanted prayers for the dead.

Exercises

1. Review the major action of the story as it affects both Leo and Salzman.

2. For what is Leo searching early in the story? How does his search change?

3. What happens in the meeting between Leo and Lily Hirschorn? What does this crisis reveal about Leo?

4. Cite two or three complications that temporarily restrain Leo's progress.

5. At what exact point in the story is the obstacle removed, thereby allowing Leo to gain his prize? Specifically, what does he achieve?

6. What do you think is the point of the story?

7. How does the concluding scene contribute to a fuller understanding of the story?

Topics for Writing

1. Draw a diagram that illustrates the plot line (see the beginning of this chapter), and explain each point in detail.

2. Describe the nature of Leo's quest, and how it changes and develops.

3. Using several important events in the plot, explain how each grows logically from something else and works with other elements to achieve artistic unity.

4. Comment on Salzman as both saint and sinner.

Selected Bibliography Bernard Malamud

Alter, Robert. "Bernard Malamud: Jewishness as Metaphor." In *After The Tradition: Essays on Modern Jewish Writing*. New York: Dutton, 1969, pp. 116–130.

Bellman, Samuel Irving. "Women, Children, and Idiots First: The Transformation Psychology of Bernard Malamud." *Critique,* 7 (Winter 1964–1965), 123–138.

Bluefarb, Sam. "Bernard Malamud: The Scope of Caricature." *English Journal,* 53 (May 1964), 319–326, 335.

Friedman, Alan Warren. "Bernard Malamud: The Hero as Schnook." *Southern Review,* n.s. 4 (October 1968), 927–944.

Reynolds, Richard. " 'The Magic Barrel': Pinye Salzman's Kaddish." *Studies in Short Fiction* 10 (1973), 100–102.

Richman, Sidney. *Bernard Malamud.* New York: Twayne, 1966.

Rovit, Earl H. "Bernard Malamud and the Jewish Literary Tradition." *Critique,* 3 (Winter–Spring, 1960), 3–10.

Solotaroff, Theodore. "Bernard Malamud's Fiction: The Old Life and the New." *Commentary,* 33 (March 1962), 197–204.

Storey, Michael L., "Pinye Salzman, Pan, and 'The Magic Barrel.' " *Studies in Short Fiction,* 18, No. 2 (Spring 1981), 180–183.

Weiss, Samuel. "Passion and Purgation in Bernard Malamud." *University of Wisconsin Review,* 2, no. 1 (1966), 93–99.

Edith Wharton (1862–1937)

Roman Fever

From the table at which they had been lunching two American ladies of ripe but well-cared-for middle age moved across the lofty terrace of the Roman restaurant and, leaning on its parapet, looked first at each other, and then down on the outspread glories of the Palatine and the Forum,[1] with the same expression of vague but benevolent approval.

As they leaned there a girlish voice echoed up gaily from the stairs leading to the court below. "Well, come along, then," it cried, not to them but to an invisible companion, "and let's leave the young things to their knitting"; and a voice as fresh laughed back: "Oh, look here, Babs, not actually *knitting* — " "Well, I mean figuratively," rejoined the first. "After all, we haven't left our poor parents much else to do . . ." and at that point the turn of the stairs engulfed the dialogue.

The two ladies looked at each other again, this time with a tinge of smiling embarrassment, and the smaller and paler one shook her head and coloured slightly.

"Barbara!" she murmured, sending an unheard rébuke after the mocking voice in the stairway.

The other lady, who was fuller, and higher in colour, with a small determined nose supported by vigorous black eyebrows, gave a good-humoured laugh. "That's what our daughters think of us!"

Her companion replied by a deprecating gesture. "Not of us individually.

1. Palatine . . . Forum: Palace of Roman caesars and center of government.

We must remember that. It's just the collective modern idea of Mothers. And you see — " Half guiltily she drew from her handsomely mounted black hand-bag a twist of crimson silk run through by two fine knitting needles. "One never knows," she murmured. "The new system has certainly given us a good deal of time to kill; and sometimes I get tired just looking — even at this." Her gesture was now addressed to the stupendous scene at their feet.

The dark lady laughed again, and they both relapsed upon the view, con-templating it in silence, with a sort of diffused serenity which might have been borrowed from the spring effulgence of the Roman skies. The luncheon-hour was long past, and the two had their end of the vast terrace to themselves. At this opposite extremity a few groups, detained by a lingering look at the out-spread city, were gathering up guide-books and fumbling for tips. The last of them scattered, and the two ladies were alone on the air-washed height.

"Well, I don't see why we shouldn't just stay here," said Mrs. Slade, the lady of the high colour and energetic brows. Two derelict basket-chairs stood near, and she pushed them into the angle of the parapet, and settled herself in one, her gaze upon the Palatine. "After all, it's still the most beautiful view in the world."

"It always will be, to me," assented her friend Mrs. Ansley, with so slight a stress on the "me" that Mrs. Slade, though she noticed it, wondered if it were not merely accidental, like the random underlinings of old-fashioned letter-writers.

"Grace Ansley was always old-fashioned," she thought; and added aloud, with a retrospective smile: "It's a view we've both been familiar with for a good many years. When we first met here we were younger than our girls are now. You remember?"

"Oh, yes, I remember," murmured Mrs. Ansley, with the same undefinable stress. — "There's that head-waiter wondering," she interpolated. She was evi-dently far less sure than her companion of herself and of her rights in the world.

"I'll cure him of wondering," said Mrs. Slade, stretching her hand toward a bag as discreetly opulent-looking as Mrs. Ansley's. Signing to the head-waiter, she explained that she and her friend were old lovers of Rome, and would like to spend the end of the afternoon looking down on the view — that is, if it did not disturb the service? The head-waiter, bowing over her gratuity, assured her that the ladies were most welcome, and would be still more so if they would condescend to remain for dinner. A full moon night, they would remember. . . .

Mrs. Slade's black brows drew together, as though references to the moon were out-of-place and even unwelcome. But she smiled away her frown as the head-waiter retreated. "Well, why not? We might do worse. There's no know-ing, I suppose, when the girls will be back. Do you even know back from *where?* I don't!"

Mrs. Ansley again coloured slightly. "I think those young Italian aviators we met at the Embassy invited them to fly to Tarquinia[2] for tea. I suppose they'll want to wait and fly back by moonlight."

"Moonlight — moonlight! What a part it still plays. Do you suppose they're as sentimental as we were?"

"I've come to the conclusion that I don't in the least know what they are," said Mrs. Ansley. "And perhaps we didn't know much more about each other."

2. Tarquinia: Town in central Italy.

"No; perhaps we didn't."

Her friend gave her a shy glance. "I never should have supposed you were sentimental, Alida."

"Well, perhaps I wasn't." Mrs. Slade drew her lids together in retrospect; and for a few moments the two ladies, who had been intimate since childhood, reflected how little they knew each other. Each one, of course, had a label ready to attach to the other's name; Mrs. Delphin Slade, for instance, would have told herself, or any one who asked her, that Mrs. Horace Ansley, twenty-five years ago, had been exquisitely lovely — no, you wouldn't believe it, would you? . . . though, of course, still charming, distinguished . . . Well, as a girl she had been exquisite; far more beautiful than her daughter Barbara, though certainly Babs, according to the new standards at any rate, was more effective — had more edge, as they say. Funny where she got it, with those two nullities as parents. Yes; Horace Ansley was — well, just the duplicate of his wife. Museum specimens of old New York. Good-looking, irreproachable, exemplary. Mrs. Slade and Mrs. Ansley had lived opposite each other — actually as well as figuratively — for years. When the drawing-room curtains in No. 20 East 73rd Street were renewed, No. 23, across the way, was always aware of it. And of all the movings, buyings, travels, anniversaries, illnesses — the tame chronicle of an estimable pair. Little of it escaped Mrs. Slade. But she had grown bored with it by the time her husband made his big *coup* in Wall Street, and when they bought in upper Park Avenue had already begun to think: "I'd rather live opposite a speak-easy for a change; at least one might see it raided." The idea of seeing Grace raided was so amusing that (before the move) she launched it at a woman's lunch. It made a hit, and went the rounds — she sometimes wondered if it had crossed the street, and reached Mrs. Ansley. She hoped not, but didn't much mind. Those were the days when respectability was at a discount, and it did the irreproachable no harm to laugh at them a little.

A few years later, and not many months apart, both ladies lost their husbands. There was an appropriate exchange of wreaths and condolences, and a brief renewal of intimacy in the half-shadow of their mourning; and now, after another interval, they had run across each other in Rome, at the same hotel, each of them the modest appendage of a salient daughter. The similarity of their lot had again drawn them together, lending itself to mild jokes, and the mutual confession that, if in old days it must have been tiring to "keep up" with daughters, it was now, at times, a little dull not to.

No doubt, Mrs. Slade reflected, she felt her unemployment more than poor Grace ever would. It was a big drop from being the wife of Delphin Slade to being his widow. She had always regarded herself (with a certain conjugal pride) as his equal in social gifts, as contributing her full share to the making of the exceptional couple they were: but the difference after his death was irremediable. As the wife of the famous corporation lawyer, always with an international case or two on hand, every day brought its exciting and unexpected obligation: the impromptu entertaining of eminent colleagues from abroad, the hurried dashes on legal business to London, Paris or Rome, where the entertaining was so handsomely reciprocated; the amusement of hearing in her wake: "What, that handsome woman with the good clothes and eyes is Mrs. Slade — *the* Slade's wife? Really? Generally the wives of celebrities are such frumps."

Yes; being *the* Slade's widow was a dullish business after that. In living up to such a husband all her faculties had been engaged; now she had only her daughter to live up to, for the son who seemed to have inherited his father's gifts had died suddenly in boyhood. She had fought through that agony because her husband was there, to be helped and to help; now, after the father's death, the thought of the boy had become unbearable. There was nothing left but to mother her daughter; and dear Jenny was such a perfect daughter that she needed no excessive mothering. "Now with Babs Ansley I don't know that I *should* be so quiet," Mrs. Slade sometimes half-enviously reflected; but Jenny, who was younger than her brilliant friend, was that rare accident, an extremely pretty girl who somehow made youth and prettiness seem as safe as their absence. It was all perplexing — and to Mrs. Slade a little boring. She wished that Jenny would fall in love — with the wrong man, even; that she might have to be watched, out-maneuvered, rescued. And instead, it was Jenny who watched her mother, kept her out of draughts, made sure that she had taken her tonic . . .

Mrs. Ansley was much less articulate than her friend, and her mental portrait of Mrs. Slade was slighter, and drawn with fainter touches. "Alida Slade's awfully brilliant; but not as brilliant as she thinks," would have summed it up; though she would have added, for the enlightenment of strangers, that Mrs. Slade had been an extremely dashing girl; much more so than her daughter, who was pretty, of course, and clever in a way, but had none of her mother's — well, "vividness," some one had once called it. Mrs. Ansley would take up current words like this, and cite them in quotation marks, as unheard-of audacities. No; Jenny was not like her mother. Sometimes Mrs. Ansley thought Alida Slade was disappointed; on the whole she had had a sad life. Full of failures and mistakes; Mrs. Ansley had always been rather sorry for her . . .

So these two ladies visualized each other, each through the wrong end of her little telescope.

2.

For a long time they continued to sit side by side without speaking. It seemed as though, to both, there was a relief in laying down their somewhat futile activities in the presence of the vast Memento Mori[3] which faced them. Mrs. Slade sat quite still, her eyes fixed on the golden slope of the Palace of the Caesars, and after a while Mrs. Ansley ceased to fidget with her bag, and she too sank into meditation. Like many intimate friends, the two ladies had never before had occasion to be silent together, and Mrs. Ansley was slightly embarrassed by what seemed, after so many years, a new stage in their intimacy, and one with which she did not yet know how to deal.

Suddenly the air was full of that deep clangour of bells which periodically covers Rome with a roof of silver. Mrs. Slade glanced at her wrist-watch. "Five o'clock already," she said, as though surprised.

Mrs. Ansley suggested interrogatively: "There's bridge at the Embassy at five." For a long time Mrs. Slade did not answer. She appeared to be lost in contemplation, and Mrs. Ansley thought the remark had escaped her. But after a while she said, as if speaking out of a dream: "Bridge, did you say? Not unless you want to . . . But I don't think I will, you know."

"Oh, no," Mrs. Ansley hastened to assure her. "I don't care to at all. It's

3. Memento Mori: Object or figure of an object, usually emblematic, used as a memento of death.

so lovely here; and so full of old memories, as you say." She settled herself in her chair, and almost furtively drew forth her knitting. Mrs. Slade took sideway note of this activity, but her own beautifully cared-for hands remained motionless on her knee.

"I was just thinking," she said slowly, "what different things Rome stands for to each generation of travellers. To our grandmothers, Roman fever; to our mothers, sentimental dangers — how we used to be guarded! — to our daughters, no more dangers than the middle of Main Street. They don't know it — but how much they're missing!"

The long golden light was beginning to pale, and Mrs. Ansley lifted her knitting a little closer to her eyes. "Yes; how we were guarded!"

"I always used to think," Mrs. Slade continued, "that our mothers had a much more difficult job than our grandmothers. When Roman fever stalked the streets it must have been comparatively easy to gather in the girls at the danger hour; but when you and I were young, with such beauty calling us, and the spice of disobedience thrown in, and no worse risk than catching cold during the cool hour after sunset, the mothers used to be put to it to keep us in — didn't they?"

She turned again toward Mrs. Ansley, but the latter had reached a delicate point in her knitting. "One, two, three — slip two; yes, they must have been," she assented, without looking up.

Mrs. Slade's eyes rested on her with a deepened attention. "She can knit — in the face of *this!* How like her . . ."

Mrs. Slade leaned back, brooding, her eyes ranging from the ruins which faced her to the long green hollow of the Forum, the fading glow of the church fronts beyond it, and the outlying immensity of the Colosseum. Suddenly she thought: "It's all very well to say that our girls have done away with sentiment and moonlight. But if Babs Ansley isn't out to catch that young aviator — the one who's a Marchese — then I don't know anything. And Jenny has no chance beside her. I know that too. I wonder if that's why Grace Ansley likes the two girls to go everywhere together? My poor Jenny as a foil — !" Mrs. Slade gave a hardly audible laugh, and at the sound Mrs. Ansley dropped her knitting.

"Yes — ?"

"I — oh, nothing. I was only thinking how your Babs carries everything before her. That Campolieri boy is one of the best matches in Rome. Don't look so innocent, my dear — you know he is. And I was wondering, ever so respectfully, you understand . . . wondering how two such exemplary characters as you and Horace had managed to produce anything quite so dynamic." Mrs. Slade laughed again, with a touch of asperity.

Mrs. Ansley's hands lay inert across her needles. She looked straight out at the great accumulated wreckage of passion and splendour at her feet. But her small profile was almost expressionless. At length she said: "I think you overrate Babs, my dear."

Mrs. Slade's tone grew easier. "No; I don't. I appreciate her. And perhaps envy you. Oh, my girl's perfect; if I were a chronic invalid I'd — well, I think I'd rather be in Jenny's hands. There must be times . . . but there! I always wanted a brilliant daughter . . . and never quite understood why I got an angel instead."

Mrs. Ansley echoed her laugh in a faint murmur. "Babs is an angel too."

"Of course — of course! But she's got rainbow wings. Well, they're wandering by the sea with their young men; and here we sit . . . and it all brings back the past a little too acutely."

Mrs. Ansley had resumed her knitting. One might almost have imagined (if one had known her less well, Mrs. Slade reflected) that, for her also, too many memories rose from the lengthening shadows of those august ruins. But no; she was simply absorbed in her work. What was there for her to worry about? She knew that Babs would almost certainly come back engaged to the extremely eligible Campolieri. "And she'll sell the New York house, and settle down near them in Rome, and never be in their way . . . she's much too tactful. But she'll have an excellent cook, and just the right people in for bridge and cocktails . . . and a perfectly peaceful old age among her grandchildren."

Mrs. Slade broke off this prophetic flight with a recoil of self-disgust. There was no one of whom she had less right to think unkindly than of Grace Ansley. Would she never cure herself of envying her? Perhaps she had begun too long ago.

She stood up and leaned against the parapet, filling her troubled eyes with the tranquilizing magic of the hour. But instead of tranquilizing her the sight seemed to increase her exasperation. Her gaze turned toward the Colosseum. Already its golden flank was drowned in purple shadow, and above it the sky curved crystal clear, without light or colour. It was the moment when afternoon and evening hang balanced in mid-heaven.

Mrs. Slade turned back and laid her hand on her friend's arm. The gesture was so abrupt that Mrs. Ansley looked up, startled.

"The sun's set. You're not afraid, my dear?"

"Afraid — ?"

"Of Roman fever or pneumonia? I remember how ill you were that winter. As a girl you had a very delicate throat, hadn't you?"

"Oh, we're all right up here. Down below, in the Forum, it does get deathly cold, all of a sudden . . . but not here."

"Ah, of course you know because you had to be so careful." Mrs. Slade turned back to the parapet. She thought: "I must make one more effort not to hate her." Aloud she said: "Whenever I look at the Forum from up here, I remember that story about a great-aunt of yours, wasn't she? A dreadfully wicked great-aunt?"

"Oh, yes; Great-aunt Harriet. The one who was supposed to have sent her young sister out to the Forum after sunset to gather a night-blooming flower for her album. All our great-aunts and grandmothers used to have albums of dried flowers."

Mrs. Slade nodded. "But she really sent her because they were in love with the same man — "

"Well, that was the family tradition. They said Aunt Harriet confessed it years afterward. At any rate, the poor little sister caught the fever and died. Mother used to frighten us with the story when we were children."

"And you frightened *me* with it, that winter when you and I were here as girls. The winter I was engaged to Delphin."

Mrs. Ansley gave a faint laugh. "Oh, did I? Really frightened you? I don't believe you're easily frightened."

"Not often; but I was then. I was easily frightened because I was too happy. I wonder if you know what that means?"

"I — yes . . ." Mrs. Ansley faltered.

"Well, I suppose that was why the story of your wicked aunt made such an impression on me. And I thought: 'There's no more Roman fever, but the Forum is deathly cold after sunset — especially after a hot day. And the Colosseum's even colder and damper'."

"The Colosseum — ?"

"Yes. It wasn't easy to get in, after the gates were locked for the night. Far from easy. Still, in those days it could be managed; it was managed, often. Lovers met there who couldn't meet elsewhere. You knew that?"

"I — I daresay. I don't remember."

"You don't remember? You don't remember going to visit some ruins or other one evening, just after dark, and catching a bad chill? You were supposed to have gone to see the moon rise. People always said that expedition was what caused your illness."

There was a moment's silence; then Mrs. Ansley rejoined: "Did they? It was all so long ago."

"Yes. And you got well again — so it didn't matter. But I suppose it struck your friends — the reason given for your illness, I mean — because everybody knew you were so prudent on account of your throat, and your mother took such care of you . . . You *had* been out late sightseeing, hadn't you, that night?"

"Perhaps I had. The most prudent girls aren't always prudent. What made you think of it now?"

Mrs. Slade seemed to have no answer ready. But after a moment she broke out: "Because I simply can't bear it any longer — !"

Mrs. Ansley lifted her head quickly. Her eyes were wide and very pale. "Can't bear what?"

"Why — your not knowing that I've always known why you went."

"Why I went — ?"

"Yes. You think I'm bluffing, don't you? Well, you went to meet the man I was engaged to — and I can repeat every word of the letter that took you there."

While Mrs. Slade spoke Mrs. Ansley had risen unsteadily to her feet. Her bag, her knitting and gloves, slid in a panic-stricken heap to the ground. She looked at Mrs. Slade as though she were looking at a ghost.

"No, no — I don't," she faltered out.

"Why not? Listen, if you don't believe me. 'My one darling, things can't go on like this. I must see you alone. Come to the Colosseum immediately after dark tomorrow. There will be somebody to let you in. No one whom you need fear will suspect' — but perhaps you've forgotten what the letter said?"

Mrs. Ansley met the challenge with an unexpected composure. Steadying herself against the chair she looked at her friend, and replied: "No, I know it by heart too."

"And the signature? 'Only *your* D.S.' Was that it? I'm right, am I? That was the letter that took you out that evening after dark?"

Mrs. Ansley was still looking at her. It seemed to Mrs. Slade that a slow struggle was going on behind the voluntarily controlled mask of her small quiet face. "I shouldn't have thought she had herself so well in hand," Mrs. Slade reflected, almost resentfully. But at this moment Mrs. Ansley spoke. "I don't know how you knew. I burnt that letter at once."

"Yes; you would, naturally — you're so prudent!" The sneer was open now.

"And if you burnt the letter you're wondering how on earth I know what was in it. That's it, isn't it?"

Mrs. Slade waited, but Mrs. Ansley did not speak.

"Well, my dear, I know what was in that letter because I wrote it!"

"You wrote it?"

"Yes."

The two women stood for a minute staring at each other in the last golden light. Then Mrs. Ansley dropped back into her chair. "Oh," she murmured, and covered her face with her hands.

Mrs. Slade waited nervously for another word or movement. None came, and at length she broke out: "I horrify you."

Mrs. Ansley's hands dropped to her knee. The face they uncovered was streaked with tears. "I wasn't thinking of you. I was thinking — it was the only letter I ever had from him!"

"And I wrote it. Yes; I wrote it! But I was the girl he was engaged to. Did you happen to remember that?"

Mrs. Ansley's head dropped again. "I'm not trying to excuse myself . . . I remembered . . ."

"And still you went?"

"Still I went."

Mrs. Slade stood looking down on the small bowed figure at her side. The flame of her wrath had already sunk, and she wondered why she had ever thought there would be any satisfaction in inflicting so purposeless a wound on her friend. But she had to justify herself.

"You do understand? I found out — and I hated you, hated you. I knew you were in love with Delphin — and I was afraid; afraid of you, of your quiet ways, your sweetness . . . your . . . well, I wanted you out of the way, that's all. Just for a few weeks; just till I was sure of him. So in a blind fury I wrote that letter . . . I don't know why I'm telling you now."

"I suppose," said Mrs. Ansley slowly, "it's because you've always gone on hating me."

"Perhaps. Or because I wanted to get the whole thing off my mind." She paused. "I'm glad you destroyed the letter. Of course I never thought you'd die."

Mrs. Ansley relapsed into silence, and Mrs. Slade, leaning above her, was conscious of a strange sense of isolation, of being cut off from the warm current of human communion. "You think me a monster!"

"I don't know . . . It was the only letter I had, and you say he didn't write it?"

"Ah, how you care for him still!"

"I cared for that memory," said Mrs. Ansley.

Mrs. Slade continued to look down on her. She seemed physically reduced by the blow — as if, when she got up, the wind might scatter her like a puff of dust. Mrs. Slade's jealousy suddenly leapt up again at the sight. All these years the woman had been living on that letter. How she must have loved him, to treasure the mere memory of its ashes! The letter of the man her friend was engaged to. Wasn't it she who was the monster?

"You tried your best to get him away from me, didn't you? But you failed; and I kept him. That's all."

"Yes. That's all."

"I wish now I hadn't told you. I'd no idea you'd feel about it as you do; I thought you'd be amused. It all happened so long ago, as you say; and you must do me the justice to remember that I had no reason to think you'd ever taken it seriously. How could I, when you were married to Horace Ansley two months afterward? As soon as you could get out of bed your mother rushed you off to Florence and married you. People were rather surprised — they wondered at its being done so quickly; but I thought I knew. I had an idea you did it out of *pique* — to be able to say you'd got ahead of Delphin and me. Girls have such silly reasons for doing the most serious things. And your marrying so soon convinced me that you'd never really cared."

"Yes, I suppose it would," Mrs. Ansley assented.

The clear heaven overhead was emptied of all its gold. Dusk spread over it, abruptly darkening the Seven Hills. Here and there lights began to twinkle through the foliage at their feet. Steps were coming and going on the deserted terrace — waiters looking out of the doorway at the head of the stairs, then reappearing with trays and napkins and flasks of wine. Tables were moved, chairs straightened. A feeble string of electric lights flickered out. Some vases of faded flowers were carried away, and brought back replenished. A stout lady in a dust-coat suddenly appeared, asking in broken Italian if any one had seen the elastic band which held together her tattered Baedeker. She poked with her stick under the table at which she had lunched, the waiters assisting.

The corner where Mrs. Slade and Mrs. Ansley sat was still shadowy and deserted. For a long time neither of them spoke. At length Mrs. Slade began again: "I suppose I did it as a sort of joke — "

"A joke?"

"Well, girls are ferocious sometimes, you know. Girls in love especially. And I remember laughing to myself all that evening at the idea that you were waiting around there in the dark, dodging out of sight, listening for every sound, trying to get in — . Of course I was upset when I heard you were so ill afterward."

Mrs. Ansley had not moved for a long time. But now she turned slowly toward her companion. "But I didn't wait. He'd arranged everything. He was there. We were let in at once," she said.

Mrs. Slade sprang up from her leaning position. "Delphin there? They let you in? — Ah, now you're lying!" she burst out with violence.

Mrs. Ansley's voice grew clearer, and full of surprise. "But of course he was there. Naturally he came — "

"Came? How did he know he'd find you there? You must be raving!"

Mrs. Ansley hesitated, as though reflecting. "But I answered the letter. I told him I'd be there. So he came."

Mrs. Slade flung her hands up to her face. "Oh, God — you answered! I never thought of your answering . . ."

"It's odd you never thought of it, if you wrote the letter."

"Yes. I was blind with rage."

Mrs. Ansley rose, and drew her fur scarf about her. "It is cold here. We'd better go . . . I'm sorry for you," she said, as she clasped the fur about her throat.

The unexpected words sent a pang through Mrs. Slade. "Yes; we'd better go." She gathered up her bag and cloak. "I don't know why you should be sorry for me," she muttered.

Mrs. Ansley stood looking away from her toward the dusky secret mass of the Colosseum. "Well — because I didn't have to wait that night."

Mrs. Slade gave an unquiet laugh. "Yes; I was beaten there. But I oughtn't to begrudge it to you, I suppose. At the end of all these years. After all, I had everything; I had him for twenty-five years. And you had nothing but that one letter that he didn't write."

Mrs. Ansley was again silent. At length she turned toward the door of the terrace. She took a step, and turned back, facing her companion.

"I had Barbara," she said, and began to move ahead of Mrs. Slade toward the stairway.

Exercises

1. Compare and contrast the characters of Mrs. Slade and Mrs. Ansley.

2. Which of the women controls or forces the important action? Who opposes whom? Who wins, and what is the price?

3. Give examples of Mrs. Slade's attacks on Mrs. Ansley. What motivates Mrs. Slade?

4. Account for the reader's sympathy for Mrs. Ansley.

5. Discuss the role of Great-aunt Harriet.

6. How much action and emotional intensity does "Roman Fever" contain? Is the story effective? Why or why not?

7. What is the function of the last sentence? Why does the author have Mrs. Ansley "move ahead" of Mrs. Slade?

8. What truths about life and human relationships are expressed in the story?

Topics for Writing

1. Examine the plot for revelation of character and meaning.

2. Describe the author's central purpose and evaluate how well it has been achieved.

3. Compare and contrast the values associated with the upper levels of society as they are presented in this story and in "Babylon Revisited" (Chapter 3).

4. Plausibility is more difficult to achieve in a story that depends chiefly on plot. Agree or disagree, supporting your comments with references to the stories you have read so far.

Selected Bibliography   Edith Wharton

McDowell, M. B. "Viewing the Custom of Her Country: Edith Wharton's Feminism." *Contemporary Literature,* 15 (August 1974), 521–538.
Rehder, Jessie, ed. *The Story at Work.* New York: Odyssey, 1963.

Sasaki, Miyoko. "The Dance of Death: A Study of Edith Wharton's Short
Stories." *Studies in English Literature,* 51 (1974), 67–90.
Satin, Joseph, ed. *Reading Prose Fiction.* Boston: Houghton Mifflin, 1964.

Guy deMaupassant *(1850–1893)*

The Necklace

Translated by Marjorie Laurie

She was one of those pretty and charming girls who are sometimes, as if by
a mistake of destiny, born in a family of clerks. She had no dowry, no expectations, no means of being known, understood, loved, wedded by any rich and
distinguished man; and she let herself be married to a little clerk at the Ministry
of Public Instruction.

She dressed plainly because she could not dress well, but she was as unhappy
as though she had really fallen from her proper station, since with women there
is neither caste nor rank: and beauty, grace, and charm act instead of family and
birth. Natural fineness, instinct for what is elegant, suppleness of wit, are the
sole hierarchy, and make from women of the people the equals of the very
greatest ladies.

She suffered ceaselessly, feeling herself born for all the delicacies and all the
luxuries. She suffered from the poverty of her dwelling, from the wretched look
of the walls, from the worn-out chairs, from the ugliness of the curtains. All
those things, of which another woman of her rank would never even have been
conscious, tortured her and made her angry. The sight of the little Breton peasant who did her humble housework aroused in her regrets which were despairing,
and distracted dreams. She thought of the silent antechambers hung with Oriental tapestry, lit by tall bronze candelabra, and of the two great footmen in
knee breeches who sleep in the big armchairs, made drowsy by the heavy
warmth of the hot-air stove. She thought of the long *salons* fitted up with ancient
silk, of the delicate furniture carrying priceless curiosities, and of the coquettish
perfumed boudoirs made for talks at five o'clock with intimate friends, with
men famous and sought after, whom all women envy and whose attention they
all desire.

When she sat down to dinner, before the round table covered with a table-
cloth three days old, opposite her husband, who uncovered the soup tureen and
declared with an enchanted air, "Ah, the good *pot-au-feu!* I don't know anything better than that," she thought of dainty dinners, of shining silverware, of
tapestry which peopled the walls with ancient personages and with strange birds
flying in the midst of a fairy forest; and she thought of delicious dishes served
on marvelous plates, and of the whispered gallantries which you listen to with a
sphinxlike smile, while you are eating the pink flesh of a trout or the wings of a
quail.

She had no dresses, no jewels, nothing. And she loved nothing but that; she
felt made for that. She would so have liked to please, to be envied, to be charming, to be sought after.

She had a friend, a former schoolmate at the convent, who was rich, and whom she did not like to go and see any more, because she suffered so much when she came back.

But one evening, her husband returned home with a triumphant air, and holding a large envelope in his hand.

"There," said he. "Here is something for you."

She tore the paper sharply, and drew out a printed card which bore these words:

"The Minister of Public Instruction and Mme. Georges Ramponneau request the honor of M. and Mme. Loisel's company at the palace of the Ministry on Monday evening, January eighteenth."

Instead of being delighted, as her husband hoped, she threw the invitation on the table with disdain, murmuring:

"What do you want me to do with that?"

"But, my dear, I thought you would be glad. You never go out, and this is such a fine opportunity. I had awful trouble to get it. Everyone wants to go; it is very select, and they are not giving many invitations to clerks. The whole official world will be there."

She looked at him with an irritated glance, and said, impatiently:

"And what do you want me to put on my back?"

He had not thought of that; he stammered:

"Why, the dress you go to the theater in. It looks very well, to me."

He stopped, distracted, seeing his wife was crying. Two great tears descended slowly from the corners of her eyes toward the corners of her mouth. He stuttered:

"What's the matter? What's the matter?"

But, by violent effort, she had conquered her grief, and she replied, with a calm voice, while she wiped her wet cheeks:

"Nothing. Only I have no dress and therefore I can't go to this ball. Give your card to some colleague whose wife is better equipped than I."

He was in despair. He resumed:

"Come, let us see, Mathilde. How much would it cost, a suitable dress, which you could use on other occasions, something very simple?"

She reflected several seconds, making her calculations and wondering also what sum she could ask without drawing on herself an immediate refusal and a frightened exclamation from the economical clerk.

Finally, she replied, hesitatingly:

"I don't know exactly, but I think I could manage it with four hundred francs."

He had grown a little pale, because he was laying aside just that amount to buy a gun and treat himself to a little shooting next summer on the plain of Nanterre, with several friends who went to shoot larks down there, of a Sunday.

But he said:

"All right. I will give you four hundred francs. And try to have a pretty dress."

The day of the ball drew near, and Mme. Loisel seemed sad, uneasy, anxious. Her dress was ready, however. Her husband said to her one evening:

"What is the matter? Come, you've been so queer these last three days."

And she answered:

"It annoys me not to have a single jewel, not a single stone, nothing to put on. I shall look like distress. I should almost rather not go at all."

He resumed:

"You might wear natural flowers. It's very stylish at this time of the year. For ten francs you can get two or three magnificent roses."

She was not convinced.

"No; there's nothing more humiliating than to look poor among other women who are rich."

But her husband cried:

"How stupid you are! Go look up your friend Mme. Forestier, and ask her to lend you some jewels. You're quite thick enough with her to do that."

She uttered a cry of joy:

"It's true. I never thought of it."

The next day she went to her friend and told her of her distress.

Mme. Forestier went to a wardrobe with a glass door, took out a large jewel-box, brought it back, opened it, and said to Mme. Loisel:

"Choose, my dear."

She saw first of all some bracelets, then a pearl necklace, then a Venetian cross, gold and precious stones of admirable workmanship. She tried on the ornaments before the glass, hesitated, could not make up her mind to part with them, to give them back. She kept asking:

"Haven't you any more?"

"Why, yes. Look. I don't know what you like."

All of a sudden, she discovered, in a black satin box, a superb necklace of diamonds, and her heart began to beat with an immoderate desire. Her hands trembled as she took it. She fastened it around her throat, outside her high-necked dress, and remained lost in ecstasy at the sight of herself.

Then she asked, hesitating, filled with anguish:

"Can you lend me that, only that?"

"Why, yes, certainly."

She sprang upon the neck of her friend, kissed her passionately, then fled with her treasure.

The day of the ball arrived. Mme. Loisel made a great success. She was prettier than them all, elegant, gracious, smiling, and crazy with joy. All the men looked at her, asked her name, endeavored to be introduced. All the attachés of the Cabinet wanted to waltz with her. She was remarked by the minister himself.

She danced with intoxication, with passion, made drunk by pleasure, forgetting all, in the triumph of her beauty, in the glory of her success, in a sort of cloud of happiness composed of all this homage, of all this admiration, of all these awakened desires, and of that sense of complete victory which is so sweet to a woman's heart.

She went away about four o'clock in the morning. Her husband had been sleeping since midnight, in a little deserted anteroom, with three other gentlemen whose wives were having a very good time. He threw over her shoulders the wraps which he had brought, modest wraps of common life, whose poverty contrasted with the elegance of the ball dress. She felt this, and wanted to escape so as not to be remarked by the other women, who were enveloping themselves in costly furs.

Loisel held her back.

"Wait a bit. You will catch cold outside. I will go and call a cab."

But she did not listen to him, and rapidly descended the stairs. When they were in the street they did not find a carriage; and they began to look for one, shouting after the cabmen whom they saw passing by at a distance.

They went down toward the Seine, in despair, shivering with cold. At last they found on the quay one of those ancient noctambulant coupés which, exactly as if they were ashamed to show their misery during the day, are never seen round Paris until after nightfall.

It took them to the door in the Rue des Martyrs, and once more, sadly, they climbed up homeward. All was ended, for her. And as to him, he reflected that he must be at the Ministry at ten o'clock.

She removed the wraps which covered her shoulders, before the glass, so as once more to see herself in all her glory. But suddenly she uttered a cry. She no longer had the necklace around her neck!

Her husband, already half undressed, demanded:

"What is the matter with you?"

She turned madly towards him:

"I have — I have — I've lost Mme. Forestier's necklace."

He stood up, distracted.

"What! — how? — impossible!"

And they looked in the folds of her dress, in the folds of her cloak, in her pockets, everywhere. They did not find it.

He asked:

"You're sure you had it on when you left the ball?"

"Yes, I felt it in the vestibule of the palace."

"But if you had lost it in the street we should have heard it fall. It must be in the cab."

"Yes. Probably. Did you take his number?"

"No. And you, didn't you notice it?"

"No."

They looked, thunderstruck, at one another. At last Loisel put on his clothes.

"I shall go back on foot," said he, "over the whole route which we have taken to see if I can find it."

And he went out. She sat waiting on a chair in her ball dress, without strength to go to bed, overwhelmed, without fire, without a thought.

Her husband came back about seven o'clock. He had found nothing.

He went to Police Headquarters, to the newspaper offices, to offer a reward; he went to the cab companies — everywhere, in fact, whither he was urged by the least suspicion of hope.

She waited all day, in the same condition of mad fear before this terrible calamity.

Loisel returned at night with a hollow, pale face; he had discovered nothing.

"You must write to your friend," said he, "that you have broken the clasp of her necklace and that you are having it mended. That will give us time to turn round."

She wrote at his dictation.

At the end of a week they had lost all hope.

And Loisel, who had aged five years, declared:

"We must consider how to replace that ornament."

The next day they took the box which had contained it, and they went to the jeweler whose name was found within. He consulted his books.

"It was not I, madame, who sold that necklace; I must simply have furnished the case."

Then they went from jeweler to jeweler, searching for a necklace like the other, consulting their memories, sick both of them with chagrin and anguish.

They found, in a shop at the Palais Royal, a string of diamonds which seemed to them exactly like the one they looked for. It was worth forty thousand francs. They could have it for thirty-six.

So they begged the jeweler not to sell it for three days yet. And they made a bargain that he should buy it back for thirty-four thousand francs, in case they found the other one before end of February.

Loisel possessed eighteen thousand francs which his father had left him. He would borrow the rest.

He did borrow, asking a thousand francs of one, five hundred of another, five louis here, three louis there. He gave notes, took up ruinous obligations, dealt with usurers and all the race of lenders. He compromised all the rest of his life, risked his signature without even knowing if he could meet it; and, frightened by the pains yet to come, by the black misery which was about to fall upon him, by the prospect of all the physical privation and of all the moral tortures which he was to suffer, he went to get the new necklace, putting down upon the merchant's counter thirty-six thousand francs.

When Mme. Loisel took back the necklace, Mme. Forestier said to her, with a chilly manner:

"You should have returned it sooner; I might have needed it."

She did not open the case, as her friend had so much feared. If she had detected the substitution, what would she have thought, what would she have said? Would she not have taken Mme. Loisel for a thief?

Mme. Loisel now knew the horrible existence of the needy. She took her part, moreover, all of a sudden, with heroism. That dreadful debt must be paid. She would pay it. They dismissed their servant; they changed their lodgings; they rented a garret under the roof.

She came to know what heavy housework meant and the odious cares of the kitchen. She washed the dishes, using her rosy nails on the greasy pots and pans. She washed the dirty linen, the shirts, and the dishcloths, which she dried upon a line; she carried the slops down to the street every morning, and carried up the water, stopping for breath at every landing. And, dressed like a woman of the people, she went to the fruiterer, the grocer, the butcher, her basket on her arm, bargaining, insulted, defending her miserable money sou by sou.

Each month they had to meet some notes, renew others, obtain more time.

Her husband worked in the evening making a fair copy of some tradesman's accounts, and late at night he often copied manuscript for five sous a page.

And this life lasted for ten years.

At the end of ten years, they had paid everything, everything, with the rates of usury, and the accumulations of the compound interest.

Mme. Loisel looked old now. She had become the woman of impoverished households — strong and hard and rough. With frowsy hair, skirts askew, and red hands, she talked loud while washing the floor with great swishes of water. But sometimes, when her husband was at the office, she sat down near the window, and she thought of that gay evening of long ago, of that ball where she had been so beautiful and so fêted.

What would have happened if she had not lost that necklace? Who knows?

Who knows? How life is strange and changeful! How little a thing is needed for us to be lost or to be saved!

But, one Sunday, having gone to take a walk in the Champs Elysées to refresh herself from the labor of the week, she suddenly perceived a woman who was leading a child. It was Mme. Forestier, still young, still beautiful, still charming.

Mme. Loisel felt moved. Was she going to speak to her? Yes, certainly. And now that she had paid, she was going to tell her all about it. Why not?

She went up.

"Good-day, Jeanne."

The other, astonished to be familiarly addressed by this plain goodwife, did not recognize her at all, and stammered:

"But — madam! — I do not know — You must be mistaken."

"No. I am Mathilde Loisel."

Her friend uttered a cry.

"Oh, my poor Mathilde! How you are changed!"

"Yes, I have had days hard enough, since I have seen you, days wretched enough — and that because of you!"

"Of me! How so?"

"Do you remember that diamond necklace which you lent me to wear at the ministerial ball?"

"Yes. Well?"

"Well, I lost it."

"What do you mean? You brought it back."

"I brought you back another just like it. And for this we have been ten years paying. You can understand that it was not easy for us, us who had nothing. At last it is ended, and I am very glad."

Mme. Forestier had stopped.

"You say that you bought a necklace of diamonds to replace mine?"

"Yes. You never noticed it, then! They were very like."

And she smiled with a joy which was proud and naïve at once.

Mme. Forestier, strongly moved, took her two hands.

"Oh, my poor Mathilde! Why, my necklace was paste. It was worth at most five hundred francs!"

Exercises

1. Briefly summarize the plot.

2. Middle-class values, to which Mme. Loisel subscribes, have not changed over the years. Identify these values.

3. Cite evidence from the character and actions of Mme. Loisel that makes it plausible for her to lose the necklace.

4. Is it credible that Mme. Loisel should receive an invitation from a wealthy friend? Support your answers with specific references to the story.

5. What kind of person is M. Loisel? What function does he have in the story?

6. After discovering the loss of the necklace, the Loisels consider themselves trapped. Why?

7. Compare the type of person Mme. Loisel is at the beginning of the story and the type of person she becomes by its end. How has she changed? Why?

8. Prepare an eight-point analysis of the story. (See pp. 6–9.)

9. Is the ending of the story happy or sad? Explain.

10. Consider what meaning the story would have were the last sentence deleted. What, then, does the final sentence contribute to meaning?

Topics for Writing

1. Compare and contrast the way that plot is handled in "The Necklace" and in "The Catbird Seat." Which ending is more of a surprise and what purpose does surprise serve in each story?

2. How do incidents of plot help to reveal characters in this story and in "The Magic Barrel"?

3. Let the story dictate an essay on the particular values of society found in the story.

Selected Bibliography   Guy deMaupassant

Bates, H. E. *The Modern Short Story: A Critical Survey*. London: Nelson, 1943.
Bement, Douglas. *Weaving the Short Story*. New York: Richard R. Smith, 1931.
Brooks, Cleanth, and Robert P. Warren. *Understanding Fiction*. 2nd ed. New York: Appleton-Century-Crofts, 1955.
Jaffe, Adrian, and Virgil Scott. *Studies in the Short Story*. 2nd ed. New York: Holt, Rinehart & Winston, 1960.
O'Faolain, Sean. *The Short Story*. New York: Devin-Adair, 1951.
Orvis, Mary B. *The Art of Writing Fiction*. New York: Prentice-Hall, 1948.
Steegmuller, Francis. *Maupassant: A Lion in the Path*. New York: Random House, 1949.
Sullivan, Edward D. *Maupassant: The Short Story*. Great Neck: Barron, 1962.

2. CHARACTER

Characters are people who make things happen in fiction. Although a writer may reveal one character more completely than another or designate a larger function for one than for another, we should get to know them all rather well, however significant or trivial their roles, for the study of character can both delight and enlighten us.

In a broad sense, we can readily identify two main types of characters: the **three-dimensional** and the **one-dimensional.** The first the author delineates more fully as dynamic or developing characters, and presents to us chiefly through the dramatic method. That is, the author shows us the characters talking and acting, and lets their words and actions reveal their natures and motives. The one-dimensional characters, on the other hand, are static and underdeveloped. The author simply sketches them as flat, stock, or stereotyped characters, presenting them to us either dramatically or by the summary method — that is, by telling us about them. Whether fully developed or not, however, every character is important because each performs a role in the process of depicting life and examining what it means to be human.

In short stories, the three-dimensional characters are usually the protagonist and the antagonist, or sometimes just one of them, for at best there is room for only two fully developed characters in so few pages. Short-story writers usually focus on a small segment of life and on relatively few aspects of character. Rather than telling or showing us everything there is to know about a central character, they judiciously select those details that can reveal *who* and *what* that character is, *how* that character acts, and *why* he or she acts in that particular fashion. The responsibility for sifting such details in order to arrive at a total picture rests with the reader.

Let us examine the three dimensions of a major character. First, there are **physical attributes:** young, old, short, tall, slim, obese, beautiful, handsome, big-eared, or freckled. Physical makeup can influence character in many ways. It may change attitudes, color outlook on life, deepen convictions, or create tolerance, recklessness, or superstition. The star center on the basketball team is not likely to have the same attitudes as the clumsy clod does. The young woman with a brace on her leg may develop frustrations not shared by most of her friends.

Second, a three-dimensional character possesses a **background:** parents who are poor, rich, happy, or miserable; friends, enemies; talents, skills, hobbies; habits, likes, and dislikes. A background presupposes a past. A knowledge of whether a character was reared in an orphanage or at home, slept in a crowded, bug-infested room or in the private suite of a mansion, was loved, neglected, or merely tolerated can provide clues that help us understand the character's nature and behavior and make us aware of the influences that have been shaping his or her life.

Third, a principal character has a dimension that we will call **psychology.** As used here, the term refers to the traits, emotions, and behavioral patterns that characterize a person as an individual. Impressions and influences from the past (for example, heredity and environment) make the characters what they are and determine their actions. These influences give birth to ambition in some people and kill it in others; they make one person's disposition easygoing and another's contentious; they produce introverted and extroverted personalities, beget frustrations and disappointments, and engender obsessions, neuroses, manias, and phobias.

Only as we try to understand the complex nature of a character's physiological, sociological, and psychological makeup can we expect to know why a woman shuts herself up in her house for some forty years, as happens in Faulkner's "A Rose for Emily," or why a young rabbinical student discovers his love for God only after having fallen in love with a prostitute, as we saw in Malamud's "The Magic Barrel."

The three-dimensional character is a **dynamic** or developing character; he or she is not the same person at the end of the story as at the beginning. The conflict through which the character moves brings about a lasting change in personality, basic values, or concept of human nature. In the first story in this chapter, John Steinbeck's "The Chrysanthemums," Elisa, after her experience with the peddler, has perhaps gained strength of character and can more easily accept her life with a husband who has proven insensitive to her needs. At the end of "Everything That Rises Must Converge," a story by Flannery O'Connor (also in this chapter), Julian is no longer an angry young man, confident that he has a right to treat his mother callously. The young boy in Sherwood Anderson's "I Want to Know Why" (Chapter 3) finds ugliness, prejudice, and false values in the adult world; he is growing up. And Mabel Pervin in D. H. Lawrence's "The Horse Dealer's Daughter" (also in Chapter 3) is regenerated through a baptism of love. Whatever the change — whether it is a dislodgement of settled beliefs, a discovery, a revelation, or a new awareness — a dynamic character emerges from conflict with a new set of eyes, never again to see the world as he or she once saw it.

Ordinarily, the author chooses to disclose the more important aspects of a three-dimensional character by the **dramatic method,** using action to give information and provide details. Often such action lets us deduce the reasons for the character's behavior and mental state. Thus, the artist creates a lifelike character who becomes real for us on the printed page.

As noted earlier, the author depicts one-dimensional characters — the flat, stock, or stereotyped persons — fairly simply. The flat character is drawn with only surface facts and details; the stock or stereotyped character (the braggart, the bully, the mad scientist, the absent-minded professor) is sketched lightly and furnished with just one or two easily recognizable traits. There is little depth to the portrayal of minor characters. We learn virtually nothing about their family or background, and their behavior is familiar or predictable. Indeed, we are given only as much information about such characters as the author deems necessary for the immediate purpose. That purpose may be to provide a contrast to another character, to furnish a clue to a motive behind an action, or to present another side of an argument; there are many possibilities. Such characters are Alix, the bartender, Lincoln Peters, and Claude Fessenden in "Babylon Revisited" by F. Scott Fitzgerald (Chapter 3); Old Man Warner, Mr. Summers, Mr. and Mrs. Adams, and Mrs. Hutchinson in "The Lottery" by Shirley Jackson (Chapter 4); Lily Hirschorn in "The Magic Barrel," which you have just studied; and Bildad in "I Want to Know Why." Minor characters generally remain static. Unmoved by the major conflict, they are usually the same people at the end of a story as at its beginning. They have served their purpose, and the author has revealed that purpose to us dramatically, or through summary, direct discussion, or description.

As we have noted, a standard requirement of good fiction is that a character be convincing — believable as a human being. Characters, like people, sometimes behave foolishly and incredibly, but however unusual or fantastic their actions, we can be convinced of the characters' reality if these actions have clearly identifiable, legitimate motivation.

Motivation is the term given to the reasons that make a character's actions plausible. When we say that a character's behavior is well motivated, we mean that it accords with the character's nature as it has been established by the author, and with the circumstances to which the character is responding. In "Roman Fever" (Edith Wharton; Chapter 1), Mrs. Slade is moved to take vengeance on Mrs. Ansley out of longstanding hatred for her. That hatred is compounded by the frustrations of widowhood and finally brought to the surface by her envy of Mrs. Ansley because Mrs. Ansley's daughter outshines her own daughter.

When characters obey the laws of their own being and behave according to the dictates of their established natures — when they act *in character* even as they develop and change — they are said to be **consistent.** Mathilde Loisel in "The Necklace" (Chapter 1) may be flighty, but she is not dishonest. She and her husband are people who care about their good name and take responsibility for what they do. Thus they act with consistency when they replace the lost necklace, at the cost of ten years of hardship.

Authors create every conceivable type of character, pattern of thought, and attitude and emotion, all in the name of humanity. In the four stories contained in this chapter, the characters range from a woman who when we first see her seems happily in tune with nature, to a youth just out of college who despairs of any future for himself. Each of the characters faces, or has faced, a crisis, and we as readers must decide whether that crisis makes the character grow and gain self-knowledge, or whether its effect is destructive.

Questions for Evaluating Character

1. Who is the chief character, and how is he or she revealed?

2. What traits, emotions, and patterns of behavior characterize that person as an individual?

3. Is the protagonist a dynamic character? How does the person change? What causes that change?

4. Is the main character convincing, believable, consistent, and adequately motivated? What means does the author use to these ends?

5. Which characters are types? What is their function in the story?

6. What is the author's attitude toward different characters? What purposes are served?

7. How suitable or significant are the names of characters?

John Steinbeck *(1902–1968)*

The Chrysanthemums

The high grey-flannel fog of winter closed off the Salinas Valley from the sky and from all the rest of the world. On every side it sat like a lid on the mountains and made of the great valley a closed pot. On the broad, level land floor the gang plows bit deep and left the black earth shining like metal where the shares had cut. On the foothill ranches across the Salinas River, the yellow stubble fields seemed to be bathed in pale cold sunshine, but there was no sunshine in the valley now in December. The thick willow scrub along the river flamed with sharp and positive yellow leaves.

It was a time of quiet and of waiting. The air was cold and tender. A light wind blew up from the southwest so that the farmers were mildly hopeful of a good rain before long; but fog and rain do not go together.

Across the river, on Henry Allen's foothill ranch there was little work to be done, for the hay was cut and stored and the orchards were plowed up to receive the rain deeply when it should come. The cattle on the higher slopes were becoming shaggy and rough-coated.

Elisa Allen, working in her flower garden, looked down across the yard and saw Henry, her husband, talking to two men in business suits. The three of them stood by the tractor shed, each man with one foot on the side of the little Fordson. They smoked cigarettes and studied the machine as they talked.

Elisa watched them for a moment and then went back to her work. She was thirty-five. Her face was lean and strong and her eyes were as clear as water. Her figure looked blocked and heavy in her gardening costume, a man's black hat pulled low down over her eyes, clod-hopper shoes, a figured print dress almost completely covered by a big corduroy apron with four big pockets to hold the snips, the trowel and scratcher, the seeds and the knife she worked with. She wore heavy leather gloves to protect her hands while she worked.

She was cutting down the old year's chrysanthemum stalks with a pair of short and powerful scissors. She looked down toward the men by the tractor shed now and then. Her face was eager and mature and handsome; even her work with the scissors was over-eager, over-powerful. The chrysanthemum stems seemed too small and easy for her energy.

She brushed a cloud of hair out of her eyes with the back of her glove, and left a smudge of earth on her cheek in doing it. Behind her stood the neat white farm house with red geraniums close-banked around it as high as the windows.

It was a hard-swept looking little house, with hard-polished windows, and a clean mud-mat on the front steps.

Elisa cast another glance toward the tractor shed. The strangers were getting into their Ford coupe. She took off a glove and put her strong fingers down into the forest of new green chrysanthemum sprouts that were growing around the old roots. She spread the leaves and looked down among the close-growing stems. No aphids were there, no sowbugs or snails or cutworms. Her terrier fingers destroyed such pests before they could get started.

Elisa started at the sound of her husband's voice. He had come near quietly, and he leaned over the wire fence that protected her flower garden from cattle and dogs and chickens.

"At it again," he said. "You've got a strong new crop coming."

Elisa straightened her back and pulled on the gardening glove again. "Yes. They'll be strong this coming year." In her tone and on her face there was a little smugness.

"You've got a gift with things," Henry observed. "Some of those yellow chrysanthemums you had this year were ten inches across. I wish you'd work out in the orchard and raise some apples that big."

Her eyes sharpened. "Maybe I could do it, too. I've a gift with things, all right. My mother had it. She could stick anything in the ground and make it grow. She said it was having planters' hands that knew how to do it."

"Well, it sure works with flowers," he said.

"Henry, who were those men you were talking to?"

"Why, sure, that's what I came to tell you. They were from the Western Meat Company. I sold those thirty head of three-year-old steers. Got nearly my own price, too."

"Good," she said. "Good for you."

"And I thought," he continued, "I thought how it's Saturday afternoon, and we might go to Salinas for dinner at a restaurant, and then to a picture show — to celebrate, you see."

"Good," she repeated. "Oh, yes. That will be good."

Henry put on his joking tone. "There's fights tonight. How'd you like to go to the fights?"

"Oh, no," she said breathlessly. "No, I wouldn't like fights."

"Just fooling, Elisa. We'll go to a movie. Let's see. It's two now. I'm going to take Scotty and bring down those steers from the hill. It'll take us maybe two hours. We'll go in town about five and have dinner at the Cominos Hotel. Like that?"

"Of course I'll like it. It's good to eat away from home."

"All right, then. I'll go get up a couple of horses."

She said, "I'll have plenty of time to transplant some of these sets, I guess."

She heard her husband calling Scotty down by the barn. And a little later she saw the two men ride up the pale yellow hillside in search of the steers.

There was a little square sandy bed kept for rooting the chrysanthemums. With her trowel she turned the soil over and over, and smoothed it and patted it firm. Then she dug ten parallel trenches to receive the sets. Back at the chrysanthemum bed she pulled out the little crisp shoots, trimmed off the leaves of each one with her scissors and laid it on a small orderly pile.

A squeak of wheels and plod of hoofs came from the road. Elisa looked up. The country road ran along the dense bank of willows and cottonwoods that bordered the river, and up this road came a curious vehicle, curiously drawn. It was an old spring-wagon, with a round canvas top on it like the cover of a prairie schooner. It was drawn by an old bay horse and a little grey-and-white burro. A big stubble-bearded man sat between the cover flaps and drove the crawling team. Underneath the wagon, between the hind wheels, a lean and rangy mongrel dog walked sedately. Words were painted on the canvas, in clumsy, crooked letters. "Pots, pans, knives, sisors, lawn mores, Fixed." Two rows of articles, and the triumphantly definitive "Fixed" below. The black paint had run down in little sharp points beneath each letter.

Elisa, squatting on the ground, watched to see the crazy, loose-jointed wagon pass by. But it didn't pass. It turned into the farm road in front of her house, crooked old wheels skirling and squeaking. The rangy dog darted from between the wheels and ran ahead. Instantly the two ranch shepherds flew out at him. Then all three stopped, and with stiff and quivering tails, with taut straight legs, with ambassadorial dignity, they slowly circled, sniffing daintily. The caravan pulled up to Elisa's wire fence and stopped. Now the newcomer dog, feeling outnumbered, lowered his tail and retired under the wagon with raised hackles and bared teeth.

The man on the wagon seat called out, "That's a bad dog in a fight when he gets started."

Elisa laughed. "I see he is. How soon does he generally get started?"

The man caught up her laughter and echoed it heartily. "Sometimes not for weeks and weeks," he said. He climbed stiffly down, over the wheel. The horse and the donkey drooped like unwatered flowers.

Elisa saw that he was a very big man. Although his hair and beard were greying, he did not look old. His worn black suit was wrinkled and spotted with grease. The laughter had disappeared from his face and eyes the moment his laughing voice ceased. His eyes were dark, and they were full of the brooding that gets in the eyes of teamsters and of sailors. The calloused hands he rested on the wire fence were cracked, and every crack was a black line. He took off his battered hat.

"I'm off my general road, ma'am," he said. "Does this dirt road cut over across the river to the Los Angeles highway?"

Elisa stood up and shoved the thick scissors in her apron pocket. "Well, yes, it does, but it winds around and then fords the river. I don't think your team could pull through the sand."

He replied with some asperity, "It might surprise you what them beasts can pull through."

"When they get started?" she asked.

He smiled for a second. "Yes. When they get started."

"Well," said Elisa, "I think you'll save time if you go back to the Salinas road and pick up the highway there."

He drew a big finger down the chicken wire and made it sing. "I ain't in any hurry, ma'am. I go from Seattle to San Diego and back every year. Takes all my time. About six months each way. I aim to follow nice weather."

Elisa took off her gloves and stuffed them in the apron pocket with the scissors. She touched the under edge of her man's hat, searching for fugitive hairs. "That sounds like a nice kind of a way to live," she said.

He leaned confidentially over the fence. "Maybe you noticed the writing on my wagon. I mend pots and sharpen knives and scissors. You got any of them things to do?"

"Oh, no," she said quickly. "Nothing like that." Her eyes hardened with resistance.

"Scissors is the worst thing," he explained. "Most people just ruin scissors trying to sharpen 'em, but I know how. I got a special tool. It's a little bobbit kind of thing, and patented. But it sure does the trick."

"No. My scissors are all sharp."

"All right, then. Take a pot," he continued earnestly, "a bent pot, or a pot with a hole. I can make it like new so you don't have to buy no new ones. That's a saving for you."

"No," she said shortly. "I tell you I have nothing like that for you to do."

His face fell to an exaggerated sadness. His voice took on a whining under-tone. "I ain't had a thing to do today. Maybe I won't have no supper tonight. You see I'm off my regular road. I know folks on the highway clear from Seattle to San Diego. They save their things for me to sharpen up because they know I do it so good and save them money."

"I'm sorry," Elisa said irritably. "I haven't anything for you to do."

His eyes left her face and fell to searching the ground. They roamed about until they came to the chrysanthemum bed where she had been working. "What's them plants, ma'am?"

The irritation and resistance melted from Elisa's face. "Oh, those are chrysanthemums, giant whites and yellows. I raise them every year, bigger than anybody around here."

"Kind of a long-stemmed flower? Looks like a quick puff of colored smoke?" he asked.

"That's it. What a nice way to describe them."

"They smell kind of nasty till you get used to them," he said.

"It's a good bitter smell," she retorted, "not nasty at all."

He changed his tone quickly. "I like the smell myself."

"I had ten-inch blooms this year," she said.

The man leaned farther over the fence. "Look. I know a lady down the road a piece, has got the nicest garden you ever seen. Got nearly every kind of flower but no chrysanthemums. Last time I was mending a copper-bottom washtub for her (that's a hard job but I do it good), she said to me, 'If you ever run acrost some nice chrysanthemums I wish you'd try to get me a few seeds.' That's what she told me."

Elisa's eyes grew alert and eager. "She couldn't have known much about chrysanthemums. You *can* raise them from seed, but it's much easier to root the little sprouts you see there."

"Oh," he said. "I s'pose I can't take none to her, then."

"Why yes you can," Elisa cried. "I can put some in damp sand, and you can carry them right along with you. They'll take root in the pot if you keep them damp. And then she can transplant them."

"She'd sure like to have some, ma'am. You say they're nice ones?"

"Beautiful," she said. "Oh, beautiful." Her eyes shone. She tore off the battered hat and shook out her dark pretty hair. "I'll put them in a flower pot, and you can take them right with you. Come into the yard."

While the man came through the picket gate Elisa ran excitedly along the geranium-bordered path to the back of the house. And she returned carrying a big red flower pot. The gloves were forgotten now. She kneeled on the ground by the starting bed and dug up the sandy soil with her fingers and scooped it into the bright new flower pot. Then she picked up the little pile of shoots she had prepared. With her strong fingers she pressed them into the sand and tamped around them with her knuckles. The man stood over her. "I'll tell you what to do," she said. "You remember so you can tell the lady."

"Yes, I'll try to remember."

"Well, look. These will take root in about a month. Then she must set them out, about a foot apart in good rich earth like this, see?" She lifted a handful of dark soil for him to look at. "They'll grow fast and tall. Now remember this. In July tell her to cut them down, about eight inches from the ground."

"Before they bloom?" he asked.

"Yes, before they bloom." Her face was tight with eagerness. "They'll grow right up again. About the last of September the buds will start."

She stopped and seemed perplexed. "It's the budding that takes the most care," she said hesitantly. "I don't know how to tell you." She looked deep into his eyes, searchingly. Her mouth opened a little, and she seemed to be listening. "I'll try to tell you," she said. "Did you ever hear of planting hands?"

"Can't say I have, ma'am."

"Well, I can only tell you what it feels like. It's when you're picking off the buds you don't want. Everything goes right down into your fingertips. You watch your fingers work. They do it themselves. You can feel how it is. They pick and pick the buds. They never make a mistake. They're with the plant. Do you see? Your fingers and the plant. You can feel that, right up your arm. They know. They never make a mistake. You can feel it. When you're like that you can't do anything wrong. Do you see that? Can you understand that?"

She was kneeling on the ground looking up at him. Her breast swelled passionately.

The man's eyes narrowed. He looked away self-consciously. "Maybe I know," he said. "Sometimes in the night in the wagon there — "

Elisa's voice grew husky. She broke in on him. "I've never lived as you do, but I know what you mean. When the night is dark — why, the stars are sharp-pointed, and there's quiet. Why, you rise up and up! Every pointed star gets driven into your body. It's like that. Hot and sharp and — lovely."

Kneeling there, her hand went out toward his legs in the greasy black trousers. Her hesitant fingers almost touched the cloth. Then her hand dropped to the ground. She crouched low like a fawning dog.

He said, "It's nice, just like you say. Only when you don't have no dinner, it ain't."

She stood up then, very straight, and her face was ashamed. She held the flower pot out to him and placed it gently in his arms. "Here. Put it in your wagon, on the seat, where you can watch it. Maybe I can find something for you to do."

At the back of the house she dug in the can pile and found two old and battered aluminum saucepans. She carried them back and gave them to him. "Here, maybe you can fix these."

His manner changed. He became professional. "Good as new I can fix them." At the back of his wagon he set a little anvil, and out of an oily tool box dug a small machine hammer. Elisa came through the gate to watch him while he pounded out the dents in the kettles. His mouth grew sure and knowing. At a difficult part of the work he sucked his under-lip.

"You sleep right in the wagon?" Elisa asked.

"Right in the wagon, ma'am. Rain or shine I'm dry as a cow in there."

"It must be nice," she said. "It must be very nice. I wish women could do such things."

"It ain't the right kind of a life for a woman."

Her upper lip raised a little, showing her teeth. "How do you know? How can you tell?" she said.

"I don't know, ma'am," he protested. "Of course I don't know. Now here's your kettles, done. You don't have to buy no new ones."

"How much?"

"Oh, fifty cents'll do. I keep my prices down and my work good. That's why I have all them satisfied customers up and down the highway."

Elisa brought him a fifty-cent piece from the house and dropped it in his hand. "You might be surprised to have a rival some time. I can sharpen scissors, too. And I can beat the dents out of little pots. I could show you what a woman might do."

He put his hammer back in the oily box and shoved the little anvil out of sight. "It would be a lonely life for a woman, ma'am, and a scarey life, too, with animals creeping under the wagon all night." He climbed over the singletree, steadying himself with a hand on the burro's white rump. He settled himself in the seat, picked up the lines. "Thank you kindly, ma'am," he said. "I'll do like you told me; I'll go back and catch the Salinas road."

"Mind," she called, "if you're long in getting there, keep the sand damp."

"Sand, ma'am? . . . Sand? Oh, sure. You mean around the chrysanthemums. Sure I will." He clucked his tongue. The beasts leaned luxuriously into their collars. The mongrel dog took his place between the back wheels. The wagon turned and crawled out the entrance road and back the way it had come, along the river.

Elisa stood in front of her wire fence watching the slow progress of the caravan. Her shoulders were straight, her head thrown back, her eyes half-closed, so that the scene came vaguely into them. Her lips moved silently, forming the words "Good-bye — good-bye." Then she whispered, "That's a bright direction. There's a glowing there." The sound of her whisper startled her. She shook herself free and looked about to see whether anyone had been listening. Only the dogs had heard. They lifted their heads toward her from their sleeping in the dust, and then stretched out their chins and settled asleep again. Elisa turned and ran hurriedly into the house.

In the kitchen she reached behind the stove and felt the water tank. It was full of hot water from the noonday cooking. In the bathroom she tore off her soiled clothes and flung them into the corner. And then she scrubbed herself with a little block of pumice, legs and thighs, loins and chest and arms, until her skin was scratched and red. When she had dried herself she stood in front of a mirror in her bedroom and looked at her body. She tightened her stomach and threw out her chest. She turned and looked over her shoulder at her back.

After a while she began to dress, slowly. She put on her newest underclothing and her nicest stockings and the dress which was the symbol of her prettiness. She worked carefully on her hair, penciled her eyebrows and rouged her lips.

Before she was finished she heard the little thunder of hoofs and the shouts of Henry and his helper as they drove the red steers into the corral. She heard the gate bang shut and set herself for Henry's arrival.

His step sounded on the porch. He entered the house calling, "Elisa, where are you?"

"In my room, dressing. I'm not ready. There's hot water for your bath. Hurry up. It's getting late."

When she heard him splashing in the tub, Elisa laid his dark suit on the bed, and shirt and socks and tie beside it. She stood his polished shoes on the floor beside the bed. Then she went to the porch and sat primly and stiffly down. She looked toward the river road where the willow-line was still yellow with frosted leaves so that under the high grey fog they seemed a thin band of sunshine. This was the only color in the grey afternoon. She sat unmoving for a long time. Her eyes blinked rarely.

Henry came banging out of the door, shoving his tie inside his vest as he came. Elisa stiffened and her face grew tight. Henry stopped short and looked at her. "Why — why, Elisa. You look so nice!"

"Nice? You think I look nice? What do you mean by 'nice'?"

Henry blundered on. "I don't know. I mean you look different, strong and happy."

"I am strong? Yes, strong. What do you mean 'strong'?"

He looked bewildered. "You're playing some kind of a game," he said helplessly. "It's a kind of a play. You look strong enough to break a calf over your knee, happy enough to eat it like a watermelon."

For a second she lost her rigidity. "Henry! Don't talk like that. You didn't know what you said." She grew complete again. "I'm strong," she boasted. "I never knew before how strong."

Henry looked down toward the tractor shed, and when he brought his eyes back to her, they were his own again. "I'll get out the car. You can put on your coat while I'm starting."

Elisa went into the house. She heard him drive to the gate and idle down his motor, and then she took a long time to put on her hat. She pulled it here and pressed it there. When Henry turned the motor off she slipped into her coat and went out.

The little roadster bounced along on the dirt road by the river, raising the birds and driving the rabbits into the brush. Two cranes flapped heavily over the willow-line and dropped into the river-bed.

Far ahead on the road Elisa saw a dark speck. She knew.

She tried not to look as they passed it, but her eyes would not obey. She whispered to herself sadly, "He might have thrown them off the road. That wouldn't have been much trouble, not very much. But he kept the pot," she explained. "He had to keep the pot. That's why he couldn't get them off the road."

The roadster turned a bend and she saw the caravan ahead. She swung full around toward her husband so she could not see the little covered wagon and the mismatched team as the car passed them.

In a moment it was over. The thing was done. She did not look back.

She said loudly, to be heard above the motor, "It will be good, tonight, a good dinner."

"Now you're changed again," Henry complained. He took one hand from the wheel and patted her knee. "I ought to take you in to dinner oftener. It would be good for both of us. We get so heavy out on the ranch."

"Henry," she asked, "could we have wine at dinner?"

"Sure we could. Say! That will be fine."

She was silent for a while; then she said, "Henry, at those prize fights, do the men hurt each other very much?"

"Sometimes a little, not often. Why?"

"Well, I've read how they break noses, and blood runs down their chests. I've read how the fighting gloves get heavy and soggy with blood."

He looked around at her. "What's the matter, Elisa? I didn't know you read things like that." He brought the car to a stop, then turned to the right over the Salinas River bridge.

"Do any women ever go to the fights?" she asked.

"Oh, sure, some. What's the matter, Elisa? Do you want to go? I don't think you'd like it, but I'll take you if you really want to go."

She relaxed limply in the seat. "Oh, no. No. I don't want to go. I'm sure I don't." Her face was turned away from him. "It will be enough if we can have wine. It will be plenty." She turned up her coat collar so he could not see that she was crying weakly — like an old woman.

Exercises

1. What impression does Steinbeck create with his initial physical description of Elisa? How does environment affect her?

2. Cite one or two incidents, dramatically presented, that unveil some aspect of Elisa's character.

3. What is the significance of Elisa's careful preparation for the trip to town?

4. What is Elisa's conflict? How is it resolved?

5. What role does the tinker play?

6. Has the experience of conflict produced any permanent change in Elisa? If so, discuss the change.

7. How much do we know about Henry? Is he a dynamic or static character? What function does he serve?

8. Explain the meaning of the following episodes: (a) Shortly after having met the peddler, Elisa removes her gloves, searches for displaced hairs under her man's hat, and moves about with palpitating excitement. (b) After the tinker leaves, Elisa tears off her soiled clothes and scrubs herself until her skin is scratched and red. (c) "I'm strong," she boasted [addressing Henry]. "I never knew before how strong."

Topics for Writing

1. Discuss the significance of the chrysanthemums in Elisa's life.

2. What do you see as Elisa's problem? Does Henry understand it? Consider these points in an essay, making specific references to the text to support your comments.

3. Using the Questions for Evaluating Character that precede the story as an aid, write an essay analyzing Elisa's character and discuss the means Steinbeck uses to portray it.

4. Analyze the means used to keep our interest in this story as compared to "The Catbird Seat" and "Roman Fever."

Selected Bibliography John Steinbeck

Calverton, V. F. "Steinbeck, Hemingway, and Faulkner." *Modern Quarterly,* 11 (1939), 36–44.

Carpenter, F. I. "John Steinbeck: American Dreamer." *Sewanee Review,* 26 (1941), 454–467.

Champney, Freeman. "John Steinbeck, Californian." *Antioch Review,* 7 (1947), 345–362.

Davis, Elmer. "The Steinbeck Country." *Saturday Review of Literature,* 24 (September 1938), 11.

Gibbs, L. R. "John Steinbeck, Moralist." *Antioch Review,* 2 (1942), 172–184.

McMahan, Elizabeth E. " 'The Chrysanthemums': Study of a Woman's Sexuality." *Modern Fiction Studies,* 14 (1968), 453–458.

Marcus, Mordecai. "The Lost Dream of Sex and Childbirth in 'The Chrysanthemums.' " *Modern Fiction Studies,* 11 (1965), 54–58.

Miller, William V. "Sexual and Spiritual Ambiguity in 'The Chrysanthemums,' " *Steinbeck Quarterly,* 5 (1972), 68–75.

Noonan, Gerald. "A Note on 'The Chrysanthemums.' " *Modern Fiction Studies,* 15 (1969), 542.

Osborne, William R. "The Texts of Steinbeck's 'The Chrysanthemums.' " *Modern Fiction Studies,* 12 (1966), 479–484.

Sweet, Charles A. "Ms. Elisa Allen and Steinbeck's 'The Chrysanthemums,' " *Modern Fiction Studies,* 20 (1974), 210–214.

William Faulkner (1897–1962)
A Rose for Emily

1.

When Miss Emily Grierson died, our whole town went to her funeral: the men through a sort of respectful affection for a fallen monument, the women mostly out of curiosity to see the inside of her house, which no one save an old manservant — a combined gardener and cook — had seen in at least ten years.

It was a big, squarish frame house that had once been white, decorated with cupolas and spires and scrolled balconies in the heavily lightsome style of the seventies, set on what had once been our most select street. But garages and cotton gins had encroached and obliterated even the august names of that neighborhood, only Miss Emily's house was left, lifting its stubborn and coquettish decay above the cotton wagons and the gasoline pumps — an eyesore among eyesores. And now Miss Emily had gone to join the representatives of those august names where they lay in the cedar-bemused cemetery among the ranked and anonymous graves of Union and Confederate soldiers who fell at the battle of Jefferson.[1]

---

1. Jefferson: Faulkner's name for Oxford, Mississippi.

Alive, Miss Emily had been a tradition, a duty, and a care; a sort of hereditary obligation upon the town, dating from that day in 1894 when Colonel Sartoris,[2] the mayor — he who fathered the edict that no Negro woman should appear on the streets without an apron — remitted her taxes, the dispensation dating from the death of her father on into perpetuity. Not that Miss Emily would have accepted charity. Colonel Sartoris invented an involved tale to the effect that Miss Emily's father had loaned money to the town, which the town, as a matter of business, preferred this way of repaying. Only a man of Colonel Sartoris' generation and thought could have invented it, and only a woman could have believed it.

When the next generation, with its more modern ideas, became mayors and aldermen, this arrangement created some little dissatisfaction. On the first of the year they mailed her a tax notice. February came, and there was no reply. They wrote her a formal letter, asking her to call at the sheriff's office at her convenience. A week later the mayor wrote her himself, offering to call or to send his car for her, and received in reply a note on paper of an archaic shape, in a thin, flowing calligraphy in faded ink, to the effect that she no longer went out at all. The tax notice was also enclosed, without comment.

They called a special meeting of the Board of Aldermen. A deputation waited upon her, knocked at the door through which no visitor had passed since she ceased giving china-painting lessons eight or ten years earlier. They were admitted by the old Negro into a dim hall from which a stairway mounted into still more shadow. It smelled of dust and disuse — a close, dank smell. The Negro led them into the parlor. It was furnished in heavy, leather-covered furniture. When the Negro opened the blinds of one window, they could see that the leather was cracked; and when they sat down, a faint dust rose sluggishly about their thighs, spinning with slow motes in the single sun-ray. On a tarnished gilt easel before the fireplace stood a crayon portrait of Miss Emily's father.

They rose when she entered — a small, fat woman in black, with a thin gold chain descending to her waist and vanishing into her belt, leaning on an ebony cane with a tarnished gold head. Her skeleton was small and spare; perhaps that was why what would have been merely plumpness in another was obesity in her. She looked bloated, like a body long submerged in motionless water, and of that pallid hue. Her eyes, lost in the fatty ridges of her face, looked like two small pieces of coal pressed into a lump of dough as they moved from one face to another while the visitors stated their errand.

She did not ask them to sit. She just stood in the door and listened quietly until the spokesman came to a stumbling halt. Then they could hear the invisible watch ticking at the end of the gold chain.

Her voice was dry and cold. "I have no taxes in Jefferson. Colonel Sartoris explained it to me. Perhaps one of you can gain access to the city records and satisfy yourselves."

"But we have. We are the city authorities, Miss Emily. Didn't you get a notice from the sheriff, signed by him?"

"I received a paper, yes," Miss Emily said. "Perhaps he considers himself the sheriff. . . . I have no taxes in Jefferson."

"But there is nothing on the books to show that, you see. We must go by the — "

2. Colonel Sartoris: Major fictional figure, one of many, inhabiting legendary Yoknapatawpha County.

"See Colonel Sartoris. I have no taxes in Jefferson."

"But, Miss Emily — "

"See Colonel Sartoris." (Colonel Sartoris had been dead almost ten years.) "I have no taxes in Jefferson. Tobe!" The Negro appeared. "Show these gentlemen out."

2.

So she vanquished them, horse and foot, just as she had vanquished their fathers thirty years before about the smell. That was two years after her father's death and a short time after her sweetheart — the one we believed would marry her — had deserted her. After her father's death she went out very little; after her sweetheart went away, people hardly saw her at all. A few ladies had the temerity to call, but were not received, and the only sign of life about the place was the Negro man — a young man then — going in and out with a market basket.

"Just as if a man — any man — could keep a kitchen properly," the ladies said; so they were not surprised when the smell developed. It was another link between the gross, teeming world and the high and mighty Griersons.

A neighbor, a woman, complained to the mayor, Judge Stevens, eighty years old.

"But what will you have me do about it, madam?" he said.

"Why, send her word to stop it," the woman said. "Isn't there a law?"

"I'm sure that won't be necessary," Judge Stevens said. "It's probably just a snake or a rat that nigger of hers killed in the yard. I'll speak to him about it."

The next day he received two more complaints, one from a man who came in diffident deprecation. "We really must do something about it, Judge. I'd be the last one in the world to bother Miss Emily, but we've got to do something." That night the Board of Aldermen met — three graybeards and one younger man, a member of the rising generation.

"It's simple enough," he said. "Send her word to have her place cleaned up. Give her a certain time to do it in, and if she don't . . ."

"Dammit, sir," Judge Stevens said, "will you accuse a lady to her face of smelling bad?"

So the next night, after midnight, four men crossed Miss Emily's lawn and slunk about the house like burglars, sniffing along the base of the brickwork and at the cellar openings while one of them performed a regular sowing motion with his hand out of a sack slung from his shoulder. They broken open the cellar door and sprinkled lime there, and in all the outbuildings. As they recrossed the lawn, a window that had been dark was lighted and Miss Emily sat in it, the light behind her, and her upright torso motionless as that of an idol. They crept quietly across the lawn and into the shadow of the locusts that lined the street. After a week or two the smell went away.

That was when people had begun to feel really sorry for her. People in our town, remembering how old lady Wyatt, her great-aunt, had gone completely crazy at last, believed that the Griersons held themselves a little too high for what they really were. None of the young men were quite good enough for Miss Emily and such. We had long thought of them as a tableau: Miss Emily a slender figure in white in the background, her father a spraddled silhouette in the foreground, his back to her and clutching a horsewhip, the two of them framed by the back-flung front door. So when she got to be thirty and was still single, we were not pleased exactly, but vindicated; even with insanity in the family she wouldn't have turned down all of her chances if they had really materialized.

When her father died, it got about that the house was all that was left to her; and in a way, people were glad. At last they could pity Miss Emily. Being left alone, and a pauper, she had become humanized. Now she too would know the old thrill and the old despair of a penny more or less.

The day after his death all the ladies prepared to call at the house and offer condolence and aid, as is our custom. Miss Emily met them at the door, dressed as usual and with no trace of grief on her face. She told them that her father was not dead. She did that for three days, with the ministers calling on her, and the doctors, trying to persuade her to let them dispose of the body. Just as they were about to resort to law and force, she broke down, and they buried her father quickly.

We did not say she was crazy then. We believed she had to do that. We remembered all the young men her father had driven away, and we knew that with nothing left, she would have to cling to that which had robbed her, as people will.

3.

She was sick for a long time. When we saw her again, her hair was cut short, making her look like a girl, with a vague resemblance to those angels in colored church windows — sort of tragic and serene.

The town had just let the contracts for paving the sidewalks, and in the summer after her father's death they began the work. The construction company came with niggers and mules and machinery, and a foreman named Homer Barron, a Yankee — a big, dark, ready man, with a big voice and eyes lighter than his face. The little boys would follow in groups to hear him cuss the niggers, and the niggers singing in time to the rise and fall of picks. Pretty soon he knew everybody in town. Whenever you heard a lot of laughing anywhere about the square, Homer Barron would be in the center of the group. Presently we began to see him and Miss Emily on Sunday afternoons driving in the yellow-wheeled buggy and the matched team of bays from the livery stable.

At first we were glad that Miss Emily would have an interest, because the ladies all said, "Of course a Grierson would not think seriously of a Northerner, a day laborer." But there were still others, older people, who said that even grief could not cause a real lady to forget *noblesse oblige*[3] — without calling it *noblesse oblige*. They just said, "Poor Emily. Her kinsfolk should come to her." She had some kin in Alabama; but years ago her father had fallen out with them over the estate of old lady Wyatt, the crazy woman, and there was no communication between the two families. They had not even been represented at the funeral.

And as soon as the old people said, "Poor Emily," the whispering began. "Do you suppose it's really so?" they said to one another. "Of course it is. What else could . . ." This behind their hands; rustling of craned silk and satin behind jalousies closed upon the sun of Sunday afternoon as the thin, swift clop-clop-clop of the matched team passed: "Poor Emily."

3. *Noblesse oblige:* Obligation of the higher class.

She carried her head high enough — even when we believed that she was fallen. It was as if she demanded more than ever the recognition of her dignity as the last Grierson; as if it had wanted that touch of earthiness to reaffirm her imperviousness. Like when she bought the rat poison, the arsenic. That was over a year after they had begun to say "Poor Emily," and while the two female cousins were visiting her.

"I want some poison," she said to the druggist. She was over thirty then, still a slight woman, though thinner than usual, with cold, haughty black eyes in a face the flesh of which was strained across the temples and about the eyesockets as you imagine a lighthouse-keeper's face ought to look. "I want some poison," she said.

"Yes, Miss Emily. What kind? For rats and such? I'd recom — "

"I want the best you have. I don't care what kind."

The druggist named several. "They'll kill anything up to an elephant. But what you want is — "

"Arsenic," Miss Emily said. "Is that a good one?"

"Is . . . arsenic? Yes, ma'am. But what you want — "

"I want arsenic."

The druggist looked down at her. She looked back at him, erect, her face like a strained flag. "Why, of course," the druggist said. "If that's what you want. But the law requires you to tell what you are going to use it for."

Miss Emily just stared at him, her head tilted back in order to look him eye for eye, until he looked away and went and got the arsenic and wrapped it up. The Negro delivery boy brought her the package; the druggist didn't come back. When she opened the package at home there was written on the box, under the skull and bones: "For rats."

4.

So the next day we all said, "She will kill herself"; and we said it would be the best thing. When she had first begun to be seen with Homer Barron, we had said, "She will marry him." Then we said, "She will persuade him yet," because Homer himself had remarked — he liked men, and it was known that he drank with the younger men in the Elk's Club — that he was not a marrying man. Later we said, "Poor Emily," behind the jalousies as they passed on Sunday afternoon in the glittering buggy, Miss Emily with her head high and Homer Barron with his hat cocked and a cigar in his teeth, reins and whip in a yellow glove.

Then some of the ladies began to say that it was a disgrace to the town and a bad example to the young people. The men did not want to interfere, but at last the ladies forced the Baptist minister — Miss Emily's people were Episcopal — to call upon her. He would never divulge what happened during that interview, but he refused to go back again. The next Sunday they again drove about the streets, and the following day the minister's wife wrote to Miss Emily's relations in Alabama.

So she had blood-kin under her roof again and we sat back to watch developments. At first nothing happened. Then we were sure that they were to be married. We learned that Miss Emily had been to the jeweler's and ordered a man's toilet set in silver, with the letters H.B. on each piece. Two days later we learned that she had bought a complete outfit of men's clothing, including a nightshirt, and we said, "They are married." We were really glad. We were glad because the two female cousins were even more Grierson than Miss Emily had ever been.

So we were not surprised when Homer Barron — the streets had been finished some time since — was gone. We were a little disappointed that there was not a public blowing-off, but we believed that he had gone on to prepare for Miss Emily's coming, or to give her a chance to get rid of the cousins. (By that time it was a cabal, and we were all Miss Emily's allies to help circumvent the cousins.) Sure enough, after another week they departed. And, as we had expected all along, within three days Homer Barron was back in town. A neighbor saw the Negro man admit him at the kitchen door at dusk one evening.

And that was the last we saw of Homer Barron. And of Miss Emily for some time. The Negro man went in and out with the market basket, but the front door remained closed. Now and then we would see her at a window for a moment, as the men did that night when they sprinkled the lime, but for almost six months she did not appear on the streets. Then we knew that this was to be expected too; as if that quality of her father which had thwarted her woman's life so many times had been too virulent and too furious to die.

When we next saw Miss Emily, she had grown fat and her hair was turning gray. During the next few years it grew grayer and grayer until it attained an even pepper-and-salt iron-gray, when it ceased turning. Up to the day of her death at seventy-four it was still that vigorous iron-gray, like the hair of an active man.

From that time on her front door remained closed, save for a period of six or seven years, when she was about forty, during which she gave lessons in china-painting. She fitted up a studio in one of the downstairs rooms, where the daughters and granddaughters of Colonel Sartoris' contemporaries were sent to her with the same regularity and in the same spirit that they were sent on Sundays with a twenty-five cent piece for the collection plate. Meanwhile her taxes had been remitted.

Then the newer generation became the backbone and the spirit of the town, and the painting pupils grew up and fell away and did not send their children to her with boxes of color and tedious brushes and pictures cut from the ladies' magazines. The front door closed upon the last one and remained closed for good. When the town got free postal delivery Miss Emily alone refused to let them fasten the metal numbers above her door and attach a mailbox to it. She would not listen to them.

Daily, monthly, yearly we watched the Negro grow grayer and more stooped, going in and out with the market basket. Each December we sent her a tax notice, which would be returned by the post office a week later, unclaimed. Now and then we would see her in one of the downstairs windows — she had evidently shut up the top floor of the house — like the carven torso of an idol in a niche, looking or not looking at us, we could never tell which. Thus she passed from generation to generation — dear, inescapable, impervious, tranquil, and perverse.

And so she died. Fell ill in the house filled with dust and shadows, with only a doddering Negro man to wait on her. We did not even know she was sick; we had long since given up trying to get any information from the Negro. He talked to no one, probably not even to her, for his voice had grown harsh and rusty, as if from disuse.

She died in one of the downstairs rooms, in a heavy walnut bed with a curtain, her gray head propped on a pillow yellow and moldy with age and lack of sunlight.

5.

The Negro met the first of the ladies at the front door and let them in, with their hushed, sibilant voices and their quick, curious glances, and then he disappeared. He walked right through the house and out the back and was not seen again.

The two female cousins came at once. They held the funeral on the second day, with the town coming to look at Miss Emily beneath a mass of bought flowers, with the crayon face of her father musing profoundly above the bier and the ladies sibilant and macabre; and the very old men — some in their brushed Confederate uniforms — on the porch and the lawn, talking of Miss Emily as if she had been a contemporary of theirs, believing that they had danced with her and courted her perhaps, confusing time with its mathematical progression, as the old do, to whom all the past is not a diminishing road, but, instead, a huge meadow which no winter ever quite touches, divided from them now by the narrow bottleneck of the most recent decade of years.

Already we knew that there was one room in that region above stairs which no one had seen in forty years, and which would have to be forced. They waited until Miss Emily was decently in the ground before they opened it.

The violence of breaking down the door seemed to fill this room with pervading dust. A thin, acrid pall as of the tomb seemed to lie everywhere upon this room decked and furnished as for a bridal: upon the valance curtains of faded rose color, upon the rose-shaded lights, upon the dressing table, upon the delicate array of crystal and the man's toilet things backed with tarnished silver, silver so tarnished that the monogram was obscured. Among them lay a collar and tie, as if they had just been removed, which, lifted, left upon the surface a pale crescent in the dust. Upon a chair hung the suit, carefully folded; beneath it the two mute shoes and the discarded socks.

The man himself lay in the bed.

For a long while we just stood there, looking down at the profound and fleshless grin. The body had apparently once lain in the attitude of an embrace, but now the long sleep that outlasts love, that conquers even the grimace of love, had cuckolded him. What was left of him, rotted beneath what was left of the nightshirt, had become inextricable from the bed in which he lay; and upon him and upon the pillow beside him lay that even coating of the patient and biding dust.

Then we noticed that in the second pillow was the indentation of a head. One of us lifted something from it, and leaning forward, that faint and invisible dust dry and acrid in the nostrils, we saw a long strand of iron-gray hair.

Exercises

1. Discuss the conflict and how it is resolved.

2. Describe Miss Emily's personality. What kind of person is she?

3. Detail both the physical and historical setting of the story. To what extent do they influence Miss Emily?

4. What social and psychological forces have helped shape Miss Emily's character?

5. Explain the credibility of her psychotic behavior. Is it plausible for her to sleep with the corpse of the lover she murdered? Explain.

6. What is there about the Old South and Miss Emily that leads you to an understanding of what the story means?

7. In a few sentences summarize the meaning of the story.

8. What is Homer Barron's function in the story?

9. Comment on the relationship between the subject matter or theme of the story and its title.

Topics for Writing

1. Examine Faulkner's attitude toward the declining Southern aristocratic tradition as expressed in this story.

2. Discuss the means Faulkner uses to characterize Miss Emily.

3. In an essay, consider how minor characters are depicted in this story.

4. Compare the past as characters in this story and in "Babylon Revisited" in Chapter 3.

5. The story is divided into five sections. Determine what each section contributes to the whole.

Selected Bibliography   William Faulkner

Adams, Richard P. "The Apprenticeship of William Faulkner." *Tulane Studies in English,* 12 (1962), 113–156.

———. *Faulkner: Myth and Motion.* Princeton: Princeton University Press, 1968.

Arthos, John. "Ritual and Humor in the Writing of William Faulkner." *Accent,* 9 (1948), 17–30.

Bowling, Lawrence E. "Faulkner and the Theme of Innocence." *Kenyon Review,* 20 (1958), 466–487.

Brooks, Cleanth. "William Faulkner: Vision of Good and Evil." In *The Hidden God: Studies in Hemingway, Faulkner, Yeats, Eliot, and Warren.* New Haven and London: Yale University Press, 1963, pp. 22–43.

Clements, Arthur L., and Sister Mary Bride. "Faulkner's 'A Rose for Emily.'" *Explicator,* 20 (1972), 78.

Davis, William V. "Another Flower for Faulkner's Bouquet: Theme and Structure in 'A Rose for Emily.'" *Notes on Mississippi Writers,* 7 (Fall 1974), 34–38.

Going, W. T. "Faulkner's 'A Rose for Emily.' " *Explicator,* 16 (1958), 27.

Grenier, Cynthia. "The Art of Fiction: An Interview with William Faulkner — September, 1955." *Accent,* 16 (1956), 167–177.

Hagopian, John V., and Martin Dolch. "Faulkner's 'A Rose for Emily.' " *Explicator,* 22 (1964), 68.

Heller, Terry. "The Telltale Hair: A Critical Study of William Faulkner's 'A Rose for Emily.' " *Arizona Quarterly,* 28 (1972), 301–318.

Hoffman, Frederick J., and Olga W. Vickery, eds. *William Faulkner: Three Decades of Criticism.* Lansing: Michigan State University Press, 1960.

Holland, Norman. "Fantasy and Defense in Faulkner's 'A Rose for Emily.' " *Hartford Studies in Literature,* 4, no. 1 (1972), 1–36.

Howell, Elmo. "Faulkner's 'A Rose for Emily.' " *Explicator,* 19 (1961), 26.

Johnson, C. W. M. "Faulkner's 'A Rose for Emily.' " *Explicator,* 6 (1948), 45.

Kobler, J. F. "Faulkner's 'A Rose for Emily.' " *Explicator,* 32 (1974), Item 65.

Litz, Walton. "William Faulkner's Moral Vision." *Southwest Review,* 37 (1952), 200–209.

Slatoff, Walter J. *Quest For Failure: A Study of William Faulkner.* Ithaca, N.Y.: Cornell University Press, 1960.

Stein, Jean. "The Art of Fiction XII: William Faulkner." *Paris Review,* 4 (1956), 28–52.

Sullivan, Ruth. "The Narrator in 'A Rose for Emily.' " *Journal of Narrative Technique,* 1 (1971), 159–178.

Waggoner, Hyatt H. *William Faulkner: From Jefferson to the World.* Lexington: University of Kentucky Press, 1959.

Warren, Robert Penn, ed. *Faulkner: A Collection of Critical Essays.* Englewood Cliffs, N.J.: Prentice-Hall, 1966.

Watkins, Floyd C. "The Structure of 'A Rose for Emily.' " *Modern Language Notes,* 69 (1954), 508–510.

West, R. B. "Atmosphere and Theme in Faulkner's 'A Rose for Emily.' " *Perspective,* 2 (1949), 239–245.

———. "Faulkner's 'A Rose for Emily.' " *Explicator,* 7 (1948), 8.

Wilson, G. R. "The Chronology of Faulkner's 'A Rose for Emily.' " *Notes on Mississippi Writers,* 5 (1972), 56, 58–62.

Flannery O'Connor (1925–1964)

Everything That Rises Must Converge

Her doctor had told Julian's mother that she must lose twenty pounds on account of her blood pressure, so on Wednesday nights Julian had to take her downtown on the bus for a reducing class at the Y. The reducing class was designed for working girls over fifty, who weighed from 165 to 200 pounds. His mother was one of the slimmer ones, but she said ladies did not tell their age or weight. She would not ride the buses by herself at night since they had been integrated, and because the reducing class was one of her few pleasures, necessary for her health, and *free,* she said Julian could at least put himself out to take her, considering all she did for him. Julian did not like to consider all she did for him, but every Wednesday night he braced himself and took her.

She was almost ready to go, standing before the hall mirror, putting on her hat, while he, his hands behind him, appeared pinned to the door frame, waiting like Saint Sebastian[1] for the arrows to begin piercing him. The hat was new and had cost over seven dollars and a half. She kept saying, "Maybe I shouldn't have paid that for it. No, I shouldn't have. I'll take it off and return it tomorrow. I shouldn't have bought it."

Julian raised his eyes to heaven. "Yes, you should have bought it," he said. "Put it on and let's go." It was a hideous hat. A purple velvet flap came down on one side of it and stood up on the other; the rest of it was green and looked like a cushion with the stuffing out. He decided it was less comical than jaunty and pathetic. Everything that gave her pleasure was small and depressed him.

She lifted the hat one more time and set it down slowly on top of her head. Two wings of gray hair protruded on either side of her florid face, but her eyes, sky-blue, were as innocent and untouched by experience as they must have been when she was ten. Were it not that she was a widow who had struggled fiercely to feed and clothe and put him through school and who was supporting him still, "until he got on his feet," she might have been a little girl that he had to take to town.

"It's all right, it's all right," he said. "Let's go." He opened the door himself and started down the walk to get her going. The sky was a dying violet and the houses stood out darkly against it, bulbous liver-colored monstrosities of a uniform ugliness though no two were alike. Since this had been a fashionable neighborhood forty years ago, his mother persisted in thinking they did well to have an apartment in it. Each house had a narrow collar of dirt around it in which sat, usually, a grubby child. Julian walked with his hands in his pockets, his head down and thrust forward and his eyes glazed with the determination to make himself completely numb during the time he would be sacrificed to her pleasure.

The door closed and he turned to find the dumpy figure, surmounted by the atrocious hat, coming toward him. "Well," she said, "you only live once and paying a little more for it, I at least won't meet myself coming and going."

"Some day I'll start making money," Julian said gloomily — he knew he never would — "and you can have one of those jokes whenever you take the fit." But first they would move. He visualized a place where the nearest neighbors would be three miles away on either side.

"I think you're doing fine," she said, drawing on her gloves. "You've only been out of school a year. Rome wasn't built in a day."

She was one of the few members of the Y reducing class who arrived in hat and gloves and who had a son who had been to college. "It takes time," she said, "and the world is in such a mess. This hat looked better on me than any of the others, though when she brought it out I said, 'Take that thing back. I wouldn't have it on my head,' and she said, 'Now wait till you see it on,' and when she put it on me, I said, 'We-ull,' and she said, 'If you ask me, that hat does something for you and you do something for the hat, and besides,' she said, 'with that hat, you won't meet yourself coming and going.'"

Julian thought he could have stood his lot better if she had been selfish, if she had been an old hag who drank and screamed at him. He walked along,

1. Saint Sebastian: Roman defender of Christian faith, martyred for his beliefs.

saturated in depression, as if in the midst of his martyrdom he had lost his faith. Catching sight of his long, hopeless, irritated face, she stopped suddenly with a grief-stricken look, and pulled back on his arm. "Wait on me," she said. "I'm going back to the house and take this thing off and tomorrow I'm going to return it. I was out of my head. I can pay the gas bill with that seven-fifty."

He caught her in a vicious grip. "You are not going to take it back," he said. "I like it."

"Well," she said, "I don't think I ought . . ."

"Shut up and enjoy it," he muttered, more depressed than ever.

"With the world in the mess it's in," she said, "it's a wonder we can enjoy anything. I tell you, the bottom rail is on the top."

Julian sighed.

"Of course," she said, "if you know who you are, you can go anywhere." She said this every time he took her to the reducing class. "Most of them in it are not our kind of people," she said, "but I can be gracious to anybody. I know who I am."

"They don't give a damn for your graciousness," Julian said savagely. "Knowing who you are is good for one generation only. You haven't the foggiest idea where you stand now or who you are."

She stopped and allowed her eyes to flash at him. "I most certainly do know who I am," she said, "and if you don't know who you are, I'm ashamed of you."

"Oh hell," Julian said.

"Your great-grandfather was a former governor of this state," she said. "Your grandfather was a prosperous landowner. Your grandmother was a Godhigh."

"Will you look around you," he said tensely, "and see where you are now?" and he swept his arm jerkily out to indicate the neighborhood, which the growing darkness at least made less dingy.

"You remain what you are," she said. "Your great-grandfather had a plantation and two hundred slaves."

"There are no more slaves," he said irritably.

"They were better off when they were," she said. He groaned to see that she was off on that topic. She rolled onto it every few days like a train on an open track. He knew every stop, every junction, every swamp along the way, and knew the exact point at which her conclusion would roll majestically into the station: "It's ridiculous. It's simply not realistic. They should rise, yes, but on their own side of the fence."

"Let's skip it," Julian said.

"The ones I feel sorry for," she said, "are the ones that are half white. They're tragic."

"Will you skip it?"

"Suppose we were half white. We would certainly have mixed feelings."

"I have mixed feelings now," he groaned.

"Well, let's talk about something pleasant," she said. "I remember going to Grandpa's when I was a little girl. Then the house had double stairways that went up to what was really the second floor — all the cooking was done on the first. I used to like to stay down in the kitchen on account of the way the walls smelled. I would sit with my nose pressed against the plaster and take deep breaths. Actually the place belonged to the Godhighs but your grandfather

Chestny paid the mortgage and saved it for them. They were in reduced circumstances," she said, "but reduced or not, they never forgot who they were."

"Doubtless that decayed mansion reminded them," Julian muttered. He never spoke of it without contempt or thought of it without longing. He had seen it once when he was a child before it had been sold. The double stairways had rotted and been torn down. Negroes were living in it. But it remained in his mind as his mother had known it. It appeared in his dreams regularly. He would stand on the wide porch, listening to the rustle of oak leaves, then wander through the high-ceilinged hall into the parlor that opened onto it and gaze at the worn rugs and faded draperies. It occurred to him that it was he, not she, who could have appreciated it. He preferred its threadbare elegance to anything he could name and it was because of it that all the neighborhoods they had lived in had been a torment to him — whereas she had hardly known the difference. She called her insensitivity "being adjustable."

"And I remember the old darky who was my nurse, Caroline. There was no better person in the world. I've always had a great respect for my colored friends," she said. "I'd do anything in the world for them and they'd . . ."

"Will you for God's sake get off that subject?" Julian said. When he got on a bus by himself, he made it a point to sit down beside a Negro, in reparation as it were for his mother's sins.

"You're mighty touchy tonight," she said. "Do you feel all right?"

"Yes I feel all right," he said. "Now lay off."

She pursed her lips. "Well, you certainly are in a vile humor," she observed. "I just won't speak to you at all."

They had reached the bus stop. There was no bus in sight and Julian, his hands still jammed in his pockets and his head thrust forward, scowled down the empty street. The frustration of having to wait on the bus as well as ride on it began to creep up his neck like a hot hand. The presence of his mother was borne in upon him as she gave a pained sigh. He looked at her bleakly. She was holding herself very erect under the preposterous hat, wearing it like a banner of her imaginary dignity. There was in him an evil urge to break her spirit. He suddenly unloosened his tie and pulled it off and put it in his pocket.

She stiffened. "Why must you look like *that* when you take me to town?" she said. "Why must you deliberately embarrass me?"

"If you'll never learn where you are," he said, "you can at least learn where I am."

"You look like a — thug," she said.

"Then I must be one," he murmured.

"I'll just go home," she said. "I will not bother you. If you can't do a little thing like that for me . . ."

Rolling his eyes upward, he put his tie back on. "Restored to my class," he muttered. He thrust his face toward her and hissed, "True culture is in the mind, the *mind*," he said, and tapped his head, "the mind."

"It's in the heart," she said, "and in how you do things and how you do things is because of who you *are*."

"Nobody in the damn bus cares who you are."

"I care who I am," she said icily.

The lighted bus appeared on top of the next hill and as it approached, they moved out into the street to meet it. He put his hand under her elbow and hoisted her up on the creaking step. She entered with a little smile, as if she were going into a drawing room where everyone had been waiting for her. While he put in the tokens, she sat down on one of the broad front seats for three which faced the aisle. A thin woman with protruding teeth and long yellow hair was sitting on the end of it. His mother moved up beside her and left room for Julian beside herself. He sat down and looked at the floor across the aisle where a pair of thin feet in red and white canvas sandals were planted.

His mother immediately began a general conversation meant to attract anyone who felt like talking. "Can it get any hotter?" she said and removed from her purse a folding fan, black with a Japanese scene on it, which she began to flutter before her.

"I reckon it might could," the woman with the protruding teeth said, "but I know for a fact my apartment couldn't get no hotter."

"It must get the afternoon sun," his mother said. She sat forward and looked up and down the bus. It was half filled. Everybody was white. "I see we have the bus to ourselves," she said. Julian cringed.

"For a change," said the woman across the aisle, the owner of the red and white canvas sandals. "I come on one the other day and they were thick as fleas — up front and all through."

"The world is in a mess everywhere," his mother said. "I don't know how we've let it get in this fix."

"What gets my goat is all those boys from good families stealing automobile tires," the woman with the protruding teeth said. "I told my boy, I said you may not be rich but you been raised right and if I ever catch you in any such mess, they can send you on to the reformatory. Be exactly where you belong."

"Training tells," his mother said. "Is your boy in high school?"

"Ninth grade," the woman said.

"My son just finished college last year. He wants to write but he's selling typewriters until he gets started," his mother said.

The woman leaned forward and peered at Julian. He threw her such a malevolent look that she subsided against the seat. On the floor across the aisle there was an abandoned newspaper. He got up and got it and opened it out in front of him. His mother discreetly continued the conversation in a lower tone but the woman across the aisle said in a loud voice, "Well that's nice. Selling typewriters is close to writing. He can go right from one to the other."

"I tell him," his mother said, "that Rome wasn't built in a day."

Behind the newspaper Julian was withdrawing into the inner compartment of his mind where he spent most of his time. This was a kind of mental bubble in which he established himself when he could not bear to be a part of what was going on around him. From it he could see out and judge but in it he was safe from any kind of penetration from without. It was the only place where he felt free of the general idiocy of his fellows. His mother had never entered it but from it he could see her with absolute clarity.

The old lady was clever enough and he thought that if she had started from any of the right premises, more might have been expected of her. She lived according to the laws of her own fantasy world, outside of which he had never seen her set foot. The law of it was to sacrifice herself for him after she had first created the necessity to do so by making a mess of things. If he had permitted her sacrifices, it was only because her lack of foresight had made them necessary. All of her life had been a struggle to act like a Chestny without the Chestny goods, and to give him everything she thought a Chestny ought to have;

but since, said she, it was fun to struggle, why complain? And when you had won, as she had won, what fun to look back on the hard times! He could not forgive her that she had enjoyed the struggle and that she thought *she* had won.

What she meant when she said she had won was that she had brought him up successfully and had sent him to college and that he had turned out so well — good-looking (her teeth had gone unfilled so that his could be straightened), intelligent (he realized he was too intelligent to be a success), and with a future ahead of him (there was of course no future ahead of him). She excused his gloominess on the grounds that he was still growing up and his radical ideas on his lack of practical experience. She said he didn't yet know a thing about "life," that he hadn't even entered the real world — when already he was as disenchanted with it as a man of fifty.

The further irony of all this was that in spite of her, he had turned out so well. In spite of going to only a third-rate college, he had, on his own initiative, come out with a first-rate education; in spite of growing up dominated by a small mind, he had ended up with a large one; in spite of all her foolish views, he was free of prejudice and unafraid to face facts. Most miraculous of all, instead of being blinded by love for her as she was for him, he had cut himself emotionally free of her and could see her with complete objectivity. He was not dominated by his mother.

The bus stopped with a sudden jerk and shook him from his meditation. A woman from the back lurched forward with little steps and barely escaped falling in his newspaper as she righted herself. She got off and a large Negro got on. Julian kept his paper lowered to watch. It gave him a certain satisfaction to see injustice in daily operation. It confirmed his view that with a few exceptions there was no one worth knowing within a radius of three hundred miles. The Negro was well dressed and carried a briefcase. He looked around and then sat down on the other end of the seat where the woman with the red and white canvas sandals was sitting. He immediately unfolded a newspaper and obscured himself behind it. Julian's mother's elbow at once prodded insistently into his ribs. "Now you see why I won't ride on these buses by myself," she whispered.

The woman with the red and white canvas sandals had risen at the same time the Negro sat down and had gone further back in the bus and taken the seat of the woman who had got off. His mother leaned forward and cast her an approving look.

Julian rose, crossed the aisle, and sat down in the place of the woman with the canvas sandals. From this position, he looked serenely across at his mother. Her face had turned an angry red. He stared at her, making his eyes the eyes of a stranger. He felt his tension suddenly lift as if he had openly declared war on her.

He would have liked to get in conversation with the Negro and to talk with him about art or politics or any subject that would be above the comprehension of those around them, but the man remained entrenched behind his paper. He was either ignoring the change of seating or had never noticed it. There was no way for Julian to convey his sympathy.

His mother kept her eyes fixed reproachfully on his face. The woman with the protruding teeth was looking at him avidly as if he were a type of monster new to her.

"Do you have a light?" he asked the Negro.

Without looking away from his paper, the man reached in his pocket and handed him a packet of matches.

"Thanks," Julian said. For a moment he held the matches foolishly. A NO SMOKING sign looked down upon him from over the door. This alone would not have deterred him; he had no cigarettes. He had quit smoking some months before because he could not afford it. "Sorry," he muttered and handed back the matches. The Negro lowered the paper and gave him an annoyed look. He took the matches and raised the paper again.

His mother continued to gaze at him but she did not take advantage of his momentary discomfort. Her eyes retained their battered look. Her face seemed to be unnaturally red, as if her blood pressure had risen. Julian allowed no glimmer of sympathy to show on his face. Having got the advantage, he wanted desperately to keep it and carry it through. He would have liked to teach her a lesson that would last her a while, but there seemed no way to continue the point. The Negro refused to come out from behind his paper.

Julian folded his arms and looked stolidly before him, facing her but as if he did not see her, as if he had ceased to recognize her existence. He visualized a scene in which, the bus having reached their stop, he would remain in his seat and when she said, "Aren't you going to get off?" he would look at her as at a stranger who had rashly addressed him. The corner they got off on was usually deserted, but it was well lighted and it would not hurt her to walk by herself the four blocks to the Y. He decided to wait until the time came and then decide whether or not he would let her get off by herself. He would have to be at the Y at ten to bring her back, but he could leave her wondering if he was going to show up. There was no reason for her to think she could always depend on him.

He retired again into the high-ceilinged room sparsely settled with large pieces of antique furniture. His soul expanded momentarily but then he became aware of his mother across from him and the vision shriveled. He studied her coldly. Her feet in little pumps dangled like a child's and did not quite reach the floor. She was training on him an exaggerated look of reproach. He felt completely detached from her. At that moment he could with pleasure have slapped her as he would have slapped a particularly obnoxious child in his charge.

He began to imagine various unlikely ways by which he could teach her a lesson. He might make friends with some distinguished Negro professor or lawyer and bring him home to spend the evening. He would be entirely justified but her blood pressure would rise to 300. He could not push her to the extent of making her have a stroke, and moreover, he had never been successful at making any Negro friends. He had tried to strike up an acquaintance on the bus with some of the better types, with ones that looked like professors or ministers or lawyers. One morning he had sat down next to a distinguished-looking dark brown man who had answered his questions with a sonorous solemnity but who had turned out to be an undertaker. Another day he had sat down beside a cigar-smoking Negro with a diamond ring on his finger, but after a few stilted pleasantries, the Negro had rung the buzzer and risen, slipping two lottery tickets into Julian's hand as he climbed over him to leave.

He imagined his mother lying desperately ill and his being able to secure only a Negro doctor for her. He toyed with that idea for a few minutes and then dropped it for a momentary vision of himself participating as a sympathizer in a sit-in demonstration. This was possible but he did not linger with it. Instead, he approached the ultimate horror. He brought home a beautiful suspiciously Negroid woman. Prepare yourself, he said. There is nothing you can do about it. This is the woman I've chosen. She's intelligent, dignified, even good, and she's suffered and she hasn't thought it *fun*. Now persecute us, go ahead and persecute us. Drive her out of here, but remember, you're driving me too. His eyes were narrowed and through the indignation he had generated, he saw his mother across the aisle, purple-faced, shrunken to the dwarf-like proportions of her moral nature, sitting like a mummy beneath the ridiculous banner of her hat.

He was tilted out of his fantasy again as the bus stopped. The door opened with a sucking hiss and out of the dark a large, gaily dressed, sullen-looking colored woman got on with a little boy. The child, who might have been four, had on a short plaid suit and a Tyrolean hat with a blue feather in it. Julian hoped that he would sit down beside him and that the woman would push in beside his mother. He could think of no better arrangement.

As she waited for her tokens, the woman was surveying the seating possibilities — he hoped with the idea of sitting where she was least wanted. There was something familiar-looking about her but Julian could not place what it was. She was a giant of a woman. Her face was set not only to meet opposition but to seek it out. The downward tilt of her large lower lip was like a warning sign: DON'T TAMPER WITH ME. Her bulging figure was encased in a green crepe dress and her feet overflowed in red shoes. She had on a hideous hat. A purple velvet flap came down on one side of it and stood up on the other; the rest of it was green and looked like a cushion with the stuffing out. She carried a mammoth red pocketbook that bulged throughout as if it were stuffed with rocks.

To Julian's disappointment, the little boy climbed up on the empty seat beside his mother. His mother lumped all children, black and white, into the common category "cute," and she thought little Negroes were on the whole cuter than little white children. She smiled at the little boy as he climbed on the seat.

Meanwhile the woman was bearing down upon the empty seat beside Julian. To his annoyance, she squeezed herself into it. He saw his mother's face change as the woman settled herself next to him and he realized with satisfaction that this was more objectionable to her than it was to him. Her face seemed almost gray and there was a look of dull recognition in her eyes, as if suddenly she had sickened at some awful confrontation. Julian saw that it was because she and the woman had, in a sense, swapped sons. Though his mother would not realize the symbolic significance of this, she would feel it. His amusement showed plainly on his face.

The woman next to him muttered something unintelligible to herself. He was conscious of a kind of bristling next to him, a muted growling like that of an angry cat. He could not see anything but the red pocketbook upright on the bulging green thighs. He visualized the woman as she had stood waiting for her tokens — the ponderous figure, rising from the red shoes upward over the solid hips, the mammoth bosom, the haughty face, to the green and purple hat.

His eyes widened.

The vision of the two hats, identical, broke upon him with the radiance of a brilliant sunrise. His face was suddenly lit with joy. He could not believe that Fate had thrust upon his mother such a lesson. He gave a loud chuckle so that she would look at him and see that he saw. She turned her eyes on him slowly. The blue in them seemed to have turned a bruised purple. For a moment he had an uncomfortable sense of her innocence, but it lasted only a second before principle rescued him. Justice entitled him to laugh. His grin hardened until it said to her as plainly as if he were saying aloud: Your punishment exactly fits your pettiness. This should teach you a permanent lesson.

Her eyes shifted to the woman. She seemed unable to bear looking at him and to find the woman preferable. He became conscious again of the bristling presence at his side. The woman was rumbling like a volcano about to become active. His mother's mouth began to twitch slightly at one corner. With a sinking heart, he saw incipient signs of recovery on her face and realized that this was going to strike her suddenly as funny and was going to be no lesson at all. She kept her eyes on the woman and an amused smile came over her face as if the woman were a monkey that had stolen her hat. The little Negro was looking up at her with large fascinated eyes. He had been trying to attract her attention for some time.

"Carver!" the woman said suddenly. "Come heah!"

When he saw that the spotlight was on him at last, Carver drew his feet up and turned himself toward Julian's mother and giggled.

"Carver!" the woman said. "You heah me? Come heah!"

Carver slid down from the seat but remained squatting with his back against the base of it, his head turned slyly around toward Julian's mother, who was smiling at him. The woman reached a hand across the aisle and snatched him to her. He righted himself and hung backwards on her knees, grinning at Julian's mother. "Isn't he cute?" Julian's mother said to the woman with the protruding teeth.

"I reckon he is," the woman said without conviction.

The Negress yanked him upright but he eased out of her grip and shot across the aisle and scrambled, giggling wildly, onto the seat beside his love.

"I think he likes me," Julian's mother said, and smiled at the woman. It was the smile she used when she was being particularly gracious to an inferior. Julian saw everything lost. The lesson had rolled off her like rain on a roof.

The woman stood up and yanked the little boy off the seat as if she were snatching him from contagion. Julian could feel the rage in her at having no weapon like his mother's smile. She gave the child a sharp slap across his leg. He howled once and then thrust his head into her stomach and kicked his feet against her shins. "Be-have," she said vehemently.

The bus stopped and the Negro who had been reading the newspaper got off. The woman moved over and set the little boy down with a thump between herself and Julian. She held him firmly by the knee. In a moment he put his hands in front of his face and peeped at Julian's mother through his fingers.

"I see yooooooo!" she said and put her hand in front of her face and peeped at him.

The woman slapped his hand down. "Quit yo' foolishness," she said, "before I knock the living Jesus out of you!"

Julian was thankful that the next stop was theirs. He reached up and pulled the cord. The woman reached up and pulled it at the same time. Oh my God, he thought. He had the terrible intuition that when they got off the bus together, his mother would open her purse and give the little boy a nickel. The gesture would be as natural to her as breathing. The bus stopped and the woman got up and lunged to the front, dragging the child, who wished to stay on, after her. Julian and his mother got up and followed. As they neared the door, Julian tried to relieve her of her pocketbook.

"No," she murmured, "I want to give the little boy a nickel."

"No!" Julian hissed. "No!"

She smiled down at the child and opened her bag. The bus door opened and the woman picked him up by the arm and descended with him, hanging at her hip. Once in the street she set him down and shook him.

Julian's mother had to close her purse while she got down the bus step but as soon as her feet were on the ground, she opened it again and began to rummage inside. "I can't find but a penny," she whispered, "but it looks like a new one."

"Don't do it!" Julian said fiercely between his teeth. There was a streetlight on the corner and she hurried to get under it so that she could better see into her pocketbook. The woman was heading off rapidly down the street with the child still hanging backward on her hand.

"Oh little boy!" Julian's mother called and took a few quick steps and caught up with them just beyond the lamppost. "Here's a bright new penny for you," and she held out the coin, which shone bronze in the dim light.

The huge woman turned and for a moment stood, her shoulders lifted and her face frozen with frustrated rage, and stared at Julian's mother. Then all at once she seemed to explode like a piece of machinery that had been given one ounce of pressure too much. Julian saw the black fist swing out with the red pocketbook. He shut his eyes and cringed as he heard the woman shout, "He don't take nobody's pennies!" When he opened his eyes, the woman was disappearing down the street with the little boy staring wide-eyed over her shoulder. Julian's mother was sitting on the sidewalk.

"I told you not to do that," Julian said angrily. "I told you not to do that!"

He stood over her for a minute, gritting his teeth. Her legs were stretched out in front of her and her hat was on her lap. He squatted down and looked her in the face. It was totally expressionless. "You got exactly what you deserved," he said. "Now get up."

He picked up her pocketbook and put what had fallen out back in it. He picked her hat up off her lap. The penny caught his eye on the sidewalk and he picked that up and let it drop before her eyes into the purse. Then he stood up and leaned over and held his hands out to pull her up. She remained immobile. He sighed. Rising above them on either side were black apartment buildings, marked with irregular rectangles of light. At the end of the block a man came out of a door and walked off in the opposite direction. "All right," he said, "suppose somebody happens by and wants to know why you're sitting on the sidewalk?"

She took the hand and, breathing hard, pulled heavily up on it and then stood for a moment, swaying slightly as if the spots of light in the darkness were circling around her. Her eyes, shadowed and confused, finally settled on his face. He did not try to conceal his irritation. "I hope this teaches you a lesson," he said. She leaned forward and her eyes raked his face. She seemed trying to determine his identity. Then, as if she found nothing familiar about him, she started off with a headlong movement in the wrong direction.

"Aren't you going on to the Y?" he asked.

"Home," she muttered.

"Well, are we walking?"

For answer she kept going. Julian followed along, his hands behind him. He saw no reason to let the lesson she had had go without backing it up with an explanation of its meaning. She might as well be made to understand what had happened to her. "Don't think that was just an uppity Negro woman," he said. "That was the whole colored race which will no longer take your condescending pennies. That was your black double. She can wear the same hat as you, and to be sure," he added gratuitously (because he thought it was funny), "it looked better on her than it did on you. What all this means," he said, "is that the old world is gone. The old manners are obsolete and your graciousness is not worth a damn." He thought bitterly of the house that had been lost for him. "You aren't who you think you are," he said.

She continued to plow ahead, paying no attention to him. Her hair had come undone on one side. She dropped her pocketbook and took no notice. He stooped and picked it up and handed it to her but she did not take it.

"You needn't act as if the world had come to an end," he said, "because it hasn't. From now on you've got to live in a new world and face a few realities for a change. Buck up," he said, "it won't kill you."

She was breathing fast.

"Let's wait on the bus," he said.

"Home," she said thickly.

"I hate to see you behave like this," he said. "Just like a child. I should be able to expect more of you." He decided to stop where he was and make her stop and wait for a bus. "I'm not going any farther," he said, stopping. "We're going on the bus."

She continued to go on as if she had not heard him. He took a few steps and caught her arm and stopped her. He looked into her face and caught his breath. He was looking into a face he had never seen before. "Tell Grandpa to come get me," she said.

He stared, stricken.

"Tell Caroline to come get me," she said.

Stunned, he let her go and she lurched forward again, walking as if one leg were shorter than the other. A tide of darkness seemed to be sweeping her from him. "Mother!" he cried. "Darling, sweetheart, wait!" Crumpling, she fell to the pavement. He dashed forward and fell at her side, crying, "Mamma, Mamma!" He turned her over. Her face was fiercely distorted. One eye, large and staring, moved slightly to the left as if it had become unmoored. The other remained fixed on him, raked his face again, found nothing and closed.

"Wait here, wait here!" he cried and jumped up and began to run for help toward a cluster of lights he saw in the distance ahead of him. "Help, help!" he shouted, but his voice was thin, scarcely a thread of sound. The lights drifted farther away the faster he ran and his feet moved numbly as if they carried him nowhere. The tide of darkness seemed to sweep him back to her, postponing from moment to moment his entry into the world of guilt and sorrow.

Exercises

1. What influences in the background and psychological make-up of Julian's mother have determined her lifestyle, attitudes, and patterns of behavior?

2. Julian's mother admits to knowing precisely who she is. How does she perceive herself? How does Julian perceive her?

3. How does Julian see himself? What do you feel for him? sympathy? pity? disgust? Why?

4. Cite examples of childish behavior on the part of Julian's mother.

5. Without any other modification and loss of effect, do you believe the setting could be changed to Detroit? Why, or why not?

6. What special meaning does the hat have for Julian's mother? for Julian? What significance do you attach to the black woman's wearing a similar hat?

7. Corroborate how the complications in the story grow logically from the point at which the conflict is introduced and lead naturally to another incident that further complicates the chief problem.

8. Retell in your words what happens to Julian's mother in the climactic scene. What early information (foreshadowing) prepares the reader to accept the fact that she is having an attack?

9. What do you discover about Julian from his cries to his afflicted mother?

Topics for Writing

1. Which character, Julian or his mother, would you judge to be more fully developed as a dynamic character? Justify your choice in an essay.

2. Compare and contrast Julian's experience of initiation with that of the boy in "I Want to Know Why" in Chapter 3.

3. In a letter dated July 27, 1963, to Sister M. Bernetta Quinn, a friend, the author admits having touched the subject of justice only once by way of fiction in this story and offers the comment: "Justice is justice and should not be appealed to along racial lines. The problem is not abstract for the Southerner, it's concrete; he sees it in terms of persons, not races — which way of seeing does away with easy answers."

Using the quotation from the letter as your starting point, discuss the author's treatment of the issue of justice in this story.

4. How does Flannery O'Connor's attitude toward tradition in the Old South differ from Faulkner's as shown in their respective stories? What similarities do you discern?

Selected Bibliography   Flannery O'Connor

Brittain, Joan T. "Flannery O'Connor — Addenda." *Bulletin of Bibliography*, 25 (1968), 142.
———. "Flannery O'Connor: A Bibliography." *Bulletin of Bibliography*, 25 (1968), 98–100, 123–124.

Browning, Preston M. *Flannery O'Connor.* Carbondale: Southern Illinois University Press, 1974.

Burns, Stuart L. "Flannery O'Connor's Literary Apprenticeship." *Renascence,* 22 (Autumn 1969), 3–16.

Cheney, Brainard. "Miss O'Connor Creates Unusual Humor Out of Ordinary Sin." *Sewanee Review,* 71 (Autumn 1963), 644–652.

Detweiler, Robert. "The Curse of Christ in Flannery O'Connor's Fiction." *Comparative Literature Studies,* 3 (1966), 235–245.

Dowell, Bob. "The Moment of Grace in the Fiction of Flannery O'Connor." *College English,* 27 (December 1965), 235–239.

Drake, Robert Y., Jr. "The Bleeding, Stinking, Mad Shadow of Jesus in the Fiction of Flannery O'Connor." *Comparative Literature Studies,* 3, no. 2 (1966), 183–196.

————. "The Paradigm of Flannery O'Connor's True Country." *Studies in Short Fiction,* 6 (Summer 1969), 433–442.

Driskell, Leon V., and Joan T. Brittain. *The Eternal Crossroads: The Art of Flannery O'Connor.* Lexington: University of Kentucky Press, 1971.

Eggenschwiler, David. *The Christian Humanism of Flannery O'Connor.* Detroit: Wayne State University Press, 1972.

Feeley, M. Kathleen, S.S.N.D. "Thematic Imagery in the Fiction of Flannery O'Connor." *Southern Humanities Review,* 3 (Winter 1968), 14–32.

Fitzgerald, Robert. "The Countryside and the True Country." *Sewanee Review,* 70, no. 3 (1962), 380–394.

Friedman, Melvin J., and Lewis A. Lawson, eds. *The Added Dimension: The Art and Mind of Flannery O'Connor.* New York: Fordham University Press, 1966.

Hendin, Josephine. *The World of Flannery O'Connor.* Bloomington: Indiana University Press, 1970.

Lorch, Thomas M. "Flannery O'Connor: Christian Allegorist." *Critique,* 10, no. 2 (1968), 69–80.

McFarland, Dorothy Tuck. *Flannery O'Connor.* New York: Ungar, 1976.

Martin, Carter W. "Flannery O'Connor's Early Fiction." *Southern Humanities Review,* 7 (Spring 1973), 210–214.

————. *The True Country: Themes in the Fiction of Flannery O'Connor.* Nashville: Vanderbilt University Press, 1969.

May, John R. *The Pruning Word: The Parables of Flannery O'Connor.* Notre Dame, Ind.: University of Notre Dame Press, 1976.

Montgomery, Marion. "Beyond Symbol and Surface: The Fiction of Flannery O'Connor." *Georgia Review,* 22 (Summer 1968), 188–193.

————. "Miss O'Connor and the Christ-Haunted." *Southern Review,* 4 (Summer 1968), 665–672.

Muller, Gilbert H. *Nightmares and Visions: Flannery O'Connor and the Catholic Grotesque.* Athens: University of Georgia Press, 1972.

Orvell, Miles. *Invisible Parade: The Fiction of Flannery O'Connor.* Philadelphia: Temple University Press, 1972.

Smith, J[oyce Carol] Oates. "Ritual and Violence in Flannery O'Connor." *Thought,* 41 (Winter 1966), 545–560.

Walters, Dorothy. *Flannery O'Connor.* New York: Twayne, 1973.

W. Somerset Maugham (1874–1965)

The Colonel's Lady

All this happened two or three years before the outbreak of the war.

The Peregrines were having breakfast. Though they were alone and the table was long they sat at opposite ends of it. From the walls George Peregrine's ancestors, painted by the fashionable painters of the day, looked down upon them. The butler brought in the morning post. There were several letters for the Colonel, business letters, the *Times* and a small parcel for his wife Evie. He looked at his letters and then, opening the *Times,* began to read it. They finished breakfast and rose from the table. He noticed that his wife hadn't opened the parcel.

"What's that?" he asked.

"Only some books."

"Shall I open it for you?"

"If you like."

He hated to cut string and so with some difficulty untied the knots.

"But they're all the same," he said when he had unwrapped the parcel. "What on earth d'you want six copies of the same book for?" He opened one of them. "Poetry." Then he looked at the title page. *When Pyramids Decay,* he read, by E. K. Hamilton. Eva Katherine Hamilton: that was his wife's maiden name. He looked at her with smiling surprise. "Have you written a book, Evie? You are a slyboots."

"I didn't think it would interest you very much. Would you like a copy?"

"Well, you know poetry isn't much in my line, but — yes, I'd like a copy; I'll read it. I'll take it along to my study. I've got a lot to do this morning."

He gathered up the *Times,* his letters and the book and went out. His study was a large and comfortable room, with a big desk, leather armchairs and what he called "trophies of the chase" on the walls. In the bookshelves were works of reference, books on farming, gardening, fishing and shooting, and books on the last war, in which he had won an M.C. and a D.S.O. For before his marriage he had been in the Welsh Guards. At the end of the war he retired and settled down to the life of a country gentleman in the spacious house, some twenty miles from Sheffield, which one of his forebears had built in the reign of George II. George Peregrine had an estate of some fifteen hundred acres which he managed with ability; he was a justice of the peace and performed his duties conscientiously. During the season he rode to hounds two days a week. He was a good shot, a golfer and though now a little over fifty could still play a hard game of tennis. He could describe himself with propriety as an all-around sportsman.

He had been putting on weight lately, but was still a fine figure of a man; tall, with gray curly hair, only just beginning to grow thin on the crown, frank blue eyes, good features and a high colour. He was a public-spirited man, chairman of any number of local organizations and, as became his class and station, a loyal member of the Conservative party. He looked upon it as his duty to see to the welfare of the people on his estate and it was a satisfaction to him to know that Evie could be trusted to tend the sick and succour the poor. He had built a cottage hospital on the outskirts of the village and paid the wages of a nurse out of his own pocket. All he asked of the recipients of his bounty was that at elections, county or general, they should vote for his candidate. He was a friendly man, affable to his inferiors, considerate with his tenants and popular with the neighbouring gentry. He would have been pleased and at the same time slightly embarrassed if someone had told him he was a jolly good fellow. That was what he wanted to be. He desired no higher praise.

It was hard luck that he had no children. He would have been an excellent father, kindly but strict, and would have brought up his sons as a gentleman's sons should be brought up, sent them to Eton, you know, taught them to fish, shoot and ride. As it was, his heir was a nephew, son of his brother killed in a motor accident, not a bad boy, but not a chip off the old block, no, sir, far from it; and would you believe it, his fool of a mother was sending him to a co-educational school. Evie had been a sad disappointment to him. Of course she was a lady, and she had a bit of money of her own; she managed the house uncommonly well and she was a good hostess. The village people adored her. She had been a pretty little thing when he married her, with a creamy skin, light brown hair and a trim figure, healthy too and not a bad tennis player; he couldn't understand why she'd had no children; of course she was faded now, she must be getting on for five and forty; her skin was drab, her hair had lost its sheen and she was as thin as a rail. She was always neat and suitably dressed, but she didn't seem to bother how she looked, she wore no make-up and didn't even use lipstick; sometimes at night when she dolled herself up for a party you could tell that once she'd been quite attractive, but ordinarily she was — well, the sort of woman you simply didn't notice. A nice woman, of course, a good wife, and it wasn't her fault if she was barren, but it was tough on a fellow who wanted an heir of his own loins; she hadn't any vitality, that's what was the matter with her. He supposed he'd been in love with her when he asked her to marry him, at least sufficiently in love for a man who wanted to marry and settle down, but with time he discovered that they had nothing much in common. She didn't care about hunting, and fishing bored her. Naturally they'd drifted apart. He had to do her the justice to admit that she'd never bothered him. There'd been no scenes. They had no quarrels. She seemed to take it for granted that he should go his own way. When he went up to London now and then she never wanted to come with him. He had a girl there, well, she wasn't exactly a girl, she was thirty-five if she was a day, but she was blonde and luscious and he only had to wire ahead of time and they'd dine, do a show and spend the night together. Well, a man, a healthy normal man had to have some fun in his life. The thought crossed his mind that if Evie hadn't been such a good woman she'd have been a better wife; but it was not the sort of thought that he welcomed and he put it away from him.

George Peregrine finished his *Times* and being a considerate fellow rang the bell and told the butler to take the paper to Evie. Then he looked at his watch. It was half-past ten and at eleven he had an appointment with one of his tenants. He had half an hour to spare.

"I'd better have a look at Evie's book," he said to himself.

He took it up with a smile. Evie had a lot of highbrow books in her sitting room, not the sort of books that interested him, but if they amused her he had no objection to her reading them. He noticed that the volume he now held in his hand contained no more than ninety pages. That was all to the good. He shared Edgar Allan Poe's opinion that poems should be short. But as he turned the pages he noticed that several of Evie's had long lines of irregular length and didn't rhyme. He didn't like that. At his first school, when he was a little boy, he remembered learning a poem that began: *The boy stood on the burning deck* and later, at Eton, one that started: *Ruin seize thee, ruthless king;* and then there was Henry V; they'd had to take that one half. He stared at Evie's pages with consternation.

"That's not what I call poetry," he said.

Fortunately it wasn't all like that. Interspersed with the pieces that looked so odd, lines of three or four words and then a line of ten or fifteen, there were little poems, quite short, that rhymed, thank God, with the lines all the same length. Several of the pages were just headed with the word *Sonnet,* and out of curiosity he counted the lines; there were fourteen of them. He read them. They seemed all right, but he didn't quite know what they were all about. He repeated to himself: *Ruin seize thee, ruthless king.*

"Poor Evie," he sighed.

At that moment the farmer he was expecting was ushered into the study, and putting the book down he made him welcome. They embarked on their business.

"I read your book, Evie," he said as they sat down to lunch. "Jolly good. Did it cost you a packet to have it printed?"

"No, I was lucky. I sent it to a publisher and he took it."

"Not much money in poetry, my dear," he said in his good-natured, hearty way.

"No, I don't suppose there is. What did Bannock want to see you about this morning?"

Bannock was the tenant who had interrupted his reading of Evie's poems.

"He's asked me to advance the money for a pedigree bull he wants to buy. He's a good man and I've half a mind to do it."

George Peregrine saw that Evie didn't want to talk about her book and he was not sorry to change the subject. He was glad she had used her maiden name on the title page; he didn't suppose anyone would ever hear about the book, but he was proud of his own unusual name and he wouldn't have liked it if some damned penny-a-liner had made fun of Evie's effort in one of the papers.

During the few weeks that followed he thought it tactful not to ask Evie any questions about her venture into verse and she never referred to it. It might have been a discreditable incident that they had silently agreed not to mention. But then a strange thing happened. He had to go to London on business and he took Daphne out to dinner. That was the name of the girl with whom he was in the habit of passing a few agreeable hours whenever he went to town.

"Oh, George," she said, "is that your wife who's written a book they're all talking about?"

"What on earth d'you mean?"

"Well, there's a fellow I know who's a critic. He took me out to dinner the other night and he had a book with him. 'Got anything for me to read?' I said. 'What's that?' 'Oh, I don't think that's your cup of tea,' he said. 'It's poetry. I've just been reviewing it.' 'No poetry for me,' I said. 'It's about the hottest stuff I ever read,' he said. 'Selling like hot cakes. And it's damned good.' "

"Who's the book by?" asked George.

"A woman called Hamilton. My friend told me that wasn't her real name. He said her real name was Peregrine. 'Funny,' I said, 'I know a fellow called Peregrine.' 'Colonel in the army,' he said. 'Lives near Sheffield.' "

"I'd just as soon you didn't talk about me to your friends," said George with a frown of vexation.

"Keep your shirt on, dearie. Who'd you take me for? I just said, 'It's not the same one.' " Daphne giggled. "My friend said: 'They say he's a regular Colonel Blimp.' "

George had a keen sense of humour.

"You could tell them better than that," he laughed. "If my wife had written a book I'd be the first to know about it, wouldn't I?"

"I suppose you would."

Anyhow the matter didn't interest her and when the Colonel began to talk of other things she forgot about it. He put it out of his mind too. There was nothing to it, he decided, and that silly fool of a critic had just been pulling Daphne's leg. He was amused at the thought of her tackling that book because she had been told it was hot stuff and then finding it just a lot of stuff cut up into unequal lines.

He was a member of several clubs and next day he thought he'd lunch at one in St. James's Street. He was catching a train back to Sheffield early in the afternoon. He was sitting in a comfortable armchair having a glass of sherry before going into the dining-room when an old friend came up to him.

"Well, old boy, how's life?" he said. "How d'you like being the husband of a celebrity?"

George Peregrine looked at his friend. He thought he saw an amused twinkle in his eyes.

"I don't know what you're talking about," he answered.

"Come off it, George. Everyone knows E. K. Hamilton is your wife. Not often a book of verse has a success like that. Look here, Henry Dashwood is lunching with me. He'd like to meet you."

"Who the devil is Henry Dashwood and why should he want to meet me?"

"Oh, my dear fellow, what do you do with yourself all the time in the country? Henry's about the best critic we've got. He wrote a wonderful review of Evie's book. D'you mean to say she didn't show it you?"

Before George could answer his friend had called a man over. A tall, thin man, with a high forehead, a beard, a long nose and a stoop, just the sort of man whom George was prepared to dislike at first sight. Introductions were effected. Henry Dashwood sat down.

"Is Mrs. Peregrine in London by any chance? I should very much like to meet her," he said.

"No, my wife doesn't like London. She prefers the country," said George stiffly.

"She wrote me a very nice letter about my review. I was pleased. You know, we critics get more kicks than halfpence. I was simply bowled over by her book. It's so fresh and original, very modern without being obscure. She seems to be as much at her ease in free verse as in the classical metres." Then because he was a critic he thought he should criticize. "Sometimes her ear is a trifle at fault, but you can say the same of Emily Dickinson. There are several of those short lyrics of hers that might have been written by Landor."

All this was gibberish to George Peregrine. The man was nothing but a disgusting highbrow. But the Colonel had good manners and he answered with proper civility: Henry Dashwood went on as though he hadn't spoken.

"But what makes the book so outstanding is the passion that throbs in every line. So many of these young poets are so anaemic, cold, bloodless, dully intellectual, but here you have real naked, earthy passion; of course deep, sincere emotion like that is tragic — ah, my dear Colonel, how right Heine was when he said that the poet makes little songs out of his great sorrows. You know, now and then, as I read and reread those heart-rending pages I thought of Sappho."

This was too much for George Peregrine and he got up.

"Well, it's jolly nice of you to say such nice things about my wife's little book. I'm sure she'll be delighted. But I must bolt, I've got to catch a train and I want to get a bite of lunch."

"Damned fool," he said irritably to himself as he walked upstairs to the dining-room.

He got home in time for dinner and after Evie had gone to bed he went into his study and looked for her book. He thought he'd just glance through it again to see for himself what they were making such a fuss about, but he couldn't find it. Evie must have taken it away.

"Silly," he muttered.

He'd told her he thought it jolly good. What more could a fellow be expected to say? Well, it didn't matter. He lit his pipe and read the *Field* till he felt sleepy. But a week or so later it happened that he had to go into Sheffield for the day. He lunched there at his club. He had nearly finished when the Duke of Haverel came in. This was the great local magnate and of course the Colonel knew him, but only to say how d'you do to; and he was surprised when the Duke stopped at his table.

"We're so sorry your wife couldn't come to us for the week end," he said, with a sort of shy cordiality. "We're expecting rather a nice lot of people."

George was taken aback. He guessed that the Haverels had asked him and Evie over for the week end and Evie, without saying a word to him about it, had refused. He had the presence of mind to say he was sorry too.

"Better luck next time," said the Duke pleasantly and moved on.

Colonel Peregrine was very angry and when he got home he said to his wife:

"Look here, what's this about our being asked over to Haverel? Why on earth did you say we couldn't go? We've never been asked before and it's the best shooting in the county."

"I didn't think of that. I thought it would only bore you."

"Damn it all, you might at least have asked me if I wanted to go."

"I'm sorry."

He looked at her closely. There was something in her expression that he didn't quite understand. He frowned.

"I suppose *I* was asked?" he barked.

Evie flushed a little.

"Well, in point of fact you weren't."

"I call it damned rude of them to ask you without asking me."

"I suppose they thought it wasn't your sort of party. The Duchess is rather fond of writers and people like that, you know. She's having Henry Dashwood, the critic, and for some reason he wants to meet me."

"It was damned nice of you to refuse, Evie."

"It's the least I could do," she smiled. She hesitated a moment. "George, my publishers want to give a little dinner party for me one day towards the end of the month and of course they want you to come too."

"Oh, I don't think that's quite my mark. I'll come up to London with you if you like. I'll find someone to dine with."

Daphne.

"I expect it'll be very dull, but they're making rather a point of it. And the day after, the American publisher who's taken my book is giving a cocktail party at Claridge's. I'd like you to come to that if you wouldn't mind."

"Sounds like a crashing bore, but if you really want me to come I'll come."

"It would be sweet of you."

George Peregrine was dazed by the cocktail party. There were a lot of people. Some of them didn't look so bad, a few of the women were decently turned out, but the men seemed to him pretty awful. He was introduced to everybody as Colonel Peregrine, E. K. Hamilton's husband, you know. The men didn't seem to have anything to say to him, but the women gushed.

"You *must* be proud of your wife. Isn't it *wonderful?* You know, I read it right through at a sitting, I simply couldn't put it down, and when I'd finished I started again at the beginning and read it right through a second time. I was simply *thrilled.*"

The English publisher said to him:

"We've not had a success like this with a book of verse for twenty years. I've never seen such reviews."

The American publisher said to him:

"It's swell. It'll be a smash hit in America. You wait and see."

The American publisher had sent Evie a great spray of orchids. Damned ridiculous, thought George. As they came in, people were taken up to Evie and it was evident that they said flattering things to her, which she took with a pleasant smile and a word or two of thanks. She was a trifle flushed with the excitement, but seemed quite at her ease. Though he thought the whole thing a lot of stuff and nonsense George noted with approval that his wife was carrying it off in just the right way.

"Well, there's one thing," he said to himself, "you can see she's a lady and that's a damned sight more than you can say of anyone else here."

He drank a good many cocktails. But there was one thing that bothered him. He had a notion that some of the people he was introduced to looked at him in rather a funny sort of way, he couldn't quite make out what it meant, and once when he strolled by two women who were sitting together on a sofa he had the impression that they were talking about him and after he passed he was almost certain they tittered. He was very glad when the party came to an end.

In the taxi on their way back to their hotel Evie said to him:

"You were wonderful, dear. You made quite a hit. The girls simply raved about you; they thought you so handsome."

"Girls," he said bitterly. "Old hags."

"Were you bored, dear?"

"Stiff."

She pressed his hand in a gesture of sympathy.

"I hope you won't mind if we wait and go down by the afternoon train. I've got some things to do in the morning."

"No, that's all right. Shopping?"

"I do want to buy one or two things, but I've got to go and be photographed. I hate the idea, but they think I ought to be. For America, you know."

He said nothing. But he thought. He thought it would be a shock to the American public when they saw the portrait of the homely, desiccated little woman who was his wife. He'd always been under the impression that they liked glamour in America.

He went on thinking and next morning when Evie had gone out he went to his club and up to the library. There he looked up recent numbers of the *Times Literary Supplement*, the *New Statesman* and the *Spectator*. Presently he found reviews of Evie's book. He didn't read them very carefully, but enough to see that they were extremely favourable. Then he went to the bookseller's in Piccadilly where he occasionally bought books. He'd make up his mind that he had to read this damned thing of Evie's properly, but he didn't want to ask her what she'd done with the copy she'd given him. He'd buy one for himself. Before going in he looked in the window and the first thing he saw was a display of *When Pyramids Decay*. Damned silly title! He went in. A young man came forward and asked if he could help him.

"No, I'm just having a look round." It embarrassed him to ask for Evie's book and he thought he'd find it for himself and then take it to the salesman. But he couldn't see it anywhere and at last, finding the young man near him, he said in a carefully casual tone: "By the way, have you got a book called *When Pyramids Decay?*"

"The new edition came in this morning. I'll get a copy."

In a moment the young man returned with it. He was a short, rather stout young man, with a shock of untidy carroty hair and spectacles. George Peregrine, tall, upstanding, very military, towered over him.

"Is this a new edition then?" he asked.

"Yes, sir. The fifth. It might be a novel the way it's selling."

George Peregrine hesitated a moment.

"Why d'you suppose it's such a success? I've always been told no one reads poetry."

"Well, it's good, you know. I've read it meself." The young man, though obviously cultured, had a slight Cockney accent, and George quite instinctively adopted a patronizing attitude. "It's the story they like. Sexy, you know, but tragic."

George frowned a little. He was coming to the conclusion that the young man was rather impertinent. No one had told him anything about there being a story in the damned book and he had not gathered that from reading the reviews. The young man went on.

"Of course it's only a flash in the pan, if you know what I mean. The way I look at it, she was sort of inspired like by a personal experience, like Housman was with *The Shropshire Lad*. She'll never write anything else."

"How much is the book?" said George coldly to stop his chatter. "You needn't wrap it up, I'll just slip it in my pocket."

The November morning was raw and he was wearing a greatcoat.

At the station he bought the evening papers and magazines and he and Evie settled themselves comfortably in opposite corners of a first-class carriage and read. At five o'clock they went along to the restaurant car to have tea and chatted a little. They arrived. They drove home in the car which was waiting for them. They bathed, dressed for dinner, and after dinner Evie, saying she was tired out, went to bed. She kissed him, as was her habit, on the forehead. Then he went into the hall, took Evie's book out of his greatcoat pocket and going into the study began to read it. He didn't read verse very easily and though he read with attention, every word of it, the impression he received was far from clear. Then he began at the beginning again and read it a second time. He read with increasing malaise, but he was not a stupid man and when he had finished he had a distinct understanding of what it was all about. Part of the book was in free verse, part in conventional metres, but the story it related was coherent and plain to the meanest intelligence. It was the story of a passionate love affair between an older woman, married, and a young man. George Peregrine made out the steps of it as easily as if he had been doing a sum in simple addition.

Written in the first person, it began with the tremulous surprise of the woman, past her youth, when it dawned upon her that the young man was in love with her. She hesitated to believe it. She thought she must be deceiving herself. And she was terrified when on a sudden she discovered that she was passionately in love with him. She told herself it was absurd; with the disparity of age between them nothing but unhappiness could come to her if she yielded to her emotion. She tried to prevent him from speaking, but the day came when he told her that he loved her and forced her to tell him that she loved him too. He begged her to run away with him. She couldn't leave her husband, her home; and what life could they look forward to, she an ageing woman, he so young? How could she expect his love to last? She begged him to have mercy on her. But his love was impetuous. He wanted her, he wanted her with all his heart, and at last trembling, afraid, desirous, she yielded to him. Then there was a period of ecstatic happiness. The world, the dull, humdrum world of every day, blazed with glory. Love songs flowed from her pen. The woman worshipped the young, virile body of her lover. George flushed darkly when she praised his broad chest and slim flanks, the beauty of his legs and the flatness of his belly.

Hot stuff, Daphne's friend had said. It was that all right. Disgusting.

There were sad little pieces in which she lamented the emptiness of her life when as must happen he left her, but they ended with a cry that all she had to suffer would be worth it for the bliss that for a while had been hers. She wrote of the long, tremulous nights they passed together and the languor that lulled them to sleep in one another's arms. She wrote of the rapture of brief stolen moments when, braving all danger, their passion overwhelmed them and they surrendered to its call.

She thought it would be an affair of a few weeks, but miraculously it lasted. One of the poems referred to three years having gone by without lessening the love that filled their hearts. It looked as though he continued to press her to go away with him, far away, to a hill town in Italy, a Greek island, a walled city in Tunisia, so that they could be together always, for in another of the poems she besought him to let things be as they were. Their happiness was precarious. Perhaps it was owing to the difficulties they had to encounter and the rarity of their meetings that their lover had retained for so long its first enchanting ardour. Then on a sudden the young man died. How, when or where George could not discover. There followed a long, heartbroken cry of bitter grief, grief she could not indulge in, grief that had to be hidden. She had to be cheerful, give dinner parties and go out to dinner, behave as she had always behaved, though the light had gone out of her life and she was bowed down with anguish. The last poem of all was a set of four short stanzas in which the writer, sadly resigned to her loss, thanked the dark powers that rule man's destiny that she had been privileged at least for a while to enjoy the greatest happiness that we poor human beings can ever hope to know.

It was three o'clock in the morning when George Peregrine finally put the book down. It had seemed to him that he heard Evie's voice in every line, over and over again he came upon turns of phrase he had heard her use, there were details that were as familiar to him as to her: there was no doubt about it; it was her own story she had told, and it was as plain as anything could be that she had had a lover and her lover had died. It was not anger so much that he felt, nor horror or dismay, though he was dismayed and he was horrified, but amazement. It was as inconceivable that Evie should have had a love affair, and a wildly passionate one at that, as that the trout in a glass case over the chimney piece in his study, the finest he had ever caught, should suddenly wag its tail. He understood now the meaning of the amused look he had seen in the eyes of that man he had spoken with at the club, he understood why Daphne when she was talking about the book had seemed to be enjoying a private joke and why those two women at the cocktail party had tittered when he strolled past them.

He broke out into a sweat. Then on a sudden he was seized with fury and he jumped up to go and awake Evie and ask her sternly for an explanation. But he stopped at the door. After all what proof had he? A book. He remembered that he'd told Evie he thought it jolly good. True, he hadn't read it, but he'd pretended he had. He would look a perfect fool if he had to admit that.

"I must watch my step," he muttered.

He made up his mind to wait for two or three days and think it all over. Then he'd decide what to do. He went to bed, but he couldn't sleep for a long time.

"Evie," he kept on saying to himself. "Evie, of all people."

They met at breakfast next morning as usual. Evie was as she always was, quiet, demure and self-possessed, a middle-aged woman, who made no effort to look younger than she was, a woman who had nothing of what he still called It. He looked at her as he hadn't looked at her for years. She had her usual placid serenity. Her pale blue eyes were untroubled. There was no sign of guilt on her candid brow. She made the same little casual remarks she always made.

"It's nice to get back to the country again after those two hectic days in London. What are you going to do this morning?"

It was incomprehensible.

Three days later he went to see his solicitor. Henry Blane was an old friend of George's as well as his lawyer. He had a place not far from Peregrine's and for years they had shot over one another's preserves. For two days a week he was a country gentleman and for the other five a busy lawyer in Sheffield. He was a tall, robust fellow, with a boisterous manner and a jovial laugh, which suggested that he liked to be looked upon essentially as a sportsman and a good fellow and only incidentally as a lawyer. But he was shrewd and worldly-wise.

"Well, George, what's brought you here today?" he boomed as the Colonel was shown into his office. "Have a good time in London? I'm taking my missus up for a few days next week. How's Evie?"

"It's about Evie I've come to see you," said Peregrine, giving him a suspicious look. "Have you read her book?"

His sensitivity had been sharpened during those last days of troubled thought and he was conscious of a faint change in the lawyer's expression. It was as though he were suddenly on his guard.

"Yes, I've read it. Great success, isn't it? Fancy Evie breaking out into poetry. Wonders will never cease."

George Peregrine was inclined to lose his temper.

"It's made me look a perfect damned fool."

"Oh, what nonsense, George! There's no harm in Evie's writing a book. You ought to be jolly proud of her."

"Don't talk such rot. It's her own story. You know it and everyone else knows it. I suppose I'm the only one who doesn't know who her lover was."

"There is such a thing as imagination, old boy. There's no reason to suppose the whole thing isn't just made up."

"Look here, Henry, we've known one another all our lives. We've had all sorts of good times together. Be honest with me. Can you look me in the face and tell me you believe it's a made-up story,"

Henry Blane moved uneasily in his chair. He was disturbed by the distress in old George's voice.

"You've got no right to ask me a question like that. Ask Evie."

"I daren't," George answered after an anguished pause. "I'm afraid she'd tell me the truth."

There was an uncomfortable silence.

"Who was the chap?"

Henry Blane looked at him straight in the eye.

"I don't know, and if I did I wouldn't tell you."

"You swine. Don't you see what a position I'm in? Do you think it's very pleasant to be made absolutely ridiculous?"

The lawyer lit a cigarette and for some moments silently puffed it.

"I don't see what I can do for you," he said at last.

"You've got private detectives you employ, I suppose. I want you to put them on the job and let them find everything out."

"It's not very pretty to put detectives on one's wife, old boy; and besides, taking for granted for a moment that Evie had an affair, it was a good many years ago and I don't suppose it would be possible to find out a thing. They seem to have covered their tracks pretty carefully."

"I don't care. You put the detectives on. I want to know the truth."

"I won't, George. If you're determined to do that you'd better consult some-one else. And look here, even if you got evidence that Evie had been unfaithful to you what would you do with it? You'd look rather silly divorcing your wife because she'd committed adultery ten years ago."

"At all events I could have it out with her."

"You can do that now, but you know just as well as I do, that if you do she'll leave you. D'you want her to do that?"

George gave him an unhappy look.

"I don't know. I always thought she'd been a damned good wife to me. She runs the house perfectly, we never have any servant trouble; she's done wonders with the garden and she's splendid with all the village people. But damn it, I have my self-respect to think of. How can I go on living with her when I know that she was grossly unfaithful to me?"

"Have you always been faithful to her?"

"More or less, you know. After all we've been married for nearly twenty-four years and Evie was never much for bed."

The solicitor slightly raised his eyebrows, but George was too intent on what he was saying to notice.

"I don't deny that I've had a bit of fun now and then. A man wants it. Women are different."

"We only have men's word for that," said Henry Blane, with a faint smile.

"Evie's absolutely the last woman I'd have suspected of kicking over the traces. I mean, she's a very fastidious, reticent woman. What on earth made her write the damned book?"

"I suppose it was a very poignant experience and perhaps it was a relief to her to get it off her chest like that."

"Well, if she had to write it why the devil didn't she write it under an assumed name?"

"She used her maiden name. I suppose she thought that was enough and it would have been if the book hadn't had this amazing boom."

George Peregrine and the lawyer were sitting opposite one another with a desk between them. George, his elbow on the desk, his cheek resting on his hand, frowned at his thought.

"It's so rotten not to know what sort of a chap he was. One can't even tell if he was by way of being a gentleman. I mean, for all I know he may have been a farmhand or a clerk in a lawyer's office."

Henry Blane did not permit himself to smile and when he answered there was in his eyes a kindly, tolerant look.

"Knowing Evie so well I think the probabilities are that he was all right. Anyhow I'm sure he wasn't a clerk in my office."

"It's been such a shock to me," the Colonel sighed. "I thought she was fond of me. She couldn't have written that book unless she hated me."

"Oh, I don't believe that. I don't think she's capable of hatred."

"You're not going to pretend that she loves me."

"No."

"Well, what does she feel for me?"

Henry Blane leaned back in his swivel chair and looked at George reflectively.

"Indifference, I should say."

The Colonel gave a little shudder and reddened.

"After all, you're not in love with her, are you?"

George Peregrine did not answer directly.

"It's been a great blow to me not to have any children, but I've never let her see that I think she's let me down. I've always been kind to her. Within reasonable limits I've tried to do my duty by her."

The lawyer passed a large hand over his mouth to conceal the smile that trembled on his lips.

"It's been such an awful shock to me," Peregrine went on. "Damn it all, even ten years ago Evie was no chicken and God knows, she wasn't much to look at. It's so ugly." He sighed deeply. "What would *you* do in my place?"

"Nothing."

George Peregrine drew himself bolt upright in his chair and he looked at Henry with the stern set face that he must have worn when he inspected his regiment.

"I can't overlook a thing like this. I've been made a laughingstock. I can never hold up my head again."

"Nonsense," said the lawyer sharply, and then in a pleasant, kindly manner:

"Listen, old boy: the man's dead; it all happened a long while back. Forget it. Talk to people about Evie's book, rave about it, tell 'em how proud you are of her. Behave as though you had so much confidence in her, you *knew* she could never have been unfaithful to you. The world moves so quickly and people's memories are so short. They'll forget."

"I shan't forget."

"You're both middle-aged people. She probably does a great deal more for you than you think and you'd be awfully lonely without her. I don't think it matters if you don't forget. It'll be all to the good if you can get it into that thick head of yours that there's a lot more in Evie than you ever had the gumption to see."

"Damn it all, you talk as if *I* was to blame."

"No, I don't think you were to blame, but I'm not so sure that Evie was either. I don't suppose she wanted to fall in love with this boy. D'you remember those verses right at the end? The impression they gave me was that though she was shattered by his death, in a strange sort of way she welcomed it. All through she'd been aware of the fragility of the tie that bound them. He died in the full flush of his first love and had never known that love so seldom endures; he'd only known its bliss and beauty. In her own bitter grief she found solace in the thought that he'd been spared all sorrow."

"All that's a bit above my head, old boy. I see more or less what you mean."

George Peregrine stared unhappily at the inkstand on the desk. He was silent and the lawyer looked at him with curious, yet sympathetic eyes.

"Do you realize what courage she must have had never by a sign to show how dreadfully unhappy she was," he said gently.

Colonel Peregrine sighed.

"I'm broken. I suppose you're right; it's no good crying over spilt milk and it would only make things worse if I made a fuss."

"Well?"

George Peregrine gave a pitiful little smile.

"I'll take your advice. I'll do nothing. Let them think me a damned fool and to hell with them. The truth is, I don't know what I'd do without Evie. But I'll tell you what, there's one thing I shall never understand till my dying day: What in the name of heaven did the fellow ever see in her?"

Exercises

1. Describe George Peregrine's psychological make-up, that is, the traits, emotions, and patterns of behavior that characterize him as an individual.

2. Compare and contrast the characterizations of George and Evie Peregrine.

3. What is George's major flaw as a person? How is it shown in the story?

4. How is sympathy for Evie achieved?

5. How does society view George?

6. What is Maugham's attitude toward George and society as expressed in the story?

7. Is George a static or a dynamic character? Has the conflict through which he has passed changed him in any way? What, if anything, has he learned?

8. What is gained or lost by Maugham's intrusion into the action of the story?

9. Critics contend that Maugham often wrote stories from a moral point of view. What do you think is the moral of this story?

Topics for Writing

1. Discuss the double standard of morality in this story. Focus on the one standard for George, another for Evie, and explain how George accepts the double standard and how Evie rejects it.

2. Argue for or against the notion that this story belongs to George Peregrine.

3. Evaluate the interdependence of plot and character, making specific references to the text.

3. POINT OF VIEW

We observe the action of a story through the eyes and mind of the character or the community of characters the author designates to tell the story. We call this awareness, through which we view the unfolding of events, the **point of view.**

There are many potential vantage points and combinations for looking at a situation, but generally a story can be told from one of four basic positions: the omniscient point of view, the limited omniscient point of view, the first-person point of view, and the dramatic point of view.

With the **omniscient** point of view, sometimes called panoramic, shifting, or multiple, the author employs a narrator who speaks in the third person and knows just about all there is to know about each character and event in the story.

The all-knowing raconteur can disclose as much or as little about the backgrounds, trials, failures, successes, prejudices, loves, and hates of as few or as many of the characters as the author permits; omniscience allows the narrator to enter into the minds of some or all of the characters, revealing what the author wishes to reveal about their innermost thoughts and feelings.

Through the omniscient narrator, writers are freed to move at will in the arena of conflict. They may easily shift from the consciousness of one character to that of another and change the viewpoint from the subjective to the objective. They may speculate on the significance of certain events and pass judgment on the behavior of the characters. Such godlike omnipresence and omniscience allow authors great scope and freedom in presenting their fictional worlds.

The following excerpt illustrates the omniscient point of view. Note the periodic shifts from the objective to the subjective point of view and the fact that we not only see the action from the perspective of each character but also have access to the consciousness of each. This allows the writer to communicate the characters' most secret attitudes and emotions.

Gordon J. Taylor, a tall, angry, meticulously dressed advertising executive, walked resolutely up the busy street, glanced about irritably, and pushed his large frame through the door into a pawn shop.

Behind the counter, an undersized, beggarly-looking, cigar-chewing clerk stood undisturbed, glued to a radio blaring with a twitter of emotional excitement — produced apparently by a killing.

Apprised finally of the customer's interest in guns, the pawnbroker dawdled toward the gentleman.

"What's your handle, mister?" the clerk asked, glaring at the stranger as if he were a rank criminal.

"What?" Gordon asked, his thoughts lingering nervously on the painful events just passed.

"Your handle — your name?" the clerk insisted. He began to lose patience.

"Taylor . . . Gordon J.," he answered, still preoccupied with the matter of his wife and partner.

"Your racket — what do you do with the gems?" the pawnbroker asked shrewdly, determined to trap his man.

"Salesman." Gordon feared this line of questioning.

"In or outer?" the clerk persisted, barely concealing his contempt.

Gordon trembled. He could take it no longer. "Why all the questions?"

The pawnbroker, seizing what he felt was a capital opportunity to close the matter at hand, uttered sharply, "You want a gun or not?"

Gordon's need being absolute, he replied with apologetic nervousness. "I don't appreciate this third-degree business."

"Listen, buster," the clerk said, taking the remark as a personal affront, "what kinda place you think we run here? We're legit. We can't sell no weapons to every joker that comes off the street. How do I know you ain't gonna pull a sheist or knock off somebody? That's why the questions, see. We gotta know an' the cops gotta know."

"The police?" Gordon asked, visibly shaken and doing a bad job of trying to hide his inner disturbance.

"Yeah, they wanna know. They wanna know make, serial number, who buys, why, address an' proof," the clerk said authoritatively. "You got some I.D.?"

The **limited omniscient** point of view, also known as the selective or limited third-person point of view, uses a third-person narrator and limits our perception to that of a single character, who may be the protagonist, a minor character, or an outside observer. We invade only one mind and no other. By using a central intelligence to transmit the story and the action to us, the author draws us more intimately into that one character and his or her discoveries and experiences. Limiting the point of view to a single consciousness provides the story with a built-in unity. Furthermore, since the narrator does not know everything — just as in life one person does not know everything — the limited omniscient point of view creates a stronger illusion of reality than the omniscient viewpoint does.

The following version of the excerpt exemplifies the limited omniscient point of view; it clearly restricts our perspective to a single character's consciousness — the pawnbroker's. What the clerk sees and feels, we see and feel — no more, no less. We are given absolutely no knowledge of Gordon's thoughts.

"What's your handle, mister?" the clerk asked, glaring at the stranger as if he were a rank criminal.

"What?" Gordon asked.

"Your handle — your name?" the clerk insisted. He began to lose patience.

"Taylor . . . Gordon J."

"Your racket — what do you do with the gems?" the pawnbroker asked shrewdly, determined to trap his man.

"Salesman."

"In or outer?" the clerk persisted, barely concealing his contempt.

"Why all the questions?"

The pawnbroker, seizing what he felt was a capital opportunity to close the matter at hand, uttered sharply, "You want a gun or not?"

"I don't appreciate this third-degree business."

"Listen, buster," the clerk said, taking the remark as a personal affront, "what kinda place you think we run here? We're legit. We can't sell no weapons to every joker that comes off the street. How do I know you ain't gonna pull a sheist or knock off somebody? That's why the questions, see. We gotta know an' the cops gotta know."

"The police?"

"Yeah, they wanna know. They wanna know make, serial number, who buys, why, address an' proof," the clerk said authoritatively. "You got some I.D.?"

The **first-person,** or personal, point of view, which has many attributes of the limited omniscient viewpoint, means that the story is told in the first person and filtered through the consciousness of one narrator. The narrative "I" can be the protagonist, a minor character, or an outside observer. While the use of the first-person pronoun helps to foster intimacy between the reader and the narrator, the personal point of view is quite restrictive. We are confined to one character's reporting, views, and commentaries, however biased they might be. But this restricted viewpoint may enhance the sense of reality in the story and, by virtue of the single, consistent outlook, create a natural unity.

As an outside observer, the first-person narrator gains in reliability because he or she is not involved in the events of the story. Such a character is likely to be more objective than a first-person narrator who is one of the actors and who tends to display prejudicial judgment because of his or her involvement in the action. However, a first-person narrator who is a crucial character, and especially a protagonist, is likely to secure our empathy and draw us more intimately into the action. The gains and losses produced by this point of view are obvious.

Finally, after what must have been thirty minutes of grunts for attention, the dripping cigar wafted toward me.

"What's your handle, mister?" he asked, accusing me with his large, black, piercing eyes.

I immediately took a dislike to him. For one thing, I failed to understand his English; for another, I thought he was a stupid little man.

"What?" I asked, my thoughts still lingering nervously on the painful events just passed.

"Your handle — your name?" he insisted, in as rude a manner as one could expect from an idiot.

"Taylor . . . Gordon J.," I answered, thinking it wiser to give him my real name.

"Your racket — what do you do with the gems?" he asked.

"Salesman," I said quickly, dismissing the line of questioning, which I did not at all like.

"In or outer?" he persisted.

I could take it no longer. I was afraid. He might find out more than he needed to know.

"Why all the questions?" I asked.

"You want a gun or not?"

I found myself at the mercy of this undaunted fool. I surely needed a gun, I thought.

"I don't appreciate this third-degree business," I told him.

That really jarred him. He took it as a personal attack on his integrity. What integrity? For a minute I imagined he was going to punch me in the mouth. He was mad; but he soon cooled off.

"Listen, buster," he said, "what kinda place you think we run here? We're legit. We can't sell no weapons to every joker that comes off the street. How do I know you ain't gonna pull a sheist or knock off somebody? That's why the questions, see. We gotta know an' the cops gotta know."

"The police?" I asked, visibly shaken and trying to conceal my anxiety.

"Yeah, they wanna know. They wanna know make, serial number, who buys, why, address an' proof," the little man said. "You got some I.D.?"

"Yes," I answered, haughtily displaying my awesome collection of credit cards. At long last I had my gun. And I knew it.

In the **dramatic** point of view, also referred to as the objective or the scenic viewpoint, we have no access to the consciousness of any character. We must view everything from outside the story, as a spectator at the theater watches a play, through the externals of developing physical action, the appearance or description of the characters, and their speech. We see only what is happening and hear only what is being spoken. Consequently, we must rely almost exclusively on our own powers of deductive reasoning to grasp the full meaning of the story.

The dramatic point of view presents an action that moves swiftly and gives the impression of immediacy. More than any other viewpoint, it affords an objective insight into the characters and events and produces the greatest illusion of reality in a story.

The next segment illustrates the dramatic point of view. Observe the differences in effects between this version and the previous ones.

"What's your handle, mister?" the clerk asked.

"What?"

"Your handle — your name?"

"Taylor . . . Gordon J."

"Your racket — what do you do with the gems?"

"Salesman."

"In or outer?"

"Why all the questions?"

"You want a gun or not?"

"I don't appreciate this third-degree business."

"Listen, buster," the clerk said, "what kinda place you think we run here? We're legit. We can't sell no weapons to every joker that comes off the street. How do I know you ain't gonna pull a sheist or knock off somebody? That's why the questions, see. We gotta know an' the cops gotta know."

"The police?" Gordon asked.

"Yeah, they wanna know. They wanna know make, serial number, who buys, why, address an' proof," the clerk said. "You got some I.D.?"

As frequently as we find an author who adheres strictly to a single basic point of view, we discover another who prefers to mix his or her own salmagundi. Almost certainly the creative writer will select a point of view or a mixture of two or three that is best suited to serve the artistic design or to complement the materials.

As you read the stories in this chapter, keep asking yourself the first question on page 98 — through whose consciousness is the story experienced? — and then apply the other questions to each story. Consider, too, how well the author succeeds in establishing a given viewpoint, and how the author's choice affects your grasp of plot and character in each instance.

Four Basic Positions of Point of View

	I. Omniscient	*II. Limited Omniscient*
Voice	Third-person pronouns *he, she* mostly; first-person pronoun rarely	Third-person pronouns
Consciousness	Access to consciousness of more than one character, perhaps all	Access to consciousness of one character
Position and Presence	Story seen through eyes of outside observer, whose presence is pervasive	Story seen through eyes of outside observer, protagonist, or minor character whose presence dominates
Reliability	Reliable as implied author's voice	Reliable when observer used; less reliable when character used
Usage in Modern Fiction	Infrequently used	Frequently used
Other Features	1. Allows great scope and flexibility 2. Permits author intrusions, editorializing, evaluations, and comments	1. Fosters illusion of reality 2. Allows author comments 3. Establishes intimate relationship between reader and narrator

	I. Omniscient	II. Limited Omniscient
Other Features (*cont.*)	3. Creates distance between reader and characters	4. Provides structural unity 5. Combines scope of omniscient and immediacy of first-person narration

	III. First-Person	IV. Dramatic
Voice	First-person pronouns *I, my, mine,* etc.	Third-person pronouns
Consciousness	Access to narrator's consciousness	No access to any consciousness
Position and Presence	Story told through eyes of outside observer, protagonist, or minor character whose presence dominates	Story seen through eyes of outside observer whose presence is unobtrusive
Reliability	Reliable when observer used; less reliable when character used	Reliable when "teller" remains neutral
Usage in Modern Fiction	Frequently used	Infrequently used
Other Features	1. Fosters illusion of reality 2. Allows author comments 3. Establishes intimate relationship between reader and narrator 4. Provides structural unity	1. Permits great flexibility 2. Forbids author comments 3. Places reader in position of spectator 4. Allows action to move swiftly 5. Creates strongest illusion of reality

Questions for Evaluating Point of View

1. Through whose consciousness is the story experienced?

2. Is one point of view used, or a combination of two or more?

3. How effective is the use of this particular point of view?

4. What are the advantages and the disadvantages of presenting the story through this point of view?

5. Do we have access to the consciousness of one, two, or more characters?

6. How effective is this approach?

Carson McCullers (1917–1967)

A Tree, a Rock, a Cloud

It was raining that morning, and still very dark. When the boy reached the streetcar café he had almost finished his route and he went in for a cup of coffee. The place was an all-night café owned by a bitter and stingy man called Leo. After the raw, empty street, the café seemed friendly and bright: along the counter there were a couple of soldiers, three spinners from the cotton mill, and in a corner a man who sat hunched over with his nose and half his face down in a beer mug. The boy wore a helmet such as aviators wear. When he went into the café he unbuckled the chin strap and raised the right flap up over his pink little ear; often as he drank his coffee someone would speak to him in a friendly way. But this morning Leo did not look into his face and none of the men were talking. He paid and was leaving the café when a voice called out to him:

"Son! Hey Son!"

He turned back and the man in the corner was crooking his finger and nodding to him. He had brought his face out of the beer mug and he seemed suddenly very happy. The man was long and pale, with a big nose and faded orange hair.

"Hey Son!"

The boy went toward him. He was an undersized boy of about twelve, with one shoulder drawn higher than the other because of the weight of the paper sack. His face was shallow, freckled, and his eyes were round child eyes.

"Yeah Mister?"

The man laid one hand on the paper boy's shoulders, then grasped the boy's chin and turned his face slowly from one side to the other. The boy shrank back uneasily.

"Say! What's the big idea?"

The boy's voice was shrill; inside the café it was suddenly very quiet.

The man said slowly, "I love you."

All along the counter the men laughed. The boy, who had scowled and sidled away, did not know what to do. He looked over the counter at Leo, and

Leo watched him with a weary, brittle jeer. The boy tried to laugh also. But the man was serious and sad.

"I did not mean to tease you, Son," he said. "Sit down and have a beer with me. There is something I have to explain."

Cautiously, out of the corner of his eye, the paper boy questioned the men along the counter to see what he should do. But they had gone back to their beer or their breakfast and did not notice him. Leo put a cup of coffee on the counter and a little jug of cream.

"He is a minor," Leo said.

The paper boy slid himself up onto the stool. His ear beneath the upturned flap of the helmet was very small and red. The man was nodding at him soberly. "It is important," he said. Then he reached in his hip pocket and brought out something which he held up in the palm of his hand for the boy to see.

"Look very carefully," he said.

The boy stared, but there was nothing to look at very carefully. The man held in his big, grimy palm a photograph. It was the face of a woman, but blurred, so that only the hat and the dress she was wearing stood out clearly.

"See?" the man asked.

The boy nodded and the man placed another picture in his palm. The woman was standing on the beach in a bathing suit. The suit made her stomach very big, and that was the main thing you noticed.

"Got a good look?" He leaned over closer and finally asked: "You ever seen her before?"

The boy sat motionless, staring slantwise at the man. "Not so I know of."

"Very well." The man blew on the photographs and put them back into his pocket. "That was my wife."

"Dead?" the boy asked.

Slowly the man shook his head. He pursed his lips as though about to whistle and answered in a long-drawn way: "Nuuu—" he said. "I will explain."

The beer on the counter before the man was in a large brown mug. He did not pick it up to drink. Instead he bent down and, putting his face over the rim, he rested there for a moment. Then with both hands he tilted the mug and sipped.

"Some night you'll go to sleep with your big nose in a mug and drown," said Leo. "Prominent transient drowns in beer. That would be a cute death."

The paper boy tried to signal to Leo. While the man was not looking he screwed up his face and worked his mouth to question soundlessly: "Drunk?" But Leo only raised his eyebrows and turned away to put some pink strips of bacon on the grill. The man pushed the mug away from him, straightened himself, and folded his loose crooked hands on the counter. His face was sad as he looked at the paper boy. He did not blink, but from time to time the lids closed down with delicate gravity over his pale green eyes. It was nearing dawn and the boy shifted the weight of the paper sack.

"I am talking about love," the man said. "With me it is a science."

The boy half slid down from the stool. But the man raised his forefinger, and there was something about him that held the boy and would not let him go away.

"Twelve years ago I married the woman in the photograph. She was my wife for one year, nine months, three days, and two nights. I loved her. Yes. . . ." He tightened his blurred, rambling voice and said again: "I loved her. I thought also that she loved me. I was a railroad engineer. She had all home comforts and luxuries. It never crept into my brain that she was not satisfied. But do you know what happened?"

"Mgneeow!" said Leo.

The man did not take his eyes from the boy's face. "She left me. I came in one night and the house was empty and she was gone. She left me."

"With a fellow?" the boy asked.

Gently the man placed his palm down on the counter. "Why naturally, Son. A woman does not run off like that alone."

The café was quiet, the soft rain black and endless in the street outside. Leo pressed down the frying bacon with the prongs of his long fork. "So you have been chasing the floozie for eleven years. You frazzled old rascal!"

For the first time the man glanced at Leo. "Please don't be vulgar. Besides, I was not speaking to you." He turned back to the boy and said in a trusting and secretive undertone, "Let's not pay any attention to him. O.K.?"

The paper boy nodded doubtfully.

"It was like this," the man continued. "I am a person who feels many things. All my life one thing after another has impressed me. Moonlight. The leg of a pretty girl. One thing after another. But the point is that when I had enjoyed anything there was a peculiar sensation as though it was laying around loose in me. Nothing seemed to finish itself up or fit in with the other things. Women? I had my portion of them. The same. Afterwards laying around loose in me. I was a man who had never loved."

Very slowly he closed his eyelids, and the gesture was like a curtain drawn at the end of a scene in a play. When he spoke again his voice was excited and the words came fast — the lobes of his large, loose ears seemed to tremble.

"Then I met this woman. I was fifty-one years old and she always said she was thirty. I met her at a filling station and we were married within three days. And do you know what it was like? I just can't tell you. All I had ever felt was gathered together around this woman. Nothing lay around loose in me any more but was finished up by her."

The man stopped suddenly and stroked his long nose. His voice sank down to a steady and reproachful undertone: "I'm not explaining this right. What happened was this. There were these beautiful feelings and loose little pleasures inside me. And this woman was something like an assembly line for my soul. I run these little pieces of myself through her and I come out complete. Now do you follow me?"

"What was her name?" the boy asked.

"Oh," he said. "I called her Dodo. But that is immaterial."

"Did you try to make her come back?"

The man did not seem to hear. "Under the circumstances you can imagine how I felt when she left me."

Leo took the bacon from the grill and folded two strips of it between a bun. He had a gray face, with slitted eyes, and a pinched nose saddled by faint blue shadows. One of the mill workers signaled for more coffee and Leo poured it. He did not give refills on coffee free. The spinner ate breakfast there every morning, but the better Leo knew his customers the stingier he treated them. He nibbled his own bun as though he grudged it to himself.

"And you never got hold of her again?"

The boy did not know what to think of the man, and his child's face was uncertain with mingled curiosity and doubt. He was new on the paper route; it was still strange to him to be out in the town in the black, queer early morning.

"Yes," the man said. "I took a number of steps to get her back. I went around trying to locate her. I went to Tulsa where she had folks. And to Mobile. I went to every town she had ever mentioned to me, and I hunted down every man she had formerly been connected with. Tulsa, Atlanta, Chicago, Cheehaw, Memphis. . . . For the better part of two years I chased around the country trying to lay hold of her."

"But the pair of them had vanished from the face of the earth!" said Leo.

"Don't listen to him," the man said confidentially. "And also just forget those two years. They are not important. What matters is that around the third year a curious thing begun to happen to me."

"What?" the boy asked.

The man leaned down and tilted his mug to take a sip of beer. But as he hovered over the mug his nostrils fluttered slightly; he sniffed the staleness of the beer and did not drink. "Love is a curious thing to begin with. At first I thought only of getting her back. It was a kind of mania. But then as time went on I tried to remember her. But do you know what happened?"

"No," the boy said.

"When I laid myself down on a bed and tried to think about her my mind became a blank. I couldn't see her. I would take out her pictures and look. No good. Nothing doing. A blank. Can you imagine it?"

"Say Mac!" Leo called down the counter. "Can you imagine this bozo's mind a blank!"

Slowly, as though fanning away flies, the man waved his hand. His green eyes were concentrated and fixed on the shallow little face of the paper boy.

"But a sudden piece of glass on a sidewalk. Or a nickel tune in a music box. A shadow on a wall at night. And I would remember. It might happen in a street and I would cry or bang my head against a lamppost. You follow me?"

"A piece of glass . . ." the boy said.

"Anything. I would walk around and I had no power of how and when to remember her. You think you can put up a kind of shield. But remembering don't come to a man face forward — it corners around sideways. I was at the mercy of everything I saw and heard. Suddenly instead of me combing the countryside to find her she begun to chase me around in my very soul. *She* chasing *me,* mind you! And in my soul."

The boy asked finally: "What part of the country were you in then?"

"Ooh," the man groaned. "I was a sick mortal. It was like smallpox. I confess, Son, that I boozed. I fornicated. I committed any sin that suddenly appealed to me. I am loath to confess it but I will do so. When I recall that period it is all curdled in my mind, it was so terrible."

The man leaned his head down and tapped his forehead on the counter. For a few seconds he stayed bowed over in this position, the back of his stringy neck covered with orange furze, his hands with their long warped fingers held palm to palm in an attitude of prayer. Then the man straightened himself; he was smiling and suddenly his face was bright and tremulous and old.

"It was in the fifth year that it happened," he said. "And with it I started my science."

Leo's mouth jerked with a pale, quick grin. "Well none of we boys are getting any younger," he said. Then with sudden anger he balled up a dishcloth he was holding and threw it down hard on the floor. "You draggle-tailed old Romeo!"

"What happened?" the boy asked.

The old man's voice was high and clear: "Peace," he answered.

"Huh?"

"It is hard to explain scientifically, Son," he said. "I guess the logical explanation is that she and I had fleed around from each other for so long that finally we just got tangled up together and lay down and quit. Peace. A queer and beautiful blankness. It was spring in Portland and the rain came every afternoon. All evening I just stayed there on my bed in the dark. And that is how the science came to me."

The windows in the streetcar were pale blue with light. The two soldiers paid for their beers and opened the door — one of the soldiers combed his hair and wiped off his muddy puttees before they went outside. The three mill workers bent silently over their breakfasts. Leo's clock was ticking on the wall.

"It is this. And listen carefully. I meditated on love and reasoned it out. I realized what is wrong with us. Men fall in love for the first time. And what do they fall in love with?"

The boy's soft mouth was partly open and he did not answer.

"A woman," the old man said, "without science, with nothing to go by, they undertake the most dangerous and sacred experience in God's earth. They fall in love with a woman. Is that correct, Son?"

"They start at the wrong end of love. They begin at the climax. Can you wonder it is so miserable? Do you know how men should love?"

The old man reached over and grasped the boy by the collar of his leather jacket. He gave him a gentle little shake and his green eyes gazed down unblinking and grave.

"Son, do you know how love should be begun?"

The boy sat small and listening and still. Slowly he shook his head. The old man leaned closer and whispered:

"A tree. A rock. A cloud."

It was still raining outside in the street: a mild, gray, endless rain. The mill whistle blew for the six o'clock shift and the three spinners paid and went away. There was no one in the café but Leo, the old man, and the little paper boy.

"The weather was like this in Portland," he said. "At the time my science was begun. I meditated and I started very cautious. I would pick up something from the street and take it home with me. I bought a goldfish and I concentrated on the goldfish and I loved it. I graduated from one thing to another. Day by day I was getting this technique. On the road from Portland to San Diego — "

"Aw shut up!" screamed Leo suddenly. "Shut up! Shut up!"

The old man still held the collar of the boy's jacket; he was trembling and his face was earnest and bright and wild. "For six years now I have gone around by myself and built up my science. And now I am a master. Son. I can love anything. No longer do I have to think about it even. I see a street full of people and a beautiful light comes in me. I watch a bird in the sky. Or I meet a traveler on the road. Everything, Son. And anybody. All stranger and all loved! Do you realize what a science like mine can mean?"

The boy held himself stiffly, his hands curled tight around the counter edge. Finally he asked: "Did you ever really find that lady?"

"What? What say, Son?"

"I mean," the boy asked timidly. "Have you fallen in love with a woman again?"

The old man loosened his grasp on the boy's collar. He turned away and for the first time his green eyes had a vague and scattered look. He lifted the mug from the counter, drank down the yellow beer. His head was shaking slowly from side to side. Then finally he answered: "No, Son. You see that is the last step in my science. I go cautious. And I am not quite ready yet."

"Well!" said Leo. "Well well well!"

The old man stood in the open doorway. "Remember," he said. Framed there in the gray damp light of the early morning he looked shrunken and seedy and frail. But his smile was bright. "Remember I love you," he said with a last nod. And the door closed quietly behind him.

The boy did not speak for a long time. He pulled down the bangs on his forehead and slid his grimy little forefinger around the rim of his empty cup. Then without looking at Leo he finally asked:

"Was he drunk?"

"No," said Leo shortly.

The boy raised his clear voice higher. "Then was he a dope fiend?"

"No."

The boy looked up at Leo, and his flat little face was desperate, his voice urgent and shrill. "Was he crazy? Do you think he was a lunatic?" The paper boy's voice dropped suddenly with doubt. "Leo? Or not?"

But Leo would not answer him. Leo had run a night café for fourteen years, and he held himself to be a critic of craziness. There were the town characters and also the transients who roamed in from the night. He knew the manias of all of them. But he did not want to satisfy the questions of the waiting child. He tightened his pale face and was silent.

So the boy pulled down the right flap of his helmet and as he turned to leave he made the only comment that seemed safe to him, the only remark that could not be laughed down and despised:

"He sure has done a lot of traveling."

Exercises

1. How effective is the use of the narrator's point of view in this story? Why cannot the transient, Leo, or the boy narrate the story?

2. Precisely what is the transient trying to do? Does he achieve his goal? Explain.

3. What is Leo's function? Why does the boy turn to Leo for his answers? Why does Leo refuse to answer him?

4. Are the three main characters dynamic? Does anyone change or experience a moment of illumination?

5. Is the setting significant? What do you make of the contrasting play of light and dark?

6. What attitude toward love does the story express?

7. Prepare an eight-point analysis of the story.

Topics for Writing

1. Discuss, in an essay, whether the dramatic point of view works well in this story. Does it allow for sufficient development of the characters?

2. Interpret the transient's system of scientific love.

3. Write a short story from the objective point of view dramatizing an event in your adolescent life that you feel has profoundly influenced your outlook or changed your character.

Selected Bibliography Carson McCullers

Baldanza, Frank. "Plato in Dixie." *Georgia Review*, 12 (1958), 151–167.
Evans, Oliver. "The Achievement of Carson McCullers. *English Journal*, 51 (1962), 301–308.
——. "The Case of Carson McCullers." *Georgia Review*, 18 (1964), 40–45.
Fletcher, Mary D. "Carson McCullers' 'Ancient Mariner.'" *South Central Bulletin*, 35 (1975), 123–125.
Folk, Barbara Nauer. "The Sad Sweet Music of Carson McCullers." *Georgia Review*, 16 (1962), 202–209.
Graner, Lawrence. "Carson McCullers." *University of Minnesota Pamphlets on American Writers*, no. 84. Minneapolis: University of Minnesota Press, 1969.
Griffith, Albert J. "Carson McCullers' Myth of the Sad Cafe." *Georgia Review*, 21 (1957), 46–56.
Hamilton, Alice. "Loneliness and Alienation: The Life and Works of Carson McCullers." *Dalhousie Review*, 50 (1970), 215–229.
Hart, Jane. "Carson McCullers, Pilgrim of Loneliness." *Georgia Review*, 11 (1957), 53–58.
Hassan, Ihab H. "Carson McCullers: The Alchemy of Love and Aesthetics of Pain." *Modern Fiction Studies*, 5 (1959–60), 311–326.
Hughes, Catherine. "A World of Outcasts." *Commonweal*, 13 (October 1961), 73–75.
Phillips, Robert S. "Painful Love: Carson McCullers' Parable." *Southwest Review*, 51 (1966), 80–86.

Sherwood Anderson (1876–1941)

I Want to Know Why

We got up at four in the morning, that first day in the east. On the evening before we had climbed off a freight train at the edge of town, and with the true instinct of Kentucky boys had found our way across town and to the race track and the stables at once. Then we knew we were all right. Hanley Turner right away found a nigger we knew. It was Bildad Johnson who in the winter works at Ed Becker's livery barn in our home town, Beckersville. Bildad is a good cook as almost all our niggers are and of course he, like everyone in our part of

Kentucky who is anyone at all, likes the horses. In the spring Bildad begins to scratch around. A nigger from our country can flatter and wheedle anyone into letting him do most anything he wants. Bildad wheedles the stable men and the trainers from the horse farms in our country around Lexington. The trainers come into town in the evening to stand around and talk and maybe get into a poker game. Bildad gets in with them. He is always doing little favors and telling about things to eat, chicken browned in a pan, and how is the best way to cook sweet potatoes and corn bread. It makes your mouth water to hear him.

When the racing season comes on and the horses go to the races and there is all the talk on the streets in the evenings about the new colts, and everyone says when they are going over to Lexington or to the spring meeting at Churchill Downs or to Latonia, and the horsemen that have been down to New Orleans or maybe at the winter meeting at Havana in Cuba come home to spend a week before they start out again, at such a time when everything talked about in Beckersville is just horses and nothing else and the outfits start out and horse racing is in every breath of air you breathe, Bildad shows up with a job as cook for some outfit. Often when I think about it, his always going all season to the races and working in the livery barn in the winter where horses are and where men like to come and talk about horses, I wish I was a nigger. It's a foolish thing to say, but that's the way I am about being around horses, just crazy. I can't help it.

Well, I must tell you about what we did and let you in on what I'm talking about. Four of us boys from Beckersville, all whites and sons of men who live in Beckersville regular, made up our minds we were going to the races, not just to Lexington or Louisville, I don't mean, but to the big eastern track we were always hearing our Beckersville men talk about, to Saratoga. We were all pretty young then. I was just turned fifteen and I was the oldest of the four. It was my scheme. I admit that and I talked the others into trying it. There was Hanley Turner and Henry Rieback and Tom Tumberton and myself. I had thirty-seven dollars I had earned during the winter working nights and Saturdays in Enoch Myer's grocery. Henry Rieback had eleven dollars and the others, Hanley and Tom, had only a dollar or two each. We fixed it all up and laid low until the Kentucky spring meetings were over and some of our men, the sportiest ones, the ones we envied the most, had cut out — then we cut out, too.

I won't tell you the trouble we had beating our way on freights and all. We went through Cleveland and Buffalo and other cities and saw Niagara Falls. We bought things there, souvenirs and spoons and cards and shells with pictures of the falls on them for our sisters and mothers, but thought we had better not send any of the things home. We didn't want to put the folks on our trail and maybe be nabbed.

We got into Saratoga as I said at night and went to the track. Bildad fed us up. He showed us a place to sleep in hay over a shed and promised to keep still. Niggers are all right about things like that. They won't squeal on you. Often a white man you might meet, when you had run away from home like that, might appear to be all right and give you a quarter or a half dollar or something, and then go right and give you away. White men will do that, but not a nigger. You can trust them. They are squarer with kids. I don't know why.

At the Saratoga meeting that year there were a lot of men from home. Dave Williams and Arthur Mulford and Jerry Myers and others. Then there was a lot from Louisville and Lexington Henry Rieback knew but I didn't.

They were professional gamblers and Henry Rieback's father is one too. He is what is called a sheet writer and goes away most of the year to tracks. In the winter when he is home in Beckersville he don't stay there much but goes away to cities and deals faro. He is a nice man and generous, is always sending Henry presents, a bicycle and a gold watch and a boy scout suit of clothes and things like that.

My own father is a lawyer. He's all right, but don't make much money and can't buy me things and anyway I'm getting so old now I don't expect it. He never said nothing to me against Henry, but Hanley Turner and Tom Tumberton's fathers did. They said to their boys that money so come by is no good and they didn't want their boys brought up to hear gamblers' talk and be thinking about such things and maybe embrace them.

That's all right and I guess the men know what they are talking about, but I don't see what it's got to do with Henry or with horses either. That's what I'm writing this story about. I'm puzzled. I'm getting to be a man and want to think straight and be O.K., and there's something I saw at the race meeting at the eastern track I can't figure out.

I can't help it, I'm crazy about thoroughbred horses. I've always been that way. When I was ten years old and saw I was growing to be big and couldn't be a rider I was so sorry I nearly died. Harry Hellinfinger in Beckersville, whose father is Postmaster, is grown up and too lazy to work, but likes to stand around in the street and get up jokes on boys like sending them to a hardware store for a gimlet to bore square holes and other jokes like that. He played one on me. He told me that if I would eat half a cigar I would be stunted and not grow any more and maybe could be a rider. I did it. When father wasn't looking I took a cigar out of his pocket and gagged it down some way. It made me awful sick and the doctor had to be sent for, and then it did no good. I kept right on growing. It was a joke. When I told what I had done and why most fathers would have whipped me but mine didn't.

Well, I didn't get stunted and didn't die. It serves Harry Hellinfinger right. Then I made up my mind I would like to be a stable boy, but had to give that up too. Mostly niggers do that work and I knew father wouldn't let me go into it. No use to ask him.

If you've never been crazy about thoroughbreds it's because you've never been around where they are much and don't know any better. They're beautiful. There isn't anything so lovely and clean and full of spunk and honest and everything as some race horses. On the big horse farms that are all around our town Beckersville there are tracks and the horses run in the early morning. More than a thousand times I've got out of bed before daylight and walked two or three miles to the tracks. Mother wouldn't of let me go but father always says, "Let him alone." So I got some bread out of the bread box and some butter and jam, gobbled it and lit out.

At the tracks you sit on the fence with men, whites and niggers, and they chew tobacco and talk, and then the colts are brought out. It's early and the grass is covered with shiny dew and in another field a man is plowing and they are frying things in a shed where the track niggers sleep, and you know how a nigger can giggle and laugh and say things that make you laugh. A white man can't do it and some niggers can't but a track nigger can every time.

And so the colts are brought out and some are just galloped by stable boys, but almost every morning on a big track owned by a rich man who lives maybe in New York, there are always, nearly every morning, a few colts and some of the old race horses and geldings and mares that are cut loose.

It brings a lump up into my throat when a horse runs. I don't mean all horses but some. I can pick them nearly every time. It's in my blood like in the blood of race track niggers and trainers. Even when they just go slop-jogging along with a little nigger on their backs I can tell a winner. If my throat hurts and it's hard for me to swallow, that's him. He'll run like Sam Hill when you let him out. If he don't win every time it'll be a wonder and because they've got him in a pocket behind another or he was pulled or got off bad at the post or something. If I wanted to be a gambler like Henry Rieback's father I could get rich. I know I could and Henry says so too. All I would have to do is wait 'til that hurt comes when I see a horse and then bet every cent. That's what I would do if I wanted to be a gambler, but I don't.

When you're at the tracks in the morning — not the race tracks but the training tracks around Beckersville — you don't see a horse, the kind I've been talking about, very often, but it's nice anyway. Any thoroughbred, that is sired right and out of a good mare and trained by a man that knows how, can run. If he couldn't what would he be there for and not pulling a plow?

Well, out of the stables they come and the boys are on their backs and it's lovely to be there. You hunch down on top of the fence and itch inside you. Over in the sheds the niggers giggle and sing. Bacon is being fried and coffee made. Everything smells lovely. Nothing smells better than coffee and manure and horses and niggers and bacon frying and pipes being smoked out of doors on a morning like that. It just gets you, that's what it does.

But about Saratoga. We was there six days and not a soul from home seen us and everything came off just as we wanted it to, fine weather and horses and races and all. We beat our way home and Bildad gave us a basket with fried chicken and bread and other eatables in it, and I had eighteen dollars when we got back to Beckersville. Mother jawed and cried but Pop didn't say much. I told everything we done except one thing. I did and saw that alone. That's what I'm writing about. It got me upset. I think about it at night. Here it is.

At Saratoga we laid up nights in the hay in the shed Bildad had showed us and ate with the niggers early and at night when the race people had all gone away. The men from home stayed mostly in the grandstand and betting field, and didn't come out around the places where the horses are kept except to the paddocks just before a race when the horses are saddled. At Saratoga they don't have paddocks under an open shed as at Lexington and Churchill Downs and other tracks down in our country, but saddle the horses right out in an open place under trees on a lawn as smooth and nice as Banker Bohon's front yard here in Beckersville. It's lovely. The horses are sweaty and nervous and shine and the men come out and smoke cigars and look at them and the trainers are there and the owners, and your heart thumps so you can hardly breathe.

Then the bugle blows for post and the boys that ride come running out with their silk clothes on and you run to get a place by the fence with the niggers.

I always am wanting to be a trainer or owner, and at the risk of being seen and caught and sent home I went to the paddocks before every race. The other boys didn't but I did.

We got to Saratoga on a Friday and on Wednesday the next week the big Mullford Handicap was to be run. Middlestride was in it and Sunstreak. The weather was fine and the track fast. I couldn't sleep the night before.

What had happened was that both these horses are the kind it makes my throat hurt to see. Middlestride is long and looks awkward and is a gelding. He belongs to Joe Thompson, a little owner from home who only has a half dozen horses. The Mullford Handicap is for a mile and Middlestride can't untrack fast. He goes away slow and is always way back at the half, then he begins to run and if the race is a mile and a quarter he'll just eat up everything and get there.

Sunstreak is different. He is a stallion and nervous and belongs on the biggest farm we've got in our country, the Van Riddle place that belongs to Mr. Van Riddle of New York. Sunstreak is like a girl you think about sometimes but never see. He is hard all over and lovely too. When you look at his head you want to kiss him. He is trained by Jerry Tillford who knows me and has been good to me lots of times, lets me walk into a horse's stall to look at him close and other things. There isn't anything as sweet as that horse. He stands at the post quiet and not letting on, but he is just burning up inside. Then when the barrier goes up he is off like his name, Sunstreak. It makes you ache to see him. It hurts you. He just lays down and runs like a bird dog. There isn't anything I ever see run like him except Middlestride when he gets untracked and stretches himself.

Gee! I ached to see that race and those two horses run, ached and dreaded it too. I didn't want to see either of our horses beaten. We had never sent a pair like that to the races before. Old men in Beckersville said so and the niggers said so. It was a fact.

Before the race I went over to the paddocks to see. I looked a last look at Middlestride, who isn't such a much standing in a paddock that way, then I went to see Sunstreak.

It was his day. I knew when I see him. I forgot all about being seen myself and walked right up. All the men from Beckersville were there and no one noticed me except Jerry Tillford. He saw me and something happened. I'll tell you about that.

I was standing looking at that horse and aching. In some way, I can't tell how, I knew just how Sunstreak felt inside. He was quiet and letting the niggers rub his legs and Mr. Van Riddle himself put the saddle on, but he was just a raging torrent inside. He was like the water in the river at Niagara Falls just before it goes plunk down. That horse wasn't thinking about running. He don't have to think about that. He was just thinking about holding himself back 'til the time for the running came. I knew that. I could just in a way see right inside him. He was going to do some awful running and I knew it. He wasn't bragging or letting on much or prancing or making a fuss, but just waiting. I knew it and Jerry Tillford his trainer knew. I looked up and then that man and I looked into each other's eyes. Something happened to me. I guess I loved the man as much as I did the horse because he knew what I knew. Seemed to me there wasn't anything in the world but that man and the horse and me. I cried and Jerry Tillford had a shine in his eyes. Then I came away to the fence to wait for the race. The horse was better than me, more steadier, and now I know better than Jerry. He was the quietest and he had to do the running.

Sunstreak ran first of course and he busted the world's record for a mile. I've seen that if I never see anything more. Everything came out just as I expected. Middlestride got left at the post and was way back and closed up to be second, just as I knew he would. He'll get a world's record too some day. They can't skin the Beckersville country on horses.

I watched the race calm because I knew what would happen. I was sure. Hanley Turner and Henry Rieback and Tom Tumberton were all more excited than me.

A funny thing had happened to me. I was thinking about Jerry Tillford the trainer and how happy he was all through the race. I liked him that afternoon even more than I ever liked my own father. I almost forgot the horses thinking that way about him. It was because of what I had seen in his eyes as he stood in the paddocks beside Sunstreak before the race started. I knew he had been watching and working with Sunstreak since the horse was a baby colt, had taught him to run and be patient and when to let himself out and not to quit, never. I knew that for him it was like a mother seeing her child do something brave or wonderful. It was the first time I ever felt for a man like that.

After the race that night I went out from Tom and Hanley and Henry. I wanted to be by myself and I wanted to be near Jerry Tillford if I could work it. Here is what happened.

The track in Saratoga is near the edge of town. It is all polished up and trees around, the evergreen kind, and grass and everything painted and nice. If you go past the track you get to a hard road made of asphalt for automobiles, and if you go along this for a few miles there is a road turns off to a little rummy-looking farm house set in a yard.

That night after the race I went along that road because I had seen Jerry and some other men go that way in an automobile. I didn't expect to find them. I walked for a ways and then sat down by a fence to think. It was the direction they went in. I wanted to be as near Jerry as I could. I felt close to him. Pretty soon I went up the side road — I don't know why — and came to the rummy farm house. I was just lonesome to see Jerry, like wanting to see your father at night when you were a young kid. Just then an automobile came along and turned in. Jerry was in it and Henry Rieback's father, and Arthur Bedford from home, and Dave Williams and two other men I didn't know. They got out of the car and went into the house, all but Henry Rieback's father who quarreled with them and said he wouldn't go. It was only about nine o'clock, but they were all drunk and the rummy-looking farm house was a place for bad women to stay in. That's what it was. I crept up along a fence and looked through a window and saw.

It's what gives me the fantods. I can't make it out. The women in the house were all ugly mean-looking women, not nice to look at or be near. They were homely too, except one who was tall and looked a little like the gelding Middlestride, but not clean like him, but with a hard ugly mouth. She had red hair. I saw everything plain. I got up by an old rose bush by an open window and looked. The women had on loose dresses and sat around in chairs. The men came in and some sat on the women's laps. The place smelled rotten and there was rotten talk, the kind a kid hears around a livery stable in a town like Beckersville in the winter but don't ever expect to hear talked when there are women around. It was rotten. A nigger wouldn't go into such a place.

I looked at Jerry Tillford. I've told you how I had the feeling about him on account of his knowing what was going on inside of Sunstreak in the minute before he went to the post for the race in which he made a world's record.

Jerry bragged in that bad woman house as I know Sunstreak wouldn't never have bragged. He said that he made that horse, that it was him that won the race and made the record. He lied and bragged like a fool. I never heard such silly talk.

And then, what do you suppose he did! He looked at the woman in there, the one that was lean and hard-mouthed and looked a little like the gelding Middlestride, but not clean like him, and his eyes began to shine just as they did when he looked at me and at Sunstreak in the paddocks at the track in the afternoon. I stood there by the window — gee! — but I wished I hadn't gone away from the tracks, but had stayed with the boys and the niggers and the horses. The tall rotten-looking woman was between us just as Sunstreak was in the paddocks in the afternoon.

Then, all of a sudden, I began to hate that man. I wanted to scream and rush in the room and kill him. I never had such a feeling before. I was so mad clean through that I cried and my fists were doubled up so my finger nails cut my hands.

And Jerry's eyes kept shining and he waved back and forth, and then he went and kissed that woman and I crept away and went back to the tracks and to bed and didn't sleep hardly any, and then next day I got the other kids to start home with me and never told them anything I seen.

I been thinking about it ever since. I can't make it out. Spring has come again and I'm nearly sixteen and go to the tracks mornings same as always, and I see Sunstreak and Middlestride and a new colt named Strident I'll bet will lay them all out, but no one thinks so but me and two or three niggers.

But things are different. At the tracks the air don't taste as good or smell as good. It's because a man like Jerry Tillford, who knows what he does, could see a horse like Sunstreak run, and kiss a woman like that the same day. I can't make it out. Darn him, what did he want to do like that for? I keep thinking about it and it spoils looking at horses and smelling things and hearing niggers laugh and everything. Sometimes I'm so mad about it I want to fight someone. It gives me the fantods. What did he do it for? I want to know why.

Exercises

1. What kind of person is the narrator? When is he reliable and when is he not?

2. The use of the first-person narrator often allows the author to establish an intimate relationship between the reader and the characters. Does Anderson accomplish this feat here? If so, how?

3. Is the boy a static or dynamic character? What is his dilemma? How is sympathy for him achieved?

4. Study the plot of the story. Explain how unity is achieved by showing how the episodes are interrelated.

5. How helpful is the title of the story? What is the meaning of the boy's final statement?

6. What exactly does the boy want to know?

7. For what purpose does the author give admirable human qualities to the horses?

8. Characterize Bildad. Explain his role in the story.

Topics for Writing

1. Making specific references to the text, discuss the plight of the young, naive boy who inevitably loses his innocence in the course of discovering evil in the world.

2. Write a comparison that points to the similarities and differences in the characters of the two boys in "A Tree, a Rock, a Cloud" and "I Want to Know Why."

3. Discuss the advantages of the first-person-protagonist point of view as used in this story.

Selected Bibliography   Sherwood Anderson

Flanagan, J. T. "The Permanence of Sherwood Anderson." *Southeast Review,* 35 (1970), 170–177.
Gold, Herbert. "The Purity and Cunning of Sherwood Anderson." *Hudson Review,* 10 (1957–58), 548–557.
Howe, Irving. "Sherwood Anderson: An American as Artist." *Kenyon Review,* 13 (1951), 193–203.
O'Connor, Frank. *The Lonely Voice: A Study of the Short Story.* Cleveland and New York: World, 1963, pp. 39–41.
Sherbo, Arthur. "I Want to Know Why and Brooks and Warren." *College English,* 15 (1954), 350–351.
Trilling, Lionel. *The Liberal Imagination.* New York: Viking, 1950, pp. 23–33.
Weber, Brom. "Anderson and 'The Essence of Things.'" *Sewanee Review,* 59 (1951), 678–692.
White, Ray Lewis, ed. *The Achievement of Sherwood Anderson: Essays in Criticism.* Chapel Hill: University of North Carolina Press, 1966.
Winther, S. K. "The Aura of Loneliness in Sherwood Anderson." *Modern Fiction Studies,* 5 (1959), 145–152.

D. H. Lawrence (1885–1930)

The Horse Dealer's Daughter

"Well, Mabel, and what are you going to do with yourself?" asked Joe, with foolish flippancy. He felt quite safe himself. Without listening for an answer, he turned aside, worked a grain of tobacco to the tip of his tongue and spat it out. He did not care about anything, since he felt safe himself.

The three brothers and the sister sat round the desolate breakfast table, attempting some sort of desultory consultation. The morning's post had given the final tap to the family fortune, and all was over. The dreary dining-room itself, with its heavy mahogany furniture, looked as if it were waiting to be done away with.

But the consultation amounted to nothing. There was a strange air of ineffectuality about the three men, as they sprawled at table, smoking and reflecting vaguely on their own condition. The girl was alone, a rather short, sullen-looking young woman of twenty-seven. She did not share the same life as her brothers. She would have been good-looking, save for the impassive fixity of her face, "bull-dog," as her brothers called it.

There was a confused tramping of horses' feet outside. The three men all sprawled round in their chairs to watch. Beyond the dark holly-bushes that separated the strip of lawn from the highroad, they could see a cavalcade of shire horses swinging out of their own yard, being taken for exercise. This was the last time. These were the last horses that would go through their hands. The young men watched with critical, callous look. They were all frightened at the collapse of their lives, and the sense of disaster in which they were involved left them no inner freedom.

Yet they were three fine, well-set fellows enough. Joe, the eldest, was a man of thirty-three, broad and handsome in a hot, flushed way. His face was red, he twisted his black mustache over a thick finger, his eyes were shallow and restless. He had a sensual way of uncovering his teeth when he laughed, and his bearing was stupid. Now he watched the horses with a glazed look of helplessness in his eyes, a certain stupor of downfall.

The great draught-horses swung past. They were tied head to tail, four of them, and they heaved along to where a lane branched off from the highroad, planting their great hoofs floutingly in the fine black mud, swinging their great rounded haunches sumptuously, and trotting a few sudden steps as they were led into the lane, round the corner. Every movement showed a massive, slumbrous strength, and a stupidity which held them in subjection. The groom at the head looked back, jerking the leading rope. And the cavalcade moved out of sight up the lane, the tail of the last horse, bobbed up tight and stiff, held out taut from the swinging great haunches as they rocked behind the hedges in a motion-like sleep.

Joe watched with glazed hopeless eyes. The horses were almost like his own body to him. He felt he was done for now. Luckily he was engaged to a woman as old as himself, and therefore her father, who was steward of a neighboring estate, would provide him with a job. He would marry and go into harness. His life was over, he would be a subject animal now.

He turned uneasily aside, the retreating steps of the horses echoing in his ears. Then, with foolish restlessness, he reached for the scraps of bacon-rind from the plates, and making a faint whistling sound, flung them to the terrier that lay against the fender. He watched the dog swallow them, and waited till the creature looked into his eyes. Then a faint grin came on his face, and in a high, foolish voice he said:

"You won't get much more bacon, shall you, you little bitch?"

The dog faintly and dismally wagged its tail, then lowered its haunches, circled round, and lay down again.

There was another helpless silence at the table. Joe sprawled uneasily in his seat, not willing to go till the family conclave was dissolved. Fred Henry, the second brother, was erect, clean-limbed, alert. He had watched the passing of the horses with more *sang-froid*. If he was an animal, like Joe, he was an animal which controls, not one which is controlled. He was master of any horse, and he carried himself with a well-tempered air of mastery. But he was not master of the situations of life. He pushed his coarse brown mustache upwards, off his lip, and glanced irritably at his sister, who sat impassive and inscrutable.

"You'll go and stop with Lucy for a bit, shan't you?" he asked. The girl did not answer.

"I don't see what else you can do," persisted Fred Henry.

"Go as a skivvy," Joe interpolated laconically.

The girl did not move a muscle.

"If I was her, I should go in for training for a nurse," said Malcolm, the youngest of them all. He was the baby of the family, a young man of twenty-two, with a fresh, jaunty *museau*.

But Mabel did not take any notice of him. They had talked at her and round her for so many years, that she hardly heard them at all.

The marble clock on the mantelpiece softly chimed the half-hour, the dog rose uneasily from the hearthrug and looked at the party at the breakfast table. But still they sat on in ineffectual conclave.

"Oh, all right," said Joe suddenly, apropos of nothing. "I'll get a move on."

He pushed back his chair, straddled his knees with a downward jerk, to get them free, in horsey fashion, and went to the fire. Still he did not go out of the room; he was curious to know what the others would do or say. He began to charge his pipe, looking down at the dog and saying, in a high, affected voice:

"Going wi' me? Going wi' me are ter? Tha'rt goin' further than that counts on just now, dost hear?"

The dog faintly wagged its tail, the man stuck out his jaw and covered his pipe with his hands, and puffed intently, losing himself in the tobacco, looking down all the while at the dog with an absent brown eye. The dog looked at him in mournful distrust. Joe stood with his knees stuck out, in real horsey fashion.

"Have you had a letter from Lucy?" Fred Henry asked his sister.

"Last week," came the neutral reply.

"And what does she say?"

There was no answer.

"Does she *ask* you to go and stop there?" persisted Fred Henry.

"She says I can if I like."

"Well, then, you'd better. Tell her you'll come on Monday."

This was received in silence.

"That's what you'll do then, is it?" said Fred Henry, in some exasperation.

But she made no answer. There was a silence of futility and irritation in the room. Malcolm grinned fatuously.

"You'll have to make up your mind between now and next Wednesday," said Joe loudly, "or else find yourself lodgings on the curbstone."

The face of the young woman darkened, but she sat on immutable.

"Here's Jack Fergusson!" exclaimed Malcolm, who was looking aimlessly out of the window.

"Where?" exclaimed Joe, loudly.

"Just gone past."

"Coming in?"

Malcolm craned his neck to see the gate.

"Yes," he said.

There was a silence. Mabel sat on like one condemned, at the head of the table. Then a whistle was heard from the kitchen. The dog got up and barked sharply. Joe opened the door and shouted:

"Come on."

After a moment a young man entered. He was muffled up in overcoat and a purple woolen scarf, and his tweed cap, which he did not remove, was pulled down on his head. He was of medium height, his face was rather long and pale, his eyes looked tired.

"Hello, Jack! Well, Jack!" exclaimed Malcolm and Joe. Fred Henry merely said "Jack!"

"What's doing?" asked the newcomer, evidently addressing Fred Henry.

"Same. We've got to be out by Wednesday. — Got a cold?"

"I have — got it bad, too."

"Why don't you stop in?"

"*Me* stop in? When I can't stand on my legs, perhaps I shall have a chance." The young man spoke huskily. He had a slight Scotch accent.

"It's a knock-out, isn't it," said Joe boisterously, "if a doctor goes round croaking with a cold. Looks bad for the patients, doesn't it?"

The young doctor looked at him slowly.

"Anything the matter with *you,* then?" he asked sarcastically.

"Not as I know of. Damn your eyes, I hope not. Why?"

"I thought you were very concerned about the patients, wondered if you might be one yourself."

"Damn it, no, I've never been patient to no flaming doctor, and hope I never shall be," returned Joe.

At this point Mabel rose from the table, and they all seemed to become aware of her existence. She began putting the dishes together. The young doctor looked at her, but did not address her. He had not greeted her. She went out of the room with the tray, her face impassive and unchanged.

"When are you off then, all of you?" asked the doctor.

"I'm catching the eleven-forty," replied Malcolm. "Are you goin' down wi' th' trap, Joe?"

"Yes, I've told you I'm going down wi' th' trap, haven't I?"

"We'd better be getting her in then. So long, Jack, if I don't see you before I go," said Malcolm, shaking hands.

He went out, followed by Joe, who seemed to have his tail between his legs.

"Well, this is the devil's own," exclaimed the doctor, when he was left alone with Fred Henry. "Going before Wednesday, are you?"

"That's the orders," replied the other.

"Where, to Northampton?"

"That's it."

"The devil!" exclaimed Fergusson, with quiet chagrin.

And there was silence between the two.

"All settled up, are you?" asked Fergusson.

"About."

There was another pause.

"Well, I shall miss yer, Freddy boy," said the young doctor.

"And I shall miss thee, Jack," returned the other.

"Miss you like hell," mused the doctor.

Fred Henry turned aside. There was nothing to say. Mabel came in again, to finish clearing the table.

"What are *you* going to do, then, Miss Pervin?" asked Fergusson. "Going to your sister's, are you?"

Mabel looked at him with her steady, dangerous eyes, that always made him uncomfortable, unsettling his superficial ease.

"No," she said.

"Well, what in the name of fortune *are* you going to do? Say what you *mean* to do," cried Fred Henry, with futile intensity.

But she only averted her head, and continued her work. She folded the white table-cloth, and put on the chenille cloth.

"The sulkiest bitch that ever trod!" muttered her brother.

But she finished her task with perfectly impassive face, the young doctor watching her interestedly all the while. Then she went out.

Fred Henry stared after her, clenching his lips, his blue eyes fixing in sharp antagonism, as he made a grimace of sour exasperation.

"You could bray her into bits, and that's all you'd get out of her," he said in a small, narrowed tone.

The doctor smiled faintly.

"What's she *going* to do, then?" he asked.

"Strike me if *I* know!" returned the other.

There was a pause. Then the doctor stirred.

"I'll be seeing you to-night, shall I" he said to his friend.

"Ay — where's it to be? Are we going over to Jessdale?"

"I don't know. I've got such a cold on me. I'll come round to the Moon and Stars, anyway."

"Let Lizzie and May miss their night for once, eh?"

"That's it — if I feel as I do now."

"All's one — "

The two young men went through the passage and down to the back door together. The house was large, but it was servantless now, and desolate. At the back was a small bricked house-yard, and beyond that a big square, graveled fine and red, and having stables on two sides. Sloping, dank, winter-dark fields stretched away on the open sides.

But the stables were empty. Joseph Pervin, the father of the family, had been a man of no education, who had become a fairly large horse dealer. The stables had been full of horses, there was a great turmoil and come-and-go of horses and of dealers and grooms. Then the kitchen was full of servants. But of late things had declined. The old man had married a second time, to retrieve his fortunes. Now he was dead and everything was gone to the dogs, there was nothing but debt and threatening.

For months, Mabel had been servantless in the big house, keeping the home together in penury for her ineffectual brothers. She had kept house for ten years. But previously, it was with unstinted means. Then, however brutal and coarse everything was, the sense of money had kept her proud, confident. The men might be foul-mouthed, the women in the kitchen might have bad reputations, her brothers might have illegitimate children. But so long as there was money, the girl felt herself established, and brutally proud, reserved.

No company came to the house, save dealers and coarse men. Mabel had no associates of her own sex, after her sister went away. But she did not mind. She went regularly to church, she attended to her father. And she lived in the memory of her mother, who had died when she was fourteen, and whom she had loved. She had loved her father, too, in a different way, depending upon him, and feeling secure in him, until at the age of fifty-four he married again. And then she had set hard against him. Now he had died and left them all hopelessly in debt.

She had suffered badly during the period of poverty. Nothing, however, could shake the curious sullen, animal pride that dominated each member of the family. Now, for Mabel, the end had come. Still she would not cast about her. She would follow her own way just the same. She would always hold the keys of her own situation. Mindless and persistent, she endured from day to day. Why should she think? Why should she answer anybody? It was enough that this was the end, and there was no way out. She need not pass any more darkly along the main street of the small town, avoiding every eye. She need not demean herself any more, going into the shops and buying the cheapest food. This was at an end. She thought of nobody, not even of herself. Mindless and persistent, she seemed in a sort of ecstasy to becoming nearer to her fulfillment, her own glorification, approaching her dead mother, who was glorified.

In the afternoon she took a little bag, with shears and sponge and a small scrubbing brush, and went out. It was a gray, wintry day, with saddened, dark-green fields and an atmosphere blackened by the smoke of foundries not far off. She went quickly, darkly along the causeway, heeding nobody, through the town to the churchyard.

There she always felt secure, as if no one could see her, although as a matter of fact she was exposed to the stare of everyone who passed along under the churchyard wall. Nevertheless, once under the shadow of the great looming church, among the graves, she felt immune from the world, reserved within the thick churchyard wall as in another country.

Carefully she clipped the grass from the grave, and arranged the pinky-white, small chrysanthemums in the tin cross. When this was done, she took an empty jar from a neighboring grave, brought water, and carefully, most scrupulously sponged the marble headstone and the coping-stone.

It gave her sincere satisfaction to do this. She felt in immediate contact with the world of her mother. She took minute pains, went through the park in a state bordering on pure happiness, as if in performing this task she came into a subtle, intimate connection with her mother. For the life she followed here in the world was far less real than the world of death she inherited from her mother.

The doctor's house was just by the church. Fergusson, being a mere hired assistant, was slave to the countryside. As he hurried now to attend to the out-patients in the surgery, glancing across the graveyard with his quick eye, he saw the girl at her task at the grave. She seemed so intent and remote, it was like looking into another world. Some mystical element was touched in him. He slowed down as he walked, watching her as if spellbound.

She lifted her eyes, feeling him looking. Their eyes met. And each looked away again at once, each feeling, in some way, found out by the other. He lifted his cap and passed on down the road. There remained distinct in his consciousness, like a vision, the memory of her face, lifted from the tombstone in the churchyard, and looking at him with slow, large, portentous eyes. It *was* portentous, her face. It seemed to mesmerize him. There was a heavy power in her eyes which laid hold of his whole being, as if he had drunk some powerful drug. He had been feeling weak and done before. Now the life came back into him, he felt delivered from his own fretted, daily self.

He finished his duties at the surgery as quickly as might be, hastily filling up the bottle of the waiting people with cheap drugs. Then, in perpetual haste, he set off again to visit several cases in another part of his round, before teatime. At all times he preferred to walk if he could, but particularly when he was not well. He fancied the motion restored him.

The afternoon was falling. It was gray, deadened, and wintry, with a slow, moist, heavy coldness sinking in and deadening all the faculties. But why should he think or notice? He hastily climbed the hill and turned across the dark-green fields, following the black cinder-track. In the distance, across a shallow dip in the country, the small town was clustered like smoldering ash, a tower, a spire, a heap of low, raw, extinct houses. And on the nearest fringe of the town, sloping into the dip, was Oldmeadow, the Pervins' house. He could see the stables and the outbuildings distinctly, as they lay towards him on the slope. Well, he would not go there many more times! Another resource would be lost to him, another place gone: the only company he cared for in the alien, ugly little town he was losing. Nothing but work, drudgery, constant hastening from dwelling to dwelling among the colliers and the iron-workers. It wore him out, but at the same time he had a craving for it. It was a stimulant to him to be in the homes of the working people, moving as it were through the innermost body of their life. His nerves were excited and gratified. He could come so near, into the very lives of the rough, inarticulate, powerfully emotional men and women. He grumbled, he said he hated the hellish hole. But as a matter of fact it excited him, the contact with the rough, strongly-feeling people was a stimulant applied direct to his nerves.

Below Oldmeadow, in the green, shallow, soddened hollow of fields, lay a square, deep pond. Roving across the landscape, the doctor's quick eye detected a figure in black passing through the gate of the field, down towards the pond. He looked again. It would be Mabel Pervin. His mind suddenly became alive and attentive.

Why was she going down there? He pulled up on the path on the slope above, and stood staring. He could just make sure of the small black figure moving in the hollow of the failing day. He seemed to see her in the midst of such obscurity, that he was like a clairvoyant, seeing rather with the mind's eye than with ordinary sight. Yet he could see her positively enough, while he kept his eye attentive. He felt, if he looked away from her, in the thick, ugly falling dusk, he would lose her altogether.

He followed her minutely as she moved, direct and intent, like something transmitted rather than stirring in voluntary activity, straight down the field towards the pond. There she stood on the bank for a moment. She never raised her head. Then she waded slowly into the water.

He stood motionless as the small black figure walked slowly and deliberately towards the center of the pond, very slowly, gradually moving deeper into the motionless water, and still moving forward as the water got up to her breast. Then he could see her no more in the dusk of the dead afternoon.

"There!" he exclaimed. "Would you believe it?"

And he hastened straight down, running over the wet, soddened fields, pushing through the hedges, down into the depression of callous wintry obscurity. It took him several minutes to come to the pond. He stood on the bank, breathing heavily. He could see nothing. His eyes seemed to penetrate the dead water. Yes, perhaps that was the dark shadow of her black clothing beneath the surface of the water.

He slowly ventured into the pond. The bottom was deep, soft clay, he sank in, and the water clasped dead cold round his legs. As he stirred he could smell the cold, rotten clay that fouled up into the water. It was objectionable in his lungs. Still, repelled and yet not heeding, he moved deeper into the pond. The cold water rose over his thighs, over his loins, upon his abdomen. The lower part of his body was all sunk in the hideous cold element. And the bottom was so deeply soft and uncertain, he was afraid of pitching with his mouth underneath. He could not swim, and was afraid.

He crouched a little, spreading his hands under the water and moving them round, trying to feel for her. The dead cold pond swayed upon his chest. He moved again, a little deeper, and again, with his hands underneath, he felt all around under the water. And he touched her clothing. But it evaded his fingers. He made a desperate effort to grasp it.

And so doing he lost his balance and went under, horribly, suffocating in the foul earthy water, struggling madly for a few moments. At last, after what seemed an eternity, he got his footing, rose again into the air and looked around. He gasped, and knew he was in the world. Then he looked at the water. She had risen near him. He grasped her clothing, and drawing her nearer, turned to take his way to land again.

He went very slowly, carefully, absorbed in the slow progress. He rose higher, climbing out of the pond. The water was now only about his legs; he was thankful, full of relief to be out of the clutches of the pond. He lifted her and staggered onto the bank, out of the horror of wet, gray clay.

He laid her down on the bank. She was quite unconscious and running with water. He made the water come from her mouth, he worked to restore her. He did not have to work very long before he could feel the breathing begin again in her; she was breathing naturally. He worked a little longer. He could feel her live beneath his hands; she was coming back. He wiped her face, wrapped her in his overcoat, looked round into the dim, dark-gray world, the lifted her and staggered down the bank and across the fields.

It seemed an unthinkably long way, and his burden so heavy he felt he would never get to the house. But at last he was in the stableyard, and then in the house-yard. He opened the door and went into the house. In the kitchen he laid her down on the hearthrug, and called. The house was empty. But the fire was burning in the grate.

Then again he kneeled to attend to her. She was breathing regularly, her eyes were wide open and as if conscious, but there seemed something missing in her look. She was conscious in herself, but unconscious of her surroundings.

He ran upstairs, took blankets from a bed, and put them before the fire to warm. Then he removed her saturated, earthy-smelling clothing, rubbed her dry with a towel, and wrapped her naked in the blankets. Then he went into the dining-room, to look for spirits. There was a little whisky. He drank a gulp himself, and put some into her mouth.

The effect was instantaneous. She looked full into his face, as if she had been seeing him for some time, and yet had only just become conscious of him.

"Dr. Fergusson?" she said.

"What?" he answered.

He was divesting himself of his coat, intending to find some dry clothing upstairs. He could not bear the smell of the dead, clayey water, and he was mortally afraid for his own health.

"What did I do?" she asked.

"Walked into the pond," he replied. He had begun to shudder like one sick, and could hardly attend to her. Her eyes remained full on him, he seemed to be going dark in his mind, looking back at her helplessly. The shuddering became quieter in him, his life came back in him, dark and unknowing, but strong again.

"Was I out of my mind?" she asked, while her eyes were fixed on him all the time.

"Maybe, for the moment," he replied. He felt quiet, because his strength had come back. The strange fretful strain had left him.

"Am I out of my mind now?" she asked.

"Are you?" he reflected a moment. "No," he answered truthfully, "I don't see that you are." He turned his face aside. He was afraid now, because he felt dazed, and felt dimly that her power was stronger than his, in this issue. And she continued to look at him fixedly all the time. "Can you tell me where I shall find some dry things to put on?" he asked.

"Did you dive into the pond for me?" she asked.

"No," he answered. "I walked in. But I went in overhead as well."

There was silence for a moment. He hesitated. He very much wanted to go upstairs to get into dry clothing. But there was another desire in him. And she seemed to hold him. His will seemed to have gone to sleep, and left him, standing there slack before her. But he felt warm inside himself. He did not shudder at all, though his clothes were sodden on him.

"Why did you?" she asked.

"Because I didn't want you to do such a foolish thing," he said.

"It wasn't foolish," she said, still gazing at him as she lay on the floor, with a sofa cushion under her head. "It was the right thing to do. *I* knew best, then."

"I'll go and shift these wet things," he said. But still he had not the power to move out of her presence, until she sent him. It was as if she had the life of his body in her hands, and he could not extricate himself. Or perhaps he did not want to.

Suddenly she sat up. Then she became aware of her own immediate condition. She felt the blankets about her, she knew her own limbs. For a moment it seemed as if her reason were going. She looked round, with wild eye, as if seeking something. He stood still with fear. She saw her clothing lying scattered.

"Who undressed me?" she asked, her eyes resting full and inevitable on his face.

"I did," he replied, "to bring you round."

For some moments she sat and gazed at him awfully, her lips parted.

"Do you love me, then?" she asked.

He only stood and stared at her, fascinated. His soul seemed to melt.

She shuffled forward on her knees, and put her arms round him, round his legs, as he stood there, pressing her breasts against his knees and thighs, clutching him with strange, convulsive certainty, pressing his thighs against her, drawing him to her face, her throat, as she looked up at him with flaring, humble eyes of transfiguration, triumphant in first possession.

"You love me," she murmured, in strange transport, yearning and triumphant and confident. "You love me. I know you love me, I know."

And she was passionately kissing his knees, through the wet clothing, passionately and indiscriminately kissing his knees, his legs, as if unaware of everything.

He looked down at the tangled wet hair, the wild, bare, animal shoulders. He was amazed, bewildered, and afraid. He had never thought of loving her. He had never wanted to love her. When he rescued her and restored her, he was a doctor, and she was a patient. He had had no single personal thought of her. Nay, this introduction of the personal element was very distasteful to him, a violation of his professional honor. It was horrible to have her there embracing his knees. It was horrible. He revolted from it, violently. And yet — and yet — he had not the power to break away.

She looked at him again, with the same supplication of powerful love, and that same transcendent, frightening light of triumph. In view of the delicate flame which seemed to come from her face like a light, he was powerless. And yet he had never intended to love her. He had never intended. And something stubborn in him could not give way.

"You love me," she repeated, in a murmur of deep, rhapsodic assurance. "You love me."

Her hands were drawing him, drawing him down to her. He was afraid, even a little horrified. For he had, really, no intention of loving her. Yet her hands were drawing him towards her. He put out his hand quickly to steady himself, and grasped her bare shoulder. A flame seemed to burn the hand that grasped her soft shoulder. He had no intention of loving her: his whole will was against his yielding. It was horrible. And yet wonderful was the touch of her shoulders, beautiful the shining of her face. Was she perhaps mad? He had a horror of yielding to her. Yet something in him ached also.

He had been staring away at the door, away from her. But his hand remained on her shoulder. She had gone suddenly very still. He looked down at her. Her eyes were now wide with fear, with doubt, the light was dying from her face, a shadow of terrible grayness was returning. He could not bear the touch of her eyes' question upon him, and the look of death behind the question.

With an inward groan he gave way, and let his heart yield towards her. A sudden gentle smile came on his face. And her eyes, which never left his face, slowly, slowly filled with tears. He watched the strange water rise in her eyes, like some slow fountain coming up. And his heart seemed to burn and melt away in his breast.

He could not bear to look at her any more. He dropped on his knees and caught her head with his arms and pressed her face against his throat. She was very still. His heart, which seemed to have broken, was burning with a kind of agony in his breast. And he felt her slow, hot tears wetting his throat. But he could not move.

He felt the hot tears wet his neck and the hollows of his neck, and he remained motionless, suspended through one of man's eternities. Only now it had become indispensable to him to have her face pressed close to him; he could never let her go again. He could never let her head go away from the close clutch of his arm. He wanted to remain like that forever, with his heart hurting him in a pain that was also life to him. Without knowing, he was looking down on her damp, soft brown hair.

Then, as it were suddenly, he smelt the horrid stagnant smell of that water. And at the same moment she drew away from him and looked at him. Her eyes were wistful and unfathomable. He was afraid of them, and he fell to kissing her, not knowing what he was doing. He wanted her eyes not to have that terrible, wistful, unfathomable look.

When she turned her face to him again, a faint delicate flush was glowing, and there was again dawning that terrible shining of joy in her eyes, which really terrified him, and yet which he now wanted to see, because he feared the look of doubt still more.

"You love me?" she said, rather faltering.

"Yes." The word cost him a painful effort. Not because it wasn't true. But because it was too newly true, the *saying* seemed to tear open again his newly-torn heart. And he hardly wanted it to be true, even now.

She lifted her face to him, and he bent forward and kissed her on the mouth, gently, with the one kiss that is an eternal pledge. And as he kissed her his heart strained again in his breast. He never intended to love her. But now it was over. He had crossed over the gulf to her, and all that he had left behind had shriveled and become void.

After the kiss, her eyes again slowly filled with tears. She sat still, away from him, with her face drooped aside, and her hands folded in her lap. The tears fell very slowly. There was complete silence. He too sat there motionless and silent on the hearthrug. The strange pain of his heart that was broken seemed to consume him. That he should love her? That this was love! That he should be ripped open in this way! — Him, a doctor! — How they would all jeer if they knew! — It was agony to him to think they might know.

In the curious naked pain of the thought he looked again to her. She was sitting there drooped into a muse. He saw a tear fall, and his heart flared hot. He saw for the first time that one of her shoulders was quite uncovered, one arm bare, he could see one of her small breasts; dimly, because it had become almost dark in the room.

"Why are you crying?" he asked, in an altered voice.

She looked up at him, and behind her tears the consciousness of her situation for the first time brought a dark look of shame to her eyes.

"I'm not crying, really," she said, watching him half frightened.

He reached his hand, and softly closed it on her bare arm.

"I love you! I love you!" he said in a soft, low, vibrating voice, unlike himself.

She shrank, and dropped her head. The soft, penetrating grip of his hand on her arm distressed her. She looked up at him.

"I want to go," she said. "I want to go and get you some dry things."

"Why?" he said. "I'm all right."

"But I want to go," she said. "And I want you to change your things."

He released her arm, and she wrapped herself in the blanket, looking at him rather frightened. And still she did not rise.

"Kiss me," she said wistfully.

He kissed her, but briefly, half in anger.

Then, after a second, she rose nervously, all mixed up in the blanket. He watched her in her confusion, as she tried to extricate herself and wrap herself up so that she could walk. He watched her relentlessly, as she knew. And as she went, the blanket trailing, and as he saw a glimpse of her feet and her white leg, he tried to remember her as she was when he had wrapped her in the blanket. But then he didn't want to remember, because she had been nothing to him then, and his nature revolted from remembering her as she was when she was nothing to him.

A tumbling, muffled noise from within the dark house startled him. Then he heard her voice: — "There are clothes." He rose and went to the foot of the stairs, and gathered up the garments she had thrown down. Then he came back to the fire, to rub himself down and dress. He grinned at his own appearance, when he had finished.

The fire was sinking, so he put on coal. The house was now quite dark, save for the light of a street-lamp that shone in faintly from beyond the holly trees. He lit the gas with matches he found on the mantelpiece. Then he emptied the pockets of his own clothes, and threw all his wet things in a heap into the scullery. After which he gathered up her sodden clothes, gently, and put them in a separate heap on the copper-top in the scullery.

It was six o'clock on the clock. His own watch had stopped. He ought to go back to the surgery. He waited, and still she did not come down. So he went to the foot of the stairs and called:

"I shall have to go."

Almost immediately he heard her coming down. She had on her best dress of black voile, and her hair was tidy, but still damp. She looked at him — and in spite of herself, smiled.

"I don't like you in those clothes," she said.

"Do I look a sight?" he answered.

They were shy of one another.

"I'll make you some tea," she said.

"No, I must go."

"Must you?" And she looked at him again with the wide, strained, doubtful eyes. And again, from the pain of his breast, he knew how he loved her. He went and bent to kiss her, gently, passionately, with his heart's painful kiss.

"And my hair smells so horrible," she murmured in distraction. "And I'm so awful, I'm so awful! Oh, no, I'm too awful." And she broke into bitter, heartbroken sobbing. "You can't want to love me, I'm horrible."

"Don't be silly, don't be silly," he said, trying to comfort her, kissing her, holding her in his arms. "I want you, I want to marry you, we're going to be married, quickly, quickly — tomorrow if I can."

But she only sobbed terribly, and cried:

"I feel awful. I feel awful. I feel I'm horrible to you."

"No, I want you, I want you," was all he answered, blindly, with that terrible intonation which frightened her almost more than her horror lest he should *not* want her.

Exercises

1. What author's intentions are served by the first two paragraphs?

2. What point of view is used in this story?

3. List the incidents that move the story forward.

4. Identify and explain one scene, incident, or speech that illustrates each of the following: (a) objective point of view; (b) subjective point of view; (c) dramatic mode of presentation; (d) summary method of presentation.

5. Do you find one protagonist or two? Do these characters change? Which one better fits our earlier definition of a protagonist? Why?

6. How is Dr. Fergusson characterized? What is his chief motivation? Is it plausible?

7. Is there sufficient preparation for Dr. Fergusson's falling in love?

8. Explain the importance of the final love scene.

Topics for Writing

1. Explore the thesis that this story is about rebirth.

2. Articulate a definition of love based on the delightful and horrible aspects of love that the story seems to suggest.

3. Discuss the point of view used in the story and comment on its appropriateness to the author's purpose and the effects he achieves.

Selected Bibliography   D. H. Lawrence

Amon, Frank. "D. H. Lawrence and the Short Story." In *The Achievement of D. H. Lawrence,* ed. Frederick J. Hoffman and Harry T. Moore. Norman: University of Oklahoma Press, 1953, pp. 222–234.

Ford, George H. *Double Measure: A Study of the Novels and Stories of D. H. Lawrence.* New York: Holt, 1965.

Frye, Northrop. "The Archetypes of Literature." *Kenyon Review,* 13 (1951), 92–110.

Junkins, Donald. "D. H. Lawrence's 'The Horse Dealer's Daughter.'" *Studies in Short Fiction,* 6 (1969), 210–212.

McCabe, Thomas H. "Rhythm as Form in Lawrence: 'The Horse Dealer's Daughter.'" *PMLA,* 87 (1972), 64–68.

O'Connor, Frank. *The Lonely Voice: A Study of the Short Story.* Cleveland and New York: World, 1963, pp. 143–155.

Phillips, Steven R. "The Double Pattern of D. H. Lawrence's 'The Horse Dealer's Daughter,'" *Studies in Short Fiction,* 10 (1973), 94–97.

Spilka, Mark. *The Love Ethic of D. H. Lawrence.* Bloomington: Indiana University Press, 1955.

Tedlock, E. W. *D. H. Lawrence, Artist & Rebel.* Albuquerque: University of New Mexico Press, 1963.

Vickery, John B. "Myth and Ritual in the Shorter Fiction of D. H. Lawrence." *Modern Fiction Studies,* 5 (1959), 65–82.

F. Scott Fitzgerald (1896–1940)

Babylon Revisited[1]

I.

"And where's Mr. Campbell?" Charlie asked.

"Gone to Switzerland. Mr. Campbell's a pretty sick man, Mr. Wales."

"I'm sorry to hear that. And George Hardt?" Charlie inquired.

"Back in America, gone to work."

"And where is the Snow Bird?" [2]

"He was in here last week. Anyway, his friend, Mr. Schaeffer, is in Paris."

Two familiar names from the long list of a year and a half ago. Charlie scribbled an address in his notebook and tore out the page.

"If you see Mr. Schaeffer, give him this," he said. "It's my brother-in-law's address. I haven't settled on a hotel yet."

He was not really disappointed to find Paris was so empty. But the stillness in the Ritz bar[3] was strange and portentous. It was not an American bar any more — he felt polite in it, and not as if he owned it. It had gone back into France. He felt the stillness from the moment he got out of the taxi and saw the doorman, usually in a frenzy of activity at this hour, gossiping with a *chasseur*[4] by the servants' entrance.

Passing through the corridor, he heard only a single, bored voice in the once-clamorous women's room. When he turned into the bar he traveled the twenty feet of green carpet with his eyes fixed straight ahead by old habit; and then, with his foot firmly on the rail, he turned and surveyed the room, encountering only a single pair of eyes that fluttered up from a newspaper in the corner. Charlie asked for the head barman, Paul, who in the latter days of the bull market[5] had come to work in his own custom-built car — disembarking, however, with due nicety at the nearest corner. But Paul was at his country house today and Alix giving him information.

"No, no more," Charlie said, "I'm going slow these days."

Alix congratulated him: "You were going pretty strong a couple of years ago."

"I'll stick to it all right," Charlie assured him. "I've stuck to it for over a year and a half now."

1. "Babylon Revisited": Babylon, an ancient city, symbolized decadence. The story is Fitzgerald's final criticism in fiction of a generation he himself came to represent.
2. Snow Bird: Slang for a user or peddler of heroin or cocaine.
3. Ritz bar: A popular rendezvous for wealthy Americans.
4. *Chasseur:* Errand boy for the hotel.
5. Latter days . . . market: The period of opulence immediately preceding the stock market crash of 1929 that ushered in the Great Depression.

"How do you find conditions in America?"

"I haven't been to America for months. I'm in business in Prague, representing a couple of concerns there. They don't know about me down there."

Alix smiled.

"Remember the night of George Hardt's bachelor dinner here?" said Charlie. "By the way, what's become of Claude Fessenden?"

Alix lowered his voice confidentially: "He's in Paris, but he doesn't come here any more. Paul doesn't allow it. He ran up a bill of thirty thousand francs, charging all his drinks and his lunches, and usually his dinner, for more than a year. And when Paul finally told him he had to pay, he gave him a bad check."

Alix shook his head sadly.

"I don't understand it, such a dandy fellow. Now he's all bloated up — " He made a plump apple of his hands.

Charlie watched a group of strident queens installing themselves in a corner.

"Nothing affects them," he thought. "Stocks rise and fall, people loaf or work, but they go on forever." The place oppressed him. He called for the dice and shook with Alix for the drink.

"Here for long, Mr. Wales?"

"I'm here for four or five days to see my little girl."

"Oh-h! You have a little girl?"

Outside, the fire-red, gas-blue, ghost-green signs shone smokily through the tranquil rain. It was late afternoon and the streets were in movement; the bistros[6] gleamed. At the corner of the Boulevard des Capucines he took a taxi. The Place de la Concorde moved by in pink majesty; they crossed the logical Seine, and Charlie felt the sudden provincial quality of the left bank.[7]

Charlie directed his taxi to the Avenue de l'Opera, which was out of his way. But he wanted to see the blue hour spread over the magnificent facade, and imagine that the cab horns, playing endlessly the first few bars of *Le Plus que Lent*,[8] were the trumpets of the Second Empire.[9] They were closing the iron grill in front of Brentano's Bookstore, and people were already at dinner behind the trim little bourgeois hedge of Duval's. He had never eaten at a really cheap restaurant in Paris. Five-course dinner, four francs fifty, eighteen cents, wine included. For some odd reason he wished that he had.

As they rolled on to the Left Bank and he felt its sudden provincialism, he thought, "I spoiled this city for myself. I didn't realize it, but the days came along one after another, and then two years were gone, and everything was gone, and I was gone."

He was thirty-five, and good to look at. The Irish mobility of his face was sobered by a deep wrinkle between his eyes. As he rang his brother-in-law's bell in the Rue Palatine, the wrinkle deepened till it pulled down his brows; he felt a cramping sensation in his belly. From behind the maid who opened the door darted a lovely little girl of nine who shrieked "Daddy!" and flew up, struggling like a fish, into his arms. She pulled his head around by one ear and set her cheek against his.

6. *Bistros:* Small cafés that also serve alcoholic beverages.
7. Left bank: A section of Paris on the south side of the Seine, famous as a haven for artists and writers identified as "bohemians."
8. *Le Plus que Lent:* A slow waltz by Debussy.
9. Second Empire: The reign of Napoleon III of France, a nineteenth-century period of wealthy ostentation.

"My old pie," he said.

"Oh, daddy, daddy, daddy, daddy, dads, dads, dads!"

She drew him into the salon, where the family waited, a boy and a girl his daughter's age, his sister-in-law and her husband. He greeted Marion with his voice pitched carefully to avoid either feigned enthusiasm or dislike, but her response was more frankly tepid, though she minimized her expression of unalterable distrust by directing her regard toward his child. The two men clasped hands in a friendly way and Lincoln Peters rested his for a moment on Charlie's shoulder.

The room was warm and comfortably American. The three children moved intimately about, playing through the yellow oblongs that led to other rooms; the cheer of six o'clock spoke in the eager smacks of the fire and the sounds of French activity in the kitchen. But Charlie did not relax; his heart sat up rigidly in his body and he drew confidence from his daughter, who from time to time came close to him, holding in her arms the doll he had brought.

"Really extremely well," he declared in answer to Lincoln's question. "There's a lot of business there that isn't moving at all, but we're doing even better than ever. In fact, damn well. I'm bringing my sister over from America next month to keep house for me. My income last year was bigger than it was when I had money. You see, the Czechs — "

His boasting was for a specific purpose; but after a moment, seeing a faint restiveness in Lincoln's eye, he changed the subject:

"Those are fine children of yours, well brought up, good manners."

"We think Honoria's a great little girl too."

Marion Peters came back from the kitchen. She was a tall woman with worried eyes, who had once possessed a fresh American loveliness. Charlie had never been sensitive to it and was always surprised when people spoke of how pretty she had been. From the first there had been an instinctive antipathy between them.

"Well, how do you find Honoria?" she asked.

"Wonderful. I was astonished how much she's grown in ten months. All the children are looking well."

"We haven't had a doctor for a year. How do you like being back in Paris?"

"It seems very funny to see so few Americans around."

"I'm delighted," Marion said vehemently. "Now at least you can go into a store without their assuming you're a millionaire. We've suffered like everybody, but on the whole it's a good deal pleasanter."

"But it was nice while it lasted," Charlie said. "We were a sort of royalty, almost infallible, with a sort of magic around us. In the bar this afternoon" — he stumbled, seeing his mistake — "there wasn't a man I knew."

She looked at him keenly. "I should think you'd have had enough of bars."

"I only stayed a minute. I take one drink every afternoon, and no more."

"Don't you want a cocktail before dinner?" Lincoln asked.

"I take only one drink every afternoon, and I've had that."

"I hope you keep to it," said Marion.

Her dislike was evident in the coldness with which she spoke, but Charlie only smiled; he had larger plans. Her very aggressiveness gave him an advantage, and he knew enough to wait. He wanted them to initiate the discussion of what they knew had brought him to Paris.

At dinner he couldn't decide whether Honoria was most like them or her mother. Fortunate if she didn't combine the traits of both that had brought them to disaster. A great wave of protectiveness went over him. He thought he knew what to do for her. He believed in character; he wanted to jump back a whole generation and trust in character again as the eternally valuable element. Everything else wore out.

He left soon after dinner, but not to go home. He was curious to see Paris by night with clearer and more judicious eyes than those of other days. He bought a *strapontin*[10] for the Casino and watched Josephine Baker[11] go through her chocolate arabesques.

After an hour he left and strolled toward Montmartre,[12] up the Rue Pigalle into the Place Blanche. The rain had stopped and there were a few people in evening clothes disembarking from taxis in front of cabarets, and *cocottes*[13] prowling singly or in pairs, and many Negroes. He passed a lighted door from which issued music, and stopped with the sense of familiarity; it was Bricktop's, where he had parted with so many hours and so much money. A few doors farther on he found another ancient rendezvous and incautiously put his head inside. Immediately an eager orchestra burst into sound, a pair of professional dancers leaped to their feet and a maître d'hôtel [14] swooped toward him, crying, "Crowd just arriving, sir!" But he withdrew quickly.

"You have to be damn drunk," he thought.

Zelli's was closed, the bleak and sinister cheap hotels surrounding it were dark; up in the Rue Blanche there was more light and a local, colloquial French crowd. The Poet's Cave[15] had disappeared, but the two great mouths of the Café of Heaven and the Café of Hell still yawned — even devoured, as he watched, the meager contents of a tourist bus — a German, a Japanese, and an American couple who glanced at him with frightened eyes.

So much for the effort and ingenuity of Montmartre. All the catering to vice and waste was on an utterly childish scale, and he suddenly realized the meaning of the word "dissipate" — to dissipate into thin air; to make nothing out of something. In the little hours of the night every move from place to place was an enormous human jump, an increase of paying for the privilege of slower and slower motion.

He remembered thousand-franc notes given to an orchestra for playing a single number, hundred-franc notes tossed to a doorman for calling a cab.

But it hadn't been given for nothing.

It had been given, even the most wildly squandered sum, as an offering to destiny that he might not remember the things most worth remembering, the things that now he would always remember — his child taken from his control, his wife escaped to a grave in Vermont.

In the glare of a *brasserie*[16] a woman spoke to him. He bought her some eggs and coffee, and then, eluding her encouraging stare, gave her a twenty-franc note and took a taxi to his hotel.

---

10. *Strapontin:* Folding seat that opens in the aisle.
11. Josephine Baker: Black dancer and singer; toast of Parisian night life during the late twenties.
12. Montmartre: Famous bohemian district in northern Paris catering to persons of artistic or literary interests.
13. *Cocottes:* Prostitutes.
14. Maître d'hôtel: Headwaiter.
15. Cave: Literally, "wine vault"; often identifying a carbaret found below ground level.
16. *Brasserie:* Small restaurant that serves alcoholic beverages.

II.

He woke upon a fine fall day — football weather. The depression of yesterday was gone and he liked the people on the streets. At noon he sat opposite Honoria at Le Grand Vatel, the only restaurant he could think of not reminiscent of champagne dinners and long luncheons that began at two and ended in a blurred and vague twilight.

"Now, how about vegetables? Oughtn't you to have some vegetables?"

"Well, yes."

"Here's *épinards* and *chou-fleur* and carrots and *haricots*." [17]

"I'd like *chou-fleur*."

"Wouldn't you like to have two vegetables?"

"I usually only have one at lunch."

The waiter was pretending to be inordinately fond of children. *"Qu'elle est mignonne la petite! Elle parle exactement comme une Française."* [18]

"How about dessert? Shall we wait and see?"

The waiter disappeared. Honoria looked at her father expectantly.

"What are we going to do?"

"First, we're going to that toy store in the Rue Saint-Honoré and buy you anything you like. And then we're going to the vaudeville at the Empire."

She hesitated. "I like it about the vaudeville, but not the toy store."

"Why not?"

"Well, you brought me this doll." She had it with her. "And I've got lots of things. And we're not rich any more, are we?"

"We never were. But today you are to have anything you want."

"All right," she agreed resignedly.

When there had been her mother and a French nurse he had been inclined to be strict; now he extended himself, reached out for a new tolerance; he must be both parents to her and not shut any of her out of communication.

"I want to get to know you," he said gravely. "First let me introduce myself. My name is Charles J. Wales, of Prague."

"Oh, daddy!" her voice cracked with laughter.

"And who are you, please?" he persisted, and she accepted a rôle immediately: "Honoria Wales, Rue Palatine, Paris."

"Married or single?"

"No, not married. Single."

He indicated the doll. "But I see you have a child, madame."

Unwilling to disinherit it, she took it to her heart and thought quickly: "Yes, I've been married, but I'm not married now. My husband is dead."

He went on quickly, "And the child's name?"

"Simone. That's after my best friend at school."

"I'm very pleased that you're doing so well at school."

"I'm third this month," she boasted. "Elsie" — that was her cousin — "is only about eighteenth, and Richard is about at the bottom."

"You like Richard and Elsie, don't you?"

"Oh, yes. I like Richard quite well and I like her all right."

Cautiously and casually he asked: "And Aunt Marion and Uncle Lincoln — which do you like best?"

---

17. *Épinards . . . chou-fleur . . . haricots.* Spinach, cauliflowers, beans.
18. *"Qu'elle . . . Française"*: "What a darling little one! She speaks precisely like a French girl."

"Oh, Uncle Lincoln, I guess."

He was increasingly aware of her presence. As they came in, a murmur of
"...adorable" followed them, and now the people at the next table bent all their
silences upon her, staring as if she were something no more conscious than a
flower.

"Why don't I live with you?" she asked suddenly. "Because mamma's
dead?"

"You must stay here and learn more French. It would have been hard for
daddy to take care of you so well."

"I don't really need much taking care of any more. I do everything for myself."

Going out of the restaurant, a man and a woman unexpectedly hailed him.

"Well, the old Wales!"

"Hello there, Lorraine . . . Dunc."

Sudden ghosts out of the past: Duncan Schaeffer, a friend from college.
Lorraine Quarrles, a lovely, pale blonde of thirty; one of a crowd who had
helped them make months into days in the lavish times of three years ago.

"My husband couldn't come this year," she said, in answer to his question.
"We're poor as hell. So he gave me two hundred a month and told me I could
do my worst on that. . . . This your little girl?"

"What about coming back and sitting down?" Duncan asked.

"Can't do it." He was glad for an excuse. As always, he felt Lorraine's
passionate, provocative attraction, but his own rhythm was different now.

"Well, how about dinner?" she asked.

"I'm not free. Give me your address and let me call you."

"Charlie, I believe you're sober," she said judicially. "I honestly believe he's
sober, Dunc. Pinch him and see if he's sober."

Charlie indicated Honoria with his head. They both laughed.

"What's your address?" said Duncan skeptically.

He hesitated, unwilling to give the name of his hotel.

"I'm not settled yet. I'd better call you. We're going to see the vaudeville
at the Empire."

"There! That's what I want to do," Lorraine said. "I want to see some
clowns and acrobats and jugglers. That's just what we'll do, Dunc."

"We've got to do an errand first," said Charlie. "Perhaps we'll see you
there."

"All right, you snob. . . . Good-by, beautiful little girl."

"Good-by."

Honoria bobbed politely.

Somehow, an unwelcome encounter. They liked him because he was functioning, because he was serious, they wanted to see him, because he was stronger
than they were now, because they wanted to draw a certain sustenance from his
strength.

At the Empire, Honoria proudly refused to sit upon her father's folded coat.
She was already an individual with a code of her own, and Charlie was more
and more absorbed by the desire of putting a little of himself into her before
she crystallized utterly. It was hopeless to try to know her in so short a time.

Between the acts they came upon Duncan and Lorraine in the lobby where
the band was playing.

"Have a drink?"

"All right, but not up at the bar. We'll take a table."

"The perfect father."

Listening abstractedly to Lorraine, Charlie watched Honoria's eyes leave their table, and he followed them wistfully about the room, wondering what they saw. He met her glance and she smiled.

"I liked that lemonade," she said.

What had she said? What had he expected? Going home in a taxi afterward, he pulled her over until her head rested against his chest.

"Darling, do you ever think about your mother?"

"Yes, sometimes," she answered vaguely.

"I don't want you to forget her. Have you got a picture of her?"

"Yes, I think so. Anyhow, Aunt Marion has. Why don't you want me to forget her?"

"She loved you very much."

"I loved her too."

They were silent for a moment.

"Daddy, I want to come and live with you," she said suddenly.

His heart leaped; he had wanted it to come like this.

"Aren't you perfectly happy?"

"Yes, but I love you better than anybody. And you love me better than anybody, don't you, now that mummy's dead?"

"Of course I do. But you won't always like me best, honey. You'll grow up and meet somebody your own age and go marry him and forget you ever had a daddy."

"Yes, that's true," she agreed tranquilly.

He didn't go in. He was coming back at nine o'clock and he wanted to keep himself fresh and new for the thing he must say then.

"When you're safe inside, just show yourself in that window."

"All right. Good-by, dads, dads, dads, dads."

He waited in the dark street until she appeared, all warm and glowing, in the window above and kissed her fingers out into the night.

III.

They were waiting. Marion sat behind the coffee service in a dignified black dinner dress that just faintly suggested mourning. Lincoln was walking up and down with the animation of one who had already been talking. They were as anxious as he was to get into the question. He opened it almost immediately:

"I suppose you know what I want to see you about — why I really came to Paris."

Marion played with the black stars on her necklace and frowned.

"I'm awfully anxious to have a home," he continued. "And I'm awfully anxious to have Honoria in it. I appreciate your taking in Honoria for her mother's sake, but things have changed now" — he hesitated and then continued more forcibly — "changed radically with me, and I want to ask you to reconsider the matter. It would be silly for me to deny that about three years ago I was acting badly — "

Marion looked up at him with hard eyes.

" — but all that's over. As I told you, I haven't had more than a drink a day for over a year, and I take that drink deliberately, so that the idea of alcohol won't get too big in my imagination. You see the idea?"

"No," said Marion succinctly.

"It's a sort of stunt I set myself. It keeps the matter in proportion."

"I get you," said Lincoln. "You don't want to admit it's got any attraction for you."

"Something like that. Sometimes I forget and don't take it. But I try to take it. Anyhow, I couldn't afford to drink in my position. The people I represent are more than satisfied with what I've done, and I'm bringing my sister over from Burlington to keep house for me, and I want awfully to have Honoria too. You know that even when her mother and I weren't getting along well we never let anything that happened touch Honoria. I know she's fond of me and I know I'm able to take care of her and — well, there you are. How do you feel about it?"

He knew that now he would have to take a beating. It would last an hour or two hours, and it would be difficult, but if he modulated his inevitable resentment to the chastened attitude of the reformed sinner, he might win his point in the end.

Keep your temper, he told himself. You don't want to be justified. You want Honoria.

Lincoln spoke first: "We've been talking it over ever since we got your letter last month. We're happy to have Honoria here. She's a dear little thing, and we're glad to be able to help her, but of course that isn't the question — "

Marion interrupted suddenly. "How long are you going to stay sober, Charlie?" she asked.

"Permanently, I hope."

"How can anybody count on that?"

"You know I never did drink heavily until I gave up business and came over here with nothing to do. Then Helen and I began to run around with — "

"Please leave Helen out of it. I can't bear to hear you talk about her like that."

He stared at her grimly; he had never been certain how fond of each other the sisters were in life.

"My drinking only lasted about a year and a half — from the time we came over until I — collapsed."

"It was time enough."

"It was time enough," he agreed.

"My duty is entirely to Helen," she said. "I try to think what she would have wanted me to do. Frankly, from the night you did that terrible thing you haven't really existed for me. I can't help that. She was my sister."

"Yes."

"When she was dying she asked me to look out for Honoria. If you hadn't been in a sanitarium then, it might have helped matters."

He had no answer.

"I'll never in my life be able to forget the morning when Helen knocked at my door, soaked to the skin and shivering, and said you'd locked her out."

Charlie gripped the sides of the chair. This was more difficult than he expected; he wanted to launch out into a long expostulation and explanation, but he only said: "The night I locked her out — " and she interrupted, "I don't feel up to going over that again."

After a moment's silence Lincoln said: "We're getting off the subject. You want Marion to set aside her legal guardianship and give you Honoria. I think the main point for her is whether she has confidence in you or not."

"I don't blame Marion," Charlie said slowly, "but I think she can have entire confidence in me. I had a good record up to three years ago. Of course, it's within human possibilities I might go wrong any time. But if we wait much longer I'll lose Honoria's childhood and my chance for a home." He shook his head. "I'll simply lose her, don't you see?"

"Yes, I see," said Lincoln.

"Why didn't you think of all this before?" Marion asked.

"I suppose I did, from time to time, but Helen and I were getting along badly. When I consented to the guardianship, I was flat on my back in a sanitarium and the market had cleaned me out. I knew I'd acted badly, and I thought if it would bring any peace to Helen, I'd agree to anything. But now it's different. I'm functioning. I'm behaving damn well, so far as — "

"Please don't swear at me," Marion said.

He looked at her, startled. With each remark the force of her dislike became more and more apparent. She had built up all her fear of life into one wall and faced it toward him. This trivial reproof was possibly the result of some trouble with the cook several hours before. Charlie became increasingly alarmed at leaving Honoria in this atmosphere of hostility against himself; sooner or later it would come out, in a word here, a shake of the head there, and some of that distrust would be irrevocably implanted in Honoria. But he pulled his temper down out of his face and shut it up inside him; he had won a point, for Lincoln realized the absurdity of Marion's remark and asked her lightly since when she had objected to the word "damn."

"Another thing," Charlie said: "I'm able to give her certain advantages now. I'm going to take a French governess to Prague with me. I've got a lease on a new apartment — "

He stopped, realizing that he was blundering. They couldn't be expected to accept with equanimity the fact that his income was again twice as large as their own.

"I suppose you can give her more luxuries than we can," said Marion. "When you were throwing away money we were living along watching every ten francs.... I suppose you'll start doing it again."

"Oh, no," he said. "I've learned. I worked hard for ten years, you know — until I got lucky in the market, like so many people. Terribly lucky. It didn't seem any use working any more, so I quit."

There was a long silence. All of them felt their nerves straining, and for the first time in a year Charlie wanted a drink. He was sure now that Lincoln Peters wanted him to have his child.

Marion shuddered suddenly; part of her saw that Charlie's feet were planted on the earth now, and her own maternal feeling recognized the naturalness of his desire; but she had lived for a long time with a prejudice — a prejudice founded on a curious disbelief in her sister's happiness, and which, in the shock of one terrible night, had turned to hatred for him. It had all happened at a point in her life where the discouragement of ill health and adverse circumstances made it necessary for her to believe in tangible villainy and a tangible villain.

"I can't help what I think!" she cried out suddenly. "How much you were responsible for Helen's death, I don't know. It's something you'll have to square with your own conscience."

An electric current of agony surged through him; for a moment he was almost on his feet, an unuttered sound echoing in his throat. He hung on to himself for a moment, another moment.

"Hold on there," said Lincoln uncomfortably. "I never thought you were responsible for that."

"Helen died of heart trouble," Charlie said dully.

"Yes, heart trouble." Marion spoke as if the phrase had another meaning for her.

Then, in the flatness that followed her outburst, she saw him plainly and she knew he had somehow arrived at control over the situation. Glancing at her husband, she found no help from him, and as abruptly as if it were a matter of no importance, she threw up the sponge.

"Do what you like!" she cried, springing up from her chair. "She's your child. I'm not the person to stand in your way. I think if it were my child I'd rather see her — " She managed to check herself. "You two decide it. I can't stand this. I'm sick. I'm going to bed."

She hurried from the room; after a moment Lincoln said:

"This has been a hard day for her. You know how strongly she feels — " His voice was almost apologetic: "Where a woman gets an idea in her head."

"Of course."

"It's going to be all right. I think she sees now that you — can provide for the child, and so we can't very well stand in your way or Honoria's way."

"Thank you, Lincoln."

"I'd better go along and see how she is."

"I'm going."

He was still trembling when he reached the street, but a walk down the Rue Bonaparte to the *quais*[19] set him up, and as he crossed the Seine, fresh and new by the *quai* lamps, he felt exultant. But back in his room he couldn't sleep. The image of Helen haunted him. Helen whom he had loved so until they had senselessly begun to abuse each other's love, tear it into shreds. On that terrible February night that Marion remembered so vividly, a slow quarrel had gone on for hours. There was a scene at the Florida, and then he attempted to take her home, and then she kissed young Webb at a table; after that there was what she had hysterically said. When he arrived home alone he turned the key in the lock in wild anger. How could he know she would arrive an hour later alone, that there would be a snowstorm in which she wandered about in slippers, too confused to find a taxi? Then the aftermath, her escaping pneumonia by a miracle, and all the attendant horror. They were "reconciled," but that was the beginning of the end, and Marion, who had seen with her own eyes and who imagined it to be one of many scenes from her sister's martyrdom, never forgot.

Going over it again brought Helen nearer, and in the white, soft light that steals upon the half sleep near morning he found himself talking to her again. She said that he was perfectly right about Honoria and that she wanted Honoria to be with him. She said she was glad he was being good and doing better. She said a lot of other things — very friendly things — but she was in a swing in a white dress, and swinging faster and faster all the time, so that at the end he could not hear clearly all that she said.

19. *Quais:* Paved embankments along the river.

IV.

He woke up feeling happy. The door of the world was open again. He made plans, vistas, futures for Honoria and himself, but suddenly he grew sad, remembering all the plans he and Helen had made. She had not planned to die. The present was the thing — work to do and someone to love. But not to love too much, for he knew the injury that a father can do to a daughter or a mother to a son by attaching them too closely: afterward, out in the world, the child would seek in the marriage partner the same blind tenderness and, failing probably to find it, turn against love and life.

It was another bright, crisp day. He called Lincoln Peters at the bank where he worked and asked if he could count on taking Honoria when he left for Prague. Lincoln agreed that there was no reason for delay. One thing — the legal guardianship. Marion wanted to retain that a while longer. She was upset by the whole matter, and it would oil things if she felt that the situation was still in her control for another year. Charlie agreed, wanting only the tangible, visible child.

Then the question of a governess. Charles sat in a gloomy agency and talked to a cross Béarnaise and to a buxom Breton peasant, neither of whom he could have endured. There were others whom he would see tomorrow.

He lunched with Lincoln Peters at Griffons, trying to keep down his exultation.

"There's nothing quite like your own child," Lincoln said. "But you understand how Marion feels too."

"She's forgotten how hard I worked for seven years there," Charlie said. "She just remembers one night."

"There's another thing." Lincoln hesitated. "While you and Helen were tearing around Europe throwing money away, we were just getting along. I didn't touch any of the prosperity because I never got ahead enough to carry anything but my insurance. I think Marion felt there was some of kind of injustice in it — you not even working toward the end, and getting richer and richer."

"It went just as quick as it came," said Charlie.

"Yes, a lot of it stayed in the hands of *chasseurs* and saxophone players and maîtres d'hôtel — well, the big party's over now. I just said that to explain Marion's feeling about those crazy years. If you drop in about six o'clock tonight before Marion's too tired, we'll settle the details on the spot."

Back at his hotel, Charlie found a *pneumatique*[20] that had been redirected from the Ritz bar where Charlie had left his address for the purpose of finding a certain man.

Dear Charlie: You were so strange when we saw you the other day that I wondered if I did something to offend you. If so, I'm not conscious of it. In fact, I have thought about you too much for the last year, and it's always been in the back of my mind that I might see you if I came over here. We *did* have such good times that crazy spring, like the night you and I stole the butcher's tricycle, and the time we tried to call on the president and you had the old derby rim and the wire cane. Everybody seems so old lately,

20. *Pneumatique:* Message delivered by pneumatic tube.

but I don't feel old a bit. Couldn't we get together some time today for old time's sake? I've got a vile hang-over for the moment, but will be feeling better this afternoon and will look for you about five in the sweat-shop at the Ritz.

Always devotedly,

Lorraine.

His first feeling was one of awe that he had actually, in his mature years, stolen a tricycle and pedaled Lorraine all over the Etoile[21] between the small hours and dawn. In retrospect it was a nightmare. Locking out Helen didn't fit in with any other act of his life, but the tricycle incident did — it was one of many. How many weeks or months of dissipation to arrive at that condition of utter irresponsibility?

He tried to picture how Lorraine had appeared to him then — very attractive; Helen was unhappy about it, though she said nothing. Yesterday, in the restaurant, Lorraine had seemed trite, blurred, worn away. He emphatically did not want to see her, and he was glad Alix had not given away his hotel address. It was a relief to think, instead, of Honoria, to think of Sundays spent with her and of saying good morning to her and of knowing she was there in his house at night, drawing her breath in the darkness.

At five he took a taxi and bought presents for all the Peters — a piquant cloth doll, a box of Roman soldiers, flowers for Marion, big linen handkerchiefs for Lincoln.

He saw, when he arrived in the apartment, that Marion had accepted the inevitable. She greeted him now as though he were a recalcitrant member of the family, rather than a menacing outsider. Honoria had been told she was going; Charlie was glad to see that her tact made her conceal her excessive happiness. Only on his lap did she whisper her delight and the question "When?" before she slipped away with the other children.

He and Marion were alone for a minute in the room, and on an impulse he spoke out boldly:

"Family quarrels are bitter things. They don't go according to any rules. They're not like aches or wounds; they're more like splits in the skin that won't heal because there's not enough material. I wish you and I could be on better terms."

"Some things are hard to forget," she answered. "It's a question of confidence." There was no answer to this and presently she asked, "When do you propose to take her?"

"As soon as I can get a governess. I hoped the day after tomorrow."

"That's impossible. I've got to get her things in shape. Not before Saturday."

He yielded. Coming back into the room, Lincoln offered him a drink.

"I'll take my daily whisky," he said.

It was warm here, it was a home, people together by a fire. The children felt very safe and important; the mother and father were serious, watchful. They had things to do for the children more important than his visit here. A spoonful of medicine was, after all, more important than the strained relations

---

21. Etoile: Open square in Paris; site of the Arc de Triomphe.

between Marion and himself. They were not dull people, but they were very much in the grip of life and circumstances. He wondered if he couldn't do something to get Lincoln out of his rut at the bank.

A long peal at the door-bell; the *bonne à tout faire*[22] passed through and went down the corridor. The door opened upon another long ring, and then voices, and the three in the salon looked up expectantly; Richard moved to bring the corridor within his range of vision, and Marion rose. Then the maid came back along the corridor, closely followed by the voices, which developed under the light into Duncan Schaeffer and Lorraine Quarrles.

They were gay, they were hilarious, they were roaring with laughter. For a moment Charlie was astounded; unable to understand how they ferreted out the Peters' address.

"Ah-h-h!" Duncan wagged his finger roguishly at Charlie. "Ah-h-h!"

They both slid down another cascade of laughter. Anxious and at a loss, Charlie shook hands with them quickly and presented them to Lincoln and Marion. Marion nodded, scarcely speaking. She had drawn back a step toward the fire; her little girl stood beside her, and Marion put an arm about her shoulder.

With growing annoyance at the intrusion, Charlie waited for them to explain themselves. After some concentration Duncan said:

"We came to invite you out to dinner. Lorraine and I insist that all this chi-chi, cagy business 'bout your address got to stop."

Charlie came closer to them, as if to force them backward down the corridor.

"Sorry, but I can't. Tell me where you'll be and I'll phone you in half an hour."

This made no impression. Lorraine sat down suddenly on the side of a chair, and focusing her eyes on Richard, cried, "Oh, what a nice little boy! Come here, little boy." Richard glanced at his mother, but did not move. With a perceptible shrug of her shoulders, Lorraine turned back to Charlie:

"Come and dine. Sure your cousins won' mine. See you so sel'om. Or solemn."

"I can't," said Charlie sharply. "You two have dinner and I'll phone you."

Her voice became suddenly unpleasant. "All right, we'll go. But I remember once you hammered on my door at four A.M. I was enough of a good sport to give you a drink. Come on, Dunc."

Still in slow motion, with blurred, angry faces, with uncertain feet, they retired along the corridor.

"Good night," Charlie said.

"Good night!" responded Lorraine emphatically.

When he went back into the salon Marion had not moved, only now her son was standing in the circle of her other arm. Lincoln was still swinging Honoria back and forth like a pendulum from side to side.

"What an outrage!" Charlie broke out. "What an absolute outrage!"

Neither of them answered. Charlie dropped into an armchair, picked up his drink, set it down again and said:

"People I haven't seen for two years having the colossal nerve — "

22. *Bonne...faire:* All-purpose maid.

He broke off. Marion had made the sound "Oh!" in one swift, furious breath, turned her body from him with a jerk, and left the room.

Lincoln set down Honoria carefully.

"You children go in and start your soup," he said, and when they obeyed, he said to Charlie:

"Marion's not well and she can't stand shocks. That kind of people make her really physically sick."

"I didn't tell them to come here. They wormed your name out of somebody. They deliberately — "

"Well, it's too bad. It doesn't help matters. Excuse me a minute."

Left alone, Charlie sat tense in his chair. In the next room he could hear the children eating, talking in monosyllables, already oblivious to the scene between their elders. He heard a murmur of conversation from a farther room and then the ticking bell of a telephone receiver picked up, and in a panic he moved to the other side of the room and out of earshot.

In a minute Lincoln came back. "Look here, Charlie, I think we'd better call off dinner for tonight. Marion's in bad shape."

"Is she angry with me?"

"Sort of," he said, almost roughly. "She's not strong and — "

"You mean she's changed her mind about Honoria?"

"She's pretty bitter right now. I don't know. You phone me at the bank tomorrow."

"I wish you'd explain to her I never dreamed these people would come here. I'm just as sore as you are."

"I couldn't explain anything to her now."

Charlie got up. He took his coat and hat and started down the corridor. Then he opened the door of the dining room and said in a strange voice, "Good night, children."

Honoria rose and ran around the table to hug him.

"Good night, sweetheart," he said vaguely, and then trying to make his voice more tender, trying to conciliate something, "Good night, dear children."

V.

Charlie went directly to the Ritz bar with the furious idea of finding Lorraine and Duncan, but they were not there, and he realized that in any case there was nothing he could do. He had not touched his drink at the Peters', and now he ordered a whisky-and-soda. Paul came over to say hello.

"It's a great change," he said sadly. "We do about half the business we did. So many fellows I hear about back in the States lost everything, maybe not in the first crash, but then in the second. Your friend George Hardt lost every cent, I hear. Are you back in the States?"

"No, I'm in business in Prague."

"I heard that you lost a lot in the crash."

"I did," and he added grimly, "but I lost everything I wanted in the boom."

"Selling short."

"Something like that."

Again the memory of those days swept over him like a nightmare — the people they had met travelling; then people who couldn't add a row of figures or speak a coherent sentence. The little man Helen had consented to dance with at the ship's party, who had insulted her ten feet from the table; the women and girls carried screaming with drink or drugs out of public places —

— The men who locked their wives out in the snow, because the snow of twenty-nine wasn't real snow. If you didn't want it to be snow, you just paid some money.

He went to the phone and called the Peters' apartment; Lincoln answered.

"I called up because this thing is on my mind. Has Marion said anything definite?"

"Marion's sick," Lincoln answered shortly. "I know this thing isn't altogether your fault, but I can't have her go to pieces about it. I'm afraid we'll have to let it slide for six months; I can't take the chance of working her up to this state again."

"I see."

"I'm sorry, Charlie."

He went back to his table. His whisky glass was empty, but he shook his head when Alix looked at it questioningly. There wasn't much he could do now except send Honoria some things; he would send her a lot of things tomorrow. He thought rather angrily that this was just money — he had given so many people money. . . .

"No, no more," he said to another waiter. "What do I owe you?"

He would come back some day; they couldn't make him pay forever. But he wanted his child, and nothing was much good now, beside that fact. He wasn't young any more, with a lot of nice thoughts and dreams to have by himself. He was absolutely sure Helen wouldn't have wanted him to be so alone.

Exercises

1. Prepare an eight-point analysis of this story.

2. Describe Charlie Wales. Identify his strengths and weaknesses.

3. What kind of person is Marion Peters? Define the role of Duncan Schaeffer and Lorraine Quarrles.

4. Clarify the function of each of the following minor characters: the bartender, Alix; the head barman, Paul; Lincoln Peters; and Claude Fessenden.

5. Charlie is a lonely person. Why? How does setting serve to emphasize his loneliness?

6. What does Part II accomplish? Does it furnish information, advance the story-line, or reveal character?

7. What do the proper names Honoria, Wales, and Quarrles suggest? What purpose is served by the use of proper names and places? Relate the significance of the title to the story.

8. What chief effect does Fitzgerald achieve by associating people with certain colors?

9. Define the point of view used in this story. Identify voice, consciousness, position and presence, reliability, and several other features.

Topics for Writing

1. Write a detailed analysis of Charlie Wales and his conflict.

2. Fitzgerald's story and Steinbeck's "The Chrysanthemums" rely heavily on the author's use of setting — all that time and place implies — for their effects. Compare the use of setting in these two stories.

3. Write an essay about the ghosts from Charlie's past and discuss their role in the portrayal of character and the development of a central theme.

4. Render a valid interpretation incorporating all of the following topics: loneliness, parenthood, the inescapable past, money, and alcohol.

5. Compare and contrast the way point of view works in this story and in one other story you have read so far. Do you find that each of the two authors has chosen the right point of view for his or her purpose? Support your comments with detailed references to the text.

Selected Bibliography   F. Scott Fitzgerald

Eble, Kenneth. *F. Scott Fitzgerald*. New York: Twayne, 1963.

Edenbaum, Robert I. " 'Babylon Revisited': A Psychological Note on F. Scott Fitzgerald." *Literature & Psychology*, 18 (1968), 27–29.

Griffith, Richard R. "A Note on Fitzgerald's 'Babylon Revisited.' " *American Literature*, 35 (1963), 236–239.

Gross, Seymour L. "Fitzgerald's 'Babylon Revisited.' " *College English*, 25 (1963), 128–135.

Hagopian, John V. " 'Babylon Revisited.' " In *Insight I: Analyses of American Literature*. 3rd ed. Eds. John V. Hagopian and Martin Dolch. Frankfort: Hirschgraben Verlag, 1962, pp. 60–63.

———. "A Prince in Babylon." *Fitzgerald Newsletter*, 19 (Fall 1962), 1–3.

Harrison, James M. "Fitzgerald's 'Babylon Revisited.' " *Explicator*, 16 (1958), Item 20.

Heiney, Donald. *Recent American Literature*. Great Neck, N.Y.: Barron, 1958.

Hoffman, Frederick J. *The Twenties: American Writing in the Postwar Decade*. New York: Viking, 1955, Free Press, New York: Macmillan, 1965.

Johnson, Ira. "Roundheads and Royalty in 'Babylon.' " *English Record*, 14 (October 1963), 32–35.

Lehan, Richard D. *F. Scott Fitzgerald and the Craft of Fiction*. Carbondale: Southern Illinois University Press, 1966, 144–146.

Lynskey, Winifred, ed. *Reading Modern Fiction: Thirty-one Stories With Critical Aids*. 4th ed. New York: Charles Scribner's Sons, 1968.

Male, Roy A. " 'Babylon Revisited': A Story of the Exile's Return." *Studies in Short Fiction*, 2 (1965), 270–277.

Murphy, Garry N., and William C. Slattery. "The Flawed Text of 'Babylon Revisited': A Challenge to Editors, A Warning to Readers." *Studies in Short Fiction*, 18, No. 3 (Summer 1981), 315–318.

Osborne, William R. "The Wounds of Charlie Wales in Fitzgerald's 'Babylon Revisited.' " *Studies in Short Fiction,* 2 (1964), 86–87.

Perosa, Sergio. *The Art of F. Scott Fitzgerald.* Translated by Charles Fatz and Sergio Perosa. Ann Arbor: University of Michigan Press, 1965.

Savage, D. S. "The Significance of F. Scott Fitzgerald." *Arizona Quarterly,* 8 (1952), 208–209.

Schramm, Wilbur L. " 'Babylon Revisited.' " In *Fifty Best American Short Stories, 1915–1939.* Ed. Edward J. O'Brien. Boston: Houghton Mifflin Company, 1939, p. 839.

Sklar, Robert. *F. Scott Fitzgerald; the Last Laocoön.* New York: Oxford University Press, 1967, pp. 243–245.

Staley, Thomas F. "Time and Structure in Fitzgerald's 'Babylon Revisited.' " *Modern Fiction Studies,* 10 (1964), 386–388.

Toor, David. "Guilt and Retribution in 'Babylon Revisited.' " In *Fitzgerald/ Hemingway Annual 1973,* Eds. Matthew J. Bruccoli and C. E. Fraser Clark, pp. 155–164.

West, Ray B. *The Short Story in America, 1900–1950.* Chicago: Regnery, 1952.

4. THEME OR MEANING

Although not all stories necessarily make a philosophical statement or deliver a sermon, a serious story does have something to say, a meaning to impart. We may call this meaning the main idea, central insight, thesis, premise, statement, judgment, or opinion. But the preferred critical term is **theme.** By means of its theme, a story offers us a comment about some aspect of life, expresses a truth about human affairs, or convey an insight into character. Theme is the controlling idea of a story.

Interpretative fiction (and each story in this text fits the description) does more than exhibit personality, pose a problem, create a mood, give readers a vicarious thrill, make us chuckle or shed a tear. It supports a view, an idea, or an attitude toward something. As long as fiction deals with love and fear and suffering and hope, stories will have something to say about these emotions and experiences.

Occasionally an author will state the theme more or less explicitly somewhere in the action, through the voice of an articulate character or narrator who acts as the spokesman. Crane points to at least two possible interpretations in the statements made by characters and the narrator in "The Open Boat." One of these assertions, appearing at the beginning of section 3 of the story, reads: "It would be difficult to describe the subtle brotherhood of men that was here established on the seas." By expressing this universal truth about human nature here and throughout the narrative, Crane leads us to infer that tragedy and suffering contribute to our common humanity. A second possible meaning can be deduced from the characters' changing attitudes toward nature. The refrain in section 4 that begins with "If I am going to drown . . ." and is again repeated at the beginning of section 6 recapitulates Crane's condemnation of the "old ninny-woman Fate" for gross mismanagement of human fortunes and for not regarding human beings as important.

More often than not, however, at least in modern fiction, readers must discover the theme for themselves, synthesizing meaning by inference, much as they complete the picture of the protagonist. To arrive at the theme, we should examine every element of the short story — plot, character, point of view, and even title — for each contributes its portion to the total thematic communication of the story.

The search for **meaning** is hardly a free-for-all of message-hunting. Not all stories tackle the matter of good versus evil. We must therefore guard against relying on supposed facts, details, and notions extraneous to the story, or leap-frogging to conclusions that derive from personal experience. To be whole and valid, interpretation must emerge from the story itself and take into account all the significant events, relationships, and details we can perceive. A story is an organic whole in which all the parts serve the whole. Total interpretation is possible only with total analysis. However, prominent actions or notable details, and in some stories symbols, allusions, or imagery, may direct us toward meaning.

Consider, for example, the three **key incidents** in "The Magic Barrel" (Chapter 1). Recall Leo's crisis following his encounter with Lily Hirschorn; after that meeting, Leo's attitude toward God and his concept of love and marriage change. Then re-examine the final scene, which produces at least two significant actions. First is Salzman's chant for the "dead." Who has died? Salzman? Or has something died in Leo or Stella? Second is Leo's reaction to the sight of Stella posing as a prostitute against a lamppost. Leo sees in her eyes "desperate innocence" and his own redemption. In a sense, Leo is ordained in this scene with Stella.

In D. H. Lawrence's view, the urge to love and be loved is the ruling obsession of man, while the absence, denial, or loss of love has a pernicious effect. This attitude permeates much of his work, including "The Horse Dealer's Daughter" (Chapter 3). To arrive at the theme in this story, we need to discover the significance of the incident at the pond, in which Dr. Fergusson rescues Mabel from drowning. This action brings together two lonely people. Love transfigures their lives. Therein lies the central meaning of the story.

An incident can crystallize in a very special way. Many of James Joyce's stories contain such incidents, which he called **epiphanies** and we may define as moments of awareness, revelation, or insight for the reader and sometimes for the characters in the story. An epiphany is usually an isolated, intense moment that occurs near the end of a story. If there is an epiphany for the reader in "Araby" (this chapter), it occurs in the scene at the bazaar. To find out the nature of this epiphany, we need to ask what precisely the boy learns.

Objects, as well as incidents, can generate epiphanies. Indeed, any significant physical **details** evoked in a story can furnish clues to its meaning. For example, the flowers in "The Chrysanthemums" (John Steinbeck; Chapter 2) represent more than the color and beauty lacking in Elisa's appearance. To some readers they may suggest female potency or creativity, which in Elisa's case has been suppressed. We need only to watch her handle the chrysanthemums with such loving care to determine that they are perhaps substitutes for the children this strong young woman does not have.

A **topic** discussed by the characters or brought into the story in some other fashion may well indicate the theme. In "A Tree, a Rock, a Cloud" (Carson McCullers; Chapter 3), the old man talks about love. Before he found love, his life was disorganized and purposeless; after he finds love, his life takes on order and meaning. In the narrative, the man tries to share his "science of love" with the young newspaper boy. Surely one of the major themes of the story must relate to the matter of love.

Titles, too, may give us hints about an author's purpose and the theme of his or her work. Knowing what *Araby* means, being aware of the ancient civilization of Babylon, understanding how the hills are like white elephants to the young woman, and perhaps grasping the reason that Faulkner may have wanted to present a rose (a symbol of love) for Emily will help us discover the meaning of each of these stories.

Sometimes **plot** may furnish the best insight. What is Thurber's "The Catbird Seat" (Chapter 1) about? A battle between the sexes in which the male triumphs? A man who has been pushed to the limit so that he feels he must retaliate? The tidy Mr. Martin, who has a mind that operates like a filing cabinet, considers himself efficient. However, Mr. Fitweiler, convinced that Martin's office needs overhauling, hires Mrs. Barrows as an efficiency expert. After due consideration, Martin decides to "rub her out." In a mock trial, he acts as Mrs. Barrows's judge, jury, and executioner. She tells the truth about Martin's crazy, out-of-character behavior, but she is not believed. Instead, Mrs. Barrows is considered irrational and fired from her job. What comment about human nature can you make from this synopsis?

In a story such as "A Rose for Emily" (Chapter 2), **setting** might give us a key to an important theme. The physical and historical setting of this story — the picture of the Grierson house as a shrine to former aristocratic Southern grandeur in the context of a complex set of attitudes toward a declining tradition — must lead us to some conclusions about a way of life that has disappeared.

Elsewhere **character** may best elucidate the theme. Knowing *who* the young boy is and *what* he is in "I Want to Know Why" (Chapter 3) will direct us toward the story's meaning. The young boy is an idealist, immature and sensitive. He loves horses and begins to question certain accepted values of the adult world. The boy wants to know why parents place an "off limits" sign on racetracks because gambling goes on there; he wants to know what standard gives blacks inferior positions in society; he wants to know why adults have prejudices and false values, and he wants to know why his close friend Jerry Tillford, who loves beauty (horses), would lie and embrace ugliness (the girl) and not "think straight and be O.K." Is Anderson suggesting prerequisites for growing up in this story?

Another workable approach to theme involves a review of the answers posed by the **eight-point analysis** mentioned in Chapter 1. In particular, the reader should get to know the protagonist, explore the conflict, and determine the outcome of the story. What kind of person is the central character? What is she or he contending for or against? What forces resist him? Does she achieve her goal? Why or why not? Do you find a change in this character at the conclusion of the story? Is he or she the wiser for the experience? This kind of questioning will unearth facts and particulars that can lead to the central meaning of the story.

We might consider using this approach to arrive at the theme of "The Chrysanthemums." Nearly everything in this story serves to characterize Elisa. The setting of Salinas Valley, obviously a man's domain, separates Elisa from the rest of the world and heightens her sense of isolation. Her manly garb hides her femininity. The environment molds her character. Early in the story, when Elisa cuts down the old chrysanthemum stalks, Steinbeck describes her as a young woman of great energy. She is gardening, handling chrysanthemums with adoring care instead of rearing children. The peddler also exposes Elisa's character. He flirts with her. His youthfulness and carefree life attract her. She reacts by removing her masculine mask. She feels like a woman again and reaches out toward him; but he breaks the spell and later discards her gift of the flowers. Elisa's husband also contributes to the total characterization. He is insensitive to her needs and fails to grasp her potential. The fifth and sixth paragraphs of the story convey the idea of this unrealized potential within her.

Elisa's major conflict is clearly within herself, between her desire to express her feminine potential or womanliness and her resigned acceptance of her present way of life in the masculine world of the valley. The resolution shows Elisa accepting her life for what it is, but with some regret.

When a writer expends much energy delineating a central figure and gives her or him an urgent problem to solve, the emphasis invariably converges upon that character and that dilemma. Logically speaking, doesn't it follow that the central significance of a story — whatever it is that the author is trying to tell us — must emanate from the same source? If theme has any connection at all with the protagonist, as surely it must, then what that character says, thinks, and does can reveal to us the author's chief concerns.

Theme exists in fiction because characters live in a world like ours and face problems like ours. We hate, love, suffer, and die; and all of us at one time or another contemplate the nature of man and woman, life and death and what lies beyond, good and evil, reality and fantasy, and the existence of God.

These concerns relate to universal human experience and consequently permeate fiction. Some of the better-known themes recurring frequently in serious fiction are (1) love heals or gives new life; (2) evil corrupts; (3) fate controls human destiny; (4) people cannot escape their past; (5) one cannot cure real-world problems with dream-world remedies.

There are, of course, variations of these common themes, and you might look for them as you read the next four stories. Note that the stories all have suggestive titles. However, the full significance of each title and its link to the theme may not become apparent until you have analyzed the story. As a start toward such analysis, once you have finished reading a story, try to express its theme in a single sentence. Your statement will not be conclusive and probably will not cover the whole theme, but it will give you a point from which to penetrate more deeply into the story's meaning.

Questions for Evaluating Theme

1. What is the major theme of the story? Is there more than one theme?

2. What is the chief means by which the theme is revealed?

3. What incidents and actions help to develop the theme?

4. What elements in the story contribute most to total meaning?

5. How does character, point of view, setting, and title reveal, amplify, or reinforce the theme?

6. Are there any elements at odds with the major theme?

Stephen Crane *(1871–1900)*

The Open Boat

A Tale Intended to Be After the Fact.
Being the Experience of Four Men from
the Sunk Steamer "Commodore." [1]

1.

None of them knew the color of the sky. Their eyes glanced level, and were fastened upon the waves that swept toward them. These waves were of the hue of slate, save for the tops, which were of foaming white, and all of the men know the colors of the sea. The horizon narrowed and widened, and dipped and rose, and at all times its edge was jagged with waves that seemed thrust up in points like rocks. Many a man ought to have a bath-tub larger than the boat which here rode upon the sea. These waves were most wrongfully and barbarously abrupt and tall, and each froth-top was a problem in small-boat navigation.

The cook squatted in the bottom and looked with both eyes at the six inches of gunwale which separated him from the ocean. His sleeves were rolled over his fat forearms, and the two flaps of his unbuttoned vest dangled as he bent to bail out the boat. Often he said: "Gawd! That was a narrow clip." As he remarked it he invariably gazed eastward over the broken sea.

The oiler, steering with one of the two oars in the boat, sometimes raised himself suddenly to keep clear of water that swirled in over the stern. It was a thin little oar and it seemed often ready to snap.

The correspondent, pulling at the other oar, watched the waves and wondered why he was there.

The injured captain, lying in the bow, was at this time buried in that profound dejection and indifference which comes, temporarily at least, to even the bravest and most enduring when, willy nilly, the firm fails, the army loses, the ship goes down. The mind of the master of a vessel is rooted deep in the timbers of her, though he commands for a day or a decade, and this captain had on him the stern impression of a scene in the greys of dawn of seven turned faces, and later a stump of a top-mast with a white ball on it that slashed to and fro at the waves, went low and lower, and down. Thereafter there was something strange in his voice. Although steady, it was deep with mourning, and of a quality beyond oration or tears.

"Keep 'er a little more south, Billie," said he.

" 'A little more south,' sir," said the oiler in the stern.

A seat in this boat was not unlike a seat upon a bucking broncho, and by the same token, a broncho is not much smaller. The craft pranced and reared, and plunged like an animal. As each wave came, and she rose for it, she seemed like a horse making at a fence outrageously high. The manner of her scramble over these walls of water is a mystic thing, and, moreover, at the top of them were ordinarily these problems in white water, the foam racing down from the summit of each wave, requiring a new leap, and a leap from the air. Then,

---

1. Crane, who actually experienced the encounter at sea, published his account of the adventure in the New York *Press* on January 7, 1897.

after scornfully bumping a crest, she would slide, and race, and splash down a long incline, and arrive bobbing and nodding in front of the next menace.

A singular disadvantage of the sea lies in the fact that after successfully surmounting one wave you discover that there is another behind it just as important and just as nervously anxious to do something effective in the way of swamping boats. In a ten-foot dinghy one can get an idea of the resources of the sea in the line of waves that is not probable to the average experience which is never at sea in a dinghy. As each slatey wall of water approached, it shut all else from the view of the men in the boat, and it was not difficult to imagine that this particular wave was the final outburst of the ocean, the last effort of the grim water. There was a terrible grace in the move of the waves, and they came in silence, save for the snarling of the crests.

In the wan light, the faces of the men must have been grey. Their eyes must have glinted in strange ways as they gazed steadily astern. Viewed from a balcony, the whole thing would doubtless have been weirdly picturesque. But the men in the boat had no time to see it, and if they had had leisure there were other things to occupy their minds. The sun swung steadily up the sky, and they knew it was broad day because the color of the sea changed from slate to emerald-green, streaked with amber lights, and the foam was like tumbling snow. The process of the breaking day was unknown to them. They were aware only of this effect upon the color of the waves that rolled toward them.

In disjointed sentences the cook and the correspondent argued as to the difference between a life-saving station and a house of refuge. The cook had said: "There's a house of refuge just north of the Mosquito Inlet Light, and as soon as they see us, they'll come off in their boat and pick us up."

"As soon as who see us?" said the correspondent.

"The crew," said the cook.

"Houses of refuge don't have crews," said the correspondent. "As I understand them, they are only places where clothes and grub are stored for the benefit of shipwrecked people. They don't carry crews."

"Oh, yes, they do," said the cook.

"No, they don't," said the correspondent.

"Well, we're not there yet, anyhow," said the oiler, in the stern.

"Well," said the cook, "perhaps it's not a house of refuge that I'm thinking of as being near Mosquito Inlet Light. Perhaps it's a life-saving station."

"We're not there yet," said the oiler, in the stern.

2.

As the boat bounced from the top of each wave, the wind tore through the hair of the hatless men, and as the craft plopped her stern down again the spray splashed past them. The crest of each of these waves was a hill, from the top of which the men surveyed, for a moment, a broad tumultuous expanse, shining and wind-riven. It was probably splendid. It was probably glorious, this play of the free sea, wild with lights of emerald and white and amber.

"Bully good thing it's an on-shore wind," said the cook. "If not, where would we be? Wouldn't have a show."

"That's right," said the correspondent.

The busy oiler nodded his assent.

Then the captain, in the bow, chuckled in a way that expressed humor, contempt, tragedy, all in one. "Do you think we've got much of a show now, boys?" said he.

Whereupon the three were silent, save for a trifle of hemming and hawing. To express any particular optimism at this time they felt to be childish and stupid, but they all doubtless possessed this sense of the situation in their mind. A young man thinks doggedly at such times. On the other hand, the ethics of their condition was decidedly against any open suggestions of hopelessness. So they were silent.

"Oh, well," said the captain, soothing his children, "we'll get ashore all right."

But there was that in his tone which made them think, so the oiler quoth: "Yes! If this wind holds!"

The cook was bailing: "Yes! If we don't catch hell in the surf."

Canton flannel [2] gulls flew near and far. Sometimes they sat down on the sea, near patches of brown seaweed that rolled on the waves with a movement like carpets on a line in a gale. The birds sat comfortably in groups, and they were envied by some in the dinghy, for the wrath of the sea was no more to them than it was to a covey of prairie chickens a thousand miles inland. Often they came very close and stared at the men with black bead-like eyes. At these times they were uncanny and sinister in their unblinking scrutiny, and the men hooted angrily at them, telling them to be gone. One came, and evidently decided to alight on the top of the captain's head. The bird flew parallel to the boat and did not circle, but made short sidelong jumps in the air in chicken-fashion. His black eyes were wistfully fixed upon the captain's head. "Ugly brute," said the oiler to the bird. "You look as if you were made with a jack-knife." The cook and the correspondent swore darkly at the creature. The captain naturally wished to knock it away with the end of the heavy painter; but he did not dare do it, because anything resembling an emphatic gesture would have capsized this freighted boat, and so with his open hand, the captain gently and carefully waved the gull away. After it had been discouraged from the pursuit the captain breathed easier on account of his hair, and others breathed easier because the bird struck their minds at this time as being somehow gruesome and ominous.

In the meantime the oiler and the correspondent rowed. And also they rowed.

They sat together in the same seat, and each rowed an oar. Then the oiler took both oars; then the correspondent took both oars; then the oiler; then the correspondent. They rowed and they rowed. The very ticklish part of the business was when the time came for the reclining one in the stern to take his turn at the oars. By the very last star of truth, it is easier to steal eggs from under a hen than it was to change seats in the dinghy. First the man in the stern slid his hand along the thwart and moved with care, as if he were of Sèvres. [3] Then the man in the rowing seat slid his hand along the other thwart. It was all done with the most extraordinary care. As the two sidled past each other, the whole party kept watchful eyes on the coming wave, and the captain cried: "Look out now! Steady there!"

The brown mats of seaweed that appeared from time to time were like islands, bits of earth. They were traveling, apparently, neither one way nor the other. They were, to all intents, stationary. They informed the men in the boat that it was making progress slowly toward the land.

2. Canton flannel: A plain-woven   3. Sèvres: A type of quality china.
cotton fabric.

The captain, rearing cautiously in the bow, after the dinghy soared on a great swell, said that he had seen the lighthouse at Mosquito Inlet. Presently the cook remarked that he had seen it. The correspondent was at the oars then, and for some reason he too wished to look at the lighthouse, but his back was toward the far shore and the waves were important, and for some time he could not seize an opportunity to turn his head. But at last there came a wave more gentle than the others, and when at the crest of it he swiftly scoured the western horizon.

"See it?" said the captain.

"No," said the correspondent slowly, "I didn't see anything."

"Look again," said the captain. He pointed. "It's exactly in that direction."

At the top of another wave, the correspondent did as he was bid, and this time his eyes chanced on a small still thing on the edge of the swaying horizon. It was precisely like the point of a pin. It took an anxious eye to find a lighthouse so tiny.

"Think we'll make it, captain?"

"If this wind holds and the boat don't swamp, we can't do much else," said the captain.

The little boat, lifted by each towering sea, and splashed viciously by the crests, made progress that in the absence of seaweed was not apparent to those in her. She seemed just a wee thing wallowing, miraculously top-up, at the mercy of five oceans. Occasionally, a great spread of water, like white flames, swarmed into her.

"Bail her, cook," said the captain serenely.

"All right, captain," said the cheerful cook.

3.

It would be difficult to describe the subtle brotherhood of men that was here established on the seas. No one said that it was so. No one mentioned it. But it dwelt in the boat, and each man felt it warm him. They were a captain, an oiler, a cook, and a correspondent, and they were friends, friends in a more curiously iron-bound degree than may be common. The hurt captain, lying against the water-jar in the bow, spoke always in a low voice and calmly, but he could never command a more ready and swiftly obedient crew than the motley three of the dinghy. It was more than a mere recognition of what was best for the common safety. There was surely in it a quality that was personal and heartfelt. And after this devotion to the commander of the boat there was this comradeship that the correspondent, for instance, who had been taught to be cynical of men, knew even at the time was the best experience of his life. But no one said that it was so. No one mentioned it.

"I wish we had a sail," remarked the captain. "We might try my overcoat on the end of an oar and give you two boys a chance to rest." So the cook and the correspondent held the mast and spread wide the overcoat. The oiler steered, and the little boat made good way with her new rig. Sometimes the oiler had to scull sharply to keep a sea from breaking into the boat, but otherwise sailing was a success.

Meanwhile the lighthouse had been growing slowly larger. It had now almost assumed color, and appeared like a little grey shadow on the sky. The man at the oars could not be prevented from turning his head rather often to try for a glimpse of this little grey shadow.

At last, from the top of each wave the men in the tossing boat could see land. Even as the lighthouse was an upright shadow on the sky, this land seemed but a long black shadow on the sea. It certainly was thinner than paper. "We must be about opposite New Smyrna,"[4] said the cook, who had coasted this shore often in schooners. "Captain, by the way, I believe they abandoned that life-saving station there about a year ago."

"Did they?" said the captain.

The wind slowly died away. The cook and the correspondent were not now obliged to slave in order to hold high the oar. But the waves continued their old impetuous swooping at the dinghy, and the little craft, no longer under way, struggled woundily over them. The oiler or the correspondent took the oars again.

Shipwrecks are *à propos* of nothing. If men could only train for them and have them occur when the men had reached pink condition, there would be less drowning at sea. Of the four in the dinghy none had slept any time worth mentioning for two days and two nights previous to embarking in the dinghy, and in the excitement of clambering about the deck of a foundering ship they had also forgotten to eat heartily.

For these reasons, and for others, neither the oiler nor the correspondent was fond of rowing at this time. The correspondent wondered ingenuously how in the name of all that was sane could there be people who thought it amusing to row a boat. It was not an amusement; it was a diabolical punishment, and even a genius of mental aberrations could never conclude that it was anything but a horror to the muscles and a crime against the back. He mentioned to the boat in general how the amusement of rowing struck him, and the weary-faced oiler smiled in full sympathy. Previously to the foundering, by the way, the oiler had worked double-watch in the engine-room of the ship.

"Take her easy, now, boys," said the captain. "Don't spend yourselves. If we have to run a surf you'll need all your strength, because we'll sure have to swim for it. Take your time."

Slowly the land arose from the sea. From a black line it became a line of black and a line of white, trees and sand. Finally, the captain said that he could make out a house on the shore. "That's the house of refuge, sure," said the cook. "They'll see us before long, and come out after us."

The distant lighthouse reared high. "The keeper ought to be able to make us out now, if he's looking through a glass," said the captain. "He'll notify the life-saving people. "

"None of those other boats could have got ashore to give word of the wreck," said the oiler, in a low voice. "Else the lifeboat would be out hunting us."

Slowly and beautifully the land loomed out of the sea. The wind came again. It had veered from the north-east to the south-east. Finally, a new sound struck the ears of the men in the boat. It was the low thunder of the surf on the shore. "We'll never be able to make the lighthouse now," said the captain. "Swing her head a little more north, Billie," said he.

" 'A little more north,' sir," said the oiler.

Whereupon the little boat turned her nose once more down the wind, and

4. New Smyrna: A town on the
northern Florida coast.

all but the oarsman watched the shore grow. Under the influence of this expansion doubt and direful apprehension was leaving the minds of the men. The management of the boat was still most absorbing, but it could not prevent a quiet cheerfulness. In an hour, perhaps, they would be ashore.

Their backbones had become thoroughly used to balancing in the boat, and they now rode this wild colt of a dinghy like circus men. The correspondent thought that he had been drenched to the skin, but happening to feel in the top pocket of his coat, he found therein eight cigars. Four of them were soaked with sea-water; four were perfectly scathless. After a search, somebody produced three dry matches, and thereupon the four waifs rode impudently in their little boat, and with an assurance of an impending rescue shining in their eyes, puffed at the big cigars and judged well and ill of all men. Everybody took a drink of water.

4.

"Cook," remarked the captain, "there don't seem to be any signs of life about your house of refuge."

"No," replied the cook. "Funny they don't see us!"

A broad stretch of lowly coast lay before the eyes of the men. It was of dunes topped with dark vegetation. The roar of the surf was plain, and sometimes they could see the white lip of a wave as it spun up the beach. A tiny house was blocked out black upon the sky. Southward, the slim lighthouse lifted its little gray length.

Tide, wind, and waves were swinging the dinghy northward. "Funny they don't see us," said the men.

The surf's roar was here dulled, but its tone was, nevertheless, thunderous and mighty. As the boat swam over the great rollers, the men sat listening to this roar. "We'll swamp sure," said everybody.

It is fair to say here that there was not a life-saving station within twenty miles in either direction, but the men did not know this fact, and in consequence they made dark and opprobrious remarks concerning the eyesight of the nation's life-savers. Four scowling men sat in the dinghy and surpassed records in the invention of epithets.

"Funny they don't see us."

The lightheartedness of a former time had completely faded. To their sharpened minds it was easy to conjure pictures of all kinds of incompetency and blindness and, indeed, cowardice. There was the shore of the populous land, and it was bitter and bitter to them that from it came no sign.

"Well," said the captain, ultimately, "I suppose we'll have to make a try for ourselves. If we stay out here too long, we'll none of us have strength left to swim after the boat swamps."

And so the oiler, who was at the oars, turned the boat straight for the shore. There was a sudden tightening of muscle. There was some thinking.

"If we don't all get ashore — " said the captain. "If we don't all get ashore, I suppose you fellows know where to send news of my finish?"

They then briefly exchanged some addresses and admonitions. As for the reflections of the men, there was a great deal of rage in them. Perchance they might be formulated thus: "If I am going to be drowned — if I am going to be drowned — if I am going to be drowned, why in the name of the seven mad gods who rule the sea, was I allowed to come thus far and contemplate sand

and trees? Was I brought here merely to have my nose dragged away as I was about to nibble the sacred cheese of life? It is preposterous. If this old ninny-woman, Fate, cannot do better than this, she should be deprived of the management of men's fortunes. She is an old hen who knows not her intention. If she has decided to drown me, why did she not do it in the beginning and save me all this trouble? The whole affair is absurd. . . . But no, she cannot mean to drown me. She dare not drown me. She cannot drown me. Not after all this work." Afterward the man might have had an impulse to shake his fist at the clouds: "Just you drown me, now, and then hear what I call you!"

The billows that came at this time were more formidable. They seemed always just about to break and roll over the little boat in a turmoil of foam. There was a preparatory and long growl in the speech of them. No mind un-used to the sea would have concluded that the dinghy could ascend these sheer heights in time. The shore was still afar. The oiler was a wily surfman. "Boys," he said swiftly, "she won't live three minutes more, and we're too far out to swim. Shall I take her to sea again, captain?"

"Yes! Go ahead!" said the captain.

This oiler, by a series of quick miracles, and fast and steady oarsmanship, turned the boat in the middle of the surf and took her safely to sea again.

There was a considerable silence as the boat bumped over the furrowed sea to deeper water. Then somebody in gloom spoke. "Well, anyhow, they must have seen us from the shore by now."

The gulls went in slanting flight up the wind toward the grey desolate east. A squall, marked by dingy clouds, and clouds brick-red, like smoke from a burning building, appeared from the south-east.

"What do you think of those life-saving people? Ain't they peaches?"

"Funny they haven't seen us."

"Maybe they think we're out here for sport! Maybe they think we're fishin'. Maybe they think we're damned fools."

It was a long afternoon. A changed tide tried to force them southward, but the wind and wave said northward. Far ahead, where coastline, sea, and sky formed their mighty angle, there were little dots which seemed to indicate a city on the shore.

"St. Augustine?"

The captain shook his head. "Too near Mosquito Inlet."

And the oiler rowed, and then the correspondent rowed. Then the oiler rowed. It was a weary business. The human back can become the seat of more aches and pains than are registered in books for the composite anatomy of a regiment. It is a limited area, but it can become the theatre of innumerable muscular conflicts, tangles, wrenches, knots, and other comforts.

"Did you ever like to row, Billie?" asked the correspondent.

"No," said the oiler. "Hang it!"

When one exchanged the rowing-seat for a place in the bottom of the boat, he suffered a bodily depression that caused him to be careless of everything save an obligation to wiggle one finger. There was cold sea-water swashing to and fro in the boat, and he lay in it. His head, pillowed on a thwart, was within an inch of the swirl of a wave crest, and sometimes a particularly obstreperous sea came in-board and drenched him once more. But these matters did not annoy him. It is almost certain that if the boat had capsized he would have tumbled comfortably out upon the ocean as if he felt sure that it was a great soft mattress.

"Look! There's a man on the shore!"

"Where?"

"There! See 'im? See 'im?"

"Yes, sure! He's walking along."

"Now he's stopped. Look! He's facing us!"

"He's waving at us!"

"So he is! By thunder!"

"Ah, now we're all right! Now we're all right! There'll be a boat out here for us in half-an-hour."

"He's going on. He's running. He's going up to that house there."

The remote beach seemed lower than the sea, and it required a searching glance to discern the little black figure. The captain saw a floating stick and they rowed to it. A bath-towel was by some weird chance in the boat, and tying this on the stick, the captain waved it. The oarsman did not dare turn his head, so he was obliged to ask questions.

"What's he doing now?"

"He's standing still again. He's looking, I think. . . . There he goes again. Toward the house. . . . Now he's stopped again."

"Is he waving at us?"

"No, not now! He was, though."

"Look! There comes another man!"

"He's running."

"Look at him go, would you."

"Why, he's on a bicycle. Now he's met the other man. They're both waving at us. Look!"

"There comes something up the beach."

"What the devil is that thing?"

"Why, it looks like a boat."

"Why, certainly, it's a boat."

"No; it's on wheels."

"Yes, so it is. Well, that must be the life-boat. They drag them along shore on a wagon."

"That's the life-boat sure."

"No, by — , it's — it's an omnibus."

"I tell you it's a life-boat."

"It is not! It's an omnibus. I can see it plain. See? One of these big hotel omnibuses."

"By thunder, you're right. It's an omnibus, sure as fate. What do you suppose they are doing with an omnibus? Maybe they are going around collecting the life-crew, hey?"

"That's it, likely. Look! There's a fellow waving a little black flag. He's standing on the steps of the omnibus. There come those other two fellows. Now they're all talking together. Look at the fellow with the flag. Maybe he ain't waving it!"

"That ain't a flag, is it? That's his coat: Why, certainly, that's his coat."

"So it is; it's his coat. He's taken it off and is waving it around his head. But would you look at him swing it!"

"Oh, say, there isn't any life-saving station there. That's just a winter-resort hotel omnibus that has brought over some of the boarders to see us drown."

"What's that idiot with the coat mean? What's he signaling, anyhow?"

"It looks as if he were trying to tell us to go north. There must be a life-saving station up there."

"No; he thinks we're fishing. Just giving us a merry hand. See? Ah, there, Willie."

"Well, I wish I could make something out of those signals. What do you suppose he means?"

"He don't mean anything; he's just playing."

"Well, if he'd just signal us to try the surf again, or to go to sea and wait, or go north, or go south, or go to hell, there would be some reason in it. But look at him! He just stands there and keeps his coat revolving like a wheel! The ass!"

"There come more people."

"Now there's quite a mob. Look! Isn't that a boat?"

"Where? Oh, I see where you mean. No, that's no boat."

"That fellow is still waving his coat."

"He must think we like to see him do that. Why don't he quit it? It don't mean anything."

"I don't know. I think he is trying to make us go north. It must be that there's a life-saving station there somewhere."

"Say, he ain't tired yet. Look at 'im wave!"

"Wonder how long he can keep that up. He's been revolving his coat ever since he caught sight of us. He's an idiot. Why aren't they getting men to bring a boat out? A fishing boat — one of those big yawls — could come out here all right. Why don't he do something?"

"Oh, it's all right now."

"They'll have a boat out here for us in less than no time, now that they've seen us."

A faint yellow tone came into the sky over the low land. The shadows on the sea slowly deepened. The wind bore coldness with it, and the men began to shiver.

"Holy smoke!" said one, allowing his voice to express his impious mood, "if we keep on monkeying out here! If we've got to flounder out here all night!"

"Oh, we'll never have to stay here all night! Don't you worry. They've seen us now, and it won't be long before they'll come chasing out after us."

The shore grew dusky. The man waving a coat blended gradually into this gloom, and it swallowed in the same manner the omnibus and the group of people. The spray, when it dashed uproariously over the side, made the voyagers shrink and swear like men who were being branded.

"I'd like to catch the chump who waved the coat. I feel like soaking him one, just for luck."

"Why? What did he do?"

"Oh, nothing, but then he seemed so damned cheerful."

In the meantime the oiler rowed, and then the correspondent rowed, and then the oiler rowed. Gray-faced and bowed forward, they mechanically, turn by turn, plied the leaden oars. The form of the lighthouse had vanished from the southern horizon, but finally a pale star appeared, just lifting from the sea. The streaked saffron in the west passed before the all-merging darkness, and the sea to the east was black. The land had vanished, and was expressed only by the low and drear thunder of the surf.

"If I am going to be drowned — if I am going to be drowned — if I am going to be drowned, why, in the name of the seven mad gods who rule the sea, was I allowed to come thus far and contemplate sand and trees? Was I brought here merely to have my nose dragged away as I was about to nibble the sacred cheese of life?"

The patient captain, drooped over the water-jar, was sometimes obliged to speak to the oarsman.

"Keep her head up! Keep her head up!"

"Keep her head up, sir." The voices were weary and low.

This was surely a quiet evening. All save the oarsman lay heavily and list-lessly in the boat's bottom. As for him, his eyes were just capable of noting the tall black waves that swept forward in a most sinister silence, save for an occasional subdued growl of a crest.

The cook's head was on a thwart, and he looked without interest at the water under his nose. He was deep in other scenes. Finally he spoke. "Billie," he murmured dreamfully, "what kind of pie do you like best?"

5.

"Pie!" said the oiler and the correspondent, agitatedly. "Don't talk about those things, blast you!"

"Well," said the cook, "I was just thinking about ham sandwiches, and — "

A night on the seas in an open boat is a long night. As darkness settled finally, the shine of the light, lifting from the sea in the south, changed to full gold. On the northern horizon a new light appeared, a small bluish gleam on the edge of the waters. These two lights were the furniture of the world. Otherwise there was nothing but waves.

Two men huddled in the stern, and distances were so magnificent in the dinghy that the rower was enabled to keep his feet partly warm by thrusting them under his companions. Their legs indeed extended far under the rowing-seat until they touched the feet of the captain forward. Sometimes, despite the efforts of the tired oarsman, a wave came piling into the boat, an icy wave of the night, and the chilling water soaked them anew. They would twist their bodies for a moment and groan, and sleep the dead sleep once more, while the water in the boat gurgled about them as the craft rocked.

The plan of the oiler and the correspondent was for one to row until he lost the ability, and then arouse the other from his sea-water couch in the bottom of the boat.

The oiler plied the oars until his head drooped forward and the overpowering sleep blinded him; and he rowed yet afterward. Then he touched a man in the bottom of the boat, and called his name. "Will you spell me for a little while?" he said meekly.

"Sure, Billie," said the correspondent, awaking and dragging himself to a sitting position. They exchanged places carefully, and the oiler, cuddling down in the sea-water at the cook's side, seemed to go to sleep instantly.

The particular violence of the sea had ceased. The waves came without snarling. The obligation of the man at the oars was to keep the boat headed so that the tilt of the rollers would not capsize her, and to preserve her from filling when the crests rushed past. The black waves were silent and hard to be seen in the darkness. Often one was almost upon the boat before the oarsman was aware.

In a low voice the correspondent addressed the captain. He was not sure that the captain was awake, although this iron man seemed to be always awake. "Captain, shall I keep her making for that light north, sir?"

The same steady voice answered him. "Yes. Keep it about two points off the port bow."

The cook had tied a life-belt around himself in order to get even the warmth which this clumsy cork contrivance could donate, and he seemed almost stove-like when a rower, whose teeth invariably chattered wildly as soon as he ceased his labor, dropped down to sleep.

The correspondent, as he rowed, looked down at the two men sleeping under-foot. The cook's arm was around the oiler's shoulders, and, with their frag-mentary clothing and haggard faces, they were the babes of the sea — a gro-tesque rendering of the old babes in the wood.

Later he must have grown stupid at his work, for suddenly there was a growl-ing of water, and a crest came with a roar and a swash into the boat, and it was a wonder that it did not set the cook afloat in his life-belt. The cook continued to sleep, but the oiler sat up, blinking his eyes and shaking with the new cold.

"Oh, I'm awful sorry, Billie," said the correspondent, contritely.

"That's all right, old boy," said the oiler, and lay down again and was asleep.

Presently it seemed that even the captain dozed, and the correspondent thought that he was the one man afloat on all the oceans. The wind had a voice as it came over the waves, and it was sadder than the end.

There was a long, loud swishing astern of the boat, and a gleaming trail of phosphorescence, like blue flame, was furrowed on the black waters. It might have been made by a monstrous knife.

Then there came a stillness, while the correspondent breathed with the open mouth and looked at the sea.

Suddenly there was another swish and another long flash of bluish light, and this time it was alongside the boat, and might almost have been reached with an oar. The correspondent saw an enormous fin speed like a shadow through the water, hurling the crystalline spray and leaving the long glowing trail.

The correspondent looked over his shoulder at the captain. His face was hidden, and he seemed to be asleep. He looked at the babes of the sea. They certainly were asleep. So, being bereft of sympathy, he leaned a little way to one side and swore softly into the sea.

But the thing did not then leave the vicinity of the boat. Ahead or astern, on one side or the other, at intervals long or short, fled the long sparkling streak, and there was to be heard the whiroo of the dark fin. The speed and power of the thing was greatly to be admired. It cut the water like a gigantic and keen projectile.

The presence of this biding thing did not affect the man with the same horror that it would if he had been a picnicker. He simply looked at the sea dully and swore in an undertone.

Nevertheless, it is true that he did not wish to be alone with the thing. He wished one of his companions to awake by chance and keep him company with it. But the captain hung motionless over the water-jar, and the oiler and the cook in the bottom of the boat were plunged in slumber.

"If I am going to be drowned — if I am going to be drowned — if I am going to be drowned, why, in the name of the seven mad gods who rule the sea, was I allowed to come thus far and contemplate sand and trees?"

During this dismal night, it may be remarked that a man would conclude that it was really the intention of the seven mad gods to drown him, despite the abominable injustice of it. For it was certainly an abominable injustice to drown a man who had worked so hard, so hard. The man felt it would be a crime most unnatural. Other people had drowned at sea since galleys swarmed with painted sails, but still —

When it occurs to a man that nature does not regard him as important, and that she feels she would not maim the universe by disposing of him, he at first wishes to throw bricks at the temple, and he hates deeply the fact that there are no bricks and no temples. Any visible expression of nature would surely be pelleted with his jeers.

Then, if there be no tangible thing to hoot, he feels, perhaps, the desire to confront a personification and indulge in pleas, bowed to one knee, and with hands supplicant, saying, "Yes, but I love myself."

A high cold star on a winter's night is the word he feels that she says to him. Thereafter he knows the pathos of his situation.

The men in the dinghy had not discussed these matters, but each had, no doubt, reflected upon them in silence and according to his mind. There was seldom any expression upon their faces save the general one of complete weariness. Speech was devoted to the business of the boat.

To chime the notes of his emotion, a verse mysteriously entered the correspondent's head. He had even forgotten that he had forgotten this verse, but it suddenly was in his mind.

> A soldier of the Legion lay dying in Algiers;
> There was a lack of woman's nursing, there was dearth of woman's
>   tears;
> But a comrade stood beside him, and he took that comrade's hand,
> And he said, "I never more shall see my own, my native land." [5]

In his childhood the correspondent had been made acquainted with the fact that a soldier of the Legion lay dying in Algiers, but he had never regarded it as important. Myriads of his school-fellows had informed him of the soldier's plight, but the dinning had naturally ended by making him perfectly indifferent. He had never considered it his affair that a soldier of the Legion lay dying in Algiers, nor had it appeared to him as a matter for sorrow. It was less to him than the breaking of a pencil's point.

Now, however, it quaintly came to him as a human, living thing. It was no longer merely a picture of a few throes in the breast of a poet, meanwhile drinking tea and warming his feet at the grate; it was an actuality — stern, mournful, and fine.

The correspondent plainly saw the soldier. He lay on the sand with his feet out straight and still. While his pale left hand was upon his chest in an attempt

---

5. From "Bingen on the Rhine,"
a poem written by Caroline Norton (1808–1877).

to thwart the going of his life, the blood came between his fingers. In the far Algerian distance, a city of low square forms was set against a sky that was faint with the last sunset hues. The correspondent, plying the oars and dreaming of the slow and slower movements of the lips of the soldier, was moved by a profound and perfectly impersonal comprehension. He was sorry for the soldier of the Legion who lay dying in Algiers.

The thing which had followed the boat and waited had evidently grown bored at the delay. There was no longer to be heard the slash of the cutwater, and there was no longer the flame of the long trail. The light in the north still glimmered, but it was apparently no nearer to the boat. Sometimes the beam of the surf rang in the correspondent's ears, and he turned the craft seaward then and rowed harder. Southward, some one had evidently built a watch-fire on the beach. It was too low and too far to be seen, but it made a shimmering, roseate reflection upon the bluff back of it, and this could be discerned from the boat. The wind came stronger, and sometimes a wave suddenly raged out like a mountain-cat, and there was to be seen the sheen and sparkle of a broken crest.

The captain, in the bow, moved on his water-jar and sat erect. "Pretty long night," he observed to the correspondent. He looked at the shore. "Those life-saving people take their time."

"Did you see that shark playing around?"

"Yes, I saw him. He was a big fellow, all right."

"Wish I had known you were awake."

Later the correspondent spoke into the bottom of the boat.

"Billie!" There was a slow and gradual disentanglement. "Billie, will you spell me?"

"Sure," said the oiler.

As soon as the correspondent touched the cold, comfortable sea-water in the bottom of the boat and had huddled close to the cook's life-belt he was deep in sleep, despite the fact that his teeth played all the popular airs. This sleep was so good to him that it was but a moment before he heard a voice call his name in a tone that demonstrated the last stages of exhaustion. "Will you spell me?"

"Sure, Billie."

The light in the north had mysteriously vanished, but the correspondent took his course from the wide-awake captain.

Later in the night they took the boat farther out to sea, and the captain directed the cook to take one oar at the stern and keep the boat facing the seas. He was to call out if he should hear the thunder of the surf. This plan enabled the oiler and the correspondent to get respite together. "We'll give those boys a chance to get into shape again," said the captain. They curled down and, after a few preliminary chatterings and trembles, slept once more the dead sleep. Neither knew they had bequeathed to the cook the company of another shark, or perhaps the same shark.

As the boat caroused on the waves, spray occasionally bumped over the side and gave them a fresh soaking, but this had no power to break their repose. The ominous slash of the wind and the water affected them as it would have affected mummies.

"Boys," said the cook, with the notes of every reluctance in his voice, "she's drifted in pretty close. I guess one of you had better take her to sea again." The correspondent, aroused, heard the crash of the toppled crests.

As he was rowing, the captain gave him some whiskey and water, and this steadied the chills out of him. "If I ever get ashore and anybody shows me even a photograph of an oar — "

At last there was a short conversation.

"Billie! . . . Billie, will you spell me?"

"Sure," said the oiler.

7.

When the correspondent again opened his eyes, the sea and the sky were each of the gray hue of the dawning. Later, carmine and gold was painted upon the waters. The morning appeared finally, in its splendor, with a sky of pure blue, and the sunlight flamed on the tips of the waves.

On the distant dunes were set many little black cottages, and a tall white windmill reared above them. No man, nor dog, nor bicycle appeared on the beach. The cottages might have formed a deserted village.

The voyagers scanned the shore. A conference was held in the boat. "Well," said the captain, "if no help is coming, we might better try a run through the surf right away. If we stay out here much longer we will be too weak to do anything for ourselves at all." The others silently acquiesced in this reasoning. The boat was headed for the beach. The correspondent wondered if none ever ascended the tall wind-tower, and if then they never looked seaward. This tower was a giant, standing with its back to the plight of the ants. It represented in a degree, to the correspondent, the serenity of nature amid the struggles of the individual — nature in the wind, and nature in the vision of men. She did not seem cruel to him then, nor beneficent, nor treacherous, nor wise. But she was indifferent, flatly indifferent. It is, perhaps, plausible that a man in this situation, impressed with the unconcern of the universe, should see the innumerable flaws of his life and have them taste wickedly in his mind and wish for another chance. A distinction between right and wrong seems absurdly clear to him, then, in this new ignorance of the grave-edge, and he understands that if he were given another opportunity he would mend his conduct and his words, and be better and brighter during an introduction or at a tea.

"Now, boys," said the captain, "she is going to swamp sure. All we can do is to work her in as far as possible, and then when she swamps, pile out and scramble for the beach. Keep cool now, and don't jump until she swamps sure."

The oiler took the oars. Over his shoulders he scanned the surf. "Captain," he said, "I think I'd better bring her about, and keep her head-on to the seas, and back her in."

"All right, Billie," said the captain. "Back her in." The oiler swung the boat then, and seated in the stern, the cook and the correspondent were obliged to look over their shoulders to contemplate the lonely and indifferent shore.

The monstrous inshore rollers heaved the boat high until the men were again enabled to see the white sheets of water scudding up the slanted beach. "We won't get in very close," said the captain. Each time a man could wrest his attention from the rollers, he turned his glance toward the shore, and in the expression of the eyes during this contemplation there was a singular quality. The correspondent, observing the others, knew that they were not afraid, but the full meaning of their glances was shrouded.

As for himself, he was too tired to grapple fundamentally with the fact. He tried to coerce his mind into thinking of it, but the mind was dominated at this time by the muscles, and the muscles said they did not care. It merely occurred to him that if he should drown it would be a shame.

There were no hurried words, no pallor, no plain agitation. The men simply looked at the shore. "Now, remember to get well clear of the boat when you jump," said the captain.

Seaward the crest of a roller suddenly fell with a thunderous crash, and the long white comber came roaring down upon the boat.

"Steady now," said the captain. The men were silent. They turned their eyes from the shore to the comber and waited. The boat slid up the incline, leaped at the furious top, bounced over it, and swung down the long back of the wave. Some water had been shipped, and the cook bailed it out.

The next crest crashed also. The tumbling, boiling flood of white water caught the boat and whirled it almost perpendicular. Water swarmed in from all sides. The correspondent had his hands on the gunwale at this time, and when the water entered at that place he swiftly withdrew his fingers, as if he objected to wetting them.

The little boat, drunken with this weight of water, reeled and snuggled deeper into the sea.

"Bail her out, cook! Bail her out!" said the captain.

"All right, Captain," said the cook.

"Now, boys, the next one will do for us sure," said the oiler. "Mind to jump clear of the boat."

The third wave moved forward, huge, furious, implacable. It fairly swallowed the dinghy, and almost simultaneously the men tumbled into the sea. A piece of life-belt had lain in the bottom of the boat, and as the correspondent went overboard he held this to his chest with his left hand.

The January water was icy, and he reflected immediately that it was colder than he had expected to find it off the coast of Florida. This appeared to his dazed mind as a fact important enough to be noted at the time. The coldness of the water was sad; it was tragic. This fact was somehow mixed and confused with his opinion of his own situation so that it seemed almost a proper reason for tears. The water was cold.

When he came to the surface he was conscious of little but the noisy water. Afterward he saw his companions in the sea. The oiler was ahead in the race. He was swimming strongly and rapidly. Off to the correspondent's left, the cook's great white and corked back bulged out of the water; and in the rear the captain was hanging with his one good hand to the keel of the overturned dinghy.

There is a certain immovable quality to a shore, and the correspondent wondered at it amid the confusion of the sea.

It seemed also very attractive; but the correspondent knew that it was a long journey, and he paddled leisurely. The piece of life-preserver lay under him, and sometimes he whirled down the incline of a wave as if he were on a hand-sled.

But finally he arrived at a place in the sea where travel was beset with difficulty. He did not pause swimming to inquire what manner of current had caught him, but there his progress ceased. The shore was set before him like a bit of scenery on a stage, and he looked at it, and understood with his eyes each detail of it.

As the cook passed, much farther to the left, the captain was calling to him, "Turn over on your back, cook! Turn over on your back and use the oar."

"All right, sir." The cook turned on his back, and, paddling with an oar, went ahead as if he were a canoe.

Presently the boat also passed to the left of the correspondent, with the captain clinging with one hand to the keel. He would have appeared like a man raising himself to look over a board fence if it were not for the extraordinary gymnastics of the boat. The correspondent marveled that the captain could still hold to it.

They passed on nearer to shore — the oiler, the cook, the captain — and following them went the water-jar, bouncing gaily over the seas.

The correspondent remained in the grip of this strange new enemy, a current. The shore, with its white slope of sand and its green bluff, topped with little silent cottages, was spread like a picture before him. It was very near to him then, but he was impressed as one who, in a gallery, looks at a scene from Brittany or Algiers.

He thought: "I am going to drown? Can it be possible? Can it be possible? Can it be possible?" Perhaps an individual must consider his own death to be the final phenomenon of nature.

But later a wave perhaps whirled him out of this small deadly current, for he found suddenly that he could again make progress toward the shore. Later still he was aware that the captain, clinging with one hand to the keel of the dinghy, had his face turned away from the shore and toward him, and was calling his name. "Come to the boat! Come to the boat!"

In his struggle to reach the captain and the boat, he reflected that when one gets properly wearied drowning must really be a comfortable arrangement — a cessation of hostilities accompanied by a large degree of relief; and he was glad of it, for the main thing in his mind for some moments had been horror of the temporary agony; he did not wish to be hurt.

Presently he saw a man running along the shore. He was undressing with most remarkable speed. Coat, trousers, shirt, everything flew magically off him.

"Come to the boat!" called the captain.

"All right, Captain." As the correspondent paddled, he saw the captain let himself down to bottom and leave the boat. Then the correspondent performed his one little marvel of the voyage. A large wave caught him and flung him with ease and supreme speed completely over the boat and far beyond it. It struck him even then as an event in gymnastics and a true miracle of the sea. An overturned boat in the surf is not a plaything to a swimming man.

The correspondent arrived in water that reached only to his waist, but his condition did not enable him to stand for more than a moment. Each wave knocked him into a heap, and the under-tow pulled at him.

Then he saw the man who had been running and undressing, and undressing and running, come bounding into the water. He dragged ashore the cook, and then waded towards the captain, but the captain waved him away, and sent him to the correspondent. He was naked, naked as a tree in winter, but a halo was about his head, and he shone like a saint. He gave a strong pull, and a long drag, and a bully heave at the correspondent's hand. The correspondent, schooled in the minor formulae, said: "Thanks, old man." But suddenly the man cried: "What's that?" He pointed a swift finger. The correspondent said: "Go."

In the shallows, face downward, lay the oiler. His forehead touched sand that was periodically, between each wave, clear of the sea.

The correspondent did not know all that transpired afterward. When he achieved safe ground he fell, striking the sand with each particular part of his body. It was as if he had dropped from a roof, but the thud was grateful to him.

It seemed that instantly the beach was populated with men with blankets, clothes, and flasks, and women with coffeepots and all the remedies sacred to their minds. The welcome of the land to the men from the sea was warm and generous, but a still and dripping shape was carried slowly up the beach, and the land's welcome for it could only be the different and sinister hospitality of the grave.

When it came night, the white waves paced to and fro in the moonlight, and the wind brought the sound of the great sea's voice to the men on shore, and they felt that they could then be interpreters.

Exercises

1. What is the chief emphasis of each of the seven parts of Crane's story? Consider plot, character, or theme.

2. Who is the protagonist? What is the conflict?

3. What can be inferred from the fact that the oiler, seemingly the fittest, drowns?

4. What is the correspondent's early attitude toward the dying Algerian soldier? What motivates his change of feelings?

5. Interpret the meaning of (a) the naked rescuer; (b) the survivors hearing "the sound of the great sea's voice" and feeling that "they could then be interpreters"; (c) the correspondent's description of the comradeship of the four shipwrecked men as "the best experience of his life."

6. What view of nature do the four men hold at the beginning of the story? To what view have they converted at the end?

7. How does the resolution help you to discover meaning? State two possible themes.

8. Interpret the final sentence of the story.

9. Discuss the theme of brotherhood as expressed in the story.

Topics for Writing

1. Explain how this story, written many years ago in an era vastly different from our own, transcends time. What comments does the author make about human nature that remain applicable today?

2. Compare man's condition in life to that of man in a ten-foot dinghy on the menacing sea.

3. Supporting your discussion with details from the story, substantiate the premise that misfortune and suffering make men brothers.

Adams, Richard P. "Naturalistic Fiction: 'The Open Boat.' " *Tulane Studies in English,* 4 (1954), 137–146.

Autrey, Max L. "The World Out of the Sea: A View of Crane's 'The Open Boat.' " *Arizona Quarterly,* 30 (1974), 101–110.

Berryman, John. "Commentary." In Ralph Ross, John Berryman, and Allen Tate, *The Arts of Reading.* New York: Thomas Y. Crowell, 1960, pp. 279–288.

Brennan, Joseph X. "Stephen Crane and the Limits of Irony." *Criticism,* 11 (1969), 183–200.

Buitenhuis, Peter. "The Essentials of Life." *Modern Fiction Studies,* 5 (1959), 243–250.

Burns, Landon C. "On 'The Open Boat.' " *Studies in Short Fiction,* 3 (1966), 455–457.

Colvert, James B. "Style and Meaning in Stephen Crane: *The Open Boat.*" *Texas Studies in English,* 37 (1958), 34–45.

Frederick, John T. "The Fifth Man in 'The Open Boat,' " *CEA Critic,* 30 (May 1968), 1–14.

Garnett, Edward. "Stephen Crane and His Work." In *Friday Nights.* New York: Knopf, 1922, pp. 201–217.

Gerstenberger, Donna. " 'The Open Boat': Additional Perspective." *Modern Fiction Studies,* 17 (1972), 557–561.

Gibson, Donald B. *The Fiction of Stephen Crane.* Carbondale and Edwardsville: Southern Illinois University Press, 1968.

Going, William T. "William Higgins and Crane's 'The Open Boat': A Note About Fact and Fiction." *Papers on Language and Literature,* 1 (Winter 1965), 79–82.

Gordon, Caroline. "Stephen Crane." *Accent,* 9(1949), 72.

Griffith, Clark. "Stephen Crane and the Ironic Last Word." *Philological Quarterly,* 47 (1968), 83–91.

Gullason, Thomas A. "The New Criticism and the Older Ones: Another Ride in 'The Open Boat,' " *CEA Critic,* 32 (June 1969), 8.

Hagemann, E. R. "Crane's 'Real' War in His Short Stories." *American Quarterly,* 8 (1956), 356–367.

Kissane, Leedice. "Interpretation Through Language: A Study of Metaphors in Stephen Crane's 'The Open Boat.' " *Rendezvous,* 1 (1966), 18–22.

Kwiat, Joseph J. "Stephen Crane and Painting." *American Quarterly,* 4 (1952), 331–338.

Labor, Earle. "Crane and Hemingway: Anatomy of Trauma." *Renascence,* 11 (1959), 189–196.

LaFrance, Marston. *A Reading of Stephen Crane.* New York: Oxford University Press, 1971, pp. 195–205.

Leaver, Florence. "Isolation in the Work of Stephen Crane." *South Atlantic Quarterly,* 61 (1962), 521–532.

Marcus, Mordecai. "The Three-fold View of Nature in 'The Open Boat.' " *Philological Quarterly,* 41 (1962), 511–515.

Metzger, Charles R. "Realistic Devices in Stephen Crane's 'The Open Boat.' " *Midwest Quarterly,* 4 (1962), 47–54.

Meyers, Robert. "Crane's 'The Open Boat.' " *Explicator,* 21 (1963), 60.

Monteiro, George. "The Logic Beneath 'The Open Boat.' " *Georgia Review,* 26 (1972), 326–335.

Parks, Edd Winfield. "Crane's 'The Open Boat.' " *Nineteenth-Century Fiction,* 8 (1953), 77.

Randel, William. "The Cook in 'The Open Boat.' " *American Literature,* 34 (1962), 405–411.

Roth, Russell. "A Tree in Winter: The Short Fiction of Stephen Crane." *New Mexico Quarterly,* 23 (1953), 188–196.

Stallman, R. W. "Crane's Short Stories." In *The Houses That James Built and Other Literary Studies.* Lansing: Michigan State University Press, 1961, pp. 103–110.

————. "The Land-Sea Irony in 'The Open Boat.' " *CEA Critic,* 30 (May 1968), 15.

Stein, William Bysshe. "Stephen Crane's *Homo Absurdus.*" *Bucknell Review,* 8 (1959), 168–188.

Walcutt, Charles Child. "Stephen Crane: Naturalist and Impressionist." In *American Literary Naturalism: A Divided Stream.* Minneapolis: University of Minnesota Press, 1956, pp. 66–86.

James Joyce (1882–1941)

Araby

North Richmond Street, being blind, was a quiet street except at the hour when the Christian Brothers' School set the boys free. An uninhabited house of two storeys stood at the blind end, detached from its neighbours in a square ground. The other houses of the street, conscious of decent lives within them, gazed at one another with brown imperturbable faces.

The former tenant of our house, a priest, had died in the back drawing-room. Air, musty from having been long enclosed, hung in all the rooms, and the waste room behind the kitchen was littered with old useless papers. Among these I found a few paper-covered books, the pages of which were curled and damp: *The Abbot,* by Walter Scott, *The Devout Communicant* and *The Memoirs of Vidocq.*[1] I liked the last best because its leaves were yellow. The wild garden behind the house contained a central apple-tree and a few straggling bushes under one of which I found the late tenant's rusty bicycle-pump. He had been a very charitable priest; in his will he had left all his money to institutions and the furniture of his house to his sister.

When the short days of winter came dusk fell before we had well eaten our dinners. When we met in the street the houses had grown sombre. The space of sky above us was the colour of ever-changing violet and towards it the lamps of the street lifted their feeble lanterns. The cold air stung us and we played till

---

1. *The Abbot:* A novel about a brief period in the life of Mary Queen of Scots, written by Sir Walter Scott (1771–1832), an English romantic novelist. *The Devout Communicant:* A variant title for *Pious Meditations* (1813), a religious pamphlet written by Pacificus Baker, a Franciscan friar. *The Memoirs of Vidocq:* The autobiography of a French policeman, soldier of fortune, and writer (1775–1857).

our bodies glowed. Our shouts echoed in the silent street. The career of our play brought us through the dark muddy lanes behind the houses where we ran the gauntlet of the rough tribes from the cottages, to the back doors of the dark dripping gardens where odours arose from the ashpits, to the dark odorous stables where a coachman smoothed and combed the horse or shook music from the buckled harness. When we returned to the street light from the kitchen windows had filled the areas. If my uncle was seen turning the corner we hid in the shadow until we had seen him safely housed. Or if Mangan's sister came out on the doorstep to call her brother in to his tea we watched her from our shadow peer up and down the street. We waited to see whether she would remain or go in and, if she remained, we left our shadow and walked up to Mangan's steps resignedly. She was waiting for us, her figure defined by the light from the half-opened door. Her brother always teased her before he obeyed and I stood by the railings looking at her. Her dress swung as she moved her body and the soft rope of her hair tossed from side to side.

Every morning I lay on the floor in the front parlour watching her door. The blind was pulled down to within an inch of the sash so that I could not be seen. When she came out on the doorstep my heart leaped. I ran to the hall, seized my books and followed her. I kept her brown figure always in my eye and, when we came near the point at which our ways diverged, I quickened my pace and passed her. This happened morning after morning. I had never spoken to her, except for a few casual words, and yet her name was like a summons to all my foolish blood.

Her image accompanied me even in places the most hostile to romance. On Saturday evenings when my aunt went marketing I had to go to carry some of the parcels. We walked through the flaring streets, jostled by drunken men and bargaining women, amid the curses of labourers, the shrill litanies of shop-boys who stood on guard by the barrels of pigs' cheeks, the nasal chanting of street-singers, who sang a *come-all-you*[2] about O'Donovan Rossa,[3] or a ballad about the troubles in our native land. These noises converged in a single sensation of life for me: I imagined that I bore my chalice[4] safely through a throng of foes. Her name sprang to my lips at moments in strange prayers and praises which I myself did not understand. My eyes were often full of tears (I could not tell why) and at times a flood from my heart seemed to pour itself out into my bosom. I thought little of the future. I did not know whether I would ever speak to her or not or, if I spoke to her, how I could tell her of my confused adoration. But my body was like a harp and her words and gestures were like fingers running upon the wires.

One evening I went into the back drawing-room in which the priest had died. It was a dark rainy evening and there was no sound in the house. Through one of the broken panes I heard the rain impinge upon the earth, the fine incessant needles of water playing in the sodden beds. Some distant lamp or lighted window gleamed below me. I was thankful that I could see so little. All my senses seemed to desire to veil themselves and, feeling that I was about to slip from

2. *Come-all-you:* Any popular song beginning with "Come all you Irishmen."
3. O'Donovan Rossa: Real name Jeremiah O'Donovan (1831–1915), an Irish nationalist whose revolutionary activities sent him into exile to the United States in 1870.
4. Chalice: The cup used to celebrate the Eucharist (or Holy Communion) during the Catholic mass.

them, I pressed the palms of my hands together until they trembled, murmuring: "*O love! O love!*" many times.

At last she spoke to me. When she addressed the first words to me I was so confused that I did not know what to answer. She asked me was I going to *Araby.*[5] I forgot whether I answered yes or no. It would be a splendid bazaar, she said she would love to go.

"And why can't you?" I asked.

While she spoke she turned a silver bracelet round and round her wrist. She could not go, she said, because there would be a retreat that week in her convent.[6] Her brother and two other boys were fighting for their caps and I was alone at the railings. She held one of the spikes, bowing her head towards me. The light from the lamp opposite our door caught the white curve of her neck, lit up her hair that rested there and, falling, lit up the hand upon the railing. It fell over one side of her dress and caught the white border of a petticoat, just visible as she stood at ease.

"It's well for you," she said.

"If I go," I said, "I will bring you something."

What innumerable follies laid waste my waking and sleeping thoughts after that evening! I wished to annihilate the tedious intervening days. I chafed against the work of school. At night in my bedroom and by day in the classroom her image came between me and the page I strove to read. The syllables of the word *Araby* were called to me through the silence in which my soul luxuriated and cast an Eastern enchantment over me. I asked for leave to go to the bazaar on Saturday night. My aunt was surprised and hoped it was not some Freemason[7] affair. I answered few questions in class. I watched my master's face pass from amiability to sternness; he hoped I was not beginning to idle. I could not call my wandering thoughts together. I had hardly any patience with the serious work of life which, now that it stood between me and my desire, seemed to me child's play, ugly monotonous child's play.

On Saturday morning I reminded my uncle that I wished to go to the bazaar in the evening. He was fussing at the hallstand, looking for the hat-brush, and answered me curtly:

"Yes, boy, I know."

As he was in the hall I could not go into the front parlour and lie at the window. I left the house in bad humour and walked slowly towards the school. The air was pitilessly raw and already my heart misgave me.

When I came home to dinner my uncle had not yet been home. Still it was early. I sat staring at the clock for some time and, when its ticking began to irritate me, I left the room. I mounted the staircase and gained the upper part of the house. The high cold empty gloomy rooms liberated me and I went from room to room singing. From the front window I saw my companions playing below in the street. Their cries reached me weakened and indistinct and, leaning my forehead against the cool glass, I looked over at the dark house where she lived. I may have stood there for an hour, seeing nothing but the brown-clad

5. *Araby:* A billboard sign of that period which read as follows: "Araby in DUBLIN Official Catalogue GRAND ORIENTAL FETE May 14th to 19th in aid of Jervis St. Hospital. Admission one shilling."

6. Convent: An establishment housing nuns bound by vows to a religious life.

7. Freemason: Catholics considered the Masonic Order an enemy of the church.

figure cast by my imagination, touched discreetly by the lamplight at the curved neck, at the hand upon the railings and at the border below the dress.

When I came downstairs again I found Mrs. Mercer sitting at the fire. She was an old garrulous woman, a pawnbroker's widow, who collected used stamps for some pious purpose. I had to endure the gossip of the tea-table. The meal was prolonged beyond an hour and still my uncle did not come. Mrs. Mercer stood up to go: she was sorry she couldn't wait any longer, but it was after eight o'clock and she did not like to be out late, as the night air was bad for her. When she had gone I began to walk up and down the room, clenching my fists. My aunt said:

"I'm afraid you may put off your bazaar for this night of Our Lord."

At nine o'clock I heard my uncle's latchkey in the halldoor. I heard him talking to himself and heard the hallstand rocking when it had received the weight of his overcoat. I could interpret these signs. When he was midway through his dinner I asked him to give me the money to go to the bazaar. He had forgotten.

"The people are in bed and after their first sleep now," he said.

I did not smile. My aunt said to him energetically:

"Can't you give him the money and let him go? You've kept him late enough as it is."

My uncle said he was very sorry he had forgotten. He said he believed in the old saying: "All work and no play makes Jack a dull boy." He asked me where I was going and, when I had told him a second time he asked me did I know *The Arab's Farewell to his Steed*.[8] When I left the kitchen he was about to recite the opening lines of the piece to my aunt.

I held a florin[9] tightly in my hand as I strode down Buckingham Street towards the station. The sight of the streets thronged with buyers and glaring with gas recalled to me the purpose of my journey. I took my seat in a third-class carriage of a deserted train. After an intolerable delay the train moved out of the station slowly. It crept onward among ruinous houses and over the twinkling river. At Westland Row Station a crowd of people pressed to the carriage doors; but the porters moved them back, saying that it was a special train for the bazaar. I remained alone in the bare carriage. In a few minutes the train drew up beside an improvised wooden platform. I passed out on to the road and saw by the lighted dial of a clock that it was ten minutes to ten. In front of me was a large building which displayed the magical name.

I could not find any sixpenny entrance and, fearing that the bazaar would be closed, I passed in quickly through a turnstile, handing a shilling to a weary-looking man. I found myself in a big hall girdled at half its height by a gallery. Nearly all the stalls were closed and the greater part of the hall was in darkness. I recognised a silence like that which pervades a church after a service. I walked into the centre of the bazaar timidly. A few people were gathered about the stalls which were still open. Before a curtain, over which the words *Café Chantant*[10] were written in coloured lamps, two men were counting money on a salver. I listened to the fall of the coins.

8. *The . . . Steed:* A poem by Caroline Norton (1808–1877), treating of an Arab's heavy heart after the sale of his favorite horse.

9. Florin: A British coin worth two shillings.

10. *Café Chantant:* A café offering musical entertainment.

Remembering with difficulty why I had come I went over to one of the stalls and examined porcelain vases and flowered teasets. At the door of the stall a young lady was talking and laughing with two young gentlemen. I remarked their English accents and listened vaguely to their conversation.

"O, I never said such a thing!"

"O, but you did!"

"O, but I didn't!"

"Didn't she say that?"

"Yes. I heard her."

"O, there's a . . . fib!"

Observing me the young lady came over and asked me did I wish to buy anything. The tone of her voice was not encouraging; she seemed to have spoken to me out of a sense of duty. I looked humbly at the great jars that stood like eastern guards at either side of the dark entrance to the stall and murmured:

"No, thank you."

The young lady changed the position of one of the vases and went back to the two young men. They began to talk of the same subject. Once or twice the young lady glanced at me over her shoulder.

I lingered before her stall, though I knew my stay was useless, to make my interest in her wares seem the more real. Then I turned away slowly and walked down the middle of the bazaar. I allowed the two pennies to fall against the sixpence in my pocket. I heard a voice call from one end of the gallery that the light was out. The upper part of the hall was now completely dark.

Gazing up into the darkness I saw myself as a creature driven and derided by vanity; and my eyes burned with anguish and anger.

Exercises

1. The story begins and concludes by showing the emptiness of the world. Why?

2. What is accomplished by the first two paragraphs?

3. How is the boy's neighborhood described?

4. Describe the function of the scene at the bazaar.

5. What did the boy expect to find at Araby? What does he find instead?

6. What significant episodes in the story furnish clues to its meaning?

7. The story is narrated by a mature person who recounts an experience that happened in his youth. What would be gained or lost were the story told by the young boy?

8. Identify the religious references in the story and comment on their importance to the story.

9. Express the theme. What does the word *Araby* suggest? How does it relate to the theme?

10. Comment on the significance of the final sentence.

Topics for Writing

1. What is "Araby" about: A boy's dream of finding romance at a Dublin fair? A quest for meaning? What kind of meaning? Make a case to support your view.

2. Compare the use of setting in "Araby" with that in Steinbeck's "The Chrysanthemums."

3. Compare and contrast the boy's disillusionment in "Araby" and in Anderson's "I Want to Know Why."

4. Joyce's story deals with the world of reality and the world of fantasy as represented by the boy's vivid imagination. How does each contribute to the story's effectiveness?

Selected Bibliography   James Joyce

Beck, Warren. *Joyce's "Dubliners": Substance, Vision, and Art.* Durham, N.C.: Duke University Press, 1969.

Benstock, Bernard. "Arabesques: Third Position of Concord." *James Joyce Quarterly,* 5 (1967), 30–39.

Brooks, Cleanth, and Robert P. Warren. *Understanding Fiction,* 2nd ed. New York: Appleton-Century-Crofts, Inc., 1959, pp. 189–192.

Burto, William. "Joyce's 'Araby.'" *Explicator,* 25 (1967), item 67.

Collins, Ben L. "Joyce's 'Araby' and the 'Extended Simile.'" *James Joyce Quarterly,* 4 (1967), 84–90.

Dadufalza, Concepcion D. "The Quest of the Chalice-Bearer in James Joyce's 'Araby.'" *Diliman Review,* 7 (1959), 317–325.

Freimarck, John. "'Araby': A Quest for Meaning." *James Joyce Quarterly,* 7 (1970), 366–368.

Friedman, Stanley. "Joyce's 'Araby.'" *Explicator,* 24 (1966), item 43.

Fuller, James A. "A Note on Joyce's 'Araby.'" *College English Association Critic,* 20 (1958), 8.

Garrison, Joseph M. "The Adult Consciousness of the Narrator in Joyce's 'Araby.'" *Studies in Short Fiction,* 10 (1973), 416–419.

Going, William T. "Joyce's 'Araby.'" *Explicator,* 26 (1968), item 39.

Lyons, John O. "James Joyce and Chaucer's Prioress." *English Language Notes,* 2 (1964), 127–132.

Peterson, Richard F. "Joyce's Use of Time in Dubliners." *Ball State University Forum,* 14, no. 1 (1973), 44–45.

Russell, John. "From Style to Meaning in 'Araby.'" *College English,* 28 (1966), 170–171.

San Juan, Epifanio. *James Joyce and the Craft of Fiction: An Interpretation of "Dubliners."* Cranbury, N.J.: Associated University Presses, for Fairleigh Dickinson University Press, 1972.

Stein, William B. "Joyce's 'Araby': Paradise Lost." *Perspective,* 12 (1962), 215–222.

Stone, Harry. "'Araby' and the Writings of James Joyce." *Antioch Review,* 25 (Fall 1965), 375–410.

Thorn, Eric. "James Joyce: Early Imitations of Structural Unity." *Costerus,* 9 (1973), 232–234.

Walzl, Florence L. "The Liturgy of the Epiphany Season and the Epiphanies of Joyce." *PMLA,* 80 (1965), 445.

West, Ray B. *The Art of Writing Fiction.* New York: Thomas Y. Crowell, 1968.

Shirley Jackson (1919–1965)

The Lottery

The morning of June 27th was clear and sunny, with the fresh warmth of a full-summer day; the flowers were blossoming profusely and the grass was richly green. The people of the village began to gather in the square, between the post office and the bank, around ten o'clock; in some towns there were so many people that the lottery took two days and had to be started on June 26th, but in this village, where there were only about three hundred people, the whole lottery took less than two hours, so it could begin at ten o'clock in the morning and still be through in time to allow the villagers to get home for noon dinner.

The children assembled first, of course. School was recently over for the summer, and the feeling of liberty sat uneasily on most of them; they tended to gather together quietly for a while before they broke into boisterous play, and their talk was still of the classroom and the teacher, of books and reprimands. Bobby Martin had already stuffed his pockets full of stones, and the other boys soon followed his example, selecting the smoothest and roundest stones; Bobby and Harry Jones and Dickie Delacroix — the villagers pronounced this name "Dellacroy" — eventually made a great pile of stones in one corner of the square and guarded it against the raids of the other boys. The girls stood aside, talking among themselves, looking over their shoulders at the boys, and the very small children rolled in the dust or clung to the hands of their older brothers or sisters.

Soon the men began to gather, surveying their own children, speaking of planting and rain, tractors and taxes. They stood together, away from the pile of stones in the corner, and their jokes were quiet and they smiled rather than laughed. The women, wearing faded house dresses and sweaters, came shortly after their menfolk. They greeted one another and exchanged bits of gossip as they went to join their husbands. Soon the women, standing by their husbands, began to call to their children, and the children came reluctantly, having to be called four or five times. Bobby Martin ducked under his mother's grasping hand and ran, laughing, back to the pile of stones. His father spoke up sharply, and Bobby came quickly and took his place between his father and his oldest brother.

The lottery was conducted — as were the square dances, the teen-age club, the Halloween program — by Mr. Summers, who had time and energy to devote to civic activities. He was a round-faced jovial man and he ran the coal business, and people were sorry for him, because he had no children and his wife was a scold. When he arrived in the square, carrying the black wooden box, there was a murmur of conversation among the villagers, and he waved and called, "Little late today, folks." The postmaster, Mr. Graves, followed him, carrying a three-legged stool, and the stool was put in the center of the square and Mr. Summers set the black box down on it. The villagers kept their distance, leaving a space between themselves and the stool, and when Mr. Summers said, "Some of you fellows want to give me a hand?" there was a hesitation before two men, Mr. Martin and his oldest son, Baxter, came forward to hold the box steady on the stool while Mr. Summers stirred up the papers inside it.

The original paraphernalia for the lottery had been lost long ago, and the black box now resting on the stool had been put into use even before Old Man Warner, the oldest man in town, was born. Mr. Summers spoke frequently to the villagers about making a new box, but no one liked to upset even as much tradition as was represented by the black box. There was a story that the present box had been made with some pieces of the box that had preceded it, the one that had been constructed when the first people settled down to make a village here. Every year, after the lottery, Mr. Summers began talking again about a new box, but every year the subject was allowed to fade off without anything's being done. The black box grew shabbier each year; by now it was no longer completely black but splintered badly along one side to show the original wood color, and in some places faded or stained.

Mr. Martin and his oldest son, Baxter, held the black box securely on the stool until Mr. Summers had stirred the papers thoroughly with his hand. Because so much of the ritual had been forgotten or discarded, Mr. Summers had been successful in having slips of paper substituted for the chips of wood that had been used for generations. Chips of wood, Mr. Summers had argued, had been all very well when the village was tiny, but now that the population was more than three hundred and likely to keep on growing, it was necessary to use something that would fit more easily into the black box. The night before the lottery, Mr. Summers and Mr. Graves made up the slips of paper and put them in the box, and it was then taken to the safe of Mr. Summers' coal company and locked up until Mr. Summers was ready to take it to the square next morning. The rest of the year, the box was put away, sometimes one place, sometimes another; it had spent one year in Mr. Graves's barn and another year underfoot in the post office, and sometimes it was set on a shelf in the Martin grocery and left there.

There was a great deal of fussing to be done before Mr. Summers declared the lottery open. There were the lists to make up — of heads of families, heads of households in each family, members of each household in each family. There was the proper swearing-in of Mr. Summers by the postmaster, as the official of the lottery; at one time, some people remembered, there had been a recital of some sort, performed by the official of the lottery, a perfunctory, tuneless chant that had been rattled off duly each year; some people believed that the official of the lottery used to stand just so when he said or sang it, others believed that he was supposed to walk among the people, but years and years ago this part of the ritual had been allowed to lapse. There had been, also, a ritual salute, which the official of the lottery had had to use in addressing each person who came up to draw from the box, but this also had changed with time, until now it was felt necessary only for the official to speak to each person approaching. Mr. Summers was very good at all this; in his clean white shirt and blue jeans, with one hand resting carelessly on the black box, he seemed very proper and important as he talked interminably to Mr. Graves and the Martins.

Just as Mr. Summers finally left off talking and turned to the assembled villagers, Mrs. Hutchinson came hurriedly along the path to the square, her sweater thrown over her shoulders, and slid into place in the back of the crowd. "Clean forgot what day it was," she said to Mrs. Delacroix, who stood next to her, and they both laughed softly. "Thought my old man was out back stacking wood," Mrs. Hutchinson went on, "and then I looked out the window and the kids was gone, and then I remembered it was the twenty-seventh and came a-running." She dried her hands on her apron, and Mrs. Delacroix said, "You're in time, though. They're still talking away up there."

Mrs. Hutchinson craned her neck to see through the crowd and found her husband and children standing near the front. She tapped Mrs. Delacroix on the arm as a farewell and began to make her way through the crowd. The people separated good-humoredly to let her through; two or three people said, in voices just loud enough to be heard across the crowd, "Here comes your Missus, Hutchinson," and "Bill, she made it after all." Mrs. Hutchinson reached her husband, and Mr. Summers, who had been waiting, said cheerfully, "Thought we were going to have to get on without you, Tessie." Mrs. Hutchinson said, grinning, "Wouldn't have me leave m'dishes in the sink, now, would you Joe?," and soft laughter ran through the crowd as the people stirred back into position after Mrs. Hutchinson's arrival.

"Well, now," Mr. Summers said soberly, "guess we better get started, get this over with, so's we can go back to work. Anybody ain't here?"

"Dunbar," several people said. "Dunbar, Dunbar."

Mr. Summers consulted his list. "Clyde Dunbar," he said. "That's right. He's broke his leg, hasn't he? Who's drawing for him?"

"Me, I guess," a woman said, and Mr. Summers turned to look at her. "Wife draws for her husband," Mr. Summers said. "Don't you have a grown boy to do it for you, Janey?" Although Mr. Summers and everyone else in the village knew the answer perfectly well, it was the business of the official of the lottery to ask such questions formally. Mr. Summers waited with an expression of polite interest while Mrs. Dunbar answered.

"Horace's not but sixteen yet," Mrs. Dunbar said regretfully. "Guess I gotta fill in for the old man this year."

"Right," Mr. Summers said. He made a note on the list he was holding. Then he asked, "Watson boy drawing this year?"

A tall boy in the crowd raised his hand. "Here," he said. "I'm drawing for m'mother and me." He blinked his eyes nervously and ducked his head as several voices in the crowd said things like "Good fellow, Jack," and "Glad to see your mother's got a man to do it."

"Well," Mr. Summers said, "guess that's everyone. Old Man Warner make it?"

"Here," a voice said, and Mr. Summers nodded.

A sudden hush fell on the crowd as Mr. Summers cleared his throat and looked at the list. "All ready?" he called. "Now, I'll read the names — heads of families first — and the men come up and take a paper out of the box. Keep the paper folded in your hand without looking at it until everyone has had a turn. Everything clear?"

The people had done it so many times that they only half listened to the directions; most of them were quiet, wetting their lips, not looking around.

Then Mr. Summers raised one hand high and said, "Adams." A man disengaged himself from the crowd and came forward. "Hi, Steve," Mr. Summers said, and Mr. Adams said, "Hi, Joe." They grinned at one another humorously and nervously. Then Mr. Adams reached into the black box and took out a folded paper. He held it firmly by one corner as he turned and went hastily back to his place in the crowd, where he stood a little apart from his family, not looking down at his hand.

"Allen," Mr. Summers said. "Anderson. . . . Bentham."

"Seems like there's no time at all between lotteries any more," Mrs. Delacroix said to Mrs. Graves in the back row. "Seems like we got through with the last one only last week."

"Time sure goes fast," Mrs. Graves said.

"Clark. . . . Delacroix."

"There goes my old man," Mrs. Delacroix said. She held her breath while her husband went forward.

"Dunbar," Mr. Summers said, and Mrs. Dunbar went steadily to the box while one of the women said, "Go on, Janey," and another said, "There she goes."

"We're next," Mrs. Graves said. She watched while Mr. Graves came around from the side of the box, greeted Mr. Summers gravely, and selected a slip of paper from the box. By now, all through the crowd there were men holding the small folded papers in their large hands, turning them over and over nervously. Mrs. Dunbar and her two sons stood together, Mrs. Dunbar holding the slip of paper.

"Harburt. . . . Hutchinson."

"Get up there, Bill," Mrs. Hutchinson said, and the people near her laughed.

"Jones."

"They do say," Mr. Adams said to Old Man Warner, who stood next to him, "that over in the north village they're talking of giving up the lottery."

Old Man Warner snorted. "Pack of crazy fools," he said. "Listening to the young folks, nothing's good enough for *them.* Next thing you know, they'll be wanting to go back to living in caves, nobody work any more, live *that* way for a while. Used to be a saying about 'Lottery in June, corn be heavy soon.' First thing you know, we'd all be eating stewed chickweed and acorns. There's *always* been a lottery," he added petulantly. "Bad enough to see young Joe Summers up there joking with everybody."

"Some places have already quit lotteries," Mrs. Adams said.

"Nothing but trouble in *that,*" Old Man Warner said stoutly. "Pack of young fools."

"Martin." And Bobby Martin watched his father go forward. "Overdyke. . . . Percy."

"I wish they'd hurry," Mrs. Dunbar said to her older son. "I wish they'd hurry."

"They're almost through," her son said.

"You get ready to run tell Dad," Mrs. Dunbar said.

Mr. Summers called his own name and then stepped forward precisely and selected a slip from the box. Then he called, "Warner."

"Seventy-seventh year I been in the lottery," Old Man Warner said as he went through the crowd. "Seventy-seventh time."

"Watson." The tall boy came awkwardly through the crowd. Someone said,

"Don't be nervous, Jack," and Mr. Summers said, "Take your time, son."

"Zanini."

After that, there was a long pause, a breathless pause, until Mr. Summers, holding his slip of paper in the air, said, "All right, fellows." For a minute, no one moved, and then all the slips of paper were opened. Suddenly, all the women began to speak at once, saying, "Who is it?," "Who's got it?," "Is it the Dunbars?," "Is it the Watsons?" Then the voices began to say, "It's Hutchinson. It's Bill," "Bill Hutchinson's got it."

"Go tell your father," Mrs. Dunbar said to her older son.

People began to look around to see the Hutchinsons. Bill Hutchinson was standing quiet, staring down at the paper in his hand. Suddenly, Tessie Hutchinson shouted to Mr. Summers, "You didn't give him time enough to take any paper he wanted. I saw you. It wasn't fair!"

"Be a good sport, Tessie," Mr. Delacroix called, and Mrs. Graves said, "All of us took the same chance."

"Shut up, Tessie," Bill Hutchinson said.

"Well, everyone," Mr. Summers said, "that was done pretty fast, and now we've got to be hurrying a little more to get done in time." He consulted his next list. "Bill," he said, "you draw for the Hutchinson family. You got any other households in the Hutchinsons?"

"There's Don and Eva," Mrs. Hutchinson yelled. "Make *them* take their chance!"

"Daughters draw with their husbands' families, Tessie," Mr. Summers said gently. "You know that as well as anyone else."

"It wasn't *fair*," Tessie said.

"I guess not, Joe," Bill Hutchinson said regretfully. "My daughter draws with her husband's family, that's only fair. And I've got no other family except the kids."

"Then, as far as drawing for families is concerned, it's you," Mr. Summers said in explanation, "and as far as drawing for households is concerned, that's you, too. Right?"

"Right," Bill Hutchinson said.

"How many kids, Bill?" Mr. Summers asked formally.

"Three," Bill Hutchinson said. "There's Bill, Jr., and Nancy, and little Dave. And Tessie and me."

"All right, then," Mr. Summers said. "Harry, you got their tickets back?"

Mr. Graves nodded and held up the slips of paper. "Put them in the box, then," Mr. Summers directed. "Take Bill's and put it in."

"I think we ought to start over," Mrs. Hutchinson said, as quietly as she could. "I tell you it wasn't *fair*. You didn't give him time enough to choose. Everybody saw that."

Mr. Graves had selected the five slips and put them in the box, and he dropped all the papers but those onto the ground, where the breeze caught them and lifted them off.

"Listen, everybody," Mrs. Hutchinson was saying to the people around her.

"Ready, Bill?" Mr. Summers asked, and Bill Hutchinson, with one quick glance around at his wife and children, nodded.

"Remember," Mr. Summers said, "take the slips and keep them folded until each person has taken one. Harry, you help little Dave." Mr. Graves took the hand of the little boy, who came willingly with him up to the box. "Take a paper out of the box, Davy," Mr. Summers said. Davy put his hand into the box and laughed. "Take just *one* paper," Mr. Summers said. "Harry, you hold it for him." Mr. Graves took the child's hand and removed the folded paper from the tight fist and held it while little Dave stood next to him and looked up at him wonderingly.

"Nancy next," Mr. Summers said. Nancy was twelve, and her school friends breathed heavily as she went forward, switching her skirt, and took a slip daintily from the box. "Bill, Jr.," Mr. Summers said, and Billy, his face red and his feet over-large, nearly knocked the box over as he got a paper out. "Tessie," Mr. Summers said. She hesitated for a minute, looking around defiantly, and then set her lips and went up to the box. She snatched a paper out and held it behind her.

"Bill," Mr. Summers said, and Bill Hutchinson reached into the box and felt around, bringing his hand out at last with the slip of paper in it.

The crowd was quiet. A girl whispered, "I hope it's not Nancy," and the sound of the whisper reached the edges of the crowd.

"It's not the way it used to be," Old Man Warner said clearly. "People ain't the way they used to be."

"All right," Mr. Summers said. "Open the papers. Harry, you open little Dave's."

Mr. Graves opened the slip of paper and there was a general sigh through the crowd as he held it up and everyone could see that it was blank. Nancy and Bill, Jr., opened theirs at the same time, and both beamed and laughed, turning around to the crowd and holding their slips of paper above their heads.

"Tessie," Mr. Summers said. There was a pause, and then Mr. Summers looked at Bill Hutchinson, and Bill unfolded his paper and showed it. It was blank.

"It's Tessie," Mr. Summers said, and his voice was hushed. "Show us her paper, Bill."

Bill Hutchinson went over to his wife and forced the slip of paper out of her hand. It had a black spot on it, the black spot Mr. Summers had made the night before with the heavy pencil in the coal-company office. Bill Hutchinson held it up, and there was a stir in the crowd.

"All right, folks," Mr. Summers said. "Let's finish quickly."

Although the villagers had forgotten the ritual and lost the original black box, they still remembered to use stones. The pile of stones the boys had made earlier was ready; there were stones on the ground with the blowing scraps of paper that had come out of the box. Mrs. Delacroix selected a stone so large she had to pick it up with both hands and turned to Mrs. Dunbar. "Come on," she said. "Hurry up."

Mrs. Dunbar had small stones in both hands, and she said, gasping for breath, "I can't run at all. You'll have to go ahead and I'll catch up with you."

The children had stones already, and someone gave little Davey Hutchinson a few pebbles.

Tessie Hutchinson was in the center of a cleared space by now, and she held her hands out desperately as the villagers moved in on her. "It isn't fair," she said. A stone hit her on the side of the head.

Old Man Warner was saying, "Come on, come on, everyone." Steve Adams was in the front of the crowd of villagers, with Mrs. Graves beside him.

"It isn't fair, it isn't right," Mrs. Hutchinson screamed, and then they were upon her.

Exercises

1. Who is the protagonist? Why? Is the prize escape from death or death itself?

2. Examine the author's view of tradition. What does it have to do with conflict and theme?

3. What important statement about the human condition does the story make? What important events and details lead you to this conclusion?

4. Identify the stock characters. Why are there so many one-dimensional characters?

5. How is suspense achieved?

6. Compare the person of Tessie before she is selected for sacrifice and after she is chosen.

7. What special effects might have been gained or lost had the story been told from the point of view of one of the characters?

8. How does the author lend plausibility to an idea that seems improbable?

9. Comment on your emotional and your intellectual reaction to the story.

Topics for Writing

1. Compare the role of the entire community as protagonist with the role of the four men as composite protagonist in Crane's "The Open Boat."

2. Seymour Lainoff ("Jackson's 'The Lottery,'" *Explicator,* 12 [March 1954], item 34) sees the theme of the story as a commentary on the nature of human behavior. He describes that nature as "civilized" on the surface but "savage" within the depths. Using evidence from the story, write an essay that supports this statement.

3. Discuss the story as one dealing with "scapegoating."

Selected Bibliography   Shirley Jackson

Brooks, Cleanth, and Robert P. Warren. *Understanding Fiction,* 2nd ed. New York: Appleton-Century-Crofts, 1955.

Gordon, Caroline, and Allen Tate. *The House of Fiction,* 2nd ed. New York: Scribner's, 1960.

Nebeker, Helen E. " 'The Lottery': Symbolic Tour de Force." *American Literature,* 46 (1974), 100–107.

Robert Fontaine[1] *(1912–   )*

Six Beauties

My Uncle Desmonde announced abruptly one day that he expected to die presently. This was a common announcement in our family, of course, and no one paid much attention.

Desmonde, however, persisted, and in time we began to consider his case with a certain amount of seriousness.

"It is true," Papa said, "that the blood pressure of Desmonde is greatly elevated."

"That's dangerous," *Maman* said. "You never can tell in cases like that. I hate to mention it, but you remember Jean Dubuc went like that."

"Jean Dubuc," Papa observed, "went *comme ça*[2] only after he had filled himself with ale and fallen into a lake."

"Still," *Maman* insisted, "if his blood pressure had been low . . ."

She shook her head as if to say we might still have had Jean Dubuc with us.

"The sideboard of Desmonde is forever empty," I said.

"Yes," my father agreed. "He eats all the time. Still, it is better than robbing a bank or marrying a woman with twelve children."

"Who is doing that?" *Maman* inquired nervously.

"No one," Papa replied. "I merely make a comparison."

"Anyway," *Maman* said, "to eat so much rich food as Desmonde does is to encourage sudden death."

A few days later, surely enough, Desmonde had a fainting spell. He fell suddenly to the floor while reaching for a bottle of *vin ordinaire*.[3] For a while we left him undisturbed, thinking him merely tired.

Soon Papa noticed, as did I, that Desmonde's face had become a peculiar color, and we called the doctor.

The doctor immediately ordered Desmonde to a diet of wet toast and warm milk plus, here and there, a mushed egg, barely cooked.

It was like taking wings from a bird.

"Begone, vulture!" Desmonde exclaimed. "The medicine is worse than the malady."

"Take my word for it," the doctor said. "Your blood pressure is like the weather in Ecuador."

"Go! faker, quack, medicine man."

The doctor shrugged and fastened up his small black bag.

"My fee is four dollars," he said coldly.

"Why?" Desmonde inquired with narrowed eyes.

"Why?" the doctor repeated, puzzled.

"Yes. Did I steal your stethoscope?"

"Very well," the doctor agreed. "Three dollars. Let us have no arguments. I don't feel very well myself."

Desmonde handed him two dollars.

---

1. Robert Fontaine was raised in Ottawa, Canada; his bilingual family background is evidenced in this story.
2. *Comme ça:* Like that.
3. *Vin ordinaire:* Ordinary wine.

"You may keep the change," he explained, leading the medico to the door. "Believe me," said the doctor, "I hope you drop dead before I get home." When the doctor was gone, Desmonde regarded us all plaintively.

"Why," he inquired, "does he not wish me to eat hay, which will dry me up and make my blood pressure zero?"

He continued to eat highly spiced foods and to drink too much wine and to insist daily that he was dying and that he did not care since to live on wet toast, warm milk, and mushed eggs was a fate worse than death.

After a while the wine and the food and the pressure seemed to rise to Desmonde's head, because he began to confide to us the strange manner in which he wished to die. Only my mother, whom he did not wish to shock too much, remained innocent of his dream.

We quickly called a family conference.

Desmonde was not present, so we spoke freely around the table with the red-fringed cloth.

"Consider," Uncle Felix announced, after the preliminaries had been dispensed with, "the scandal."

"The scandal," Papa replied, "is more important to you than the death of your brother. Consider *this*. If he remains quietly seated on the wet toast and mushed eggs he will live perhaps to a great age. If he attempts to carry out his plan, his teeth will surely stop aching permanently!"

Felix stretched out his hands helplessly.

"Make no mistake; he will kill himself, anyway. Is it necessary he do it with such fervor and publicity?"

He looked at me, as if for help. I shrugged.

"I don't know," I said. I did not know much about these things and I was interested only in the outcome, as at a cinema serial.

My mother spoke now, gently: "If he is bent on dying, then he should have his last wishes granted, I think."

Uncle Louis scratched his red nose.

"*J'en suis tout bleu,*" [4] he said.

I sat up at this. For Uncle Louis to be flabbergasted was indeed a rarity.

"It is also doubtful," Felix explained, pointing a fork at Papa, "that Desmonde can find six of the most beautiful girls in Canada for such a venture."

"Pouf!" Papa scoffed. "Desmonde can hire artists' models. Who is more beautiful? What is the difference to an artists' model if she poses for a picture or eats dinner? It is enough if she receives her fee and is not harmed in any way. *N'est-ce pas?*" [5]

"Why," I inquired earnestly, "should Desmonde harm anybody?"

"You are too young," Papa replied. "How old are you?"

"Haha! *Mon père!* [6] He asks me how many years I have!"

"I cannot remember everything," my father said. "Anyway, beyond a doubt you are too young to know."

Uncle Louis ran his fingers around the curves of his ears.

"And Desmonde is too old," he said. "So we do not have to worry about that."

4. *J'en suis tout bleu:* I am flabbergasted.

5. *N'est-ce-pas?:* Is it not?

6. *Mon père!:* My father!

"Desmonde is not so old," *Maman* observed from across the room.

"He is past one hundred in the glands," Felix said. "With a tree it is the rings of the trunk, with a horse it is the teeth, with a man it is the glands."

"And with a woman?" *Maman* laughed.

"A woman," said Papa, "is never over thirty-nine. If she is your wife, she is never over thirty."

"Anyway," said *Maman,* flushing with pleasure, "Desmonde is not so old. He is still young enough to enjoy the normal activities of life. I don't see him in a wheel chair."

"Listen to her sing!" Papa chuckled. "She does not know of what we are speaking, yet she sings and sings. She is like a bird. A bird sings and has no idea of what it is singing."

"Then *tell* me," my mother said coldly. She put down a pair of my knicker-bockers she was mending. "I know, of course, that there is a secret."

My father looked around carefully at the others. There seemed to be no objection, so he said: "Desmonde has it in his head to die, as you know. He now has arrived at the point where he wishes to die in style. It is not enough for my brother to merely die. With him there must be a pageant."

"If he dies in the true Christian manner what is the difference?" *Maman* asked.

"Sing on!" Papa laughed. "The true Christian manner, eh? 'The Beautiful Ending,' eh? Do not imagine any such thing to yourself, my hummingbird."

"Hummingbirds," I said, "do not sing."

"With their feet," Felix corrected, "they sing."

"Are we," my father asked, somewhat irked, "to discuss the beautiful death of Desmonde or the feet of hummingbirds?"

Everyone was silent. My father spoke once more to my mother: "Desmonde wishes to have a fine dinner on his last day on earth. The main dish of this dinner will consist of brook trout, whole brook trout cooked in wine and served with iced grapes. There will also be hot cheesecake, truffles, leek soup, and so forth. The Last Menu is quite complete, believe me!"

Maman moistened her lips.

"It sounds good," she said.

"The rest," said Papa ominously, "does not sound so good."

He looked around at the others, and they all smiled mysteriously.

Papa's glance fell on me again and he raised his brows with a certain hesitation.

"How old did you say you were?"

"Since I have no glands," I laughed, "what difference?"

"Hmm," murmured my father. "Well, you are too young for this to harm you. Eh, *mes frères?*" [7]

He looked around at the others again. They nodded in agreement. I took a deep, satisfactory breath.

Papa went on: "Desmonde wishes, you understand, to have a wine with each course. The finest wines, and the most correct. He has not yet named the wines, since he is not on certain ground when it comes to the wines, which must be exactly right. This banquet, you see, is to be exquisite in all respects. How many times in his life does a man die? Eh?"

---

7. *Mes frères:* My brothers.

"I myself," interrupted Felix, "am a good judge of wines. It is a wonder Desmonde does not consult me. To judge wines one needs a tongue of the rarest sort. To judge exquisite wines one needs an exquisite tongue."

"One needs also the exquisite wines," Papa laughed.

"To tell you the truth," *Maman* said. "It all sounds quite pleasant to me."

"Ah, but wait . . . wait, my dove. Imagine *this* to yourself? Desmonde wishes as his dinner companions the six most beautiful girls in Canada. Or perhaps not the six most beautiful. Perhaps six *of* the most beautiful. Anyway, six beauties to dine with him while he overeats, elevates the blood pressure, and dies. Ha!"

"And why not?" *Maman* smiled. "Beautiful girls, I understand, are the best appetizers at dinner."

"And why not!" my father mocked, leaning back in his chair and winking at the others.

"Listen to her!" Felix chided.

"Oho!" said Uncle Louis, "they are moving the furniture out of her head. Soon will come in the butterflies!"

Papa now spoke softly and mysteriously.

"It is the way Desmonde wishes the beautiful girls to dress!"

"And how is that?" *Maman* encouraged.

My father took a deep breath and swallowed hard.

"They must wear," he said in a precise tone, "a large picture hat of the garden-party type. The hat they must keep on while eating."

He spoke slowly, relishing the details of his presentation.

Maman said: "That is the old fashion, but it is, nonetheless, charming."

"Ah, charming, eh? So! Imagine this, then: they must wear long black gloves which reach up past the elbows, and long black silk stockings of what is called the opera length."

He showed with a gesture on his trousers about where the stockings would reach.

Maman became slightly pink, but she spoke gaily: "It all sounds very delightful. What else?"

"What else what?" Papa asked, grinning broadly.

"What else must the beautiful girls wear?"

"Haha!" laughed Felix. "What else!"

"Oho!" said Louis. "What else!"

I squirmed in my chair anxiously.

"Well," I demanded, "*what* else?"

"You are too young," Papa said.

Everybody laughed at this, except, of course, *Maman*.

"I do wish you would tell me what else," she remarked crisply.

Papa leaned back and downed a large glass of red wine. When he was finished he wiped his lips slowly with the serviette and replied calmly: "Nothing."

"Nothing?" *Maman* repeated.

"Nothing," said Papa, Louis, and Felix in unison.

There was a long silence. *Maman* spoke after a while and without looking at us.

"Perhaps," she suggested uneasily and with a sharp and wondering glance at me, "perhaps we had better have the Reverend McKintosh speak to Desmonde."

"McKintosh?" repeated Felix. "McKintosh? There was a McKintosh who invented a mechanism for tipping the hat at a lady without removing the hands from the pockets. It worked, I believe, by steam. Although this seems impossible. Then there was . . ."

"The minister of the Presbyterian church, of course," *Maman* stated. "Where *bibi*[8] used to go to Sunday school. *Bibi,* perhaps, had better start again."

"In the winter," I agreed. "When come the Christmas parties."

"No McKintosh," Papa said. "*Mais non!*[9] McKintosh will drone to Desmonde that he must live the rest of his life on scones and breakfast tea and read, every day, a dozen chapters from the New Testament. To sit on wet toast first . . . and then to lay on scones[10] and tea, reading the New Testament . . . bah! Why should a man live at all if that is what he must do? Also, a Presbyterian would not be expected to know about the subtleties of wines, truffles, hot cheesecake, and beautiful girls in picture hats and opera-length, black silk stockings."

"Who then?" asked *Maman.*

"Only a priest," my father replied, "would know if this is good. A priest is compassionate. A priest has the understanding of human frailty without the dryness in the heart of the Protestant clergy."

"Ah. *Bon! Bon!*"[11] exclaimed Felix. "Always, in the history of the world, the priest has stood . . ."

"Good," interrupted Louis. "Father Sebastian!"

"Father Sebastian it is," agreed Felix. "Father Sebastian knows everything . . ."

"Except which is the right way to Paradise," Louis amended.

"Tomorrow, then," Papa said, "I will invite Father Sebastian to discuss with us Uncle Desmonde's farewell banquet."

We were, of course, all gathered together while my father told the story to Father Sebastian.

The Father listened attentively, solemnly tapping a finger to his under lip every now and then, and murmuring frequent "ahs."

"And so," my father concluded, "we wish your advice. What do you think of it? Is it bad? Is it an evil thing to do? Or is it good?"

The priest reflected a long time, crossing and uncrossing his legs, tapping his mouth thoughtfully, looking often into nowhere, dreamily, a faint smile flickering on his shining face.

"Hmmmmmm," he murmured finally. I tugged nervously on my stocking. My mother moistened her lips. Papa lit a cigar, and Felix and Louis stared fixedly at Father Sebastian.

"Hmmmmmmmmmmmmmm!" he repeated. "Wine . . . brook trout . . . truffles . . . hot cheesecake . . . iced grapes . . . and so forth. Hmmmm . . . picture hats . . . black gloves to the elbow . . . stockings of the opera length . . . Hmmmmmm."

"So?" questioned my father, eagerly and solemnly. "Will it be good?"

"It will all depend . . ." Father Sebastian ordained at length.

---

8. *Bibi:* Way of addressing a small boy, meaning dear or darling.
9. *Mais non:* But no.
10. scones: Flat, round, leavened cakes.
11. *Bon!:* Good!

"On what?" asked my father nervously.

"On the choice of wines," Father Sebastian concluded.

Exercises

1. Retell the main points of the story.

2. Characterize Uncle Desmonde.

3. Does the protagonist win or lose? How?

4. Explain the roles of Maman and Uncle Felix.

5. How is suspense achieved?

6. What is the central theme and how is it revealed?

7. Do you find the story amusing? What makes it so?

Topics for Writing

1. Compare the means Fontaine uses to achieve humor with those Thurber relies on in "The Catbird Seat."

2. Discuss Fontaine's method of characterizing Uncle Desmonde.

3. Analyze Maman's sense of humor. What do the things that amuse her reveal about her character?

5. STYLE

A good writer evolves an individualized way of telling a story. **Style** is the author's distinct manner of writing; it is how the author expresses his or her materials. Style differentiates one author from another.

Broadly speaking, style comprises a writer's every technique and application of language. In addition to such aspects of language as diction, syntax, dialogue, imagery, allusion, tone, irony, and symbol (to list a few), style includes all the elements explored in previous chapters: development of plot, delineation of characters, execution of point of view, and treatment of theme.

A narrower definition of style describes it as a writer's management of language.

The author's choice of words, or **diction,** can ordinarily be classified as either formal or informal. An author may rely on high-flown and esoteric words, use foreign terms, or favor a richly connotative vocabulary and devices often associated with poetry — simile, metaphor, alliteration, personification, and so on. Another writer's diction may be drawn from everyday discourse, lean on denotative words and terms more popular than learned, and borrow from dialect and slang.

For instance, William Dean Howells, an American editor, critic, and novelist who was also a friend of Mark Twain, indulged in high-flown diction and ornate phraseology. He has one character "striving to propitiate the conductor by a dastardly amiability"; another shifting himself from one foot to another "with saltatory briskness"; and others uttering such expressions as "I would make a *point d'appui*," "I'm a *huite de mon siècle*," "I am not a mere *doppelgänger*," "*sotto voce* to her husband," and "O Parthian Shaft!"

A more informal style would favor *learned* or *smart* over *erudite; stout* or *fat* over *corpulent* or *obese; drunk* or the slang *smashed* or *plastered* over *inebriated;* and *cop* or *fuzz* over *police officer* or *gendarme.*

As a contrast to the work of Howells, let us look at Sherwood Anderson's simple vocabulary when he has a young boy narrate the events of "I Want to Know Why": "There isn't anything so lovely and clean and full of spunk and honest and everything as some race horses." After watching Jerry Tillford kissing the "tall rotten-looking woman" in the "bad woman house," the boy narrates: "Then, all of a sudden, I began to hate that man. I wanted to scream and rush in the room and kill him." Note that while the boy's words about horses are simple, they are not very precise. We get a sense of his feeling about "some race horses" rather than a description of any of them. The boy is telling us not what a racehorse is but what it connotes to him; the adjectives *lovely* and *clean* express his private associations with the word *racehorse.*

However, many words have **connotations** — implied or suggested meanings beyond the denotation, or dictionary definition — that are generally known and accepted. For example, *slender* and *emaciated* mean approximately the same thing denotatively, but how sharply different are their connotative meanings! *Slender* suggests someone slight of frame in a polite and graceful manner, but *emaciated* implies a wasting away of the body and is not at all attractive.

Sentence structure, or **syntax,** the arrangement of words in sentences, is as important to a writer's style as diction is. Sentences may be elaborate, making use of balance and parallel and periodic structure. Balance is exemplified by this line:

> To err is human, to forgive divine.
> *Alexander Pope,* "An Essay on Man"

Parallel structure characterizes this sentence fragment:

> . . . and then he was shooting at the bull as he moved away, hearing the bullets whunk into him, emptying his rifle at him as he moved steadily away, finally remembering to get his shots forward into the shoulder . . .
> *Ernest Hemingway,* "The Short Happy
> Life of Francis Macomber"

Periodic structure — that is, putting the most important words just before the period — gives emphasis here.

> On the breast of her gown, in red cloth, surrounded with an elaborate embroidery and fantastic flourishes of gold thread, appeared the letter A.
> *Nathaniel Hawthorne,* The Scarlet Letter

At the other extreme are sentences constructed in the simplest way:

> I had shut the door to. Then I turned around, and there he was. I used to be scared of him all the time, he tanned me so much. I reckoned I was scared now, too; but in a minute I see I was mistaken.
> *Mark Twain,* The Adventures of Huckleberry Finn

Of course, an author is likely to vary the length and complexity of sentences, if only to avoid monotony. His or her choices may also depend on the character who is speaking or on the narrator through whose consciousness we experience the action. But despite such variations, there is usually enough of a pattern in an author's choices to distinguish them from the choices of others. By taking note of this pattern, we learn to recognize and describe a given author's style.

Two writers with sharply contrasting styles are Ernest Hemingway and Henry James. Observe the obvious differences in their diction and syntax in the following two sentences, the first from Hemingway's "The Short Happy Life of Francis Macomber" and the second from James's "The Real Thing."

> The car was going a wild forty-five miles an hour across the open and as Macomber watched, the buffalo got bigger and bigger until he could see the gray, hairless, scabby look of one huge bull and how his neck was a part of his shoulders and the shiny black of his horns as he galloped a little behind

the others that were strung out in that steady plunging gait; and then, the car swaying as though it had just jumped a road, they drew up close and he could see the plunging hugeness of the bull, and the dust in his parsely haired hide, the wide boss of horn and his outstretched, wide-nostrilled muzzle, and he was raising his rifle when Wilson shouted, "Not from the car, you fool!" and he had no fear, only hatred of Wilson, while the brakes clamped on and the car skidded, plowing sideways to an almost stop and Wilson was out on one side and he on the other, stumbling as his feet hit the still speeding by of the earth, and then he was shooting at the bull as he moved away, hearing the bullets whunk into him, emptying his rifle at him as he moved steadily away, finally remembering to get his shots forward into the shoulder, and as he fumbled to re-load, he saw the bull was down.

I hadn't then visited his country, nor was I proficient in his tongue; but as he was not so meanly constituted — what Italian is? — as to depend only on that member for expression he conveyed to me, in familiar but graceful mimicry, that he was in search of exactly the employment in which the lady before me was engaged.

Hemingway's sentence is certainly much longer, but if you examine it, you will find familiar, concrete, monosyllabic words and short, direct, uncomplicated clauses that could have been short, independent sentences but instead are joined by the connective *and*. James, on the other hand, employs a rather formal vocabulary and complex sentence structure, interrupted by modification and qualification. Further reading of Hemingway and James shows us that these stylistic differences are characteristic of the two writers.

The speech of characters, used profusely by some authors and sparingly by others, serves to advance action, explain motivation, and reveal thoughts and feelings. It is commonly described as natural, lively, stilted, witty, or dull. Unquestionably, **dialogue** must be appropriate to the region, profession or trade, character, and state of mind of the speaker.

In "I Want to Know Why," Anderson clearly employs the speaking mannerisms of a fifteen-year-old boy in 1919.

Gee! I ached to see that race and those two horses run, ached and dreaded it too.

In "The Magic Barrel," Bernard Malamud captures Yiddish speech patterns.

"I have for you a first-class bride."

"Yiddishe kinder, what can I say to somebody that he is not interested in high school teachers? So what then you are interested?"

In "A Worn Path," which you will find in this chapter, Eudora Welty re-creates the dialect of an old black woman in Mississippi.

"Old woman," she said to herself, "that black dog come up out of the weeds to stall you off, and now there he sitting on his fine tail, smiling at you."

When you come to read that story, the woman's name, Phoenix, should give you pause. In bestowing that name on her protagonist, Welty is making an **allusion** to a mythological phenomenon, and you should look up the name in a dictionary and consider its significance for the story. Allusions are general or specific hints or references to persons, places, events, or objects that exist outside the time and space of the story. Authors use them to support their views or heighten the meaning of character and action. Their chief sources are the Bible, mythology, literature, and history. In another story in this chapter, James Joyce's "Araby," we can find allusions to Irish history and to the ritual of the Roman Cathloic Church. F. Scott Fitzgerald draws on the Bible for the title of his story "Babylon Revisited," Carson McCullers, in "A Tree, a Rock, a Cloud," hints at a well-known poem by Samuel Taylor Coleridge, "The Rime of the Ancient Mariner," by having the transient's message to the boy parallel Coleridge's mariner's message to the wedding guest.

If we read carefully, we can usually discern a writer's attitude toward his or her subject matter and readers. **Tone** identifies or describes that attitude. It may be humorous, nostalgic, affectionate, serious, melancholy, sarcastic, elated, angry, or have as many other variations as there are emotions. Just as the painter conveys tone with shades of color and light, so the writer conveys tone with choice of words and their arrangement in sentences.

Can you easily identify the tone of these two excerpts from stories in earlier chapters? What specific words, phrases, and clauses provide you with clues in each instance?

Mr. Martin could no longer doubt that the finger was on his beloved department. Her pickaxe was on the upswing, poised for the first blow. It had not come yet; he had received no blue memo from the enchanted Mr. Fitweiler bearing nonsensical instructions deriving from the obscene woman. . . . Mr. Martin stood up in his living room, still holding his milk glass. "Gentlemen of the jury," he said to himself, "I demand the death penalty for this horrible person."

    James Thurber, "The Catbird Seat"

The three brothers and the sister sat round the desolate breakfast table, attempting some sort of desultory consultation. The morning's post had given the final tap to the family fortune, and all was over. The dreary dining-room itself, with its heavy mahogany furniture, looked as if it were waiting to be done away with.

    D. H. Lawrence, "The Horse Dealer's Daughter"

Irony is a relatively simple and economical device by which a writer can suggest tone or meaning without elaborate explanations. It involves both an incongruity and the opposite of what one expects.

When using **verbal irony**, a speaker says one thing but means another. In "The Catbird Seat," when Mr. Fitweiler tells Mr. Martin that Mrs. Barrows has "worked hard" and "suffered a severe breakdown," Martin says, "I am very sorry, sir." Since he has engineered her downfall and has shown no signs of remorse, he is obviously saying the opposite of what he feels.

An author creates **dramatic irony** by giving readers a piece of knowledge that a character lacks, so they realize that the character's actions or expectations are inappropriate to the actual circumstances. For instance, we know that Mr. Martin has judged Mrs. Barrows, found her guilty, and "sentenced" her. Mrs. Barrows does not know this, however, and so she walks into the trap he baits for her. In her ignorance, she acts in a way that ensures her dismissal from her job, and we watch her move unwittingly to that outcome. Here, of course, dramatic irony serves a comic purpose, but as you will see when you read *Oedipus Rex* and *Othello* in the drama section, it can also have tragic implications.

Another type of irony, **irony of situation,** involves a discrepancy between what one expects or deems appropriate and what actually happens. In "The Magic Barrel," the protagonist, Leo Finkle, a theological student, does not find love until he sees Stella Salzman, a prostitute; in "A Rose for Emily," readers, as well as Miss Emily's neighbors, learn with shock that she slept for years with the corpse of her lover in a bridal chamber that had become his tomb.

We might also mention **irony of fate, or cosmic irony.** This occurs in stories in which God, fate, or some cosmic power seems to control human events, arranging them in such a way that the characters' hopes are raised and then cruelly dashed or mocked. The four men in "The Open Boat" survive the hardships they suffer in the dinghy after their shipwreck. But when they are within reach of land and swimming to safety, the oiler, who seemed the likeliest to make it to shore, dies in the shallows.

Though we often associate **imagery** with poetry, it is very much a part of fiction as well. Imagery and figures of speech are fully discussed in Chapters 9 and 10 of the poetry section, and you should consult those chapters for a thorough understanding of both images and figurative language. All we will say here is that *imagery* is the term we apply to words used to communicate a sensory experience or to render a mental or emotional experience by appealing to our senses. An image can be visual ("Each house had a narrow collar of dirt around it," from "Everything That Rises Must Converge"), auditory ("The air was full of that deep clangour of bells," from "Roman Fever"), tactile ("The cold air stung him," from "Araby"), or indeed involve any of the senses.

In "Everything That Rises Must Converge," Julian's mental and emotional state is evoked by an image: "The frustration of having to wait on the bus as well as ride on it began to creep up his neck like a hot hand." This illustrates rather well how imagery is created by figures of speech. The most common types of figures of speech in fiction are *simile, metaphor,* and *personification.* In brief, *simile* involves an explicit comparison between dissimilar things, generally using *like* or *as.* For instance, in the quoted sentence, "frustration" creeps "like a hot hand." In "The King of the Bingo Game," a short story by Ralph Ellison which is included in this chapter, the protagonist at one point feels as though he has become "like a long thin black wire that was being stretched and wound upon the bingo wheel." (When a simile is elaborated beyond the basic comparison, as here, it is called an *extended simile.*) If Ellison had not used *like* but written "he was a thin black wire," we would have had a *metaphor,* a figure that involves an implicit comparison between dissimilar things, suggesting an identification of one with the other. Metaphors can be created with verbs as well as nouns. In "The Chrysanthemums," as the story opens, "The thick willow scrub along the river *flamed* with sharp and positive yellow leaves." In the example from "Everything That Rises," the verb *creep* gives concreteness to the abstraction *frustration.* Later in that story, when Julian's mother is near death, "her eyes *raked* his face."

When a figure of speech gives human attributes to an abstraction or an inanimate object, it is called *personification.* In "A Worn Path," the "dead corn" through which Phoenix must make her way "whispered." And in our initial example from "Everything That Rises," the abstract noun *frustration,* having gained both concreteness and animation from the verb *creep,* is personified by the simile "like a hot hand." Broadly speaking, personification also covers instances in which the author gives an inanimate object, a force of nature, or an abstraction the characteristics of a living being that is not human. "The Magic Barrel" yields a rather charming humorous example. Leo Finkle looks out the window during the matchmaker's first visit:

> He now observed the round white moon, moving high in the sky through a cloud menagerie, and watched with half-open mouth as it penetrated a huge hen, and dropped out of her like an egg laying itself.

Since the figure here is amplified and elaborated, it too can be termed *extended.*

Simile, metaphor, and personification (in the broader sense of the term) all appear in the following passage from "The Open Boat" — more than once. How many similes and examples of personification can you discover in Crane's paragraph?

> A seat in this boat was not unlike a seat upon a bucking broncho, and, by the same token, a broncho is not much smaller. The craft pranced and reared, and plunged like an animal. As each wave came, and she rose for it, she seemed like a horse making a fence outrageously high. The manner of her scramble over these walls of water is a mystic thing, and, moreover, at the top of them were ordinarily these problems in white water, the foam racing down from the summit of each wave, requiring a new leap, and a leap from the air. Then, after scornfully bumping a crest, she would incline, and arrive bobbing and nodding in front of the next menace.

Not only in this passage but throughout "The Open Boat," Crane uses personification to intensify the effects of his imagery: "the lighthouse had been growing slowly larger"; later, "the distant lighthouse reared high"; and "slowly and beautifully the land loomed out of the sea." He also gives the wind a voice, he compares fate to an "old ninny-woman," and (toward the end of the story) he describes nature as not "cruel; nor beneficent, nor treacherous, nor wise" but "indifferent."

Like imagery, **symbols** work economically to heighten the meaning of a story by means of suggestion. A symbol is a word, an object, a place, a person, or an incident that stands for itself as well as for something else. A symbol, then, is both itself and something more significant than itself.

Symbols abound in many of our stories. Some we may miss; some we may misinterpret; and some the writer may not have selected consciously. But if symbols are recognizable as symbols, and if they fit the context of the story, they can emphasize its salient points as well as underscore, and even reveal, its meaning.

Frequently names of people and places serve as symbols. Phoenix ("A Worn Path") symbolizes love, endurance, immortality, and even perhaps Christ. Titles also may represent larger meanings. "A Worn Path" suggests, at least to an older person, the much-traveled road of life and all its trials and tribulations. "A Tree, a Rock, a Cloud" incorporates the transient's message concerning the science of love. In considering the title "A Rose for Emily," we need to ask why Faulkner offers Emily a *rose,* a symbol of love. In "The Horse Dealer's Daughter," doesn't the pond become a place of baptism, and the story itself a tale of rebirth?

Steinbeck's story "The Chrysanthemums" yields an opulence of sexual imagery and color, representing the passionate desires of Elisa: the sharp-pointed stars "driven into the body — hot and sharp and — lovely," the *blood* that comes from broken noses at fights, scratching her skin *red* after scrubbing herself once the tinker has gone, and the *wine* that will suffice.

Finally, the young newspaper boy in "A Tree, a Rock, a Cloud" enters a café "friendly and bright" from the outside, where it is raining and dark. Symbolically, the boy enters a place where enlightenment is possible, where an important lesson in life can be learned. He comes from the outside world, a place unenlightened, gloomy, and perhaps even sinister. At the beginning of the story the boy "raised the right flap up over his pink little ear," perhaps to hear something significant; at the end of the story, the boy "pulled down the right flap of his helmet," which signals the end of the transient's revelations.

An entire chapter in the poetry section, Chapter 13, is devoted to symbol and allusion, while Chapter 14 deals at length with irony and tone. Refer to those chapters, too, as you try to evaluate style.

One measure of success and effectiveness of a story as a work of art is the degree of coherence it achieves. The prize in this case is **unity,** the coalescing of all the components we have discussed in these chapters — components of style, structure, and content — into a design where all the parts fit together in an unforced, seemingly natural way. That kind of design is often described as an organic whole. Within it, each element has a capacity to unite, react, and interact with other elements in order to achieve the author's artistic purpose. The title may be linked with the protagonist and the setting, which in turn may help characterize the protagonist. All three of these components, as well as others we have discussed, may have a bearing on the conflict and its progress toward the climax. Their roles and their significance grow clear in the resolution, which not only reveals or sums up the meaning of the story but also lets us see the nature of its total design. And that design, as well as the meaning it embodies, is communicated to us through the shape and texture of language.

Questions for Evaluating Style

1. What are the outstanding stylistic features of the story?

2. Do you like the author's style? Why or why not?

3. Is the style formal, informal, simple, complex, literal, figurative, concrete, abstract, richly suggestive, or original? What characteristics of its diction and syntax place it in one of these categories?

4. Does the author make use of humor, irony, or symbolism? In what way and for what purpose?

5. Are you moved emotionally or intellectually?

6. Do all components cohere to form an organic whole?

7. What, in your opinion, are the author's strengths and weaknesses?

Ernest Hemingway (1899–1961)

Hills Like White Elephants

The hills across the valley of the Ebro[1] were long and white. On this side there was no shade and no trees and the station was between two lines of rails in the sun. Close against the side of the station there was the warm shadow of the building and a curtain, made of strings of bamboo beads, hung across the open door into the bar, to keep out flies. The American and the girl with him sat at a table in the shade, outside the building. It was very hot and the express from Barcelona would come in forty minutes. It stopped at this junction for two minutes and went on to Madrid.

"What should we drink?" the girl asked. She had taken off her hat and put it on the table.

"It's pretty hot," the man said.

"Let's drink beer."

"Dos cervezas," the man said into the curtain.

"Big ones?" a woman asked from the doorway.

"Yes. Two big ones."

The woman brought two glasses of beer and two felt pads. She put the felt pads and the beer glasses on the table and looked at the man and the girl. The girl was looking off at the line of hills. They were white in the sun and the country was brown and dry.

"They look like white elephants," she said.

"I've never seen one," the man drank his beer.

"No, you wouldn't have."

"I might have," the man said. "Just because you say I wouldn't have doesn't prove anything."

The girl looked at the bead curtain. "They've painted something on it," she said. "What does it say?"

"Anis del Toro. It's a drink."

"Could we try it?"

The man called "Listen" through the curtain. The woman came out from the bar.

"Four reales." [2]

"We want two Anis del Toro."

"With water?"

"Do you want it with water?"

"I don't know," the girl said. "Is it good with water?"

"It's all right."

---

1. Ebro: A river in northern Spain.   2. Reales: Spanish coins.

"You want them with water?" asked the woman.

"Yes, with water."

"It tastes like licorice," the girl said and put the glass down.

"That's the way with everything."

"Yes," said the girl. "Everything tastes of licorice. Especially all the things you've waited so long for, like absinthe."

"Oh, cut it out."

"You started it," the girl said. "I was being amused. I was having a fine time."

"Well, let's try and have a fine time."

"All right. I was trying. I said the mountains looked like white elephants. Wasn't that bright?"

"That was bright."

"I wanted to try this new drink. That's all we do, isn't it — look at things and try new drinks?"

"I guess so."

The girl looked across at the hills.

"They're lovely hills," she said. "They don't really look like white elephants. I just meant the coloring of their skin through the trees."

"Should we have another drink?"

"All right."

The warm wind blew the bead curtain against the table.

"The beer's nice and cool," the man said.

"It's lovely," the girl said.

"It's really an awfully simple operation, Jig," the man said. "It's not really an operation at all."

The girl looked at the ground the table legs rested on.

"I know you wouldn't mind it, Jig. It's really not anything. It's just to let the air in."

The girl did not say anything.

"I'll go with you and I'll stay with you all the time. They just let the air in and then it's all perfectly natural."

"Then what will we do afterward?"

"We'll be fine afterward. Just like we were before."

"What makes you think so?"

"That's the only thing that bothers us. It's the only thing that's made us unhappy."

The girl looked at the bead curtain, put her hand out and took hold of two of the strings of beads.

"And you think then we'll be all right and be happy."

"I know we will. You don't have to be afraid. I've known lots of people that have done it."

"So have I," said the girl. "And afterward they were all so happy."

"Well," the man said, "if you don't want to you don't have to. I wouldn't have you do it if you didn't want to. But I know it's perfectly simple."

"And you really want to?"

"I think it's the best thing to do. But I don't want you to do it if you don't really want to."

"And if I do it you'll be happy and things will be like they were and you'll love me?"

"I love you now. You know I love you."

"I know. But if I do it, then it will be nice again if I say things are like white elephants, and you'll like it?"

"I'll love it. I love it now but I just can't think about it. You know how I get when I worry."

"If I do it you won't ever worry?"

"I won't worry about that because it's perfectly simple."

"Then I'll do it. Because I don't care about me."

"What do you mean?"

"I don't care about me."

"Well, I care about you."

"Oh, yes. But I don't care about me. And I'll do it and then everything will be fine."

"I don't want you to do it if you feel that way."

The girl stood up and walked to the end of the station. Across, on the other side, were fields of grain and trees along the banks of the Ebro. Far away, beyond the river, were mountains. The shadow of a cloud moved across the field of grain and she saw the river through the trees.

"And we could have all this," she said. "And we could have everything and every day we make it more impossible."

"What did you say?"

"I said we could have everything."

"We can have everything."

"No, we can't."

"We can have the whole world."

"No, we can't."

"We can go everywhere."

"No, we can't. It isn't ours any more."

"It's ours."

"No, it isn't. And once they take it away, you never get it back."

"But they haven't taken it away."

"We'll wait and see."

"Come on back in the shade," he said. "You mustn't feel that way."

"I don't feel any way," the girl said. "I just know things."

"I don't want you to do anything that you don't want to do — "

"Nor that isn't good for me," she said. "I know. Could we have another beer?"

"All right. But you've got to realize — "

"I realize," the girl said. "Can't we maybe stop talking?"

They sat down at the table and the girl looked across at the hills on the dry side of the valley and the man looked at her and at the table.

"You've got to realize," he said, "that I don't want you to do it if you don't want to. I'm perfectly willing to go through with it if it means anything to you."

"Doesn't it mean anything to you? We could get along."

"Of course it does. But I don't want anybody but you. I don't want anyone else. And I know it's perfectly simple."

"Yes, you know it's perfectly simple."

"It's all right for you to say that, but I do know it."

"Would you do something for me now?"

"I'd do anything for you."

"Would you please please please please please please please stop talking?"

He did not say anything but looked at the bags against the wall of the station. There were labels on them from all the hotels where they had spent nights.

"But I don't want you to," he said. "I don't care anything about it."

"I'll scream," the girl said.

The woman came out through the curtains with two glasses of beer and put them down on the damp felt pads. "The train comes in five minutes," she said.

"What did she say?" asked the girl.

"That the train is coming in five minutes."

The girl smiled brightly at the woman, to thank her.

"I'd better take the bags over to the other side of the station," the man said. She smiled at him.

"All right. Then come back and we'll finish the beer."

He picked up the two heavy bags and carried them around the station to the other tracks. He looked up the tracks but could not see the train. Coming back, he walked through the barroom, where people waiting for the train were drinking. He drank an Anis at the bar and looked at the people. They were all waiting reasonably for the train. He went out through the bead curtain. She was sitting at the table and smiled at him.

"Do you feel better?" he asked.

"I feel fine," she said. "There's nothing wrong with me. I feel fine."

Exercises

1. Hemingway unfolds the story much like a playwright, with abundant dialogue and a few stage directions. He divulges little or no information about the characters, their appearance, background, and thoughts. What advantages and disadvantages do you see in this method?

2. To what extent is dialogue used? How would you describe it?

3. What does the girl eventually discover about the man?

4. By insisting on an abortion and avoiding the responsibility of rearing a family, what kind of life is the man accepting and rejecting?

5. Are the man and the girl compatible? What evidence do you find in the text to support your view?

6. Explain the significance of the setting.

7. Hemingway is noted for his use of understatement. Cite a few examples of this technique and comment on their effectiveness.

8. Does the title have any significance? Does it shed any light on the meaning of the story?

9. What is the theme of the story?

10. Many of Hemingway's early stories, including "Hills Like White Elephants," were rejected by magazine editors of the 1920s and called mere sketches or anecdotes. What elements or techniques of fiction are missing from this story if you compare it to other stories you have read so far?

Topics for Writing

1. Hemingway's story relies almost exclusively on dialogue, whereas Faulkner's "A Rose for Emily" depends very little on direct discourse. Compare and contrast the effects achieved by the two different techniques of storytelling.

2. Discuss the point of view in "Hills Like White Elephants." How well does it work in this story?

3. Describe Hemingway's style. What are its special traits in this story? Support your comments with specific references to the text.

Selected Bibliography   Ernest Hemingway

Bates, H. E. *The Modern Short Story: A Critical Survey.* London: Nelson, 1943.

DeFalco, Joseph. *The Hero in Hemingway's Short Stories.* Pittsburgh: University of Pittsburgh Press, 1963.

Friedman, Norman. "What Makes a Short Story Short?" *Modern Fiction Studies,* 4 (1958), 107–108.

Gurko, Leo. *Ernest Hemingway and the Pursuit of Heroism.* New York: Thomas Y. Crowell, 1968.

Hovey, Richard B. *Hemingway: The Inward Terrain.* Seattle: University of Washington Press, 1968.

Jain, S. P. " 'Hills Like White Elephants': A Study." *Indian Journal of American Studies,* 1, no. 3 (1970), 33–38.

Lid, Richard W. "Hemingway and the Need for Speech." *Modern Fiction Studies,* 8 (1962), 403–406.

Maynard, Reid. "Leitmotif and Irony in Hemingway's 'Hills Like White Elephants.' " *University Review,* 37 (1971), 273–275.

Rodrigues, Eusebio L. " 'Hills Like White Elephants': An Analysis." *Literary Criterion,* 5 (1962), 105–109.

Trilling, Lionel. *The Experience of Literature.* New York: Holt, 1967.

Wright, Austin M. *The American Short Story of the Twenties.* Chicago: University of Chicago Press, 1961.

Ralph Ellison (1914–)

King of the Bingo Game[1]

The woman in front of him was eating roasted peanuts that smelled so good that he could barely contain his hunger. He could not even sleep and wished they'd hurry and begin the bingo game. There, on his right, two fellows were

1. This story, published in 1944, appeared eight years before Ellison's celebrated novel, *Invisible Man.*

drinking wine out of a bottle wrapped in a paper bag, and he could hear soft gurgling in the dark. His stomach gave a low, gnawing growl. "If this was down South," he thought, "all I'd have to do is lean over, and say, 'Lady, gimme a few of those peanuts, please ma'am,' and she'd pass me the bag and never think nothing of it." Or he could ask the fellows for a drink in the same way. Folks down South stuck together that way; they didn't even have to know you. But up here it was different. Ask somebody for something, and they'd think you were crazy. Well, I ain't crazy. I'm just broke, 'cause I got no birth certificate to get a job, and Laura 'bout to die 'cause we got no money for a doctor. But I ain't crazy. And yet a pinpoint of doubt was focused in his mind as he glanced toward the screen and saw the hero stealthily entering a dark room and sending the beam of a flashlight along a wall of bookcases. This is where he finds the trapdoor, he remembered. The man would pass abruptly through the wall and find the girl tied to a bed, her legs and arms spread wide, and her clothing torn to rags. He laughed softly to himself. He had seen the picture three times, and this was one of the best scenes.

On his right the fellow whispered wide-eyed to his companion, "Man, look a-yonder!"

"Damn!"

"Wouldn't I like to have her tied up like that . . ."

"Hey! That fool's letting her loose!"

"Aw, man, he loves her."

"Love or no love!"

The man moved impatiently beside him, and he tried to involve himself in the scene. But Laura was on his mind. Tiring quickly of watching the picture he looked back to where the white beam filtered from the projection room above the balcony. It started small and grew large, specks of dust dancing in its whiteness as it reached the screen. It was strange how the beam always landed right on the screen and didn't mess up and fall somewhere else. But they had it all fixed. Everything was fixed. Now suppose when they showed that girl with her dress torn the girl started taking off the rest of her clothes, and when the guy came in he didn't untie her but kept her there and went to taking off his own clothes? *That* would be something to see. If a picture got out of hand like that those guys up there would go nuts. Yeah, and there'd be so many folks in here you couldn't find a seat for nine months! A strange sensation played over his skin. He shuddered. Yesterday he'd seen a bedbug on a woman's neck as they walked out into the bright street. But exploring his thigh through a hole in his pocket he found only goose pimples and old scars.

The bottle gurgled again. He closed his eyes. Now a dreamy music was accompanying the film and train whistles were sounding in the distance, and he was a boy again walking along a railroad trestle down South, and seeing the train coming, and running back as fast as he could go, and hearing the whistle blowing, and getting off the trestle to solid ground just in time, with the earth trembling beneath his feet, and feeling relieved as he ran down the cinder-strewn embankment onto the highway, and looking back and seeing with terror that the train had left the track and was following him right down the middle of the street, and all the white people laughing as he ran screaming . . .

"Wake up there, buddy! What the hell do you mean hollering like that? Can't you see we trying to enjoy this here picture?"

He stared at the man with gratitude.

"I'm sorry, old man," he said. "I musta been dreaming."

"Well, here, have a drink. And don't be making no noise like that, damn!"

His hands trembled as he tilted his head. It was not wine, but whiskey. Cold rye whiskey. He took a deep swoller, decided it was better not to take another, and handed the bottle back to its owner.

"Thanks, old man," he said.

Now he felt the cold whiskey breaking a warm path straight through the middle of him, growing hotter and sharper as it moved. He had not eaten all day, and it made him light-headed. The smell of the peanuts stabbed him like a knife, and he got up and found a seat in the middle aisle. But no sooner did he sit than he saw a row of intense-faced young girls, and got up again, thinking, "You chicks musta been Lindy-hopping somewhere." He found a seat several rows ahead as the lights came on, and he saw the screen disappear behind a heavy red and gold curtain; then the curtain rising, and the man with the microphone and a uniformed attendant coming on the stage.

He felt for his bingo cards, smiling. The guy at the door wouldn't like it if he knew about his having *five* cards. Well, not everyone played the bingo game; and even with five cards he didn't have much of a chance. For Laura, though, he had to have faith. He studied the cards, each with its different numerals, punching the free center hole in each and spreading them neatly across his lap; and when the lights faded he sat slouched in his seat so that he could look from his cards to the bingo wheel with but a quick shifting of his eyes.

Ahead, at the end of the darkness, the man with the microphone was pressing a button attached to a long cord and spinning the bingo wheel and calling out the number each time the wheel came to rest. And each time the voice rang out his finger raced over the cards for the number. With five cards he had to move fast. He became nervous; there were too many cards, and the man went too fast with his grating voice. Perhaps he should just select one and throw the others away. But he was afraid. He became warm. Wonder how much Laura's doctor would cost? Damn that, watch the cards! And with despair he heard the man call three in a row which he missed on all five cards. This way he'd never win . . .

When he saw the row of holes punched across the third card, he sat paralyzed and heard the man call three more numbers before he stumbled forward, screaming,

"Bingo! Bingo!"

"Let that fool up there," someone called.

"Get up there, man!"

He stumbled down the aisle and up the steps to the stage into a light so sharp and bright that for a moment it blinded him, and he felt that he had moved into the spell of some strange, mysterious power. Yet it was as familiar as the sun, and he knew it was the perfectly familiar bingo.

The man with the microphone was saying something to the audience as he held out his card. A cold light flashed from the man's finger as the card left his hand. His knees trembled. The man stepped closer, checking the card against the numbers chalked on the board. Suppose he had made a mistake? The pomade on the man's hair made him feel faint, and he backed away. But the man was checking the card over the microphone now, and he had to stay. He stood tense, listening.

"Under the O, forty-four," the man chanted. "Under the I, seven. Under the G, three. Under the B, ninety-six. Under the N, thirteen!"

His breath came easier as the man smiled at the audience.

"Yessir, ladies and gentlemen, he's one of the chosen people!"

The audience rippled with laughter and applause.

"Step right up to the front of the stage."

He moved slowly forward, wishing that the light was not so bright.

"To win tonight's jackpot of $36.90 the wheel must stop between the double zero, understand?"

He nodded, knowing the ritual from the many days and nights he had watched the winners march across the stage to press the button that controlled the spinning wheel and receive the prizes. And now he followed the instructions as though he'd crossed the slippery stage a million prize-winning times.

The man was making some kind of a joke, and he nodded vacantly. So tense had he become that he felt a sudden desire to cry and shook it away. He felt vaguely that his whole life was determined by the bingo wheel; not only that which would happen now that he was at last before it, but all that had gone before, since his birth, and his mother's birth and the birth of his father. It had always been there, even though he had not been aware of it, handing out the unlucky cards and numbers of his days. The feeling persisted, and he started quickly away. I better get down from here before I make a fool of myself, he thought.

"Here, boy," the man called. "You haven't started yet."

Someone laughed as he went hesitantly back.

"Are you all reet?"

He grinned at the man's jive talk, but no words would come, and he knew it was not a convincing grin. For suddenly he knew that he stood on the slippery brink of some terrible embarrassment.

"Where are you from, boy?" the man asked.

"Down South."

"He's from down South, ladies and gentlemen," the man said. "Where from? Speak right into the mike."

"Rocky Mont," he said. "Rock' Mont, North Car'lina."

"So you decided to come down off that mountain to the U.S.," the man laughed. He felt that the man was making a fool of him, but then something cold was placed in his hand, and the lights were no longer behind him.

Standing before the wheel he felt alone, but that was somehow right, and he remembered his plan. He would give the wheel a short quick twirl. Just a touch of the button. He had watched it many times, and always it came close to double zero when it was short and quick. He steeled himself; the fear had left, and he felt a profound sense of promise, as though he were about to be repaid for all the things he'd suffered all his life. Trembling, he pressed the button. There was a whirl of lights, and in a second he realized with finality that though he wanted to, he could not stop. It was as though he held a high-powered line in his naked hand. His nerves tightened. As the wheel increased its speed it seemed to draw him more and more into its power, as though it held his fate; and with it came a deep need to submit, to whirl, to lose himself in its swirl of color. He could not stop it now, he knew. So let it be.

The button rested snugly in his palm where the man had placed it. And now he became aware of the man beside him, advising him through the microphone, while behind the shadowy audience hummed with noisy voices. He shifted his feet. There was still that feeling of helplessness within him, making part of him desire to turn back, even now that the jackpot was right in his hand. He squeezed the button until his fist ached. Then, like the sudden shriek of a subway whistle, a doubt tore through his head. Suppose he did not spin the wheel long enough? What could he do, and how could he tell? And then he knew, even as he wondered, that as long as he pressed the button, he could control the jackpot. He and only he could determine whether or not it was to be his. Not even the man with the microphone could do anything about it now. He felt drunk. Then, as though he had come down from a high hill into a valley of people, he heard the audience yelling.

"Come down from there, you jerk!"

"Let somebody else have a chance . . ."

"Ole Jack thinks he done found the end of the rainbow . . ."

The last voice was not unfriendly, and he turned and smiled dreamily into the yelling mouths. Then he turned his back squarely on them.

"Don't take too long, boy," a voice said.

He nodded. They were yelling behind him. Those folks did not understand what had happened to him. They had been playing the bingo game day in and night out for years, trying to win rent money or hamburger change. But not one of those wise guys had discovered this wonderful thing. He watched the wheel whirling past the numbers and experienced a burst of exaltation: This is God! This is the really truly God! He said it aloud, "This is God!"

He said it with such absolute conviction that he feared he would fall fainting into the footlights. But the crowd yelled so loud that they could not hear. Those fools, he thought. I'm here trying to tell them the most wonderful secret in the world, and they're yelling like they gone crazy. A hand fell upon his shoulder.

"You'll have to make a choice now, boy. You've taken too long."

He brushed the hand violently away.

"Leave me alone, man. I know what I'm doing!"

The man looked surprised and held on to the microphone for support. And because he did not wish to hurt the man's feelings he smiled, realizing with a sudden pang that there was no way of explaining to the man just why he had to stand there pressing the button forever.

"Come here," he called tiredly.

The man approached, rolling the heavy microphone across the stage.

"Anybody can play this bingo game, right?" he said.

"Sure, but . . ."

He smiled, feeling inclined to be patient with this slick looking white man with his blue sport shirt and his sharp gabardine suit.

"That's what I thought," he said. "Anybody can win the jackpot as long as they get the lucky number, right?"

"That's the rule, but after all . . ."

"That's what I thought," he said. "And the big prize goes to the man who knows how to win it?"

The man nodded speechlessly.

"Well then, go on over there and watch me win like I want to. I ain't going to hurt nobody," he said, "and I'll show you how to win. I mean to show the whole world how it's got to be done."

And because he understood, he smiled again to let the man know that he held nothing against him for being white and impatient. Then he refused to see the man any longer and stood pressing the button, the voices of the crowd reaching him like sounds in distant streets. Let them yell. All the Negroes down there were just ashamed because he was black like them. He smiled inwardly, knowing how it was. Most of the time he was ashamed of what Negroes did himself. Well, let them be ashamed for something this time. Like him. He was like a long thin black wire that was being stretched and wound upon the bingo wheel; wound until he wanted to scream; wound, but this time himself controlling the winding and the sadness and the shame, and because he did, Laura would be all right. Suddenly the lights flickered. He staggered backwards. Had something gone wrong? All this noise. Didn't they know that although he controlled the wheel, it also controlled him, and unless he pressed the button forever and forever and ever it would stop, leaving him high and dry, dry and high on this hard high slippery hill and Laura dead? There was only one chance; he had to do whatever the wheel demanded. And gripping the button in despair, he discovered with surprise that it imparted a nervous energy. His spine tingled. He felt a certain power.

Now he faced the raging crowd with defiance, its screams penetrating his eardrums like trumpets shrieking from a jukebox. The vague faces glowing in the bingo lights gave him a sense of himself that he had never known before. He was running the show, by God! They had to react to him, for he was their luck. This is *me,* he thought. Let the bastards yell. Then someone was laughing inside him, and he realized that somehow he had forgotten his own name. It was a sad, lost feeling to lose your name, and a crazy thing to do. That name had been given him by the white man who had owned his grandfather a long lost time ago down South. But maybe those wise guys knew his name.

"Who am I?" he screamed.

"Hurry up and bingo, you jerk!"

They didn't know either, he thought sadly. They didn't even know their own names, they were all poor nameless bastards. Well, he didn't need that old name; he was reborn. For as long as he pressed the button he was The-man-who-pressed-the-button-who-held-the-prize-who-was-the-King-of-Bingo. That was the way it was, and he'd have to press the button even if nobody understood, even though Laura did not understand.

"Live!" he shouted.

The audience quieted like the dying of a huge fan.

"Live, Laura, baby. I got holt of it now, sugar. Live!"

He screamed it, tears streaming down his face. "I got nobody but YOU!"

The screams tore from his very guts. He felt as though the rush of blood to his head would burst out in baseball seams of small red droplets, like a head beaten by police clubs. Bending over he saw a trickle of blood splashing the toe of his shoe. With his free hand he searched his head. It was his nose. God, suppose something has gone wrong? He felt that the whole audience had somehow entered him and was stamping its feet in his stomach and he was unable to throw them out. They wanted the prize, that was it. They wanted the secret for themselves. But they'd never get it; he would keep the bingo wheel whirling forever, and Laura would be safe in the wheel. But would she? It had to be, because if she were not safe the wheel would cease to turn; it could not go on. He had to get away, *vomit* all, and his mind formed an image of himself running with Laura in his arms down the tracks of the subway just ahead of an A train, running desperately *vomit* with people screaming for him to come out but knowing no way of leaving the tracks because to stop would bring the train crushing down upon him and to attempt to leave across the other tracks would mean to run into a hot third rail as high as his waist which threw blue sparks that blinded his eyes until he could hardly see.

He heard singing and the audience was clapping its hands.

Shoot the liquor to him, Jim, boy!
Clap-clap-clap
Well a-calla the cop
He's blowing his top!
Shoot the liquor to him, Jim, boy!

Bitter anger grew within him at the singing. They think I'm crazy. Well let 'em laugh. I'll do what I got to do.

He was standing in an attitude of intense listening when he saw that they were watching something on the stage behind him. He felt weak. But when he turned he saw no one. If only his thumb did not ache so. Now they were applauding. And for a moment he thought that the wheel had stopped. But that was impossible, his thumb still pressed the button. Then he saw them. Two men in uniform beckoned from the end of the stage. They were coming toward him, walking in step, slowly, like a tap-dance team returning for a third encore. But their shoulders shot forward, and he backed away, looking wildly about. There was nothing to fight them with. He had only the long black cord which led to a plug somewhere back stage, and he couldn't use that because it operated the bingo wheel. He backed slowly, fixing the men with his eyes as his lips stretched over his teeth in a tight, fixed grin; moved toward the end of the stage and realizing that he couldn't go much further, for suddenly the cord became taut and he couldn't afford to break the cord. But he had to do something. The audience was howling. Suddenly he stopped dead, seeing the men halt, their legs lifted as in an interrupted step of a slow-motion dance. There was nothing to do but run in the other direction and he dashed forward, slipping and sliding. The men fell back, surprised. He struck out violently going past.

"Grab him!"

He ran, but all too quickly the cord tightened, resistingly, and he turned and ran back again. This time he slipped them, and discovered by running in a circle before the wheel he could keep the cord from tightening. But this way he had to flail his arms to keep the men away. Why couldn't they leave a man alone? He ran, circling.

"Ring down the curtain," someone yelled. But they couldn't do that. If they did the wheel flashing from the projection room would be cut off. But they had him before he could tell them so, trying to pry open his fist, and he was wrestling and trying to bring his knees into the fight and holding on to the button, for it was his life. And now he was down, seeing a foot coming down, crushing his wrist cruelly, down, as he saw the wheel whirling serenely above.

"I can't give it up," he screamed. Then quietly, in a confidential tone, "Boys, I really can't give it up."

It landed hard against his head. And in the blank moment they had it away from him, completely now. He fought them trying to pull him up from the stage as he watched the wheel spin slowly to a stop. Without surprise he saw it rest at double-zero.

"You see," he pointed bitterly.

"Sure, boy, sure, it's O.K.," one of the the men said smiling.

And seeing the man bow his head to someone he could not see, he felt very, very happy; he would receive what all the winners received.

But as he warmed in the justice of the man's tight smile he did not see the man's slow wink, nor see the bow-legged man behind him step clear of the swiftly descending curtain and set himself for a blow. He only felt the dull pain exploding in his skull, and he knew even as it slipped out of him that his luck had run out on the stage.

Exercises

1. Define Ellison's central purpose for the story. What broad, deep issue is being addressed? How effective is the story in its design? By what means has the purpose been achieved?

2. Although "the jackpot was right in his hand," the young black has a feeling of helplessness early in the story and he considers turning back. Why do you think he has this feeling? What meaning is there in his forgetting his name?

3. Symbolically, what does the bingo wheel stand for? How can you tell?

4. Before the singing, "Shoot the liquor to him, Jim, boy!" there is a long sentence which begins "He had to get away. . . ." What special effect does the lengthy sentence achieve?

5. Describe the crowd at the theater and explain its function.

6. Interpret the following passages:
   a. "He felt vaguely that his whole life was determined by the bingo wheel; not only that which would happen now that he was at last before it, but all that had gone before, since birth, and his mother's birth and the birth of his father."
   b. "Didn't they know that although he controlled the wheel, it also controlled him, and unless he pressed the button forever and forever and ever it would stop, leaving him high and dry, dry and high on this hard high slippery hill and Laura dead?"
   c. "For as long as he pressed the button he was The-man-who-pressed-the-button-who-held-the-prize-who-was-the-King-of-Bingo."

7. What kind of victory has the bingo player achieved?

8. What is the purpose of the wheel stopping on the double-zero at the end of the story?

9. Who is the real king of the bingo game? Explain.

Topics for Writing

1. Discuss the language of this story. Is the diction appropriate to the subject and characters? Is there any imagery? If so, how important and effective is it?

2. During an acceptance speech on the occasion of receiving the National Book

Award for his novel *Invisible Man,* Ralph Ellison suggested that writers of the period (the 1950s) should take a personal moral responsibility for the condition of democracy. Demonstrate how Ellison has responded to his own challenge in this story.

3. Discuss the importance of ritual in "The Lottery" and "The King of the Bingo Game," comparing and contrasting the two stories as appropriate.

4. Write an essay contrasting the styles of Ellison and Hemingway in the two stories you have read. Make specific references to the texts to support your points.

Selected Bibliography   Ralph Ellison

Deutsch, L. J. "Ellison's Early Fiction." *Negro American Literature Forum,* 7 (Summer 1973), 53–59.

Doyle, M. E. "In Need of Folk: The Alienated Protagonists in Ralph Ellison's Short Fiction.'" *College Language Association Journal,* 19 (1975), 165–172.

Gayle, Addison, Jr. " 'The Harlem Renaissance': Towards a Black Aesthetic." *Midcontinent American Studies Journal,* 11 (Fall 1970), 78–87.

Kaiser, Ernest. "A Critical Look at Ellison's Fiction and at Social and Literary Criticism by and About the Author." *Negro Digest,* 20 (1970), 53–59, 81–97.

Schafer, W. F. "Ralph Ellison and the Birth of the Anti-Hero." *Critique,* 10 (Spring 1968), 81–93.

West, Hollie. "Ralph Ellison: The Man and His Views." *Topic,* 83 (1974), 38–41.

Eudora Welty (1909–   )

A Worn Path

It was December — a bright frozen day in the early morning. Far out in the country there was an old Negro woman with her head tied in a red rag, coming along a path through the pinewoods. Her name was Phoenix Jackson. She was very old and small and she walked slowly in the dark pine shadows, moving a little from side to side in her steps, with the balanced heaviness and lightness of a pendulum in a grandfather clock. She carried a thin, small cane made from an umbrella, and with this she kept tapping the frozen earth in front of her. This made a grave and persistent noise in the still air, that seemed meditative, like the chirping of a solitary little bird.

She wore a dark striped dress reaching down to her shoetops, and an equally long apron of bleached sugar sacks, with a full pocket; all neat and tidy, but every time she took a step she might have fallen over her shoe-laces, which dragged from her unlaced shoes. She looked straight ahead. Her eyes were blue with age. Her skin had a pattern all its own of numberless branching wrinkles and as though a whole little tree stood in the middle of her forehead, but a golden color ran underneath, and the two knobs of her cheeks were illuminated by a yellow burning under the dark. Under the red rag her hair came down on her neck in the frailest of ringlets, still black, and with an odor like copper.

Now and then there was a quivering in the thicket. Old Phoenix said, "Out of my way, all you foxes, owls, beetles, jack rabbits, coons, and wild animals! . . . Keep out from under these feet, little bobwhites. . . . Keep the big wild hogs out of my path. Don't let none of those come running my direction. I got a long way." Under her small black-freckled hand her cane, limber as a buggy whip, would switch at the brush as if to rouse up any hiding things.

On she went. The woods were deep and still. The sun made the pine needles almost too bright to look at, up where the wind rocked. The cones dropped as light as feathers. Down in the hollow was the mourning dove — it was not too late for him.

The path ran up a hill. "Seems like there is chains about my feet, time I get this far," she said, in the voice of argument old people keep to use with themselves. "Something always take a hold on this hill — pleads I should stay."

After she got to the top she turned and gave a full, severe look behind her where she had come. "Up through pines," she said at length. "Now down through oaks."

Her eyes opened their widest and she started down gently. But before she got to the bottom of the hill a bush caught her dress.

Her fingers were busy and intent, but her skirts were full and long, so that before she could pull them free in one place they were caught in another. It was not possible to allow the dress to tear. "I in the thorny bush," she said. "Thorns, you doing your appointed work. Never want to let folks pass — no sir. Old eyes thought you was a pretty little green bush."

Finally, trembling all over, she stood free, and after a moment dared to stoop for her cane.

"Sun so high!" she cried, leaning back and looking, while the thick tears went over her eyes. "The time getting all gone here."

At the foot of this hill was a place where a log was laid across the creek.

"Now comes the trial," said Phoenix.

Putting her right foot out, she mounted the log and shut her eyes. Lifting her skirt, levelling her cane fiercely before her, like a festival figure in some parade, she began to march across. Then she opened her eyes and she was safe on the other side.

"I wasn't as old as I thought," she said.

But she sat down to rest. She spread her skirts on the bank around her and folded her hands over her knees. Up above her was a tree in a pearly cloud of mistletoe. She did not dare to close her eyes, and when a little boy brought her a little plate with a slice of marble-cake on it she spoke to him. "That would be acceptable," she said. But when she went to take it there was just her own hand in the air.

So she left that tree, and had to go through a barbed-wire fence. There she had to creep and crawl, spreading her knees and stretching her fingers like a baby trying to climb the steps. But she talked loudly to herself: she could not let her dress be torn now, so late in the day, and she could not pay for having her arm or her leg sawed off if she got caught fast where she was.

At last she was safe through the fence and risen up out in the clearing. Big dead trees, like black men with one arm, were standing in the purple stalks of the withered cotton field. There sat a buzzard.

"Who you watching?"

In the burrow she made her way along.

"Glad this not the season for bulls," she said, looking sideways, "and the good Lord made his snakes to curl up and sleep in the winter. A pleasure I don't see no two-headed snake coming around that tree, where it come once. It took a while to get by him, back in the summer."

She passed through the old cotton and went into a field of dead corn. It whispered and shook, and was taller than her head. "Through the maze now," she said, for there was no path.

Then there was something tall, black, and skinny there, moving before her.

At first she took it for a man. It could have been a man dancing in the field. But she stood still and listened, and it did not make a sound. It was as silent as a ghost.

"Ghost," she said sharply, "who be you the ghost of? For I have heard of nary death close by."

But there was no answer, only the ragged dancing in the wind.

She shut her eyes, reached out her hand, and touched a sleeve. She found a coat and inside that an emptiness, cold as ice.

"You scarecrow," she said. Her face lighted. "I ought to be shut up for good," she said with laughter. "My senses is gone. I too old. I the oldest people I ever know. Dance, old scarecrow," she said, "while I dancing with you."

She kicked her foot over the furrow, and with mouth drawn down shook her head once or twice in a little strutting way. Some husks blew down and whirled in streamers about her skirts.

Then she went on, parting her way from side to side with the cane, through the whispering field. At last she came to the end, to a wagon track, where the silver grass blew between the red ruts. The quail were walking around like pullets, seeming all dainty and unseen.

"Walk pretty," she said. "This the easy place. This the easy going."

She followed the track, swaying through the quiet bare fields, through the little strings of trees silver in their dead leaves, past cabins silver from weather, with the doors and windows boarded shut, all like old women under a spell sitting there. "I walking in their sleep," she said, nodding her head vigorously.

In a ravine she went where a spring was silently flowing through a hollow log. Old Phoenix bent and drank. "Sweetgum makes the water sweet," she said, and drank more. "Nobody knows who made this well, for it was here when I was born."

The track crossed a swampy part where the moss hung as white as lace from every limb. "Sleep on, alligators, and blow your bubbles." Then the track went into the road.

Deep, deep the road went down between the high green-colored banks. Overhead the live-oaks met, and it was as dark as a cave.

A black dog with a lolling tongue came up out of the weeds by the ditch. She was meditating, and not ready, and when he came at her she only hit him a little with her cane. Over she went in the ditch, like a little puff of milk-weed.

Down there, her senses drifted away. A dream visited her, and she reached her hand up, but nothing reached down and gave her a pull. So she lay there and presently went to talking. "Old woman," she said to herself, "that black dog came up out of the weeds to stall you off, and now there he sitting on his fine tail, smiling at you."

A white man finally came along and found her — a hunter, a young man, with his dog on a chain.

"Well, Granny!" he laughed. "What are you doing there?"

"Lying on my back like a June-bug waiting to be turned over, mister," she said, reaching up her hand.

He lifted her up, gave her a swing in the air, and set her down, "Anything broken, Granny?"

"No sir, them old dead weeds is springy enough," said Phoenix, when she had got her breath. "I thank you for your trouble."

"Where do you live, Granny?" he asked, while the two dogs were growling at each other.

"Away back yonder, sir, behind the ridge. You can't even see it from here."

"On your way home?"

"No, sir, I going to town."

"Why, that's too far! That's as far as I walk when I come out myself, and I get something for my trouble." He patted the stuffed bag he carried, and there hung down a little closed claw. It was one of the bobwhites, with its beak hooked bitterly to show it was dead. "Now you go on home, Granny!"

"I bound to go to town, mister," said Phoenix. "The time come around."

He gave another laugh, filling the whole landscape. "I know you colored people! Wouldn't miss going to town to see Santa Claus!"

But something held Old Phoenix very still. The deep lines in her face went into a fierce and different radiation. Without warning she had seen with her own eyes a flashing nickel fall out of the man's pocket on to the ground.

"How old are you, Granny?" he was saying.

"There is no telling, mister," she said, "no telling."

Then she gave a little cry and clapped her hands, and said, "Git on away from here, dog! Look! Look at that dog!" She laughed as if in admiration. "He ain't scared of nobody. He a big black dog." She whispered, "Sick him!"

"Watch me get rid of that cur," said the man. "Sick him, Pete! Sick him!"

Phoenix heard the dogs fighting and heard the man running and throwing sticks. She even heard a gunshot. But she was slowly bending forward by that time, further and further forward, the lids stretched down over her eyes, as if she were doing this in her sleep. Her chin was lowered almost to her knees. The yellow palm of her hand came out from the fold of her apron. Her fingers slid down and along the ground under the piece of money with the grace and care they would have in lifting an egg from under a sitting hen. Then she slowly straightened up, she stood erect, and the nickel was in her apron pocket. A bird flew by. Her lips moved. "God watching me the whole time. I come to stealing."

The man came back, and his own dog panted about them. "Well, I scared him off that time," he said, and then he laughed and lifted his gun and pointed it at Phoenix.

She stood straight and faced him.

"Doesn't the gun scare you?" he said, still pointing it.

"No, sir, I seen plenty go off closer by, in my day, and for less than what I done," she said, holding utterly still.

He smiled, and shouldered the gun. "Well, Granny," he said, "you must be a hundred years old and scared of nothing. I'd give you a dime if I had any money with me. But you take my advice and stay home, and nothing will happen to you."

"I bound to go on my way, mister," said Phoenix. She inclined her head in the red rag. Then they went in different directions, but she could hear the gun shooting again and again over the hill.

She walked on. The shadows hung from the oak trees to the road like curtains. Then she smelled wood-smoke, and smelled the river, and she saw a steeple and the cabins on their steep steps. Dozens of little black children whirled around her. There ahead was Natchez shining. Bells were ringing. She walked on.

In the paved city it was Christmas time. There were red and green electric lights strung and crisscrossed everywhere, and all turned on in the daytime. Old Phoenix would have been lost if she had not distrusted her eyesight and depended on her feet to know where to take her.

She paused quietly on the sidewalk, where people were passing by. A lady came along in the crowd, carrying an armful of red-, green-, and silver-wrapped presents; she gave off perfume like the red roses in hot summer, and Phoenix stopped her.

"Please, missy, will you lace up my shoe?" She held up her foot.

"What do you want, Grandma?"

"See my shoe," said Phoenix. "Do all right for out in the country, but wouldn't look right to go in a big building."

"Stand still then, Grandma," said the lady. She put her packages down carefully on the sidewalk beside her and laced and tied both shoes tightly.

"Can't lace 'em with a cane," said Phoenix. "Thank you, missy. I doesn't mind asking a nice lady to tie up my shoe when I gets out on the street."

Moving slowly and from side to side, she went into the stone building and into a tower of steps, where she walked up and around and around until her feet knew to stop.

She entered a door, and there she saw nailed up on the wall the document that had been stamped with the gold seal and framed in the gold frame which matched the dream that was hung up in her head.

"Here I be," she said. There was a fixed and ceremonial stiffness over her body.

"A charity case, I suppose," said an attendant who sat at the desk before her.

But Phoenix only looked above her head. There was sweat on her face; the wrinkles shone like a bright net.

"Speak up, Grandma," the woman said. "What's your name? We must have your history, you know. Have you been here before? What seems to be the trouble with you?"

Old Phoenix only gave a twitch to her face as if a fly were bothering her.

"Are you deaf?" cried the attendant.

But then the nurse came in.

"Oh, that's just old Aunt Phoenix," she said. "She doesn't come for herself — she has a little grandson. She makes these trips just as regular as clockwork.

She lives away back off the Old Natchez Trace." She bent down. "Well, Aunt Phoenix, why don't you just take a seat? We won't keep you standing after your long trip." She pointed.

The old woman sat down, bolt upright in the chair.

"Now, how is the boy?" asked the nurse.

Old Phoenix did not speak.

"I said, how is the boy?"

But Phoenix only waited and stared straight ahead, her face very solemn and withdrawn into rigidity.

"Is his throat any better?" asked the nurse. "Aunt Phoenix, don't you hear me? Is your grandson's throat any better since the last time you came for the medicine?"

With her hand on her knees, the old woman waited, silent, erect and motionless, just as if she were in armor.

"You mustn't take up our time this way, Aunt Phoenix," the nurse said. "Tell us quickly about your grandson, and get it over. He isn't dead, is he?"

At last there came a flicker and then a flame of comprehension across her face, and she spoke.

"My grandson. It was my memory had left me. There I sat and forgot why I made my long trip."

"Forgot?" The nurse frowned. "After you came so far?"

Then Phoenix was like an old woman begging a dignified forgiveness for waking up frightened in the night. "I never did go to school — I was too old at the Surrender," [1] she said in a soft voice. "I'm an old woman without an education. It was my memory fail me. My little grandson, he is just the same, and I forgot it in the coming."

"Throat never heals, does it?" said the nurse, speaking in a loud, sure voice to Old Phoenix. By now she had a card with something written on it, a little list. "Yes. Swallowed lye. When was it — January — two — three years ago — "

Phoenix spoke unasked now. "No, missy, he not dead, he just the same. Every little while his throat begin to close up again, and he not able to swallow. He not get his breath. He not able to help himself. So the time come around, and I go on another trip for the soothing-medicine."

"All right. The doctor said as long as you came to get it you could have it," said the nurse. "But it's an obstinate case."

"My little grandson, he sit up there in the house all wrapped up, waiting by himself," Phoenix went on. "We is the only two left in the world. He suffer and it don't seem to put him back at all. He got a sweet look. He going to last. He wear a little patch quilt and peep out, holding his mouth open like a little bird. I remembers so plain now. I not going to forget him again, no, the whole enduring time. I could tell him from all the others in creation."

"All right." The nurse was trying to hush her now. She brought her a bottle of medicine. "Charity," she said, making a check mark in a book.

Old Phoenix held the bottle close to her eyes and then carefully put it into her pocket.

---

1. Surrender: General Robert E. Lee of the Confederacy surrendered on April 9, 1865, to General Ulysses S. Grant of the Union, thus ending the Civil War.

"I thank you," she said.

"It's Christmas time, Grandma," said the attendant. "Could I give you a few pennies out of my purse?"

"Five pennies is a nickel," said Phoenix stiffly.

"Here's a nickel," said the attendant.

Phoenix rose carefully and held out her hand. She received the nickel and then fished the other nickel out of her pocket and laid it beside the new one. She stared at her palm closely, with her head on one side.

Then she gave a tap with her cane on the floor.

"This is what come to me to do," she said. "I going to the store and buy my child a little windmill they sells, made out of paper. He going to find it hard to believe there such a thing in the world. I'll march myself back where he waiting, holding it straight up in this hand."

She lifted her free hand, gave a little nod, turned round, and walked out of the doctor's office. Then her slow step began on the stairs, going down.

Exercises

1. In his *Histories,* Herodotus reveals the legend of the phoenix, a sacred bird with gold and red plumage, which consumes itself by fire and renews itself out of its own ashes to return whole and young again every five hundred years to the Egyptian city of the sun. The mythical bird symbolizes the sun; its rebirth suggests immortality. How is the black woman an appropriate symbol of the phoenix bird?

2. What is the protagonist's goal? What is the conflict?

3. Enumerate the various crises that threaten Phoenix along her journey. What do they reveal about her character?

4. Along the worn path Phoenix is perceptive, imaginative, courageous, wise, and talkative; at the clinic she is ceremonially stiff and reticent. What accounts for this change in behavior?

5. Discuss the implications of the episode with the hunter.

6. Interpret the Christmas symbolism in the story.

7. Cite instances of humor and tell what they contribute to the story.

8. How is unity achieved?

9. How does Phoenix's capacity of self-sacrifice, endurance, and love suggest the theme? What is the central theme?

Topics for Writing

1. Describe the story's effectiveness as it derives chiefly from a blend of character, setting, and action.

2. Discuss Phoenix as a Christ-figure, making specific references to the imagery and other elements in the story that suggest such a comparison.

3. Write an essay citing and discussing several aspects of Welty's style, focusing particularly on the description of setting and people.

4. Compare and contrast the function of humor in "A Worn Path" and in Thurber's "The Catbird Seat."

Selected Bibliography   Eudora Welty

Daniel, Robert. "The World of Eudora Welty." *Hopkins Review,* 7 (1953), 49–58.
Donlan, Dan. " 'A Worn Path': Immortality of Stereotype," *English Journal,* 62 (1973), 549–550.
Glenn, Eunice. "Fantasy in the Fiction of Eudora Welty." In *A Southern Vanguard,* ed. Allen Tate. New York: Prentice-Hall, 1947, pp. 78–91.
Hartley, Lodwick. "Proserpina and the Old Ladies." *Modern Fiction Studies,* 3 (1957–58), 350–354.
Hicks, Granville. "Eudora Welty." *College English,* 14 (1952), 69–76. Also in *English Journal,* 41 (1952), 461–468.
Howell, Elmo. "Eudora Welty's Negroes: A Note on 'A Worn Path.' " *Xavier University Studies,* 9 (1970), 28–32.
Isaacs, Neil D. "Life of Phoenix." *Sewanee Review,* 71 (1963), 75–81.
Jones, William M. "Name and Symbol in the Prose of Eudora Welty." *Southern Folklore Quarterly,* 22 (1958), 173–185.
Moss, Grant. " 'A Worn Path' Retrod," *College Language Association Journal,* 15 (1971), 144–152.
Rubin, Louis D., Jr. "Two Ladies of the South." *Sewanee Review,* 63 (1955), 671–681.
Seidl, Frances. "Eudora Welty's Phoenix." *Notes on Mississippi Writers,* 6 (1973), 53–55.
Vande Kieft, Ruth M. *Eudora Welty.* New York: Twayne, 1962.
Warren, Robert Penn. "The Love and the Separateness in Miss Welty." *Kenyon Review,* 6 (1944), 246–259.
Welty, Eudora. "How I Write." *Virginia Quarterly,* 31 (1955), 240–251.
———. "Is Phoenix Jackson's Grandson Really Dead?" *Critical Inquiry,* 1 (1974), 219–221.

Kurt Vonnegut, Jr. (1922–   )

The Manned Missiles

I, Mikhail Ivankov, stone mason in the village of Ilba in the Ukrainian Soviet Socialist Republic, greet you and pity you, Charles Ashland, petroleum merchant in Titusville, Florida, in the United States of America. I grasp your hand.

The first true space man was my son, Major Stepan Ivankov. The second was your son, Captain Bryant Ashland. They will be forgotten only when men no longer look up at the sky. They are like the moon and the planets and the sun and the stars.

I do not speak English. I speak these words in Russian, from my heart, and my surviving son, Alexei, writes them down in English. He studies English in school and German also. He likes English best. He admires Jack London and your O. Henry and your Mark Twain. Alexei is seventeen. He is going to be a scientist like his brother Stepan.

He wants me to tell you that he is going to work on science for peace, not war. He wants me to tell you also that he does not hate the memory of your son. He understands that your son was ordered to do what he did. He is talking very much, and would like to compose this letter himself. He thinks that a man forty-nine is a very old man, and he does not think that a very old man who can do nothing but put one stone on top of another can say the right things about young men who die in space.

If he wishes, he can write a letter of his own about the deaths of Stepan and your son. This is my letter, and I will get Aksinia, Stepan's widow, to read it to me to make sure Alexei has made it say exactly what I wish it to say. Aksinia, too, understands English very well. She is a physician for children. She is beautiful. She works very hard so she can forget sometimes her grief for Stepan.

I will tell you a joke, Mr. Ashland. When the second baby moon of the U.S.S.R. went up with a dog in it, we whispered that it was not really a dog inside, but Prokhor Ivanoff, a dairy manager who had been arrested for theft two days before. It was only a joke, but it made me think what a terrible punishment it would be to send a human being up there. I could not stop thinking about that. I dreamed about it at night, and I dreamed that it was myself who was being punished.

I would have asked my elder son Stepan about life in space, but he was far away in Guryev, on the Caspian Sea. So I asked my younger son. Alexei laughed at my fears of space. He said that a man could be made very comfortable up there. He said that many young men would be going up there soon. First they would ride in baby moons. Then they would go to the moon itself. Then they would go to other planets. He laughed at me, because only an old man would worry about such simple trips.

Alexei told me that the only inconvenience would be the lack of gravity. That seemed like a great lack to me. Alexei said one would have to drink out of nursing bottles, and one would have to get used to the feeling of falling constantly, and one would have to learn to control one's movements because gravity would no longer offer resistance to them. That was all. Alexei did not think such things would be bothersome. He expected to go to Mars soon.

Olga, my wife, laughed at me, too, because I was too old to understand the great new Age of Space. "Two Russian moons shine overhead," she said, "and my husband is the only man on earth who does not yet believe it!"

But I went on dreaming bad dreams about space, and now I had information to make my bad dreams truly scientific. I dreamed of nursing bottles and falling, falling, falling, and the strange movements of my limbs. Perhaps the dreams were supernatural. Perhaps something was trying to warn me that Stepan would soon be suffering in space as I had suffered in dreams. Perhaps something was trying to warn me that Stepan would be murdered in space.

Alexei is very embarrassed that I should say that in a letter to the United

States of America. He says that you will think that I am a superstitious peasant. So be it. I think that scientific persons of the future will scoff at scientific persons of the present. They will scoff because scientific persons of the present thought so many important things were superstitions. The things I dreamed about space all came true for my son. Stepan suffered very much up there. After the fourth day in space, Stepan sometimes cried like a baby. I had cried like a baby in my dreams.

I am not a coward, and I do not love comfort more than the improvement of human life. I am not a coward for my sons, either. I knew great suffering in the war, and I understand that there must be great suffering before great joy. But when I thought of the suffering that must surely come to a man in space, I could not see the joy to be earned by it. This was long before Stepan went up in his baby moon.

I went to the library and read about the moon and the planets, to see if they were truly desirable places to go. I did not ask Alexei about them, because I knew he would tell me what fine times we would have on such places. I found out for myself in the library that the moon and the planets were not fit places for men or for any life. They were much too hot or much too cold or much too poisonous.

I said nothing at home about my discoveries at the library, because I did not wish to be laughed at again. I waited quietly for Stepan to visit us. He would not laugh at my questions. He would answer them scientifically. He had worked on rockets for years. He would know everything that was known about space.

Stepan at last came to visit us, and brought his beautiful wife. He was a small man, but strong and broad and wise. He was very tired. His eyes were sunken. He knew already that he was to be shot into space. First had come the baby moon with the radio. Next had come the baby moon with the dog. Next would come the baby moons with the monkeys and the apes. After them would come the baby moon with Stepan. Stepan had been working night and day, designing his home in space. He could not tell me. He could not even tell his wife.

Mr. Ashland, you would have liked my son. Everybody liked Stepan. He was a man of peace. He was not a major because he was a great warrior. He was a major because he understood rockets so well. He was a thoughtful man. He often said that he wished that he could be a stone mason like me. He said a stone mason would have time and peace in which to think things out. I did not tell him that a stone mason thinks of little but stones and mortar.

I asked him my question about space, and he did not laugh. Stepan was very serious when he answered me. He had reason to be serious. He was telling me why he was himself willing to suffer in space.

He told me I was right. A man would suffer greatly in space, and the moon and the planets were bad places for men. There might be good places, but they were too far for men to reach in a lifetime.

"Then, what is this great new Age of Space, Stepan?" I asked him.

"It will be an age of baby moons for a long time," he said. "We will reach the moon itself soon, but it would be very difficult to stay there more than a few hours."

"Then why go into space, if there is so little good out there?" I asked him.

"There is so much to be learned and seen out there," he said. "A man could look at other worlds without a curtain of air between himself and them. A man could look at his own world, study the flow of weather over it, measure its true dimensions." This last surprised me. I thought the dimensions of our world were well known. "A man out there could learn much about the wonderful showers of matter and energy in space," said Stepan. And he spoke of many other poetic and scientific joys out there.

I was satisfied. Stepan had made me feel his own great joy at the thought of all the beauty and truth in space. I understood at last, Mr. Ashland, why the suffering would be worthwhile. When I dreamed of space again, I would dream of looking down at our own lovely green ball, dream of looking up at other worlds and seeing them more clearly than they had ever been seen.

It was not for the Soviet Union but for the beauty and truth in space, Mr. Ashland, that Stepan worked and died. He did not like to speak of the warlike uses of space. It was Alexei who liked to speak of such things, of the glory of spying on earth from baby moons, of guiding missiles to their targets from baby moons, of mastering the earth with weapons fired from the moon itself. Alexei expected Stepan to share his excitement about thoughts of such childish violence.

Stepan smiled, but only because he loved Alexei. He did not smile about war, or the things a man in a baby moon or on the moon itself could do to an enemy. "It is a use of science that we may be forced to make, Alexei," he said. "But if such a war happens, nothing will matter any more. Our world will become less fit for life than any other in the solar system."

Alexei has not spoken well of war since.

Stepan and his wife left late that night. He promised to come back before another year had passed, but I never saw him alive again.

When news came that the Soviet Union had fired a man-carrying baby moon into space, I did not know that the man was Stepan. I did not dare to suspect it. I could not wait to see Stepan again, to ask him what the man had said before he took off, how he was dressed, what his comforts were. We were told that we would be able to hear the man speak from space at eight o'clock that night on the radio.

We listened. We heard the man speak. The man was Stepan.

Stepan sounded strong. He sounded happy. He sounded proud and decent and wise. We laughed until we cried, Mr. Ashland. We danced. Our Stepan was the most important man alive. He had risen above everyone, and now he was looking down, telling us what our world looked like; looking up, telling us what the other worlds looked like.

Stepan made pleasant jokes about his little house in the sky. He said it was a cylinder ten meters long and four meters in diameter. It could be very cozy. And Stepan told us that there were little windows in his house, and a television camera, and a telescope, and radar, and all manner of instruments. How delightful to live in a time when such things could be! How delightful to be the father of the man who was the eyes, ears, and heart in space for all mankind!

He would remain up there for a month, he said. We began to count the days. Every night we listened to a broadcast of recordings of things Stepan had said. We heard nothing about his nosebleeds and his nausea and his crying. We heard only the calm, brave things he had said. And then, on the tenth night, there were no more recordings of Stepan. There was only music at eight o'clock. There was no news of Stepan at all, and we knew he was dead.

Only now, a year later, have we learned how Stepan died and where his body is. When I became accustomed to the horror of it, Mr. Ashland, I said, "So be it. May Major Stepan Ivankov and Captain Bryant Ashland serve to reproach us, whenever we look at the sky, for making a world in which there is no trust. May the two men be the beginning of trust between peoples. May they mark the end of the time when science sent out good, brave young men hurtling to meet in death."

I enclose a photograph of my family, taken during Stepan's last visit to us. It is an excellent picture of Stepan. The body of water in the background is the Black Sea.

Mikhail Ivankov

Dear Mr. Ivankov:

Thank you for the letter about our sons. I never did get it in the mail. It was in all the papers after your Mr. Koshevoi read it out loud in the United Nations. I never did get a copy just for me. I guess Mr. Koshevoi forgot to drop it in the mailbox. That's all right. I guess that's the modern way to deliver important letters, just hand them to reporters. They say your letter to me is just about the most important thing that's happened lately, outside of the fact we didn't go to war over what happened between our two boys.

I don't speak Russian, and I don't have anybody right close by who does, so you'll have to excuse the English. Alexei can read it to you. You tell him he writes English very well — better than I do.

Oh, I could have had a lot of expert help with this letter, if I'd wanted it — people happy to write to you in perfect Russian or perfect English or perfect anything at all. Seems like everybody in this country is like your boy Alexei. They all know better than I do what I should say to you. They say I have a chance to make history, if I answer you back the right things. One big magazine in New York offered me two thousand dollars for my letter back to you, and then it turned out I wasn't even supposed to write a letter for all that money. The magazine people had already written it, and all I had to do was sign it. Don't worry. I didn't.

I tell you, Mr. Ivankov, I have had a bellyful of experts. If you ask me, our boys were experted to death. Your experts would do something, then our experts would answer back with some fancy billion-dollar stunt, and then your experts would answer that back with something fancier, and what happened finally happened. It was just like a bunch of kids with billions of dollars or billions or rubles or whatever.

You are lucky you have a son left, Mr. Ivankov. Hazel and I don't. Bryant was the only son Hazel and I had. We didn't call him Bryant after he was christened. We called him Bud. We have one daughter, named Charlene. She works for the telephone company in Jacksonville. She called up when she saw your letter in the paper, and she is the only expert about what I ought to say I've listened to. She's a real expert, I figure, because she is Bud's twin. Bud never married, so Charlene is as close as you can get to Bud. She said you did a good job, showing how your Stepan was a good-hearted man, trying to do what was right, just like anybody else. She said I should show you the same about Bud. And then she started to cry, and she said for me to tell you about Bud and the goldfish, I said, "What's the sense of writing somebody in Russia a story like that?" The story doesn't prove anything. It's just one of those silly stories a family will keep telling when ever they get together. Charlene said that was why I should tell it to you, because it would be cute and silly in Russia, too, and you would laugh and like us better.

So here goes. When Bud and Charlene were about eight, why I came home one night with a fish bowl and two goldfish. There was one goldfish for each twin, only it was impossible to tell one fish from the other one. They were exactly alike. So one morning Bud got up early, and there was one goldfish floating on top of the water dead. So Bud went and woke up Charlene, and he said, "Hey, Charlene — your goldfish just died." That's the story Charlene asked me to tell you, Mr. Ivankov.

I think it is interesting that you are a mason. That is a good trade. You talk as if you lay up mostly stone. There aren't many people left in America who can really lay up stone. It's almost all cement-block work and bricks here. It probably is over there, too. I don't mean to say Russia isn't modern. I know it is.

Bud and I laid up quite a bit of block when we built the gas station here, with an apartment up over it. If you looked at the first course of block along the back wall, you would have to laugh, because you can see how Bud and I learned as we went. It's strong enough, but it sure looks lousy. One thing wasn't so funny. When we were hanging the rails for the overhead door, Bud slipped on the ladder, and he grabbed a sharp edge on the mounting bracket, and he cut a tendon on his hand. He was scared to death his hand would be crippled, and that would keep him out of the Air Force. His hand had to be operated on three times before it was right again, and every operation hurt something awful. But Bud would have let them operate a hundred times, if they had to, because there was just one thing he wanted to be, and that was a flyer.

One reason I wish your Mr. Koshevoi had thought to mail me your letter was the picture you sent with it. The newspapers got that, too, and it didn't come out too clear in the papers. But one thing we couldn't get over was all that beautiful water behind you. Somehow, when we think about Russia, we never think about any water around. I guess that shows how ignorant we are. Hazel and I live up over the gas station, and we can see water, too. We can see the Atlantic Ocean, or an inlet of it they call Indian River. We can see Merritt Island, too, out in the water, and we can see the place Bud's rocket went up from. It is called Cape Canaveral. I guess you know that. It isn't any secret where he went up from. They couldn't keep that tremendous missile secret any more than they could keep the Empire State Building secret. Tourists came from miles around to take pictures of it.

The story was, its warhead was filled with flash powder, and it was going to hit the moon and make a big show. Hazel and I thought that's what the story was, too. When it took off, we got set for a big flash on the moon. We didn't know it was our Bud up in the warhead. We didn't even know he was in Florida. He couldn't get in touch with us. We thought he was up at Otis Air Force Base on Cape Cod. That was the last place we heard from him. And then that thing went up, right in the middle of our view out the picture window.

You say you're superstitious sometimes, Mr. Ivankov. Me too. Sometimes I can't help thinking it was all meant to be right from the very first — even the way our picture window is aimed. There weren't any rockets going up down here when we built. We moved down here from Pittsburgh, which maybe you know is the center of our steel industry. And we figured we maybe weren't going to break any records for pumping gas, but at least we'd be way far away from any bomb targets, in case there was another war. And the next thing we know, a rocket center goes up almost next door, and our little boy is a man, and he goes up in a rocket and dies.

The more we think about it, the more we're sure it was meant to be. I never got it straight in my mind about religion in Russia. You don't mention it. Anyway, we are religious, and we think God singled out Bud and your boy, too, to die in a special way for a special reason. When everybody was asking, "How is it going to end?" — well, maybe this is how God meant for it to end. I don't see how it can keep on.

Mr. Ivankov, one thing that threw me as much as anything was the way Mr. Koshevoi kept telling the U.N. that Bud was a killer. He called Bud a mad dog and a gangster. I'm glad you don't feel that way, because that's the wrong way to feel about Bud. It was flying and not killing he liked. Mr. Koshevoi made a big thing out of how cultured and educated and all your boy was, and how wild and ignorant mine was. He made it sound as though a juvenile delinquent had murdered a college professor.

Bud never was in any trouble with the police, and he didn't have a cruel streak. He never went hunting, for instance, and he never drove like a crazy man, and he got drunk only one time I know of, and that was an experiment. He was proud of his reflexes, see? His health was on his mind all the time, because he had to be healthy to be a great flyer. I keep looking around for the right word for Bud, and I guess the one Hazel suggested is the best one. It sounded kind of stuffed-up to me at first, but now I'm used to it, and it sounds right. Hazel says Bud was dignified. Man and boy, that's what he was — straight and serious and polite and pretty much alone.

I think he knew he was going to die young. That one time he got drunk, just to find out what alcohol was, he talked to me more than he'd ever talked before. He was nineteen then. And then was the only time he let me know he knew death was all balled up in what he wanted to do with his life. It wasn't other people's deaths he was talking about, Mr. Ivankov. It was his own. "One nice thing about flying," he said to me that night. "What's that?" I said. "You never know how bad it is till it's too late," he said, "and when it happens, it happens so fast you never know what hit you."

That was death he was talking about, and a special, dignified, honorable kind of death. You say you were in the war and had a hard time. Same here, so I guess we both know about what kind of death it was that Bud had in mind. It was a soldier's death.

We got the news he was dead three days after the big rocket went up across the water. The telegram said he had died on a secret mission, and we couldn't have any details. We had our Congressman, Earl Waterman, find out what he could about Bud. Mr. Waterman came and talked to us personally and he looked like he had seen God. He said he couldn't tell us what Bud had done, but it was one of the most heroic things in United States history.

The word they put out on the big rocket we saw launched was that the firing was satisfactory, the knowledge gained was something wonderful, and the missile had been blown up over the ocean somewhere. That was that.

Then the word came that the man in the Russian baby moon was dead. I tell you honestly, Mr. Ivankov, that was good news to us, because that man sailing way up there with all those instruments meant just one thing, and that was a terrible weapon of war.

Then we heard the Russian baby moon had turned into a bunch of baby moons, all spreading apart. Then, this last month, the cat was out of the bag. Two of the baby moons were men. One was your boy, the other was mine.

I'm crying now, Mr. Ivankov. I hope some good comes of the death of our two boys. I guess that's what millions of fathers have hoped for as long as there have been people. There in the U.N. they're still arguing about what happened way up in the sky. I'm glad they've got around to where everybody, including your Mr. Koshevoi, agrees it was an accident. Bud was up there to get pictures of what your boy was riding in, and to show off for the United States some. He got too close. I like to think they lived a little while after the crash and tried to save each other.

They say they'll be up there for hundreds of years, long after you and I are gone. In their orbits they will meet and part and meet again and the astronomers know exactly where their next meeting place will be. Like you say, they are up there like the sun and the moon and the stars.

I enclose a photograph of my boy in his uniform. He was twenty-one when the picture was taken. He was only twenty-two when he died. Bud was picked for that mission on account of he was the finest flyer in the United States Air Force. That's what he always wanted to be. That's what he was.

Charles M. Ashland
Petroleum Merchant
Titusville, Florida
U.S.A.

Exercises

1. Describe the conflict. Which forces are warring against one another?

2. What significant information does the first letter reveal? What does the second letter reveal? What does the symmetrical design of the letters accomplish?

3. What is achieved by the fathers' display of strong emotions? What might have been gained, as well as lost, had the author chosen to be callous instead of being sentimental?

4. Does Vonnegut achieve suspense? How? Does he achieve unity? How?

5. What chief point is Vonnegut trying to make in this story?

6. If Vonnegut's intention is to be satirical, what is he satirizing?

7. What does the use of irony contribute to the meaning of the story?

8. Vonnegut appears to have something to say about the win, lose, or tie syndrome. What does he suggest as an alternative?

Topics for Writing

1. Write an essay discussing the elements of plot used in the story. Tell how they are used and evaluate the effectiveness of Vonnegut's design.

2. Study and compare the writing styles of Hemingway and Vonnegut, focusing on three or four aspects of style.

3. Compare and contrast the two fathers, the two sons, the two countries and their ideologies.

6. OTHER STORIES TO READ

James Baldwin *(1924–   )*

Sonny's Blues

I read about it in the paper, in the subway, on my way to work. I read it, and I couldn't believe it, and I read it again. Then perhaps I just stared at it, at the newsprint spelling out his name, spelling out the story. I stared at it in the swinging lights of the subway car, and in the faces and bodies of the people, and in my own face, trapped in the darkness which roared outside.

It was not to be believed and I kept telling myself that, as I walked from the subway station to the high school. And at the same time I couldn't doubt it. I was scared, scared for Sonny. He became real to me again. A great block of ice got settled in my belly and kept melting there slowly all day long, while I taught my classes algebra. It was a special kind of ice. It kept melting, sending trickles of ice water all up and down my veins, but it never got less. Sometimes it hardened and seemed to expand until I felt my guts were going to come spilling out or that I was going to choke or scream. This would always be at a moment when I was remembering some specific thing Sonny had once said or done.

When he was about as old as the boys in my classes his face had been bright and open, there was a lot of copper in it; and he'd had wonderfully direct brown eyes, and great gentleness and privacy. I wondered what he looked like now. He had been picked up, the evening before, in a raid on an apartment downtown, for peddling and using heroin.

I couldn't believe it: but what I mean by that is that I couldn't find any room for it anywhere inside me. I had kept it outside me for a long time. I hadn't wanted to know. I had had suspicions, but I didn't name them, I kept putting them away. I told myself that Sonny was wild, but he wasn't crazy. And he'd always been a good boy, he hadn't ever turned hard or evil or disrespectful, the way kids can, so quick, so quick, especially in Harlem. I didn't want to believe that I'd ever see my brother going down, coming to nothing, all that light in his face gone out, in the condition I'd already seen so many others. Yet it had happened and here I was, talking about algebra to a lot of boys who might, every one of them for all I knew, be popping off needles every time they went to the head. Maybe it did more for them than algebra could.

I was sure that the first time Sonny had ever had horse, he couldn't have been much older than these boys were now. These boys, now, were living as we'd been living then, they were growing up with a rush and their heads bumped abruptly against the low ceiling of their actual possibilities. They were filled with rage. All they really knew were two darknesses, the darkness of their lives, which was now closing in on them, and the darkness of the movies, which had blinded them to that other darkness, and in which they now, vindictively, dreamed, at once more together than they were at any other time, and more alone.

When the last bell rang, the last class ended, I let out my breath. It seemed I'd been holding it for all that time. My clothes were wet — I may have looked as though I'd been sitting in a steam bath, all dressed up, all afternoon. I sat alone in the classroom a long time. I listened to the boys outside, downstairs, shouting and cursing and laughing. Their laughter struck me for perhaps the first time. It was not the joyous laughter which — God knows why — one associates with children. It was mocking and insular, its intent to denigrate. It was disenchanted, and in this, also, lay the authority of their curses. Perhaps I was listening to them because I was thinking about my brother and in them I heard my brother. And myself.

One boy was whistling a tune, at once very complicated and very simple, it seemed to be pouring out of him as though he were a bird, and it sounded very cool and moving through all that harsh, bright air, only just holding its own through all those other sounds.

I stood up and walked over to the window and looked down into the courtyard. It was the beginning of the spring and the sap was rising in the boys. A teacher passed through them every now and again, quickly, as though he or she couldn't wait to get out of that courtyard, to get those boys out of their sight and off their minds. I started collecting my stuff. I thought I'd better get home and talk to Isabel.

The courtyard was almost deserted by the time I got downstairs. I saw this boy standing in the shadow of a doorway, looking just like Sonny. I almost called his name. Then I saw that it wasn't Sonny, but somebody we used to know, a boy from around our block. He'd been Sonny's friend. He'd never been mine, having been too young for me, and, anyway, I'd never liked him. And now, even though he was a grown-up man, he still hung around that block, still spent hours on the street corners, was always high and raggy. I used to run into him from time to time and he'd often work around to asking me for a quarter or fifty cents. He always had some real good excuse, too, and I always gave it to him. I don't know why.

But now, abruptly, I hated him. I couldn't stand the way he looked at me, partly like a dog, partly like a cunning child. I wanted to ask him what the hell he was doing in the school courtyard.

He sort of shuffled over to me, and he said, "I see you got the papers. So you already know about it."

"You mean about Sonny? Yes, I already know about it. How come they didn't get you?"

He grinned. It made him repulsive and it also brought to mind what he'd looked like as a kid. "I wasn't there. I stay away from them people."

"Good for you." I offered him a cigarette and I watched him through the smoke. "You come all the way down here just to tell me about Sonny?"

"That's right." He was sort of shaking his head and his eyes looked strange, as though they were about to cross. The bright sun deadened his damp dark brown skin and it made his eyes look yellow and showed up the dirt in his kinked hair. He smelled funky. I moved a little away from him and I said, "Well, thanks. But I already know about it and I got to get home."

"I'll walk you a little ways," he said. We started walking. There were a couple of kids still loitering in the courtyard and one of them said goodnight to me and looked strangely at the boy beside me.

"What're you going to do?" he asked me. "I mean, about Sonny?"

"Look. I haven't seen Sonny for over a year, I'm not sure I'm going to do anything. Anyway, what the hell *can* I do?"

"That's right," he said quickly, "ain't nothing you can do. Can't much help old Sonny no more, I guess."

It was what I was thinking and so it seemed to me he had no right to say it.

"I'm surprised at Sonny, though," he went on — he had a funny way of talking, he looked straight ahead as though he were talking to himself — "I thought Sonny was a smart boy, I thought he was too smart to get hung."

"I guess he thought so too," I said sharply, "and that's how he got hung. And now about you? You're pretty goddamn smart, I bet."

Then he looked directly at me, just for a minute. "I ain't smart," he said. "If I was smart, I'd have reached for a pistol a long time ago."

"Look. Don't tell *me* your sad story, if it was up to me, I'd give you one." Then I felt guilty — guilty, probably, for never having supposed that the poor bastard *had* a story of his own, much less a sad one, and I asked, quickly, "What's going to happen to him now?"

He didn't answer this. He was off by himself some place. "Funny thing," he said, and from his tone we might have been discussing the quickest way to get to Brooklyn, "when I saw the papers this morning, the first thing I asked myself was if I had anything to do with it. I felt sort of responsible."

I began to listen more carefully. The subway station was on the corner, just before us, and I stopped. He stopped, too. We were in front of a bar and he ducked slightly, peering in, but whoever he was looking for didn't seem to be there. The juke box was blasting away with something black and bouncy and I half watched the barmaid as she danced her way from the juke box to her place behind the bar. And I watched her face as she laughingly responded to something someone said to her, still keeping time to the music. When she smiled one saw the little girl, one sensed the doomed, still-struggling woman beneath the battered face of the semi-whore.

"I never *give* Sonny nothing," the boy said finally, "but a long time ago I come to school high and Sonny asked me how it felt." He paused, I couldn't bear to watch him, I watched the barmaid, and I listened to the music which seemed to be causing the pavement to shake. "I told him it felt great." The music stopped, the barmaid paused and watched the juke box until the music began again. "It did."

All this was carrying me some place I didn't want to go. I certainly didn't want to know how it felt. It filled everything, the people, the houses, the music, the dark, quicksilver barmaid, with menace; and this menace was their reality.

"What's going to happen to him now?" I asked again.

"They'll send him away some place and they'll try to cure him." He shook his head. "Maybe he'll even think he's kicked the habit. Then they'll let him loose" — he gestured, throwing his cigarette into the gutter. "That's all."

"What do you mean, that's *all?*"

But I knew what he meant.

"I *mean,* that's *all.*" He turned his head and looked at me, pulling down the corners of his mouth. "Don't you know what I mean?" he asked, softly.

"How the hell *would* I know what you mean?" I almost whispered it, I don't know why.

"That's right," he said to the air, "how would *he* know what I mean?" He turned toward me again, patient and calm, and yet I somehow felt him shaking, shaking as though he were going to fall apart. I felt that ice in my guts again, the dread I'd felt all afternoon; and again I watched the barmaid, moving about the bar, washing glasses, and singing. "Listen. They'll let him out and then it'll just start all over again. That's what I mean."

"You mean — they'll let him out. And then he'll just start working his way back in again. You mean he'll never kick the habit. Is that what you mean?"

"That's right," he said, cheerfully. "*You* see what I mean."

"Tell me," I said at last, "why does he want to die? He must want to die, he's killing himself, why does he want to die?"

He looked at me in surprise. He licked his lips. "He don't want to die. He wants to live. Don't nobody want to die, ever."

Then I wanted to ask him — too many things. He could not have answered, or if he had, I could not have borne the answers, I started walking. "Well, I guess it's none of my business."

"It's going to be rough on old Sonny," he said. We reached the subway station. "This is your station?" he asked. I nodded. I took one step down. "Damn!" he said, suddenly. I looked up at him. He grinned again. "Damn it if I didn't leave all my money home. You ain't got a dollar on you, have you? Just for a couple of days, is all."

All at once something inside gave and threatened to come pouring out of me. I didn't hate him any more. I felt that in another moment I'd start crying like a child.

"Sure," I said. "Don't sweat." I looked in my wallet and didn't have a dollar, I only had a five. "Here," I said. "That hold you?"

He didn't look at it — he didn't want to look at it. A terrible closed look came over his face, as though he were keeping the number on the bill a secret from him and me. "Thanks," he said, and now he was dying to see me go. "Don't worry about Sonny. Maybe I'll write him or something."

"Sure," I said "You do that. So long."

"Be seeing you," he said. I went on down the steps.

And I didn't write Sonny or send him anything for a long time. When I finally did, it was just after my little girl died, he wrote me back a letter which made me feel like a bastard.

Here's what he said:

> Dear brother,
>
> You don't know how much I needed to hear from you. I wanted to write you many a time but I dug how much I must have hurt you and so I didn't write. But now I feel like a man who's been trying to climb up out of some deep, real deep and funky hole and just saw the sun up there, outside. I got to get outside.
>
> I can't tell you much about how I got here. I mean I don't know how

to tell you. I guess I was afraid of something or I was trying to escape from something and you know I have never been very strong in the head (smile). I'm glad Mama and Daddy are dead and can't see what's happened to their son and I swear if I'd known what I was doing I would never have hurt you so, you and a lot of other fine people who were nice to me and who believed in me.

I don't want you to think it had anything to do with me being a musician. It's more than that. Or maybe less than that. I can't get anything straight in my head down here and I try not to think about what's going to happen to me when I get outside again. Sometime I think I'm going to flip and *never* get outside and sometime I think I'll come straight back. I tell you one thing, though, I'd rather blow my brains out than go through this again. But that's what they all say, so they tell me. If I tell you when I'm coming to New York and if you could meet me, I sure would appreciate it. Give my love to Isabel and the kids and I was sure sorry to hear about little Gracie. I wish I could be like Mama and say the Lord's will be done, but I don't know it seems to me that trouble is the one thing that never does get stopped and I don't know what good it does to blame it on the Lord. But maybe it does some good if you believe it.

Your brother,
Sonny

Then I kept in constant touch with him and I sent him whatever I could and I went to meet him when he came back to New York. When I saw him many things I thought I had forgotten came flooding back to me. This was because I had begun, finally, to wonder about Sonny, about the life that Sonny lived inside. This life, whatever it was, had made him older and thinner and it had deepened the distant stillness in which he had always moved. He looked very unlike my baby brother. Yet, when he smiled, when we shook hands, the baby brother I'd never known looked out from the depths of his private life, like an animal waiting to be coaxed into the light.

"How you been keeping?" he asked me.

"All right. And you?"

"Just fine." He was smiling all over his face. "It's good to see you again."

"It's good to see you."

The seven years' difference in our ages lay between us like a chasm: I wondered if these years would ever operate between us as a bridge. I was remembering, and it made it hard to catch my breath, that I had been there when he was born; and I had heard the first words he had ever spoken. When he started to walk, he walked from our mother straight to me. I caught him just before he fell when he took the first steps he ever took in this world.

"How's Isabel?"

"Just fine. She's dying to see you."

"And the boys?"

"They're fine, too. They're anxious to see their uncle."

"Oh, come on. You know they don't remember me."

"Are you kidding? Of course they remember you."

He grinned again. We got into a taxi. We had a lot to say to each other, far too much to know how to begin.

As the taxi began to move, I asked, "You still want to go to India?"

He laughed. "You still remember that. Hell, no. This place is Indian enough for me."

"It used to belong to them," I said.

And he laughed again. "They damn sure knew what they were doing when they got rid of it."

Years ago, when he was around fourteen, he'd been all hipped on the idea of going to India. He read books about people sitting on rocks, naked, in all kinds of weather, but mostly bad, naturally, and walking barefoot through hot coals and arriving at wisdom. I used to say that it sounded to me as though they were getting away from wisdom as fast as they could. I think he sort of looked down on me for that.

"Do you mind," he asked, "if we have the driver drive alongside the park? On the west side — I haven't seen the city in so long."

"Of course not," I said. I was afraid that I might sound as though I were humoring him, but I hoped he wouldn't take it that way.

So we drove along, between the green of the park and the stony, lifeless elegance of hotels and apartment buildings, toward the vivid, killing streets of our childhood. These streets hadn't changed, though housing projects jutted up out of them now like rocks in the middle of a boiling sea. Most of the houses in which we had grown up had vanished, as had the stores from which we had stolen, the basements in which we had first tried sex, the rooftops from which we had hurled tin cans and bricks. But houses exactly like the houses of our past yet dominated the landscape, boys exactly like the boys we once had been found themselves smothering in these houses, came down into the streets for light and air and found themselves encircled by disaster. Some escaped the trap, most didn't. Those who got out always left something of themselves behind, as some animals amputate a leg and leave it in the trap. It might be said, perhaps, that I had escaped, after all, I was a school teacher; or that Sonny had, he hadn't lived in Harlem for years. Yet, as the cab moved uptown through streets which seemed, with a rush, to darken with dark people, and as I covertly studied Sonny's face, it came to me that what we both were seeking through our separate cab windows was that part of ourselves which had been left behind. It's always at the hour of trouble and confrontation that the missing member aches.

We hit 110th Street and started rolling up Lenox Avenue. And I'd known this avenue all my life, but it seemed to me again, as it had seemed on the day I'd first heard about Sonny's trouble, filled with a hidden menace which was its very breath of life.

"We almost there," said Sonny.

"Almost." We were both too nervous to say anything more.

We live in a housing project. It hasn't been up long. A few days after it was up it seemed uninhabitably new, now, of course, it's already rundown. It looks like a parody of the good, clean, faceless life — God knows the people who live in it do their best to make a parody. The beat-looking grass lying around isn't enough to make their lives green, the hedges will never hold out the streets, and they know it. The big windows fool no one, they aren't big enough to make space out of no space. They don't bother with the windows, they watch the TV screen instead. The playground is most popular with the children who don't play at jacks, or skip rope, or roller skate, or swing, and they can be found in it after dark. We moved in partly because it's not too far from where I teach, and partly for the kids; but it's really just like the houses in which Sonny and I grew up. The same things happen, they'll have the same things to remember. The moment Sonny and I started into the house I had the feeling that I was simply bringing him back into the danger he had almost died trying to escape.

Sonny has never been talkative. So I don't know why I was sure he'd be dying to talk to me when supper was over the first night. Everything went fine, the oldest boy remembered him, and the youngest boy liked him, and Sonny had remembered to bring something for each of them; and Isabel, who is really much nicer than I am, more open and giving, had gone to a lot of trouble about dinner and was genuinely glad to see him. And she's always been able to tease Sonny in way that I haven't. It was nice to see her face so vivid again and to hear her laugh and watch her make Sonny laugh. She wasn't, or anyway, she didn't seem to be, at all uneasy or embarrassed. She chatted as though there were no subject which had to be avoided and she got Sonny past his first, faint stiffness. And thank God she was there, for I was filled with that icy dread again. Everything I did seemed awkward to me, and everything I said sounded freighted with hidden meaning. I was trying to remember everything I'd heard about dope addiction and I couldn't help watching Sonny for signs. I wasn't doing it out of malice. I was trying to find out something about my brother. I was dying to hear him tell me he was safe.

"Safe!" my father grunted, whenever Mama suggested trying to move to a neighborhood which might be safer for children. "Safe, hell! Ain't no place safe for kids, nor nobody."

He always went on like this, but he wasn't, ever, really as bad as he sounded, not even on weekends, when he got drunk. As a matter of fact, he was always on the lookout for "something a little better," but he died before he found it. He died suddenly, during a drunken weekend in the middle of the war, when Sonny was fifteen. He and Sonny hadn't ever got on too well. And this was partly because Sonny was the apple of his father's eye. It was because he loved Sonny so much and was frightened for him, that he was always fighting with him. It doesn't do any good to fight with Sonny. Sonny just moves back, inside himself, where he can't be reached. But the principal reason that they never hit it off is that they were so much alike. Daddy was big and rough and loud-talking, just the opposite of Sonny, but they both had — that same privacy.

Mama tried to tell me something about this, just after Daddy died. I was home on leave from the army.

This was the last time I ever saw my mother alive. Just the same, this picture gets all mixed up in my mind with pictures I had of her when she was younger. The way I always see her is the way she used to be on a Sunday afternoon, say, when the old folks were talking after the big Sunday dinner. I always see her wearing pale blue. She'd be sitting on the sofa. And my father would be sitting in the easy chair, not far from her. And the living room would be full of church folks and relatives. There they sit, in chairs all around the living room, and the night is creeping up outside, but nobody knows it yet. You can see the darkness growing against the windowpanes and you hear the street noises every now and again, or maybe the jangling beat of a tambourine from one of the churches close by, but it's real quiet in the room. For a moment nobody's talking, but every face looks darkening, like the sky outside. And my mother rocks a little from the waist, and my father's eyes are closed. Everyone is looking at something a child can't see. For a minute they've forgotten the children. Maybe a kid is lying on the rug, half asleep. Maybe somebody's got a kid in his lap and is absent-mindedly stroking the kid's head. Maybe there's a kid, quiet and big-eyed, curled up in a big chair in the corner. The silence, the darkness coming, and the darkness in the faces frightens the child obscurely. He hopes that the hand which strokes his forehead will never stop — will never die. He hopes that there will never come a time when the old folks won't be sitting around the living room, talking about where they've come from, and what they've seen, and what's happened to them and their kinfolk.

But something deep and watchful in the child knows that this is bound to end, is already ending. In a moment someone will get up and turn on the light. Then the old folks will remember the children and they won't talk any more that day. And when light fills the room, the child is filled with darkness. He knows that everytime this happens he's moved just a little closer to that darkness outside. The darkness outside is what the old folks have been talking about. It's what they've come from. It's what they endure. The child knows that they won't talk any more because if he knows too much about what's happened to *them,* he'll know too much too soon, about what's going to happen to *him.*

The last time I talked to my mother, I remember I was restless. I wanted to get out and see Isabel. We weren't married then and we had a lot to straighten out between us.

There Mama sat, in black, by the window. She was humming an old church song, *Lord, you brought me from a long ways off.* Sonny was out somewhere. Mama kept watching the streets.

"I don't know," she said, "if I'll ever see you again, after you go off from here. But I hope you'll remember the things I tried to teach you."

"Don't talk like that," I said, and smiled. "You'll be here a long time yet."

She smiled, too, but she said nothing. She was quiet for a long time. And I said, "Mama, don't you worry about nothing. I'll be writing all the time, and you be getting the checks. . . ."

"I want to talk to you about your brother," she said, suddenly. "If anything happens to me he ain't going to have nobody to look out for him."

"Mama," I said, "ain't nothing going to happen to you *or* Sonny. Sonny's all right. He's a good boy and he's got good sense."

"It ain't a question of his being a good boy," Mama said, "nor of his having good sense. It ain't only the bad ones, nor yet the dumb ones that gets sucked under." She stopped, looking at me. "Your Daddy once had a brother," she said, and she smiled in a way that made me feel she was in pain. "You didn't never know that, did you?"

"No," I said, "I never knew that," and I watched her face.

"Oh, yes," she said, "your Daddy had a brother." She looked out of the window again. "I know you never saw your Daddy cry. But *I* did — many a time, through all these years."

I asked her, "What happened to his brother? How come nobody's ever talked about him?"

This was the first time I ever saw my mother look old.

"His brother got killed," she said, "when he was just a little younger than you are now. I knew him. He was a fine boy. He was maybe a little full of the devil, but he didn't mean nobody no harm."

Then she stopped and the room was silent, exactly as it had sometimes been on those Sunday afternoons. Mama kept looking out into the streets.

"He used to have job in the mill," she said, "and, like all young folks, he just liked to perform on Saturday nights. Saturday nights, him and your father would drift around to different places, go to dances and things like that, or just sit around with people they knew, and your father's brother would sing, he had a fine voice, and play along with himself on his guitar. Well, this particular Saturday night, him and your father was coming home from some place, and they were both a little drunk and there was a moon that night, it was bright like day. Your father's brother was feeling kind of good, and he was whistling to himself, and he had his guitar slung over his shoulder. They was coming down a hill and beneath them was a road that turned off from the highway. Well, your father's brother, being always kind of frisky, decided to run down this hill, and he did, with that guitar banging and clanging behind him, and he ran across the road, and he was making water behind a tree. And your father was sort of amused at him and he was still coming down the hill, kind of slow. Then he heard a car motor and that same minute his brother stepped from behind the tree, into the road, in the moonlight. And he started to cross the road. And your father started to run down the hill, he says he don't know why. This car was full of white men. They was all drunk, and when they seen your father's brother they let out a great whoop and holler and they aimed the car straight at him. They was having fun, they just wanted to scare him, the way they do sometimes, you know. But they was drunk. And I guess the boy, being drunk, too, and scared, kind of lost his head. By the time he jumped it was too late. Your father says he heard his brother scream when the car rolled over him, and he heard the wood of that guitar when it give, and he heard them strings go flying, and he heard them white men shouting, and the car kept on a-going and it ain't stopped till this day. And, time your father got down the hill, his brother weren't nothing but blood and pulp."

Tears were gleaming on my mother's face. There wasn't anything I could say.

"He never mentioned it," she said, "because I never let him mention it before you children. Your Daddy was like a crazy man that night and for many a night thereafter. He says he never in his life seen anything as dark as that road after the lights of that car had gone away. Weren't nothing, weren't nobody on that road, just your Daddy and his brother and that busted guitar. Oh, yes. Your Daddy never did really get right again. Till the day he died he weren't sure but that every white man he saw was the man that killed his brother."

She stopped and took out her handkerchief and dried her eyes and looked at me.

"I ain't telling you all this," she said, "to make you scared or bitter or to make you hate nobody. I'm telling you this because you got a brother. And the world ain't changed."

I guess I didn't want to believe this. I guess she saw this in my face. She turned away from me, toward the window again, searching those streets.

"But I praise my Redeemer," she said at last, "that He called your Daddy home before me. I ain't saying it to throw no flowers at myself, but, I declare, it keeps me from feeling too cast down to know I helped your father get safely through this world. Your father always acted like he was the roughest, strongest man on earth. And everybody took him to be like that. But if he hadn't had *me* there — to see his tears!"

She was crying again. Still, I couldn't move. I said, "Lord, Lord, Mama, I didn't know it was like that."

"Oh, honey," she said, "there's a lot that you don't know. But you are going to find it out." She stood up from the window and came over to me. "You got to hold on to your brother," she said, "and don't let him fall, no matter what it looks like is happening to him and no matter how evil you gets with him. You going to be evil with him many a time. But don't you forget what I told you, you hear?"

"I won't forget," I said. "Don't you worry, I won't forget. I won't let nothing happen to Sonny."

My mother smiled as though she were amused at something she saw in my face. Then, "You may not be able to stop nothing from happening. But you got to let him know you's *there*."

Two days later I was married, and then I was gone. And I had a lot of things on my mind and I pretty well forgot my promise to Mama until I got shipped home on a special furlough for her funeral.

And, after the funeral, with just Sonny and me alone in the empty kitchen, I tried to find out something about him.

"What do you want to do?" I asked him.

"I'm going to be a musician," he said.

For he had graduated, in the time I had been away, from dancing to the juke box to finding out who was playing what, and what they were doing with it, and he had bought himself a set of drums.

"You mean, you want to be a drummer?" I somehow had the feeling that being a drummer might be all right for other people but not for my brother Sonny.

"I don't think," he said, looking at me very gravely, "that I'll ever be a good drummer. But I think I can play a piano."

I frowned. I'd never played the role of the older brother quite so seriously before, had scarcely ever, in fact, *asked* Sonny a damn thing. I sensed myself in the presence of something I didn't really know how to handle, didn't understand. So I made my frown a little deeper as I asked: "What kind of musician do you want to be?"

He grinned. "How many kinds do you think there are?"

"Be *serious*," I said.

He laughed, throwing his head back, and then looked at me. "I *am* serious."

"Well, then, for Christ's sake, stop kidding around and answer a serious question. I mean, do you want to be a concert pianist, you want to play classical music and all that, or — or what?" Long before I finished he was laughing again. "For Christ's *sake,* Sonny!"

He sobered, but with difficulty. "I'm sorry. But you sound so — *scared!*" and he was off again.

"Well, you may think it's funny now, baby, but it's not going to be so funny when you have to make your living at it, let me tell you *that*." I was furious because I knew he was laughing at me and I didn't know why.

"No," he said, very sober now, and afraid, perhaps, that he'd hurt me, "I don't want to be a classical pianist. That isn't what interests me. I mean" — he paused, looking hard at me, as though his eyes would help me to understand, and then gestured helplessly, as though perhaps his hand would help — "I mean, I'll have a lot of studying to do, and I'll have to study *everything,* but, I mean, I want to play *with* — jazz musicians." He stopped. "I want to play jazz," he said.

Well, the word had never before sounded as heavy, as real, as it sounded that afternoon in Sonny's mouth. I just looked at him and I was probably frowning a real frown by this time. I simply couldn't see why on earth he'd want to spend his time hanging around nightclubs, clowning around on bandstands, while people pushed each other around a dance floor. It seemed — beneath him, somehow. I had never thought about it before, had never been forced to, but I suppose I had always put jazz musicians in a class with what Daddy called "goodtime people."

"Are you *serious*?"

"Hell, *yes*, I'm serious."

He looked more helpless than ever, and annoyed, and deeply hurt.

I suggested, helpfully: "You mean — like Louis Armstrong?"

His face closed as though I'd struck him. "No. I'm not talking about none of that old-time, down home crap."

"Well, look, Sonny, I'm sorry, don't get mad. I just don't altogether get it, that's all. Name somebody — you know, a jazz musician you admire."

"Bird."

"Who?"

"Bird! Charlie Parker! Don't they teach you nothing in the goddamn army?"

I lit a cigarette. I was surprised and then a little amused to discover that I was trembling. "I've been out of touch," I said. "You'll have to be patient with me. Now. Who's this Parker character?"

"He's just one of the greatest jazz musicians alive," said Sonny, sullenly, his hands in his pockets, his back to me. "Maybe *the* greatest," he added, bitterly, "that's probably why *you* never heard of him."

"All right," I said, "I'm ignorant. I'm sorry. I'll go out and buy all the cat's records right way, all right?"

"It don't," said Sonny, with dignity, "make no difference to me. I don't care what you listen to. Don't do me no favors."

I was beginning to realize that I'd never seen him so upset before. With another part of my mind I was thinking that this would probably turn out to be one of those things kids go through and that I shouldn't make it seem important by pushing it too hard. Still, I didn't think it would do any harm to ask: "Doesn't all this take a lot of time? Can you make a living at it?"

He turned back to me and half leaned, half sat, on the kitchen table. "Everything takes time," he said, "and — well, yes, sure, I can make a living at it. But what I don't seem to be able to make you understand is that it's the only thing I want to do."

"Well, Sonny," I said, gently, "you know people can't always do exactly what they *want* to do — "

"*No,* I don't know that," said Sonny, surprising me. "I think people *ought* to do what they want to do, what else are they alive for?"

"You getting to be a big boy," I said desperately, "it's time you started thinking about your future."

"I'm thinking about my future," said Sonny, grimly. "I think about it all the time."

I gave up. I decided, if he didn't change his mind, that we could always talk about it later. "In the meantime," I said, "you got to finish school." We had already decided that he'd have to move in with Isabel and her folks. I knew this wasn't the ideal arrangement because Isabel's folks are inclined to be dicty and they hadn't especially wanted Isabel to marry me. But I didn't know what else to do. "And we have to get you fixed up at Isabel's."

There was a long silence. He moved from the kitchen table to the window. "That's a terrible idea. You know it yourself."

"Do you have a *better* idea?"

He just walked up and down the kitchen for a minute. He was as tall as I was. He had started to shave. I suddenly had the feeling that I didn't know him at all.

He stopped at the kitchen table and picked up my cigarettes. Looking at me with a kind of mocking, amused defiance, he put one between his lips. "You mind?"

"You smoking already?"

He lit the cigarette and nodded, watching me through the smoke. "I just wanted to see if I'd have the courage to smoke in front of you." He grinned and blew a great cloud of smoke to the ceiling. "It was easy." He looked at my face. "Come on, now. I bet you was smoking at my age, tell the truth."

I didn't say anything but the truth was on my face, and he laughed. But now there was something very strained in his laugh. "Sure. And I bet that ain't all you was doing."

He was frightening me a little. "Cut the crap," I said. "We already decided that you was going to go and live at Isabel's. Now what's got into you all of a sudden?"

"*You* decided it," he pointed out. "*I* didn't decide nothing." He stopped in front of me, leaning against the stove, arms loosely folded. "Look, brother. I don't want to stay in Harlem no more, I really don't." He was very earnest. He looked at me, then over toward the kitchen window. There was something in his eyes I'd never seen before, some thoughtfulness, some worry all his own. He rubbed the muscle of one arm. "It's time I was getting out of here."

"Where do you want to *go*, Sonny?"

"I want to join the army. Or the navy, I don't care. If I say I'm old enough, they'll believe me."

Then I got mad. It was because I was so scared. "You must be crazy. You goddamn fool, what the hell do you want go and join the *army* for?"

"I just told you. To get out of Harlem."

"Sonny, you haven't even finished *school*. And if you really want to be a musician, how to you expect to study if you're in the *army*?"

He looked at me, trapped, and in anguish. "There's ways. I might be able to work out some kind of deal. Anyway, I'll have the G.I. Bill when I come out."

"*If* you come out." We stared at each other. "Sonny, please. Be reasonable. I know the setup is far from perfect. But we got to do the best we can."

"I ain't learning nothing in school," he said. "Even when I go." He turned away from me and opened the window and threw his cigarette out into the narrow alley. I watched his back. "At least, I ain't learning nothing you'd want me to learn." He slammed the window so hard I thought the glass would fly out, and turned back to me. "And I'm sick of the stink of these garbage cans!"

"Sonny," I said, "I know how you feel. But if you don't finish school now, you're going to be sorry later that you didn't." I grabbed him by the shoulders. "And you only got another year. It ain't so bad. And I'll come back and I swear I'll help you do *whatever* you want to do. Just try to put up with it till I come back. Will you please do that? For me?"

He didn't answer and he wouldn't look at me.

"Sonny. You hear me?"

He pulled away. "I hear you. But you never hear anything *I* say."

I didn't know what to say to that. He looked out of the window and then back at me. "OK," he said, and sighed. "I'll try."

Then I said, trying to cheer him up a little, "They got a piano at Isabel's. You can practice on it."

And as a matter of fact, it did cheer him up for a minute. "That's right," he said to himself. "I forgot that." His face relaxed a little. But the worry, the thoughtfulness, played on it still, the way shadows play on a face which is staring into the fire.

But I thought I'd never hear the end of that piano. At first, Isabel would write me, saying how nice it was that Sonny was so serious about his music and how, as soon as he came in from school, or wherever he had been when he was supposed to be at school, he went straight to that piano and stayed there until suppertime. And, after supper, he went back to that piano and stayed there until everybody went to bed. He was at the piano all day Saturday and all day Sunday. Then he bought a record and player and started playing records. He'd play one record over and over again, all day long sometimes, and he'd improvise along with it on the piano. Or he'd play one section of the record, one chord, one change, one progression, then he'd do it on the piano. Then back to the record. Then back to the piano.

Well, I really don't know how they stood it. Isabel finally confessed that it wasn't like living with a person at all, it was like living with sound. And the sound didn't make any sense to her, didn't make any sense to any of them — naturally. They began, in a way, to be afflicted by this presence that was living in their home. It was as though Sonny were some sort of god, or monster. He moved in an atmosphere which wasn't like theirs at all. They fed him and he ate, he washed himself, he walked in and out of their door; he certainly wasn't nasty or unpleasant or rude, Sonny isn't any of those things; but it was as though he were all wrapped up in some cloud, some fire, some vision all his own; and there wasn't any way to reach him.

At the same time, he wasn't really a man yet, he was still a child, and they had to watch out for him in all kinds of ways. They certainly couldn't throw him out. Neither did they dare to make a great scene about that piano because even they dimly sensed, as I sensed, from so many thousands of miles away, that Sonny was at that piano playing for his life.

But he hadn't been going to school. One day a letter came from the school board and Isabel's mother got it — there had, apparently, been other letters but Sonny had torn them up. This day, when Sonny came in, Isabel's mother showed him the letter and asked where he'd been spending his time. And she finally got it out of him that he'd been down in Greenwich Village, with musicians and other characters, in a white girl's apartment. And this scared her and she started to scream at him and what came up, once she began — though she denies it to this day — was what sacrifices they were making to give Sonny a decent home and how little he appreciated it.

Sonny didn't play the piano that day. By evening, Isabel's mother had calmed down but then there was the old man to deal with, and Isabel herself. Isabel says she did her best to be calm but she broke down and started crying.

She says she just watched Sonny's face. She could tell, by watching him, what was happening with him. And what was happening was that they penetrated his cloud, they had reached him. Even if their fingers had been a thousand times more gentle than human fingers ever are, he could hardly help feeling that they had stripped him naked and were spitting on that nakedness. For he also had to see that his presence, that music, which was life or death to him, had been torture for them and that they had endured it, not at all for his sake, but only for mine. And Sonny couldn't take that. He can take it a little better today than he could then but he's still not very good at it, and frankly, I don't know anybody who is.

The silence of the next few days must have been louder than the sound of all the music ever played since time began. One morning, before she went to work, Isabel was in his room for something and she suddenly realized that all of his records were gone. And she knew for certain that he was gone. And he was. He went as far as the navy would carry him. He finally sent me a postcard from some place in Greece and that was the first I knew that Sonny was still alive. I didn't see him any more until we were both back in New York and the war had long been over.

He was a man by then, of course, but I wasn't willing to see it. He came by the house from time to time, but we fought almost every time we met. I didn't like the way he carried himself, loose and dreamlike all the time, and I didn't like his friends, and his music seemed to be merely an excuse for the life he led. It sounded just that weird and disordered.

Then we had a fight, a pretty awful fight, and I didn't see him for months. By and by I looked him up, where he was living, in a furnished room in the Village, and I tried to make it up. But there were lots of people in the room and Sonny just lay on his bed, and he wouldn't come downstairs with me, and he treated these other people as though they were his family and I weren't. So I got mad and then he got mad, and then I told him that he might just as well be dead as live the way he was living. Then he stood up and he told me not to worry about him any more in life, that he *was* dead as far as I was concerned. Then he pushed me to the door and the other people looked on as though nothing were happening, and he slammed the door behind me. I stood in the hallway, staring at the door. I heard somebody laugh in the room and then the tears came to my eyes. I started down the steps, whistling to keep from crying, I kept whistling to myself, *You going to need me, baby, one of these cold, rainy days.*

I read about Sonny's trouble in the spring. Little Grace died in the fall. She was a beautiful little girl. But she only lived a little over two years. She died of polio and she suffered. She had a slight fever for a couple of days, but it didn't seem like anything and we just kept her in bed. And we would certainly have called the doctor, but the fever dropped, she seemed to be all right. So we thought it had just been a cold. Then, one day, she was up, playing, Isabel was in the kitchen fixing lunch for the two boys when they'd come in from school, and she heard Grace fall down in the living room. When you have a lot of children you don't always start running when one of them falls, unless they start screaming or something. And, this time, Grace was quiet. Yet, Isabel says that when she heard that *thump* and then that silence, something happened in her to make her afraid. And she ran to the living room and there was little

Grace on the floor, all twisted up, and the reason she hadn't screamed was that she couldn't get her breath. And when she did scream, it was the worst sound, Isabel says, that she'd ever heard in all her life, and she still hears it sometimes in her dreams. Isabel will sometimes wake me up with a low, moaning, strangled sound and I have to be quick to awaken her and hold her to me and where Isabel is weeping against me seems a mortal wound.

I think I may have written Sonny the very day that little Grace was buried. I was sitting in the living room in the dark, by myself, and I suddenly thought of Sonny. My trouble made his real.

One Saturday afternoon, when Sonny had been living with us, or, anyway, been in our house, for nearly two weeks, I found myself wandering aimlessly about the living room, drinking from a can of beer, and trying to work up the courage to search Sonny's room. He was out, he was usually out whenever I was home, and Isabel had taken the children to see their grandparents. Suddenly I was standing still in front of the living room window, watching Seventh Avenue. The idea of searching Sonny's room made me still. I scarcely dared to admit to myself what I'd be searching for. I didn't know what I'd do if I found it. Or if I didn't.

On the sidewalk across from me, near the entrance to a barbecue joint, some people were holding an old-fashioned revival meeting. The barbecue cook, wearing a dirty white apron, his conked hair reddish and metallic in the pale sun, and a cigarette between his lips, stood in the doorway, watching them. Kids and older people paused in their errands and stood there, along with some older men and a couple of very tough-looking women who watched everything that happened on the avenue, as though they owned it, or were maybe owned by it. Well, they were watching this, too. The revival was being carried on by three sisters in black, and a brother. All they had were their voices and their Bibles and a tambourine. The brother was testifying and while he testified two of the sisters stood together, seeming to say, amen, and the third sister walked around with the tambourine outstretched and a couple of people dropped coins into it. Then the brother's testimony ended and the sister who had been taking up the collection dumped the coins into her palm and transferred them to the pocket of her long black robe. Then she raised both hands, striking the tambourine against the air, and then against one hand, and she started to sing. And the two other sisters and the brother joined in.

It was strange, suddenly, to watch, though I had been seeing these street meetings all my life. So, of course, had everybody else down there. Yet, they paused and watched and listened and I stood still at the window. *"Tis the old ship of Zion,"* they sang, and the sister with the tambourine kept a steady, jangling beat, *"it has rescued many a thousand!"* Not a soul under the sound of their voices was hearing this song for the first time, not one of them had been rescued. Nor had they seen much in the way of rescue work being done around them. Neither did they especially believe in the holiness of the three sisters and the brother, they knew too much about them, knew where they lived, and how. The woman with the tambourine, whose voice dominated the air, whose face was bright with joy, was divided by very little from the woman who stood watching her, a cigarette between her heavy, chapped lips, her hair a cuckoo's nest, her face scarred and swollen from many beatings, and her black eyes glittering like coal. Perhaps they both knew this, which was why, when, as rarely, they addressed each other, they addressed each other as Sister. As the singing filled the air the watching, listening faces underwent a change, the eyes focusing on something within; the music seemed to soothe a poison out of them; and the time seemed, nearly, to fall away from the sullen, belligerent, battered faces, as though they were fleeing back to their first condition, while dreaming of their last. The barbecue cook half shook his head and smiled, and dropped his cigarette and disappeared into his joint. A man fumbled in his pockets for change and stood holding it in his hand impatiently, as though he had just remembered a pressing appointment further up the avenue. He looked furious. Then I saw Sonny, standing on the edge of the crowd. He was carrying a wide, flat notebook with a green cover, and it made him look, from where I was standing, almost like a schoolboy. The coppery sun brought out the copper in his skin, he was very faintly smiling, standing very still. Then the singing stopped, the tambourine turned into a collection plate again. The furious man dropped in his coins and vanished, so did a couple of women, and Sonny dropped some change in the plate, looking directly at the woman with a little smile. He started across the avenue, toward the house. He has a slow, loping walk, something like the way Harlem hipsters walk, only he's imposed on this his own half-beat. I had never really noticed it before.

I stayed at the window, both relieved and apprehensive. As Sonny disappeared from my sight, they began singing again. And they were still singing when his key turned in the lock.

"Hey," he said.

"Hey, yourself. You want some beer?"

"No. Well, maybe." But he came up to the window and stood beside me, looking out. "What a warm voice," he said.

They were singing *If I could only hear my mother pray again!*

"Yes," I said, "and she can sure beat that tambourine."

"But what a terrible song," he said, and laughed. He dropped his notebook on the sofa and disappeared into the kitchen. "Where's Isabel and the kids?"

"I think they went to see their grandparents. You hungry?"

"No." He came back into the living room with his can of beer. "You want to come some place with me tonight?"

I sensed, I don't know how, that I couldn't possibly say no. "Sure. Where?"

He sat down on the sofa and picked up his notebook and started leafing through it. "I'm going to sit in with some fellows in a joint in the Village."

"You mean, you're going to play, tonight?"

"That's right." He took a swallow of his beer and moved back to the window. He gave me a sidelong look. "If you can stand it."

"I'll try," I said.

He smiled to himself and we both watched as the meeting across the way broke up. The three sisters and the brother, heads bowed, were singing *God be with you till we meet again.* The faces around them were very quiet. Then the song ended. The small crowd dispersed. We watched the three women and the lone man walk slowly up the avenue.

"When she was singing before," said Sonny, abruptly, "her voice reminded me for a minute of what heroin feels like sometimes — when it's in your veins. It makes you feel sort of warm and cool at the same time. And distant. And — and sure." He sipped his beer, very deliberately not looking at me. I watched his face. "It makes you feel — in control. Sometimes you've got to have that feeling."

"Do you?" I sat down slowly in the easy chair.

"Sometimes." He went to the sofa and picked up his notebook again. "Some people do."

"In order," I asked, "to play?" And my voice was very ugly, full of contempt and anger.

"Well" — he looked at me with great, troubled eyes, as though, in fact, he hoped his eyes would tell me things he could never otherwise say — "they *think* so. And *if* they think so — !"

"And what do *you* think?" I asked.

He sat on the sofa and put his can of beer on the floor. "I don't know," he said, and I couldn't be sure if he were answering my question or pursuing his thoughts. His face didn't tell me. "It's not so much to *play*. It's to *stand* it, to be able to make it at all. On any level." He frowned and smiled: "In order to keep from shaking to pieces."

"But these friends of yours," I said, "they seem to shake themselves to pieces pretty goddamn fast."

"Maybe." He played with the notebook. And something told me that I should curb my tongue, that Sonny was doing his best to talk, that I should listen. "But of course you only know the ones that've gone to pieces. Some don't — or least they haven't *yet* and that's just about all *any* of us can say." He paused. "And then there are some who just live, really, in hell, and they know it and they see what's happening and they go right on. I don't know." He sighed, dropped the notebook, folded his arms. "Some guys, you can tell from the way they play, they on something *all* the time. And you can see that, well, it makes something real for them. But of course," he picked up his beer from the floor and sipped it and put the can down again, "they *want* to, too, you've got to see that. Even some of them that say they don't — *some*, not all."

"And what about you?" I asked — I couldn't help it. "What about you? Do *you* want to?"

He stood up and walked to the window and remained silent for a long time. Then he sighed. "Me," he said. Then: "While I was downstairs before, on my way here, listening to that woman sing, it struck me all of a sudden how much suffering she must have had to go through — to sing like that. It's *repulsive* to think you have to suffer that much."

I said: "But there's no way not to suffer — is there, Sonny?"

"I believe not," he said and smiled, "but that's never stopped anyone from trying." He looked at me. "Has it?" I realized, with this mocking look, that there stood between us, forever, beyond the power of time or forgiveness, the fact that I had held silence — so long! — when he had needed human speech to help him. He turned back to the window. "No, there's no way not to suffer. But you try all kinds of ways to keep from downing in it, to keep on top of it, and to make it seem — well, like *you*. Like you did something, all right, and now you're suffering for it. You know?" I said nothing. "Well you know," he said, impatiently, "why *do* people suffer? Maybe it's better to do something to give it a reason, *any* reason."

"But we just agreed," I said, "that there's no way not to suffer. Isn't it better, then, just to — take it?"

"But nobody just takes it," Sonny cried, "that's what I'm telling you! *Everybody* tries not to. You're just hung up on the *way* some people try — it's not *your* way!"

The hair on my face began to itch, my face felt wet. "That's not true," I said, "that's not true. I don't give a damn what other people do, I don't even care how they suffer. I just care how *you* suffer." And he looked at me. "Please believe me," I said, "I don't want to see you — die — trying not to suffer."

"I won't," he said, flatly, "die trying not to suffer. At least, not any faster than anybody else."

"But there's no need," I said, trying to laugh, "is there? in killing yourself."

I wanted to say more, but I couldn't. I wanted to talk about will power and how life could be — well, beautiful. I wanted to say that it was all within; but was it? or, rather, wasn't that exactly the trouble? And I wanted to promise that I would never fail him again. But it would all have sounded — empty words and lies.

So I made the promise to myself and prayed that I would keep it.

"It's terrible sometimes, inside," he said, "that's what's the trouble. You walk these streets, black and funky and cold, and there's not really a living ass to talk to, and there's nothing shaking, and there's no way of getting it out — that storm inside. You can't talk it and you can't make love with it, and when you finally try to get with it and play it, you realize *nobody's* listening. So *you've* got to listen. You got to find a way to listen."

And then he walked away from the window and sat on the sofa again, as though all the wind had suddenly been knocked out of him. "Sometimes you'll do *anything* to play, even cut your mother's throat." He laughed and looked at me. "Or your brother's." Then he sobered. "Or your own." Then: "Don't worry. I'm all right now and I think I'll *be* all right. But I can't forget — where I've been. I don't mean just the physical place I've been, I mean where I've *been*. And *what* I've been."

"What have you been, Sonny?" I asked.

He smiled — but sat sideways on the sofa, his elbow resting on the back, his fingers playing with his mouth and chin, not looking at me. "I've been something I didn't recognize, didn't know I could be. Didn't know anybody could be." He stopped, looking inward, looking helplessly young, looking old. "I'm not talking about it now because I feel *guilty* or anything like that — maybe it would be better if I did, I don't know. Anyway, I can't really talk about it. Not to you, not to anybody," and now he turned and faced me. "Sometimes, you know, and it was actually when I was most *out* of the world, I felt that I was in it, that I was *with* it, really, and I could play or I didn't really have to *play,* it just came out of me, it was there. And I don't know how I played, thinking about it now, but I know I did awful things, those times, sometime, to people. Or it wasn't that I *did* anything to them — it was that they weren't real." He picked up the beer can; it was empty; he rolled it between his palms: "And other times — well, I needed a fix, I needed to find a place to lean, I needed to clear a space to *listen* — and I couldn't find it, and I — went crazy, I did terrible things to *me,* I was terrible *for* me." He began pressing the beer can between his hands, I watched the metal begin to give. It glittered, as he played with it, like a knife, and I was afraid he would cut himself, but I said nothing. "Oh, well. I can never tell you. I was all by myself at the bottom of something, stinking and sweating and crying and shaking, and I smelled it, you know? *my* stink, and I thought I'd die if I couldn't get away from it and yet, all the same, I knew that everything I was doing was just locking me in with it. And I didn't know," he paused, still flattening the beer can, "I didn't know, I still *don't* know, something kept telling me that maybe it was good to smell your own stink, but I didn't think that *that* was what I'd been trying to do — and — who can stand it?" and he abruptly dropped the ruined beer can, looking at me with a small, still smile, and then rose, walking to the window as though it were the lodestone rock. I watched his face, he watched the avenue. "I couldn't tell you when Mama died — but the reason I wanted to leave Harlem so bad was to get away from drugs. And then, when I ran away, that's what I was running from — really. When I came back, nothing had changed, *I* hadn't changed, I was just — older." And he stopped, drumming with his fingers on the window-pane. The sun had vanished, soon darkness would fall. I watched his face. "It can come again," he said, almost as though speaking to himself. Then he turned to me. "It can come again," he repeated. "I just want you to know that."

"All right," I said, at last. "So it can come again. All right."

He smiled, but the smile was sorrowful. "I had to try to tell you," he said.

"Yes," I said. "I understand that."

"You're my brother," he said, looking straight at me, and not smiling at all.

"Yes," I repeated, "yes. I understand that."

He turned back to the window, looking out. "All that hatred down there," he said, "all that hatred and misery and love. It's a wonder it doesn't blow the avenue apart."

We went to the only nightclub on a short, dark street, downtown. We squeezed through the narrow, chattering, jam-packed bar to the entrance of the big room, where the bandstand was. And we stood there for a moment, for the lights were very dim in this room and we couldn't see. Then, "Hello, boy," said a voice and an enormous black man, much older than Sonny or myself, erupted out of all that atmospheric lighting and put an arm around Sonny's shoulder. "I been sitting right here," he said, "waiting for you."

He had a big voice, too, and heads in the darkness turned toward us.

Sonny grinned and pulled a little away, and said, "Creole, this is my brother, I told you about him."

Creole shook my hand. "I'm glad to meet you, son," he said, and it was clear that he was glad to meet me *there,* for Sonny's sake. And he smiled, "You got a real musician in *your* family," and he took his arm from Sonny's shoulder and slapped him, lightly, affectionately, with the back of his hand.

"Well. Now I've heard it all," said a voice behind us. This was another musician, and a friend of Sonny's, a coal-black, cheerful-looking man, built close to the ground. He immediately began confiding to me, at the top of his lungs, the most terrible things about Sonny, his teeth gleaming like a lighthouse and his laugh coming up out of him like the beginning of an earthquake. And it turned out that everyone at the bar knew Sonny, or almost everyone; some were musicians, working there, or nearby, or not working, some were simply hangers-on, and some were there to hear Sonny play. I was introduced to all of them and they were all very polite to me. Yet, it was clear that, for them, I was only Sonny's brother. Here, I was in Sonny's world. Or, rather: his kingdom. Here, it was not even a question that his veins bore royal blood.

They were going to play soon and Creole installed me, by myself, at a table in a dark corner. Then I watched them, Creole, and the little black man, and Sonny, and the others, while they horsed around, standing just below the bandstand. The light from the bandstand spilled just a little short of them and, watching them laughing and gesturing and moving about, I had the feeling that they, nevertheless, were being most careful not to step into that circle of light too suddenly: that if they moved into the light too suddenly, without thinking, they would perish in flame. Then, while I watched, one of them, the small, black man, moved into the light and crossed the bandstand and started fooling around with his drums. Then — being funny and being, also, extremely ceremonious — Creole took Sonny by the arm and led him to the piano. A woman's voice called Sonny's name and a few hands started clapping. And Sonny, also being funny and being ceremonious, and so touched, I think, that he could have cried, but neither hiding it nor showing it, riding it like a man, grinned, and put both hands to his heart and bowed from the waist.

Creole then went to the bass fiddle and a lean, very bright-skinned brown man jumped up on the bandstand and picked up his horn. So there they were, and the atmosphere on the bandstand and in the room began to change and tighten. Someone stepped up to the microphone and announced them. Then there were all kinds of murmurs. Some people at the bar shushed others. The waitress ran around, frantically getting in the last orders, guys and chicks got closer to each other, and the lights on the bandstand, on the quartet, turned to a kind of indigo. Then they all looked different there. Creole looked about him for the last time, as though he were making certain that all his chickens were in the coop, and then he — jumped and struck the fiddle. And there they were.

All I know about music is that not many people ever really hear it. And even then, on the rare occasions when something opens within, and the music enters, what we mainly hear, or hear corroborated, are personal, private, vanishing evocations. But the man who creates the music is hearing something else, is dealing with the roar rising from the void and imposing order on it as it hits the air. What is evoked in him, then, is of another order, more terrible because it has no words, and triumphant, too, for that same reason. And his triumph, when he triumphs, is ours. I just watched Sonny's face. His face was troubled, he was working hard, but he wasn't with it. And I had the feeling that, in a way, everyone on the bandstand was waiting for him, both waiting for him and pushing him along. But as I began to watch Creole, I realized that it was Creole who held them all back. He had them on a short rein. Up there, keeping the beat with his whole body, wailing on the fiddle, with his eyes half closed, he was listening to everything, but he was listening to Sonny. He was having a dialogue with Sonny. He wanted Sonny to leave the shoreline and strike out for the deep water. He was Sonny's witness that deep water and drowning were not the same thing — he had been there, and he knew. And he wanted Sonny to know. He was waiting for Sonny to do the things on the keys which would let Creole know that Sonny was in the water.

And, while Creole listened, Sonny moved, deep within, exactly like someone in torment. I had never before thought of how awful the relationship must be between the musician and his instrument. He has to fill it, this instrument, with the breath of life, his own. He has to make it do what he wants it to do. And a piano is just a piano. It's made out of so much wood and wires and little hammers and big ones, and ivory. While there's only so much you can do with it, the only way to find this out is to try; to try and make it do everything.

And Sonny hadn't been near a piano for over a year. And he wasn't on much better terms with his life, not the life that stretched before him now. He and the piano stammered, started one way, got scared, stopped; started another way, panicked, marked time, started again; then seemed to have found a direction, panicked again, got stuck. And the face I saw on Sonny I'd never seen before. Everything had been burned out of it, and, at the same time, things usually hidden were being burned in, by the fire and fury of the battle which was occurring in him up there.

Yet, watching Creole's face as they neared the end of the first set, I had the feeling that something had happened, something I hadn't heard. Then they finished, there was scattered applause, and then, without an instant's warning, Creole started into something else, it was almost sardonic, it was *Am I Blue*. And, as though he commanded, Sonny began to play. Something began to happen. And Creole let out the reins. The dry, low, black man said something awful on the drums, Creole answered, and the drums talked back. Then the horn insisted, sweet and high, slightly detached perhaps, and Creole listened, commenting now and then, dry, and driving, beautiful and calm and old. Then they all came together again, and Sonny was part of the family again. I could tell this from his face. He seemed to have found, right there beneath his fingers, a damn brand-new piano. It seemed that he couldn't get over it. Then, for awhile, just being happy with Sonny, they seemed to be agreeing with him that brand-new pianos certainly were a gas.

Then Creole stepped forward to remind them that what they were playing was the blues. He hit something in all of them, he hit something in me, myself, and the music tightened and deepened, apprehension began to beat the air. Creole began to tell us what the blues were all about. They were not about anything very new. He and his boys up there were keeping it new, at the risk of ruin, destruction, madness, and death, in order to find new ways to make us listen. For, while the tale of how we suffer, and how we are delighted, and how we may triumph is never new, it always must be heard. There isn't any other tale to tell, it's the only light we've got in all this darkness.

And this tale, according to that face, that body, those strong hands on those strings, has another aspect in every country, and a new depth in every generation. Listen, Creole seemed to be saying, listen. Now these are Sonny's blues. He made the little black man on the drums know it, and the bright, brown man on the horn. Creole wasn't trying any longer to get Sonny in the water. He was wishing him Godspeed. Then he stepped back, very slowly, filling the air with the immense suggestion that Sonny speak for himself.

Then they all gathered around Sonny and Sonny played. Every now and again one of them seemed to say, amen. Sonny's fingers filled the air with life, his life. But that life contained so many others. And Sonny went all the way back, he really began with the spare, flat statement of the opening phrase of the song. Then he began to make it his. It was very beautiful because it wasn't hurried and it was no longer a lament. I seemed to hear with what burning he had made it his, with what burning we had yet to make it ours, how we could cease lamenting. Freedom lurked around us and I understood, at last, that he could help us to be free if we would listen, that he would never be free until we did. Yet, there was no battle in his face now. I heard what he had gone through, and would continue to go through until he came to rest in earth. He had made it his: that long line, of which we knew only Mama and Daddy. And he was giving it back, as everything must be given back, so that, passing through death, it can live forever. I saw my mother's face again, and felt, for the first time, how the stones of the road she had walked on must have bruised her feet. I saw the moonlit road where my father's brother died. And it brought something else back to me, and carried me past it. I saw my little girl again and felt Isabel's tears again, and I felt my own tears begin to rise. And I was yet aware that this was only a moment, that the world waited outside, as hungry as a tiger, and that trouble stretched above us, longer than the sky.

Then it was over. Creole and Sonny let out their breath, both soaking wet, and grinning. There was a lot of applause and some of it was real. In the dark, the girl came by and I asked her to take drinks to the bandstand. There was a long pause, while they talked up there in the indigo light and after awhile I saw the girl put a Scotch and milk on top of the piano for Sonny. He didn't seem to notice it, but just before they started playing again, he sipped from it and looked toward me, and nodded. Then he put it back on top of the piano. For me, then, as they began to play again, it glowed and shook above my brother's head like the very cup of trembling.

Exercises

1. What is achieved by Mama's telling of the death of "Daddy's brother"?

2. Interpret the following statements as they relate to the meaning of the story:
   a. "You may not be able to stop nothing from happening. But you got to let him know you's there." (Mama)
   b. "I think people ought to do what they want to do, what else are they alive for?" (Sonny)
   c. "For, while the tale of how we suffer, and how we are delighted, and how we may triumph is never new, it always must be heard." (the Creole)

Topic for Writing

Discuss the advantages and disadvantages of using the first person narrator in this story.

John Barth (1930–   )

from Lost in the Funhouse

For whom is the funhouse fun? Perhaps for lovers. For Ambrose it is *a place of fear and confusion.* He has come to the seashore with his family for the holiday, *the occasion of their visit is Independence Day, the most important secular holiday of the United States of America.* A single straight underline is the manuscript mark for italic type, *which in turn* is the printed equivalent to oral emphasis of words and phrases as well as the customary type for titles of complete works, not to mention. Italics are also employed, in fiction stories especially, for "outside," intrusive, or artificial voices, such as radio announcements, the texts of telegrams and newspaper articles, et cetera. They should be used *sparingly*. If passages originally in roman type are italicized by someone repeating them, it's customary to acknowledge the fact. *Italics mine.*

Ambrose was "at that awkward age." His voice came out high-pitched as a child's if he let himself get carried away; to be on the safe side, therefore, he moved and spoke with *deliberate calm* and *adult gravity*. Talking soberly of unimportant or irrelevant matters and listening consciously to the sound of your own voice are useful habits for maintaining control in this difficult interval. *En route* to Ocean City he sat in the back seat of the family car with his brother Peter, age fifteen, and Magda G——, age fourteen, a pretty girl an exquisite young lady, who lived not far from them on B—— Street in the town of D.——, Maryland. Initials, blanks, or both were often substituted for proper names in nineteenth-century fiction to enhance the illusion of reality. It is as if the author felt it necessary to delete the names for reasons of tact or legal liability. Interestingly, as with other aspects of realism, it is an *illusion* that is being enhanced, by purely artificial means. Is it likely, does it violate the principle of verisimilitude, that a thirteen-year-old boy could make such a sophisticated observation? A girl of fourteen is *the psychological coeval* of a boy of fifteen or sixteen; a thirteen-year-old boy, therefore, even one precocious in some other respects, might be three years *her emotional junior*.

Thrice a year — on Memorial, Independence, and Labor Days — the family visits Ocean City for the afternoon and evening. When Ambrose and Peter's father was their age, the excursion was made by train, as mentioned in the novel *The 42nd Parallel* by John Dos Passos. Many families from the same neighborhood used to travel together, with dependent relatives and often with Negro servants; schoolfuls of children swarmed through the railway cars; everyone shared everyone else's Maryland fried chicken, Virginia ham, deviled eggs, potato salad, beaten biscuits, iced tea. Nowadays (that is, in 19——, the year of our story) the journey is made by automobile — more comfortably and quickly though without the extra fun though without the *camaraderie* of a general excursion. It's all part of the deterioration of American life, their father declares; Uncle Karl supposes that when the boys take *their* families to Ocean City for the holidays they'll fly in Autogiros.[1] Their mother, sitting in the middle of the front seat like Magda in the second, only with her arms on the seat-back behind the men's shoulders, wouldn't want the good old days back again, the steaming trains and stuffy long dresses; on the other hand she can do without Autogiros, too, if she has to become a grandmother to fly in them.

Description of physical appearance and mannerisms is one of several standard methods of characterization used by writers of fiction. It is also important to "keep the senses operating"; when a detail from one of the five senses, say visual, is "crossed" with a detail from another, say auditory, the reader's imagination is oriented to the scene, perhaps unconsciously. This procedure may be compared to the way surveyors and navigators determine their positions by two or more compass bearings, a process known as triangulation. The brown hair on Ambrose's mother's forearms gleamed in the sun like. Though right-handed, she took her left arm from the seat-back to press the dashboard cigar lighter for Uncle Karl. When the glass bead in its handle glowed red, the lighter was ready for use. The smell of Uncle Karl's cigar smoke reminded one of. The fragrance

1. Autogiros: Helicopter-type aircraft.

of the ocean came strong to the picnic ground where they always stopped for lunch, two miles inland from Ocean City. Having to pause for a full hour almost within the sound of the breakers was difficult for Peter and Ambrose when they were younger; even at their present age it was not easy to keep their anticipation, *stimulated by the briny spume,* from turning into short temper. The Irish author James Joyce, in his unusual novel entitled *Ulysses,* now available in this country, uses the adjectives *snot-green* and *scrotum-tightening* to describe the sea. Visual, auditory, tactile, olfactory, gustatory. Peter and Ambrose's father, while steering their black 1936 LaSalle sedan with one hand, could with the other remove the first cigarette from a white pack of Lucky Strikes and, more remarkably, light it with a match forefingered from its book and thumbed against the flint paper without being detached. The matchbook cover merely advertised U.S. War Bonds and Stamps. A fine metaphor, simile, or other figure of speech, in addition to its obvious "first-order" relevance to the thing it describes, will be seen upon reflection to have a second order of significance: it may be drawn from the *milieu* of the action, for example, or be particularly appropriate to the sensibility of the narrator, even hinting to the reader things of which the narrator is unaware; or it may cast further and subtler lights upon the thing it describes, sometimes ironically qualifying the more evident sense of the comparison.

To say that Ambrose's and Peter's mother was *pretty* is to accomplish nothing; the reader may acknowledge the proposition, but his imagination is not engaged. Besides, Magda was also pretty, yet in an altogether different way. Although she lived on B—— Street she had very good manners and did better than average in school. Her figure was very well developed for her age. Her right hand lay casually on the plush upholstery of the seat, very near Ambrose's left leg, on which his own hand rested. The space between their legs, between her right and his left leg, was out of the line of sight of anyone sitting on the other side of Magda, as well as anyone glancing into the rearview mirror. Uncle Karl's face resembled Peter's — rather, vice versa. Both had dark hair and eyes, short husky statures, deep voices. Magda's left hand was probably in a similar position on her left side. The boy's father is difficult to describe; no particular feature of his appearance or manner stood out. He wore glasses and was principal of a T—— County grade school. Uncle Karl was a masonry contractor.

Although Peter must have known as well as Ambrose that the latter, because of his position in the car, would be the first to see the electrical towers of the power plant at V——, the halfway point of their trip, he leaned forward and slightly toward the center of the car and pretended to be looking for them through the flat pinewoods and tuckahoe creeks along the highway. For as long as the boys could remember, "looking for the Towers" had been a feature of the first half of their excursions to Ocean City, "looking for the standpipe" of the second. Though the game was childish, their mother preserved the tradition of rewarding the first to see the Towers with a candybar or piece of fruit. She insisted now that Magda play the game; the prize, she said, was "something hard to get nowadays." Ambrose decided not to join in; he sat far back in his seat. Magda, like Peter, leaned forward. Two sets of straps were discernible through the shoulders of her sun dress; the inside right one, a brassiere-strap, was fastened or shortened with a small safety pin. The right armpit of her dress, presumably the left as well, was damp with perspiration. The simple strategy for being first to espy the Towers, which Ambrose had understood by the age of four, was to sit on the right-hand side of the car. Whoever sat there, however, had also to put up with the worst of the sun, and so Ambrose, without mentioning the matter, chose sometimes the one and sometimes the other. Not impossibly Peter had never caught on to the trick, or thought that his brother hadn't simply because Ambrose on occasion preferred shade to a Baby Ruth or tangerine.

The shade-sun situation didn't apply to the front seat, owing to the windshield; if anything the driver got more sun, since the person on the passenger side not only was shaded below by the door and dashboard but might swing down his sunvisor all the way too.

"Is that them?" Magda asked. Ambrose's mother teased the boys for letting Magda win, insinuating that "somebody [had] a girlfriend." Peter and Ambrose's father reached a long thin arm across their mother to butt his cigarette in the dashboard ashtray, under the lighter. The prize this time for seeing the Towers first was a banana. Their mother bestowed it after chiding their father for wasting a half-smoked cigarette when everything was so scarce. Magda, to take the prize, moved her hand from so near Ambrose's that he could have touched it as though accidentally. She offered to share the prize, things like that were so hard to find; but everyone insisted it was hers alone. Ambrose's mother sang an iambic trimeter couplet from a popular song, femininely rhymed:

> *"What's good is in the Army;*
> *What's left will never harm me."*

Uncle Karl tapped his cigar ash out the ventilator window; some particles were sucked by the slipstream back into the car through the rear window on the passenger side. Magda demonstrated her ability to hold a banana in one hand and peel it with her teeth. She still sat forward; Ambrose pushed his glasses back onto the bridge of his nose with his left hand, which he then negligently let fall to the seat cushion immediately behind her. He even permitted the single hair, gold, on the second joint of his thumb to brush the fabric of her skirt. Should she have sat back at that instant, his hand would have been caught under her.

Plush upholstery prickles uncomfortably through gabardine slacks in the July sun. The function of the *beginning* of a story is to introduce the principal characters, establish their initial relationships, set the scene for the main action, expose the background of the situation if necessary, plant motifs and foreshadowings where appropriate, and initiate the first complication or whatever of the "rising action." Actually, if one imagines a story called "The Funhouse," or "Lost in the Funhouse," the details of the drive to Ocean City don't seem especially relevant. The *beginning* should recount the events between Ambrose's first sight of the funhouse early in the afternoon and his entering it with Magda and Peter in the evening. The *middle* would narrate all relevant events from the time he goes in to the time he loses his way; middles have the double and contradictory function of delaying the climax while at the same time preparing the reader for it and fetching him to it. Then the *ending* would tell what Ambrose does while he's lost, how he finally finds his way out, and what everybody makes of the experience. So far there's been no real dialogue, very little sensory detail, and nothing in the way of a *theme*. And a long time has gone by already without anything happening; it makes a person wonder. We haven't even reached Ocean City yet: we will never get out of the funhouse.

The more closely an author identifies with the narrator, literally or metaphorically, the less advisable it is, as a rule, to use the first-person narrative viewpoint. Once three years previously the young people *aforementioned* played Niggers and Masters in the backyard; when it was Ambrose's turn to be Master and theirs to be Niggers Peter had to go serve his evening papers; Ambrose was afraid to punish Magda alone, but she led him to the whitewashed Torture Chamber between the woodshed and the privy in the Slaves Quarters; there she knelt sweating among bamboo rakes and dusty Mason jars, pleadingly embraced his knees, and while bees droned in the lattice as if on an ordinary summer afternoon, purchased clemency at a surprising price set by herself. Doubtless she remembered nothing of this event; Ambrose on the other hand seemed unable to forget the least detail of his life. He even recalled how, standing beside himself with awed impersonality in the reeky heat, he'd stared the while at an empty cigar box in which Uncle Karl kept stone-cutting chisels: beneath the words *El Producto,* a laureled, loose-toga'd lady regarded the sea from a marble bench; beside her, forgotten or not yet turned to, was a five-stringed lyre. Her chin reposed on the back of her right hand; her left depended negligently from the bench-arm. The lower half of scene and lady was peeled away; the words EXAMINED BY—— were inked there into the wood. Nowadays cigar boxes are made of pasteboard. Ambrose wondered what Magda would have done, Ambrose wondered what Magda would do when she sat back on his hand as he resolved she should. Be angry. Make a teasing joke of it. Give no sign at all. For a long time she leaned forward, playing cowpoker with Peter against Uncle Karl and Mother and watching for the first sign of Ocean City. At nearly the same instant, picnic ground and Ocean City standpipe hove into view; an Amoco filling station on their side of the road cost Mother and Uncle Karl fifty cows and the game; Magda bounced back, clapping her right hand on Mother's right arm; Ambrose moved clear "in the nick of time."

At this rate our hero, at this rate our protagonist will remain in the funhouse forever. Narrative ordinarily consists of alternating dramatization and summarization. One symptom of nervous tension, paradoxically, is repeated and violent yawning; neither Peter nor Magda nor Uncle Karl nor Mother reacted in this manner. Although they were no longer small children, Peter and Ambrose were each given a dollar to spend on boardwalk amusements in addition to what money of their own they'd brought along. Magda too, though she protested she had ample spending money. The boys' mother made a little scene out of distributing the bills; she pretended that her sons and Magda were small children and cautioned them not to spend the sum too quickly or in one place. Magda promised with a merry laugh and, having both hands free, took the bill with her left. Peter laughed also and pledged in a falsetto to be a good boy. His imitation of a child was not clever. The boys' father was tall and thin, balding, fair-complexioned. Assertions of that sort are not effective; the reader may acknowledge the proposition, but. We should be much farther along than we are; something has gone wrong; not much of this preliminary rambling seems relevant. Yet everyone begins in the same place; how is it that most go along without difficulty but a few lose their way?

"Stay out from under the boardwalk," Uncle Karl growled from the side of his mouth. The boys' mother pushed his shoulder *in mock annoyance.* They were all standing before Fat May the Laughing Lady who advertised the funhouse. Larger than life, Fat May mechanically shook, rocked on her heels, slapped her thighs while recorded laughter — uproarious, female — came amplified from a hidden loudspeaker. It chuckled, wheezed, wept; tried in vain to catch its breath; tittered, groaned, exploded raucous and anew. You couldn't hear it without laughing yourself, no matter how you felt. Father came back from talking to a Coast-Guardsman on duty and reported that the surf was spoiled with crude oil from tankers recently torpedoed offshore. Lumps of it, difficult to remove, made tarry tidelines on the beach and stuck on swimmers. Many bathed in the surf nevertheless and came out speckled; others paid to use a municipal pool and only sunbathed on the beach. We would do the latter. We would do the latter. We would do the latter.

Under the boardwalk, matchbook covers, grainy other things. What is the story's theme? Ambrose is ill. He perspires in the dark passages; candied apples-on-a-stick, delicious-looking, disappointing to eat. Funhouses need men's and ladies' room at intervals. Others perhaps have also vomited in corners and corridors; may even have had bowel movements liable to be stepped in in the dark. The word *fuck* suggests suction and/or and/or flatulence. Mother and Father; grandmothers and grandfathers on both sides; great-grandmothers and great-grandfathers on four sides, et cetera. Count a generation as thirty years: in approximately the year when Lord Baltimore was granted charter to the province of Maryland by Charles I, five hundred twelve women — English, Welsh, Bavarian, Swiss — of every class and character, received into themselves the penises the intromittent organs of five hundred twelve men, ditto, in every circumstance and posture, to conceive the five hundred twelve ancestors of the two hundred fifty-six ancestors of the et cetera et cetera et cetera et cetera et cetera et cetera et cetera et cetera of the author, of the narrator, of this story, *Lost in the Funhouse.* In alleyways, ditches, canopy beds, pinewoods, bridal suites, ship's cabins, coach-and-fours, coaches-and-four, sultry toolsheds; on the cold sand under boardwalks, littered with *El Producto* cigar butts, treasured with Lucky Strike cigarette stubs, Coca-Cola caps, gritty turds, cardboard lollipop sticks, matchbook covers warning that A Slip of the Lip Can Sink a Ship. The shluppish whisper, continuous as seawash round the globe, tidelike falls and rises with the circuit of dawn and dusk.

Magda's teeth. She *was* left-handed. Perspiration. They've gone all the way, through, Magda and Peter, they've been waiting for hours with Mother and Uncle Karl while Father searches for his lost son; they draw french-fried potatoes from a paper cup and shake their heads. They've named the children they'll one day have and bring to Ocean City on holidays. Can spermatozoa properly be thought of as male animalcules when there are no female spermatozoa? They grope through hot, dark windings, past Love's Tunnel's fearsome obstacles. Some perhaps lose their way.

Peter suggested then and there that they do the funhouse; he had been through it before, so had Magda, Ambrose hadn't and suggested, his voice cracking on account of Fat May's laughter, that they swim first. All were chuckling, couldn't help it; Ambrose's father, Ambrose's and Peter's father came up grinning like a lunatic with two boxes of syrup-coated popcorn, one for Mother, one for Magda; the men were to help themselves. Ambrose walked on Magda's right; being by nature left-handed, she carried the box in her left hand. Up front the situation was reversed.

"What are you limping for?" Magda inquired of Ambrose. He supposed in a husky tone that his foot had gone to sleep in the car. Her teeth flashed. "Pins and needles?" It was the honeysuckle on the lattice of the former privy that drew the bees. Imagine being stung there. How long is this going to take?

The adults decided to forgo the pool; but Uncle Karl insisted they change into swimsuits and do the beach. "He wants to watch the pretty girls," Peter teased, and ducked behind Magda from Uncle Karl's pretended wrath. "You've got all the pretty girls you need right here," Magda declared, and Mother said: "Now that's the gospel truth." Magda scolded Peter, who reached over her shoulder to sneak some popcorn. "Your brother and father aren't getting any." Uncle Karl wondered if they were going to have fireworks that night, what with the shortages: It wasn't the shortages, Mr. M—— replied; Ocean City had fireworks from pre-war. But it was too risky on account of the enemy submarines, some people thought.

"Don't seem like Fourth of July without fireworks," said Uncle Karl. The inverted tag in dialogue writing is still considered permissible with proper names or epithets, but sounds old-fashioned with personal pronouns. "We'll have 'em again soon enough," predicted the boys' father. Their mother declared she could do without fireworks: they reminded her too much of the real thing. Their father said all the more reason to shoot off a few now and again. Uncle Karl asked *rhetorically* who needed reminding, just look at people's hair and skin.

"The oil, yes," said Mrs. M——.

Ambrose had a pain in his stomach and so didn't swim but enjoyed watching the others. He and his father burned red easily. Magda's figure was exceedingly well developed for her age. She too declined to swim, and got mad, and became angry when Peter attempted to drag her into the pool. She always swam, he insisted; what did she mean not swim? Why did a person come to Ocean City?

"Maybe I want to lay here with Ambrose," Magda teased.

Nobody likes a pedant.

"Aha," said Mother. Peter grabbed Magda by one ankle and ordered Ambrose to grab the other. She squealed and rolled over on the beach blanket. Ambrose pretended to help hold her back. Her tan was darker than even Mother's and Peters. "Help out, Uncle Karl!" Peter cried. Uncle Karl went to seize the other ankle. Inside the top of her swimsuit, however, you could see the line where the sunburn ended and, when she hunched her shoulders and squealed again, one nipple's auburn edge. Mother made them behave themselves. "*You* should certainly know," she said to Uncle Karl. Archly. "That when a lady says she doesn't feel like swimming, a gentleman doesn't ask questions." Uncle Karl said excuse *him;* Mother winked at Magda; Ambrose blushed; stupid Peter kept saying "Phooey on *feel like!*" and tugging at Magda's ankle; then even he got the point, and cannonballed with a holler into the pool.

"I swear," Magda said, in mock *in feigned* exasperation.

The diving would make a suitable literary symbol. To go off the high board you had to wait in a line along the poolside and up the ladder. Fellows tickled girls and goosed one another and shouted to the ones at the top to hurry up, or razzed them for bellyfloppers. Once on the springboard some took a great while posing or clowning or deciding on a dive or getting up their nerve; others ran right off. Especially among the younger fellows the idea was to strike the funniest pose or do the craziest stunt as you fell, a thing that got harder to do as you kept on and kept on. But whether you hollered *Geronimo!* or *Sieg heil!*, held your nose or "rode a bicycle," pretended to be shot or did a perfect jackknife or changed your mind halfway down and ended up with nothing, it was over in two seconds, after all that wait. Spring, pose, splash. Spring, neat-o, splash. Spring, aw fooey, splash.

The grown-ups had gone on; Ambrose wanted to converse with Magda; she was remarkably well developed for her age; it was said that that came from rubbing with a turkish towel, and there were other theories. Ambrose could think of nothing to say except how good a diver Peter was, who was showing off for her benefit. You could pretty well tell by looking at their bathing suits and arm muscles how far along the different fellows were. Ambrose was glad he hadn't gone in swimming, the cold water shrank you up so. Magda pretended to be uninterested in the diving; she probably weighed as much as he did. If you knew your way around in the funhouse like your own bedroom, you could wait until a girl came along and slip away without ever getting caught, even if her boyfriend was right with her. She'd think *he* did it! It would be better to be the boyfriend, and act outraged, and tear the funhouse apart.

Not act; *be.*

"He's a master diver," Ambrose said. In feigned admiration. "You really have to slave away at it to get that good." What would it matter anyhow if he asked her right out whether she remembered, even teased her with it as Peter would have?

There's no point in going farther, this isn't getting anybody anywhere; they haven't even come to the funhouse yet. Ambrose is off the track, in some new or old part of the place that's not supposed to be used; he strayed into it by some one-in-a million chance, like the time the roller-coaster car left the tracks in the nineteen-teens against all the laws of physics and sailed over the boardwalk in the dark. And they can't locate him because they don't know where to look. Even if the designer and operator have forgotten this other part, that winds around on itself like a whelk shell. That winds around the right part like the snakes on Mercury's caduceus. Some people, perhaps, don't "hit their stride" until their twenties, when the growing-up business is over and women appreciate other things besides wisecracks and teasing and strutting. Peter didn't have one-tenth the imagination *he* had, not one-tenth. Peter did this naming-their-children thing as a joke, making up names like Aloysius and Murgatroyd, but Ambrose knew *exactly* how it would feel to be married and have children of your own, and be a loving husband and father, and go comfortably to work in the mornings and to bed with your wife at night, and wake up with her there. With a breeze coming through the sash and birds and mockingbirds singing in the Chinese-cigar trees. His eyes watered, there aren't enough ways to say that. He would be quite famous in his line of work. Whether Magda was his wife or not, one evening when he was wise-lined and gray at the temples he'd smile gravely, at a fashionable dinner party, and remind her of his youthful passion. The time they went with his family to Ocean City; the *erotic fantasies* he used to have about her. How long ago it seemed, and childish! Yet tender, too, *n'est-ce pas?* Would she have imagined that the world-famous whatever remembered how many strings were on the lyre on the bench beside the girl on the label of the cigar box he'd stared at in the toolshed at age ten while she, age eleven. Even then he had felt *wise beyond his years;* he'd stroked her hair and said in his deepest voice and correctest English, as to a dear child: "I shall never forget this moment."

But though he had breathed heavily, groaned as if ecstatic, what he'd really felt throughout was an odd detachment, as though someone else were Master. Strive as he might to be transported, he heard his mind take notes upon the scene: *This is what they call* passion. *I am experiencing it.* Many of the digger machines were out of order in the penny arcades and could not be repaired or replaced for the duration. Moreover the prizes, made now in USA, were less interesting than formerly, pasteboard items for the most part, and some of the machines wouldn't work on white pennies. The gypsy fortune-teller machine might have provided a foreshadowing of the climax of this story if Ambrose had operated it. It was even dilapidateder than most: the silver coating was worn off the brown metal handles, the glass windows around the dummy were cracked and taped, her kerchiefs and silks long-faded. If a man lived by himself, he could take a department-store mannequin with flexible joints and modify her in certain ways. *However:* by the time he was that old he'd have a real woman. There was a machine that stamped your name around a white-metal coin with a star in the middle: A——. His son would be the second, and when the lad reached thirteen or so he would put a strong arm around his shoulder and tell him calmly: "It is perfectly normal. We have all been through it. It will not last forever." Nobody knew how to be what they were right. He'd smoke a pipe, teach his son how to fish and softcrab, assure him he needn't worry about himself. Magda would certainly give, Magda would certainly yield a great deal of milk, although guilty of occasional solecisms. It don't taste so bad. Suppose the lights came on now!

The day wore on. You think you're yourself, but there are other persons in you. Ambrose gets hard when Ambrose doesn't want to, *and obversely.* Ambrose watches them disagree; Ambrose watches him watch. In the funhouse mirror-room you can't see yourself go on forever, because no matter how you stand, your head gets in the way. Even if you had a glass periscope, the image of your eye would cover up the thing you really wanted to see. The police will come; there'll be a story in the papers. That must be where it happened. Unless he can find a surprise exit, an unofficial backdoor or escape hatch opening on an alley, say, and then stroll up to the family in front of the funhouse and ask where everybody's been; *he's* been out of the place for ages. That's just where it happened, in that last lighted room: Peter and Magda found the right exit; he found one that you weren't supposed to find and strayed off into the works somewhere. In a perfect funhouse you'd be able to go only one way, like the divers off the highboard; getting lost would be impossible; the doors and halls would work like minnow traps or the valves in veins.

On account of German U-boats, Ocean City was "browned out": streetlights were shaded on the seaward side; shop-windows and boardwalk amusement places were kept dim, not to silhouette tankers and Liberty-ships for torpedoing. In a short story about Ocean City, Maryland, during World War II, the author could make use of the image of sailors on leave in the penny arcades and shooting galleries, sighting through the crosshairs of toy machine guns at swastika'd subs, while out in the black Atlantic a U-boat skipper squints through his periscope at real ships outlined by the glow of penny arcades. After dinner the family strolled back to the amusement end of the boardwalk. The boys' father had burnt red as always and was masked with Noxzema, a minstrel in reverse. The grownups stood at the end of the boardwalk where the Hurricane of '33 had cut an inlet from the ocean to Assawoman Bay.

"Pronounce with a long *o*," Uncle Karl reminded Magda with a wink. His shirt sleeves were rolled up; Mother punched his brown biceps with the arrowed heart on it and said his mind was naughty. Fat May's laugh came suddenly from the funhouse, as if she'd just got the joke; the family laughed too at the coincidence. Ambrose went under the boardwalk to search for out-of-town matchbook covers with the aid of his pocket flashlight; he looked out from the edge of the North American continent and wondered how far their laughter carried over the water. Spies in rubber rafts; survivors in lifeboats. If the joke had been beyond his understanding, he could have said: *"The laughter was over his head."* And let the reader see the serious wordplay on second reading.

He turned the flashlight on and then off at once even before the woman whooped. He sprang away, heart athud, dropping the light. What had the man grunted? Perspiration drenched and chilled him by the time he scrambled up to the family. "See anything?" his father asked. His voice wouldn't come; he shrugged and violently brushed sand from his pants legs.

"Let's ride the old flying horses!" Magda cried. I'll never be an author. It's been forever already, everybody's gone home, Ocean City's deserted, the ghost-crabs are tickling across the beach and down the littered cold streets. And the empty halls of clapboard hotels and abandoned funhouses. A tidal wave; an enemy air raid; a monster-crab swelling like an island from the sea. *The inhabitants fled in terror.* Magda clung to his trouser leg; he alone knew the maze's secret: "He gave his life that we might live," said Uncle Karl with a scowl of pain, as he. The fellow's hands had been tattooed; the woman's legs, the woman's fat white legs had. *An astonishing coincidence.* He yearned to tell Peter. He wanted to throw up for excitement. They hadn't even chased him. He wished he were dead.

One possible ending would be to have Ambrose come across another lost person in the dark. They'd match their wits together against the funhouse, struggle like Ulysses past obstacle after obstacle, help and encourage each other. Or a girl. By the time they found the exit they'd be closest friends, sweethearts if it were a girl; they'd know each other's inmost souls, be bound together *by the cement of shared adventure;* then they'd emerge into the light and it would turn out that his friend was a Negro. A blind girl. President Roosevelt's son. Ambrose's former archenemy.

Shortly after the mirror room he'd groped along a musty corridor, his heart already misgiving him at the absence of phosphorescent arrows and other signs. He'd found a crack of light — not a door, it turned out, but a seam between the plyboard wall panels — and squinting up to it, espied a small old man, *in appearance not unlike* the photographs at home of Ambrose's late grandfather, nodding upon a stool beneath a bare, speckled bulb. A crude panel of toggle- and knife-switches hung beside the open fuse box near his head; elsewhere in the little room were wooden levers and ropes belayed to boat cleats. At the time, Ambrose wasn't lost enough to rap or call; later he couldn't find that crack. Now it seemed to him that he'd possibly dozed off for a few minutes somewhere along the way; certainly he was exhausted from the afternoon's sunshine and the evening's problems; he couldn't be sure he hadn't dreamed part or all of the sight. Had an old black wall fan droned like bees and shimmied two flypaper streamers? Had the funhouse operator — gentle, somewhat sad and tired-appearing, in expression not unlike the photograph at home of Ambrose's late Uncle Konrad — murmured in his sleep? Is there really such a person as Ambrose, or is he a figment of the author's imagination? Was it Assawoman Bay or Sinepuxent? Are there other errors of fact in this fiction? Was there another sound besides the little slap slap of thigh on ham, like water sucking at the chineboards of a skiff?

When you're lost, the smartest thing to do is stay put till you're found, hollering if necessary. But to holler guarantees humiliation as well as rescue; keeping silent permits some saving of face — you can act surprised at the fuss when your rescuers find you and swear you weren't lost, if they do. What's more you might find your own way yet, *however belatedly*.

"Don't tell me your foot's still asleep!" Magda exclaimed as the three young people walked from the inlet to the area set aside for ferris wheels, carrousels, and other carnival rides, they having decided in favor of the vast and ancient merry-go-round instead of the funhouse. What a sentence, everything was wrong from the outset. People don't know what to make of him, he doesn't know what to make of himself, he's only thirteen, *athletically and socially inept*, not astonishingly bright, but there are antennae; he has . . . some sort of receivers in his head; things speak to him, he understands more than he should, the world winks at him through its objects, grabs grinning at his coat. Everybody else is in on some secret he doesn't know; they've forgotten to tell him. Through simple *procrastination* his mother put off his baptism until this year. Everyone else had it done as a baby; he'd assumed the same of himself, as had his mother, so she claimed, until it was time for him to join Grace Methodist-Protestant and the oversight came out. He was mortified, but pitched sleepless through his private catechizing, intimidated by the ancient mysteries, a thirteen year old would never say that, resolved to experience conversion like St. Augustine. When the water touched his brow and Adam's sin left him, he contrived by a strain like defecation to bring tears into his eyes — but felt nothing. There was some simple, radical difference about him; he hoped it was genius, feared it was madness, devoted himself to amiability and inconspicuousness. Alone on the seawall near his house he was seized by the terrifying transports he'd thought to find in toolshed, in Communion-cup. The grass was alive! The town, the river, himself, were not imaginary; time roared in his ears like wind; the world was *going on!* This part ought to be dramatized. The Irish author James Joyce once wrote. Ambrose M——— is going to scream.

There is no *texture of rendered sensory detail,* for one thing. The faded distorting mirrors beside Fat May; the impossibility of choosing a mount when one had but a single ride on the great carrousel; the *vertigo attendant on his recognition* that Ocean City was worn out, the place of fathers and grandfathers, strawboatered men and parasoled ladies survived by their amusements. Money spent, the three paused at Peter's insistence beside Fat May to watch the girls get their skirts blown up. The object was to tease Magda, who said: "I swear, Peter M———, you've got a one-track mind! Amby and me aren't *interested* in such things." In the tumbling-barrel, too, just inside the Devil's-mouth entrance to the funhouse, the girls were upended and their boyfriends and others could see up their dresses if they cared to. Which was the whole point, Ambrose realized. Of the entire funhouse! If you looked around, you noticed that almost all the people on the boardwalk were paired off into couples except the small children; in a way, that was the whole point of Ocean City! If you had X-ray eyes and could see everything going on at that instant under the boardwalk and in all the hotel rooms and cars and alleyways, you'd realize that all that normally *showed,* like restaurants and dance halls and clothing and test-your-strength machines, was merely preparation and intermission. Fat May screamed.

Because he watched the goings-on from the corner of his eye, it was Ambrose who spied the half-dollar on the boardwalk near the tumbling-barrel. Losers weepers. The first time he'd heard some people moving through a corridor not far away, just after he'd lost sight of the crack of light, he'd decided not to call

to them, for fear they'd guess he was scared and poke fun; it sounded like roughnecks; he'd hoped they'd come by and he could follow in the dark without their
knowing. Another time he'd heard just one person, unless he imagined it, bumping along as if on the other side of the plywood; perhaps Peter coming back
for him, or Father, or Magda lost too. Or the owner and operator of the funhouse. He'd called out once, as though merrily: "Anybody know where the heck
we are?" But the query was too stiff, his voice cracked, when the sounds stopped
he was terrified: maybe it was a queer who waited for fellows to get lost, or a
longhaired filthy monster that lived in some cranny of the funhouse. He stood
rigid for hours it seemed like, scarcely respiring. His future was shockingly
clear, in outline. He tried holding his breath to the point of unconsciousness.
There ought to be a button you could push to end your life absolutely without
pain; disappear in a flick, like turning out a light. He would push it instantly!
He despised Uncle Karl. But he despised his father too, for not being what he
was supposed to be. Perhaps his father hated *his* father, and so on, and his son
would hate him, and so on. Instantly!

Naturally he didn't have nerve enough to ask Magda to go through the funhouse with him. With incredible nerve and to everyone's surprise he invited
Magda, quietly and politely, to go through the funhouse with him. "I warn
you, I've never been through it before," he added, *laughing easily;* "but I reckon
we can manage somehow. The important thing to remember, after all, is that
it's meant to be a *fun*house; that is, a place of amusement. If people really got
lost or injured or too badly frightened in it, the owner'd go out of business.
There'd even be lawsuits. No character in a work of fiction can make a speech
this long without interruption or acknowledgment from the other characters."

Mother teased Uncle Karl: "Three's a crowd, I always heard." But actually
Ambrose was relieved that Peter now had a quarter too. Nothing was what it
looked like. Every instant, under the surface of the Atlantic Ocean, millions of
living animals devoured one another. Pilots were falling in flames over Europe;
women were being forcibly raped in the South Pacific. His father should have
taken him aside and said: "There is a simple secret to getting through the funhouse, as simple as being first to see the Towers. Here it is. Peter does not know
it; neither does your Uncle Karl. You and I are different. Not surprisingly,
you've often wished you weren't. Don't think I haven't noticed how unhappy your
childhood has been! But you'll understand, when I tell you, why it had to be
kept secret until now. And you won't regret not being like your brother and
your uncle. *On the contrary!"* If you knew all the stories behind all the people
on the boardwalk, you'd see that *nothing* was what it looked like. Husbands and
wives often hated each other; parents didn't necessarily love their children; et
cetera. A child took things for granted because he had nothing to compare his
life to and everybody acted as if things were as they should be. Therefore each
saw himself as the hero of the story, when the truth might turn out to be that he's
the villain, or the coward. And there wasn't one thing you could do about it!

Hunchbacks, fat ladies, fools — that no one chose what he was was unbearable. In the movies he'd meet a beautiful young girl in the funhouse; they'd
have hairs-breadth escapes from real dangers; he'd do and say the right things;
she also; in the end they'd be lovers; their dialogue lines would match up; he'd
be perfectly at ease; she'd not only like him well enough, she'd think he was
marvelous; she'd lie awake thinking about *him,* instead of vice versa — the way
his face looked in different lights and how he stood and exactly what he'd said

— and yet that would be only one small episode in his wonderful life, among many many others. Not a *turning point* at all. What had happened in the tool-shed was nothing. He hated, he loathed his parents! One reason for not writing a lost-in-the-funhouse story is that either everybody's felt what Ambrose feels, in which case it goes without saying, or else no normal person feels such things, in which case Ambrose is a freak. "Is anything more tiresome, in fiction, than the problems of sensitive adolescents?" And it's all too long and rambling, as if the author. For all a person knows the first time through, the end could be just around any corner; perhaps, *not impossibly* it's been within reach any number of times. On the other hand he may be scarcely past the start, with everything yet to get through, an intolerable idea.

Fill in: His father's raised eyebrows when he announced his decision to do the funhouse with Magda. Ambrose understands now, but didn't then, that his father was wondering whether he knew what the funhouse was *for* — especially since he didn't object, as he should have, when Peter decided to come along too. The ticket-woman, witchlike, mortifying him when inadvertently he gave her his name-coin instead of the half-dollar, then unkindly calling Magda's attention to the birthmark on his temple: "Watch out for him, girlie, he's a marked man!" She wasn't even cruel, he understood, only vulgar and insensitive. Somewhere in the world there was a young woman with such splendid understanding that she'd see him entire, like a poem or story, and find his words so valuable after all that when he confessed his apprehensions she would explain why they were in fact the very things that made him precious to her . . . and to Western Civilization! There was no such girl, the simple truth being. Violent yawns as they approached the mouth. Whispered advice from an old-timer on a bench near the barrel: "Go crabwise and ye'll get an eyeful without upsetting!" Composure vanished at the first pitch: Peter hollered joyously, Magda tumbled, shrieked, clutched her skirt; Ambrose scrambled crabwise, tight-lipped with terror, was soon out, watched his dropped name-coin slide among the couples. Shame-faced he saw that to get through expeditiously was not the point; Peter feigned assistance in order to trip Magda up, shouted "I see Christmas!" when her legs went flying. The old man, his latest betrayer, cackled approval. A dim hall then of black-thread cobwebs and recorded gibber: he took Magda's elbow to steady her against revolving discs set in the slanted floor to throw your feet out from under, and explained to her in a calm, deep voice his theory that each phase of the funhouse was triggered either automatically, by a series of photo-electric devices, or else manually by operators stationed at peepholes. But he lost his voice thrice as the discs unbalanced him; Magda was anyhow squealing; but at one point she clutched him about the waist to keep from falling, and her right cheek pressed for a moment against his belt-buckle. Heroically he drew her up, it was his chance to clutch her close as if for support and say: "I love you." He even put an arm lightly about the small of her back before a sailor-and-girl pitched into them from behind, sorely treading his left big toe and knocking Magda asprawl with them. The sailor's girl was a string-haired hussy with a loud laugh and light blue drawers; Ambrose realized that he wouldn't have said "I love you" anyhow, and was smitten with self-contempt. How much better it would be to be that common sailor! A wiry little Seaman 3rd, the fellow squeezed a girl to each side and stumbled hilarious into the mirror room, closer to Magda in thirty seconds than Ambrose had got in thirteen years. She giggled at something the fellow said to Peter; she drew her hair from her eyes with a movement so womanly it struck Ambrose's heart; Peter's smacking her backside then seemed particularly coarse. But Magda made a pleased indignant face and cried, "All right for *you,* mister!" and pursued Peter into the maze without a backward glance. The sailor followed after, leisurely, drawing his girl against his hip; Ambrose understood not only that they were all so relieved to be rid of his burdensome company that they didn't even notice his absence, but that he himself shared their relief. Stepping from the treacherous passage at last into the mirror-maze, he saw once again, more clearly than ever, how readily he deceived himself into supposing he was a person. He even foresaw, wincing at his dreadful self-knowledge, that he would repeat the deception, at ever-rarer intervals, all his wretched life, so fearful were the alternatives. Fame, madness, suicide; perhaps all three. It's not believable that so young a boy could articulate that reflection, and in fiction the merely true must always yield to the plausible. Moreover, the symbolism is in places heavy-footed. Yet Ambrose M—— understood, as few adults do, that the famous loneliness of the great was no popular myth but a general truth — furthermore, that it was as much cause as effect.

All the preceding except the last few sentences is exposition that should've been done earlier or interspersed with the present action instead of lumped together. No reader would put up with so much with such *prolixity.* It's interesting that Ambrose's father, though presumably an intelligent man (as indicated by his role as grade-school principal), neither encouraged nor discouraged his sons at all in any way — as if he either didn't care about them or cared all right but didn't know how to act. If this fact should contribute to one of them's becoming a celebrated but wretchedly unhappy scientist, was it a good thing or not? He too might someday face the question; it would be useful to know whether it had tortured his father for years, for example, or never once crossed his mind.

In the maze two important things happened. First, our hero found a name-coin someone else had lost or discarded: *AMBROSE,*[2] suggestive of the famous lightship and of his late grandfather's favorite dessert, which his mother used to prepare on special occasions out of coconut, oranges, grapes, and what else. Second, as he wondered at the endless replication of his image in the mirrors, second, as he *lost himself in the reflection* that the necessity for an observer makes perfect observation impossible, better make him eighteen at least, yet that would render other things unlikely, he heard Peter and Magda chuckling somewhere together in the maze. "Here!" "No, here!" they shouted to each other; Peter said, "Where's Amby?" Magda murmured. "Amb?" Peter called. In a pleased, friendly voice. He didn't reply. The truth was, his brother was a *happy-go-lucky youngster* who'd've been better off with a regular brother of his own, but who seldom complained of his lot and was generally cordial. Ambrose's throat ached; there aren't enough different ways to say that. He stood quietly while the two young people giggled and thumped through the glittering maze, hurrah'd their discovery of its exit, cried out in joyful alarm at what next beset them. Then he set his mouth and followed after, as he supposed, took a wrong turn, strayed into the pass *wherein he lingers yet.*

2. Saint Ambrose: A bishop (340?–397 A.D.) of Milan, Italy, and composer of hymns.

The action of conventional dramatic narrative may be represented by a diagram called Freitag's Triangle:

or more accurately by a variant of that diagram:

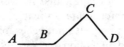

in which *AB* represents the exposition, *B* the introduction of conflict, *BC* the "rising action," complication, or development of the conflict, *C* the climax, or turn of the action, *CD* the dénouement, or resolution of the conflict. While there is no reason to regard this pattern as an absolute necessity, like many other conventions it became conventional because great numbers of people over many years learned by trial and error that it was effective; one ought not to forsake it, therefore, unless one wishes to forsake as well the effect of drama or has clear cause to feel that deliberate violation of the "normal" pattern can better effect that effect. This can't go on much longer; it can go on forever. He died telling stories to himself in the dark; years later, when that vast unsuspected area of the funhouse came to light, the first expedition found his skeleton in one of its labyrinthine corridors and mistook it for part of the entertainment. He died of starvation telling himself stories in the dark; but unbeknownst to him, an assistant operator of the funhouse, happening to overhear him, crouched just behind the plyboard partition and wrote down his every word. The operator's daughter, an exquisite young woman with a figure unusually well developed for her age, crouched just behind the partition and transcribed his every word. Though she had never laid eyes on him, she recognized that here was one of Western Culture's truly great imaginations, the eloquence of whose suffering would be an inspiration to unnumbered. And her heart was torn between her love for the misfortunate young man (yes, she loved him, though she had never laid though she knew him only — but how well! — through his words, and the deep, calm voice in which he spoke them) between her love et cetera and her womanly intuition that only in suffering and isolation could he give voice et cetera. Lone dark dying. Quietly she kissed the rough plyboard, and a tear fell upon the page. Where she had written in shorthand *Where she had written in shorthand* Where she had written in shorthand *Where she* et cetera. A long time ago we should have passed the apex of Freitag's Triangle and made brief work of the *dénouement;* the plot doesn't rise by meaningful steps but winds upon itself, digresses, retreats, hesitates, sighs, collapses, expires. The climax of the story must be its protagonist's discovery of a way to get through the funhouse. But he has found none, may have ceased to search.

What relevance does the war have to the story? Should there be fireworks outside or not?

Ambrose wandered, languished, dozed. Now and then he fell into his habit of rehearsing to himself the unadventurous story of his life, narrated from the third-person point of view, from his earliest memory parenthesis of maple leaves stirring in the summer breath of tidewater Maryland end of parenthesis to the present moment. Its principal events, on this telling, would appear to have been *A, B, C,* and *D*.

He imagined himself years hence, successful, at ease in the world, the trials of his adolescence far behind him. He has come to the seashore with his family for the holiday: how Ocean City has changed! But at one seldom at one ill-frequented end of the boardwalk a few derelict amusements survive from times gone by: the great carrousel from the turn of the century, with its monstrous griffins and mechanical concert band; the roller coaster rumored since 1916 to have been condemned; the mechanical shooting gallery in which only the image of our enemies changed. His own son laughs with Fat May and wants to know what a funhouse is; Ambrose hugs the sturdy lad close and smiles around his pipestem at his wife.

The family's going home. Mother sits between Father and Uncle Karl, who teases him good-naturedly who chuckles over the fact that the comrade with whom he'd fought his way shoulder to shoulder through the funhouse had turned out to be a blind Negro girl — to their mutual discomfort, as they'd opened their souls. But such are the walls of custom, which even. Whose arm is where? How must it feel. He dreams of a funhouse vaster by far than any yet constructed; but by then they may be out of fashion, like steamboats and excursion trains. Already quaint and seedy: the draperied ladies on the frieze of the carrousel are his father's father's mooncheeked dreams; if he thinks of it more he will vomit his apple-on-a-stick.

He wonders: will he become a regular person? Something has gone wrong; his vaccination didn't take; at the Boy-Scout initiation campfire he only pretended to be deeply moved, as he pretends to this hour that it is not so bad after all in the funhouse, and that he has a little limp. How long will it last? He envisions a truly astonishing funhouse, incredibly complex yet utterly controlled from a great central switchboard like the console of a pipe organ. Nobody had enough imagination. He could design such a place himself, wiring and all, and he's only thirteen years old. He would be its operator; panel lights would show what was up in every cranny of its cunning of its multifarious vastness; a switch-flick would ease this fellow's way, complicate that's, to balance things out; if anyone seemed lost or frightened, all the operator had to do was.

He wishes he had never entered the funhouse. But he has. Then he wishes he were dead. But he's not. Therefore he will construct funhouses for others and be their secret operator — though he would rather be among the lovers for whom funhouses are designed.

Jorge Luis Borges (1899–   )

The Shape of the Sword

A spiteful scar crossed his face: an ash-colored and nearly perfect arc that creased his temple at one tip and his cheek at the other. His real name is of no importance; everyone in Tacuarembó called him the "Englishman from La Colorada." Cardoso, the owner of those fields, refused to sell them: I understand that the Englishman resorted to an unexpected argument: he confided to Cardoso the secret of the scar. The Englishman came from the border, from Rio Grande del Sur; there are many who say that in Brazil he had been a smuggler. The fields were overgrown with grass, the waterholes brackish; the Englishman, in order to correct those deficiencies, worked fully as hard as his laborers. They say that he was severe to the point of cruelty, but scrupulously just. They say also that he drank: a few times a year he locked himself into an upper room, not to emerge until two or three days later as if from a battle or from vertigo, pale, trembling, confused and as authoritarian as ever. I remember the glacial eyes, the energetic leanness, the gray mustache. He had no dealings with anyone; it is a fact that his Spanish was rudimentary and cluttered with Brazilian. Aside from a business letter or some pamphlet, he received no mail.

The last time I passed through the northern provinces, a sudden overflowing of the Caraguatá stream compelled me to spend the night at La Colorada. Within a few moments, I seemed to sense that my appearance was inopportune; I tried to ingratiate myself with the Englishman; I resorted to the least discerning of passions: patriotism. I claimed as invincible a country with such spirits as England's. My companion agreed, but added with a smile that he was not English. He was Irish, from Dungarvan. Having said this, he stopped short, as if he had revealed a secret.

After dinner we went outside to look at the sky. It had cleared up, but beyond the low hills the southern sky, streaked and gashed by lightning, was conceiving another storm. Into the cleared up dining room the boy who had served dinner brought a bottle of rum. We drank for some time, in silence.

I don't know what time it must have been when I observed that I was drunk; I don't know what inspiration or what exultation or tedium made me mention the scar. The Englishman's face changed its expression; for a few seconds I thought he was going to throw me out of the house. At length he said in his normal voice:

"I'll tell you the history of my scar under one condition: that of not mitigating one bit of the opprobrium, of the infamous circumstances."

I agreed. This is the story that he told me, mixing his English with Spanish, and even with Portuguese:

"Around 1922, in one of the cities of Connaught, I was one of the many who were conspiring for the independence of Ireland. Of my comrades, some are still living, dedicated to peaceful pursuits; others, paradoxically, are fighting on desert and sea under the English flag; another, the most worthy, died in the courtyard of a barracks, at dawn, shot by men filled with sleep; still others (not the most unfortunate) met their destiny in the anonymous and almost secret battles of the civil war. We were Republicans, Catholics; we were, I suspect, Romantics. Ireland was for us not only the utopian future and the intolerable present; it was a bitter and cherished mythology, it was the circular towers and the red marshes, it was the repudiation of Parnell and the enormous epic poems which sang of the robbing of bulls which in another incarnation were heroes and in others fish and mountains . . . One afternoon I will never forget, an affiliate from Munster joined us: one John Vincent Moon.

"He was scarcely twenty years old. He was slender and flaccid at the same time; he gave the uncomfortable impression of being invertebrate. He had studied with fervor and with vanity nearly every page of Lord knows what Communist manual; he made use of dialectical materialism to put an end to any discussion whatever. The reasons one can have for hating another man, or for loving him, are infinite: Moon reduced the history of the universe to a sordid economic conflict. He affirmed that the revolution was predestined to succeed. I told him that for a gentleman only lost causes should be attractive ... Night had already fallen; we continued our disagreement in the hall, on the stairs, then along the vague streets. The judgments Moon emitted impressed me less than his irrefutable, apodictic note. The new comrade did not discuss: he dictated opinions with scorn and with a certain anger.

"As we were arriving at the outlying houses, a sudden burst of gunfire stunned us. (Either before or afterwards we skirted the blank wall of a factory or barracks.) We moved into an unpaved street; a soldier, huge in the firelight, came out of a burning hut. Crying out, he ordered us to stop. I quickened my pace; my companion did not follow. I turned around: John Vincent Moon was motionless, fascinated, as if eternized by fear. I then ran back and knocked the soldier to the ground with one blow, shook Vincent Moon, insulted him and ordered him to follow. I had to take him by the arm; the passion of fear had rendered him helpless. We fled, into the night pierced by flames. A rifle volley reached out for us, and a bullet nicked Moon's right shoulder; as we were fleeing amid pines, he broke out in weak sobbing.

"In that fall of 1923 I had taken shelter in General Berkeley's country house. The general (whom I had never seen) was carrying out some administrative assignment or other in Bengal; the house was less than a century old, but it was decayed and shadowy and flourished in puzzling corridors and in pointless antechambers. The museum and the huge library usurped the first floor: controversial and uncongenial books which in some manner are the history of the nineteenth century; scimitars from Nishapur, along whose captured arcs there seemed to persist still the wind and violence of battle. We entered (I seem to recall) through the rear. Moon, trembling, his mouth parched, murmured that the events of the night were interesting; I dressed his wound and brought him a cup of tea; I was able to determine that his 'wound' was superficial. Suddenly he stammered in bewilderment:

" 'You know, you ran a terrible risk.'

"I told him not to worry about it. (The habit of the civil war had incited me to act as I did; besides, the capture of a single member could endanger our cause.)

"By the following day Moon had recovered his poise. He accepted a cigarette and subjected me to a severe interrogation on the 'economic resources of our revolutionary party.' His questions were very lucid; I told him (truthfully) that the situation was serious. Deep bursts of rifle fire agitated the south. I told Moon our comrades were waiting for us. My overcoat and my revolver were in my room; when I returned, I found Moon stretched out on the sofa, his eyes closed. He imagined he had a fever; he invoked a painful spasm in his shoulder.

"At that moment I understood that his cowardice was irreparable. I clumsily entreated him to take care of himself and went out. This frightened man mortified me, as if I were the coward, not Vincent Moon. Whatever one man does, it is as if all men did it. For that reason it is not unfair that one disobedience in a garden should contaminate all humanity; for that reason it is not unjust that the crucifixion of a single Jew should be sufficient to save it. Perhaps Schopenhauer was right: I am all other men, any man is all men, Shakespeare is in some manner the miserable John Vincent Moon.

"Nine days we spent in the general's enormous house. Of the agonies and the successes of the war I shall not speak: I propose to relate the history of the scar that insults me. In my memory, those nine days form only a single day, save for the next to the last, when our men broke into a barracks and we were able to avenge precisely the sixteen comrades who had been machinegunned in Elphin. I slipped out of the house towards dawn, in the confusion of daybreak. At nightfall I was back. My companion was waiting for me upstairs: his wound did not permit him to descend to the ground floor. I recall him having some volume of strategy in his hand, F. N. Maude or Clausewitz. 'The weapon I prefer is the artillery,' he confessed to me one night. He inquired into our plans; he liked to censure them or revise them. He also was accustomed to denouncing 'our deplorable economic basis'; dogmatic and gloomy, he predicted the disastrous end. *'C'est une affaire flambée,'* [1] he murmured. In order to show that he was indifferent to being a physical coward, he magnified his mental arrogance. In this way, for good or for bad, nine days elapsed.

"On the tenth day the city fell definitely to the Black and Tans. Tall, silent horsemen patrolled the roads; ashes and smoke rode on the wind; on the corner I saw a corpse thrown to the ground, an impression less firm in my memory than that of a dummy on which the soldiers endlessly practiced their marksmanship, in the middle of the square ... I had left when dawn was in the sky; before noon I returned. Moon, in the library, was speaking with someone; the tone of his voice told me he was talking on the telephone. Then I heard my name; then, that I would return at seven; then, the suggestion that they should arrest me as I was crossing the garden. My reasonable friend was reasonably selling me out. I heard him demand guarantees of personal safety.

"Here my story is confused and becomes lost. I know that I pursued the informer along the black, nightmarish halls and along deep stairways of dizziness. Moon knew the house very well, much better than I. One or two times I lost him. I cornered him before the soldiers stopped me. From one of the general's collections of arms I tore a cutlass: with that half moon I carved into his face forever a half moon of blood. Borges, to you, a stranger, I have made this confession. Your contempt does not grieve me so much."

Here the narrator stopped. I noticed that his hands were shaking.

"And Moon?" I asked him.

"He collected his Judas money and fled to Brazil. That afternoon, in the square, he saw a dummy shot up by some drunken men."

I waited in vain for the rest of the story. Finally I told him to go on.

Then a sob went through his body; and with a weak gentleness he pointed to the whitish curved scar.

"You don't believe me?" he stammered. "Don't you see that I carry written on my face the mark of my infamy? I have told you the story thus so that you would hear me to the end. I denounced the man who protected me: I am Vincent Moon. Now despise me."

To E. H. M.

1. *C'est une affaire flambée:* It is
a risky affair.

Exercises

1. How is surprise achieved in this story?

2. What do you learn from the first paragraph of the story on a *second* reading, after you have heard the "Englishman's" confession?

3. The author gives his own name to the narrator of this story, telling us in effect that he is the narrator. Does this fact enhance the credibility of the story? Justify your answer with specific references to the text.

4. Is Moon repentant? How do you know?

Topics for Writing

1. Consider the metaphorical, as well as the literal, significance of the title and its relation to the story.

2. Discuss the importance of the biblical allusions in "The Shape of the Sword."

Ray Bradbury (1920–   )

There Will Come Soft Rains

In the living room the voice-clock sang, *Tick-tock, seven o'clock, time to get up, time to get up, seven o'clock!* as if it were afraid that nobody would. The morning house lay empty. The clock ticked on, repeating and repeating its sound into the emptiness. *Seven-nine, breakfast time, seven-nine!*

In the kitchen the breakfast stove gave a hissing sigh and ejected from its warm interior eight pieces of perfectly browned toast, eight eggs sunny-side up, sixteen slices of bacon, two coffees, and two cool glasses of milk.

"Today is August 4, 2026," said a second voice from the kitchen ceiling, "in the city of Allendale, California." It repeated the date three times for memory's sake. "Today is Mr. Featherstone's birthday. Today is the anniversary of Tilita's marriage. Insurance is payable, as are the water, gas, and light bills."

Somewhere in the walls, relays clicked, memory tapes glided under electric eyes.

Eight-one, tick-tock, eight-one o'clock, off to school, off to work, run, run, eight-one! But no doors slammed, no carpets took the soft tread of rubber heels. It was raining outside. The weather box on the front door sang quietly: "Rain, rain, go away; rubbers, raincoats for today . . ." And the rain tapped on the empty house, echoing.

Outside, the garage chimed and lifted its door to reveal the waiting car. After a long wait the door swung down again.

At eight-thirty the eggs were shriveled and the toast was like stone. An aluminum wedge scraped them into the sink, where hot water whirled them down a metal throat which digested and flushed them away to the distant sea. The dirty dishes were dropped into a hot washer and emerged twinkling dry.

Nine-fifteen, sang the clock, *time to clean.*

Out of warrens in the wall, tiny robot mice darted. The rooms were acrawl with the small cleaning animals, all rubber and metal. They thudded against chairs, whirling their mustached runners, kneading the rug nap, sucking gently at hidden dust. Then, like mysterious invaders, they popped into their burrows. Their pink electric eyes faded. The house was clean.

Ten o'clock. The sun came out from behind the rain. The house stood alone in a city of rubble and ashes. This was the one house left standing. At night the ruined city gave off a radioactive glow which could be seen for miles.

Ten-fifteen. The garden sprinklers whirled up in golden founts, filling the soft morning air with scatterings of brightness. The water pelted windowpanes, running down the charred west side where the house had been burned evenly free of its white paint. The entire west face of the house was black, save for five places. Here the silhouette in paint of a man mowing a lawn. Here, as in a photograph, a woman bent to pick flowers. Still farther over, their images burned on wood in one titanic instant, a small boy, hands flung into the air; higher up, the image of a thrown ball, and opposite him a girl, hands raised to catch a ball which never came down.

The five spots of paint — the man, the woman, the children, the ball — remained. The rest was a thin charcoaled layer.

The gentle sprinkler rain filled the garden with falling light.

Until this day, how well the house had kept its peace. How carefully it had inquired, "Who goes there? What's the password?" and, getting no answer from lonely foxes and whining cats, it had shut up its windows and drawn shades in an old-maidenly preoccupation with self-protection which bordered on a mechanical paranoia.

It quivered at each sound, the house did. If a sparrow brushed a window, the shade snapped up. The bird, startled, flew off! No, not even a bird must touch the house!

The house was an altar with ten thousand attendants, big, small, servicing, attending, in choirs. But the gods had gone away, and the ritual of the religion continued senselessly, uselessly.

Twelve noon.

A dog whined, shivering, on the front porch.

The front door recognized the dog voice and opened. The dog, once huge and fleshy, but now gone to bone and covered with sores, moved in and through the house, tracking mud. Behind it whirred angry mice, angry at having to pick up mud, angry at inconvenience.

For not a leaf fragment blew under the door but what the wall panels flipped open and the copper scrap rats flashed swiftly out. The offending dust, hair, or paper, seized in miniature steel jaws, was raced back to the burrows. There, down tubes which fed into the cellar, it was dropped into the sighing vent of an incinerator which sat like evil Baal in a dark corner.

The dog ran upstairs, hysterically yelping to each door, at last realizing, as the house realized, that only silence was here.

It sniffed the air and scratched the kitchen door. Behind the door, the stove was making pancakes which filled the house with a rich baked odor and the scent of maple syrup.

The dog frothed at the mouth, lying at the door, sniffing, its eyes turned to fire. It ran wildly in circles, biting at its tail, spun in a frenzy, and died. It lay in the parlor for an hour.

Two o'clock, sang a voice.

Delicately sensing decay at last, the regiments of mice hummed out as softly as blown gray leaves in an electrical wind.

Two-fifteen.

The dog was gone.

In the cellar, the incinerator glowed suddenly and a whirl of sparks leaped up the chimney.

Two thirty-five.

Bridge tables sprouted from patio walls. Playing cards fluttered onto pads in a shower of pips. Martinis manifested on an oaken bench with egg-salad sandwiches. Music played.

But the tables were silent and the cards untouched.

At four o'clock the tables folded like great butterflies back through the paneled walls.

Four-thirty.

The nursery walls glowed.

Animals took shape: yellow giraffes, blue lions, pink antelopes, lilac panthers cavorting in crystal substance. The walls were glass. They looked out upon color and fantasy. Hidden films clocked through well-oiled sprockets, and the walls lived. The nursery floor was woven to resemble a crisp, cereal meadow. Over this ran aluminum roaches and iron crickets, and in the hot still air butterflies of delicate red tissue wavered among the sharp aroma of animal spoors! There was the sound like a great matted yellow hive of bees within a dark bellows, the lazy bumble of a purring lion. And there was the patter of okapi feet and the murmur of a fresh jungle rain, like other hoofs, falling upon the summer-starched grass. Now the walls dissolved into distances of parched weed, mile on mile, and warm endless sky. The animals drew away into thorn brakes and water holes.

It was the children's hour.

Five o'clock. The bath filled with clear hot water.

Six, seven, eight o'clock. The dinner dishes manipulated like magic tricks, and in the study a *click.* In the metal stand opposite the hearth where a fire now blazed up warmly, a cigar popped out, half an inch of soft gray ash on it, smoking, waiting.

Nine o'clock. The beds warmed their hidden circuits, for nights were cool here.

Nine-five. A voice spoke from the study ceiling:

"Mrs. McClellan, which poem would you like this evening?"

The house was silent.

The voice said at last, "Since you express no preference, I shall select a poem at random." Quiet music rose to back the voice. "Sara Teasdale. As I recall, your favorite. . . .

"There will come soft rains and the smell of the ground,
And swallows circling with their shimmering sound;

And frogs in the pools singing at night,
And wild plum-trees in tremulous white;

Ray Bradbury 259

Robins will wear their feathery fire
Whistling their whims on a low fence-wire;

And not one will know of the war, not one
Will care at last when it is done.

Not one would mind, either bird nor tree
If mankind perished utterly;

And Spring herself, when she woke at dawn,
Would scarcely know that we were gone." [1]

The fire burned on the stone hearth and the cigar fell away into a mound of quiet ash on its tray. The empty chairs faced each other between the silent walls, and the music played.

At ten o'clock the house began to die.
The wind blew. A falling tree bough crashed through the kitchen window. Cleaning solvent, bottled, shattered over the stove. The room was ablaze in an instant!
"Fire!" screamed a voice. The house lights flashed, water pumps shot water from the ceilings. But the solvent spread on the linoleum, licking, eating under the kitchen door, while the voices took it up in chorus: "Fire, fire, fire!"

The house tried to save itself. Doors sprang tightly shut, but the windows were broken by the heat and the wind blew and sucked upon the fire.
The house gave ground as the fire in ten billion angry sparks moved with flaming ease from room to room and then up the stairs. While scurrying water rats squeaked from the walls, pistoled their water, and ran for more. And the wall sprays let down showers of mechanical rain.
But too late. Somewhere, sighing, a pump shrugged to a stop. The quenching rain ceased. The reserve water supply which had filled baths and washed dishes for many quiet days was gone.
The fire crackled up the stairs. It fed upon Picassos and Matisses in the upper halls, like delicacies, baking off the oily flesh, tenderly crisping the canvases into black shavings.
Now the fire lay in beds, stood in windows, changed the colors of drapes!
And then, reinforcements.
From attic trapdoors, blind robot faces peered down with faucet mouths gushing green chemical.
The fire backed off, as even an elephant must at the sight of a dead snake. Now there were twenty snakes whipping over the floor, killing the fire with a clear cold venom of green froth.
But the fire was clever. It had sent flame outside the house, up through the attic to the pumps there. An explosion! The attic brain which directed the pumps was shattered into bronze shrapnel on the beams.
The fire rushed back into every closet and felt of the clothes hung there.
The house shuddered, oak bone on bone, its bared skeleton cringing from

1. " 'There Will Come Soft Rains,' "
in Sara Teasdale, *Collected Poems*
(New York: Macmillan, 1920).

the heat, its wire, its nerves revealed as if a surgeon had torn the skin off to let the red veins and capillaries quiver in the scalded air. Help, help! Fire! Run, run! Heat snapped mirrors like the first brittle winter ice. And the voices wailed Fire, fire, run, run, like a tragic nursery rhyme, a dozen voices, high, low, like children dying in a forest, alone, alone. And the voices fading as the wires popped their sheathings like hot chestnuts. One, two, three, four, five voices died.

In the nursery the jungle burned. Blue lions roared, purple giraffes bounded off. The panthers ran in circles, changing color, and ten million animals, running before the fire, vanished off toward a distant steaming river. . . .

Ten more voices died. In the last instant under the fire avalanche, other choruses, oblivious, could be heard announcing the time, playing music, cutting the lawn by remote-control mower, or setting an umbrella frantically out and in the slamming and opening front door, a thousand things happening, like a clock shop when each clock strikes the hour insanely before or after the other, a scene of maniac confusion, yet unity; singing, screaming, a few last cleaning mice darting bravely out to carry the horrid ashes away! And one voice, with sublime disregard for the situation, read poetry aloud in the fiery study, until all the film spools burned, until all the wires withered and the circuits cracked.

The fire burst the house and let it slam flat down, puffing out skirts of spark and smoke.

In the kitchen, an instant before the rain of fire and timber, the stove could be seen making breakfasts at a psychopathic rate, ten dozen eggs, six loaves of toast, twenty dozen bacon strips, which, eaten by fire, started the stove working again, hysterically hissing!

The crash. The attic smashing into kitchen and parlor. The parlor into cellar, cellar into sub-cellar. Deep freeze, armchair, film tapes, circuits, beds, and all like skeletons thrown in a cluttered mound deep under.

Smoke and silence. A great quantity of smoke.

Dawn showed faintly in the east. Among the ruins, one wall stood alone. Within the wall, a last voice said, over and over again and again, even as the sun rose to shine upon the heaped rubble and steam:

"Today is August 5, 2026, today is August 5, 2026, today is . . ."

Kate Chopin (1851–1904)

The Story of an Hour

Knowing that Mrs. Mallard was afflicted with a heart trouble, great care was taken to break to her as gently as possible the news of her husband's death.

It was her sister Josephine who told her, in broken sentences; veiled hints that revealed in half concealing. Her husband's friend Richards was there, too, near her. It was he who had been in the newspaper office when intelligence of the railroad disaster was received, with Brently Mallard's name leading the list of "killed." He had only taken the time to assure himself of its truth by a second telegram, and had hastened to forestall any less careful, less tender friend in bearing the sad message.

She did not hear the story as many women have heard the same, with a paralyzed inability to accept its significance. She wept at once, with sudden, wild abandonment, in her sister's arms. When the storm of grief had spent itself she went away to her room alone. She would have no one follow her.

There stood, facing the open window, a comfortable, roomy armchair. Into this she sank, pressed down by a physical exhaustion that haunted her body and seemed to reach into her soul.

She could see in the open square before her house the tops of trees that were all aquiver with the new spring life. The delicious breath of rain was in the air. In the street below a peddler was crying his wares. The notes of a distant song which some one was singing reached her faintly, and countless sparrows were twittering in the eaves.

There were patches of blue sky showing here and there through the clouds that had met and piled one above the other in the west facing her window.

She sat with her head thrown back upon the cushion of the chair, quite motionless, except when a sob came up into her throat and shook her, as a child who has cried itself to sleep continues to sob in its dreams.

She was young, with a fair, calm face, whose lines bespoke repression and even a certain strength. But now there was a dull stare in her eyes, whose gaze was fixed away off yonder on one of those patches of blue sky. It was not a glance of reflection, but rather indicated a suspension of intelligent thought.

There was something coming to her and she was waiting for it, fearfully. What was it? She did not know; it was too subtle and elusive to name. But she felt it, creeping out of the sky, reaching toward her through the sounds, the scents, the color that filled the air.

Now her bosom rose and fell tumultuously. She was beginning to recognize this thing that was approaching to possess her, and she was striving to beat it back with her will — as powerless as her two white slender hands would have been.

When she abandoned herself a little whispered word escaped her slightly parted lips. She said it over and over under her breath: "free, free, free!" The vacant stare and the look of terror that had followed it went from her eyes. They stayed keen and bright. Her pulses beat fast, and the coursing blood warmed and relaxed every inch of her body.

She did not stop to ask if it were or were not a monstrous joy that held her. A clear and exalted perception enabled her to dismiss the suggestion as trivial.

She knew that she would weep again when she saw the kind, tender hands folded in death; the face that had never looked save with love upon her, fixed and gray and dead. But she saw beyond that bitter moment a long procession of years to come that would belong to her absolutely. And she opened and spread her arms out to them in welcome.

There would be no one to live for her during those coming years; she would live for herself. There would be no powerful will bending hers in that blind persistence with which men and women believe they have a right to impose a private will upon a fellow-creature. A kind intention or a cruel intention made the act seem no less a crime as she looked upon it in that brief moment of illumination.

And yet she had loved him — sometimes. Often she had not. What did it matter! What could love, the unsolved mystery, count for in face of this possession of self-assertion which she suddenly recognized as the strongest impulse of her being!

"Free! Body and soul free!" she kept whispering.

Josephine was kneeling before the closed door with her lips to the keyhole, imploring for admission. "Louise, open the door! I beg; open the door — you will make yourself ill. What are you doing, Louise? For heaven's sake open the door."

"Go away. I am not making myself ill." No; she was drinking in a very elixir of life through that open window.

Her fancy was running riot along those days ahead of her. Spring days, and summer days, and all sorts of days that would be her own. She breathed a quick prayer that life might be long. It was only yesterday she had thought with a shudder that life might be long.

She rose at length and opened the door to her sister's importunities. There was a feverish triumph in her eyes, and she carried herself unwittingly like a goddess of Victory. She clasped her sister's waist, and together they descended the stairs. Richards stood waiting for them at the bottom.

Some one was opening the front door with a latchkey. It was Brently Mallard who entered, a little travel-stained, composedly carrying his grip-sack and umbrella. He had been far from the scene of the accident, and did not even know there had been one. He stood amazed at Josephine's piercing cry; at Richards' quick motion to screen him from the view of his wife.

But Richards was too late.

When the doctors came they said she had died of heart disease — of joy that kills.

Exercises

1. Describe the kind of relationship Mrs. Mallard has had with her husband. What does it reveal about her view of herself?

2. Explain why Mrs. Mallard suddenly feels "free."

3. Is the reader prepared for the ending? If so, how? Consider other possible endings and their different effects.

Topics for Writing

1. Compare and contrast the thematic effects of the endings in "The Necklace" and "The Story of an Hour."

2. Discuss the type (or types) of irony present in this story.

Guadalupe Valdés Fallis (*1941–*   )

Recuerdo[1]

It was noon. It was dusty. And the sun, blinding in its brightness, shone unmercifully on the narrow dirty street.

It was empty. And to Rosa, walking slowly past the bars and the shops and the curio stands, it seemed as if they all were peering out at her, curiously watching what she did.

She walked on . . . toward the river, toward the narrow, muddy strip of land that was the dry Rio Grande; and she wished suddenly that it were night and that the tourists had come across, making the street noisy and gay and full of life.

But it was noon. And there were no happy or laughing Americanos; no eager girls painted and perfumed and waiting for customers; no blaring horns or booming bongos . . . only here and there a hungry dog, a crippled beggar, or a drunk, thirsty and broke from the night before.

She was almost there. She could see the narrow door and the splintered wooden steps. And instinctively she stopped. Afraid suddenly, feeling the hollow emptiness again, and the tightness when she swallowed.

And yet, it was not as if she did not know why he had wanted her to come, why he had sent for her. It was not as though she were a child. Her reflection in a smudged and dirty window told her that she was no longer even a girl.

And still, it was not as if she were old, she told herself, it was only that her body was rounded and full, and her eyes in the dark smooth face were hard and knowing, mirroring the pain and the disappointment and the tears of thirty-five years . . .

She walked to the narrow door slowly, and up the stairs . . . thumping softly on the creaking swollen wood. At the top, across a dingy hallway, she knocked softly at a door. It was ajar, and Rosa could see the worn chairs and the torn linoleum and the paper-littered desk. But she did not go in. Not until the man came to the door and looked out at her impatiently.

He saw her feet first and the tattered sandals. Then her dress clean but faded, a best dress obviously, because it was not patched. Finally, after what seemed to Rosa an eternity, he looked at her face, at her dark black hair knotted neatly on top of her head; and at last, into her eyes.

"Come in, Rosa," he said slowly, "I am glad that you could come."

"*Buenas tardes*[2] Don Lorenzo," Rosa said meekly, looking up uneasily at the bulky smelly man. "I am sorry I am late."

"Yes," he said mockingly; and turning, he walked back into the small and dirty room.

Rosa followed him, studying him, while he ·could not see her, seeing the wrinkled trousers, the sweat stained shirt, and the overgrown greasy hair on the back of his pudgy neck.

He turned suddenly, his beady eyes surveying his domain smugly; then deliberately, he walked to the window and straightened the sign that said:

DIVORCES . . . LORENZO PEREZ SAUZA . . . ATTORNEY AT LAW

1. *Recuerdo:* Recollection.   2. *Buenas tardes:* Good afternoon.

It was not as important as the neon blinking sign, of course, but sometimes people came from the side street, and it was good to be prepared.

"Well, Rosa," he said, looking at her again, "and where is Maruca?"

"She is sick, señor."

"Sick?"

"Yes, she has had headaches and she is not well . . . she . . ."

"Has she seen a doctor, Rosa?" The question was mocking again.

"No . . . she . . . it will pass, señor. . . . It's only that now . . . I do not think that she should come to work."

"Oh?" He was looking out of the window distractedly, ignoring her.

"I am sorry, I should have come before," she continued meekly . . .

"Maruca is very pretty, Rosa," Don Lorenzo said suddenly.

"Thank you, señor, you are very kind." She was calmer now . . .

"She will make a man very happy, someday," he continued.

"Yes."

"Do you think she will marry soon then?" he asked her, watching her closely.

"No," she hesitated, "that is, I don't know, she . . . there isn't anyone yet."

"Ah!" It was said quietly but somehow triumphantly . . .

And Rosa waited, wondering what he wanted, sensing something and suddenly suspicious.

"Do you think she likes me, Rosa?" he asked her deliberately, baiting her.

And she remembered Maruca's face, tear-stained, embarrassed telling her: "I can't go back, Mama. He does not want me to help in his work. He touches me, Mother . . . and smiles. And today, he put his large sweaty hand on my breast, and held it, smiling, like a cow. Ugly!"

"Why, yes, Don Lorenzo," she lied quickly. "She thinks you are very nice." Her heart was racing now, hoping and yet not daring to —

"I am much of a man, Rosa," he went on slowly, "and the girl is pretty. . . . I would take care of her . . . if she let me."

"Take care of her?" Rosa was praying now, her fingers crossed behind her back.

"Yes, take care of her," he repeated. "I would be good to her, you would have money. And then, perhaps, if there is a child . . . she would need a house . . ."

"A house." Rosa repeated dully. A house for Maruca. That it might be. That it might be, really, was unbelievable. To think of the security, of the happy future frightened her suddenly, and she could only stare at the fat man, her eyes round and very black.

"Think about it, Rosita," he said smiling benevolently . . . "You know me . . ." And Rosa looked at him angrily, remembering, and suddenly feeling very much like being sick.

The walk home was long; and in the heat Rosa grew tired. She wished that she might come to a tree, so that she could sit in the shade and think. But the hills were bare and dry, and there were no trees. There were only shacks surrounded by hungry crying children.

And Rosa thought about her own, about the little ones. The ones that still depended on her even for something to eat. And she felt it again, the strange despair of wanting to cry out: "Don't, don't depend on me! I can hardly depend on myself."

But they had no one else; and until they could beg or steal a piece of bread and a bowl of beans, they would turn to her, only to her, not ever to Pablo.

And it wasn't because he was drunk and lazy, or even because only the last two children belonged to him. He was kind enough to all of them. It was, though, as if they sensed that he was only temporary.

And still it was not that Pablo was bad. He was better actually than the others. He did not beat her when he drank, or steal food from the children. He was not even too demanding. And it gave them a man, after all, a man to protect them. . . . It was enough, really.

True, he had begun to look at Maruca, and it had bothered Rosa. But perhaps it WAS really time for Maruca to leave. For the little ones, particularly. Because men are men, she said to herself, and if there is a temptation . . .

But she was not fooling anyone, and when at last she saw the tin and cardboard shack against the side of the hill, with its cluttered front and screaming children, she wanted to turn back.

Maruca saw her first.

"There's Mama," she told the others triumphantly, and at once they took up the shout: "Mama! Mama! Mama!"

The other girl, standing with Maruca, turned to leave as Rosa came closer.

"Buenas tardes," she said uncomfortably, sensing the dislike and wanting to hurry away.

"What did Petra want?" Rosa asked Maruca angrily, even before Petra was out of earshot.

"Mama, por favor, she'll hear you."

"I told you I did not want her in this house."

"We were only talking, Mama. She was telling me about her friends."

"Her friends!" Rosa cut in sharply, "as if we did not know that she goes with the first American that looks at her. Always by the river that one, with one soldier and another, her friends indeed!"

"But she says she has fun, Mama, and they take her to dance and buy her pretty things."

"Yes, yes, and tomorrow, they will give her a baby. . . . And where is the fun then . . . eh? She is in the streets . . . no?"

Rosa was shaking with anger. "Is that what you want? Do you?"

"No, Mama," Maruca said meekly, "I was just listening to her talk."

"Well, remember it,' Rosa snapped furiously, but then seeing Maruca's face, she stopped suddenly. "There, there, it's alright," she said softly. "We will talk about it later."

And Rosa watched her, then, herding the children into the house gently, gracefully; slim and small, angular still, with something perhaps a little doltish in the way she held herself, impatient, and yet distrusting, not quite daring to go forward.

And she thought of Don Lorenzo, and for a moment, she wished that he were not so fat, or so ugly, and especially, so sweaty.

But it was an irrecoverable chance! Old men with money did not often come into their world, and never to stay.

To Rosa, they had been merely far away gods at whose houses she had worked as a maid or as a cook; faultless beings who were to be obeyed without question; powerful creatures who had commanded her to come when they needed variety or adventure . . .

But only that.

She had never been clever enough, or even pretty enough to make it be more. But Maruca! Maruca could have the world.

No need for her to marry a poor young bum who could not even get a job. No need for her to have ten children all hungry and crying. No need for her to dread, even, that the bum might leave her. No need at all.

"Maruca," Rose said decidedly, turning to where she sat playing with the baby, "I went to see Don Lorenzo."

"Oh?" There was fear in the bright brown eyes.

"And he wants to take care of you," Rosa continued softly. "He thinks you're pretty, and he likes you."

"Take care of me?" It was more of a statement than a question.

"He wants to make an arrangement with you, Maruca." Rosa too was afraid now. "He would come to see you . . . and . . . well . . . if there is a baby, there might very well be a house."

"A baby?" The face was pale now, the eyes surprised and angry. "You want me to go to bed with Don Lorenzo? You want me to let him put his greasy hands all over me, and make love to me? You want that? Is that how much better I can do than Petra?"

"Don't you see, I want you to happy, to be safe. I want you to have pretty things and not to be afraid. I want you to love your babies when you have them, to hear them laugh with full fat stomachs . . . I want you to love life, to be glad that you were born."

"To be happy?" Maruca repeated slowly, as if it had never occurred to her that she was not.

"Yes, to be happy."

"And sleeping with Don Lorenzo," Maruca asked uncertainly, "will that make me glad that I was born?"

And Rosa looked at her, saw her waiting for an answer, depending on it . . .

And she wanted to scream out. "No, no! You will hate it probably, and you will dread his touch on you and his breath smelling of garlic. But it isn't HE, that will make you happy. It's the rest of it. Don't you see, can't you understand how important HE is?"

But the brown eyes stared at her pleadingly, filling with tears, like a child's, and Rosa said quietly: "Yes, Maruca, it will make you happy."

But then suddenly, unexpectedly, she felt alone and very very tired.

"Go on to church now," she said slowly, "it's time for benediction and you have the novena to complete." And Rosa watched her go, prayer book clutched tightly in one hand, hopeful still, trusting still, and so very, very young still. And she wondered if she would change much, really, after Don Lorenzo, and the baby and the house. She wondered if she would still be gay and proud and impatient.

But then suddenly Maruca was out of sight, and Rosa turned to the others, kissing one, patting another's head, and hurrying to have the beans hot and the house tidy for the time that Pablo would come home.

Shirley Ann Grau (1929–)

The Black Prince

*"How art thou fallen from heaven,
O Lucifer, son of the morning!"*

Winters are short and very cold; sometimes there is even a snow like heavy frost on the ground. Summers are powdery hot; the white ball sun goes rolling around and around in a sky behind the smoke from the summer fires. There is always a burning somewhere in summer; the pines are dry and waiting; the sun itself starts the smoldering. A pine fire is quiet; there is only a kind of rustle from the flames inside the trunks until the branches and needles go up with a whistling. A whole hill often burns that way, its smoke rising straight up to the white sun, and quiet.

In the plowed patches, green things grow quickly: the ground is rich and there are underground rivers. But there are no big farms: only patches of corn, green beans, and a field or two of cotton (grown for a little cash to spend on Saturdays at Luther's General Store or Willie's Café; these are the only two places for forty miles in any direction). There is good pasture: the green places along the hillsides with pines for shade and sure water in the streams that come down from the Smokies to the north; even in the burnt-out land of five seasons back, shrubs are high. But in the whole county there are only fifty cows, gone wild most of them and dry because they were never milked. They are afraid of men and feed in the farthest ridges and the swamps that are the bottoms of some littlest of the valleys. Their numbers are slowly increasing because no one bothers them. Only once in a while some man with a hankering for cow meat takes his rifle and goes after them. But that is not often; the people prefer pork. Each family keeps enough razorbacks in a run of bark palings.

It is all colored people here, and it is the poorest part of the smallest and worst county in the state. The place at the end of the dirt road leading from the state highway, the place where Luther's Store and Willie's Café stand, does not even have a name in the county records.

The only cool time of the summer day is very early, before the mists have shriveled away. There is a breeze then, a good stiff one out of the Smokies. During the day there is no sound: it is dead hot. But in the early mornings, when the breeze from the north is blowing, it is not so lonesomely quiet: crickets and locusts and the birds that flutter about hunting them, calling frantically as if they had something of importance to settle quick before the heat sets in. (By seven they are quiet again, in the invisible places they have chosen to wait out the day.)

A pine cone rattled down on Alberta's head and bounced from her shoulder. She scooped it from the ground and threw it upward through the branches. "You just keep your cone, mister birds. I got no cause to want it." With a pumping of wings the birds were gone, their cries sliding after them, back down the air. "You just yell your head off. I can hit you any time I want. Any time I want." There was a small round piece of granite at her feet and she tossed it, without particular aim, into the biggest of the bay trees: a gray squirrel with a thin rattail tumbled from the branches and peeped at her from behind the trunk with a pointed little rat face. She jammed her hands in the pockets of her dress and went on, swaggering slightly, cool and feeling good.

She was a handsome girl, taller than most people in her part of the county, and light brown — there had been a lot of white blood in her family, back somewhere, they'd forgot where exactly. She was not graceful — not as a woman is — but light on her feet and supple as a man. Her dress, which the sun had bleached to a whitish color, leaving only a trace of pink along the seams, had shrunk out of size for her: it pulled tight across her broad, slightly hunched, muscled back, even though she had left all the front buttons open down to the waist.

As she walked along, the birds were making even more of a row, knocking loose cones and dry pine needles and old broad bay leaves, and twice she stopped, threw back her head, and called up to them: "Crazy fool birds. Can't do nothing to me. Fool jackass birds." Up ahead, a couple of minutes' walk, was the field and the cotton, bursting white out of the brown cups and waiting to be picked. And she did not feel like working. She leaned against a tree, stretching so that the bark crumbled in her fingers, listening to the birds.

Something different was in their calling. She listened, her head bent forward, her eyes closed, as she sorted the sounds. One jay was wrong: its long sustained note ended with the cluck of a quail. No bird did that. Alberta opened her eyes and looked slowly around. But the pines were thick and close and full of blue night shadow and wrapped with fog that moved like bits of cloth in the wind. Leaving the other bird calls, the whistle became distinct, high, soaring, mocking, like some rare bird, proudly, insolently.

Alberta moved a few steps out from the tree and turned slowly on her heels. The whistle was going around her now, in slow circles, and she turned with it, keeping her eye on the sound, seeing nothing. The birds were still calling and fluttering in the branches, sending bits of twig and bark tumbling down.

Alberta said: "A fool thing you doing. A crazy fool jackass thing." She sat down on a tumbled pile of bricks that had been the chimney of a sugarhouse burned during the Civil War. She spoke in her best tone, while the whistling went round and round her faster. "I reckon you got nothing better to do than go around messing up folks. You got me so riled up I don't reckon I know what way I'm heading in." The sound went around her and around her, but she held her head steady, talking to the pine directly in front of her. "I don't reckon there's nothing for me but set here till you tires out and goes away." The whistle circled her twice and then abruptly stopped, the last high clear note running off down the breeze. Alberta stood up, pulling down her faded dress. "I am mighty glad you come to stopping. I reckon now I can tell what direction I got to go in."

He was right there, leaning on the same pine she had been staring at, cleaning his front teeth with a little green twig and studying her, and she told him to his face: "That was a crazy mean thing, and you ain't got nothing better to do."

"Reckon not," he said, moving the little green twig in and out of the hole between his lower front teeth.

She pushed her hands in the pockets of her dress and looked him over. "Where you come from?"

"Me?" The little green twig went in and out of his teeth with each breath. "I just come straight out the morning."

She turned and walked away. "I be glad to see you go."

He stood in front of her: he had a way of moving without a sound, of popping up in places. "I be sorry to see you go, Alberta Lacy."

She studied him before she answered: tall, not too big or heavy, and black (no other blood but his own in him, she thought). He was dressed nice — a leather jacket with fringe on the sleeves, a red plaid shirt, and new blue denim pants. "How you know what I'm called?" she asked him politely.

He grinned, and his teeth were white and perfect. "I done seen it in the fire," he said. "I done seen it in the fire and I read it clear: Alberta Lacy."

She frowned. "I don't see as how I understand."

He blew the little green twig out of his mouth. "I might could be seeing you again real soon, Alberta Lacy." Then he slipped around the tree like the last trail of night shadow and disappeared.

Alberta stood listening: only the birds and the insects and the wind. Then everything got quiet, and the sun was shining white all around, and she climbed down the slope to the field.

A little field — just a strip of cotton tucked in between two ridges. Her father and her two biggest brothers had planted it with half a morning's work, and they hadn't gone back to tend it once. They didn't even seem to remember it: whatever work they did was in the older fields closer to home. So Alberta had taken it over. Sometimes she brought along the twins: Sidney and Silvia; they were seven: young enough for her to order around and big enough to be a help. But usually she couldn't find them; they were strange ones, gone out of the house for a couple of days at a time in summer, sleeping out somewhere, always sticking together. They were strange little ones and not worth trouble looking for. So most times Alberta worked with Maggie Mary Evans, who was Josh Evans's daughter and just about the only girl her age she was friendly with. From the field there'd be maybe three bales of real early stuff; and they'd split the profit. They worked all morning, pulling off the bolls and dropping them in the sacks they slung crosswise across their shoulders. They worked very slowly, so slowly that at times their hands seemed hardly to move, dozing in the heat. When it got to be noon, when they had no shadow any more, they slipped off the sacks, leaving them between the furrows, and turned to the shade to eat their lunch.

He was waiting for them there, stretched out along the ground with his head propped up on the slender trunk of a little bay tree. He winked lazily at Alberta; his eyes were big and shiny black as oil. "How you, Miss Alberta Lacy?"

Alberta looked down at him, crooking her lips. "You got nothing to do but pester me?"

"Sure I got something to do, but ain't nothing nice like this."

Alberta looked at him through half-closed lids, then sat down to the lunch.

"You hungry, mister?" Maggie Mary asked. She had stood watching, both hands jammed into the belt of her dress, and her eyes moving from one to the other with the quickness and the color of a sparrow.

The man rolled over and looked up at her. "Reckon I am."

"You can have some of our lunch," Maggie Mary said.

Crazy fool, Alberta thought, standing so close with him on the ground like that. He must can see all the way up her. And from the way he lay there, grinning, he must be enjoying it.

"That real nice," he said to Maggie Mary, and crawled over on his stomach to where the lunch bucket was.

Alberta watched his smooth, black hand reaching into the bucket and suddenly she remembered. "How you called?"

He put a piece of corn bread in his mouth, chewed it briefly, and swallowed it with a gulp. "I got three names."

"No fooling," Maggie Mary said, and giggled in her hand. "I got three names, too."

"Stanley Albert Thompson."

"That a good-sounding name," Alberta said. She began to eat her lunch quickly, her mouth too full to talk. Stanley Albert was staring at her, but she didn't raise her eyes. Then he began to sing, low, pounding time with the flat of his hand against the ground.

> "Alberta, let you hair hang low,
> Alberta, let you hair hang low,
> I'll give you more gold than you apron can hold
> If you just let you hair hang low."

Alberta got up slowly, not looking at him. "We got work to finish."

Stanley Albert turned over so that his face was pressed in the grass and pine needles. "All you get's the muscles in you arm."

"That right." Maggie Mary nodded quickly. "That right."

"Maggie Mary," Alberta said, "iffen you don't come with me I gonna bop you so hard you land in the middle of tomorrow."

"Good-bye, Mr. Stanley Albert Thompson," Maggie Mary said, but he had fallen asleep.

By the time they finished work he was gone; there wasn't even a spot in the pine needles and short grass to show where he had been.

"Ain't that the strangest thing?" Maggie Mary said.

Alberta picked up the small bucket they carried their lunch in. "I reckon not."

"Seemed like he was fixing to wait for us."

"He ain't fixing to wait for nobody, that kind." Alberta rubbed one hand across her shoulders, sighing slightly. "I got a pain fit to kill."

Maggie Mary leaned one arm against a tree and looked off across the little field where they had spent the day. "You reckon he was in here most all morning watching us?"

"Maybe." Alberta began to walk home. Maggie Mary followed slowly, her head still turned, watching the field.

"He musta spent all morning just watching."

"Nothing hard about doing that, watching us break our back out in the sun."

Maggie Mary took one long, loping step and came up with Alberta. "You reckon he coming back?"

Alberta stared full at her, head bent, chewing on her lower lip. "Maggie Mary Evans," she said, "you might could get a thought that you be wanting him — "

Maggie Mary bent down and brushed the dust off her bare feet carefully, not answering.

"You a plain crazy fool." Alberta planted both hands on her hips and bent her body forward slightly. "A plain crazy fool. You wouldn't be forgetting Jay Mastern?" Jay Mastern had gone off to Ramsey to work at the mill and never come back, but left Maggie Mary to have his baby. So one day Maggie Mary took her pa's best mule and put a blanket on it for a saddle and rode over to Blue Goose Lake, where the old woman lived who could tell her what to do. The old woman gave her medicine in a beer can: whisky and calomel and other things that were a secret. Maggie Mary took the medicine in one gulp, because it tasted so bad, waded way out into Blue Goose Lake so that the water came up to her neck, then dripping wet got up on the mule and whipped him up to a good fast pace all the way home. The baby had come off all right: there wasn't one. And Maggie Mary nearly died. It was something on to three months before she was able to do more than walk around, her arms hanging straight down and stiff and her black skin overtinged with gray.

"You wouldn't be forgetting Jay Mastern?"

"Sure," Maggie Mary said, brushing the dust off her bare feet lightly. "I clean forgot about him."

"Don't you be having nothing to do with this here Stanley Albert Thompson."

Maggie Mary began to walk again, slowly, smiling just a little bit with one corner of her mouth. "Sounds like you been thinking about him for yourself."

Alberta jammed both hands down in the pockets of her dress. "I been thinking nothing of the sort."

"Willie'll kill him."

Alberta chewed on one finger. "I reckon he could care for himself."

Maggie Mary smiled to herself softly, remembering. "I reckon he could; he's real fine-appearing man."

"He was dressed good."

"Where you reckon he come from?" Maggie Mary asked.

Alberta shrugged. "He just come walking out of the morning fog."

That was how he came into this country: he appeared one day whistling a bird call in the woods in high summer. And he stayed on. The very first Saturday night he went down to Willie's and had four fights and won them all.

Willie's was an ordinary house made of pine slabs, older than most of the other houses, but more solid. There were two rooms: a little one where Willie lived (a heavy scrolled ironwork bed, a square oak dresser, a chest, a three-footed table, and on its cracked marble top a blue-painted mandolin without strings). And a big room: the café. Since anybody could remember, the café had been there with Willie's father or his grandfather, as long as there had been people in these parts. And that had been a long while: long before the Civil War even, runaways were settling here, knowing they'd be safe and hidden in the rough, uneven hills and the pines.

Willie had made some changes in the five or six years since his father died. He painted the counter that was the bar with varnish; that had not been a good idea: the whisky took the varnish off in a few weeks. And he painted the walls: bright blue. Then he went over them again, shaking his brush so that the walls were flecked like a mockingbird's eggs. But Willie used red to fleck — red against blue. And the mirror, gilt-edged, and hanging from a thick gold cord: that had been Willie's idea, too. He'd found it one day, lying on the shoulder alongside the state highway; it must have fallen from a truck somehow. So he took it home. It was cracked in maybe two dozen pieces. Anyone who looked into it would see his face split up into a dozen different parts, all separate. But Willie hung it right over the shelves where he kept his whisky and set one of the kerosene lamps in front of it so that the light should reflect yellow-bright from all the pieces. One of them fell out (so that Willie had to glue it back with flour and water) the night Stanley Albert had his fourth fight, which he won like the other three. Not a man in the country would stand up like that, because fighting at Willie's on Saturday night is a rough affair with razors, or knives, or bottles.

Not a man in the country could have matched the way Stanley Albert fought that night, his shirt off, and his black body shining with sweat, the muscles along his neck and shoulders twisting like grass snakes. There wasn't a finer-looking man and there wasn't a better: he proved that.

The first three fights were real orderly affairs. Everybody could see what was coming minutes ahead, and Willie got the two of them out in the yard before they got at each other. And everybody who was sober enough to walk went out on the porch and watched Stanley Albert pound first Ran Carey's and then Henry Johnson's head up and down in the dust. Alberta sat on the porch (Willie had brought her a chair from inside) and watched Stanley Albert roll around the dust of the yard and didn't even blink an eye, not even during the third fight when Tim Evans, who was Maggie Mary's brother, pull a razor. The razor got Stanley Albert all down one cheek, but Tim didn't have any teeth left and one side of his face got punched in so that it looked peculiar always afterward. Maggie Mary went running down into the yard, not bothering with her brother, to press her finger up against the little cut across Stanley Albert's cheek.

The fourth fight came up so suddenly nobody had time hardly to get out of the way: Joe Turner got one arm hooked around Stanley Albert's neck from behind. There wasn't any reason for it, except maybe that Joe was so drunk he didn't see who he had and that once there's been a couple of fights there's always more. Stanley Albert swung a bottle over his shoulder to break the hold and then nobody could see exactly what was happening: they were trying so hard to get clear. Willie pulled Alberta over the bar and pushed her down behind it and crouched alongside her, grinning. "That some fighter." And when it was all over they stood up again; first thing they saw was Joe Turner down on the floor and Stanley Albert leaning on a chair with Maggie dabbing at a cut on his hand with the edge of her petticoat.

He got a reputation from that Saturday night, and everybody was polite to him, and he could have had just about any of the girls he wanted. But he didn't seem to want them; at least he never took to coming to the houses to see them or to taking them home from Willie's. Maggie Mary Evans swore up and down that he had got her one day when she was fishing in Scanos River, but nobody paid her much attention. She liked to make up stories that way.

He had a little house in a valley to the east. Some boys who had gone out to shoot a cow for Christmas meat said they saw it. But they didn't go close even if there was three of them with a shotgun while Stanley Albert only carried a razor. Usually people only saw him on Saturday nights, and after a while they got used to him, though none of the men ever got to be friendly with him. There wasn't any mistaking the way the girls watched him. But after four or five Saturdays, by the time the summer was over, everybody expected him and waited for him, the way you'd wait for a storm to come or a freeze: not liking it, but not being able to do anything either. That's the way it went along: he'd buy his food for the coming week at Luther's Store, and then he'd come next door to Willie's.

He never stood up at the counter that was the bar. He'd take his glass and walk over to a table and sit down, and pull out a little bottle from his pocket, and add white lightning to the whisky. There wasn't anything could insult Willie more. He made the whisky and it was the best stuff in the county. He even had some customers drive clear out from Montgomery to buy some of his corn, and, being good stuff, there wasn't any call to add anything: it had enough kick of its own; raw and stinging to the throat. It was good stuff; nobody added anything to it — except Stanley Albert Thompson, while Willie looked at him and said things under his breath. But nothing ever came of it, because everybody remembered how good a job Stanley Albert had done the first night he came.

Stanley Albert always had money, enough of it to pay for the groceries and all the whisky he wanted. There was always the sound of silver jingling in his trouser pocket. Everybody could hear that. Once when Willie was standing behind the bar, shuffling a pack of cards with a wide fancy twirl — just for amusement — Stanley Albert, who had had a couple of drinks and was feeling especially good, got up and pulled a handful of coins out of his pocket. He began to shuffle them through the air, the way Willie had done with the cards. Stanley Albert's black hands flipped the coins back and forth, faster and faster, until there was a solid silver ring hanging and shining in the air. Then Stanley Albert let one of his hands drop to his side and the silver ring poured back into the other hand and disappeared with a little clinking sound. And he dropped the money into his pocket with a short quick laugh.

That was the way Stanley Albert used his money: he had fun with it. Only thing, one night when Stanley Albert had had maybe a bit too much and sat dozing at his table, Morris Henry slipped a hand into the pocket. He wouldn't have ever dared to do that if Stanley Albert hadn't been dozing, leaning back in his chair, the bottle of white lightning empty in one hand. And Morris Henry slipped his little hand in the pocket and felt all around carefully. Then he turned his head slowly in a circle, looking at everybody in the room. He was a little black monkey Negro and his eyes were shiny and flat as mirrors. He slipped his hand back and scurried out into the yard and hid in the blackberry bushes. He wouldn't move until morning came; he just sat there, chewing on his little black fingers with his wide flaring yellow teeth. Anybody who wanted to know what was happening had to go out there and ask him. And ever afterwards Morris Henry swore that there hadn't been anything at all in Stanley Albert Thompson's pocket. But then everybody knew Morris Henry was crazy because just a few minutes later when Stanley Albert woke up and walked across to the bar, the change jingled in the pocket and he laid five quarters on the counter. And the money was good enough because Willie bounced it on the counter and it gave the clear ring of new silver.

Stanley Albert had money all right and he spent it; there wasn't anything short about him. He'd buy drinks for anybody who'd come over to his table; the only ones who came were the girls. And he didn't seem to care how much they drank. He'd just sit there, leaning way back in his chair, grinning, his teeth white and big behind his black lips, and matching them drink for drink, and every now and then running his eye up and down their length just to let them know he was appreciating their figures. Most often it was Maggie Mary who would be sitting there, warning all the other girls away with a little slanting of her eyes when they got near. And sometimes he'd sing a song: a song about whisky that would make everyone forget they didn't like him and laugh; or a song about poor boys who were going to be hanged in the morning. He had a good voice, strong and clear, and he pounded time with the flat of his hand on the table. And he'd always be looking at Alberta when he was singing until she'd get up, holding her head high and stiff, and march over to where Willie was and take hold of his arm real sweet and smile at him. And Willie would give Stanley Albert a quick mean look and then pour her a drink of his best whisky.

Stanley Albert had a watch, a big heavy gold one, round almost as a tomato, that would strike the hours. (That was how you could tell he was around sometimes — hearing his watch strike.) It was attached to a broad black ribbon and sometimes he held it up, let it swing before the eyes of whatever girl it happened to be at the time, let it swing slowly back and forth, up and down, so that her head moved with it. He had a ring too, on his right little finger: a white-colored band with a stone big as a chip of second coal and dark green. And when he fought, the first time he came into Willie's, the ring cut the same as a razor in his hand; it was maybe a little more messy, because its edges were jagged.

Those were two things — the watch and the ring — that must have cost more than all the money around here in a year. That was why all the women liked him so; they kept thinking of the nice things he could give them if he got interested. And that was why the men hated him. Things can go as smooth as glass if everybody's got about the same things and the same amount of money knocking around in a jean pocket on Saturday night. But when they don't, things begin happening. It would have been simpler maybe if they could have fought Stanley Albert Thompson, but there wasn't any man keen to fight him. That was how they started fighting each other. A feud that nobody'd paid any mind to for eight or ten years started up again.

It began one Sunday morning along toward dawn when everyone was feeling tired and leaving Willie's. Stanley Albert had gone out first and was sitting aside the porch railing. Jim Mastern was standing on the lowest step not moving, just staring across the fields, not being able to see anything in the dark, except maybe the bright-colored patterns the whisky set shooting starwise before his eyes. And Randall Stevens was standing in the doorway, looking down at his own foot, which he kept moving in a little circle around and around on the floor boards. And Stanley Albert was looking hard at him. Randall Stevens didn't lift his head; he just had his razor out and was across the porch in one minute, bringing down his arm in a sweeping motion to get at Jim Mastern's neck. But he was too drunk to aim very straight and he missed; but he did cut the ear away so that it fell on the steps. Jim Mastern was off like a bat in the daylight, running fast, crashing into things, holding one hand to the side of his head. And Randall Stevens folded up the razor and slipped it back in his pocket and walked off slowly, his head bent over, as if he was sleepy. There wasn't any more sense to it than that, but it started the feud again.

Stanley Albert swung his legs over the railing and stretched himself and yawned. Nobody noticed except Alberta, they were so busy listening to the way Jim Mastern was screaming and running across the fields, and watching Randall Stevens march off, solemnly, like a priest.

And the next night Randall Stevens tumbled down the steps of his cabin with his head full of scatter shot. It was a Monday night in November. His mother came out to see and stepped square on him, and his blood spattered on the hoarfrost. Randall Stevens had six brothers, and the next night they rode their lanky burred horses five miles south and tried to set fire to the Mastern house. That was the beginning; the fighting kept up, off and on, all through the winter.

The sheriff from Gloverston came down to investigate. He came driving down the road in the new shiny white state police patrol car — the only one in the county — stopped in Willie's Café for a drink and went back taking two gallons of home brew with him. That wasn't exactly right, maybe, seeing that he had taken an oath to uphold the law; but he couldn't have done much, except get killed. And that was certain.

The Stevenses and their friends took to coming to Willie's on Friday nights; the Masterns kept on coming on Saturday. That just made two nights Willie had to keep the place open and the lamps filled with kerosene; the crowd was smaller; shotguns were leaning against the wall.

That's the way it went all winter. Everybody got on one side or the other — everybody except Stanley Albert Thompson. They both wanted him: they had seen what he could do in a fight. But Stanley Albert took to coming a night all by himself: Sunday night, and Willie had to light all the lamps for just him and stand behind the counter and watch him sit at the table adding lightning to the whisky.

Once along toward the end of February when Cy Mastern was killed and the roof of his house started burning with pine knots tossed from the ground, Stanley Albert was standing just on the rim of the light, watching. He helped the Masterns carry water, but Ed Stevens, who was hiding up in top of a pine to watch, swore that the water was like kerosene in his hands. Wherever he'd toss a bucketful, the fire would shoot up, brighter and hotter than before.

By March the frosts stopped, and there weren't any more cold winds. The farmers came out every noon, solemnly, and laid their hands on the bare ground to see if it was time to put in their earliest corn and potatoes. But the ground stayed cold a long time that year so that there wasn't any plowing until near May. All during that time from March till May there wasn't anything doing; that was the worst time for the fighting. In the winter your hand shakes so with the cold that you aren't much good with a gun or knife. But by March the air is warmer and you don't have any work to get you tired, so you spend all the time thinking.

That spring things got bad. There wasn't a crowd any more at Willie's though he kept the place open and the lights on for the three nights of the week-end. Neither the Stevenses nor the Masterns would come; they were too easy targets in a house with wall lamps burning. And on Sunday night the only person who ever came was Stanley Albert Thompson. He'd sit and drink his whisky and lightning and maybe sing a song or two for the girls who came over to see him. By the end of April that was changed too. He finally got himself the girl he wanted; the one he'd been waiting around nearly all winter for. And his courting was like this:

Thomas Henry Lacy and his sons, Luke and Tom, had gone for a walk, spoiling for a fight. They hadn't seen anything all evening, just some of the cows that had gone wild and went crashing away through the blueberry bushes. Alberta had taken herself along with them, since she was nearly as good as a man in a fight. They had been on the move all night but keeping in the range of a couple of miles and on the one side of the Scanos River. They were for Stevens and there was no telling what sort of affair the Masterns had rigged up on their ground. They rested for a while on the bluff of the river. Tom had some bread in his pocket and they ate it there, wondering if there was any-body in the laurels across the river just waiting for them to show themselves.

Then they walked on again, not saying very much, seeing nothing but the moon flat against the sky and its light shiny on the heavy dew.

Alberta didn't particularly care when they left her behind. She turned her head to listen to the plaintive gargling call of a night quail, and when she looked again her father and the boys were gone. She knew where she was: on the second ridge away from home. There was just the big high ridge there to the left. The house was maybe twenty minutes away, but a hard walk, and Alberta was tired. She'd been washing all day, trying to make the clear brook water carry off the dirt and grease from the clothes, her mother standing behind her, yelling at each spot that remained, her light face black almost as her husband's with temper, and her gray fuzzy hair tied into knots like a pickaninny's. The boys had spent the whole day dozing in the shed while they put a new shoe on the mule.

Alberta listened carefully; there was nothing but night noises; her father and the boys would be halfway home by now, scrambling down the rain-washed sides of the ridge. For a moment she considered following them. "Ain't no raving rush, girl," she told herself aloud. The night was cool, but there wasn't any wind. With her bare feet she felt the dry pine needles, then sat down on them, propping her back against a tree. She slipped the razor from the cord around her neck and held it open loosely in the palm of her hand; then she fell asleep.

She woke when the singing started, opening her eyes but not moving. The moon was right overhead, shining down so that the trunks of the pines stuck straight up out of the white shiny ground. There wasn't a man could hide behind a pine, yet she didn't see him. Only the singing going round and round her.

> "Alberta, what's on you mind,
> Alberta, why you treat me so unkind?
> You keep me worried; you keep me blue
> All the time,
> Alberta, why you treat me so unkind?"

She pushed herself up to a sitting position, still looking straight ahead, not following the song around and around. She let the hand that held the razor fall in her lap, so that the moon struck on the blade.

> "Alberta, why you treat me so unkind?"

Nothing grows under pines, not much grass even, not any bushes big enough to hide a man. Only pine trees, like black matches stuck in the moonlight. Black like matches, and thin like matches. There wasn't a man could hide behind a pine under a bright moon. There wasn't a man could pass a bright open space and not be seen.

> "Alberta, let you hair hang low,
> Alberta, let you hair hang low.
> I'll give you more gold
> Than you apron can hold."

"That ain't a very nice song," she said.

> "I'll give you more gold
> Than you apron can hold."

She lifted her right hand and turned the razor's edge slowly in the light.
"I got silver of my own right here," she said. "That enough for me."

The song went round in a circle, round and round, weaving in and out of
the pines, passing invisible across the open moon filled spaces.

> *"Alberta, let you hair hang low,*
> *I'll give you more gold*
> *Than you apron can hold.*
> *If you just let you hair hang low."*

There wasn't a man alive could do that. Go round and round.

> *"Alberta, why you treat me so unkind?"*

Round and round, in and out the thin black trees. Alberta stood up, following the sound, turning on her heel.

> *"You keep me worried, you keep me blue*
> *All the time."*

"I plain confused," she said. "I don't reckon I understand."

> *"I'll give you more gold*
> *Than you apron can hold."*

"I ain't got no apron," she said.

> *"Alberta, let you hair hang low,*
> *Just let you hair hang low."*

The song stopped and Stanley Albert Thompson came right out of a patch
of bright moon ground, where there were only brown pine needles.

Alberta forgot she was tired; the moon-spotted ground rolled past her feet
like the moon in the sky — effortless. She recognized the country they passed
through: Blue Goose Lake, Scanos River, and the steeper rough ground of the
north part of the country, toward the Tennessee border. It was a far piece to
walk and she wondered at the lightness of her feet. By moonset they had got
there — the cabin that the boys had seen one day while they were hunting cows.
She hesitated a little then, not afraid, not reluctant, but just not sure how to go
on. Stanley Albert Thompson had been holding her hand all evening; he still
held it. Right at the beginning when he had first taken her along with him,
she'd shook her head, no, she could walk; no man needed to lead her. But he'd
grinned at her, and shook his head, imitating her gesture, so that the moon
sparkled on his black curly hair, and his black broad forehead, and he took her
hand and led her so that the miles seemed nothing and the hours like smooth
water.

He showed her the cabin, from the outside first: mustard color, trimmed with
white, like the cabins the railroad company builds. One room with high peaked
roof.

"A real fine house," she said. "A real fine house. You work for the railroad?"

"No."

He took her inside. "You light with candles," she said.

"I ain't ever been able to stand the smell of lamps," he said.

"But it's a real nice house. I might could learn to like it."

"No might could about it." He smoothed the cloth on the table with his fingers. "You going to like it."

She bent her head and looked at him through her eyelashes. "Now I don't rightly know. Seems as how I don't know you."

"Sure you do," he said. "I'm standing right here."

"Seems as how I don't know nothing. You might could have a dozen girls all over this here state."

"I reckon there's a dozen," he said.

She glared at him, hands on hips. "You old fool jackass," she said. "I reckon you can just keep everything."

He jammed his hands into the back pockets of his denim pants and bent backward staring at the ceiling.

"Ain't you gonna try to stop me?"

"Nuh-uh."

She leaned against the doorjamb and twisted her neck to look at him. "Ain't you sorry I going?"

"Sure." He was still staring upward at the ceiling with its four crossed beams. "Sure, I real sorry."

"I don't see as how I could stay though."

"Sure you could." He did not look at her.

"I don't see as how. You ain't give me none of the things you said."

"You a driving woman," he said, and grinned, his mouth wide and white in the dark of his face.

Then he sat down at the table. There were five candles there, stuck in bottles, but only one was lighted, the one in the center. Wax had run all down the side of the candle and down the bottle in little round blobs, nubby like gravel. He picked one off, dirty white between his black fingers. He rolled it slowly between his flat palms, back and forth. Then he flipped it toward Alberta. It flashed silvery through the circle of lamplight and thudded against her skirt. She bent forward to pick it up: a coin, new silver. As she bent there, another one struck her shoulder, and another. Stanley Albert Thompson sat at the table, grinning and tossing the coins to her, until she had filled both pockets of her dress.

He pushed the candle away from him. "You all right, I reckon, now."

She held one coin in her hands, turning it over and over.

"That ain't what you promised. I remember how you came and sang:

> *"I give you more gold*
> *Than you apron can hold.'"*

"Sure," he said and lifted a single eyebrow, very high. "I can do that all right, iffen you want it. I reckon I can do that."

She stood for a moment studying him. And Stanley Albert Thompson, from where he still sat at the table, curled up one corner of his mouth.

And very slowly Alberta began to smile. "I might could like it here," she said. "If you was real nice."

He got up then and rubbed her cheek very gently with his first finger. "I might could do that," he said. "I don't reckon it would be too heavy a thing to do."

The candle was on the table to one side. It caught the brightness of Alberta's eyes as she stood smiling at Stanley Albert Thompson. The steady yellow light threw her shadow over his body, a dark shadow that reached to his chin. His own shadow was on the wall behind. She glanced at it over his shoulder and giggled. "You better do something about your shadow there, Mr. Thompson. That there is a ugly shadow, sure."

He turned his head and glanced at it briefly. "Reckon so," he said.

It was an ugly shadow, sure. Alberta looked at Stanley Albert Thompson and shook her head. "I can't hardly believe it," she said. "You a right pretty man."

He grinned at her and shook himself so that the shadow on the wall spun around in a wild turn.

"I don't reckon you can do anything about it?"

"No," he said briefly. "I can't go changing my shadow." He hunched his back so that the figure on the wall seemed to jump up and down in anger.

She stepped over to him, putting her hands behind her, leaning backward to see his face. "If he don't do any more than dance on a wall, I ain't complaining."

Stanley Albert stood looking down at her, looking down the length of his face at her, and rocking slowly back and forth on his heels. "No," he said. "He ain't gonna do more than wiggle around the wall sometimes. But you can bet I am."

The coins weighed down the pockets of her dress, and his hands were warm against her skin. "I reckon I'm satisfied," she said.

That was the way it began. That was the courting. The woman was young and attractive and strong. The man could give her whatever she wanted. There were other courtings like that in this country. Every season there were courtings like that.

People would see them around sometimes; or sometimes they'd only hear them when they were still far off. Sometimes it would be Stanley Albert Thompson singing:

> "*Alberta, let you hair hang low,*
> *Alberta, let you hair hang low.*
> *I'll give you more gold*
> *Than you apron can hold*
> *If you just let you hair hang low.*"

He had a strong voice. It could carry far in a quiet day or night. And if any of the people heard it, they'd turn and look at each other and nod their heads toward it, not saying anything, but just being sure that everyone was listening. And whenever Willie heard it, he'd close his eyes for a minute, seeing Alberta; and then he'd rub his hands all over his little black kinky head and whistle: "Euuuu," which meant that he was very, very sorry she had left him.

And sometimes all you could hear of them would be the chiming of Stanley Albert's watch every quarter-hour. One night that August, when the moon was heavy and hot and low, Maggie Mary was out walking with Jack Belden. She heard the clear high chime and remembered the nights at Willie's and the dangling gold watch. And she turned to Jack Belden, who had just got her comfortable in one arm, and jammed her fingers in his eyes and ran off after the sound. She didn't find them; and it wouldn't have much mattered if she had.

Stanley Albert was much too gone on Alberta to notice any other woman in more than a passing appraising way.

And sometimes people would come on them walking alone, arms around each other's waist; or sitting in a shady spot during the day's heat, his head on her lap and both of them dozing and smiling a little. And everybody who saw them would turn around and get out of there fast; but neither of them turned a head or looked up: there might not have been anyone there.

And then every night they'd go down to Willie's. The first night they came — it was on a Thursday — the place was closed up tight. There wasn't ever anybody came on Thursday. Stanley Albert went around back to where Willie lived and pounded on the door, and when Willie didn't answer he went around to the front again where Alberta was waiting on the steps and kicked in the front panel of the wood door. Willie came scuttling out, his eyes round and bewildered like a suckling's and saw them sitting at one of the tables drinking his home brew, only first putting lightning into it. After that they came every night, just them. It was all most people could do to afford a drink on Saturday or the week-end, but some of them would walk over to Willie's just to look at Stanley Albert and Alberta sitting there. They'd stand at the windows and look in, sweating in the hot summer nights and looking. Maybe a few of them would still be there waiting when Stanley and Alberta got ready to go, along toward morning.

That's what they did every single night of the year or so they were together. If they fell asleep, Willie would just have to stand waiting. They'd go out with their arms around each other's waist, staggering some, but not falling. And an hour or so later, people who were going out before dawn to get a little work done in the cool would see them clear over on the other side of the county, at Goose Lake, maybe, a good three hours' walk for a man cold sober. Willie had his own version of how they got around. They just picked up their feet, he said, and went sliding off down the winds. Once, he said, when they were sitting over on the bench against the wall, Stanley Albert flat on it with his head on her lap, when the whisky made the man in him come up sudden, so he couldn't wait, they went straight out the window, up the air, like a whistle sound. Willie had the broken glass to show the next morning, if you wanted to believe him.

Willie hated them, the two of them, maybe because they broke his glass, maybe because they made him stay up late every single night of the week, so that he had to hold his eyes open with his fingers, and watch them pour lightning into his very best whiskey, maybe because he had wanted Alberta mighty bad himself. He'd been giving her presents — bottles of his best stuff — but he just couldn't match Stanley Albert. Those are three reasons; maybe he had others. And Maggie Mary hated them; and she had only one reason.

Once Pete Stokes shot at Stanley Albert Thompson. He hadn't wanted to: he was scared like everybody else. But Maggie Mary Evans talked him into it. She was a fine-looking girl: she could do things like that. He hid behind the privy and got a perfect bead on Stanley Albert as he came out the door. The bullet just knocked off a piece of Willie's doorframe. When Pete saw what happened he dropped the gun and began to run, jumping the rail fence and crashing face-first through the thick heavy berry bushes. Stanley Albert pursed his lips together and rubbed his hands on his chin, slow, like he was deciding what to do. Then he jumped down from the porch and went after Pete. He ran through the hackberries too; only with him it did not seem difficult: none of the crackling and crashing and waving arms. Stanley Albert just put his head down and moved his legs, and the sprays of the bushes, some of them thick as a rooster's spur, seemed to pull back and make way. Nobody saw the fight: the brave ones were too drunk to travel fast; and the sober ones didn't want to mix with a man like Stanley Albert, drunk and mad. Alberta, she just ran her hand across her mouth and then wiped it along the side of her green satin dress, yawning like she was tired. She stood listening for a while, her head cocked a little, though there wasn't anything to hear, then walked off, pulling down the dress across her hips. And the next night she and Stanley Albert were back at Willie's, and Pete never did turn up again. Willie used to swear that he ended up in the Scanos River and that if the water wasn't so yellow muddy, that if you could see to the bottom, you would see Pete lying there, along with all the others Stanley Albert had killed.

At the last it was Willie who got the idea. For a week, carefully, he put aside the coins Stanley Albert gave him. There were a lot of them, all new silver, because Stanley Albert always paid in silver. Then one morning very early, just after Stanley Albert and Alberta left, Willie melted the coins down, and using the molds he kept for his old outsized pistol, he cast four bullets.

He made a special little shelf for the pistol under the counter so that it would be near at hand. And he waited all evening, sometimes touching the heavy black handle with the tips of his fingers; and he waited, hoping that Stanley Albert would drink enough to pass out. But of course nothing like that happened. So Willie poured himself three or four fingers of his best stuff and swallowed it fast as his throat would stand, then he blinked his little eyes fast for a second or so to clear his vision, and he reached for the gun. He got two shots over the bar, two good ones: the whole front of Stanley Albert's plaid shirt folded together and sank in, after the silver bullets went through. He got up, holding the table edge, unsteady, bending over, looking much smaller, his black skin gray-filmed and dull. His eyes were larger: they reached almost across his face — and they weren't dark any more; they were silver, two polished pieces of silver. Willie was afraid to fire again; the pistol shook where he held it in his two hands.

Then Stanley Albert walked out, not unsteady any more, but bent over the hole in his chest, walked out slowly with his eyes shining like flat metal, Alberta a few steps behind. They passed right in front of Willie, who still hadn't moved; his face was stiff with fear. Quietly, smoothly, in a single motion, almost without interrupting her step, Alberta picked up a bottle (the same one from which he had poured his drink moments before) and swung it against Willie's head. He slipped down in a quiet little heap, his legs folded under him, his black kinky head on top. But his idea had worked: over by Stanley Albert's chair there was a black pool of blood.

All that was maybe eight or ten years ago. People don't see them any more — Stanley and Alberta. They don't think much about them, except when something goes wrong — like weevils getting in the cotton, or Willie's burning down and Willie inside it — then they begin to think that those two had a hand in it. Brad Tedrow swore that he had seen Stanley Albert that night, just for a second, standing on the edge of the circle of light, with a burning faggot in his hand. And the next morning Brad went back to look, knowing that your eyes play tricks at night in firelight; he went back to look for footprints or some sign. All he found was a burnt-out stick of pine wood that anybody could have dropped.

And kids sometimes think they hear the jingle of silver in Stanley Albert's pocket, or the sound of his watch. And when women talk — when there's been a miscarriage or a stillbirth — they remember and whisper together.

And they all wonder if that's not the sort of work they do, the two of them. Maybe so; maybe not. The people themselves are not too sure. They don't see them around any more.

Nathaniel Hawthorne (1804–1864)

Rappaccini's Daughter

(From the Writings of Aubépine)

A young man, named Giovanni Guasconti, came, very long ago, from the more southern region of Italy, to pursue his studies at the University of Padua. Giovanni, who had but a scanty supply of gold ducats in his pocket, took lodgings in a high and gloomy chamber of an old edifice which looked not unworthy to have been the palace of a Paduan noble, and which, in fact, exhibited over its entrance the armorial bearings of a family long since extinct. The young stranger, who was not unstudied in the great poem of his country, recollected that one of the ancestors of this family, and perhaps an occupant of this very mansion, had been pictured by Dante as a partaker of the immortal agonies of his Inferno. These reminiscences and associations, together with the tendency to heartbreak natural to a young man for the first time out of his native sphere, caused Giovanni to sigh heavily as he looked around the desolate and ill-furnished apartment.

"Holy Virgin, signor!" cried old Dame Lisabetta, who, won by the youth's remarkable beauty of person, was kindly endeavoring to give the chamber a habitable air, "what a sigh was that to come out of a young man's heart! Do you find this old mansion gloomy? For the love of Heaven, then, put your head out of the window, and you will see as bright sunshine as you have left in Naples."

Guasconti mechanically did as the old woman advised, but could not quite agree with her that the Paduan sunshine was as cheerful as that of southern Italy. Such as it was, however, it fell upon a garden beneath the window and expended its fostering influences on a variety of plants, which seemed to have been cultivated with exceeding care.

"Does this garden belong to the house?" asked Giovanni.

"Heaven forbid, signor, unless it were fruitful of better pot herbs than any that grow there now," answered old Lisabetta. "No; that garden is cultivated by the own hands of Signor Giacomo Rappaccini, the famous doctor, who, I warrant him, has been heard of as far as Naples. It is said that he distils these plants into medicines that are as potent as a charm. Oftentimes you may see the signor doctor at work, and perchance the signora, his daughter, too, gathering the strange flowers that grow in the garden."

The old woman had now done what she could for the aspect of the chamber; and, commending the young man to the protection of the saints, took her departure.

Giovanni still found no better occupation than to look down into the garden beneath his window. From its appearance, he judged it to be one of those botanic gardens which were of earlier date in Padua than elsewhere in Italy or in the world. Or, not improbably, it might once have been the pleasure-place of an opulent family; for there was the ruin of a marble fountain in the center, sculptured with rare art, but so wofully shattered that it was impossible to trace the original design from the chaos of remaining fragments. The water, however, continued to gush and sparkle into the sunbeams as cheerfully as ever. A little gurgling sound ascended to the young man's window and made him feel as if the fountain were an immortal spirit, that sung its song unceasingly and without heeding the vicissitudes around it, while one century embodied it in marble and another scattered the perishable garniture on the soil. All about the pool into which the water subsided grew various plants, that seemed to require a plentiful supply of moisture for the nourishment of gigantic leaves, and, in some instances, flowers gorgeously magnificent. There was one shrub in particular, set in a marble vase in the midst of the pool, that bore a profusion of purple blossoms, each of which had the lustre and richness of a gem; and the whole together made a show so resplendent that it seemed enough to illuminate the garden, even had there been no sunshine. Every portion of the soil was peopled with plants and herbs, which, if less beautiful, still bore tokens of assiduous care, as if all had their individual virtues, known to the scientific mind that fostered them. Some were placed in urns, rich with old carving, and others in common garden pots; some crept serpent-like along the ground or climbed on high, using whatever means of ascent was offered them. One plant had wreathed itself round a statue of Vertumnus, which was thus quite veiled and shrouded in a drapery of hanging foliage, so happily arranged that it might have served a sculptor for a study.

While Giovanni stood at the window he heard a rustling behind a screen of leaves, and became aware that a person was at work in the garden. His figure soon emerged into view, and showed itself to be that of no common laborer, but a tall, emaciated, sallow, and sickly-looking man, dressed in a scholar's garb of black. He was beyond the middle term of life, with gray hair, a thin, gray beard, and a face singularly marked with intellect and cultivation, but which could never, even in his more youthful days, have expressed much warmth of heart.

Nothing could exceed the intentness with which this scientific gardener examined every shrub which grew in his path: it seemed as if he was looking into their inmost nature, making observations in regard to their creative essence, and discovering why one leaf grew in this shape and another in that, and wherefore such and such flowers differed among themselves in hue and perfume. Nevertheless, in spite of this deep intelligence on his part, there was no approach to intimacy between himself and these vegetable existences. On the contrary, he avoided their actual touch or the direct inhaling of their odors with a caution that impressed Giovanni most disagreeably; for the man's demeanor was that of one walking among malignant influences, such as savage beasts, or deadly snakes, or evil spirits, which, should he allow them one moment of license, would wreak upon him some terrible fatality. It was strangely frightful to the young man's imagination to see this air of insecurity in a person cultivating a garden, that most simple and innocent of human toils, and which had been alike the joy and labor of the unfallen parents of the race. Was this garden, then, the Eden of the present world? And this man, with such perception of harm in what his own hands caused to grow — was he the Adam?

The distrustful gardener, while plucking away the dead leaves or pruning the too luxuriant growth of the shrubs, defended his hands with a pair of thick gloves. Nor were these his only armor. When, in his walk through the garden, he came to the magnificent plant that hung its purple gems beside the marble fountain, he placed a kind of mask over his mouth and nostrils, as if all this beauty did but conceal a deadlier malice; but, finding his task still too dangerous, he drew back, removed the mask, and called loudly, but in the infirm voice of a person affected with inward disease —

"Beatrice! Beatrice!"

"Here am I, my father. What would you?" cried a rich and youthful voice from the window of the opposite house — a voice as rich as a tropical sunset, and which made Giovanni, though he knew not why, think of deep hues of purple or crimson and of perfumes heavily delectable, "Are you in the garden?"

"Yes, Beatrice," answered the gardener, "and I need your help."

Soon there emerged from under a sculptured portal the figure of a young girl, arrayed with as much richness of taste as the most splendid of the flowers, beautiful as the day, and with a bloom so deep and vivid that one shade more would have been too much. She looked redundant with life, health, and energy; all of which attributes were bound down and compressed, as it were, and girdled tensely, in their luxuriance, by her virgin zone. Yet Giovanni's fancy must have grown morbid while he looked down into the garden; for the impression which the fair stranger made upon him was as if here were another flower, the human sister of those vegetable ones, as beautiful as they, more beautiful than the richest of them, but still to be touched only with a glove, nor to be approached without a mask. As Beatrice came down the garden path, it was observable that she handled and inhaled the odor of several of the plants which her father had most sedulously avoided.

"Here, Beatrice," said the latter, "see how many needful offices require to be done to our chief treasure. Yet, shattered as I am, my life might pay the penalty of approaching it so closely as circumstances demand. Henceforth, I fear, this plant must be consigned to your sole charge."

"And gladly will I undertake it," cried again the rich tones of the young lady, as she bent towards the magnificent plant and opened her arms as if to embrace it. "Yes, my sister, my splendor, it shall be Beatrice's task to nurse and serve thee; and thou shalt reward her with thy kisses and perfumed breath, which to her is as the breath of life."

Then, with all the tenderness in her manner that was so strikingly expressed in her words, she busied herself with such attentions as the plant seemed to require; and Giovanni, at his lofty window, rubbed his eyes, and almost doubted whether it were a girl tending her favorite flower, or one sister performing the duties of affection to another. The scene soon terminated. Whether Dr. Rappaccini had finished his labors in the garden, or that his watchful eye had caught the stranger's face, he now took his daughter's arm and retired. Night was already closing in; oppressive exhalations seemed to proceed from the plants and steal upward past the open window; and Giovanni, closing the lattice, went to his couch and dreamed of a rich flower and beautiful girl. Flower and maiden were different, and yet the same, and fraught with some strange peril in either shape.

But there is an influence in the light of morning that tends to rectify whatever errors of fancy, or even of judgment, we may have incurred during the sun's decline, or among the shadows of the night, or in the less wholesome glow of moonshine. Giovanni's first movement, on starting from sleep, was to throw open the window and gaze down into the garden which his dreams had made so fertile of mysteries. He was surprised, and a little ashamed, to find how real and matter-of-fact an affair it proved to be, in the first rays of the sun which gilded the dewdrops that hung upon leaf and blossom, and, while giving a brighter beauty to each rare flower, brought everything within the limits of ordinary experience. The young man rejoiced that, in the heart of the barren city, he had the privilege of overlooking this spot of lovely and luxuriant vegetation. It would serve, he said to himself, as symbolic language to keep him in communion with Nature. Neither the sickly and thoughtworn Dr. Giacomo Rappaccini, it is true, nor his brilliant daughter, were now visible; so that Giovanni could not determine how much of the singularity which he attributed to both was due to their own qualities and how much to his wonder-working fancy; but he was inclined to take a most rational view of the whole matter.

In the course of the day he paid his respects to Signor Pietro Baglioni, professor of medicine in the university, a physician of eminent repute, to whom Giovanni had brought a letter of introduction. The professor was an elderly personage, apparently of genial nature and habits that might almost be called jovial. He kept the young man to dinner, and made himself very agreeable by the freedom and liveliness of his conversation, especially when warmed by a flask or two of Tuscan wine. Giovanni, conceiving that men of science, inhabitants of the same city, must needs be on familiar terms with one another, took an opportunity to mention the name of Dr. Rappaccini. But the professor did not respond with so much cordiality as he had anticipated.

"Ill would it become a teacher of the divine art of medicine," said Professor Pietro Baglioni, in answer to a question of Giovanni, "to withhold due and well-considered praise of a physician so eminently skilled as Rappaccini; but, on the other hand, I should answer it but scantily to my conscience were I to permit a worthy youth like yourself, Signor Giovanni, the son of an ancient friend, to imbibe erroneous ideas respecting a man who might hereafter chance to hold your life and death in his hands. The truth is, our worshipful Dr. Rappaccini has as much science as any member of the faculty — with perhaps one single exception — in Padua, or all Italy; but there are certain grave objections to his professional character."

"And what are they?" asked the young man.

"Has my friend Giovanni any disease of body or heart, that he is so inquisitive about physicians?" said the professor, with a smile. "But as for Rappaccini, it is said of him — and I, who know the man well, can answer for its truth — that he cares infinitely more for science than for mankind. His patients are interesting to him only as subjects for some new experiment. He would sacrifice human life, his own among the rest, or whatever else was dearest to him, for the sake of adding so much as a grain of mustard seed to the great heap of his accumulated knowledge."

"Methinks he is an awful man indeed," remarked Guasconti, mentally recalling the cold and purely intellectual aspect of Rappaccini. "And yet, worshipful professor, is it not a noble spirit? Are there many men capable of so spiritual a love of science?"

"God forbid," answered the professor, somewhat testily; "at least, unless they take sounder views of the healing art than those adopted by Rappaccini. It is his theory that all medicinal virtues are comprised within those substances which we term vegetable poisons. These he cultivates with his own hands, and is said even to have produced new varieties of poison, more horribly deleterious than Nature, without the assistance of this learned person, would ever have plagued the world withal. That the signor doctor does less mischief than might be expected with such dangerous substances is undeniable. Now and then, it must be owned, he has effected, or seemed to effect, a marvellous cure; but, to tell you my private mind, Signor Giovanni, he should receive little credit for such instances of success — they being probably the work of chance — but should be held strictly accountable for his failures, which may justly be considered his own work."

The youth might have taken Baglioni's opinions with many grains of allowance had he known that there was a professional warfare of long continuance between him and Dr. Rappaccini, in which the latter was generally thought to have gained the advantage. If the reader be inclined to judge for himself, we refer him to certain black-letter tracts on both sides, preserved in the medical department of the University of Padua.

"I know not, most learned professor," returned Giovanni, after musing on what had been said of Rappaccini's exclusive zeal for science — "I know not how dearly this physician may love his art; but surely there is one object more dear to him. He has a daughter."

"Aha!" cried the professor, with a laugh. "So now our friend Giovanni's secret is out. You have heard of this daughter, whom all the young men in Padua are wild about, though not half a dozen have ever had the good hap to see her face. I know little of the Signora Beatrice save that Rappaccini is said to have instructed her deeply in his science, and that, young and beautiful as fame reports her, she is already qualified to fill a professor's chair. Perchance her father destines her for mine! Other absurd rumors there be, not worth talking about or listening to. So now, Signor Giovanni, drink off your glass of lachryma."

Guasconti returned to his lodgings somewhat heated with the wine he had quaffed, and which caused his brain to swim with strange fantasies in reference to Dr. Rappaccini and the beautiful Beatrice. On his way, happening to pass by a florist's, he bought a fresh bouquet of flowers.

Ascending to his chamber, he seated himself near the window, but within the shadow thrown by the depth of the wall, so that he could look down into the garden with little risk of being discovered. All beneath his eye was a solitude. The strange plants were basking in the sunshine, and now and then nodding gently to one another, as if in acknowledgment of sympathy and kindred. In the midst, by the shattered fountain, grew the magnificent shrub, with its purple gems clustering all over it; they glowed in the air, and gleamed back again out of the depths of the pool, which thus seemed to overflow with colored radiance from the rich reflection that was steeped in it. At first, as we have said, the garden was a solitude. Soon, however — as Giovanni had half hoped, half feared, would be the case — a figure appeared beneath the antique sculptured portal, and came down between the rows of plants, inhaling their various perfumes as if she were one of those beings of old classic fable that lived upon sweet odors. On again beholding Beatrice, the young man was even startled to perceive how much her beauty exceeded his recollection of it; so brilliant, so vivid, was its character, that she glowed amid the sunlight, and, as Giovanni whispered to himself, positively illuminated the more shadowy intervals of the garden path.

Her face being now more revealed than on the former occasion, he was struck by its expression of simplicity and sweetness — qualities that had not entered into his idea of her character, and which made him ask anew what manner of mortal she might be. Nor did he fail again to observe, or imagine, an analogy between the beautiful girl and the gorgeous shrub that hung its gemlike flowers over the fountain — a resemblance which Beatrice seemed to have indulged a fantastic humor in heightening, both by the arrangement of her dress and the selection of its hues.

Approaching the shrub, she threw open her arms, as with a passionate ardor, and drew its branches into an intimate embrace — so intimate that her features were hidden in its leafy bosom and her glistening ringlets all intermingled with the flowers.

"Give me thy breath, my sister," exclaimed Beatrice; "for I am faint with common air. And give me this flower of thine, which I separate with gentlest fingers from the stem and place it close beside my heart."

With these words the beautiful daughter of Rappaccini plucked one of the richest blossoms of the shrub, and was about to fasten it in her bosom. But now, unless Giovanni's draughts of wine had bewildered his senses, a singular incident occurred. A small orange-colored reptile, of the lizard or chameleon species, chanced to be creeping along the path, just at the feet of Beatrice. It appeared to Giovanni — but, at the distance from which he gazed, he could scarcely have seen anything so minute — it appeared to him, however, that a drop or two of moisture from the broken stem of the flower descended upon the lizard's head. For an instant the reptile contorted itself violently, and then lay motionless in the sunshine. Beatrice observed this remarkable phenomenon, and crossed herself, sadly, but without surprise; nor did she therefore hesitate to arrange the fatal flower in her bosom. There it blushed, and almost glimmered with the dazzling effect of a precious stone, adding to her dress and aspect the one appropriate charm which nothing else in the world could have supplied. But Giovanni, out of the shadow of his window, bent forward and shrank back, and murmured and trembled.

"Am I awake? Have I my senses?" said he to himself. "What is this being? Beautiful shall I call her, or inexpressibly terrible?"

Beatrice now strayed carelessly through the garden, approaching closer beneath Giovanni's window, so that he was compelled to thrust his head quite out of its concealment in order to gratify the intense and painful curiosity which she excited. At this moment there came a beautiful insect over the garden wall: it had, perhaps, wandered through the city, and found no flowers or verdure among those antique haunts of men until the heavy perfumes of Dr. Rappaccini's shrubs had lured it from afar. Without alighting on the flowers, this winged brightness seemed to be attracted by Beatrice, and lingered in the air and fluttered about her head. Now, here it could not be but that Giovanni Guasconti's eyes deceived him. Be that as it might, he fancied that, while Beatrice was gazing at the insect with childish delight, it grew faint and fell at her feet; its bright wings shivered; it was dead — from no cause that he could discern, unless it were the atmosphere of her breath. Again Beatrice crossed herself and sighed heavily as she bent over the dead insect.

An impulsive movement of Giovanni drew her eyes to the window. There she beheld the beautiful head of the young man — rather a Grecian than an Italian head, with fair, regular features, and a glistening of gold among his ringlets — gazing down upon her like a being that hovered in mid air. Scarcely knowing what he did, Giovanni threw down the bouquet which he had hitherto held in his hand.

"Signora," said he, "there are pure and healthful flowers. Wear them for the sake of Giovanni Guasconti."

"Thanks, signor," replied Beatrice, with her rich voice, that came forth as it were like a gush of music, and with a mirthful expression half childish and half womanlike. "I accept your gift, and would fain recompense it with this precious purple flower; but, if I toss it into the air, it will not reach you. So Signor Guasconti must even content himself with my thanks."

She lifted the bouquet from the ground, and then, as if inwardly ashamed at having stepped aside from her maidenly reserve to respond to a stranger's greeting, passed swiftly homeward through the garden. But few as the moments were, it seemed to Giovanni, when she was on the point of vanishing beneath the sculptured portal, that his beautiful bouquet was already beginning to wither in her grasp. It was an idle thought; there could be no possibility of distinguishing a faded flower from a fresh one at so great a distance.

For many days after this incident the young man avoided the window that looked into Dr. Rappaccini's garden, as if something ugly and monstrous would have blasted his eyesight had he been betrayed into a glance. He felt conscious of having put himself, to a certain extent, within the influence of an unintelligible power by the communication which he had opened with Beatrice. The wisest course would have been, if his heart were in any real danger, to quit his lodgings and Padua itself at once; the next wiser, to have accustomed himself, as far as possible, to the familiar and daylight view of Beatrice — thus bringing her rigidly and systematically within the limits of ordinary experience. Least of all, while avoiding her sight, ought Giovanni to have remained so near this extraordinary being that the proximity and possibility even of intercourse should give a kind of substance and reality to the wild vagaries which his imagination ran riot continually in producing. Guasconti had not a deep heart — or, at all events, its depths were not sounded now; but he had a quick fancy, and an ardent southern temperament, which rose every instant to a higher fever pitch. Whether or no Beatrice possessed those terrible attributes, that fatal breath, the affinity with those so beautiful and deadly flowers which were indicated by what Giovanni had witnessed, she had at least instilled a fierce and subtle poison into his system. It was not love, although her rich beauty was a madness to him; nor horror, even while he fancied her spirit to be imbued with the same baneful essence that seemed to pervade her physical frame; but a wild offspring of both love and horror that had each parent in it, and burned like one and shivered like the other. Giovanni knew not what to dread; still less did he know what to hope; yet hope and dread kept a continual warfare in his breast, alternately vanquishing one another and starting up afresh to renew the contest. Blessed are all simple emotions, be they dark or bright! It is the lurid intermixture of the two that produces the illuminating blaze of the infernal regions.

Sometimes he endeavored to assuage the fever of his spirit by a rapid walk through the streets of Padua or beyond its gates: his footsteps kept time with the throbbings of his brain, so that the walk was apt to accelerate itself to a race. One day he found himself arrested; his arm was seized by a portly personage, who had turned back on recognizing the young man and expended much breath in overtaking him.

"Signor Giovanni! Stay, my young friend!" cried he. "Have you forgotten me? That might well be the case if I were as much altered as yourself."

It was Baglioni, whom Giovanni had avoided ever since their first meeting, from a doubt that the professor's sagacity would look too deeply into his secrets. Endeavoring to recover himself, he started forth wildly from his inner world into the outer one and spoke like a man in a dream.

"Yes; I am Giovanni Guasconti. You are Professor Pietro Baglioni. Now let me pass!"

"Not yet, not yet, Signor Giovanni Guasconti," said the professor, smiling, but at the same time scrutinizing the youth with an earnest glance. "What! did I grow up side by side with your father? and shall his son pass me like a stranger in these old streets of Padua? Stand still, Signor Giovanni; for we must have a word or two before we part."

"Speedily, then, most worshipful professor, speedily," said Giovanni, with feverish impatience. "Does not your worship see that I am in haste?"

Now, while he was speaking there came a man in black along the street, stooping and moving feebly like a person in inferior health. His face was all overspread with a most sickly and sallow hue, but yet so pervaded with an expression of piercing and active intellect that an observer might easily have overlooked the merely physical attributes and have seen only this wonderful energy. As he passed, this person exchanged a cold and distant salutation with Baglioni, but fixed his eyes upon Giovanni with an intentness that seemed to bring out whatever was within him worthy of notice. Nevertheless, there was a peculiar quietness in the look, as if taking merely a speculative, not human, interest in the young man.

"It is Dr. Rappaccini!" whispered the professor when the stranger had passed. "Has he ever seen your face before?"

"Not that I know," answered Giovanni, starting at the name.

"He *has* seen you! he must have seen you!" said Baglioni, hastily. "For some purpose or other, this man of science is making a study of you. I know that look of his! It is the same that coldly illuminates his face as he bends over a bird, a mouse, or a butterfly, which, in pursuance of some experiment, he has killed by the perfume of a flower; a look as deep as Nature itself, but without Nature's warmth of love. Signor Giovanni, I will stake my life upon it, you are the subject of one of Rappaccini's experiments!"

"Will you make a fool of me?" cried Giovanni, passionately. "*That,* signor professor, were an untoward experiment."

"Patience! patience!" replied the imperturbable professor. "I tell thee, my poor Giovanni, that Rappaccini has a scientific interest in thee. Thou hast fallen into fearful hands! And the Signora Beatrice, — what part does she act in this mystery?"

But Guasconti, finding Baglioni's pertinacity intolerable, here broke away, and was gone before the professor could again seize his arm. He looked after the young man intently and shook his head.

"This must not be," said Baglioni to himself. "The youth is the son of my old friend, and shall not come to any harm from which the arcana of medical science can preserve him. Besides, it is too insufferable an impertinence in Rappaccini thus to snatch the lad out of my own hands, as I may say, and make use of him for his infernal experiments. This daughter of his! It shall be looked to. Perchance, most learned Rappaccini, I may foil you where you little dream of it!"

Meanwhile Giovanni had pursued a circuitous route, and at length found himself at the door of his lodgings. As he crossed the threshold he was met by old Lisabetta, who smirked and smiled, and was evidently desirous to attract his attention; vainly, however, as the ebullition of his feelings had momentarily subsided into a cold and dull vacuity. He turned his eyes full upon the withered face that was puckering itself into a smile, but seemed to behold it not. The old dame, therefore, laid her grasp upon his cloak.

"Signor! signor!" whispered she, still with a smile over the whole breadth of her visage, so that it looked not unlike a grotesque carving in wood, darkened by centuries. "Listen, signor! There is a private entrance into the garden!"

"What do you say?" exclaimed Giovanni, turning quickly about, as if an inanimate thing should start into feverish life. "A private entrance into Dr. Rappaccini's garden?"

"Hush! hush! not so loud!" whispered Lisabetta, putting her hand over his mouth. "Yes, into the worshipful doctor's garden, where you may see all his fine shrubbery. Many a young man in Padua would give gold to be admitted among those flowers."

Giovanni put a piece of gold into her hand.

"Show me the way," said he.

A surmise, probably excited by his conversation with Baglioni, crossed his mind, that this interposition of old Lisabetta might perchance be connected with the intrigue, whatever were its nature, in which the professor seemed to suppose that Dr. Rappaccini was involving him. But such a suspicion, though it disturbed Giovanni, was inadequate to restrain him. The instant that he was aware of the possibility of approaching Beatrice, it seemed an absolute necessity of his existence to do so. It mattered not whether she were angel or demon; he was irrevocably within her sphere, and must obey the law that whirled him onward, in ever-lessening circles, towards a result which he did not attempt to foreshadow; and yet, strange to say, there came across him a sudden doubt whether this intense interest on his part were not delusory; whether it were really of so deep and positive a nature as to justify him in now thrusting himself into an incalculable position; whether it were not merely the fantasy of a young man's brain, only slightly or not at all connected with his heart.

He paused, hesitated, turned half about, but again went on. His withered guide led him along several obscure passages, and finally undid a door, through which, as it was opened, there came the sight and sound of rustling leaves, with the broken sunshine glimmering among them. Giovanni stepped forth, and, forcing himself through the entanglement of a shrub that wreathed its tendrils over the hidden entrance, stood beneath his own window in the open area of Dr. Rappaccini's garden.

How often is it the case that, when impossibilities have come to pass and dreams have condensed their misty substance into tangible realities, we find ourselves calm, and even coldly self-possessed, amid circumstances which it would have been a delirium of joy or agony to anticipate! Fate delights to thwart us thus. Passion will choose his own time to rush upon the scene, and lingers sluggishly behind when an appropriate adjustment of events would seem to summon his appearance. So was it now with Giovanni. Day after day his pulses had throbbed with feverish blood at the improbable idea of an interview with Beatrice, and of standing with her, face to face, in this very garden, basking in the Oriental sunshine of her beauty, and snatching from her full gaze the mystery which he deemed the riddle of his own existence. But now there was a singular and untimely equanimity within his breast. He threw a glance around the garden to discover if Beatrice or her father were present, and, perceiving that he was alone, began a critical observation of the plants.

The aspect of one and all of them dissatisfied him; their gorgeousness seemed fierce, passionate, and even unnatural. There was hardly an individual shrub which a wanderer, straying by himself through a forest, would not have been startled to find growing wild, as if an unearthly face had glared at him out of the thicket. Several also would have shocked a delicate instinct by an appearance of artificialness indicating that there had been such commixture, and, as it were, adultery, of various vegetable species, that the production was no longer of God's making, but the monstrous offspring of man's depraved fancy, glowing with only an evil mockery of beauty. They were probably the result of experiment, which in one or two cases had succeeded in mingling plants individually lovely into a compound possessing the questionable and ominous character that distinguished the whole growth of the garden. In fine, Giovanni recognized but two or three plants in the collection, and those of a kind that he well knew to be poisonous. While busy with these contemplations he heard the rustling of a silken garment, and, turning, beheld Beatrice emerging from beneath the sculptured portal.

Giovanni had not considered with himself what should be his deportment; whether he should apologize for his intrusion into the garden, or assume that he was there with the privity at least, if not by the desire, of Dr. Rappaccini or his daughter; but Beatrice's manner placed him at his ease, though leaving him still in doubt by what agency he had gained admittance. She came lightly along the path and met him near the broken fountain. There was surprise in her face, but brightened by a simple and kind expression of pleasure.

"You are a connoisseur in flowers, signor," said Beatrice, with a smile, alluding to the bouquet which he had flung her from the window. "It is no marvel, therefore, if the sight of my father's rare collection has tempted you to take a nearer view. If he were here, he could tell you many strange and interesting facts as to the nature and habits of these shrubs; for he has spent a lifetime in such studies, and this garden is his world."

"And yourself, lady," observed Giovanni, "if fame says true, — you likewise are deeply skilled in the virtues indicated by these rich blossoms and these spicy perfumes. Would you deign to be my instructress, I should prove an apter scholar than if taught by Signor Rappaccini himself."

"Are there such idle rumors?" asked Beatrice, with the music of a pleasant laugh. "Do people say that I am skilled in my father's science of plants? What a jest is there! No; though I have grown up among these flowers, I know no more of them than their hues and perfume; and sometimes methinks I would fain rid myself of even that small knowledge. There are many flowers here, and those not the least brilliant, that shock and offend me when they meet my eye. But pray, signor, do not believe these stories about my science. Believe nothing of me save what you see with your own eyes."

"And must I believe all that I have seen with my own eyes?" asked Giovanni, pointedly, while the recollection of former scenes made him shrink. "No, signora, you demand too little of me. Bid me believe nothing save what comes from your own lips."

It would appear that Beatrice understood him. There came a deep flush to her cheek; but she looked full into Giovanni's eyes, and responded to his gaze of uneasy suspicion with a queenlike haughtiness.

"I do so bid you, signor," she replied. "Forget whatever you may have fancied in regard to me. If true to the outward senses, still it may be false in its essence; but the words of Beatrice Rappaccini's lips are true from the depths of the heart outward. Those you may believe."

A fervor glowed in her whole aspect and beamed upon Giovanni's consciousness like the light of truth itself; but while she spoke there was a fragrance in the atmosphere around her, rich and delightful, though evanescent, yet which the young man, from an indefinable reluctance, scarcely dared to draw into his lungs. It might be the odor of the flowers. Could it be Beatrice's breath which thus embalmed her words with a strange richness, as if by steeping them in her heart? A faintness passed like a shadow over Giovanni and flitted away; he seemed to gaze through the beautiful girl's eyes into her transparent soul, and felt no more doubt or fear.

The tinge of passion that had colored Beatrice's manner vanished; she became gay, and appeared to derive a pure delight from her communion with the youth not unlike what the maiden of a lonely island might have felt conversing with a voyager from the civilized world. Evidently her experience of life had been confined within the limits of that garden. She talked now about matters as simple as the daylight or summer clouds, and now asked questions in reference to the city, or Giovanni's distant home, his friends, his mother, and his sister — questions indicating such seclusion, and such lack of familiarity with modes and forms, that Giovanni responded as if to an infant. Her spirit gushed out before him like a fresh rill that was just catching its first glimpse of the sunlight and wondering at the reflections of earth and sky which were flung into its bosom. There came thoughts, too, from a deep source, and fantasies of a gemlike brilliancy, as if diamonds and rubies sparkled upward among the bubbles of the fountain. Ever and anon there gleamed across the young man's mind a sense of wonder that he should be walking side by side with the being who had so wrought upon his imagination, whom he had idealized in such hues of terror, in whom he had positively witnessed such manifestations of dreadful attributes — that he should be conversing with Beatrice like a brother, and should find her so human and so maidenlike. But such reflections were only momentary; the effect of her character was too real not to make itself familiar at once.

In this free intercourse they had strayed through the garden, and now, after many turns among its avenues, were come to the shattered fountain, beside which grew the magnificent shrub, with its treasury of glowing blossoms. A fragrance was diffused from it which Giovanni recognized as identical with that which he had attributed to Beatrice's breath, but incomparably more powerful. As her eyes fell upon it, Giovanni beheld her press her hand to her bosom as if her heart were throbbing suddenly and painfully.

"For the first time in my life," murmured she, addressing the shrub, "I had forgotten thee."

"I remember, signora," said Giovanni, "that you once promised to reward

me with one of these living gems for the bouquet which I had the happy bold-
ness to fling to your feet. Permit me now to pluck it as a memorial of this
interview."

He made a step towards the shrub with extended hand; but Beatrice darted
forward, uttering a shriek that went through his heart like a dagger. She caught
his hand and drew it back with the whole force of her slender figure. Giovanni
felt her touch thrilling through his fibres.

"Touch it not!" exclaimed she, in a voice of agony. "Not for thy life! It
is fatal!"

Then, hiding her face, she fled from him and vanished beneath the sculptured
portal. As Giovanni followed her with his eyes, he beheld the emaciated figure
and pale intelligence of Dr. Rappaccini, who had been watching the scene, he
knew not how long, within the shadow of the entrance.

No sooner was Guasconti alone in his chamber than the image of Beatrice
came back to his passionate musings, invested with all the witchery that had
been gathering around it ever since his first glimpse of her, and now likewise
imbued with a tender warmth of girlish womanhood. She was human; her nature was endowed with all gentle and feminine qualities; she was worthiest to be
worshipped; she was capable, surely, on her part, of the height and heroism of
love. Those tokens which he had hitherto considered as proofs of a frightful
peculiarity in her physical and moral system were now either forgotten or by
the subtle sophistry of passion transmitted into a golden crown of enchantment,
rendering Beatrice the more admirable by so much as she was the more unique.
Whatever had looked ugly was now beautiful; or, if incapable of such a change,
it stole away and hid itself among those shapeless half ideas which throng the
dim region beyond the daylight of our perfect consciousness. Thus did he spend
the night, nor fell asleep until the dawn had begun to awake the slumbering
flowers in Dr. Rappaccini's garden, whither Giovanni's dreams doubtless led him.
Up rose the sun in his due season, and, flinging his beams upon the young man's
eyelids, awoke him to a sense of pain. When thoroughly aroused, he became
sensible of a burning and tingling agony in his hand — in his right hand — the
very hand which Beatrice had grasped in her own when he was on the point of
plucking one of the gemlike flowers. On the back of that hand there was now a
purple print like that of four small fingers, and the likeness of a slender thumb
upon his wrist.

O, how stubbornly does love, — or even that cunning semblance of love
which flourishes in the imagination, but strikes no depth of root into the heart, —
how stubbornly does it hold its faith until the moment comes when it is doomed
to vanish into thin mist! Giovanni wrapped a handkerchief about his hand and
wondered what evil thing had stung him, and soon forgot his pain in a reverie
of Beatrice.

After the first interview, a second was in the inevitable course of what we
call fate. A third; a fourth; and a meeting with Beatrice in the garden was no
longer an incident in Giovanni's daily life, but the whole space in which he
might be said to live; for the anticipation and memory of that ecstatic hour made
up the remainder. Nor was it otherwise with the daughter of Rappaccini. She
watched for the youth's appearance and flew to his side with confidence as un-
reserved as if they had been playmates from early infancy — as if they were
such playmates still. If, by any unwonted chance, he failed to come at the appointed moment, she stood beneath the window and sent up the rich sweetness

of her tones to float around him in his chamber and echo and reverberate throughout his heart: "Giovanni! Giovanni! Why tarriest thou? Come down!" And down he hastened into that Eden of poisonous flowers.

But, with all this intimate familiarity, there was still a reserve in Beatrice's demeanor, so rigidly and invariably sustained that the idea of infringing it scarcely occurred to his imagination. By all appreciable signs, they loved; they had looked love with eyes that conveyed the holy secret from the depths of one soul into the depths of the other, as if it were too sacred to be whispered by the way; they had even spoken love in those gushes of passion when their spirits darted forth in articulated breath like tongues of long hidden flame; and yet there had been no seal of lips, no clasp of hands, nor any slightest caress such as love claims and hallows. He had never touched one of the gleaming ringlets of her hair; her garment — so marked was the physical barrier between them — had never been waved against him by a breeze. On the few occasions when Giovanni had seemed tempted to overstep the limit, Beatrice grew so sad, so stern, and withal wore such a look of desolate separation, shuddering at itself, that not a spoken word was requisite to repel him. At such times he was startled at the horrible suspicions that rose, monster-like, out of the caverns of his heart and stared him in the face; his love grew thin and faint as the morning mist; his doubts alone had substance. But, when Beatrice's face brightened again after the momentary shadow, she was transformed at once from the mysterious, questionable being whom he had watched with so much awe and horror; she was now the beautiful and unsophisticated girl whom he felt that his spirit knew with a certainty beyond all other knowledge.

A considerable time had now passed since Giovanni's last meeting with Baglioni. One morning, however, he was disagreeably surprised by a visit from the professor, whom he had scarcely thought of for whole weeks, and would willingly have forgotten still longer. Given up as he had long been to a pervading excitement, he could tolerate no companions except upon condition of their perfect sympathy with his present state of feeling. Such sympathy was not to be expected from Professor Baglioni.

The visitor chatted carelessly for a few moments about the gossip of the city and the university, and then took up another topic.

"I have been reading an old classic author lately," said he, "and met with a story that strangely interested me. Possibly you may remember it. It is of an Indian prince, who sent a beautiful woman as a present to Alexander the Great. She was as lovely as the dawn and gorgeous as the sunset; but what especially distinguished her was a certain rich perfume in her breath — richer than a garden of Persian roses. Alexander, as was natural to a youthful conqueror, fell in love at first sight with this magnificent stranger; but a certain sage physician, happening to be present, discovered a terrible secret in regard to her."

"And what was that?" asked Giovanni, turning his eyes downward to avoid those of the professor.

"That this lovely woman," continued Baglioni, with emphasis, "had been nourished with poisons from her birth upward, until her whole nature was so imbued with them that she herself had become the deadliest poison in existence. Poison was her element of life. With that rich perfume of her breath she blasted the very air. Her love would have been poison — her embrace death. Is not this a marvellous tale?"

"A childish fable," answered Giovanni, nervously starting from his chair.

"I marvel how your worship finds time to read such nonsense among your graver studies."

"By the by," said the professor, looking uneasily about him, "what singular fragrance is this in your apartment? Is it the perfume of your gloves? It is faint, but delicious; and yet, after all, by no means agreeable. Were I to breathe it long, methinks it would make me ill. It is like the breath of a flower; but I see no flowers in the chamber."

"Nor are there any," replied Giovanni, who had turned pale as the professor spoke; "nor, I think, is there any fragrance except in your worship's imagination. Odors, being a sort of element combined of the sensual and the spiritual, are apt to deceive us in this manner. The recollection of a perfume, the bare idea of it, may easily be mistaken for a present reality."

"Ay; but my sober imagination does not often play such tricks," said Baglioni; "and, were I to fancy any kind of odor, it would be that of some vile apothecary drug, wherewith my fingers are likely enough to be imbued. Our worshipful friend Rappaccini, as I have heard, tinctures his medicaments with odors richer than those of Araby. Doubtless, likewise, the fair and learned Signora Beatrice would minister to her patients with draughts as sweet as a maiden's breath; but woe to him that sips them!"

Giovanni's face evinced many contending emotions. The tone in which the professor alluded to the pure and lovely daughter of Rappaccini was a torture to his soul; and yet the intimation of a view of her character, opposite to his own, gave instantaneous distinctness to a thousand dim suspicions, which now grinned at him like so many demons. But he strove hard to quell them and to respond to Baglioni with a true lover's perfect faith.

"Signor professor," said he, "you were my father's friend; perchance, too, it is your purpose to act a friendly part towards his son. I would fain feel nothing towards you save respect and deference; but I pray you to observe, signor, that there is one subject on which we must not speak. You know not the Signora Beatrice. You cannot, therefore, estimate the wrong — the blasphemy, I may even say — that is offered to her character by a light or injurious word."

"Giovanni! my poor Giovanni!" answered the professor, with a calm expression of pity, "I know this wretched girl far better than yourself. You shall hear the truth in respect to the poisoner Rappaccini and his poisonous daughter; yes, poisonous as she is beautiful. Listen; for, even should you do violence to my gray hairs, it shall not silence me. That old fable of the Indian woman has become a truth by the deep and deadly science of Rappaccini and in the person of the lovely Beatrice."

Giovanni groaned and hid his face.

"Her father," continued Baglioni, "was not restrained by natural affection from offering up his child in this horrible manner as the victim of his insane zeal for science; for, let us do him justice, he is as true a man of science as ever distilled his own heart in an alembic. What, then, will be your fate? Beyond a doubt you are selected as the material of some new experiment. Perhaps the result is to be death; perhaps a fate more awful still. Rappaccini, with what he calls the interest of science before his eyes, will hesitate at nothing."

"It is a dream," muttered Giovanni to himself; "surely it is a dream."

"But," resumed the professor, "be of good cheer, son of my friend. It is not yet too late for the rescue. Possibly we may even succeed in bringing back this miserable child within the limits of ordinary nature, from which her father's madness has estranged her. Behold this little silver vase! It was wrought by the hands of the renowned Benvenuto Cellini, and is well worthy to be a love gift to the fairest dame in Italy. But its contents are invaluable. One little sip of this antidote would have rendered the most virulent poisons of the Borgias innocuous. Doubt not that it will be as efficacious against those of Rappaccini. Bestow the vase, and the precious liquid within it, on your Beatrice, and hopefully await the result."

Baglioni laid a small, exquisitely wrought silver vial on the table and withdrew, leaving what he had said to produce its effects upon the young man's mind.

"We will thwart Rappaccini yet," thought he, chuckling to himself, as he descended the stairs; "but, let us confess the truth of him, he is a wonderful man — a wonderful man indeed; a vile empiric, however, in his practice, and therefore not to be tolerated by those who respect the good old rules of the medical profession."

Throughout Giovanni's whole acquaintance with Beatrice, he had occasionally, as we have said, been haunted by dark surmises as to her character; yet so thoroughly had she made herself felt by him as a simple, natural, most affectionate, and guileless creature, that the image now held up by Professor Baglioni looked as strange and incredible as if it were not in accordance with his own original conception. True, there were ugly recollections connected with his first glimpses of the beautiful girl; he could not quite forget the bouquet that withered in her grasp, and the insect that perished amid the sunny air, by no ostensible agency save the fragrance of her breath. These incidents, however, dissolving in the pure light of her character, had no longer the efficacy of facts, but were acknowledged as mistaken fantasies, by whatever testimony of the senses they might appear to be substantiated. There is something truer and more real than what we can see with the eyes and touch with the finger. On such better evidence had Giovanni founded his confidence in Beatrice, though rather by the necessary force of her high attributes than by any deep and generous faith on his part. But now his spirit was incapable of sustaining itself at the height to which the early enthusiasm of passion had exalted it; he fell down, grovelling among earthly doubts, and defiled therewith the pure whiteness of Beatrice's image. Not that he gave her up; he did but distrust. He resolved to institute some decisive test that should satisfy him, once for all, whether there were those dreadful peculiarities in her physical nature which could not be supposed to exist without some corresponding monstrosity of soul. His eyes, gazing down afar, might have deceived him as to the lizard, the insect, and the flowers; but if he could witness, at the distance of a few paces, the sudden blight of one fresh and healthful flower in Beatrice's hand, there would be room for no further question. With this idea he hastened to the florist's and purchased a bouquet that was still gemmed with the morning dewdrops.

It was now the customary hour of his daily interview with Beatrice. Before descending into the garden, Giovanni failed not to look at his figure in the mirror — a vanity to be expected in a beautiful young man, yet, as displaying itself at that troubled and feverish moment, the token of a certain shallowness of feeling and insincerity of character. He did gaze, however, and said to himself that his features had never before possessed so rich a grace, nor his eyes such vivacity, nor his cheeks so warm a hue of super-abundant life.

"At least," thought he, "her poison has not yet insinuated itself into my system. I am no flower to perish in her grasp."

With that thought he turned his eyes on the bouquet, which he had never once laid aside from his hand. A thrill of indefinable horror shot through his frame on perceiving that those dewy flowers were already beginning to droop; they wore the aspect of things that had been fresh and lovely yesterday. Giovanni grew white as marble, and stood motionless before the mirror, staring at his own reflection there as at the likeness of something frightful. He remembered Baglioni's remark about the fragrance that seemed to pervade the chamber. It must have been the poison in his breath! Then he shuddered — shuddered at himself. Recovering from his stupor, he began to watch with curious eye a spider that was busily at work hanging its web from the antique cornice of the apartment, crossing and recrossing the artful system of interwoven lines — as vigorous and active a spider as ever dangled from an old ceiling. Giovanni bent towards the insect, and emitted a deep, long breath. The spider suddenly ceased its toil; the web vibrated with a tremor originating in the body of the small artisan. Again Giovanni sent forth a breath, deeper, longer, and imbued with a venomous feeling out of his heart: he knew not whether he were wicked, or only desperate. The spider made a convulsive gripe with his limbs and hung dead across the window.

"Accursed! accursed!" muttered Giovanni, addressing himself. "Hast thou grown so poisonous that this deadly insect perishes by thy breath?"

At that moment a rich, sweet voice came floating up from the garden.

"Giovanni! Giovanni! It is past the hour! Why tarriest thou? Come down!"

"Yes," muttered Giovanni again. "She is the only being whom my breath may not slay! Would that it might!"

He rushed down, and in an instant was standing before the bright and loving eyes of Beatrice. A moment ago his wrath and despair had been so fierce that he could have desired nothing so much as to wither her by a glance; but with her actual presence there came influences which had too real an existence to be at once shaken off; recollections of the delicate and benign power of her feminine nature, which had so often enveloped him in a religious calm; recollections of many a holy and passionate outgush of her heart, when the pure fountain had been unsealed from its depths and made visible in its transparency to his mental eye; recollections which, had Giovanni known how to estimate them, would have assured him that all this ugly mystery was but an earthly illusion, and that, whatever mist of evil might seem to have gathered over her, the real Beatrice was a heavenly angel. Incapable as he was of such high faith, still her presence had not utterly lost its magic. Giovanni's rage was quelled into an aspect of sullen insensibility. Beatrice, with a quick spiritual sense, immediately felt that there was a gulf of blackness between them which neither he nor she could pass. They walked on together, sad and silent, and came thus to the marble fountain and to its pool of water on the ground, in the midst of which grew the shrub that bore gemlike blossoms. Giovanni was affrighted at the eager enjoyment — the appetite, as it were — with which he found himself inhaling the fragrance of the flowers.

"Beatrice," asked he, abruptly, "whence came this shrub?"

"My father created it," answered she, with simplicity.

"Created it! created it!" repeated Giovanni. "What mean you, Beatrice?"

"He is a man fearfully acquainted with the secrets of Nature," replied Beatrice; "and at the hour when I first drew breath, this plant sprang from the soil, the offspring of his science, of his intellect, while I was but his earthly child.

Approach it not!" continued she, observing with terror that Giovanni was drawing nearer to the shrub. "It has qualities that you little dream of. But I, dearest Giovanni, — I grew up and blossomed with the plant and was nourished with its breath. It was my sister, and I loved it with a human affection; for, alas! — hast thou not suspected it? — there was an awful doom."

Here Giovanni frowned so darkly upon her that Beatrice paused and trembled. But her faith in his tenderness reassured her, and made her blush that she had doubted for an instant.

"There was an awful doom," she continued, "the effect of my father's fatal love of science, which estranged me from all society of my kind. Until Heaven sent thee, dearest Giovanni, O, how lonely was thy poor Beatrice!"

"Was it a hard doom?" asked Giovanni fixing his eyes upon her.

"Only of late have I known how hard it was," answered she, tenderly. "O, yes; but my heart was torpid, and therefore quiet."

Giovanni's rage broke forth from his sullen gloom like a lightning flash out of a dark cloud.

"Accursed one!" cried he, with venomous scorn and anger. "And, finding thy solitude wearisome, thou has severed me likewise from all the warmth of life and enticed me into thy region of unspeakable horror!"

"Giovanni!" exclaimed Beatrice, turning her large bright eyes upon his face. The force of his words had not found its way into her mind; she was merely thunderstruck.

"Yes, poisonous thing!" repeated Giovanni, beside himself with passion. "Thou hast done it! Thou hast blasted me! Thou hast filled my veins with poison! Thou hast made me as hateful, as ugly, as loathsome and deadly a creature as thyself — a world's wonder of hideous monstrosity! Now, if our breath be happily as fatal to ourselves as to all others, let us join our lips in one kiss of unutterable hatred, and so die!"

"What has befallen me?" murmured Beatrice, with a low moan out of her heart. "Holy Virgin, pity me, a poor heart-broken child!"

"Thou — dost thou pray?" cried Giovanni, still with the same fiendish scorn. "Thy very prayers, as they come from thy lips, taint the atmosphere with death. Yes, yes; let us pray! Let us to church and dip our fingers in the holy water at the portal! They that come after us will perish as by a pestilence! Let us sign crosses in the air! It will be scattering curses abroad in the likeness of holy symbols!"

"Giovanni," said Beatrice, calmly, for her grief was beyond passion, "why dost thou join thyself with me thus in those terrible words? I, it is true, am the horrible thing thou namest me. But thou, — what hast thou to do, save with one other shudder at my hideous misery to go forth out of the garden and mingle with thy race, and forget that there ever crawled on earth such a monster as poor Beatrice?"

"Dost thou pretend ignorance?" asked Giovanni, scowling upon her. "Behold! this power have I gained from the pure daughter of Rappaccini."

There was a swarm of summer insects flitting through the air in search of the food promised by the flower odors of the fatal garden. They circled round Giovanni's head, and were evidently attracted towards him by the same influence which had drawn them for an instant within the sphere of several of the shrubs. He sent forth a breath among them, and smiled bitterly at Beatrice as at least a score of the insects fell dead upon the ground.

"I see it! I see it!" shrieked Beatrice. "It is my father's fatal science! No, no, Giovanni; it was not I! Never! never! I dreamed only to love thee and be with thee a little time, and so to let thee pass away, leaving but thine image in my heart; for, Giovanni, believe it, though my body be nourished with poison, my spirit is God's creature, and craves love as its daily food. But my father, — he has united us in this fearful sympathy. Yes; spurn me, tread upon me, kill me! O, what is death after such words as thine? But it was not I. Not for a world of bliss would I have done it."

Giovanni's passion had exhausted itself in its outburst from his lips. There now came across him a sense, mournful, and not without tenderness, of the intimate and peculiar relationship between Beatrice and himself. They stood, as it were, in an utter solitude, which would be made none the less solitary by the densest throng of human life. Ought not, then, the desert of humanity around them to press this insulated pair closer together? If they should be cruel to one another, who was there to be kind to them? Besides, thought Giovanni, might there not still be a hope of his returning within the limits of ordinary nature, and leading Beatrice, the redeemed Beatrice, by the hand? O, weak, and selfish, and unworthy spirit, that could dream of an earthly union and earthly happiness as possible, after such deep love had been so bitterly wronged as was Beatrice's love by Giovanni's blighting words! No, no; there could be no such hope. She must pass heavily, with that broken heart, across the borders of Time — she must bathe her hurts in some fount of paradise, and forget her grief in the light of immortality, and *there* be well.

But Giovanni did not know it.

"Dear Beatrice," said he approaching her, while she shrank as always at his approach, but now with a different impulse, "dearest Beatrice, our fate is not yet so desperate. Behold! there is a medicine, potent as a wise physician has assured me, and almost divine in its efficacy. It is composed of ingredients the most opposite to those by which thy awful father has brought this calamity upon thee and me. It is distilled of blessed herbs. Shall we not quaff it together, and thus be purified from evil?"

"Give it me!" said Beatrice, extending her hand to receive the little silver vial which Giovanni took from his bosom. She added, with a peculiar emphasis, "I will drink; but do thou await the result."

She put Baglioni's antidote to her lips; and, at the same moment, the figure of Rappaccini emerged from the portal and came slowly towards the marble fountain. As he drew near, the pale man of science seemed to gaze with a triumphant expression at the beautiful youth and maiden, as might an artist who should spend his life in achieving a picture or a group of statuary and finally be satisfied with his success. He paused; his bent form grew erect with conscious power; he spread out his hands over them in the attitude of a father imploring a blessing upon his children; but those were the same hands that had thrown poison into the stream of their lives. Giovanni trembled. Beatrice shuddered nervously, and pressed her hand upon her heart.

"My daughter," said Rappaccini, "thou art no longer lonely in the world. Pluck one of those precious gems from thy sister shrub and bid thy bridegroom wear it in his bosom. It will not harm him now. My science and the sympathy between thee and him have so wrought within his system that he now stands apart from common men, as thou dost, daughter of my pride and triumph, from ordinary women. Pass on, then, through the world, most dear to one another and dreadful to all besides!"

"My father," said Beatrice, feebly — and still as she spoke she kept her hand upon her heart — "wherefore didst thou inflict this miserable doom upon thy child?"

"Miserable!" exclaimed Rappaccini. "What mean you, foolish girl? Dost thou deem it misery to be endowed with marvelous gifts against which no power nor strength could avail an enemy — misery, to be able to quell the mightiest with a breath — misery, to be as terrible as thou art beautiful? Wouldst thou, then, have preferred the condition of a weak woman, exposed to all evil and capable of none?"

"I would fain have been loved, not feared," murmured Beatrice, sinking down upon the ground. "But now it matters not. I am going, father, where the evil which thou hast striven to mingle with my being will pass away like a dream — like the fragrance of these poisonous flowers, which will no longer taint my breath among the flowers of Eden. Farewell, Giovanni! Thy words of hatred are like lead within my heart; but they, too, will fall away as I ascend. O, was there not, from the first, more poison in thy nature than in mine?"

To Beatrice — so radically had her earthly part been wrought upon by Rappaccini's skill — as poison had been life, so the powerful antidote was death; and thus the poor victim of man's ingenuity and of thwarted nature, and of the fatality that attends all such efforts of perverted wisdom, perished there, at the feet of her father and Giovanni. Just at that moment Professor Pietro Baglioni looked forth from the window, and called loudly, in a tone of triumph mixed with horror, to the thunderstricken man of science —

"Rappaccini! Rappaccini! and is *this* the upshot of your experiment!"

Exercises

1. Prepare an eight-point analysis of this story. (Refer to Chapter 1.)

2. What means does Hawthorne use to establish credibility? Does he succeed?

3. Is irony present in the story? If so, what type of irony, and what purpose does it serve?

4. Compare and contrast the character of Giovanni with that of Beatrice.

5. Is the imagery consistent and is it appropriate to the theme? Explain.

Topics for Writing

1. Early in the story, Rappaccini's garden is compared to the Garden of Eden. Note other images and allusions that reinforce this comparison and discuss, in an essay, its importance to the theme of the story.

2. Among other things, both "Rappaccini's Daughter" and the next story in this chapter, "The Tree of Knowledge" by Henry James, could be said to deal with the misuse of art, for though Dr. Rappaccini is a scientist, his garden is an artistic creation. Write an essay discussing the ways in which Dr. Rappaccini and Morgan Mallow misuse art and the consequences of their misuse.

Henry James (1843–1916)

The Tree of Knowledge

I.

It was one of the secret opinions, such as we all have, of Peter Brench that his main success in life would have consisted in his never having committed himself about the work, as it was called, of his friend Morgan Mallow. This was a subject on which it was, to the best of his belief, impossible with veracity to quote him, and it was nowhere on record that he had, in the connexion, on any occasion and in any embarrassment, either lied or spoken the truth. Such a triumph had its honour even for a man of other triumphs — a man who had reached fifty, who had escaped marriage, who had lived within his means, who had been in love with Mrs. Mallow for years without breathing it, and who, last but not least, had judged himself once for all. He had so judged himself in fact that he felt an extreme and general humility to be his proper portion; yet there was nothing that made him think so well of his parts as the course he had steered so often through the shallows just mentioned. It became thus a real wonder that the friends in whom he had most confidence were just those with whom he had most reserves. He couldn't tell Mrs. Mallow — or at least he supposed, excellent man, he couldn't — that she was the one beautiful reason he had never married; any more than he could tell her husband that the sight of the multiplied marbles in that gentleman's studio was an affliction of which even time had never blunted the edge. His victory, however, as I have intimated, in regard to these productions, was not simply in his not having let it out that he deplored them; it was, remarkably, in his not having kept it in by anything else.

The whole situation, among these good people, was verily a marvel, and there was probably not such another for a long way from the spot that engages us — the point at which the soft declivity of Hampstead began at that time to confess in broken accents to Saint John's Wood.[1] He despised Mallow's statues and adored Mallow's wife, and yet was distinctly fond of Mallow, to whom, in turn, he was equally dear. Mrs. Mallow rejoiced in the statues — though she preferred, when pressed, the busts; and if she was visibly attached to Peter Brench it was because of his affection for Morgan. Each loved the other moreover for the love borne in each case to Lancelot, whom the Mallows respectively cherished as their only child and whom the friend of their fireside identified as the third — but decidedly the handsomest — of his godsons. Already in the old years it had come to that — that no one, for such a relation, could possibly have occurred to any of them, even to the baby itself, but Peter. There was luckily a certain independence, of the pecuniary sort, all round: the Master could never otherwise have spent his solemn Wanderjahre[2] in Florence and Rome, and continued by the Thames as well as by the Arno and the Tiber[3] to add unpurchased group to group and model, for what was too apt to prove in the event mere love, fancy-heads of celebrities either too busy or too buried — too much of the age

---

1. Saint John's Wood: A heavily wooded district, near Hampstead, in northwest London.
2. Wanderjahre: Years of travel required of a novice learning a trade.

3. Arno and Tiber: Rivers traversing Florence and Rome, respectively.

or too little of it — to sit. Neither could Peter, lounging in almost daily, have found time to keep the whole complicated tradition so alive by his presence. He was massive but mild, the depositary of these mysteries — large and loose and ruddy and curly, with deep tones, deep eyes, deep pockets, to say nothing of the habit of long pipes, soft hats and brownish greyish weather-faded clothes, apparently always the same.

He had "written," it was known, but had never spoken, never spoken in particular of that; and he had the air (since, as was believed, he continued to write) of keeping it up in order to have something more — as if he hadn't at the worst enough — to be silent about. Whatever his air, at any rate, Peter's occasional unmentioned prose and verse were quite truly the result of an impulse to maintain the purity of his taste by establishing still more firmly the right relation of fame to feebleness. The little green door of his domain was in a garden-wall on which the discolored stucco made patches, and in the small detached villa behind it everything was old, the furniture, the servants, the books, the prints, the immemorial habits and the new improvements. The Mallows, at Carrara Lodge, were within ten minutes, and the studio there was on their little land, to which they had added, in their happy faith, for building it. This was the good fortune, if it was not the ill, of her having brought him in marriage a portion that put them in a manner at their ease and enabled them thus, on their side, to keep it up. And they did keep it up — they always had — the infatuated sculptor and his wife, for whom nature had refined on the impossible by relieving them of the sense of the difficult. Morgan had at all events everything of the sculptor but the spirit of Phidias — the brown velvet, the becoming *beretto,* the "plastic" presence, the fine fingers, the beautiful accent in Italian and the old Italian factotum.[4] He seemed to make up for everything when he addressed Egidio with the "tu"[5] and waved him to turn one of the rotary pedestals of which the place was full. They were tremendous Italians at Carrara Lodge, and the secret of the part played by this fact in Peter's life was in a large degree that it gave him, sturdy Briton as he was, just the amount of "going abroad" he could bear. The Mallows were all his Italy, but it was in a measure for Italy he liked them. His one worry was that Lance — to which they had shortened his godson — was, in spite of a public school, perhaps a shade too Italian. Morgan meanwhile looked like somebody's flattering idea of somebody's own person as expressed in the great room provided at the Uffizi Museum[6] for the general illustration of that idea by eminent hands. The Master's sole regret that he hadn't been born rather to the brush than to the chisel[7] sprang from his wish that he might have contributed to that collection.

It appeared with time at any rate to be to the brush that Lance had been born; for Mrs. Mallow, one day when the boy was turning twenty, broke it to their friend, who shared, to the last delicate morsel, their problems and pains, that it seemed as if nothing would really do but that he should embrace the career. It had been impossible longer to remain blind to the fact that he was gaining no glory at Cambridge, where Brench's own college had for a year

4. Factotum: Assistant who performs a wide range of functions.
5. Tu: The informal, second-person pronoun.
6. Uffizi Museum: World-knowned art museum in Florence.

7. The brush . . . the chisel: Reference to a vocation as painter instead of as sculptor.

tempered its tone to him as for Brench's own sake. Therefore why renew the vain form of preparing him for the impossible? The impossible — it had become clear — was that he should be anything but an artist.

"Oh dear, dear!" said poor Peter.

"Don't you believe in it?" asked Mrs. Mallow, who still, at more than forty, had her violet velvet eyes, her creamy satin skin and her silken chestnut hair.

"Believe in what?"

"Why in Lance's passion."

"I don't know what you mean by 'believing in it.' I've never been unaware, certainly, of his disposition, from his earliest time, to daub and draw; but I confess I've hoped it would burn out."

"But why should it," she sweetly smiled, "with his wonderful heredity? Passion is passion — though of course indeed *you*, dear Peter, know nothing of that. Has the Master's ever burned out?"

Peter looked off a little and, in his familiar formless way, kept up for a moment, a sound between a smothered whistle and a subdued hum. "Do you think he's going to be another Master?"

She seemed scarce prepared to go that length, yet she had on the whole a marvellous trust. "I know what you mean by that. Will it be a career to incur the jealousies and provoke the machinations that have been at times almost too much for his father? Well — say it may be, since nothing but clap-trap, in these dreadful days, *can*, it would seem, make its way, and since, with the curse of refinement and distinction, one may easily find one's self begging one's bread. Put it at the worst — say he *has* the misfortune to wing his flight further than the vulgar taste of his stupid countrymen can follow. Think, all the same, of the happiness — the same the Master has had. He'll *know*."

Peter looked rueful. "Ah but *what* will he know?"

"Quiet joy!" cried Mrs. Mallow, quite impatient and turning away.

II.

He had of course before long to meet the boy himself on it and to hear that practically everything was settled. Lance was not to go up again, but to go instead to Paris where, since the die was cast, he would find the best advantages. Peter had always felt he must be taken as he was, but had never perhaps found him so much of that pattern as on this occasion. "You chuck Cambridge then altogether? Doesn't that seem rather a pity?"

Lance would have been like his father, to his friend's sense, had he had less humour, and like his mother had he had more beauty. Yet it was a good middle way for Peter that, in the modern manner, he was, to the eye, rather the young stockbroker than the young artist. The youth reasoned that it was a question of time — there was such a mill to go through, such an awful lot to learn. He had talked with fellows and had judged. "One has got, today," he said, "don't you see? to know."

His interlocutor, at this, gave a groan. "Oh hang it, *don't* know!"

Lance wondered. " 'Don't? Then what's the use — ?"

"The use of what?"

"Why of anything. Don't you think I've talent?"

Peter smoked away for a little in silence; then went on: "It isn't knowledge, it's ignorance that — as we've been beautifully told — is bliss."

"Don't you think I've talent?" Lance repeated.

Peter, with his trick of queer kind demonstration, passed his arm round his godson and held him a moment. "How do I know?"

"Oh," said the boy, "if it's your own ignorance you're defending — !"

Again, for a pause, on the sofa, his godfather smoked. "It isn't. I've the misfortune to be omniscient."

"Oh well," Lance laughed again, "if you know *too* much — !"

"That's what I do, and it's why I'm so wretched."

Lance's gaity grew. "Wretched? Come, I say!"

"But I forgot," his companion went on — "you're not to know about that. It would indeed for you to make the too much. Only I'll tell you what I'll do." And Peter got up from the sofa. "If you'll go up again I'll pay your way at Cambridge."

Lance stared, a little rueful in spite of being still more amused. "Oh Peter! You disapprove so of Paris?"

"Well, I'm afraid of it."

"Ah I see!"

"No, you don't see — yet. But you will — that is you would. And you mustn't."

The young man thought more gravely. "But one's innocence, already — !"

"Is considerably damaged? Ah that won't matter," Peter persisted — "we'll patch it up here."

"Here? Then you want me to stay at home?"

Peter almost confessed to it. "Well, we're so right — we four together — just as we are. We're so safe. Come, don't spoil it."

The boy, who had turned to gravity, turned from this, on the real pressure in his friend's tone, to consternation. "Then what's a fellow to be?"

"My particular care. Come, old man" — and Peter now fairly pleaded — "*I'll* look out for you."

Lance, who had remained on the sofa with his legs out and his hands in his pockets, watched him with eyes that showed suspicion. Then he got up. "You think there's something the matter with me — that I can't make a success."

"Well, what do you call a success?"

Lance thought again. "Why, the best sort, I suppose, is to please one's self. Isn't that the sort that, in spite of cabals and things, is — in his own peculiar line — the Master's?"

There were so much too many things in this question to be answered at once that they practically checked the discussion, which became particularly difficult in the light of such renewed proof that, though the young man's innocence might, in the course of his studies, as he contended, somewhat have shrunken, the finer essence of it still remained. That was indeed exactly what Peter had assumed and what above all he desired; yet perversely enough it gave him a chill. The boy believed in the cabals and things, believed in the peculiar line, believed, to be brief, in the Master. What happened a month or two later wasn't that he went up again at the expense of his godfather, but that a fortnight after he had got settled in Paris this personage sent him fifty pounds.

He had meanwhile at home, this personage, made up his mind to the worst; and what that might be had never yet grown quite so vivid to him as when, on his presenting himself one Sunday night, as he never failed to do, for supper, the mistress of Carrara Lodge met him with an appeal as to — of all things in the world — the wealth of the Canadians. She was earnest, she was even excited. "Are many of them *really* rich?"

He had to confess he knew nothing about them, but he often thought afterwards of that evening. The room in which they sat was adorned with sundry specimens of the Master's genius, which had the merit of being, as Mrs. Mallow herself frequently suggested, of an unusually convenient size. They were indeed of dimensions not customary in the products of the chisel, and they had the singularity that, if the objects and features intended to be small looked too large, the objects and features intended to be large looked too small. The Master's idea, either in respect to this matter or to any other, had in almost any case, even after years, remained undiscoverable to Peter Brench. The creations that so failed to reveal it stood about on pedestals and brackets, on tables and shelves, a little staring white population, heroic, idyllic, allegoric, mythic, symbolic, in which "scale" had so strayed and lost itself that the public square and the chimney-piece seemed to have changed places, the monumental being all diminutive and the diminutive all monumental; branches at any rate, markedly, of a family in which stature was rather oddly irrespective of function, age, and sex. They formed, like the Mallows themselves, poor Brench's own family — having at least to such a degree the note of familiarity. The occasion was one of those he had long ago learnt to know and to name — short flickers of the faint flame, soft gusts of a kinder air. Twice a year regularly the Master believed in his fortune, in addition to believing all the year round in his genius. This time it was to be made by a bereaved couple from Toronto, who had given him the handsomest order for a tomb to three lost children, each of whom they desired to see, in the composition, emblematically and characteristically represented.

Such was naturally the moral of Mrs. Mallow's question: if their wealth was to be assumed, it was clear, from the nature of their admiration, as well as from mysterious hints thrown out (they were a little odd!) as to other possibilities of the same mortuary sort, that their further patronage might be; and not less evident that should The Master become at all known in those climes nothing would be more inevitable than a run of Canadian custom. Peter had been present before at runs of custom, colonial and domestic — present at each of those of which the aggregation had left so few gaps in the marble company round him; but it was his habit never at these junctures to prick the bubble in advance. The fond illusion, while it lasted, eased the wound of elections never won, the long ache of medals and diplomas carried off, on every chance, by every one but the Master; it moreover lighted the lamp that would glimmer through the next eclipse. They lived, however, after all — as it was always beautiful to see — at a height scarce susceptible of ups and downs. They strained a point at times charmingly, strained it to admit that the public was here and there not too bad to buy; but they would have been nowhere without their attitude that the Master was always too good to sell. They were at all events deliciously formed, Peter often said to himself, for their fate; the Master had a vanity, his wife had a loyalty, of which success, depriving these things of innocence, would have diminished the merit and the grace. Any one could be charming under a charm, and as he looked about him at a world of prosperity more void of proportion even than the Master's museum he wondered if he knew another pair that so completely escaped vulgarity.

"What a pity Lance isn't with us to rejoice!" Mrs. Mallow on this occasion sighed at supper.

"We'll drink to the health of the absent," her husband replied, filling his friend's glass and his own and giving a drop to their companion; "but we must hope he's preparing himself for a happiness much less like this of ours this evening — excusable as I grant it to be! — than like the comfort we have always (whatever has happened or has not happened) been able to trust ourselves to enjoy. The comfort," the Master explained, leaning back in the pleasant lamplight and firelight, holding up his glass and looking round at his marble family, quartered more or less, a monstrous brood, in every room — "the comfort of art in itself!"

Peter looked a little shyly at his wine. "Well — I don't care what you may call it when a fellow doesn't — but Lance must learn to *sell,* you know. I drink to his acquisition of the secret of a base popularity!"

"Oh, yes, *he* must sell," the boy's mother, who was still more, however, this seemed to give out, the Master's wife, rather artlessly allowed.

"Ah," the sculptor after a moment confidently pronounced, "Lance *will.* Don't be afraid. He'll have learnt."

"Which is exactly what Peter," Mrs. Mallow gaily returned — "why in the world were you so perverse, Peter? — wouldn't when he told him hear of."

Peter, when this lady looked at him with accusatory affection — a grace on her part not infrequent — could never find a word; but the Master, who was always all amenity and tact, helped him out now as he had often helped him before. "That's his old idea, you know — on which we've so often differed: his theory that the artist should be all impulse and instinct. *I* go in of course for a certain amount of school. Not too much — but a due proportion. There's where his protest came in," he continued to explain to his wife, "as against what *might,* don't you see? be in question for Lance."

"Ah, well!" — and Mrs. Mallow turned the violet eyes across the table at the subject of this discourse — "he's sure to have meant of course nothing but good. Only that wouldn't have prevented him, if Lance *had* taken his advice, from being in effect horribly cruel."

They had a sociable way of talking of him to his face as if he had been in the clay or — at most — in the plaster, and the Master was unfailingly generous. He might have been waving Egidio to make him revolve. "Ah but poor Peter wasn't so wrong as to what it may after all come to that he *will* learn."

"Oh but nothing artistically bad," she urged — still, for poor Peter, arch and dewy.

"Why just the little French tricks," said the Master: on which their friend had to pretend to admit, when pressed by Mrs. Mallow, that these aesthetic vices had been the objects of his dread.

III.

"I know now," Lance said to him the next year, "why you were so much against it." He had come back supposedly for a mere interval and was looking about him at Carrara Lodge, where indeed he had already on two or three occasions since his expatriation briefly reappeared. This had the air of a longer holiday. "Something rather awful has happened to me. It *isn't* so very good to know."

"I'm bound to say high spirits don't show in your face," Peter was rather ruefully forced to confess. "Still, are you very sure you do know?"

"Well, I at least know about as much as I can bear." These remarks were exchanged in Peter's den, and the young man, smoking cigarettes, stood before the fire with his back against the mantel. Something of his bloom seemed really to have left him.

Poor Peter wondered. "You're clear then as to what in particular I wanted you not to go for?"

"In particular?" Lance thought. "It seems to me that in particular there can have been only one thing."

They stood for a little sounding like each other. "Are you quite sure?"

"Quite sure I'm a beastly duffer? Quite — by this time."

"Oh!" — and Peter turned away as if almost with relief.

"It's *that* that isn't pleasant to find out."

"Oh I don't care for 'that,' " said Peter, presently coming round again. "I mean I personally don't."

"Yet I hope you can understand a little that I myself should!"

"Well, what do you mean by it?" Peter sceptically asked.

And on this Lance had to explain — how the upshot of his studies in Paris had inexorably proved a mere deep doubt of his means. These studies had so waked him up that a new light was in his eyes; but what the new light did was really to show him too much. "Do you know what's the matter with me? I'm too horribly intelligent. Paris was really the last place for me. I've learnt what I can't do."

Poor Peter stared — it was a staggerer; but even after they had had, on the subject, a longish talk in which the boy brought out to the full the hard truth of his lesson, his friend betrayed less pleasure than usually breaks into a face to the happy tune of "I told you so!" Poor Peter himself made now indeed so little a point of having told him so that Lance broke ground in a different place a day or two after. "What was it then that — before I went — you were afraid I should find out?" This, however, Peter refused to tell him — on the ground that if he hadn't yet guessed perhaps he never would, and that in any case nothing at all for either of them was to be gained by giving the thing a name. Lance eyed him on this an instant with the bold curiosity of youth — with the air indeed of having in his mind two or three names, of which one or other would be right. Peter nevertheless, turning his back again, offered no encouragement, and when they parted afresh it was with some show of impatience on the side of the boy. Accordingly on their next encounter Peter saw at a glance that he had now, in the interval, divined and that, to sound his note, he was only waiting till they should find themselves alone. This he had soon arranged and he then broke straight out. "Do you know your conundrum has been keeping me awake? But in the watches of the night the answer came over me — so that, upon my honour, I quite laughed out. Had you been supposing I had to go to Paris to learn *that?*" Even now, to see him still so sublimely on his guard, Peter's young friend had to laugh afresh. "You won't give a sign till you're sure? Beautiful old Peter!" But Lance at last produced it. "Why, hang it, the truth about the Master."

It made between them for some minutes a lively passage, full of wonder for each at the wonder of the other. "Then how long have you understood — "

"The true value of his work? I understood it," Lance recalled, "as soon as I began to understand anything. But I didn't begin fully to do that, I admit, till I got *là-bas*." [8]

8. *Là-bas:* Down there.

"Dear, dear!" — Peter gasped with retrospective dread.

"But for what have you taken me? I'm a hopeless muff — that I *had* to have rubbed in. But I'm not such a muff as the Master!" Lance declared.

"Then why did you never tell me — ?"

"That I hadn't after all" — the boy took him up — "remained such an idiot? Just because I never dreamed *you* knew. But I beg your pardon. I only wanted to spare you. And what I don't now understand is how the deuce then for so long you've managed to keep bottled."

Peter produced his explanation, but only after some delay and with a gravity not void of embarrassment. "It was for your mother."

"Oh!" said Lance.

"And that's the great thing now — since the murder *is* out. I want a promise from you. I mean" — and Peter almost feverishly followed it up — "a vow from you, solemn and such as you owe me here on the spot, that you'll sacrifice anything rather than let her ever guess — "

"That *I've* guessed?" — Lance took it in. "I see." He evidently after a moment had taken in much. "But what is it you've in mind that I may have a chance to sacrifice?"

"Oh one has always something."

Lance looked at him hard. "Do you mean that *you've* had — ?" The look he received back, however, so put the question by that he found soon enough another. "Are you really sure my mother doesn't know?"

Peter, after renewed reflexion, was really sure. "If she does he's too wonderful."

"But aren't we all too wonderful?"

"Yes," Peter granted — "but in different ways. The thing's so desperately important because your father's little public consists only, as you know then," Peter developed — "well, of how many?"

"First of all," the Master's son risked, "of himself. And last of all too. I don't quite see of whom else."

Peter had an approach to impatience. "Of your mother, I say — *always*."

Lance cast it all up. "You absolutely feel that?"

"Absolutely."

"Well then with yourself that makes three."

"Oh *me!*" — and Peter, with a wag of his kind old head, modestly excused himself. "The number's at any rate small enough for any individual dropping out to be too dreadfully missed. Therefore, to put it in a nutshell, take care, my boy — that's all — that *you're* not!"

"I've got to keep on humbugging?" Lance wailed.

"It's just to warn you of the danger of your failing of that that I've seized this opportunity."

"And what do you regard in particular," the young man asked, "as the danger?"

"Why this certainty: that the moment your mother, who feels so strongly, should suspect your secret — well," said Peter desperately, "the fat would be on the fire."

Lance for a moment seemed to stare at the blaze. "She'd throw me over?"

"She'd throw *him* over."

"And come round to us?"

Peter, before he answered, turned away. "Come round to *you*." But he had said enough to indicate — and, as he evidently trusted, to avert — the horrid contingency.

IV.

Within six months again, none the less, his fear was on more occasions than one all before him. Lance had returned to Paris for another trial; then had reappeared at home and had had, with his father, for the first time in his life, one of the scenes that strike sparks. He described it with much expression to Peter, touching whom (since they had never done so before) it was the sign of a new reserve on the part of the pair at Carrara Lodge that they at present failed, on a matter of intimate interest, to open themselves — if not in joy then in sorrow — to their good friend. This produced perhaps practically between the parties a shade of alienation and a slight intermission of commerce — marked mainly indeed by the fact that to talk at his ease with his old playmate Lance had in general to come to see him. The closest if not quite the gayest relation they had yet known together was thus ushered in. The difficulty for poor Lance was a tension at home — begotten by the fact that his father wished him to be at least the sort of success he himself had been. He hadn't "chucked" Paris — though nothing appeared more vivid to him than that Paris had chucked him: he would go back again because of the fascination in trying, in seeing, in sounding the depths — in learning one's lesson, briefly, even if the lesson were simply that of one's impotence in the presence of one's larger vision. But what did the Master, all aloft in his senseless fluency, know of impotence, and what vision — to be called such — had he in all his blind life ever had? Lance, heated and indignant, frankly appealed to his godparent on this score.

His father, it appeared, had come down on him for having, after so long, nothing to show, and hoped that on his next return this deficiency would be repaired. *The* thing, the Master complacently set forth was — for any artist, however inferior to himself — at least to "do" something. "What can you do? That's all I ask!" *He* had certainly done enough, and there was no mistake about what he had to show. Lance had tears in his eyes when it came thus to letting his old friend know how great the strain might be on the "sacrifice" asked of him. It wasn't so easy to continue humbugging — as from son to parent — after feeling one's self despised for not grovelling in mediocrity. Yet a noble duplicity was what, as they intimately faced the situation, Peter went on requiring; and it was still for a time what his young friend, bitter and sore, managed loyally to comfort him with. Fifty pounds more than once again, it was true, rewarded both in London and in Paris the young friend's loyalty; none the less sensibly, doubtless, at the moment, that the money was a direct advance on a decent sum for which Peter had long since privately prearranged an ultimate function. Whether by these arts or others, at all events, Lance's just resentment was kept for a season — but only for a season — at bay. The day arrived when he warned his companion that he could hold out — or hold in — no longer. Carrara Lodge had had to listen to another lecture delivered from a great height — an infliction really heavier at last than, without striking back or in some way letting the Master have the truth, flesh and blood could bear.

"And what I don't see is," Lance observed with a certain irritated eye for what was after all, if it came to that, owing to himself too; "what I don't see is, upon my honour, how *you,* as things are going, can keep the game up."

"Oh the game for me is only to hold my tongue," said placid Peter. "And I have my reason."

"Still my mother?"

Peter showed a queer face as he had often shown it before — that is by turning it straight away. "What will you have? I haven't ceased to like her."

"She's beautiful — she's a dear of course," Lance allowed; "but what is she to you, after all, and what is it to you that, as to anything whatever, she should or she shouldn't?"

Peter, who had turned red, hung fire a little. "Well — it's all simply what I make of it."

There was now, however, in his young friend a strange, an adopted insistence. "What are you after all to *her*?"

"Oh nothing. But that's another matter."

"She cares only for my father," said Lance the Parisian.

"Naturally — and that's just why."

"Why you've wished to spare her?"

"Because she cares so tremendously much."

Lance took a turn about the room, but with his eyes still on his host. "How awfully — always — you must have liked her!"

"Awfully. Always," said Peter Brench.

The young man continued for a moment to muse — then stopped again in front of him. "Do you know how much she cares?" Their eyes met on it, but Peter, as if his own found something new in Lance's, appeared to hesitate, for the first time in an age, to say he did know. "*I've* only just found out," said Lance. "She came to my room last night, after being present, in silence and only with her eyes on me, at what I had had to take from him; she came — and she was with me an extraordinary hour."

He had paused again and they had again for a while sounded each other. Then something — and it made him suddenly turn pale — came to Peter. "She *does* know?"

"She does know. She let it all out to me — so as to demand of me no more than 'that,' as she said, of which she herself had been capable. She has always, always known," said Lance without pity.

Peter was silent a long time; during which his companion might have heard him gently breathe, and on touching him might have felt within him the vibration of a long low sound suppressed. By the time he spoke at last he had taken everything in. "Then I do see how tremendously much."

"Isn't it wonderful?" Lance asked.

"Wonderful," Peter mused.

"So that if your original effort to keep me from Paris was to keep me from knowledge! —" Lance exclaimed as if with a sufficient indication of this futility.

It might have been at the futility Peter appeared for a little to gaze. "I think it must have been — without my quite at the time knowing it — to keep *me!*" he replied at last as he turned away.

Frank O'Connor (1903–1966)

Guests of the Nation

I.

At dusk the big Englishman, Belcher, would shift his long legs out of the ashes and say "Well, chums, what about it?" and Noble or me would say "All right, chum" (for we had picked up some of their curious expressions), and the little Englishman, Hawkins, would light the lamp and bring out the cards. Sometimes Jeremiah Donovan would come up and supervise the game and get excited over Hawkins's cards, which he always played badly, and shout at him as if he was one of our own "Ah, you divil, you, why didn't you play the tray?"

But ordinarily Jeremiah was a sober and contented poor devil like the big Englishman, Belcher, and was looked up to only because he was a fair hand at documents, though he was slow enough even with them. He wore a small cloth hat and big gaiters over his long pants, and you seldom saw him with his hands out of his pockets. He reddened when you talked to him, tilting from toe to heel and back, and looking down all the time at his big farmer's feet. Noble and me used to make fun of his broad accent, because we were from the town.

I couldn't at the time see the point of me and Noble guarding Belcher and Hawkins at all, for it was my belief that you could have planted that pair down anywhere from this to Claregalway and they'd have taken root there like a native weed. I never in my short experience seen two men to take to the country as they did.

They were handed on to us by the Second Battalion when the search for them became too hot, and Noble and myself, being young, took over with a natural feeling of responsibility, but Hawkins made us look like fools when he showed that he knew the country better than we did.

"You're the bloke they calls Bonaparte," he says to me. "Mary Brigid O'Connell told me to ask you what you done with the pair of her brother's socks you borrowed."

For it seemed, as they explained it, that the Second used to have little evenings and some of the girls of the neighbourhood turned in, and, seeing they were such decent chaps, our fellows couldn't leave the two Englishmen out of them. Hawkins learned to dance "The Walls of Limerick," "The Siege of Ennis," and "The Waves of Tory" [1] as well as any of them, though, naturally, he couldn't return the compliment, because our lads at that time did not dance foreign dances on principle.

So whatever privileges Belcher and Hawkins had with the Second they just naturally took with us, and after the first day or two we gave up all pretence of keeping a close eye on them. Not that they could have got far, for they had accents you could cut with a knife and wore khaki tunics and overcoats with civilian pants and boots. But it's my belief that they never had any idea of escaping and were quite content to be where they were.

It was a treat to see how Belcher got off with the old woman of the house where we were staying. She was a great warrant to scold, and cranky even with us, but before ever she had a chance of giving our guests, as I may call them, a

1. "The Walls ... Waves of Tory":
Irish dances.

lick of her tongue, Belcher had made her his friend for life. She was breaking sticks, and Belcher, who hadn't been more than ten minutes in the house, jumped up from his seat and went over to her.

"Allow me, madam," he says, smiling his queer little smile, "please allow me"; and he takes the bloody hatchet. She was struck too paralytic to speak, and after that, Belcher would be at her heels, carrying a bucket, a basket, or a load of turf, as the case might be. As Noble said, he got into looking before she leapt, and hot water, or any little thing she wanted, Belcher would have it ready for her. For such a huge man (and though I am five foot ten myself I had to look up at him) he had an uncommon shortness — or should I say lack? — of speech. It took us some time to get used to him, walking in and out, like a ghost, without a word. Especially because Hawkins talked enough for a platoon, it was strange to hear big Belcher with his toes in the ashes come out with a solitary "Excuse me, chum," or "That's right, chum." His one and only passion was cards, and I will say for him that he was a good card-player. He could have fleeced myself and Noble, but whatever we lost to him Hawkins lost to us, and Hawkins played with the money Belcher gave him.

Hawkins lost to us because he had too much old gab, and we probably lost to Belcher for the same reason. Hawkins and Noble would spit at one another about religion into the early hours of the morning, and Hawkins worried the soul out of Noble, whose brother was a priest, with a string of questions that would puzzle a cardinal. To make it worse even in treating of holy subjects, Hawkins had a deplorable tongue. I never in all my career met a man who could mix such a variety of cursing and bad language into an argument. He was a terrible man, and a fright to argue. He never did a stroke of work, and when he had no one else to talk to, he got stuck in the old woman.

He met his match in her, for one day when he tried to get her to complain profanely of the drought, she gave him a great comedown by blaming it entirely on Jupiter Pluvius[2] (a deity neither Hawkins nor I had ever heard of, though Noble said that among the pagans it was believed that he had something to do with the rain). Another day he was swearing at the capitalists for starting the German war[3] when the old lady laid down her iron, puckered up her little crab's mouth, and said: "Mr. Hawkins, you can say what you like about the war, and think you'll deceive me because I'm only a simple poor countrywoman, but I know what started the war. It was the Italian Count that stole the heathen divinity out of the temple in Japan. Believe me, Mr. Hawkins, nothing but sorrow and want can follow the people that disturb the hidden powers."

A queer old girl, all right.

II.

We had our tea one evening, and Hawkins lit the lamp and we all sat into cards. Jeremiah Donovan came in too, and sat down and watched us for a while, and it suddenly struck me that he had no great love for the two Englishmen. It came as a great surprise to me, because I hadn't noticed anything about him before.

2. Jupiter: Roman king of the gods whose many activities included generating rain for crops; Pluvius: rain.
3. German war: World War I.

Late in the evening a really terrible argument blew up between Hawkins and Noble, about capitalists and priests and love of your country.

"The capitalists," says Hawkins with an angry gulp, "pays the priests to tell you about the next world so as you won't notice what the bastards are up to in this."

"Nonsense, man!" says Noble, losing his temper. "Before ever a capitalist was thought of, people believed in the next world."

Hawkins stood up as though he was preaching a sermon.

"Oh, they did, did they?" he says with a sneer. "They believed all the things you believe, isn't that what you mean? And you believe that God created Adam, and Adam created Shem, and Shem created Jehoshophat.[4] You believe all that silly old fairytale about Eve and Eden and the apple. Well, listen to me, chum. If you're entitled to hold a silly belief like that, I'm entitled to hold my silly belief — which is that the first thing your God created was a bleeding capitalist, with morality and Rolls-Royce complete. Am I right, chum?" he says to Belcher.

"You're right, chum," says Belcher with his amused smile, and got up from the table to stretch his long legs into the fire and stroke his moustache. So, seeing that Jeremiah Donovan was going, and that there was no knowing when the argument about religion would be over, I went out with him. We strolled down to the village together, and then he stopped and started blushing and mumbling and saying I ought to be behind, keeping guard on the prisoners. I didn't like the tone he took with me, and anyway I was bored with life in the cottage, so I replied by asking him what the hell we wanted guarding them at all for. I told him I'd talked it over with Noble, and that we'd both rather be out with a fighting column.

"What use are those fellows to us?" says I.

He looked at me in surprise and said: "I thought you knew we were keeping them as hostages."

"Hostages?" I said.

"The enemy have prisoners belonging to us," he says, "and now they're talking of shooting them. If they shoot our prisoners, we'll shoot theirs."

"Shoot them?" I said.

"What else did you think we were keeping them for?" he says.

"Wasn't it very unforeseen of you not to warn Noble and myself of that in the beginning?" I said.

"How was it?" says he. "You might have known it."

"We couldn't know it, Jeremiah Donovan," says I. "How could we when they were on our hands so long?"

"The enemy have our prisoners as long and longer," says he.

"That's not the same thing at all," says I.

"What difference is there?" says he.

I couldn't tell him, because I knew he wouldn't understand. If it was only an old dog that was going to the vet's, you'd try and not get too fond of him, but Jeremiah Donovan wasn't a man that would ever be in danger of that.

"And when is this thing going to be decided?" says I.

"We might hear tonight," he says. "Or tomorrow or the next day at latest. So if it's only hanging round here that's a trouble to you, you'll be free soon enough."

---

4. Shem: Second son of Noah, progenitor of the Semitic race; Jehoshophat: Son of Ahilud and chronicler in the time of David.

It wasn't the hanging round that was a trouble to me at all by this time. I had worse things to worry about. When I got back to the cottage the argument was still on. Hawkins was holding forth in his best style, maintaining that there was no next world, and Noble was maintaining that there was; but I could see that Hawkins had had the best of it.

"Do you know what, chum?" he was saying with a saucy smile. "I think you're just as big a bleeding unbeliever as I am. You say you believe in the next world, and you know just as much about the next world as I do, which is sweet damn-all. What's heaven? You don't know. Where's heaven? You don't know. You know sweet damn-all! I ask you again, do they wear wings?"

"Very well, then," says Noble, "they do. Is that enough for you? They do wear wings."

"Where do they get them, then? Who makes them? Have they a factory for wings? Have they a sort of store where you hands in your chit and takes your bleeding wings?"

"You're an impossible man to argue with," says Noble. "Now, listen to me — " And they were off again.

It was long after midnight when we locked up and went to bed. As I blew out the candle I told Noble what Jeremiah Donovan was after telling me. Noble took it very quietly. When we'd been in bed about an hour he asked me did I think we ought to tell the Englishmen. I didn't think we should, because it was more than likely that the English wouldn't shoot our men, and even if they did, the brigade officers, who were always up and down with the Second Battalion and knew the Englishmen well, wouldn't be likely to want them plugged. "I think so too," says Noble. "It would be great cruelty to put the wind up them now."

"It was very unforeseen of Jeremiah Donovan anyhow," says I.

It was next morning that we found it so hard to face Belcher and Hawkins. We went about the house all day scarcely saying a word. Belcher didn't seem to notice; he was stretched into the ashes as usual, with his usual look of waiting in quietness for something unforeseen to happen, but Hawkins noticed and put it down to Noble's being beaten in the argument of the night before.

"Why can't you take a discussion in the proper spirit?" he says severely. "You and your Adam and Eve! I'm a Communist, that's what I am. Communist or anarchist, it all comes to much the same thing." And for hours he went round the house, muttering when the fit took him. "Adam and Eve! Adam and Eve! Nothing better to do with their time than picking bleeding apples!"

III.

I don't know how we got through that day, but I was very glad when it was over, the tea things were cleared away, and Belcher said in his peaceable way: "Well, chums, what about it?" We sat round the table and Hawkins took out the cards, and just then I heard Jeremiah Donovan's footstep on the path and a dark presentiment crossed my mind. I rose from the table and caught him before he reached the door:

"What do you want?" I asked.

"I want those two soldier friends of yours," he says, getting red.

"Is that the way, Jeremiah Donovan?" I asked.

"That's the way. There were four of our lads shot this morning, one of them a boy of sixteen."

"That's bad," I said.

At that moment Noble followed me out, and the three of us walked down the path together, talking in whispers. Feeney, the local intelligence officer, was standing by the gate.

"What are you going to do about it?" I asked Jeremiah Donovan.

"I want you and Noble to get them out; tell them they're being shifted again; that'll be the quietest way."

"Leave me out of that," says Noble under his breath.

Jeremiah Donovan looks at him hard.

"All right," he says. "You and Feeney get a few tools from the shed and dig a hole by the far end of the bog. Bonaparte and myself will be after you. Don't let anyone see you with the tools. I wouldn't like it to go beyond ourselves."

We saw Feeney and Noble go round to the shed and went in ourselves. I left Jeremiah Donovan to do the explanations. He told them that he had orders to send them back to the Second Battalion. Hawkins let out a mouthful of curses, and you could see that though Belcher didn't say anything, he was a bit upset too. The old woman was for having them stay in spite of us, and she didn't stop advising them until Jeremiah Donovan lost his temper and turned on her. He had a nasty temper, I noticed. It was pitch-dark in the cottage by this time, but no one thought of lighting the lamp, and in the darkness the two Englishmen fetched their topcoats and said good-bye to the old woman.

"Just as a man makes a home of a bleeding place, some bastard at head-quarters thinks you're too cushy and shunts you off," says Hawkins, shaking her hand.

"A thousand thanks, madam," says Belcher. "A thousand thanks for every-thing" — as though he'd made it up.

We went round to the back of the house and down towards the bog. It was only then that Jeremiah Donovan told them. He was shaking with excitement.

"There were four of our fellows shot in Cork this morning and now you're to be shot as a reprisal."

"What are you talking about?" snaps Hawkins. "It's bad enough being mucked about as we are without having to put up with your funny jokes."

"It isn't a joke," says Donovan. "I'm sorry, Hawkins, but it's true," and be-gins on the usual rigmarole about duty and how unpleasant it is.

I never noticed that people who talk a lot about duty find it much of a trouble to them.

"Oh, cut it out!" says Hawkins.

"Ask Bonaparte," says Donovan, seeing that Hawkins isn't taking him seri-ously. "Isn't it true, Bonaparte?"

"It is," I say, and Hawkins stops.

"Ah, for Christ's sake, chum!"

"I mean it, chum," I say.

"You don't sound as if you meant it."

"If he doesn't mean it, I do," says Donovan, working himself up.

"What have you against me, Jeremiah Donovan?"

"I never said I had anything against you. But why did your people take out four of our prisoners and shoot them in cold blood?"

He took Hawkins by the arm and dragged him on, but it was impossible to make him understand that we were in earnest. I had the Smith and Wesson[5] in

5. Smith and Wesson: A revolver.

my pocket and I kept fingering it and wondering what I'd do if they put up a fight for it or ran, and wishing to God they'd do one or the other. I knew if they did run for it, that I'd never fire on them. Hawkins wanted to know was Noble in it, and when we said yes, he asked us why Noble wanted to plug him. Why did any of us want to plug him? What had he done to us? Weren't we all chums? Didn't we understand him and didn't he understand us? Did we imagine for an instant that he'd shoot us for all the so-and-so officers in the so-and-so British Army?

By this time we'd reached the bog, and I was so sick I couldn't even answer him. We walked along the edge of it in the darkness, and every now and then Hawkins would call a halt and begin all over again, as if he was wound up, about our being chums, and I knew that nothing but the sight of the grave would convince him that we had to do it. And all the time I was hoping that something would happen; that they'd run for it or that Noble would take over the responsibility from me. I had the feeling that it was worse on Noble than on me.

IV.

At last we saw the lantern in the distance and made towards it. Noble was carrying it, and Feeney was standing somewhere in the darkness behind him, and the picture of them so still and silent in the bogland brought it home to me that we were in earnest, and banished the last bit of hope I had.

Belcher, on recognizing Noble, said: "Hallo, chum," in his quiet way, but Hawkins flew at him at once, and the argument began all over again, only this time Noble had nothing to say for himself and stood with his head down, holding the lantern between his legs.

It was Jeremiah Donovan who did the answering. For the twentieth time, as though it was haunting his mind, Hawkins asked if anybody thought he'd shoot Noble.

"Yes, you would," says Jeremiah Donovan.

"No, I wouldn't, damn you!"

"You would, because you'd know you'd be shot for not doing it."

"I wouldn't, not if I was to be shot twenty times over. I wouldn't shoot a pal. And Belcher wouldn't — isn't that right, Belcher?"

"That's right, chum," Belcher said, but more by way of answering the question than of joining in the argument. Belcher sounded as though whatever unforeseen thing he'd always been waiting for had come at last.

"Anyway, who says Noble would be shot if I wasn't? What do you think I'd do if I was in his place, out in the middle of a blasted bog?"

"What would you do?" asks Donovan.

"I'd go with him wherever he was going, of course. Share my last bob with him and stick by him through thick and thin. No one can ever say of me that I let down a pal."

"We had enough of this," says Jeremiah Donovan, cocking his revolver. "Is there any message you want to send?"

"No, there isn't."

"Do you want to say your prayers?"

Hawkins came out with a cold-blooded remark that even shocked me and turned on Noble again.

"Listen to me, Noble," he says. "You and me are chums. You can't come over to my side, so I'll come over to your side. That show you I mean what I say? Give me a rifle and I'll go along with you and the other lads."

Nobody answered him. We knew that was no way out.

"Hear what I'm saying?" he says. "I'm through with it. I'm a deserter or anything else you like. I don't believe in your stuff, but it's no worse than mine. That satisfy you?"

Noble raised his head, but Donovan began to speak and he lowered it again without replying.

"For the last time, have you any messages to send?" says Donovan in a cold, excited sort of voice.

"Shut up, Donovan! You don't understand me, but these lads do. They're not the sort to make a pal and kill a pal. They're not the tools of any capitalist."

I alone of the crowd saw Donovan raise his Webley to the back of Hawkins's neck, and as he did so I shut my eyes and tried to pray. Hawkins had begun to say something else when Donovan fired, and as I opened my eyes at the bang, I saw Hawkins stagger at the knees and lie out flat at Noble's feet, slowly and as quiet as a kid falling asleep, with the lantern-light on his lean legs and bright farmer's boots. We all stood very still, watching him settle out in the last agony.

Then Belcher took out a handkerchief and began to tie it about his own eyes (in our excitement we'd forgotten to do the same for Hawkins), and, seeing it wasn't big enough, turned and asked for the loan of mine. I gave it to him and he knotted the two together and pointed with his foot at Hawkins.

"He's not quite dead," he says. "Better give him another."

Sure enough, Hawkins's left knee is beginning to rise. I bend down and put my gun to his head; then, recollecting myself, I get up again. Belcher understands what's in my mind.

"Give him his first," he says. "I don't mind. Poor bastard, we don't know what's happening to him now."

I knelt and fired. By this time I didn't seem to know what I was doing. Belcher, who was fumbling a bit awkwardly with the handkerchiefs, came out with a laugh as he heard the shot. It was the first time I heard him laugh and it sent a shudder down my back; it sounded so unnatural.

"Poor bugger!" he said quietly. "And last night he was so curious about it all. It's very queer, chums, I always think. Now he knows as much about it as they'll ever let him know, and last night he was all in the dark."

Donovan helped him to tie the handkerchiefs about his eyes. "Thanks, chum," he said. Donovan asked if there were any messages he wanted sent.

"No, chum," he says. "Not for me. If any of you would like to write to Hawkins's mother, you'll find a letter from her in his pocket. He and his mother were great chums. But my missus left me eight years ago. Went away with another fellow and took the kid with her. I like the feeling of a home, as you may have noticed, but I couldn't start again after that."

It was an extraordinary thing, but in those few minutes Belcher said more than in all the weeks before. It was just as if the sound of the shot had started a flood of talk in him and he could go on the whole night like that, quite happily, talking about himself. We stood round like fools now that he couldn't see us any longer. Donovan looked at Noble, and Noble shook his head. Then Donovan raised his Webley, and at that moment Belcher gives his queer laugh again. He may have thought we were talking about him, or perhaps he noticed the same thing I'd noticed and couldn't understand it.

"Excuse me, chums," he says. "I feel I'm talking the hell of a lot, and so silly, about my being so handy about a house and things like that. But this thing came on me suddenly. You'll forgive me, I'm sure."

"You don't want to say a prayer?" asks Donovan.

"No, chum," he says. "I don't think it would help. I'm ready, and you boys want to get it over."

"You understand that we're only doing our duty?" says Donovan.

Belcher's head was raised like a blind man's, so that you could only see his chin and the tip of his nose in the lantern-light.

"I never could make out what duty was myself," he said. "I think you're all good lads, if that's what you mean. I'm not complaining."

Noble, just as if he couldn't bear any more of it, raised his fist at Donovan, and in a flash Donovan raised his gun and fired. The big man went over like a sack of meal, and this time there was no need of a second shot.

I don't remember much about the burying, but that it was worse than all the rest because we had to carry them to the grave. It was all mad lonely with nothing but a patch of lantern-light between ourselves and the dark, and birds hooting and screeching all round, disturbed by the guns. Noble went through Hawkins's belongings to find the letter from his mother, and then joined his hands together. He did the same with Belcher. Then, when we'd filled in the grave, we separated from Jeremiah Donovan and Feeney and took our tools back to the shed. All the way we didn't speak a word. The kitchen was dark and cold as we'd left it, and the old woman was sitting over the hearth, saying her beads. We walked past her into the room, and Noble struck a match to light the lamp. She rose quietly and came to the doorway with all her cantankerousness gone.

"What did ye do with them?" she asked in a whisper, and Noble started so that the match went out in his hand.

"What's that?" he asked without turning round.

"I heard ye," she said.

"What did you hear?" asked Noble.

"I heard ye. Do ye think I didn't hear ye, putting the spade back in the houseen?" [6]

Noble struck another match and this time the lamp lit for him.

"Was that what ye did to them?" she asked.

Then, by God, in the very doorway, she fell on her knees and began praying, and after looking at her for a minute or two Noble did the same by the fireplace. I pushed my way out past her and left them at it. I stood at the door, watching the stars and listening to the shrieking of the birds dying out over the bogs. It is so strange what you feel at times like that that you can't describe it. Noble says he saw everything ten times the size, as though there were nothing in the whole world but that little patch of bog with the two Englishmen stiffening into it, but with me it was as if the patch of bog where the Englishmen were was a million miles away, and even Noble and the old woman, mumbling behind me, and the birds and the bloody stars were all far away, and I was somehow very small and very lost and lonely like a child astray in the snow. And anything that happened me afterwards, I never felt the same about again.

6. Houseen: Storehouse.

Ann Petry (1912–   )

Doby's Gone

When Doby first came into Sue Johnson's life her family were caretakers on a farm way up in New York State. And because Sue had no one else to play with, the Johnsons reluctantly accepted Doby as a member of the family.

The spring that Sue was six they moved to Wessex, Connecticut — a small New England town whose neat colonial houses cling to a group of hills overlooking the Connecticut River. All that summer Mrs. Johnson had hoped that Doby would vanish long before Sue entered school in the fall. He would only complicate things in school.

For Doby wasn't real. He existed only in Sue's mind. He had been created out of her need for a friend her own age — her own size. And he had gradually become an escape from the very real world that surrounded her. She first started talking about him when she was two and he had been with her ever since. He always sat beside her when she ate and played with her during the day. At night he slept in a chair near her bed so that they awoke at the same time in the morning. A place had to be set for him at mealtime. A seat had to be saved for him on trains and buses.

After they moved to Wessex, he was still her constant companion just as he had been when she was three and four and five.

On the morning that Sue was to start going to school she said, "Doby has a new pencil, too. And he's got a red plaid shirt just like my dress."

"Why can't Doby stay home?" Mrs. Johnson asked.

"Because he goes everywhere I go," Sue said in amazement. "Of course he's going to school. He's going to sit right by me."

Sue watched her mother get up from the breakfast table and then followed her upstairs to the big front bedroom. She saw with surprise that her mother was putting on her going-out clothes.

"You have to come with me, Mommy?" she asked anxiously. She had wanted to go with Doby. Just the two of them. She had planned every step of the way since the time her mother told her she would start school in the fall.

"No, I don't have to, but I'm coming just the same. I want to talk to your teacher." Mrs. Johnson fastened her coat and deftly patted a loose strand of hair in place.

Sue looked at her and wondered if the other children's mothers would come to school, too. She certainly hoped so because she wouldn't want to be the only one there who had a mother with her.

Then she started skipping around the room holding Doby by the hand. Her short black braids jumped as she skipped. The gingham dress she wore was starched so stiffly that the hemline formed a wide circular frame for her sturdy dark brown legs as she bounced up and down.

"Ooh," she said suddenly. "Doby pulled off one of my hair ribbons." She reached over and picked it up from the floor and came to stand in front of her mother while the red ribbon was retied into a crisp bow.

Then she was walking down the street hand in hand with her mother. She held Doby's hand on the other side. She decided it was good her mother had come. It was better that way. The street would have looked awfully long and awfully big if she and Doby had been by themselves, even though she did know exactly where the school was. Right down the street on this side. Past the post office and town hall that sat so far back with green lawn in front of them. Past the town pump and the old white house on the corner, past the big empty lot. And there was the school.

It had a walk that went straight down between the green grass and was all brown-yellow gravel stuff — coarser than sand. One day she had walked past there with her mother and stopped to finger the stuff the walk was made of, and her mother had said, "It's gravel."

She remembered how they'd talk about it. "What's gravel?" she asked.

"The stuff in your hand. It's like sand, only coarser. People use it for driveways and walks," her mother had said.

"Gravel. She liked the sound of the word. It sounded like pebbles. Gravel. Pebble. She said the words over to herself. You gravel and pebble. Pebble said to gravel. She started making up a story. Gravel said to pebble, "You're a pebble." Pebble said back, "You're a gravel."

"Sue, throw it away. It's dirty and your hands are clean," her mother said.

She threw it down on the sidewalk. But she kept looking back at it as she walked along. It made a scattered yellow, brown color against the rich brown-black of the dirt-path.

She held on to Doby's hand a little more tightly. Now she was actually going to walk up that long gravel walk to the school. She and Doby would play there every day when school was out.

The school yard was full of children. Sue hung back a little looking at them. They were playing ball under the big maple trees near the back of the yard. Some small children were squatting near the school building, letting gravel trickle through their fingers.

"I want to play, too." She tried to free her hand from her mother's firm grip.

"We're going inside to see your teacher first." And her mother went on walking up the school steps holding on to Sue's hand.

Sue stared at the children on the steps. "Why are they looking so hard?" she asked.

"Probably because you're looking at them so hard. Now come on," and her mother pulled her through the door. The hall inside was dark and very long. A neat white sign over a door to the right said FIRST GRADE in bold black letters.

Sue peered inside the room while her mother knocked on the door. A pretty lady with curly yellow hair got up from a desk and invited them in. While the teacher and her mother talked grown-up talk, Sue looked around. She supposed she'd sit at one of those little desks. There were a lot of them and she wondered if there would be a child at each desk. If so then Doby would have to squeeze in beside her.

"Sue, you can go outside and play. When the bell rings you must come in," the teacher said.

"Yes, teacher," Sue started out the door in a hurry.

"My name is Miss Whittier," the teacher said, "You must call me that."

"Yes, Miss Whittier. Good-bye, Mommy," she said, and went quickly down the hall and out the door.

"Hold my hand, Doby," she said softly under her breath.

Now she and Doby would play in the gravel. Squeeze it between their fingers, pat it into shapes like those other children were doing. Her short starched skirt stood out around her legs as she skipped down the steps. She watched the children as long as she could without saying anything.

"Can we play, too?" she asked finally.

A boy with a freckled face and short stiff red hair looked up at her and frowned. He didn't answer but kept ostentatiously patting at a little mound of gravel.

Sue walked over a little closer, holding Doby tightly by the hand. The boy ignored her. A little girl in a blue and white checked dress stuck her tongue out.

"Your legs are black," she said suddenly. And then when the others looked up she added, "Why, look, she's black all over. Looky, she's black all over."

Sue retreated a step away from the building. The children got up and followed her. She took another backward step and they took two steps forward. The little girl who had stuck her tongue out began a chant, "Look, look. Her legs are black. Her legs are black."

The children were all saying it. They formed a ring around her and they were dancing up and down and screaming, "Her legs are black. Her legs are black."

She stood in the middle of the circle completely bewildered. She wanted to go home where it was safe and quiet and where her mother would hold her tight in her arms. She pulled Doby nearer to her. What did they mean her legs were black? Of course they were. Not black but dark brown. Just like these children were white some other children were dark like her. Her mother said so. But her mother hadn't said anyone would make her feel bad about being a different color. She didn't know what to do; so she just stood there watching them come closer and closer to her — their faces red with excitement, their voices hoarse with yelling.

Then the school bell rang. And the children suddenly plunged toward the building. She was left alone with Doby. When she walked into the school room she was crying.

"Don't you mind, Doby," she whispered. "Don't you mind. I won't let them hurt you."

Miss Whittier gave her a seat near the front of the room. Right near her desk. And she smiled at her. Sue smiled back and carefully wiped away the wet on her eyelashes with the back of her hand. She turned and looked around the room. There were no empty seats. Doby would have to stand up.

"You stand right close to me and if you get tired just sit on the edge of my seat," she said.

She didn't go out for recess. She stayed in and helped Miss Whittier draw on the blackboard with colored chalk — yellow and green and red and purple and brown. Miss Whittier drew the flowers and Sue colored them. She put a small piece of crayon out for Doby to use. And Miss Whittier noticed it. But she didn't say anything, she just smiled.

"I love her," Sue thought. "I love my teacher." And then again, "I love Miss Whittier, my teacher."

At noon the children followed her halfway home from school. They called after her and she ran so fast and so hard that the pounding in her ears cut off the sound of their voices.

"Go faster, Doby," she said. "You have to go faster." And she held his hand and ran until her legs ached.

"How was school, Sue?" asked her mother.

"It was all right," she said slowly. "I don't think Doby likes it very much. He likes Miss Whittier though."

"Do you like her?"

"Oh, yes," Sue let her breath come out with a sigh.

"Why are you panting like that?" her mother asked.

"I ran all the way home," she said.

Going back after lunch wasn't so bad. She went right in to Miss Whittier. She didn't stay put in the yard and wait for the bell.

When school was out, she decided she'd better hurry right home and maybe the children wouldn't see her. She walked down the gravel path taking quick little looks over her shoulder. No one paid any attention and she was so happy that she gave Doby's hand a squeeze.

And then she saw that they were waiting for her right by the vacant lot. She hurried along trying not to hear what they were saying.

"My mother says you're a little nigger girl," the boy with the red hair said.

And then they began to shout: "Her legs are black. Her legs are black."

It changed suddenly. "Run. Go ahead and run." She looked over her shoulder. A boy was coming toward her with a long switch in his hand. He raised it in a threatening gesture and she started running.

For two days she ran home from school like that. Ran until her short legs felt as though they couldn't move another step.

"Sue," her mother asked anxiously, watching her try to catch her breath on the front steps, "what makes you run home from school like this?"

"Doby doesn't like the other children very much," she said panting.

"Why?"

"I don't think they understand about him," she said thoughtfully. "But he loves Miss Whittier."

The next day the children waited for her right where the school's gravel walk ended. Sue didn't see them until she was close to them. She was coming slowly down the path hand in hand with Doby trying to see how many of the big pebbles they could step on without stepping on any of the finer, sandier gravel.

She was in the middle of the group of children before she realized it. They started off slowly at first. "How do you comb that kind of hair?" "Does that black color wash off?" And then the chant began and it came faster and faster: "Her legs are black. Her legs are black."

A little girl reached out and pulled one of Sue's braids. Sue tried to back away and the other children closed in around her. She rubbed the side of her head — it hurt where her hair had been pulled. Someone pushed her. Hard. In the middle of her back. She was suddenly outraged. She planted her feet firmly on the path. She started hitting out with her fists. Kicking. Pulling hair. Tearing at clothing. She reached down and picked up handfuls of gravel and aimed it at eyes and ears and noses.

While she was slapping and kicking at the small figures that encircled her she became aware that Doby had gone. For the first time in her life he had left her. He had gone when she started to fight.

She went on fighting — scratching and biting and kicking — with such passion and energy that the space around her slowly cleared. The children backed away. And she stood still. She was breathing fast as though she had been running.

The children ran off down the street — past the big empty lot, past the old white house with the green shutters. Sue watched them go. She didn't feel victorious. She didn't feel anything except an aching sense of loss. She stood there panting, wondering about Doby.

And then, "Doby," she called softly. Then louder, "Doby! Doby! Where are you?"

She listened — cocking her head on one side. He didn't answer. And she felt certain he would never be back because he had never left her before. He had gone for good. And she didn't know why. She decided it probably had something to do with growing up. And she looked down at her legs hoping to find they had grown as long as her father's. She saw instead that her dress was torn in three different places, her socks were down around her ankles, there were long angry scratches on her legs and on her arms. She felt for her hair — the red hair ribbons were gone and her braids were coming undone.

She started looking for the hair ribbons. And as she looked she saw that Daisy Bell, the little girl who had stuck her tongue out that first day of school, was leaning against the oak tree at the end of the path.

"Come on, let's walk home together," Daisy Bell said matter-of-factly.

"All right," Sue said.

As they started past the empty lot, she was conscious that someone was tagging along behind them. It was Jimmie Piebald, the boy with the stiff red hair. When she looked back he came up and walked on the other side of her.

They walked along in silence until they came to the town pump. They stopped and looked deep down into the well. And spent a long time hallooing down into it and listening delightedly to the hollow funny sound of their voices.

It was much later than usual when Sue got home. Daisy Bell and Jimmie walked up to the door with her. Her mother was standing on the front steps waiting for her.

"Sue," her mother said in a shocked voice. "What's the matter? What happened to you?"

Daisy Bell put her arm around Sue. Jimmie started kicking at some stones in the path.

Sue stared at her mother, trying to remember. There was something wrong but she couldn't think what it was. And then it came to her. "Oh," she wailed, "Doby's gone. I can't find him anywhere."

Exercises

1. What point of view obtains in this story? Is it effective? Explain.

2. What does Doby stand for, do you think? What in the story supports your view?

3. After the fight, Sue is immediately accepted by two classmates who have been nasty to her. Are you convinced? Why, or why not?

4. Is there any indication in the story why Sue does not tell her mother about her classmates' attacks?

Topic for Writing

From among the selections in this book, choose two other stories about the crises of growing up, and compare and contrast their treatment of the crises with that in "Doby's Gone." Be sure to identify the crisis in each case and to consider what knowledge, if any, the protagonist gains.

Edgar Allan Poe *(1809–1849)*

The Fall of the House of Usher

Son cœur est un luth suspendu;
Sitôt qu'on le touche il résonne.[1]
De Béranger

During the whole of a dull, dark, and soundless day in the autumn of the year, when the clouds hung oppressively low in the heavens, I had been passing alone, on horseback, through a singularly dreary tract of country; and at length found myself, as the shades of the evening drew on, within view of the melancholy House of Usher. I know not how it was — but, with the first glimpse of the building, a sense of insufferable gloom pervaded my spirit. I say insufferable; for the feeling was unrelieved by any of that half-pleasurable, because poetic, sentiment, with which the mind usually receives even the sternest natural images of the desolate or terrible. I looked upon the scene before me — upon the mere house, and the simple landscape features of the domain, upon the bleak walls, upon the vacant eye-like windows, upon a few rank sedges, and upon a few white trunks of decayed trees — with an utter depression of soul which I can compare to no earthly sensation more properly than to the after-dream of the reveller upon opium: the bitter lapse into everyday life, the hideous dropping off of the veil. There was an iciness, a sinking, a sickening of the heart, an unredeemed dreariness of thought which no goading of the imagination could torture into aught of the sublime. What was it — I paused to think — what was it that so unnerved me in the contemplation of the House of Usher? It was a mystery all insoluble; nor could I grapple with the shadowy fancies that crowded upon me as I pondered. I was forced to fall back upon the unsatisfactory conclusion, that while, beyond doubt, there *are* combinations of very simple natural objects which have the power of thus affecting us, still the analysis of this power lies among considerations beyond our depth. It was possible, I reflected, that a mere different arrangement of the particulars of the scene, of the details of the picture, would be sufficient to modify, or perhaps to annihilate its capacity for sorrowful impression; and, acting upon this idea, I reined my horse to the precipitous brink of a black and lurid tarn[2] that lay in unruffled lustre by the dwelling, and gazed down — but with a shudder even more thrilling than before —

1. "His heart is a lute suspended; / As soon as it is touched it resounds." From "Le Refus" by the French poet Jean De Béranger (1780–1857).   2. Tarn: A small mountain lake or pool.

upon the remodelled and inverted images of the gray sedge, and the ghastly tree-stems, and the vacant and eye-like windows.

Nevertheless, in this mansion of gloom I now proposed to myself a sojourn of some weeks. Its proprietor, Roderick Usher, had been one of my boon companions in boyhood; but many years had elapsed since our last meeting. A letter, however, had lately reached me in a distant part of the country — a letter from him — which, in its wildly importunate nature, had admitted of no other than a personal reply. The MS. gave evidence of nervous agitation. The writer spoke of acute bodily illness, of a mental disorder which oppressed him, and of an earnest desire to see me, as his best, and indeed his only personal friend, with a view of attempting, by the cheerfulness of my society, some alleviation of his malady. It was the manner in which all this, and much more, was said — it was the apparent *heart* that went with his request — which allowed me no room for hesitation; and I accordingly obeyed forthwith what I still considered a very singular summons.

Although, as boys, we had been even intimate associates, yet I really knew little of my friend. His reserve had been always excessive and habitual. I was aware, however, that his very ancient family had been noted, time out of mind, for a peculiar sensibility of temperament, displaying itself, through long ages, in many works of exalted art, and manifested, of late, in repeated deeds of munificent yet unobtrusive charity, as well as in a passionate devotion to the intricacies, perhaps even more than to the orthodox and easily recognizable beauties, of musical science. I had learned, too, the very remarkable fact, that the stem of the Usher race, all time-honored as it was, had put forth, at no period, any enduring branch; in other words, that the entire family lay in the direct line of descent, and had always, with very trifling and very temporary variation, so lain. It was this deficiency, I considered, while running over in thought the perfect keeping of the character of the premises with the accredited character of the people, and while speculating upon the possible influence which the one, in the long lapse of centuries, might have exercised upon the other — it was this deficiency, perhaps, of collateral issue, and the consequent undeviating transmission, from sire to son, of the patrimony with the name, which had, at length, so identified the two as to merge the original title of the estate in the quaint and equivocal appellation of the "House of Usher" — an appellation which seemed to include, in the minds of the peasantry who used it, both the family and the family mansion.

I have said that the sole effect of my somewhat childish experiment, that of looking down within the tarn, had been to deepen the first singular impression. There can be no doubt that the consciousness of the rapid increase of my superstition — for why should I not so term it? — served mainly to accelerate the increase itself. Such, I have long known, is the paradoxical law of all sentiments having terror as a basis. And it might have been for this reason only, that, when I again uplifted my eyes to the house itself, from its image in the pool, there grew in my mind a strange fancy — a fancy so ridiculous, indeed, that I but mention it to show the vivid force of the sensations which oppressed me. I had so worked upon my imagination as really to believe that about the whole mansion and domain there hung an atmosphere peculiar to themselves and their immediate vicinity: an atmosphere which had no affinity with the air of heaven, but which had reeked up from the decayed trees, and the gray wall, and the silent tarn: a pestilent and mystic vapor, dull, sluggish, faintly discernible, and leaden-hued.

Shaking off from my spirit what *must* have been a dream, I scanned more narrowly the real aspect of the building. Its principal feature seemed to be that of an excessive antiquity. The discoloration of ages had been great. Minute fungi overspread the whole exterior, hanging in a fine tangled webwork from the eaves. Yet all this was apart from any extraordinary dilapidation. No portion of the masonry had fallen; and there appeared to be a wild inconsistency between its still perfect adaptation of parts and the crumbling condition of the individual stones. In this there was much that reminded me of the specious totality of old wood-work which has rotted for long years in some neglected vault, with no disturbance from the breath of the external air. Beyond this indication of extensive decay, however, the fabric gave little token of instability. Perhaps the eye of a scrutinizing observer might have discovered a barely perceptible fissure, which, extending from the roof of the building in front, made its way down the wall in a zigzag direction, until it became lost in the sullen waters of the tarn.

Noticing these things, I rode over a short causeway to the house. A servant in waiting took my horse, and I entered the Gothic archway of the hall. A valet, of stealthy step, thence conducted me, in silence, through many dark and intricate passages in my progress to the *studio* of his master. Much that I encountered on the way contributed, I know not how, to heighten the vague sentiments of which I have already spoken. While the objects around me — while the carvings of the ceilings, the sombre tapestries of the walls, the ebon blackness of the floors, and the phantasmagoric armorial trophies which rattled as I strode, were but matters to which, or to such as which, I had been accustomed from my infancy — while I hesitated not to acknowledge how familiar was all this — I still wondered to find how unfamiliar were the fancies which ordinary images were stirring up. On one of the staircases, I met the physician of the family. His countenance, I thought, wore a mingled expression of low cunning and perplexity. He accosted me with trepidation and passed on. The valet now threw open a door and ushered me into the presence of his master.

The room in which I found myself was very large and lofty. The windows were long, narrow, and pointed, and at so vast a distance from the black oaken floor as to be altogether inaccessible from within. Feeble gleams of encrimsoned light made their way through the trellised panes, and served to render sufficiently distinct the more prominent objects around; the eye, however, struggled in vain to reach the remoter angles of the chamber, or the recesses of the vaulted and fretted ceiling. Dark draperies hung upon the walls. The general furniture was profuse, comfortless, antique, and tattered. Many books and musical instruments lay scattered about, but failed to give any vitality to the scene. I felt that I breathed an atmosphere of sorrow. An air of stern, deep, and irredeemable gloom hung over and pervaded all.

Upon my entrance, Usher arose from a sofa on which he had been lying at full length, and greeted me with a vivacious warmth which had much in it, I at first thought, of an overdone cordiality — of the constrained effort of the *ennuyé*[3] man of the world. A glance, however, at his countenance, convinced me of his perfect sincerity. We sat down; and for some moments, while he spoke not, I gazed upon him with a feeling half of pity, half of awe. Surely, man had never before so terribly altered, in so brief a period, as had Roderick Usher! It was with difficulty that I could bring myself to admit the identity of the wan

3. *Ennuyé:* Bored.

being before me with the companion of my early boyhood. Yet the character of his face had been at all times remarkable. A cadaverousness of complexion; an eye large, liquid, and luminous beyond comparison, lips somewhat thin and very pallid, but of a surpassingly beautiful curve; a nose of a delicate Hebrew model, but with a breadth of nostril unusual in similar formations; a finely moulded chin, speaking, in its want of prominence, of a want of moral energy; hair of a more than web-like softness and tenuity; these features, with an inordinate expansion above the regions of the temple, made up altogether a countenance not easily to be forgotten. And now in the mere exaggeration of the prevailing character of these features, and of the expression they were wont to convey, lay so much of change that I doubted to whom I spoke. The now ghastly pallor of the skin, and the now miraculous lustre of the eye, above all things startled and even awed me. The silken hair, too, had been suffered to grow all unheeded, and as, in its wild gossamer texture, it floated rather than fell about the face, I could not, even with effort, connect its Arabesque[4] expression with any idea of simple humanity.

In the manner of my friend I was at once struck with an incoherence, an inconsistency; and I soon found this to arise from a series of feeble and futile struggles to overcome an habitual trepidancy, an excessive nervous agitation. For something of this nature I had indeed been prepared, no less by his letter, than by reminiscences of certain boyish traits, and by conclusions deduced from his peculiar physical conformation and temperament. His action was alternately vivacious and sullen. His voice varied rapidly from a tremulous indecision (when the animal spirits seemed utterly in abeyance) to that species of energetic concision — that abrupt, weighty, unhurried, and hollow-sounding enunciation — that leaden, self-balanced and perfectly modulated guttural utterance, which may be observed in the lost drunkard, or the irreclaimable eater of opium, during the periods of his most intense excitement.

It was thus that he spoke of the object of my visit, of his earnest desire to see me, and of the solace he expected me to afford him. He entered, at some length, into what he conceived to be the nature of his malady. It was, he said, a constitutional and a family evil, and one for which he despaired to find a remedy — a mere nervous affection, he immediately added, which would undoubtedly soon pass off. It displayed itself in a host of unnatural sensations. Some of these, as he detailed them, interested and bewildered me; although, perhaps, the terms, and the general manner of the narration had their weight. He suffered much from a morbid acuteness of the senses; the most insipid food was alone endurable; he could wear only garments of certain texture; the odors of all flowers were oppressive; his eyes were tortured by even a faint light; and there were but peculiar sounds, and these from stringed instruments, which did not inspire him with horror.

To an anomolous species of terror I found him a bounden slave. 'I shall perish,' said he, 'I *must* perish in this deplorable folly. Thus, thus, and not otherwise, shall I be lost. I dread the events of the future, not in themselves, but in their results. I shudder at the thought of any, even the most trivial, incident, which may operate upon this intolerable agitation of soul. I have, indeed, no abhorrence of danger, except in its absolute effect — in terror. In this

4. Arabesque: Formed a complex
geometrical figure.

unnerved — in this pitiable condition, I feel that the period will sooner or later arrive when I must abandon life and reason together, in some struggle with the grim phantasm, FEAR.'

I learned, moreover, at intervals, and through broken and equivocal hints, another singular feature of his mental condition. He was enchained by certain superstitious impressions in regard to the dwelling which he tenanted, and whence, for many years, he had never ventured forth — in regard to an influence whose suppositious force was conveyed in terms too shadowy here to be re-stated — an influence which some peculiarities in the mere form and substance of his family mansion, had, by dint of long sufferance, he said, obtained over his spirit — an effect which the *physique* of the gray walls and turrets, and of the dim tarn into which they all looked down, had, at length, brought about upon the *morale* of his existence.

He admitted, however, although with hesitation, that much of the peculiar gloom which thus afflicted him could be traced to a more natural and far more palpable origin — to the severe and long-continued illness, indeed to the evidently approaching dissolution, of a tenderly beloved sister — his sole companion for long years, his last and only relative on earth. 'Her decease,' he said, with a bitterness which I can never forget, 'would leave him (him the hopeless and the frail) the last of the ancient race of the Ushers.' While he spoke, the lady Madeline (for so was she called) passed slowly through a remote portion of the apartment, and, without having noticed my presence, disappeared. I regarded her with an utter astonishment not unmingled with dread, and yet I found it impossible to account for such feelings. A sensation of stupor oppressed me, as my eyes followed her retreating steps. When a door, at length, closed upon her, my glance sought instinctively and eagerly the countenance of the brother; but he had buried his face in his hands, and I could only perceive that a far more than ordinary wanness had overspread the emaciated fingers through which trickled many passionate tears.

The disease of the lady Madeline had long baffled the skill of her physicians. A settled apathy, a gradual wasting away of the person, and frequent although transient affections of a partially cataleptical [5] character, were the unusual diagnosis. Hitherto she had steadily borne up against the pressure of her malady, and had not betaken herself finally to bed; but, on the closing in of the evening of my arrival at the house, she succumbed (as her brother told me at night with inexpressible agitation) to the prostrating power of the destroyer; and I learned that the glimpse I had obtained of her person would thus probably be the last I should obtain — that the lady, at least while living, would be seen by me no more.

For several days ensuing, her name was unmentioned by either Usher or myself: and during this period I was busied in earnest endeavors to alleviate the melancholy of my friend. We painted and read together; or I listened, as if in a dream, to the wild improvisations of his speaking guitar. And thus, as a closer and still closer intimacy admitted me more unreservedly into the recesses of his spirit, the more bitterly did I perceive the futility of all attempt at cheering a mind from which darkness, as if an inherent positive quality, poured forth upon

5. Cataleptical: Lacking awareness
and ability to respond to outward
stimuli; with muscular rigidity.

all objects of the moral and physical universe, in one unceasing radiation of gloom.

I shall ever bear about me a memory of the many solemn hours I thus spent alone with the master of the House of Usher. Yet I should fail in any attempt to convey an idea of the exact character of the studies, or of the occupations, in which he involved me, or led me the way. An excited and highly distempered ideality threw a sulphureous lustre over all. His long improvised dirges will ring forever in my ears. Among other things, I hold painfully in mind a certain singular perversion and amplification of the wild air of the last waltz of Von Weber.[6] From the paintings over which his elaborate fancy brooded, and which grew, touch by touch, into vaguenesses at which I shuddered the more thrillingly, because I shuddered knowing not why; — from these paintings (vivid as their images now are before me) I would in vain endeavor to educe more than a small portion which should lie within the compass of merely written words. By the utter simplicity, by the nakedness of his designs, he arrested and overawed attention. If ever mortal painted an idea, that mortal was Roderick Usher. For me at least, in the circumstances then surrounding me, there arose out of the pure abstractions which the hypochondriac contrived to throw upon his canvas, an intensity of intolerable awe, no shadow of which felt I ever yet in the contemplation of the certainly glowing yet too concrete reveries of Fuseli.[7]

One of the phantasmagoric conceptions of my friend, partaking not so rigidly of the spirit of abstraction, may be shadowed forth, although feebly, in words. A small picture presented the interior of an immensely long and rectangular vault or tunnel, with low walls, smooth, white, and without interruption or device. Certain accessory points of the design served well to convey the idea that this excavation lay at an exceeding depth below the surface of the earth. No outlet was observed in any portion of its vast extent, and no torch, or other artificial source of light was discernible; yet a flood of intense rays rolled throughout, and bathed the whole in a ghastly and inappropriate splendor.

I have just spoken of that morbid condition of the auditory nerve which rendered all music intolerable to the sufferer, with the exception of certain effects of stringed instruments. It was, perhaps, the narrow limits to which he thus confined himself upon the guitar, which gave birth, in great measure, to the fantastic character of his performances. But the fervid *facility* of his *impromptus*[8] could not be so accounted for. They must have been, and were, in the notes, as well as in the words of his wild fantasias (for he not unfrequently accompanied himself with rhymed verbal improvisations), the result of that intense mental collectedness and concentration to which I have previously alluded as observable only in particular moments of the highest artificial excitement. The words of one of these rhapsodies I have easily remembered. I was, perhaps, the more forcibly impressed with it, as he gave it, because, in the under or mystic current of its meaning, I fancied that I perceived, and for the first time, a full consciousness on the part of Usher, of the tottering of his lofty reason upon

6. Von Weber: German composer Carl Maria Von Weber (1786–1826).
7. Fuseli: Real name Johann Heinrich Füssli, Swiss painter (1741–1825).

8. *Impromptus:* Spontaneous performances, without rehearsal.

her throne. The verses, which were entitled 'The Haunted Palace,' ran very nearly, if not accurately, thus:

In the greenest of our valleys
        By good angels tenanted,
Once a fair and stately palace —
        Radiant palace — reared its head.
In the monarch Thought's dominion,
        It stood there!
Never seraph spread a pinion
        Over fabric half so fair!

Banners yellow, glorious, golden,
        On its roof did float and flow
(This — all this — was in the olden
        Time long ago)
And every gentle air that dallied,
        In that sweet day,
Along the ramparts plumed and pallid,
        A wingèd odor went away.

Wanderers in that happy valley,
        Through two luminous windows, saw
Spirits moving musically
        To a lute's well-tunèd law,
Round about a throne where, sitting,
        Porphyrogene! [9]
In state his glory well befitting,
        The ruler of the realm was seen.

And all with pearl and ruby glowing
        Was the fair palace door,
Through which came flowing, flowing, flowing,
        And sparkling evermore,
A troop of Echoes, whose sweet duty
        Was but to sing,
In voices of surpassing beauty,
        The wit and wisdom of their king.

But evil things, in robes of sorrow,
        Assailed the monarch's high estate;
(Ah, let us mourn! — for never morrow
        Shall dawn upon him, desolate!)
And round about his home the glory
        That blushed and bloomed
Is but a dim-remembered story
        Of the old time entombed.

And travellers, now, within that valley,
        Through the red-litten[10] windows see

9. Porphyrogene: One born of royal lineage.   10. Red-litten: Red-lighted.

> Vast forms that move fantastically
>   To a discordant melody;
> While, like a ghastly rapid river,
>   Through the pale door
> A hideous throng rush out forever,
>   And laugh — but smile no more.

I well remember that suggestions arising from this ballad led us into a train of thought wherein there became manifest an opinion of Usher's which I mention not so much on account of its novelty, (for other men have thought thus), as on account of the pertinacity with which he maintained it. This opinion, in its general form, was that of the sentience of all vegetable things. But, in his disordered fancy, the idea had assumed a more daring character, and trespassed, under certain conditions, upon the kingdom of inorganization. I lack words to express the full extent, or the earnest *abandon* of his persuasion. The belief, however, was connected (as I have previously hinted) with the gray stones of the home of his forefathers. The conditions of the sentience had been here, he imagined, fulfilled in the method of collocation of these stones — in the order of their arrangement, as well as in that of the many *fungi* which overspread them, and of the decayed trees which stood around — above all, in the long undisturbed endurance of this arrangement, and in its reduplication in the still waters of the tarn. Its evidence — the evidence of the sentience — was to be seen, he said, (and I here started as he spoke), in the gradual yet certain condensation of an atmosphere of their own about the waters and the walls. The result was discoverable, he added, in that silent, yet importunate and terrible influence which for centuries had moulded the destinies of his family, and which made *him* what I now saw him — what he was. Such opinions need no comment, and I will make none.

Our books — the books which, for years, had formed no small portion of the mental existence of the invalid — were, as might be supposed, in strict keeping with this character of phantasm. We pored together over such works as the *Ververt et Chartreuse* of Gresset; the *Belphegor* of Machiavelli; the *Heaven and Hell* of Swedenborg; the *Subterranean Voyage of Nicholas Klimm* by Holberg; the *Chiromancy* of Robert Flud, of Jean D'Indaginé, and of De la Chambre; the *Journey into the Blue Distance* of Tieck; and the *City of the Sun* of Campanella. One favorite volume was a small octavo edition of the *Directorium Inquisitorum,* by the Dominican Eymeric de Gironne; and there were passages in Pomponius Mela, about the old African Satyrs and Aegipans, over which Usher would sit dreaming for hours.[11] His chief delight, however, was found in the perusal of an exceedingly rare and curious book in quarto Gothic — the manual of a forgotten church — the *Vigilæ Mortuorum Secundum Chorum Ecclesiæ Maguntinæn.*[12]

I could not help thinking of the wild ritual of this work, and of its probable influence upon the hypochondriac, when, one evening, having informed me abruptly that the lady Madeline was no more, he stated his intention of pre-

---

11. Books treating chiefly of demons, damnation, the afterlife, voyages to other worlds, the art of reading palms, and various techniques of torture.

12. *Vigilæ ... Maguntinæn:* "Vigils for the Dead According to the Choir of the Church of Maguntinæ."

serving her corpse for a fortnight, (previously to its final interment), in one of the numerous vaults within the main walls of the building. The worldly reason, however, assigned for this singular proceeding, was one which I did not feel at liberty to dispute. The brother had been led to his resolution (so he told me) by consideration of the unusual character of the malady of the deceased, of certain obtrusive and eager inquiries on the part of her medical men, and of the remote and exposed situation of the burial-ground of the family. I will not deny that when I called to mind the sinister countenance of the person whom I met upon the staircase, on the day of my arrival at the house, I had no desire to oppose what I regarded as at best but a harmless, and by no means an unnatural, precaution.

At the request of Usher, I personally aided him in the arrangements for the temporary entombment. The body having been encoffined, we two alone bore it to its rest. The vault in which we placed it (and which had been so long unopened that our torches, half smothered in its oppressive atmosphere, gave us little opportunity for investigation) was small, damp, and entirely without means of admission for light; lying, at great depth, immediately beneath that portion of the building in which was my own sleeping apartment. It had been used, apparently, in remote feudal times, for the worst purposes of a donjon-keep, and, in later days, as a place of deposit for powder, or some other highly combustible substance, as a portion of its floor, and the whole interior of a long archway through which we reached it, were carefully sheathed with copper. The door, of massive iron, had been, also, similarly protected. Its immense weight caused an unusually sharp grating sound, as it moved upon its hinges.

Having deposited our mournful burden upon tressels within this region of horror, we partially turned aside the yet unscrewed lid of the coffin, and looked upon the face of the tenant. A striking similitude between the brother and sister now first arrested my attention; and Usher, divining, perhaps, my thoughts, murmured out some few words from which I learned that the deceased and himself had been twins, and that sympathies of a scarcely intelligible nature had always existed between them. Our glances, however, rested not long upon the dead — for we could not regard her unawed. The disease which had thus entombed the lady in the maturity of youth, had left, as usual in all maladies of a strictly cataleptical character, the mockery of a faint blush upon the bosom and the face, and that suspiciously lingering smile upon the lip which is so terrible in death. We replaced and screwed down the lid, and, having secured the door of iron, made our way, with toil, into the scarcely less gloomy apartments of the upper portion of the house.

And now, some days of bitter grief having elapsed, an observable change came over the features of the mental disorder of my friend. His ordinary manner had vanished. His ordinary occupations were neglected or forgotten. He roamed from chamber to chamber with hurried, unequal, and objectless step. The pallor of his countenance had assumed, if possible, a more ghastly hue — but the luminousness of his eye had utterly gone out. The once occasional huskiness of his tone was heard no more; and a tremulous quaver, as if of extreme terror, habitually characterized his utterance. There were times, indeed, when I thought his unceasingly agitated mind was laboring with some oppressive secret, to divulge which he struggled for the necessary courage. At times, again, I was obliged to resolve all into the mere inexplicable vagaries of madness, for I beheld him gazing upon vacancy for long hours, in an attitude of the profoundest attention, as if listening to some imaginary sound. It was no wonder that his condition terrified — that it infected me. I felt creeping upon me, by slow yet certain degrees, the wild influences of his own fantastic yet impressive superstitions.

It was, especially, upon retiring to bed late in the night of the seventh or eighth day after the placing of the lady Madeline within the donjon, that I experienced the full power of such feelings. Sleep came not near my couch, while the hours waned and waned away. I struggled to reason off the nervousness which had dominion over me. I endeavored to believe that much, if not all of what I felt, was due to the bewildering influence of the gloomy furniture of the room — of the dark and tattered draperies, which, tortured into motion by the breath of a rising tempest, swayed fitfully to and fro upon the walls, and rustled uneasily about the decorations of the bed. But my efforts were fruitless. An irrepressible tremor gradually pervaded my frame; and, at length, there sat upon my very heart an incubus[13] of utterly causeless alarm. Shaking this off with a gasp and a struggle, I uplifted myself upon the pillows, and, peering earnestly within the intense darkness of the chamber, hearkened — I know not why, except that an instinctive spirit prompted me — to certain low and indefinite sounds which came, through the pauses of the storm, at long intervals I knew not whence. Overpowered by an intense sentiment of horror, unaccountable yet unendurable, I threw on my clothes with haste (for I felt that I should sleep no more during the night), and endeavored to arouse myself from the pitiable condition into which I had fallen, by pacing rapidly to and fro through the apartment.

I had taken but few turns in this manner, when a light step on an adjoining staircase arrested my attention. I presently recognized it as that of Usher. In an instant afterward he rapped, with a gentle touch, at my door, and entered, bearing a lamp. His countenance was, as usual, cadaverously wan — but, moreover, there was a species of mad hilarity in his eyes — an evidently restrained *hysteria* in his whole demeanor. His air appalled me — but anything was preferable to the solitude which I had so long endured, and I even welcomed his presence as a relief.

'And you have not seen it?' he said abruptly, after having stared about him for some moments in silence — 'you have not then seen it? — but, stay! you shall.' Thus speaking, and having carefully shaded his lamp, he hurried to one of the casements and threw it freely open to the storm.

The impetuous fury of the entering gust nearly lifted us from our feet. It was, indeed, a tempestuous yet sternly beautiful night, and one wildly singular in its terror and its beauty. A whirlwind had apparently collected its force in our vicinity; for there were frequent and violent alterations in the direction of the wind; and the exceeding density of the clouds (which hung so low as to press upon the turrets of the house) did not prevent our perceiving the life-like velocity with which they flew careering from all points against each other, without passing away into the distance. I say that even their exceeding density did not prevent our perceiving this; yet we had no glimpse of the moon or stars, nor was there any flashing forth of the lightning. But the under surfaces of the

13. Incubus: Someone like an evil spirit or something that oppresses nightmarishly.

huge masses of agitated vapor, as well as all terrestrial objects immediately around us, were glowing in the unnatural light of a faintly luminous and distinctly visible gaseous exhalation which hung about and enshrouded the mansion.

'You must not — you shall not behold this!' said I, shudderingly, to Usher, as I led him, with a gentle violence, from the window to a seat. 'These appearances, which bewilder you, are merely electrical phenomena not uncommon — or it may be that they have their ghastly origin in the rank miasma of the tarn. Let us close this casement; the air is chilling and dangerous to your frame. Here is one of your favorite romances. I will read, and you shall listen; — and so we will pass away this terrible night together.'

The antique volume which I had taken up was the *Mad Trist* of Sir Launcelot Canning; but I had called it a favorite of Usher's more in sad jest than in earnest; for, in truth, there is little in its uncouth and unimaginative prolixity which could have had interest for the lofty and spiritual ideality of my friend. It was, however, the only book immediately at hand; and I indulged a vague hope that the excitement which now agitated the hypochondriac might find relief (for the history of mental disorder is full of similar anomalies) even in the extremeness of the folly which I should read. Could I have judged, indeed, by the wild overstrained air of vivacity with which he hearkened, or apparently hearkened, to the words of the tale, I might well have congratulated myself upon the success of my design.

I had arrived at that well-known portion of the story where Ethelred, the hero of the *Trist,* having sought in vain for peaceable admission into the dwelling of the hermit, proceeds to make good an entrance by force. Here, it will be remembered, the words of the narrative run thus:

> And Ethelred, who was by nature of a doughty heart, and who was now mighty withal, on account of the powerfulness of the wine which he had drunken, waited no longer to hold parley with the hermit, who, in sooth, was of an obstinate and maliceful turn, but, feeling the rain upon his shoulders, and fearing the rising of the tempest, uplifted his mace outright, and, with blows, made quickly room in the plankings of the door for his gauntleted hand; and now pulling therewith sturdily, he so cracked, and ripped, and tore all asunder, that the noise of the dry and hollow-sounding wood alarumed and reverberated throughout the forest.

At the termination of this sentence I started, and for a moment, paused; for it appeared to me (although I at once concluded that my excited fancy had deceived me) — it appeared to me that, from some very remote portion of the mansion, there came, indistinctly, to my ears, what might have been, in its exact similarity of character, the echo (but a stifled and dull one certainly) of the very cracking and ripping sound which Sir Launcelot had so particularly described. It was, beyond doubt, the coincidence alone which had arrested my attention; for, amid the rattling of the sashes of the casements, and the ordinary commingled noises of the still increasing storm, the sound, in itself, had nothing, surely, which should have interested or disturbed me. I continued the story:

> But the good champion Ethelred, now entering within the door, was sore enraged and amazed to perceive no signal of the maliceful hermit; but, in the stead thereof, a dragon of a scaly and prodigious demeanor, and of a

fiery tongue, which sate in guard before a palace of gold, with a floor of silver; and upon the wall there hung a shield of shining brass with this legend enwritten —

> *Who entereth herein, a conqueror hath bin;*
> *Who slayeth the dragon, the shield he shall win;*

And Ethelred uplifted his mace, and struck upon the head of the dragon, which fell before him, and gave up his pesty breath, with a shriek so horrid and harsh, and withal so piercing, that Ethelred had fain to close his ears with his hands against the dreadful noise of it, the like whereof was never before heard.

Here again I paused abruptly, and now with a feeling of wild amazement — for there could be no doubt whatever that, in this instance, I did actually hear (although from what direction it proceeded I found it impossible to say) a low and apparently distant, but harsh, protracted, and most unusual screaming or grating sound — the exact counterpart of what my fancy had already conjured up for the dragon's unnatural shriek as described by the romancer.

Oppressed, as I certainly was, upon the occurrence of the second and most extraordinary coincidence, by a thousand conflicting sensations, in which wonder and extreme terror were predominant, I still retained sufficient presence of mind to avoid exciting, by any observation, the sensitive nervousness of my companion. I was by no means certain that he had noticed the sounds in question; although, assuredly, a strange alteration had, during the last few minutes, taken place in his demeanor. From a position fronting my own, he had gradually brought round his chair, so as to sit with his face to the door of the chamber; and thus I could but partially perceive his features, although I saw that his lips trembled as if he were murmuring inaudibly. His head had dropped upon his breast — yet I knew that he was not asleep, from the wide and rigid opening of the eye as I caught a glance of it in profile. The motion of his body, too, was at variance with this idea — for he rocked from side to side with a gentle yet constant and uniform sway. Having rapidly taken notice of all this, I resumed the narrative of Sir Launcelot, which thus proceeded:

> And now, the champion, having escaped from the terrible fury of the dragon, bethinking himself of the brazen shield, and of the breaking up of the enchantment which was upon it, removed the carcass from out of the way before him, and approached valorously over the silver pavement of the castle to where the shield was upon the wall; which in sooth tarried not for his full coming, but fell down at his feet upon the silver floor, with a mighty great and terrible ringing sound.

No sooner had these syllables passed my lips, than — as if a shield of brass had indeed, at the moment, fallen heavily upon a floor of silver — I became aware of a distinct, hollow, metallic and clangorous yet apparently muffled reverberation. Completely unnerved, I leaped to my feet; but the measured rocking movement of Usher was undisturbed. I rushed to the chair in which he sat. His eyes were bent fixedly before him, and throughout his whole countenance there reigned a stony rigidity. But as I placed my hand upon his shoulder, there came a strong shudder over his whole person; a sickly smile quivered about his lips; and I saw that he spoke in a low, hurried, and gibbering murmur, as if unconscious of my presence. Bending closely over him, I at length drank in the hideous import of his words.

'Not hear it? — yes, I hear it, and *have* heard it. Long — long — long — many minutes, many hours, many days, have I heard it — yet I dared not — oh, pity me, miserable wretch that I am! — I dared not — I *dared* not speak! *We have put her living in the tomb!* Said I not that my senses were acute? I *now* tell you that I heard her first feeble movements in the hollow coffin. I heard them — many, many days ago — yet I dared not — *I dared not speak!* And now — to-night — Ethelred — ha! ha! — the breaking of the hermit's door, and the death-cry of the dragon, and the clangor of the shield! — say, rather, the rending of her coffin, and the grating of the iron hinges of her prison, and her struggles within the coppered archway of the vault! Oh whither shall I fly? Will she not be here anon? Is she not hurrying to upbraid me for my haste? Have I not heard her footstep on the stair? Do I not distinguish that heavy and horrible beating of her heart? MADMAN!' here he sprang furiously to his feet, and shrieked out his syllables, as if in the effort he were giving up his soul — *'Madman! I tell you that she now stands without the door!'*

As if in the superhuman energy of his utterance there had been found the potency of a spell. the huge antique panels to which the speaker pointed, threw slowly back, upon the instant, their ponderous and ebony jaws. It was the work of the rushing gust — but then without those doors there DID stand the lofty and enshrouded figure of the lady Madeline of Usher. There was blood upon her white robes, and the evidence of some bitter struggle upon every portion of her emaciated frame. For a moment she remained trembling and reeling to and fro upon the threshold — then, with a low moaning cry, fell heavily inward upon the person of her brother, and in her violent and now final death-agonies, bore him to the floor a corpse, and a victim to the terrors he had anticipated.

From that chamber, and from that mansion, I fled aghast. The storm was still abroad in all its wrath as I found myself crossing the old causeway. Suddenly there shot along the path a wild light, and I turned to see whence a gleam so unusual could have issued; for the vast house and its shadows were alone behind me. The radiance was that of the full, setting, and blood-red moon which now shone vividly through that once barely-discernible fissure of which I have before spoken as extending from the roof of the building, in a zigzag direction, to the base. While I gazed, this fissure rapidly widened — there came a fierce breath of the whirlwind — the entire orb of the satellite burst at once upon my sight — my brain reeled as I saw the mighty walls rushing asunder — there was a long tumultuous shouting sound like the voice of a thousand waters — and the deep and dank tarn at my feet closed sullenly and silently over the fragments of the HOUSE OF USHER.

Philip Roth (1933–   )

Defender of The Faith

In May of 1945, only a few weeks after the fighting had ended in Europe, I was rotated back to the States, where I spent the remainder of the war with a training company at Camp Crowder, Missouri. Along with the rest of the Ninth Army, I had been racing across Germany so swiftly during the late winter and spring that when I boarded the plane, I couldn't believe its destination lay to the west. My mind might inform me otherwise, but there was an inertia of the spirit that told me we were flying to a new front, where we would disembark and continue our push eastward — eastward until we'd circled the globe, marching through villages along whose twisting, cobbled streets crowds of the enemy would watch us take possession of what, up till then, they'd considered their own. I had changed enough in two years not to mind the trembling of the old people, the crying of the very young, the uncertainty and fear in the eyes of the once arrogant. I had been fortunate enough to develop an infantryman's heart, which, like his feet, at first aches and swells but finally grows horny enough for him to travel the weirdest paths without feeling a thing.

Captain Paul Barrett was my C.O. in Camp Crowder. The day I reported for duty, he came out of his office to shake my hand. He was short, gruff, and fiery, and — indoors or out — he wore his polished helmet liner pulled down to his little eyes. In Europe, he had received a battlefield commission and a serious chest wound, and he'd been returned to the States only a few months before. He spoke easily to me, and at the evening formation he introduced me to the troops. "Gentlemen," he said, "Sergeant Thurston, as you know, is no longer with this company. Your new first sergeant is Sergeant Nathan Marx, here. He is a veteran of the European theater, and consequently will expect to find a company of soldiers here, and not a company of *boys*."

I sat up late in the orderly room that evening, trying halfheartedly to solve the riddle of duty rosters, personnel forms, and morning reports. The Charge of Quarters slept with his mouth open on a mattress on the floor. A trainee stood reading the next day's duty roster, which was posted on the bulletin board just inside the screen door. It was a warm evening, and I could hear radios playing dance music over in the barracks. The trainee, who had been staring at me whenever he thought I wouldn't notice, finally took a step in my direction.

"Hey Sarge — we having a G.I. party tomorrow night?" he asked. A G.I. party is a barracks cleaning.

"You usually have them on Friday nights?" I asked him.

"Yes," he said, and then he added, mysteriously, "that's the whole thing."

"Then you'll have a G.I. party."

He turned away, and I heard him mumbling. His shoulders were moving, and I wondered if he was crying.

"What's your name, soldier?" I asked.

He turned, not crying at all. Instead, his green-speckled eyes, long and narrow, flashed like fish in the sun. He walked over to me and sat on the edge of my desk. He reached out a hand. "Sheldon," he said.

"Stand on your feet, Sheldon."

Getting off the desk, he said, "Sheldon Grossbart." He smiled at the familiarity into which he'd led me.

"You against cleaning the barracks Friday night, Grossbart?" I said. "Maybe we shouldn't have G.I. parties. Maybe we should get a maid." My tone startled me. I felt I sounded like every top sergeant I had ever known.

"No, Sergeant." He grew serious, but with a seriousness that seemed to be only the stifling of a smile. "It's just — G.I. parties on Friday night, of all nights."

He slipped up onto the corner of the desk again — not quite sitting, but not quite standing, either. He looked at me with those speckled eyes flashing, and then made a gesture with his hand. It was very slight — no more than a movement back and forth of the wrist — and yet it managed to exclude from our affairs everything else in the orderly room, to make the two of us the center of the world. It seemed, in fact, to exclude everything even about the two of us except our hearts.

"Sergeant Thurston was one thing," he whispered, glancing at the sleeping C.Q., "but we thought that with you here things might be a little different."

"We?"

"The Jewish personnel."

"Why?" I asked, harshly. "What's on your mind?" Whether I was still angry at the "Sheldon" business, or now at something else, I hadn't time to tell, but clearly I was angry.

"We thought you — Marx, you know, like Karl Marx. The Marx Brothers. Those guys are all — M-a-r-x. Isn't that how *you* spell it, Sergeant?"

"M-a-r-x."

"Fishbein said — " He stopped. "What I mean to say, Sergeant — " His face and neck were red, and his mouth moved but no words came out. In a moment, he raised himself to attention, gazing down at me. It was as though he had suddenly decided he could expect no more sympathy from me than from Thurston, the reason being that I was of Thurston's faith, and not his. The young man had managed to confuse himself as to what my faith really was, but I felt no desire to straighten him out. Very simply, I didn't like him.

When I did nothing but return his gaze, he spoke, in an altered tone. "You see, Sergeant," he explained to me, "Friday nights, Jews are supposed to go to services."

"Did Sergeant Thurston tell you you couldn't go to them when there was a G.I. party?"

"No."

"Did he say you had to stay and scrub the floors?"

"No, Sergeant."

"Did the Captain say you had to stay and scrub the floors?"

"That isn't it, Sergeant. It's the other guys in the barracks." He leaned toward me. "They think we're goofing off. But we're not. That's when Jews go to services, Friday night. We have to."

"Then go."

"But the other guys make accusations. They have no right."

"That's not the Army's problem, Grossbart. It's a personal problem you'll have to work out yourself."

"But it's un*fair*."

I got up to leave. "There's nothing I can do about it," I said.

Grossbart stiffened and stood in front of me. "But this is a matter of *religion,* sir."

"Sergeant," I said.

"I mean 'Sergeant,' " he said, almost snarling.

"Look, go see the chaplain. You want to see Captain Barrett, I'll arrange an appointment."

"No, no. I don't want to make trouble, Sergeant. That's the first thing they throw up to you. I just want my rights!"

"Damn it, Grossbart, stop whining. You have your rights. You can stay and scrub floors or you can go to shul — "

The smile swam in again. Spittle gleamed at the corners of his mouth. "You mean church, Sergeant."

"I mean shul, Grossbart!"

I walked past him and went outside. Near me, I heard the scrunching of a guard's boots on gravel. Beyond the lighted windows of the barracks, young men in T shirts and fatigue pants were sitting on their bunks, polishing their rifles. Suddenly there was a light rustling behind me. I turned and saw Grossbart's dark frame fleeing back to the barracks, racing to tell his Jewish friends that they were right — that, like Karl and Harpo, I was one of them.

The next morning, while chatting with Captain Barrett, I recounted the incident of the previous evening. Somehow, in the telling, it must have seemed to the Captain that I was not so much explaining Grossbart's position as defending it. "Marx, I'd fight side by side with a nigger if the fella proved to me he was a man. I pride myself," he said, looking out the window, "that I've got an open mind. Consequently, Sergeant, nobody gets special treatment here, for the good *or* the bad. All a man's got to do is prove himself. A man fires well on the range, I give him a weekend pass. He scores high in P.T., he gets a weekend pass. He *earns* it." He turned from the window and pointed a finger at me. "You're a Jewish fella, am I right, Marx?"

"Yes, sir."

"And I admire you. I admire you because of the ribbons on your chest. I judge a man by what he shows me on the field of battle, Sergeant. It's what he's got *here*," he said, and then, though I expected he would point to his heart, he jerked a thumb toward the buttons straining to hold his blouse across his belly. "Guts," he said.

"O.K., sir. I only wanted to pass on to you how the men felt."

"Mr. Marx, you're going to be old before your time if you worry about how the men feel. Leave that stuff to the chaplain — that's his business, not yours. Let's us train these fellas to shoot straight. If the Jewish personnel feels the other men are accusing them of goldbricking — well, I just don't know. Seems awful funny that suddenly the Lord is calling so loud in Private Grossman's ear he's just got to run to church."

"Synagogue," I said.

"Synagogue is right, Sergeant. I'll write that down for handy reference. Thank you for stopping by."

That evening, a few minutes before the company gathered outside the orderly room for the chow formation, I called the C.Q., Corporal Robert LaHill, in to see me. LaHill was a dark, burly fellow whose hair curled out of his clothes wherever it could. He had a glaze in his eyes that made one think of caves and dinosaurs. "LaHill," I said, "when you take the formation, remind the men that they're free to attend church services *whenever* they are held, provided they report to the orderly room before they leave the area."

LaHill scratched his wrist, but gave no indication that he'd heard or understood.

"LaHill," I said, "*church.* You remember? Church, priest, Mass, confession."

He curled one lip into a kind of smile; I took it for a signal that for a second he had flickered back up into the human race.

"Jewish personnel who want to attend services this evening are to fall out in front of the orderly room at 1900," I said. Then, as an afterthought, I added, "By order of Captain Barrett."

A little while later, as the day's last light — softer than any I had seen that year — began to drop over Camp Crowder, I heard LaHill's thick, inflectionless voice outside my window: "Give me your ears, troopers. Toppie says for me to tell you that at 1900 hours all Jewish personnel is to fall out in front, here, if they want to attend the Jewish Mass."

At seven o'clock, I looked out the orderly-room window and saw three soldiers in starched khakis standing on the dusty quadrangle. They looked at their watches and fidgeted while they whispered back and forth. It was getting dimmer, and, alone on the otherwise deserted field, they looked tiny. When I opened the door, I heard the noises of the G.I. party coming from the surrounding barracks — bunks being pushed to the walls, faucets pounding water into buckets, brooms whisking at the wooden floors, cleaning the dirt away for Saturday's inspection. Big puffs of cloth moved round and round on the windowpanes. I walked outside, and the moment my foot hit the ground I thought I heard Grossbart call to the others, " 'Ten-*hut!*" Or maybe, when they all three jumped to attention, I imagined I heard the command.

Grossbart stepped forward. "Thank you, sir," he said.

" 'Sergeant,' Grossbart," I reminded him. "You call officers 'sir.' I'm not an officer. You've been in the Army three weeks — you know that."

He turned his palms out at his sides to indicate that, in truth, he and I lived beyond convention. "Thank you, anyway," he said.

"Yes," a tall boy behind him said. "Thanks a lot."

And the third boy whispered, "Thank you," but his mouth barely fluttered, so that he did not alter by more than a lip's movement his posture of attention.

"For what?" I asked.

Grossbart snorted happily. "For the announcement. The Corporal's announcement. It helped. It made it — "

"Fancier." The tall boy finished Grossbart's sentence.

Grossbart smiled. "He means formal, sir. Public," he said to me. "Now it won't seem as though we're just taking off — goldbricking because the work has begun."

"It was by order of Captain Barrett," I said.

"Aaah, but you pull a little weight," Grossbart said. "So we thank you." Then he turned to his companions. "Sergeant Marx, I want you to meet Larry Fishbein."

The tall boy stepped forward and extended his hand. I shook it. "You from New York?" he asked.

"Yes."

"Me, too." He had a cadaverous face that collapsed inward from his cheekbone to his jaw, and when he smiled — as he did at the news of our communal attachment — revealed a mouthful of bad teeth. He was blinking his eyes a good deal, as though he were fighting back tears. "What borough?" he asked.

I turned to Grossbart. "It's five after seven. What time are services?"

"Shul," he said, smiling, "is in ten minutes. I want you to meet Mickey Halpern. This is Nathan Marx, our sergeant."

The third boy hopped forward. "Private Michael Halpern." He saluted.

"Salute officers, Halpern," I said. The boy dropped his hand, and, on its way down, in his nervousness, checked to see if his shirt pockets were buttoned.

"Shall I march them over, sir?" Grossbart asked. "Or are you coming along?"

From behind Grossbart, Fishbein piped up. "Afterward, they're having refreshments. A ladies' auxiliary from St. Louis, the rabbi told us last week."

"The chaplain," Halpern whispered.

"You're welcome to come along," Grossbart said.

To avoid his plea, I looked away, and saw, in the windows of the barracks, a cloud of faces staring out at the four of us. "Hurry along, Grossbart," I said.

"O.K., then," he said. He turned to the others. "Double time, *march!*"

They started off, but ten feet away Grossbart spun around and, running backward, called to me, "Good *shabbus,* sir!" And then the three of them were swallowed into the alien Missouri dusk.

Even after they had disappeared over the parade ground, whose green was now a deep blue, I could hear Grossbart singing the double-time cadence, and as it grew dimmer and dimmer, it suddenly touched a deep memory — as did the slant of the light — and I was remembering the shrill sounds of a Bronx playground where, years ago, beside the Grand Concourse, I had played on long spring evenings such as this. It was a pleasant memory for a young man so far from peace and home, and it brought so many recollections with it that I began to grow exceedingly tender about myself. In fact, I indulged myself in a reverie so strong that I felt as though a hand were reaching down inside me. It had to reach so very far to touch me! It had to reach past those days in the forests of Belgium, and past the dying I'd refused to weep over; past the nights in German farmhouses whose books we'd burned to warm us; past endless stretches when I had shut off all softness I might feel for my fellows, and had managed even to deny myself the posture of a conqueror — the swagger that I, as a Jew, might well have worn as my boots whacked against the rubble of Wesel, Münster, and Braunschweig.

But now one night noise, one rumor of home and time past, and memory plunged down through all I had anesthetized, and came to what I suddenly remembered was myself. So it was not altogether curious that, in search of more of me, I found myself following Grossbart's tracks to Chapel No. 3, where the Jewish services were being held.

I took a seat in the last row, which was empty. Two rows in front of me sat Grossbart, Fishbein, and Halpern, holding little white Dixie cups. Each row of seats was raised higher than the one in front of it, and I could see clearly what was going on. Fishbein was pouring the contents of his cup into Grossbart's, and Grossbart looked mirthful as the liquid made a purple arc between Fishbein's hand and his. In the glaring yellow light, I saw the chaplain standing on the platform at the front; he was chanting the first line of the responsive reading. Grossbart's prayer book remained closed on his lap; he was swishing the cup around. Only Halpern responded to the chant by praying. The fingers of his right hand were spread wide across the cover of his open book. His cap was pulled down low onto his brow, which made it round, like a yarmulke. From time to time, Grossbart wet his lips at the cup's edge; Fishbein, his long yellow face a dying light bulb, looked from here to there, craning forward to catch sight of the faces down the row, then of those in front of him, then behind. He saw me, and his eyelids beat a tattoo. His elbow slid into Grossbart's side, his neck inclined toward his friend, he whispered something, and then, when the congregation next responded to the chant, Grossbart's voice was among the others. Fishbein looked into his book now, too; his lips, however, didn't move.

Finally, it was time to drink the wine. The chaplain smiled down at them as Grossbart swigged his in one long gulp, Halpern sipped, meditating, and Fishbein faked devotion with an empty cup. "As I look down amongst the congregation" — the chaplain grinned at the word — "this night, I see many new faces, and I want to welcome you to Friday-night services here at Camp Crowder. I am Major Leo Ben Ezra, your chaplain." Though an American, the chaplain spoke deliberately — syllable by syllable, almost — as though to communicate, above all, with the lip readers in his audience. "I have only a few words to say before we adjourn to the refreshment room, where the kind ladies of the Temple Sinai, St. Louis, Missouri, have a nice setting for you."

Applause and whistling broke out. After another momentary grin, the chaplain raised his hands, palms out, his eyes flicking upward a moment, as if to remind the troops where they were and Who Else might be in attendance. In the sudden silence that followed, I thought I heard Grossbart cackle, "Let the goyim clean the floors!" Were those the words? I wasn't sure, but Fishbein, grinning, nudged Halpern. Halpern looked dumbly at him, then went back to his prayer book, which had been occupying him all through the rabbi's talk. One hand tugged at the black kinky hair that stuck out under his cap. His lips moved.

The rabbi continued. "It is about the food that I want to speak to you for a moment. I know, I know, I know," he intoned, wearily, "how in the mouths of most of you the *trafe* food tastes like ashes. I know how you gag, some of you, and how your parents suffer to think of their children eating foods unclean and offensive to the palate. What can I tell you? I can only say, close your eyes and swallow as best you can. Eat what you must to live, and throw away the rest. I wish I could help more. For those of you who find this impossible, may I ask that you try and try, but then come to see me in private. If your revulsion is so great, we will have to seek aid from those higher up."

A round of chatter rose and subsided. Then everyone sang "Ain Kelohainu"; after all those years, I discovered I still knew the words. Then, suddenly, the service over, Grossbart was upon me. "Higher up? He means the General?"

"Hey, Shelly," Fishbein said, "he means God." He smacked his face and looked at Halpern. "How high can you go!"

"Sh-h-h!" Grossbart said. "What do you think, Sergeant?"

"I don't know," I said. "You better ask the chaplain."

"I'm going to. I'm making an appointment to see him in private. So is Mickey."

Halpern shook his head. "No, no, Sheldon — "

"You have rights, Mickey," Grossbart said. "They can't push us around."

"It's O.K.," said Halpern. "It bothers my mother, not me."

Grossbart looked at me. "Yesterday he threw up. From the hash. It was all ham and God knows what else."

"I have a cold — that was why," Halpern said. He pushed his yarmulke back into a cap.

"What about you, Fishbein?" I asked. "You kosher, too?"

He flushed. "A little. But I'll let it ride. I have a very strong stomach, and I don't eat a lot anyway." I continued to look at him, and he held up his wrist to reinforce what he'd just said; his watch strap was tightened to the last hole, and he pointed that out to me.

"But services are important to you?" I asked him.

He looked at Grossbart. "Sure, sir."

"'Sergeant.'"

"Not so much at home," said Grossbart, stepping between us, "but away from home it gives one a sense of his Jewishness."

"We have to stick together," Fishbein said.

I started to walk toward the door; Halpern stepped back to make way for me.

"That's what happened in Germany," Grossbart was saying, loud enough for me to hear. "They didn't stick together. They let themselves get pushed around."

I turned. "Look, Grossbart. This is the Army, not summer camp."

He smiled. "So?"

Halpern tried to sneak off, but Grossbart held his arm.

"Grossbart, how old are you?" I asked.

"Nineteen."

"And you?" I said to Fishbein.

"The same. The same month, even."

"And what about him?" I pointed to Halpern, who had by now made it safely to the door.

"Eighteen," Grossbart whispered. "But like he can't tie his shoes or brush his teeth himself. I feel sorry for him."

"I feel sorry for all of us, Grossbart," I said, "but just act like a man. Just don't overdo it."

"Overdo what, sir?"

"The 'sir' business, for one thing. Don't overdo that," I said.

I left him standing there. I passed by Halpern, but he did not look at me. Then I was outside, but, behind, I heard Grossbart call, "Hey, Mickey, my *leben*, come on back. Refreshments!"

"*Leben!*" My grandmother's word for me!

One morning a week later, while I was working at my desk, Captain Barrett shouted for me to come into his office. When I entered, he had his helmet liner squashed down so far on his head that I couldn't even see his eyes. He was on the phone, and when he spoke to me, he cupped one hand over the mouthpiece. "Who the hell is Grossbart?"

"Third platoon, Captain," I said. "A trainee."

"What's all this stink about food? His mother called a goddam congressman about the food." He uncovered the mouthpiece and slid his helmet up until I could see his bottom eyelashes. "Yes, sir," he said into the phone. "Yes, sir. I'm still here, sir. I'm asking Marx, here, right now — "

He covered the mouthpiece again and turned his head back toward me. "Lightfoot Harry's on the phone," he said, between his teeth. "This congressman calls General Lyman, who calls Colonel Sousa, who calls the Major, who calls me. They're just dying to stick this thing on me. Whatsa matter?" He shook the phone at me. "I don't feed the troops? What the hell is this?"

"Sir, Grossbart is strange — " Barrett greeted that with a mockingly indulgent smile. I altered my approach. "Captain, he's a very orthodox Jew, and so he's only allowed to eat certain foods."

"He throws up, the congressman said. Every time he eats something, his mother says, he throws up!"

"He's accustomed to observing the dietary laws, Captain."

"So why's his old lady have to call the White House?"

"Jewish parents, sir — they're apt to be more protective than you expect. I mean, Jews have a very close family life. A boy goes away from home, sometimes the mother is liable to get very upset. Probably the boy mentioned something in a letter, and his mother misinterpreted."

"I'd like to punch him one right in the mouth," the Captain said. "There's a goddam war on, and he wants a silver platter!"

"I don't think the boy's to blame, sir. I'm sure we can straighten it out by just asking him. Jewish parents worry — "

"*All* parents worry, for Christ's sake. But they don't get on their high horse and start pulling strings — "

I interrupted, my voice higher, tighter than before. "The home life, Captain, is very important — but you're right, it may sometimes get out of hand. It's a very wonderful thing, Captain, but because it's so close, this kind of thing . . ."

He didn't listen any longer to my attempt to present both myself and Lightfoot Harry with an explanation for the letter. He turned back to the phone. "Sir?" he said. "Sir — Marx, here, tells me Jews have a tendency to be pushy. He says he thinks we can settle it right here in the company. . . . Yes, sir. . . . I *will* call back, sir, soon as I can." He hung up. "Where are the men, Sergeant?"

"On the range."

With a whack on the top of his helmet, he crushed it down over his eyes again, and charged out of his chair. "We're going for a ride," he said.

The Captain drove, and I sat beside him. It was a hot spring day, and under my newly starched fatigues I felt as though my armpits were melting down onto my sides and chest. The roads were dry, and by the time we reached the firing range, my teeth felt gritty with dust, though my mouth had been shut the whole trip. The Captain slammed the brakes on and told me to get the hell out and find Grossbart.

I found him on his belly, firing wildly at the five-hundred-feet target. Waiting their turns behind him were Halpern and Fishbein. Fishbein, wearing a pair of steel-rimmed G.I. glasses I hadn't seen on him before, had the appearance of an old peddler who would gladly have sold you his rifle and the cartridges that were slung all over him. I stood back by the ammo boxes, waiting for Grossbart to finish spraying the distant targets. Fishbein straggled back to stand near me.

"Hello, Sergeant Marx," he said.

"How are you?" I mumbled.

"Fine, thank you. Sheldon's really a good shot."

"I didn't notice."

"I'm not so good, but I think I'm getting the hang of it now. Sergeant, I don't mean to, you know, ask what I shouldn't — " The boy stopped. He was trying to speak intimately, but the noise of the shooting forced him to shout at me.

"What is it?" I asked. Down the range, I saw Captain Barrett standing up in the jeep, scanning the line for me and Grossbart.

"My parents keep asking and asking where we're going," Fishbein said. "Everybody says the Pacific. I don't care, but my parents — If I could relieve their minds, I think I could concentrate more on my shooting."

"I don't know where, Fishbein. Try to concentrate anyway."

"Sheldon says you might be able to find out."

"I don't know a thing, Fishbein. You just take it easy, and don't let Sheldon — "

"*I'm* taking it easy, Sergeant. It's at home — "

Grossbart had finished on the line, and was dusting his fatigues with one hand. I called to him. "Grossbart, the Captain wants to see you."

He came toward us. His eyes blazed and twinkled. "Hi!"

"Don't point that goddam rifle!" I said.

"I wouldn't shoot you, Sarge." He gave me a smile as wide as a pumpkin, and turned the barrel aside.

"Damn you, Grossbart, this is no joke! Follow me."

I walked ahead of him, and had the awful suspicion that, behind me, Grossbart was *marching*, his rifle on his shoulder, as though he were a one-man detachment. At the jeep, he gave the Captain a rifle salute. "Private Sheldon Grossbart, sir."

"At ease, Grossman." The Captain sat down, slid over into the empty seat, and, crooking a finger, invited Grossbart closer.

"Bart, sir. Sheldon Gross*bart*. It's a common error." Grossbart nodded at me; *I* understood, he indicated. I looked away just as the mess truck pulled up to the range, disgorging a half-dozen K.P.s with rolled-up sleeves. The mess sergeant screamed at them while they set up the chow-line equipment.

"Grossbart, your mama wrote some congressman that we don't feed you right. Do you know that?" the Captain said.

"It was my father, sir. He wrote to Representative Franconi that my religion forbids me to eat certain foods."

"What religion is that, Grossbart?"

"Jewish."

" 'Jewish, *sir*,' " I said to Grossbart.

"Excuse me, sir. Jewish, sir."

"What have you been living on?" the Captain asked. "You've been in the Army a month already. You don't look to me like you're falling to pieces."

"I eat because I have to, sir. But Sergeant Marx will testify to the fact that I don't eat one mouthful more than I need to in order to survive."

"Is that so, Marx?" Barrett asked.

"I've never seen Grossbart eat, sir," I said.

"But you heard the rabbi," Grossbart said. "He told us what to do, and I listened."

The Captain looked at me. "Well, Marx?"

"I still don't know what he eats and doesn't eat, sir."

Grossbart raised his arms to plead with me, and it looked for a moment as though he were going to hand me his weapon to hold. "But, Sergeant — "

"Look, Grossbart, just answer the Captain's questions," I said sharply.

Barrett smiled at me, and I resented it. "All right, Grossbart," he said. "What is it you want? The little piece of paper? You want out?"

"No, sir. Only to be allowed to live as a Jew. And for the others, too."

"What others?"

"Fishbein, sir, and Halpern."

"They don't like the way we serve, either?"

"Halpern throws up, sir. I've seen it."

"I thought *you* throw up."

"Just once, sir. I didn't know the sausage was sausage."

"We'll give menus, Grossbart. We'll show training films about the food, so you can identify when we're trying to poison you."

Grossbart did not answer. The men had been organized into two long show lines. At the tail end of one, I spotted Fishbein — or, rather, his glasses spotted me. They winked sunlight back at me. Halpern stood next to him, patting the inside of his collar with a khaki handkerchief. They moved with the line as it began to edge up toward the food. The mess sergeant was still screaming at the K.P.s. For a moment, I was actually terrified by the thought that somehow the mess sergeant was going to become involved in Grossbart's problem.

"Marx," the Captain said, "you're a Jewish fella — am I right?"

I played straight man. "Yes, sir."

"How long you been in the Army? Tell this boy."

"Three years and two months."

"A year in combat, Grossbart. Twelve goddam months in combat all through Europe. I admire this man." The Captain snapped a wrist against his chest. "Do you hear him peeping about the food? Do you? I want an answer, Grossbart. Yes or no."

"No, sir."

"And why not? He's a Jewish fella."

"Some things are more important to some Jews than other things to other Jews."

Barrett blew up. "Look, Grossbart. Marx, here, is a good man — a goddam hero. When you were in high school, Sergeant Marx was killing Germans. Who does more for the Jews — you, by throwing up over a lousy piece of sausage, a piece of first-cut meat, or Marx, by killing those Nazi bastards? If I was a Jew, Grossbart, I'd kiss this man's feet. He's a goddam hero, and *he* eats what we give him. Why do you have to cause trouble is what I want to know! What is it you're buckin' for — a discharge?"

"No, sir."

"I'm talking to a wall! Sergeant, get him out of my way." Barrett swung himself back into the driver's seat. "I'm going to see the chaplain." The engine roared, the jeep spun around in a whirl of dust, and the Captain was headed back to camp.

For a moment, Grossbart and I stood side by side, watching the jeep. Then he looked at me and said, "I don't want to start trouble. That's the first thing they toss up to us."

When he spoke, I saw that his teeth were white and straight, and the sight of them suddenly made me understand that Grossbart actually did have parents — that once upon a time someone had taken little Sheldon to the dentist. He was their son. Despite all the talk about his parents, it was hard to believe in Grossbart as a child, an heir — as related by blood to anyone, mother, father, or, above all, to me. This realization led me to another.

"What does your father do, Grossbart?" I asked as we started to walk back toward the chow line.

"He's a tailor."

"An American?"

"Now, yes. A son in the Army," he said, jokingly.

"And your mother?" I asked.

He winked. "A *ballabusta*. She practically sleeps with a dustcloth in her hand."

"She's also an immigrant?"

"All she talks is Yiddish, still."

"And your father, too?"

"A little English. 'Clean,' 'Press,' 'Take the pants in.' That's the extent of it. But they're good to me."

"Then, Grossbart —" I reached out and stopped him. He turned toward me, and when our eyes met, his seemed to jump back, to shiver in their sockets. "Grossbart — you were the one who wrote that letter, weren't you?"

It took only a second or two for his eyes to flash happy again. "Yes." He walked on, and I kept pace. "It's what my father *would* have written if he had known how. It was his name, though. *He* signed it. He even mailed it. I sent it home. For the New York postmark."

I was astonished, and he saw it. With complete seriousness, he thrust his right arm in front of me. "Blood is blood, Sergeant," he said, pinching the blue vein in his wrist.

"What the hell *are* you trying to do, Grossbart?" I asked. "I've seen you eat. Do you know that? I told the Captain I don't know what you eat, but I've seen you eat like a hound at chow."

"We work hard, Sergeant. We're in training. For a furnace to work, you've got to feed it coal."

"Why did you say in the letter that you threw up all the time?"

"I was really talking about Mickey there. I was talking *for* him. He would never write, Sergeant, though I pleaded with him. He'll waste away to nothing if I don't help. Sergeant, I used my name — my father's name — but it's Mickey, and Fishbein, too, I'm watching out for."

"You're a regular Messiah, aren't you?"

We were at the chow line now.

"That's a good one, Sergeant," he said, smiling. "But who knows? Who can tell? Maybe you're the Messiah — a little bit. What Mickey says is the Messiah is a collective idea. He went to Yeshiva, Mickey, for a while. He says *together* we're the Messiah. Me a little bit, you a little bit. You should hear that kid talk, Sergeant, when he gets going."

"Me a little bit, you a little bit," I said. "You'd like to believe that, wouldn't you, Grossbart? That would make everything so clean for you."

"It doesn't seem too bad a thing to believe, Sergeant. It only means we should all *give* a little, is all."

I walked off to eat my rations with the other noncoms.

Two days later, a letter addressed to Captain Barrett passed over my desk. It had come through the chain of command — from the office of Congressman Franconi, where it had been received, to General Lyman, to Colonel Sousa, to Major Lamont, now to Captain Barrett. I read it over twice. It was dated May 14, the day Barrett had spoken with Grossbart on the rifle range.

Dear Congressman:

First let me thank you for your interest in behalf of my son, Private Sheldon Grossbart. Fortunately, I was able to speak with Sheldon on the phone the other night, and I think I've been able to solve our problem. He is, as I mentioned in my last letter, a very religious boy, and it was only with the greatest difficulty that I could persuade him that the religious thing to do — what God Himself would want Sheldon to do — would be to suffer the pangs of religious remorse for the good of his country and all mankind. It took some doing, Congressman, but finally he saw the light. In fact, what he said (and I wrote down the words on a scratch pad so as never to forget), what he said was "I guess you're right, Dad. So many millions of my fellow-Jews gave up their lives to the enemy, the least I can do is live for a while minus a bit of my heritage so as to help end this struggle and regain for all the children of God dignity and humanity." That, Congressman, would make any father proud.

By the way, Sheldon wanted me to know — and to pass on to you — the name of a soldier who helped him reach this decision. SERGEANT NATHAN MARX. Sergeant Marx is a combat veteran who is Sheldon's first sergeant. This man has helped Sheldon over some of the first hurdles he's had to face in the Army, and is in part responsible for Sheldon's changing his mind about the dietary laws. I know Sheldon would appreciate any recognition Marx could receive.

Thank you and good luck. I look forward to seeing your name on the next election ballot.

Respectfully,
Samuel E. Grossbart

Attached to the Grossbart communiqué was another, addressed to General Marshall Lyman, the post commander, and signed by Representative Charles E. Franconi, of the House of Representatives. The communiqué informed General Lyman that Sergeant Nathan Marx was a credit to the U.S. Army and the Jewish people.

What was Grossbart's motive in recanting? Did he feel he'd gone too far? Was the letter a strategic retreat — a crafty attempt to strengthen what he considered our alliance? Or had he actually changed his mind, via an imaginary dialogue between Grossbart père and Grossbart fils? I was puzzled, but only for a few days — that is, only until I realized that, whatever his reasons, he had actually decided to disappear from my life; he was going to allow himself to become just another trainee. I saw him at inspection, but he never winked; at chow formations, but he never flashed me a sign. On Sundays, with the other trainees, he would sit around watching the noncoms' softball team, for which I pitched, but not once did he speak an unnecessary word to me. Fishbein and Halpern retreated, too — at Grossbart's command, I was sure. Apparently he had seen that wisdom lay in turning back before he plunged over into the ugliness of privilege undeserved. Our separation allowed me to forgive him our past encounters, and, finally, to admire him for his good sense.

Meanwhile, free of Grossbart, I grew used to my job and my administrative tasks. I stepped on a scale one day, and discovered I had truly become a noncombatant; I had gained seven pounds. I found patience to get past the first three pages of a book. I thought about the future more and more, and wrote letters to girls I'd known before the war. I even got a few answers. I sent away to Columbia for a Law School catalogue. I continued to follow the war in the Pacific, but it was not my war. I thought I could see the end, and sometimes, at night, I dreamed that I was walking on the streets of Manhattan — Broadway, Third Avenue, 116th Street, where I had lived the three years I attended Columbia. I curled myself around these dreams and I began to be happy.

And then, one Saturday, when everybody was away and I was alone in the orderly room reading a month-old copy of the *Sporting News,* Grossbart reappeared.

"You a baseball fan, Sergeant?"

I looked up. "How are you?"

"Fine," Grossbart said. "They're making a soldier out of me."

"How are Fishbein and Halpern?"

"Coming along," he said. "We've got no training this afternoon. They're at the movies."

"How come you're not with them?"

"I wanted to come over and say hello."

He smiled — a shy, regular-guy smile, as though he and I well knew that our friendship drew its sustenance from unexpected vists, remembered birthdays, and borrowed lawnmowers. At first it offended me, and then the feeling was swallowed by the general uneasiness I felt at the thought that everyone on the post was locked away in a dark movie theater and I was here alone with Grossbart. I folded up my paper.

"Sergeant," he said, "I'd like to ask a favor. It is a favor, and I'm making no bones about it."

He stopped, allowing me to refuse him a hearing — which, of course, forced me into a courtesy I did not intend. "Go ahead."

"Well, actually it's two favors."

I said nothing.

"The first one's about these rumors. Everybody says we're going to the Pacific."

"As I told your friend Fishbein, I don't know," I said. "You'll just have to wait to find out. Like everybody else."

"You think there's a chance of any of us going East?"

"Germany?" I said. "Maybe."

"I meant New York."

"I don't think so, Grossbart. Offhand."

"Thanks for the information, Sergeant," he said.

"It's not information, Grossbart. Just what I surmise."

"It certainly would be good to be near home. My parents — you know." He took a step toward the door and then turned back. "Oh, the other thing. May I ask the other?"

"What is it?"

"The other thing is — I've got relatives in St. Louis, and they say they'll give me a whole Passover dinner if I can get down. God, Sergeant, that'd mean an awful lot to me."

I stood up. "No passes during basic, Grossbart."

"But we're off from now till Monday morning, Sergeant. I could leave the post and no one would even know."

"I'd know. You'd know."

"But that's all. Just the two of us. Last night, I called my aunt, and you should have heard her. 'Come — come,' she said. 'I got gefilte fish, *chrain* — the works!' Just a day, Sergeant. I'd take the blame if anything happened."

"The Captain isn't here to sign a pass."

"You could sign."

"Look, Grossbart — "

"Sergeant, for two months, practically, I've been eating *trafe* till I want to die."

"I thought you'd made up your mind to live with it. To be minus a little bit of heritage."

He pointed a finger at me. "You!" he said. "That wasn't for you to read."

"I read it. So what?"

"That letter was addressed to a congressman."

"Grossbart, don't feed me any baloney. You *wanted* me to read it."

"Why are you persecuting me, Sergeant?"

"Are you kidding!"

"I've run into this before," he said, "but never from my own!"

"Get out of here, Grossbart! Get the hell out of my sight!"

He did not move. "Ashamed, that's what you are," he said. "So you take it out on the rest of us. They say Hitler himself was half a Jew. Hearing you, I wouldn't doubt it."

"What are you trying to do with me, Grossbart?" I asked him. "What are you after? You want me to give you special privileges, to change the food, to find out about your orders, to give you weekend passes."

"You even talk like a goy!" Grossbart shook his fist. "Is this just a weekend pass I'm asking for? Is a Seder sacred, or not?"

Seder! It suddenly occurred to me that Passover had been celebrated weeks before. I said so.

"That's right," he replied. "Who says no? A month ago — and I was in the field eating hash! And now all I ask is a simple favor. A Jewish boy I thought would understand. My aunt's willing to go out of her way — to make a Seder a month later. . . ." He turned to go, mumbling.

"Come back here!" I called. He stopped and looked at me. "Grossbart, why can't you be like the rest? Why do you have to stick out like a sore thumb?"

"Because I'm a Jew, Sergeant. I *am* different. Better, maybe not. But different."

"This is a war, Grossbart. For the time being *be* the same."

"I refuse."

"What?"

"I refuse. I can't stop being me, that's all there is to it." Tears came to his eyes. "It's a hard thing to be a Jew. But now I understand what Mickey says — it's a harder thing to stay one." He raised a hand sadly toward me. "Look at *you*."

"Stop crying!"

"Stop this, stop that, stop the other thing! *You* stop, Sergeant. Stop closing your heart to your own!" And, wiping his face with his sleeve, he ran out the door. "The least we can do for one another — the least . . ."

An hour later, looking out of the window, I saw Grossbart headed across the field. He wore a pair of starched khakis and carried a little leather ditty bag. I went out into the heat of the day. It was quiet; not a soul was in sight except, over by the mess hall, four K.P.s sitting around a pan, sloped forward from their waists, gabbing and peeling potatoes in the sun.

"Grossbart!" I called.

He looked toward me and continued walking.

"Grossbart, get over here!"

He turned and came across the field. Finally, he stood before me.

"Where are you going?" I asked.

"St. Louis. I don't care."

"You'll get caught without a pass."

"So I'll get caught without a pass."

"You'll go to the stockade."

"I'm *in* the stockade." He made an about-face and headed off.

I let him go only a step or two. "Come back here," I said and he followed me into the office, where I typed out a pass and signed the Captain's name, and my own initials after it.

He took the pass and then, a moment later, reached out and grabbed my hand. "Sergeant, you don't know how much this means to me."

"O.K.," I said. "Don't get in any trouble."

"I wish I could show you how much this means to me."

"Don't do me any favors. Don't write any more congressmen for citations."

He smiled. "You're right. I won't. But let me do something."

"Bring me a piece of that gefilte fish. Just get out of here."

"I will!" he said. "With a slice of carrot and a little horseradish. I won't forget."

"All right. Just show your pass at the gate. And don't tell *anybody*."

"I won't. It's a month late, but a good Yom Tov to you."

"Good Yom Tov, Grossbart," I said.

"You're a good Jew, Sergeant. You like to think you have a hard heart, but underneath you're a fine, decent man. I mean that."

Those last three words touched me more than any words from Grossbart's mouth had the right to. "All right, Grossbart," I said. "Now call me 'sir,' and get the hell out of here."

He ran out the door and was gone. I felt very pleased with myself; it was a great relief to stop fighting Grossbart, and it had cost me nothing. Barrett would never find out, and if he did, I could manage to invent some excuse. For a while, I sat at my desk, comfortable in my decision. Then the screen door flew back and Grossbart burst in again. "Sergeant!" he said. Behind him I saw Fishbein and Halpern, both in starched khakis, both carrying ditty bags like Grossbart's.

"Sergeant, I caught Mickey and Larry coming out of the movies. I almost missed them."

"Grossbart — did I say to tell no one?" I said.

"But my aunt said I could bring friends. That I should, in fact."

"*I'm* the Sergeant, Grossbart — not your aunt!"

Grossbart looked at me in disbelief. He pulled Halpern up by his sleeve. "Mickey, tell the Sergeant what this would mean to you."

Halpern looked at me and, shrugging, said, "A lot."

Fishbein stepped forward without prompting. "This would mean a great deal to me and my parents, Sergeant Marx."

"No!" I shouted.

Grossbart was shaking his head. "Sergeant, I could see you denying me, but how can you deny Mickey, a Yeshiva boy — that's beyond me."

"I'm not denying Mickey anything," I said. "You just pushed a little too hard, Grossbart. *You* denied him."

"I'll give him my pass, then," Grossbart said. "I'll give him my aunt's address and a little note. At least let him go."

In a second, he had crammed the pass into Halpern's pants pockets. Halpern looked at me, and so did Fishbein. Grossbart was at the door, pushing it open. "Mickey, bring me a piece of gefilte fish, at least," he said, and then he was outside again.

The three of us looked at one another, and then I said, "Halpern, hand that pass over."

He took it from his pocket and gave it to me. Fishbein had now moved to the doorway, where he lingered. He stood there for a moment with his mouth slightly open, and then he pointed to himself. "And me?" he asked.

His utter ridiculousness exhausted me. I slumped down in my seat and felt pulses knocking at the back of my eyes. "Fishbein," I said, "you understand I'm not trying to deny you anything, don't you? If it was my Army, I'd serve gefilte fish in the mess hall. I'd sell *kugel* in the PX, honest to God."

Halpern smiled.

"You understand, don't you, Halpern?"

"Yes, Sergeant."

"And you, Fishbein? I don't want enemies. I'm just like you — I want to serve my time and go home. I miss the same things you miss."

"Then, Sergeant," Fishbein said, "why don't you come, too?"

"Where?"

"To St. Louis. To Shelly's aunt. We'll have a regular Seder. Play hide-the-matzoh." He gave me a broad, blacktoothed smile.

I saw Grossbart again, on the other side of the screen.

"Pst!" He waved a piece of paper. "Mickey, here's the address. Tell her I couldn't get away."

Halpern did not move. He looked at me, and I saw the shrug moving up his arms into his shoulders again. I took the cover off my typewriter and made out passes for him and Fishbein. "Go," I said. "The three of you."

I thought Halpern was going to kiss my hand.

That afternoon, in a bar in Joplin, I drank beer and listened with half an ear to the Cardinal game. I tried to look squarely at what I'd become involved in, and began to wonder if perhaps the struggle with Grossbart wasn't as much my fault as his. What was I that I had to *muster* generous feelings? Who was I to have been feeling so grudging, so tight-hearted? After all, I wasn't being asked to move the world. Had I a right, then, or a reason, to clamp down on Grossbart, when that meant clamping down on Halpern, too? And Fishbein — that ugly, agreeable soul? Out of the many recollections of my childhood that had tumbled over me these past few days I heard my grandmother's voice: "What are you making a *tsimmes?*" It was what she would ask my mother when, say, I had cut myself while doing something I shouldn't have done, and her daughter was busy bawling me out. I needed a hug and a kiss, and my mother would moralize. But my grandmother knew — mercy overrides justice. I should have known it, too. Who was Nathan Marx to be such a penny pincher with kindness? Surely, I thought, the Messiah himself — if He should ever come — won't niggle over nickles and dimes. God willing, he'll hug and kiss.

The next day, while I was playing softball over on the parade ground, I decided to ask Bob Wright, who was noncom in charge of Classification and Assignment, where he thought our trainees would be sent when their cycle ended, in two weeks. I asked casually, between innings, and he said, "They're pushing them all into the Pacific. Shulman cut the orders on your boys the other day."

The news shocked me, as though I were the father of Halpern, Fishbein, and Grossbart.

That night, I was just sliding into sleep when someone tapped on my door. "Who is it?" I asked.

"Sheldon."

He opened the door and came in. For a moment, I felt his presence without being able to see him. "How was it?" I asked.

He popped into sight in the near-darkness before me. "Great, Sergeant." Then he was sitting on the edge of the bed. I sat up.

"How about you?" he asked. "Have a nice weekend?"

"Yes."

"The others went to sleep." He took a deep, paternal breath. We sat silent for a while, and a homey feeling invaded my ugly little cubicle; the door was locked, the cat was out, the children were safely in bed.

"Sergeant, can I tell you something? Personal?"

I did not answer, and he seemed to know why. "Not about me. About Mickey. Sergeant, I never felt for anybody like I feel for him. Last night I heard Mickey in the bed next to me. He was crying so, it could have broken your heart. Real sobs."

"I'm sorry to hear that."

"I had to talk to him to stop him. He held my hand, Sergeant — he wouldn't let it go. He was almost hysterical. He kept saying if he only knew where we were going. Even if he knew it *was* the Pacific, that would be better than nothing. Just to know."

Long ago, someone had taught Grossbart the sad rule that only lies can get the truth. Not that I couldn't believe in the fact of Halpern's crying; his eyes *always* seemed red-rimmed. But, fact or not, it became a lie when Grossbart uttered it. He was entirely strategic. But then — it came with the force of indictment — so was I! There are strategies of aggression, but there are strategies of retreat as well. And so, recognizing that I myself had not been without craft and guile, I told him what I knew. "It is the Pacific."

He let out a small gasp, which was not a lie. "I'll tell him. I wish it was otherwise."

"So do I."

He jumped on my words. "You mean you think you could do something? A change, maybe?"

"No. I couldn't do a thing."

"Don't you know anybody over at C. and A.?"

"Grossbart, there's nothing I can do," I said. "If your orders are for the Pacific, then it's the Pacific."

"But Mickey — "

"Mickey, you, me — everybody, Grossbart. There's nothing to be done. Maybe the war'll end before you go. Pray for a miracle."

"But — "

"Good night, Grossbart." I settled back, and was relieved to feel the springs unbend as Grossbart rose to leave. I could see him clearly now; his jaw had dropped, and he looked like a dazed prizefighter. I noticed for the first time a little paper bag in his hand.

"Grossbart." I smiled. "My gift?"

"Oh, yes, Sergeant. Here — from all of us." He handed me the bag. "It's egg roll."

"Egg roll?" I accepted the bag and felt a damp grease spot on the bottom. I opened it, sure that Grossbart was joking.

"We thought you'd probably like it. You know — Chinese egg roll. We thought you'd probably have a taste for — "

"Your aunt served egg roll?"

"She wasn't home."

"Grossbart, she invited you. You told me she invited you and your friends."

"I know," he said. "I just reread the letter. *Next* week."

I got out of bed and walked to the window. "Grossbart," I said. But I was not calling to him.

"What?"

"What are you, Grossbart? Honest to God, what are you?"

I think it was the first time I'd asked him a question for which he didn't have an immediate answer.

"How can you do this to people?" I went on.

"Sergeant, the day away did us all a world of good. Fishbein, you should see him, he *loves* Chinese food."

"But the Seder," I said.

"We took second best, Sergeant."

Rage came charging at me. I didn't sidestep. "Grossbart, you're a liar!" I said. "You're a schemer and a crook. You've got no respect for anything. Nothing at all. Not for me, for the truth — not even for poor Halpern! You use us all — "

"Sergeant, Sergeant, I feel for Mickey. Honest to God, I do. I *love* Mickey. I try — "

"You try! You feel!" I lurched toward him and grabbed his shirt front. I shook him furiously. "Grossbart, get out! Get out and stay the hell away from me. Because if I see you, I'll make your life miserable. *You understand that?*"

"Yes."

I let him free, and when he walked from the room, I wanted to spit on the floor where he had stood. I couldn't stop the fury. It engulfed me, owned me, till it seemed I could only rid myself of it with tears or an act of violence. I snatched from the bed the bag Grossbart had given me and, with all my strength, threw it out the window. And the next morning, as the men policed the area around the barracks, I heard a great cry go up from one of the trainees, who had been anticipating only his morning handful of cigarette butts and candy wrappers. "Egg roll!" he shouted. "Holy Christ, Chinese goddam egg roll!"

A week later, when I read the orders that had come down from C. and A., I couldn't believe my eyes. Every single trainee was to be shipped to Camp Stoneman, California, and from there to the Pacific — every trainee but one. Private Sheldon Grossbart. He was to be sent to Fort Monmouth, New Jersey. I read the mimeographed sheet several times. Dee, Farrell, Fishbein, Fuselli,

Fylypowycz, Glinicki, Gromke, Gucwa, Halpern, Hardy, Helebrandt, right down to Anton Zygadlo — all were to be headed West before the month was out. All except Grossbart. He had pulled a string, and I wasn't it.

I lifted the phone and called C. and A.

The voice on the other end said smartly, "Corporal Shulman, sir."

"Let me speak to Sergeant Wright."

"Who is this calling, sir?"

"Sergeant Marx."

And, to my surprise, the voice said, *"Oh!"* Then, "Just a minute, Sergeant." Shulman's *"Oh!"* stayed with me while I waited for Wright to come to the phone. Why *"Oh!"*? Who was Shulman? And then, so simply, I knew I'd discovered the string that Grossbart had pulled. In fact, I could hear Grossbart the day he'd discovered Shulman in the PX, or in the bowling alley, or maybe even at services. "Glad to meet you. Where you from? Bronx? Me, too. Do you know So-and-So? And So-and-So? Me, too! You work at C. and A.? Really? Hey, how's chances of getting East? Could you do something? Change something? Swindle, cheat, lie? We gotta help each other, you know. If the Jews in Germany . . ."

Bob Wright answered the phone. "How are you, Nate? How's the pitching arm?"

"Good. Bob, I wonder if you could do me a favor." I heard clearly my own words, and they so reminded me of Grossbart that I dropped more easily than I could have imagined into what I had planned. "This may sound crazy, Bob, but I got a kid here on orders to Monmouth who wants them changed. He had a brother killed in Europe, and he's hot to go to the Pacific. Says he'd feel like a coward if he wound up Stateside. I don't know, Bob — can anything be done? Put somebody else in the Monmouth slot?"

"Who?" he asked cagily.

"Anybody. First guy in the alphabet. I don't care. The kid just asked if something could be done."

"What's his name?"

"Grossbart, Sheldon."

Wright didn't answer.

"Yeah," I said. "He's a Jewish kid, so he thought I could help him out. You know."

"I guess I can do something," he finally said. "The Major hasn't been around here for weeks. Temporary duty to the golf course. I'll try, Nate, that's all I can say."

"I'd appreciate it, Bob. See you Sunday." And I hung up, perspiring.

The following day, the corrected orders appeared: Fishbein, Fuselli, Fylypowycz, Glinicki, Gromke, Grossbart, Gucwa, Halpern, Hardy . . . Lucky Private Harley Alton was to go to Fort Monmouth, New Jersey, where for some reason or other, they wanted an enlisted man with infantry training.

After chow that night, I stopped back at the orderly room to straighten out the guard-duty roster. Grossbart was waiting for me. He spoke first.

"You son of a bitch!"

I sat down at my desk, and while he glared at me, I began to make the necessary alterations in the duty roster.

"What do you have against me?" he cried. "Against my family? Would it kill you for me to be near my father, God knows how many months he has left to him?"

"Why so?"

"His heart," Grossbart said. "He hasn't had enough troubles in a lifetime, you've got to add to them. I curse the day I ever met you, Marx! Shulman told me what happened over there. There's no limit to your anti-Semitism, is there? The damage you've done here isn't enough. You have to make a special phone call! You really want me dead!"

I made the last few notations in the duty roster and got up to leave. "Good night, Grossbart."

"You owe me an explanation!" He stood in my path.

"Sheldon, you're the one who owes explanations."

He scowled. "To *you?*"

"To me, I think so — yes. Mostly to Fishbein and Halpern."

"That's right, twist things around. I owe nobody nothing, I've done all I could do for them. Now I think I've got the right to watch out for myself."

"For each other we have to learn to watch out, Sheldon. You told me yourself."

"You call this watching out for me — what you did?"

"No. For all of us."

I pushed him aside and started for the door. I heard his furious breathing behind me, and it sounded like steam rushing from an engine of terrible strength.

"*You'll* be all right," I said from the door. And, I thought, so would Fishbein and Halpern be all right, even in the Pacific, if only Grossbart continued to see — in the obsequiousness of the one, the soft spirituality of the other — some profit for himself.

I stood outside the orderly room, and I heard Grossbart weeping behind me. Over in the barracks, in the lighted windows, I could see the boys in their T shirts sitting on their bunks talking about their orders, as they'd been doing for the past two days. With a kind of quiet nervousness, they polished shoes, shined belt buckles, squared away underwear, trying as best they could to accept their fate. Behind me, Grossbart swallowed hard, accepting his. And then, resisting with all my will an impulse to turn and seek pardon for my vindictiveness, I accepted my own.

Exercises

1. Compare and contrast the characters of Sergeant Marx and Grossbart.

2. How is Grossbart a stereotype to the white, Anglo-Saxon Protestant, or WASP, of the early 1940s?

3. Identify the protagonist, the conflict, and the obstacle standing in the way of a solution until the dénouement.

Topic for Writing

Evaluate either Grossbart's or Marx's role as the "defender of the faith," or, if you prefer, prove that each man represents a different kind of defender of the faith.

Leslie Marmon Silko (1948–   )

Storyteller

I.

Every day the sun came up a little lower on the horizon, moving more slowly until one day she got excited and started calling the jailer. She realized she had been sitting there for many hours, yet the sun had not moved from the center of the sky. The color of the sky had not been good lately; it had been pale blue, almost white, even when there were no clouds. She told herself it wasn't a good sign for the sky to be indistinguishable from the river ice, frozen solid and white against the earth. The tundra rose up behind the river but all the boundaries between the river and hills and sky were lost in the density of the pale ice.

She yelled again, this time some English words which came randomly into her mouth, probably swear words she'd heard from the oil drilling crews last winter. The jailer was an Eskimo, but he would not speak Yupik to her. She had watched people in the other cells; when they spoke to him in Yupik he ignored them until they spoke English.

He came and stared at her. She didn't know if he understood what she was telling him until he glanced behind her at the small high window. He looked at the sun, and turned and walked away. She could head the buckles on his heavy snowmobile boots jingle as he walked to the front of the building.

It was like the other buildings that white people, the Gussucks, brought with them: BIA and school buildings, portable buildings that arrived sliced in halves, on barges coming up the river. Squares of metal panelling bulged out with the layers of insulation stuffed inside. She had asked once what it was and someone told her it was to keep out the cold. She had not laughed then, but she did now. She walked over to the small double-pane window and she laughed out loud. They thought they could keep out the cold with stringy yellow wadding. Look at the sun. It wasn't moving; it was frozen, caught in the middle of the sky. Look at the sky, solid as the river with ice which had trapped the sun. It had not moved for a long time; in a few more hours it would be weak, and heavy frost would begin to appear on the edges and spread across the face of the sun like a mask. Its light was pale yellow, worn thin by the winter.

She could see people walking down the snow-packed roads, their breath steaming out from their parka hoods, faces hidden and protected by deep ruffs of fur. There were no cars or snowmobiles that day so she calculated it was fifty below zero, the temperature which silenced their machines. The metal froze; it split and shattered. Oil hardened and moving parts jammed solidly. She had seen it happen to their big yellow machines and the giant drill last winter when they came to drill their test holes. The cold stopped them, and they were helpless against it.

Her village was many miles upriver from this town, but in her mind she could see it clearly. Their house was not near the village houses. It stood alone on the bank upriver from the village. Snow had drifted to the eaves of the roof on the north side, but on the west side, by the door, the path was almost clear. She had nailed scraps of red tin over the logs last summer. She had done it for the bright red color, not for added warmth the way the village people had done.

This final winter had been coming down even then; there had been signs of its approach for many years.

II.

She went because she was curious about the big school where the Government sent all the other girls and boys. She had not played much with the village children while she was growing up because they were afraid of the old man, and they ran when her grandmother came. She went because she was tired of being alone with the old woman whose body had been stiffening for as long as the girl could remember. Her knees and knuckles were swollen grotesquely, and the pain had squeezed the brown skin of her face tight against the bones; it left her eyes hard like river stone. The girl asked once, what it was that did this to her body, and the old woman had raised up from sewing a sealskin boot, and stared at her.

"The joints," the old woman said in a low voice, whispering like wind across the roof, "the joints are swollen with anger."

Sometimes she did not answer and only stared at the girl. Each year she spoke less and less, but the old man talked more — all night sometimes, not to anyone but himself; in a soft deliberate voice, he told stories, moving his smooth brown hands above the blankets. He had not fished or hunted with the other men for many years although he was not crippled or sick. He stayed in his bed, smelling like dry fish and urine, telling stories all winter; and when warm weather came, he went to his place on the river bank. He sat with a long willow stick, poking at the smoldering moss he burned against the insects while he continued with the stories.

The trouble was that she had not recognized the warnings in time. She did not see what the Gussuck school would do to her until she walked into the dormitory and realized that the old man had not been lying about the place. She thought he had been trying to scare her as he used to when she was very small and her grandmother was outside cutting up fish. She hadn't believed what he told her about the school because she knew he wanted to keep her there in the log house with him. She knew what he wanted.

The dormitory matron pulled down her underpants and whipped her with a leather belt because she refused to speak English.

"Those backwards village people," the matron said, because she was an Eskimo who had worked for the BIA a long time, "they kept this one until she was too big to learn." The other girls whispered in English. They knew how to work the showers, and they washed and curled their hair at night. They ate Gussuck food. She laid on her bed and imagined what her grandmother might be sewing, and what the old man was eating in his bed. When summer came, they sent her home.

The way her grandmother had hugged her before she left for school had been a warning too, because the old woman had not hugged or touched her for many years. Not like the old man, whose hands were always hunting, like ravens circling lazily in the sky, ready to touch her. She was not surprised when the priest and the old man met her at the landing strip, to say that the old lady was gone. The priest asked her where she would like to stay. He referred to the old man as her grandfather, but she did not bother to correct him. She had already been thinking about it; if she went with the priest, he would send her away to a school. But the old man was different. She knew he wouldn't send her back to school. She knew he wanted to keep her.

III.

He told her one time that she would get too old for him faster than he got too old for her; but again she had not believed him because sometimes he lied. He had lied about what he would do with her if she came into his bed. But as the years passed, she realized what he said was true. She was restless and strong. She had no patience with the old man who had never changed his slow smooth motions under the blankets.

The old man was in his bed for the winter; he did not leave it except to use the slop bucket in the corner. He was dozing with his mouth open slightly; his lips quivered and sometimes they moved like he was telling a story even while he dreamed. She pulled on the sealskin boots, the mukluks with the bright red flannel linings her grandmother had sewn for her, and she tied the braided red yarn tassels around her ankles over the gray wool pants. She zipped the wolf-skin parka. Her grandmother had worn it for many years, but the old man said that before she died, she instructed him to bury her in an old black sweater, and to give the parka to the girl. The wolf pelts were creamy colored and silver, almost white in some places, and when the old lady had walked across the tundra in the winter, she disappeared into the snow.

She walked toward the village, breaking her own path through the deep snow. A team of sled dogs tied outside a house at the edge of the village leaped against their chains to bark at her. She kept walking, watching the dusky sky for the first evening stars. It was warm and the dogs were alert. When it got cold again, the dogs would lie curled and still, too drowsy from the cold to bark or pull at the chains. She laughed loudly because it made them howl and snarl. Once the old man had seen her tease the dogs and he shook his head. "So that's the kind of woman you are," he said, "in the wintertime the two of us are no different from those dogs. We wait in the cold for someone to bring us a few dry fish."

She laughed out loud again, and kept walking. She was thinking about the Gussuck oil drillers. They were strange; they watched her when she walked near their machines. She wondered what they looked like underneath their quilted goosedown trousers; she wanted to know how they moved. They would be something different from the old man.

The old man screamed at her. He shook her shoulders so violently that her head bumped against the log wall. "I smelled it!" he yelled, "as soon as I woke up! I am sure of it now. You can't fool me!" His thin legs were shaking inside the baggy wool trousers; he stumbled over her boots in his bare feet. His toe nails were long and yellow like bird claws; she had seen a gray crane last summer fighting another in the shallow water on the edge of the river. She laughed out loud and pulled her shoulder out of his grip. He stood in front of her. He was breathing hard and shaking; he looked weak. He would probably die next winter.

"I'm warning you," he said, "I'm warning you." He crawled back into his bunk then, and reached under the old soiled feather pillow for a piece of dry fish. He lay back on the pillow, staring at the ceiling and chewed dry strips of salmon. "I don't know what the old woman told you," he said, "but there will be trouble." He looked over to see if she was listening. His face suddenly relaxed into a smile, his dark slanty eyes were lost in wrinkles of brown skin. "I could tell you, but you are too good for warnings now. I can smell what you did all night with the Gussucks."

She did not understand why they came there, because the village was small and so far upriver that even some Eskimos who had been away to school would not come back. They stayed downriver in the town. They said the village was too quiet. They were used to the town where the boarding school was located, with electric lights and running water. After all those years away at school, they had forgotten how to set nets in the river and where to hunt seals in the fall. Those who left did not say it, but their confidence had been destroyed. When she asked the old man why the Gussucks bothered to come to the village, his narrow eyes got bright with excitement.

"They only come when there is something to steal. The fur animals are too difficult for them to get now, and the seals and fish are hard to find. Now they come for oil deep in the earth. But this is the last time for them." His breathing was wheezy and fast; his hands gestured at the sky. "It is approaching. As it comes, ice will push across the sky." His eyes were open wide and he stared at the low ceiling rafters for hours without blinking. She remembered all this clearly because he began the story that day, the story he told from that time on. It began with a giant bear which he described muscle by muscle, from the curve of the ivory claws to the whorls of hair at the top of the massive skull. And for eight days he did not sleep, but talked continuously of the giant bear whose color was pale blue glacier ice.

IV.

The snow was dirty and worn down in a path to the door. On either side of the path, the snow was higher than her head. In front of the door there were jagged yellow stains melted into the snow where men had urinated. She stopped in the entry way and kicked the snow off her boots. The room was dim; a kerosene lantern by the cash register was burning low. The long wooden shelves were jammed with cans of beans and potted meats. On the bottom shelf a jar of mayonnaise was broken open, leaking oily white clots on the floor. There was no one in the room except the yellowish dog sleeping in front of the long glass display case. A reflection made it appear to be lying on the knives and ammunition inside the case. Gussucks kept dogs inside their houses with them; they did not seem to mind the odors which seeped out of the dogs. "They tell us we are dirty for the food we eat — raw fish and fermented meat. But we do not live with dogs," the old man once said. She heard voices in the back room, and the sound of bottles set down hard on tables.

They were always confident. The first year they waited for the ice to break up on the river, and then they brought their big yellow machines up river on barges. They planned to drill their test holes during the summer to avoid the freezing. But the imprints and graves of their machines were still there, on the edge of the tundra above the river, where the summer mud had swallowed them before they ever left sight of the river. The village people had gathered to watch the white men, and to laugh as they drove the giant machines, one by one, off the steel ramp into the bogs; as if sheer numbers of vehicles would somehow make the tundra solid. But the old man said they behaved like desperate people, and they would come back again. When the tundra was frozen solid, they returned.

Village women did not even look through the door to the back room. The priest had warned them. The storeman was watching her because he didn't let Eskimos or Indians sit down at the tables in the back room. But she knew he couldn't throw her out if one of his Gussuck customers invited her to sit with him. She walked across the room. They stared at her, but she had the feeling she was walking for someone else, not herself, so their eyes did not matter. The red-haired man pulled out a chair and motioned for her to sit down. She looked back at the storeman while the red-haired man poured her a glass of red sweet wine. She wanted to laugh at the storeman the way she laughed at the dogs, straining against their chains, howling at her.

The red-haired man kept talking to the other Gussucks sitting around the table, but he slid one hand off the top of the table to her thigh. She looked over at the storeman to see if he was still watching her. She laughed out loud at him and the red-haired man stopped talking and turned to her. He asked if she wanted to go. She nodded and stood up.

Someone in the village had been telling him things about her, he said as they walked down the road to his trailer. She understood that much of what he was saying, but the rest she did not hear. The whine of the big generators at the construction camp sucked away the sound of his words. But English was of no concern to her anymore, and neither was anything the Christians in the village might say about her or the old man. She smiled at the effect of the subzero air on the electric lights around the trailers; they did not shine. They left only flat yellow holes in the darkness.

It took him a long time to get ready, even after she had undressed for him. She waited in the bed with the blankets pulled close, watching him. He adjusted the thermostat and lit candles in the room, turning out the electric lights. He searched through a stack of record albums until he found the right one. She was not sure about the last thing he did: he taped something on the wall behind the bed where he could see it while he laid on top of her. He was shrivelled and white from the cold; he pushed against her body for warmth. He guided her hands to his thighs; he was shivering.

She had returned a last time because she wanted to know what it was he stuck on the wall above the bed. After he finished each time, he reached up and pulled it loose, folding it carefully so that she could not see it. But this time she was ready; she waited for his fast breathing and sudden collapse on top of her. She slid out from under him and stood up beside the bed. She looked at the picture while she got dressed. He did not raise his face from the pillow, and she thought she heard teeth rattling together as she left the room.

She heard the old man move when she came in. After the Gussuck's trailer, the log house felt cool. It smelled like dry fish and cured meat. The room was dark except for the blinking yellow flame in the mica window of the oil stove. She squatted in front of the stove and watched the flames for a long time before she walked to the bed where her grandmother had slept. The bed was covered with a mound of rags and fur scraps the old woman had saved. She reached into the mound until she felt something cold and solid wrapped in a wool blanket. She pushed her fingers around it until she felt smooth stone. Long ago, before the Gussucks came, they had burned whale oil in the big stone lamp which made light and heat as well. The old woman had saved everything they would need when the time came.

In the morning, the old man pulled a piece of dry caribou meat from under the blankets and offered it to her. While she was gone, men from the village had brought a bundle of dry meat. She chewed it slowly, thinking about the way they still came from the village to take care of the old man and his stories. But she had a story now, about the red-haired Gussuck. The old man knew what she was thinking, and his smile made his face seem more round than it was.

"Well," he said, "what was it?"

"A woman with a big dog on top of her."

He laughed softly to himself and walked over to the water barrel. He dipped the tin cup into the water.

"It doesn't surprise me," he said.

V.

"Grandma," she said, "there was something red in the grass that morning. I remember." She had not asked about her parents before. The old woman stopped splitting the fish bellies open for the willow drying racks. Her jaw muscles pulled so tightly against her skull, the girl thought the old woman would not be able to speak.

"They bought a tin can full of it from the storeman. Late at night. He told them it was alcohol safe to drink. They traded a rifle for it." The old woman's voice sounded like each word stole strength from her. "It made no difference about the rifle. That year the Gussuck boats had come, firing big guns at the walrus and seals. There was nothing left to hunt after that anyway. "So," the old lady said, in a low soft voice the girl had not heard for a long time, "I didn't say anything to them when they left that night."

"Right over there," she said, pointing at the fallen poles, half buried in the river sand and tall grass, "in the summer shelter. The sun was high half the night then. Early in the morning when it was still low, the policeman came around. I told the interpreter to tell him that the storeman had poisoned them." She made outlines in the air in front of her, showing how their bodies laid twisted on the sand; telling the story was like laboring to walk through deep snow; sweat shone in the white hair around her forehead. "I told the priest too, after he came. I told him the storeman lied." She turned away from the girl. She held her mouth even tighter, set solidly, not in sorrow or anger, but against the pain, which was all that remained. "I never believed," she said, "not much anyway. I wasn't surprised when the priest did nothing."

The wind came off the river and folded the tall grass into itself like river waves. She could feel the silence the story left, and she wanted to have the old woman go on.

"I heard sounds that night, grandma. Sounds like someone was singing. It was light outside. I could see something red on the ground." The old woman did not answer her; she moved to the tub full of fish on the ground beside the work bench. She stabbed her knife into the belly of a whitefish and lifted it onto the bench. "The Gussuck storeman left the village right after that," the old woman said as she pulled the entrails from the fish, "otherwise, I could tell you more." The old woman's voice flowed with the wind blowing off the river; they never spoke of it again.

When the willows got their leaves and the grass grew tall along the river banks and around the sloughs, she walked early in the morning. While the sun was still low on the horizon, she listened to the wind off the river; its sound was like the voice that day long ago. In the distance, she could hear the engines of the machinery the oil drillers had left the winter before, but she did not go near the village or the store. The sun never left the sky and the summer became the same long day, with only the winds to fan the sun into brightness or allow it to slip into twilight.

She sat beside the old man at his place on the river bank. She poked the smoky fire for him, and felt herself growing wide and thin in the sun as if she had been split from belly to throat and strung on the willow pole in preparation for the winter to come. The old man did not speak anymore. When men from the village brought him fresh fish he hid them deep in the river grass where it was cool. After he went inside, she split the fish open and spread them to dry on the willow frame the way the old woman had done. Inside, he dozed and talked to himself. He had talked all winter, softly and incessantly about the giant polar bear stalking a lone man across Bering Sea ice. After all the months the old man had been telling the story, the bear was within a hundred feet of the man; but the ice fog had closed in on them now and the man could only smell the sharp ammonia odor of the bear, and hear the edge of the snow crust crack under the giant paws.

One night she listened to the old man tell the story all night in his sleep, describing each crystal of ice and the slightly different sounds they made under each paw; first the left and then the right paw, then the hind feet. Her grandmother was there suddenly, a shadow around the stove. She spoke in her low wind voice and the girl was afraid to sit up to hear more clearly. Maybe what she said had been to the old man because he stopped telling the story and began to snore softly the way he had long ago when the old woman had scolded him for telling his stories while others in the house were trying to sleep. But the last words she heard clearly: "It will take a long time, but the story must be told. There must not be any lies." She pulled the blanket up around her chin, slowly, so that her movements would not be seen. She thought her grandmother was talking about the old man's bear story; she did not know about the other story then.

She left the old man wheezing and snoring in his bed. She walked through river grass glistening with frost; the bright green summer color was already fading. She watched the sun move across the sky, already lower on the horizon, already moving away from the village. She stopped by the fallen poles of the summer shelter where her parents had died. Frost glittered on the river sand too; in a few more weeks there would be snow. The predawn light would be the color of an old woman. An old woman sky full of snow. There had been something red lying on the ground the morning they died. She looked for it again, pushing aside the grass with her foot. She knelt in the sand and looked under the fallen structure for some trace of it. When she found it, she would know what the old woman had never told her. She squatted down close to the gray poles and leaned her back against them. The wind made her shiver.

The summer rain had washed the mud from between the logs; the sod blocks stacked as high as her belly next to the log walls had lost their square-cut shape and had grown into soft mounds of tundra moss and stiff-bladed grass bending with clusters of seed bristles. She looked at the northwest, in the direction of the

Bering Sea. The cold would come down from there to find narrow slits in the mud, rainwater holes in the outer layer of sod which protected the log house. The dark green tundra stretched away flat and continuous. Somewhere the sea and the land met; she knew by their dark green colors there were no boundaries between them. That was how the cold would come: when the boundaries were gone the polar ice would range across the land into the sky. She watched the horizon for a long time. She would stand in that place on the north side of the house and she would keep watch on the northwest horizon, and eventually she would see it come. She would watch for its approach in the stars, and hear it come with the wind. These preparations were unfamiliar, but gradually she recognized them as she did her own footprints in the snow.

She emptied the slop jar beside his bed twice a day and kept the barrel full of water melted from river ice. He did not recognize her anymore, and when he spoke to her, he called her by her grandmother's name and talked about people and events from long ago, before he went back to telling the story. The giant bear was creeping across the new snow on its belly, close enough now that the man could hear the rasp of its breathing. On and on in a soft singing voice, the old man caressed the story, repeating the words again and again like gentle strokes.

The sky was gray like a river crane's egg; its density curved into the thin crust of frost already covering the land. She looked at the bright red color of the tin against the ground and the sky and she told the village men to bring the pieces for the old man and her. To drill the test holes in the tundra, the Gussucks had used hundreds of barrels of fuel. The village people split open the empty barrels that were abandoned on the river bank, and pounded the red tin into flat sheets. The village people were using the strips of tin to mend walls and roofs for winter. But she nailed it on the log walls for its color. When she finished, she walked away with the hammer in her hand, not turning around until she was far away, on the ridge above the river banks, and then she looked back. She felt a chill when she saw how the sky and the land were already losing their boundaries, already becoming lost in each other. But the red tin penetrated the thick white color of earth and sky; it defined the boundaries like a wound revealing the ribs and heart of a great caribou about to bolt and be lost to the hunter forever. That night the wind howled and when she scratched a hole through the heavy frost on the inside of the window, she could see nothing but the impenetrable white; whether it was blowing snow or snow that had drifted as high as the house, she did not know.

It had come down suddenly, and she stood with her back to the wind looking at the river, its smoky water clotted with ice. The wind had blown the snow over the frozen river, hiding thin blue streaks where fast water ran under ice translucent and fragile as memory. But she could see shadows of boundaries, outlines of paths which were slender branches of solidity reaching out from the earth. She spent days walking on the river, watching the colors of ice that would safely hold her, kicking the heel of her boot into the snow crust, listening for a solid sound. When she could feel the paths through the soles of her feet, she went to the middle of the river where the fast gray water churned under a thin pane of ice. She looked back. On the river bank in the distance she could see the red tin nailed to the log house, something not swallowed up by the heavy white belly of the sky or caught in the folds of the frozen earth. It was time.

The wolverine fur around the hood of her parka was white with the frost from her breathing. The warmth inside the store melted it, and she felt tiny drops of water on her face. The storeman came in from the back room. She unzipped the parka and stood by the oil stove. She didn't look at him, but stared instead at the yellowish dog, covered with scabs of matted hair, sleeping in front of the stove. She thought of the Gussuck's picture, taped on the wall above the bed and she laughed out loud. The sound of her laughter was piercing; the yellow dog jumped to its feet and the hair bristled down its back. The storeman was watching her. She wanted to laugh again because he didn't know about the ice. He did not know that it was prowling the earth, or that it had already pushed its way into the sky to seize the sun. She sat down in the chair by the stove and shook her long hair loose. He was like a dog tied up all winter, watching while the others got fed. He remembered how she had gone with the oil drillers, and his blue eyes moved like flies crawling over her body. He held his thin pale lips like he wanted to spit on her. He hated the people because they had something of value, the old man said, something which the Gussucks could never have. They thought they could take it, suck it out of the earth or cut it from the mountains; but they were fools.

There was a matted hunk of dog hair on the floor by her foot. She thought of the yellow insulation coming unstuffed: their defense against the freezing going to pieces as it advanced on them. The ice was crouching on the northwest horizon like the old man's bear. She laughed out loud again. The sun would be down now; it was time.

The first time he spoke to her, she did not hear what he said, so she did not answer or even look up at him. He spoke to her again but his words were only noises coming from his pale mouth, trembling now as his anger began to unravel. He jerked her up and the chair fell over behind her. His arms were shaking and she could feel his hands tense up, pulling the edges of the parka tighter. He raised his fist to hit her, his thin body quivering with rage; but the fist collapsed with the desire he had for the valuable things, which, the old man had rightly said, was the only reason they came. She could hear his heart pounding as he held her close and arched his hips against her, groaning and breathing in spasms. She twisted away from him and ducked under his arms.

She ran with a mitten over her mouth, breathing through the fur to protect her lungs from the freezing air. She could hear him running behind her, his heavy breathing, the occasional sound of metal jingling against metal. But he ran without his parka or mittens, breathing the frozen air; its fire squeezed the lungs against the ribs and it was enough that he could not catch her near his store. On the river bank he realized how far he was from his stove, and the wads of yellow stuffing that held off the cold. But the girl was not able to run very fast through the deep drifts at the edge of the river. The twilight was luminous and he could still see clearly for a long distance; he knew he could catch her so he kept running.

When she neared the middle of the river she looked over her shoulder. He was not following her tracks; he went straight across the ice, running the shortest distance to reach her. He was close then; his face was twisted and scarlet from the exertion and the cold. There was satisfaction in his eyes; he was sure he could outrun her.

She was familiar with the river, down to the instant the ice flexed into hairline fractures, and the cracking bone-sliver sounds gathered momentum with the opening ice until the sound of the churning gray water was set free. She stopped and turned to the sound of the river and the rattle of swirling ice fragments where he fell through. She pulled off a mitten and zipped the parka to her throat. She was conscious then of her own rapid breathing.

She moved slowly, kicking the ice ahead with the heel of her boot, feeling for sinews of ice to hold her. She looked ahead and all around herself; in the twilight, the dense white sky had merged into the flat snow-covered tundra. In the frantic running she had lost her place on the river. She stood still. The east bank of the river was lost in the sky; the boundaries had been swallowed by the freezing white. And then, in the distance, she saw something red, and suddenly it was as she had remembered it all those years.

VI.

She sat on her bed and while she waited, she listened to the old man. The man had found a small jagged knoll on the ice. He pulled his beaver fur cap off his head; the fur inside it steamed with his body heat and sweat. He left it upside down on the ice for the great bear to stalk, and he waited downwind on top of the ice knoll; he was holding the jade knife.

She thought she could see the end of his story in the way he wheezed out the words; but still he reached into his cache of dry fish and dribbled water into his mouth from the tin cup. All night she listened to him describe each breath the man took, each motion of the bear's head as it tried to catch the sound of the man's breathing, and tested the wind for his scent.

The state trooper asked her questions, and the woman who cleaned house for the priest translated them into Yupik. They wanted to know hat happened to the storeman, the Gussuck who had been seen running after her down the road onto the river late last evening. He had not come back, and the Gussuck boss in Anchorage was concerned about him. She did not answer for a long time because the old man suddenly sat up in his bed and began to talk excitedly, looking at all of them — the trooper in his dark glasses and the housekeeper in her corduroy parka. He kept saying, "The story! The story! Eh-ya! The great bear! The hunter!"

They asked her again, what happened to the man from the Northern Commercial store. "He lied to them. He told them it was safe to drink. But I will not lie." She stood up and put on the gray wolfskin parka. "I killed him," she said, "but I don't lie."

The attorney came back again, and the jailer slid open the steel doors and opened the cell to let him in. He motioned for the jailer to stay to translate for him. She laughed when she saw how the jailer would be forced by this Gussuck to speak Yupik to her. She liked the Gussuck attorney for that, and for the thinning hair on his head. He was very tall, and she liked to think about the exposure of his head to the freezing; she wondered if he would feel the ice descending from the sky before the others did. He wanted to know why she told the state trooper she had killed the storeman. Some village children had seen it happen, he said, and it was an accident. "That's all you have to say to the judge: it was an accident." He kept repeating it over and over again to her. slowly in a loud but gentle voice: "It was an accident. He was running after you and he fell through the ice. That's all you have to say in court. That's all. And they will let you go home. Back to your village." The jailer translated the words sullenly, staring down at the floor. She shook her head. "I will not change the story, not even to escape this place and go home. I intended that he die. The story must be told as it is." The attorney exhaled loudly; his eyes looked tired. "Tell her that she could not have killed him that way. He was a white man. He ran after her without a parka or mittens. She could not have planned that." He paused and turned toward the cell door. "Tell her I will do all I can for her. I will explain to the judge that her mind is confused." She laughed out loud when the jailer translated what the attorney said. The Gussucks did not understand the story; they could not see the way it must be told, year after year as the old man had done, without lapse or silence.

She looked out the window at the frozen white sky. The sun had finally broken loose from the ice but it moved like a wounded caribou running on strength which only dying animals find, leaping and running on bullet-shattered lungs. Its light was weak and pale; it pushed dimly through the clouds. She turned and faced the Gussuck attorney.

"It began a long time ago," she intoned steadily, "in the summertime. Early in the morning, I remember, something red in the tall river grass. . . ."

The day after the old man died, men from the village came. She was sitting on the edge of her bed, across from the woman the trooper hired to watch her. They came into the room slowly and listened to her. At the foot of her bed they left a king salmon that had been split open wide and dried last summer. But she did not pause or hesitate; she went on with the story, and she never stopped not even when the woman got up to close the door behind the village men.

The old man would not change the story even when he knew the end was approaching. Lies could not stop what was coming. He thrashed around on the bed, pulling the blankets loose, knocking bundles of dried fish and meat on the floor. The man had been on the ice for many hours. The freezing winds on the ice knoll had numbed his hands in the mittens, and the cold had exhausted him. He felt a single muscle tremor in his hand that he could not suppress, and the jade knife fell; it shattered on the ice, and the blue glacier bear turned slowly to face him.

Wakako Yamauchi (1924–   )

The Boatmen on Toneh River

Kimi Sumida knew the end was near. The bed she'd lived in for many months now ceased to resist the bony protuberances of her body and prolonged attitudes of discomfort reached a stage of stone-like numbness. The cancer that ate at her lungs had no more on which to feed.

Where once the long day steadily, slowly, inexorably moved into night, now darkness descended without warning — dark and light, dark and light, and dreams, always dreams. Sometimes daylight and reality seemed just beyond a door of pain — now near, now distant — on the other side of pain. "Mari, do I have to remind a 7-year-old every day to brush her teeth? What will your teacher say?" "Give me time, Daddy, you never give me enough time." "Shshsh. Not so loud." "Mommy still sleeping?" "Shshsh . . ." Like a stone at the bottom of the sea, Kimi lay on the ocean floor and the tide flowed over her. "Ryo! Mari! Me: wife and mother! Do you not need me?" Did she cry out?

The door opened and a thin light poured into the room with Ryo. A warped sandwich on the night-stand indicated to Kimi it was still day — late afternoon. "How do you feel now, dear?"

Did I feel worse before? How long before? His mien is one of enormous cheer: he has on his cheer face. What happened to your other face, Ryo, the one that mirrors your heart? Did you discard it along with hope for my recovery? Honor me with a little honesty, the reality of my disease. Despair a little; feel free to despair a little with me. This is the time to be yourself. I hear the things you tell Mari: that I am going away; that we will all meet again some day; that this is not the time of sorrow; that flowers are sometimes broken in the bud, or plucked in bloom, or sometimes mature to seed and fruition and seed again. Are these words to take the edge off the rawness of death, or do you really believe, or do you only wish to believe? But you haven't known this desperate reluctance to leave life — you don't know the terror of the things I face. You don't even see me any more; you turn your back while the doctor presses, turns, and probes me like a vegetable, and mutters, "Comatose; can't see what keeps her here."

Once you looked at me with eyes soft and tender; eyes dull with desire. Now only this cheer. You won't acknowledge me. I'm the woman who moved you through those many dark streets hurrying, rushing to meet me; the woman who brought words and unspoken dreams from your lips; I'm the woman who brought the fire to your loins. I'm the one! Wasted now; my hair is too black against the fearful pallor of my skin. Do I frighten you? Do you drop your cheerful mask in alarm when you close my door? Do you keep my Mari from me to protect her from the horror of seeing me? Are you afraid I will sear the color from her warm lips, sow seeds of my disease in her tender body? But she's mine. Mine. And I have the right to insist she share my experience, just as, yes, just as my mother had shared hers with me. And she will no doubt travel the lonely channels I've charted; paths like the narrow canals on my cracked ceiling that angle off here, stop abruptly there, by-ways I've come to know as well as I know the palm of my hand. I'm at one of those dead ends now.

The door closed but the light remained and turned blood-red with pain. Slowly the red tide subsided and throbbing with the beat of her pulse, Kimi heard her own mother's voice call: "Kimi, Kimi . . ." Warm, a mother's voice. She opened her eyes.

This is the country kitchen of my childhood: furniture of raw unfinished wood, bare floors, sweaters on pegs, grey dishcloths drying on the sink rim, cosmic dust slowly sifting. And beyond the windows, the stretch of desert, broken nearby with rows of furrowed earth. All there. Am I mother or am I the child; am I the caller or the called?

"Kimi, go fix the bath for Father. He'll be back from the fields and will want his bath."

"Not now, Mother, I'll be back soon, and I will do it then."

"Now. Now. Every evening you go off when I need you. What's in this compulsion to commune with this nothing land. I need your help here; do you think this wild desert changes a whit for your walking through a piece of it? Stay here and use the strength God gave you where it'd do some good. Make the bath."

My Kimi, where do you go; what do you dream? Fancy clothes? Glittering lights? Love? There're none of these here. I was seventeen, the caress of my mother's fingers still warm in my hair, when they married me to a stranger from the next province. He must have a young healthy woman to help him in America, they said; and soon I would return, a rich, proud, honored lady. I looked forward to this promise in dewy-eyed innocence — unaware of even the conjugal night that lay before me. The years have devoured me with work and poverty and anxieties: early frost, fluctuating market, price of rice — what chance had love? They told me with this black mole on my ear lobe, I couldn't fail, a black mole on the ear lobe is a sure sign of fame and fortune, they said. I waited for this fortune; worked and waited and when finally my time was up, I counted my fortune. Fifty years of living and what was there to show? Ten thousand nights I lay there remembering my Japan; clear lakes, lonely shrines, the lyric of flowering cherry trees, street vendors' calls, plaintive and sweet as a mother's lullabyes, the sound of a flute on a summer evening. I spent a life-time waiting to return to these. I thought my happiness was bound to these. I reached too far for what was always here, in the dust, in the sunrise, in the sunset, in you.

"Kimi, make the bath."

"Yes, I'll do it now."

I'm going now to heat the bath with sage that you and I gathered and spread out to dry in early summer. It will shoot up in crackling flames and tiny sparks and I'll think of your fireflies in Japan. Though you may not believe it, I've found something here in this arid desert that is gentle and sweet too. I want to ask you about it, but to put it to words or to your critical eye may be to pro-fane it. And now the tall summer reeds bend in the wind, cicadas hum, shadows lengthen, cottonwood leaves catch the last flutter of sunlight, and the lad who peddles down the warm dusty road each evening at this time is passing by, and I am not there. I shall not see the wind move through his black hair, and touch his smooth brown cheeks and fill his blouse with air. I want to be as close to him as that wind. Where he comes from, where he peddles to, I don't know; but when I watch him, I see west winds in the sage, I see tumbleweeds lope across the prairie, and primrose petals fall, and I am moved. From my hiding place in the reeds, I watch him scan the horizon, and I wonder if he looks for me. Does he watch for me? Does he yearn for me?

Kimi, how extravagantly you dream; what disenchantment you court. What loneliness you will know.

The room was dark and cold. Night had come; the sandwich on the night-stand had been removed and a covered tray replaced it. This is Ryo's acknowl-edgement of me, Kimi thought; ashes of dreams he prepares for me. I am still here.

"Still here! Kimi, drat it! I tell you, put the dog out. He's still here!"

Three days of steady rain now; one more day and the tiny seedlings that last week pushed their tender shoots from the over-worked earth will rot. The kitchen is dank and murky with smoke from Bull Durhams and the smell of *sake* warming on the coal-oil stove. The patriarch sits at the table with Mr. Nagata, one of a legion of shifting rootless men who follow crops along the length of California. They sip the warm rice wine and talk, tugging exaggeratedly at one another's sleeve. They laugh; they sing half-remembered songs.

"Kimi, I tell you, put the dog out! If there's anything that annoys me, it's the smell of a wet dog. I've got troubles enough without that. The stench comes from the floor like something stepped on in the dark. Eh, Nagata-*kun?* Heh, heh. What a life, eh? Heh, heh."

Yah, those seedlings. A month's work destroyed. You sow one more row before sundown, pull one more weed before nightfall, for what? Rain, more seeding, more weeding. Don't look at me like that, Kimi; I didn't order this rain. I didn't ask for this kind of life. What would you have me do? Run out and stop the rain with my bare hands? I can't change the shape of fate. I know. I tried. I left my native shore to tread these "gold-paved" streets, heh, heh; to live and die, unseen, among aliens. And I've found when it rains there's nothing to do but jump into bed and pull the covers over your head, or find a friend and drink a little wine, sing a few songs, and explore those feelings you've forgotten you'd had; so remote, so beautiful, so fragile they are. And then you can pull out your *koto* (chin-chiri-rin) and close your eyes and leave this soggy life-style. Heh, heh. What would you have me do?

The smell of a wet dog isn't bad. There's hardly any smell sadder than the smell of *sake* and rain together. I read in school books where fathers return from work and kiss their wives and toss their children in the air, their pockets bulging with candies and balloons, and the smell of supper cooking on the range permeates the air. Warm smells and good sounds. Here rain drums on the tar-paper roof, and you and your crony sit and drink and you close your eyes and with this expression of tender sorrow, you pluck your imaginary *koto*, brown hands moving on the air; thick fingers touching phantom strings (chin-chiri-rin).

I am a dying reed by the river bed
As thou, a drying dying reed
Alas, our lives together lie,
Blossomless, on the river bed.

Whether we live, or whether die
Tides will ebb and flow
Come then, thou with me, to dwell
As boatmen on Toneh River.

Now you come to me. You come to haunt me as I had never permitted you to do when I was stronger. Sly old man. You waited until there was only a membrane between you and me. Is there still unfinished business? What do you want to tell me? That you are me and I am you and today is the same as yesterday, and tomorrow will be the same as today? I thought I could change the pattern of my life; I thought I could deny your existence, deny our lonely past together, but alas, I had preserved it carefully and when all the frills and furbelows are stripped away, you are here, the backbone of my life, the bleached hull of my shipwreck. And here between yesterday and today, I sing the same lonely song as you. I should not have denied you; I should have woven my life within the framework of our past. I should have loved you. Now my guilt comes home to me.

It's all right, Kimi. The pattern doesn't change, and the guilt doesn't change. It's too late now; too late for might-have-been and would-have-liked. Give yourself to the tide, give yourself to the river; the sun is setting, the desert is cooling. . . .

Kimi.

A nebulous anticipation filled Kimi's bowels as she drifted to a cold dimension. She surrendered to the chill that enveloped her, her lips twisted in a pain akin to joy as she moved with a wind that carried her out, back to the country road, and against the smooth brown cheeks of a lad on a bicycle, and into the blouse that billowed behind him.

Exercises

1. What is the purpose of the frequent shifts of scene in the story?

2. What role does Kimi's mother play?

3. How important are the descriptions of nature? Why?

4. What is the role of Kimi's father?

5. Prepare an eight-point analysis of this story. (See Chapter 1.)

Topics for Writing

1. Water is a recurrent image in this story. Discuss its significance and its appropriateness to the theme.

2. Kimi Sumida relives her life in the hours before her death depicted here. In an essay, consider what she learns about herself and her life during those hours.

3. Discuss the attitude toward life expressed here and in Eudora Welty's "A Worn Path," making specific references to both texts to support your comments.

7. *THE LONGER STORY*

Perhaps the greatest difference between short stories and novels is scope. As a longer and ampler work of prose narrative, a novel can offer a greater variety of characters and develop them more thoroughly. If they so choose, novelists may complicate the plot or plots by introducing a greater number of incidents than a short story could bear. They may also expand the setting, elaborate the situations, and develop extensively several characters and episodes, as short-story writers normally cannot do without diluting their works.

Of course, many authors try their hand at both the novel and the short story, as well as at prose fiction of intermediate lengths. Most of the writers whose stories you have been reading in this book are also novelists of considerable stature, and you may well have encountered the novels of D. H. Lawrence, F. Scott Fitzgerald, Ernest Hemingway, Ralph Ellison, or Kurt Vonnegut before you came across their short stories.

Although Joseph Conrad liked to view even his major novels as tales (*Lord Jim* is subtitled "A Tale," and *Nostromo,* "A Tale of the Seaboard"), he, too, straddles the worlds of short and long fiction. In fact, *Heart of Darkness* started out as a short story that was to have been published in a single issue of *Blackwood's Magazine* in London. Instead, it grew into three installments, appearing early in 1899. In his Author's Note to the book edition, Conrad continues to call *Heart of Darkness* a story. Given its scope, however, critics and scholars have preferred to place it in the category of intermediate-length fiction, although they do not always agree on the best slot for it. Generally, they term it a short novel. But Ian Watt, author of a now classic work, *The Rise of the Novel,*[1] and more recently of an illuminating study of Conrad's fiction, suggests that *Heart of Darkness* should be ranked as a long novella rather than as a short novel. "*Heart of Darkness,*" he writes in his *Conrad in the Nineteenth Century,* "is essentially composed of a single and unbroken narrative movement. This seamless continuity is particularly characteristic of the *novella,* whose length falls between that of the novel and the short story."[2]

While Conrad develops the situation and setting in *Heart of Darkness* far beyond what he could have done in a short story, he does not introduce subplots, or bring in complications that might deflect our attention, even temporarily, from the main line of the story. But although it is not a full-fledged

1. Ian Watt, *The Rise of the Novel: Studies in Defoe, Richardson, and Fielding* (Berkeley: University of California Press, 1959).

2. (Berkeley and Los Angeles: University of California Press, 1979), p. 224.

novel itself, *Heart of Darkness* anticipates the direction that the modern novel would take in terms of both theme and form. The themes of alienation and moral defeatism that weave through this work are among the major concerns of the twentieth-century novel. Yet to deal with these issues, Conrad brings in a narrator who cannot provide all the answers. Marlow belongs in the category of first-person narrator considered in the discussion of point of view in Chapter 3. He is both an observer and a participant. The commentary we get from him is subjective and therefore not entirely reliable; it is colored by his values, his expectations and convictions, and the impact of the events upon him. But his recollection is a precise rendering of what he has experienced, and consequently we ourselves can judge, and try to make sense of, the raw material of his tale, so to speak, just as he is trying to make sense of it in the remembrance.

Marlow can recall, but not necessarily explain, what has happened, and we must contend with the enigmas of the experience as much as he. Furthermore, Marlow does not talk to us directly. Although we hear his very words and may feel that we are present at the telling of the story, his tale is actually transmitted to us by one of the listeners with whom he had shared it. The listener is another first-person narrator, whose words begin and end *Heart of Darkness* and evoke the setting of the Thames estuary that frames the tale of Marlow's journey up the Congo River. Thus, along with its various thematic challenges, enigmas of character, and the symbolic value of the setting — both the setting framing Marlow's story and that within the tale itself — *Heart of Darkness* also offers us an anomaly that turns into a remarkable artistic feat. Even though the main story is kept at two removes from the reader, because the unsettling experience is recalled by someone who heard the tale from a participant, the main story nevertheless achieves extraordinary immediacy and a strong illusion of reality.

Joseph Conrad (1857–1924)

Heart of Darkness

I.

The *Nellie,* a cruising yawl, swung to her anchor without a flutter of the sails, and was at rest. The flood had made, the wind was nearly calm, and being bound down the river, the only thing for it was to come to and wait for the turn of the tide.

The sea-reach of the Thames stretched before us like the beginning of an interminable waterway. In the offing the sea and the sky were welded together without a joint, and in the luminous space the tanned sails of the barges drifting up with the tide seemed to stand still in red clusters of canvas sharply peaked, with gleams of varnished sprits. A haze rested on the low shores that ran out to sea in vanishing flatness. The air was dark above Gravesend, and farther back still seemed condensed into a mournful gloom, brooding motionless over the biggest, and the greatest, town on earth.

The Director of Companies was our captain and our host. We four affectionately watched his back as he stood in the bows looking to seaward. On the whole river there was nothing that looked half so nautical. He resembled a pilot, which to a seaman is trustworthiness personified. It was difficult to realize his work was not out there in the luminous estuary, but behind him, within the brooding gloom.

Between us there was, as I have already said somewhere, the bond of the sea. Besides holding our hearts together through long periods of separation, it had the effect of making us tolerant of each other's yarns — and even convictions. The Lawyer — the best of old fellows — had, because of his many years and many virtues, the only cushion on deck, and was lying on the only rug. The Accountant had brought out already a box of dominoes, and was toying architecturally with the bones. Marlow sat cross-legged right aft, leaning against the mizzen-mast. He had sunken cheeks, a yellow complexion, a straight back, an ascetic aspect, and, with his arms dropped, the palms of hands outwards, resembled an idol. The director, satisfied the anchor had good hold, made his way aft and sat down amongst us. We exchanged a few words lazily. Afterwards there was silence on board the yacht. For some reason or other we did not begin that game of dominoes. We felt meditative, and fit for nothing but placid staring. The day was ending in a serenity of still and exquisite brilliance. The water shone pacifically; the sky, without a speck, was a benign immensity of unstained light; the very mist on the Essex marshes was like a guazy and radiant fabric, hung from the wooded rises inland, and draping the low shores in diaphanous folds. Only the gloom to the west, brooding over the upper reaches, became more sombre every minute, as if angered by the approach of the sun.

And at last, in its curved and imperceptible fall, the sun sank low, and from glowing white changed to a dull red without rays and without heat, as if about to go out suddenly, stricken to death by the touch of that gloom brooding over a crowd of men.

Forthwith a change came over the waters, and the serenity became less brilliant but more profound. The old river in its broad reach rested unruffled at the decline of day, after ages of good service done to the race that peopled its banks, spread out in the tranquil dignity of a waterway to the uttermost ends of the earth. We looked at the venerable stream not in the vivid flush of a short day that comes and departs forever, but in the august light of abiding memories. And indeed nothing is easier for a man who has, as the phrase goes, "followed the sea" with reverence and affection, than to evoke the great spirit of the past upon the lower reaches of the Thames. The tidal current runs to and fro in its unceasing service, crowded with memories of men and ships it had borne to the rest of home or to the battles of the sea. It had known and served all the men of whom the nation is proud, from Sir Francis Drake to Sir John Franklin,[1] knights all, titled and untitled — the great knights-errant of the sea. It had borne all the ships whose names are like jewels flashing in the night of time, from the *Golden Hind* returning with her round flanks full of treasure, to be visited by the Queen's Highness and thus pass out of the gigantic tale, to the *Erebus* and *Terror,* bound in other conquests — and that never returned. It had known the ships and the men. They had sailed from Deptford, from Greenwich, from Erith — the adventurers and the settlers; kings' ships and the ships of men on 'Change; captains, admirals, the dark "interlopers" of the

1. Sir John Franklin: A British explorer of the artic.

Eastern trade, and the commissioned "generals" of East India fleets. Hunters for gold or pursuers of fame, they all had gone out on that stream, bearing the sword, and often the torch, messengers of the might within the land, bearers of a spark from the sacred fire. What greatness had not floated on the ebb of that river into the mystery of an unknown earth! . . . The dreams of men, the seed of commonwealths, the germs of empires.

The sun set; the dusk fell on the stream, and lights began to appear along the shore. The Chapman lighthouse, a three-legged thing erect on a mud-flat, shone strongly. Lights of ships moved in the fairway — a great stir of lights going up and going down. And farther west on the upper reaches the place of the monstrous town was still marked ominously on the sky, a brooding gloom in sunshine, a lurid glare under the stars.

"And this also," said Marlow suddenly, "has been one of the dark places on the earth."

He was the only man of us who still "followed the sea." The worst that could be said of him was that he did not represent his class. He was a seaman, but he was a wanderer, too, while most seamen lead, if one may so express it, a sedentary life. Their minds are of the stay-at-home order, and their home is always with them — the ship; and so is their country — the sea. One ship is very much like another, and the sea is always the same. In the immutability of their surroundings the foreign shores, the foreign faces, the changing immensity of life, glide past, veiled not by a sense of mystery but by a slightly disdainful ignorance; for there is nothing mysterious to a seaman unless it be the sea itself, which is the mistress of his existence and as inscrutable as Destiny. For the rest, after his hours of work, a casual stroll or a casual spree on shore suffices to unfold for him the secret of a whole continent, and generally he finds the secret not worth knowing. The yarns of seamen have a direct simplicity, the whole meaning of which lies within the shell of a cracked nut. But Marlow was not typical (if his propensity to spin yarns be excepted), and to him the meaning of an episode was not inside like a kernel but outside, enveloping the tale which brought it out only as a glow brings out a haze, in the likeness of one of these misty halos that sometimes are made visible by the spectral illumination of moonshine.

His remark did not seem at all surprising. It was just like Marlow. It was accepted in silence. No one took the trouble to grunt even; and presently he said, very slow —

"I was thinking of very old times, when the Romans first came here, nineteen hundred years ago — the other day. . . . Light came out of this river since — you say Knights? Yes; but it is like a running blaze on a plain, like a flash of lightning in the clouds. We live in the flicker — may it last as long as the old earth keeps rolling! But darkness was here yesterday. Imagine the feelings of a commander of a fine — what d'ye call 'em? — trireme in the Mediterranean, ordered suddenly to the north; run overland across the Gauls in a hurry; put in charge of one of these craft the legionaries — a wonderful lot of handy men they must have been, too — used to build, apparently by the hundred, in a month or two, if we may believe what we read. Imagine him here — the very end of the world, a sea the colour of lead, a sky the colour of smoke, a kind of ship about as rigid as a concertina — and going up this river with stores, or orders, or what you like. Sand-banks, marshes, forests, savages, — precious little to eat fit for a civilized man, nothing but Thames water to drink. No

Falernian wine here, no going ashore. Here and there a military camp lost in a wilderness, like a needle in a bundle of hay — cold, fog, tempests, disease, exile, and death, — death skulking in the air, in the water, in the bush. They must have been dying like flies here. Oh, yes — he did it. Did it very well, too, no doubt, and without thinking much about it either, except afterwards to brag of what he had gone through in his time, perhaps. They were men enough to face the darkness. And perhaps he was cheered by keeping his eye on a chance of promotion to the fleet at Ravenna by and by, if he had good friends in Rome and survived the awful climate. Or think of a decent young citizen in a toga — perhaps too much dice, you know — coming out here in the train of some prefect, or tax-gatherer, or trader even, to mend his fortunes. Land in a swamp, march through the woods, and in some inland post feel the savagery, the utter savagery, had closed round him, — all that mysterious life of the wilderness that stirs in the forest, in the jungles, in the hearts of wild men. There's no initiation either into such mysteries. He has to live in the midst of the incomprehensible, which is also detestable. And it has a fascination, too, that goes to work upon him. The fascination of the abomination — you know, imagine the growing regrets, the longing to escape, the powerless disgust, the surrender, the hate."

He paused.

"Mind," he began again, lifting one arm from the elbow, the palm of the hand outwards, so that, with his legs folded before him, he had the pose of a Buddha preaching in European clothes and without a lotus-flower — "Mind, none of us would feel exactly like this. What saves us is efficiency — the devotion to efficiency. But these chaps were not much account, really. They were no colonists; their administration were merely a squeeze, and nothing more, I suspect. They were conquerors, and for that you want only brute force — nothing to boast of, when you have it, since your strength is just an accident arising from the weakness of others. They grabbed what they could get for the sake of what was to be got. It was just robbery with violence, aggravated murder on a great scale, and men going at it blind — as is very proper for those who tackle a darkness. The conquest of the earth, which mostly means the taking it away from those who have a different complexion or slightly flatter noses than ourselves, is not a pretty thing when you look into it too much. What redeems it is the idea only. An idea at the back of it; not a sentimental pretence but an idea; and an unselfish belief in the idea — something you can set up, and bow down before, and offer a sacrifice to. . . ."

He broke off. Flames glided in the river, small green flames, red flames, white flames, pursuing, overtaking, joining, crossing each other — then separating slowly or hastily. The traffic of the great city went on in the deepening night upon the sleepless river. We looked on, waiting patiently — there was nothing else to do till the end of the flood; but it was only after a long silence, when he said, in a hesitating voice, "I suppose you fellows remember I did once turn fresh-water sailor for a bit," that we knew we were fated, before the ebb began to run, to hear about one of Marlow's inconclusive experiences.

"I don't want to bother you much with what happened to me personally," he began, showing in this remark the weakness of many tellers of tales who seem so often unaware of what their audience would best like to hear; "yet to understand the effect of it on me you ought to know how I got out there, what I saw, how I went up that river to the place where I first met the poor chap. It was the farthest point of navigation and the culminating point of my experience. It seemed somehow to throw a kind of light on everything about me — and into my thoughts. It was sombre enough, too — and pitiful — not extraordinary in any way — not very clear either. No, not very clear. And yet it seemed to throw a kind of light.

"I had then, as you remember, just returned to London after a lot of Indian Ocean, Pacific, China Seas — a regular dose of the East — six years or so, and I was loafing about, hindering you fellows in your work and invading your homes, just as though I had got a heavenly mission to civilize you. It was very fine for a time, but after a bit I did get tired of resting. Then I began to look for a ship — I should think the hardest work on earth. But the ships wouldn't even look at me. And I got tired of that game, too.

"Now when I was a little chap I had a passion for maps. I would look for hours at South America, or Africa, or Australia, and lose myself in all the glories of exploration. At the time there were many blank spaces on the earth, and when I saw one that looked particularly inviting on a map (but they all look that) I would put my finger on it and say, When I grow up I will go there. The North Pole was one of these places, I remember. Well, I haven't been there yet, and shall not try now. The glamour's off. Other places were scattered about the Equator, and in every sort of latitude all over the two hemispheres. I have been in some of them, and . . . well, we won't talk about that. But there was one yet — the biggest, the most blank, so to speak — that I had a hankering after.

"True, by this time it was not a blank space any more. It had got filled since my boyhood with rivers and lakes and names. It had ceased to be a blank space of delightful mystery — a white patch for a boy to dream gloriously over. It had become a place of darkness. But there was in it one river especially, a mighty big river, that you could see on the map, resembling an immense snake uncoiled, with its head in the sea, its body at rest curving afar over a vast country, and its tail lost in the depths of the land. And as I looked at the map of it in a shop-window, it fascinated me as a snake would a bird — a silly little bird. Then I remembered there was a big concern, a Company for trade on that river. Dash it all! I thought to myself, they can't trade without using some kind of craft on that lot of fresh water — steamboats! Why shouldn't I try to get charge of one? I went on along Fleet Street, but could not shake off the idea. The snake had charmed me.

"You understand it was a Continental concern, that Trading society; but I have a lot of relations living on the Continent, because it's cheap and not so nasty as it looks, they say.

"I am sorry to own I began to worry them. This was already a fresh departure for me. I was not used to get things that way, you know. I always went my own road and on my own legs where I had a mind to go. I wouldn't have believed it of myself; but, then — you see — I felt somehow I must get there by hook or by crook. So I worried them. The men said 'My dear fellow,' and did nothing. Then — would you believe it? — I tried the women. I, Charlie Marlow, set the women to work — to get a job. Heavens! Well, you see, the notion drove me. I had an aunt, a dear enthusiastic soul. She wrote: 'It will be delightful. I am ready to do anything, anything for you. It is a glorious idea. I know the wife of a very high personage in the Administration, and also a man who has lots of influence with,' etc., etc. She was determined to make no end of fuss to get me appointed skipper of a river steamboat, if such was my fancy.

"I got my appointment — of course; and I got it very quick. It appears the Company had received news that one of their captains had been killed in a scuffle with the natives. This was my chance, and it made me the more anxious to go. It was only months and months afterwards, when I made the attempt to recover what was left of the body, that I heard the original quarrel arose from a misunderstanding about some hens. Yes, two black hens. Fresleven — that was the fellow's name, a Dane — thought himself wronged somehow in the bargain, so he went ashore and started to hammer the chief of the village with a stick. Oh, it didn't surprise me in the least to hear this, and at the same time to be told that Fresleven was the gentlest, quietest creature that ever walked on two legs. No doubt he was; but he had been a couple of years already out there engaged in the noble cause, you know, and he probably felt the need at last of asserting his self-respect in some way. Therefore he whacked the old nigger mercilessly, while a big crowd of his people watched him, thunderstruck, till some man — I was told the chief's son — in desperation at hearing the old chap yell, made a tentative jab with a spear at the white man — and of course it went quite easy between the shoulder-blades. Then the whole population cleared into the forest, expecting all kinds of calamities to happen, while, on the other hand, the steamer Fresleven commanded left also in a bad panic, in charge of the engineer, I believe. Afterwards nobody seemed to trouble much about Fresleven's remains, till I got out and stepped into his shoes. I couldn't let it rest, though; but when an opportunity offered at last to meet my predecessor, the grass growing through his ribs was tall enough to hide his bones. They were all there. The supernatural being had not been touched after he fell. And the village was deserted, the huts gaped black, rotting, all askew within the fallen enclosures. A calamity had come to it, sure enough. The people had vanished. Mad terror had scattered them, men, women, and children, through the bush, and they had never returned. What became of the hens I don't know either. I should think the cause of progress got them, anyhow. However, through this glorious affair I got my appointment, before I had fairly begun to hope for it.

"I flew around like mad to get ready, and before forty-eight hours I was crossing the Channel to show myself to my employers, and sign the contract. In a very few hours I arrived in a city that always makes me think of a whited sepulchre. Prejudice no doubt. I had no difficulty in finding the Company's offices. It was the biggest thing in the town, and everybody I met was full of it. They were going to run an over-sea empire, and make no end of coin by trade.

"A narrow and deserted street in deep shadow, high houses, innumerable windows with venetian blinds, a dead silence, grass sprouting between the stones, imposing carriage archways right and left, immense double doors standing ponderously ajar. I slipped through one of these cracks, went up a swept and ungarnished staircase, as arid as a desert, and opened the first door I came to. Two women, one fat and the other slim, sat on straw-bottomed chairs, knitting black wool. The slim one got up and walked straight at me — still knitting with down-cast eyes — and only just as I began to think of getting out of her way, as you would for a somnambulist, stood still, and looked up. Her dress was as plain as an umbrella-cover, and she turned round without a word and preceded me into a waiting-room. I gave my name, and looked about. Deal table in the middle, plain chairs all round the walls, on one end a large shining map, marked with all the colours of a rainbow. There was a vast amount of red — good to see at any time, because one knows that some real work is done in there, a deuce of a lot of blue, a little green, smears of orange, and, on the East Coast, a purple patch, to show where the jolly pioneers of progress drink the jolly lager-beer. However, I wasn't going into any of these. I was going into the yellow. Dead in the centre. And the river was there — fascinating — deadly — like a snake. Ough! A door opened, a white-haired secretarial head, but wearing a compassionate expression, appeared, and a skinny forefinger beckoned me into the sanctuary. Its light was dim, and a heavy writing-desk squatted in the middle. From behind that structure came out an impression of pale plumpness in a frock-coat. The great man himself. He was five feet six, I should judge, and had his grip on the handle-end of ever so many millions. He shook hands, I fancy, murmured vaguely, was satisfied with my French. *Bon voyage.*

"In about forty-five seconds I found myself again in the waiting-room with the compassionate secretary, who, full of desolation and sympathy, made me sign some document. I believe I undertook amongst other things not to disclose any trade secrets. Well, I am not going to.

"I began to feel slightly uneasy. You know I am not used to such ceremonies, and there was something ominous in the atmosphere. It was just as though I had been let into some conspiracy — I don't know — something not quite right; and I was glad to get out. In the outer room the two women knitted black wool feverishly. People were arriving, and the younger one was walking back and forth introducing them. The old one sat on her chair. Her flat cloth slippers were propped up on a foot-warmer, and a cat reposed on her lap. She wore a starched white affair on her head, had a wart on one cheek, and silver-rimmed spectacles hung on the tip of her nose. She glanced at me above the glasses. The swift and indifferent placidity of that look troubled me. Two youths with foolish and cheery countenances were being piloted over, and she threw at them the same quick glance of unconcerned wisdom. She seemed to know all about them and about me, too. An eerie feeling came over me. She seemed uncanny and fateful. Often far away there I thought of these two, guarding the door of Darkness, knitting black wool as for a warm pall, one introducing, introducing continuously to the unknown, the other scrutinizing the cheery and foolish faces with unconcerned old eyes. *Ave!* Old knitter of black wool. *Morituri te salutant.*[2] Not many of those she looked at ever saw her again — not half, by a long way.

"There was yet a visit to the doctor. 'A simple formality,' assured me the secretary, with an air of taking an immense part in all my sorrows. Accordingly a young chap wearing his hat over the left eyebrow, some clerk I suppose, — there must have been clerks in the business, though the house was as still as a house in a city of the dead — came from somewhere up-stairs, and led me forth. He was shabby and careless, with ink-stains on the sleeves of his jacket, and his cravat was large and billowy, under a chin shaped like the toe of an old boot. It was a little too early for the doctor, so I proposed a drink, and thereupon he

2. *Ave!...Morituri te salutant:* Hail! They who are about to die salute you.

developed a vein of joviality. As we sat over our vermuths he glorified the Company's business, and by and by I expressed casually my surprise at him not going out there. He became very cool and collected all at once. 'I am not such a fool as I look, quoth Plato to his disciples,' he said sententiously, emptied his glass with great resolution, and we rose.

"The old doctor felt my pulse, evidently thinking of something else the while. 'Good, good for there,' he mumbled, and then with a certain eagerness asked me whether I would let him measure my head. Rather surprised, I said Yes, when he produced a thing like calipers and got the dimensions back and front and every way, taking notes carefully. He was an unshaven little man in a threadbare coat like a gaberdine, with his feet in slippers, and I thought him a harmless fool. 'I always ask leave, in the interests of science, to measure the crania of those going out there,' he said. 'And when they come back, too?' I asked. 'Oh, I never see them,' he remarked; 'and, moreover, the changes take place inside, you know.' He smiled, as if at some quiet joke. 'So you are going out there. Famous. Interesting, too.' He gave me a searching glance, and made another note. 'Ever any madness in your family?' he asked, in a matter-of-fact tone. I felt very annoyed. 'Is that question in the interests of science, too?' 'It would be,' he said, without taking notice of my irritation, 'interesting for science to watch the mental changes of individuals, on the spot, but . . .' 'Are you an alienist?' I interrupted. 'Every doctor should be — a little,' answered that original, imperturbably. 'I have a little theory which you Messieurs who go out there must help me to prove. This is my share in the advantages my country shall reap from the possession of such a magnificent dependency. The mere wealth I leave to others. Pardon my questions, but you are the first Englishman coming under my observation . . .' I hastened to assure him I was not in the least typical. 'If I were,' said I, 'I wouldn't be talking like this with you.' 'What you say is rather profound, and probably erroneous,' he said, with a laugh. 'Avoid irritation more than exposure to the sun. Adieu. How do you English say, eh? Good-bye. Ah! Good-bye. Adieu. In the tropics one must before everything keep calm.' . . . He lifted a warning forefinger. . . . *'Du calme, du calme. Adieu.'*

"One thing more remained to do — say good-bye to my excellent aunt. I found her triumphant. I had a cup of tea — the last decent cup of tea for many days — and in a room that most soothingly looked just as you would expect a lady's drawing-room to look, we had a long quiet chat by the fireside. In the course of these confidences it became quite plain to me I had been represented to the wife of the high dignitary, and goodness knows to how many more people besides, as an exceptional and gifted creature — a piece of good fortune for the Company — a man you don't get hold of every day. Good heavens! and I was going to take charge of a two-penny-half-penny river-steamboat with a penny whistle attached! It appeared, however, I was also one of the Workers, with a capital — you know. Something like an emissary of light, something like a lower sort of apostle. There had been a lot of such rot let loose in print and talk just about that time, and the excellent woman, living right in the rush of all that humbug, got carried off her feet. She talked about 'weaning those ignorant millions from their horrid ways,' till, upon my word, she made me quite uncomfortable. I ventured to hint that the Company was run for profit.

" 'You forget, dear Charlie, that the labourer is worthy of his hire,' she said, brightly. It's queer how out of touch with truth women are. They live in a world of their own, and there has never been anything like it, and never can be. It is too beautiful altogether, and if they were to set it up it would go to pieces before the first sunset. Some confounded fact we men have been living contentedly with ever since the day of creation would start up and knock the whole thing over.

"After this I got embraced, told to wear flannel, be sure to write often, and so on — and I left. In the street — I don't know why — a queer feeling came to me that I was an impostor. Odd thing that I, who used to clear out for any part of the world at twenty-four hours' notice, with less thought than most men give to the crossing of a street, had a moment — I won't say of hesitation, but of startled pause, before this commonplace affair. The best way I can explain it to you is by saying that, for a second or two, I felt as though, instead of going to the centre of a continent, I were about to set off for the centre of the earth.

"I left in a French steamer, and she called in every blamed port they have out there, for, as far as I could see, the sole purpose of landing soldiers and custom-house officers. I watched the coast. Watching a coast as it slips by the ship is like thinking about an enigma. There it is before you — smiling, frowning, inviting, grand, mean, insipid, or savage, and always mute with an air of whispering. Come and find out. This one was almost featureless, as if still in the making, with an aspect of monotonous grimness. The edge of a colossal jungle, so dark-green as to be almost black, fringed with white surf, ran straight, like a ruled line, far, far away along a blue sea whose glitter was blurred by a creeping mist. The sun was fierce, the land seemed to glisten and drip with steam. Here and there grayish-whitish specks showed up clustered inside the white surf, with a flag flying above them perhaps. Settlements some centuries old, and still no bigger than pinheads on the untouched expanse of their background. We pounded along, stopped, landed soldiers; went on, landed custom-house clerks to levy toll in what looked like a God-forsaken wilderness, with a tin shed and a flag-pole lost in it; landed more soldiers — to take care of the custom-house clerks, presumably. Some, I heard, got drowned in the surf; but whether they did or not, nobody seemed particularly to care. They were just flung out there, and on we went. Every day the coast looked the same, as though we had not moved; but we passed various places — trading places — with names like Gran' Bassam, Little Popo; names that seemed to belong to some sordid farce acted in front of a sinister back-cloth. The idleness of a passenger, my isolation amongst all these men with whom I had no point of contact, the oily and languid sea, the uniform sombreness of the coast, seemed to keep me away from the truth of things, within the toil of a mournful and senseless delusion. The voice of the surf heard now and then was a positive pleasure, like the speech of a brother. It was something natural, that had its reason, that had a meaning. Now and then a boat from the shore gave one a momentary contact with reality. It was paddled by black fellows. You could see from afar the white of their eyeballs glistening. They shouted, sang; their bodies streamed with perspiration; they had faces like grotesque masks — these chaps; but they had bone, muscle, a wild vitality, an intense energy of movement, that was as natural and true as the surf along their coast. They wanted no excuse for being there. They were a great comfort to look at. For a time I would feel I belonged still to a world of straightforward facts; but the feeling would not last long. Something would turn up to scare it away. Once, I remember, we came upon a man-of-war anchored off the coast. There wasn't even a shed there, and she was shelling the bush. It appears the French had one of their wars going on thereabouts. Her ensign dropped limp like a rag; the muzzles of the long six-inch guns stuck out all over the low hull; the greasy, slimy swell swung her up lazily and let her down, swaying her thin masts. In the empty immensity of earth, sky, and water, there she was, incomprehensible, firing into a continent. Pop, would go one of the six-inch guns; a small flame would dart and vanish, a little white smoke would disappear, a tiny projectile would give a feeble screech — and nothing happened. Nothing could happen. There was a touch of insanity in the proceeding, a sense of lugubrious drollery in the sight; and it was not dissipated by somebody on board assuring me earnestly there was a camp of natives — he called them enemies! — hidden out of sight somewhere.

"We gave her her letters (I heard the men in that lonely ship were dying of fever at the rate of three a day) and went on. We called at some more places with farcical names, where the merry dance of death and trade goes on in a still and earthy atmosphere as of an overheated catacomb; all along the formless coast bordered by dangerous surf, as if Nature herself had tried to ward off intruders; in and out of rivers, streams of death in life, whose banks were rotting into mud, whose waters, thickened into slime, invaded the contorted mangroves, that seemed to writhe at us in the extremity of an impotent despair, Nowhere did we stop long enough to get a particularized impression, but the general sense of vague and oppressive wonder grew upon me. It was like a weary pilgrimage amongst hints for nightmares.

"It was upward of thirty days before I saw the mouth of the big river. We anchored off the seat of the government. But my work would not begin till some two hundred miles farther on. So as soon as I could I made a start for a place thirty miles higher up.

"I had my passage on a little sea-going steamer. Her captain was a Swede, and knowing me for a seaman, invited me on the bridge. He was a young man, lean, fair, and morose, with lanky hair and a shuffling gait. As we left the miserable little wharf, he tossed his head contemptuously at the shore. 'Been living there?' he asked. I said, 'Yes.' 'Fine lot these government chaps — are they not?' he went on, speaking English with great precision and considerable bitterness. 'It is funny what some people will do for a few francs a month. I wonder what becomes of that kind when it goes up country?' I said to him I expected to see that soon. 'So-o-o!' he exclaimed. He shuffled athwart, keeping one eye ahead vigilantly. 'Don't be too sure,' he continued. 'The other day I took up a man who hanged himself on the road. He was a Swede, too.' 'Hanged himself! Why, in God's name?' I cried. He kept on looking out watchfully. 'Who knows? The sun too much for him, or the country perhaps.'

"At last we opened a reach. A rocky cliff appeared, mounds of turned-up earth by the shore, houses on a hill, others with iron roofs, amongst a waste of excavations, or hanging to the declivity. A continuous noise of the rapids above hovered over this scene of inhabited devastation. A lot of people, mostly black and naked, moved about like ants. A jetty projected into the river. A blinding sunlight drowned all this at times in a sudden recrudescence of glare. 'There's your Company's station,' said the Swede, pointing to three wooden barrack-like structures on the rocky slope. 'I will send your things up. Four boxes did you say? So. Farewell.'

"I came upon a boiler wallowing in the grass, then found a path leading up the hill. It turned aside for the boulders, and also for an undersized railway-truck lying there on its back with its wheels in the air. One was off. The thing looked as dead as the carcass of some animal. I came upon more pieces of decaying machinery, a stack of rusty rails. To the left a clump of trees made a shady spot, where dark things seemed to stir feebly. I blinked, the path was steep. A horn tooted to the right, and I saw the black people run. A heavy and dull detonation shook the ground, a puff of smoke came out of the cliff, and that was all. No change appeared on the face of the rock. They were building a railway. The cliff was not in the way or anything; but this objectless blasting was all the work going on.

"A slight clinking behind me made me turn my head. Six black men advanced in a file, toiling up the path. They walked erect and slow, balancing small baskets full of earth on their heads, and the clink kept time with their footsteps. Black rags were wound round their loins, and the short ends behind waggled to and fro like tails. I could see every rib, the joints of their limbs were like knots in a rope; each had an iron collar on his neck, and all were connected together with a chain whose bights swung between them, rhythmically clinking. Another report from the cliff made me think suddenly of that ship of war I had seen firing into a continent. It was the same kind of ominous voice; but these men could by no stretch of imagination be called enemies. They were called criminals, and the outraged law, like the bursting shells, had come to them, an insoluble mystery from the sea. All their meagre breasts panted together, the violently dilated nostrils quivered, the eyes stared stonily up-hill. They passed me within six inches, without a glance, with that complete, death-like indifference of unhappy savages. Behind this raw matter one of the reclaimed, the product of the new forces at work, strolled despondently, carrying a rifle by its middle. He had a uniform jacket with one button off, and seeing a white man on the path, hoisted his weapon to his shoulder with alacrity. This was simple prudence, white men being so much alike at a distance that he could not tell who I might be. He was speedily reassured, and with a large, white, rascally grin, and a glance at his charge, seemed to take me into partnership in his exalted trust. After all, I also was a part of the great cause of these high and just proceedings.

"Instead of going up, I turned and descended to the left. My idea was to let that chain-gang get out of sight before I climbed the hill. You know I am not particularly tender; I've had to strike and to fend off. I've had to resist and to attack sometimes — that's only one way of resisting — without counting the exact cost, according to the demands of such sort of life as I had blundered into. I've seen the devil of violence, and the devil of greed, and the devil of hot desire; but, by all the stars! these were strong, lusty, red-eyed devils, that swayed and drove men — men, I tell you. But as I stood on this hillside, I foresaw that in the blinding sunshine of that land I would become acquainted with a flabby, pretending, weak-eyed devil of a rapacious and pitiless folly. How insidious he could be, too, I was only to find out several months later and a thousand miles farther. For a moment I stood appalled, as though by a warning. Finally I descended the hill, obliquely, towards the trees I had seen.

"I avoided a vast artificial hole somebody had been digging on the slope, the purpose of which I found it impossible to divine. It wasn't a quarry or a sandpit, anyhow. It was just a hole. It might have been connected with the philanthropic desire of giving the criminals something to do. I don't know. Then I nearly fell into a very narrow ravine, almost no more than a scar in the hillside. I discovered that a lot of imported drainage-pipes for the settlement had been tumbled in there. There wasn't one that was not broken. It was a wanton smash-up. At last I got under the trees. My purpose was to stroll into the shade for a moment; but no sooner within than it seemed to me I had stepped into the gloomy circle of some Inferno. The rapids were near, and an uninterrupted, uniform, headlong, rushing noise filled the mournful stillness of the grove, where not a breath stirred, not a leaf moved, with a mysterious sound — as though the tearing pace of the launched earth had suddenly become audible.

"Black shapes crouched, lay, sat between the trees leaning against the trunks, clinging to the earth, half coming out, half effaced within the dim light, in all the attitudes of pain, abandonment, and despair. Another mine on the cliff went off, followed by a slight shudder of the soil under my feet. The work was going on. The work! And this was the place where some of the helpers had withdrawn to die.

"They were dying slowly — it was very clear. They were not enemies, they were not criminals, they were nothing earthly now, — nothing but black shadows of disease and starvation, lying confusedly in the greenish gloom. Brought from all the recesses of the coast in all the legality of time contracts, lost in uncongenial surroundings, fed on unfamiliar food, they sickened, became inefficient, and were then allowed to crawl away and rest. These moribund shapes were free as air — and nearly as thin. I began to distinguish the gleam of the eyes under the trees. Then, glancing down, I saw a face near my hand. The black bones reclined at full length with one shoulder against the tree, and slowly the eyelids rose and the sunken eyes looked up at me, enormous and vacant, a kind of blind, white flicker in the depths of the orbs, which died out slowly. The man seemed young — almost a boy — but you know with them it's hard to tell. I found nothing else to do but to offer him one of my good Swede's ship's biscuits I had in my pocket. The fingers closed slowly on it and held — there was no other movement and no other glance. He had tied a bit of white worsted round his neck — Why? Where did he get it? Was it a badge — an ornament — a charm — a propitiatory act? Was there any idea at all connected with it? It looked startling round his black neck, this bit of white thread from beyond the seas.

"Near the same tree two more bundles of acute angles sat with their legs drawn up. One, with his chin propped on his knees, stared at nothing, in an intolerable and appalling manner: his brother phantom rested its forehead, as if overcome with a great weariness; and all about others were scattered in every pose of contorted collapse, as in some picture of a massacre or a pestilence. While I stood horror-struck, one of these creatures rose to his hands and knees, and went off on all-fours towards the river to drink. He lapped out of his hand, then sat up in the sunlight, crossing his shins in front of him, and after a time let his woolly head fall on his breastbone.

"I didn't want any more loitering in the shade, and I made haste towards the station. When near the buildings I met a white man, in such an unexpected elegance of get-up that in the first moment I took him for a sort of vision. I saw a high starched collar, white cuffs, a light alpaca jacket, snowy trousers, a clean necktie, and varnished boots. No hat. Hair parted, brushed, oiled, under a green-lined parasol held in a big white hand. He was amazing, and had a penholder behind his ear.

"I shook hands with this miracle, and I learned he was the Company's chief accountant, and that all the book-keeping was done at this station. He had come out for a moment, he said, 'to get a breath of fresh air.' The expression sounded wonderfully odd, with its suggestion of sedentary desk-life. I wouldn't have mentioned the fellow to you at all, only it was from his lips that I first heard the name of the man who is so indissolubly connected with the memories of that time. Moreover, I respected the fellow. Yes; I respected his collars, his vast cuffs, his brushed hair. His appearance was certainly that of a hairdresser's dummy; but in the great demoralization of the land he kept up his appearance. That's backbone. His starched collars and got-up shirt-fronts were achievements of character. He had been out nearly three years; and, later, I could not help asking him how he managed to sport such linen. He had just the faintest blush, and said modestly, 'I've been teaching one of the native women about the station. It was difficult. She had a distaste for the work.' Thus this man had verily accomplished something. And he was devoted to his books, which were in apple-pie order.

"Everything else in the station was in a muddle, — heads, things, buildings. Strings of dusty niggers with splay feet arrived and departed; a stream of manufactured goods, rubbishy cottons, beads, and brass-wire set into the depths of darkness, and in return came a precious trickle of ivory.

"I had to wait in the station for ten days — an eternity. I lived in a hut in the yard, but to be out of the chaos I would sometimes get into the accountant's office. It was built of horizontal planks, and so badly put together that, as he bent over his high desk, he was barred from neck to heels with narrow strips of sunlight. There was no need to open the big shutter to see. It was hot there, too; big flies buzzed fiendishly, and did not sting, but stabbed. I sat generally on the floor, while, of faultless appearance (and even slightly scented), perching on a high stool, he wrote, he wrote. Sometimes he stood up for exercise. When a trucklebed with a sick man (some invalid agent from up-country) was put in there, he exhibited a gentle annoyance. 'The groans of this sick person,' he said, 'distract my attention. And without that it is extremely difficult to guard against clerical errors in this climate.'

"One day he remarked, without lifting his head, 'In the interior you will no doubt meet Mr. Kurtz.' On my asking who Mr. Kurtz was, he said he was a first-class agent; and seeing my disappointment at this information, he added slowly, laying down his pen, 'He is a very remarkable person.' Further questions elicited from him that Mr. Kurtz was at present in charge of a trading post, a very important one, in the true ivory-country, at 'the very bottom of there. Sends in as much ivory as all the others put together . . .' He began to write again. The sick man was too ill to groan. The flies buzzed in a great peace.

"Suddenly there was a growing murmur of voices and a great tramping of feet. A caravan had come in. A violent babble of uncouth sounds burst out on the other side of the planks. All the carriers were speaking together, and in the midst of the uproar the lamentable voice of the chief agent was heard 'giving it up' tearfully for the twentieth time that day. . . . He rose slowly. 'What a frightful row,' he said. He crossed the room gently to look at the sick man, and returning, said to me, 'He does not hear.' 'What! Dead?' I asked, startled.

'No, not yet,' he answered, with great composure. Then, alluding with a toss of the head to the tumult in the station-yard, 'When one has got to make correct entries, one comes to hate those savages — hate them to the death." He remained thoughtful for a moment. 'When you see Mr. Kurtz,' he went on, 'tell him from me that everything here' — he glanced at the desk — 'is very satisfactory. I don't like to write to him — with those messengers of ours you never know who may get hold of your letter — at that Central Station.' He stared at me for a moment with his mild, bulging eyes. 'Oh, he will go far, very far,' he began again. 'He will be a somebody in the Administration before long. They, above — the Council in Europe, you know — mean him to be.'

"He turned to his work. The noise outside had ceased, and presently in going out I stopped at the door. In the steady buzz of flies the homeward-bound agent was lying flushed and insensible; the other, bent over his books, was making correct entries of perfectly correct transactions; and fifty feet below the doorstep I could see the still tree-tops of the grove of death.

"Next day I left that station at last, with a caravan of sixty men, for a two-hundred-mile tramp.

"No use telling you much about that. Paths, paths, everywhere; a stamped-in network of paths spreading over the empty land, through long grass, through burnt grass, through thickets, down and up chilly ravines, up and down stony hills ablaze with heat; and a solitude, a solitude, nobody, not a hut. The population had cleared out a long time ago. Well, if a lot of mysterious niggers armed with all kinds of fearful weapons suddenly took to travelling on the road between Deal and Gravesend, catching the yokels right and left to carry heavy loads for them, I fancy every farm and cottage thereabouts would get empty very soon. Only here the dwellings were gone, too. Still I passed through several abandoned villages. There's something pathetically childish in the ruins of grass walls. Day after day, with the stamp and shuffle of sixty pair of bare feet behind me, each pair under a 60-lb. load. Camp, cook, sleep, strike camp, march. Now and then a carrier dead in harness, at rest in the long grass near the path, with an empty water-gourd and his long staff lying by his side. A great silence around and above. Perhaps on some quiet night the tremor of far-off drums, sinking, swelling, a tremor vast, faint; a sound weird, appealing, suggestive, and wild — and perhaps with as profound a meaning as the sound of bells in a Christian country. Once a white man in an unbuttoned uniform, camping on the path with an armed escort of lank Zanzibaris, very hospitable and festive — not to say drunk. Was looking after the upkeep of the road, he declared. Can't say I saw any road or any upkeep, unless the body of a middle-aged negro, with a bullet-hole in the forehead, upon which I absolutely stumbled three miles farther on, may be considered as a permanent improvement. I had a white companion, too, not a bad chap, but rather too fleshy and with the exasperating habit of fainting on the hot hillsides, miles away from the least bit of shade and water. Annoying, you know, to hold your own coat like a parasol over a man's head while he is coming-to. I couldn't help asking him once what he meant by coming there at all. 'To make money, of course. What do you think?' he said, scornfully. Then he got fever, and had to be carried in a hammock slung under a pole. As he weighed sixteen stone I had no end of rows with the carriers. They jibbed, ran away, sneaked off with their loads in the night — quite a mutiny. So, one evening, I made a speech in English with gestures, not one of which was lost to the sixty pairs of eyes before me, and the next morning I started the hammock off in front all right. An hour afterwards I came upon the whole concern wrecked in a bush — man, hammock, groans, blankets, horrors. The heavy pole had skinned his poor nose. He was very anxious for me to kill somebody, but there wasn't the shadow of a carrier near. I remembered the old doctor — 'It would be interesting for science to watch the mental changes of individuals, on the spot.' I felt I was becoming scientifically interesting. However, all that is to no purpose. On the fifteenth day I came in sight of the big river again, and hobbled into the Central Station. It was on a back water surrounded by scrub and forest, with a pretty border of smelly mud on one side, and on the three others enclosed by a crazy fence of rushes. A neglected gap was all the gate it had, and the first glance at the place was enough to let you see the flabby devil was running that show. White men with long staves in their hands appeared languidly from amongst the buildings, strolling up to take a look at me, and then retired out of sight somewhere. One of them, a stout, excitable chap with black moustaches, informed me with great volubility and many digressions, as soon as I told him who I was, that my steamer was at the bottom of the river. I was thunderstruck. What, how, why? Oh, it was 'all right.' The 'manager himself' was there. All quite correct. 'Everybody had behaved splendidly! splendidly!' — 'you must,' he said in agitation, 'go and see the general manager at once. He is waiting!'

"I did not see the real significance of that wreck at once. I fancy I see it now, but I am not sure — not at all. Certainly the affair was too stupid — when I think of it — to be altogether natural. Still . . . But at the moment it presented itself simply as a confounded nuisance. The steamer was sunk. They had started two days before in a sudden hurry up the river with the manager on board, in charge of some volunteer skipper, and before they had been out three hours they tore the bottom out of her on stones, and she sank near the south bank. I asked myself what I was to do there, now my boat was lost. As a matter of fact, I had plenty to do in fishing my command out of the river. I had to set about it the very next day. That, and the repairs when I brought the pieces to the station, took some months.

"My first interview with the manager was curious. He did not ask me to sit down after my twenty-mile walk that morning. He was commonplace in complexion, in feature, in manners, and in voice. He was of middle size and of ordinary build. His eyes, of the usual blue, were perhaps remarkably cold, and he certainly could make his glance fall on one as trenchant and heavy as an axe. But even at these times the rest of his person seemed to disclaim the intention. Otherwise there was only an indefinable, faint expression of his lips, something stealthy — a smile — not a smile — I remember it, but I can't explain. It was unconscious, this smile was, though just after he had said some thing it got intensified for an instant. It came at the end of his speeches like a seal applied on the words to make the meaning of the commonest phrase appear absolutely inscrutable. He was a common trader, from his youth up employed in these parts — nothing more. He was obeyed, yet he inspired neither love nor fear, nor even respect. He inspired uneasiness. That was it! Uneasiness. Not a definite mistrust — just uneasiness — nothing more. You have no idea how effective such a . . . a . . . faculty can be. He had no genius for organizing, for initiative, or for order even. That was evident in such things as the deplorable state of the station. He had no learning, and no intelligence. His position had come to him — why? Perhaps because he was never ill . . . He had served three terms of three years out there . . . Because triumphant health in the general rout of constitutions is a kind of power in itself. When he went home on leave he rioted on a large scale — pompously. Jack ashore — with a difference — in externals only. This one could gather from his casual talk. He originated nothing, he could keep the routine going — that's all. But he was great. He was great by this little thing that it was impossible to tell what could control such a man. He never gave that secret away. Perhaps there was nothing within him. Such a suspicion made one pause — for out there there were no external checks. Once when various tropical diseases had laid low almost every 'agent' in the station, he was heard to say, 'Men who come out here should have no entrails.' He sealed the utterance with that smile of his, as though it had been a door opening into a darkness he had in his keeping. You fancied you had seen things — but the seal was on. When annoyed at meal-times by the constant quarrels of the white men about precedence, he ordered an immense round table to be made, for which a special house had to be built. This was the station's mess-room. Where he sat was the first place — the rest were nowhere. One felt this to be his unalterable conviction. He was neither civil nor uncivil. He was quiet. He allowed his 'boy' — an overfed young negro from the coast — to treat the white men, under his very eyes, with provoking insolence.

He began to speak as soon as he saw me. I had been very long on the road. He could not wait. Had to start without me. The up-river stations had to be relieved. There had been so many delays already that he did not know who was dead and who was alive, and how they got on — and so on, and so on. He paid no attention to my explanations, and, playing with a stick of sealing-wax, repeated several times that the situation was 'very grave, very grave.' There were rumours that a very important station was in jeopardy, and its chief, Mr. Kurtz, was ill. Hoped it was not true. Mr. Kurtz was . . . I felt weary and irritable. Hang Kurtz, I thought. I interrupted him by saying I had heard of Mr. Kurtz on the coast. 'Ah! So they talk of him down there,' he murmured to himself. Then he began again, assuring me Mr. Kurtz was the best agent he had, an exceptional man, of the greatest importance to the Company; therefore I could understand his anxiety. He was, he said, 'very, very uneasy.' Certainly he fidgeted on his chair a good deal, exclaimed, 'Ah, Mr. Kurtz!' broke the stick of sealing-wax and seemed dumbfounded by the accident. Next thing he wanted to know 'how long it would take to' . . . I interrupted him again. Being hungry, you know, and kept on my feet too, I was getting savage. 'How can I tell? I said. 'I haven't even seen the wreck yet — some months, no doubt.' All this talk seemed to me so futile. 'Some months,' he said. 'Well, let us say three months before we can make a start. Yes. That ought to do the affair.' I flung out of his hut (he lived all alone in a clay hut with a sort of verandah) muttering to myself my opinion of him. He was a chattering idiot. Afterwards I took it back when it was borne in upon me startlingly with what extreme nicety he had estimated the time requisite for the 'affair.'

"I went to work the next day, turning, so to speak, my back on that station. In that way only it seemed to me I could keep my hold on the redeeming facts of life. Still, one must look about sometimes; and then I saw this station, these men strolling aimlessly about in the sunshine of the yard. I asked myself sometimes what it all meant. They wandered here and there with their absurd long staves in their hands, like a lot of faithless pilgrims bewitched inside a rotten fence. The word 'ivory' rang in the air, was whispered, was sighed. You would think they were praying to it. A tint of imbecile rapacity blew through it all, like a whiff from some corpse. By Jove! I've never seen anything so unreal in my life. And outside, the silent wilderness surrounding this cleared speck on the earth struck me as something great and invincible, like evil or truth, waiting patiently for the passing away of this fantastic invasion.

"Oh, these months! Well, never mind. Various things happened. One evening a grass shed full of calico, cotton prints, beads, and I don't know what else, burst into a blaze so suddenly that you would have thought the earth had opened to let an avenging fire consume all that trash. I was smoking my pipe quietly by my dismantled steamer, and saw them all cutting capers in the light, with their arms lifted high, when the stout man with moustaches came tearing down to the river, a tin pail in his hand, assured me that everybody was 'behaving splendidly, splendidly,' dipped about a quart of water and tore back again. I noticed there was a hole in the bottom of his pail.

"I strolled up. There was no hurry. You see the thing had gone off like a box of matches. It had been hopeless from the very first. The flame had leaped high, driven everybody back, lighted up everything — and collapsed. The shed was already a heap of embers glowing fiercely. A nigger was being beaten near by. They said he had caused the fire in some way; be that as it may, he was screeching most horribly. 'I saw him, later, for several days, sitting in a bit of shade looking very sick and trying to recover himself: afterwards he arose and went out — and the wilderness without a sound took him into its bosom again. As I approached the glow from the dark I found myself at the back of two men, talking. I heard the name of Kurtz pronounced, then the words, 'take advantage of this unfortunate accident.' One of the men was the manager. I wished him a good evening. 'Did you ever see anything like it — eh? it is incredible,' he said, and walked off. The other man remained. He was a first-class agent, young, gentlemanly, a bit reserved, with a forked little beard and a hooked nose. He was stand-offish with the other agents, and they on their side said he was the manager's spy upon them. As to me, I had hardly ever spoken to him before. We got into talk, and by and by we strolled away from the hissing ruins. Then he asked me to his room, which was in the main building of the station. He struck a match, and I perceived that this young aristocrat had not only a silver-mounted dressing-case but also a whole candle all to himself. Just at that time the manager was the only man supposed to have any right to candles. Native mats covered the clay walls; a collection of spears, assegais, shields, knives was hung up in trophies. The business intrusted to this fellow was the making of bricks — so I had been informed; but there wasn't a fragment of a brick anywhere in the station, and he had been there more than a year — waiting. It seems he could not make bricks without something, I don't know what — straw maybe. Anyways, it could not be found there, and as it was not likely to be sent from Europe, it did not appear clear to me what he was waiting for. An act of special creation perhaps. However, they were all waiting — all the sixteen or twenty pilgrims of them — for something; and upon my word it did not seem an uncongenial occupation, from the way they took it, though the only thing that ever came to them was disease — as far as I could see. They beguiled the time by backbiting and intriguing against each other in a foolish kind of way. There was an air of plotting about that station, but nothing came of it, of course. It was as unreal as everything else — as the philanthropic pretence of the whole concern, as their talk, as their government, as their show of work. The only real feeling was a desire to get appointed to a trading-post where ivory was to be had, so that they could earn percentages. They intrigued and slandered and hated each other only on that account, — but as to effectually lifting a little finger — oh, no. By heavens! there is something after all in the world allowing one man to steal a horse while another must not look at a halter. Steal a horse straight out. Very well. He has done it. Perhaps he can ride. But there is a way of looking at a halter that would provoke the most charitable of saints into a kick.

"I had no idea why he wanted to be sociable, but as we chatted in there it suddenly occurred to me the fellow was trying to get at something — in fact, pumping me. He alluded constantly to Europe, to the people I was supposed to know there — putting leading questions as to my acquaintances in the sepulchral city, and so on. His little eyes glittered like mica discs — with curiosity — though he tried to keep up a bit of superciliousness. At first I was astonished, but very soon I became awfully curious to see what he would find out from me. I couldn't possibly imagine what I had in me to make it worth his while. It was very pretty to see how he baffled himself, for in truth my body was full only of chills, and my head had nothing in it but that wretched steamboat business. It was evident he took me for a perfectly shameless prevaricator. At last he got angry, and, to conceal a movement of furious annoyance. he yawned. I rose. Then I noticed a small sketch in oils, on a panel, representing a woman, draped and blindfolded, carrying a lighted torch. The background was sombre — almost black. The movement of the woman was stately, and the effect of the torch-light on the face was sinister.

"It arrested me, and he stood civilly, holding an empty half-pint champagne bottle (medical comforts) with the candle stuck in it. To my question he said Mr. Kurtz had painted this — in this very station more than a year ago — while waiting for means to go to his trading-post. 'Tell me, pray,' said I, 'who is this Mr. Kurtz?'

" 'The chief of the Inner Station,' he answered in a short tone, looking away. 'Much obliged,' I said, laughing. 'And you are the brickmaker of the Central Station. Everyone knows that.' He was silent for a while. 'He is a prodigy,' he said at last. 'He is an emissary of pity, and science, and progress, and devil knows what else. We want,' he began to declaim suddenly, 'for the guidance of the cause intrusted to us by Europe, so to speak, higher intelligence, wide sympathies, a singleness of purpose.' 'Who says that?' I asked. 'Lots of them,' he replied. 'Some even write that; and so *he* comes here, a special being, as you ought to know.' 'Why ought I to know?' I interrupted, really surprise. He paid no attention. 'Yes. To-day he is chief of the best station, next year he will be assistant-manager, two years more and . . . but I daresay you know what he will be in two years' time. You are of the new gang — the gang of virtue. The same people who sent him specially also recommended you. Oh, don't say no. I've my own eyes to trust.' 'Light dawned upon me. My dear aunt's influential acquaintances were producing an unexpected effect upon that young man. I nearly burst into a laugh. 'Do you read the Company's confidential correspondence?' I asked. He hadn't a word to say. It was great fun. 'When Mr. Kurtz,' I continued, severely, 'is General Manager, you won't have the opportunity.'

"He blew the candle out suddenly, and we went outside. The moon had risen. Black figures strolled about listlessly, pouring water on the glow, whence proceeded a sound of hissing; steam ascended in the moonlight, the beaten nigger groaned somewhere. 'What a row the brute makes!' said the indefatigable man with the moustaches, appearing near us. 'Serve him right. Transgression — punishment — bang! Pitiless, pitiless. That's the only way. This will prevent all conflagrations for the future. I was just telling the manager . . .' He noticed my companion, and became crestfallen all at once. 'Not in bed yet,' he said, with a kind of servile heartiness; 'it's so natural. Ha! Danger — agitation.' He vanished. I went on to the river-side, and the other followed me. I heard a scathing murmur at my ear, 'Heap of muffs — go to.' The pilgrims could be seen in knots gesticulating, discussing. Several had still their staves in their hands. I verily believe they took these sticks to bed with them. Beyond the fence the forest stood up spectrally in the moonlight, and through the dim stir, through the faint sounds of that lamentable courtyard, the silence of the land went home to one's very heart — its mystery, its greatness, the amazing reality of its concealed life. The hurt nigger moaned feebly somewhere near by, and then fetched a deep sigh that made me mend my pace away from there. I felt a hand introducing itself under my arm. 'My dear sir,' said the fellow, 'I don't want to be misunderstood, and especially by you, who will see Mr. Kurtz long before I can have that pleasure. I wouldn't like him to get a false idea of my disposition. . . .'

"I let him run on, this papier-maché Mephistopheles, and it seemed to me that if I tried I could poke my forefinger through him, and would find nothing inside but a little loose dirt, maybe. He, don't you see, had been planning to be assistant-manager by and by under the present man, and I could see that the coming of that Kurtz had upset them both not a little. He talked precipitately, and I did not try to stop him. I had my shoulders against the wreck of my steamer, hauled up on the slope like a carcass of some big river animal. The smell of mud, of primeval mud, by Jove! was in my nostrils, the high stillness of primeval forest was before my eyes; there were shiny patches on the black creek. The moon had spread over everything a thin layer of silver — over the rank grass, over the mud, upon the wall of matted vegetation standing higher than the wall of a temple, over the great river I could see through a sombre gap glittering, glittering, as it flowed broadly by without a murmur. All this was great, expectant, mute, while the man jabbered about himself. I wondered whether the stillness on the face of the immensity looking at us two were meant as an appeal or as a menace. What were we who had strayed in here? Could we handle that dumb thing, or would it handle us? I felt how big, how confoundedly big, was that thing that couldn't talk, and perhaps was deaf as well. What was in there? I could see a little ivory coming out from there, and I had heard Mr. Kurtz was in there. I had heard enough about it, too — God knows! Yet somehow it didn't bring any image with it — no more than if I had been told an angel or a fiend was in there. I believed it in the same way one of you might believe there are inhabitants in the planet Mars. I knew once a Scotch sailmaker who was certain, dead sure, there were people in Mars. If you asked him for some idea how they looked and behaved, he would get shy and mutter something about 'walking on all-fours.' If you as much as smiled, he would — though a man of sixty — offer to fight you. I would not have gone so far as to fight for Kurtz, but I went for him near enough to a lie. You know I hate, detest, and can't bear a lie, not because I am straighter than the rest of us, but simply because it appalls me. There is a taint of death, a flavour of mortality in lies — which is exactly what I hate and detest in the world — what I want to forget. It makes me miserable and sick, like biting something rotten would do. Temperament, I suppose. Well, I went near enough to it by letting the young fool there believe anything he liked to imagine as to my influence in Europe. I became in an instant as much of a pretence as the rest of the bewitched pilgrims. This simply because I had a notion it somehow would be of help to that Kurtz whom at the time I did not see — you understand. He was just a word for me. I did not see the man in the name any more than you do. Do you see him? Do you see the story? Do you see anything? It seems to me I am trying to tell you a dream — making a vain attempt, because no relation of a dream can convey the dream-sensation, that commingling of absurdity, surprise, and bewilderment in a tremor of struggling revolt, that notion of being captured by the incredible which is of the very essence of dreams. . . ."

He was silent for a while.

". . . No, it is impossible; it is impossible to convey the life-sensation of any given epoch of one's existence — that which makes its truth, its meaning — its subtle and penetrating essence. It is impossible. We live, as we dream — alone. . . ."

He paused again as if reflecting, then added —

"Of course in this you fellows see more than I could then. You see me, whom you know. . . ."

It had become so pitch dark that we listeners could hardly see one another. For a long time already he, sitting apart, had been no more to us than a voice. There was not a word from anybody. The others might have been asleep, but I was awake. I listened, I listened on the watch for the sentence, for the word, that would give me the clue to the faint uneasiness inspired by this narrative that seemed to shape itself without human lips in the heavy night-air of the river.

". . . Yes — I let him run on " Marlow began again, "and think what he pleased about the powers that were behind me. I did! And there was nothing behind me! There was nothing but that wretched, old, mangled steamboat I was leaning against, while he talked fluently about 'the necessity for every man to get on.' 'And when one comes out here, you conceive, it is not to gaze at the moon.' Mr. Kurtz was a 'universal genius,' but even a genius would find it easier to work with 'adequate tools — intelligent men.' He did not make bricks — why, there was a physical impossibility in the way — as I was well aware; and if he did secretarial work for the manager, it was because 'no sensible man rejects wantonly the confidence of his superiors.' Did I see it? I saw it. What more did I want? What I really wanted was rivets, by heaven! Rivets. To get on with the work — to stop the hole. Rivets I wanted. There were cases of them down at the coast — cases — piled up — burst — split! You kicked a loose rivet at every second step in that station yard on the hillside. Rivets had rolled into the grove of death. You could fill your pockets with rivets for the trouble of stooping down — and there wasn't one rivet to be found where it was wanted. We had plates that would do, but nothing to fasten them with. And every week the messenger, a lone negro, letter-bag on shoulder and staff in hand, left our station for the coast. And several times a week a coast caravan came in with trade goods — ghastly glazed calico that made you shudder only to look at it, glass beads valued about a penny a quart, confounded spotted cotton handker-chiefs. And no rivets. Three carriers could have brought all that was wanted to set that steamboat afloat.

"He was becoming confidential now, but I fancy my unresponsive attitude must have exasperated him at last, for he judged it necessary to inform me he feared neither God nor devil, let alone any mere man. I said I could see that very well, but what I wanted was a certain quantity of rivets — and rivets were what really Mr. Kurtz wanted, if he had only known it. Now letters went to the coast every week.... 'My dear sir,' he cried, 'I write from dictation.' I demanded rivets. There was a way — for an intelligent man. He changed his manner; became very cold, and suddenly began to talk about a hippopotamus; wondered whether sleeping on board the steamer (I stuck to my salvage night and day) I wasn't disturbed. There was an old hippo that had the bad habit of getting out on the bank and roaming at night over the station grounds. The pilgrims used to turn out in a body and empty every rifle they could lay hands on at him. Some even had sat up o' nights for him. All this energy was wasted, though. 'That animal has a charmed life,' he said; 'but you can say this only of brutes in this country. No man — you apprehend me? — no man here bears a charmed life.' He stood there for a moment in the moonlight with his delicate hooked nose set a little askew, and his mica eyes glittering without a wink, then, with a curt good-night, he strode off. I could see he was disturbed and considerably puzzled, which made me feel more hopeful than I had been for days. It was a great comfort to turn from that chap to my influential friend, the battered, twisted, ruined tin-pot steamboat. I clambered on board. She rang under my feet like an empty Huntley & Palmer biscuit-tin kicked along a gutter; she was nothing so solid in make, and rather less pretty in shape, but I had expended enough hard work on her to make me love her. No influential friend would have served me better. She had given me a chance to come out a bit — to find out what I could do. No, I don't like work. I had rather laze about and think of all the fine things that can be done. I don't like work — no man does — but I like what is in the work, — the chance to find yourself. Your own reality — for yourself, not for others — what no other man can ever know. They can only see the mere show, and never can tell what it really means.

"I was not surprised to see somebody sitting aft, on the deck, with his legs dangling over the mud. You see I rather chummed with the few mechanics there were in that station, whom the other pilgrims naturally despised — on account of their imperfect manners, I suppose. This was the foreman — a boiler-maker by trade — a good worker. He was a lank, bony, yellow-faced man, with big intense eyes. His aspect was worried, and his head was as bald as the palm of my hand; but his hair in falling seemed to have stuck to his chin, and has prospered in the new locality for his beard hung down to his waist. He was a widower with six young children (he had left them in charge of a sister of his to come out there), and the passion of his life was pigeon-flying. He was an enthusiast and a connoisseur. He would rave about pigeons. After work hours he used sometimes to come over from his hut for a talk about his children and his pigeons; at work, when he had to crawl in the mud under the bottom of the steamboat, he would tie up that beard of his in a kind of white serviette he brought for the purpose. It had loops to go over his ears. In the evening he could be seen squatted on the bank rinsing that wrapper in the creek with great care, then spreading it solemnly on a bush to dry.

"I slapped him on the back and shouted, 'We shall have rivets!' He scrambled to his feet exclaiming, 'No! Rivets!' as though he couldn't believe his ears. Then in a low voice, 'You ... eh?' I don't know why we behaved like lunatics. I put my finger to the side of my nose and nodded mysteriously. 'Good for you!'

he cried, snapped his fingers above his head, lifting one foot. I tried a jig. We capered on the iron deck. A frightful clatter came out of that hulk, and the virgin forest on the other bank of the creek sent it back in a thundering roll upon the sleeping station. It must have made some of the pilgrims sit up in their hovels. A dark figure obscured the lighted doorway of the manager's hut, vanished, then, a second or so after, the doorway itself vanished, too. We stopped, and the silence driven away by the stamping of our feet flowed back again from the recesses of the land. The great wall of vegetation, an exuberant and entangled mass of trunks, branches, leaves, boughs, festoons, motionless in the moonlight, was like a rioting invasion of soundless life, a rolling wave of plants, piled up, crested, ready to topple over the creek, to sweep every little man of us out of his little existence. And it moved not. A deadened burst of mighty splashes and snorts reached us from afar, as though an ichthyosaurus had been taking a bath of glitter in the great river. 'After all,' said the boiler-maker in a reasonable tone, 'why shouldn't we get the rivets?' Why not, indeed! I did not know of any reason why we shouldn't. 'They'll come in three weeks,' I said, confidently.

"But they didn't. Instead of rivets there came an invasion, an infliction, a visitation. It came in sections during the next three weeks, each section headed by a donkey carrying a white man in new clothes and tan shoes, bowing from that elevation right and left to the impressed pilgrims. A quarrelsome band of footsore sulky niggers trod on the heels of the donkey; a lot of tents, camp-stools, tin boxes, white cases, brown bales would be shot down in the courtyard, and the air of mystery would deepen a little over the muddle of the station. Five such instalments came, with their absurd air of disorderly flight with the loot of innumerable outfit shops and provision stores, that, one would think, they were lugging, after a raid, into the wilderness for equitable division. It was an inextricable mess of things decent in themselves but that human folly made look like the spoils of thieving.

"This devoted band called itself the Eldorado Exploring Expedition, and I believe they were sworn to secrecy. Their talk, however, was the talk of sordid buccaneers: it was reckless without hardihood, greedy without audacity, and cruel without courage; there was not an atom of foresight or of serious intention in the whole batch of them, and they did not seem aware these things are wanted for the work of the world. To tear treasure out of the bowels of the land was their desire, with no more moral purpose at the back of it than there is in burglars breaking into a safe. Who paid the expenses of the noble enterprise I don't know; but the uncle of our manager was leader of that lot.

"In exterior he resembled a butcher in a poor neighbourhood, and his eyes had a look of sleepy cunning. He carried his fat paunch with ostentation on his short legs, and during the time his gang infested the station spoke to no one but his nephew. You could see these two roaming about all day long with their heads close together in an everlasting confab.

"I had given up worrying myself about the rivets. One's capacity for that kind of folly is more limited than you would suppose. I said Hang! — and let things slide. I had plenty of time for meditation, and now and then I would give some thought to Kurtz. I wasn't very interested in him. No. Still, I was curious to see whether this man, who had come out equipped with moral ideas of some sort, would climb to the top afterall and how he would set about his work when there."

II.

"One evening as I was lying flat on the deck of my steamboat, I heard voices approaching — and there were the nephew and the uncle strolling along the bank. I laid my head on my arm again, and had nearly lost myself in a doze, when somebody said in my ear, as it were: 'I am as harmless as a little child, but I don't like to be dictated to. Am I the manager — or am I not? I was ordered to send him there. It's incredible.' . . . I became aware that the two were standing on the shore alongside the forepart of the steamboat, just below my head. I did not move; it did not occur to me to move: I was sleepy. 'It *is* unpleasant,' grunted the uncle. 'He has asked the Administration to be sent there,' said the other, 'with the idea of showing what he could do; and I was instructed accordingly. Look at the influence that man must have. Is it not frightful?' They both agreed it was frightful, then made several bizarre remarks: 'Make rain and fine weather — one man — the Council — by the nose' — bits of absurd sentences that got the better of my drowsiness, so that I had pretty near the whole of my wits about me when the uncle said, 'The climate may do away with this difficulty for you. Is he alone there?' 'Yes,' answered the manager; 'he sent his assistant down the river with a note to me in these terms: "Clear this poor devil out of the country, and don't bother sending more of that sort. I had rather be alone than have the kind of men you can dispose of with me." It was more than a year ago. Can you imagine such impudence!' 'Anything since then?' asked the other, hoarsely. 'Ivory,' jerked the nephew; 'lots of it — prime sort — lots — most annoying, from him.' 'And with that?' questioned the heavy rumble. 'Invoice,' was the reply fired out, so to speak. Then silence. They had been talking about Kurtz.

"I was broad awake by this time, but, lying perfectly at ease, remained still, having no inducement to change my position. 'How did that ivory come all this way?' growled the elder man, who seemed very vexed. The other explained that it had come with a fleet of canoes in charge of an English half-caste clerk Kurtz had with him; that Kurtz had apparently intended to return himself, the station being by that time bare of goods and stores, but after coming three hundred miles, had suddenly decided to go back, which he started to do alone in a small dugout with four paddlers, leaving the half-caste to continue down the river with the ivory. The two fellows there seemed astounded at anybody attempting such a thing. They were at a loss for an adequate motive. As to me, I seemed to see Kurtz for the first time. It was a distinct glimpse: the dugout, four paddling savages, and the lone white man turning his back suddenly on the headquarters, on relief, on thoughts of home — perhaps; setting his face towards the depths of the wilderness, towards his empty and desolate station. I did not know the motive. Perhaps he was just simply a fine fellow who stuck to his work for its own sake. His name, you understand, had not been pronounced once. He was 'that man.' The half-caste, who, as far as I could see, had conducted a difficult trip with great prudence and pluck, was invariably alluded to as 'that scoundrel.' The 'scoundrel' had reported that the 'man' had been very ill — had recovered imperfectly. . . . The two below me moved away then a few paces, and strolled back and forth at some little distance. I heard: 'Military post — doctor — two hundred miles — quite alone now — unavoidable delays — nine months — no news — strange rumours.' They approached again, just as the manager was saying, 'No one, as far as I know, unless a species of wandering trader — a pestilential fellow, snapping ivory from the natives.' Who was it they were talking about now? I gathered in snatches that this was some man supposed to be in Kurtz's district, and of whom the manager did not approve. 'We will not be free from unfair competition till one of these fellows is hanged for an example,' he said. 'Certainly,' grunted the other; 'get him hanged! Why not? Anything — anything can be done in this country. That's what I say; nobody here, you understand, *here,* can endanger your position. And why? You stand the climate — you outlast them all. The danger is in Europe; but there before I left I took care to——' They moved off and whispered, then their voices rose again. 'The extraordinary series of delays is not my fault. I did my best.' The fat man sighed. 'Very sad.' 'And the pestiferous absurdity of his talk,' continued the other; 'he bothered me enough when he was here. "Each station should be like a beacon on the road towards better things, a centre for trade of course, but also for humanizing, improving, instructing." Conceive you — that ass! And he wants to be manager! No, it's——' Here he got choked by excessive indignation, and I lifted my head the least bit. I was surprised to see how near they were — right under me. I could have spat upon their hats. They were looking on the ground, absorbed in thought. The manager was switching his leg with a slender twig: his sagacious relative lifted his head. 'You have been well since you came out this time?' he asked. The other gave a start. 'Who? I? Oh! Like a charm — like a charm. But the rest — oh, my goodness! All sick. They die so quick, too, that I haven't the time to send them out of the country — it's incredible!' 'H'm. Just so,' grunted the uncle. 'Ah! my boy, trust to this — I say, trust to this.' I saw him extend his short flipper of an arm for a gesture that took in the forest, the creek, the mud, the river, — seemed to beckon with a dishonouring flourish before the sunlit face of the land a treacherous appeal to the lurking death, to the hidden evil, to the profound darkness of its heart. It was so startling that I leaped to my feet and looked back at the edge of the forest, as though I had expected an answer of some sort to that black display of confidence. You know the foolish notions that come to one sometimes. The high stillness confronted these two figures with its ominous patience, waiting for the passing away of a fantastic invasion.

"They swore aloud together — out of sheer fright, I believe — then pretending not to know anything of my existence, turned back to the station. The sun was low; and leaning forward side by side, they seemed to be tugging painfully uphill their two ridiculous shadows of unequal length, that trailed behind them slowly over the tall grass without bending a single blade.

"In a few days the Eldorado Expedition went into the patient wilderness, that closed upon it as the sea closes over a diver. Long afterwards the news came that all the donkeys were dead. I know nothing as to the fate of the less valuable animals. They, no doubt, like the rest of us, found what they deserved. I did not inquire. I was then rather excited at the prospect of meeting Kurtz very soon. When I say very soon I mean it comparatively. It was just two months from the day we left the creek when we came to the bank below Kurtz's station.

"Going up that river was like travelling back to the earliest beginnings of the world, when vegetation rioted on the earth and the big trees were kings. An empty stream, a great silence, an impenetrable forest. The air was warm, thick, heavy, sluggish. There was no joy in the brilliance of sunshine. The long stretches of the waterway ran on, deserted, into the gloom of overshadowed distances. On silvery sandbanks hippos and alligators sunned themselves side by side. The broadening waters flowed through a mob of wooded islands; you lost your way on that river as you would in a desert, and butted all day long against shoals, trying to find the channel, till you thought yourself bewitched and cut off for ever from everything you had known once — somewhere — far away — in another existence perhaps. There were moments when one's past came back to one, as it will sometimes when you have not a moment to spare to yourself; but it came in the shape of an unrestful and noisy dream, remembered with wonder amongst the overwhelming realities of this strange world of plants, and water, and silence. And this stillness of life did not in the least resemble a peace. It was the stillness of an implacable force brooding over an inscrutable intention. It looked at you with a vengeful aspect. I got used to it afterwards; I did not see it any more; I had no time. I had to keep guessing at the channel; I had to discern, mostly by inspiration, the signs of hidden banks; I watched for sunken stones; I was learning to clap my teeth smartly before my heart flew out, when I shaved by a fluke some infernal sly old snag that would have ripped the life out of the tin-pot steamboat and drowned all the pilgrims; I had to keep a look-out for the signs of dead wood we could cut up in the night for next day's steaming. When you have to attend to things of that sort, to the mere incidents of the surface, the reality — the reality, I tell you — fades. The inner truth is hidden — luckily, luckily. But I felt it all the same; I felt often its mysterious stillness watching me at my monkey tricks, just as it watches you fellows performing on your respective tight-ropes for — what is it? half-a-crown a tumble——"

"Try to be civil, Marlow," growled a voice, and I knew there was at least one listener awake besides myself.

"I beg your pardon. I forgot the heartache which makes up the rest of the price. And indeed what does the price matter, if the trick be well done? You do your tricks very well. And I didn't do badly either, since I managed not to sink that steamboat on my first trip. It's a wonder to me yet. Imagine a blindfolded man set to drive a van over a bad road. I sweated and shivered over that business considerably, I can tell you. After all, for a seaman, to scrape the bottom of the thing that's supposed to float all the time under his care is the unpardonable sin. No one may know of it, but you never forget the thump — eh? A blow on the very heart. You remember it, you dream of it, you wake up at night and think of it — years after — and go hot and cold all over. I don't pretend to say that steamboat floated all the time. More than once she had to wade for a bit, with twenty cannibals splashing around and pushing. We had enlisted some of these chaps on the way for a crew. Fine fellows — cannibals — in their place. They were men one could work with, and I am grateful to them. And, after all, they did not eat each other before my face: they had brought along a provision of hippo-meat which went rotten, and made the mystery of the wilderness stink in my nostrils. Phoo! I can sniff it now. I had the manager on board and three or four pilgrims with their staves — all complete. Sometimes we came upon a station close by the bank, clinging to the skirts of the unknown, and the white men rushing out of a tumble-down hovel, with great gestures of joy and surprise and welcome, seemed very strange — had the appearance of being held there captive by a spell. The word ivory would ring in the air for a while — and on we went again into the silence, along empty reaches, round the still bends, between the high walls of our winding way, reverberating in hollow claps the ponderous beat of the stern-wheel. Trees, trees, millions of trees, massive, immense, running up high; and at their foot, hugging the bank against the stream, crept the little begrimed steamboat, like a sluggish beetle crawling on the floor of a lofty portico. It made you feel very small, very lost, and yet it was not altogether depressing, that feeling. After all, if you were small, the grimy beetle crawled on — which was just what you wanted it to do. Where the pilgrims imagined it crawled to I don't know. To some place where they expected to get something, I bet! For me it crawled towards Kurtz — exclusively; but when the steam-pipes started leaking we crawled very slow. The reaches opened before us and closed behind, as if the forest had stepped leisurely across the water to bar the way for our return. We penetrated deeper and deeper into the heart of darkness. It was very quiet there. At night sometimes the roll of drums behind the curtain of trees would run up the river and remain sustained faintly, as if hovering in the air high over our heads, till the first break of day. Whether it meant war, peace, or prayer we could not tell. The dawns were heralded by the descent of a chill stillness; the wood-cutters slept, their fires burned low; the snapping of a twig would make you start. We were wanderers on a prehistoric earth, on an earth that wore the aspect of an unknown planet. We could have fancied ourselves the first of men taking possession of an accursed inheritance, to be subdued at the cost of profound anguish and of excessive toil. But suddenly, as we struggled round a bend, there would be a glimpse of rush walls, of peaked grass-roofs, a burst of yells, a whirl of black limbs, a mass of hands clapping, of feet stamping, of bodies swaying, of eyes rolling, under the droop of heavy and motionless foliage. The steamer toiled along slowly on the edge of a black and incomprehensible frenzy. The prehistoric man was cursing us, praying to us, welcoming us — who could tell? We were cut off from the comprehension of our surroundings; we glided past like phantoms, wondering and secretly appalled, as sane men would be before an enthusiastic outbreak in a madhouse. We could not understand because we were too far and could not remember, because we were travelling in the night of first ages, of those ages that are gone, leaving hardly a sign — and no memories.

"The earth seemed unearthly. We are accustomed to look upon the shackled form of a conquered monster, but there — there you could look at a thing monstrous and free. It was unearthly, and the men were—— No, they were not inhuman. Well, you know, that was the worst of it — this suspicion of their not being inhuman. It would come slowly to one. They howled and leaped, and spun, and made horrid faces; but what thrilled you was just the thought of their humanity — like yours — the thought of your remote kinship with this wild and passionate uproar. Ugly. Yes, it was ugly enough; but if you were man enough you would admit to yourself that there was in you just the faintest trace of a response to the terrible frankness of that noise, a dim suspicion of there being a meaning in it which you — you so remote from the night of first ages — could comprehend. And why not? The mind of man is capable of anything — because everything is in it, all the past as well as all the future. What was there after all? Joy, fear, sorrow, devotion, valour, rage — who can tell? — but truth — truth stripped of its cloak of time. Let the fool gape and shudder — the man knows, and can look on without a wink. But he must at least be as much of a man as these on the shore. He must meet that truth with his own true stuff — with his own inborn strength. Principles won't do. Acquisitions, clothes, pretty rags — rags that would fly off at the first good shake. No; you want a deliberate belief. An appeal to me in this fiendish row — is there? Very well; I hear; I admit, but I have a voice, too, and for good or evil mine is the speech that cannot be silenced. Of course, a fool, what with sheer fright and fine sentiments, is always safe. Who's that grunting? You wonder I didn't go ashore for a howl and a dance? Well, no — I didn't. Fine sentiments, you say? Fine sentiments, be hanged! I had no time. I had to mess about with white-lead and strips of woollen blanket helping to put bandages on those leaky steam-pipes — I tell you. I had to watch the steering, and circumvent those snags, and get the tin-pot along by hook or by crook. There was surface-truth enough in these things to save a wiser man. And between whiles I had to look after the savage who was fireman. He was an improved specimen; he could fire up a vertical boiler. He was there below me, and, upon my word, to look at him was as edifying as seeing a dog in a parody of breeches and a feather hat, walking on his hind-legs. A few months of training had done for that really fine chap. He squinted at the steam-gauge and at the water-gauge with an evident effort of intrepidity — and he had filed teeth, too, the poor devil, and the wool of his pate shaved into queer patterns, and three ornamental scars on each of his cheeks. He ought to have been clapping his hands and stamping his feet on the bank, instead of which he was hard at work, a thrall to strange witchcraft, full of improving knowledge. He was useful because he had been instructed; and what he knew was this — that should the water in that transparent thing disappear, the evil spirit inside the boiler would get angry through the greatness of his thirst, and take a terrible vengeance. So he sweated and fired up and watched the glass fearfully (with an impromptu charm, made of rags, tied to his arm, and a piece of polished bone, as big as a watch, stuck flat-ways through his lower lip), while the wooded banks slipped past us slowly, the short noise was left behind, the interminable miles of silence — and we crept on, towards Kurtz. But the snags were thick, the water was treacherous and shallow, the boiler seemed indeed to have a sulky devil in it, and thus neither that fireman nor I had any time to peer into our creepy thoughts.

"Some fifty miles below the Inner Station we came upon a hut of reeds, an inclined and melancholy pole, with the unrecognizable tatters of what had been a flag of some sort flying from it, and a neatly stacked wood-pile. This was unexpected. We came to the bank, and on the stack of firewood found a flat piece of board with some faded pencil-writing on it. When deciphered it said: 'Wood for you. Hurry up. Approach cautiously.' There was a signature, but it was illegible — not Kurtz — a much longer word. 'Hurry up.' Where? Up the river? 'Approach cautiously.' We had not done so. But the warning could not have been meant for the place where it could be only found after approach. Something was wrong above. But what — and how much? That was the question. We commented adversely upon the imbecility of that telegraphic style. The bush around said nothing, and would not let us look very far, either. A torn curtain of red twill hung in the doorway of the hut, and flapped sadly in our faces. The dwelling was dismantled; but we could see a white man had lived there not very long ago. There remained a rude table — a plank on two posts; a heap of rubbish reposed in a dark corner, and by the door I picked up a book. It had lost its covers, and the pages had been thumbed into a state of extremely dirty softness; but the back had been lovingly stitched afresh with white cotton thread, which looked clean yet. It was an extraordinary find. Its title was, *An Inquiry into some Points of Seamanship*, by a man Towser, Towson — some such name — Master in his Majesty's Navy. The matter looked dreary reading enough, with illustrative diagrams and repulsive tables of figures, and the copy was sixty years old. I handled this amazing antiquity with the greatest possible tenderness, lest it should dissolve in my hands. Within, Towson or Towser was inquiring earnestly into the breaking strain of ships' chains and tackle, and other such matters. Not a very enthralling book; but at the first glance you could see there a singleness of intention, an honest concern for the right way of going to work, which made these humble pages, thought out so many years ago, luminous with another than a professional light. The simple old sailor, with his talk of chains and purchases, made me forget the jungle and the pilgrims in a delicious sensation of having come upon something unmistakably real. Such a book being there was wonderful enough; but still more astounding were the notes pencilled in the margin, and plainly referring to the text. I couldn't believe my eyes! They were in cipher! Yes, it looked like cipher. Fancy a man lugging with him a book of that description into this nowhere and studying it — and making notes — in cipher at that! It was an extravagant mystery.

"I had been dimly aware for some time of a worrying noise, and when I lifted my eyes I saw the wood-pile was gone, and the manager, aided by all the pilgrims, was shouting at me from the river-side. I slipped the book into my pocket. I assure you to leave off reading was like tearing myself away from the shelter of an old and solid friendship.

"I started the lame engine ahead. 'It must be this miserable trader — this intruder,' exclaimed the manager, looking back malevolently at the place we had left. 'He must be English,' I said. 'It will not save him from getting into trouble if he is not careful,' muttered the manager darkly. I observed with assumed innocence that no man was safe from trouble in this world.

"The current was more rapid now, the steamer seemed at her last gasp, the stern-wheel flopped languidly, and I caught myself listening on tiptoe for the next beat of the boat, for in sober truth I expected the wretched thing to give up every moment. It was like watching the last flickers of a life. But still we crawled. Sometimes I would pick out a tree a little way ahead to measure our progress towards Kurtz by, but I lost it invariably before we got abreast. To keep the eyes so long on one thing was too much for human patience. The manager displayed a beautiful resignation. I fretted and fumed and took to arguing with myself whether or no I would talk openly with Kurtz; but before I could come to any conclusion it occurred to me that my speech or my silence, indeed any action of mine, would be a mere futility. What did it matter what any one knew or ignored? What did it matter who was manager? One gets sometimes such a flash of insight. The essentials of this affair lay deep under the surface, beyond my reach, and beyond my power of meddling.

"Towards the evening of the second day we judged ourselves about eight miles from Kurtz's station. I wanted to push on; but the manager looked grave, and told me the navigation up there was so dangerous that it would be advisable, the sun being very low already, to wait where we were till next morning. Moreover, he pointed out that if the warning to approach cautiously were to be followed, we must approach in daylight — not at dusk, or in the dark. This was sensible enough. Eight miles meant nearly three hours' steaming for us, and I could also see suspicious ripples at the upper end of the reach. Nevertheless, I was annoyed beyond expression at the delay, and most unreasonably, too, since one night more could not matter much after so many months. As we had plenty of wood, and caution was the word, I brought up in the middle of the stream. The reach was narrow, straight, with high sides like a railway cutting. The dusk came gliding into it long before the sun had set. The current ran smooth and swift, but a dumb immobility sat on the banks. The living trees, lashed together by the creepers and every living bush of the undergrowth, might have been changed into stone, even to the slenderest twig, to the lightest leaf. It was not sleep — it seemed unnatural, like a state of trance. Not the faintest sound of any kind could be heard. You looked on amazed, and began to suspect yourself of being deaf — then the night came suddenly, and struck you blind as well. About three in the morning some large fish leaped, and the loud splash made me jump as though a gun had been fired. When the sun rose there was a white fog, very warm and clammy, and more blinding than the night. It did not shift or drive; it was just there, standing all round you like something solid. At eight or nine, perhaps, it lifted as a shutter lifts. We had a glimpse of the towering multitude of trees, of the immense matted jungle, with the blazing little ball of the sun hanging over it — all perfectly still — and then the white shutter came down again, smoothly, as if sliding in greased grooves. I ordered the chain, which we had begun to heave in, to be paid out again. Before it stopped running with a muffled rattle, a cry, a very loud cry, as of infinite desolation, soared slowly in the opaque air. It ceased. A complaining clamour, modulated in savage discords, filled our ears. The sheer unexpectedness of it made my hair stir under my cap. I don't know how it struck the others: to me it seemed as though the mist itself had screamed, so suddenly, and apparently from all sides at once, did this tumultuous and mournful uproar arise. It culminated in a hurried outbreak of almost intolerably excessive shrieking, which stopped short, leaving us stiffened in a variety of silly attitudes, and obstinately listening to the nearly as appalling and excessive silence. 'Good God! What is the meaning——' stammered at my elbow one of the pilgrims, — a little fat man, with sandy hair and red whiskers, who wore side-spring boots, and pink pyjamas tucked into his socks. Two others remained open-mouthed a whole minute, then dashed into the little cabin, to rush out incontinently and stand darting scared glances, with Winchesters at 'ready' in their hands. What we could see was just the steamer we were on, her outlines blurred as though she had been on the point of dissolving, and a misty strip of water, perhaps two feet broad, around her — and that was all. The rest of the world was nowhere, as far as our eyes and ears were concerned. Just nowhere. Gone, disappeared; swept off without leaving a whisper or a shadow behind.

"I went forward, and ordered the chain to be hauled in short, so as to be ready to trip the anchor and move the steamboat at once if necessary. 'Will they attack?' whispered an awed voice. 'We will be all butchered in this fog,' murmured another. The faces twitched with the strain, the hands trembled slightly, the eyes forgot to wink. It was very curious to see the contrast of expressions of the white men and of the black fellows of our crew, who were as much strangers to that part of the river as we, though their homes were only eight hundred miles away. The whites, of course greatly discomposed, had besides a curious look of being painfully shocked by such an outrageous row. The others had an alert, naturally interested expression; but their faces were essentially quiet, even those of the one or two who grinned as they hauled at the chain. Several exchanged short, grunting phrases, which seemed to settle the matter to their satisfaction. Their headman, a young, broad-chested black, severely draped in dark-blue fringed cloths, with fierce nostrils and his hair all done up artfully in oily ringlets, stood near me. 'Aha!' I said, just for good fellowship's sake. 'Catch 'im,' he snapped, with a bloodshot widening of his eyes and a flash of sharp teeth — 'catch 'im. Give 'im to us.' 'To you, eh?' I asked; 'what would you do with them?' 'Eat 'im!' he said, curtly, and, leaning his elbow on the rail, looked out into the fog in a dignified and profoundly pensive attitude. I would no doubt have been properly horrified, had it not occurred to me that he and his chaps must be very hungry: that they must have been growing increasingly hungry for at least this month past. They had been engaged for six months (I don't think a single one of them had any clear idea of time, as we at the end of countless ages have. They still belonged to the beginnings of time — had no inherited experience to teach them as it were), and of course, as long as there was a piece of paper written over in accordance with some farcical law or other made down the river, it didn't enter anybody's head to trouble how they would live. Certainly they had brought with them some rotten hippo-meat, which couldn't have lasted very long, anyway, even if the pilgrims hadn't, in the midst of a shocking hullabaloo, thrown a considerable quantity of it overboard. It looked like a high-handed proceeding: but it was really a case of legitimate self-defence. You can't breathe dead hippo waking, sleeping, and eating, and at the same time keep your precarious grip on existence. Besides that, they had given them every week three pieces of brass wire, each about nine inches long; and the theory was they were to buy their provisions with that currency in river-side villages. You can see how *that* worked. There were either no villages, or the people were hostile, or the director, who like the rest of us fed out of tins, with an occasional old he-goat thrown in, didn't want to stop the steamer for some more or less recondite reason. So, unless they swallowed the wire itself, or made loops of it to snare the fishes with, I don't see what good their extravagant salary could be to them. I must say it was paid with a regularity worthy of a large and honourable trading company. For the rest, the only thing to eat — though it didn't look eatable in the least — I saw in their possession was a few lumps of some stuff like half-cooked dough, of a dirty lavender colour, they kept wrapped in leaves, and now and then swallowed a piece of, but so small that it seemed done more for the looks of the thing than for any serious purpose of sustenance. Why in the name of all the gnawing devils of hunger they didn't go for us — they were thirty to five — and have a good tuck-in for once, amazes me now when I think of it. They were big powerful men, with not much capacity to weigh the consequences, with courage, with strength, even yet, though their skins were no longer glossy and their muscles no longer hard. And I saw that something restraining, one of those human secrets that baffle probability, had come into play there. I looked at them with a swift quickening of interest — not because it occurred to me I might be eaten by them before very long, though I own to you that just then I perceived — in a new light, as it were — how unwholesome the pilgrims looked, and I hoped, yes, I positively hoped, that my aspect was not so — what shall I say? — so — unappetizing: a touch of fantastic vanity which fitted well with the dream-sensation that pervaded all my days at that time. Perhaps I had a little fever, too. One can't live with one's finger everlastingly on one's pulse. I had often 'a little fever,' or a little touch of other things — the playful paw-strokes of the wilderness, the preliminary trifling before the more serious onslaught which came in due course. Yes; I looked at them as you would on any human being, with a curiosity of their impulses, motives, capacities, weaknesses, when brought to the test of an inexorable physical necessity. Restraint! What possible restraint? Was it superstition, disgust, patience, fear — or some kind of primitive honour? No fear can stand up to hunger, no patience can wear it out, disgust simply does not exist where hunger is; and as to superstition, beliefs, and what you may call principles, they are less than chaff in a breeze. Don't you know the devilry of lingering starvation, its exasperating torment, its black thoughts, its sombre and brooding ferocity? Well, I do. It takes a man all his inborn strength to fight hunger properly. It's really easier to face bereavement, dishonour, and the perdition of one's soul — than this kind of prolonged hunger. Sad, but true. And these chaps, too, had no earthly reason for any kind of scruple. Restraint! I would just as soon have expected restraint from a hyena prowling amongst the corpses of a battlefield. But there was the fact facing me — the fact dazzling, to be seen, like the foam on the depths of the sea, like a ripple on an unfathomable enigma, a mystery greater — when I thought of it — than the curious, inexplicable note of desperate grief in this savage clamour that had swept by us on the river-bank, behind the blind whiteness of the fog.

"Two pilgrims were quarrelling in hurried whispers as to which bank. 'Left.' 'No, no; how can you? Right, right, of course.' 'It is very serious,' said the manager's voice behind me; 'I would be desolated if anything should happen to Mr. Kurtz before we came up.' I looked at him, and had not the slightest doubt he was sincere. He was just the kind of man who would wish to preserve appearances. That was his restraint. But when he muttered something about going on at once, I did not even take the trouble to answer him. I knew, and he knew, that it was impossible. Were we to let go our hold of the bottom, we would be absolutely in the air — in space. We wouldn't be able to tell where we were going to — whether up or down stream, or across — till we fetched against one bank or the other, — and then we wouldn't know at first which it was. Of course I made no move. I had no mind for a smash-up. You couldn't imagine a more deadly place for a shipwreck. Whether drowned at once or not, we were sure to perish speedily in one way or another. 'I authorize you to take all the risks,' he said, after a short silence. 'I refuse to take any,' I said, shortly; which was just the answer he expected, though its tone might have surprised him. 'Well, I must defer to your judgment. You are captain,' he said, with marked civility. I turned my shoulder to him in sign of my appreciation, and looked into the fog. How long would it last? It was the most hopeless look-out. The approach to this Kurtz grubbing for ivory in the wretched bush was beset by as many dangers as though he had been an enchanted princess sleeping in a fabulous castle. 'Will they attack, do you think?' asked the manager, in a confidential tone.

"I did not think they would attack, for several obvious reasons. The thick fog was one. If they left the bank in their canoes they would get lost in it, as we would be if we attempted to move. Still, I had also judged the jungle of both banks quite impenetrable — and yet eyes were in it, eyes that had seen us. The river-side bushes were certainly very thick; but the undergrowth behind was evidently penetrable. However, during the short lift I had seen no canoes anywhere in the reach — certainly not abreast of the steamer. But what made the idea of attack inconceivable to me was the nature of the noise — of the cries we had heard. They had not the fierce character boding immediate hostile intention. Unexpected, wild, and violent as they had been, they had given me an irresistible impression of sorrow. The glimpse of the steamboat had for some reason filled those savages with unrestrained grief. The danger, if any, I expounded, was from our proximity to a great human passion let loose. Even extreme grief may ultimately vent itself in violence — but more generally takes the form of apathy. . . .

"You should have seen the pilgrims stare! They had no heart to grin, or even to revile me: but I believe they thought me gone mad — with fright, maybe. I delivered a regular lecture. My dear boys, it was no good bothering. Keep a look-out? Well, you may guess I watched the fog for the signs of lifting as a cat watches a mouse; but for anything else our eyes were of no more use to us than if we had been buried miles deep in a heap of cotton-wool. It felt like it, too — choking, warm, stifling. Besides, all I said, though it sounded extravagant, was absolutely true to fact. What we afterwards alluded to as an attack was really an attempt at repulse. The action was very far from being aggressive — it was not even defensive, in the usual sense: it was undertaken under the stress of desperation, and in its essence was purely protective.

"It developed itself, I should say, two hours after the fog lifted, and its commencement was at a spot, roughly speaking, about a mile and a half below Kurtz's station. We had just floundered and flopped round a bend, when I saw an islet, a mere grassy hummock of bright green, in the middle of the stream. It was the only thing of the kind; but as we opened the reach more, I perceived it was the head of a long sandbank, or rather of a chain of shallow patches stretching down the middle of the river. They were discoloured, just awash, and the whole lot was seen just under the water, exactly as a man's backbone is seen running down the middle of his back under the skin. Now, as far as I did see, I could go to the right or to the left of this. I didn't know either channel, of course. The banks looked pretty well alike, the depth appeared the same; but as I had been informed the station was on the west side, I naturally headed for the western passage.

"No sooner had we fairly entered it than I became aware it was much narrower than I had supposed. To the left of us there was the long uninterrupted shoal, and to the right a high, steep bank heavily overgrown with bushes. Above the bush the trees stood in serried ranks. The twigs overhung the current thickly, and from distance to distance a large limb of some tree projected rigidly over the stream. It was then well on in the afternoon, the face of the forest was gloomy, and a broad strip of shadow had already fallen on the water. In this shadow we steamed up — very slowly, as you may imagine. I sheered her well inshore — the water being deepest near the bank, as the sounding-pole informed me.

"One of my hungry and forbearing friends was sounding in the bows just below me. This steamboat was exactly like a decked scow. On the deck, there were two little teak-wood houses, with doors and windows. The boiler was in the fore-end, and the machinery right astern. Over the whole there was a light roof, supported on stanchions. The funnel projected through that roof, and in front of the funnel a small cabin built of light planks served for a pilot-house. It contained a couch, two camp-stools, a loaded Martini-Henry leaning in one corner, a tiny table, and the steering-wheel. It had a wide door in front and a broad shutter at each side. All these were always thrown open, of course. I spent my days perched up there on the extreme fore-end of that roof, before the door. At night I slept, or tried to, on the couch. An athletic black belonging to some coast tribe, and educated by my poor predecessor, was the helms-man. He sported a pair of brass earrings, wore a blue cloth wrapper from the waist to the ankles, and thought all the world of himself. He was the most un-stable kind of fool I had ever seen. He steered with no end of a swagger while you were by; but if he lost sight of you, he became instantly the prey of an abject funk, and would let that cripple of a steamboat get the upper hand of him in a minute.

"I was looking down at the sounding-pole, and feeling much annoyed to see at each try a little more of it stick out of that river, when I saw my poleman give up the business suddenly, and stretch himself flat on the deck, without even taking the trouble to haul his pole in. He kept hold on it though, and it trailed in the water. At the same time the fireman, whom I could also see below me, sat down abruptly before his furnace and ducked his head. I was amazed. Then I had to look at the river mighty quick, because there was a snag in the fairway. Sticks, little sticks, were flying about — thick: they were whizzing before my nose, dropping below me, striking behind me against my pilot-house. All this time the river, the shore, the woods, were very quiet — perfectly quiet. I could only hear the heavy splashing thump of the stern-wheel and the patter of these things. We cleared the snag clumsily. Arrows, by Jove! We were be-ing shot at! I stepped in quickly to close the shutter on the land-side. That fool-helmsman, his hands on the spokes, was lifting his knees high, stamping his feet, champing his mouth, like a reined-in horse. Confound him! And we were staggering within ten feet of the bank. I had to lean right out to swing the heavy shutter, and I saw a face amongst the leaves on the level with my own, looking at me very fierce and steady; and then suddenly, as though a veil had been removed from my eyes, I made out, deep in the tangled gloom, naked breasts, arms, legs, glaring eyes, — the bush was swarming with human limbs in movement, glistening, of bronze colour. The twigs shook, swayed, and rus-tled, the arrows flew out of them, and then the shutter came to. 'Steer her straight,' I said to the helmsman. He held his head rigid, face forward; but his eyes rolled, he kept on lifting and setting down his feet gently, his mouth foamed a little. 'Keep quiet!' I said in a fury. I might just as well have ordered a tree not to sway in the wind. I darted out. Below me there was a great scuffle of feet on the iron deck; confused exclamations; a voice screamed, 'Can you turn back?' I caught sight of a V-shaped ripple on the water ahead. What? Another snag! A fusillade burst out under my feet. The pilgrims had opened with their Winchesters, and were simply squirting lead into that bush. A deuce of a lot of smoke came up and drove slowly forward. I swore at it. Now I couldn't see the ripple or the snag either. I stood in the doorway, peering, and the arrows came in swarms. They might have been poisoned, but they looked as though they wouldn't kill a cat. The bush began to howl. Our wood-cutters raised a warlike whoop; the report of a rifle just at my back deafened me. I glanced over my shoulder, and the pilot-house was yet full of noise and smoke when I made a dash at the wheel. The fool-nigger had dropped everything, to throw the shutter open and let off that Martini-Henry. He stood before the wide open-ing, glaring, and I yelled at him to come back, while I straightened the sudden twist out of that steamboat. There was no room to turn even if I had wanted to, the snag was somewhere very near ahead in that confounded smoke, there was no time to lose, so I just crowded her into the bank — right into the bank, where I knew the water was deep.

"We tore slowly along the overhanging bushes in a whirl of broken twigs and flying leaves. The fusillade below stopped short, as I had foreseen it would when the squirts got empty. I threw my head back to a glinting whizz that traversed the pilot-house, in at one shutter-hole and out at the other. Looking past that mad helmsman, who was shaking the empty rifle and yelling at the shore, I saw vague forms of men running bent double, leaping, gliding, distinct, incomplete, evanescent. Something big appeared in the air before the shutter, the rifle went overboard, and the man stepped back swiftly, looked at me over his shoulder in an extraordinary, profound, familiar manner, and fell upon my feet. The side of his head hit the wheel twice, and the end of what appeared a long cane clattered round and knocked over a little camp-stool. It looked as though after wrenching that thing from somebody ashore he had lost his balance in the effort. The thin smoke had blown away, we were clear of the snag, and looking ahead I could see that in another hundred yards or so I would be free to sheer off, away from the bank; but my feet felt so very warm and wet that I had to look down. The man had rolled on his back and stared straight up at me; both his hands clutched that cane. It was the shaft of a spear that, either thrown or lunged through the opening, had caught him in the side just below the ribs; the blade had gone in out of sight, after making a frightful gash; my shoes were full; a pool of blood lay very still, gleaming dark-red under the wheel; his eyes shone with an amazing lustre. The fusillade burst out again. He looked at me anxiously, gripping the spear like something precious, with an air of being afraid I would try to take it away from him. I had to make an effort to free my eyes from his gaze and attend to the steering. With one hand I felt above my head for the line of the steam whistle, and jerked out screech after screech hurriedly. The tumult of angry and warlike yells was checked instantly, and then from the depths of the woods went out such a tremulous and prolonged wail of mournful fear and utter despair as may be imagined to follow the flight of the last hope from the earth. There was a great commotion in the bush; the shower of arrows stopped, a few dropping shots rang out sharply — then silence, in which the languid beat of the stern-wheel came plainly to my ears. I put the helm hard a-starboard at the moment when the pilgrim in pink pyjamas, very hot and agitated, appeared in the doorway. 'The manager sends me——' he began in an official tone, and stopped short. 'Good God!' he said, glaring at the wounded man.

"We two whites stood over him, and his lustrous and inquiring glance enveloped us both. I declare it looked as though he would presently put to us some question in an understandable language; but he died without uttering a sound, without moving a limb, without twitching a muscle. Only in the very last moment, as though in response to some sign we could not see, to some whisper we could not hear, he frowned heavily, and that frown gave to his black death-mask an inconceivably sombre, brooding, and menacing expression. The lustre of inquiring glance faded swiftly into vacant glassiness. 'Can you steer?' I asked the agent eagerly. He looked very dubious; but I made a grab at his arm, and he understood at once I meant him to steer whether or no. To tell you the truth, I was morbidly anxious to change my shoes and socks. 'He is dead,' murmured the fellow, immensely impressed. 'No doubt about it,' said I, tugging like mad at the shoe-laces. 'And by the way, I suppose Mr. Kurtz is dead as well by this time.'

"For the moment that was the dominant thought. There was a sense of extreme disappointment, as though I had found out I had been striving after something altogether without a substance. I couldn't have been more disgusted if I had travelled all this way for the sole purpose of talking with Mr. Kurtz. Talking with . . . I flung one shoe overboard, and became aware that that was exactly what I had been looking forward to — a talk with Kurtz. I made the strange discovery that I had never imagined him as doing, you know, but as discoursing. I didn't say to myself, 'Now I will never see him,' or 'Now I will never shake him by the hand,' but, 'now I will never hear him.' The man presented himself as a voice. Not of course that I did not connect him with some sort of action. Hadn't I been told in all the tones of jealousy and admiration that he had collected, bartered, swindled, or stolen more ivory than all the other agents together? That was not the point. The point was in his being a gifted creature, and that of all his gifts the one that stood out preëminently, that carried with it a sense of real presence, was his ability to talk, his words — the gift of expression, the bewildering, the illuminating, the most exalted and the most contemptible, the pulsating stream of light, or the deceitful flow from the heart of an impenetrable darkness.

"The other shoe went flying unto the devil-god of that river. I thought, By Jove! it's all over. We are too late; he has vanished — the gift has vanished, by means of some spear, arrow, or club. I will never hear that chap speak after all, — and my sorrow had a startling extravagance of emotion, even such as I had noticed in the howling sorrow of these savages in the bush. I couldn't have felt more of lonely desolation somehow, had I been robbed of a belief or had missed my destiny in life. . . . Why do you sigh in this beastly way, somebody? Absurd? Well, absurd. Good Lord! mustn't a man ever—— Here, give me some tobacco." . . .

There was a pause of profound stillness, then a match flared, and Marlow's lean face appeared, worn, hollow, with downward folds and dropped eyelids, with an aspect of concentrated attention; and as he took vigorous draws at his pipe, it seemed to retreat and advance out of the night in the regular flicker of the tiny flame. The match went out.

"Absurd!" he cried. "This is the worst of trying to tell. . . . Here you all are, each moored with two good addresses, like a hulk with two anchors, a butcher round one corner, a policeman round another, excellent appetites, and temperature normal — you hear — normal from year's end to year's end. And you say, Absurd! Absurd be — exploded! Absurd! My dear boys, what can you expect from a man who out of sheer nervousness had just flung overboard a pair of new shoes! Now I think of it, it is amazing I did not shed tears. I am, upon the whole, proud of my fortitude. I was cut to the quick at the idea of having lost the inestimable privilege of listening to the gifted Kurtz. Of course I was wrong. The privilege was waiting for me. Oh, yes, I heard more than enough. And I was right, too. A voice. He was very little more than a voice. And I heard — him — it — this voice — other voices — all of them were so little more than voices — and the memory of that time itself lingers around me, impalpable, like a dying vibration of one immense jabber, silly, atrocious, sordid, savage, or simply mean, without any kind of sense. Voices, voices — even the girl herself — now——"

He was silent for a long time.

"I laid the ghost of his gifts at last with a lie," he began, suddenly. "Girl! What? Did I mention a girl? Oh, she is out of it — completely. They — the women I mean — are out of it — should be out of it. We must help them to stay in that beautiful world of their own, lest ours gets worse. Oh, she had to be out of it. You should have heard the disinterred body of Mr. Kurtz saying, 'My Intended.' You would have perceived directly then how completely she was out of it. And the lofty frontal bone of Mr. Kurtz! They say the hair goes on growing sometimes, but this — ah — specimen, was impressively bald. The wilderness had patted him on the head, and, behold, it was like a ball — an ivory ball; it had caressed him, and — lo! — he had withered; it had taken him, loved him, embraced him, got into his veins, consumed his flesh, and sealed his soul to its own by the inconceivable ceremonies of some devilish initiation. He was its spoiled and pampered favourite. Ivory? I should think so. Heaps of it, stacks of it. The old mud shanty was bursting with it. You would think there was not a single tusk left either above or below the ground in the whole country. 'Mostly fossil,' the manager had remarked, disparagingly. It was no more fossil than I am; but they call it fossil when it is dug up. It appears these niggers do bury the tusks sometimes — but evidently they couldn't bury this parcel deep enough to save the gifted Mr. Kurtz from his fate. We filled the steamboat with it, and had to pile a lot on the deck. Thus he could see and enjoy as long as he could see, because the appreciation of this favour had remained with him to the last. You should have heard him say, 'My ivory.' Oh yes, I heard him. 'My Intended, my ivory, my station, my river, my——' everything belonged to him. It made me hold my breath in expectation of hearing the wilderness burst into a prodigious peal of laughter that would shake the fixed stars in their places. Everything belonged to him — but that was a trifle. The thing was to know what he belonged to, how many powers of darkness claimed him for their own. That was the reflection that made you creepy all over. It was impossible — it was not good for one either — trying to imagine. He had taken a high seat amongst the devils of the land — I mean literally. You can't understand. How could you? — with solid pavement under your feet, surrounded by kind neighbours ready to cheer you or to fall on you, stepping delicately between the butcher and the policeman, in the holy terror of scandal and gallows and lunatic asylums — how can you imagine what particular region of the first ages a man's untrammelled feet may take him into by the way of solitude — utter solitude without a policeman — by the way of silence — utter silence, where no warning voice of a kind neighbour can be heard whispering of public opinion? These little things make all the great difference. When they are gone you must fall back upon your own innate strength, upon your own capacity for faithfulness. Of course you may be too much of a fool to go wrong — too dull even to know you are being assaulted by the powers of darkness. I take it, no fool ever made a bargain for his soul with the devil: the fool is too much of a fool, or the devil too much of a devil — I don't know which. Or you may be such a thunderingly exalted creature as to be altogether deaf and blind to anything but heavenly sights and sounds. Then the earth for you is only a standing place — and whether to be like this is your loss or your gain I won't pretend to say. But most of us are neither one nor the other. The earth for us is a place to live in, where we must put up with sights, with sounds, with smells, too, by Jove! — breathe dead hippo, so to speak, and not be contaminated. And there, don't you see? your strength comes in, the faith in your ability for the digging of unostentatious holes to bury the stuff in — your power of devotion, not to yourself, but to an obscure, back-breaking business. And that's difficult enough.

Mind, I am not trying to excuse or even explain — I am trying to account to myself for — for — Mr. Kurtz — for the shade of Mr. Kurtz. This initiated wraith from the back of Nowhere honoured me with its amazing confidence before it vanished altogether. This was because it could speak English to me. The original Kurtz had been educated partly in England, and — as he was good enough to say himself — his sympathies were in the right place. His mother was half-English, his father was half-French. All Europe contributed to the making of Kurtz; and by and by I learned that, most appropriately, the International Society for the Suppression of Savage Customs had intrusted him with the making of a report, for its future guidance. And he had written it, too. I've seen it. I've read it. It was eloquent, vibrating with eloquence, but too high-strung, I think. Seventeen pages of close writing he had found time for! But this must have been before his — let us say — nerves, went wrong, and caused him to preside at certain midnight dances ending with unspeakable rites, which — as far as I reluctantly gathered from what I heard at various times — were offered up to him — do you understand? — to Mr. Kurtz himself. But it was a beautiful piece of writing. The opening paragraph, however, in the light of later information, strikes me now as ominous. He began with the argument that we whites, from the point of development we had arrived at, 'must necessarily appear to them [savages] in the nature of supernatural beings — we approach them with the might as of a deity,' and so on, and so on. 'By the simple exercise of our will we can exert a power for good practically unbounded,' etc. etc. From that point he soared and took me with him. The peroration was magnificent, though difficult to remember, you know. It gave me the notion of an exotic Immensity ruled by an august Benevolence. It made me tingle with enthusiasm. This was the unbounded power of eloquence — of words — of burning noble words. There were no practical hints to interrupt the magic current of phrases, unless a kind of note at the foot of the last page, scrawled evidently much later, in an unsteady hand, may be regarded as the exposition of a method. It was very simple, and at the end of that moving appeal to every altruistic sentiment it blazed at you, luminous and terrifying, like a flash of lightning in a serene sky: 'Exterminate all the brutes!' The curious part was that he had apparently forgotten all about that valuable postscriptum, because, later on, when he in a sense came to himself, he repeatedly entreated me to take good care of 'my pamphlet' (he called it), as it was sure to have in the future a good influence upon his career. I had full information about all these things, and, besides, as it turned out, I was to have the care of his memory. I've done enough for it to give me the indisputable right to lay it, if I choose, for an everlasting rest in the dust-bin of progress, amongst all the sweepings and, figuratively speaking, all the dead cats of civilization. But then, you see, I can't choose. He won't be forgotten. Whatever he was, he was not common. He had the power to charm or frighten rudimentary souls into an aggravated witch-dance in his honour; he could also fill the small souls of the pilgrims with bitter misgivings: he had one devoted friend at least, and he had conquered one soul in the world that was neither rudimentary nor tainted with self-seeking. No; I can't forget him, though I am not prepared to affirm the fellow was exactly worth the life we lost in getting to him. I missed my late helmsman awfully, — I missed him even while his body was still lying in the pilot-house. Perhaps you will think it passing strange this regret for a savage who was no more account than a grain of sand in a black Sahara. Well, don't you see, he had done something, he had steered; for months I had him at my back — a help — an instrument. It was a kind of partnership. He steered for me — I had to look after him, I worried about his deficiencies, and thus a subtle bond had been created, of which I only became aware when it was suddenly broken. And the intimate profundity of that look he gave me when he received his hurt remains to this day in my memory — like a claim of distant kinship affirmed in a supreme moment.

"Poor fool! If he had only left that shutter alone. He had no restraint, no restraint — just like Kurtz — a tree swayed by the wind. As soon as I had put on a dry pair of slippers, I dragged him out, after first jerking the spear out of his side, which operation I confess I performed with my eyes shut tight. His heels leaped together over the little door-step; his shoulders were pressed to my breast; I hugged him from behind desperately. Oh! he was heavy, heavy; heavier than any man on earth, I should imagine. Then without more ado I tipped him overboard. The current snatched him as though he had been a wisp of grass, and I saw the body roll over twice before I lost sight of it for ever. All the pilgrims and the manager were then congregated on the awning-deck about the pilot-house, chattering at each other like a flock of excited magpies, and there was a scandalized murmur at my heartless promptitude. What they wanted to keep that body hanging about for I can't guess. Embalm it, maybe. But I had also heard another, and a very ominous, murmur on the deck below. My friends the wood-cutters were likewise scandalized, and with a better show of reason — though I admit that the reason itself was quite inadmissible. Oh, quite! I had made up my mind that if my late helmsman was to be eaten, the fishes alone should have him. He had been a very second-rate helmsman while alive, but now he was dead he might have become a first-class temptation, and possibly cause some startling trouble. Besides, I was anxious to take the wheel, the man in pink pyjamas showing himself a hopeless duffer at the business.

"This I did directly the simple funeral was over. We were going half-speed, keeping right in the middle of the stream, and I listened to the talk about me. They had given up Kurtz, they had given up the station; Kurtz was dead, and the station had been burnt — and so on — and so on. The red-haired pilgrim was beside himself with the thought that at least this poor Kurtz had been properly avenged. 'Say! We must have made a glorious slaughter of them in the bush. Eh? What do you think? Say?' He positively danced, the bloodthirsty little gingery beggar. And he had nearly fainted when he saw the wounded man! I could not help saying, 'You made a glorious lot of smoke, anyhow.' I had seen, from the way the tops of the bushes rustled and flew, that almost all the shots had gone too high. You can't hit anything unless you take aim and fire from the shoulder; but these chaps fired from the hip with their eyes shut. The retreat, I maintained — and I was right — was caused by the screeching of the steam-whistle. Upon this they forgot Kurtz, and began to howl at me with indignant protests.

"The manager stood by the wheel murmuring confidentially about the necessity of getting well away down the river before dark at all events, when I saw in the distance a clearing on the river-side and the outlines of some sort of building. 'What's this?' I asked. He clapped his hands in wonder. 'The station!' he cried. I edged in at once, still going half-speed.

"Through my glasses I saw the slope of a hill interspersed with rare trees and perfectly free from undergrowth. A long decaying building on the summit was half buried in the high grass; the large holes in the peaked roof gaped black from afar; the jungle and the woods made a background. There was no enclosure or fence of any kind; but there had been one apparently, for near the house half-a-dozen slim posts remained in a row, roughly trimmed, and with their upper ends ornamented with round carved balls. The rails, or whatever there had been between, had disappeared. Of course the forest surrounded all that. The river-bank was clear, and on the water-side I saw a white man under a hat like a cart-wheel beckoning persistently with his whole arm. Examining the edge of the forest above and below, I was almost certain I could see movements — human forms gliding here and there. I steamed past prudently, then stopped the engines and let her drift down. The man on the shore began to shout, urging us to land. 'We have been attacked,' screamed the manager. 'I know — I know. It's all right,' yelled back the other, as cheerful as you please. 'Come along. It's all right. I am glad.'

"His aspect reminded me of something I had seen — something funny I had seen somewhere. As I manœuvred to get alongside, I was asking myself, 'What does this fellow look like?' Suddenly I got it. He looked like a harlequin. His clothes had been made of some stuff that was brown holland probably, but it was covered with patches all over, with bright patches, blue, red, and yellow, — patches on the back, patches on the front, patches on elbows, on knees; coloured binding around his jacket, scarlet edging at the bottom of his trousers; and the sunshine made him look extremely gay and wonderfully neat withal, because you could see how beautifully all this patching had been done. A beardless, boyish face, very fair, no features to speak of, nose peeling, little blue eyes, smiles and frowns chasing each other over that open countenance like sunshine and shadow on a wind-swept plain. 'Look out, captain!' he cried; 'there's a snag lodged in here last night.' What! Another snag? I confess I swore shamefully. I had nearly holed my cripple, to finish off that charming trip. The harlequin on the bank turned his little pug-nose up to me. 'You English?' he asked, all smiles. 'Are you?' I shouted from the wheel. The smiles vanished, and he shook his head as if sorry for my disappointment. Then he brightened up. 'Never mind!' he cried, encouragingly. 'Are we in time?' I asked. 'He is up there,' he replied, with a toss of the head up the hill, and becoming gloomy all of a sudden. His face was like the autumn sky, overcast one moment and bright the next.

"When the manager, escorted by the pilgrims, all of them armed to the teeth, had gone to the house this chap came on board. 'I say, I don't like this. These natives are in the bush,' I said. He assured me earnestly it was all right. 'They are simple people,' he added; 'well, I am glad you came. It took me all my time to keep them off.' 'But you said it was all right,' I cried. 'Oh, they meant no harm,' he said; and as I stared he corrected himself, 'Not exactly.' Then vivaciously, 'My faith, your pilot-house wants a clean-up!' In the next breath he advised me to keep enough steam on the boiler to blow the whistle in case of any trouble. 'One good screech will do more for you than all your rifles. They are simple people,' he repeated. He rattled away at such a rate he quite overwhelmed me. He seemed to be trying to make up for lots of silence, and actually hinted, laughing, that such was the case. 'Don't you talk with Mr. Kurtz?' I said. 'You don't talk with that man — you listen to him,' he exclaimed with severe exaltation. 'But now——' He waved his arm, and in the twinkling of an eye was in the uttermost depths of despondency. In a moment he came up again with a jump, possessed himself of both my hands, shook them continuously, while he gabbled: 'Brother sailor ... honour ... pleasure ... delight ... introduce myself ... Russian ... son of an arch-priest ... Government of Tambov ... What? Tobacco! English tobacco; the excellent English tobacco! Now, that's brotherly. Smoke? Where's a sailor that does not smoke?'

"The pipe soothed him, and gradually I made out he had run away from school, had gone to sea in a Russian ship; ran away again; served some time in English ships; was now reconciled with the arch-priest. He made a point of that. 'But when one is young one must see things, gather experience, ideas; enlarge the mind.' 'Here!' I interrupted. 'You can never tell! Here I met Mr. Kurtz,' he said, youthfully solemn and reproachful. I held my tongue after that. It appears he had persuaded a Dutch trading-house on the coast to fit him out with stores and goods, and had started for the interior with a light heart, and no more idea of what would happen to him than a baby. He had been wandering about that river for nearly two years alone, cut off from everybody and everything. 'I am not so young as I look. I am twenty-five,' he said. 'At first old Van Shuyten would tell me to go to the devil,' he narrated with keen enjoyment; 'but I stuck to him, and talked and talked, till at last he got afraid I would talk the hind-leg off his favourite dog, so he gave me some cheap things and a few guns, and told me he hoped he would never see my face again. Good old Dutchman, Van Shuyten. I've sent him one small lot of ivory a year ago, so that he can't call me a little thief when I get back. I hope he got it. And for the rest I don't care. I had some wood stacked for you. That was my old house. Did you see?'

"I gave him Towson's book. He made as though he would kiss me, but restrained himself. 'The only book I had left, and I thought I had lost it,' he said, looking at it ecstatically. 'So many accidents happen to a man going about alone, you know. Canoes get upset sometimes — and sometimes you've got to clear out so quick when the people get angry.' He thumbed the pages. 'You made notes in Russian?' I asked. He nodded. 'I thought they were written in cipher,' I said. He laughed, then became serious. 'I had lots of trouble to keep these people off,' he said. 'Did they want to kill you?' I asked. 'Oh, no!' he cried, and checked himself. 'Why did they attack us?' I pursued. He hesitated, then said shamefacedly, 'They don't want him to go.' 'Don't they?' I said, curiously. He nodded a nod full of mystery and wisdom. 'I tell you,' he cried, 'this man has enlarged my mind.' He opened his arms wide, staring at me with his little blue eyes that were perfectly round."

III.

"I looked at him, lost in astonishment. There he was before me, in motley, as though he had absconded from a troupe of mimes, enthusiastic, fabulous. His very existence was improbable, inexplicable, and altogether bewildering. He was an insoluble problem. It was inconceivable how he had existed, how he had succeeded in getting so far, how he had managed to remain — why he did not instantly disappear. 'I went a little farther,' he said, 'then still a little farther — till I had gone so far that I don't know how I'll ever get back. Never mind. Plenty time. I can manage. You take Kurtz away quick — quick — I tell you.' The glamour of youth enveloped his particoloured rags, his destitution, his loneliness, the essential desolation of his futile wanderings. For months — for years — his life hadn't been worth a day's purchase; and there he was gallantly, thoughtlessly alive, to all appearance indestructible solely by the virtue of his few years and of his unreflecting audacity. I was seduced into something like admiration — like envy. Glamour urged him on, glamour kept him unscathed. He surely wanted nothing from the wilderness but space to breathe in and to push on through. His need was to exist, and to move onwards at the greatest possible risk, and with a maximum of privation. If the absolutely pure, uncalculating, unpractical spirit of adventure had ever ruled a human being, it ruled this be-patched youth. I almost envied him the possession of this modest and clear flame. It seemed to have consumed all thought of self so completely, that even while he was talking to you, you forgot that it was he — the man before your eyes — who had gone through these things. I did not envy him his devotion to Kurtz, though. He had not meditated over it. It came to him, and he accepted it with a sort of eager fatalism. I must say that to me it appeared about the most dangerous thing in every way he had come upon so far.

"They had come together unavoidably, like two ships becalmed near each other, and lay rubbing sides at last. I suppose Kurtz wanted an audience, because on a certain occasion, when encamped in the forest, they had talked all night, or more probably Kurtz had talked. 'We talked of everything,' he said, quite transported at the recollection. 'I forgot there was such a thing as sleep. The night did not seem to last an hour. Everything! Everything! . . . Of love, too.' 'Ah, he talked to you of love!' I said, much amused. 'It isn't what you think,' he cried, almost passionately. "It was in general. He made me see things — things.'

"He threw his arms up. We were on deck at the time, and the headman of my wood-cutters, lounging near by, turned upon him his heavy and glittering eyes. I looked around, and I don't know why, but I assure you that never, never before, did this land, this river, this jungle, the very arch of this blazing sky, appear to me so hopeless and so dark, so impenetrable to human thought, so pitiless to human weakness. 'And, ever since, you have been with him, of course?' I said.

"On the contrary. It appears their intercourse had been very much broken by various causes. He had, as he informed me proudly, managed to nurse Kurtz through two illnesses (he alluded to it as you would to some risky feat), but as a rule Kurtz wandered alone, far in the depths of the forest. 'Very often coming to this station, I had to wait days and days before he would turn up,' he said. 'Ah, it was worth waiting for! — sometimes.' 'What was he doing? exploring or what?' I asked. 'Oh, yes, of course;' he had discovered lots of villages, a lake, too — he did not know exactly in what direction; it was dangerous to inquire too much — but mostly his expeditions had been for ivory. 'But he had no goods to trade with by that time,' I objected. 'There's a good lot of cartridges left even yet,' he answered, looking away. 'To speak plainly, he raided the country,' I said. He nodded. 'Not alone, surely!' He muttered something about the villages round that lake. 'Kurtz got the tribe to follow him, did he?' I suggested. He fidgeted a little. 'They adored him,' he said. The tone of these words was so extraordinary that I looked at him searchingly. It was curious to see his mingled eagerness and reluctance to speak of Kurtz. The man filled his life, occupied his thoughts, swayed his emotions. 'What can you expect?' he burst out; 'he came to them with thunder and lightning, you know — and they had never seen anything like it — and very terrible. He could be very terrible. You can't judge Mr. Kurtz as you would an ordinary man. No, no, no! Now

— just to give you an idea — I don't mind telling you, he wanted to shoot me, too, one day — but I don't judge him.' 'Shoot you!' I cried. "What for?' 'Well, I had a small lot of ivory the chief of that village near by house gave me. You see I used to shoot game for them. Well, he wanted it, and wouldn't hear reason. He declared he would shoot me unless I gave him the ivory and then cleared out of the country, because he could do so, and had a fancy for it, and there was nothing on earth to prevent him killing whom he jolly well pleased. And it was true, too. I gave him the ivory. What did I care! But I didn't clear out. No, no. I couldn't leave him. I had to be careful, of course, till we got friendly again for a time. He had his second illness then. Afterwards I had to keep out of the way; but I didn't mind. He was living for the most part in those villages on the lake. When he came down to the river, sometimes he would take to me, and sometimes it was better for me to be careful. This man suffered too much. He hated all this, and somehow he couldn't get away. When I had a chance I begged him to try and leave while there was time; I offered to go back with him. And he would say yes, and then he would remain; go off on another ivory hunt; disappear for weeks; forget himself amongst these people — forget himself — you know.' 'Why! he's mad,' I said. He protested indignantly. Mr. Kurtz couldn't be mad. If I had heard him talk, only two days ago, I wouldn't dare hint at such a thing. . . . I had taken up my binoculars while we talked, and was looking at the shore, sweeping the limit of the forest at each side and at the back of the house. The consciousness of there being people in that bush, so silent, so quiet — as silent and quiet as the ruined house on the hill — made me uneasy. There was no sign on the face of nature of this amazing tale that was not so much told as suggested to me in desolate exclamations, completed by shrugs, in interrupted phrases, in hints ending in deep sighs. The woods were unmoved, like a mask — heavy, like the closed door of a prison — they looked with their air of hidden knowledge, of patient expectation, of unapproachable silence. The Russian was explaining to me that it was only lately that Mr. Kurtz had come down to the river, bringing along with him all the fighting men of that lake tribe. He had been absent for several months — getting himself adored, I suppose — and had come down unexpectedly, with the intention to all appearance of making a raid either across the river or down stream. Evidently the appetite for more ivory had got the better of the — what shall I say? — less material aspirations. However he had got much worse suddenly. 'I heard he was lying helpless, and so I came up — took my chance,' said the Russian. 'Oh, he is bad, very bad.' I directed my glass to the house. There were no signs of life, but there was the ruined roof, the long mud wall peeping above the grass, with three little square window-holes, no two of the same size; all this brought within reach of my hand, as it were. And then I made a brusque movement, and one of the remaining posts of that vanished fence leaped up in the field of my glass. You remember I told you I had been struck at the distance by certain attempts at ornamentation, rather remarkable in the ruinous aspect of the place. Now I had suddenly a nearer view, and its first result was to make me throw my head back as if before a blow. Then I went carefully from post to post with my glass, and I saw my mistake. These round knobs were not ornamental but symbolic; they were expressive and puzzling, striking and disturbing — food for thought and also for vultures if there had been any looking down from the sky; but at all events for such ants as were industrious enough to ascend the pole. They would have been even more impressive, those heads on the stakes, if their faces had not been turned to the house. Only one, the first I had made out, was facing my way. I was not so shocked as you may think. The start back I had given was really nothing but a movement of surprise. I had expected to see a knob of wood there, you know. I returned deliberately to the first I had seen — and there it was, black, dried, sunken, with closed eyelids, — a head that seemed to sleep at the top of that pole, and, with the shrunken dry lips showing a narrow white line of the teeth, was smiling, too, smiling continuously at some endless and jocose dream of that eternal slumber.

"I am not disclosing any trade secrets. In fact, the manager said afterwards that Mr. Kurtz's methods had ruined the district. I have no opinion on that point, but I want you clearly to understand that there was nothing exactly profitable in these heads being there. They only showed that Mr. Kurtz lacked restraint in the gratification of his various lusts, that there was something wanting in him — some small matter which, when the pressing need arose, could not be found under his magnificent eloquence. Whether he knew of this deficiency himself I can't say. I think the knowledge came to him at last — only at the very last. But the wilderness had found him out early, and had taken on him a terrible vengeance for the fantastic invasion. I think it had whispered to him things about himself which he did not know, things of which he had no conception till he took counsel with this great solitude — and the whisper had proved irresistibly fascinating. It echoed loudly within him because he was hollow at the core.... I put down the glass, and the head that had appeared near enough to be spoken to seemed at once to have leaped away from me into inaccessible distance.

"The admirer of Mr. Kurtz was a bit crestfallen. In a hurried, indistinct voice he began to assure me he had not dared to take these — say, symbols — down. He was not afraid of the natives; they would not stir till Mr. Kurtz gave the word. His ascendancy was extraordinary. The camps of these people surrounded the place, and the chiefs came every day to see him. They would crawl.... 'I don't want to know anything of the ceremonies used when approaching Mr. Kurtz,' I shouted. Curious, this feeling that came over me that such details would be more intolerable than those heads drying on the stakes under Mr. Kurtz's windows. After all, that was only a savage sight, while I seemed at one bound to have been transported into some lightless region of subtle horrors, where pure, uncomplicated savagery was a positive relief, being something that had a right to exist — obviously — in the sunshine. The young man looked at me with surprise. I suppose it did not occur to him that Mr. Kurtz was no idol of mine. He forgot I hadn't heard any of these splendid monologues on, what was it? on love, justice, conduct of life — or what not. If it had come to crawling before Mr. Kurtz, he crawled as much as the veriest savage of them all. I had no idea of the conditions, he said: these heads were the heads of rebels. I shocked him excessively by laughing. Rebels! What would be the next definition I was to hear? There had been enemies, criminals, workers — and these were rebels. Those rebellious heads looked very subdued to me on their sticks. 'You don't know how such a life tries a man like Kurtz,' cried Kurtz's last disciple. 'Well, and you?' I said. 'I! I! I am a simple man. I have no great thoughts. I want nothing from anybody. How can you compare me to...?' His feelings were too much for speech, and suddenly he broke down. 'I don't understand,' he groaned. 'I've been doing my best to keep him alive, and that's enough. I had no hand in all this. I have no abilities. There hasn't been a drop of medicine or a mouthful of invalid food for months here. He was shamefully abandoned. A man like this, with such ideas. Shamefully! Shamefully! I — I — haven't slept for the last ten nights . . .'

"His voice lost itself in the calm of the evening. The long shadows of the forest had slipped down hill while we talked, had gone far beyond the ruined hovel, beyond the symbolic row of stakes. All this was in the gloom, while we down there were yet in the sunshine, and the stretch of the river abreast of the clearing glittered in a still and dazzling splendour, with a murky and over-shadowed bend above and below. Not a living soul was seen on the shore. The bushes did not rustle.

"Suddenly round the corner of the house a group of men appeared, as though they had come up from the ground. They waded waist-deep in the grass, in a compact body, bearing an improvised stretcher in their midst. In-stantly, in the emptiness of the landscape, a cry arose whose shrillness pierced the still air like a sharp arrow flying straight to the very heart of the land; and, as if by enchantment, streams of human beings — of naked human beings — with spears in their hands, with bows, with shields, with wild glances and savage movements, were poured into the clearing by the dark-faced and pensive forest. The bushes shook, the grass swayed for a time, and then everything stood still in attentive immobility.

"'Now, if he does not say the right thing to them we are all done for,' said the Russian at my elbow. The knot of men with the stretcher had stopped, too, halfway to the steamer, as if petrified. I saw the man on the stretcher sit up, lank and with an uplifted arm, above the shoulders of the bearers. 'Let us hope that the man who can talk so well of love in general will find some particular reason to spare us this time,' I said. I resented bitterly the absurd danger of our situation, as if to be at the mercy of that atrocious phantom had been a dis-honouring necessity. I could not hear a sound, but through my glasses I saw the thin arm extended commandingly, the lower jaw moving, the eyes of that apparition shining darkly far in its bony head that nodded with grotesque jerks. Kurtz — Kurtz — that means short in German — don't it? Well, the name was as true as everything else in his life — and death. He looked at least seven feet long. His covering had fallen off, and his body emerged from it pitiful and appalling as from a winding-sheet. I could see the cage of his ribs all astir, the bones of his arm waving. It was as though an animated image of death carved out of old ivory had been shaking its hand with menaces at a motionless crowd of men made of dark and glittering bronze. I saw him open his mouth wide — it gave him a weirdly voracious aspect, as though he had wanted to swallow all the air, all the earth, all the men before him. A deep voice reached me faintly. He must have been shouting. He fell back suddenly. The stretcher shook as the bearers staggered forward again, and almost at the same time I noticed that the crowd of savages was vanishing without any perceptible movement of retreat, as if the forest that had ejected these beings so suddenly had drawn them in again as the breath is drawn in a long aspiration.

"Some of the pilgrims behind the stretcher carried his arms — two shot-guns, a heavy rifle, and a light revolver-carbine — the thunderbolts of that pitiful Jupiter. The manager bent over him murmuring as he walked beside his head. They laid him down in one of the little cabins — just a room for a bedplace and a camp-stool or two, you know. We had brought his belated correspondence, and a lot of torn envelopes and open letters littered his bed. His hand roamed feebly amongst these papers. I was struck by the fire of his eyes and the composed languor of his expression. It was not so much the exhaustion of disease. He did not seem in pain. This shadow looked satiated and calm, as though for the moment it had had its fill of all the emotions.

"He rustled one of the letters, and looking straight in my face said, 'I am glad.' Somebody had been writing to him about me. These special recommendations were turning up again. The volume of tone he emitted without effort, almost without the trouble of moving his lips, amazed me. A voice! a voice! It was grave, profound, vibrating, while the man did not seem capable of a whisper. However, he had enough strength in him — factitious no doubt — to very nearly make an end of us, as you shall hear directly.

"The manager appeared silently in the doorway; I stepped out at once and he drew the curtain after me. The Russian, eyed curiously by the pilgrims, was staring at the shore. I followed the direction of his glance.

"Dark human shapes could be made out in the distance, flitting indistinctly against the gloomy border of the forest, and near the river two bronze figures, leaning on tall spears, stood in the sunlight under fantastic head-dresses of spotted skins, warlike and still in statuesque repose. And from right to left along the lighted shore moved a wild and gorgeous apparition of a woman.

"She walked with measured steps, draped in striped and fringed cloths, treading the earth proudly, with a slight jingle and flash of barbarous ornaments. She carried her head high; her hair was done in the shape of a helmet; she had brass leggings to the knee, brass wire gauntlets to the elbow, a crimson spot on her tawny cheek, innumerable necklaces of glass beads on her neck; bizarre things, charms, gifts of witch-men, that hung about her, glittered and trembled at every step. She must have had the value of several elephant tusks upon her. She was savage and superb, wild-eyed and magnificent; there was something ominous and stately in her deliberate progress. And in the hush that had fallen suddenly upon the whole sorrowful land, the immense wilderness, the colossal body of the fecund and mysterious life seemed to look at her, pensive, as though it had been looking at the image of its own tenebrous and passionate soul.

"She came abreast of the steamer, stood still, and faced us. Her long shadow fell to the water's edge. Her face had a tragic and fierce aspect of wild sorrow and of dumb pain mingled with the fear of some struggling, half-shaped resolve. She stood looking at us without a stir, and like the wilderness itself, with an air of brooding over an inscrutable purpose. A whole minute passed, and then she made a step forward. There was a low jingle, a glint of yellow metal, a sway of fringed draperies, and she stopped as if her heart had failed her. The young fellow by my side growled. The pilgrims murmured at my back. She looked at us all as if her life had depended upon the unswerving steadiness of her glance. Suddenly she opened her bared arms and threw them up rigid above her head, as though in an uncontrollable desire to touch the sky, and at the same time the swift shadows darted out on the earth, swept around on the river, gathering the steamer into a shadowy embrace. A formidable silence hung over the scene.

"She turned away slowly, walked on, following the bank, and passed into the bushes to the left. Once only her eyes gleamed back at us in the dusk of the thickets before she disappeared.

" 'If she had offered to come aboard I really think I would have tried to shoot her,' said the man of patches, nervously. 'I have been risking my life every day for the last fortnight to keep her out of the house. She got in one day and kicked up a row about those miserable rags I picked up in the storeroom to mend my clothes with. I wasn't decent. At least it must have been that, for she talked like a fury to Kurtz for an hour, pointing at me now and then. I don't understand the dialect of this tribe. Luckily for me, I fancy Kurtz felt too ill that day to care, or there would have been mischief. I don't understand. . . . No — it's too much for me. Ah, well, it's all over now.'

"At this moment I heard Kurtz's deep voice behind the curtain: 'Save me! — save the ivory, you mean. Don't tell me. Save *me!* Why, I've had to save you. You are interrupting my plans now. Sick! Sick! Not so sick as you would like to believe. Never mind. I'll carry my ideas out yet — I will return. I'll show you what can be done. You with your little peddling notions — you are interfering with me. I will return. I . . . .'

"The manager came out. He did me the honour to take me under the arm and lead me aside. 'He is very low, very low,' he said. He considered it necessary to sigh, but neglected to be consistently sorrowful. 'We have done all we could for him — haven't we? But there is no disguising the fact, Mr. Kurtz has done more harm than good to the Company. He did not see the time was not ripe for vigorous action. Cautiously, cautiously — that's my principle. We must be cautious yet. The district is closed to us for a time. Deplorable! Upon the whole, the trade will suffer. I don't deny there is a remarkable quantity of ivory — mostly fossil. We must save it, at all events — but look how precarious the position is — and why? Because the method is unsound.' 'Do you,' said I, looking at the shore, 'call it "unsound method?"' 'Without doubt,' he exclaimed, hotly. 'Don't you?' . . .

'No method at all,' I murmured after a while. 'Exactly,' he exulted. 'I anticipated this. Shows a complete want of judgment. It is my duty to point it out in the proper quarter.' 'Oh,' said I, 'that fellow — what's his name? — the brickmaker, will make a readable report for you.' He appeared confounded for a moment. It seemed to me I had never breathed an atmosphere so vile, and I turned mentally to Kurtz for relief — positively for relief. 'Nevertheless I think Mr. Kurtz is a remarkable man,' I said with emphasis. He started, dropped on me a cold heavy glance, said very quietly, 'he *was*,' and turned his back on me. My hour of favour was over; I found myself lumped along with Kurtz as a partisan of methods for which the time was not ripe: I was unsound! Ah! but it was something to have at least a choice of nightmares.

"I had turned to the wilderness really, not to Mr. Kurtz, who, I was ready to admit, was as good as buried. And for a moment it seemed to me as if I also were buried in a vast grave full of unspeakable secrets. I felt an intolerable weight oppressing my breast, the smell of the damp earth, the unseen presence of victorious corruption, the darkness of an impenetrable night. . . . The Russian tapped me on the shoulder. I heard him mumbling and stammering something about 'brother seaman — couldn't conceal — knowledge of matters that would affect Mr. Kurtz's reputation.' I waited. For him evidently Mr. Kurtz was not in his grave; I suspect that for him Mr. Kurtz was one of the immortals. 'Well!' said I at last, 'speak out. As it happens, I am Mr. Kurtz's friend — in a way.'

"He stated with a good deal of formality that had we not been 'of the same profession,' he would have kept the matter to himself without regard to consequences. 'He suspected there was an active ill will towards him on the part of these white men that——' 'You are right,' I said, remembering a certain conversation I had overheard. 'The manager thinks you ought to be hanged.' He showed a concern at this intelligence which amused me at first. 'I had better get out of the way quietly,' he said, earnestly. 'I can do no more for Kurtz now, and they would soon find some excuse. What's to stop them? There's a military post three hundred miles from here.' 'Well, upon my word,' said I, 'perhaps you had better go if you have any friends amongst the savages near by.' 'Plenty,' he said. 'They are simple people — and I want nothing, you know.' He stood biting his lip, then: 'I don't want any harm to happen to these whites here, but of course I was thinking of Mr. Kurtz's reputation — but you are a brother seaman and ——' 'All right,' said I, after a time. 'Mr. Kurtz's reputation is safe with me.' I did not know how truly I spoke.

"He informed me, lowering his voice, that it was Kurtz who had ordered the attack to be made on the steamer. 'He hated sometimes the idea of being taken away — and then again. . . . But I don't understand these matters. I am a simple man. He thought it would scare you away — that you would give it up, thinking him dead. I could not stop him. Oh, I had an awful time of it this last month.' 'Very well,' I said. 'He is all right now.' 'Ye-e-es,' he muttered, not very convinced apparently. 'Thanks,' said I; 'I shall keep my eyes open.' 'But quiet — eh?' he urged, anxiously. 'It would be awful for his reputation if any-body here ——' I promised a complete discretion with great gravity. 'I have a canoe and three black fellows waiting not very far. I am off. Could you give me a few Martini-Henry cartridges?' I could, and did, with proper secrecy. He helped himself, with a wink at me, to a handful of my tobacco. 'Between sailors — you know — good English tobacco.' At the door of the pilot-house he turned round — 'I say, haven't you a pair of shoes you could spare?' He raised one leg. 'Look.' The soles were tied with knotted strings sandal-wise under his bare feet. I rooted out an old pair, at which he looked with admiration before tucking it under his left arm. One of his pockets (bright red) was bulging with cartridges, from the other (dark blue) peeped "Towson's Inquiry,' etc., etc. He seemed to think himself excellently well equipped for a renewed encounter with the wilder-ness. 'Ah! I'll never, never meet such a man again. You ought to have heard him recite poetry — his own, too, it was, he told me. Poetry!' He rolled his eyes at the recollection of these delights. 'Oh, he enlarged my mind!' 'Good-bye,' said I. He shook hands and vanished in the night. Sometimes I ask myself whether I had ever really seen him — whether it was possible to meet such a phenomenon! . . .

"When I woke up shortly after midnight his warning came to my mind with its hint of danger that seemed, in the starred darkness, real enough to make me get up for the purpose of having a look round. On the hill a big fire burned, illuminating fitfully a crooked corner of the station-house. One of the agents with a picket of a few of our blacks, armed for the purpose, was keeping guard over the ivory; but deep within the forest, red gleams that wavered, that seemed to sink and rise from the ground amongst confused columnar shapes of intense blackness, showed the exact position of the camp where Mr. Kurtz's adorers were keeping their uneasy vigil. The monotonous beating of a big drum filled the air with muffled shocks and a lingering vibration. A steady droning sound of many men chanting each to himself some weird incantation came out from the black, flat wall of the woods as the humming of bees comes out of a hive, and had a strange narcotic effect upon my half-awake senses. I believe I dozed off leaning over the rail, till an abrupt burst of yells, an overwhelming outbreak of a pent-up and mysterious frenzy, woke me up in a bewildered wonder. It was cut short all at once, and the low droning went on with an effect of audible and soothing silence. I glanced casually into the little cabin. A light was burning within, but Mr. Kurtz was not there.

"I think I would have raised an outcry if I had believed my eyes. But I didn't believe them at first — the thing seemed so impossible. The fact is I was completely unnerved by a sheer blank fright, pure abstract terror, unconnected with any distinct shape of physical danger. What made this emotion so over-powering was — how shall I define it? — the moral shock I received, as if some-thing altogether monstrous, intolerable to thought and odious to the soul, had been thrust upon me unexpectedly. This lasted of course the merest fraction of a second, and then the usual sense of commonplace, deadly danger, the possibil-ity of a sudden onslaught and massacre, or something of the kind, which I saw impending, was positively welcome and composing. It pacified me, in fact, so much, that I did not raise an alarm.

"There was an agent buttoned up inside an ulster and sleeping on a chair on deck within three feet of me. The yells had not awakened him; he snored very slightly; I left him to his slumbers and leaped ashore. I did not betray Mr. Kurtz — it was ordered I should never betray him — it was written I should be loyal to the nightmare of my choice. I was anxious to deal with this shadow by myself alone, — and to this day I don't know why I was so jealous of shar-ing with any one the peculiar blackness of that experience.

"As soon as I got on the bank I saw a trail — a broad trail through the grass. I remember the exultation with which I said to myself, 'He can't walk — he is crawling on all-fours — I've got him.' The grass was wet with dew. I strode rapidly with clenched fists. I fancy I had some vague notion of falling upon him and giving him a drubbing. I don't know. I had some imbecile thoughts. The knitting old woman with the cat obtruded herself upon my memory as a most improper person to be sitting at the other end of such an affair. I saw a row of pilgrims squirting lead in the air out of Winchesters held to the hip. I thought I would never get back to the steamer, and imagined my-self living alone and unarmed in the woods to an advanced age. Such silly things — you know. And I remember I confounded the beat of the drum with the beating of my heart, and was pleased at its calm regularity.

"I kept to the track though — then stopped to listen. The night was very clear; a dark blue space, sparkling with dew and starlight, in which black things stood very still. I thought I could see a kind of motion ahead of me. I was strangely cocksure of everything that night. I actually left the track and ran in a wide semicircle (I verily believe chuckling to myself) so as to get in front of that stir, of that motion I had seen — if indeed I had seen anything. I was cir-cumventing Kurtz as though it had been a boyish game.

"I came upon him, and, if he had not heard me coming, I would have fallen over him, too, but he got up in time. He rose, unsteady, long, pale, indistinct, like a vapour exhaled by the earth, and swayed slightly, misty and silent before me; while at my back the fires loomed between the trees, and the murmur of many voices issued from the forest. I had cut him off cleverly; but when ac-tually confronting him I seemed to come to my senses, I saw the danger in its right proportion. It was by no means over yet. Suppose he began to shout? Though he could hardly stand, there was still plenty of vigour in his voice. 'Go away — hide yourself,' he said, in that profound tone. It was very awful. I glanced back. We were within thirty yards from the nearest fire. A black figure stood up, strode on long black legs, waving long black arms, across the glow. It had horns — antelope horns, I think — on its head. Some sorcerer, some witch-man, no doubt: it looked fiend-like enough. 'Do you know what you are doing?' I whispered. 'Perfectly,' he answered, raising his voice for that single word: it sounded to me far off and yet loud, like a hail through a speaking-trumpet. If he makes a row we are lost, I thought to myself. This clearly was not a case for fisticuffs, even apart from the very natural aversion I had to beat that Shadow — this wandering and tormented thing. 'You will be lost,' I said — 'utterly lost.' One gets sometimes such a flash of inspiration, you know. I did say the right thing, though indeed he could not have been more irretrievably lost than he was at this very moment, when the foundations of our intimacy were being laid — to endure — to endure — even to the end — even beyond.

" 'I had immense plans,' he muttered irresolutely. 'Yes,' said I; 'but if you try to shout I'll smash your head with ——' There was not a stick or a stone near. 'I will throttle you for good,' I corrected myself. 'I was on the threshold of great things,' he pleaded, in a voice of longing, with a wistfulness of tone that made my blood run cold. 'And now for this stupid scoundrel ——' 'Your success in Europe is assured in any case,' I affirmed, steadily. I did not want to have the throttling of him, you understand — and indeed it would have been very little use for any practical purpose. I tried to break the spell — the heavy, mute spell of the wilderness — that seemed to draw him to its pitiless breast by the awakening of forgotten and brutal instincts, by the memory of gratified and monstrous passions. This alone, I was convinced, had driven him out to the edge of the forest, to the bush, towards the gleam of fires, the throb of drums, the drone of weird incantations; this alone had beguiled his unlawful soul beyond the bounds of permitted aspirations. And, don't you see, the terror of the position was not in being knocked on the head — though I had a very lively sense of that danger, too — but in this, that I had to deal with a being to whom I could not appeal in the name of anything high or low. I had, even like the niggers, to invoke him — himself — his own exalted and incredible degradation. There was nothing either above or below him, and I knew it. He had kicked himself loose of the earth. Confound the man! he had kicked the very earth to pieces. He was alone, and I before him did not know whether I stood on the ground or floated in the air. I've been telling you what we said — repeating the phrases we pronounced — but what's the good? They were common everyday words — the familiar, vague sounds exchanged on every waking day of life. But what of that? They had behind them, to my mind, the terrific suggestiveness of words heard in dreams, of phrases spoken in nightmares. Soul! If anybody had ever struggled with a soul, I am the man. And I wasn't arguing with a lunatic either. Believe me or not, his intelligence was perfectly clear — concentrated, it is true, upon himself with horrible intensity, yet clear; and therein was my only chance — barring, of course, the killing him there and then, which wasn't so good, on account of unavoidable noise. But his soul was mad. Being alone in the wilderness, it had looked within itself, and, by heavens! I tell you, it had gone mad. I had — for my sins, I suppose — to go through the ordeal of looking into it myself. No eloquence could have been so withering to one's belief in mankind as his final burst of sincerity. He struggled with himself, too. I saw it, — I heard it. I saw the inconceivable mystery of a soul that knew no restraint, no faith, and no fear, yet struggling blindly with itself.

I kept my head pretty well; but when I had him at last stretched on the couch, I wiped my forehead, while my legs shook under me as though I had carried half a ton on my back down that hill. And yet I had only supported him, his bony arm clasped round my neck — and he was not much heavier than a child.

"When next day we left at noon, the crowd, of whose presence behind the curtain of trees I had been acutely conscious all the time, flowed out of the woods again, filled the clearing, covered the slope with a mass of naked, breathing, quivering, bronze bodies. I steamed up a bit, then swung downstream, and two thousand eyes followed the evolutions of the splashing, thumping, fierce river-demon beating the water with its terrible tail and breathing black smoke into the air. In front of the first rank, along the river, three men, plastered with bright red earth from head to foot, strutted to and fro restlessly. When we came abreast again, they faced the river, stamped their feet, nodded their horned heads, swayed their scarlet bodies; they shook towards the fierce river-demon a bunch of black feathers, a mangy skin with a pendent tail — something that looked like a dried gourd; they shouted periodically together strings of amazing words that resembled no sounds of human language; and the deep murmurs of the crowd, interrupted suddenly, were like the responses of some satanic litany.

"We had carried Kurtz into the pilot-house: there was more air there. Lying on the couch, he stared through the open shutter. There was an eddy in the mass of human bodies, and the woman with helmeted head and tawny cheeks rushed out to the very brink of the stream. She put out her hands, shouted something, and all that wild mob took up the shout in a roaring chorus of articulated, rapid, breathless utterance.

"Do you understand this?' I asked.

"He kept on looking out past me with fiery, longing eyes, with a mingled expression of wistfulness and hate. He made no answer, but I saw a smile, a smile of indefinable meaning, appear on his colourless lips that a moment after twitched convulsively. 'Do I not?' he said slowly, gasping, as if the words had been torn out of him by a supernatural power.

"I pulled the string of the whistle, and I did this because I saw the pilgrims on deck getting out their rifles with an air of anticipating a jolly lark. At the sudden screech there was a movement of abject terror through that wedged mass of bodies. 'Don't! don't you frighten them away,' cried someone on deck disconsolately. I pulled the string time after time. They broke and ran, they leaped, they crouched, they swerved, they dodged the flying terror of the sound. The three red chaps had fallen flat, face down on the shore, as though they had been shot dead. Only the barbarous and superb woman did not so much as flinch, and stretched tragically her bare arms after us over the sombre and glittering river.

"And then that imbecile crowd down on the deck started their little fun, and I could see nothing more for smoke.

"The brown current ran swiftly out of the heart of darkness, bearing us down towards the sea with twice the speed of our upward progress; and Kurtz's life was running swiftly, too, ebbing, ebbing out of his heart into the sea of inexorable time. The manager was very placid, he had no vital anxieties now, he took us both in with a comprehensive and satisfied glance: the 'affair' had come off as well as could be wished. I saw the time approaching when I would be left alone of the party of 'unsound method.' The pilgrims looked upon me with disfavour. I was, so to speak, numbered with the dead. It is strange how I accepted this unforeseen partnership, this choice of nightmares forced upon me in the tenebrous land invaded by these mean and greedy phantoms.

"Kurtz discoursed. A voice! a voice! It rang deep to the very last. It survived his strength to hide in the magnificent folds of eloquence the barren darkness of his heart. Oh, he struggled! he struggled! The wastes of his weary brain were haunted by shadowy images now — images of wealth and fame revolving obsequiously round his unextinguishable gift of noble and lofty expression. My Intended, my station, my career, my ideas — these were the subjects for the occasional utterances of elevated sentiments. The shade of the original Kurtz frequented the bedside of the hollow sham, whose fate it was to be buried presently in the mould of primeval earth. But both the diabolic love and the unearthly hate of the mysteries it had penetrated fought for the possession of that soul satiated with primitive emotions, avid of lying fame, of sham distinction, of all the appearances of success and power.

"Sometimes he was contemptibly childish. He desired to have kings meet him at railway-stations on his return from some ghastly Nowhere, where he intended to accomplish great things. 'You show them you have in you something that is really profitable, and then there will be no limits to the recognition of your ability,' he would say. 'Of course you must take care of the motives — right motives — always.' The long reaches that were like one and the same reach, monotonous bends that were exactly alike, slipped past the steamer with their multitude of secular trees looking patiently after this grimy fragment of another world, the forerunner of change, of conquest, of trade, of massacres, of blessings. I looked ahead — piloting. 'Close the shutter,' said Kurtz suddenly one day; 'I can't bear to look at this.' I did so. There was a silence. 'Oh, but I will wring your heart yet!' he cried at the invisible wilderness.

"We broke down — as I had expected — and had to lie up for repairs at the head of an island. This delay was the first thing that shook Kurtz's confidence. One morning he gave me a packet of papers and a photograph — the lot tied together with a shoe-string. 'Keep this for me,' he said. 'This noxious fool' (meaning the manager) 'is capable of prying into my boxes when I am not looking.' In the afternoon I saw him. He was lying on his back with closed eyes, and I withdrew quietly, but I heard him mutter, 'Live rightly, die, die . . .' I listened. There was nothing more. Was he rehearsing some speech in his sleep, or was it a fragment of a phrase from some newspaper article? He had been writing for the papers and meant to do so again, 'for the furthering of my ideas. It's a duty.'

His was an impenetrable darkness. I looked at him as you peer down at a man who is lying at the bottom of a precipice where the sun never shines. But I had not much time to give him, because I was helping the engine-driver to take to pieces the leaky cylinders, to straighten a bent connecting-rod, and in other such matters. I lived in an infernal mess of rust, filings, nuts, bolts, spanners, hammers, ratchet-drills — things I abominate, because I don't get on with them. I tended the little forge we fortunately had aboard; I toiled wearily in a wretched scrap-heap — unless I had the shakes too bad to stand.

"One evening coming in with a candle I was startled to hear him say a little tremulously, 'I am lying here in the dark waiting for death.' The light was within a foot of his eyes. I forced myself to murmur, 'Oh, nonsense!' and stood over him as if transfixed.

"Anything approaching the change that came over his features I have never seen before, and hope never to see again. Oh, I wasn't touched. I was fascinated. It was as though a veil had been rent. I saw on that ivory face the expression of sombre pride, of ruthless power, of craven terror — of an intense and hopeless despair. Did he live his life again in every detail of desire, temptation, and surrender during that supreme moment of complete knowledge? He cried in a whisper at some image, at some vision — he cried out twice, a cry that was no more than a breath —

" 'The horror! The horror!'

"I blew the candle out and left the cabin. The pilgrims were dining in the mess-room, and I took my place opposite the manager, who lifted his eyes to give me a questioning glance, which I successfully ignored. He leaned back, serene, with that peculiar smile of his sealing the unexpressed depths of his meanness. A continuous shower of small flies streamed upon the lamp, upon the cloth, upon our hands and faces. Suddenly the manager's boy put his insolent black head in the doorway, and said in a tone of scathing contempt —

" 'Mistah Kurtz — he dead.'

"All the pilgrims rushed out to see. I remained, and went on with my dinner. I believe I was considered brutally callous. However, I did not eat much. There was a lamp in there — light, don't you know — and outside it was so beastly, beastly dark. I went no more near the remarkable man who had pronounced a judgment upon the adventures of his soul on this earth. The voice was gone. What else had been there? But I am of course aware that next day the pilgrims buried something in a muddy hole.

"And then they very nearly buried me.

"However, as you see, I did not go to join Kurtz there and then. I did not. I remained to dream the nightmare out to the end, and to show my loyalty to Kurtz once more. Destiny. My destiny! Droll thing life is — that mysterious arrangement of merciless logic for a futile purpose. The most you can hope from it is some knowledge of yourself — that comes too late — a crop of unextinguishable regrets. I have wrestled with death. It is the most unexciting contest you can imagine. It takes place in an impalpable grayness, with nothing underfoot, with nothing around, without spectators, without clamour, without glory, without the great desire of victory, without the great fear of defeat, in a sickly atmosphere of tepid scepticism, without much belief in your own right, and still less in that of your adversary. If such is the form of ultimate wisdom, then life is a greater riddle than some of us think it to be. I was within a hair's breadth of the last opportunity for pronouncement, and I found with humiliation that probably I would have nothing to say. This is the reason why I affirm that Kurtz was a remarkable man. He had something to say. He said it. Since I had peeped over the edge myself, I understand better the meaning of his stare, that could not see the flame of the candle, but was wide enough to embrace the whole universe, piercing enough to penetrate all the hearts that beat in the darkness. He had summed up — he had judged. 'The horror!' He was a remarkable man. After all, this was the expression of some sort of belief; it had candour, it had conviction, it had a vibrating note of revolt in its whisper, it had the appalling face of a glimpsed truth — the strange commingling of desire and hate. And it is not my own extremity I remember best — a vision of grayness without form filled with physical pain, and a careless contempt for the evanescence of all things — even of this pain itself. No! It is his extremity that

I seem to have lived through. True, he had made that last stride, he had stepped over the edge, while I had been permitted to draw back my hesitating foot. And perhaps in this is the whole difference; perhaps all the wisdom, and all truth, and all sincerity, are just compressed into that inappreciable moment of time in which we step over the threshold of the invisible. Perhaps! I like to think my summing-up would not have been a word of careless contempt. Better his cry — much better. It was an affirmation, a moral victory paid for by innumerable defeats, by abominable terrors, by abominable satisfactions. But it was a victory! That is why I have remained loyal to Kurtz to the last, and even beyond, when a long time after I heard once more, not his own voice, but the echo of his magnificent eloquence thrown to me from a soul as translucently pure as a cliff of crystal.

"No, they did not bury me, though there is a period of time which I remember mistily, with a shuddering wonder, like a passage through some inconceivable world that had no hope in it and no desire. I found myself back in the sepulchral city resenting the sight of people hurrying through the streets to filch a little money from each other, to devour their infamous cookery, to gulp their unwholesome beer, to dream their insignificant and silly dreams. They trespassed upon my thoughts. They were intruders whose knowledge of life was to me an irritating pretence, because I felt so sure they could not possibly know the things I knew. Their bearing, which was simply the bearing of commonplace individuals going about their business in the assurance of perfect safety, was offensive to me like the outrageous flauntings of folly in the face of a danger it is unable to comprehend. I had no particular desire to enlighten them, but I had some difficulty in restraining myself from laughing in their faces, so full of stupid importance. I daresay I was not very well at that time. I tottered about the streets — there were various affairs to settle — grinning bitterly at perfectly respectable persons. I admit my behaviour was inexcusable, but then my temperature was seldom normal in these days. My dear aunt's endeavours to 'nurse up my strength' seemed altogether beside the mark. It was not my strength that wanted nursing, it was my imagination that wanted soothing. I kept the bundle of papers given me by Kurtz, not knowing exactly what to do with it. His mother had died lately, watched over, as I was told, by his Intended. A clean-shaved man, with an official manner and wearing gold-rimmed spectacles, called on me one day and made inquiries, at first circuitous, afterwards suavely pressing, about what he was pleased to denominate certain 'documents.' I was not surprised, because I had had two rows with the manager on the subject out there. I had refused to give up the smallest scrap out of that package, and I took the same attitude with the spectacled man. He became darkly menacing at last, and with much heat argued that the Company had the right to every bit of information about its 'territories.' And said he, 'Mr. Kurtz's knowledge of unexplored regions must have been necessarily extensive and peculiar — owing to his great abilities and to the deplorable circumstances in which he had been placed: therefore ——' I assured him Mr. Kurtz's knowledge, however extensive, did not bear upon the problems of commerce or administration. He invoked then the name of science. 'It would be an incalculable loss if,' etc., etc. I offered him the report on the 'Suppression of Savage Customs,' with the postscriptum torn off. He took it up eagerly, but ended by sniffing at it with an air of contempt. 'This is not what we had a right to expect,' he remarked. 'Expect nothing else,' I said. 'There are only private letters.' He withdrew upon some threat of legal proceedings, and I saw him no more; but another fellow, calling himself Kurtz's cousin, appeared two days later, and was anxious to hear all the details about his dear relative's last moments. Incidentally he gave me to understand that Kurtz had been essentially a great musician. 'There was the making of an immense success,' said the man, who was an organist, I believe, with lank gray hair flowing over a greasy coat-collar. I had no reason to doubt his statement; and to this day I am unable to say what was Kurtz's profession, whether he ever had any — which was the greatest of his talents. I had taken him for a painter who wrote for the papers, or else for a journalist who could paint — but even the cousin (who took snuff during the interview) could not tell me what he had been — exactly. He was a universal genius — on that point I agreed with the old chap, who thereupon blew his nose noisily into a large cotton handkerchief and withdrew in senile agitation, bearing off some family letters and memoranda without importance. Ultimately a journalist anxious to know something of the fate of his 'dear colleague' turned up. This visitor informed me Kurtz's proper sphere ought to have been politics 'on the popular side.' He had furry straight eyebrows, bristly hair cropped short, an eye-glass on a broad ribbon, and, becoming expansive, confessed his opinion that Kurtz really couldn't write a bit — 'but heavens! how that man could talk. He electrified large meetings. He had faith — don't you see? — he had the faith. He could get himself to believe anything — anything. He would have been a splendid leader of an extreme party.' 'What party?' I asked. 'Any party,' answered the other. 'He was an — an — extremist.' Did I not think so? I assented. Did I know, he asked, with a sudden flash of curiosity, 'what it was that had induced him to go out there?' 'Yes,' said I, and forthwith handed him the famous Report for publication, if he thought fit. He glanced through it hurriedly, mumbling all the time, judged 'it would do,' and took himself off with this plunder.

"Thus I was left at last with a slim packet of letters and the girl's portrait. She struck me as beautiful — I mean she had a beautiful expression. I know that the sunlight can be made to lie, too, yet one felt that no manipulation of light and pose could have conveyed the delicate shade of truthfulness upon those features. She seemed ready to listen without mental reservation, without suspicion, without a thought for herself. I concluded I would go and give her back her portrait and those letters myself. Curiosity? Yes; and also some other feeling perhaps. All that had been Kurtz's had passed out of my hands: his soul, his body, his station, his plans, his ivory, his career. There remained only his memory and his Intended — and I wanted to give that up, too, to the past, in a way — to surrender personally all that remained of him with me to that oblivion which is the last word of our common fate. I don't defend myself. I had no clear perception of what it was I really wanted. Perhaps it was an impulse of unconscious loyalty, or the fulfilment of one of those ironic necessities that lurk in the facts of human existence. I don't know. I can't tell. But I went.

"I thought his memory was like the other memories of the dead that accumulate in every man's life — a vague impress on the brain of shadows that had fallen on it in their swift and final passage; but before the high and ponderous door, between the tall houses of a street as still and decorous as a well-kept alley in a cemetery, I had a vision of him on the stretcher, opening his mouth voraciously, as if to devour all the earth with all its mankind. He lived then before me; he lived as much as he had ever lived — a shadow insatiable of splendid appearances, of frightful realities; a shadow darker than the shadow of the night, and draped nobly in the folds of a gorgeous eloquence. The vision seemed to enter the house with me — the stretcher, the phantom-bearers, the wild crowd of obedient worshippers, the gloom of the forests, the glitter of the reach between the murky bends, the beat of the drum, regular and muffled like the beating of a heart — the heart of a conquering darkness. It was a moment of triumph for the wilderness, an invading and vengeful rush which, it seemed to me, I would have to keep back alone for the salvation of another soul. And the memory of what I had heard him say afar there, with the horned shapes stirring at my back, in the glow of fires, within the patient woods, those broken phrases came back to me, were heard again in their ominous and terrifying simplicity. I remembered his abject pleading, his abject threats, the colossal scale of his vile desires, the meanness, the torment, the tempestuous anguish of his soul. And later on I seemed to see his collected languid manner, when he said one day, 'This lot of ivory now is really mine. The Company did not pay for it. I collected it myself at a very great personal risk. I am afraid they will try to claim it as theirs though. H'm. It is a difficult case. What do you think I ought to do — resist, Eh? I want no more than justice.' . . . He wanted no more than justice — no more than justice. I rang the bell before a mahogany door on the first floor, and while I waited he seemed to stare at me out of the glassy panel — stare with that wide and immense stare embracing, condemning, loathing all the universe. I seemed to hear the whispered cry, 'The horror! The horror!'

"The dusk was falling. I had to wait in a lofty drawing-room with three long windows from floor to ceiling that were like three luminous and bedraped columns. The bent gilt legs and backs of the furniture shone in indistinct curves. The tall marble fireplace had a cold and monumental whiteness. A grand piano stood massively in a corner; with dark gleams on the flat surfaces like a sombre and polished sarcophagus. A high door opened — closed. I rose.

"She came forward, all in black, with a pale head, floating towards me in the dusk. She was in mourning. It was more than a year since his death, more than a year since the news came; she seemed as though she would remember and mourn for ever. She took both my hands in hers and murmured, 'I had heard you were coming.' I noticed she was not very young — I mean not girlish. She had a mature capacity for fidelity, for belief, for suffering. The room seemed to have grown darker, as if all the sad light of the cloudy evening had taken refuge on her forehead. This fair hair, this pale visage, this pure brow, seemed surrounded by an ashy halo from which the dark eyes looked out at me. Their glance was guileless, profound, confident, and trustful. She carried her sorrowful head as though she were proud of that sorrow, as though she would say, I — I alone know how to mourn for him as he deserves. But while we were still shaking hands, such a look of awful desolation came upon her face that I perceived she was one of those creatures that are not the playthings of Time. For her he had died only yesterday. And, by Jove! the impression was so powerful that for me, too, he seemed to have died only yesterday — nay, this very minute. I saw her and him in the same instant of time — his death and her sorrow — I saw her sorrow in the very moment of his death. Do you understand? I saw them together — I heard them together. She had said, with a deep catch of the breath, 'I have survived' while my strained ears seemed to hear distinctly, mingled with her tone of despairing regret, the summing up whisper of his eternal condemnation. I asked myself what I was doing there, with a sensation of panic in my heart as though I had blundered into a place of cruel and absurd mysteries not fit for a human being to behold. She motioned me to a chair. We sat down. I laid the packet gently on the little table, and she put her hand over it.... 'You knew him well,' she murmured, after a moment of mourning silence.

" 'Intimacy grows quickly out there,' I said. 'I knew him as well as it is possible for one man to know another.'

" 'And you admired him,' she said. 'It was impossible to know him and not to admire him. Was it?'

" 'He was a remarkable man,' I said, unsteadily. Then before the appealing fixity of her gaze, that seemed to watch for more words on my lips, I went on, 'It was impossible not to ——'

" 'Love him,' she finished eagerly, silencing me into an appalled dumbness. 'How true! how true! But when you think that no one knew him so well as I! I had all his noble confidence. I knew him best.'

" 'You knew him best,' I repeated. And perhaps she did. But with every word spoken the room was growing darker, and only her forehead, smooth and white, remained illumined by the unextinguishable light of belief and love.

" 'You were his friend,' she went on. 'His friend,' she repeated, a little louder. 'You must have been, if he had given you this, and sent you to me. I feel I can speak to you — and oh! I must speak. I want you — you who have heard his last words — to know I have been worthy of him.... It is not pride. ... Yes! I am proud to know I understood him better than any one on earth — he told me so himself. And since his mother died I have had no one — no one — to — to ——'

"I listened. The darkness deepened. I was not even sure whether he had given me the right bundle. I rather suspect he wanted me to take care of another batch of his papers which, after his death, I saw the manager examining under the lamp. And the girl talked, easing her pain in the certitude of my sympathy; she talked as thirsty men drink. I had heard that her engagement with Kurtz had been disapproved by her people. He wasn't rich enough or something. And indeed I don't know whether he had not been a pauper all his life. He had given me some reason to infer that it was his impatience of comparative poverty that drove him out there.

" '... Who was not his friend who had heard him speak once?' she was saying. 'He drew men towards him by what was best in them.' She looked at me with intensity. 'It is the gift of the great,' she went on, and the sound of her low voice seemed to have the accompaniment of all the other sounds, full of mystery, desolation, and sorrow, I had ever heard — the ripple of the river, the soughing of the trees swayed by the wind, the murmurs of the crowds, the faint ring of incomprehensible words cried from afar, the whisper of a voice speaking from beyond the threshold of an eternal darkness. 'But you have heard him! You know!' she cried.

" 'Yes, I know,' I said with something like despair in my heart, but bowing my head before the faith that was in her, before that great and saving illusion that shone with an unearthly glow in the darkness, in the triumphant darkness from which I could not have defended her — from which I could not even defend myself.

" 'What a loss to me — to us!' — she corrected herself with beautiful generosity; then added in a murmur, 'To the world. ' By the last gleams of twilight I could see the glitter of her eyes, full of tears — of tears that would not fall.

" 'I have been very happy — very fortunate — very proud,' she went on. 'Too fortunate. Too happy for a little while. And now I am unhappy for — for life.'

"She stood up; her fair hair seemed to catch all the remaining light in a glimmer of gold. I rose, too.

" 'And of all this,' she went on, mournfully, 'of all his promise, and of all his greatness, of his generous mind, of his noble heart, nothing remains — nothing but a memory. You and I ——'

" 'We shall always remember him,' I said, hastily.

" 'No!' she cried. 'It is impossible that all this should be lost — that such a life should be sacrificed to leave nothing — but sorrow. You know what vast plans he had. I knew of them, too — I could not perhaps understand — but others knew of them. Something must remain. His words, at least, have not died.'

" 'His words will remain,' I said.

" 'And his example,' she whispered to herself. 'Men looked up to him — his goodness shone in every act. His example ——'

" 'True,' I said; 'his example, too. Yes, his example. I forgot that.'

" 'But I do not. I cannot — I cannot believe — not yet. I cannot believe that I shall never see him again, that nobody will see him again, never, never, never.'

"She put out her arms as if after a retreating figure, stretching them black and with clasped pale hands across the fading and narrow sheen of the window. Never see him! I saw him clearly enough then. I shall see this eloquent phantom as long as I live, and I shall see her, too, a tragic and familiar Shade, resembling in this gesture another one, tragic also, and bedecked with powerless charms, stretching bare brown arms over the glitter of the infernal stream, the stream of darkness. She said suddenly very low, 'He died as he lived.'

" 'His end,' said I, with dull anger stirring in me, 'was in every way worthy of his life.'

" 'And I was not with him,' she murmured. My anger subsided before a feeling of infinite pity.

" 'Everything that could be done ——' I mumbled.

" 'Ah, but I believed in him more than any one on earth — more than his own mother, more than — himself. He needed me! Me! I would have treasured every sigh, every word, every sign, every glance.'

"I felt like a chill grip on my chest. 'Don't,' I said, in a muffled voice.

" 'Forgive me. I — I — have mourned so long in silence — in silence. . . . You were with him — to the last? I think of his loneliness. Nobody near to understand him as I would have understood. Perhaps no one to hear. . . .'

" 'To the very end,' I said, shakily. 'I heard his very last words. . . .' I stopped in a fright.

" 'Repeat them,' she murmured in a heart-broken tone. 'I want — I want — something — something — to — to live with.'

"I was on the point of crying at her, 'Don't you hear them?' The dusk was repeating them in a persistent whisper all around us, in a whisper that seemed to swell menacingly like the first whisper of a rising wind. 'The horror! the horror!'

" 'His last word — to live with,' she insisted. 'Don't you understand I loved him — I loved him — I loved him!'

"I pulled myself together and spoke slowly.

" 'The last word he pronounced was — your name.'

"I heard a light sigh and then my heart stood still, stopped dead short by an exulting and terrible cry, by the cry of inconceivable triumph and of unspeakable pain. 'I knew it — I was sure!' . . . She knew. She was sure. I heard her weeping; she had hidden her face in her hands. It seemed to me that the house would collapse before I could escape, that the heavens would fall upon my head. But nothing happened. The heavens do not fall for such a trifle. Would they have fallen, I wonder, if I had rendered Kurtz that justice which was his due? Hadn't he said he wanted only justice? But I couldn't. I could not tell her. It would have been too dark — too dark altogether. . . ."

Marlow ceased, and sat apart, indistinct and silent, in the pose of a meditating Buddha. Nobody moved for a time. "We have lost the first of the ebb," said the Director, suddenly. I raised my head. The offing was barred by a black bank of clouds, and the tranquil waterway leading to the uttermost ends of the earth flowed sombre under an overcast sky — seemed to lead into the heart of an immense darkness.

Exercises

1. Why does Marlow go to the Congo?

2. What comments on the human condition do you discover in Marlow's generalizations?

3. How well is Kurtz drawn as a character? Support your conclusion.

4. What is the Russian's function?

5. Why doesn't Marlow tell the Intended Kurtz's last words?

6. Do you find any symbolic elements in Marlow's journey?

7. Is Marlow changed by his Congo experience? Explain.

Topics for Writing

1. Conrad uses two narrators in *Heart of Darkness*. Discuss the function and significance of the first narrator, who begins and ends this work.

2. Discuss the importance of the setting to the theme or themes with which the work deals.

3. Choose one of the longer descriptive passages and analyze its style.

4. Trace the imagery of light and darkness. Is it used in a conventional fashion, dark and black standing for evil and white for good? What does this imagery and the way it is used contribute to the meaning of the work?

5. Analyze Kurtz's character, trying to identify the flaw within him that causes his downfall.

Baines, Jocelyn. *Joseph Conrad: A Critical Biography*. New York: McGraw-Hill, 1960.

Conrad, Joseph. *Congo Diary and Other Uncollected Pieces*. Ed. Zdzisław Najder. Garden City, N.Y.: Doubleday, 1978.

Dean, Leonard F., ed. *Joseph Conrad's Heart of Darkness: Backgrounds and Criticisms*. Englewood Cliffs, N.J.: Prentice-Hall, 1960.

Graver, Lawrence. *Conrad's Short Fiction*. Berkeley and Los Angeles: University of California Press, 1969.

Guerard, Albert. *Conrad the Novelist*. Cambridge, Mass.: Harvard University Press, 1958.

Guetti, James L. *The Limits of Metaphor: A Study of Melville, Conrad, and Faulkner*. Ithaca, N.Y.: Cornell University Press, 1967.

Harkness, Bruce, ed. *Conrad's "Heart of Darkness" and the Critics*. San Francisco: Wadsworth Publishing Co., 1960.

———. "The Young Roman Trader in 'Heart of Darkness.'" *Conradiana*, 12 (1980), 227–229.

Hewitt, Douglas. *Conrad: A Reassessment*. 2nd ed. London: Bowes and Bowes, 1969.

Karl, Frederick. *A Reader's Guide to Joseph Conrad*. New York: Farrar, Straus and Giroux, 1969.

Kimbrough, Robert, ed. *Heart of Darkness*. Norton Critical Edition. New York: Norton, 1963.

McClure, John A. *Kipling and Conrad: The Colonial Fiction*. Cambridge, Mass.: Harvard University Press, 1981.

Martin, David M. "The Function of the Intended in Conrad's *Heart of Darkness*." *Studies in Short Fiction*, 11 (1974), 227–233.

Moser, Thomas. *Joseph Conrad: Achievement and Decline*. Cambridge, Mass.: Harvard University Press, 1957.

Nettels, Elsa. *James and Conrad*. Athens, Ga.: The University of Georgia Press, 1977.

Roussel, Royal. *The Metaphysics of Darkness: A Study in the Unity and Development of Conrad's Fiction*. Baltimore: The Johns Hopkins Press, 1971.

Schwarz, Daniel R. *Conrad: Almayer's Folly to Under Western Eyes*. Ithaca, N.Y.: Cornell University Press, 1980.

Sherry, Norman. *Conrad's Western World*. Cambridge: University Press, 1971.

Stallman, Robert W., ed. *The Art of Joseph Conrad: A Critical Symposium*. East Lansing, Mich.: Michigan State University Press, 1960.

Stark, Bruce H. "Kurtz's Intended: The Heart of *Heart of Darkness*." *Texas Studies in Literature and Language*, 16 (1974), 535–555.

Stewart, Garrett. "Lying as Dying in 'Heart of Darkness.'" *PMLA*, 95 (1980), 319–331.

Watt, Ian. *Conrad in the Nineteenth Century*. Berkeley and Los Angeles: University of California Press, 1979.

Yelton, Donald. *Mimesis and Metaphor: An Inquiry into the Genesis and Scope of Conrad's Symbolic Imagery*. The Hague: Mouton, 1967.

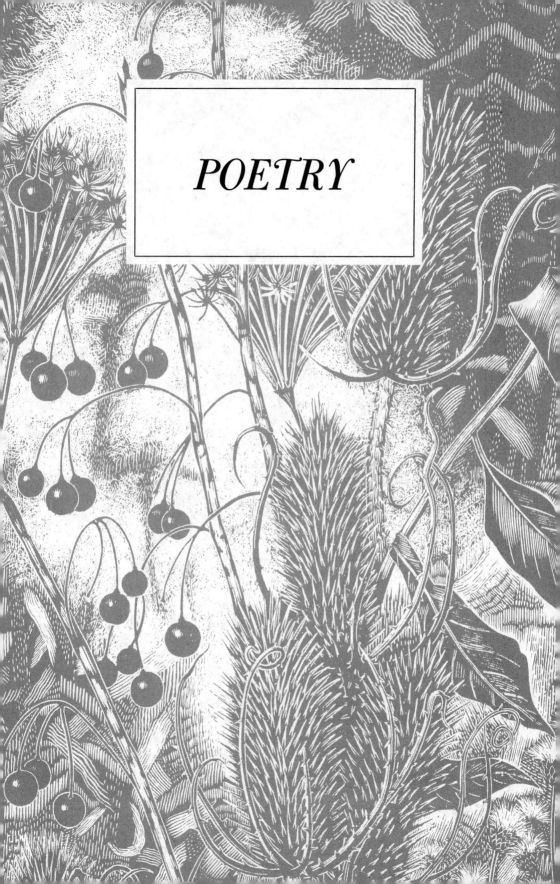

POETRY

Good poetry has a certain enchantment that is not easily defined. If we are deeply affected by a poem — if we think about it for weeks after reading it — we will sense this enchanting power. The following poem, although a simple one, demonstrates such strength.

William Carlos Williams *(1883–1963)*

Young Woman at a Window

She sits with
tears on

her cheek
her cheek on

her hand   5
the child

in her lap
his nose

pressed
to the glass   10

With the sure hand of a skilled artist, Williams has drawn a poignant picture of loneliness and grief. The few details can be summarized in a sentence: a young woman sits crying by a window while the child in her lap peers out, putting his face to the glass, as small children are wont to do. This prose statement, however, lacks the impact, the depth of emotion, and the power we feel in the poetic version, even though the details are the same. By using just the right language and form, Williams has created a forceful impression, especially of the child. What impression does the next poem make on you?

Nikki Giovanni *(1943–   )*

Poem for Flora

when she was little
and colored and ugly with short
straightened hair
and a very pretty smile
she went to sunday school to hear   5

435

'bout nebuchadnezzar the king
of the jews†

and she would listen

shadrach, meshach and abednego in the fire†

and she would learn   10

how god was neither north
nor south east or west
with no color but all
she remembered was that
Sheba was Black and comely†   15

and she would think

i want to be
like that

we got important things to pick up on personal things & feelings [handwritten marginalia]

The aspirations of this black girl and the grief of the young woman in Williams's poem are universal human feelings. Most poetry centers on common human emotions — joys and sorrows, hopes and fears, likes and dislikes. Poets often reveal new insights into these feelings, and so we read their works with increasing awareness of self, of others, and of the world, as well as with a sense of emotional and intellectual adventure.

Occasionally we find in a poem an explanation of what certain kinds of poetry aim to do. As you read aloud the three poems below, note the sense of serious delight in poetry that each conveys, even though each offers a different perception of poetry's aims.

Victor Hernandez Cruz (1949–   )

Today Is a Day of Great Joy

when they stop poems
in the mail   & clap
their hands & dance to
them
when women become pregnant   5
by the side of poems
the strongest sounds   making
the river go along

it is a great day

7. *Nebuchadnezzar:* the most powerful of Babylonian kings, whose reign (605–562 B.C.) spanned the major captivity of the Jews.
9. *Shadrach, Meshach, Abednego:* three Jews who were cast into a furnace for refusing to worship an idol set up by Nebuchadnezzar, but who emerged unharmed (recorded in the Old Testament, Daniel 1–3).
15. *Sheba:* the queen of Sheba (a region in southern Arabia), who visited King Solomon in Jerusalem about the tenth century B.C., ostensibly to test his wisdom.

as poems fall down to   10
movie crowds   in restaurants
in bars

when poems start to
knock down walls   to
choke politicians   15
when poems scream &
begin to break the air

that is the time of
true poets   that is
the time of greatness   20

a true poet   aiming
poems   & watching things
fall to the ground

it is a great day.

Denise Levertov (1923–   )

The Secret

Two girls discover
the secret of life
in a sudden line of
poetry.

I who don't know the   5
secret wrote
the line. They
told me

(through a third person)
they had found it   10
but not what it was
not even

what line it was. No doubt
by now, more than a week
later, they have forgotten   15
the secret,

the line, the name of
the poem. I love them
for finding what
I can't find,   20

and for loving me
for the line I wrote,

and for forgetting it
so that

a thousand times, till death   25
finds them, they may
discover it again, in other
lines

in other
happenings. And for   30
wanting to know it,
for

assuming there is
such a secret, yes,
for that   35
most of all.

Christopher Logue *(1926–   )*

from the foreword to **New Numbers**

If this book doesn't change you
give it no house space;
if having read it you
are the same person you
were before picking it up,   5
then throw it away.
Not enough for me
that my poems shine in your eye;
not enough for me
that they look from your walls   10
or lurk on your shelves;
I want my poems to be in your mind
so you can say them when you are in love
so you can say them when the plane takes off
and death comes near;   15
I want my poems to come between
the raised stick and the cowering back,
I want my poems to become
a weapon in your trembling hands,
a sword whose blade both makes and mirrors change;   20
but most of all I want my poems sung
unthinkingly between your lips like air.

Whether we expect poetry to give us the joy and power that Cruz suggests, whether we seek from it the secrets of life, which Levertov says it contains; whether we explore it for ways to change ourselves, as Logue hopes we might; or whether we enjoy it for its appeal to our senses and emotions, we will discover many delights of the heart as well as the mind in this multifaceted art.

Not all the aspects, forms, and techniques found in poetry can be described in this introduction. The chapters that follow explain and illustrate the most important of these to help you to respond more fully to them. Perhaps the most fundamental characteristic of poetry is that it deals with truth, beauty, and emotion. In doing so, it relies heavily on the careful, concentrated use of words and on their emotional associations (the topic of Chapter 8). It appeals to the senses (Chapter 9). It frequently compares one subject to another in order to clarify and illuminate (Chapter 10). Often poetry is written in meter (or regularly recurring accented syllables) and is strikingly rhythmic, even if written in free verse, which has irregular meter (Chapter 11). It may be rhymed or unrhymed, and in a variety of stanzaic (paragraph) patterns, such as the ballad stanza. And the whole poem may follow a fixed form (such as the sonnet), or it may avoid traditional forms altogether (Chapter 12). Finally, it may speak of one subject but allude to another, and these allusions may be symbolic, containing several levels and aspects of meaning (Chapters 13 and 14). But whatever its form, technique, and complexity, each poem is an attempt to say something significant in a highly memorable way, as shown by the following example:

Wilfred Owen (1893–1918)

Arms and the Boy

Let the boy try along this bayonet-blade
How cold steel is, and keen with hunger of blood;
Blue with all malice, like a madman's flash;
And thinly drawn with famishing for flesh.

Lend him to stroke these blind, blunt bullet-heads   5
Which long to nuzzle in the hearts of lads,
Or give him cartridges of fine zinc teeth,
Sharp with the sharpness of grief and death.

For his teeth seem for laughing round an apple.
There lurk no claws behind his fingers supple;   10
And God will grow no talons at his heels,
Nor antlers through the thickness of his curls.

    Of course, not all poems are significant or memorable. We should consider, then, how we can discern quality in poetry. If you have written poems, you have sensed the difficulty of selecting just the right word or phrase and finding the right balance and emphasis. When a poet spends weeks writing a short poem, does this investment guarantee quality? Is a poem good, or great, just because the lines sound smooth? Or rhyme? Or contain exotic words, hidden meanings, symbolic allusions? If a particular poem sounds sincere, does the sincerity alone make it good? The answer to all these questions is, of course, no. Poetic quality results when many elements are appropriately employed and combined. Literary evaluators, or critics, generally agree that good poetry nearly always exhibits the following traits (among others of lesser importance), and that great poetry often contains these characteristics in especially powerful and memorable combinations:

1. *Insight.* Poetry is a way of asking and answering important questions about the human condition, the world, the universe. Are the questions asked by the poem significant ones? Do the answers lead us to understand fundamental and vital truths?

2. *Beauty.* Is the picture presented in the poem vivid, striking, memorable? Are the sounds harmonious, rhythmic? Is the form symmetrical, balanced? If the poem lacks some of these traits, is there a compelling reason, in terms of subject matter, for their absence? Is the poem appealing even if it deals with an ugly situation, character, or emotion?

3. *Emotion.* Are the feelings expressed by the speaker and the characters in the poem genuine, realistic, truthful, deep? If the feelings are false, unbelievable, or shallow, is there an appropriate reason?

Exercises

1. Symmetry, one of the elements of beauty, can be observed in "Young Woman at a Window," at the beginning of this chapter. Find the center of the poem by line count (excluding the title), then tell what simple symmetry governs Williams's portrayal of the mother and child.

2. Explain the beauty found in Wilfred Owen's use of rhyme in "Arms and the Boy." How well do the lines rhyme? Is there a consistency in how well they rhyme? Why do you think the poet chose this rhyming approach? In your answer, consider the subject of the poem. What connection can you find between the rhyming technique and the subject? Are the rhymes effective and appropriate in this situation?

3. What important truths about people of all races and ages can you discover in Giovanni's "Poem for Flora"?

4. Levertov's "The Secret" contains an insight into a discovery made by two girls. Explain what insight the speaker gains from the insight earlier discovered by the girls.

5. After identifying the *insight* gained by the speaker in Imamu Amiri Baraka's poem below, evaluate its significance. What has the speaker learned that might be important to him or her?

6. Tell what emotions find expression in "Out, Out — " by Robert Frost, at the end of this chapter. In your opinion, are they genuine, realistic, truthful, deep? How do you know?

Throughout the following chapters, including a final chapter entitled "Other Poems to Read," you will find a great variety of poetic expression. You will be invited to increase both your understanding of poetic art and your ability to evaluate it through explanations, examples, exercises, and topics for essays. As you read aloud the poems below, ask yourself whether you like them, what you think they mean, how they affect you, and what elements of insight, beauty, and emotion they contain.

Imamu Amiri Baraka (LeRoi Jones, 1934–   )

Preface to a Twenty Volume Suicide Note

Lately, I've become accustomed to the way
The ground opens up and envelops me
Each time I go out to walk the dog.
Or the broad edged silly music the wind
Makes when I run for a bus —   5

Things have come to that.

And now, each night I count the stars,
And each night I get the same number.
And when they will not come to be counted
I count the holes they leave.   10

Nobody sings anymore.

And then last night, I tiptoed up
To my daughter's room and heard her
Talking to someone, and when I opened
The door, there was no one there . . .   15
Only she on her knees,
Peeking into her own clasped hands.

Carol Lynn Pearson (1939–   )

Optical Illusion

Time is a stage magician
Pulling sleight-of-hand tricks
To make you think things go.

There —
Eclipsed by the quick scarf —   5
A lifetime of loves.

Zip —
The child is man.
Zip —
The friend in your arms   10
Is earth.
Zip —
The green tree is gold, is white,
Is smoking ash, is gone.

Zip —   15
Time's trick goes on.
All things loved —
Now you see them, now you don't.

Oh, this world has more
Of coming and of going   *20*
Than I can bear.
I guess it's eternity I want,
Where all things are
And always will be,
Where I can hold my loves   *25*
A little looser,
Where finally we realize —
Time
Is the only thing that really dies.

John Keats (*1795–1821*)

When I Have Fears

When I have fears that I may cease to be
   Before my pen has gleaned my teeming brain,
Before high-pilèd books, in charactery,†
   Hold like rich garners† the full-ripened grain;
When I behold, upon the night's starred face,   *5*
   Huge cloudy symbols of a high romance,
And think that I may never live to trace
   Their shadows, with the magic hand of chance;
And when I feel, fair creature of an hour,
   That I shall never look upon thee more,   *10*
Never have relish† in the fairy† power
   Of unreflecting love; then on the shore
Of the wide world I stand alone and think
Till love and fame to nothingness do sink.

Robert Frost (*1874–1963*)

Out, Out —

The buzz saw snarled and rattled in the yard
And made dust and dropped stove-length sticks of wood,
Sweet-scented stuff when the breeze drew across it.
And from there those that lifted eyes could count
Five mountain ranges one behind the other   *5*
Under the sunset far into Vermont.
And the saw snarled and rattled, snarled and rattled,

3. *charactery:* printing or hand-   11. *relish:* enjoyment; *fairy:* mag-
writing.   ical.
4. *rich garners:* full storage bins.

As it ran light, or had to bear a load.
And nothing happened: day was all but done.
Call it a day, I wish they might have said   *10*
To please the boy by giving him the half hour
That a boy counts so much when saved from work.
His sister stood beside them in her apron
To tell them "Supper." At the word, the saw,
As if to prove saws knew what supper meant,   *15*
Leaped out at the boy's hand, or seemed to leap —
He must have given the hand. However it was,
Neither refused the meeting. But the hand!
The boy's first outcry was a rueful laugh,
As he swung toward them holding up the hand,   *20*
Half in appeal, but half as if to keep
The life from spilling. Then the boy saw all —
Since he was old enough to know, big boy
Doing a man's work, though a child at heart —
He saw all spoiled. "Don't let him cut my hand off —   *25*
The doctor, when he comes. Don't let him, sister!"
So. But the hand was gone already.
The doctor put him in the dark of ether.
He lay and puffed his lips out with his breath.
And then — the watcher at his pulse took fright.   *30*
No one believed. They listened at his heart.
Little — less — nothing! — and that ended it.
No more to build on there. And they, since they
Were not the one dead, turned to their affairs.

Topics for Writing

1. Select the poem in this introduction that you enjoyed the most, or the least, or the one you believe you will remember the longest, and write an essay explaining why you feel as you do about it. Organize the essay into two, three, or four categories, and quote from the poem to support each statement.

2. Compose an essay describing your personal experiences with poetry and your feelings and ideas about it, grouping your comments into several unified categories.

3. Using the title, the general form, and the style of a poem in this introduction, write a poem of your own in which you strive to say something significant about yourself or someone you know.

4. Evaluate a poem in this introduction, focusing your judgment on one of the three fundamental characteristics of good poetry discussed in these pages. Point to specific words, phrases, lines, and ideas in the poem as evidence.

8. DENOTATION AND CONNOTATION

When poets circulate their work among friends, publish it, or share it with an audience at a poetry reading, they initiate a potentially delightful collaboration with the readers or listeners. To take part in this collaboration, we must train ourselves to read poetry sensitively and intelligently. If we don't, we may find poems incomprehensible, or misunderstand them. As a seventeenth-century poet put it,

> Thou say'st my lines are hard;
>   And I the truth will tell;
> They are both hard, and marr'd,
>   If thou not read'st them well.
>   *Robert Herrick*, "To My Ill Reader"

Because the range of poetic creation is immense, the challenges and delights of individual poems vary considerably. Certain poems yield their fruits at a first reading; others, only after repeated attempts.

Although you may encounter unfamiliar words and phrases, you should be able to establish on the first or second reading of most short poems who the characters are, what they are like, where they are located, what kind of person the speaker is, and what emotions are being expressed. To participate fully, however, you should know the meanings, or **denotations,** of all words in a poem. For this reason you may need to consult a dictionary or other reference work, or you may find that the context of the poem itself enables you to discover denotations of words you do not know. In the insightful poem below, only *tanager* might be unfamiliar to you; as you summarize the poem, though, you will readily understand its meaning.

Marge Piercy (1936–   )

The Crippling

I used to watch
it on the ledge:
a crippled bird.
Surely it would
die soon.   5

Then I saw a man
at one of the windows
fed it a few seeds,
a crust from lunch.
Often he forgot   10
and it went hopping on the ledge
a starving scurvy sparrow.
Every couple of weeks
he caught it in his hand
and clipped back one wing.   15
I call it a sparrow.
The plumage was sooty.
Sometimes in the sun
the feathers might have
been scarlet like a tanager.   20
He never
let it fly.
He never took it in.
Perhaps he was starving himself.

When you come to understand the situation in "The Crippling," you appreciate the speaker's reaction to the bird's mutilation and imprisonment more fully if you realize what a tanager is, and that the "starving scurvy sparrow" (line 12) might be a lovely scarlet tanager covered with soot.

   You may encounter more than one unfamiliar word in the next poem, but if you read it aloud carefully, you will clarify many of its difficulties. The poem contains clues enabling us to perceive the situation and to understand the feelings of the speaker.

Raymond Carver (1938–   )

Photograph of My Father in His Twenty-second Year

October. Here in this dank, unfamiliar kitchen
I study my father's embarrassed young man's face.
Sheepish grin, he holds in one hand a string
Of spiny yellow perch, in the other
A bottle of Carlsbad beer.   5

In jeans and denim shirt, he leans
Against the front fender of a Ford circa 1934.
He would like to pose bluff and hearty for his posterity,
Wear his old hat cocked over his ear, stick out his tongue . . .
All his life my father wanted to be bold.   10

But the eyes give him away, and the hands
That limply offer the string of dead perch
And the bottle of beer. Father, I loved you,
Yet how can I say thank you, I who cannot hold my liquor either
And do not even know the places to fish?   15

Exercises

1. Who is involved in this poem? Where is the speaker? What is he like? About how old is he?

2. What feelings, insights, and ideas is the speaker trying to communicate?

3. Relying only on the poem and your own vocabulary, define the following words as used by the poet and describe the hints in the poem (if any) that help to define them: *dank* kitchen, *sheepish* grin, *circa* 1934, *bluff* and *hearty*. Then consult a college dictionary to verify your definitions.

4. After you have defined the specified words in question 3, tell what information they provide about the scene, the situation, the speaker, and the speaker's feelings about his father and about himself.

5. Does the poem communicate these feelings effectively? Explain, referring to specific words and phrases.

As illustrated by Carver's lines, a poem can be a valuable source of information about itself, especially if read with patience and sensitivity. The reader must resist the impulse to cast a poem aside because it contains unfamiliar words or ideas, and instead cultivate a careful approach necessary in dealing with challenging works. For assistance with crucial words or phrases that are unfamiliar and insufficiently clarified by context, naturally you should consult a good dictionary. When looking up a word, you will often find several denotations, and you must evaluate the appropriateness of each for the context of the poem you are considering. In the poem below, underline unfamiliar words and phrases and also recognizable words and phrases used in unusual ways.

John Crowe Ransom *(1888–1974)*

Bells for John Whiteside's Daughter

There was such speed in her little body,
And such lightness in her footfall,
It is no wonder her brown study
Astonishes us all.

Her wars were bruited in our high window.   5
We looked among orchard trees and beyond
Where she took arms against her shadow,
Or harried unto the pond

The lazy geese, like a snow cloud
Dripping their snow on the green grass,   10
Tricking and stopping, sleepy and proud,
Who cried in goose, Alas,

For the tireless heart within the little
Lady with rod that made them rise
From their noon apple-dreams and scuttle   *15*
Goose-fashion under the skies!

But now go the bells, and we are ready,
In one house we are sternly stopped
To say we are vexed at her brown study,
Lying so primly propped.   *20*

Exercises

1. As you attempt to summarize the situation in Ransom's poem (Who are the characters? Where are they located? What is happening? What message is being presented?), you may discover that you are puzzled by words not often used in ordinary conversation. Define as well as you can the following italicized words, using a dictionary if necessary to supplement information provided by the poem: her *brown study;* her wars being *bruited; harried* unto the pond; to *scuttle* goose-fashion; being *vexed.*

2. Define the following familiar words used in unusual ways: her *wars;* taking *arms* against her shadow; dripping their *snow* on the green grass; crying in *goose,* Alas; the little lady with *rod.*

3. After you have identified appropriate denotations for these words and phrases, very likely you will recognize more clearly who the characters are, what they are doing, and why they feel as they do. In a paragraph, explain what is happening in the scene described in the present tense and what has happened prior to this scene.

Topics for Writing

1. In an essay, characterize John Whiteside's daughter, focusing on such topics as her probable age, activities, and interests; her relationships with others, including her effect upon them; her present state, and the probable causes of that state. Support your conclusions with specific evidence from the poem.

2. Write an essay characterizing the speaker of the poem. Answer such questions as these: Is the speaker male or female? Is that person one of the girl's parents? Does he or she like children? About how old is the speaker? How does he or she feel about the present situation?

Like Ransom's poem, the one below contains both familiar and unfamiliar words, but it is simpler to assimilate than "Bells for John Whiteside's Daughter," partly because the situation is more quickly understandable and partly because more information is supplied.

Phyllis McGinley (1905–   )
Intimations of Mortality

*On being told by the dentist that "this will
be over soon"*

Indeed, it will soon be over, I shall be done
    With the querulous drill, the forceps, the clove-smelling cotton.
I can go forth into fresher air, into sun,
    This narrow anguish forgotten.

In twenty minutes or forty or half an hour,   *5*
    I shall be easy, and proud of my hard-got gold.
But your apple of comfort is eaten by worms, and sour.
    Your consolation is cold.

This will not last, and the day will be pleasant after.
    I'll dine tonight with a witty and favorite friend.   *10*
No doubt tomorrow I shall rinse my mouth with laughter.
    And also that will end.

The handful of time that I am charily granted
    Will likewise pass, to oblivion duly apprenticed.
Summer will blossom and autumn be faintly enchanted.   *15*
    Then time for the grave, or the dentist.

Because you are shrewd, my man, and your hand is clever,
    You must not believe your words have a charm to spell me.
There was never a half of an hour that lasted forever.
    Be quiet. You need not tell me.   *20*

Exercises

1. Give appropriate denotations for *querulous, anguish, charily, oblivion, apprenticed,* and *shrewd.*

2. We usually think of *narrow* in terms of width. What does *narrow anguish* mean in this poem?

3. State the dentist's admonition to his patient, and give the patient's unspoken reply.

4. Who is master of the situation? Why?

As the preceding poems and exercises have shown, readers of poetry sometimes are challenged not only to deal with difficult diction, but to select appropriate denotations for words in specific contexts. With many of the most skillful poets, the challenge of definition does not end there. Because most words have several denotations, a poet may intend a word to convey more than one meaning — a kind of poetic economy. This resourcefulness in using words is a type of literary **ambiguity,** or **multiple meaning.** An invaluable aid in dealing with such richness is the *Oxford English Dictionary* (or *OED*), a multivolume reference work available in most libraries. This unabridged dictionary provides historical samples of specific denotations, enabling the reader to determine when a specific meaning has been in use.

The word *carbuncle* in the passage below is a striking example of the use of multiple meaning; the lines describe the biblical Satan, disguised as a serpent, approaching Eve in the Garden of Eden.

John Milton *(1608–1674)*

from **Paradise Lost (Book IX)**

Toward Eve

[He] addressed his way, not with indented wave,
Prone on the ground, as since, but on his rear,
Circular base of rising folds, that towered
Fold above fold a surging maze, his head   5
Crested aloft,† and carbuncle his eyes;
With burnished† neck of verdant† gold, erect
Amidst his circling spires,† that on the grass
Floated redundant:† pleasing was his shape,
And lovely, never since of serpent kind   10
Lovelier ...

If you consult the *OED* for a suitable denotation of *carbuncle,* you will find several that are appropriate to a description of the Devil and that were in use during Milton's time: a fiery-red stone, a stone said to emit supernatural light, a malignant and inflamed tumor, and a red pimple or sore on the face caused by intemperance. All of these denotations are apt descriptions of the Devil's eyes — red, inflamed (with malevolence toward God and toward mankind, his immediate prey), hypnotic, malignant (evil and infected with a fatal spiritual disease), and intemperate (given to excess). In Milton's passage, the single supercharged word *carbuncle* conveys them all.

With respect to multiple meaning, consider the following sonnet about a handsome young man.

6. *crested aloft:* with a peak on top, suggesting the plume of a battle helmet.

7. *burnished:* shiny; *verdant:* green.
8. *circling spires:* coils.
9. *redundant:* like swelling waves.

William Shakespeare *(1564–1616)*

Sonnet 12

When I do count the clock that tells the time,
And see the brave day sunk in hideous night;
When I behold the violet past prime,
And sable† curls [all] silver'd o'er with white;
When lofty trees I see barren of leaves   5
Which erst† from heat did canopy the herd,
And summer's green† all girded up in sheaves
Borne on the bier† with white and bristly beard;
Then of thy beauty do I question make†
That thou among the wastes of time must go,   10
Since sweets and beauties† do themselves forsake
And die as fast as they see others grow;
    And nothing 'gainst Time's scythe can make defence
    Save breed, to brave† him when he takes thee hence.

Exercises

1. Identify at least six references to the passage of time in this sonnet (one of 154 by Shakespeare, printed in 1609). What do they cause the speaker to think about?

2. After consulting a dictionary (if necessary) for an appropriate denotation of *breed* as a noun (line 14), tell what the speaker claims is man's only defense against aging and death.

3. Search for suitable denotations of *brave* (line 2) in the *OED* (locate the first boldface entry, then check under *brave* as an adjective). What denotations are applicable to this poem? What insights are provided by an awareness of these denotations? For instance, how do the meanings of *brave* correlate with the beauty and vitality of youth in contrast to the loss of these qualities through aging?

Poets also rely on **connotation,** or the associations of a word beyond its literal sense, to communicate their impressions, feelings, and insights. The essential difference between denotation and connotation can be observed in this line by a minor but often-quoted American poet, Edgar A. Guest (1881–1959): "It takes a heap o' livin' in a house t' make it home." Both *house* and *home* denote a domicile or dwelling, but a home is a house for which specific individuals have strong, usually positive feelings. The word *home* connotes security, comfort, acceptance, love. When poets select this word, they are generally relying on it to suggest these attributes. (Readers should guard against interpreting a word in terms of their private connotations if their experience relating to that word is

4. *sable:* black.
6. *erst:* earlier.
7. *summer's green:* wheat.
8. *bier:* harvest wagon; also, the stand on which a coffin is placed.
9. *question make:* ponder.
11. *sweets and beauties:* flowers.
14. *brave:* defy.

not typical; if *home* has negative connotations for a certain reader, that person clearly must make an adjustment in interpretation when reading a line like Guest's.)

By developing a sensitivity to connotation, we can participate more completely in the richness of good poetry. Often the attitudes and feelings of the poet as well as of the poem's speaker are carried largely by connotation. For this reason, understanding the denotation(s) of each word and phrase is only a preliminary step toward experiencing the poem fully. The next poem depends on familiar connotations to characterize certain situations and suggest the feelings of those involved.

—*John Lennon* (1940–1980)
Paul McCartney (1942–   )

She's Leaving Home

Wednesday morning at five o'clock as the day begins
Silently closing her bedroom door
Leaving the note that she hoped would say more
She goes downstairs to the kitchen clutching her handkerchief
Quietly turning the backdoor key   5
Stepping outside she is free.
She (We gave her most of our lives) is leaving (Sacrificed most
    of our lives) home (We gave her everything money could
    buy)
She's leaving home after living alone
For so many years. Bye, bye.

Father snores as his wife gets into her dressing gown   10
Picks up the letter that's lying there
Standing alone at the top of the stairs
She breaks down and cries to her husband
Daddy our baby's gone.
How would she treat us so thoughtlessly   15
How could she do this to me.
She (We never thought of ourselves) is leaving (Never a thought
    for ourselves) home (We struggled all of our lives to get by)
She's leaving home after living alone
For so many years. Bye, bye.

Friday morning at nine o'clock she is far away.   20
Waiting to keep the appointment she made
Meeting a man from the motor trade
She (What did we do that was wrong) is having (We didn't know
what was wrong) fun (Fun is the one thing that money can't buy)
Something inside that was always denied
For so many years. Bye, bye.   25
She's leaving home bye bye.

1. If *home* generally connotes a place of love and security, why is *home* used in this poem to describe a place of loneliness and alienation?

2. Some of the parental responses in this poem are contained within parentheses. What do the parents' words tell us about their feelings? For example, what does "We gave her most of our lives" (line 7) connote that a substitute, such as "most of our attention" or "most of our time and money," does not? Why does the mother call her daughter "our baby" (line 14)? Why not "our girl" or "Brenda" (or whatever her name is), or even perhaps "that sneak"?

3. Find evidence of parental selfishness in these lyrics. Do you believe that the daughter leaves home because of these attitudes, because of selfishness on her own part, or because of the "man from the motor trade" (line 22)?

Widely held connotations pertaining to family life heighten the emotional impact of this poem about a kitten.

Nikki Giovanni (1943–)

A Poem for Carol

(*May she always wear red ribbons*)

when i was very little
though it's still true today
there were no sidewalks in lincoln heights†
and the home we had on jackson street
was right next to a bus stop and a sewer   5
which didn't really ever become offensive
but one day from the sewer a little kitten
with one eye gone
came crawling out
though she never really came into our yard but just   10
sort of hung by to watch the folk
my sister who was always softhearted but able
to act effectively started taking milk
out to her while our father would only say
don't bring *him* home and everyday   15
after school i would rush home to see if she was still
there and if gary had fed her but i could never
bring myself to go near her
she was so loving
and so hurt and so singularly beautiful and i knew   20
i had nothing to give that would
replace her one gone eye

and if i had named her which i didn't i'm sure
i would have called her carol

3. *Lincoln Heights:* a black sub-
urb of Cincinnati.

Exercises

1. What do the following words from the poem connote: *red ribbons* (subtitle), *lincoln heights* (line 3), *sewer* (lines 5, 7), *little kitten* (line 7)? Try to think of connotations that would be familiar to most people.

2. Why does the speaker think of naming the kitten Carol? List all the denotations and connotations of *carol* — both as a noun and as a verb — that you can think of, then check the *OED* and a recently published college dictionary. Which definitions seem to you appropriate to the poem? Why? What attributes of the kitten and feelings of the speaker justify a name with these meanings and associations? How does the subtitle relate to these meanings?

3. Write a paragraph explaining the importance of this kitten to the scene described. Ordinarily a kitten in a city would be of little significance. In your answer, consider the point of view from which the poem is presented.

Topics for Writing

1. Compose an essay telling why you think the speaker of "A Poem for Carol" apparently never feeds this kitten and never goes near it, yet is fascinated by it. Point to specific evidence in the poem as you describe the speaker's relationship with the kitten.

2. In a personal essay, compare this childhood experience with one you have had concerning the treatment of and attitudes toward pets such as Carol.

3. Using *comparison* (similarities) and *contrast* (differences), write an essay about this poem and "The Crippling" at the beginning of this chapter. Select several (two to five) areas for comparison and contrast, such as adult attitudes toward animals, attitudes of the speakers, or effects of the bird and the kitten on those around them.

Robert Browning (1812–1889)

Meeting at Night

1.

The gray sea and the long black land;
And the yellow half-moon large and low;
And the startled little waves that leap
In fiery ringlets from their sleep,
As I gain the cove with pushing prow,   5
And quench its speed i' the slushy sand.

2.

Then a mile of warm sea-scented beach;
Three fields to cross till a farm appears;

A tap at the pane, the quick sharp scratch
And blue spurt of a lighted match,   *10*
And a voice less loud, through its joys and fears,
Than the two hearts beating each to each!

Exercises

1. List the words and phrases the poet uses to suggest, either denotatively or connotatively, the sense of haste and urgency.

2. What words suggest fire, heat?

3. Identify the specific lines in which the poet fuses haste and heat into a single emotional sensation. What is that sensation?

4. Why are haste and heat appropriate connotations for this particular love situation?

Carol Lynn Pearson (1939–   )

Of Places Far

To me Istanbul
Was only a name,
Until a picture
You took
Of the Blue Mosque   *5*
Came.

I don't receive
Postcards from heaven
Showing Saint Peter
At prayer,   *10*
But, oh — that place
Is real enough,
Now that
You are there.

Exercise

What connotations does the Blue Mosque (line 5) of Istanbul, Turkey, have for you? Do you believe that the speaker feels about the mosque as you do? In a paragraph, specify how and why the speaker's connotations of this distant place have changed, then explain the change in the speaker's perception of heaven (line 8).

Claude McKay (1890–1948)

The White House

Your door is shut against my tightened face,
And I am sharp as steel with discontent;
But I possess the courage and the grace
To bear my anger proudly and unbent.
The pavement slabs burn loose beneath my feet,   5
And passion rends my vitals as I pass,
A chafing savage, down the decent street,
Where boldly shines your shuttered door of glass.
Oh, I must search for wisdom every hour,
Deep in my wrathful bosom sore and raw,   10
And find in it the superhuman power
To hold me to the letter of your law!
Oh, I must keep my heart inviolate
Against the poison of your deadly hate.

Exercises

After defining *vitals, chafing, wrathful,* and *inviolate,* do the following exercises.

1. When we know that Claude McKay is a black poet, we should not be surprised that the title is weighted with connotation. Define what house or houses the title refers to, giving evidence to support your answer.

2. Compare this poem to William Blake's "A Poison Tree" in "Other Poems to Read." How are the themes of the poems similar?

3. Compose a poem describing any experience you have had with racial, religious, or sexual discrimination or bigotry.

John Milton (1608–1674)

On the Late Massacre in Piedmont†

Avenge, O Lord, thy slaughtered saints, whose bones
Lie scattered on the Alpine mountains cold;
Even them who kept thy truth so pure of old,
When all our fathers worshiped stocks and stones,
Forget not: in thy book record their groans   5
Who were thy sheep, and in their ancient fold
Slain by the bloody Piedmontese, that rolled
Mother with infant down the rocks. Their moans

Piedmont: the mountainous region in northwest Italy where a thousand men, women, and children of a primitive Protestant sect were massacred in 1655 as a result of political and religious bigotry.

The vales redoubled to the hills, and they
To heaven. Their martyred blood and ashes sow   *10*
Over all the Italian fields, where still doth sway
The triple Tyrant: that from these may grow
A hundredfold who, having learned thy way,
Early may fly the Babylonian woe.†

Exercises

1. Literary critics have called this sonnet the most powerful in the English language. The Protestant Milton's feelings are conveyed partly by connotation. Identify words and phrases connoting his reaction to the atrocities.

2. Had Milton favored the military action, what substitutions might he have made for the words and phrases you listed above? In answering, observe how readily the connotations of a poet's diction communicate attitudes and emotions.

Percy Bysshe Shelley (1792–1822)

Song to the Men of England

Men of England, wherefore† plough
For the lords who lay ye low?
Wherefore weave with toil and care
The rich robes your tyrants wear?

Wherefore feed, and clothe, and save,   *5*
From the cradle to the grave,
Those ungrateful drones who would
Drain your sweat — nay, drink your blood?

Wherefore, Bees of England, forge
Many a weapon, chain, and scourge,†   *10*
That these stingless drones may spoil
The forced produce of your toil?

Have ye leisure, comfort, calm,
Shelter, food, love's gentle balm?
Or what is it ye buy so dear   *15*
With your pain and with your fear?

14. *Babylonian woe:* an allusion to the capture of the Jews by Babylonian armies in about the seventh century B.C.; in a broader sense, all tyrannical oppression, particularly that which results in the death of those who oppose it.

1. *wherefore:* why.

10. *scourge:* whip used to inflict punishment.

The seed ye sow, another reaps;
The wealth ye find, another keeps;
The robes ye weave, another wears;
The arms ye forge, another bears.   20

Sow seed, — but let no tyrant reap;
Find wealth, — let no impostor heap;
Weave robes, — let not the idle wear;
Forge arms, — in your defence to bear.

Shrink to your cellars, holes, and cells;   25
In halls ye deck another dwells.
Why shake the chains ye wrought? Ye see
The steel ye tempered glance on ye.

With plough and spade, and hoe and loom,
Trace your grave, and build your tomb,   30
And weave your winding-sheet, till fair
England be your sepulchre.

Topics for Writing

1. Discuss in an essay Shelley's use of connotation in this poem. What do you believe was his purpose in writing the poem?

2. Consult an encyclopedia, book, or article on Shelley's life and write an essay on the poem as it reflects his political and social concerns in early nineteenth-century England. Specify several of the problems he was disturbed about and the solutions he proposed. Then explain how the poem focuses on those concerns.

3. How appropriate and effective are Shelley's comparisons between men and honeybees? If you are unfamiliar with the details of a beehive and the functions of the queen, workers, and drones, consult an encyclopedia as an aid in evaluating the poet's references.

4. Select the poem in this chapter that you consider the most successful (or the least successful) in terms of what it attempts to convey. In an essay, evaluate the poem, using the three fundamental criteria of poetic quality described in the previous chapter — insight, beauty, and emotion.

9. IMAGERY

In discussions of literature, the term *image* often refers to the rendering of a sensory experience, although images can also be used to communicate perceptions and ideas. An image need not be visual. It can involve any of the senses: hearing, taste, smell, and touch as well as sight. It can also involve the sensations of temperature, pressure, distance, movement, and so forth. **Imagery** is any combination of these sensory representations.

The great Roman poet Horace (65–8 B.C.) was perhaps the first to call poetry a "speaking picture." His definition firmly implies that images are the very heart of poetic expression. Undoubtedly many of the sensory references in poems previously presented in this book remain in your memory: the picture of a boy's nose pressed to the window, the snarl of a New England buzz saw, the tastes and smells associated with the dentist, the cold roughness of the Alpine slopes in Piedmont. A moment's reflection will convince you that much of the enjoyment of good poetry derives from the vividness of such imagery. Each image stimulates us to recall our own experiences with similar sensations, or at least to gain a vicarious awareness of them. As a result, we often undergo a renewal of earlier sensations; our experience with the poem becomes both intensely personal and emotionally complex, for in a sense we join with the poet in the poetic creation.

Before discussing the value of giving close attention to imagery, we should note important distinctions among types of images. Images can be either literal or figurative. A **literal image** involves no shift in basic meaning. A **figurative image** is one to which a subject is compared, usually to render that subject more perceptible; it therefore requires a change in meaning. Elinor Wylie first uses literal imagery, then employs figurative imagery as she communicates the sensations of a winter walk.

Elinor Wylie *(1885–1928)*

Velvet Shoes

Let us walk in the white snow
   In a soundless space;
With footsteps quiet and slow,
   At a tranquil pace,
Under veils of white lace.

5

I shall go shod in silk,
    And you in wool,
White as a white cow's milk, *simile*
    More beautiful *simile*
    Than the breast of a gull.   *10*

We shall walk through the still town
    In a windless peace; *imagery*
We shall step upon white down, *metaphor*
    Upon silver fleece, *metaphor*
    Upon softer than these.   *15*

We shall walk in velvet shoes: — *metaphor*
    Wherever we go
Silence will fall like dews — *simile*
    On white silence below. — *metaphor*
    We shall walk in the snow. — *imagery*   *20*

"The white snow" (line 1) is not compared to anything, but when the poet describes the snow and ice on tree limbs as "veils of white lace" (line 5), we know instantly that she is not being literal. As image after image follows, involving a remarkable array of sensory appeals combined into a harmonious whole, we should be aware that many of these images, such as "white as a white cow's milk," are figurative. Such similes and metaphors, part of figurative language, are discussed in the next chapter.

As you read the poem below — a summer scene contrasting with Wylie's picture of a winter day — observe both literal and figurative imagery. Note, too, how the idea of peace — an experience of the mind rather than of the senses — is conveyed to us in sensory terms.

William Butler Yeats (1865–1939)

The Lake Isle of Innisfree†

I will arise and go now, and go to Innisfree,
And a small cabin build there, of clay and wattles made:
Nine bean-rows will I have there, a hive for the honeybee,
And live alone in the bee-loud glade.

And I shall have some peace there, for peace comes dropping slow,   *5*
Dropping from the veils of the morning to where the cricket sings;
There midnight's all a glimmer, and noon a purple glow,
And evening full of the linnet's wings.

I will arise and go now, for always night and day
I hear lake water lapping with low sounds by the shore;   *10*
While I stand on the roadway, or on the pavements grey,
I hear it in the deep heart's core.

    Innisfree: a small island in Lough
Gill in northwestern Ireland.

Exercises

1. Locate at least four literal and four figurative images in Yeats's poem.

2. Which images in the poem appeal to the sense of hearing? touch? taste?

3. Which place is described more vividly: where the speaker is, or where he wishes to go?

The final question above draws attention to another important distinction among images: in addition to being literal or figurative, imagery can be fixed or free. A **fixed image** is one for which the meaning and associations are approximately the same for all readers. In "Velvet Shoes," most of the imagery is fixed, and whoever reads the poem will visualize more or less the same scene and experience similar sensations. Fixed imagery also dominates Yeats's description of Innisfree, but his portrayal of the speaker's position ("on the roadway, or on the pavements grey") is much less specific. The following poem also describes a fairly fixed experience, yet the ending moves away from fixed imagery to a freer representation.

Theodore Roethke (1908–1963)

Snake

I saw a young snake glide
Out of the mottled shade
And hang, limp on a stone:
A thin mouth, and a tongue
Stayed, in the still air.   5

It turned; it drew away;
Its shadow bent in half;
It quickened, and was gone.

I felt my slow blood warm.
I longed to be that thing,   10
The pure, sensuous form.

And I may be, some time.

A fixed image helps us to feel secure. Because it is specific, all we are required to do is respond. But often poets use fixed images to prepare for a later complexity, in which we are drawn into the unusual, the intricate, perhaps the inexplicable. Notice how this is the case in "Snake." When the speaker tells us that after the snake disappeared he felt his "slow blood warm," he implies that the experience has been a chilling one, as though he has become, for a moment, cold-blooded like the snake. When in the final lines he expresses the abstract desire to become a serpent, we may have difficulty perceiving so radical a transformation. Yet the fixed imagery in the first stanza, an exquisite, concrete evocation of the "pure, sensuous form" of the third stanza, assists us toward that perception.

A **free image** is not as specific. It is open to various interpretations and emotional responses. It requires more of its readers, who must use their imaginations to a greater extent and probe for meaning, rather than merely respond. Understandably, free imagery is particularly prominent in existential poetry, which sees the world beyond the self as absurd and meaningless; the discovery and improvement of the self thus become the primary focuses. We may be uncomfortable with the task imposed on us by free imagery, and for this reason, in part, good poets are restrained in their use of it. They recognize, as Roethke does in "Snake," that a fixed frame of reference, a definite picture and recognizable sounds, smells, and other sensations, is needed, especially at the beginning of a poem.

As you read the following poem, watch for fixed and free imagery, realizing there are varying degrees of each type.

Paul Vesey (Samuel W. Allen, 1917–   )

In My Father's House

A Reverie

In my father's house, when dusk had fallen
I was alone on the dim first floor
I sensed someone, a power, desirous
Of forcing the outer door.
                    How shall I explain —   5

I bolted it securely
And was locking the inner when
Somehow I was constrained to turn
To see it quietly open again.

Transfixed before the panther night   10
My heart gave one tremendous bound
Paralyzed, my feet refused
The intervening ground.
                    How shall I say —

I was in the house and dusk had fallen   15
I was alone on the earthen floor
I knew there was a power
Lurking beyond the door.

I bolted the outside
And was closing the inner when   20
I noticed the first had swung open again
My heart bound and I knew it would be upon me I rushed to the door
It came upon me out of the night and I rushed to the yard
If I could throw the ball the stone the spear in my hand
Against the wall my father would be warned but now   25
Their hands had fallen on me and they had taken me and I tried
To cry out but O I could not cry out and the cold grey waves
Came over me O stifling me and drowning me.

Exercises

1. When Samuel W. Allen, a black poet who writes under the pseudonym of Paul Vesey, wishes to describe his speaker's fear, which type of imagery does he use, literal or figurative? Identify examples of each type.

2. Generally speaking, is Vesey's imagery fixed or free? Which type is used in referring to the "power" that assaults the speaker? How effective is this type of imagery in describing the antagonists in this poem?

3. What sensory images does Vesey use besides visual ones? Do not limit your answer to the five basic senses.

Topics for Writing

1. Compose a poem in which you describe a terrifying experience like that in Vesey's poem. You may wish to write about an actual experience, a fictitious one, or a nightmare.

2. In an essay, analyze the antagonists in Vesey's poem. Are they real persons, supernatural beings, figments of the speaker's imagination, hallucinations? Or is there a more feasible identification?

3. Write a short essay on one of the following topics.

a. The title and subtitle. What significance does each have in helping us to understand the poem? Is there a correlation between the title and the following words of Jesus to his disciples?

"In my Father's house are many mansions: if it were not so, I would have told you. I go to prepare a place for you." (John 14:2)

b. The speaker's repeated bolting of the doors. What does this imply about the reality of his nocturnal experience?

c. The cumulative effect of the fixed imagery, literal and figurative, on the reader, particularly when the poem is read aloud.

Whenever a single image involving any of the senses dominates an extensive passage or an entire poem, that image is called a **controlling image.** Notice that although the following poem appeals both to the sense of sight and to the sense of touch, and contains other sensory images as well, the visual image of the hand rules it.

John Keats (1795–1821)

This Living Hand

This living hand, now warm and capable
Of earnest grasping, would, if it were cold
And in the icy silence of the tomb,
So haunt thy days and chill thy dreaming nights

That thou wouldst wish thine own heart dry of blood   5
So in my veins red life might stream again,
And thou be conscience-calmed — see here it is —
I hold it towards you.

Exercises

1. In a sentence or two, summarize the situation described in this poem, including the message of the speaker to the person being addressed.

2. Identify as many sensory images as you can that are directly associated with the image of the speaker's hand. Your list should illustrate the dominance of the hand imagery in this particular poem.

3. In a paragraph, evaluate this poem with respect to realistic, truthful emotion. Given the implied relationship between the two persons in the poem, do you believe the emotional appeal is justified? effective? melodramatic? Point to the methods Keats uses to evoke an emotional response.

If a poet groups similar images — several kinds of flowers, for example — in a short passage, such concentration is called an **image cluster.** In the second stanza of the next poem, insects form this type of cluster.

Robert Graves (1895–   )

Lost Love

His eyes are quickened so with grief,
He can watch a grass or leaf
Every instant grow; he can
Clearly through a flint wall see,
Or watch the startled spirit flee   5
From the throat of a dead man.
    Across two counties he can hear
And catch your words before you speak.
The woodlouse or the maggot's weak
Clamor rings in his sad ear,   10
And noise so slight it would surpass
Credence — drinking sound of grass,
Worm talk, clashing jaws of moth
Chumbling holes in cloth;
The groan of ants who undertake   15
Gigantic loads for honor's sake
(Their sinews creak, their breath comes thin);
Whir of spiders when they spin,
And minute whispering, mumbling, sighs
Of idle grubs and flies.   20

This man is quickened so with grief,
He wanders god-like or like thief
Inside and out, below, above,
Without relief seeking lost love.

Topics for Writing

1. In a poem about love, focusing on insect noises might appear bizarre. Write an essay expressing your opinion of the image cluster in Graves's poem as a vehicle for describing a man grieving over lost love.

2. The final stanza of the poem, which contains freer imagery than those preceding it, is more challenging. In an essay, tell why this particular speaker wanders "god-like or like thief," since the two terms appear to be opposites.

3. Do the insects actually make the noises the man hears? After consulting the library for specific information about some of these insect noises, write a report on the accuracy of the speaker's claims.

Often poets and their readers are not fully aware of the patterns formed by the chosen imagery. But in discerning the **image patterns,** we can recognize more clearly why a poem affects us as it does. Note the patterns of color imagery used as a device for capturing the magic of romantic love in this poem:

William Butler Yeats (1865–1939)

The Song of Wandering Aengus†

I went out to the hazel wood,
Because a fire was in my head,
And cut and peeled a hazel wand,
And hooked a berry to a thread;
And when white moths were on the wing,   5
And moth-like stars were flickering out,
I dropped the berry in a stream
And caught a little silver trout.

When I had laid it on the floor
I went to blow the fire aflame,   10
But something rustled on the floor,
And some one called me by my name:

Aengus (Oengus Mac Ind Oc): mythological god in Irish folklore who falls in love with a beautiful girl he sees in a dream. According to one version, Oengus eventually identifies the girl as Caer, daughter of Ethal, but her father refuses to relinquish her. Every other year she and her maids turn into birds — she the loveliest, with a golden necklace — and Oengus finds her in this form on the seashore. He changes into a bird himself, flies off with her, and later, in his natural form, claims her as his bride.

It had become a glimmering girl
With apple blossom in her hair
Who called me by my name and ran   15
And faded through the brightening air.

Though I am old with wandering
Through hollow lands and hilly lands,
I will find out where she has gone,
And kiss her lips and take her hands;   20
And walk among long dappled grass,
And pluck till time and times are done
The silver apples of the moon,
The golden apples of the sun.

Exercises

1. In addition to the green implied by "hazel wood" (line 1) and "dappled grass" (line 21), what two basic colors does Yeats use? After listing (line by line) the visual images incorporating these two colors, tell what image pattern is evident in the poem.

2. The color image pattern, as your list for question 1 should demonstrate, is a shifting one, invoking first one, then another color. How does a recognition of this image pattern help us understand the mental, emotional, and sexual nature of the speaker?

3. Compare and contrast the speaker of this poem with that of Robert Browning's "Meeting at Night" (Chapter 8), John Keats's "This Living Hand," or Robert Graves's "Lost Love" (both in this chapter).

As the next lines show, a single poem may appeal to the senses in a variety of ways: through figurative and literal imagery, fixed and free imagery, image clusters, and image patterns. Such a concentration of images produces a rich sensory experience.

Gwendolyn Brooks (1917–   )

kitchenette building

We are things of dry hours and the involuntary plan,
Grayed in, and gray. "Dream" makes a giddy sound, not strong
Like "rent," "feeding a wife," "satisfying a man."

But could a dream send up through onion fumes
Its white and violet, fight with fried potatoes   5
And yesterday's garbage ripening in the hall,
Flutter, or sing an aria down these rooms

Even if we were willing to let it in,
Had time to warm it, keep it very clean,
Anticipate a message, let it begin?   *10*

We wonder. But not well! not for a minute!
Since Number Five is out of the bathroom now,
We think of lukewarm water, hope to get in it.

Exercises

1. To which senses does the poem appeal most strongly? Justify your answer.

2. Characterize the speaker, then tell what she wishes to but cannot do.

3. What sort of life cycle is suggested by the image pattern in the first and last lines? In formulating an answer, consider what the speaker wishes to "warm" and "keep...clean" (line 9), and what her circumstances force her to warm and keep clean instead.

Several types of imagery can be discerned in the three poems below. The first, by a native American, a Creek, is about a telephone call to a lover in Albuquerque; the second, by a seventeenth-century English poet, is about Puritans landing in the tropical Bermudas; and the third is by an eighteenth-century English poet who provides a dreadful picture of winter, in startling contrast to Elinor Wylie's soft portrait in the beginning of this chapter.

Joy Harjo (1951–   )

"Are You Still There"

there are sixty-five miles
of telephone wire
between acoma†
      and albuquerque

i dial the number   *5*
and listen for the sound
of his low voice
      on the other side

"hello"
      is a gentle motion of a western wind   *10*
cradling tiny purple flowers
that grow near the road
      towards laguna†

3. *Acoma* (pronounced A' coma): pueblo and mission in the Acoma Indian Reservation, west of Albuquerque in west-central New Mexico.

13. *Laguna:* small New Mexican town northeast of Acoma and immediately north of Interstate Highway 40.

i smell them
as i near the rio puerco bridge†   *15*
my voice stumbles
returning over sandstone
          as it passes the cañocito exit†

"i have missed you"   he says
the rhythm circles the curve   *20*
of mesita cliffs†
              to meet me

but my voice is caught
shredded on a barbed wire fence
at the side of the road   *25*
and flutters soundless
in the wind

Topics for Writing

1. To participate fully in this poem, consult a recent, detailed road atlas of New Mexico (your library should have one) for locations of the following: *Acoma, Laguna, Rio Puerco Bridge, Cañocito Exit* (Canoncito). Then write an essay in which you describe geographically the journey of each word and phrase in this telephone conversation. Conclude by explaining why the speaker employs a geographical image pattern that repeatedly changes direction.

2. In an essay, use evidence from the imagery of the poem to describe the two persons involved: how they feel toward one another, possible reasons for their being apart, why one is nearly unable to speak, what we might expect of the conversation after the poem closes, and whether the title might be an appropriate last line.

3. Do you like this poem? Write an essay about your reactions to it, organizing your response into several clear categories.

Andrew Marvell (1621–1678)

Bermudas

Where the remote Bermudas ride
In the ocean's bosom unespied,
From a small boat that rowed along,
The listening winds received this song:
          "What should we do but sing His praise,   5

---

15. *Rio Puerco Bridge:* Interstate 40 bridge over the Rio Puerco, a river.
18. *Cañocito Exit:* Interstate 40 exit to Canoncito Indian Reservation.

21. *Mesita cliffs:* from Spanish *meseta* (mesa), a flat-topped mountain with steep sides, typical of the American Southwest.

That led us through the watery maze
Unto an isle so long unknown,
And yet far kinder than our own?
Where He the huge sea monsters wracks,†
That lift the deep upon their backs;   *10*
He lands us on a grassy stage,
Safe from the storms, and prelate's rage.†
He gave us this eternal spring
Which here enamels everything,
And sends the fowls to us in care,   *15*
On daily visits through the air;
He hangs in shades the orange bright,
Like golden lamps in a green night,
And does in the pomegranates close
Jewels more rich than Ormus† shows;   *20*
He makes the figs our mouths to meet,
And throws the melons at our feet;
But apples† plants of such a price,
No tree could ever bear them twice;
With cedars, chosen by His hand,   *25*
From Lebanon, He stores the land;
And makes the hollow seas, that roar,
Proclaim the ambergris† on shore;
He cast (of which we rather boast)
The Gospel's pearl upon our coast,   *30*
And in these rocks for us did frame
A temple, where to sound His name.
O! let our voice His praise exalt,
Till it arrive at heaven's vault,
Which, thence (perhaps) rebounding, may   *35*
Echo beyond the Mexique Bay."†
      Thus sung they in the English boat,
An holy and a cheerful note;
And all the way, to guide their chime,
With falling oars they kept the time.   *40*

Exercise

In this poem, which is particularly rich in imagery, locate both an image cluster
and an image pattern in the song of the rowing Puritans (lines 5 through 36).
What are the effects of these two image devices in the poem?

9. *the huge sea monsters wracks:*
casts whales ashore.
12. *prelate's rage:* the intolerance
of many Anglican bishops toward
the Puritans.
20. *Ormus* (today spelled *Hormuz*
or *Hormoz*): an island off the
southern coast of Iran on which
precious gems were mined.

23. *apples:* probably pineapples
(although pineapples do not grow
on trees).
28. *ambergris:* a waxy substance
secreted by the sperm whale,
found floating on or near the
shores of tropical waters and used
in perfumes.
36. *Mexique Bay:* Gulf of Mexico.

from **Winter**

As thus the snows arise, and, foul and fierce,
All Winter drives along the darkened air,
In his own loose-revolving fields, the Swain†
Disastered stands; sees other hills ascend,
Of unknown joyless brow; and other Scenes,   *5*
Of horrid prospect, shag† the trackless plain:
Nor finds the river, nor the forest, hid
Beneath the formless wild; but wanders on
From hill to dale, still more and more astray;
Impatient flouncing through the drifted heaps,   *10*
Stung with the thoughts of Home; the thoughts of Home
Rush on his nerves, and call their vigour forth
In many a vain attempt. How sinks his soul!
What black despair, what horror fills his heart!
When for the dusky spot, which fancy feigned   *15*
His tufted Cottage, rising through the snow,
He meets the roughness of the middle waste,
Far from the track and blessed abode of man;
While round him Night resistless closes fast,
And every tempest, howling over his head,   *20*
Renders the savage wilderness more wild.
Then throng the busy shapes into his Mind,
Of covered pits, unfathomably deep,
A dire descent! beyond the power of frost;
Of faithless bogs; of precipices huge,   *25*
Smoothed up with snow; and, what is land unkown,
What water, of the still unfrozen spring,
In the loose marsh or solitary lake,
Where the fresh fountain from the bottom boils.
These check his fearful steps; and down he sinks,   *30*
Beneath the shelter of the shapeless drift,
Thinking over all the bitterness of Death;
Mixed with the tender anguish nature shoots
Through the wrung bosom of the dying man,
His wife, his children, and his friends unseen.   *35*
In vain for him the officious Wife prepares
The fire fair-blazing, and the vestment warm;
In vain his little Children, peeping out
Into the mingling storm, demand their sire,
With tears of artless innocence. Alas!   *40*
Nor wife, nor children more shall he behold,
Nor friends, nor sacred home. On every nerve
The deadly Winter seizes; shuts up sense;
And, over his inmost vitals creeping cold,
Lays him along the snows, a stiffened Corse,   *45*
Stretched out, and bleaching in the northern blast.

3. *Swain:* peasant farmer.   6. *shag:* break the smoothness of.

Exercises

1. Are most of the images in this passage fixed or free? Why do you think the poet fashioned them as he did? What, in short, seems to be his purpose?

2. This scene is packed with images reflecting particular human fears. Locate as many negative images as you can, then tell what fears they help to communicate.

3. Generally we think of fear as a product of the mind and the emotions — for example, fear of failure or fear of the unknown. Which of the farmer's fears relate to or derive from the senses and are communicated to us through imagery?

10. FIGURATIVE LANGUAGE

Much poetic communication is achieved through comparisons, especially if the feelings, sensations, and ideas to be communicated are abstract or complex. When poets wish to describe their perceptions of time and eternity, for example, they will often compare these abstractions to more imaginable subjects, as Carol Lynn Pearson does in comparing time to a magician ("Optical Illusion," introduction to Part II). The poet below uses the same device.

Henry Vaughan (1622–1695)

from **The World**

> I saw eternity the other night
> Like a great ring of pure and endless light,
>   All calm as it was bright;
> And round beneath it, time, in hours, days, years,
>   Driven by the spheres,   5
> Like a vast shadow moved, in which the world
> And all her train were hurled.

By comparing time to "a vast shadow" and eternity to "a great ring of pure and endless light," Vaughan achieves an effective description of what he has thought and felt while observing the stars. Here are the opening lines of another poem about time, without such comparisons:

T. S. Eliot (1888–1965)

from **Burnt Norton**

> Time present and time past
> Are both perhaps present in time future,
> And time future contained in time past.
> If all time is eternally present
> All time is unredeemable.   5

These lines are not as vivid as Vaughan's, although they may be easier to grasp, since Eliot states his point explicitly. But later in the poem, when he needs to engage our senses and our emotions, Eliot too employs figurative language that creates images.

As we have seen in the previous chapter, imagery can help suggest the intensity of the feelings being experienced by the poet or by the characters. Note the vivid image in this comparison used by Samuel Taylor Coleridge (1772–1834) in "Dejection: An Ode" (the complete poem appears in Chapter 15): "Hence, viper thoughts, that coil around my mind." Coleridge was aware that we might be better able to imagine how troubled thoughts make him feel if he described them in sensory terms. Thus he implicitly compared his thoughts to poisonous snakes infecting his mind and soul.

Such comparisons are part of **figurative language,** a nonliteral mode of expression that employs devices called **figures of speech.** Figures of speech are by no means peculiar to poetry. Because our language is by nature highly figurative, we employ figures of speech in nearly all types of communication. They include *antithesis, apostrophe, hyperbole, irony, metaphor, metonymy, personification, simile,* and *synecdoche,* as well as others that are less well known. Although we will deal with six basic figures of speech in this chapter — simile, metaphor, personification, apostrophe, metonymy, and synecdoche — and with two additional ones deriving from them, the *conceit* and the *pathetic fallacy,* all of those listed are defined in the glossary.

A **simile** explicitly compares two unlike objects, an object and an abstraction, or two abstractions. Although these things are essentially incompatible, the poet's invitation to compare them stimulates us to perceive illuminating similarities and may lead to new insights. Vaughan's lines from "The World" contain two similes, each connected with the term of comparison *like:* "eternity . . . / Like a great ring of pure and endless light," and "time . . . / Like a vast shadow." Other terms of comparison often used in similes are *as, than,* and *so.* In figurative comparisons, the central object being described is called the *tenor* ("eternity" and "time" are the tenors in Vaughan's verse), and that to which the tenor is compared is the *vehicle.* Often the vehicle will contain subtenors and subvehicles. Differentiate between tenors and vehicles in these similes by D. H. Lawrence:

D. H. Lawrence (1885–1930)

Baby Running Barefoot

When the white feet of the baby beat across the grass
The little white feet nod like white flowers in a wind,
They poise and run like puffs of wind that pass
Over water where the weeds are thinned.

And the sight of their white playing in the grass   5
Is winsome as a robin's song, so fluttering;
Or like two butterflies that settle on a glass
Cup for a moment, soft little wing-beats uttering.

And I wish that the baby would tack across here to me
Like a wind-shadow running on a pond, so she could stand   10

With two little bare white feet upon my knee
And I could feel her feet in either hand

Cool as syringa buds in morning hours,
Or firm and silken as young peony flowers.

Exercises

1. After circling all the similes in this winsome poem, tell what purposes they serve and what value they contribute to this vignette of sensations, emotions, and thoughts.

2. Usually when a number of vehicles are brought together (as in this poem) to describe a single tenor, those vehicles will have much in common in order to present a unified picture. What is the common denominator in Lawrence's similes describing the baby's feet?

3. Describe the poet's use of connotation in this poem. Establish appropriate denotations for *tack* (line 9), *syringa* buds (line 13), and *peony* flowers (line 14) as you define connotative levels.

Topics for Writing

1. Analyze the speaker's character.

2. In an essay, explain the appropriateness of the imagery in this poem, giving particular attention to the speaker's feelings about the child.

3. If you have read a novel by D. H. Lawrence, write a comparison between it and aspects of this poem. Focus your comparison on several clearly defined topics pertaining to choice of imagery, character types, or ideas.

4. Compare and contrast this poem with John Crowe Ransom's "Bells for John Whiteside's Daughter" (Chapter 8). Focus on a single aspect of the two poems, such as the speakers, the children, or the effects of the children on the speakers.

If the vehicle of a simile is described at such length that it temporarily eclipses the tenor, as it does in the next poem, the simile is called **extended.**

Edmund Spenser (1552?–1599)

Sonnet 54

Of this world's theater in which we stay,
My love like the spectator idly sits,
Beholding me that all the pageants play,
Disguising diversely my troubled wits.
Sometimes I joy when glad occasion fits   5

And mask in mirth like to a comedy;
Soon after, when my joy to sorrow flits,
I wail and make my woes a tragedy.
Yet she beholding me with constant eye
Delights not in my mirth nor rues my smart;   10
But when I laugh she mocks, and when I cry
She laughs, and hardens evermore her heart.
What then can move her? If nor mirth nor moan,
She is no woman, but a senseless stone.

In *The Iliad, The Odyssey,* and more recent epic poems such as John Milton's *Paradise Lost,* the extended similes often invoke the past, or nature, in a comparison with a character or event in the poem. Such extended similes are properly called **epic** or **Homeric similes.**

A **metaphor** resembles a simile, except that the comparison between tenor and vehicle is *implied* rather than stated by means of such words as *like* or *as.* A metaphor thus suggests an identification between two unlike subjects, the most common purpose being the same as that of similes — to illuminate the tenor. James Russell Lowell gives an overused (or *dead*) metaphor about life new vigor in this poem about aging:

James Russell Lowell (1819–1891)

Sixty-eighth Birthday

As life runs on, the road grows strange
With faces new, and near the end
The milestones into headstones change,
'Neath every one a friend.

The following well-known poem contains an **extended metaphor,** drawing our attention to more than a simple correlation between tenor and vehicle. Because it begins with the vehicle, the poem leads us to realize that we must consider context when differentiating between tenor and vehicle.

Walt Whitman (1819–1892)

A Noiseless Patient Spider

A noiseless patient spider,
I marked where on a little promontory it stood isolated,
Marked how to explore the vacant vast surrounding,
It launched forth filament, filament, filament, out of itself,
Ever unreeling them, ever tirelessly speeding them.   5

And you O my soul where you stand,
Surrounded, detached, in measureless oceans of space,
Ceaselessly musing, venturing, throwing, seeking the spheres to con-
    nect them,
Till the bridge you will need be formed, till the ductile anchor hold,
Till the gossamer thread you fling catch somewhere, O my soul.   *10*

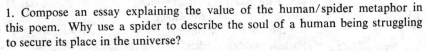

you can't make a mare till you get one thing that holds to start out on other things

Topics for Writing

1. Compose an essay explaining the value of the human/spider metaphor in this poem. Why use a spider to describe the soul of a human being struggling to secure its place in the universe?

2. Would you classify this poem as optimistic or pessimistic about humans' future? Develop your answer into an essay, considering such topics as the connections implied between the spider ("patient," "noiseless," "tireless") and a person (patient? noiseless? tireless?).

The following antiwar poem employs the extended metaphor in a narrative setting:

Henry Taylor (1942–   )

Speech

1.

I crouch over my radio
to tune in the President,
thinking how lucky I am
not to own a television.

2.

Now the rich, cultivated voice   *5*
with its cautious, measured pauses
fills my living room, fills
the wastebasket, the vase
on the mantel, the hurricane
lamps, and even fills   *10*
the antique pottery whiskey jug
beside the fireplace, nourishing
the dried flowers I have put in it.

3.

"I had a responsibility,"
he says; the phrase pours   *15*
from the speaker like molasses,

flows to the rug, spreads
into a black, shining puddle,
slowly expands, covers
the rug with dark sweetness.   20
It begins to draw flies;
they eat all the syrup
and clamor for more.

4.

I can barely hear the speech
above the buzzing of their wings.   25
But the Commander-in-Chief
has the solution: another
phrase, sweeter, thicker,
blacker, oozes out
over my living room floor: 30
"I have personal reasons
for wanting peace." This is more
than the flies will be able to eat;
they will stay quiet
for the rest of the speech.   35

5.

Now, you are thinking, comes
the Good Part, the part
where the syrup proves poisonous
and kills all the flies.
My fellow Americans, that   40
is not at all what happened.
The flies grew fat on the phrases,
grew as large as bullfrogs.

6.

They are everywhere in the house,
and the syrup continues   45
to feed and fatten them;
in the pottery whiskey jug,
sprouting new leaves and buds,
even the dried flowers thrive.

7.

The speech   50
has been over for weeks now;
they go on eating
but they stay quiet
and seem peaceful enough.
At night, sometimes,   55
I can hear them
making soft liquid sounds
of contentment.

1. In an essay, discuss the use of figurative language in this poem. Be certain to identify the major tenor and vehicle, then subordinate tenors and vehicles. Finally, explain the message conveyed largely by the extended metaphor.

2. Evaluate this poem with respect to beauty by focusing on questions such as these: Is the picture vivid, striking, memorable? Is the fantasy rooted in reality well enough to make us believe, if only for a moment, that this experience really happened?

Additional figures of comparison that bear a close relationship to similes and metaphors yet are distinctive enough to have labels of their own are illustrated in the poems that follow. The **conceit** is an elaborate and inventive simile or metaphor that makes a comparison between radically different subjects. Eccentric, yet often ingenious when used by a masterful poet, conceits surprise or even shock us, forcing us to consider potentially insightful similarities we would probably never imagine on our own. The next poem, from Herbert's collection of religious poems that use many parts of an English chapel as metaphors, compares the minister to a stained-glass window.

George Herbert (1593–1633)

The Windows

Lord, how can man preach thy eternal word?
  He is a brittle crazy† glass:
Yet in thy temple† thou dost him afford
  This glorious and transcendent place,
  To be a window, through thy grace.   *5*

But when thou dost anneal in glass† thy story,
  Making thy life to shine within
The holy preachers; then the light and glory
  More reverend grows, & more doth win:
  Which else shows waterish, bleak, & thin.   *10*

Doctrine and life, colors and light, in one
  When they combine and mingle, bring
A strong regard and awe: but speech alone
  Doth vanish like a flaring thing,
  And in the ear, not conscience ring.   *15*

2. *crazy:* full of cracks and flaws.   6. *anneal in glass:* fix colors on
3. *temple:* chapel.   glass by heating.

Exercises

1. According to the poet, how is a minister like a church window?

2. In these metaphorical terms, what constitutes a good and a bad preacher (line 8)?

3. Identify and paraphrase the tenors and vehicles in the conceits found in a poem of the same period as this one, John Donne's "A Valediction: Forbidding Mourning" (Chapter 15).

The poem below relies for its effectiveness on **personification,** a figure of speech in which a nonhuman subject is given human characteristics.

personification

Molly Holden (1927–   )

Giant Decorative Dahlia

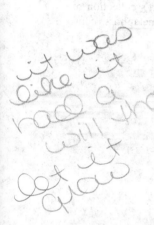
it was like it had a will that let it grow

It is easy enough to love flowers but these
had never appealed to me before, so
out of proportion above my garden's
other colored heads and steady stems.

This spring though, in warm soil, I set   5
an unnamed tuber, offered cheap, and,
when August came and still no sign,
assumed the slugs had eaten it.

     Suddenly it showed;
began to grow, became a small tree.   10
It was a race between the dingy bud
and the elements. It has beaten
the frost, rears now three feet above
the muddled autumn bed, barbaric petals
pink quilled with tangerine, turning *like a child*   15
its great (innocent face) towards me
triumphantly through the damp afternoon.

I could not deny it love if I tried.

Exercises

1. How is this remarkable dahlia likened to a person, and what effect do these human characteristics have on the speaker, who cannot "deny it love"?

2. Write several paragraphs evaluating the effectiveness of this personification, or that of Wilfred Owen's "Arms and the Boy" (introduction to Part II) or John Keats's "Ode on a Grecian Urn" (Chapter 15).

If in using personification the poet gives human emotions to objects in nature, or to nature in general, that figure of speech is called a **pathetic fallacy,** a term coined by the Victorian author John Ruskin. In "Great Decorative Dahlia" above, the flower triumphs against odds in nature, but it exhibits few human emotions. In contrast, note the human feelings attributed to the flowers, birds, and even twigs in these lines:

William Wordsworth (1770–1850)

Lines Written in Early Spring

I heard a thousand blended notes,
While in a grove I sate reclined,
In that sweet mood when pleasant thoughts
Bring sad thoughts to the mind.

To her fair works did Nature link   5
The human soul that through me ran;
And much it grieved my heart to think
What man has made of man.

Through primrose tufts, in that green bower,
The periwinkle trailed its wreaths;   10
And 'tis my faith that every flower   — pathetic
Enjoys the air it breathes.   fallacy

The birds around me hopped and played,   pathetic
Their thoughts I cannot measure —   fallacy
But the least motion which they made,   15
It seemed a thrill of pleasure.   their motion thrills them

The budding twigs spread out their fan,   pathetic fallacy
To catch the breezy air;   the buds enjoyed
And I must think, do all I can,   opening
That there was pleasure there.   20

If this belief from heaven be sent,
If such be Nature's holy plan,
Have I not reason to lament
What man has made of man?

Exercise

Wordsworth is often called the most philosophic of English poets. What philosophy does he express here about the lesson nature can teach human beings?

Whenever a poet addresses someone or something that is absent, that expression is labeled an **apostrophe.** A contemporary Chicana poet uses this figure of speech in her poem about work in a Texas city.

Carmen Tafolla (1951–   )

San Antonio

San Antonio,
　　They called you lazy.
They saw your silent, subtle, screaming eyes,
　　And called you lazy.
They saw your lean bronzed workmaid's arms,　　　　　　　　5
　　And called you lazy.
They saw your centuries-secret sweet-night song,
　　And called you lazy.

San Antonio,
　　They saw your skybirth and sunaltar,　　　　　　　　　　10
　　Your corn-dirt soul and mute bell-toll,
　　Your river-ripple heart, soft with life,
　　Your ancient shawl of sigh on strife,
　　　　And didn't see.
San Antonio,　　　　　　　　　　　　　　　　　　　　　　15
　　They called you lazy.

Exercises

1. In the double apostrophe in this poem, who is addressing the city now and who has addressed it previously?

2. Who is "San Antonio"? Why has it been judged "lazy"? Is the judgment valid, according to the speaker? Why?

3. To which senses do the poem's images appeal? Are the images unified by common denominators?

4. What figures of speech discussed so far do you find here besides the apostrophe?

　　Another unusual device for comparison is **metonymy,** a figure of speech in which something closely associated with the main subject is substituted for it. Your answer to question 2 above should reveal an example of metonymy: Because many Mexican-Americans live in San Antonio, and the city is thus closely associated with them, the poet merely uses the name of the city to refer to them. If we use the cliché "from the cradle to the grave" when we mean "from birth to death," we are using metonymy. Can you identify examples of this figure of speech in the following poem?

James Shirley (1596–1666)

The Glories of Our Blood and State

The glories of our blood and state
Are shadows, not substantial things;

There is no armor against fate;
Death lays his icy hand on kings.
    Scepter and crown   5
    Must tumble down
And in the dust be equal made
With the poor crooked scythe and spade.

Some men with swords may reap the field
And plant fresh laurels where they kill,   10
But their strong nerves at last must yield;
They tame but one another still.
    Early or late
    They stoop to fate
And must give up their murmuring breath,   15
When they, pale captives, creep to death.

The garlands wither on your brow,
Then boast no more your mighty deeds;
Upon death's purple altar now
See where the victor-victim bleeds.   20
    Your heads must come
    To the cold tomb;
Only the actions of the just
Smell sweet and blossom in their dust.

Although Shirley's poem contains many metaphors, the comparisons in lines 5 and 8 stand out as distinctive examples of metonymy: "scepter and crown" are substitutes for king or monarch, and "scythe and spade" for the poor laborer.

The comparison suggested in lines 21 and 22, "Your heads must come/To the cold tomb," might at first appear to be metonymy, the head being substituted for the whole body. When a part (typically the most important part) is substituted for the whole, however, the expression is called **synecdoche**. The "head" in Shirley's poem is an example of this figure. The synecdoche in the next poem is easily identifiable.

Dylan Thomas (1914–1953)

The hand that signed the paper felled a city†

The hand that signed the paper felled a city;
Five sovereign fingers taxed the breath,
Doubled the globe of dead and halved a country;
These five kings did a king to death.

Title: this poem, dated August 17, 1933, might have been prompted by political events in Germany, where Hitler had come to power earlier in the year. Paul Ferris suggests that the poem has more "a flavour of far-off tyrants, perhaps from the Bible" (*Dylan Thomas,* New York: Dial Press, 1977, p. 88).

The mighty hand leads to a sloping shoulder,   *5*
The finger joints are cramped with chalk;
A goose's quill has put an end to murder
That put an end to talk.

The hand that signed the treaty bred a fever,
And famine grew, and locusts came;   *10*
Great is the hand that holds dominion over
Man by a scribbled name.

The five kings count the dead but do not soften
The crusted wound nor stroke the brow;
A hand rules pity as a hand rules heaven;   *15*
Hands have no tears to flow.

Topics for Writing

1. Write an essay explaining the events described in this poem, published in 1936, then summarize the speaker's feelings about them. As you work out each line, answer such questions as these: Who signs the paper? Does he or she also sign the treaty (line 9)? Is he the king of line 4? Who are the five kings of lines 4 and 13? What is the significance of the murder (line 7)? What has happened to the country (line 3)?

2. Compare and contrast the speaker's feelings in this poem with those in John Milton's "On the Late Massacre in Piedmont" (Chapter 8). Pay close attention to connotation and imagery.

3. Write an essay about war, power, and oppression as depicted in two or more of the following poems, focusing on specific aspects of these three topics: Wilfred Owen, "Arms and the Boy" (introduction to Part II); Milton, "On the Late Massacre in Piedmont" (Chapter 8); Percy Bysshe Shelley, "Song to the Men of England" (Chapter 8); Lord Byron, "The Destruction of Sennacherib" (Chapter 11).

As you read the two poems below, note the poetic power that the figurative devices exert on the process of poetic communication.

Denise Levertov (1923–)

Scenes from the Life of the Peppertrees

1.

The peppertrees, the peppertrees!

Cats are stretching in the doorways,
sure of everything. It is morning.
     But the peppertrees
stand aside in diffidence, with berries   *5*
of modest red.

Branch above branch, an air
of lightness; of shadows
scattered lightly.
                  A cat   *10*
closes upon its shadow.
Up and up goes the sun,
sure of everything.
      The peppertrees
            shiver a little.   *15*
Robust
and soot-black, the cat
leaps to a low branch. Leaves
close about him.

2.

The yellow moon dreamily   *20*
tipping buttons of light
down among the leaves. Marimba,
marimba — from beyond the
black street.
                  Somebody dancing,   *25*
somebody
            getting the hell
outta here. Shadows of cats
weave around the treetrunks,
the exposed knotty roots.   *30*

3.

The man on the bed sleeping
defenseless. Look —
his bare long feet together
sideways, keeping each other
warm. And the foreshortened shoulders,   *35*
the head
barely visible. He is good.
Let him sleep.
                  But the third peppertree
      is restless, twitching   *40*
thin leaves in the light
of afternoon. After a while
it walks over and taps
on the upstairs window with a bunch
of red berries. Will he wake?   *45*

Exercises

1. In what ways are the peppertrees said to be like people? Unlike people?
Point to examples of the pathetic fallacy in this poem.

2. In what important way are the trees unlike the cats and the sun in part 1 of the poem?

3. How might you correlate this difference with the action of the third peppertree in part 3 of the poem?

4. Why does a peppertree tap on the window?

John Milton (1608–1674)

from **Paradise Lost (Book IX)**

For now, and since first break of dawn, the fiend,
Mere serpent in appearance, forth was come,
And on his quest, where likeliest he might find
The only two of mankind, but in them
The whole included race, his purposed prey.   *5*
In bower and field he sought, where any tuft
Of grove or garden-plot more pleasant lay,
Their tendance or plantation for delight;
By fountain or by shady rivulet
He sought them both, but wished his hap might find   *10*
Eve separate; he wished, but not with hope
Of what so seldom chanced; when to his wish,
Beyond his hope, Eve separate he spies,
Veiled in a cloud of fragrance, where she stood,
Half spied, so thick the roses bushing round   *15*
About her glowed, oft stooping to support
Each flower of slender stalk, whose head though gay
Carnation, purple, azure, or specked with gold,
Hung drooping unsustained, them she upstays
Gently with myrtle band, mindless the while   *20*
Herself, though fairest unsupported flower,
From her best prop so far, and storm so nigh.

Exercises

1. In this scene, Adam and Eve are separated for the morning, each performing a task in the Garden. Satan, the "fiend" (line 1), approaches Eve to lure her into sin. Explain the metaphor used to describe Eve and Adam.

2. Evaluate the effectiveness of this metaphor by pointing to similarities between Eve (the tenor) and the vehicle used to describe her, then those between Adam (another tenor) and the vehicle used to describe him.

3. How might Adam and Eve be viewed as metaphorical representatives of all mankind? In considering them as figurative types, you may wish to review the brief biblical account of them in Genesis, Chapters 2 and 3.

Like other artists and performers, poets open new worlds to us as they communicate their passions, sensations, experiences, and insights. Figurative language is a powerful means of poetic communication, comparing the puzzling to the knowable, the complex to the simple, the abstract to the concrete, the inhuman to the human. Figures of speech may startle us with a bold new outlook; they may lead us toward heightened awareness of ourselves and of others; they may cause us to consider the world from a fresh perspective. Therein lies much of poetry's power to instruct as well as to delight us.

11. RHYTHM AND METER

Students in literature classes often ask why we need to study rhythm and meter in poetry at all. They ask if it isn't just confusing and if ultimately the study of technicalities doesn't hamper us in understanding what the poet meant to say. Questions of this kind really demand — and deserve — answers. Poets too have fostered such questions by their seeming casualness about organization and details. Byron and Dylan Thomas, for example, give the impression that they were able to sit down and, in a single burst of inspiration, produce a poem. Actually, they were great technicians who labored long and hard over what others might call irrelevant details in order to make their poems as nearly perfect as they could be.

Maybe the best way to answer for ourselves questions about the need to study meter and other poetic devices is to be sure that we understand what poetry is. A poem has being as an entity, and this entity is made up of many parts. Poetry is not just an arrangement of words on paper. It is words in action: patterns of sounds and meanings and rhythms at work in our minds, whether the poem is recited or read silently; patterns that show us, suggest to us, or tell us of objects and emotions, thoughts and moods. Poetry is the totality of these patterns, and to ignore any one of them is to deny ourselves complete understanding. Because rhythm and meter are parts of the total poem, we need to look carefully at this aspect of poetry in order to understand the sum. Rhythm and meter provide for us another way of seeing the poem, and another opportunity for seeing it whole. To understand the basics of the metrical side of poetry is not a difficult task. Although some unfamiliar nomenclature is used occasionally, it is easily mastered.

Nearly all language involves **rhythm.** Listen to a child chanting while skipping rope, to the auctioneer's melodic voice trying to drive up the price of an old cabinet, or even to the television newscaster reciting the day's events at six o'clock. While one type of spoken language may have a more pronounced rhythm than another type — a nursery rhyme, say, compared to a stock-market report — still, each has its own cadence or beat. The language of poetry is no exception: it contains a wide range of beats and rhythms, as varied as those we find in music. Read the following poem aloud and try to get a sense of the poem's rhythm.

Langston Hughes *(1902–1967)*

The Weary Blues

Droning a drowsy syncopated tune,
Rocking back and forth to a mellow croon,
   I heard a Negro play.
Down on Lenox Avenue† the other night
By the pale dull pallor of an old gas light   *5*
   He did a lazy sway. . . .
   He did a lazy sway. . . .
To the tune o' those Weary Blues.
With his ebony hands on each ivory key
He made that poor piano moan with melody.   *10*
   O Blues!
Swaying to and fro on his rickety stool
He played that sad raggy tune like a musical fool.
   Sweet Blues!
Coming from a black man's soul.   *15*
   O Blues!
In a deep song voice with a melancholy tone
I heard that Negro sing, that old piano moan —
   "Ain't got nobody in all this world,
   Ain't got nobody but ma self.   *20*
   I's gwine to quit ma frownin'
   And put ma troubles on the shelf."
Thump, thump, thump, went his foot on the floor.
He played a few chords then he sang some more —
   "I got the Weary Blues   *25*
   And I can't be satisfied.
   Got the Weary Blues
   And can't be satisfied —
   I ain't happy no mo'
   And I wish that I had died."   *30*
And far into the night he crooned that tune.
The stars went out and so did the moon.
The singer stopped playing and went to bed
While the Weary Blues echoed through his head.
He slept like a rock or a man that's dead.   *35*

Exercises

1. Would you say that the poem has a definite rhythm? Is the beat illusive and hard to pin down?

2. Does the poem seem to have a regular rhythm?

3. How do you account for any sense of rhythm you find in the poem?

    4. *Lenox Avenue:* a street in the Harlem section of New York City.

Rhythm in poetry, or in any kind of language for that matter, depends on the relationship between stressed words and syllables and those that are unstressed. Stressed words or syllables are often called accented, and the unstressed words are referred to as unaccented or slack. When the relationship between accented and slack syllables forms a regular pattern in a poem, we call it **meter.** Most poetry in English is metrical, although the rhythmic patterns in some poems are less obvious than in others. Many poets, too, have experimented with meter, and the results are often unsual.

The first step in determining the meter of a poem is locating the stresses. This process often comes naturally as you read poetry, especially if you read it aloud; but sometimes it helps to exaggerate slightly. Read the following two poems and pencil in an accent mark over every stressed syllable.

A. E. Housman *(1859–1936)*

R. L. S.

Home is the sailor, home from sea:
Her far-borne canvas furled
The ship pours shining on the quay
The plunder of the world.

Home is the hunter from the hill: 5
Fast in the boundless snare
All flesh lies taken at his will
And every fowl of air.

'Tis evening on the moorland free,
The starlit wave is still: 10
Home is the sailor from the sea,
The hunter from the hill.

Henry David Thoreau *(1817–1862)*

Haze

Woof of the sun, ethereal gauze,
Woven of Nature's richest stuffs,
Visible heat, air-water and dry sea,
Last conquest of the eye;
Toil of the day displayed, sun-dust,   5
Aerial surf upon the shores of earth,
Ethereal estuary, frith of light,
Breakers of air, billows of heat,
Fine summer spray on inland seas;   10
Bird of the sun, transparent-winged
Owlet of noon, soft-pinioned,
From heath or stubble rising without song,
Establish thy serenity o'er the fields.

1. Look at the accent marks you have made over the stressed syllables in "R. L. S." Do the marked syllables occur in any sort of pattern? What about the unaccented, or slack, syllables?

2. Which poem has the more regular meter? How can you tell?

3. Thoreau describes the haze as being "ethereal gauze," "aerial surf," and "sun-dust" — an illusive and fleeting thing. Is the lack of a strong, regular beat compatible with this idea? Explain.

When we analyze a line of poetry in order to determine its meter, we are said to be **scanning** the line. In scanning, we usually break the line down into groups of two or three syllables called *feet.* Theoretically, a line may have any number of feet, but usually poetry has from one to six or seven feet per line. These groups of syllables, for the most part, have one stressed syllable and one or more unstressed syllables. The position of the stressed syllable in relation to the unstressed one theoretically remains the same, although frequently there are variations in this pattern to avoid monotony and to keep the meter from seeming forced.

The meter of English poetry falls into four basic patterns: the *iambic,* which consists of one unstressed syllable followed by a stressed one; the *trochaic,* a stressed syllable followed by an unstressed one; the *anapestic,* which has two unstressed and then a stressed syllable; and finally the *dactylic,* whose single stressed syllable is followed by two unstressed ones. Here are some examples of metrically regular verses marked above the lines to show the stressed and unstressed syllables. The diagonal lines separate the poetic feet.

Iambic

How rare/ly Rea/son guides / the stub/born Choice.
　　　　　　Samuel Johnson, "The Vanity of Human Wishes"

Trochaic

Golden / branch a/mong the / shadows
　　　Alfred Tennyson, "To Virgil"

Anapestic

Twas the night / before Christ/mas, when all /

through the house
　　　Clement Moore, "A Visit from Saint Nicholas"

Dactylic

Ye who be/lieve in af/fection that / hopes, and

en/dures, and is / patient
　　　Henry Wadsworth Longfellow, "Evangeline"

Just as **metric feet** are classified according to stress patterns, so lines of poetry are divided into types according to the number of feet they contain. A one-foot line is called *monometer*. A line of two feet is termed *dimeter;* of three feet, *trimeter;* of four feet, *tetrameter;* of five feet, *pentameter;* and of six feet, *hexameter*. Each line of regular poetry, then, can be identified first by the type of foot that is dominant in it, and second by the number of feet in the line. Thus, after scanning the following line, we can identify it as iambic pentameter.

> Forth reaching to the fruit, she plucked, she eat.
> *John Milton,* Paradise Lost

This next line is trochaic tetrameter.

> Worlds on worlds are rolling ever.
> *Percy Bysshe Shelley,* "Hellas"

The meter in a poem often reinforces the theme, and in good poetry the sense and the form are in harmony. Consider the following poem.

George Gordon, Lord Byron (1788–1824)

The Destruction of Sennacherib†

1.

The Assyrian came down like the wolf on the fold,
And his cohorts were gleaming in purple and gold;
And the sheen of their spears was like stars on the sea,
When the blue wave rolls nightly on deep Galilee.

2.

Like the leaves of the forest when summer is green,   5
That host with their banners at sunset were seen;
Like the leaves of the forest when autumn hath blown,
That host on the morrow lay withered and strown.

3.

For the Angel of Death spread his wings on the blast,
And breathed in the face of the foe as he passed;   10
And the eyes of the sleepers waxed deadly and chill,
And their hearts but once heaved, and forever grew still!

Sennacherib: an Assyrian king who attempted an invasion of Israel in 701 B.C. He was defeated when his army was wiped out by a plague.

4.

And there lay the steed with his nostril all wide,
But through it there rolled not the breath of his pride;
And the foam of his gasping lay white on the turf,   *15*
And cold as the spray of the rock-beating surf.

5.

And there lay the rider distorted and pale,
With the dew on his brow, and the rust on his mail;
And the tents were all silent, the banners alone,
The lances unlifted, the trumpet unblown.   *20*

[handwritten note: Clint Eastwood took the name of the movie "PALE RIDER" from that line]

6.

And the widows of Ashur† are loud in their wail,
And the idols are broke in the temple of Baal;†
And the might of the Gentile, unsmote by the sword,
Hath melted like snow in the glance of the Lord!

Exercises

1. Scan the poem and identify the meter.

2. This poem describes a great battle between armies of horsemen. How does the meter help in this description?

3. Discuss the simile in the last line of the fourth stanza. What effect does meter have on a comparison of this kind?

Topic for Writing

There is a good deal of repetition in "The Destruction of Sennacherib." What purpose do you think it serves? Evaluate its function, discussing specific words, phrases, and lines in your answer.

Strict adherence to a regular meter is not necessarily a sign of merit in a poem. In fact, a poet who writes in a regular meter and never varies from it is likely to be accused of monotony. Most poets recognize the need for introducing some variety into their metric pattern. John Milton, for instance, wrote *Paradise Lost,* an epic poem of more than ten thousand lines, in iambic pentameter, but he was able, skillfully and, for us, happily, to vary his meter from the standard five-foot pattern. Had he stuck tenaciously to strict pentameter, the result would no doubt have been as sleep-provoking as any pill on the market, no matter how interesting and exciting the other aspects of the poem.

One of the primary functions meter serves is to establish a sense of anticipation in the reader or listener. In our mind's ear we recognize the beat and expect this rhythm to continue, but if we are surprised by a sudden variation, the effect

21. *Ashur:* another name for Assyria.
22. *Baal:* the Assyrians' chief god.

is often aesthetically pleasing. The poet, like the musician, can startle us out of our ennui; for the most part, we enjoy this sensation. There are practical considerations, too. Sometimes a multisyllabic word or phrase used in a poem has its own natural rhythm, which doesn't happen to fit into the meter of the poem. Trying to force the word or phrase into the metrical pattern would create an artificiality that would be heard immediately by the reader-listener. And this artificiality would to some extent destroy the integrity of the poem. In other cases, the placement of the accent determines the very meaning of the phrase. Insisting in every case that the rhythmic pattern of the phrase follow the poem's basic meter could alter the meaning and destroy or make ambiguous the sense of the line.

Therefore, variation from the standard meter is often necessary to preserve the meaning of the poem, to avoid artificiality and monotony, and to add the spice of surprise to our total appreciation of the poem. Read the following poem and then go back and scan it.

Thomas Wyatt (1503?–1542)

If thou wilt mighty be

    If thou wilt mighty be, flee from the rage
        Of cruel will, and see thou keep thee free
    From the foul yoke of sensual bondage;
        For though thy empire stretch to Indian sea,
        And for thy fear trembleth the fardest Thule,†   *5*
If thy desire have over thee the power,
Subject then art thou and no governor.

    If to be noble and high thy mind be moved,
        Consider well thy ground and thy beginning;
    For he that hath each star in heaven fixed,   *10*
        And gives the moon her horns and her
        eclipsing,
        Alike hath made thee noble in his working;
So that wretched no way thou may be,
Except foul lust and vice do conquer thee.

        All were it so thou had a flood of gold   *15*
            Unto thy thirst, yet should it not suffice;
        And though with Indian stones, a thousand fold
          More precious than can thyself devise,
          Ycharged† were thy back, thy covetise
    And busy biting yet should never let   *20*
    Thy wretched life, ne do thy death profet.

5. *fardest Thule* (pronounced Tóo-lee): the northernmost point in the ancient world.

19. *ycharged:* an old form of the word *charged.*

Exercises

1. What is the meter?

2. Are there variations in the meter? Give some examples. Can you give reasons for these variations? Do the variations detract from the poem? Explain.

So far we have been looking at poems that are fairly regular and can be scanned according to the standard accentual syllabic system we have discussed. Not all poetry, however, can be analyzed metrically according to this method. Poets do experiment and as a consequence have produced some unusual metric results — unusual at least for the time in which they were introduced. One of these experiments is called **free verse**, or in French, *vers libre*. This is not to be confused with *blank verse*, which is unrhymed iambic pentameter. The free-verse line does not conform to any predetermined configurations based on accents or syllables; it uses no conventional metrical devices. The result is that, at least to some extent, this kind of poetry resembles prose, except that the line and not the sentence or the paragraph remains the basic unit. Justifications for this kind of poetry include the claim that the poet is free to operate according to the demands of the subject or theme without the distraction of having to conform to any set meter. Several excellent poets, especially some of the modern or contemporary ones, have chosen to write free verse. The following is an example.

William Carlos Williams (1883–1963)

Queen-Ann's-Lace

Her body is not so white as
anemone petals nor so smooth — nor
so remote a thing. It is a field
of the wild carrot taking
the field by force; the grass   5
does not raise above it.
Here is no question of whiteness,
white as can be, with a purple mole
at the center of each flower.
Each flower is a hand's span   10
of her whiteness. Wherever
his hand has lain there is
a tiny purple blemish. Each part
is a blossom under his touch
to which the fibres of her being   15
stem one by one, each to its end,
until the whole field is a
white desire, empty, a single stem,
a cluster, flower by flower,
a pious wish to whiteness gone over —   20
or nothing.

Exercises

1. Do you think that the absence of a regular meter detracts from or enhances the poem? Why?

2. Does the poem have any rhythm at all? Support your answer with references to specific lines.

In addition to developments such as free verse, there have been many experiments with the theory of **prosody**, the very inexact science that studies metrics, or versification. Ever since human beings have been creating poetry, it seems, they have been trying to articulate exactly what it is that makes poetry different from what is termed prose. One way of attempting to arrive at this definition over the years has been to try to develop a satisfactory theory of prosody. There have been many efforts to discover the principle on which the poetic line is based. Some prosodists, as we have seen, contend that the scansion of a poetic line depends on discernible patterns based on the relationship between stressed and unstressed syllables. Others, such as the nineteenth-century poet Coventry Patmore, developed theories around the idea that a poetic line is based on time, much as the measure in music is based on isochronous intervals. Still others, grounding their arguments in studies of classical Greek and Old English poetry, maintain that a poetic line is organized according to a fixed number of stressed syllables, the number of unstressed syllables being immaterial. Gerard Manley Hopkins, one of the great innovators in this area, developed a theory of prosody that he called **sprung rhythm.** The basis for the organization of the poetic line, Hopkins said, is a fixed number of stressed syllables in the line. Look at the following poem and see if you can tell how he organizes his lines.

Gerard Manley Hopkins (1844–1889)

The Windhover†

To Christ Our Lord

I caught this morning morning's minion,† king-
dom of daylight's dauphin,† dapple-dawn-drawn Falcon, in his riding
Of the rolling level underneath him steady air, and striding
High there, how he rung upon the rein of a wimpling wing
In his ecstasy! then off, off forth on swing,   5
As a skate's heel sweeps smooth on a bow-bend: the hurl and gliding
Rebuffed the big wind. My heart in hiding
Stirred for a bird, — the achieve of, the mastery of the thing!

Brute beauty and valour and act, oh, air, pride, plume here —
Buckle! AND the fire that breaks from thee then, a billion   10
Times told lovelier, more dangerous, O my chevalier!

Title: a windhover is a kestrel, or small Old World falcon, which keeps its head to the wind as it hovers in the air.

1. *minion:* a servant.
2. *dauphin:* French for crown prince.

No wonder of it: shéer plód makes plough down sillion†
Shine, and blue-bleak embers, ah my dear,
    Fall, gall themselves, and gash gold-vermilion.

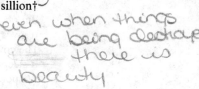
even mud shines
even when things are being destroyed there is beauty

Exercises

1. Is Hopkins's poetry identical with free verse? Why or why not?

2. Is sprung rhythm too sprung? Is it so unstructured that it ceases to be rhythmic at all? Defend your answer.

3. Does Hopkins's vocabulary seem to have anything to do with the way the line is organized?

Topics for Writing

1. Consider the connection between the windhover and Christ in this poem by examining the imagery in which the bird is depicted.

2. This poem is clearly a joyous one. Discuss Hopkins's use of figurative language in creating a sense of joy. Does the rhythm of the lines contribute to this impression?

3. Movement is very important in both "The Windhover" and Byron's "The Destruction of Sennacherib." Discuss the words and figures of speech that each author uses to suggest it. Notice which words get a metrical stress, and consider how rhythm helps to enhance the impression of movement.

    It is important to remember that merit in poetry, like merit in all things, is determined by the evaluation of a total entity; we need to look at the poem from all sides and to respond to it in as many ways as we can before we make any final critical decisions about it. The meter and its interaction with the rest of the poem are only one facet of understanding and appreciating the work.

    Read and scan the following poems. Identify their meter and tell if and why you think the meter is an integral part of each poem.

A. E. Housman (1859–1936)

"Terence, this is stupid stuff"†

    "Terence, this is stupid stuff:
    You eat your victuals fast enough;
    There can't be much amiss, 'tis clear,

12. *sillion:* the earth between furrows on a plowed field.

Title: Housman's original title for the book of poems in which this work first appeared was *The Poems of Terence Hearsay.*

To see the rate you drink your beer.
But oh, good Lord, the verse you make,   5
It gives a chap the belly-ache.
The cow, the old cow, she is dead;
It sleeps well, the hornéd head:
We poor lads, 'tis our turn now
To hear such tunes as killed the cow.   10
Pretty friendship 'tis to rhyme
Your friends to death before their time
Moping melancholy mad:
Come, pipe a tune to dance to, lad."

    Why, if 'tis dancing you would be,   15
There's brisker pipes than poetry.
Say, for what were hop-yards meant
Or why was Burton built on Trent,†
Oh many a peer of England brews
Livelier liquor than the Muse,   20
And malt does more than Milton can
To justify God's ways to man.
Ale, man, ale's the stuff to drink
For fellows whom it hurts to think:
Look into the pewter pot   25
To see the world as the world's not.
And faith, 'tis pleasant till 'tis past:
The mischief is that 'twill not last.
Oh I have been to Ludlow† fair
And left my necktie God knows where,   30
And carried halfway home, or near,
Pints and quarts of Ludlow beer:
Then the world seemed none so bad,
And I myself a sterling lad;
And down in lovely muck I've lain,   35
Happy till I woke again.
Then I saw the morning sky:
Heigho, the tale was all a lie;
The world, it was the old world yet,
I was I, my things were wet,   40
And nothing now remained to do
But begin the game anew.

    Therefore, since the world has still
Much good, but much less good than ill,
And while the sun and moon endure   45
Luck's a chance, but trouble's sure,
I'd face it as a wise man would,
And train for ill and not for good.
'Tis true, the stuff I bring for sale

18. *Burton-on-Trent:* an English   29. *Ludlow:* an English town.
town famous for its breweries.

Is not so brisk a brew as ale: 50
Out of a stem that scored the hand
I wrung it in a weary land.
But take it: if the smack is sour,
The better for the embittered hour;
It should do good to heart and head   55
When your soul is in my soul's stead;
And I will friend you, if I may,
In the dark and cloudy day.

  There was a king reigned in the East:
There, when kings will sit to feast,   60
They get their fill before they think
With poisoned meat and poisoned drink.
He gathered all that springs to birth
From the many-venomed earth;
First a little, thence to more,   65
He sampled all her killing store;
And easy, smiling, seasoned sound,
Sate the king when healths went round.
They put arsenic in his meat
And stared aghast to watch him eat;   70
They poured strychnine in his cup
And shook to see him drink it up:
They shook, they stared as white's their shirt:
Them it was their poison hurt.
— I tell the tale that I heard told.   75
Mithridates,† he died old.

Exercises

1. Who are the two speakers in the poem? Why do they disagree?

2. Discuss the relationship among beer, poison, and poetry in this poem.

Thomas Hardy (1840–1928)

The Ruined Maid

"O 'Melia, my dear, this does everything crown!
Who could have supposed I should meet you in Town?
And whence such fair garments, such prosperi-ty?"
"O didn't you know I'd been ruined?" said she.

76. *Mithridates:* an ancient king in Asia Minor who feared that his enemies were trying to poison him. He made himself immune by taking small doses of poison over a period of time; those who intended to murder Mithridates ended up poisoning themselves.

"You left us in tatters, without shoes or socks,
Tired of digging potatoes, and spudding up docks;†
And now you've gay bracelets and bright feathers three!"
"Yes: that's how we dress when we're ruined," said she.   *5*

"At home in the barton† you said 'thee' and 'thou,'
And 'thik oon,' and 'theäs oon,' and 't'other'; but now   *10*
Your talking quite fits 'ee for high compa-ny!"
"Some polish is gained with one's ruin," said she.

"Your hands were like paws then, your face blue and bleak
But now I'm bewitched by your delicate cheek,
And your little gloves fit as on any la-dy!"   *15*
"We never do work when we're ruined," said she.

"You used to call home-life a hag-ridden dream,
And you'd sigh, and you'd sock; but at present you seem
To know not of megrims† or melancho-ly!"
"True. One's pretty lively when ruined," said she.   *20*

"I wish I had feathers, a fine sweeping gown,
And a delicate face, and could strut about Town!"
"My dear — a raw country girl, such as you be,
Cannot quite expect that. You ain't ruined," said she.

Exercises

1. Identify the speakers. Would you expect two such persons to address each other in such metrical language? Why do you suppose Hardy has them do this?

2. Is the meter "forced" at times? Give specific examples. Does this add or detract from the poem's effect? Why?

3. What attitudes is Hardy ridiculing in this poem? How do you know?

Emily Dickinson (1830–1886)

I like to see it lap the Miles —

I like to see it lap the Miles —
And lick the Valleys up —
And stop to feed itself at Tanks —
And then — prodigious step

Around a Pile of Mountains —   *5*
And supercilious peer
In Shanties — by the sides of Roads —
And then a Quarry pare

6. *spudding up docks:* digging up   9. *barton:* a farm.
weeds.   19. *megrims:* low spirits.

To fit its sides
And crawl between   *10*
Complaining all the while
In horrid — hooting stanza —
Then chase itself down Hill —

And neigh like Boanerges† —
Then — prompter than a Star   *15*
Stop — docile and omnipotent
At its own stable door —

Exercises

1. What is the "it" referred to in the first line? Is there a central metaphor in the poem? What is it?

2. How does the meter relate to the theme and organizing metaphor of the poem?

Henry Wadsworth Longfellow (1807–1882)

The tide rises, the tide falls

The tide rises, the tide falls,
The twilight darkens, the curlew calls,
Along the sea-sands damp and brown
The traveler hastens toward the town,
    And the tide rises, the tide falls.   *5*

Darkness settles on roofs and walls,
But the sea, the sea in the darkness calls;
The little waves, with their soft, white hands,
Efface the footprints in the sands,
    And the tide rises, the tide falls.   *10*

The morning breaks; the steeds in their stalls
Stamp and neigh, as the hostler calls;
The day returns, but nevermore
Returns the traveler to the shore,
    And the tide rises, the tide falls.   *15*

Exercises

1. What are the "sea-sands" the traveler hastens upon? Who is the traveler? Why are the footprints erased, and why are we sure the traveler will never return?

14. *Boanerges:* the name Jesus
gave to the sons of Zebedee; any
loud preacher.

2. What is the role of time in this poem? Why is the first line repeated three times?

3. What can you say about the meter as it affects the total poem? Is it effective?

4. What does the rising and falling of the tide suggest?

Christina Rossetti (1830–1894)

Song

When I am dead, my dearest,
   Sing no sad songs for me;
Plant thou no roses at my head,
   Nor shady cypress tree:
Be the green grass above me   5
   With showers and dewdrops wet:
And if thou wilt, remember,
   And if thou wilt, forget.

I shall not see the shadows,
   I shall not feel the rain;   10
I shall not hear the nightingale
   Sing on as if in pain:
And dreaming through the twilight
   That doth not rise nor set,
Haply I may remember,   15
   And haply may forget.

Exercises

1. How does the meter serve to amplify the distinction between the two main elements of the theme, remembering and forgetting?

2. How do particular objects mentioned in the poem contribute to the mood? Is the mood too contrived? Explain.

3. Does the speaker in the poem seem to have a realistic view of death? Justify your answer.

4. Does the speaker in the poem feel sorry for himself or herself? Discuss.

Marnie Walsh (?–   )

The Red Fox

A winter day on the prairie
finds me in a bus
going nowhere

though a nowhere
of grey snow   *5*
the bus grey also
only the road ahead
real enough
to lead somewhere

It is cold   *10*
prairie cold
and the prairie runs grey
up hills not there
runs over the bus and down
crossing the dark windrow   *15*
following us

My breath is a wet
circle of existence
against the window
through which I glimpse   *20*
the fox
sitting in his singular sunset
the wind sleeking his fur

Exercises

1. Comment on the meter of the poem. Does it reinforce the theme? In what
way?

2. Discuss the contrast of color in the poem. What does the choice of colors
indicate about the speaker's attitude toward the day, the bus, the prairie, and the
fox?

3. What is the attitude of the rider in the warm bus toward the animal of the
bleak prairie? Sympathy? Admiration? Puzzlement? Envy?

Matthew Arnold (1822–1888)

Dover Beach

The sea is calm tonight.
The tide is full, the moon lies fair
Upon the straits; on the French coast the light
Gleams and is gone; the cliffs of England stand,
Glimmering and vast, out in the tranquil bay.   *5*
Come to the window, sweet is the night-air!
Only, from the long line of spray
Where the sea meets the moon-blanched land,

Listen! you hear the grating roar
Of pebbles which the waves draw back, and fling,   *10*
At their return, up the high strand,
Begin, and cease, and then again begin,
With tremulous cadence slow, and bring
The eternal note of sadness in.

Sophocles† long ago   *15*
Heard it on the Aegean, and it brought
Into his mind the turbid ebb and flow
Of human misery; we
Find also in the sound a thought,
Hearing it by this distant northern sea.   *20*

The Sea of Faith
Was once, too, at the full, and round earth's shore
Lay like the folds of a bright girdle furled.
But now I only hear
Its melancholy, long, withdrawing roar,   *25*
Retreating, to the breath
Of the night-wind, down the vast edges drear
And naked shingles of the world.

Ah, love, let us be true
To one another! for the world, which seems   *30*
To lie before us like a land of dreams,
So various, so beautiful, so new,
Hath really neither joy, nor love, nor light,
Nor certitude, nor peace, nor help for pain;
And we are here as on a darkling plain   *35*
Swept with confused alarms of struggle and flight,
Where ignorant armies clash by night.

Exercises

1. What is the thought Arnold finds in the sound at line 19? Does the meter of the poem contribute to this thought? How?

2. What did Sophocles hear long ago that Arnold now hears? What is cadence? What does cadence have to do with the theme of the poem?

3. The last five lines of the poem offer a description of the intellectual climate of the nineteenth century. What does the poem suggest people can do in the face of such a situation?

4. What does the poem suggest about appearance and reality?

15. *Sophocles:* a Greek dramatist of the fifth century B.C.

Walt Whitman (1819–1892)

Beat! beat! drums!

Beat! beat! drums! blow! bugles! blow!
Through the windows — through doors — burst like a ruthless force,
Into the solemn church, and scatter the congregation,
Into the school where the scholar is studying;
Leave not the bridegroom quiet — no happiness must he have now
    with his bride,   5
Nor the peaceful farmer any peace, ploughing his field or gathering
    his grain,
So fierce you whirr and pound you drums — so shrill you bugles
    blow.

Beat! beat! drums! — blow! bugles! blow!
Over the traffic of cities — over the rumble of wheels in the streets;
Are beds prepared for sleepers at night in the houses? no sleepers
    must sleep in those beds,   10
No bargainers' bargains by day — no brokers or speculators —
    would they continue?
Would the talkers be talking? would the singer attempt to sing?
Would the lawyer rise in the court to state his case before the judge?

Then rattle quicker, heavier drums — you bugles wilder blow.
Beat! beat! drums! — blow! bugles! blow!   15
Make no parley — stop for no expostulation,
Mind not the timid — mind not the weeper or prayer,
Mind not the old man beseeching the young man,
Let not the child's voice be heard, nor the mother's entreaties,
Make even the trestles to shake the dead where they lie awaiting the
    hearses,   20
So strong you thump O terrible drums — so loud you bugles blow.

Exercises

1. Is the poem more rhythmic than others you have read? Less rhythmic?
Explain.

2. Whitman, it has been said, writes in cadences rather than in meter. From
your perception of the rhythmic structure of this poem, attempt to distinguish
between meter and cadence.

3. What do the drums and bugles represent in the poem?

Topics for Writing

1. In an essay, discuss the main elements, including rhythm, that help to establish the mood in Arnold's "Dover Beach" and Whitman's "Beat! beat! drums!"

2. Scan one of Shakespeare's sonnets, noticing departures from iambic pentameter. Examine each variation and discuss its purpose or effectiveness.

3. Examine a poem written in free verse, such as Whitman's "Beat! beat! drums!" or William Carlos Williams's "Queen-Ann's-Lace." Point out metrical symmetries that distinguish this writing from prose, or show that the poem you have chosen does not differ significantly from a prose passage of your choice.

12. SOUND DEVICES AND STANZA PATTERNS

Since early childhood, most of us have been familiar with what rhyme is, although undoubtedly some time passed before we consciously knew the definition: the correspondence of terminal sounds in words. We have all heard rhyming devices used in nursery rhymes and weather saws like this one:

> Red sky at night —
> Sailors' delight.
> Red sky at morning —
> Sailors' warning.

Rhyme involves the repetition of sound patterns, and poets have used it through the years to make their poetry appealing to the reader's ear. Poets use many other sound devices for emphasis, effect, and organization — for instance, alliteration, assonance, and consonance — but these will be discussed later.

Rhyme is usually most noticeable when it occurs at the ends of the lines of a poem. In the following stanza we have two rhymes, or what for the sake of convenience we call **a rhyme** and **b rhyme.**

> I hear the noise about thy keel;   *a*
> I hear the bell struck in the night: *b*
> I see the cabin window bright;   *b*
> I see the sailor at the wheel.   *a*

In this stanza from Tennyson's *In Memoriam,* rhyme, or corresponding sounds at the ends of words, helps organize the poetry. The poet has taken his *a* rhyme and his *b* rhyme and used them to organize his stanza vertically, in the same way he has used meter to organize his poetry horizontally. The result is a tight, two-dimensional effect; the rhyme serves to hold together a section of the poem and give it unity.

Many different rhyming units are used in poetry. The simplest and one of the most popular is the **couplet.** As the name implies, the couplet's organization depends upon the rhyming of words at the end of a pair of lines. These from William Blake's "Auguries of Innocence" provide an example:

The Emmets Inch and Eagles Mile
Make Lame Philosophy to Smile

The **heroic couplet** is a refinement of this form. It consists of two rhymed lines of iambic pentameter (see Chapter 10) that are end-stopped; that is, that finish with a strong punctuation mark such as a period or a colon. Each line is usually balanced, with a caesura (a rest, a pause) somewhere in the middle. These couplets are called *heroic* because the form was widely used in the seventeenth and eighteenth centuries in English translations of classical epic, or heroic, poems, as well as in mock-heroic poems (mock epics) such as Alexander Pope's "The Rape of the Lock." The following lines form heroic couplets:

> Thus man by his own strength to heaven would soar,
> And would not be obliged to God for more.
> Vain wretched creature, how art thou misled,
> To think thy wit these god-like notions bred!
> These truths are not the product of thy mind,
> But dropt from heaven and of a nobler kind.
> > *John Dryden,* "Religio Laici"

As we have seen in the example from Tennyson, rhyme is also used to organize poetic units longer than couplets. A **stanza** is the name for a group of lines arranged in a regular pattern, usually involving both meter and rhyme. Stanzas are parts of a larger poetic structure, and their type depends on the total conception of the poem. Down through the years poets used many different types of stanzas, and certain conventions or expectations have come to be associated with the various stanzaic patterns. The **ballad stanza,** for instance, is familiar to nearly everyone. Many of us have heard it since infancy.

> "Mistress Mary, quite contrary,
> How does your garden grow?"
> "With silver bells and cockle shells
> And pretty maids all in a row."

The ballad stanza, in its most widely used variation, has four lines — the first and third written in iambic tetrameter and the second and fourth in iambic trimeter. In this formation, often called *common meter,* the second and the fourth lines are rhymed. Because its roots are in the folk songs and poems of the distant past, the ballad stanza is most often used in narratives that deal with such topics as old legends, tragic love stories, and adventures of folk heroes. The form is also used in literary ballads such as Coleridge's "The Rime of the Ancient Mariner," in which the poet intends to capture the feeling of an old folk legend while writing an original, serious poem.

> About, about, in reel and rout   *a*
> The death-fires danced at night;   *b*
> The water, like a witch's oils,   *c*
> Burnt green, and blue and white.   *b*
> > *Samuel Taylor Coleridge,*
> > "The Rime of the Ancient Mariner"

The ballad stanza is also said to be a **quatrain,** a word referring to any stanza or poem of four lines. Other quatrains have a variety of meters and rhyme schemes. Two of the commoner types, the **elegiac stanza** and the *In Memoriam* **stanza,** are given here as examples:

So once it would have been — 'tis so no more;   *a*
I have submitted to a new control: *b*
A power is gone, which nothing can restore;   *a*
A deep distress hath humanized my Soul.   *b*
    William Wordsworth, "Elegiac Stanzas"

So now I sit here quite alone.   *a*
   Blinded with tears; nor grieve for that,   *b*
   For nought is left worth looking at   *b*
Since my delightful land is gone.   *a*
    Christina Rossetti, "Shut Out"

Many poets are given to more complex stanzaic forms. Some of these forms were discovered in continental European literature and adapted to English, while others, like the **Spenserian stanza,** are native to England. Ever since it was first used by Edmund Spenser in his *Faerie Queene* (1590), the Spenserian stanza has come to be associated with voluptuousness of language and lushness of imagery. It is a nine-line stanza, with eight lines of iambic pentameter and a last line of iambic hexameter, called an Alexandrine. The rhyme scheme is *ababbcbcc.* The following is an example from *The Faerie Queene* (Book III, Canto IX, Stanza 1):

Redoubted knights, and honorable Dames,   *a*
   To whom I levell all my labours end,   *b*
   Right sore I feare, least with unworthy blames   *a*
   This odious argument my rimes should shend,†   *b*
   Or ought your goodly patience offend,   *b*
   Whiles of a wanton Lady I do write,   *c*
   Which with her loose incontinence doth blend   *b*
   The shyning glory of your soveraigne light,   *c*
And knighthood fowle defacéd by a faithlesse knight.   *c*

Another stanza form often found in English is the **ottava rima.** Used widely in Italian romances, it has been adapted by various poets writing in English. The stanza consists of eight lines of iambic pentameter with a rhyme scheme of *abababcc.* The concluding couplet provides an epigrammatical impact at the end of each stanza.

This may seem strange, but yet 'tis very common;   *a*
   For instance — gentlemen, whose ladies take   *b*

4. *shend:* disgrace.

Leave to o'erstep the written rights of Woman,   *a*
 And break the —— Which commandment is't they break?   *b*
(I have forgot the number, and think no man   *a*
 Should rashly quote, for fear of a mistake;)   *b*
I say, when these same gentlemen are jealous,   *c*
 They make some blunder, which their ladies tell us.   *c*
   George Gordon, Lord Byron,
   Don Juan, *Canto I, Stanza 98*

Rhyme royal is a stanza form used by Chaucer and Shakespeare, among others. It consists of seven lines of iambic pentameter rhymed *ababbcc*.

Of heaven or hell I have no power to sing,   *a*
I cannot ease the burden of your fears,   *b*
Or make quick-coming death a little thing,   *a*
Or bring again the pleasure of past years,   *b*
Nor for my words shall ye forget your tears,   *b*
Or hope again for aught that I can say,   *c*
The idle singer of an empty day.   *c*
   William Morris, "The Earthly Paradise"

A particularly fascinating stanza form is the **terza rima.** Used by Dante in *The Divine Comedy,* this three-line stanza rhymes *aba* and is in iambic pentameter. Each terza rima stanza interlocks with the next stanza by means of rhyme, and the result is a tight verse form which still allows for a progression of ideas.

The sun by now o'er that horizon's rim   *a*
Was sinking, whose meridian circle stands   *b*
With its mid-arch above Jerusalem   *a*

While night, who wheels opposed to him, from sands   *b*
Of Ganges mounted with the Scales, whose weight   *c*
Drops in her hour of victory from her hands   *b*

So that, where we were, fair Aurora, late   *c*
Flushing from white to rose-vermilion,   *d*
Grew sallow with ripe age and matron state.   *c*
   Dante, The Divine Comedy (*as*
   translated by Dorothy L. Sayers)

Sometimes an entire poem, as distinguished from a stanza, has its own poetic form. An important one is the **sonnet.** The sonnet is a fourteen-line poem written in iambic pentameter usually following one of two rhyme schemes. The **Petrarchan** (or **Italian**) **sonnet** is divided into two parts: an octave (eight-line stanza) usually rhymed *abbaabba,* and a sestet (six-line stanza) rhyming much as the poet chooses. Often there is a rhetorical turn or shift between the octave and the sestet. The poet gives a proposition or raises a question in the first eight lines, and then presents a solution or answer in the sestet. Thus the octave prepares for the statement made by the sestet.

Dante Gabriel Rossetti *(1828–1882)*

A Sonnet from The House of Life

A Sonnet is a moment's monument, —	*a*
Memorial from the Soul's eternity	*b*
To one dead deathless hour. Look that it be,	*b*
Whether for lustral rite or dire portent,	*a*
Of its own arduous fulness reverent:	*a*
Carve it in ivory or in ebony,	*b*
As Day or Night may rule; and let Time see	*b*
Its flowering crest impearled and orient.	*a*
A Sonnet is a coin: its face reveals	*c*
The soul — its converse, to what Power 'tis due.	*d*
Whether for tribute to the august appeals	*c*
O Life, or dower in Love's high retinue,	*d*
It serve; or, 'mid the dark wharf's cavernous breath,	*e*
In Charon's palm it pay the toll to Death.	*e*

The **Shakespearean** (also called **English,** or **Elizabethan**) **sonnet** is divided into three quatrains and ends with a rhymed couplet.

William Shakespeare *(1564–1616)*

Sonnet 106

When in the chronicle of wasted time	*a*
I see descriptions of the fairest wights,†	*b*
And beauty making beautiful old rhyme	*a*
In praise of ladies dead and lovely knights,	*b*
Then, in the blazon† of sweet beauty's best,	*c*
Of hand, of foot, of lip, of eye, of brow,	*d*
I see their antique pen would have expressed	*c*
Even such a beauty as you master now.	*d*
So all their praises are but prophecies	*e*
Of this our time, all you prefiguring;	*f*
And, for they looked but with divining eyes,	*e*
They had not skill enough your worth to sing:	*f*
For we, which now behold these present days,	*g*
Have eyes to wonder, but lack tongues to praise.	*g*

Despite its difficult and demanding form, the sonnet is used by many poets because it is concise and tight. Shakespeare's Sonnet 106, for instance, is a self-contained, logical construction. The three quatrains take us from point to point until we reach the couplet, which furnishes the conclusion.

2. *wights:* persons.   5. *blazon:* a record of virtues or excellencies.

The **villanelle** is another familiar poetic form, although not as widely used as the sonnet. Its line length can vary, but it runs on only two rhymes and consists of five tercets (three-line stanzas) rhyming *aba,* with a quatrain at the end rhyming *abaa.* In addition, the first and third lines are repeated: line 1 is repeated in lines 6, 12, and 18, while line 3 is repeated in 9, 15, and 19. The following poem illustrates the form:

gentleman
polite controlled
proper
manerly

Dylan Thomas (1914–1953)

Do not go gentle into that good night

have
courage
when
facing
it

Do not go gentle into that good night,　　　　　*even though*
Old age should burn and rave at close of day;　*you weren't*
Rage, rage against the dying of the light.　　　*famous you*
　　　　　　　　　　　　　　　　　　　　shouldn't go
Though wise men at their end know dark is right,　*meekly*
Because their words had forked no lightning they　　　　5
Do not go gentle into that good night.　*do give up*
　　　　　　　　　　　　　　　　　　once it
Good men, the last wave by, crying how bright　*manly*
Their frail deeds might have danced in a green bay,
Rage, rage against the dying of the light.
　　　　　　　　　　　　they didn't do
Wild men who caught and sang the sun in flight,　*anything* 10
And learn, too late, they grieved it on its way,　*significant*
Do not go gentle into that good night.　*don't go*
　　　　　　　　　　　　　　　　　meekly
Grave men, near death, who see with blinding sight
Blind eyes could blaze like meteors and be gay,
Rage, rage against the dying of the light.　　　　　　15

And you, my father, there on the sad height,
Curse, bless, me now with your fierce tears, I pray.
Do not go gentle into that good night.
Rage, rage against the dying of the light.

death
to
father

couplet
no matter
who you are
or what you
did you can die
with dignity

Exercises

1. What advice does the poem offer people who are dying? Why?

2. Mark up the rhyme scheme. What is the effect of the repeated lines? Boredom? Emphasis? A sense of symmetry?

3. Consider the images of light in this poem. What do they tell us about life and death? What do you think the phrase "dark is right" means?

In addition to rhyme, other poetic devices depend on the repetition of certain sound patterns. Rhyme, as we have seen, occurs when there is a duplication of sounds at the ends of words. **Alliteration** is the repetition of initial consonants in words — for instance, *the weary way-worn wanderer,* or *daylight's dauphin, dapple-dawn-drawn Falcon.* Alliteration has played an important part in English poetry, and in fact served as the basis for organizing the poetic line in early English verse. Still common today, it occurs most often in conjunction with other devices of sound, such as rhyme and assonance.

Assonance involves the close repetition of the same vowels followed by different consonants. Stephen Crane has examples in his poetry, such as *rolled over* and *champing and mouthing of hats*. **Consonance,** on the other hand, is the recurrence of consonant sounds without a corresponding repetition of vowel sounds. Hopkins often turns to this device in his poetry, as when he uses the *r* sound in this series of words: *original, spare, strange*. **Internal rhyme,** another of the poetic devices involving sound, is the repetition of terminal sounds in words, as in *c*at and *r*at, when they occur within a line of poetry rather than at the end. *The flower's leaf, the sheaf of grain* is an example.

The sound devices — rhyme, alliteration, consonance, internal rhyme, and assonance — are all items in the poet's toolbox. Like skilled artisans, poets use these tools to create the best possible piece of work. Like cabinetmakers or stonemasons, they are always aware of the scope and limitations of each tool. The master poet uses them accordingly.

Read the following poems and excerpts and determine the stanzaic pattern or the poetic form. Then identify the devices of sound the poet uses to make a point, to spotlight or enhance an idea, or simply to make the poetry more appealing to our mind's ear.

Paula Gunn Allen (1939–   )

Hoop Dancer

It's hard to enter
circling clockwise and counter
clockwise moving no
regard for time, metrics
irrelevant to this dance where pain   5
is the prime counter and soft
stepping feet praise water from the skies:
I have seen the face of triumph
the winding line stare down all moves to desecration
guts not cut from arms, fingers joined to minds,   10
together Sky and Water one dancing one
circle of a thousand turning lines beyond the march of years —
out of time, out of
time, out
of time.   15

Exercises

1. What is "hard to enter" (line 1) here? Merely the circle of dancers?

2. Are metrics irrelevant to the poem? Explain.

3. How is the dance "out of time"?

Ulysses†

It little profits that an idle king,
By this still hearth, among these barren crags,
Matched with an aged wife, I mete and dole
Unequal laws unto a savage race,
That hoard, and sleep, and feed, and know not me.   *5*

I cannot rest from travel; I will drink
Life to the lees. All times I have enjoyed
Greatly, have suffered greatly, both with those
That loved me, and alone; on shore, and when
Through scudding drifts the rainy Hyades†   *10*
Vexed the dim sea. I am become a name;
For always roaming with a hungry heart
Much have I seen and known — cities of men
And manners, climates, councils, governments,
Myself not least, but honored of them all —   *15*
And drunk delight of battle with my peers,
Far on the ringing plains of windy Troy.
I am a part of all that I have met;
Yet all experience is an arch wherethrough
Gleams that untraveled world whose margin fades   *20*
Forever and forever when I move.
How dull it is to pause, to make an end,
To rust unburnished, not to shine in use!
As though to breathe were life! Life piled on life
Were all too little, and of one to me   *25*
Little remains; but every hour is saved
From that eternal silence, something more,
A bringer of new things; and vile it were
For some three suns to store and hoard myself,
And this gray spirit yearning in desire   *30*
To follow knowledge like a sinking star,
Beyond the utmost bound of human thought.

This is my son, mine own Telemachus,
To whom I leave the scepter and the isle —
Well-loved of me, discerning to fulfill   *35*
This labor, by slow prudence to make mild
A rugged people, and through soft degrees
Subdue them to the useful and the good.
Most blameless is he, centered in the sphere
Of common duties, decent not to fail   *40*

Title: Ulysses, a character in *The Iliad* and the hero of *The Odyssey,* has returned home to Ithaca.
10. *Hyades:* a cluster of stars in the constellation Taurus; when they rise in the sky, sailors expect rain.

In offices of tenderness, and pay
Meet adoration to my household gods,
When I am gone. He works his work, I mine.

    There lies the port; the vessel puffs her sail;
There gloom the dark, broad seas. My mariners,   45
Souls that have toiled, and wrought, and thought with me —
That ever with a frolic welcome took
The thunder and the sunshine, and opposed
Free hearts, free foreheads — you and I are old;
Old age hath yet his honor and his toil.   50
Death closes all; but something ere the end,
Some work of noble note, may yet be done,
Not unbecoming men that strove with Gods.
The lights begin to twinkle from the rocks;
The long day wanes; the slow moon climbs; the deep   55
Moans round with many voices. Come, my friends,
'Tis not too late to seek a newer world.
Push off, and sitting well in order smite
The sounding furrows; for my purpose holds
To sail beyond the sunset, and the baths   60
Of all the western stars, until I die.
It may be that the gulfs will wash us down;
It may be we shall touch the Happy Isles,†
And see the great Achilles, whom we knew.
Though much is taken, much abides; and though   65
We are not now that strength which in old days
Moved earth and heaven, that which we are, we are —
One equal temper of heroic hearts,
Made weak by time and fate, but strong in will
To strive, to seek, to find, and not to yield.   70

Exercises

1. The speaker in this poem is clearly Ulysses. But whom is he speaking to?

2. Is Ulysses a heroic figure here, or a silly old man?

3. What is Ulysses' idea of eternity, or the afterlife?

---

63. *Happy Isles:* Elysium, placed by Homer in the western sea, or Atlantic Ocean, and described by him as a happy land to which favored heroes could pass without dying.

Tithonus†

The woods decay, the woods decay and fall,
The vapors weep their burthen to the ground,
Man comes and tills the field and lies beneath,
And after many a summer dies the swan.
Me only cruel immortality   *5*
Consumes; I wither slowly in thine arms,
Here at the quiet limit of the world,
A white-haired shadow roaming like a dream
The ever-silent spaces of the East,
Far-folded mists, and gleaming halls of morn.   *10*
    Alas! for this gray shadow, once a man —
So glorious in his beauty and thy choice,
Who madest him thy chosen, that he seemed
To his great heart none other than a God!
I asked thee, "Give me immortality."   *15*
Then didst thou grant mine asking with a smile,
Like wealthy men who care not how they give.
But thy strong Hours† indignant worked their wills,
And beat me down and marred and wasted me,
And though they could not end me, left me maimed   *20*
To dwell in presence of immortal youth,
Immortal age beside immortal youth,
And all I was in ashes. Can they love,
Thy beauty, make amends, though even now,
Close over us, the silver star, thy guide,   *25*
Shines in those tremulous eyes that fill with tears
To hear me? Let me go; take back thy gift.†
Why should a man desire in any way
To vary from the kindly race of men,
Or pass beyond the goal of ordinance   *30*
Where all should pause, as is most meet for all?
    A soft air fans the cloud apart; there comes
A glimpse of that dark world where I was born.
Once more the old mysterious glimmer steals
From thy pure brows, and from thy shoulders pure,   *35*
And bosom beating with a heart renewed.
Thy cheek begins to redden through the gloom,
Thy sweet eyes brighten slowly close to mine,
Ere yet they blind the stars, and the wild team†
Which love thee, yearning for thy yoke, arise,   *40*
And shake the darkness from their loosened manes,
And beat the twilight into flakes of fire.

Title: Tithonus was a Trojan prince loved by Eos, goddess of the dawn, who obtained for him the gift of eternal life. She neglected to ask the gods for eternal youth as well, so Tithonus continued to shrivel and wither away with age.

18. *Hours:* also called Horae; they regulate the days and the seasons.
27. *thy gift:* Eos is unable to rescind the gift of immortality.
39. *wild team:* the horses that pull Eos' chariot into the sky at dawn.

Lo! ever thus thou growest beautiful
In silence, then before thine answer given
Departest, and thy tears are on my cheek.   45
    Why wilt thou ever scare me with thy tears,
And make me tremble lest a saying learnt,
In days far-off, on that dark earth, be true?
"The Gods themselves cannot recall their gifts."
    Ay me! ay me! with what another heart   50
In days far-off, and with what other eyes
I used to watch — if I be he that watched —
The lucid outline forming round thee; saw
The dim curls kindle into sunny rings;
Changed with thy mystic change, and felt my blood   55
Glow with the glow that slowly crimsoned all
Thy presence and thy portals, while I lay,
Mouth, forehead, eyelids, growing dewy-warm
With kisses balmier than half-opening buds
Of April, and could hear the lips that kissed   60
Whispering I knew not what of wild and sweet,
Like that strange song I heard Apollo sing,
While Ilion like a mist rose into towers.†
    Yet hold me not forever in thine East;
How can my nature longer mix with thine?   65
Coldly thy rosy shadows bathe me, cold
Are all thy lights, and cold my wrinkled feet
Upon thy glimmering thresholds, when the steam
Floats up from those dim fields about the homes
Of happy men that have the power to die,   70
And grassy barrows of the happier dead.
Release me, and restore me to the ground.
Thou seest all things, thou wilt see my grave;
Thou wilt renew thy beauty morn by morn,
I earth in earth forget these empty courts,   75
And thee returning on thy silver wheels.

Exercises

1. Discuss the horror and incongruity of Tithonus' position. See especially lines 5–6, 20–23, 28–31, and 70–71.

2. What is "the goal of ordinance" referred to in line 30?

3. Is Tithonus being punished? For what?

Topic for Writing

"Ulysses" and "Tithonus" are companion poems that present contrasting viewpoints. In an essay, discuss the varying points of view of these Tennyson poems

63. *rose into towers:* according to   by Apollo's song; Ilion is an-
legend, Troy's walls were raised   other name for Troy.

or the contrasting elements of the two parts of Geary Hobson's poem "Deer Hunting," printed below.

Geary Hobson (1941–   )

Deer Hunting

1.

"God dammit, Al. Are you gonna help me
cut up this deer, or
are you gonna stand there all day
drinking beer and yakking?"
    Knives flash in savage motion   5
flesh from hide quickly severs
as the two men rip the pelt tail downwards
from the head. The hide but not
the head is kept. Guts spew forth
in a riot of heat and berries and shit,   10
and is quickly kicked into the trash hole.
    Hooves are whacked off,
and thrown also to the waste hole —
a rotted hollow stump.
But the antler rack is saved,   15
sawed from the crown with a hand-saw,
trophy of the hunt,
like gold teeth carried home
from the wars
in small cigar boxes.   20
    Men stand around in little groups,
bragging how the deer fell to their rifles
and throw their empties into the stump-hole.
    Al walks to the stump, unzips his pants.
"Hell, Bob, you're so fucking slow,   25
I could skin ten deer while you're doing one
and I'll show you up just as soon
as I take a piss."
    The hounds,
tired from the slaughter,   30
watch the men. They whine
for flesh denied them
and turn to pans filled with Purina.

2.

"Now, watch me, *ungilisi*, grandson,
as I prepare this deer   35
which the Great Spirit has given to us
for meat."

The old man hangs the carcass
feet-first from the pecan tree
with gentleness   40
like the handling of spider-webbing
for curing purposes.
    Slow cuts around the hooves,
quick slices of the knives as
the grandfather and father   45
part the hide from the meat.
The young boy — now a man —
stands shy and proud,
his initiating kill before him,
like a prayer unexpected,   50
his face still smeared
with the deer's blood of blessing.
    The hide is taken softly,
the head and antlers brought easily with it,
in a downward pull by the two men.   55
    Guts in a tumbling rush
fall into the bucket
to be cooked with the hooves
into a strength stew
for the hunting dogs   60
brothers who did their part in the chase.
    The three men share the raw liver,
eating it to become
part of the deer.
    The older man cuts   65
a small square of muscle
from the deer's dead flank,
and tosses it solemnly into the bushes
behind him, giving back part of the deer's
swiftness   70
to the place from which it came.
    Softly, thankfully, the older man
breathes to the woods,
and turns and smiles at his grandson,
now become a man.   75

Exercises

1. Compare and contrast the attitudes of the two sets of hunters toward their quarry.

2. Point out the ways (word choice is one) in which the poet conveys the ethos, or guiding beliefs, of the two groups.

3. Point out the ritualistic elements of both parts of the poem.

A Villanelle   _Theodore Roethke_ (1908–1963)

The Waking

awaking
_to a_
different
conciousness +
"going to
sleep"

— A I wake to sleep, and take my waking slow.
    B I feel my fate in what I cannot fear.
    A I learn by going where I have to go.

    A We think by feeling. What is there to know?
    B I hear my being dance from ear to ear.   5
— A I wake to sleep, and take my waking slow.

    A Of those so close beside me, which are you?
    B God bless the Ground! I shall walk softly there,
 * A And learn by going where I have to go.

    A Light takes the Tree; but who can tell us how?   10
    B The lowly worm climbs up a winding stair;
— A I wake to sleep, and take my waking slow.

    A Great Nature has another thing to do
    B To you and me; so take the lively air,
 * A And, lovely, learn by going where to go.   15

    A This shaking keeps me steady. I should know.
    B What falls away is always. And is near.
— A I wake to sleep, and take my waking slow.
 * A I learn by going where I have to go.

Exercises

1. What is the poetic form here? Is this form appropriate to the theme and to any kind of logical progression you find? Explain.

2. Comment on line 5: "I hear my being dance from ear to ear." What do you think it means in the context of the poem? What figure or figures of speech does it involve?

Percy Bysshe Shelley (1792–1822)

Ode to the West Wind

1.

O wild West Wind, thou breath of Autumn's being,
Thou, from whose unseen presence the leaves dead
Are driven, like ghosts from an enchanter fleeing,

Yellow, and black, and pale, and hectic red,
Pestilence-stricken multitudes: O thou,   5
Who chariotest to their dark wintry bed

The wingéd seeds, where they lie cold and low,
Each like a corpse within its grave, until
Thine azure sister of the Spring shall blow

Her clarion o'er the dreaming earth, and fill   *10*
(Driving sweet buds like flocks to feed in air)
With living hues and odors plain and hill:

Wild Spirit, which art moving everywhere;
Destroyer and preserver; hear, oh, hear!

2.

Thou on whose stream, mid the steep sky's commotion,   *15*
Loose clouds like earth's decaying leaves are shed,
Shook from the tangled boughs of Heaven and Ocean,

Angels of rain and lightning: there are spread
On the blue surface of thine aëry surge,
Like the bright hair uplifted from the head   *20*

Of some fierce Maenad,† even from the dim verge
Of the horizon to the zenith's height,
The locks of the approaching storm. Thou dirge

Of the dying year, to which this closing night
Will be the dome of a vast sepulcher,   *25*
Vaulted with all thy congregated might

Of vapors, from whose solid atmosphere
Black rain, and fire, and hail will burst: oh, hear!

3.

Thou who didst waken from his summer dreams
The blue Mediterranean, where he lay,   *30*
Lulled by the coil of his crystalline streams,

Beside a pumice isle in Baiae's† bay,
And saw in sleep old palaces and towers
Quivering within the wave's intenser day,

All overgrown with azure moss and flowers   *35*
So sweet, the sense faints picturing them! Thou
For whose path the Atlantic's level powers

Cleave themselves into chasms, while far below
The sea-blooms and the oozy woods which wear
The sapless foliage of the ocean, know   *40*

Thy voice, and suddenly grow gray with fear,
And tremble and despoil themselves: oh, hear!

---

21. *Maenad:* one of the female followers of Dionysius, under whose influence they were said to go mad.

32. *Baiae:* an Italian town near Naples.

If I were a dead leaf thou mightest bear;
If I were a swift cloud to fly with thee;
A wave to pant beneath thy power, and share   *45*

The impulse of thy strength, only less free
Than thou, O uncontrollable! If even
I were as in my boyhood, and could be

The comrade of thy wanderings over Heaven,
As then, when to outstrip thy skyey speed   *50*
Scarce seemed a vision; I would ne'er have striven

As thus with thee in prayer in my sore need.
Oh, lift me as a wave, a leaf, a cloud!
I fall upon the thorns of life! I bleed!

A heavy weight of hours has chained and bowed   *55*
One too like thee: tameless, and swift, and proud.

5.

Make me thy lyre, even as the forest is:
What if my leaves are falling like its own!
The tumult of thy mighty harmonies

Will take from both a deep, autumnal tone,   *60*
Sweet though in sadness. Be thou, Spirit fierce,
My spirit! Be thou me, impetuous one!

Drive my dead thoughts over the universe
Like withered leaves to quicken a new birth!
And, by the incantation of this verse,   *65*

Scatter, as from an unextinguished hearth
Ashes and sparks, my words among mankind!
Be through my lips to unawakened earth

The trumpet of a prophecy! O Wind,
If Winter comes, can Spring be far behind?   *70*

Exercises

1. There is a sense of movement or progression in the poem. How does the stanzaic pattern contribute to this progression?

2. The seasons of the year as well as such natural phenomena as clouds, leaves, and the sea play an important part in this poem. Discuss these natural elements and show how they are integral to the theme.

3. Why does the speaker suffer from life, as is stated in line 54?

Jonathan Swift *(1667–1745)*

A Description of a City Shower

Careful observers may foretell the hour
(By sure prognostics) when to dread a shower:
While rain depends, the pensive cat gives o'er
Her frolics, and pursues her tail no more.
Returning home at night, you'll find the sink   5
Strike your offended sense with double stink.
If you be wise, then go not far to dine;
You'll spend in coach hire more than save in wine.
A coming shower your shooting corns presage,
Old aches throb, your hollow tooth will rage.   10
Sauntering in coffeehouse is Dulman† seen;
He damns the climate and complains of spleen.
    Meanwhile the South, rising with dabbled wings,
A sable cloud athwart the welkin† flings,
That swilled more liquor than it could contain,   15
And, like a drunkard, gives it up again.
Brisk Susan whips her linen from the rope,
While the first drizzling shower is borne aslope:
Such is that sprinkling which some careless quean
Flirts on you from her mop, but not so clean: 20
You fly, invoke the gods; then turning, stop
To rail; she singing, still whirls on her mop.
Not yet the dust had shunned the unequal strife,
But, aided by the wind, fought still for life,
And wafted with its foe by violent gust,   25
'Twas doubtful which was rain and which was dust.
Ah! where must needy poet seek for aid,
When dust and rain at once his coat invade?
Sole coat, where dust cemented by the rain
Erects the nap, and leaves a mingled stain.   30
    Now in contiguous drops the flood comes down,
Threatening with deluge this devoted town.
To shops in crowds the daggled† females fly,
Pretend to cheapen goods,† but nothing buy.
The Templar spruce,† while every spout's abroach,   35
Stays till 'tis fair, yet seems to call a coach.
The tucked-up sempstress walks with hasty strides,
While streams run down her oiled umbrella's sides.
Here various kinds, by various fortunes led,
Commence acquaintance underneath a shed.   40
Triumphant Tories and desponding Whigs†

11. *Dulman:* any dull man.
14. *welkin:* the sky.
33. *daggled:* bedraggled.
34. *cheapen goods:* bargain for them.
35. *Templar spruce:* a well-dressed laywer.
41. *Tories and . . . Whigs:* members of opposing political parties.

Forget their feuds, and join to save their wigs.
Boxed in a chair the beau impatient sits,
While spouts run clattering o'er the roof by fits,
And ever and anon with frightful din   45
The leather sounds; he trembles from within.
So when Troy chairmen bore the wooden steed,
Pregnant with Greeks impatient to be freed
(Those bully Greeks who, as the moderns do,
Instead of paying chairmen, run them through),   50
Laocoön† struck the outside with his spear,
And each imprisoned hero quaked for fear.
   Now from all parts the swelling kennels flow,
And bear their trophies with them as they go:
Filth of all hues and odors seem to tell   55
What street they sailed from, by their sight and smell.
They, as each torrent drives with rapid force,
From Smithfield or St. Pulchre's shape their course,
And in huge confluence joined at Snow Hill ridge,
Fall from the conduit prone to Holborn Bridge.†   60
Sweepings from butchers' stalls, dung, guts, and blood,
Drowned puppies, stinking sprats, all drenched in mud,
Dead cats, and turnip tops, come tumbling down the flood.

Exercises

1. In broad terms, we can say that realism is telling the story straight, rather than telling it as we want it to be. Given this definition, can we call Swift's poem a realistic one? What details can you point out to support your case?

2. How well does the couplet work in this poem?

William Wordsworth (1770–1850)

I wandered lonely as a cloud

I wandered lonely as a cloud
That floats on high o'er vales and hills,
When all at once I saw a crowd,
A host, of golden daffodils;
Beside the lake, beneath the trees,   5
Fluttering and dancing in the breeze.

Continuous as the stars that shine
And twinkle on the milky way,

---

51. *Laocoön:* a Greek priest who warned of the dangers of the Trojan horse.

58–60. *Smithfield . . . Holborn Bridge:* areas of London.

They stretched in never-ending line
Along the margin of a bay: *10*
Ten thousand saw I at a glance,
Tossing their heads in sprightly dance.

The waves beside them danced; but they
Outdid the sparkling waves in glee;
A poet could not but be gay,   *15*
In such a jocund company;
I gazed — and gazed — but little thought
What wealth the show to me had brought:

For oft, when on my couch I lie
In vacant or in pensive mood,   *20*
They flash upon that inward eye
Which is the bliss of solitude;
And then my heart with pleasure fills,
And dances with the daffodils.

Exercises

1. How does Wordsworth here synthesize two common stanzaic patterns to create a third?

2. The poem contains musings on the perception and recollection of beauty. When is beauty most appreciated, according to the speaker in the poem? Isn't the bloom of daffodils transitory and fleeting? Of what value is such short-lived pleasure? Explain.

Richard Hugo *(1923–1982)*

2433 Agnes, First Home, Last House in Missoula

It promises quiet here. A green Plymouth
has been a long time sitting across the street.
The lady in 2428 limps with a cane
and west of me fields open all the way
to the mountains, all the way I imagine   *5*
to the open sea. A three colored dog
doesn't bark, and between 2428
and 24 I see blocks away a chicken coop
in disrepair, what in the distance seems
moss on the roof and for certain   *10*
the windows out, for terribly certain
no chickens, and for beautifully sure
a gray pile of lumber in a vacant lot.

My first morning is cloudy. A rumpled
dirty sheet of clouds is crawling northeast,   *15*

not threatening rain, but obscuring
the Rattlesnake range. In 2430
a woman is moving, muted to ghost behind
dotted swiss curtains. She drives
a pale green Falcon. This neighborhood   *20*
seems a place where lives, like cars, go on
a long time. It has few children.

I'm somewhat torn. On one hand, I believe
no one should own land. You can't respect
what you own. Better we think of spirits   *25*
as owning the land, and use it wisely, giving
back at least as much as we take, repaying
land with Indian rituals of thanks.
And I think when we buy, just the crude fact
of money alone means we really pay out   *30*
some part of self we should have retained.
On the other hand, at least fifty buntings
are nervously pecking my lawn.

Exercises

1. What can you say about Hugo's perception of beauty as compared with
Wordsworth's in "I wandered lonely as a cloud"?

2. What points does the poem make about the ownership of land?

3. Do the birds use the land wisely and give back at least as much as they take?
Explain.

Gerard Manley Hopkins *(1844–1889)*

Felix Randal

Felix Randal the farrier,† O is he dead then? my duty all ended,
Who have watched his mould of man, big-boned and hardy-
    handsome
Pining, pining, till time when reason rambled in it and some
Fatal four disorders, fleshed there, all contended?

Sickness broke him. Impatient, he cursed at first, but mended   *5*
Being anointed and all; though a heavenlier heart began some
Months earlier, since I had our sweet reprieve and ransom†
Tendered to him. Ah well, God rest him all road ever he offended!

This seeing the sick endears them to us, us too it endears.
My tongue had taught thee comfort, touch had quenched thy tears,   *10*

1. *farrier:* one who shoes horses.   7. *sweet reprieve and ransom:* the
                                      Eucharist, or Holy Communion.

Thy tears that touched my heart, child, Felix, poor Felix Randal;
How far from then forethought of, all thy more boisterous years,
When thou at the random grim forge, powerful amidst peers,
Didst fettle† for the great grey drayhorse his bright and battering
     sandal!

Exercises

1. What is the poetic form? Is there a shift of emphasis from the first part of the poem to the second?

2. What devices of sound does Hopkins use? Do they provide emphasis? How?

3. What is the most powerful line in the poem? Why?

Patricia Washington McGraw (1940–   )

BluesBlack

Lord-I-got-the
Last-hired-first-fired
Catch-a-nigger-by-the-toe
White-is-right-brown-stick-around
Black-get-back   5
Integration-segregation-tokenism
We-got-one-in-our-office
Things-is-better-for-yawl
Welfare-foodstamps-housing-project
First-of-the-month-come-see-me   10
I-can-feel-you-but-I-can't-see-you
Soup-line-jive-time-dudes-cats
Pool-shark-lurking-in-the-dark
Long-time-no-see
Superfly-I-can't-cope   15
Things-is-tough-all-over
Roach-infested-rat-gnawing-babies
Blues —
And-I-don't-know-what-to-do.

14. *fettle:* to make ready, shape.

1. The poem consists of a series of images provoked into being by a word or a phrase. Look at some of these words or phrases and discuss what images come to mind.

2. The last line of this poem is commonly used in the lyrics of blues songs. In view of this fact, is the last line trite or poignant? Defend your answer.

3. What does line 11 mean?

Elizabeth Jennings (1926–   )

Answers

I kept my answers small and kept them near;
Big questions bruised my mind but still I let
Small answers be a bulwark to my fear.

The huge abstractions I kept from the light;
Small things I handled and caressed and loved.   5
I let the stars assume the whole of night.

But the big answers clamored to be moved
Into my life. Their great audacity
Shouted to be acknowledged and believed.

Even when all small answers build up to   10
Protection of my spirit, still I hear
Big answers striving for their overthrow

And all the great conclusions coming near.

Exercises

1. Scan the lines and identify the rhyme scheme of the poem. How does the meter contribute to the overall effect?

2. What are the small answers? The large answers? How can the small ones protect against the onslaught of the large?

3. What do you think the poem says about the practice of shutting out the large answers?

Joy Harjo (1951–

Someone Talking

Language is movement.
They watch the glittering moon
from the front porch in Oxford, Iowa.
Which reservation
in this river of star motion? 5
The man of words sits next to
Nonnie Daylight,
listening this time.
                    Tequila, a little wine, and she
                    remembers some Old Crow, yellow 10
                    in a fifth on the drainboard. She
                    thinks of Hobson in Oklahoma. And
                    how he ducked behind the truck with
                    her the summer powwow for a drink.
                    Where is the word for a warm night 15
                    and how it continues to here, a
                    thousand miles from that time?

Milky Way.
And there are other words
in other languages. Always 20
in movement. He touches
her back where her hair
reaches to the middle. There
is that gesture and the
cricket's voice beginning. 25
All in the same circle of space.
Maybe the man of words speaks
like the cricket.
Nonnie Daylight
hears him that way. 30
                    It is along the Turner Turnpike
                    between Tulsa and Oklahoma City, she
                    tells him,
                    where they have all those signs,
                    Kickapoo, Creek, 35
                    Sac and Fox.
                    Dating the beginning and end
                    of the United States recognition
                    of tribal histories.
                    And hell, 40
                    where is Hobson now
                    when she needs and tastes
                    the Old Crow.
                    Yellow fire all the way into
                    her belly. 45
                    The way they meant it.

They have maps
named after Africa and the blue oceans.
Sky circles the other way
but she doesn't feel dizzy.   50
Stars in the dark are clear
not blurred, and the earth's movement
is a whirring current in the grass.
The man of words outlines wet islands
with his lips   55
on Nonnie Daylight's neck.

          She got stopped outside
          of Anadarko once.
          Red lights.
          You must be Indian, said   60
          the Oklahoma Highway Patrol.
          Of course they knew the history
          before switching on the lights.
          And when they rolled open the truck
          in the moist night,   65
          Was only going home,
          She said.

What voice
in the warm grass of her belly,
What planet?   70

Exercises

1. What is meant by the expression "language is movement" (line 1)?

2. Who is the speaker? What is being said?

3. Comment on the final image of the poem.

Topics for Writing

1. Compare a Petrarchan sonnet and a Shakespearean sonnet to show how
structure controls content.

2. Examine the following passage from Pope's *Essay on Criticism*.

True ease in writing comes from art, not chance,
As those move easiest who have learned to dance.
'Tis not enough no harshness gives offense,
The sound must seem an echo to the sense:
Soft is the strain when Zephyr gently blows,
And the smooth stream in smoother numbers flows;
But when loud surges lash the sounding shore,

The hoarse, rough verse should like the torrent roar;
When Ajax strives some rock's vast weight to throw,
The line too labors, and the words move slow;
Not so, when swift Camilla scours the plain,
Flies o'er the unbending corn, and skims along the main.

Show how the sound echoes the sense in this passage. What structural limits has the poet imposed upon himself? Do the restrictions of poetic form limit what the poet can say?

3. In an essay, consider the interrelation of meaning, imagery, rhythm, stanzaic patterns, and sound devices in two or three poems from this chapter. Evaluate the poems in terms of the criteria of insight, beauty, and emotion given in the introduction to the poetry section.

13. ALLUSION* AND SYMBOL

*a reference to a well known person, place or thing that adds its significance to the writer's meaning

T. S. Eliot said that the poet puts meaning in a poem "to satisfy one habit of the reader, to keep his mind diverted and quiet, while the poem does its work upon him: much as the imaginary burglar is always provided with a bit of nice meat for the house-dog." What Eliot meant is that, while there may be more important issues than meaning in poetry, we readers expect to find meaning, and the good poet tries to satisfy our expectations.

The poet has several ways of providing meaning, and the best is usually the one that makes it as unobtrusive as possible. That is to say, the poet works by indirection. Rather than announcing the poem's "meaning" with a moral tag at the end, the poet drops clues throughout that lead us to discover the meaning on our own. The poem as meaningful statement becomes a test of the best sort, for it is a test we cannot fail. The more we understand how the poet develops meaning, the better we can enjoy the test of feeling and intellect that each poem offers.

One favorite device that poets use to provide clues for their readers is **allusion.** While talking about one subject, the poet alludes to or plays upon another. We do not need to recognize the allusion to appreciate the poem, but it stands to reason that just as allusions add further dimensions to the experience in the poem, our recognition of them enriches our experience of the poem. There are as many types of allusions as of fields of human activity, but generally we can speak of four major categories: the historical, the classical, the biblical, and the literary. The following poem provides an interesting example of the first type, the historical allusion:

He didn't read the Illiad etc by Homer until Chapman translated it. He is the astronomer who finds a new planet / poet.

John Keats (1795–1821)

On First Looking into Chapman's Homer

Much have I traveled in the realms of gold,
   And many goodly states and kingdoms seen;
   Round many western islands have I been
Which bards in fealty to Apollo hold.
Oft of one wide expanse had I been told   5
   That deep-browed Homer ruled as his demesne;
   Yet did I never breathe its pure serene

Till I heard Chapman speak out loud and bold:
Then felt I like some watcher of the skies
When a new planet swims into his ken;   *10*
Or like stout Cortez when with eagle eyes
He stared at the Pacific — and all his men
Looked at each other with a wild surmise —
Silent, upon a peak in Darien.

Because Keats's poem is about reading George Chapman's Elizabethan translation of Homer's *Iliad,* we cannot really call references to Apollo and Homer
classical allusions; rather, they are part of the announced subject of the poem.
Keats *does* use an allusion in his reference to a historical incident, the European
discovery of the Pacific Ocean. By drawing a comparison between the new
world that he has discovered in a book and an important moment in the discovery of the New World, Keats emphasizes his own excitement. We have to
recognize the allusion, which simply requires that we know something of history.
Once that recognition is made, we sense more fully the excitement that Keats
must have felt, and because we make a discovery (solving a poetic clue) ourselves, we perhaps share in that excitement.

Exercises

1. There can be no doubt that Keats is making a historical allusion in his reference to Cortez standing on a peak in Darien and staring at the Pacific, an ocean
that until that moment had not existed for the European mind. However, Keats
had his facts wrong. It was not Cortez but Balboa, another early Spanish explorer, who discovered the Pacific Ocean in 1513. How might Keats's mistake
detract from the effectiveness of the allusion? How factually accurate should a
historical allusion be?

2. If we miss Keats's historical allusion altogether, does he still convey a measure of his excitement to us? By what means?

William Butler Yeats is especially renowned for using all manner of allusions
in his poetry. Allusions to classical mythology, ancient and contemporary history and historical figures, the Old Testament and the New, and literature —
sometimes his own earlier poems — abound in his work, creating a fabric of
reference and cross-reference so rich that we find in them an endless source of
fascination and discovery. The following poem is just one example:

William Butler Yeats (1865–1939)

Long-legged Fly

That civilization may not sink,
Its great battle lost,
Quiet the dog, tether the pony
To a distant post;
Our master Caesar is in the tent   5

Where the maps are spread,
His eyes fixed upon nothing,
A hand under his head.
Like a long-legged fly upon the stream
His mind moves upon silence.   *10*

That the topless towers be burnt
And men recall that face,
Move most gently if move you must
In this lonely place.
She thinks, part woman, three parts a child,   *15*
That nobody looks; her feet
Practice a tinker shuffle
Picked up on a street.
Like a long-legged fly upon the stream
Her mind moves upon silence.   *20*

That girls at puberty may find
The first Adam in their thought,
Shut the door of the Pope's chapel,†
Keep those children out.
There on that scaffolding reclines   *25*
Michael Angelo.
With no more sound than the mice make
His hand moves to and fro.
Like a long-legged fly upon the stream
His mind moves upon silence.   *30*

We could argue that since "our master Caesar" is mentioned in no specific historical context (for example, which of any number of Roman Caesars does Yeats mean?), that reference carries more of the symbolic than the allusive. (We shall consider symbols later.) But "the topless towers" that are to "be burnt" in the second stanza might remind us of the burning towers of Troy. The destruction of Troy, we now know, was a historical event; we are further reminded of Homer's *Iliad,* a classical work of literature that mythologizes that historical event. If we feel that we are letting ourselves get carried away by reading too much into a single line, the next line — "And men recall that face" — assures us that we are not wrong, but only if we catch the further allusion. It ought to remind us of the beautiful Helen, for whom the Trojan War was fought. Notice, however, that this is not only a historical allusion or simply a classical allusion to Homer, in whose great poem Helen appears. The very way in which Yeats phrases those two lines could remind us of another literary treatment of the same theme. From Christopher Marlowe's *Doctor Faustus,* a play written in the late sixteenth century, come these two lines:

Was this the face that launched a thousand ships
And burnt the topless towers of Ilium?

23. *Pope's chapel:* the Sistine
Chapel in the Vatican.

These lines are spoken by Faustus when he beholds Helen, whose spirit has been summoned up for him by Mephistophilis, a henchman of the Devil. The main thing for us to notice is how richly Yeats has combined historical, classical, and literary allusions in just two lines of poetry. As readers, we are given many points of entry to his meaning, depending on the extent of our knowledge of history and our experiences with literature. Again, once we recognize the allusions, even if only on one level, we can begin to work toward understanding Yeats's meaning.

Exercises

1. "The first Adam," "the Pope's chapel," and "Michael Angelo" appear in the third stanza. Are they allusions? If so, what type or types of allusions are they? How do they work upon one another to create meaning within the stanza?

2. Must we recognize the wealth of allusions in "Long-legged Fly" to be able to interpret its meaning? How, for example, does Yeats provide us with a tool for understanding his meaning with that image of a "long-legged fly upon a stream"? Furthermore, that image is presented to us as a simile. What comparisons are being made?

T. S. Eliot is another poet who works extensively with allusion, though he relies primarily upon literary allusions in much of his poetry. While we cannot possibly deal with the vast extent of those allusions, we can examine one aspect of them. We will look at a seventeenth-century poem that captured the imagination of many later poets, including Eliot.

Andrew Marvell (1621–1678)

To His Coy Mistress

Had we but world enough, and time,
This coyness, lady, were no crime.
We would sit down, and think which way
To walk, and pass our long love's day.
Thou by the Indian Ganges' side   5
Shoudst rubies find; I by the tide
Of Humber† would complain. I would
Love you ten years before the flood,
And you should, if you please, refuse
Till the conversion of the Jews.   10
My vegetable love should grow
Vaster than empires and more slow;
An hundred years should go to praise
Thine eyes, and on thy forehead gaze;

7. *Humber:* a river in England, near the poet's birthplace.

Two hundred to adore each breast,   *15*
But thirty thousand to the rest;
An age at least to every part,
And the last age should show your heart.
For, lady, you deserve this state,
Nor would I love at lower rate.   *20*
        But at my back I always hear
Time's wingéd chariot hurrying near;
And yonder all before us lie
Deserts of vast eternity.
Thy beauty shall no more be found;   *25*
Nor, in thy marble vault, shall sound
My echoing song; then worms shall try
That long-preserved virginity,
And your quaint honor† turn to dust,
And into ashes all my lust: *30*
The grave's a fine and private place,
But none, I think, do there embrace.
        Now therefore, while the youthful hue
Sits on thy skin like morning dew,
And while thy willing soul transpires   *35*
At every pore with instant fires,
Now let us sport us while we may,
And now, like amorous birds of prey,
Rather at once our time devour
Than languish in his slow-chapped† power.   *40*
Let us roll all our strength and all
Our sweetness up into one ball,†
And tear our pleasures with rough strife
Through the iron gates of life:
Thus, though we cannot make our sun   *45*
Stand still, yet we will make him run.

[handwritten margin notes: "death at the door (life expectancy is 40)" and "& it will no good when were dead" and "do it while we have the chance" and "hard times in life" and "you have to fight for pleasure through the hard times of life"]

Exercises

1. There are biblical allusions in Marvell's poem. How many can you identify? Discuss their significance.

2. "To His Coy Mistress" proceeds in the manner of a logical argument: major premise, minor premise, conclusion. Using Marvell's own logical connectives (*if, but, therefore*) to introduce each statement, paraphrase the argument in three brief statements of your own. From a purely logical point of view, is Marvell's conclusion valid? Why or why not?

3. How do the many references to time work with the geographical allusions to reinforce Marvell's argument?

29. *quaint honor:* sexual virtue.   42. *one ball:* a cannonball.
40. *slow-chapped:* slowly chewing.

"To His Coy Mistress" is a masterful and somewhat ironic statem[...]
age-old poetic theme, the *carpe diem* motif. Quite briefly, this motif [...]
questions of love and death, time's passage, and what use we should [...]
what little time we have. Once a statement as definitive as Marvell's [...]
later poets can return to it again and again in their own treatments o[...]
themes. The following poem is a modern variation:

T. S. Eliot (1888–1965)

The Love Song of J. Alfred Prufrock

> *S'io credesse che mia risposta fosse*
> *A persona che mai tornasse al mondo,*
> *Questa fiamma staria senza piu scosse.*
> *Ma perciocche giammai di questo fondo*
> *Non torno vivo alcun, s'i'odo il vero,*
> *Senza tema d'infamia ti rispondo.*

Let us go then, you and I,
When the evening is spread out against the sky
Like a patient etherized upon a table;
Let us go, through certain half-deserted streets,
The muttering retreats
Of restless nights in one-night cheap hotels
And sawdust restaurants with oyster-shells:
Streets that follow like a tedious argument
Of insidious intent
To lead you to an overwhelming question . . .
Oh, do not ask, "What is it?"
Let us go and make our visit.

In the room the women come and go
Talking of Michelangelo.

The yellow fog that rubs its back upon the window-panes
The yellow smoke that rubs its muzzle on the window-panes
Licked its tongue into the corners of the evening,
Lingered upon the pools that stand in drains,
Let fall upon its back the soot that falls from chimneys,
Slipped by the terrace, made a sudden leap,
And seeing that it was a soft October night,
Curled once about the house, and fell asleep.

And indeed there will be time
For the yellow smoke that slides along the street,
Rubbing its back upon the window-panes;
There will be time, there will be time
To prepare a face to meet the faces that you meet;
There will be time to murder and create,

And time for all the works and days† of hands
That lift and drop a question on your plate;   *30*
Time for you and time for me,
And time yet for a hundred indecisions,
And for a hundred visions and revisions,
Before the taking of a toast and tea.

In the room the women come and go   *35*
Talking of Michelangelo.

And indeed there will be time
To wonder, "Do I dare?" and, "Do I dare?"
Time to turn back and descend the stair,
With a bald spot in the middle of my hair —   *40*
[They will say: "How his hair is growing thin!"]
My morning coat, my collar mounting firmly to the chin,
My necktie rich and modest, but asserted by a simple pin —
[They will say: "But how his arms and legs are thin!"]
Do I dare   *45*
Disturb the universe?
In a minute there is time
For decisions and revisions which a minute will reverse.

For I have known them all already, known them all:
Have known the evenings, mornings, afternoons,   *50*
I have measured out my life with coffee spoons;
I know the voices dying with a dying fall
Beneath the music from a farther room.
      So how should I presume?

And I have known the eyes already, known them all —   *55*
The eyes that fix you in a formulated phrase,
And when I am formulated, sprawling on a pin,
When I am pinned and wriggling on the wall,
Then how should I begin
To spit out all the butt-ends of my days and ways?   *60*
      And how should I presume?

And I have known the arms already, known them all —
Arms that are braceleted and white and bare
[But in the lamplight, downed with light brown hair!]
Is it perfume from a dress   *65*
That makes me so digress?
Arms that lie along a table, or wrap about a shawl.
      And should I then presume?
      And how should I begin?

                     .   .   .   .   .   .

Shall I say, I have gone at dusk through narrow streets   *70*
And watched the smoke that rises from the pipes

    29. *works and days:* title of a
    poem on rural life by Hesiod.

Of lonely men in shirt-sleeves, leaning out of windows? . . .

I should have been a pair of ragged claws
Scuttling across the floors of silent seas.

> . . . . . .

And the afternoon, the evening, sleeps so peacefully!   75
Smoothed by long fingers,
Asleep . . . tired . . . or it malingers,
Stretched on the floor, here beside you and me.
Should I, after tea and cakes and ices,
Have the strength to force the moment to its crisis?   80
But though I have wept and fasted, wept and prayed,
Though I have seen my head [grown slightly bald] brought in upon a
    platter,
I am no prophet† — and here's no great matter;
I have seen the moment of my greatness flicker,
And I have seen the eternal Footman hold my coat, and snicker,   85
And in short, I was afraid.

And would it have been worth it, after all,
After the cups, the marmalade, the tea,
Among the porcelain, among some talk of you and me,
Would it have been worth while,   90
To have bitten off the matter with a smile,
To have squeezed the universe into a ball
To roll it toward some overwhelming question,
To say: "I am Lazarus, come from the dead,
Come back to tell you all, I shall tell you all" —   95
If one, settling a pillow by her head,
    Should say: "That is not what I meant at all.
    That is not it, at all."

And would it have been worth it, after all,
Would it have been worth while,   100
After the sunsets and the dooryards and the sprinkled streets,
After the novels, after the teacups, after the skirts that trail along the
    floor —
And this, and so much more? —
It is impossible to say just what I mean!
But as if a magic lantern threw the nerves in patterns on a screen: 105
Would it have been worth while
If one, settling a pillow or throwing off a shawl,
And turning toward the window, should say:
    "That is not it at all,
    That is not what I meant, at all."   110

> . . . . . .

No! I am not Prince Hamlet, nor was meant to be;
Am an attendant lord, one that will do

83. *prophet:* John the Baptist
(Matthew 14).

To swell a progress, start a scene or two,
Advise the prince; no doubt, an easy tool,
Deferential, glad to be of use,   *115*
Politic, cautious, and meticulous;
Full of high sentence, but a bit obtuse;
At times, indeed, almost ridiculous —
Almost, at times, the Fool.†

I grow old . . . I grow old . . .   *120*
I shall wear the bottoms of my trousers rolled.

Shall I part my hair behind? Do I dare to eat a peach?
I shall wear white flannel trousers, and walk upon the beach.
I have heard the mermaids singing, each to each.

I do not think that they will sing to me.   *125*

I have seen them riding seaward on the waves
Combing the white hair of the waves blown back
When the wind blows the water white and black.

We have lingered in the chambers of the sea
By sea-girls wreathed with seaweed red and brown   *130*
Till human voices wake us, and we drown.

Exercises

1. "The Love Song of J. Alfred Prufrock" obviously deals with the question of love and time. Where in this unquestionably complex poem does Eliot allude to Marvell's poem on the same theme? What use does Eliot make of Marvell's imagery?

2. There is also a reference to Lazarus in "Prufrock." What type of allusion does that reference constitute? What does it tell us about Prufrock's view of himself? How does Prufrock's idea of what the women's reaction would be give us still further insights into his character?

3. Is the Michelangelo the women in "Prufrock" talk about the same Michael Angelo we met in Yeats's poem? If we find each poet making different use of the same historical figure, how does each poet nevertheless require that we have some general sense of who Michelangelo is?

Even the epigraph to "Prufrock" is a literary allusion. The verses are taken from Dante's *Inferno* (Canto XXVII, lines 61–66). Translated, they read:

If I thought my answer were given
To anyone who would ever return to the world,
This flame would stand still without moving any further.
But since never from this abyss

119. *the Fool:* a frequent figure in
Shakespeare's plays.

Has anyone ever returned alive, if what I hear is true,
Without fear of infamy I answer you.
>   *Dante,* The Divine Comedy (*as*
>   *translated by Russell E. Murphy*)

These words are spoken for Dante by Guido da Montefeltro, who is being punished in the Eighth Circle of Hell for giving false counsel.

Exercise

Though Eliot quotes Dante, on what grounds might we argue that the lines translated above are actually a literary allusion, that is, a reference that we must recognize if it is to create meaning? How do those lines comment on the character of Prufrock? On the poem "The Love Song of J. Alfred Prufrock"?

By now, we might conclude that poets ask a lot of us in their use of allusions, whatever their sources. They seem to demand a great deal of reading and a wide knowledge of our history and culture. It would be foolish to deny that with poets such as Yeats and Eliot, that is precisely the point. To understand their poetry, we must have other experience in literature. Without that experience, such poetry is difficult, but not inaccessible, as we shall see in our discussion of the symbol. Some poets, however, make allusions that we can understand from watching television, listening to the radio, going to the movies, and keeping abreast of contemporary events.

Sylvia Plath (*1932–1963*)

Daddy

You do not do, you do not do
Any more, black shoe
In which I have lived like a foot
For thirty years, poor and white,
Barely daring to breathe or Achoo.   5

Daddy, I have had to kill you.
You died before I had time —
Marble-heavy, a bag full of God,
Ghastly statue with one grey toe
Big as a Frisco seal   10

And a head in the freakish Atlantic
Where it pours bean green over blue
In the waters off beautiful Nauset.
I used to pray to recover you.
Ach, du.   15

In the German tongue, in the Polish town
Scraped flat by the roller

Of wars, wars, wars.
But the name of the town is common.
My Polack friend   *20*

Says there are a dozen or two.
So I never could tell where you
Put your foot, your root,
I never could talk to you.
The tongue stuck in my jaw.   *25*

It stuck in a barb wire snare.
Ich, ich, ich, ich,
I could hardly speak.
I thought every German was you.
And the language obscene   *30*

An engine, an engine
Chuffing me off like a Jew.
A Jew to Dachau, Auschwitz, Belsen.
I began to talk like a Jew.
I think I may well be a Jew.   *35*

The snows of the Tyrol, the clear beer of Vienna
Are not very pure or true.
With my gypsy ancestress and my weird luck
And my Taroe pack† and my Taroe pack
I may be a bit of a Jew.   *40*

I have always been scared of *you*,
With your Luftwaffe, your gobbledygoo.
And your neat moustache
And your Aryan eye, bright blue,
Panzer-man, panzer-man, O You —   *45*

Not God but a swastika
So black no sky could squeak through.
Every woman adores a Fascist,
The boot in the face, the brute
Brute heart of a brute like you.   *50*

You stand at the blackboard, daddy,
In the picture I have of you,
A cleft in your chin instead of your foot
But no less a devil for that, no not
Any less the black man who   *55*

Bit my pretty red heart in two.
I was ten when they buried you.
At twenty I tried to die
And get back, back, back to you.
I thought even the bones would do.   *60*

39. *Taroe pack:* cards used for
telling the future.

But they pulled me out of the sack,
And they stuck me together with glue,
And then I knew what to do.
I made a model of you,
A man in black with a Meinkampf† look   65

And a love of the rack and the screw.
And I said I do, I do.
So daddy, I'm finally through.
The black telephone's off at the root,
The voices just can't worm through.   70

If I've killed one man, I've killed two —
The vampire who said he was you
And drank my blood for a year,
Seven years, if you want to know.
Daddy, you can lie back now.   75

There's a stake in your fat black heart
And the villagers never liked you.
They are dancing and stamping on you.
They always *knew* it was you.
Daddy, daddy, you bastard, I'm through.   80

Exercises

1. What is Plath alluding to with her mention of "Dachau, Auschwitz, Belsen"? Identify the other allusions to the same historical events and discuss how they establish a basis of meaning in the poem.

2. Plath also talks about "a vampire" and "a stake in your fat black heart." To what is she alluding? How does that mode of allusion comment upon the other allusions? What do both have to do with the fact that the poem is apparently addressed to her father?

Imamu Amiri Baraka   *(LeRoi Jones, 1934–   )*

In Memory of Radio

Who has ever stopped to think of the divinity of Lamont Cranston?
(Only Jack Kerouac, that I know of: & me.
The rest of you probably had on WCBS and Kate Smith,
Or something equally unattractive.)

65. *Meinkampf:* title of an anti-Semitic treatise by Adolf Hitler.

What can I say?   5
It is better to have loved and lost
Than to put linoleum in your living rooms?

Am I a sage or something?
Mandrake's hypnotic gesture of the week?
(Remember, I do not have the healing powers of Oral Roberts . . .   10
I cannot, like F. J. Sheen, tell you how to get saved & *rich!*
I cannot even order you to gaschamber satori like Hitler or Goody
    Knight

& Love is an evil word.
Turn it backwards/see, what I mean?
An evol word. & besides   15
Who understands it?
I certainly wouldn't like to go out on that kind of limb.

Saturday mornings we listened to *Red Lantern* & his undersea folk.
At 11, *Let's Pretend*/& we did/& I, the poet, still do, Thank God!

What was it he used to say (after the transformation, when he was
    safe   20
& invisible & the unbelievers couldn't throw stones?) "Heh, heh, heh,
Who knows what evil lurks in the hearts of men? The Shadow
    knows."

O, yes he does
O, yes he does.
An evil word it is,   25
This Love.

Exercises

1. Baraka makes many open allusions to old radio programs and to relatively
recent celebrities. How many are related to radio as a vehicle for entertainment? How are the others connected with radio? How does Baraka use the
first group to comment on the second? What meaning is thus derived from the
poem?

2. Though they are all allusions to events in his own lifetime (within less than
the last half-century), some of Baraka's allusions may seem as obscure to you
as those of Yeats and Eliot. How do you account for that apparent obscurity?
Does Baraka imply an awareness of such a limitation to his allusions?

   Very often a poem's allusive quality can be caught in its title. The following
poem is richer and more rewarding for us if we catch the allusions in the names
"Patrice" and "Cuchulain."

Michael S. Harper (1938–

Love Medley: Patrice Cuchulain

"Stirrups, leggings, a stainless
steel slide, a dishpan, sheet,
a thread spool, scissors,
three facemasks, smocks, paper
overshoes, a two-way mirror, dials:"   5
the head and left arm
cruise out, almost together,
and you drop into gloves,
your own ointment
pulling your legs   10
binding your cord; the cheesed
surface skin, your dark
hairless complexion, the metallic room,
orchestrate and blow up your lungs,
clogged on protein and vitamins,   15
for the sterile whine of the delivery
room and your staff of attendants.
It is free exercise when the cord's
cut; you weigh in for the clean up
as your mother gets her local   20
for her stitches: boy, 6′ 13″.

As you breathe easily, your mother's
mother is tubed and strapped,
hemorrhaging slowly from her varices;†
your two dead brothers who could   25
not breathe are berries
gone to rot at our table:
what is birth but death
with complexity: blood, veins,
machinery and love: our names.   30

Clearly, this poem is about the birth of a male child. It does not really matter whether the baby was actually ever christened "Patrice Cuchulain." What does matter are the hopes and aspirations the poet expresses for the infant by alluding to two heroic personages in the title of a poem written to celebrate the child's birth. The first is a figure out of very recent history: Patrice Lumumba (1925–1961). An African nationalist, Lumumba was instrumental in the early political development of Zaire, formerly the Belgian Congo; he was assassinated in 1961 by fellow Africans opposed to his dream of making Zaire a self-sufficient Third World nation, independent of its former white colonial overlords. Cuchulain, on the other hand, is a figure from old Irish myth. A king and warrior, Cuchulain too is a model of fierce and heroic independence, as well as of visionary zeal for his people's well-being in the face of their enemies. Once you

---

24. *varices:* varicose veins.

are made aware of Cuchulain's Irish roots, the name Patrice might further remind you of Ireland's patron saint, Patrick — yet another figure that personifies courage and self-sacrifice for the sake of a cause the hero believes in.

Exercises

1. What do the allusions in the poem's title suggest the speaker's expectations are for the newborn child? Harper is black and American. Do these facts make his expectations and hopes much more justified and understandable to you? Why do you suppose the allusions cross both cultural and racial barriers?

2. How does the poem illustrate the fact that the newborn infant, like the heroes his name will encourage him to emulate, is "larger than life"?

3. A miraculous birth is often an attribute of the mythical hero. Although this birth clearly took place in a modern hospital, what statements in the poem indicate that this infant's birth is regarded as a miraculous event?

"Love Medley: Patrice Cuchulain" reminds us that even our names can contain allusions to the dreams our parents had for us when we were born. As we grow to maturity, we may try to live up to those great expectations, or perhaps we find that another name and the sort of life it signifies sum up the aspirations that have become ours, and ours alone. We would do well to remember that allusions are ways of *naming* concepts that would otherwise remain vague and abstract, the subject more of the philosopher than of the poet. The next poem, too, is built around the significance attached to a name.

alta (1942–

The Vow

for Anne Hutchinson

```
sister,
your name is not a household word.
maybe you had a 2 line description
in 8th grade history.
more likely you were left out,                              5
as i am when men converse in my presence.
Anne Hutchinson:
"a woman of haughty & free carriage."
my shoulders staighten.
you are dead, but not as dead as you                      10
have been, we will avenge you.
you and all the nameless brave spirits,
my mother, my grandmothers,
great grandmothers (Breen Northcott, butcher's wife,
the others forgotten.) who bore me?                         15
```

generations of denial & misuse
who bore those years of waste? sisters & mothers
it is too late for all of you. waste
& waste again, life after life,
shot to hell. it will take more   *20*
than a husband with a nation behind him
to stop me now.

Anne Hutchinson (1591?–1643), to whom the poem is dedicated and to whom the poet alludes in the text, was among the earliest settlers of the Massachusetts Bay Colony. Like Roger Williams, she and a small band of followers split with the original group over questions of religious freedom, which the Pilgrims had come to the New World to establish. Celebrated now as an early advocate of freedom of religion —one of the principles on which our nation was subsequently founded —Hutchinson is also credited with founding the city of Newport, Rhode Island.

Exercises

1. Why does the poet, who is a woman, say that now Anne Hutchinson is "not as dead as you/have been" (lines 10 and 11)? What specific attitudes and values does Hutchinson represent for the poet? What particular social phenomenon does Hutchinson's relative obscurity signify for the poet?

2. What is the vow that the poet makes? Does she make it only to Anne Hutchinson? Does she see Anne Hutchinson only as an advocate of religious freedom, as the history books do?

3. "Your name is not a household word" (line 2) is both a pun on the traditional role of women in our society and an allusion to a very recent figure on the American political scene. What is the pun? Who is that political figure? How does alta's allusion to him further underscore the poem's general theme: that women have had little say in the affairs of nations?

If we were to define allusion in poetry now, we might say that it is any reference to a piece of information or to an experience that we readers may have had. The poet has the right to assume that the general reader has read parts of the Bible, is familiar with other works of literature, and knows some bare-bone facts of history. At the very least, that general reader goes to the movies, watches old movies on television, listens to the radio, and reads the newspaper. Still, we might argue, the poet *is* asking a lot, and such a general reader is more of an ideal than any particular one of us. However, there are allusions that require only that we are alive and reasonably aware of the world around us. When the poet refers to the sun and the moon, to the seasons, to flowers and birds, trees, the sea, or any number of other natural objects or occurrences, he or she is, in a manner of speaking, alluding to them. The poet expects us to bring our own experiences of nature to bear on the poem as we read it. Because these natural phenomena, like some historical and biblical figures, are common knowledge, we call them **symbols** rather than allusions, which sometimes require specialized knowledge. For our purposes, then, let us call a symbol an allusion to something or someone whose significance has become a part of our common human and cultural store.

The particular strength of a symbol as a poetic device lies partly in the fact that we do not need to be especially well informed or literary to appreciate it. Furthermore, while the symbol is suggestive, working more on implication (connotation) than on explicit meaning (denotation), its strength lies also in our ability to identify it immediately for what it is, whether we all agree on its symbolic value or meaning. For example, if we turn back to Yeats's "Long-legged Fly," we find that "the Pope's chapel" and the image of Michael Angelo lying on a scaffold ask us to have some special knowledge of history. We have to know that Pope Julius commissioned Michelangelo to paint scenes from providential history on the ceiling of the Sistine Chapel and that Michelangelo had to set up an elaborate scaffolding to do so. The references to "our master Caesar" and even to "the first Adam," however, are hardly obscure to us as the inheritors of Judaic and Roman culture. Although those references are equally laden with meaning, that meaning is more symbolic than allusive in quality.

All we really need know to begin to interpret what Yeats means is that "the first Adam" is indeed the first Adam, the Adam of the Garden of Eden. All the significance that comes to mind when each of us thinks of the story of Adam and Eve, the Garden, the Tree of the Knowledge of Good and Evil, the Temptation, the Fall, the expulsion from the Garden, and so forth is compacted into the one simple reference; and Yeats can so compress his meaning because Adam is a name immediately identifiable with the story of the Creation. The same holds true for "our master Caesar." The word *Caesar* has become such a symbol for vast secular authority that both the Germans and the Russians have used it as a title for their own secular leaders, the Kaiser and the czar. With that one reference, Yeats again compresses an unlimited number of potential meanings related to worldly power, the glory of kings, the responsibilities of leadership, the bounds of duty and allegiance, and the transient nature of all secular states and leaders. Reconsidering Yeats's poems, we should find its meaning becoming more accessible, though more open-ended as well. Because symbols compact their meanings with an incredible intensity, we cannot easily reduce symbolic statement to any neat formulation of meaning, a prose paraphrase. Yeats called poetic symbolism "hints too subtle for the intellect," and we would do well to keep his warning in mind.

A further warning is necessary at this point. Once students are introduced to symbols and symbolic statements, they sometimes tend not to take a poet's words at their face, or literal, value. Never leap to the conclusion that a particular reference in a poem is intended wholly symbolically unless the symbolic meaning you attach to it coheres with all the other thematic and symbolic considerations that the poem brings to mind.

Exercises

1. We have discussed "the first Adam" as both allusion and symbol. How does it directly relate to Michelangelo and the Sistine Chapel?

2. In view of the foregoing discussion, how might both the long-legged fly and the stream in Yeats's poem be regarded as symbols? For what?

Topic for Writing

While it is not the best mode of critical interpretation, paraphrase can often help us discern the difference between the literal and the figurative, or symbolic. Stanza by stanza, write a paraphrase of Yeats's "Long-legged Fly." Work out the literal meaning for each stanza before you go on to consider its symbolic significance.

Traditionally, poets have relied on the commonality of human experiences through history and varying cultures to provide them with their stock of symbols. These symbols originate in folklore and folk customs — and, Carl Jung would argue, in our collective unconscious when we dream. The poet appropriates them later, thereby establishing a literary tradition for each symbol. Unaware that these traditions began in the streets, so to speak, and not in the academies, the average reader is often intimidated by a poem that seems to depend on symbols for its meaning. Yet symbols, we should remember, are always accessible to us because they are derived from countless human encounters with the object or concept being symbolized. We only need to trust our own experiences, as well as our general understanding of the connotative value of the symbol in question. A sewer rat, for example, is very unlikely to have a positive meaning for any of us, whether we encounter one in our own back yard or in someone else's poem. A unicorn, on the other hand, can only mean something positive, wherever we encounter it. If we come to believe that a poet means to use a given symbol because he or she shares our attitudes toward it, we will find ourselves much less puzzled by poetic symbols. They are really *human* symbols.

The following sonnet illustrates how a poet relies on the symbolic or connotative values of words to imply meaning without foisting a particular meaning upon us.

Robert Frost (1874–1963)

Design

I found a dimpled spider, fat and white,
On a white heal-all,† holding up a moth
Like a white piece of rigid satin cloth —
Assorted characters of death and blight
Mixed ready to begin the morning right,   5
Like the ingredients of a witches' broth —
A snow-drop spider, a flower like froth,
And dead wings carried like a paper kite.

What had that flower to do with being white,
The wayside blue and innocent heal-all?   10
What brought the kindred spider to that height,
Then steered the white moth thither in the night?
What but design of darkness to appall? —
If design govern in a thing so small.

2. *heal-all:* a wildflower, generally blue.

Exercises

1. By the end of the octave, has Frost made us think of the spider, the flower, and the moth as something more than a spider, a flower, and a moth? If so, have they gained a symbolic significance? Explain.

2. How do simile and metaphor function in the octave? To what extent do they help to establish the spider, the flower, and the moth as symbols?

3. Whiteness and darkness are usually viewed as opposites. Are they opposites here?

Topic for Writing

In an essay, discuss Frost's use of the spider as a symbol in comparison with Walt Whitman's use in "A Noiseless Patient Spider" (Chapter 10). How does each poet indicate a symbolic meaning in his statements? One thing we must decide is whether the phrase "assorted characters of blight and death" in Frost's poem is a symbolic statement or a direct statement of the meaning the poet wants us to derive from his symbols.

The next poem could not have been written before the recent development of inexpensive pocket calculators; it could not have been written, either, if the past fifty years and more of literary practice and studies had not made us all more conscious of the nature of symbolic statement as a poetic device.

Miller Williams (1930–

Believing in Symbols

1.

One morning I put in the pocket of my shirt
not having put two and two together
a little calculator. That afternoon
it lay on my desk and turned out 8s for hours,
shorted through by those rippling shocks   5
the sinus node sends out, now beat, now beat.

So what do we say for science and the heart?
So with reason the heart will have its way?

Believeing in symbols has led us into war,
if sometimes into bed with interesting people.   10

2.

8 becomes in the time of solid state
the figure all the figures are made from,
the enabling number, the all-fathering 8;

1 through 7, also nothing and 9,
are all pieces of 8 which is only itself.   *15*

This makes a certain sense if you look at the sign
that says infinity, the Mobius strip,
a lazy 8 hung on the gates of Heaven.

The pterodactyl, Pompeii, the Packard;
things take their turns. 3 and 7 are only   *20*
numbers again. Nothing stays for long.
Not to say that physics will ever fail us
or plain love, either, for that matter.
Like the sides of a coin, they may take turns,
or flipping fast enough, may seem to merge.   *25*

Call it, if you call it, in the air.
When the coin comes down, the tent comes down.
You look around, and there is nothing there.
Not even the planets. Not even the names of the planets.

Exercises

1. What does the poet mean when he says that symbols have "led us into war"? "Into bed with interesting people"? (Think of what you mean when you call someone a sex symbol.)

2. What does the poet ask us to make of his insight that "8 becomes in the time of solid state/the figure all the figures are made from" (lines 11 and 12)? Do you accept his conclusion that, with regard to symbols, "nothing stays for long"? Does the poet think that that is true only of symbols? How does the poem make it quite clear that he does not? (Look for several allusions.)

3. Williams also talks about the way in which symbols enable us to connect the real (the planets) with the imaginary (the names of the planets). Finally, he implies that without our penchant for symbols, we would have little understanding of the relationship between ourselves and the rest of the universe. How does Williams make a coin a symbol for the connections that he feels exist between us and other created objects, as well as between symbols and the objects symbolized? What does he imagine would happen if those connections were severed?

Topic for Writing

Think of another modern invention or development — space flight, for example, or heart-transplant operations — that has altered a traditional symbol or symbols. Then discuss in an essay how that alteration has changed our sense of the relationships and meanings those symbols previously suggested. What does the moon mean to those who have seen people walking on it? Do we still regard the heart as the center of an individual's emotions? (Like poetry, science alters our view of reality.)

Judith Moffett (1942–

Biology Lesson

The wet glass of cover slip and slide
sandwiches a world. Spiraling
blunt creatures live in it
whose beating cilia outstrip
thick thumbs that orbit them from side to side   5
under a colossal eye.

The Paramecium's† *Sex Life!* Ordinary
fission — anticlimactic thing,
a latitudinal split
athwart that homely length of lip   10
the "buccal groove" — comes later, and is very
ordinary.

But first these beasts, dumb, unicellular,
mindless, achieve by blind desire
what we who speak and think   15
must fight for: two by two they press
their buccal grooves together; then each pair
exchanges nucleoplasm.

They do. They do. One animal gives up part
of itself and gets an equivalent share   20
out of the other. The link
breaks after this, the deep long kiss
unseals. So fortified, they separate,
each to its schism.

Williams's poem may appear to be difficult if you fail to recognize that notions of symbolic relationships between mankind and nature are as old as the first
Homo sapiens who worshiped the sun or the ocean or a volcano. Our symbols,
and our continuing belief in their aptness, are ways to put a human face on actions and events that are really quite indifferent to humans. The yew tree in the
cemetery does not know that it is symbolic of life's triumph over death; the sun
does not know that shrines and temples have been built in its honor. Nevertheless, symbols are important, because they enhance our understanding of our
place in the scheme of things and of the relationship among all things. In "Biology Lesson," a real act — the reproduction of paramecia — becomes symbolic
of another, no less real action, that series of events called lovemaking, which in
many cases leads humans to perform the same biological function as these two
paramecia.

7. *paramecium:* a single-cell animal.

Exercises

1. The poet makes much of the paramecium's "buccal groove." What is a buccal groove, in plain English? What is the groove's relationship to "the deep long kiss"? How do both object and action become symbolic of human aspects of love and lovemaking? (Keep in mind that symbols are often not the thing itself but representative of it; for example, a lion is not a king but a representation of kingliness. Sometimes, however, the line is blurred; for instance, the Caesars, symbolic now of immense earthly power, were in fact kings.)

2. What word in the last two lines, which on the surface merely describe the separation of the paramecia, adds a symbolically human and emotional quality to that action? Is that word a symbol? What passage in the poem makes it quite clear that the poet does want us to think of human love as she describes the paramecia in clinical detail?

3. "The Paramecium's Sex Life" is a direct allusion to a famous 1930s comedy sketch by Robert Benchley, who parodied boring public lectures made to sound interesting and enticing. How does that allusion underscore the poem's real subject, which is not paramecia but the sexual aspects of human love?

No doubt the best way to conclude this discussion of symbols would be to allow you to trace the development of a particular symbol for the purposes of comparison and contrast. As we have been discovering, some objects are so readily susceptible to symbolic interpretations that poets do not need to invent those objects' symbolic significance but only need to make use of it. Common usage allows us to see how the eagle and the lion have come to symbolize royalty, fierce independence, and the pride of power; how the cross has come to represent self-sacrifice, suffering, humility, and spiritual salvation; how clouds are synonymous with vagueness and bewilderment, while blue skies mean clarity and bright prospects; or how the ocean reminds us of vast power, tranquil in its own self-knowledge or mindless in its rage. The list of natural objects and phenomena that have come to acquire rather specific and virtually universal symbolic significance is not endless, but it is certainly very long, and we can add an equally long list of manmade objects and events.

High on any list of symbols is a simple flower, the rose. The following selection of poems, which begins in the sixteenth century and ends in the 1970s, demonstrates only a smattering of the symbolic significance which that flower has obtained among our poets. While you will ask individual questions about each poem, you should read and study them as a group to realize the full benefit of the concluding exercise.

Edmund Spenser (ca. 1552–1599)

Sonnet 81

Fayre is my love, when her fayre golden heares,
With the loose wynd ye waving chance to marke:
Fayre when the rose in her red cheekes appeares,

Or in her eyes the fyre of love does sparke.
Fayre when her brest lyke a rich laden barke,   5
With pretious merchandize she forth doth lay:
Fayre when that cloud of pryde, which oft doth dark
Her goodly light with smiles she drives away.
But fayrest she, when so she doth display,
The gate with pearles and rubyes richly dight: 10
Throgh which her words so wise do make their way
To beare the message of her gentle spright.
The rest be works of natures wonderment,
But this the worke of harts astonishment.

Exercises

1. What does "the rose in her red cheekes" (line 3) mean? The poem as a whole
is a conceit, an extended figure of speech often hinging on exaggeration. In
that context, do you see any symbolic value in the rose? Explain.

2. How does the poet finally make what appears to be a catalogue of his beloved's physical attributes into a comment on her spiritual being? Does the rose
play any part in that process?

William Shakespeare (1564–1616)

Sonnet 130

My mistress' eyes are nothing like the sun;
Coral is far more red than her lips' red;
If snow be white, why then her breasts are dun;
If hairs be wires, black wires grow on her head.
I have seen roses damasked, red and white.   5
But no such roses see I in her cheeks;
And in some perfumes is there more delight
Than in the breath that from my mistress reeks.
I love to hear her speak, yet well I know
That music hath a far more pleasing sound;   10
I grant I never saw a goddess go;
My mistress, when she walks, treads on the ground.
And yet, by heaven, I think my love as rare
As any she belied with false compare.

Exercises

1. What does the absence of roses from Shakespeare's mistress's cheeks suggest
to you? What conditioned reflex in his readers is Shakespeare depending on in
order to achieve his final effect?

2. Sonnet 130 is a fine example of a poet's eschewing the figurative for the sake of a sincere literalism. Does he convince you of his sincerity? How? How much does his success depend on other poets, Edmund Spenser among them, who used "false compare"?

3. Consider how Shakespeare makes fun here of the "false compare" that poets of his time indulged in. Is exaggeration as much a part of this sonnet as it is of Spenser's? Note the figures of speech in Sonnet 130. Do any of them suggest to you that the poet is engaged in mockery?

Topic for Writing

Evaluate Spenser's sonnet as a tribute and Shakespeare's sonnet as a piece of literary criticism.

William Blake (1757–1827)

The Sick Rose

O Rose, thou art sick.
The invisible worm
That flies in the night
In the howling storm

Has found out thy bed   5
Of crimson joy,
And his dark secret love
Does thy life destroy

Exercise

Granted that it is a real rose, what else might Blake's sick rose represent? In formulating your answer, you should consider what "the invisible worm" symbolizes.

Paul Laurence Dunbar (1872–1906)

Promise

I grew a rose within a garden fair,
And, tending it with more than loving care,
I thought how, with the glory of its bloom,
I should the darkness of my life illume;

And, watching, ever smiled to see the lusty bud   *5*
Drink freely in the summer sun to tinct its blood.

My rose began to open, and its hue
Was sweet to me as to it sun and dew;
I watched it taking on its ruddy flame
Until the day of perfect blooming came,   *10*
Then hasted I with smiles to find it blushing red —
Too late! Some thoughtless child had plucked my rose and fled!

Exercises

1. Is there anything in Dunbar's poem to suggest that the rose is not just a rose? If you were tempted to find symbols in the poem, you have just had an excellent lesson in the dangers of reading poetry for symbolic statements. What are those dangers?

2. Whatever your response to question 1, what are some other, less literal interpretations we can find when we think of the symbolic values assigned to the rose?

Topic for Writing

Develop an interpretation for Dunbar's "Promise," assigning symbolic values not only to the rose but to the garden in which it was planted, the thoughtless child, etc. Let your imagination run free.

John Crowe Ransom   (1888–1974)

Piazza Piece†

— I am a gentleman in a dustcoat trying
To make you hear. Your ears are soft and small
And listen to an old man not at all,
They want the young men's whispering and sighing.
But see the roses on your trellis dying   *5*
And hear the spectral singing of the moon;
For I must have my lovely lady soon,
I am a gentleman in a dustcoat trying.

— I am a lady young in beauty waiting
Until my truelove comes, and then we kiss.   *10*
But what gray man among the vines is this

Title: a piazza is a spacious front
porch.

Whose words are dry and faint as in a dream?
Back from my trellis, Sir, before I scream!
I am a lady young in beauty waiting.

Exercises

1. What is a dustcoat? Does it acquire a figurative or symbolic value as the poem continues? If so, what is that value? Do you think that the poet wants us to take the dustcoat literally or figuratively? Is there any way that you can be certain? How?

2. Why does the old man call the young woman's attention to "the roses on your trellis dying" (line 5)?

Topic for Writing

Compare Ransom's treatment of the *carpe diem* theme to Marvell's treatment of that same theme in "To His Coy Mistress," found earlier in this chapter.

William Carlos Williams (1883–1963)

The Rose

The rose is obsolete
but each petal ends in
an edge, the double facet
cementing the grooved
columns of air — The edge   5
cuts without cutting
meets — nothing — renews
itself in metal or porcelain —

wither? It ends —

But if it ends   10
the start is begun
so that to engage roses
becomes a geometry —

Sharper, neater, more cutting
figured in majolica —   15
the broken plate
glazed with a rose

Somewhere the sense
makes copper roses
steel roses —   20

The rose carried weight of love
but love is at an end — of roses
It is at the edge of the
petal that love waits

Crips, worked to defeat   *25*
laboredness — fragile
plucked, moist, half-raised
cold, precise, touching

What

The place between the petal's   *30*
edge and the

From the petal's edge a line starts
that being of steel
infinitely fine, infinitely
rigid penetrates   *35*

the Milky Way
without contact — lifting
from it — neither hanging
nor pushing —

The fragility of the flower   *40*
unbruised
penetrates space.

Exercises

1. What does Williams mean when he says that "the rose is obsolete"? How can a flower become obsolete?

2. How do you interpret the final lines, "The fragility of the flower/unbruised/penetrates space"? Look for a figurative as well as a literal level of the statement, and think of both inner and outer spaces.

Marcela Christine Lucero

Roseville, Minn., U.S.A.

In Roseville, one notices
    a speck on a white wall
    a moustache on a brown face
and listens to right wing dilemmas
    of another race.   *5*

Turn that corrido† record down,
    walk softly in ponchos,

6. *corrido:* a border folk song.

Speak Spanish in whispers
 or they'll approach you to say,
  "I've been to Spain too, ¡Ole!"   *10*
 (even if you never have),
In Roseville, U.S.A.

Start the stove fan,
 close the windows on a summer day,
  'cause the neighbors might say,   *15*
  "Do they eat beans everyday, even on Sundays?"
In Roseville, U.S.A.

At the sign of the first snowflake
 Inquiring eyes will pursue you,
  asking why you haven't returned with the migrant stream *20*
 that went back in June, or even in September,
In Roseville, U.S.A.

My abuela† would turn in her grave
 to think that the culmination
 of her cultural perpetuation   *25*
 is Marcela at Target's food section
 searching desperately for flour tortillas,
No way — I live in ROSEVILLE, U.S.A.
My modus vivendi
 of New Mexico piñon and green chili   *30*
and my Colorado Southwest mentality
are another reality
in ROSEVILLE, U.S.A.

Exercises

1. Roseville, Minnesota, is a real city, but it becomes a symbol in this poem — a symbol of what?

2. Do the positive values we have come to associate with *rose* and *rosy* remain positive here? Explain, pointing to specific lines in the poem that support or negate the positive associations.

3. How does the poet speak of Roseville? Bitterly? Matter-of-factly? Enviously? How do you know?

Topics for Writing

1. The rose is one of the most common poetic symbols in our culture, and one of the most enduring. Readers have not become tired of hearing about roses, however, only because of the awareness of good poets that the rose as a poetic

---

23. *abuela:* grandmother.

symbol can fade just as surely as the real flower can. Put simply, any symbol, because its value rests on its commonality, can be overused. Thus, what was once a discovery of vivid resemblances can lose its freshness and vitality. In the actual beauty of the rose, its fragrance, its fragility, its need for care and cultivation, its short life, and even its protective thorns, poets have always found symbolic equivalents to the facts of human youth and beauty, life and love and death. Each of the preceding seven poems presents us with a rose; they are arranged chronologically. Having read them as a unit, consider how each poet uses the rose as a symbol. Does he or she use it in its traditional symbolic function or play games with that function? Does he or she deal with the rose on a literal level, letting your awareness of its symbolic qualities act upon you? Does the poet make you confront it as a symbol, but then try to make you see new dimensions to its enduring symbolic qualities? In an essay, compare and contrast the use of the rose as a symbol by any three poets discussed in this chapter.

2. Discuss how Eliot's allusions to Marvell in "The Love Song of J. Alfred Prufrock" function as a comment on Prufrock's character and his possible dilemma.

3. Explicate the Yeats poem, using symbolic values for the long-legged fly and the stream to determine meaning.

14. THE SCHEME OF MEANING

"If *that's* what he meant, why didn't he say it?" Once a poem has been interpreted for us, this complaint is commonly leveled at the poet. What we never stop to consider is that perhaps *that* is not what the poet *meant* at all, nor do we consider that even if *that* is what he or she meant, the poet may have meant many other things as well and may have wanted to achieve many effects besides a strictly intellectual one. We tend to regard the intellect as something apart from sensory experiences and emotions, yet as we have seen in earlier chapters, poetry appeals to our senses and to our love of rhythm and musical harmony as much as it appeals to our logical minds. Finally, too, and in ways that are often difficult to talk about, it appeals to our emotions. It can arouse us and depress us, cheer us up and agitate us, lull us into a sense of serenity, stir us, anger us, frustrate us. Not all of these effects are reducible to statements of meaning, and at this juncture we would be wise to recall T. S. Eliot's statement that meaning in poetry is intended to distract us while the poem does its work.

However, even with this kind of meaning, the poet can be a trickster who involves our minds on levels deeper than the purely intellectual. Poets love games, and because their medium is words, they especially love word games. We as readers want our meanings, and poets will provide them for us if we work hard enough. Still, as we saw in Chapter 12, after we have done all our work, how can we really be sure that the meaning we arrive at is the meaning intended? In point of fact, we cannot. Robert Frost says as much when he remarks that poetry is "the one permissible way of saying one thing and meaning another." Some poets go out of their way to do just that, and when they do, we as readers have been moved into the cloudy realm of *irony, paradox,* and *ambiguity.* There we can become confused and frustrated until we find ourselves agitated into trying to make sense of something that seems to refuse to make sense. At such times we should be reminded that even something as prosaic as meaning — a nice, pat, logical statement — can be transformed in poetry into something rich and strange. Once we accept that possibility, we can begin to enjoy the aesthetic qualities of meaning in poetry, for poetry overlays everything, including our logical minds, with emotions and sensory experience.

The following poem is an innocuously pretty love lyric:

Christopher Marlowe (1564–1593)

The Passionate Shepherd to His Love

Come live with me and be my love,
And we will all the pleasures prove
That valleys, groves, hills, and fields,
Woods, or steepy mountain yields.

And we will sit upon the rocks,   *5*
Seeing the shepherds feed their flocks,
By shallow rivers to whose falls
Melodious birds sing madrigals.

And I will make thee beds of roses
And a thousand fragrant posies,   *10*
A cap of flowers, and a kirtle†
Embroidered all with leaves of myrtle;

A gown made of the finest wool
Which from our pretty lambs we pull;
Fair lined slippers for the cold.   *15*
With buckles of the purest gold;

A belt of straw and ivy buds,
With coral clasps and amber studs:
And if these pleasures may thee move,
Come live with me, and be my love.   *20*

The shepherd swains shall dance and sing
For thy delight each May morning:
If these delights thy mind may move,
Then live with me and be my love.

We ought to feel that we would be belaboring the obvious to interpret the meaning of Marlowe's poem. It is written in a mode called *the pastoral,* which presumes that a summertime innocence can be found in the lives that shepherds live. This particular shepherd promises his love all sorts of pastoral delights to prove his love to her. If we find the poem a bit too idyllic, so did one of Marlowe's contemporaries, the English explorer Sir Walter Raleigh, who wrote a poem of his own in answer to Marlowe's shepherd.

Sir Walter Raleigh (ca. 1552–1618)

The Nymph's Reply to the Shepherd

If all the world and love were young,
And truth in every shepherd's tongue,
These pretty pleasures might me move
To live with thee and be thy love.

11. *kirtle:* a dress or skirt.

Time drives the flocks from field to fold,   5
When rivers rage and rocks grow cold,
And Philomel† becometh dumb;
The rest complains of cares to come.

The flowers do fade, and wanton fields
To wayward winter reckoning yields;   10
A honey tongue, a heart of gall,
Is fancy's spring, but sorrow's fall.

Thy gowns, thy shoes, thy beds of roses,
Thy cap, thy kirtle, and thy posies
Soon break, soon wither, soon forgotten —   15
In folly ripe, in reason rotten.

Thy belt of straw and ivy buds,
Thy coral clasps and amber studs.
All these in me no means can move
To come to thee and be thy love.   20

But could youth last and love still breed,
Had joys no date nor age no need,
Then these delights my mind might move
To live with thee and be thy love.

Offered an eternal summer of youth and love, Raleigh's nymph reminds Marlowe's shepherd of the facts of life. Flowers fade, winter comes, everything
withers — including love and love's golden promise, the lover's promises. If we
know the Marlowe poem, then the Raleigh poem is both an allusion and, paired
with Marlowe's, an ironic counterpoint to it. That is to say, everything Marlowe's shepherd promises, Raleigh's nymph counters with an opposite. The poem
begins with the statement "If all the world and love were young,/And truth in
every shepherd's tongue," but goes on to prove that the world and love are not
young and that shepherds are liars like everyone else.

In the last stanza, however, hope is held out to the shepherd.

But could youth last and love still breed
Had joys no date nor age no need,
Then these delights my mind might move
To live with thee and be thy love.

Here we encounter an apparent **paradox.** Because the rest of the poem has already shown us that the conditions of those first two lines are an earthly impossibility, the nymph's own closing promise — the conditions on which she will be
the shepherd's love — is an absurdity. But the paradox is only apparent, because
its absurdity is just the point: the promises of love are themselves absurdities,
which make no sense in the real world. The irony of the Raleigh poem com-
pounds itself into paradox only to make that paradox a part of the irony. One
part of the poem contradicts the other while at the same time the entire poem is
contradicting Marlowe's, and what we come out with at the end is a sense of the
wide gap between human aspirations and the realities of mortal experiences.

7. *Philomel:* the nightingale.

But now let us return to Marlowe's poem. We could argue that whenever a poet is clearly speaking in a voice other than his own, he may be speaking ironically. That is to say, in no way can we call Christopher Marlowe the speaker in this poem: he has clearly masked himself as a "passionate shepherd." Marlowe was many things — a poet, a playwright, a secret agent — but he was never a shepherd. Of course, the pastoral mode requires that the poet pretend to be a shepherd, and Raleigh admits as much when he has the nymph reply to the shepherd, not to Kit Marlowe.

Still, if we read Marlowe's poem very carefully, we may begin to suspect that Marlowe is as aware of the actual world's shortcomings as Raleigh's nymph would like the shepherd to be. For one thing, the world the shepherd speaks of is carefully circumscribed to include only "valleys, groves, hills, and fields,/ Woods or steepy mountains." It may be a small point, but a great deal of the world — seas, deserts, cities, jungles — is left out. Again, however, the omission is in keeping with the pastoral mode. Whoever heard of a shepherd in a city or on the seas? But as we read on, we find another indication that the shepherd is something of a realist: he promises his love "fair lined slippers for the cold." So there is winter in this ideal world. While we cannot be sure that the shepherd is aware of the implications of what he is saying, can we be sure that Marlowe is not? "A gown made of the finest wool" is also promised the nymph, but only at the expense of those "pretty lambs" whose wool will be pulled off. Pain and cold for them? Perhaps. And at the conclusion of the poem, when the shepherd promises that "swains shall dance and sing/For thy delight each May morning," a further question may come to mind. Although in the pastoral convention May is often the month of love, it is likely that a nymph as realistic as Raleigh's would catch the implication: What about the other 334 days of the year? Can we be sure that Marlowe was any less aware of his own poetry's implications? We cannot, of course, nor can we ask Marlowe about his intentions.

What we can do is assign the discrepancies we have found to the nature of **ambiguity,** a poetic device in which several possible meanings are implied within the same statement, and each meaning seems to expand on, if not contradict, the other. Like an optical illusion, the poem's meaning changes depending on how we look at it. Notice how this device is different from **irony,** a statement that clearly means something else than it seems to on the surface, and **paradox,** a statement that puzzles us by the fact that it seems to make both sense and non-sense simultaneously. Indeed, the truth of paradox rests in its absurdity and our emotional struggle to force the apparently absurd to make logical sense. With irony, on the other hand, our notion that the poet means the opposite of what he or she is saying is based largely on tone and context. Words that do not seem appropriate to the situation or that are perhaps even contrary to the situation or to our expectations are often intended ironically; but we can never be absolutely sure that this is the case. If you have ever found yourself laughing at an incident that no one else thought was funny, or vice versa, you have a good idea of how much irony depends upon the way a situation strikes us rather than upon some hard-and-fast rules. A word of caution: Irony is like symbolism. Once students are introduced to the concept, some tend to find irony in every statement of the poets. Beware that your own skewed view of a situation will lead you to assume irony where none is intended. In fact, the less apparent to everyone else the irony is, the more likely it is that the irony is not intended (which is not to say that it might not nevertheless be there).

These three devices, then, are as elusive as the tricks of words and the mind from which they come. For example, the statements in Raleigh's poem are not in themselves ironic; they are ironic only in the context of Marlowe's poem, and that irony is compounded when we encounter the paradoxical about-face (which is only an apparent one) at the end of the Raleigh poem. The point to remember is that the more ambivalent the poet is about the true nature of the state of the world and human beings' place in it, the more the poet is likely to rely on irony, paradox, and ambiguity. As literary devices, all they tell us is that the poet does not want us to be sure, either. Instead, we are puzzled by the same sense of uncertainty, and that uncertainty of meaning can have as much emotional impact as a well-struck image or a startling metaphor.

Exercise

Consider the fact that while *nymph* refers to a lovely woman, it can also refer to one of the female divinities inhabiting nature in classical mythology. Does that fact further confuse the issue behind Raleigh's "Reply"? Can we account for any confusions with one or more of the three devices currently being considered? (You might want to consult the Oxford English Dictionary for the various meanings that *nymph* had in Raleigh's time.)

Because the religious impulse is usually a mixture of faith and doubt, religious poetry is especially ripe with an emotional ambivalence of statement disguised as meaning. Read the next three poems with this ambivalence in mind.

John Donne *(1572–1631)*

Hymn to God My God, in My Sickness

Since I am coming to that holy room
    Where, with Thy choir of saints for evermore,
I shall be made Thy music; as I come
    I tune the instrument here at the door,
    And what I must do then, think here before.   *5*

Whilst my physicians by their love are grown
    Cosmographers, and I their map, who lie
Flat on this bed, that by them may be shown
    That this is my southwest discovery†
    Per fretum febris,† by these straits to die,   *10*

I joy, that in these straits, I see my West;
    For, though their currents yield return to none,
What shall my West hurt me? As West and East
    In all flat maps (and I am one) are one,
    So death doth touch the resurrection.   *15*

9. *southwest discovery:* the Straits   10. *per fretum febris:* through the
of Magellan.   straits of fever.

Is the Pacific Sea my home? Or are
   The Eastern riches? Is Jerusalem?
Anyan,† and Magellan, and Gibraltar,
   All straits, and none but straits, are ways to them,
   Whether where Japhet dwelt, or Cham, or Shem.†   *20*

We think that Paradise and Calvary,
   Christ's cross, and Adam's tree, stood in one place;
Look, Lord, and find both Adams met in me;
   As the first Adam's sweat surrounds my face,
   May the last Adam's blood my soul embrace.   *25*

So, in his purple wrapped, receive me, Lord;
   By these his thorns give me his other crown;
And, as to others' souls I preached Thy word,
   Be this my text, my sermon to mine own:
   Therefore that he may raise the Lord throws down.   *30*

Exercises

1. How does Donne explain the paradox "death doth touch the resurrection"? You might first decide whether the statement is paradoxical.

2. Is there irony in the question "Is the Pacific Sea my home?" Think of the metaphor Donne has established and of the wordplay often associated with ambiguity and irony.

3. The final line of the poem is irony that becomes paradox, and there is an ambiguity in the pronoun *he*. What are the possible meanings that can be assigned to that single line? How are we prepared for that verse's conundrum by the entire last two stanzas, especially the paradox that "both Adams met in me"?

4. "In his purple wrapped"? Whose purple? How wrapped? What purple? Can any of these questions be answered with a single definite response?

Topic for Writing

Donne's "Hymn to God My God, in My Sickness" is rich in symbolism, both traditional and invented by the poet for the purposes of his presentation and theme. Discuss the function of the various symbols in the poem in terms of the spirit's transit from this world to the next.

18. *Anyan:* the Bering Strait.   20. *Japhet . . . Cham . . . Shem:* Noah's sons.

George Herbert *(1593–1633)*

Virtue

Sweet day, so cool, so calm, so bright,
    The bridal of the earth and sky:
The dew shall weep thy fall tonight;
    For thou must die.

Sweet rose, whose hue, angry and brave,   *5*
    Bids the rash gazer wipe his eye:
Thy root is ever in its grave,
    And thou must die.

Sweet spring, full of sweet days and roses,
    A box where sweets compacted lie;   *10*
My music shows ye have your closes,
    And all must die.

Only a sweet and virtuous soul,
    Like seasoned timber, never gives;
But though the whole world turn to coal,   *15*
    Then chiefly lives.

Exercises

1. Once we account for the wordplay, "the dew shall weep thy fall tonight" becomes virtually a literal statement. Explain.

2. Follow the development of the poem from the first through the third stanza. There is a clear pattern in the way the statement enlarges. What is that pattern? How does that pattern create ambiguity in the line "A box where sweets compacted lie"?

3. By the time Herbert calls the soul "seasoned timber," has he established an undertone of irony and paradox that virtually makes the statement true? What patterns of irony and paradox give the poem's final paradox — for the soul to live, the world must die — a logic we cannot easily resist?

Ben Jonson *(1573–1637)*

A Hymn to God the Father

Hear me, O God!
A broken heart,
Is my best part;
Use still thy rod,
That I may prove   *5*
Therein thy love.

If thou hadst not
Been stern to me,
But left me free,
I had forgot   10
Myself and thee.

For sin's so sweet,
As minds ill bent
Rarely repent,
Until they meet   15
Their punishment.

Who more can crave
Than thou hast done,
That gav'st a Son,
To free a slave?   20
First made of naught,
With all since bought.

Sin, Death, and Hell,
His glorious Name
Quite overcame,   25
Yet I rebel,
And slight the same.

But I'll come in
Before my loss
Me farther toss,   30
As sure to win
Under his Cross.†

Exercises

1. Identify and discuss the paradox in the first stanza.

2. Identify the allusion in the final stanza. Is there irony and paradox in the
words *loss* and *toss*? The notion of winning something is double-edged as well.
In what way? First you must determine how someone can paradoxically win
and lose at the same time.

   Evidently, irony, paradox, and ambiguity are the devices by which the poet
can pretend to provide a logical meaning to matters that otherwise remain mysterious and fraught with emotion. But because that logic is only apparent and
is actually paradoxical, it is a meaning that arouses our feelings and emotions as
surely as it tricks our minds. Although it was written in the twentieth rather
than the seventeenth century, the next poem also makes connections and leaps
of logic that seem outlandish — until we consider them carefully.

28–32: Roman soldiers tossed dice
for Christ's robe.

Daniela Gioseffi (1941–   )

Wheat

I had not watched maggots closely before.
The way they squirm and burrow their way in.
What curious things.
How characteristic of sperm.
Somehow,   5
how like wheat!

Exercises

1. How are maggots similar to sperm? To wheat? Do you take offense at such
suggestions? If you do (or even if you do not), consider what common properties all three items share. (Do not limit yourself only to those that Gioseffi
has indicated.)

2. What is the poet's reaction to her discoveries? Disgust? Horror? Surprise?
Insight? Pleasure? Cite elements in the poem to support your conclusions.

Topic for Writing

"Wheat" is not unlike George Herbert's "Virtue" in its strategy of drawing connections that, when we reflect, we can see to be accurate. There are differences,
however. While Herbert compares the physical (seasoned timber) with the metaphysical (the soul, virtue), Gioseffi compares three physical things. Using that
observation for your point of departure, compare and contrast the two poems.

A poem about maggots might at first glance seem to be a sure sign that
Western culture is suffering a serious decline. Maggots are only insect larvae,
however, and thus well within the natural order of things, as are sperm and
wheat. All three items have a direct relationship with each other because they
are instrumental to life's ongoing processes of reproduction, birth, growth, and
decay. We might take offense, but nature does not, nor does nature care if we
take offense. What Gioseffi illustrates with her discovery is that from the point
of view of natural processes, nothing is awful or dirty or ugly. Because she
shares that discovery with us in a poem, we are allowed an opportunity to have
the same insight into the mysteries of life's sustenance and continuance. If, on
the other hand, the mere mention of maggots turns our stomachs or the mention
of sperm embarrasses us, we deny ourselves an appreciation both of the poem
itself and of the fullness of nature.

Not only the nature of love, our religious strivings, or the mystery of life —
which are all personal in dimension — can be treated by the poet through irony
and paradox; so too can social conditions. Consider the following pair of poems:

William Blake (1757–1827)

Holy Thursday [I]

'Twas on a Holy Thursday, their innocent faces clean,
The children walking two & two, in red & blue & green,
Grey headed beadles walkd before with wands as white as snow,
Till into the high dome of Paul's† they like Thames' waters flow.

O what a multitude they seemed, these flowers of London town!   5
Seated in companies they sit with radiance all their own.
The hum of multitudes was there, but multitudes of lambs,
Thousands of little boys & girls raising their innocent hands.

Now like a mighty wind they raise to heaven the voice of song,
Or like harmonious thunderings the seats of heaven among.   10
Beneath them sit the aged men, wise guardians of the poor;
Then cherish pity, lest you drive an angel from your door.

Holy Thursday [II]

Is this a holy thing to see,
In a rich and fruitful land,
Babes reduced to misery,
Fed with cold and usurous hand?

Is that trembling cry a song?   5
Can it be a song of joy?
And so many children poor?
It is a land of poverty!

And their sun does never shine,
And their fields and bleak & bare,   10
And their ways are fill'd with thorns;
It is eternal winter there.

For where-e'er the sun does shine,
And where-e'er rain does fall,
Babe can never hunger there,   15
Nor poverty the mind appall.

Exercises

1. Once you have read "Holy Thursday [II]," can you ever read "Holy Thursday [I]" again without sensing irony throughout it? Is the ironical tone actually in the poem, or is it the result of your having read the second poem in the pair?

4. *Paul's:* St. Paul's Cathedral, London.

For one thing, who are the "grey headed beadles" and what are their "wands as white as snow"?

2. How does the final stanza of "Holy Thursday [II]" make a straightforward statement that becomes ironical and paradoxical in the context of the entire poem?

Topic for Writing

In an essay, discuss the theme of "Holy Thursday [I]" entirely in terms of itself, and then do the same for "Holy Thursday [II]." In your conclusion, try to account for the differences in each speaker's tone and attitude toward the same subject matter.

"Holy Thursday [I]" and "Holy Thursday [II]" provide us with a fine example of how irony is established within a context, in this case the context of the two poems taken together. Naturally, poets can establish a context for irony within a single poem by giving us enough clues to make us suspect the accuracy or sincerity of what the speaker is saying. The speaker may very well mean what she or he is saying, and we should not confuse irony with the intention of being ironic. For example, an individual might walk into a room and say to others there that it is a beautiful day, simply because he has just received some very good news. Meanwhile there is a terrible storm raging outside, and the others, not knowing why the first individual is happy, laugh at his comment, thinking it is an ironic observation on the miserable weather. In this example, the speaker's intentions are confused by the context in which he is speaking — the storm outside. Similar confusions are deliberately created in some poems by skillful poets. A poem's speaker may well be sincere; it is the poet who allows us to discover the ironic underpinnings to what is being said by giving us a broader perspective on the context in which the words are being spoken. The following two poems vividly illustrate this strategy by providing us with an interesting interplay of speaker, audience, and subject, the three elements necessary to any act of communication and vital to establishing an ironic context.

Percy Bysshe Shelley (1792–1822)

Ozymandias†

I met a traveler from an antique land
Who said: Two vast and trunkless legs of stone
Stand in the desert . . . Near them, on the sand,
Half sunk, a shattered visage lies, whose frown,
And wrinkled lip, and sneer of cold command,   5
Tell that its sculptor well those passions read
Which yet survive, stamped on these lifeless things,

Title: Ozymandias was the Egyptian pharoah Ramses II (thirteenth century B.C.).

The Scheme of Meaning   569

[handwritten: from dust to dust]

The hand that mocked them, and the heart that fed: //
And on the pedestal these words appear:
"My name is Ozymandias, king of kings: *[handwritten: (Irony)]* 10
Look on my works, ye Mighty, and despair!"
Nothing beside remains. Round the decay *[handwritten: cause you to slow down]*
Of that colossal wreck, boundless and bare *[handwritten: alliteration when reading]*
The lone and level sands stretch far away.

[handwritten left margin: nothing is better than he but death took him & now he had nothing left]

[handwritten: even though you possess a great deal you will die and it will become nothing / takes a long time to read it so stretched out over the sand]

Exercises

1. Three distinct speakers appear in this poem. Identify them. Do any of the three seem to be intending irony? Is there nevertheless a very telling irony conveyed by the poem as a whole? What is that irony?

2. What do you think Ozymandias meant by the words carved on the pedestal of his statue? What do those words mean so far as the "traveler from an antique land" is concerned?

3. How did the sculptor in a sense have the last laugh on Ozymandias? Shall something have a last laugh on the sculptor? What paradox does the poem finally present?

Shelley purposely established a series of boxes within boxes in "Ozymandias": the speaker of the poem is telling us what the traveler told him, and the traveler has told him what is inscribed on the base of the statue and what the scene around it looks like. But Ozymandias ordered that those words be carved on the monument centuries before, when the surrounding scene no doubt looked quite different. The poem becomes a comment on the nature of irony in poetry: what people say in one context may come back to mock them centuries later, removed from the original context.

Through the device of the dramatic monologue, a later poet used a man's words in a similar way. But we are made to imagine the man in a live situation.

[handwritten: he was possessive very jealous of it]

Robert Browning (1812–1889)

My Last Duchess†

Ferrara†

That's my last duchess painted on the wall,
Looking as if she were alive. I call
That piece a wonder, now: Frà Pandolf's† hands
Worked busily a day, and there she stands,
Will't please you sit and look at her? I said   5
"Frà Pandolf" by design, for never read
Strangers like you that pictured countenance,

Title: Browning is said to have modeled the speaker of his poem on Alfonso II, a sixteenth-century duke of Ferrara. The phrase *my*

last duchess refers to the duke's first wife.
Subtitle: a city in northern Italy.
3. *Frà Pandolf:* a fictitious artist.

The depth and passion of its earnest glance,
But to myself they turned (since none puts by
The curtain I have drawn for you, but I)   10
And seemed as they would ask me, if they durst,
How such a glance came there; so, not the first
Are you to turn and ask thus. Sir, 'twas not
Her husband's presence only, called that spot
Of joy into the Duchess' cheek: perhaps   15
Frà Pandolf chanced to say "Her mantle laps
"Over my lady's wrist too much," or "Paint
"Must never hope to reproduce the faint
"Half-flush that dies along her throat": such stuff
Was courtesy, she thought, and cause enough   20
For calling up that spot of joy. She had
A heart — how shall I say? — too soon made glad,
Too easily impressed; she liked whate'er
She looked on, and her looks went everywhere.
Sir, 'twas all one! My favor at her breast,   25
The dropping of the daylight in the West,
The bough of cherries some officious fool
Broke in the orchard for her, the white mule
She rode with round the terrace — all and each
Would draw from her alike the approving speech,   30
Or blush, at least. She thanked men — good! but thanked
Somehow — I know not how — as if she ranked
My gift of a nine-hundred-years-old name
With anybody's gift. Who'd stoop to blame
This sort of trifling? Even had you skill   35
In speech — which I have not — to make your will
Quite clear to such an one, and say, "Just this
"Or that in you disgusts me; here you miss,
"Or there exceed the mark" — and if she let
Herself be lessoned so, nor plainly set   40
Her wits to yours, forsooth, and made excuse,
— E'en then would be some stooping; and I choose
Never to stoop. Oh sir, she smiled, no doubt,
Whene'er I passed her; but who passed without
Much the same smile? This grew; I gave commands;   45
Then all smiles stopped together. There she stands
As if alive. Will 't please you rise? We'll meet
The company below, then. I repeat,
The Count your master's known munificence
Is ample warrant that no just pretense   50
Of mine for dowry will be disallowed;
Though his fair daughter's self, as I avowed
At starting, is my object. Nay, we'll go
Together down, sir. Notice Neptune, though,
Taming a sea-horse, thought a rarity,   55
Which Claus of Innsbruck† cast in bronze for me!

56. *Claus of Innsbruck:* a fictitious sculptor.

He had lots of possessions (art, etc) now he wants a new Duchess + a dowery (money)

the old duchess was immature etc

Exercises

1. By the poem's end, do you believe the Duke when he tells the Count's emissary that he, the Duke, does not really care how large the dowry will be because the Count's "fair daughter's self . . . is my object"? Is there a potential double meaning to the word *object*? What is that double meaning, and do you think that the Duke is aware of it?

2. Point out the Duke's statements that reveal him to be an arrogant, jealous, and possessive individual. Given the context of his remarks, do you think the Duke is revealing himself knowingly? What, in his view, might his real aims be? Do you think that he will succeed in impressing the Count's emissary? If you were the emissary, would you be impressed or dismayed by the Duke's character?

3. Browning makes no comment of his own within the poem, letting the Duke speak for himself while we are permitted to eavesdrop, as it were. We can never be certain what the fate of the Duke's last duchess was, but given the character the Duke's words reveal, what would you imagine became of her?

4. What is the significance of the Duke's parting reference to the Neptune "cast in bronze for me"? How does it relate to the fact that the Duke begins his monologue when he shows the emissary a portrait of his last duchess, "looking as if she were alive"?

Topic for Writing

Pretend that you are the Count's emissary and must now make an honest report to the Count on the Duke's character and the suitability of a marriage between him and the Count's daughter. As you write your report, quote the Duke to support your conclusions.

Browning's "My Last Duchess," like all his other dramatic monologues, illustrates how we reveal ourselves — our attitudes, values, and beliefs — through every word we speak. Thus the attentive listener can gain information about us that we would otherwise not divulge even under duress. Surely reading poems like this one can help make us such listeners, for poetry is finally only language in use within very well-defined contexts, and we use language in contexts that often demand care in saying exactly what we mean. We can never be certain, however, that our words will convey an exact meaning, nor can we be certain that the other individual is saying precisely what he or she means. What Browning teaches us is how important it is to weigh carefully and astutely what is being said, both by ourselves and by others.

As we have seen, poets use irony, ambiguity, and paradox to modulate meaning as surely as organists modulate sounds with the stops on the organ. Note, however, that we are now talking not about the sound of poetry, but about its sense. Yet that sense comes through a mode of sound which we call **voice**, the tone of voice the poet uses in writing a poem. Obviously we do not hear the tone of the poet's voice; we feel it. The next poem plays what we might regard as a rather mean trick on us, but we should notice that we are cautioned in advance *not* to read the poem.

Ishmael Reed (1938–   )

beware   :   do not read this poem

tonite   ,   thriller was
abt an ol woman   , so vain she
surrounded herself w/
        many mirrors

it got so bad that finally she   5
locked herself indoors & her
whole life became the
        mirrors

one day the villagers broke
into her house   ,   but she was too   10
swift for them   .   she disappeared
        into a mirror

each tenant who bought the house
after that   ,   lost a loved one to
        the ol woman in the mirror   :   15
        first a little girl
        then a young woman
        then the young woman/s husband

the hunger of this poem is legendary
it has taken in many victims   20
back off from this poem
it has drawn in yr feet
back off from this poem
it has drawn in yr legs
back off from this poem   25
it is a greedy mirror
you are into this poem   from
        the waist down
nobody can hear you can they   ?
this poem has had you up to here   30
        belch
this poem aint got no manners
you cant call out frm this poem
relax now & go w/ this poem
move & roll on to this poem   35
do not resist this poem
this poem has yr eyes
this poem has his head
this poem has his arms
this poem has his fingers   40
this poem has his fingertips

this poem is the reader & the
reader this poem

                statistic   :   the us bureau of missing persons reports
                                  that in 1968 over 100,000 people disappeared   *45*
                                  leaving no solid clues
                                        nor trace   only
                    a space   in the lives of their friends

Exercises

1. How does the poet's loose, conversational, almost chummy tone of voice entice us? Do you think that was the effect he wanted the tone to achieve? Explain.

2. The poet calls his poem "a greedy mirror." While that statement fits the subject of the horror movie first described in the poem, how else is the poem a mirror? What does it reflect about ourselves? About our society?

3. What effect does the poet achieve by ending on a statistic which we must assume is a true one? How does the statistic directly relate to the content of the rest of the poem? Does the statisic also make an ironic comment about the rest of the poem as well as about the readers?

Reed uses the structure of his poem to get across his point that worse horrors exist than those we encounter in film thrillers and even in some poems. We humans like to be terrified as long as we can step back, if need be, to remind ourselves that the terror is all meant in fun. Reed goes as far as to use a spooky-sounding title to play upon that propensity in all of us, but then, at the end of the poem, stuns us by telling us something that is truly terrifying — that in one calendar year 100,000 Americans disappeared without a trace. The result is to jolt us into the sobriety of a different kind of reflection, the sort we engage in with our minds rather than with mirrors. Such an ironic about-face is another way for poets to work their persuasive magic on us.

By now you can understand how a poet can use our expectations in a playful manner but with a serious aim. Sometimes, like an accomplished mimic, the poet can play with a variety of voices to create a closing irony that will sober us into reflecting on some aspect of our common human experiences. Often, the poet will draw our attention to an aspect of our humanity that we might have disputed or resented having called to our attention if the poet had commented on it plainly.

Thomas Hardy (1840–1928)

"Ah, are you digging on my grave?

"Ah, are you digging on my grave,
    My loved one? — planting rue?"
— "No: yesterday he went to wed
One of the brightest wealth has bred.
'It cannot hurt her now,' he said,   5
    'That I should not be true.' "

"Then who is digging on my grave?
  My nearest dearest kin?"
— "Ah, no: they sit and think, "What use!
What good will planting flowers produce?   10
No tendance of her mound can loose
  Her spirit from Death's gin.' "

"But some one digs upon my grave?
  My enemy? — prodding sly?"
— "Nay: When she heard you had passed the Gate   15
That shuts on all flesh soon or late,
She thought you no more worth her hate,
  And cares not where you lie."

"Then, who is digging on my grave?
  Say — since I have not guessed!"   20
— "O it is I, my mistress dear,
Your little dog, who still lives near,
And much I hope my movements here
  Have not disturbed your rest?"

"Ah, yes! *You* dig upon my grave . . .   25
  Why flashed it not on me
That one true heart was left behind!
What feeling do we ever find
To equal among human kind
  A dog's fidelity!"   30

"Mistress, I dug upon your grave
  To bury a bone, in case
I should be hungry near this spot
When passing on my daily trot.
I am sorry, but I quite forgot   35
  It was your resting-place."

Exercises

1. How many voices are at work in this poem? How does the poem play those voices against each other to build toward one meaning and then undercut it?

2. The premise of this poem is so unobtrusive that we barely notice its absurdity. What is that premise? How is it absurd? How does the poet play on our emotions to reduce that absurdity to something of a truth?

Because Hardy, like Reed, makes us discover what his poem is driving toward, we find the experience of reading it pleasurable and thus do not resent his reminding us of a rather awful truth in a comic and playful manner. After all, there is nothing very funny about the fact that a person is likely to be entirely forgotten after his or her death, any more than we find anything very funny about the annual disappearance of 100,000 Americans. The poet knows that, of course, but the poet also knows that we are more likely to continue to read a poem if it entertains us. But while we are entertained, we are also made aware of some harsh truths. In the next poem, the poet, playing a mimic, brings out the hollowness of public utterances and alerts us to the dangers of Fourth of July rhetoric, for he shows us all by example that even cherished concepts can be cheapened by mindless recitation.

e. e. cummings *(1894–1962)*

"next to of course god america i

"next to of course god america i
love you land of the pilgrims' and so forth oh
say can you see by the dawn's early my
country 'tis of centuries come and go
and are no more what of it we should worry   *5*
in every language even deafanddumb
thy sons acclaim your glorious name by gorry
by jingo by gee by gosh by gum
why talk of beauty what could be more beau-
tiful than these heroic happy dead   *10*
who rushed like lions to the roaring slaughter
they did not stop to think they died instead
then shall the voice of liberty be mute?"

He spoke. And drank rapidly a glass of water

Exercises

1. What voice is cummings mimicking here? How does he make that voice sound ridiculous? Does the speaker think he sounds ridiculous? What is the effect of the final line of the poem?

2. Students love cummings because he uses no punctuation and capitalization and gets away with it. In this particular poem, how does the lack of those typographical indicators comment on the speaker? Who else does "not stop to think"? How can we tell?

Clearly, if imitation is the highest form of flattery, in poetry it is often the surest way to expose public empty-headedness for what it is. Because of its tight construction, the following poem excellently summarizes much of the foregoing discussion about the use of voice and tone to create an ironic commentary.

Gwendolyn Brooks (1915–

We Real Cool

The Pool Players.
Seven at the Golden Shovel.

We real cool. We
Left school. We

Lurk late. We
Strike straight. We

Sing sin. We   5
Thin gin. We

Jazz June. We
Die soon.

Exercises

1. Do the pool players believe that they are real cool? Does the poet believe it? Explain how you reached your conclusion in each case.

2. What comment does the constant end-of-line repetition of *we* make about the character of individuals like the pool players?

3. The poet speaks as if she is one of the pool players. If the poet had spoken about them instead, would you have been as ready to listen and to see her point? Explain.

Like Browning and cummings, in particular, Brooks realizes that in poetry one does not need to comment outright; one often needs only to record and report. If the poem's subject or subjects can do the reporting, all the better. Indeed, the best poetry allows us to form our own conclusions about the event being described or the character or ideas being presented. Obviously, the poet can convey shades of meaning and a great deal of information in very few words simply by paying close heed to *how* people speak about themselves and their world, which is not the same as paying close heed to *what* people say about themselves and their world. Thus far, however, our examples of poets' manipulation of tone and voice to create meaning and irony have been drawn from acts of spoken, or oral, communication; we have been hearing people talk exactly as if they were on a stage. (That is why we call Robert Browning's sort of poetry dramatic monologues; we hear a one-voice playlet, as it were.)

There is another kind of verbal communication, of course: the written word. In an age when it seems as though we have to fill out a form for the privilege of doing anything, our poets would miss a golden opportunity for illustrating life's ironies if they did not occasionally write poems that mimic those official-sounding forms with which we have all become much too familiar.

Naomi Lazard

Missing Father Report

Your help is urgently needed.
If you have any information
regarding the whereabouts
of the following individual
contact us immediately.   *5*

Subject is, or was, about 45
at the time of disappearance.
Last seen dissolving slowly,
first the back of his neck;
then his shoulders went away,   *10*
his legs left too. In the end
his face vanished without warning,
the mouth open, still speaking.

We have no indication why
this person, of all people,   *15*
should have disappeared.
Reliable witnesses have stated
that not even his eyes endured,
not even the tips of his fingers.

You will know him by certain signs,   *20*
by the innocent look of his hair
falling over his forehead
in moments of emotional upheaval,
by his hands which are fine
and arrive like delicate instruments   *25*
of mercy.
    You will also know him
by his eyes which have an unblinking
quality like those of a horse
or some other friendly, domesticated   *30*
animal. You will know him
if you are prepared.

There is no history of mental disease,
no police file. Disappearance was,
for all practical purposes,   *35*
voluntary. Subject's last
formal statement, for the record,
was "I love you,"
or something like that.

Exercises

1. The poem imitates several forms of public written communications. Identify them by listening carefully to the tone of the language, particularly in the opening stanzas. In what sources would you expect to find such a report?

2. Whose father, would you suppose, the speaker is reporting missing? Is he actually missing? What do you suppose really became of the father?

3. While some of the language in the poem is that of official reports, is the tone consistently impersonal? Would you find "the innocent look of his hair" and other "signs" mentioned in stanza 4 listed in official reports? What do you make of such phrases and of the entire description of the missing father? What does this description tell you about the speaker and the speaker's attitude toward the missing person?

Topic for Writing

Compare and contrast this poem with Sylvia Plath's "Daddy" (Chapter 13). In your essay, emphasize the attitude each speaker expresses toward her father through the tone she uses to speak about him.

The following poem makes perfect use of impersonal writing at its extreme. The title speaks for itself.

Ian Young (1945–   )

Poem Found in a Dime-Store Diary

Place these slips inside your diary
in the appropriate place

. . . .
Tomorrow is my wife's birthday
. . . .
Tomorrow is my husband's birthday
. . . .
Tomorrow is my wedding anniversary
. . . .
Tomorrow is my mother's birthday
. . . .
Tomorrow is my father's birthday
. . . .
Tomorrow my Holidays start
. . . .
Tomorrow is
. . . .
Tomorrow is
. . . .
Tomorrow is

1. Would it make any difference to you if you were to discover that the poet actually made this whole poem up rather than having *found* it, as he claims? Why or why not?

2. Though the poem has no more individuality to its tone than we would expect from the reported source, does it nevertheless make a point that concerns most individuals? What is that point? How does the poet's arrangement of the slips provided by the diary manufacturer help to make that point?

As we near the end of this section on poetry, we should stress that poets make every effort to give us new insights into ourselves as living, feeling, and thinking creatures. We should also have discovered that despite what we may have believed previously, poets rarely, if ever, speak in a specialized language about never-never lands; they speak in our tongue about our world. We would do well in closing, then, to hear again the poet's voice at its very best, when he or she appears to be speaking for himself or herself.

W. H. Auden (1907–1973)

Musée des Beaux Arts†

About suffering they were never wrong,
The Old Masters:† how well they understood
Its human position; how it takes place
While someone else is eating or opening a window or just walking
    dully along;
How, when the aged are reverently, passionately waiting   5
For the miraculous birth, there always must be
Children who did not specially want it to happen, skating
On a pond at the edge of the wood:
They never forgot
That even the dreadful martyrdom must run its course   10
Anyhow in a corner, some untidy spot
Where the dogs go on with their doggy life and the torturer's horse
Scratches its innocent behind on a tree.

In Breughel's† *Icarus*, for instance: how everything turns away
Quite leisurely from the disaster; the ploughman may   15
Have heard the splash, the forsaken cry,
But for him it was not an important failure; the sun shone
As it had to on the white legs disappearing into the green
Water; and the expensive delicate ship that must have seen
Something amazing, a boy falling out of the sky,   20
Had somewhere to get to and sailed calmly on.

Title: the Museum of Fine Arts in Brussels, Belgium.
2. *Old Masters:* pre–eighteenth-century European painters.
14. *Breughel:* a Flemish painter of the sixteenth century.

Exercises

1. There are several allusions in this poem. Identify them and discuss their significance.

2. How would you characterize the tone of this poem? Personal? Impersonal? Serious? Light? Ironic? Matter-of-fact? Support your comments with specific references to the poem.

3. Taking into account the poet's tone and word choices, discuss the theme of "Musée des Beaux Arts." Be sure you discuss what the poem means and not what you would like it to mean.

In Musée des Beaux Arts," Auden does not use the first-person pronoun even once. Although we hear his voice, he develops his topic without intruding into it. Our next and final poem, on the other hand, would seem to be an exercise in obscurity, if there were not a repeated use of the first-person pronoun, which we must assume represents the poet.

Johari Amini (1935–   )

Identity

(for don l. lee)

i saw a man once		
tall wearing a crown		
of natural		
a prophet/creator of		
change showing identity		5
to negroes (the whiteminded		
ones)		
a black gospel he had		
the message to save them		
his name was	Poet	10
he said	-what are you-	
i felt fear for what		
could i say or how		
should i answer what		
he asked ("a negro".no.		15
something is wrong)		
i gathered nerve and		
ventured	-i am a person-	
hoping he would ask no		
further as birth is a		20
painful process		
he said	-are you B l a c k-	
sharp pain cut like ground		

glass (should i lie/say
yes. . .no i need time)   -what do you mean-   *25*
(but i didn't want to
hear)   -do you THINK BLACK-

i knew i knew what he
meant i knew but i could
not say yes in my   *30*
imitationwhite hair
i knew but my curlfree do
said .no. without my
answering   -why Poet must you
                                                cause such pain-   *35*

he said   -Malcolm DuBois Black
                                              African Black Baldwin
                                              LeRoi Black Third World
                                              Patrice Stokely Black
                                              El-Hajj Malik   *40*
                                                      El-Shabazz-

the pain stopped i
breathed life
birth was completed
growth was begun i   *45*
was sister i had Black
            Proud   IDENTITY

Exercises

1. What is going on in the lefthand column of the poem? In the righthand column? How do these two series of actions interrelate? Would the poem have been easier or more difficult to understand if the same information had all been arranged consecutively? Why do you suppose the poet arranged the poem as she did?

2. The poem has two conclusions as well. What resolution is arrived at in the lefthand column? In the righthand column? Do the two conclusions match?

3. The Poet in the poem gives a list of names. Who are these individuals? What do they represent? How does the Poet's mention of them help bring about the poem's resolution?

4. Is the tone of voice in this poem appropriate to the subject matter? Does the use of the lower case for the first-person pronoun also lend itself to developing the poem's theme? How?

5. "Birth is a/painful process." How does the poet make us feel that pain? Is it only the speaker's identity that is coming into being? What else is being born?

   While poets do create verbal ironies, ambiguities, and paradoxes, they also confront the ironies, ambiguities, and paradoxes of human experience in their poetry. In the preceding poem, for example, the speaker painfully exposes her personal shame at being black ("in my/imitationwhite hair/ . . . my curlfree do") so that we might share more fully her final realization that being black is something to be proud of. Underlying the entire process of growth and recognition that the poem entails is the bitter irony that anyone should be ashamed for being what nature made him or her. The poet did not invent racism, but she can give us a positive perspective on its perniciousness, even if we ourselves have not been its victims, by sharing her own experiences of its effects. The poem makes the underlying irony concrete, allowing us to grow, to learn, and to feel as well as think.

A great many of the poems in earlier chapters can be just as profitably examined for the emotional qualities established by irony, paradox, and ambiguity and for the role that voice plays in establishing these poetic modes. Certainly Marvell's, Eliot's, and Ransom's poems in the preceding chapter can be reconsidered in the light of the material presented here. Furthermore, perhaps we are mindful by now that all manners and methods of poetic expression play their parts in establishing meaning in poetry. This final chapter is titled "The Scheme of Meaning" on purpose, of course. On one level the title is a pun, a weak species of ambiguity that may or may not work. But like the other puns we have seen, it is intended to point out something in the way of meaning. The devices dealt with in these last two chapters do indeed contribute a great share of the intellectual aspect of meaning to poetry. Nevertheless, no matter how excitingly puzzling we may find that intellectual meaning to be, poetry would be a rather cut-and-dried affair, more in the nature of a brain teaser, if these devices were not used in conjunction with the other devices discussed in earlier chapters. To be sure, we would not have those delightful combinations of structure and meaning that truly constitute poetry without as many poetic devices as possible acting in conjunction, and one way we can determine a good poem is to notice how many different appeals — emotional as well as intellectual, visual as well as aural — the poem makes to us.

In poetry, the scheme of meaning is just that. As we have seen, the poet has a wealth of devices to use in any attempt to entertain and to instruct us, and the beauty of poetry has always been that it leavens he latter function with the former. We may miss a poem's meaning entirely, but we may still have had the pleasure of hearing the world with the poet's ears or seeing it with the poet's eyes. We should be aware that the poet may have intended us to "miss" the meaning or may have meant other things as well.

As we learn to enjoy poetry, we learn to understand it, and we enjoy it by understanding how the poet works and how poetry works. Throughout these chapters we have attempted to introduce both aspects of an incredibly complex, rich, and rewarding art. Like everything else in life, no device in poetry can work in isolation from any others. In Frost's "Design" (Chapter 13) and Shelley's "Ozymandias" (this chapter), for example, the *pattern* of the sonnet form adds immensely to the compact statement of each theme. *Ambiguity, irony,* and *paradox* would be unknown without *connotation,* for language would then have a scientific precision that would not allow for the marvelous factual imprecisions the world permits the poet. That all things seem to exist on both a *literal* and *figurative* level makes for *allusion* and *symbol.* We could go on, but the point is probably apparent by now. The more knowledge and experience we can bring to bear when studying poetry, the richer will be our reward.

Topics for Writing

1. From among the poems in this book, select one in which the speaker is clearly not the poet. (One indication is the use of quotation marks within the poem, as in Hardy's " 'Ah, are you digging on my grave.' " Sometimes, too, a particular speaker is identified by the poem's title, as in the cases of Browning's "My Last Duchess" and Eliot's "The Love Song of J. Alfred Prufrock.") Once you have selected the poem, show how the poet manipulates the speaking voice to create irony and ambiguity or different levels of meaning, within the poem.

2. Select a poem in which you find the poet punning. (The best test: If you think he or she is, the poet probably is.) Paying special attention to those puns or ambiguous words and phrases, analyze the poem's meaning as it varies according to your reading.

3. Select a poem in which a serious subject — love, death, warfare — seems to be treated in a frivolous or at least whimsical manner. In discussing that poem, cite those lines that seem to you to prove that the poet is not being as serious as the subject might warrant. Consider too how effectively new or different meanings are thereby achieved.

15. OTHER POEMS
TO READ

Anonymous

Barbara Allan

It was in and about the Martinmas† time,
    When the green leaves were a-fallin',
That Sir John Graeme in the West Country
    Fell in love with Barbara Allan.

He sent his man down through the town   *5*
    To the place where she was dwellin':
"O haste and come to my master dear,
    Gin ye be Barbara Allan."

O slowly, slowly rase she up,
    To the place where he was lyin',   *10*
And when she drew the curtain by:
    "Young man, I think you're dyin'."

"O it's I'm sick, and very, very sick,
    And 'tis a' for Barbara Allan."
O the better for me ye sal† never be,   *15*
    Though your heart's blood were a-spillin'."

"O dinna ye mind,† young man," said she,
    "When ye the cups were fillin',
That ye made the healths gae round and round,
    And slighted Barbara Allan?"   *20*

He turned his face unto the wall,
    And death with him was dealin':
"Adieu, adieu, my dear friends all,
    And be kind to Barbara Allan."

1. *Martinmas:* November 11, the feast of St. Martin, who was martyred in 655.
15. *sal:* shall.
17. *dinna ye mind:* don't you remember.

585

And slowly, slowly, rase she up,   *25*
    And slowly, slowly left him;
And sighing said she could not stay,
    Since death of life had reft† him.

She had not gane a mile but twa,
    When she heard the dead-bell knellin',   *30*
And every jow that the dead-bell ga'ed
    It cried, "Woe to Barbara Allan!"

"O mother, mother, make my bed,
    O make it soft and narrow:
Since my love died for me today,   *35*
    I'll die for him tomorrow."

Anonymous

Lord Randall

"Oh where ha'e ye been, Lord Randall my son?
O where ha'e ye been, my handsome young man?"
    "I ha'e been to the wild wood: mother, make my bed soon,
    For I'm weary wi' hunting, and fain wald† lie down."

"Where gat ye your dinner, Lord Randall my son?   *5*
Where gat ye your dinner, my handsome young man?"
    "I dined wi' my true love; mother, make my bed soon,
    For I'm weary wi' hunting, and fain wald lie down."

"What gat ye to your dinner, Lord Randall my son?
What gat ye to your dinner, my handsome young man?"   *10*
    "I gat eels boiled in broo: mother, make my bed soon,
    For I'm weary wi' hunting and fain wald lie down."

"What became of your bloodhounds, Lord Randall my son?
What became of your bloodhounds, my handsome young man?"
    "O they swelled and they died: mother, make my bed soon,   *15*
    For I'm weary wi' hunting and fain wald lie down."

"O I fear ye are poisoned, Lord Randall my son!
O I fear ye are poisoned, my handsome young man!"
    "O yes, I am poisoned: mother, make my bed soon,
    For I'm sick at the heart, and I fain wald lie down."   *20*

28. *reft:* robbed.

---

4. *fain wald:* would like to.

Anonymous

Weep you no more, sad fountains!

Weep you no more, sad fountains!
    What need you flow so fast?
Look, how the snowy mountains
    Heaven's sun doth gently waste.
But my sun's heavenly eyes   5
    View not your weeping,
    That now lies sleeping
Softly, now softly lies
       Sleeping.

Sleep is a reconciling,   10
    A rest that peace begets.
Doth not the sun rise smiling
    When fair at even he sets?
Rest you then, rest, sad eyes,
    Melt not in weeping,   15
    While she lies sleeping
Softly, now softly lies
       Sleeping.

Anonymous

Sir Patrick Spens

The king sits in Dumferling toune,†
    Drinking the blude-reid wine:
"O whar will I get a guid sailor,
    To sail this schip of mine?"

Up and spak an eldern knicht,   5
    Sat at the kings richt kne:
"Sir Patrick Spens is the best sailor
    That sails upon the se."

The king has written a braid† letter,
    And signd it wi his hand,   10
And sent it to Sir Patrick Spens,
    Was walking on the sand.

The first line that Sir Patrick red,
    A loud lauch lauched he;
The next line that Sir Patrick red,   15
    The teir blinded his ee.

1. *toune:* town.   9. *braid:* broad.

"O wha is this has don this deid,
    This ill deid don to me,
To send me out this time o' the yeir,
    To sail upon the se!   *20*

"Mak haste, mak haste, my mirry men all,
    Our guid schip sails the morne."
"Oh say na sae, my master deir,
    For I feir a deadlie storme.

"Late late yestreen† I saw the new moone,   *25*
    Wi the auld moone in hir arme,
And I feir, I feir, my deir master,
    That we will cum to harme."

O our Scots nobles wer richt laith†
    To weet† their cork-heild schoone,†   *30*
Bot lang owre a'† the play wer playd,
    Thait hats they swam aboone.†

O lang, lang may their ladies sit,
    Wi thair fans into their hand,
Or eir† they se Sir Patrick Spens   *35*
    Cum sailing to the land.

O lang, lang may the ladies stand,
    Wi thair gold kems† in their hair,
Waiting for thair ain deir lords,
    For they'll se thame na mair.   *40*

Haf owre, half owre to Aberdour,
    It's fiftie fadom deip,
And thair lies guid Sir Patrick Spens,
    Wi the Scots lords at his feit.

Exercises

1. What is the poem's attitude toward the king and the Scots lords? How do you know?

2. Why does Sir Patrick sail off into certain danger?

3. What is the significance of the last two lines?

25. *yestreen:* yesterday evening.
29. *richt laith:* right loath.
30. *weet:* wet; *schoone:* shoes.
31. *bot lang owre a':* but long before all.

32. *Thait . . . aboone:* their hats swam above.
35. *eir:* ere.
38. *kems:* combs.

Topic for Writing

Victory in defeat is a recurring theme in literature. Explore the possibility of this idea as a theme in "Sir Patrick Spens."

Anonymous

Get Up and Bar the Door

It fell about the Martinmas† time,
    And a gay time it was then,
When our good wife got puddings to make,
    And she's boild them in the pan.

The wind sae cauld blew south and north,   *5*
    And blew into the floor;
Quoth our goodman to our goodwife,
    "Gae out and bar the door."

"My hand is in my hussyfskap,†
    Goodman, as ye may see;   *10*
An it shoud nae be barrd this hundred year,
    It's no be barrd for me."

They made a paction† tween them twa,
    They made it firm and sure,
That the first word whaeer shoud speak,   *15*
    Shoud rise and bar the door.

Then by there came two gentlemen,
    At twelve oclock at night,
And they could neither see house nor hall,
    Nor coal nor candle-light.   *20*

"Now whether is this a rich man's house,
    Or whether is it a poor?"
But neer a word wad ane o them speak,
    For barring of the door.

And first they ate the white puddings,   *25*
    And then they ate the black;
Tho muckle† thought the goodwife to hersel,
    Yet neer a word she spake.

Then said the one unto the other,
    "Here, man, tak ye my knife;   *30*
Do ye tak aff the auld man's beard,
    And I'll kiss the goodwife."

---

1. *Martinmas:* November 11, the feast of St. Martin, who was martyred in 655.

9. *hussyfskap:* duties of the housewife.

13. *paction:* agreement or pact.

27. *muckle:* much.

"But there's nae water in the house,
    And what shall we do than?"
"What ails ye at the pudding-broo,   *35*
    That boils into the pan?"

O up then started our goodman,
    An angry man was he:
"Will ye kiss my wife before my een,
    And scad me wi pudding-bree?"   *40*

Then up and started our goodwife,
    Gied three skips on the floor:
"Goodman, you've spoken the foremost word;
    Get up and bar the door."

Anonymous

There is a lady sweet and kind

There is a lady sweet and kind,
Was never face so pleased my mind;
I did but see her passing by,
And yet I love her till I die.

Her gesture, motion, and her smiles,   *5*
Her wit, her voice, my heart beguiles,
Beguiles my heart, I know not why,
And yet I love her till I die.

Her free behavior, winning looks,
Will make a lawyer burn his books;   *10*
I touched her not, alas! not I,
And yet I love her till I die.

Had I her fast betwixt mine arms,
Judge you that think such sports were harms,
Were't any harm? no, no! fie, fie!   *15*
For I will love her till I die.

Should I remain confinèd there
So long as Phoebus† in his sphere,
I to request, she to deny,
Yet would I love her till I die.   *20*

Cupid is wingèd and doth range,
Her country so my love doth change;
But change she earth, or change she sky,
Yet will I love her till I die.

18. *Phoebus:* Apollo, classical god
of the sun.

A Poem for Black Hearts

For Malcolm's eyes, when they broke
the face of some dumb white man. For
Malcolm's hands raised to bless us
all black and strong in his image
of ourselves, for Malcolm's words   5
fire darts, the victor's tireless
thrusts, words hung above the world
change as it may, he said it, and
for this he was killed, for saying,
and feeling, and being/ change, all   10
collected hot in his heart, For Malcolm's
heart, raising us above our filthy cities,
for his stride, and his beat, and his address
to the grey monsters of the world, For Malcolm's
pleas for your dignity, black men, for your life,   15
black men, for the filling of your minds
with righteousness, For all of him dead and
gone and vanished from us, and all of him which
clings to our speech black god of our time.
For all of him, and all of yourself, look up,   20
black man, quit stuttering and shuffling, look up,
black man, quit whining and stooping, for all of him,
For Great Malcolm a prince of the earth, let nothing in us rest
until we avenge ourselves for his death, stupid animals
that killed him, let us never breathe a pure breath if   25
we fail, and white men call us faggots till the end of the earth.

Exercises

1. What do you know about Malcolm X as a figure of recent history? What is Malcolm's image of black people as it is presented in this poem?

2. What are the attributes that made Malcolm "a prince of the earth"?

3. What metaphor describes Malcolm's words?

Topic for Writing

Discuss the nature of the vengeance for Malcolm's death that is called for in the poem.

William Blake *(1757–1827)*

A Poison Tree

I was angry with my friend:
I told my wrath, my wrath did end.
I was angry with my foe:
I told it not, my wrath did grow.

And I water'd it in fears,   5
Night & morning with my tears;
And I sunned it with smiles,
And with soft deceitful wiles.

And it grew both day and night,
Till it bore an apple bright;   10
And my foe beheld it shine,
And he knew that it was mine,

And into my garden stole
When the night had veil'd the pole:
In the morning glad I see   15
My foe outstretch'd beneath the tree.

The Little Black Boy

My mother bore me in the southern wild,
And I am black, but O! my soul is white;
White as an angel is the English child,
But I am black, as if bereaved of light.

My mother taught me underneath a tree,   5
And sitting down before the heat of day,
She took me on her lap and kissed me,
And, pointing to the east, began to say:

"Look on the rising sun: there God does live,
And gives his light, and gives his heat away; 10
And flowers and trees and beasts and men receive
Comfort in morning, joy in the noonday.

"And we are put on earth a little space,
That we may learn to bear the beams of love;
And these black bodies and this sunburnt face 15
Is but a cloud, and like a shady grove.

"For when our souls have learned the heat to bear,
The cloud will vanish; we shall hear his voice,
Saying: 'Come out from the grove, my love and care,
And round my golden tent like lambs rejoice.' " 20

Thus did my mother say, and kissed me;
And thus I say to little English boy:
When I from black and he from white cloud free,
And round the tent of God like lambs we joy,

I'll shade him from the heat, till he can bear   25
To lean in joy upon our Father's knee;
And then I'll stand and stroke his silver hair,
And be like him, and he will then love me.

The Tyger

Tyger! Tyger! burning bright
In the forests of the night,
What immortal hand or eye
Could frame thy fearful symmetry?

In what distant deeps or skies   5
Burnt the fire of thine eyes?
On what wings dare he aspire?
What the hand dare sieze the fire?

And what shoulder, & what art,
Could twist the sinews of thy heart?   10
And when thy heart began to beat,
What dread hand? & what dread feet?

What the hammer? what the chain?
In what furnace was thy brain?
What the anvil? what dread grasp   15
Dare its deadly terrors clasp?
When the stars threw down their spears,
And water'd heaven with their tears,
Did he smile his work to see?
Did he who made the Lamb make thee?   20

Tyger! Tyger! burning bright
In the forests of the night,
What immortal hand or eye,
Dare frame thy fearful symmetry?

Infant Sorrow

My mother groan'd! my father wept.
Into the dangerous world I leapt:
Helpless, naked, piping loud:
Like a fiend hid in a cloud.

Struggling in my father's hands,   5
Striving against my swadling bands,
Bound and weary I thought best
To sulk upon my mother's breast.

Anne Bradstreet (1612?–1672)

A Letter to Her Husband,
Absent upon Public Employment

My head, my heart, mine eyes, my life, nay, more,
My joy, my magazine of earthly store,
If two be one, as surely thou and I,
How stayest thou there, whilst I at Ipswich† lie?
So many steps, head from the heart to sever,   5
If but a neck, soon should we be together.
I, like the Earth this season, mourn in black,
My Sun is gone so far in's zodiac,
Whom whilst I 'joyed, nor storms, nor frost I felt,
His warmth such frigid colds did cause to melt.   10
My chilled limbs now numbed lie forlorn;
Return, return, sweet Sol,† from Capricorn;†
In this dead time, alas, what can I more
Than view those fruits which through thy heat I bore?
Which sweet contentment yield me for a space,   15
True living pictures of their father's face.
O strange effect! now thou art southward gone,
I weary grow the tedious day so long;
But when thou northward to me shalt return,
I wish my Sun may never set, but burn   20
Within the Cancer† of my glowing breast,
The welcome house of him my dearest guest.
Where ever, ever stay, and go not thence,
Till nature's sad decree shall call thee hence;
Flesh of thy flesh, bone of thy bone,   25
I here, thou there, yet both but one.

---

4. *Ipswich:* town in eastern England.
12. *Sol:* sun; *Capricorn:* the constellation that the sun enters in
December.
21. *Cancer:* the constellation that
the sun enters in midsummer.

Gwendolyn Brooks (1917–   )

The Chicago Picasso

August 15, 1967

"Mayor Daley tugged a white ribbon, loosing the blue percale wrap. A hearty cheer went up as the covering slipped off the big steel sculpture that looks at once like a bird and a woman."   Chicago Sun-Times

*(Seiji Ozawa leads the Symphony.
The Mayor smiles.
And 50,000 See.)*

Does man love Art? Man visits Art, but squirms.
Art hurts. Art urges voyages —
and it is easier to stay at home,
the nice beer ready.
    In commonrooms   5
we belch, or sniff, or scratch.
Are raw.

But we must cook ourselves and style ourselves for Art, who
is a requiring courtesan.†
We squirm.   10
We do not hug the Mona Lisa.
We
may touch or tolerate
an astounding fountain, or a horse-and-rider.
At most, another Lion.   15

Observe the tall cold of a Flower
which is as innocent and as guilty,
as meaningful and as meaningless as any
other flower in the western field.

Robert Browning (1812–1889)

Love Among the Ruins

1.

Where the quiet-colored end of evening smiles,
    Miles and miles
On the solitary pastures where our sheep
    Half-asleep

9. *courtesan:* a high-class prostitute.

Tinkle homeward through the twilight, stray or stop   5
    As they crop —
Was the site once of a city great and gay
    (So they say),
Of our country's very capital, its prince
    Ages since   10
Held his court in, gathered councils, wielding far
    Peace or war.

2.

Now — the country does not even boast a tree,
    As you see,
To distinguish slopes of verdure, certain rills   15
    From the hills
Intersect and give a name to (else they run
    Into one),
Where the domed and daring palace shot its spires
    Up like fires   20
O'er the hundred-gated circuit of a wall
    Bounding all,
Made of marble, men might march on nor be pressed,
    Twelve abreast.

3.

And such plenty and perfection, see, of grass   25
    Never was!
Such a carpet as, this summertime, o'erspreads
    And embeds
Every vestige of the city, guessed alone,
    Stock or stone —   30
Where a multitude of men breathed joy and woe
    Long ago;
Lust of glory pricked their hearts up, dread of shame
    Struck them tame;
And that glory and that shame alike, the gold   35
    Bought and sold.

4.

Now — the single little turret that remains
    On the plains,
By the caper overrooted, by the gourd
    Overscored,   40
While the patching houseleek's head of blossom winks
    Through the chinks —
Marks the basement whence a tower in ancient time
    Sprang sublime,
And a burning ring, all round, the chariots traced   45
    As they raced,

And the monarch and his minions† and his dames
    Viewed the games.

5.

And I know, while thus the quiet-colored eve
    Smiles to leave 50
To their folding, all our many-tinkling fleece
    In such peace,
And the slopes and rills in undistinguished gray
    Melt away —
That a girl with eager eyes and yellow hair 55
    Waits me there
In the turret whence the charioteers caught soul
    For the goal,
When the king looked, where she looks now, breathless, dumb
    Till I come. 60

6.

But he looked upon the city, every side,
    Far and wide,
All the mountains topped with temples, all the glades'
    Colonnades,
All the causeys,† bridges, aqueducts — and then, 65
    All the men!
When I do come, she will speak not, she will stand,
    Either hand
On my shoulder, give her eyes the first embrace
    Of my face, 70
Ere we rush, ere we extinguish sight and speech
    Each on each.

7.

In one year they sent a million fighters forth
    South and north,
And they built their gods a brazen pillar high 75
    As the sky,
Yet reserved a thousand chariots in full force —
    Gold, of course,
Oh heart! oh blood that freezes, blood that burns!
    Earth's returns 80
For whole centuries of folly, noise, and sin!
    Shut them in,
With their triumphs and their glories and the rest!
    Love is best.

47. *minions:* favorites.   65. *causeys:* embankments or causeways.

Exercises

1. The poem alternates between the past and the present. What is the effect of this alternation? How does it prepare us for the conclusion?

2. What role does the setting play?

3. How does Browning use time in the poem?

Topic for Writing

What is Browning's attitude toward the reader in this poem? In an essay, discuss how he presents information, and shares his insights and his view of life with the reader. Support your comments with specific references to the poem.

Respectability

1.

Dear, had the world in its caprice
    Deigned to proclaim "I know you both,
    Have recognized your plighted troth,
Am sponsor for you: live in peace!" —
How many precious months and years   5
    Of youth had passed, that speed so fast,
    Before we found it out at last,
The world, and what it fears?

2.

How much of priceless life were spent
    With men that every virtue decks,   10
    And women models of their sex,
Society's true ornament —
Ere we dared wander, nights like this,
    Through wind and rain, and watch the Seine,
    And feel the Boulevard break again   15
To warmth and light and bliss?

3.

I know! the world proscribes not love;
    Allows my fingers to caress
    Your lips' contour and downiness,
Provided it supply a glove.   20
The world's good word! — the Institute!†

21. *the Institute:* the Institut National that directed higher education in France.

Guizot receives Montalembert!†
Eh? Down the court three lampions† flare:
Put forward your best foot!

William Cullen Bryant (1794–1878)

Thanatopsis

To him who in the love of Nature holds
Communion with her visible forms, she speaks
A various language; for his gayer hours
She has a voice of gladness, and a smile
And eloquence of beauty, and she glides   5
Into his darker musings, with a mild
And healing sympathy, that steals away
Their sharpness, ere he is aware. When thoughts
Of the last bitter hour come like a blight
Over thy spirit, and sad images   10
Of the stern agony, and shroud, and pall,
And breathless darkness, and the narrow house,
Make thee to shudder and grow sick at heart; —
Go forth, under the open sky, and list
To Nature's teachings, while from all around —   15
Earth and her waters, and the depths of air —
Comes a still voice — Yet a few days, and thee
The all-beholding sun shall see no more
In all his course; nor yet in the cold ground,
Where thy pale form was laid, with many tears,   20
Nor in the embrace of ocean, shall exist
Thy image. Earth, that nourished thee, shall claim
Thy growth, to be resolved to earth again,
And, lost each human trace, surrendering up
Thine individual being, shalt thou go   25
To mix forever with the elements,
To be a brother to the insensible rock
And to the sluggish clod, which the rude swain
Turns with his share, and treads upon. The oak
Shall send his roots abroad, and pierce thy mould.   30

Yet not to thine eternal resting-place
Shalt thou retire alone, nor couldst thou wish
Couch more magnificent. Thou shalt lie down
With patriarchs of the infant world — with kings,

22. *Guizot:* François Pierre Guil-
laume Guizot (1787–1874), French
historian and statesman; *Montalembert:* Count Charles de Montalembert (1810–1870), French
statesman. Guizot stressed the importance of the middle class,
while Montalembert supported liberal policies in government.
23. *lampions:* small oil lamps.

The powerful of the earth — the wise, the good,   35
Fair forms, and hoary seers of ages past,
All in one mighty sepulchre. The hills
Rock-ribbed and ancient as the sun, — the vales
Stretching in pensive quietness between;
The venerable woods — rivers that move   40
In majesty, and the complaining brooks
That make the meadows green; and, poured round all,
Old Ocean's gray and melancholy waste, —
Are but the solemn decorations all
Of the great tomb of man. The golden sun,   45
The planets, all the infinite host of heaven,
Are shining on the sad abodes of death,
Through the still lapse of ages. All that tread
The globe are but a handful to the tribes
That slumber in its bosom. — Take the wings   50
Of morning, pierce the Barcan† wilderness,
Or lose thyself in the continuous woods
Where rolls the Oregon,† and hears no sound,
Save his own dashings — yet the dead are there:
And millions in those solitudes, since first   55
The flight of years began, have laid them down
In their last sleep — the dead reign there alone.
So shalt thou rest, and what if thou withdraw
In silence from the living, and no friend
Take note of thy departure? All that breathe   60
Will share thy destiny. The gay will laugh
When thou are gone, the solemn brood of care
Plod on, and each one as before will chase
His favorite phantom; yet all these shall leave
Their mirth and their employments, and shall come   65
And make their bed with thee. As the long train
Of ages glide away, the sons of men,
The youth in life's green spring, and he who goes
In the full strength of years, matron and maid,
The speechless babe, and the gray-headed man —   70
Shall one by one be gathered to thy side,
By those, who in their turn shall follow them.

  So live, that when thy summons comes to join
The innumerable caravan, which moves
To that mysterious realm, where each shall take   75
His chamber in the silent halls of death,
Thou go not, like the quarry-slave at night,
Scourged to his dungeon, but, sustained and soothed
By an unfaltering trust, approach thy grave,
Like one who wraps the drapery of his couch   80
About him, and lies down to pleasant dreams.

51. *Barcan:* reference to a town   53. *Oregon:* old name for the Coin Africa — hence, "eastern."   lumbia River in the northwestern
                                     United States.

1. According to the speaker of the poem, what happens after death?

2. Does the poem offer any consolation to those who contemplate death? What consolation?

3. What is the role of nature in the universe described in this poem?

Topic for Writing

Given the state of affairs described in the poem, how does a moral person live? What rules should one live by? Discuss these questions in an essay, making specific references to the poem.

To the Fringed Gentian

Thou blossom bright with autumn dew,
And colored with the heaven's own blue,
That openest when the quiet light
Succeeds the keen and frosty night —

Thou comest not when violets lean   5
O'er wandering brooks and springs unseen,
Or columbines, in purple dressed,
Nod o'er the ground-bird's hidden nest.

Thou waitest late and com'st alone,
When woods are bare and birds are flown,   10
And frosts and shortening days portend
The aged year is near his end.

Then doth thy sweet and quiet eye
Look through its fringes to the sky,
Blue — blue — as if that sky let fall   15
A flower from its cerulean wall.

I would that thus, when I shall see
The hour of death draw near to me,
Hope, blossoming within my heart,
May look to heaven as I depart.   20

Topic for Writing

In an essay explain the details of the poet's central metaphor (the speaker compared to the fringed gentian) and evaluate its effectiveness. As preparation, consult a handbook of wildflowers for information about, and a colored photograph of, the fringed gentian. Then list the elements of the metaphor employed in the final two stanzas — for example, identify the "eye" of the flower (line 13), what it corresponds to in the speaker (line 19), and why this part of the blossom is appropriate as a vehicle for the tenor it describes. Finally, explain the speaker's main point as it is expressed in the last two stanzas.

Robert Burns (1759–1796)

A Red, Red Rose

O, my luve is like a red, red rose,
    That's newly sprung in June.
O, my luve is like the melodie,
    That's sweetly played in tune.

As fair art thou, my bonnie lass,   *5*
    So deep in luve am I,
And I will luve thee still, my dear,
    Till a' the seas gang dry.

Till a' the seas gang dry, my dear,
    And the rocks melt wi' the sun!   *10*
And I will luve thee still, my dear,
    While the sands o' life shall run.

And fare thee weel, my only luve,
    And fare thee weel a while!
And I will come again, my luve,   *15*
    Tho' it were ten thousand mile!

Holy Willie's† Prayer

O Thou, wha in the heavens dost dwell,
Wha, as it pleases best thysel',
Sends ane† to heaven and ten to hell,
    A'† for thy glory,
And no for ony guid or ill   *5*
    They've done afore thee!

I bless and praise thy matchless might,
Whan thousands thou hast left in night,
That I am here afore thy sight,
    For gifts an' grace   *10*
A burnin' an' a shinin' light,
    To a' this place.

Holy Willie: William Fisher, a   3. *ane:* one.
hypocritical elder in a church near   4. *a':* all.
Burns's farm.

What was I, or my generation,
That I should get sic† exaltation?
I, wha deserve most just damnation,
   For broken laws,
Sax thousand years 'fore my creation,
   Thro' Adam's cause.

15

When frae† my mither's womb I fell,
Thou might hae plungéd me in hell,
To gnash my gums, to weep and wail,
   In burnin' lakes,
Where damnéd devils roar and yell,
   Chained to their stakes;

20

Yet I am here a chosen sample,
To show thy grace is great and ample;
I'm here a pillar in thy temple,
   Strong as a rock,
A guide, a buckler, an example
   To a' thy flock.

25

30

O Lord, thou kens† what zeal I bear,
When drinkers drink, and swearers swear.
And singin' there and dancin' here,
   Wi' great an' sma:
For I am keepit by thy fear
   Free frae them a'.

35

But yet, O Lord! confess I must
At times I'm fashed† wi' fleshy lust;
An' sometimes too, wi' warldly trust,
   Vile self gets in;
But thou remembers we are dust,
   Defiled in sin.

40

O Lord! yestreen,† thou kens, wi' Meg —
Thy pardon I sincerely beg;
O! may't ne'er be a livin' plague
   To my dishonour,
An' I'll ne'er lift a lawless leg
   Again upon her.

45

Besides I farther maun allow,
Wi' Lizzie's lass, three times I trow —
But, Lord, that Friday I was fou,†
   When I cam near her,
Or else thou kens thy servant true
   Wad never steer† her.

50

14. *sic:* such.
19. *frae:* from.
31. *kens:* knows.
38. *fashed:* bothered.

43. *yestreen:* yesterday evening.
51. *fou:* full, or drunk.
54. *steer:* stir.

May be thou lets this fleshly thorn   *55*
Beset thy servant e'en and morn
Lest he owre high and proud should turn,
      That he's sae gifted;
If sae, thy hand maun† e'en be borne,
      Until thou lift it.   *60*

Lord, bless thy chosen in this place,
For here thou hast a chosen race;
But God confound their stubborn face,
      And blast their name,
Wha bring thy elders to disgrace   *65*
      An' public shame.

Lord, mind Gawn Hamilton's† deserts,
He drinks, an' swears, an' plays at cartes,
Yet has sae mony takin' arts
      Wi' great an' sma',   *70*
Frae God's ain priest the people's hearts
      He steals awa'.

An' when we chastened him therefor,
Thou kens how he bred sic a splore†
As set the warld in a roar   *75*
      O' laughin' at us;
Curse thou his basket and his store,
      Kail† and potatoes.

Lord, hear my earnest cry an' pray'r,
Against that presbytery o' Ayr;†   *80*
Thy strong right hand, Lord, make it bare
      Upo' their heads;
Lord, weigh it down, and dinna spare,
      For their misdeeds.

O Lord my God, that glib-tongued Aiken,†   *85*
My very heart and soul are quakin',
To think how we stood sweatin', shakin',
      An' pissed wi' dread,
While he, wi' hingin lips and snakin,†
      Held up his head.   *90*

Lord in the day of vengeance try him;
Lord, visit them wha did employ him,
And pass not in thy mercy by them,
      Nor hear their pray'r:

---

59. *maun:* must.
67. *Gawn Hamilton:* Burns's friend who was accused by Fisher's church of several religious offenses.
74. *splore:* row, or argument.
78. *kail:* kale, or cabbage.

80. *Presbytery of Ayr:* Cleared Hamilton of all charges.
85. [*Robert*] *Aiken:* Hamilton's lawyer.
89. *snakin:* sneering.

But, for thy people's sake, destroy them,   95
    And dinna spare.

But, Lord, remember me and mine
Wi' mercies temp'ral and divine,
That I for gear† and grace may shine
    Excelled by nane,   100
And a' the glory shall be thine,
    Amen, Amen!

George Gordon, Lord Byron (1788–1824)

She walks in beauty

She walks in beauty, like the night
    Of cloudless climes and starry skies;
And all that's best of dark and bright
    Meet in her aspect and her eyes:
Thus mellow'd to that tender light   5
    Which heaven to gaudy day denies.

One shade the more, one ray the less,
    Had half impaired the nameless grace
Which waves in every raven tress,
    Or softly lightens o'er her face;   10
Where thoughts serenely sweet express
    How pure, how dear their dwelling-place.

And on that cheek, and o'er that brow,
    So soft, so calm, yet eloquent,
The smiles that win, the tints that glow,   15
    But tell of days in goodness spent,
A mind at peace with all below,
    A heart whose love is innocent!

Stanzas

When a man hath no freedom to fight for at home,
    Let him combat for that of his neighbors;
Let him think of the glories of Greece and of Rome,
    And get knocked on his head for his labors.
To do good to mankind is the chivalrous plan,   5
    And is always as nobly requited;
Then battle for freedom wherever you can,
    And, if not shot or hanged, you'll get knighted.

---

99. *gear:* earthly wealth.

There is a garden in her face

There is a garden in her face,
Where roses and white lilies grow;
  A heav'nly paradise is that place,
Wherein all pleasant fruits do flow.
    There cherries grow which none may buy   5
    Till cherry-ripe themselves do cry.

    Those cherries fairly do enclose
Of orient pearl a double row,
  Which when her lovely laughter shows,
They look like rosebuds filled with snow.   10
    Yet them nor peer nor prince can buy,
    Till cherry-ripe themselves do cry.

    Her eyes like angels watch them still;
Her brows like bended bows do stand,
  Threat'ning with piercing frowns to kill   15
All that attempt with eye or hand
    Those sacred cherries to come nigh,
    Till cherry-ripe themselves do cry.

Dejection: An Ode

Late, late yestreen I saw the new Moon,
With the old Moon in her arms;
And I fear, I fear, my master dear!
We shall have a deadly storm.
             Ballad of Sir Patrick Spence

1.

Well! If the bard was weather-wise, who made
  The grand old ballad of Sir Patrick Spence,
  This night, so tranquil now, will not go hence
Unroused by winds, that ply a busier trade
Than those which mold yon cloud in lazy flakes,   5
Or the dull sobbing draft, that moans and rakes
Upon the strings of this Aeolian lute,†
  Which better far were mute.
  For lo! the New-moon winter-bright!
  And overspread with phantom light,   10
  (With swimming phantom light o'erspread

7. *Aeolian lute:* harp whose strings are activated by the wind; named after Aeolus, classical god of the winds.

But rimmed and circled by a silver thread)
I see the old Moon in her lap, foretelling
    The coming-on of rain and squally blast.
And oh! that even now the gust were swelling,   15
    And the slant night shower driving loud and fast!
Those sounds which oft have raised me, whilst they awed,
    And sent my soul abroad,
Might now perhaps their wonted† impulse give,
Might startle this dull pain, and make it move and live!   20

2.

A grief without a pang, void, dark, and drear,
    A stifled, drowsy, unimpassioned grief,
    Which finds no natural outlet, no relief,
        In word, or sigh, or tear —
O Lady! in this wan and heartless mood,   25
To other thoughts by yonder throstle† wooed,
    All this long eve, so balmy and serene,
Have I been gazing on the western sky,
    And its peculiar tint of yellow green:
And still I gaze — and with how blank an eye!   30
And those thin clouds above, in flakes and bars,
That give away their motion to the stars;
Those stars, that glide behind them or between,
Now sparkling, now bedimmed, but always seen:
Yon crescent Moon, as fixed as if it grew   35
In its own cloudless, starless lake of blue;
I see them all so excellently fair,
I see, not feel, how beautiful they are!

3.

        My genial spirits† fail;
        And what can these avail   40
To lift the smothering weight from off my breast?
        It were a vain endeavor,
        Though I should gaze forever
On that green light that lingers in the west:
I may not hope from outward forms to win   45
The passion and the life, whose fountains are within.

4.

O Lady!† we receive but what we give,
And in our life alone does Nature live:
Ours is her wedding garment, ours her shroud!

19. *wonted:* usual.
26. *throstle:* thrush.
39. *genial spirits:* mental, physical, and spiritual energies and capacities.
47. *Lady:* in the original version, the poet wrote "Sara," a reference to Sara Hutchinson (with whom he was in love); later he changed it to "William" (Wordsworth), then to "Edmund," and finally to "Lady."

And would we aught behold, of higher worth,   *50*
Than that inanimate cold world allowed
To the poor loveless ever-anxious crowd,
    Ah! from the soul itself must issue forth
A light, a glory, a fair luminous cloud
      Enveloping the Earth —   *55*
And from the soul itself must there be sent
    A sweet and potent voice, of its own birth,
Of all sweet sounds the life and element!

5.

O pure of heart! thou need'st not ask of me
What this strong music in the soul may be!   *60*
What, and wherein it doth exist,
This light, this glory, this fair luminous mist,
This beautiful and beauty-making power.
    Joy, virtuous Lady! Joy that ne'er was given,
Save to the pure, and in their purest hour,   *65*
Life, and Life's effluence,† cloud at once and shower,
Joy, Lady! is the spirit and the power,
Which wedding Nature to us gives in dower
    A new Earth and new Heaven,
Undreamt of by the sensual and the proud —   *70*
Joy is the sweet voice, Joy the luminous cloud —
    We in ourselves rejoice!
And thence flows all that charms or ear or sight,
    All melodies the echoes of that voice,
All colors a suffusion from that light.   *75*

6.

There was a time when, though my path was rough,
    This joy within me dallied with distress,
And all misfortunes were but as the stuff
    Whence Fancy made me dreams of happiness:
For hope grew round me, like the twining vine,   *80*
And fruits, and foliage, not my own, seemed mine.
But now afflictions bow me down to earth:
Nor care I that they rob me of my mirth;
    But oh! each visitation
Suspends what nature gave me at my birth,   *85*
    My shaping spirit of Imagination.
For not to think of what I needs must feel,
    But to be still and patient, all I can;
And happly by abstruse research to steal
    From my own nature all the natural man —   *90*
    This was my sole resource, my only plan:
Till that which suits a part infects the whole,
And now is almost grown the habit of my soul.

66. *effluence:* vital energies.

7.

Hence, viper thoughts, that coil around my mind,
   Reality's dark dream!   95
I turn from you, and listen to the wind,
   Which long has raved unnoticed. What a scream
Of agony by torture lengthened out
That lute sent forth! Thou Wind, that rav'st without,
   Bare crag, or mountain tairn,† or blasted tree,   100
Or pine grove whither woodman never clomb,
Or lonely house, long held — the witches' home,
   Methinks were fitter instruments for thee,
Mad lutanist! who in this month of showers,
Of dark-brown gardens, and of peeping flowers,   105
Mak'st devils' yule,† with worse than wintry song,
The blossoms, buds, and timorous leaves among.
   Thou actor, perfect in all tragic sounds!
Thou mighty poet, e'en to frenzy bold!
     What tell'st thou now about?   110
   'Tis of the rushing of an host in rout,
   With groans, of trampled men, with smarting wounds —
At once they groan with pain, and shudder with the cold!
But hush! there is a pause of deepest silence!
   And all that noise, as of a rushing crowd,   115
With groans, and tremulous shudderings — all is over —
   It tells another tale, with sounds less deep and loud!
     A tale of less affright,
     And tempered with delight,
As Otway's† self had framed the tender lay† —   120
     'Tis of a little child
     Upon a lonesome wild,
Not far from home, but she hath lost her way:
And now moans low in bitter grief and fear,
And now screams loud, and hopes to make her mother hear.   125

8.

'Tis midnight, but small thoughts have I of sleep:
Full seldom may my friend such vigils keep!
Visit her, gentle Sleep! with wings of healing,
   And may this storm be but a mountain birth,
May all the stars hang bright above her dwelling,   130
   Silent as though they watched the sleeping Earth!
     With light heart may she rise,
     Gay fancy, cheerful eyes,
   Joy lift her spirit, joy attune her voice;
To her may all things live, from pole to pole,   135

100. *tairn:* tarn, small lake.
106. *devils' yule:* an unnatural Christmas caused by a winter storm in the spring.

120. *Otway's:* Thomas Otway (1652–1685), English dramatist whose tragic scenes are particularly heart-rending; *lay:* poem.

Their life the eddying of her living soul!
  O simple spirit, guided from above,
Dear Lady! friend devoutest of my choice,
Thus mayest thou ever, evermore rejoice.

Topics for Writing

1. Demonstrate the validity or falseness of the theory that first and last words, combined, sometimes capture the import of a poem. In an essay on "Dejection: An Ode," consider, in detail, the speaker's dilemma and its resolution. Then decide whether the linking of the first word ("Well") with the last ("rejoice") captures the heart of the poem, and argue the point in your discussion.

2. After reading the poem carefully, read "Sir Patrick Spens" (also in this chapter), from which Coleridge borrows for this poem. Explain what purposes this early ballad serves in "Dejection: An Ode."

3. Write an essay that answers the following questions in an organized fashion: Why is the speaker distraught? Is the poem itself evidence of what he claims to have lost? Is the poem as a whole optimistic or pessimistic? How do you know?

4. Evaluate the quality of this poem. Focus, at a minimum, on two of the three criteria for evaluation presented in the introduction to poetry.

Kubla Khan†

Or, A Vision in a Dream. A Fragment.

In Xanadu† did Kubla Khan
A stately pleasure dome decree:
Where Alph,† the sacred river, ran

Title: "Kubla Khan," according to the poet, was composed during an opium-induced dream. Coleridge claims to have taken two grains of opium for ill health and to have fallen asleep after reading the following sentence from *Purchas His Pilgrimage*, a travel book first published in 1613: "In Xamdu did Cublai Can build a stately Palace, encompassing sixteen miles of plain ground with a wall, wherein are fertile meadows, pleasant springs, delightful streams, and all sorts of beasts of chase and game, and in the middest thereof a sumptuous house of pleasure." Awakening after three hours, during which he composed in his mind two or three hundred lines, Coleridge immediately wrote down the fifty-four lines here preserved. He was interrupted for an hour, and upon returning discovered to his mortification that he could not recollect the remainder of the poem.

1. *Xanadu:* the Xamdu mentioned by Purchas. It was the summer residence of Kublai Khan, first ruler (or *khan*) of the Mongol dynasty in thirteenth-century China. Today the location is called Shang-tu.

3. *Alph:* probably suggested by the Greek river Alpheus, cited in Milton's famous elegy *Lycidas* (line 133), that runs underground in certain locations and was thought in ancient times to run unmixed beneath the sea.

Through caverns measureless to man
   Down to a sunless sea.   5
So twice five miles of fertile ground
With walls and towers were girdled round:
And there were gardens bright with sinuous rills,†
Where blossomed many an incense-bearing tree;
And here were forests ancient as the hills,   10
Enfolding sunny spots of greenery.
But oh! that deep romantic chasm which slanted
Down the green hill athwart a cedarn cover!
A savage place! as holy and enchanted
As e'er beneath a waning moon was haunted   15
By woman wailing for her demon lover!
And from this chasm, with ceaseless turmoil seething,
As if this earth in fast thick pants were breathing,
A mighty fountain momently† was forced:
Amid whose swift half-intermitted burst   20
Huge fragments vaulted like rebounding hail,
Or chaffy grain beneath the thresher's flail:
And 'mid these dancing rocks at once and ever
It flung up momently the sacred river.
Five miles meandering with a mazy motion   25
Through wood and dale the sacred river ran,
Then reached the caverns measureless to man,
And sank in tumult to a lifeless ocean:
And 'mid this tumult Kubla heard from far
Ancestral voices prophesying war!   30
   The shadow of the dome of pleasure
    Floated midway on the waves;
   Where was heard the mingled measure
    From the fountain and the caves.
It was a miracle of rare device,   35
A sunny pleasure dome with caves of ice!

   A damsel with a dulcimer†
   In a vision once I saw:
   It was an Abyssinian maid,
   And on her dulcimer she played,   40
   Singing of Mount Abora.†
Could I revive within me
Her symphony and song,
To such a deep delight 'twould win me,
That with music loud and long,   45
I would build that dome in air,
That sunny dome! those caves of ice!
And all who heard should see them there,

---

8. *sinuous rills:* winding brooks.
19. *momently:* each moment.
37. *dulcimer:* stringed instrument
played with hand-held hammers.

41. *Mount Abora:* probably the
Mount Amara in Abyssinia men-
tioned in Milton's *Paradise Lost*
(IV.281).

And all should cry, Beware! Beware!
His flashing eyes, his floating hair!   50
Weave a circle round him thrice,
And close your eyes with holy dread,
For he on honeydew hath fed,
And drunk the milk of Paradise.

e. e. cummings (1894–1962)

pity this busy monster,manunkind

pity this busy monster,manunkind,

not. Progress is a comfortable disease:
your victim(death and life safely beyond)

plays with the bigness of his littleness
— electrons deify one razorblade
into a mountainrange;lenses extend   5

unwish through curving wherewhen till unwish
returns on its unself.
                        A world of made
is not a world of born — pity poor flesh   10

and trees,poor stars and stones,but never this
fine specimen of hypermagical

ultraomnipotence. We doctors know

a hopeless case if — listen: there's a hell —
of a good universe next door;let's go   15

anyone lived in a pretty how town

anyone lived in a pretty how town
(with up so floating many bells down)
spring summer autumn winter
he sang his didn't he danced his did.

Women and men(both little and small)   5
cared for anyone not at all
they sowed their isn't they reaped their same
sun moon stars rain

children guessed(but only a few
and down they forgot as up they grew   10
autumn winter spring summer)
that noone loved him more by more

612   *Other Poems to Read*

when by now and tree by leaf
she laughed his joy she cried his grief
bird by snow and stir by still   *15*
anyone's any was all to her

someone married their everyones
laughed their cryings and did their dance
(sleep wake hope and then) they
said their nevers they slept their dream   *20*

stars rain sun moon
(and only the snow can begin to explain
how children are apt to forget to remember
with up so floating many bells down)

Emily Dickinson *(1830–1886)*

I died for Beauty — but was scarce

I died for Beauty — but was scarce
Adjusted in the Tomb
When One who died for Truth, was lain
In an adjoining Room —

He questioned softly "Why I failed"?   *5*
"For Beauty", I replied —
"And I — for Truth — Themself are One —
We Brethren, are", He said —

And so, as Kinsmen, met a Night —
We talked between the Rooms —   *10*
Until the Moss had reached our lips —
And covered up — our names —

I taste a liquor never brewed —

I taste a liquor never brewed —
From Tankards scooped in Pearl —
Not all the Frankfort Berries
Yield such an Alcohol!

Inebriate of Air — am I —   *5*
And Debauchee of Dew —
Reeling — thro endless summer days —
From inns of Molten Blue —

When "Landlords" turn the drunken Bee
Out of the Foxglove's door —   *10*

When Butterflies — renounce their "drams" —
I shall but drink the more!

Till Seraphs swing their snowy Hats —
And Saints — to windows run —
To see the little Tippler   15
From Manzanilla† come!

Because I could not stop for Death

Because I could not stop for Death —
He kindly stopped for me —
The Carriage held but just Ourselves —
And Immortality.

We slowly drove — He knew no haste   5
And I had put away
My labor and my leisure too,
For His Civility —

We passed the School, where Children strove
At Recess — in the Ring —   10
We passed the Fields of Gazing Grain —
We passed the Setting Sun —

Or rather — He passed Us —
The Dews drew quivering and chill —
For only Gossamer, my Gown —   15
My Tippet — only Tulle —

We paused before a House that seemed
A Swelling of the Ground —
The Roof was scarcely visible —
The Cornice — in the Ground —   20

Since then — 'tis Centuries — and yet
Feels shorter than the Day
I first surmised the Horses Heads
Were toward Eternity —

John Donne (1572–1631)

Death be not proud

Death be not proud, though some have callèd thee
Mighty and dreadful, for thou art not so;
For those whom thou think'st thou dost overthrow

16. *Manzanilla:* a Spanish sherry, also the name of towns in Mexico and Central America from which Monarch butterflies migrate.

Die not, poor Death, nor yet canst thou kill me.
From rest and sleep, which but thy pictures be, 5
Much pleasure; then from thee much more must flow,
And soonest our best men with thee do go,
Rest of their bones, and soul's delivery.
Thou art slave to fate, chance, kings, and desperate men,
And dost with poison, war, and sickness dwell, 10
And poppy or charms can make us sleep as well
And better than thy stroke; why swell'st thou then?
One short sleep past, we wake eternally
And death shall be no more; Death, thou shalt die.

The Triple Fool

I am two fools, I know,
For loving, and for saying so
   In whining poetry.
But where's that wise man that would not be I
   If she would not deny? 5
Then as th' earth's inward, narrow, crooked lanes
Do purge sea water's fretful salt away,
   I thought if I could draw my pains
Through rhyme's vexation, I should them allay.
Grief brought to numbers cannot be so fierce, 10
For he tames it that fetters it in verse.

   But when I have done so,
Some man, his art and voice to show,
   Doth set and sing my pain,
And by delighting many, frees again 15
   Grief, which verse did restrain.
To love and grief tribute of verse belongs,
But not of such as pleases when 'tis read;
   Both are increased by such songs,
For both their triumphs so are publishèd, 20
And I, which was two fools, do so grow three.
Who are a little wise, the best fools be.

Exercises

1. On what or whom is death dependent? Explain.

2. How are rest and sleep described? Comment on the importance of that description to Donne's argument.

3. What fact makes death impotent, according to the poem?

Topic for Writing

Compare and contrast Donne's view of death as it is presented here with Bryant's view in "Thanatopsis."

A Valediction:† Forbidding Mourning

As virtuous men pass mildly away,
   And whisper to their souls to go,
Whilst some of their sad friends do say
   The breath goes now, and some say, No;

So let us melt, and make no noise,   5
   No tear-floods, nor sigh-tempests move,
'Twere profanation of our joys
   To tell the laity our love.

Moving of the earth† brings harms and fears,
   Men reckon what it did and meant;   10
But trepidation of the spheres,†
   Though greater far, is innocent.

Dull sublunary† lovers' love
   (Whose soul is sense) cannot admit
Absence, because it doth remove   15
   Those things which elemented it.

But we by a love so much refined
   That our selves know not what it is,
Inter-assuréd of the mind,
   Care less, eyes, lips, and hands to miss.   20

Our two souls therefore, which are one,
   Though I must go, endure not yet
A breach, but an expansion,
   Like gold to airy thinness beat.

If they be two, they are two so   25
   As stiff twin compasses are two;
Thy soul, the fixed foot, makes no show
   To move, but doth, if the other do.

And though it in the center sit,
   Yet when the other far doth roam,   30

Valediction: farewell.
9. *moving of the earth:* earthquakes.
11. *trepidation of the spheres:* tremulous motion of the heavenly "spheres" or globes which, according to Ptolomaic astronomy, contained the heavenly bodies.
13. *sublunary:* beneath the moon — thus earthly, changeable, physical, low.

It leans and hearkens after it,
    And grows erect, as that comes home.

Such wilt thou be to me, who must
    Like the other foot, obliquely run;
Thy firmness makes my circle just,†   *35*
    And makes me end where I begun.

H.D. (Hilda Doolittle) (*1886–1961*)

Evening

The light passes
from ridge to ridge,
from flower to flower —
the hypaticas, wide-spread
under the light   *5*
grow faint —
the petals reach inward,
the blue tips bend
toward the bluer heart
and the flowers are lost.   *10*

The cornel-buds are still white,
but shadows dart
from the cornel-roots —
black creeps from root to root,
each leaf   *15*
cuts another leaf on the grass,
shadow seeks shadow,
then both leaf
and leaf-shadow are lost.

Exercises

1. Despite its brevity, "Evening" contains many visual images that provide a highly sensitive, perceptive description of fading light. Explain, step by step, what is happening in the poem.

2. How appropriate to the situation and mood is the botanical imagery in this poem? To answer this question, locate pictures (preferably in color) of *hypatica* (line 4, usually spelled *hepatica*) and *cornel* (line 11) in an encyclopedia of flowers and shrubs. Also locate descriptions of these plants to assist you in deciding why the poet chose them.

35. *just:* complete, exact, morally
correct and upright.

Paul Laurence Dunbar *(1872–1906)*

The Debt

This is the debt I pay
Just for one riotous day,
Years of regret and grief,
Sorrow without relief.

Pay it I will to the end —   5
Until the grave, my friend,
Gives me a true release —
Gives me the clasp of peace.

Slight was the thing I bought,
Small was the debt I thought,   10
Poor was the loan at best —
God! but the interest!

John Dryden *(1631–1700)*

A Song for St. Cecilia's Day†

1.

From harmony, from heavenly harmony
  This universal frame began;
    When Nature underneath a heap
      Of jarring atoms lay,
    And could not heave her head,   5
The tuneful Voice was heard from high,
    "Arise, ye more than dead."
Then cold and hot and moist and dry
    In order to their stations leap,
      And music's power obey.   10
From harmony, from heavenly harmony
    This universal frame began:
    From harmony to harmony
Through all the compass of the notes it ran,
The diapason† closing full in Man.   15

2.

What passion cannot music raise and quell?
  When Jubal† struck the corded shell,

St. Cecilia: patron saint of music, especially of church music; she was blind and, according to tradition, invented the organ. Her day is November 22.
15. *diapason:* the octave; an outburst of sound.

17. *Jubal:* in the Bible, a descendent of Cain, and inventor of musical instruments. He is called in Gen. 4:21, "the father of all such as handle the harp and the organ."

His listening brethren stood around,
    And, wondering, on their faces fell
To worship that celestial sound: *20*
Less than a God they thought there could not dwell
    Within the hollow of that shell,
    That spoke so sweetly and so well.
What passion cannot music raise and quell?

3.

The trumpet's loud clangor   *25*
    Excites us to arms
With shrill notes of anger
    And mortal alarms.
The double, double, double beat
    Of the thund'ring drum   *30*
Cries "Hark, the foes come;
Charge, charge, 'tis too late to retreat."

4.

The soft complaining flute
In dying notes discovers
The woes of hopeless lovers,   *35*
Whose dirge is whispered by the warbling lute.

5.

Sharp violins proclaim
Their jealous pangs and desperation,
Fury, frantic indignation,
Depth of pains and height of passion,   *40*
    For the fair, disdainful dame.

6.

But Oh! What art can teach,
What human voice can reach,
The sacred organ's praise?
Notes inspiring holy love,   *45*
Notes that wing their heavenly ways
    To mend the choirs above.

7.

Orpheus† could lead the savage race,
And trees unrooted left their place,
    Sequaceous† of the lyre;   *50*
But bright Cecilia raised the wonder higher;
When to her organ vocal breath was given,

48. *Orpheus:* the musician in Greek mythology who descended into the world of the dead to release his wife, Eurydice.

50. *sequaceous:* following, as one follows a leader.

An angel heard and straight appeared,
    Mistaking earth for heaven.

   Grand Chorus

As from the power of sacred lays   *55*
    The spheres began to move,
And sung the great Creator's praise
    To all the blest above;
So when the last and dreadful hour
This crumbling pageant shall devour,   *60*
The trumpet shall be heard on high,
The dead shall live, the living die,
And music shall untune the sky.

                     Richard Eberhart (1904–   )

If I could only live at the pitch that is near madness

If I could only live at the pitch that is near madness
When everything is as it was in my childhood
Violent, vivid, and of infinite possibility:
That the sun and the moon broke over my head.

Then I cast time out of the trees and fields,   *5*
Then I stood immaculate in the Ego;
Then I eyed the world with all delight,
Reality was the perfection of my sight.

And time has big handles on the hands,
Fields and trees a way of being themselves.   *10*
I saw battalions of the race of mankind
Standing stolid, demanding a moral answer.

I gave the moral answer and I died
And into a realm of complexity came
Where nothing is possible but necessity   *15*
And the truth wailing there like a red babe.

                    T. S. Eliot (1888–1965)

Preludes

1.

The winter evening settles down
With smell of steaks in passageways.
Six o'clock.

The burnt-out ends of smoky days.
And now a gusty shower wraps   5
The grimy scraps
Of withered leaves about your feet
And newspapers from vacant lots;
The showers beat
On broken blinds and chimney-pots,   10
And at the corner of the street
A lonely cab-horse steams and stamps.
And then the lighting of the lamps.

2.

The morning comes to consciousness
Of faint stale smells of beer   15
From the sawdust-trampled street
With all its muddy feet that press
To early coffee-stands.
With the other masquerades
That time resumes,   20
One thinks of all the hands
That are raising dingy shades
In a thousand furnished rooms.

3.

You tossed a blanket from the bed,
You lay upon your back, and waited;   25
You dozed, and watched the night revealing
The thousand sordid images
Of which your soul was constituted;
They flickered against the ceiling.
And when all the world came back   30
And the light crept up between the shutters
And you heard the sparrows in the gutters,
You had such a vision of the street
As the street hardly understands;
Sitting along the bed's edge, where   35
You curled the papers from your hair,
Or clasped the yellow soles of feet
In the palms of both soiled hands.

4.

His soul stretched tight across the skies
That fade behind a city block,   40
Or trampled by insistent feet
At four and five and six o'clock;
And short square fingers stuffing pipes,
And evening newspapers, and eyes
Assured of certain certainties,   45
The conscience of a blackened street
Impatient to assume the world.

I am moved by fancies that are curled
Around these images, and cling:
The notion of some infinitely gentle   *50*
Infinitely suffering thing.

Wipe your hands across your mouth, and laugh;
The worlds revolve like ancient women
Gathering fuel in vacant lots.

Ralph Waldo Emerson (1803–1882)

Days

Daughters of Time, the hypocritic Days,
Muffled and dumb like barefoot dervishes,†
And marching single in an endless file,
Bring diadems† and fagots† in their hands.
To each they offer gifts after his will,   *5*
Bread, kingdom, stars, and sky that holds them all.

I, in my pleached † garden, watched the pomp,
Forgot my morning wishes, hastily
Took a few herbs and apples, and the Day
Turned and departed silent. I, too late,   *10*
Under her solemn fillet† saw the scorn.

Each and All

Little thinks, in the field, yon red-cloaked clown
Of thee from the hill-top looking down;
The heifer that lows in the upland farm,
Far-heard, lows not thine ear to charm;
The sexton, tolling his bell at noon,   *5*
Deems not that great Napoleon
Stops his horse, and lists with delight,
Whilst his files sweep round yon Alpine height;
Nor knowest thou what argument
Thy life to thy neighbor's creed has lent.   *10*
All are needed by each one;
Nothing is fair or good alone.
I thought the sparrow's note from heaven,

2. *dervishes:* members of Muslim ascetic religious orders, some of which are known for body movements leading to a hypnotic trance.
4. *diadems:* crowns; *fagots* (faggots): bundle of sticks and branches; a bundle or collection of miscellaneous items.
7. *pleached:* fenced or bordered by intertwining branches.
11. *fillet:* ribbon headband.

Singing at dawn on the alder bough;
I brought him home, in his nest, at even;   15
He sings the song, but it cheers not now,
For I did not bring home the river and sky; —
He sang to my ear, — they sang to my eye.
The delicate shells lay on the shore;
The bubbles of the latest wave   20
Fresh pearls to their enamel gave,
And the bellowing of the savage sea
Greeted their safe escape to me.
I wiped away the weeds and foam,
I fetched my sea-born treasures home;   25
But the poor, unsightly, noisome things
Had left their beauty on the shore
With the sun and the sand and the wild uproar.
The lover watched his graceful maid,
As 'mid the virgin train she strayed,   30
Nor knew her beauty's best attire
Was woven still by the snow-white choir.
At last she came to his hermitage,
Like the bird from the woodlands to the cage: —
The gay enchantment was undone,   35
A gentle wife, but fairy none.
Then I said, "I covet truth;
Beauty is unripe childhood's cheat;
I leave it behind with the games of youth;" —
As I spoke, beneath my feet   40
The ground-pine curled its pretty wreath,
Running over the club-moss burrs;
I inhaled the violet's breath;
Around me stood the oaks and firs;
Pine-cones and acorns lay on the ground;   45
Over me soared the eternal sky,
Full of light and of deity;
Again I saw, again I heard,
The rolling river, the morning bird; —
Beauty through my senses stole;   50
I yielded myself to the perfect whole.

D. J. Enright (1920–   )

Buy One Now

This is a new sort of Poem,
It is Biological.
It contains a special Ingredient
(Pat. pend.) which makes it different
From other brands of poem on the market.   5

This new Poem does the work for you.
Just drop your mind into it
And leave it to soak
While you relax with the telly
Or go out to the pub   10
Or (if that is what you like)
You read a book.

It does the work for you
While (if that is what you like)
You sleep. For it is Biological   15
(Pat. pend.), it penetrates
Into the darkest recesses,
It removes the understains
Which it is difficult for us
Even to speak of.   20

Its action is so gentle
That the most delicate mind is unharmed.
This new sort of Poem
Contains an exclusive new Ingredient
(Known only to every jackass in the trade)   25
And can be found in practically any magazine
You care to mention.

Anne Finch, Countess of
Winchilsea (1661–1720)

To the Nightingale

Exert thy voice, sweet harbinger of spring!
   This moment is thy time to sing,
   This moment I attend to praise,
And set my numbers to thy lays.†
   Free as thine shall be my song,   5
   As thy music, short or long.
Poets, wild as thee, were born,
   Pleasing best when unconfined,
   When to please is least designed,
Soothing but their cares to rest;   10
   Cares do still their thoughts molest,
   And still the unhappy poet's breast,
Like thine, when best he sings, is placed against a thorn.

   She begins. Let all be still!
   Muse, thy promise now fulfil!   15

4. *my numbers to thy lays:* my
verses to your tunes.

Sweet, oh sweet! still sweeter yet!
Can thy words such accents fit,
Canst thou syllables refine,
Melt a sense that shall retain
Still some spirit of the brain,   *20*
Till with sounds like these it join?
   'Twill not be! then change thy note,
   Let division shake thy throat.
Hark! division now she tries,
Yet as far the Muse outflies.   *25*
   Cease then, prithee, cease thy tune!
   Trifler, wilt thou sing till June?
Till thy business all lies waste,
And the time of building's past?
   Thus we poets that have speech,   *30*
Unlike what thy forests teach,
   If a fluent vein be shown
   That's transcendent to our own,
Criticize, reform, or preach,
Or censure what we cannot reach.   *35*

[handwritten: aoo: being a poet is like the one road — road travelled etc.]

Robert Frost *(1874–1963)*

The Road Not Taken

Two roads diverged in a yellow wood,
And sorry I could not travel both
And be one traveler, long I stood
And looked down one as far as I could
To where it bent in the undergrowth;   *5*

Then took the other, as just as fair,
And having perhaps the better claim,
Because it was grassy and wanted wear;
Though as for that, the passing there
Had worn them really about the same,   *10*

And both that morning equally lay
In leaves no step had trodden black.
Oh, I kept the first for another day!
Yet knowing how way leads on to way,
I doubted if I should ever come back.   *15*

I shall be telling this with a sigh
Somewhere ages and ages hence:
Two roads diverged in a wood, and I —
I took the one less traveled by,
And that has made all the difference.   *20*

[handwritten margin note: life is like the road... you take one and pay the consequences. you must make a choice and you can't go back & do it all even if you say you'll come back, etc]

Stopping by Woods on a Snowy Evening

Whose woods these are I think I know.
His house is in the village, though;
He will not see me stopping here
To watch his woods fill up with snow.

My little horse must think it queer   5
To stop without a farmhouse near
Between the woods and frozen lake
The darkest evening of the year.

He gives his harness bells a shake
To ask if there is some mistake.   10
The only other sound's the sweep
Of easy wind and downy flake.

The woods are lovely, dark, and deep,
But I have promises to keep,
And miles to go before I sleep,   15
And miles to go before I sleep.

Birches

When I see birches bend to left and right
Across the lines of straighter darker trees,
I like to think some boy's been swinging them.
But swinging doesn't bend them down to stay
As ice storms do. Often you must have seen them   5
Loaded with ice a sunny winter morning
After a rain. They click upon themselves
As the breeze rises, and turn many-colored
As the stir cracks and crazes their enamel.
Soon the sun's warmth makes them shed crystal shells   10
Shattering and avalanching on the snow crust —
Such heaps of broken glass to sweep away
You'd think the inner dome of heaven had fallen.
They are dragged to the withered bracken by the load,
And they seem not to break; though once they are bowed   15
So low for long, they never right themselves:
You may see their trunks arching in the woods
Years afterwards, trailing their leaves on the ground
Like girls on hands and knees that throw their hair
Before them over their heads to dry in the sun.   20
But I was going to say when Truth broke in
With all her matter of fact about the ice storm,
I should prefer to have some boy bend them
As he went out and in to fetch the cows —
Some boy too far from town to learn baseball,   25

Whose only play was what he found himself,
Summer or winter, and could play alone.
One by one he subdued his father's trees
By riding them down over and over again
Until he took the stiffness out of them,   30
And not one but hung limp, not one was left
For him to conquer. He learned all there was
To learn about not launching out too soon
And so not carrying the tree away
Clear to the ground. He always kept his poise   35
To the top branches, climbing carefully
With the same pains you use to fill a cup
Up to the brim, and even above the brim.
Then he flung outward, feet first, with a swish,
Kicking his way down through the air to the ground.   40
So was I once myself a swinger of birches.
And so I dream of going back to be.
It's when I'm weary of considerations,
And life is too much like a pathless wood
Where your face burns and tickles with the cobwebs   45
Broken across it, and one eye is weeping
From a twig's having lashed across it open.
I'd like to get away from earth awhile
And then come back to it and begin over.
May no fate willfully misunderstand me   50
And half grant what I wish and snatch me away
Not to return. Earth's the right place for love:
I don't know where it's likely to go better.
I'd like to go by climbing a birch tree,
And climb black branches up a snow-white trunk   55
Toward heaven, till the tree could bear no more,
But dipped its top and set me down again.
That would be good both going and coming back.
One could do worse than be a swinger of birches.

Nikki Giovanni (*1943–*   )

Kidnap Poem

ever been kidnapped
by a poet
if i were a poet
i'd kidnap you
put you in my phrases and meter   5
you to jones beach
or maybe coney island
or maybe just to my house
lyric you in lilacs

dash you in the rain   *10*
blend into the beach
to complement my see
play the lyre for you
ode you with my love song
anything to win you   *15*
wrap you in the red Black green
show you off to mama
yeah if i were a poet i'd kid
nap you

Robert Graves (1895–   )

A Slice of Wedding Cake

Why have such scores of lovely, gifted girls
    Married impossible men?
Simple self-sacrifice may be ruled out,
    And missionary endeavor, nine times out of ten.

Repeat "impossible men": not merely rustic,   5
    Foul-tempered or depraved
(Dramatic foils chosen to show the world
    How well women behave, and always have behaved).

Impossible men: idle, illiterate,
    Self-pitying, dirty, sly,   10
For whose appearance even in City parks
    Excuses must be made to casual passers-by.

Has God's supply of tolerable husbands
    Fallen, in fact, so low?
Or do I always over-value woman   15
    At the expense of man?
            Do I?
               It might be so.

Thomas Gray (1716–1771)

Ode on the Death of a Favorite Cat,
Drowned in a Tub of Goldfishes

'Twas on a lofty vase's side,
Where China's gayest art had dyed
The azure flowers that blow;†

3. *blow:* bloom.

Demurest of the tabby kind,
The pensive Selima, reclined,
   Gazed on the lake below.   5

Her conscious tail her joy declared;
The fair round face, the snowy beard,
   The velvet of her paws,
Her coat, that with the tortoise vies,   10
Her ears of jet, and emerald eyes,
   She saw; and purred applause.

Still had she gazed; but 'midst the tide
Two angel forms were seen to glide,
   The genii† of the stream: 15
Their scaly armor's Tyrian hue†
Through richest purple to the view
   Betrayed a golden gleam.

The hapless nymph with wonder saw:
A whisker first and then a claw,   20
   With many an ardent wish,
She stretched in vain to reach the prize.
What female heart can gold despise?
   What cat's averse to fish?

Presumptuous maid! with looks intent   25
Again she stretched, again she bent,
   Nor knew the gulf between.
(Malignant Fate sat by and smiled)
The slippery verge her feet beguiled,
   She tumbled headlong in.   30

Eight times emerging from the flood
She mewed to every watery god,
   Some speedy aid to send.
No dolphin† came, no Nereid† stirred;
Nor cruel Tom, nor Susan† heard;   35
   A favorite has no friend!

From hence, ye beauties, undeceived,
Know, one false step is ne'er retrieved,
   And be with caution bold.
Not all that tempts your wandering eyes   40
And heedless hearts, is lawful prize;
   Nor all that glisters,† gold.

15. *genii* (plural of *genie*): spirits.
16. *Tyrian hue:* red, maroon, or purple produced by dyes associated with the ancient Phoenician city of Tyre.
34. *dolphin:* in classical mythology a dolphin saved the poet-singer Arion after he was thrown overboard; *Nereid:* sea nymph.
35. *Tom . . . Susan:* typical eighteenth-century servants' names.
42. *glisters:* glitters.

Exercises

1. Why do you think the poet calls this tub a *lake* (line 6), a *tide* (line 13), a *stream* (line 15), and a *flood* (line 31)?

2. This poem is notably rich in color imagery. List each color used, along with the object it describes. When does the poet's use of vivid colors cease (with the possible exception of the last line, which refers to the metal gold)? Why?

3. As a mock-heroic poem, this ode depicts a ridiculous event in lofty tones and inflated language. List elements from the poem that contribute to its dignified tone and, because they're linked to a trivial theme, render the poem humorous.

4. Comment on the speaker's attitude toward the hapless tabby and toward women (doubtless typical of the period). Point to examples.

Barbara Guest (1923–   )

Parachutes, My Love, Could Carry Us Higher

I just said I didn't know
And now you are holding me
In your arms,
How kind.
Parachutes, my love, could carry us higher.   5
Yet around the net I am floating
Pink and pale blue fish are caught in it,
They are beautiful,
But they are not good for eating.
Parachutes, my love, could carry us higher   10
Than this mid-air in which we tremble,
Having exercised our arms in swimming,
Now the suspension, you say,
Is exquisite. I do not know.
There is coral below the surface,   15
There is sand, and berries
Like pomegranates grow.
This wide net, I am treading water
Near it, bubbles are rising and salt
Drying on my lashes, yet I am no nearer   20
Air than water. I am closer to you
Than land and I am in a stranger ocean
Than I wished.

Thom Gunn *(1929–   )*

Considering the Snail

The snail pushes through a green
night, for the grass is heavy
with water and meets over
the bright path he makes, where rain
has darkened the earth's dark. He   *5*
moves in a wood of desire,

pale antlers barely stirring
as he hunts. I cannot tell
what power is at work, drenched there
with purpose, knowing nothing.   *10*
What is a snail's fury? All
I think is that if later

I parted the blades above
the tunnel and saw the thin
trail of broken white across   *15*
litter, I would never have
imagined the slow passion
to that deliberate progress.

Thomas Hardy *(1840–1928)*

The Convergence of the Twain

Lines on the Loss of the "Titanic"

1.

In a solitude of the sea
Deep from human vanity,
And the Pride of Life that planned her, stilly couches she.

2.

Steel chambers, late the pyres
Of her salamandrine fires,   *5*
Cold currents thrid†, and turn to rhythmic tidal lyres.

3.

Over the mirrors meant
To glass the opulent
The sea worm crawls — grotesque, slimed, dumb, indifferent.

6. *thrid:* thread.

4.

Jewels in joy designed   *10*
  To ravish the sensuous mind
Lie lightless, all their sparkles bleared and black and blind.

5.

Dim moon-eyed fishes near
  Gaze at the gilded gear
And query: "What does this vaingloriousness down here?" . . .   *15*

6.

Well: while was fashioning
  This creature of cleaving wing,
The Immanent Will† that stirs and urges everything

7.

Prepared a sinister mate
  For her — so gaily great —   *20*
A Shape of Ice, for the time far and dissociate.

8.

And as the smart ship grew
  In stature, grace, and hue,
In shadowy silent distance grew the Iceberg too.

9.

Alien they seemed to be: *25*
  No mortal eye could see
The intimate welding of their later history,

10.

Or sign that they were bent
  By paths coincident
On being anon twin halves of one august event,   *30*

11.

Till the Spinner of the Years
  Said "Now!" And each one hears,
And consummation comes, and jars two hemispheres.

---

18. *Immanent Will:* one of the terms Hardy used for the chain of causation that, he believed, operated in both human life and nature; essentially, an impersonal fate that makes a mockery of man's free will.

Exercises

1. To what are the worms "indifferent" in stanza three?
2. What is the role of "Immanent Will" in this poem?
3. Why are the ship and Iceberg described as "twin halves"?

Topic for Writing

The *Titanic,* described by its makers as unsinkable, collided with an iceberg and sank on its maiden voyage. Discuss this poem's attitude toward the *hubris,* or arrogant pride, of people who claim dominance over the world or nature.

Sara Henderson Hay (1906–   )

For a Dead Kitten

Put the rubber mouse away,
Pick the spools up from the floor,
What was velvet-shod and gay
Will not want them any more.

What was warm, is strangely cold.   5
Where dissolved the little breath?
How could this small body hold
So immense a thing as death?

Seamus Heaney (1939–   )

Poor Women in a City Church

The small wax candles melt to light,
Flicker in marble, reflect bright
Asterisks on brass candlesticks:
At the Virgin's altar on the right
Blue flames are jerking on wicks.   5

Old dough-faced women with black shawls
Drawn down tight kneel in the stalls.
Cold yellow candle-tongues, blue flame
Mince and caper as whispered calls
Take wing up to the Holy Name.   10

Thus each day in the sacred place
They kneel. Golden shrines, altar lace,
Marble columns and cool shadows
Still them. In the gloom you cannot trace
A wrinkle on their beeswax brows.   15

The Agony

Philosophers have measured mountains,
Fathomed the depths of seas, of states, and kings,
Walked with a staff to heaven, and traced fountains;
    But there are two vast, spacious things,
The which to measure it doth more behoove,   5
Yet few there are that sound them: Sin and Love.

    Who would know Sin, let him repair
Unto Mount Olivet;† there shall he see
A man so wrung with pains that all his hair,
    His skin, his garments bloody be.   10
Sin is that press and vice which forceth pain
To hunt his cruel food through every vein.

    Who knows not love, let him assay
And taste that juice which on the cross a pike
Did set again abroach; then let him say   15
    If ever he did taste the like.
Love is that liquor sweet and most divine,
Which my God feels as blood, but I as wine.

Easter-Wings†

Lord, who createdst man in wealth and store,†
    Though foolishly he lost the same,
        Decaying more and more
            Till he became
              Most poor: 5

            With thee
           Oh let me rise
        As larks, harmoniously,
    And sing this day thy victories:
Then shall the fall† further the flight in me.   10

---

8. *Mount Olivet:* the Mount of Olives, a mountain ridge on the eastern side of Jerusalem; the Garden of Gethsemane, the scene of Jesus' agony and arrest, is located there.

Title: This shaped poem was originally printed on two facing pages to enhance the suggestion of the wings of a bird.
1. *store:* abundance (in the Garden of Eden).
10. *fall:* the diving of the lark to gain momentum, but more importantly, the Fall of Man (Genesis 3), which according to Christian theology made necessary the atonement of Christ, so that humanity could rise both physically (resurrection) and spiritually (salvation).

My tender age in sorrow did begin:
And still with sicknesses and shame
Thou didst so punish sin,
That I became
Most thin. 15
With thee
Let me combine.
And feel thy victory:
For, if I imp† my wing on thine,
Affliction shall advance the flight in me. 20

Exercises

1. Using the title as a starting point, explain the meaning of this poem.

2. Aside from its correspondence to the title, does the shape of this poem visually reinforce the meaning of specific lines? Give examples and comment on them. You may wish to read the next poem, Robert Herrick's "The Pillar of Fame," which is also a shaped one.

3. Discuss the wing-grafting image (line 19). What religious significance does the poet give it?

Robert Herrick (1591–1674)

The Pillar of Fame†

Fame's pillar here, at last, we set,
Out-during† marble, brass, or jet,†
Charmed and enchanted so
As to withstand the blow
O f   overthrow: 5
Nor shall the seas
Or O U T R A G E S
Of storms   orebear
What we   up-rear
Tho kingdoms fall 10
This   pillar   never   shall
Decline or waste at all;
But stand for ever by his own
Firm and well fixed foundation.

19. *imp:* in falconry, to replace
missing feathers by grafting.

Title: "The Pillar of Fame," like   2. *out-during:* out-enduring; *jet:*
Herbert's "Easter-Wings," is a   black, polished lignite (a type of
shaped poem whose visual design   coal).
reflects its subject.

When He Would Have His Verses Read

In sober mornings, do not thou rehearse
The holy incantation of a verse;
But when that men have both well drunk, and fed,
Let my enchantments then be sung, or read.
When laurel † spirts with fire, and when the hearth   *5*
Smiles to itself, and guilds the roof with mirth;
When up the thyrse† is raised, and when the sound
Of sacred orgies† flies, A round, A round.
When the rose reigns, and locks with ointments shine,
Let rigid Cato† read these lines of mine.   *10*

Robert Hershon (1935–   )

The Cooper & Bailey Great London Circus

In 1876
The Cooper & Bailey Great London Circus
Sailing from *Tasmania* to *Australia*
Suffered *Grievous* Injuries
During A Storm of *Singular* Magnitude   *5*

The *Rhinoceros* and The *Lion*
And The *Alligator* and The *Silver Fox*
And The *Tattooed Mule* and The *Imitation*
Penguin and The *Whitewashed Elephant*
Were Among Those *Drowned*   *10*
In The *Bubbling* Pacific

Cunning James Bailey
Had The Waterlogged *Giraffe*
Stuffed by A Gentleman in Sydney
Its *Head* Equipped with A *Device*   *15*
That Made It *Nod* Slowly and Regularly
Wily Bailey
Showed The Beast in A *Darkened Cage*
And It *Appeared* to Be *Alive* Which Made
The *Australian People*   *20*

5. *laurel:* traditional evergreen associated with the writing and reciting of poetry.
7. *thyrse* (thyrsus): a staff entwined with ivy, raised in honor of Bacchus (Dionysus), classical Greek god of wine who supposedly inspired poetry by helping poets to forget their cares.

8. *sacred orgies:* songs to Bacchus (the poet's note).
10. *rigid Cato:* Roman statesman (234–149 B.C.) known for his attack on the morals of the Roman nobility, his opposition to the study of Greek culture, and his meanness in selling off his slaves when they became too old to work.

Very Very Happy
And So They *Remain* to This Day
A *Grand* Triumph for The *Grand* Bailey
Mourner of Rhino *Fisher* of Lion
Resurrector of Giraffe   25
The *Bold* and *Businesslike* Bailey
Who *Gave* The People What They *Wanted*
This Has Been A Demanding Quarter
For Your Company   Sales Decreased 14
Percent over The Corresponding Period   30
A Year Ago   Nevertheless
We Are Pleased To Tell You That
Net Earnings (There Was A Fire
In Ohio In Which Several Clowns
Burned Up) *More Than Held Their Own*   35
Hold Your Own   Hold Her Own
Hold His Own   Nod Your Head

Gerard Manley Hopkins (1844–1889)

God's Grandeur

The world is charged with the grandeur of God.
  It will flame out, like shining from shook foil;
  It gathers to a greatness, like the ooze of oil
Crushed. Why do men then now not reck his rod?
Generations have trod, have trod, have trod;   5
  And all is seared with trade; bleared, smeared with toil;
  And wears man's smudge and shares man's smell: the soil
Is bare now, nor can foot feel, being shod.

  And for all this, nature is never spent;
  There lives the dearest freshness deep down things;   10
And though the last lights off the black West went
  Oh, morning, at the brown brink eastward, springs —
Because the Holy Ghost over the bent
  World broods with warm breast and with ah! bright wings.

Exercises

1. Discuss the imagery in lines 2 and 3.

2. What sound devices does the poet use?

3. What tensions or opposing forces do you see at work in this poem?

Discuss the theme of rebirth or regeneration as presented in Hopkins's poem.

Pied Beauty

Glory be to God for dappled things —
    For skies of couple-colour as a brinded† cow;
      For rose-moles all in stipple† upon trout that swim;
Fresh-firecoal chestnut-falls; finches' wings;
    Landscape plotted and pieced — fold, fallow, and plough;   5
    And all trades, their gear and tackle and trim.

All things counter, original, spare, strange;
    Whatever is fickle, freckled (who knows how?)
      With swift, slow; sweet, sour; adazzle, dim;
He fathers-forth whose beauty is past change: Praise him.   10

A. E. Housman (1859–1936)

To an Athlete Dying Young

The time you won your town the race
We chaired you through the market place;
Man and boy stood cheering by,
And home we brought you shoulder-high.

Today, the road all runners come,   5
Shoulder-high we bring you home,
And set you at your threshold down,
Townsman of a stiller town.

Smart lad, to slip betimes away
From fields where glory does not stay   10
And early though the laurel grows
It withers quicker than the rose.

Eyes the shady night has shut
Cannot see the record cut,
And silence sounds no worse than cheers   15
After earth has stopped the ears:

Now you will not swell the rout
Of lads wore their honors out,
Runners whom renown outran
And the name died before the man.   20

2. *brinded:* brindled.
3. *stipple:* a technique in painting or engraving in which a series of dots is used to produce gradations of shading.

So set, before its echoes fade,
The fleet foot on the sill of shade,
And hold to the low lintel† up
The still defended challenge cup.

And round that early laureled head   25
Will flock to gaze the strengthless dead
And find unwithered on its curls
The garland briefer than a girl's.

Exercises

1. To what "home" is the athlete being carried in the second stanza?

2. Why is silence "no worse than cheers"?

3. Why does the poet say that at times "the name died before the man"?

Topic for Writing

Discuss the attitude toward fame expressed in the poem.

Henry Howard, Earl of Surrey (1517?–1547)

The Soote Season

The soote† season, that bud and bloom forth brings,
With green hath clad the hill and eke† the vale;
The nightingale with feathers new she sings;
The turtle† to her make† hath told her tale.
Summer is come, for every spray now springs;   5
The hart† hath hung his old head on the pale;†
The buck in brake† his winter coat he flings,
The fishes float with new repairéd scale;
The adder all her slough away she slings,
The swift swallow pursueth the flies small;   10
The busy bee her honey now she mings.†
Winter is worn, that was the flowers' bale.†
And thus I see among these pleasant things,
Each care decays, and yet my sorrow springs.

23. *lintel:* the frame at the top of
a door or window.

1. *soote:* sweet.
2. *eke:* also.
4. *turtle:* turtledove; *make:* mate.
6. *hart:* male red deer; *pale:* fence.

7. *brake:* thicket.
11. *mings:* remembers, voids.
12. *bale:* enemy.

Langston Hughes *(1902–1967)*

Dream Deferred

What happens to a dream deferred? *[handwritten: to jot off]*

Does it dry up
like a raisin in the sun?
Or fester like a sore —
And then run?   *5*

Does it stink like rotten meat?
Or crust and sugar over —
like a syrupy sweet?

Maybe it just sags
like a heavy load.   *10*

Or does it explode? — *[handwritten: talking about race w/ the blacks]*

I, too, sing America

I, too, sing America.

I am the darker brother.
They send me to eat in the kitchen
When company comes,
But I laugh,   *5*
And eat well,
And grow strong.

Tomorrow,
I'll sit at the table
When company comes.   *10*
Nobody'll dare
Say to me,
"Eat in the kitchen,"
Then.

Besides,   *15*
They'll see how beautiful I am
And be ashamed —

I, too, am America.

Exercises

1. Who is the speaker in the poem?

2. What is the central metaphor?

3. Who will be ashamed?

The first half of the poem describes the present situation while the second half makes a prediction. Comment on the present and future as seen by the speaker.

Ted Hughes (1930–   )

A Disaster

There cames news of a word.
Crow saw it killing men. He ate well.
He saw it bulldozing
Whole cities to rubble. Again he ate well.
He saw its excreta poisoning seas.   5
He became watchful.
He saw its breath burning whole lands
To dusty char.
He flew clear and peered.

The word oozed its way, all mouth,   10
Earless, eyeless.
He saw it sucking the cities
Like the nipples of a sow
Drinking out all the people
Till there were none left,   15
All digested inside the word.

Ravenous, the word tried its great lips
On the earth's bulge, like a giant lamprey —
There it started to suck.

But its effort weakened.   20
It could digest nothing but people.
So there it shrank, wrinkling weaker,
Puddling
Like a collapsing mushroom.
Finally, a drying salty lake.   25
Its era was over.
All that remained of it a brittle desert
Dazzling with the bones of earth's people

Where Crow walked and mused.

Laura Iwasaki (1950–   )

Tiger Year

new moon,
    you lie
in shadow —

traveling over the face
of silent water   5

as planets circle in the gathering dark
like pale insects
around the opened throats of flowers.

see how the stars are blossoming
one by one: 10
as if merely to breathe.

they blossom for you,
defining your way
through the clear night air
with hands as pure and bright as clouds.   15

will you hurry to my season?
it is time:
you bring the light.

Randall Jarrell (1914–1965)

The Mockingbird

Look one way and the sun is going down,
Look the other and the moon is rising.
The sparrow's shadow's longer than the lawn.
The bats squeak: "Night is here"; the birds cheep: "Day is gone."
On the willow's highest branch, monopolizing   5
Day and night, cheeping, squeaking, soaring,
The mockingbird is imitating life.

All day the mockingbird has owned the yard.
As light first woke the world, the sparrows trooped
Onto the seedy lawn: the mockingbird   10
Chased them off shrieking. Hour by hour, fighting hard
To make the world his own, he swooped
On thrushes, thrashers, jays, and chickadees —
At noon he drove away a big black cat.

Now, in the moonlight, he sits here and sings.   15
A thrush is singing, then a thrasher, then a jay —
Then, all at once, a cat begins meowing.
A mockingbird can sound like anything.
He imitates the world he drove away
So well that for a minute, in the moonlight,   20
Which one's the mockingbird? which one's the world?

1. In observing a mockingbird, the speaker of this poem develops an insight into reality versus deception. Explain that insight.

2. Why does the speaker refer several times to "sun" (an obvious representation of day) and "moon" (night)? In your answer, consider when the bird's deceptive power is greatest. What message about deception does this imagery convey?

The Orient Express

One looks from the train
Almost as one looked as a child. In the sunlight
What I see still seems to me plain,
I am safe; but at evening
As the lands darken, a questioning   5
Precariousness comes over everything.

Once after a day of rain
I lay longing to be cold; and after a while
I was cold again, and hunched shivering
Under the quilt's many colors, gray   10
With the dull ending of the winter day.
Outside me there were a few shapes
Of chairs and tables, things from a primer;
Outside the window
There were the chairs and tables of the world. . . .   15
I saw that the world
That had seemed to me the plain
Gray mask of all that was strange
Behind it — of all that *was* — was all.

But it is beyond belief.   20
One thinks, "Behind everything
An unforced joy, an unwilling
Sadness (a willing sadness, a forced joy)
Moves changelessly"; one looks from the train
And there is something, the same thing   25
Behind everything: all these little villages,
A passing woman, a field of grain,
The man who says good-bye to his wife —
A path through a wood full of lives, and the train
Passing, after all unchangeable   30
And not now ever to stop, like a heart —

It is like any other work of art.
It is and never can be changed.
Behind everything there is always
The unknown unwanted life.   35

Elizabeth Jennings (1926–   )

In Memory of Anyone Unknown to Me

At this particular time I have no one
Particular person to grieve for, though there must
Be Many, many unknown ones going to dust
Slowly, not remembered for what they have done
Or left undone. For these, then, I will grieve   5
Being impartial, unable to deceive.

How they lived or died is quite unknown,
And, by the fact gives my grief purity —
An important person quite apart from me
Or one obscure who drifted down alone.   10
Both or all I remember, have a place.
For these I never encountered face to face.

Sentiment will creep in. I cast it out
Wishing to give these classical repose,
No epitaph, no poppy and no rose   15
From me, and certainly no wish to learn about
The way they lived or died. In earth or fire
They are gone. Simply because they were human, I admire.

Exercises

1. Should grief exist if there is no "Particular person to grieve for"?

2. Why does the speaker cast out sentiment? Isn't it an integral part of grief?

3. The speaker's grief, we are told, has "purity." Does it?

Topic for Writing

The speaker makes no distinctions among the individuals who are grieved for;
they are the subjects of the speaker's sorrow "Simply because they were human."
Without commenting on the sincerity of the poem, discuss the possibility of
experiencing such an emotion.

Ben Jonson (1572–1637)

On My First Son†

Farewell, thou child of my right hand, and joy;
My sin was too much hope of thee, loved boy:

Title: The poet's son Benjamin,   "son of the right hand," died on
whose name in Hebrew means   his seventh birthday.

Seven years thou'wert lent to me, and I thee pay,
Exacted by thy fate, on the just day.
O could I lose all father now! for why   5
Will man lament the state he should envy,
To have so soon 'scaped world's and flesh's rage,
And, if no other misery, yet age?
Rest in soft peace, and asked, say, "Here doth lie
Ben Jonson his best piece of poetry."   10
For whose sake henceforth all his vows be such
As what he loves may never like too much.

Song: To Celia†

Come, my Celia, let us prove,†
While we can, the sports of love.
Time will not be ours for ever;
He, at length, our good will sever;
Spend not then his gifts in vain.   5
Suns that set may rise again;
But if once we lose this light,
'T is with us perpetual night.
Why should we defer our joys?
Fame and rumor are but toys.   10
Cannot we delude the eyes
Of a few poor household spies?
Or his easier ears beguile,
Thus removéd by our wile?
'T is no sin love's fruits to steal;   15
But the sweet theft to reveal,
To be taken, to be seen,
These have crimes accounted been.

John Keats (1795–1821)

To Autumn

Season of mists and mellow fruitfulness,
    Close bosom friend of the maturing sun:
Conspiring with him how to load and bless
    With fruit the vines that round the thatch-eaves run;
To bend with apples the mossed cottage-trees,   5
    And fill all fruit with ripeness to the core;
        To swell the gourd, and plump the hazel shells

Title: The song appears in Jonson's comedy *Volpone* and is sung by the title character to a young woman he is trying to seduce.
1. *prove:* savor or experience.

With a sweet kernel; to set budding more,
  And still more, later flowers for the bees,
  Until they think warm days will never cease,   *10*
    For Summer has o'er-brimmed their clammy cells.

Who hath not seen thee oft amid thy store?
  Sometimes whoever seeks abroad may find
Thee sitting careless on a granary floor,
  Thy hair soft-lifted by the winnowing wind;   *15*
Or on a half-reaped furrow sound asleep,
  Drowsed with the fume of poppies, while thy hook†
    Spares the next swath and all its twinèd flowers:
And sometimes like a gleaner thou dost keep
  Steady thy laden head across a brook;   *20*
Or by a cider-press, with patient look,
    Thou watchest the last oozings hours by hours.

Where are the songs of Spring? Ay, where are they?
  Think not of them, thou hast thy music too, —
While barrèd† clouds bloom the soft-dying day,   *25*
  And touch the stubble-plains with rosy hue;
Then in a wailful choir the small gnats mourn
  Among the river sallows,† borne aloft
    Or sinking as the light wind lives or dies;
And full-grown lambs loud bleat from hilly bourn;   *30*
  Hedge-crickets sing: and now with treble soft
  The red-breast whistles from a garden-croft;
    And gathering swallows twitter in the skies.

Exercises

1. Are the images in the last stanza appropriate as an ending to the poem? How do they reflect the poem's theme?

2. In the second stanza, what poetic device does the poet use to depict the activities of the fall season? What are those activities?

3. What does the closing image of "gathering swallows" that "twitter in the skies" suggest to you about the seasonal changes in nature and the poet's attitude toward them?

Topic for Writing

Evaluate the mood and tone of "To Autumn" in relation to the theme. For your focus, consider what is meant when the speaker says to autumn, "thou hast thy music too."

17. *hook:* scythe.   28. *sallows:* willow trees.
25. *barrèd:* alternating light and
dark.

Bright Star

Bright star, would I were steadfast as thou art —
    Not in lone splendor hung aloft the night
And watching, with eternal lids apart,
    Like nature's patient, sleepless Eremite,†
The moving waters at their priestlike task   5
    Of pure ablution† round earth's human shores,
Or gazing on the new soft fallen mask
    Of snow upon the mountains and the moors —
No — yet still steadfast, still unchangeable,
    Pillowed upon my fair love's ripening breast,   10
To feel forever its soft fall and swell,
    Awake forever in a sweet unrest,
Still, still to hear her tender-taken breath,
And so live ever — or else swoon to death.

La Belle Dame sans Merci†

Oh, what can ail thee, knight-at-arms,
    Alone and palely loitering?
The sedge has withered from the lake,
    And no birds sing.

Oh, what can ail thee, knight-at-arms,   5
    So haggard and so woe-begone?
The squirrel's granary† is full,
    And the harvest's done.

I see a lily on thy brow,
    With anguish moist and fever dew;   10
And on thy cheeks a fading rose
    Fast withereth too.

"I met a lady in the meads,†
    Full beautiful — a faery's child;
Her hair was long, her foot was light,   15
    And her eyes were wild.

"I made a garland for her head,
    And bracelets too, and fragrant zone;†
She looked at me as she did love,
    And made sweet moan.   20

---

4. *Eremite:* religious hermit.

6. *ablution:* ceremonial purification through washing.

Title: Literally, "The Beautiful Lady without Pity"; a temptress or seductress.

7. *granary:* a storehouse for grain.
13. *meads:* meadows.
18. *zone:* a girdle or sash.

"I set her on my pacing steed;
    And nothing else saw all day long;
For sideways would she lean, and sing
    A faery's song.

"She found me roots of relish sweet,   25
    And honey wild, and manna-dew,
And sure in language strange she said,
    'I love thee true.'

"She took me to her elfin grot,
    And there she wept, and sighed full sore,   30
And there I shut her wild, wild eyes,
    With kisses four.

"And there she lullèd me asleep,
    And there I dreamed — ah! woe betide! —
The latest dream I ever dreamed   35
    On the cold hill's side.

"I saw pale kings and princes too,
    Pale warriors, death-pale were they all,
They cried — 'La Belle Dame sans Merci
    Hath thee in thrall!'   40

"I saw their starved lips in the gloam,†
    With horrid warning gapèd wide;
And I awoke, and found me here
    On the cold hill's side.

"And this is why I sojourn here,   45
    Alone and palely loitering,
Though the sedge is withered from the lake,
    And no birds sing."

Ode on a Grecian Urn

1.

Thou still unravish'd bride of quietness,
    Thou foster-child of silence and slow time,
Sylvan historian, who canst thus express
    A flowery tale more sweetly than our rhyme:
What leaf-fring'd legend haunts about thy shape   5
    Of deities or mortals, or of both,
        In Tempe† or the dales of Arcady? †

41. *gloam:* twilight.

---

7. *Tempe; Arcady:* regions in Greece associated from ancient times with shepherds and other aspects of the pastoral ideal.

What men or gods are these? What maidens loth?
 What mad pursuit? What struggle to escape?
   What pipes and timbrels? What wild ecstasy?   *10*

2.

Heard melodies are sweet, but those unheard
 Are sweeter; therefore, ye soft pipes, play on;
Not to the sensual ear,† but, more endear'd,
 Pipe to the spirit ditties of no tone:
Fair youth, beneath the trees, thou canst not leave   *15*
 Thy song, nor ever can those trees be bare;
  Bold Lover, never, never canst thou kiss,
Though winning near the goal — yet, do not grieve;
 She cannot fade, though thou hast not thy bliss,
  For ever wilt thou love, and she be fair!   *20*

3.

Ah, happy, happy boughs! that cannot shed
 Your leaves, nor ever bid the Spring adieu;
And, happy melodist, unwearied,
 For ever piping songs for ever new;
More happy love! more happy, happy love!   *25*
 For ever warm and still to be enjoy'd,
  For ever panting, and for ever young;
All breathing human passion far above,
 That leaves a heart high-sorrowful and cloy'd,
  A burning forehead, and a parching tongue.   *30*

4.

Who are these coming to the sacrifice?
 To what green altar, O mysterious priest,
Lead'st thou that heifer lowing at the skies,
 And all her silken flanks with garlands drest?
What little town by river or sea shore,   *35*
 Or mountain-built with peaceful citadel,
  Is emptied of this folk, this pious morn?
And, little town, thy streets for evermore
 Will silent be; and not a soul to tell
  Why thou art desolate, can e'er return.   *40*

5.

O Attic† shape! Fair attitude! with brede†
 Of marble men and maidens overwrought,
With forest branches and the trodden weed;
 Thou, silent form, dost tease us out of thought

13. *sensual ear:* the ear as an organ responding to physical sensations.
41. *Attic:* the region of Greece
where Athens is located and in
general (particularly in this context) anything relating to the purity and simplicity of classical art;
brede: ornamentation worked into
an interwoven pattern.

As doth eternity: Cold Pastoral! † 45
When old age shall this generation waste,
Thou shalt remain, in midst of other woe
Than ours, a friend to man, to whom thou say'st,
"Beauty is truth, truth beauty," — that is all
Ye know on earth, and all ye need to know. 50

Exercises

1. How is Keats's urn a "still unravish'd bride of quietness"? a "Sylvan historian"? Comment on the appropriateness of these epithets.

2. In stanzas two and three, what particular aspects of the scene depicted on the urn are emphasized? How does this emphasis validate the comparisons of the urn to eternity and to a "Cold Pastoral" in stanza five?

3. The poem contrasts the "lives" depicted on the urn with the lives of mortals. Select from the text those points of contrast. What feature do they have in common? How does that feature make the lives of the figures on the urn that much more attractive?

Topic for Writing

The last two lines of "Ode on a Grecian Urn" have provoked much scholarly discussion. Although we can never be certain exactly what Keats meant by " 'Beauty is truth, truth beauty,' " that statement too is meant to "tease us out of thought." On the basis of your own understanding of the poem, attempt a definition of "beauty" and of "truth" as these two concepts are illustrated by the urn.

Sidney Keyes (1922–1943)

William Wordsworth†

No room for mourning: he's gone out
Into the noisy glen, or stands between the stones
Of the gaunt ridge, or you'll hear his shout
Rolling among the screes,† he being a boy again.
He'll never fail nor die 5

45. *cold pastoral:* the pastoral mode, which relates in highly idealized terms the lives of shepherds and their loves, is generally cast in a springtime warmth and greenery.

William Wordsworth: an English poet (1770–1850) of the Romantic period who spent much of his life observing nature.
4. *screes:* natural piles of stones.

And if they laid his bones
In the wet vaults or iron sarcophagi†
Of fame, he'd rise at the first summer rain
And stride across the hills to seek
His rest among the broken lands and clouds.
He was a stormy day, a granite peak
Spearing the sky; and look, about its base
Words flower like crocuses in the hanging woods,
Blank though the dalehead† and the bony face.

Walter Savage Landor (1775–1864)

On His Own Death

Death stands above me, whispering low
    I know not what into my ear:
Of his strange language all I know
    Is, there is not a word of fear.

Edward Lear (1812–1888)

Cold Are the Crabs

Cold are the crabs that crawl on yonder hills,
Colder the cucumbers that grow beneath,
And colder still the brazen chops that wreathe
    The tedious gloom of philosophic pills!
For when the tardy film of nectar fills   5
The ample bowls of demons and of men,
There lurks the feeble mouse, the homely hen,
    And there the porcupine with all her quills.
Yet much remains — to weave a solemn strain
That lingering sadly — slowly dies away,   10
Daily departing with departing day.
A pea-green gamut on a distant plain
When wily walruses in congress meet —
    Such such is life —

7. *sarcophagi:* coffins.
14. *dalehead:* the upper, higher end
of a river valley situated between
encompassing hills.

John Lehmann (1907–   )

This Excellent Machine

This excellent machine is neatly planned,
A child, a half-wit would not feel perplexed:
No chance to err, you simply press the button —
At once each cog in motion moves the next,
The whole revolves, and anything that lives   *5*
Is quickly sucked towards the running band,
Where, shot between the automatic knives,
It's guaranteed to finish dead as mutton.

This excellent machine will illustrate
The Modern World divided into nations: *10*
So neatly planned, that if you merely tap it
The armaments will start their devastations,
And though we're for it, though we're all convinced
Some fool will press the button soon or late,
We stand and stare, expecting to be minced, —   *15*
And very few are asking, *Why not scrap it?*

Shirley Geok-Lin Lim (1944–   )

Modern Secrets

Last night I dreamt in Chinese.
Eating Yankee shredded wheat,
I told it in English terms
To a friend who spoke
In monosyllables,   *5*
All of which I understood:
The dream shrunk
To its fiction.
I knew its end
Many years ago.   *10*
The sallow child
Eating from a rice-bowl
Hides in the cupboard
With the tea-leaves and china.

Exercises

1. Like George Herbert in "Easter-Wings" and Robert Herrick in "The Pillar of Fame," this poet uses line length as visual reinforcement of line meaning. Point to as many examples of this technique as you can.

2. Explain the correlation in this poem between the "dream" (line 1) and the child hiding "in the cupboard" (line 13). Also explain what the title means.

Vachel Lindsay *(1879–1931)*

General William Booth† Enters into Heaven

To be sung to the tune of "The Blood of the Lamb" with indicated instruments†

1.

(Bass drum beaten loudly.)
Booth led boldly with his big bass drum,
(Are you washed in the blood of the Lamb?)
The saints smiled gravely, and they said, "He's come."
(Are you washed in the blood of the Lamb?)
Walking lepers followed, rank on rank,   5
Lurching bravos from the ditches dank,
Drabs from the alleyways and drug-fiends pale —
Minds still passion-ridden, soul-powers frail: —
Vermin-eaten saints with moldy breath
Unwashed legions† with the ways of death —   10
(Are you washed in the blood of the Lamb?)

(Banjos.)
Every slum had sent its half-a-score
The round world over. (Booth had groaned for more.)
Every banner that the wide world flies
Bloomed with glory and transcendent dyes.   15
Big-voiced lasses made their banjos bang!
Tranced, fanatical, they shrieked and sang; —
"Are you washed in the blood of the Lamb?"
Hallelujah! It was queer to see
Bull-necked convicts with that land make free!   20
Loons with trumpets blowed a blare, blare, blare —
On, on, upward thro' the golden air!
(Are you washed in the blood of the Lamb?)

2.

(Bass drum slower and softer.)
Booth died blind, and still by faith he trod,
Eyes still dazzled by the ways of God.   25
Booth led boldly, and he looked the chief:
Eagle countenance in sharp relief,
Beard a-flying, air of high command
Unabated in that holy land.

(Sweet flute music.)
Jesus came from out the Courthouse door,   30

William Booth: a Briton (1829–1912) who founded the Salvation Army.
"The Blood of the Lamb": a popular spiritual associated with evangelical Christianity.

10. *legions:* cf. Luke 8:30, in which the man possessed by demons tells Jesus, who asks him his name, that his name is "Legion: because many devils were entered into him."

Stretched His hands above the passing poor.
Booth saw not, but led his queer ones there
'Round and 'round the mighty Courthouse square.
Yet in an instant all that blear review
Marched on spotless, clad in raiment new.   *35*
The lame were straightened, withered limbs uncurled,
And blind eyes opened on a new sweet world.

    (Bass drum louder.)
Drabs and vixens in a flash made whole!
Gone was the weasel-head, the snout, the jowl!
Sages and sibyls now, and athletes clean,   *40*
Rulers of empires, and of forests green!

    (Grand chorus of all instruments. Tambourines to the
      foreground.)
The hosts were sandaled and their wings were fire!
(Are you washed in the blood of the Lamb?)
But their noise played havoc with the angel-choir.
(Are you washed in the blood of the Lamb?)   *45*
Oh, shout Salvation! it was good to see
Kings and Princes by the Lamb set free.
The banjos rattled and the tambourines
Jing-jing-jingled in the hands of Queens!

    (Reverently sung, no instruments.)
And when Booth halted by the curb for prayer   *50*
He saw his Master thro' the flag-filled air.
Christ came gently with a robe and crown
For Booth the soldier, while the throng knelt down.
He saw King Jesus. They were face to face,
And he knelt a-weeping in that holy place.   *55*
Are you washed in the blood of the Lamb?

Christopher Logue (*1926–*   )

Foreword to **New Numbers**

This book was written in order to change the world
and published at 12/- (softback), 25/- (hardback) by Cape
of 30 Bedford Square, London, wc1
(a building formerly occupied by the Czarist Embassy)
in 1969.   *5*
It is generously scattered with dirty words
particularly on pages 9, 31, 37 and 45,
and was written by © Logue
a sexy young girl living among corrupted villagers
who keeps her innocence through love;   *10*
its weight is 7·926 oz,

its burning temperature is Fahrenheit 451,
and it was printed in Great Britain by
Butler & Tanner of London and Frome.
On the day of publication its price would buy   *15*
11 cut loaves,
3 yards of drip-dry nylon,
25 gallons of boiling dishwater,
5 rounds of M1 carbine ammunition,
or a cheap critic;   *20*
what do you expect for 12/- Paradise Lost?

This book will offend a number of people,
some of them influential people;
its commercial potential is slight,
the working classes will ignore it,   *25*
the middle classes will not buy it,
the ruling class will bolt it with a smile,
for I am a Western Art Treasure!
What right do I have to complain?
Nobody asked me to write it, yet   *30*
be sure I will complain.

This book is dedicated to new men,
astronauts meter-maids Chinese Ambassadors
quizmasters disc-jockeys South Vietnamese
rocket-designers thalidomide babies   *35*
anchormen skindivers African Generals
Israelis and launderette manageresses
multi-lingual porpoises left-wing doctors
draft-dodgers brainwashers bingo-queens con-
crete poets pollsters commuters computer-   *40*
programmers panels of judges gas-chamber victims
abstract expressionist chimpanzees
surfies and self-made millionaire teenagers
skydivers aquanauts working-class playwrights
industrial spies with indentikit smiles   *45*
intrusion specialists and four-minute milers
motivation researchers and systems analysts
noise abatement society members
collective farmers and war criminals
transplanted heart men and water-ski champions   *50*
the Misses World and those I love.
If this book doesn't change you
give it no house space;
if having read it you
are the same person you   *55*
were before picking it up,
then throw it away.
Not enough for me
that my poems shine in your eye;
not enough for me   *60*

that they look from your walls
or lurk on your shelves;
I want my poems to be in your mind
so you can say them when you are in love
so you can say them when the plane takes off   65
and death comes near;
I want my poems to come between
the raised stick and the cowering back,
I want my poems to become
a weapon in your trembling hands,   70
a sword whose blade both makes and mirrors change;
but most of all I want my poems sung
unthinkingly between your lips like air.

Henry Wadsworth Longfellow (1807–1882)

Milton

I pace the sounding sea-beach and behold
   How the voluminous billows roll and run,
   Upheaving and subsiding, while the sun
   Shines through their sheeted emerald far unrolled
And the ninth wave, slow gathering fold by fold   5
   All its loose-flowing garments into one,
   Plunges upon the shore, and floods the dun
   Pale reach of sands, and changes them to gold.
So in majestic cadence rise and fall
   The mighty undulations of thy song,   10
   O sightless Bard,† England's Maeonides! †
And ever and anon, high over all
   Uplifted, a ninth wave superb and strong,
   Floods all the soul with its melodious seas.

Jon Looney (1948–   )

Only the Garbage Collector

   noticed
   Old Mrs. Smith's death.
   He missed her garbage.

   (From her garbage
   he knew her.   5

11. *sightless Bard:* Milton wrote his major works, including *Paradise Lost,* after losing his eyesight at the age of forty-four; *Maeonides:* Homer, also a blind epic poet, whose birthplace was said to be Maeonia in Asia Minor.

Knew from the labels
of fish-mouthed open cans
she must keep
several cats.)

He gave   10
backdoor notice
to the retired teacher's neighbors,
suggesting
they take in the cats.

(It might take days   15
learning if any relatives survived
Mrs. Smith. In that time
the cats could starve.)

Mrs. Jones led
a rescue party   20
into the house.
But the concerned neighbors
became confused:

they found no bowl, not pet boxes,
no cats at all.   25

Robert Lovelace (1618–1658)

To Lucasta, On Going to the Wars

Tell me not, Sweet, I am unkind
That from the nunnery
Of thy chaste breast and quiet mind,
To war and arms I fly.

True, a new mistress now I chase,   5
The first foe in the field;
And with a stronger faith embrace
A sword, a horse, a shield.

Yet this inconstancy is such
As you too shall adore;   10
I could not love thee, Dear, so much,
Loved I not honor more.

Amy Lowell (1874–1925)

Patterns

I walk down the garden-paths,
And all the daffodils

Are blowing; and the bright blue squills.†
I walk down the patterned garden-paths
In my stiff, brocaded gown.   5
With my powdered hair and jewelled fan,
I too am a rare
Pattern. As I wander down
The garden-paths.

My dress is richly figured,   10
And the train
Makes a pink and silver stain
On the gravel, and the thrift
Of the borders.
Just a plate of current fashion,   15
Tripping by in high-heeled, ribboned shoes.
Not a softness anywhere about me,
Only whalebone and brocade.
And I sink on a seat in the shade
Of a lime-tree. For my passion   20
Wars against the stiff brocade.
The daffodils and squills
Flutter in the breeze
As they please.
And I weep;   25
For the lime-tree is in blossom
And one small flower has dropped upon my bosom.

And the plashing of waterdrops
In the marble fountain
Comes down the garden-paths.   30
The dripping never stops.
Underneath my stiffened gown
Is the softness of a woman bathing in a marble basin,
A basin in the midst of hedges grown
So thick, she cannot see her lover hiding,   35
But she guesses he is near,
And the sliding of the water
Seems the stroking of a dear
Hand upon her.
What is Summer in a fine brocaded gown!   40
I should like to see it lying in a heap upon the ground.
All the pink and silver crumpled up on the ground.

I would be the pink and silver as I ran along the paths,
And he would stumble after,
Bewildered by my laughter.   45
I should see the sun flashing from his sword-hilt and the buckles on
        his shoes.

3. *squills:* a genus of flowers
(*Scilla*).

I would choose
To lead him in a maze along the patterned paths,
A bright and laughing maze for my heavy-booted lover.
Till he caught me in the shade,   *50*
And the buttons of his waistcoat bruised my body as he clasped me
Aching, melting, unafraid.
With the shadows of the leaves and the sundrops,
And the plopping of the waterdrops,
All about us in the open afternoon —   *55*
I am very like to swoon
With the weight of this brocade,
For the sun sifts through the shade.

Underneath the fallen blossom
In my bosom,   *60*
Is a letter I have hid.
It was brought to me this morning by a rider from the Duke.
"Madam, we regret to inform you that Lord Hartwell
Died in action Thursday se'nnight."
As I read it in the white, morning sunlight,   *65*
The letters squirmed like snakes.
"Any answer, Madam?" said my footman.
"No," I told him.
"See that the messenger takes some refreshment.
No, no answer."   *70*
And I walked into the garden,
Up and down the patterned paths,
In my stiff, correct brocade.
The blue and yellow flowers stood up proudly in the sun,
Each one.   *75*
I stood upright too,
Held rigid to the pattern
By the stiffness of my gown.
Up and down I walked,
Up and down.   *80*

In a month he would have been my husband.
In a month, here underneath this lime,
We would have broke the pattern;
He for me, and I for him,
He as Colonel, I as Lady,   *85*
On this shady seat.
He had a whim
That sunlight carried blessing.
And I answered, "It shall be as you have said."
Now he is dead.   *90*

In Summer and in Winter I shall walk
Up and down
The patterned garden-paths
In my stiff, brocaded gown.

The squills and daffodils   95
Will give place to pillared roses, and to asters, and to snow.
I shall go
Up and down,
In my gown.
Gorgeously arrayed,   100
Boned and stayed.
And the softness of my body will be guarded from embrace
By each button, hook, and lace.
For the man who should loose me is dead,
Fighting with the Duke in Flanders,   105
In a pattern called a war.
Christ! What are patterns for?

Robert Lowell (1917–1977)

Bringing a Turtle Home

On the road to Bangor,† we spotted a domed stone,
a painted turtle petrified by fear.
I picked it up. The turtle had come a long walk,
200 millennia understudy to dinosaurs,
then their survivors. A god for the out-of-power. . . .   5
Faster gods come to Castine,† flush yachtsmen who see
hell as a city very much like New York,
these gods give a bad past and worse future to men
who never bother to set a spinnaker;†
culture without cash isn't worth their spit.   10
The laughter on Mount Olympus was always breezy. . . .
Goodnight, little Boy, little Soldier, live,
a toy to your friend, a stone of stumbling to God —
sandpaper Turtle, scratching your pail for water.

Archibald MacLeish (1892–1982)

Ars Poetica†

A poem should be palpable and mute
As a globed fruit,

Dumb
As old medallions to the thumb,

1. *Bangor:* inland city in Maine.   9. *spinnaker:* large sail used when
6. *Castine:* Maine seacoast town.   running before the wind.

Title: Literally, "poetic art," hence
any theoretical considerations on
the nature of the art of poetry.

Silent as the sleeve-worn stone   5
Of casement ledges where the moss has grown —

A poem should be wordless
As the flight of birds.

A poem should be motionless in time
As the moon climbs,   10

Leaving, as the moon releases
Twig by twig the night-entangled trees,

Leaving, as the moon behind the winter leaves,
Memory by memory the mind —

A poem should be motionless in time   15
As the moon climbs.

A poem should be equal to:
Not true.

For all the history of grief
An empty doorway and a maple leaf.   20

For love
The leaning grasses and two lights above the sea —

A poem should not mean
But be.

Exercises

1. This poem is built on similes. Identify each simile and determine what each one says about the qualities that, according to the poem, are inherent in poetry.

2. "A poem should be equal to:/Not true." If that is so, should we believe what this poem has to say about the nature of poetry? (Before formulating your response, consider what is meant when the speaker asserts, in closing, that "a poem should not mean/But be.")

3. Ultimately, "Ars Poetica" asks us to see a poem as an art object rather than as a statement. If that creates a paradox, what is the nature of that paradox? Does the poem illustrate its own definition of poetry?

Topic for Writing

Like Keats's "Ode on a Grecian Urn," "Ars Poetica" emphasizes the communicative powers of silence. Compare and contrast the two poems in terms of their emphasis on the visual and the tactile, as opposed to the strictly verbal, qualities of poetry.

You, Andrew Marvell

And here face down beneath the sun
And here upon earth's noonward height
To feel the always coming on
The always rising of the night:

To feel creep up the curving east   *5*
The earthly chill of dusk and slow
Upon those under lands the vast
And ever climbing shadow grow

And strange at Ecbatan† the trees
Take leaf by leaf the evening strange   *10*
The flooding dark about their knees
The mountains over Persia change

And now at Kermanshah† the gate
Dark empty and the withered grass
And through the twilight now the late   *15*
Few travelers in the westward pass

And Baghdad† darken and the bridge
Across the silent river gone
And through Arabia the edge
Of evening widen and steal on   *20*

And deepen on Palmyra's† street
The wheel rut in the ruined stone
And Lebanon fade out and Crete
High through the clouds and overblown

And over Sicily the air   *25*
Still flashing with the landward gulls
And loom and slowly disappear
The sails above the shadowy hulls

And Spain go under and the shore
Of Africa the gilded sand   *30*
And evening vanish and no more
The low pale light across that land

Nor now the long light on the sea:

And here face downward in the sun
To feel how swift how secretly   *35*
The shadow† of the night comes on . . .

---

9. *Ecbatan:* now Hamadan, a city in western Iran.
13. *Kermanshah:* a city in west central Iran.
17. *Baghdad:* the present-day capital of Iraq.

21. *Palmyra:* a city in Syria, located northeast of Damascus.
36. *the shadow:* as in line 8, a reference to the literal shadow cast over the earth as it rotates on its axis.

Exercises

1. Trace the course of the speaker's "ever climbing shadow" on a map of the world. What other course is traced besides the daily descent of nighttime?

2. We know from the second line that it is noon where the speaker is lying, and that dusk is simultaneously settling over the west coast of Africa (lines 29–32). Using that information, determine the speaker's location on the globe. Once you know the speaker's locale, comment on the phrase "earth's noonward height" and the lines "how swift how secretly/The shadow of the night comes on."

3. Consider how this poem does, and does not, fulfill MacLeish's own dictum, expressed in "Ars Poetica," that a poem "should not mean/But be."

Topic for Writing

Discuss how "You, Andrew Marvell" illustrates the notion that "westward the course of empire takes its way," as Bishop George Berkeley, the eighteenth-century Irish philosopher, phrased it in his "On the Prospect of Planting Arts and Learning in America."

Louis MacNeice *(1907–1963)*

Sunday Morning

Down the road someone is practicing scales,
The notes like little fishes vanish with a wink of tails,
Man's heart expands to tinker with his car
For this is Sunday morning, Fate's great bazaar,
Regard these means as ends, concentrate on this Now,   5
And you may grow to music or drive beyond Hindhead† anyhow,
Take corners on two wheels until you go so fast
That you can clutch a fringe or two of the windy past,
That you can abstract this day and make it to the week of time
A small eternity, a sonnet self-contained in rhyme.   10

But listen, up the road, something gulps, the church spire
Opens its eight bells out, skulls' mouths which will not tire
To tell how there is no music or movement which secures
Escape from the weekday time. Which deadens and endures.

6. *Hindhead:* a district in Surrey,
England, where the locals would
go on a Sunday drive.

Laureen Mar *(1953–)*

Chinatown 2

*Photograph of Eight Chinese American
Children, Ages 1½ to 10. Seattle,
Washington, 1926.*

For my father, Ling Kim

On the 19th and Jefferson block,
the trees are evenly spaced.
Sunlight falls in triangles
as regular as the trunks.
Eight Chinese children sit   5
as if they had just fallen
out of the tree they lean against,
and landed there in two neat rows,
their legs brushing the grass.
Their hair is cut like rice bowls;   10
a fringe of bangs runs high across
their foreheads, leaving eyebrows
below to umbrella somber eyes.
Dick Kim stares at shoes that overwhelm
his feet; sleeves end haphazardly   15
between Ling Kim's wrists and elbows.
Maye Kim does not like her corduroy pants.
There is one dress and one pair of suspenders.

Looking through the lens
of the heavy, borrowed camera,   20
Grandpa remembers the butterfly
resting on a stem, its thin
paper wings folding slowly together.
He had to prod himself to do more
than gawk at the bright stillness.   25
Pressing the button, he feels
the urgent beating between his fingers.
Not knowing they are the show,
his children watch the heavy, black box,
waiting for two white doves   30
to flap awkwardly into the sky,
or a brown jackrabbit to flop
on the lawn, the brown jackrabbit
my father chased for me around the dry
wheatgrass and periwinkle blue flowers.   35
Grandpa clucks his tongue to shoo them off.
They are only disappointed until they see
the neighbor's red trike waiting outside
the right corner, where sunlight
coming from the direction of the house   40
floods and fades the edge.

Edgar Lee Masters *(1868–1950)*

Margaret Fuller Slack†

I would have been as great as George Eliot†
But for an untoward fate.
For look at the photograph of me made by Penniwit,†
Chin resting on hand, and deep-set eyes —
Gray, too, and far-searching.   5
But there was the old, old problem:
Should it be celibacy, matrimony or unchastity?
Then John Slack, the rich druggist, wooed me,
Luring me with the promise of leisure for my novel,
And I married him, giving birth to eight children,   10
And had no time to write.
It was all over with me, anyway,
When I ran the needle in my hand
While washing the baby's things,
And died from lock-jaw, an ironical death.   15
Hear me, ambitious souls,
Sex is the curse of life!

Herman Melville *(1819–1891)*

The Maldive Shark

About the Shark, phlegmatical† one,
Pale sot of the Maldive sea,†
The sleek little pilot-fish,† azure and slim,
How alert in attendance be.
From his saw-pit of mouth, from his charnel of maw†   5
They have nothing of harm to dread,
But liquidly glide on his ghastly flank
Or before his Gorgonian† head;

Title: One of the many fictitious personalities in Masters's *Spoon River Anthology,* Margaret Fuller Slack, like the others, represents the bitter frustrations of otherwise ordinary lives.

1. *George Eliot:* the pen name of Mary Ann Evans (1819–1880), a major English novelist.
3. *Penniwit:* like John Slack (line 8), another resident of Spoon River.

1. *phlegmatical:* calm or sluggish in temperament.
2. *Maldive sea:* that portion of the Indian Ocean surrounding the Maldive Islands located southwest of India.
3. *pilot-fish:* smaller fish that often accompany schools of sharks.
5. *charnel of maw:* a *charnel* is a house for receiving the dead, while *maw* refers specifically to the mouth or gullet of particularly voracious animals.
8. *Gorgonian:* resembling any of the three frightful sisters in Greek mythology whose heads were covered with snakes instead of hair, and who also had wings, claws, and enormous teeth. The best known of them is Medusa; according to myth, anyone who looked at her head was turned into stone.

Or lurk in the port of serrated teeth
In white triple tiers of glittering gates,   10
And there find a haven when peril's abroad,
An asylum in jaws of the Fates!
They are friends; and friendly they guide him to prey,
Yet never partake of the treat —
Eyes and brains to the dotard lethargic and dull,   15
Pale ravener of horrible meat.

Alice Meynell (1847–1922)

Summer in England, 1914

On London fell a clearer light;
    Caressing pencils of the sun
Defined the distances, the white
    Houses transfigured one by one,
The 'long, unlovely street' impearled.   5
Oh, what a sky has walked the world!

Most happy year! And out of town
    The hay was prosperous, and the wheat;
The silken harvest climbed the down:
    Moon after moon was heavenly-sweet,   10
Stroking the bread within the sheaves,
Looking 'twixt apples and their leaves.

And while this rose made round her cup,
    The armies died convulsed. And when
This chaste young silver sun went up   15
    Softly, a thousand shattered men,
One wet corruption, heaped the plain,
After a league-long throb of pain.

Flower following tender flower; and birds,
    And berries; and benignant skies   20
Made thrive the serried flocks and herds. —
    Yonder are men shot through the eyes.
        Love, hide thy face
From man's unpardonable race.

Josephine Miles (1911–   )

Belief

Mother said to call her if the H bomb exploded
And I said I would, and it about did
When Louis my brother robbed a service station
And lay cursing on the oily cement in handcuffs.

But by that time it was too late to tell Mother,   *5*
She was too sick to worry the life out of her
Over *why why*. Causation is sequence
And everything is one thing after another.

Besides, my other brother, Eddie, had got to be President,
And you can't ask too much of one family.   *10*
The chances were as good for a good future
As bad for a bad one.

Therefore it was surprising that, as we kept the newspapers from
   Mother,
She died feeling responsible for a disaster unverified,
Murmuring, in her sleep as it seemed, the ancient slogan   *15*
Noblesse oblige.†

Edna St. Vincent Millay *(1892–1950)*

The Concert

No, I will go alone.
I will come back when it's over.
Yes, of course I love you.
No, it will not be long.
Why may you not come with me? —   *5*
You are too much my lover.
You would put yourself
Between me and song.

If I go alone,
Quiet and suavely clothed,   *10*
My body will die in its chair,
And over my head a flame,
A mind that is twice my own,
Will mark with icy mirth
The wise advance and retreat   *15*
Of armies without a country,
Storming a nameless gate,
Hurling terrible javelins down
From the shouting walls of a singing town
Where no women wait!   *20*
Armies clean of love and hate,
Marching lines of pitiless sound
Climbing hills to the sun and hurling
Golden spears to the ground!
Up the lines a silver runner   *25*
Bearing a banner whereon is scored
The milk and steel of a bloodless wound
Healed at length by the sword!

16. *Noblesse oblige:* noble birth
begets obligations.

You and I have nothing to do with music.
We may not make of music a filigree† frame,   30
Within which you and I,
Tenderly glad we came,
Sit smiling, hand in hand.

Come now, be content.
I will come back to you, I swear I will;   35
And you will know me still.
I shall be only a little taller
Than when I went.

Never May the Fruit Be Plucked

Never, never may the fruit be plucked from the bough
And gathered into barrels.
He that would eat of love must eat it where it hangs.
Though the branches bend like reeds,
Though the ripe fruit splash in the grass or wrinkle on the tree,   5
He that would eat of love may bear away with him
Only what his belly can hold,
Nothing in the apron,
Nothing in the pockets.
Never, never may the fruit be gathered from the bough   10
And harvested in barrels.
The winter of love is a cellar of empty bins,
In an orchard soft with rot.

John Milton *(1608–1674)*

When I consider how my light is spent

When I consider how my light is spent,
   Ere half my days, in this dark world and wide,
   And that one Talent† which is death to hide,
   Lodg'd with me useless, though my Soul more bent
To serve therewith my Maker, and present   5
   My true account, lest he returning chide;
   "Doth God exact day-labor, light denied,"
   I fondly† ask; But patience to prevent†

30. *filigree:* ornamental work of
delicate, intricate design.

---

3. *Talent:* Matthew 25:24–25 tells
of the servant who hid the talent,
a unit of money, that his master
gave to him.

8. *fondly:* foolishly; *prevent:* forestall.

That murmur soon replies, "God doth not need
    Either man's work or his own gifts; who best   *10*
    Bear his mild yoke, they serve him best; his State
Is Kingly. Thousands at his bidding speed
    And post o'er Land and Ocean without rest:
    They also serve who only stand and wait."

Exercises

1. What is the source of the speaker's despair expressed in the first two lines? Try not to limit yourself to a single possibility, such as the poet's physical blindness.

2. What saves the speaker from yielding to despair?

3. Now that you know the source and the context of the much-quoted line "They also serve who only stand and wait," what precise meaning would you assign to it? What relationship does it assume between God and each individual?

Topic for Writing

At the heart of Milton's sonnet is a common despair, also often felt by the young, that the individual has accomplished little or nothing and never will accomplish anything more. Discuss how Milton's treatment of this theme has a universal application, no matter what personal event in the poet's life inspired the poem.

How soon hath Time, the subtle thief of youth

How soon hath Time, the subtle thief of youth,
    Stol'n on his wing my three and twentieth year!
    My hasting days fly on with full career,
    But my late spring no bud or blossom show'th.
Perhaps my semblance might deceive the truth,   *5*
    That I to manhood am arriv'd so near,
    And inward ripeness doth much less appear,
    That some more timely-happy spirits endu'th.†
Yet be it less or more, or soon or slow,
    It shall be still in strictest measure ev'n   *10*
    To that same lot, however mean or high,
Toward which Time leads me, and the will of Heav'n;
    All is, if I have grace to use it so,
    As ever in my great task-Master's eye.

8. *endu'th:* endowed.

Marianne Moore *(1887–1972)*

Poetry

I, too, dislike it: there are things that are important beyond all this
    fiddle.
    Reading it, however, with a perfect contempt for it, one discovers
        in
    it after all, a place for the genuine.
        Hands that can grasp, eyes
            that can dilate, hair that can rise   5
                if it must, these things are important not because a

high-sounding interpretation can be put upon them but because they
    are
    useful. When they become so derivative as to become unintelli-
        gible,
    the same thing may be said for all of us, that we
        do not admire what   10
        we cannot understand: the bat
            holding on upside down or in quest of something to

eat, elephants pushing, a wild horse taking a roll, a tireless wolf under
    a tree, the immovable critic twitching his skin like a horse that
        feels a flea, the base-
    ball fan, the statistician —   15
        nor is it valid
            to discriminate against 'business documents and

school-books'; all these phenomena are important. One must make a
    distinction
    however: when dragged into prominence by half poets, the result
        is not poetry,
    nor till the poets among us can be   20
        'literalists of
        the imagination' — above
            insolence and triviality and can present

for inspection, imaginary gardens with real toads in them, shall we
    have
    it. In the meantime, if you demand on the one hand,   25
    the raw material of poetry in
        all its rawness and
        that which is on the other hand
            genuine, then you are interested in poetry.

Ogden Nash *(1902–1971)*

Inter-Office Memorandum

The only people who should really sin
Are the people who can sin with a grin,
Because if sinning upsets you,
Why, nothing at all is what it gets you.
Everybody certainly ought to eschew all offences however venial   5
As long as they are conscience's menial.
Some people suffer weeks of remorse after having committed the
     slightest peccadillo,
And other people feel perfectly all right after feeding their husbands
     arsenic or smothering their grandmother with a pillow.
Some people are perfectly self-possessed about spending their lives on
     the verge of delirium tremens,
And other people feel like hanging themselves on a coathook just
     because they took that extra cocktail and amused their fellow
     guests with recitations from the poems of Mrs. Hemans.   10
Some people calmly live a barnyard life because they find monogamy
     dull and arid,
And other people have sinking spells if they dance twice in an eve-
     ning with a lady to whom they aren't married.
Some people feel forever lost if they are riding on a bus and the
     conductor doesn't collect their fare,
And other people ruin a lot of widows and orphans, and all they
     think is, Why there's something in this business of ruining wid-
     ows and orphans, and they go out and ruin some more and get
     to be a millionaire.
Now it is not the purpose of this memorandum, or song,   15
To attempt to define the difference between right and wrong;
All I am trying to say is that if you are one of the unfortunates who
     recognize that such a difference exists,
Well, you had better oppose even the teensiest temptation with
     clenched fists,
Because if you desire peace of mind it is all right to do wrong if it
     never occurs to you that it is wrong to do it,
Because you can sleep perfectly well and look the world in the eye
     after doing anything at all so long as you don't rue it,   20
While on the other hand nothing at all is any fun
So long as you yourself know it is something you shouldn't have
     done.
There is only one way to achieve happiness on this terrestrial ball,
And that is to have either a clear conscience, or none at all.

Wilfred Owen (1893–1918)

Anthem for Doomed Youth

What passing-bells for these who die as cattle?
Only the monstrous anger of the guns.
Only the stuttering rifles' rapid rattle
Can patter out their hasty orisons.
No mockeries for them from prayers or bells,   5
Nor any voice of mourning save the choirs —
The shrill, demented choirs of wailing shells;
And bugles calling for them from sad shires.
What candles may be held to speed them all?
Not in the hands of boys, but in their eyes   10
Shall shine the holy glimmers of good-byes.
The pallor of girls' brows shall be their pall;
Their flowers the tenderness of patient minds,
And each slow dusk a drawing-down of blinds.

Carol Lynn Pearson (1939–   )

Millie's Mother's Red Dress

It hung there in the closet
While she was dying, Mother's red dress,
Like a gash in the row
Of dark, old clothes
She had worn away her life in.   5

They had called me home,
And I knew when I saw her
She wasn't going to last.

When I saw the dress, I said,
"Why, Mother — how beautiful!   10
I've never seen it on you."

"I've never worn it," she slowly said.
"Sit down, Millie — I'd like to undo
A lesson or two before I go, if I can."

I sat by her bed,   15
And she sighed a bigger breath
Than I thought she could hold.
"Now that I'll soon be gone,
I can see some things.
Oh, I taught you good — but I taught you wrong."   20

"What do you mean, Mother?"

"Well — I always thought
That a good woman never takes her turn,

That she's just for doing for somebody else.
Do here, do there, always keep 25
Everybody else's wants tended and make sure
Yours are at the bottom of the heap.
Maybe someday you'll get to them,
But of course you never do.
My life was like that — doing for your dad, 30
Doing for the boys, for your sisters, for you."

"You did — everything a mother could."

"Oh, Millie, Millie, it was no good —
For you — for him. Don't you see?
I did you the worst of wrongs. 35
I asked nothing — for me!

"Your father in the other room,
All stirred up and staring at the walls —
When the doctor told him, he took
It bad — came to my bed and all but shook 40
The life right out of me. 'You can't die,
Do you hear? What'll become of me?
What'll become of me?'
It'll be hard, all right, when I go.
He can't even find the frying pan, you know. 45

"And you children.
I was a free ride for everybody, everywhere.
I was the first one up and the last one down
Seven days out of the week.
I always took the toast that got burned, 50
And the very smallest piece of pie.
I look at how some of your brothers treat their wives now,
And it makes me sick, 'cause it was me
That taught it to them. And they learned.
They learned that a woman doesn't 55
Even exist except to give.
Why, every single penny that I could save
Went for your clothes, or your books,
Even when it wasn't necessary.
Can't even remember once when I took 60
Myself downtown to buy something beautiful —
For me.

"Except last year when I got that red dress.
I found I had twenty dollars
That wasn't especially spoke for. 65
I was on my way to pay it extra on the washer.
But somehow — I came home with this big box.
Your father really gave it to me then.
'Where you going to wear a thing like that to —
Some opera or something?' 70
And he was right, I guess.

I've never, except in the store,
Put on that dress.

"Oh, Millie — I always thought if you take
Nothing for yourself in this world,   *75*
You'd have it all in the next somehow.
I don't believe that anymore.
I think the Lord wants us to have something —
Here — and now.

"And I'm telling you, Millie, if some miracle   *80*
Could get me off this bed, you could look
For a different mother, 'cause I would be one.
Oh, I passed up my turn so long
I would hardly know how to take it.
But I'd learn, Millie.   *85*
I would learn!"

It hung there in the closet
While she was dying, Mother's red dress,
Like a gash in the row
Of dark, old clothes   *90*
She had worn away her life in.

Her last words to me were these:
"Do me the honor, Millie,
Of not following in my footsteps.
Promise me that."   *95*

I promised.
She caught her breath,
Then Mother took her turn
In death.

Sylvia Plath *(1932–1963)*

Lady Lazarus†

I have done it again.
One year in every ten
I manage it—

A sort of walking miracle, my skin
Bright as a Nazi lampshade,   *5*
My right foot

A paperweight,
My face a featureless, fine
Jew linen.

Lazarus: brother of Mary and
Martha, raised from the dead by
Jesus (John 11:1–44).

Peel off the napkin
O my enemy.
Do I terrify? —

The nose, the eye pits, the full set of teeth?
The sour breath
Will vanish in a day.

Soon, soon the flesh
The grave cave ate will be
At home on me

And I a smiling woman.
I am only thirty.
And like the cat I have nine times to die.

This is Number Three.
What a trash
To annihilate each decade.

What a million filaments.
The peanut-crunching crowd
Shoves in to see

Them unwrap me hand and foot —
The big strip tease.
Gentleman, ladies,

These are my hands,
My knees.
I may be skin and bone,

Nevertheless, I am the same, identical woman.
The first time it happened I was ten.
It was an accident.

The second time I meant
To last it out and not come back at all.
I rocked shut

As a seashell.
They had to call and call
And pick the worms off me like sticky pearls.

Dying
Is an art, like everything else.
I do it exceptionally well.

I do it so it feels like hell.
I do it so it feels real.
I guess you could say I've a call.

It's easy enough to do it in a cell.
It's easy enough to do it and stay put.
It's the theatrical

Comeback in broad day
To the same place, the same face, the same brute
Amused shout:

"A miracle!"   55
That knocks me out.
There is a charge

For the eyeing of my scars, there is a charge
For the hearing of my heart —
It really goes.   60

And there is a charge, very large charge,
For a word or a touch
Or a bit of blood

Or a piece of my hair or my clothes.
So, so, Herr Doktor.   65
So, Herr Enemy.

I am your opus,†
I am your valuable,
The pure gold baby

That melts to a shriek.   70
I turn and burn.
Do not think I underestimate your great concern.

Ash, ash —
You poke and stir.
Flesh, bone, there is nothing there —   75

A cake of soap,
A wedding ring,
A gold filling.

Herr God, Herr Lucifer,
Beware   80
Beware.

Out of the ash
I rise with my red hair
And I eat men like air.

Exercises

1. Who is the speaker in this poem? What happened to her at the age of ten
(line 35)? What is happening to her now, at the age of thirty?

2. What is the cause of the speaker's periodic deaths? How is this method of
annihilation and the identity of the annihilators indicated?

   67. *opus:* work, creation.

3. After reading the New Testament account of Lazarus raised from the dead (John 11:1–44), tell why you believe the poet relies on this Biblical allusion.

4. What is the poem telling us?

Edgar Allan Poe (1809–1849)

The Raven

Once upon a midnight dreary, while I pondered, weak and weary,
Over many a quaint and curious volume of forgotten lore —
While I nodded, nearly napping, suddenly there came a tapping,
As of some one gently rapping, rapping at my chamber door.
" 'Tis some visitor," I muttered, "tapping at my chamber door —   *5*
    Only this and nothing more."

Ah, distinctly I remember it was in the bleak December;
And each separate dying ember wrought its ghost upon the floor.
Eagerly I wished the morrow; — vainly I had sought to borrow
From my books surcease† of sorrow — sorrow for the lost Lenore —   *10*
For the rare and radiant maiden whom the angels name Lenore —
    Nameless *here* for evermore.

And the silken, sad, uncertain rustling of each purple curtain
Thrilled me — filled me with fantastic terrors never felt before;
So that now, to still the beating of my heart, I stood repeating   *15*
" 'Tis some visitor entreating entrance at my chamber door —
Some late visitor entreating entrance at my chamber door: —
    This it is and nothing more."

Presently my soul grew stronger; hesitating then no longer,
"Sir," said I, "or Madam, truly your forgiveness I implore;   *20*
But the fact is I was napping, and so gently you came rapping,
And so faintly you came tapping, tapping at my chamber door,
That I scarce was sure I heard you" — here I opened wide the
    door; —
    Darkness there and nothing more.

Deep into that darkness peering, long I stood there wondering, fearing,   *25*
Doubting, dreaming dreams no mortal ever dared to dream before;
But the silence was unbroken, and the stillness gave no token,
And the only word there spoken was the whispered word, "Lenore?"
Till I whispered, and an echo murmured back the word, "Lenore!"
    Merely this and nothing more.   *30*

Back into the chamber turning, all my soul within me burning,
Soon again I heard a tapping somewhat louder than before.
"Surely," said I, "surely that is something at my window lattice;

10. *surcease:* end or cessation.

Let me see, then, what thereat is, and this mystery explore —
Let my heart be still a moment and this mystery explore; —   *35*
    'Tis the wind and nothing more!"

Open here I flung the shutter, when, with many a flirt and flutter,
In there stepped a stately Raven of the saintly days of yore;
Not the least obeisance made he; not a minute stopped or stayed he;
But, with mien of lord or lady, perched above my chamber door —   *40*
Perched upon a bust of Pallas† just above my chamber door —
    Perched, and sat, and nothing more.

Then this ebony bird beguiling my sad fancy into smiling,
By the grave and stern decorum of the countenance it wore,
"Though thy crest be shorn and shaven, thou," I said, "art sure no
      craven,
                                                         45
Ghastly grim and ancient Raven wandering from the Nightly shore—
Tell me what thy lordly name is on the Night's Plutonian† shore!"
    Quoth the Raven, "Nevermore."

Much I marvelled this ungainly fowl to hear discourse so plainly,
Though its answer little meaning — little relevancy bore;   *50*
For we cannot help agreeing that no living human being
Ever yet was blessed with seeing bird above his chamber door —
Bird or beast upon the sculptured bust above his chamber door,
    With such name as "Nevermore."

But the Raven, sitting lonely on the placid bust, spoke only   *55*
That one word, as if his soul in that one word he did outpour.
Nothing farther then he uttered — not a feather then he fluttered —
Till I scarcely more than muttered "Other friends have flown before —
On the morrow *he* will leave me, as my Hopes have flown before."
    Then the bird said "Nevermore."   *60*

Startled at the stillness broken by reply so aptly spoken,
"Doubtless," said I, "what it utters is its only stock and store
Caught from some unhappy master whom unmerciful Disaster
Followed fast and followed faster till his songs one burden bore —
Till the dirges of his Hope that melancholy burden bore   *65*
    Of 'Never-nevermore.' "

But the Raven still beguiling my sad fancy into smiling,
Straight I wheeled a cushioned seat in front of bird, and bust and
    door;
Then, upon the velvet sinking, I betook myself to linking
Fancy unto fancy, thinking what this ominous bird of yore —   *70*
What this grim, ungainly, ghastly, gaunt, and ominous bird of yore
    Meant in croaking "Nevermore."

41. *Pallas:* Pallas Athena, Greek goddess of wisdom — a popular subject for sculptors imitating the classical style and a suitable addition to any scholar's study.

47. *Plutonian:* in Greek mythology, Pluto was the god of the underworld, or Hades, which is now synonymous with hell.

This I sat engaged in guessing, but no syllable expressing
To the fowl whose fiery eyes now burned into my bosom's core;
This and more I sat divining, with my head at ease reclining   *75*
On the cushion's velvet lining that the lamp-light gloated o'er,
But whose velvet-violet lining with the lamp-light gloating o'er,
    She shall press, ah, nevermore!

Then, methought, the air grew denser, perfumed from an unseen
        censer
Swung by seraphim whose foot-falls tinkled on the tufted floor.   *80*
"Wretch," I cried, "thy God hath lent thee — by these angels he hath
        sent thee
Respite — respite and nepenthe† from thy memories of Lenore;
Quaff, oh quaff this kind nepenthe and forget this lost Lenore!"
    Quoth the Raven "Nevermore."

"Prophet!" said I, "thing of evil! — prophet still, if bird or devil! —   *85*
Whether Tempter† sent, or whether tempest tossed thee here ashore,
Desolate yet all undaunted, on this desert land enchanted —
On this home by Horror haunted — tell me truly, I implore —
Is there — *is* there balm in Gilead?† — tell me — tell me, I implore!"
    Quoth the Raven "Nevermore."   *90*

"Prophet!" said I, "thing of evil! — prophet still, if bird devil!
By that Heaven that bends above us — by that God we both adore —
Tell this soul with sorrow laden if, within the distant Aidenn,†
It shall clasp a sainted maiden whom the angels named Lenore —
Clasp a rare and radiant maiden whom the angels name Lenore."   *95*
    Quoth the Raven "Nevermore."

"Be that word our sign of parting, bird or fiend!" I shrieked, upstarting —
"Get thee back into the tempest and the Night's Plutonian shore!
Leave no black plume as a token of that lie thy soul hath spoken!
Leave my loneliness unbroken! — quit the bust above my door!   *100*
Take thy beak from out my heart, and take thy form from off my
        door!"
    Quoth the Raven "Nevermore."

And the Raven, never flitting, still is sitting, *still* is sitting
On the pallid bust of Pallas just above my chamber door;
And his eyes have all the seeming of a demon's that is dreaming,   *105*
And the lamp-light o'er him streaming throws his shadow on the
        floor;
And my soul from out that shadow that lies floating on the floor
    Shall be lifted — nevermore!

82. *nepenthe:* a drug, which the
ancient Greeks believed enabled a
person to forget sorrow.
86. *Tempter:* Satan.
89. *balm in Gilead:* Ishmaelites
carry balm from Gilead (see Genesis 37:25).
93: *Aidenn:* Eden; in this context,
heaven.

Exercises

1. Characterize the speaker of the poem. Does he strike you as a particularly stable individual? If not, what is the cause of his instability? Is it simply this episode with the raven? Or does he appear susceptible to making more out of the encounter than a sane person would? If so, what made him susceptible?

2. Poe is renowned as a master of horrific and often macabre tales. Are the same elements to be found in this poem? Select the features of "The Raven" that invest the poem with much more horror than the incident itself supports.

3. The entire exchange between the speaker and the raven may seem improbable until we notice the single dramatic effect that makes the entire poem cohere. What is that single effect?

Topic for Writing

Poe often deals with obsessive personalities weakened by some great grief, either real or imagined. In this respect, the speaker of "The Raven" is very similar to Roderick Usher in "The Fall of the House of Usher" (pp. 325–337). Compare and contrast these two situations and characterizations to establish the methods by which Poe created the mood of horror for which he has become famous.

Alexander Pope (1688–1744)

Elegy to the Memory of an Unfortunate Lady

What beckoning ghost, along the moonlight shade
Invites my steps, and points to yonder glade?
'Tis she! — but why that bleeding bosom gored,
Why dimly gleams the visionary sword?
O ever beauteous, ever friendly! tell,   *5*
Is it, in Heaven, a crime to love too well?
To bear too tender, or too firm a heart,
To act a lover's or a Roman's part?†
Is there no bright reversion† in the sky,
For those who greatly think, or bravely die?   *10*
    Why bade ye else, ye Powers! her soul aspire
Above the vulgar flight of low desire?
Ambition first sprung from your blest abodes;
The glorious fault of angels and of gods:
Thence to their images on earth it flows,   *15*
And in the breasts of kings and heroes glows.
Most souls, 'tis true, but peep out once an age,

8. *Roman's part:* to commit suicide as prescribed by the Roman Stoics when life appears unbearable and no solution is apparent.
9. *reversion:* inheritance, reward.

Dull sullen prisoners in the body's cage:
Dim lights of life, that burn a length of years
Useless, unseen, as lamps in sepulchers;   *20*
Like Eastern kings a lazy state they keep,
And close confined to their own palace, sleep.
    From these perhaps (ere Nature bade her die)
Fate snatched her early to the pitying sky.
As into air the purer spirits flow,   *25*
And separate from their kindred dregs below;
So flew the soul to its congenial place,
Nor left one virtue to redeem her race.
    But thou, false guardian of a charge too good,
Thou, mean deserter of thy brother's blood!   *30*
See on these ruby lips the trembling breath,
These cheeks, now fading at the blast of death;
Cold is that breast which warmed the world before,
And those love-darting eyes must roll no more.
Thus, if Eternal Justice rules the ball,   *35*
Thus shall your wives, and thus your children fall:
On all the line a sudden vengeance waits,
And frequent hearses shall besiege your gates.
There passengers shall stand, and pointing say
(While the long funerals blacken all the way),   *40*
Lo these were they, whose souls the Furies steeled,
And cursed with hearts unknowing how to yield.
Thus unlamented pass the proud away,
The gaze of fools, and pageant of a day!
So perish all, whose breast ne'er learned to glow   *45*
For others' good, or melt at others' woe.
    What can atone (oh, ever-injured shade!†)
Thy fate unpitied, and thy rites unpaid?†
No friend's complaint, no kind domestic tear
Pleased thy pale ghost, or graced thy mournful bier.†   *50*
By foreign hands thy dying eyes were closed,
By foreign hands thy decent limbs composed,
By foreign hands thy humble grave adorned,
By strangers honored, and by strangers mourned!
What though no friends in sable weeds† appear,   *55*
Grieve for an hour, perhaps, then mourn a year,
And bear about the mockery of woe
To midnight dances, and the public show?
What though no weeping Loves thy ashes grace,
Nor polished marble emulate thy face?   *60*
What though no sacred earth allow thee room,
Nor hallowed dirge be muttered o'er thy tomb?

---

47. *shade:* spirit (here, of the lady).   50. *bier:* coffin stand.
48. *rites unpaid:* rites in the Chris-   55. *sable weeds:* black clothes for
tian burial service that will not be   mourning.
performed because the lady com-
mitted suicide.

Yet shall thy grave with rising flowers be dressed,
And the green turf lie lightly on thy breast:
There shall the morn her earliest tears bestow, 65
There the first roses of the year shall blow;
While angels with their silver wings o'ershade
The ground, now sacred by thy relics made.

    So peaceful rests, without a stone, a name,
What once had beauty, titles, wealth, and fame. 70
How loved, how honored once, avails thee not,
To whom related, or by whom begot;
A heap of dust alone remains of thee,
'Tis all thou art, and all the proud shall be!

    Poets themselves must fall, like those they sung, 75
Deaf the praised ear, and mute the tuneful tongue.
Even he, whose soul now melts in mournful lays,
Shall shortly want the generous tear he pays;
Then from his closing eyes thy form shall part,
And the last pang shall tear thee from his heart, 80
Life's idle business at one gasp be o'er,
The Muse forgot, and thou beloved no more!

Peter Porter (1929–   )

A Consumer's Report

The name of the product I tested is *Life*,
I have completed the form you sent me
and understand that my answers are confidential.
I had it as a gift,
I didn't feel much while using it, 5
in fact I think I'd have liked to be more excited.
It seemed gentle on the hands
but left an embarrassing deposit behind.
It was not economical
and I have used much more than I thought 10
(I suppose I have about half left
but it's difficult to tell) —
although the instructions are fairly large
there are so many of them
I don't know which to follow, especially 15
as they seem to contradict each other.
I'm not sure such a thing
should be put in the way of children —
It's difficult to think of a purpose
for it. One of my friends says 20
it's just to keep its maker in a job.
Also the price is much too high.
Things are piling up so fast,

after all, the world got by
for a thousand million years   25
without this, do we need it now?
(Incidentally, please ask your man
to stop calling me 'the respondent',
I don't like the sound of it.)
There seems to be a lot of different labels,   30
sizes and colours should be uniform,
the shape is awkward, it's waterproof
but not heat resistant, it doesn't keep
yet it's very difficult to get rid of:
whenever they make it cheaper they seem   35
to put less in — if you say you don't
want it, then it's delivered anyway.
I'd agree it's a popular product,
it's got into the language; people
even say they're on the side of it.   40
Personally I think it's overdone,
a small thing people are ready
to behave badly about. I think
we should take it for granted. If its
experts are called philosophers or market   45
researchers or historians, we shouldn't
care. We are the consumers and the last
law makers. So finally, I'd buy it.
But the question of a 'best buy'
I'd like to leave until I get   50
the competitive product you said you'd send.

Ezra Pound (1885–1972)

Ballad of the Goodly Fere†

Simon Zelotes† Speaketh It Somewhile
After the Crucifixion

Ha' we lost the goodliest fere o' all
For the priests and the gallows tree?†
Aye lover he was of brawny men,
O' ships and the open sea.

When they came wi' a host to take Our Man   5
His smile was good to see,

Fere: brother. The Goodly Fere of the title is, of course, Christ.
Simon Zelotes: also known as Simon the Canaanite, one of the twelve apostles. Little else is known about Simon. The Zealots, a Jewish sect at the time of Christ, violently opposed Roman rule in Palestine.
2. *the gallows tree:* the cross upon which Christ was crucified.

"First let these go!"† quo' our Goodly Fere,
"Or I'll see ye damned," says he.

Aye he sent us out through the crossed high spears
And the scorn of his laugh rang free,   *10*
"Why took ye not me when I walked about
Alone in the town?" says he.

Oh we drunk his "Hale" in the good red wine
When we last made company,
No capon† priest was the Goodly Fere   *15*
But a man o' men was he.

I ha' seen him drive a hundred men
Wi' a bundle o' cords swung free,
That they took the high and holy house
For their pawn and treasury.†   *20*

They'll no' get him a' in a book I think
Though they write it cunningly;
No mouse of the scrolls was the Goodly Fere
But aye loved the open sea.

If they think they ha' snared our Goodly Fere   *25*
They are fools to the last degree.
"I'll go to the feast," quo' our Goodly Fere,
"Though I go to the gallows tree."

"Ye ha' seen me heal the lame and blind,
And wake the dead," says he,   *30*
"Ye shall see one thing to master all:
'Tis how a brave man dies on the tree."

A son of God was the Goodly Fere
That bade us his brothers be.
I ha' seen him cow a thousand men.   *35*
I have seen him upon the tree.

He cried no cry when they drave the nails
And the blood gushed hot and free,
The hounds of the crimson sky gave tongue
But never a cry cried he.   *40*

I ha' seen him cow a thousand men
On the hills o' Galilee,
They whined as he walked out calm between,
Wi' his eyes like the grey o' the sea,

Like the sea that brooks no voyaging   *45*
With the winds unleashed and free,

7. *"First let these go!":* When they
came to arrest Jesus in the Garden
of Gethsemane, Jesus asked his
captors to let the others in his
company go (John 18:8).

15. *capon:* a neutered rooster.
17–20. Jesus cast the moneylenders
and merchants out of the Temple
courtyard, where they were doing
business (Matt. 21:12).

Like the sea that he cowed at Genseret†
Wi' twey words spoke' suddently.

A master of men was the Goodly Fere,
A mate of the wind and sea,   *50*
If they think they ha' slain our Goodly Fere
They are fools eternally.

I ha' seen him eat o' the honey-comb
Sin' they nailed him to the tree.

Exercises

1. Although many of us are used to Gospel stories being recounted in the language of the King James version of the Bible, Pound clearly avoids that style. Why? If he meant simply to modernize and embellish the Gospels, why didn't he use a language more familiar to twentieth-century Americans? Why did he use the ballad form?

2. What is the irony expressed in stanza six? What image of Jesus emerges from Simon Zelotes' recounting of Christ's life and death?

3. What is the significance of the last two lines of the poem? Does their implication give more strength and credence to all of Simon's earlier remarks?

Topic for Writing

Simon Zelotes does not seem to be a very religious man, although he was certainly devoted to Christ. Discuss what view of Christ Pound develops through the speaker, who is a man of the people and a political radical. Then consider how that view coincides with what you know to be the orthodox view of Christ, and account for any disparities.

John Crowe Ransom (1888–1974)

Here Lies a Lady

Here lies a lady of beauty and high degree.
Of chills and fever she died, of fever and chills,
The delight of her husband, her aunts, an infant of three,
And of medicos marvelling sweetly on her ills.

47. *Genseret:* Genneserat. After the miracle of the loaves and fish (Matt. 14), Jesus sent his disciples out in a boat while he dismissed the multitude that had gathered to hear him. That night, the disciples saw Jesus walking across the water to join them in the boat while a storm was coming up. The disciple Peter walked out to meet him; Jesus saved him from drowning and calmed the waves.

For either she burned, and her confident eyes would blaze,   5
And her fingers fly in a manner to puzzle their heads —
What was she making? Why, nothing; she sat in a maze
Of old scraps of laces, snipped into curious shreds —

Or this would pass, and the light of her fire decline
Till she lay discouraged and cold as a thin stalk white and blown,   10
And would not open her eyes, to kisses, to wine;
The sixth of these states was her last; the cold settled down.

Sweet ladies, long may ye bloom, and toughly I hope ye may thole,†
But was she not lucky? In flowers and lace and mourning,
In love and great honour we bade God rest her soul   15
After six little spaces of chill, and six of burning.

                                                    Adrienne Rich (1929–   )

Orion†

Far back when I went zig-zagging
through tamarack† pastures
you were my genius,† you
my cast-iron Viking, my helmed
lion-heart king in prison.   5
Years later now you're young

my fierce half-brother, staring
down from that simplified west
your breast open, your belt dragged down
by an oldfashioned thing, a sword   10
the last bravado you won't give over
though it weighs you down as you stride

and the stars in it are dim
and maybe have stopped burning.
But you burn, and I know it;   15
as I throw back my head to take you in
an old transfusion happens again:
divine astronomy is nothing to it.

Indoors I bruise and blunder,
break faith, leave ill enough   20
alone, a dead child born in the dark.

13. *thole:* to suffer or endure; Ransom clearly intends the second meaning.

Orion: a constellation represented on star charts by a giant hunter with a belt (three bright stars) and sword (dim stars); a winter constellation in the Northern Hemisphere.
2. *tamarack:* a species of pine tree.
3. *genius:* attendant spirit.

Night cracks up over the chimney,
pieces of time, frozen geodes†
come showering down in the grate.

A man reaches behind my eyes   25
and finds them empty
a woman's head turns away
from my head in the mirror
children are dying my death
and eating crumbs of my life.   30

Pity is not your forte.
Calmly you ache up there
pinned aloft in your crow's nest,
my speechless pirate!
You take it all for granted   35
and when I look you back

it's with a starlike eye
shooting its cold and egotistical spear
where it can do least damage.
Breathe deep! No hurt, no pardon   40
out here in the cold with you
you with your back to the wall.

Edwin Arlington Robinson (1869–1935)

Karma†

Christmas was in the air and all was well
With him, but for a few confusing flaws
In divers of God's images. Because
A friend of his would neither buy nor sell,
Was he to answer for the axe that fell?   5
He pondered; and the reason for it was,
Partly, a slowly freezing Santa Clause
Upon the corner, with his beard and bell.

Acknowledging an improvident† surprise,
He magnified a fancy that he wished   10
The friend whom he had wrecked were here again.
Not sure of that, he found a compromise;
And from the fullness of his heart he fished
A dime for Jesus who had died for man.

23. *geodes:* stones having a cavity
lined with crystals.

Title: In Buddhism and Hinduism,
karma is regarded as the accumulated moral actions in one life that
determine the level of spiritual life
in succeeding incarnations; generally, karma has come to mean fate
or destiny.
9. *improvident:* acting without foresight.

Richard Cory

Whenever Richard Cory went down town,
We people on the pavement looked at him:
He was a gentleman from sole to crown,
Clean favored, and imperially slim.

And he was always quietly arrayed,   *5*
And he was always human when he talked;
But still he fluttered pulses when he said,
"Good-morning," and he glittered when he walked.

And he was rich — yes, richer than a king —
And admirably schooled in every grace: *10*
In fine,† we thought that he was everything
To make us wish that we were in his place.

So on we worked, and waited for the light,
And went without the meat, and cursed the bread;
And Richard Cory, one calm summer night,   *15*
Went home and put a bullet through his head.

Exercises

1. After reading the poem, did you think that Richard Cory was every bit as well off as the speaker seemed to think he was? Does the poem offer any clues as to why Cory took his own life? Explain.

2. Does the speaker admire or envy Cory? Once you have answered that question, decide whether or not the speaker gives us an accurate picture of Cory. If not, consider what crucial details might be missing.

3. The speaker tells us that the townspeople all wished that they "were in his [Cory's] place." What basic flaw in human nature does Robinson illustrate here? Why didn't Robinson explicitly tell us about this flaw?

Topic for Writing

"Richard Cory" shows us Cory as others see him. On the basis of the information and attitudes provided by the speaker, write a paper in which you speculate about Cory's real life. For example, do you feel that he might have been a very lonely man? Why?

11. *in fine:* in conclusion.

Theodore Roethke *(1908–1963)*

The Meadow Mouse

1.

In a shoe box stuffed in an old nylon stocking
Sleeps the baby mouse I found in the meadow,
Where he trembled and shook beneath a stick
Till I caught him up by the tail and brought him in,
Cradled in my hand,   5
A little quaker, the whole body of him trembling,
His absurd whiskers sticking out like a cartoon-mouse,
His feet like small leaves,
Little lizard-feet,
Whitish and spread wide when he tried to struggle away,   10
Wriggling like a miniscule puppy.

Now he's eaten his three kinds of cheese and drunk from his bottle-
      cap watering-trough —
So much he just lies in one corner,
His tail curled under him, his belly big
As his head; his bat-like ears   15
Twitching, tilting toward the least sound.

Do I imagine he no longer trembles
When I come close to him?
He seems no longer to tremble.

2.

But this morning the shoe-box house on the back porch is empty.   20
Where has he gone, my meadow mouse,
My thumb of a child that nuzzled in my palm? —
To run under the hawk's wing,
Under the eye of the great owl watching from the elm-tree,
To live by courtesy of the shrike, the snake, the tom-cat.   25

I think of the nestling fallen into the deep grass,
The turtle gasping in the dusty rubble of the highway,
The paralytic stunned in the tub, and the water rising, —
All things innocent, hapless, forsaken.

I Knew a Woman

I knew a woman, lovely in her bones,
When small birds sighed, she would sigh back at them;
Ah, when she moved, she moved more ways than one:
The shapes a bright container can contain!
Of her choice virtues only gods should speak,   5

Or English poets who grew up on Greek
(I'd have them sing in chorus, cheek to cheek).

How well her wishes went! She stroked my chin,
She taught me Turn, and Counter-turn, and Stand;
She taught me Touch, that undulant white skin;   10
I nibbled meekly from her proffered hand;
She was the sickle; I, poor I the rake,
Coming behind her for her pretty sake
(But what prodigious mowing we did make).

Love likes a gander, and adores a goose: 15
Her full lips pursed, the errant note to seize;
She played it quick, she played it light and loose;
My eyes, they dazzled at her flowing knees;
Her several parts could keep a pure repose,
Or one hip quiver with a mobile nose   20
(She moved in circles, and those circles moved).

Let seed be grass, and grass turn into hay:
I'm martyr to a motion not my own;
What's freedom for? To know eternity.
I swear she cast a shadow white as stone.   25
But who would count eternity in days?
These old bones live to learn her wanton ways:
(I measure time by how a body sways).

Wendy Rose (1948–   )

For the White Poets Who Would Be Indian

just once. Just long enough
to snap up the words, fish-hooked
to your tongues: you think of us now
when you kneel on the earth, when
you turn holy in a temporary tourism   5
of our souls;
            with words you paint your faces,
            chew your doeskin, touch beast
            and tree as if sharing a mother
            were all it takes, could bring   10
instant and primal knowledge.
You think of us only when
your voice wants for roots,
when you have sat back on your heels
and   become   primitive.   15

You finish your poems
and go back.

Topics for Writing

1. In this poem by a Hopi, how effective and appropriate to the situation is the figurative language? Write an essay evaluating Rose's use of metaphor.

2. The speaker of this poem voices a sharp complaint against certain fellow poets. Explain as accurately as you can what this complaint is. Use specific words, phrases, and lines from the poem to support your position.

Christina Rossetti (1830–1894)

In an Artist's Studio

One face looks out from all his canvases,
   One selfsame figure sits or walks or leans:
   We found her hidden just behind those screens,
That mirror gave back all her loveliness.
A queen in opal or in ruby dress,   5
   A nameless girl in freshest summer-greens,
   A saint, an angel — every canvas means
The same one meaning, neither more nor less.
He feeds upon her face by day and night,
   And she with true kind eyes looks back on him,   10
Fair as the moon and joyful as the light:
   Not wan with waiting, not with sorrow dim;
Not as she is, but was when hope shone bright;
   Not as she is, but as she fills his dream.

Dante Gabriel Rossetti (1828–1882)

The Blessed Damozel†

The blessed damozel leaned out
   From the gold bar of heaven;
Her eyes were deeper than the depth
   Of waters stilled at even;
She had three lilies in her hand,   5
   And the stars in her hair were seven.

Her robe, ungirt from clasp to hem,
   No wrought flowers did adorn,
But a white rose of Mary's gift
   For service meetly worn;   10
Her hair that lay along her back
   Was yellow like ripe corn.

Damozel: a poetic way of saying
damsel, young woman.

Herseemed† she scarce had been a day
    One of God's choristers;
The wonder was not yet quite gone   *15*
    From that still look of hers;
Albeit, to them she left, her day
    Had counted as ten years.

(To *one* it is ten years of years.
    . . . Yet now, and in this place,   *20*
Surely she leaned o'er me — her hair
    Fell all about my face. . . .
Nothing: the autumn fall of leaves.
    The whole year sets apace.)

It was the rampart of God's house   *25*
    That she was standing on;
By God built over the sheer depth
    The which is Space begun;
So high, that looking downward thence
    She scarce could see the sun.   *30*

It lies in heaven, across the flood
    Of ether, as a bridge.
Beneath, the tides of day and night
    With flame and darkness ridge
The void, as low as where this earth   *35*
    Spins like a fretful midge.

Around her, lovers, newly met
    'Mid deathless love's acclaims,
Spoke evermore among themselves
    Their heart-remembered names;   *40*
And the souls mounting up to God
    Went by her like thin flames.

And still she bowed herself and stooped
    Out of the circling charm;
Until her bosom must have made   *45*
    The bar she leaned on warm,
And the lilies lay as if asleep
    Along her bended arm.

From the fixed place of heaven she saw
    Time like a pulse shake fierce   *50*
Through all the worlds. Her gaze still strove
    Within the gulf to pierce
Its path; and now she spoke as when
    The stars sang in their spheres.

13. *herseemed:* read as "to her it
seemed."

The sun was gone now; the curled moon 55
    Was like a little feather
Fluttering far down the gulf; and now
    She spoke through the still weather.
Her voice was like the voice the stars
    Had when they sang together. 60

(Ah, sweet! Even now, in that bird's song,
    Strove not her accents there,
Fain to be harkened? When those bells
    Possessed the midday air,
Strove not her steps to reach my side 65
    Down all the echoing stair?)

"I wish that he were come to me,
    For he will come," she said.
"Have I not prayed in heaven? — on earth,
    Lord, Lord, has he not prayed? 70
Are not two prayers a perfect strength?
    And shall I feel afraid?

"When round his head the aureole clings,
    And he is clothed in white,
I'll take his hand and go with him 75
    To the deep wells of light;
As unto a stream we will step down,
    And bathe there in God's sight.

"We two will stand beside that shrine,
    Occult, withheld, untrod, 80
Whose lamps are stirred continually
    With prayers sent up to God;
And see our old prayers, granted, melt
    Each like a little cloud.

"We two will lie i' the shadow of 85
    That living mystic tree
Within whose secret growth the Dove
    Is sometimes felt to be,
While every leaf that His plumes touch
    Saith His Name audibly. 90

"And I myself will teach to him,
    I myself, lying so,
The songs I sing here; which his voice
    Shall pause in, hushed and slow,
And find some knowledge at each pause, 95
    Or some new thing to know."

(Alas! We two, we two, thou say'st!
    Yea, one wast thou with me
That once of old. But shall God lift
    To endless unity 100

The soul whose likeness with thy soul
    Was but its love for thee?)

"We two," she said, "will seek the groves
    Where the lady Mary is,
With her five handmaidens, whose names   *105*
    Are five sweet symphonies,
Cecily, Gertrude, Magdalen,
    Margaret, and Rosalys.

"Circlewise sit they, with bound locks
    And foreheads garlanded;   *110*
Into the fine cloth white like flame
    Weaving the golden thread,
To fashion the birth-robes for them
    Who are just born, being dead.

"He shall fear, haply, and be dumb;   *115*
    Then will I lay my cheek
To his, and tell about our love,
    Not once abashed or weak;
And the dear Mother will approve
    My pride, and let me speak.   *120*

"Herself shall bring us, hand in hand,
    To Him round whom all souls
Kneel, the clear-ranged unnumbered heads
    Bowed with their aureoles;
And angels meeting us shall sing   *125*
    To their citherns and citoles.†

"There will I ask of Christ the Lord
    Thus much for him and me —
Only to live as once on earth
    With Love, only to be,   *130*
As then awhile, forever now,
    Together, I and he."

She gazed and listened and then said,
    Less sad of speech than mild —
"All this is when he comes." She ceased.   *135*
    The light thrilled toward her, filled
With angels in strong, level flight.
    Her eyes prayed, and she smiled.

(I saw her smile.) But soon their path
    Was vague in distant spheres;   *140*
And then she cast her arms along
    The golden barriers,
And laid her face between her hands,
    And wept. (I heard her tears.)

126. *citherns and citoles:* musical
instruments similar to the modern
guitar.

Boy with His Hair Cut Short

Sunday shuts down on this twentieth-century evening.
The El† passes. Twilight and bulb define
the brown room, the overstuffed plum sofa,
the boy, and the girl's thin hands above his head.
A neighbor radio sings stocks, news, serenade.   5

He sits at the table, head down, the young clear neck exposed.
Watching the drugstore sign from the tail of his eye;
tattoo, neon, until the eye blears, while his
solicitous tall sister, simple in blue, bending
behind him, cuts his hair with her cheap shears.   10

The arrow's electric red always reaches its mark,
successful neon! He coughs, impressed by that precision.
His child's forehead, forever protected by his cap,
is bleached against the lamplight as he turns head
and steadies to let the snippets drop.   15

Erasing the failure of weeks with level fingers,
she sleeks the fine hair, combing: "You'll look fine tomorrow!
You'll surely find something, they can't keep turning you down;
the finest gentleman's not so trim as you!" Smiling, he raises
the adolescent forehead wrinkling ironic now.   20

He sees his decent suit laid out, new-pressed,
his carfare on the shelf. He lets his head fall, meeting
her earnest hopeless look, seeing the sharp blades splitting,
the darkened room, the impersonal sign, her motion,
the blue vein, bright on her temple, pitifully beating.   25

Exercises

1. In your opinion, what is the purpose of this poem? Is it accomplished successfully? How do you know?

2. Identify correlations between the hair-cutting situation and the larger problem of the boy's failure to find a job. Note, for example, the significance of his sitting with "head down" (line 6) for the haircut, but also an attitude of defeat.

3. In terms of the boy and his dilemma, what is the significance of the neon drugstore sign that keeps flashing throughout the poem?

2. *El:* elevated railway.

Norman H. Russell (*1921–*)

indian school

in the darkness
of the house of the white brother
i go alone and am frightened
strange things touch me
i cannot breathe his air   5
or eat his tasteless food

on his walls
are pictures of the world
that his walls shut out
in his hands are leaves of words   10
from dead mens mouths

he speaks to me with only
the sounds of his mouth
for he is dumb and blind
as the staggering old bear   15
filled with many arrows
as the rocks that lie on the mountain

and in his odd robes
uglier
than any other creature i have ever seen   20

i am not wise enough to know
gods purpose in him.

Exercises

1. Describe the speaker's feelings about his "white brother" (line 2) in this poem by a part-Cherokee, noting what the speaker likes, what he does not like, and what his attitude is concerning these dislikes.

2. Compare and contrast this speaker's feelings with those of James Welch, another Native American, as he expresses them in "The Man from Washington."

3. Considering the tone and sentiment of this poem, can you explain the poet's decision not to capitalize the title nor the first word of each verse?

Delmore Schwartz (1913–1966)

For Rhoda

Calmly we walk through this April's day,
Metropolitan poetry here and there,
In the park sit pauper and rentier,†
The screaming children, the motor car
Fugitive about us, running away,   5
Between the worker and the millionaire
Number provides all distances,
It is Nineteen Thirty-Seven now,
Many great dears are taken away,
What will become of you and me   10
(This is the school in which we learn . . .)

Besides the photo and the memory?
(. . . that time is the fire in which we burn.)
(This is the school in which we learn . . .)
What is the self amid this blaze?   15
What am I now that I was then
Which I shall suffer and act again,
The theodicy† I wrote in my high school days
Restored all life from infancy,
The children shouting are bright as they run   20
(This is the school in which they learn . . .)
Ravished entirely in their passing play!
(. . . that time is the fire in which they burn.)
Avid its rush, that reeling blaze!
Where is my father and Eleanor?   25
Not where are they now, dead seven years,
But what they were then?
                        No more? No more?
From Nineteen-Fourteen to the present day,
Bert Spira and Rhoda consume, consume
Not where they are now (where are they now?)   30
But what they were then, both beautiful;
Each minute bursts in the burning room,
The great globe reels in the solar fire,
Spinning the trivial and unique away.
(How all things flash! How all things flare!)   35
What am I now that I was then?
May memory restore again and again
The smallest color of the smallest day:
Time is the school in which we learn,
Time is the fire in which we burn.   40

---

3. *rentier:* a person receiving a
fixed income from property rentals
or from investments.

18. *theodicy:* any work attempting
to explain the nature of divine justice.

Anne Sexton *(1928–1974)*

The Abortion

Somebody who should have been born
is gone.

Just as the earth puckered its mouth,
each bud puffing out from its knot,
I changed my shoes, and then drove south.   5

Up past the Blue Mountains, where
Pennsylvania humps on endlessly,
wearing, like a crayoned cat, its green hair,

its roads sunken in like a gray washboard;
where, in truth, the ground cracks evilly,   10
a dark socket from which the coal has poured,

Somebody who should have been born
is gone.

the grass as bristly and stout as chives,
and me wondering when the ground would break,   15
and me wondering how anything fragile survives;

up in Pennsylvania, I met a little man,
not Rumpelstiltskin, at all, at all . . .
he took the fullness that love began.

Returning north, even the sky grew thin   20
like a high window looking nowhere.
The road was as flat as a sheet of tin.

Somebody who should have been born
is gone.

Yes, woman, such logic will lead   25
to loss without death. Or say what you meant,
you coward . . . this baby that I bleed.

Lament

Someone is dead.
Even the trees know it,
those poor old dancers who come on lewdly,
all pea-green scarfs and spine pole.
I think . . .   5
I think I could have stopped it,
if I'd been as firm as a nurse
or noticed the neck of the driver
as he cheated the crosstown lights;

or later in the evening,   *10*
if I'd held my napkin over my mouth.
I think I could . . .
if I'd been different, or wise, or calm,
I think I could have charmed the table,
the stained dish or the hand of the dealer.   *15*
But it's done.
It's all used up.
There's no doubt about the trees
spreading their thin feet into the dry grass.
A Canada goose rides up,   *20*
spread out like a gray suede shirt,
honking his nose into the March wind.
In the entryway a cat breathes calmly
into her watery blue fur.
The supper dishes are over and the sun   *25*
unaccustomed to anything else
goes all the way down.

Exercises

1. How is this poem like "Scenes from the Life of the Peppertrees" by Denise Levertov? In several paragraphs, compare and contrast these two poems.

2. Characterize the speaker of this poem: male or female? age? urban or rural? intelligent? educated? a person of action or of contemplation? Cite evidence to support your answers.

3. How does the "someone" (line 1) die? Explain the clues that lead you to an answer.

William Shakespeare (1564–1616)

Fear No More the Heat o' th' Sun†

Fear no more the heat o' th' sun,
    Nor the furious winter's rages;
Thou thy worldly task hast done,
    Home art gone, and ta'en thy wages.
Golden lads and girls all must,   *5*
    As chimney-sweepers, come to dust.

Fear No More the Heat o' th' Sun: a lament from *Cymbeline* (IV.ii.258–281) sung by two young men, the brothers Guiderius and Arviragus, at the apparent death of Fidele, a page boy. Actually, Fidele is their royal sister Imogen — in disguise — who is merely drugged and later revives.

Fear no more the frown o' th' great;
  Thou art past the tyrant's stroke.
Care no more to clothe and eat;
  To thee the reed is as the oak.   *10*
The sceptre, learning, physic,† must
All follow this, and come to dust.

Fear no more the lightning-flash,
  Nor the all-dreaded thunder-stone;†
Fear not slander, censure rash;   *15*
  Thou hast finish'd joy and moan.
All lovers young, all lovers must
Consign to thee, and come to dust.

No exorciser harm thee!
Nor no witchcraft charm thee!   *20*
Ghost unlaid forbear thee!
Nothing ill come near thee!
Quiet consummation† have,
And renowned be thy grave!

O Mistress Mine†

O mistress mine, where are you roaming?
O, stay and hear, your true love's coming,
  That can sing both high and low.
Trip no further, pretty sweeting;
Journeys end in lovers meeting,   *5*
  Every wise man's son doth know.

What is love? 'Tis not hereafter.
Present mirth hath present laughter;
  What's to come is still unsure.
In delay there lies no plenty;   *10*
Then come kiss me, sweet and twenty,
  Youth's a stuff will not endure.

---

11. *physic:* medical arts.   23. *consummation:* end.
14. *thunder-stone:* thunderbolt.

O Mistress Mine: a seductive love   Belch in *Twelfth Night* (II.iii.40–
lyric sung by Feste the Clown in   45, 48–53).
response to the urging of Sir Toby

Sonnet 18

Shall I compare thee to a summer's day?
Thou art more lovely and more temperate:
Rough winds do shake the darling buds of May,
And summer's lease hath all too short a date:
Sometime too hot the eye of heaven shines,   5
And often is his gold complexion dimmed;
And every fair from fair sometimes declines,
By chance or nature's changing course untrimmed;†
But thy eternal summer shall not fade,
Nor lose possession of that fair thou owest;†   10
Nor shall Death brag thou wander'st in his shade,
When in eternal lines to time thou growest:
So long as men can breathe, or eyes can see,
So long lives this, and this† gives life to thee.

Exercises

1. Why does the poet decide not to compare his beloved to a summer's day?

2. What does Shakespeare mean when he says that "every fair from fair some-times declines"? Why is he nevertheless convinced that his beloved's "eternal summer shall not fade"?

Topic for Writing

Shakespeare's Sonnet 18 expresses the long-held belief that art has the capacity to preserve the object of its contemplation for all time. In this case, the object is the beauty of the poet's beloved. Using Sonnet 18 as your focal point, discuss the theme of art's preserving youth and beauty against the ravages of time and nature's decay. You might wish to consider further whether or not we continue to hold to that belief and, if not, why not.

Sonnet 29

When, in disgrace with fortune and men's eyes,
I all alone beweep my outcast state,
And trouble deaf heaven with my bootless† cries,
And look upon myself, and curse my fate,

---

8. *untrimmed:* reduced in quality
or circumstance.

10. *owest:* own.

14. *this . . . this:* the poem.

---

3. *bootless:* useless or futile.

Wishing me like to one more rich in hope,   5
Featured like him, like him with friends possessed,
Desiring this man's art and that man's scope,†
With what I most enjoy contented least;
Yet in these thoughts myself almost despising,
Haply† I think on thee — and then my state,   10
Like to the lark at break of day arising
From sullen earth, sings hymns at heaven's gate;
For thy sweet love remembered such wealth brings
That then I scorn to change my state with kings.

Sonnet 60

Like as the waves make towards the pebbled shore,
So do our minutes hasten to their end;
Each changing place with that which goes before,
In sequent† toil all forwards do contend.
Nativity, once in the main of light,   5
Crawls to maturity, wherewith being crown'd,
Crooked eclipses† 'gainst his glory fight,
And Time that gave doth now his gift confound.†
Time doth transfix the flourish† set on youth
And delves the parallels† in beauty's brow,   10
Feeds on the rarities of nature's truth,†
And nothing stands but for his scythe to mow;
         And yet to times in hope my verse shall stand,
         Praising thy worth, despite his cruel hand.

Exercises

1. How aptly does Shakespeare's initial simile (lines 1–4) indicate the passage of time? Comment not only on the imagery, but on the rhythm and sound devices as well.

2. Who is the villain possessing a "cruel hand" (line 14)? Evaluate the comparison of this antagonist to the ocean (lines 1–4). What negative attributes do they have in common?

7. *scope:* range of learning or accomplishments.

10. *haply:* by chance or accident.

4. *sequent:* one following another.
7. *crooked eclipses:* bad luck.
8. *confound:* ruin.
9. *transfix the flourish:* destroy the youthful vigor.

10. *delves the parallels:* digs the wrinkles.
11. *rarities . . . truth:* excellencies in nature (namely, the young, the growing, the vibrant, in contrast to the aging).

3. This sonnet (lines 5–12) summarizes the life of man. Indicate each stage presented, and comment on its characteristics as Shakespeare depicts them. What hope is extended to the person addressed in the sonnet?

4. Do you like this poem? Why or why not?

Sonnet 116

Let me not to the marriage of true minds
Admit impediments. Love is not love
Which alters when it alteration finds,
Or bends with the remover to remove.†
O, no! it is an ever-fixed mark   5
That looks on tempests and is never shaken;
It is the star to every wand'ring bark,†
Whose worth's unknown, although his height be taken.
Love's not Time's fool, though rosy lips and cheeks
Within his bending sickle's compass come;   10
Love alters not with his brief hours and weeks,
But bears it out even to the edge of doom.†
   If this be error and upon me proved,
   I never writ, nor no man ever loved.

Karl Shapiro (1913–   )

Drug Store

I do remember an apothecary,
And hereabouts 'a dwells†

It baffles the foreigner like an idiom,
And he is right to adopt it as a form
Less serious than the living-room or bar;
   For it disestablishes the café,
Is a collective, and on basic country.   5

Not that it praises hygiene and corrupts
The ice-cream parlor and the tobacconist's
Is it a center; but that the attractive symbols
   Watch over puberty and leer
Like rubber bottles waiting for sick-use.   10

4. *Or . . . remove:* is inconstant on demand.

7. *bark:* ship.
12. *doom:* day of final judgment.

Epigraph: William Shakespeare, *Romeo and Juliet* (V.i.37–38). Romeo speaks these words after he has been told (incorrectly) that Juliet has died. He seeks out the apothecary and buys poison for himself.

Youth comes to jingle nickels and crack wise;
The baseball scores are his, the magazines
Devoted to lust, the jazz, the Coca-Cola,
    The lending-library of love's latest.
He is the customer, he is heroized.   15

And every nook and cranny of the flesh
Is spoken to by packages with wiles.
"Buy me, buy me," they whimper and cajole;
    The hectic range of lipstick pouts,
Revealing the wicked and the simple mouth.   20

With scarcely any evasion in their eye
They smoke, undress their girls, exact a stance;
But only for a moment. The clock goes round;
    Crude fellowships are made and lost;
They slump in booths like rags, not even drunk.   25

Sir Philip Sidney (1554–1586)

My True Love Hath My Heart

My true love hath my heart and I have his,
By just exchange, one for the other given;
I hold his dear, and mine he cannot miss;
There never was a better bargain driven.
His heart in me keeps me and him in one,   5
My heart in him his thoughts and senses guides;
He loves my heart, for once it was his own;
I cherish his, because in me it bides.
His heart his wound received from my sight;
My heart was wounded with his wounded heart,   10
For as from me on him his hurt did light,
So still methought in me his hurt did smart;
Both equal hurt, in this change sought our bliss:
My true love hath my heart and I have his.

Jon Silkin (1930–   )

Creatures

Shells are now found
Of creatures not still subsisting,
Chipped from the hardened mud under
Which oil lurks.

Men came with their chipped diamonds   5
And a pole with these smelted onto it

To bore rock. Oil broke out
Into the clear American air.

Barely noticed at the time
Among the soil screwed from   10
Above the crude useful oil,
Shells, about half an inch.
They were whorled, and chipped from
What they had been hardening in,
Falling through the glistening mud   15
They filled with the spiral
Wriggling creature gone from them.
It is a spiral horn, silent;
And shaped like an inert
Clammy-skinned spring.   20
They grew property:
An amnion,† a house,
Their grave no more special,
No more particular than
A pattern, a repetition of curving   25
Continuous shape, for survival.

Death of a Son (Who Died in a Mental
Hospital Aged One)

Something has ceased to come along with me.
Something like a person: something very like one.
   And there was no nobility in it
   Or anything like that.

Something was there like a one year   5
Old house, dumb as stone. While the near buildings
   Sang like birds and laughed
   Understanding the pact

They were to have with silence. But he
Neither sang nor laughed. He did not bless silence   10
   Like bread, with words.
   He did not forsake silence.

But rather, like a house in mourning
Kept the eye turned in to watch the silence while
   The other houses like birds   15
   Sang around him.

And the breathing silence neither
Moved nor was still.

22. *amnion:* the sac immediately
around a developing mammalian
embryo.

I have seen stones: I have seen brick
But this house was made up of neither bricks nor stone   20
    But a house of flesh and blood
        With flesh of stone

And bricks for blood. A house
Of stones and blood in breathing silence with the other
    Birds singing crazy on its chimneys.   25
        But this was silence,

This was something else, this was
Hearing and speaking though he was a house drawn
    Into silence, this was
        Something religious in his silence,   30

Something shining in his quiet,
This was different this was altogether something else:
    Though he never spoke, this
        Was something to do with death.

And then slowly the eye stopped looking   35
Inward. The silence rose and became still.
The look turned to the outer place and stopped,
    With the birds still shrilling around him.
        And as if he could speak

He turned over on his side with his one year   40
Red as a wound
He turned over as if he could be sorry for this
And out of his eyes two great tears rolled, like stones, and he died.

Edmund Spenser (1552?–1599)

Sonnet 75

One day I wrote her name upon the strand,†
    But came the waves and washèd it away.
    Again I wrote it with a second hand,
    But came the tide and made my pains his prey.
"Vain man," said she, "that dost in vain essay†   5
    A mortal thing so to immortalize;
    For I myself shall like to this decay,
    And eke† my name be wipèd out likewise."
"Not so," quod† I, "let baser things devise
    To die in dust, but you shall live by fame;   10
    My verse your virtues rare shall eternize,
    And in the heavens write your glorious name:
Where, whereas death shall all the world subdue,
    Our love shall live, and later life renew."

1. *strand:* shore.   8. *eke:* also.
5. *essay:* attempt.   9. *quod:* said.

Wallace Stevens *(1879-1955)*

Disillusionment of Ten O'Clock

The houses are haunted
By white night-gowns
None are green,
Or purple with green rings,
Or green with yellow rings,   5
Or yellow with blue rings,
None of them are strange,
With socks of lace
And beaded ceintures.†
People are not going   10
To dream of baboons and periwinkles.
Only, here and there, an old sailor,
Drunk and asleep in his boots,
Catches tigers
In red weather.   15

Thirteen Ways of Looking at a Blackbird

1.

Among twenty snowy mountains,
The only moving thing
Was the eye of the blackbird.

2.

I was of three minds,
Like a tree   5
In which there are three blackbirds.

3.

The blackbird whirled in the autumn winds.
It was a small part of the pantomime.

4.

A man and a woman
Are one.   10
A man and a woman and a blackbird
Are one.

5.

I do not know which to prefer,
The beauty of inflections
Or the beauty of innuendoes,   15

9. *ceintures:* belts, girdles.

The blackbird whistling
Or just after.

6.

Icicles filled the long window
With barbaric glass.
The shadow of the blackbird   *20*
Crossed it, to and fro.
The mood
Traced in the shadow
In indecipherable cause.

7.

O thin men of Haddam,†   *25*
Why do you imagine golden birds?
Do you not see how the blackbird
Walks around the feet
Of the women about you?

8.

I know noble accents   *30*
And lucid, inescapable rhythms;
But I know, too,
That the blackbird is involved
In what I know.

9.

When the blackbird flew out of sight,   *35*
It marked the edge
Of one of many circles.

10.

At the sight of blackbirds
Flying in a green light,
Even the bawds of euphony   *40*
Would cry out sharply.

11.

He rode over Connecticut
In a glass coach.
Once, a fear pierced him,
In that he mistook   *45*
The shadow of his equipage
For blackbirds.

12.

The river is moving.
The blackbird must be flying.

25. *Haddam:* a small town in Connecticut near where the poet lived
and worked; hence, any place that
connotes small-town values.

13.

It was evening all afternoon.   *50*
It was snowing
And it was going to snow.
The blackbird sat
In the cedar-limbs.

Edward Taylor *(1642?–1729)*

Housewifery

Make me, O Lord, Thy spinning-wheel complete.
   Thy holy Word my distaff† make for me;
Make mine affections Thy swift flyers† neat;
   And make my soul Thy holy spool to be;
   My conversation make to be Thy reel,†   *5*
   And reel the yarn thereon spun of Thy wheel.

Make me Thy loom then; knit therein this twine;
   And make Thy Holy Spirit, Lord, wind quills;†
Then weave the web Thyself. The yarn is fine.
   Thine ordinances make my fulling mills.†   *10*
   Then dye the same in heavenly colors choice,
   All pinked† with varnished flowers of paradise.

Then clothe therewith mine understanding, will,
   Affections, judgment, conscience, memory,
My words and actions, that their shine may fill   *15*
   My ways with glory and Thee glorify.
   Then mine apparel shall display before Ye
   That I am clothed in holy robes for glory.

Alfred, Lord Tennyson *(1809–1892)*

Tears, Idle Tears

   Tears, idle tears, I know not what they mean,
Tears from the depth of some divine despair
Rise in the heart, and gather to the eyes,
In looking on the happy autumn-fields,
And thinking of the days that are no more.   *5*

---

2. *distaff:* in spinning, the device that holds the flax, tow, or wool to be spun.
3. *flyers:* parts of the spinning wheel that twist the spun thread and wind it on the bobbins.
5. *reel:* a rotatory instrument that takes up the finished thread.
8. *quills:* spools.
10. *fulling mills:* rolling presses that compact and clean the finished cloth.
12. *pinked:* decorated.

Fresh as the first beam glittering on a sail,
That brings our friends up from the underworld
Sad as the last which reddens over one
That sinks with all we love below the verge;
So sad, so fresh, the days that are no more.   *10*

Ah, sad and strange as in dark summer dawns
The earliest pipe of half-awakened birds
To dying ears, when unto dying eyes
The casement† slowly grows a glimmering square;
So sad, so strange, the days that are no more.   *15*

Dear as remembered kisses after death,
And sweet as those by hopeless fancy feigned
On lips that are for others; deep as love,
Deep as first love, and wild with all regret;
O Death in Life, the days that are no more!   *20*

Dylan Thomas (1914–1953)

The Hunchback in the Park

The hunchback in the park
A solitary mister
Propped between trees and water
From the opening of the garden lock
That lets the trees and water enter   *5*
Until the Sunday somber bell at dark

Eating bread from a newspaper
Drinking water from the chained cup
That the children filled with gravel
In the fountain basin where I sailed my ship   *10*
Slept at night in a dog kennel
But nobody chained him up.

Like the park birds he came early
Like the water he sat down
And Mister they called Hey mister   *15*
The truant boys from the town
Running when he had heard them clearly
On out of sound

Past lake and rockery†
Laughing when he shook his paper   *20*
Hunchbacked in mockery

14. *casement:* window.

19. *rockery:* a rock garden.

Through the loud zoo of the willow groves
Dodging the park keeper
With his stick that picked up leaves.

And the old dog sleeper   25
Alone between nurses and swans
While the boys among willows
Made the tigers jump out of their eyes
To roar on the rockery stones
And the groves were blue with sailors   30

Made all day until bell time
A woman figure without fault
Straight as a young elm
Straight and tall from his crooked bones
That she might stand in the night   35
After the locks and chains

All night in the unmade park
After the railings and shrubberies
The birds the grass the trees the lake
And the wild boys innocent as strawberries   40
Had followed the hunchback
To his kennel in the dark.

Henry Vaughan (1622–1695)

The World

I saw eternity the other night
Like a great ring of pure and endless light,
   All calm as it was bright;
And round beneath it, Time, in hours, days, years,
   Driven by the spheres,†   5
Like a vast shadow moved, in which the world
   And all her train were hurled.
The doting lover in his quaintest strain
   Did there complain;
Near him, his lute, his fancy, and his flights,   10
   Wit's sour delights,
With gloves and knots,† the silly snares of pleasure,
   Yet his dear treasure,
All scattered lay, while he his eyes did pour
   Upon a flower.   15

---

5. *spheres:* in Ptolomaic astron-   12. *knots:* decorative knots given
omy, the clear globes circling the   as love emblems.
earth that held sun, moon, and
stars.

The darksome statesman, hung with weights and woe,
Like a thick midnight fog, moved there so slow
   He did nor stay nor go;
Condemning thoughts, like sad eclipses, scowl
   Upon his soul,   20
And clouds of crying witnesses without
   Pursued him with one shout.
Yet digged the mole, and, lest his ways be found,
   Worked underground,
Where he did clutch his prey. But one did see   25
   That policy:†
Churches and altars fed him; perjuries
   Were gnats and flies;
It rained about him blood and tears; but he
   Drank them as free.   30

The fearful miser on a heap of rust
Sat pining all his life there, did scarce trust
   His own hands with the dust;
Yet would not place one piece above, but lives
   In fear of thieves.   35
Thousands there were as frantic as himself,
   And hugged each one his pelf:
The downright epicure placed heaven in sense,
   And scorned pretense;
While others, slipped into a wide excess,   40
   Said little less;
The weaker sort, slight, trivial wares enslave,
   Who think them brave;†
And poor, despiséd Truth sat counting by†
   Their victory.   45

Yet some, who all this while did weep and sing,
And sing and weep, soared up into the ring;
   But most would use no wing.
"O fools!" said I, "thus to prefer dark night
   Before true light!   50
To live in grots and caves, and hate the day
   Because it shows the way,
The way which from this dead and dark abode
   Leads up to God,
A way where you might tread the sun and be   55
   More bright than he!"
But, as I did their madness so discuss,
   One whispered thus:
"This ring the bridegroom† did for none provide,
   But for His bride." †   60

26. *policy:* strategy.
43. *brave:* lovely.
44. *counting by:* observing.

59. *bridegroom:* Christ.
60. *bride:* the Christian church
(Rev. 19:7–8 and 21:9).

Peter Viereck (1916–   )

Game Called on Account of Darkness

Once there was a friend.
He watched me from the sky.
Maybe he never lived at all.
Maybe too much friendship made him die.

When the gang played cops-and-robbers in the alley,   5
It was my friend who told me which were which,
Now he doesn't tell me any more.
(Which team am I playing for?)

My science teacher built a telescope
To show me every answer in the end.   10
I stared and stared at every star for hours.
I couldn't find my friend.

At Sunday School they said I breathe too much.
When I hold my breath within the under
Side of earth, they said I'll find my friend.   15
. . . I wonder.

He was like a kind of central heating
In the big cold house, and that was good.
One by one I have to chop my toys now,
As firewood.   20

Everytime I stood upon a crosroads,
It made me mad to feel him watch me choose.
I'm glad there's no more spying while I play.
Still, I'm sad he went away.

Diane Wakoski (1937–   )

Thanking My Mother for Piano Lessons

The relief of putting your fingers on the keyboard
as if you were walking on the beach
and found a diamond
as big as a shoe;

as if   5
you had just built a wooden table
and the smell of sawdust was in the air,
your hands dry and woody;

as if
you had eluded   10
the man in the dark hat who had been following you
all week;

the relief
of putting your fingers on the keyboard,
playing the chords of   15
Beethoven,
Bach,
Chopin
     in an afternoon when I had no one to talk to,
     when the magazine advertisement forms of soft sweaters   20
     and clean-shining Republican middle-class hair
     walked into carpeted houses
     and left me alone
     with bare floors and a few books

I want to thank my mother   25
for working every day
in a drab office
in garages and water companies
cutting the cream out of her coffee at 40
to lose weight, her heavy body   30
writing its delicate bookkeeper's ledgers
alone, with no man to look at her face,
her body, her prematurely white hair
in love
     I want to thank   35
my mother for working and always paying for
my piano lessons
before she paid the Bank of America loan
or bought the groceries
or had our old rattling Ford repaired.   40

I was a quiet child,
afraid of walking into a store alone,
afraid of the water,
the sun,
the dirty weeds in backyards,   45
afraid of my mother's bad breath
and afraid of my father's occasional visits home,
knowing he would leave again,
afraid of not having any money,
afraid of my clumsy body,   50
that I knew
     no one would ever love

But I played my way
on the old upright piano
obtained for $10   55
played my way through fear,
through ugliness
through growing up in a world of dimestore purchases,
and a desire to love
a loveless world.   60

I played my way through an ugly face
and lonely afternoons, days, evenings, nights,
mornings even, empty
as a rusty coffee can,
played my way through the rustles of spring   65
and wanted everything around me to shimmer like the narrow tide
on a flat beach at sunset in Southern California,
I played my way through
an empty father's hat in my mother's closet
and a bed she slept on only one side of,   70
Never wrinkling an inch of
the other side,
waiting,
waiting,

I played my way through honors in school   75
the only place I could
talk,
    the classroom,
    or at my piano lessons, Mrs. Hillhouse's canary always
    singing the most for my talents,   80
    as if I had thrown some part of my body away upon entering
    her house
    and was now searching every ivory case
    of the keyboard, slipping my fingers over black
    ridges and around smooth rocks,   85
    wondering where I had lost my bloody organs,
    or my mouth which sometimes opened
    like a California poppy, wide and with contrasts
    beautiful in sweeping fields,
entirely closed morning and night,   90
I played my way from age to age,
but they all seemed ageless
or perhaps always
old and lonely,

    wanting only one thing, surrounded by the dusty bitter smelling   95
leaves of orange trees,
wanting only to be touched by a man who loved me,
who would be there every night
to put his large strong hand over my shoulder,
whose hips I would wake up against in the morning   100
whose mustaches might brush a face asleep
dreaming of pianos that made the sound of Mozart
and Schubert without demanding
that life suck everything
out of you each day,   105
without demanding the emptiness
of a timid little life.

I want to thank my mother
for letting me wake her up sometimes at 6 in the morning

when I practiced my lessons 110
and for making sure I had a piano
to lay my school books down on, every afternoon.
I haven't touched the piano in 10 years
perhaps in fear that what little love I've been able to
pick, like lint, out of the corners of pockets, 115
will get lost,
slide away,
into the terribly empty cavern of me
if I ever open it all the way up again.
love is a man 120
with a mustache
gently holding me every night,
always being there when I need to touch him;
he could not know the painfully loud
music from the past that 125
his loving stops from pounding, banging,
battering through my brain,
which does its best to destroy the precarious grey matter when I am
   alone;
he does not hear Mrs. Hillhouse's canary singing for me,
liking the sound of my lesson this week, 130
telling me,
confirming what my teacher says,
that I have a gift for the piano
few of her other pupils had.

When I touch the man 135
I love,
I want to thank my mother for giving me
piano lessons
all those years,
keeping the memory of Beethoven, 140
a deaf tortured man
in mind;
        of the beauty that can come
from even an ugly
past. 145

Topics for Writing

1. In an essay, analyze the character of the speaker of this poem. What was she like as a child? as a young girl? What sort of adult is she? Cite examples from the poem as evidence.

2. Write an essay characterizing the speaker's mother — as described by her daughter. Divide your analysis into two, three, or four subtopics, such as physical characteristics, personality, attitudes, and so forth.

Edmund Waller (1606–1687)

Go, lovely rose!

Go, lovely rose!
Tell her that wastes her time and me,
That now she knows,
When I resemble her to thee,
How sweet and fair she seems to be.   5

Tell her that's young,
And shuns to have her graces spied,
That hadst thou sprung
In deserts, where no men abide,
Thou must have uncommended died.   10

Small is the worth
Of beauty from the light retired;
Bid her come forth,
Suffer herself to be desired,
And not blush so to be admired.   15

Then die! that she
The common fate of all things rare
May read in thee;
How small a part of time they share
That are so wondrous sweet and fair!   20

James Welch (1940–   )

The Man from Washington

The end came easy for most of us.
Packed away in our crude beginnings
in some far corner of a flat world,
we didn't expect much more
than firewood and buffalo robes   5
to keep us warm. The man came down,
a slouching dwarf with rainwater eyes,
and spoke to us. He promised
that life would go on as usual,
that treaties would be signed, and everyone —   10
man, woman and child — would be inoculated
against a world in which we had no part,
a world of wealth, promise and fabulous disease.

1. What is the speaker in this poem by a Blackfoot Native American telling us?

2. When the speaker describes the man from Washington, that man turns out to be a "dwarf" (line 7). Why do you think the poet describes him thus? Also explain the significance of his coming "down" to speak to the Indians (line 6). Why is he "slouching" (line 7)? Why does he have "rainwater eyes" (line 7)?

3. Discuss what you believe the poet means by the word "promise" in lines 8 and 13.

Walt Whitman *(1819–1892)*

One's-self I sing

One's-self I sing, a simple separate person,
Yet utter the word Democratic, the word En-Masse.†

Of physiology from top to toe I sing,
Not physiognomy alone nor brain alone is worthy for the Muse, I
    say the Form complete is worthier far,
The Female equally with the Male I sing.   *5*

Of Life immense in passion, pulse, and power,
Cheerful, for freest action form'd under the laws divine,
The Modern Man I sing.

When I heard the learn'd astronomer

When I heard the learn'd astronomer,
When the proofs, the figures, were ranged in columns before me,
When I was shown the charts and diagrams, to add, divide, and
    measure them,
When I sitting heard the astronomer where he lectured with much
    applause in the lecture-room,
How soon unaccountable I became tired and sick,   *5*
Till rising and gliding out I wander'd off by myself,
In the mystical moist night-air, and from time to time,
Look'd up in perfect silence at the stars.

2. *En-Masse:* literally, in a group; in a democratic society, such as the one Whitman is celebrating, the term has come to signify the united strength of the people constituting that society.

Exercises

1. Why did the speaker become "tired and sick" after hearing the astronomer's discourse? Does the fact that the speaker holds this attitude "unaccountable" suggest an embarrassment on the speaker's part, or is there a potential for irony in the adjective? What might that irony be?

2. What particular feature of the astronomer's presentation unsettled the speaker? Were the others present equally as unsettled by the information? How does the speaker finally resolve his dilemma?

3. What aspect of the stars is contrasted with the astronomer's facts and figures and charts? How does the speaker characterize that aspect? Does the speaker feel that his reaction is a common one? If not, does he nevertheless feel that it is a natural one? Why does the speaker apparently believe that the stars cannot be added and measured and divided?

Topic for Writing

Discuss this poem as it illustrates the conflicts between the explanations of science and the intuitions of the senses and between commonly held truths and individually held convictions.

Richard Wilbur (1921–   )

Juggler

A ball will bounce, but less and less. It's not
A light-hearted thing, resents its own resilience.
Falling is what it loves, and the earth falls
So in our hearts from brilliance,
Settles and is forgot.   5
It takes a sky-blue juggler with five red balls

To shake our gravity up. Whee, in the air
The balls roll round, wheel on his wheeling hands,
Learning the ways of lightness, alter to spheres
Grazing his finger ends,   10
Cling to their courses there,
Swinging a small heaven about his ears.

But a heaven is easier made of nothing at all
Than the earth regained, and still and sole within
The spin of worlds, with a gesture sure and noble   15
He reels that heaven in,
Landing it ball by ball,
And trades it all for a broom, a plate, a table.

Oh, on his toe the table is turning, the broom's
Balancing up on his nose, and the plate whirls   *20*
On the tip of the broom! Damn, what a show, we cry:
The boys stamp, and the girls
Shriek, and the drum booms
And all comes down, and he bows and says good-bye.

If the juggler is tired now, if the broom stands   *25*
In the dust again, if the table starts to drop
Through the daily dark again, and though the plate
Lies flat on the table top,
For him we batter our hands
Who has won for once over the world's weight.   *30*

Oscar Wilde (1854–1900)

The Harlot's House

We caught the tread of dancing feet,
We loitered down the moonlit street,
And stopped beneath the harlot's house.

Inside, above the din and fray,
We heard the loud musicians play   *5*
The "Treues Liebes Herz" † of Strauss.

Like strange mechanical grotesques,
Making fantastic arabesques,†
The shadows raced across the blind.

We watched the ghostly dancers spin   *10*
To sound of horn and violin,
Like black leaves wheeling in the wind.

Like wire-pulled automatons,
Slim silhouetted skeletons
Went sidling through the slow quadrille.†   *15*

They took each other by the hand,
And danced a stately saraband;†
Their laughter echoed thin and shrill.

6. *"Treues Liebes Herz"*: "True Love's Heart," a Viennese waltz. Johann Strauss (1825–1899) has been called the Waltz King.
8. *arabesques*: intricately intertwined designs; in dance, an arabesque is a particularly stylized position involving the arms and requiring one leg to be extended backward.

15. *quadrille*: an elaborate square dance performed by four couples. French in origin, it is an extremely formal ballroom dance.
17. *saraband*: a dance of Spanish origin. The ballroom version is slow and stately, although it is derived from a lively folk dance.

Sometimes a clockwork puppet pressed
A phantom lover to her breast,   *20*
Sometimes they seemed to try to sing.

Sometimes a horrible marionette
Came out, and smoked its cigarette
Upon the steps like a live thing.

Then, turning to my love, I said,   *25*
"The dead are dancing with the dead,
The dust is whirling with the dust."

But she — she heard the violin,
And left my side, and entered in:
Love passed into the house of lust.   *30*

Then suddenly the tune went false,
The dancers wearied of the waltz,
The shadows ceased to wheel and whirl.

And down the long and silent street,
The dawn, with silver-sandaled feet,   *35*
Crept like a frightened girl.

Ramona C. Wilson (1945–   )

Keeping Hair

My grandmother had braids
at the thickest, pencil wide
held with bright wool
cut from her bed shawl.
No teeth left but white hair   *5*
combed and wet carefully
early each morning.
The small wild plants found among stones
on the windy and brown plateaus
revealed their secrets to her hand   *10*
and yielded to her cooking pots.
She made a sweet amber water
from willows,
boiling the life out
to pour onto her old head.   *15*
"It will keep your hair."
She bathed my head once
rain water not sweeter.
The thought that once
when I was so very young   *20*
her work-bent hands
very gently and smoothly
washed my hair in willows
may also keep my heart.

William Wordsworth (1770–1850)

The Solitary Reaper

Behold her, single in the field,
Yon solitary Highland Lass!
Reaping and singing by herself;
Stop here, or gently pass!
Alone she cuts and binds the grain,   5
And sings a melancholy strain;
O listen! for the Vale profound
Is overflowing with the sound.

No Nightingale did ever chaunt
More welcome notes to weary bands   10
Of travellers in some shady haunt
Among Arabian sands:
A voice so thrilling ne'er was heard
In spring-time from the Cuckoo-bird,
Breaking the silence if the seas   15
Among the farthest Hebrides.†

Will no one tell me what she sings? —
Perhaps the plaintive numbers flow
For old, unhappy, far-off things,
And battles long ago: 20
Or is it some more humble lay,
Familiar matter of today?
Some natural sorrow, loss, or pain,
That has been, and may be again?

Whate'er the theme, the Maiden sang   25
As if her song could have no ending;
I saw her singing at her work,
And o'er the sickle bending;
I listened, motionless and still;
And, as I mounted up the hill,   30
The music in my heart I bore,
Long after it was heard no more.

(handwritten margin notes: why capitalization of nature, sea, & Pagan ① emphasis & add are called forces in nature & nature - God are the same ② suggests the vast need of each)

(handwritten: meter of poem - predominantly iambic pentameter. piece like narrative structure in 1st 4 lines till we get to a patterned line in 5)

The world is too much with us

The world is too much with us; late and soon, A
Getting and spending, we lay waste our powers: B
Little we see in Nature that is ours; B
We have given our hearts away, a sordid boon! A
This Sea that bares her bosom to the moon; A   5

(handwritten: the octave establishing we are not in sync. disobey nature)

(handwritten: the world takes us over since the day of birth to death & that we can't appreciate nature just the worldly possessions & their worth)

(handwritten: dirty, disrupt power / personification)

16. *Hebrides:* islands off the west
coast of Scotland.

The winds that will be howling at all hours,
And are up-gathered now like sleeping flowers;
For this, for everything, we are out of tune;
It moves us not — Great God! I'd rather be
A Pagan suckled in a creed outworn;
So might I, standing on this pleasant lea,
Have glimpses that would make me less forlorn;
Have sight of Proteus† rising from the sea;
Or hear old Triton† blow his wreathéd horn.

10

Elinor Wylie (1855–1928)

The Eagle and the Mole

Avoid the reeking herd,
Shun the polluted flock,
Live like that stoic bird,
The eagle of the rock.

The huddled warmth of crowds   5
Begets and foster hate;
He keeps, above the clouds,
His cliff inviolate.

When flocks are folded warm,
And herds to shelter run,   10
He sails above the storm,
He stares into the sun.

If in the eagle's track
Your sinews cannot leap,
Avoid the lathered pack,   15
Turn from the steaming sheep.

If you would keep your soul
From spotted sight or sound,
Live like the velvet mole;
Go burrow under ground.   20

And there hold intercourse
With roots of trees and stones,
With rivers at their source,
And disembodied bones.

13. *Proteus:* in Greek myth, a sea god who assisted Poseidon, the Greek god of the sea and earthquakes, and who could change his shape at will.

14. *Triton:* a sea god, son of Poseidon, who was half man and half fish, and carried a conch-shell horn.

DRAMA

W hat is drama?

Drama is the performance of a story by actors in front of an audience. Like fiction and poetry, it is a genre of literature. That is, when we contemplate its language as written, it is literature; but when we regard its language as spoken, it is theater.

Drama is simply one way of telling a story. All the elements of fiction — character, plot, conflict, exposition, complication, climax, resolution, and others — are also found in drama.

Playwrights share with the writers of fiction many of the problems that grow out of the process of selecting the materials that they ultimately mold into their creations. All want to create interesting, believable characters, exhibit a struggle, present complications designed to thicken the plot, sustain interest, and express some attitude toward the meaning of life.

But dramatic art is unique, because action on stage unfolds before our eyes. Conflict, of course, throbs at the center of every story, but the story dramatically enlivened on stage achieves a lifelikeness and intensity that fiction can only hope to attain. The playwright can be more direct and more powerful than the fiction writer. He or she can present conflict with the intensity and immediacy of the present, as the fiction writer rarely can. In fiction, the events are usually reported to us as having already happened, and conversation represents what characters have already said. But in drama, the events are revealed to us as they unfold, and the dialogue is what characters are saying *now*. Watching or reading a play, we feel the action as it takes place. We are there. Only drama brings us this close to characters and the significance of their actions.

For this potential vitality and power playwrights pay a price. Of necessity they fit their materials into a tight structure: they condense and compress the depiction of characters, their actions, and their speeches. At the other extreme, novelists often write a lengthy story that runs on a wider track; they may introduce long, descriptive passages, digressions, and many of the details that crowd our daily experiences.

Playwrights also must recount the story within a strict time frame — what Shakespeare called "the two-hours' traffic of our stage." The time limit usually cannot exceed three hours. A telephone conversation, a duel, a lengthy argument, or a wedding ceremony that would consume fifteen minutes or longer in real life lasts only a few minutes on stage. Because playwrights must tell their story swiftly, they must make every action and every speech count — in fact, make it indispensable.

Furthermore, playwrights are generally restricted to a single point of view, which is severely objective. They do not normally permit their own voices to be heard commenting upon an event or character, explaining motivation, or interpreting the significance of an action, except through a character or in the stage directions. By and large, we infer meaning from what the characters do and say.

Another constraint is a playwright's nearly absolute dependence on dialogue to tell the story. Dialogue is everything to drama, whereas it is one means among several in fiction.

Playwrights also must keep in mind the physical realities of the theater in which their plays will be performed. Ancient Greek drama, such as Sophocles's *Oedipus the King,* was performed before massive audiences in huge outdoor amphitheaters. The Greek theater and stage is shown on pages 730–731.

By the time of Shakespeare, the staging of drama had become considerably more versatile and intimate. In the Elizabethan theater (see pages 732–733), most of the action is presented on a platform stage, surrounded on three sides by the audience.

In the nineteenth century, as drama achieved a much higher standard of realism, a corresponding trend toward realism in staging developed. The stage in the modern proscenium theater (pages 734–735) is essentially a real room with one wall removed so that the audience can observe the action going on within. Such a stage allows for elaborate sets, props, and scene changes.

The modern approach to staging is characterized by flexibility. That is, playwrights are freed from a single, limiting stage design and can be as innovative as they wish in staging action and designing sets. One twentieth-century innovation is the arena theater (see pages 736–737). Here the action takes place on a central stage, completely surrounded by the audience. This set-up increases the proximity of the audience to the action, resulting in greater intimacy and immediacy. Contemporary sets are usually simple, functional, and suggestive arrangements that do not draw an audience's attention away from the actors. The arena theater is but one example of the modern belief that the ideal stage is one that can be easily manipulated and rearranged to meet the specific production demands of a particular play.

Taken together, the effects the dramatist achieves have large appeal, for drama enjoys the greatest popularity of all the arts, if we include the dramas presented on television to huge audiences. More people saw a single performance of *Oedipus the King* on American television than have seen the thousands of performances given throughout the world since Sophocles wrote the drama 2,400 years ago.

Drama appeals to us for no fewer reasons than fiction does. We are witnesses to a story: our emotions are stirred and our sympathies aroused. We enjoy drama because it is entertaining and because the world of make-believe affords us an opportunity to escape the monotony of the daily details of life. In addition, we may find companionship, perhaps comfort, in a play, and we may be enlightened. Finally, we take pleasure in great dramas as literary masterpieces, enjoying the stories, the ideas contained in them, or the beauty of the artistry.

Though the fullest enjoyment of a play may come from seeing it performed, pleasure and profit are also gained by reading it. As readers of drama, however, we accept an enormous responsibility; we are at once the director, the set designer, the makeup artist, all the actors, and sometimes the playwright. Any play that we read can live if we bring it to life in our imaginations. Indeed, the reader of a play may have an advantage over the viewer, who can miss some points because so much happens so fast on the stage.

A sensitive, mature reading of plays augments our knowledge of drama, cultivates our taste, refines our critical posture, and perhaps even earns us the right to be counted among those intelligent and responsive members of an audience for whom every playwright craves.

By and large, we judge the quality of drama in much the same way that we judge the quality of fiction, as long as we are assessing the form, techniques, and meaning of a story and not the acting, directing, lighting, sets, costumes, or anything else that makes for a total experience at the theater. Only one major element differs. As we have already noted, drama is usually restricted to a single point of view. While in reading fiction we may have access to the consciousness of a character, in reading drama we have to infer meaning from what the characters say and do.

Of course, there are exceptions, for a playwright may choose to make use of a narrator or a chorus. But the point of view in most dramas is objective; it is the point of view of the reader or spectator. Otherwise, the major elements that make for a good story are similar whether we are dealing with fiction or drama. If it is good, a play will doubtless have interesting, believable characters, a struggle that builds toward a point of high emotional intensity, and a comment on some aspect of life.

Greek Theater and Stage

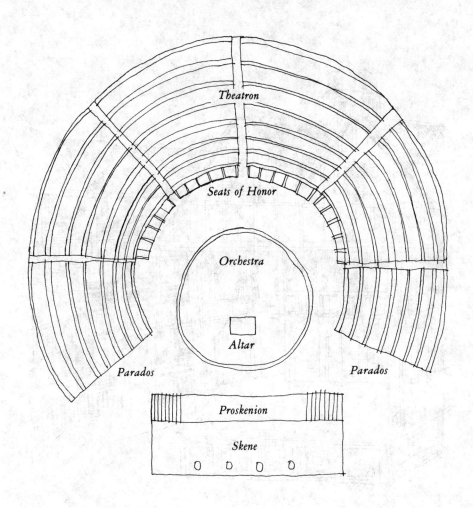

Theatron	Seating area for audience on hillside in open air
Seats of honor	Seating area for dignitaries, including priests and public officials
Orchestra	Stage or acting area and dancing place of chorus
Altar	Place for offering sacrifices
Parados	Points of entry and exit for chorus
Proskenion	Scenery, usually representing the front of a palace or temple (also called "proscenium")
Skene	Building with three doors used for background scenery, entrance and exit of actors; houses dressing rooms and stage machinery

Elizabethan Theater and Stage

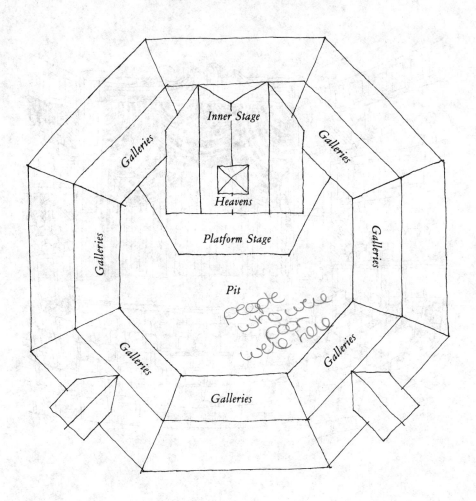

Inner Stage

Galleries

Galleries

Galleries

Galleries

Heavens

Platform Stage

Pit

people who were poor were here

Galleries

Galleries

Galleries

there was no electricity & fire was not used very often because of lighting your costume on fire

Inner stage	Acting area for intimate scenes; acting also done on one or two balconies above inner stage
Platform stage	Main acting area, raised several feet above pit
Heavens	Projecting roof, supported by pillars, half covering platform stage; underside often painted to resemble sky
Pit	Uncovered area for standing audience of about 600
Galleries	Three tiers of seats, topmost covered with a roof, seating 1,400 or more spectators

Modern Proscenium Theater and Stage

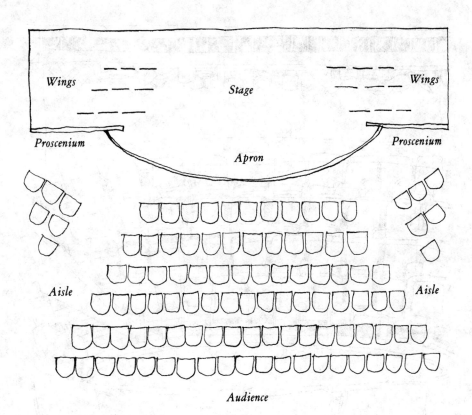

Stage	Main acting area, raised several feet above floor of audience. Size and outline of acting area is determined by placement of drops and other pieces of scenery
Wings	Parts of stage not used as acting area; house scenery and equipment and serve as entrances and exits for performers; lead to dressing rooms and other backstage facilities
Proscenium	Wall between stage and audience masking wings and fly-loft; play is viewed through a large arch in the wall
Apron	Shallow area of stage projecting out from proscenium toward audience, used chiefly to achieve intimacy with audience
Audience	First-floor seating area, usually raked upward away from the stage; spectators also view play from boxes and balconies at the sides and back of the theater
Aisle	Entrance and exit for audience and occasionally for actors

Modern Arena Theater and Stage

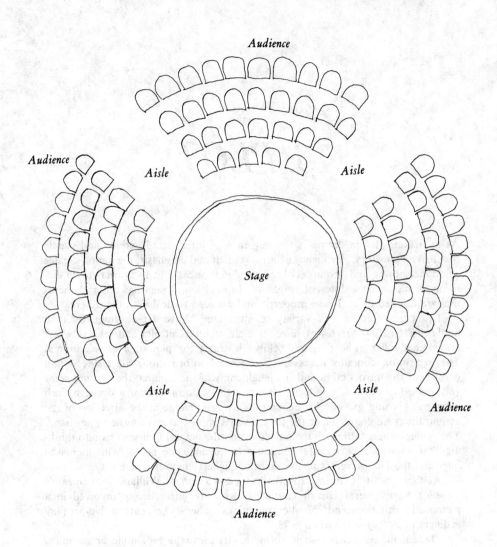

Stage	Acting area; may be any shape — round, oval, rectangular. Sets are simple, consisting primarily of props (furniture, rocks, etc.)
Audience	Seating area, raked upward away from the stage as in an amphitheater. Proximity to stage permits greater intimacy and immediacy than any other theater. Capacity is small
Aisles	Entrances and exits for performers, as well as audience; often on same level as stage

16. PLOT

As in fiction, **plot** in drama is the sequence of interrelated actions and events that make up a story. By means of arrangement and emphasis, the action creates emotional power and promotes thematic significance. But in drama, some elements of plot need a different emphasis. In addition, drama has other elements that are deemed its exclusive property, and we need to deal with them here.

Dramatic plots have a variety of structures. Most **Greek tragedies** (like Sophocles' *Oedipus the King*) have a simple, tightly knit plot and relatively few major characters. The diagram below illustrates the plot of a Greek drama. The *exposition* contains necessary background information; the *rising action* consists of the introduction and the heightening of the conflict; the *turning point* (also called *crisis*) refers to a high point in the action involving a decisive clash between opposing forces. At this point there is a change in the direction of the action; the main character or the antagonist is shown as having the upper hand. The *falling action* (although the adjective and the diagram mislead us into thinking that interest slackens off) continues to advance the action with increased intensity; the *climax* refers to the point of highest emotional intensity.

At the opposite extreme, **Elizabethan plays** (such as William Shakespeare's *Othello*) have several sets of characters who are energetically involved in a plethora of situations and complicated actions. The Shakespearean five-act play is diagrammed at the top of page 739.

Modern drama fits no single formula. Its plot may be simple or complex. The plot of a modern play can be diagrammed as shown at the bottom of page 739; however, the plots of most conventional modern dramas would be depicted as shown on page 740. The *introduction* (or *exposition*) sets the stage for the action that will follow; the *point of attack* (or *inciting force*) initiates the action, showing the main character in conflict with nature's forces, social forces, others, or the self; the *complications* make the problem more difficult to solve; the

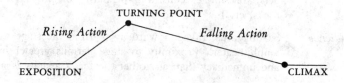

Plot Structure of Greek Drama

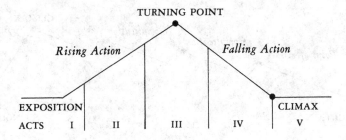

Plot Structure of Shakespearean Play

climax presents the opposing forces at the apex of their struggle; the *resolution* (or *dénouement*) settles the outcome of the conflict; and the *conclusion* (or *ending*) terminates the action.

The internal structure of a typical **three-act play** follows a fairly predictable pattern. Act I presents the preliminary exposition and introduces the characters and the main conflict (point of attack). Act II advances the action forward through any number of complications with increasing suspense. Act III raises the action to the highest point of emotional intensity (the climax) and then offers a solution to the major problem (the resolution). Plays constructed with scene divisions within acts or only with scenes function in much the same manner. For the most part, the dramatist divides the action into these segments to indicate a passage of time or to show a change in setting or character. Each act or scene contains a segment of the action; each has its own emphasis, direction, and crisis; and each contributes to the overall unity of the action.

The playwright's immediate obligation at the beginning of a play is to provide the background information **(exposition)** necessary for the audience or reader to comprehend the action that is to follow. The playwright must identify the characters, show their relationships to one another, and ignite the fuse of conflict without undue delay. *Who* these characters are and *what* they are doing must be apparent at the outset. The events in this exposition, sometimes called *antecedent action,* have actually preceded the beginning of the play. There was a time when Oedipus had not killed Laius or married his mother, a time when the dark-skinned Moor Othello was not married to the light-skinned Desdemona. All this antecedent action is important and must be introduced early in the play if the playwright is to avoid bewildering the audience.

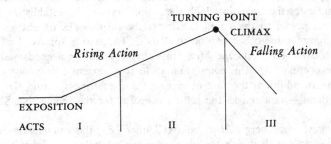

Plot Structure of Modern Play

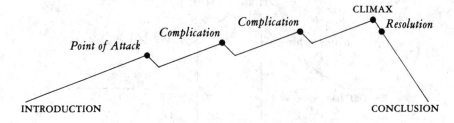

Alternate Plot Structure of Modern Play

A playwright achieves the most direct kind of exposition by making a direct statement to the audience. The vehicle of communication can be a **prologue,** a **chorus,** or a **narrator.** Each of these methods ordinarily sets the tone and atmosphere of the drama, provides background information about one or two main characters, and gives some notion of the nature of the conflict. In the seventy or so lines that Oedipus speaks in the prologue of *Oedipus the King* (in this chapter), for example, Sophocles shows him suffering with the suppliants who have come to beg their honored lord to rid their city of a devastating pestilence. In addition, we learn that Oedipus has already sent Creon, Jocasta's brother, to consult the oracle at Delphi, and that he, Oedipus, will do everything the oracle requires of him.

The soliloquy and the aside may also be used to present exposition effectively. **Soliloquy** means the act of speaking to oneself in solitude or as if one were alone. The speaker, alone on the stage, gives the appearance of talking to himself or herself, although he or she really addresses the audience with a speech that commonly reflects penetrating thoughts about that speaker's character. Similarly, the **aside,** which merely pretends to be a stage whisper, is really spoken directly to the audience or occasionally to some of the characters. Usually a single word or sentence, it tersely comments on an action or a character.

Any one of these methods (prologue, chorus, narrator, soliloquy, aside) will accomplish the dramatist's purpose of imparting preliminary information, although today they are dismissed as outmoded and infrequently used. To take care of preliminary exposition indirectly, the modern playwright customarily favors the use of a setting, an incident, or a conversation between two characters other than the protagonist and the antagonist.

Setting furnishes a great deal more material than one would reasonably expect; it indicates the times in which the action takes place, establishes tone and atmosphere, points to the conflict, mirrors the dispositions of characters, and presents innumerable other significant details. The setting for Act I of George Bernard Shaw's *Arms and the Man* (this chapter) tells us a good many things about the occupants of the house, and so to some extent foreshadows characterization. In addition, the mix of elegance and paltriness — and the contrast between them — that marks the setting prepares for the theme that Shaw will develop.

In August Strindberg's *Miss Julie* (Chapter 18), the **conversation** between the two servants with which the play opens reveals what has been happening. During the first nine exchanges, the following information is given: Miss Julie is acting crazy again; Jean took the Count to the station; Jean discovers Julie at a dance hall with the gamekeeper and waltzes with her; Miss Julie broke off an engagement two weeks earlier; the fiancé was not rich; the family is choosy in these matters; Miss Julie prefers to stay at home with the servants rather than go with her father to visit relations; Miss Julie may feel awkward as a result of the end of her engagement; she was seen "training" her fiancé, "making him jump over her riding-whip — the way you teach a dog."

Exposition is not limited, of course, to the beginnings of plays. Playwrights introduce background information throughout the play, whenever they deem it necessary. They only gradually complete the picture of the main characters, reveal all that they want us to know about them — their experiences, their thoughts, and their motives. In Arthur Miller's *Death of a Salesman* (Chapter 17), for instance, it is not until late in the play that we hear of Biff's thievery, which has lost him every job since high school.

To be sure, playwrights at their best select judiciously, revealing only those specific details absolutely vital to our understanding of the play, and at precisely the right moment. Consequently, only the significant details are likely to be incorporated into the play. The means by which playwrights disclose facts and details vary according to the times in which they write and the techniques they prefer; to those already mentioned, we can add confidants, dumb shows, charts, slides, film, music, or whatever.

There is a kind of tranquillity in drama at the beginning, before the action starts, and toward the end, after a solution is found (if one is found) for the main problem. **Conflict** disturbs this tranquillity. It is what the plot is about; conflict is the essence of drama.

Conflict is the struggle of forces in opposition to each other — for example, human beings against human beings, human beings against society, environment, or fate, or human beings against some aspect of the self. It may also be defined as the *action* and *reaction* of characters or forces opposing each other. This view of conflict resembles a good tug-of-war. First one side gains an advantage, then the other does. In between the tugs are moments of relaxation and adjustment. The climax is reached with the frantic last tug, a few moments before one side pulls down the other in defeat, at the point of relaxation. If there is a standstill, there is no resolution.

Conflict may be as simple as in Paddy Chayefsky's *Marty* (Chapter 17), as ambiguous as in *Oedipus,* as moral as in *Death of a Salesman,* or as absurd as in Edward Albee's *The Sandbox* (Chapter 19). The conflict in *Marty* is between Marty and his feelings of inferiority; in *Oedipus* it is between man and the gods of fate; in *Death of a Salesman* it is between Willy Loman and his dreams of material success.

A good approach to the analysis of conflict (or plot) is to use the following eight-point formula:

Protagonist — the chief character
Prize — the goal
Obstacle — the opposing force or forces
Point of attack — the introduction of the problem (conflict)
Complications — temporary hindrances
Climax — the moment of truth
Resolution — the solving of the problem
Theme — the main point of the story

In the face of conflict a character has one or several choices to make; he or she must decide to act in one way or another. A major character whose decisions and actions generally force and control the main action is the **protagonist.** We may or may not sympathize, but we do identify with the protagonist or the problem, and we are eager to know what will happen. In most plays, major characters are caught in decisive moments of conflict. They respond with action, seeking answers to perplexing questions, struggling to overcome difficulties, or wrestling to achieve something. What the protagonist seeks to achieve is the **prize** or goal. The opposition — the someone **(antagonist)** or something (forces of nature, fate, the ethos of society, or warring internal passions) opposing the protagonist in the pursuit of the goal — we call the **obstacle.** No conflict exists without this opposition, which persists until the outcome at the end of the play.

Conflict, then, is made up of a protagonist who struggles against great odds (obstacle) to achieve a goal (prize). Once this situation becomes known to us, the dramatic story has really begun (point of attack). Oedipus (the protagonist) decides to eradicate the cause of the blight that infects Thebes (prize and point of attack), whatever the cost. Once he has made that decision, and despite what the oracle promises (gods or fate as obstacle), he refuses to alter his course, and disaster ensues.

Plot is constructed of the building blocks of **complications.** They are unexpected problems, difficulties, or changes that usually come up temporarily to impede the protagonist's progress toward the goal. In Strindberg's play, Miss Julie's struggle to find her place in the world is further confused by her yielding to a moment of passion. Willy Loman's progress in *Death of a Salesman* toward achieving recognition as an important person is hindered by several complications, including the fact that Willy loses first his salary and then his job.

Through complications, the action moves upward and forward toward the most crucial scene in the play, which we know as the **climax.** It is the point of highest emotional intensity. For the forces in opposition, at the apex of their struggle, it is the moment of truth.

What follows is the **resolution** or dénouement, which announces the outcome of the entire sequence of events. At this point something has been decided for or against the protagonist. The struggle is won or lost. The resolution, which settles the conflict, may shed light on the theme of the play. **Theme** is the point the playwright tries to make, the central meaning or significance of the drama.

Oedipus the King, the first play in this chapter, presents us with the plot of a classic tragedy. Shaw's comedy *Arms and the Man,* dating from the end of the last century and written in prose, illustrates the modern dramatist's way with plot.

Sophocles   (495–405 B.C.)

Oedipus the King

Characters

OEDIPUS, *King of Thebes*　　　　　FIRST MESSENGER
JOCASTA, *His wife*　　　　　　　　SECOND MESSENGER
CREON, *His brother-in-law*　　　　A HERDSMAN
TEIRESIAS, *An old blind prophet*　A CHORUS OF OLD MEN OF THEBES
A PRIEST

> *Scene: In front of the palace of Oedipus at Thebes. To the right of the stage near the altar stands the* PRIEST *with a crowd of children.* OEDIPUS *emerges from the central door.*

OEDIPUS   Children, young sons and daughters of old Cadmus,
　　why do you sit here with your suppliant crowns?
　　The town is heavy with a mingled burden
　　of sounds and smells, of groans and hymns and incense;
　　I did not think it fit that I should hear
　　of this from messengers but came myself, —
　　I Oedipus whom all men call the Great.
　　(*He turns to the* PRIEST.)
　　You're old and they are young; come, speak for them.
　　What do you fear or want, that you sit here
　　suppliant? Indeed I'm willing to give all
　　that you may need; I would be very hard
　　should I not pity suppliants like these.

PRIEST   O ruler of my country, Oedipus,
　　you see our company around the altar;
　　you see our ages; some of us, like these,
　　who cannot yet fly far, and some of us
　　heavy with age; these children are the chosen
　　among the young, and I the priest of Zeus.
　　Within the market place sit others crowned
　　with suppliant garlands, at the double shrine
　　of Pallas and the temple where Ismenus
　　gives oracles by fire. King, you yourself
　　have seen our city reeling like a wreck
　　already; it can scarcely lift its prow
　　out of the depths, out of the bloody surf.
　　A blight is on the fruitful plants of the earth,
　　A blight is on the cattle in the fields,
　　a blight is on our women that no children
　　are born to them; a God that carries fire,
　　a deadly pestilence, is on our town,
　　strikes us and spares not, and the house of Cadmus
　　is emptied of its people while black Death
　　grows rich in groaning and in lamentation.

We have not come as suppliants to this altar
because we thought of you as of a God,
but rather judging you the first of men
in all the chances of this life and when
we mortals have to do with more than man.
You came and by your coming saved our city,
freed us from tribute which we paid of old
to the Sphinx, cruel singer. This you did
in virtue of no knowledge we could give you,
in virtue of no teaching; it was God
that aided you, men say, and you are held
with God's assistance to have saved our lives.
Now Oedipus, Greatest in all men's eyes,
here falling at your feet we all entreat you,
find us some strength for rescue.
Perhaps you'll hear a wise word from some God,
perhaps you will learn something from a man
(for I have seen that for the skilled of practice
the outcome of their counsels live the most).
Noblest of men, go, and raise up our city,
go, — and give heed. For now this land of ours
calls you its savior since you saved it once.
So, let us never speak about your reign
as of a time when first our feet were set
secure on high, but later fell to ruin.
Raise up our city, save it and raise it up.
Once you have brought us luck with happy omen;
be no less now in fortune.
If you will rule this land, as now you rule it,
better to rule it full of men than empty.
For neither tower nor ship is anything
when empty, and none live in it together.

OEDIPUS   I pity you, children. You have come full of longing,
but I have known the story before you told it
only too well. I know you are all sick,
yet there is not one of you, sick though you are,
that is as sick as I myself.
Your several sorrows each have single scope
and touch but one of you. My spirit groans
for city and myself and you at once.
You have not roused me like a man from sleep;
know that I have given many tears to this,
gone many ways wandering in thought,
but as I thought I found only one remedy
and that I took. I sent Menoeceus' son
Creon, Jocasta's brother, to Apollo,
to his Pythian temple,
that he might learn there by what act or word
I could save this city. As I count the days,

it vexes me what ails him; he is gone
far longer than he needed for the journey.
But when he comes, then, may I prove a villain,
if I shall not do all the God commands.

PRIEST   Thanks for your gracious words. Your servants here
signal that Creon is this moment coming.

OEDIPUS   His face is bright. O holy Lord Apollo,
grant that his news too may be bright for us
and bring us safety.

PRIEST   It is happy news,
I think, for else his head would not be crowned
with sprigs of fruitful laurel.

OEDIPUS   We will know soon,
he's within hail. Lord Creon, my good brother,
what is the word you bring us from the God?

(CREON enters.)

CREON   A good word, — for things hard to bear themselves
if in the final issue all is well
I count complete good fortune.

OEDIPUS   What do you mean?
What you have said so far
leaves me uncertain whether to trust or fear.

CREON   If you will hear my news before these others
I am ready to speak, or else to go within.

OEDIPUS   Speak it to all;
the grief I bear, I bear it more for these
than for my own heart.

CREON   I will tell you, then,
what I heard from the God.
King Phoebus in plain words commanded us
to drive out a pollution from our land,
pollution grown ingrained within the land;
drive it out, said the God, not cherish it,
till it's past cure.

OEDIPUS   What is the rite
of purification? How shall it be done?

CREON   By banishing a man, or expiation
of blood by blood, since it is murder guilt
which holds our city in this destroying storm.

OEDIPUS   Who is this man whose fate the God pronounces?

CREON   My Lord, before you piloted the state
we had a king called Laius.

OEDIPUS   I know of him by hearsay. I have not seen him.

CREON   The God commanded clearly: let some one
punish with force this dead man's murderers.

OEDIPUS   Where are they in the world? Where would a trace
of this old crime be found? It would be hard
to guess where.

CREON   The clue is in this land;
that which is sought is found;
the unheeded thing escapes:
so said the God.

OEDIPUS   Was it at home,
or in the country that death came upon him,
or in another country travelling?

CREON   He went, he said himself, upon an embassy,
but never returned when he set out from home.

OEDIPUS   Was there no messenger, no fellow traveller
who knew what happened? Such a one might tell
something of use.

CREON   They were all killed save one. He fled in terror
and he could tell us nothing in clear terms
of what he knew, nothing, but one thing only.

OEDIPUS   What was it?
If we could even find a slim beginning
in which to hope, we might discover much.

CREON   This man said that the robbers they encountered
were many and the hands that did the murder
were many; it was no man's single power.

OEDIPUS   How could a robber dare a deed like this
were he not helped with money from the city,
money and treachery?

CREON   That indeed was thought.
But Laius was dead and in our trouble
there was none to help.

OEDIPUS   What trouble was so great to hinder you
inquiring out the murder of your king?

CREON   The riddling Sphinx induced us to neglect
mysterious crimes and rather seek solution
of troubles at our feet.

OEDIPUS   I will bring this to light again. King Phoebus
fittingly took this care about the dead,
and you too fittingly.

And justly you will see in me an ally,
a champion of my country and the God.
For when I drive pollution from the land
I will not serve a distant friend's advantage,
but act in my own interest. Whoever
he was that killed the king may readily
wish to dispatch me with his murderous hand;   *Irony*
so helping the dead king I help myself.

Come, children, take your suppliant boughs and go;
up from the altars now. Call the assembly
and let it meet upon the understanding
that I'll do everything. God will decide
whether we prosper or remain in sorrow.

PRIEST   Rise, children — it was this we came to seek,
which of himself the king now offers us.
May Phoebus who gave us the oracle
come to our rescue and stay the plague.

(*Exeunt all but the* CHORUS.)

Strophe

CHORUS   What is the sweet spoken word of God from the shrine of Pytho rich
        in gold
    that has come to glorious Thebes?
    I am stretched on the rack of doubt, and terror and trembling hold
    my heart, O Delian Healer, and I worship full of fears
    for what doom you will bring to pass, new or renewed in the revolving years.
    Speak to me, immortal voice,
    child of golden Hope.

Antistrophe

First I call on you, Athene, deathless daughter of Zeus,
and Artemis, Earth Upholder,
who sits in the midst of the market place in the throne which men call Fame,
and Phoebus, the Far Shooter, three averters of Fate,
come to us now, if ever before, when ruin rushed upon the state,
you drove destruction's flame away
out of our land.

Strophe

Our sorrows defy number;
all the ship's timbers are rotten;
taking of thought is no spear for the driving away of the plague.
There are no growing children in this famous land;
there are no women bearing the pangs of childbirth.
You may see them one with another, like birds swift on the wing,
quicker than fire unmastered,
speeding away to the coast of the Western God.

Antistrophe

In the unnumbered deaths
of its people the city dies;
those children that are born lie dead on the naked earth
unpitied, spreading contagion of death; and grey haired mothers and wives
everywhere stand at the altar's edge, suppliant, moaning;
the hymn to the healing God rings out but with it the wailing voices are
    blended.
From these our sufferings grant us, O golden Daughter of Zeus, glad-
    faced deliverance.

Strophe

There is no clash of brazen shields but our fight is with the War God,
a War God ringed with the cries of men, a savage God who burns us;
grant that he turn in racing course backwards out of our country's bounds
to the great palace of Amphitrite or where the waves of the Thracian sea
deny the stranger safe anchorage.
Whatsoever escapes the night
at last the light of day revisits;
so smite the War God, Father Zeus,
beneath your thunderbolt,
for you are the Lord of the lightning, the lightning that carries fire.

Antistrophe

And your unconquered arrow shafts, winged by the golden corded bow,
Lycean King, I beg to be at our side for help;
and the gleaming torches of Artemis with which she scours the Lycean hills,
and I call on the God with the turban of gold, who gave his name to this
    country of ours,
the Bacchic God with the wind flushed face,
Evian One, who travel
with the Maenad company,
combat the God that burns us
with your torch of pine;
for the God that is our enemy is a God unhonoured among the Gods.

    (OEDIPUS *returns.*)

OEDIPUS   For what you ask me — if you will hear my words,
    and hearing welcome them and fight the plague,
    you will find strength and lightening of your load.

    Hark to me; what I say to you, I say
    as one that is a stranger to the story
    as stranger to the deed. For I would not
    be far upon the track if I alone
    were tracing it without a clue. But now,
    since after all was finished, I became
    a citizen among you, citizens —
    now I proclaim to all the men of Thebes:
    who so among you knows the murderer

by whose hand Laius, son of Labdacus,
died — I command him to tell everything
to me, — yes, though he fears himself to take the blame
on his own head; for bitter punishment
he shall have none, but leave this land unharmed.
Or if he knows the murderer, another,
a foreigner, still let him speak the truth.
For I will pay him and be grateful, too.
But if you shall keep silence, if perhaps
some one of you, to shield a guilty friend,
or for his own sake shall reject my words —
hear what I shall do then:
I forbid that man, whoever he be, my land,
my land where I hold sovereignty and throne;
and I forbid any to welcome him
or cry him greeting or make him a sharer
in sacrifice or offering to the Gods,
or give him water for his hands to wash.
I command all to drive him from their homes,
since he is our pollution, as the oracle
of Pytho's God proclaimed him now to me.
IRONY So I stand forth a champion of the God
and of the man who died.
Upon the murderer I invoke this curse —
whether he is one man and all unknown,
or one of many — may he wear out his life
in misery to miserable doom!
If with my knowledge he lives at my hearth
I pray that I myself may feel my curse.
On you I lay my charge to fulfill all this
for me, for the God, and for this land of ours
destroyed and blighted, by the God forsaken.

Even were this no matter of God's ordinance
it would not fit you so to leave it lie,
unpurified, since a good man is dead
and one that was a king. Search it out.
Since I am now the holder of his office,
and have his bed and wife that once was his, *IRONY*
and had his line not been unfortunate
we would have common children — (fortune leaped
upon his head) — because of all these things,
I fight in his defence as for my father,
and I shall try all means to take the murderer
of Laius the son of Labdacus
the son of Polydorus and before him
of Cadmus and before him of Agenor.
Those who do not obey me, may the Gods
grant no crops springing from the ground they plough
nor children to their women! May a fate

like this, or one still worse than this consume them!
For you whom these words please, the other Thebans,
may Justice as your ally and all the Gods
live with you, blessing you now and for ever!

CHORUS   As you have held me to my oath, I speak:
I neither killed the king nor can declare
the killer; but since Phoebus set the quest
it is his part to tell who the man is.

OEDIPUS   Right; but to put compulsion on the Gods
against their will — no man can do that.

CHORUS   May I then say what I think second best?

OEDIPUS   If there's a third best, too, spare not to tell it.

CHORUS   I know that what the Lord Teiresias
sees, is most often what the Lord Apollo
sees. If you should inquire of this from him
you might find out most clearly.

OEDIPUS   Even in this my actions have not been sluggard.
On Creon's word I have sent two messengers
and why the prophet is not here already
I have been wondering.

CHORUS   His skill apart
there is besides only an old faint story.

OEDIPUS   What is it?
I look at every story.

CHORUS   It was said
that he was killed by certain wayfarers.

OEDIPUS   I heard that, too, but no one saw the killer.

CHORUS   Yet if he has a share of fear at all,
his courage will not stand firm, hearing your curse.

OEDIPUS   The man who in the doing did not shrink
will fear no word.

CHORUS   Here comes his prosecutor:
led by your men the godly prophet comes
in whom alone of mankind truth is native.

(*Enter* TEIRESIAS, *led by a little boy.*)

OEDIPUS   Teiresias, you are versed in everything,
things teachable and things not to be spoken,
things of the heaven and earth-creeping things.
You have no eyes but in your mind you know
with what a plague our city is afflicted.
My lord, in you alone we find a champion,
in you alone one that can rescue us.

Perhaps you have not heard the messengers,
but Phoebus sent in answer to our sending
an oracle declaring that our freedom
from this disease would only come when we
should learn the names of those who killed King Laius,
and kill them or expel from our country.
Do not begrudge us oracles from birds,
or any other way of prophecy
within your skill; save yourself and the city,
save me; redeem the debt of our pollution
that lies on us because of this dead man.
We are in your hands; pains are most nobly taken
to help another when you have means and power.

TEIRESIAS   Alas, how terrible is wisdom when
it brings no profit to the man that's wise!
This I knew well, but had forgotten it,
else I would not have come here.

OEDIPUS   What is this?
How sad you are now you have come!

TEIRESIAS   Let me
go home. It will be easiest for us both
to bear our several destinies to the end
if you will follow my advice.

OEDIPUS   You'd rob us
of this your gift of prophecy? You talk
as one who had no care for law nor love
for Thebes who reared you.

TEIRESIAS   Yes, but I see that even your own words
miss the mark; therefore I must fear for mine.

OEDIPUS   For God's sake if you know of anything,
do not turn from us; all of us kneel to you,
all of us here, your suppliants.

TEIRESIAS   All of you here know nothing. I will not
bring to the light of day my troubles, mine —
rather than call them yours.

OEDIPUS   What do you mean?
You know of something but refuse to speak.
Would you betray us and destroy the city?

TEIRESIAS   I will not bring this pain upon us both,
neither on you nor on myself. Why is it
you question me and waste your labour? I
will tell you nothing.

OEDIPUS   You would provoke a stone! Tell us, you villain,
tell us, and do not stand there quietly
unmoved and balking at the issue.

TEIRESIAS   You blame my temper but you do not see
your own that lives within you; it is me
you chide.

OEDIPUS   Who would not feel his temper rise
at words like these with which you shame our city?

TEIRESIAS   Of themselves things will come, although I hide them
and breathe no word of them.

OEDIPUS   Since they will come
tell them to me.

TEIRESIAS   I will say nothing further.
Against this answer let your temper rage
as wildly as you will.

OEDIPUS   Indeed I am
so angry I shall not hold back a jot
of what I think. For I would have you know
I think you were complotter of the deed
and doer of the deed save in so far
as for the actual killing. Had you had eyes
I would have said alone you murdered him.

TEIRESIAS   Yes? Then I warn you faithfully to keep
the letter of your proclamation and
from this day forth to speak no word of greeting
to these nor me; you are the land's pollution.

OEDIPUS   How shamelessly you started up this taunt!
How do you think you will escape?

TEIRESIAS   I have.
I have escaped; the truth is what I cherish
and that's my strength.

OEDIPUS   And who has taught you truth?
Not your profession surely!

TEIRESIAS   You have taught me,
for you have made me speak against my will.

OEDIPUS   Speak what? Tell me again that I may learn it better.

TEIRESIAS   Did you not understand before or would you
provoke me into speaking?

OEDIPUS   I did not grasp it,
not so to call it known. Say it again.

TEIRESIAS   I say you are the murderer of the king
whose murderer you seek.

OEDIPUS   Not twice you shall
say calumnies like this and stay unpunished.

TEIRESIAS   Shall I say more to tempt your anger more?

OEDIPUS   As much as you desire; it will be said
in vain.

TEIRESIAS   I say that with those you love best
you live in foulest shame unconsciously
and do not see where you are in calamity.

OEDIPUS   Do you imagine you can always talk
like this, and live to laugh at it hereafter?

TEIRESIAS   Yes, if the truth has anything of strength.

OEDIPUS   It has, but not for you; it has no strength
for you because you are blind in mind and ears
as well as in your eyes.

TEIRESIAS   You are a poor wretch
to taunt me with the very insults which
every one soon will heap upon yourself.

OEDIPUS   Your life is one long night so that you cannot
hurt me or any other who sees the light.

TEIRESIAS   It is not fate that I should be your ruin,
Apollo is enough; it is his care
to work this out.

OEDIPUS   Was this your own design
or Creon's?

TEIRESIAS   Creon is no hurt to you,
but you are to yourself.

OEDIPUS   Wealth, sovereignty and skill outmatching skill
for the contrivance of an envied life!
Great store of jealousy fill your treasury chests,
if my friend Creon, friend from the first and loyal,
thus secretly attacks me, secretly
desires to drive me out and secretly
suborns this juggling, trick devising quack,
this wily beggar who has only eyes
for his own gains, but blindness in his skill.
For, tell me, where have you seen clear, Teiresias,
with your prophetic eyes? When the dark singer,
the sphinx, was in your country, did you speak
word of deliverance to its citizens?
And yet the riddle's answer was not the province
of a chance comer. It was a prophet's task
and plainly you had no such gift of prophecy
from birds nor otherwise from any God
to glean a word of knowledge. But I came,

Oedipus, who knew nothing, and I stopped her.
I solved the riddle by my wit alone.
Mine was no knowledge got from birds. And now
you would expel me,
because you think that you will find a place
by Creon's throne. I think you will be sorry,
both you and your accomplice, for your plot
to drive me out. And did I not regard you
as an old man, some suffering would have taught you
that what was in your heart was treason.

CHORUS   We look at this man's words and yours, my king,
and we find both have spoken them in anger.
We need no angry words but only thought
how we may best hit the God's meaning for us.

TEIRESIAS   If you are king, at least I have the right
no less to speak in my defence against you.
Of that much I am master. I am no slave
of yours, but Loxias', and so I shall not
enroll myself with Creon for my patron.
Since you have taunted me with being blind,
here is my word for you.
You have your eyes but see not where you are
in sin, nor where you live, nor whom you live with.
Do you know who your parents are? Unknowing
you are an enemy to kith and kin
in death, beneath the earth, and in this life.
A deadly footed, double striking curse,
from father and mother both, shall drive you forth
out of this land, with darkness on your eyes,
that now have such straight vision. Shall there be
a place will not be harbour to your cries,
a corner of Cithaeron will not ring
in echo to your cries, soon, soon, —
when you shall learn the secret of your marriage,
which steered you to a haven in this house, —
haven no haven, after lucky voyage?
And of the multitude of other evils
establishing a grim equality
between you and your children, you know nothing.
So, muddy with contempt my words and Creon's!
Misery shall grind no man as it will you.

OEDIPUS   Is it endurable that I should hear
such words from him? Go and a curse go with you!
Quick, home with you! Out of my house at once!

TEIRESIAS   I would not have come either had you not called me.

OEDIPUS   I did not know then you would talk like a fool —
or it would have been long before I called you.

TEIRESIAS   I am a fool then, as it seems to you —
     but to the parents who have bred you, wise.   *IRONY*

OEDIPUS   What parents? Stop! Who are they of all the world?

TEIRESIAS   This day will show your birth and will destroy you.

OEDIPUS   How needlessly your riddles darken everything.

TEIRESIAS   But it's in riddle answering you are strongest.   *riddle of the Olympth riddle of his birth*

OEDIPUS   Yes. Taunt me where you will find me great.

TEIRESIAS   It is this very luck that has destroyed you.

OEDIPUS   I do not care, if it has saved this city.

TEIRESIAS   Well, I will go. Come, boy, lead me away.

OEDIPUS   Yes, lead him off. So long as you are here,
     you'll be a stumbling block and a vexation;
     once gone, you will not trouble me again.

TEIRESIAS   I have said
     what I came here to say not fearing your
     countenance: there is no way you can hurt me.
     I tell you, king, this man, this murderer
     (whom you have long declared you are in search of,
     indicting him in threatening proclamation
     as murderer of Laius) — he is here.
     In name he is a stranger among citizens
     but soon he will be shown to be a citizen
     true native Theban, and he'll have no joy
     of the discovery: blindness for sight
     and beggary for riches his exchange,
     he shall go journeying to a foreign country
     tapping his way before him with a stick.
     He shall be proved father and brother both
     to his own children in his house; to her
     that gave him birth, a son and husband both;
     a fellow sower in his father's bed
     with that same father that he murdered.
     Go within, reckon that out, and if you find me
     mistaken, say I have no skill in prophecy.

     (*Exeunt separately* TEIRESIAS *and* OEDIPUS.)

     Strophe

CHORUS   Who is the man proclaimed
     by Delphi's prophetic rock
     as the bloody handed murderer,
     the doer of deeds that none dare name?
     Now is the time for him to run
     with a stronger foot
     than Pegasus

for the child of Zeus leaps in arms upon him
with fire and the lightning bolt,
and terribly close on his heels
are the Fates that never miss.

Antistrophe

Lately from snowy Parnassus
clearly the voice flashed forth,
bidding each Theban track him down,
the unknown murderer.
In the savage forests he lurks and in
the caverns like
the mountain bull.
He is sad and lonely, and lonely his feet
that carry him far from the navel of earth;
but its prophecies, ever living,
flutter around his head.

Strophe

The augur has spread confusion,
terrible confusion;
I do not approve what was said
nor can I deny it.
I do not know what to say;
I am in a flutter of foreboding;
I never heard in the present
nor past of a quarrel between
the sons of Labdacus and Polybus,
that I might bring as proof
in attacking the popular fame
of Oedipus, seeking
to take vengeance for undiscovered
death in the line of Labdacus.

Antistrophe

Truly Zeus and Apollo are wise
and in human things all knowing;
but amongst men there is no
distinct judgment, between the prophet
and me — which of us is right.
One man may pass another in wisdom
but I would never agree
with those that find fault with the king
till I should see the word
proved right beyond doubt. For once
in visible form the Sphinx
came on him and all of us
saw his wisdom and in that test
he saved the city. So he will not be condemned by my mind.

(Enter CREON.*)*

CREON   Citizens, I have come because I heard
         deadly words spread about me, that the king
         accuses me. I cannot take that from him.
         If he believes that in these present troubles
         he has been wronged by me in word or deed
         I do not want to live on with the burden
         of such a scandal on me. The report
         injures me doubly and most vitally —
         for I'll be called a traitor to my city
         and traitor also to my friends and you.

CHORUS   Perhaps it was a sudden gust of anger
         that forced that insult from him, and no judgment.

CREON   But did he say that it was in compliance
         with schemes of mine that the seer told him lies?

CHORUS   Yes, he said that, but why, I do not know.

CREON   Were his eyes straight in his head? Was his mind right
         when he accused me in this fashion?

CHORUS   I do not know; I have no eyes to see
         what princes do. Here comes the king himself.

(Enter OEDIPUS.*)*

OEDIPUS You, sir, how is it you come here? Have you so much
         brazen-faced daring that you venture in
         my house although you are proved manifestly
         the murderer of that man, and though you tried,
         openly, highway robbery of my crown?
         For God's sake, tell me what you saw in me,
         what cowardice or what stupidity,
         that made you lay a plot like this against me?
         Did you imagine I should not observe
         the crafty scheme that stole upon me or
         seeing it, take no means to counter it?
         Was it not stupid of you to make the attempt,
         to try to hunt down royal power without
         the people at your back or friends? For only
         with the people at your back or money can
         the hunt end in the capture of a crown.

CREON   Do you know what you're doing? Will you listen
         to words to answer yours, and then pass judgment?

OEDIPUS You're quick to speak, but I am slow to grasp you,
         for I have found you dangerous, — and my foe.

CREON   First of all hear what I shall say to that.

OEDIPUS At least don't tell me that you are not guilty.

CREON   If you think obstinacy without wisdom
a valuable possession, you are wrong.

OEDIPUS   And you are wrong if you believe that one,
a criminal, will not be punished only
because he is my kinsman.

CREON   This is but just —
but tell me, then, of what offense I'm guilty?

OEDIPUS   Did you or did you not urge me to send
to this prophetic mumbler?

CREON   I did indeed,
and I shall stand by what I told you.

OEDIPUS   How long ago is it since Laius. . . .

CREON   What about Laius? I don't understand.

OEDIPUS   Vanished — died — was murdered?

CREON   It is long,
a long, long time to reckon.

OEDIPUS   Was this prophet
in the profession then?

CREON   He was, and honoured
as highly as he is today.

OEDIPUS   At that time did he say a word about me?

CREON   Never, at least when I was near him.

OEDIPUS   You never made a search for the dead man?

CREON   We searched, indeed, but never learned of anything.

OEDIPUS   Why did our wise old friend not say this then?

CREON   I don't know; and when I know nothing, I
usually hold my tongue.

OEDIPUS   You know this much,
and can declare this much if you are loyal.

CREON   What is it? If I know, I'll not deny it.

OEDIPUS   That he would not have said that I killed Laius
had he not met you first.

CREON   You know yourself
whether he said this, but I demand that I
should hear as much from you as you from me.

OEDIPUS   Then hear, — I'll not be proved a murderer.

CREON   Well, then. You're married to my sister.

OEDIPUS   Yes,
    that I am not disposed to deny.

CREON   You rule
    this country giving her an equal share
    in the government?

OEDIPUS   Yes, everything she wants
    she has from me.

CREON   And I, as thirdsman to you,
    am rated as the equal of you two?

OEDIPUS   Yes, and it's there you've proved yourself false friend.

CREON   Not if you will reflect on it as I do.
    Consider, first, if you think any one
    would choose to rule and fear rather than rule
    and sleep untroubled by a fear if power
    were equal in both cases. I, at least,
    I was not born with such a frantic yearning
    to be a king — but to do what kings do.
    And so it is with every one who has learned
    wisdom and self-control. As it stands now,
    the prizes are all mine — and without fear.
    But if I were the king myself, I must
    do much that went against the grain.
    How should despotic rule seem sweeter to me
    than painless power and an assured authority?
    I am not so besotted yet that I
    want other honours than those that come with profit.
    Now every man's my pleasure; every man greets me;
    now those who are your suitors fawn on me, —
    success for them depends upon my favour.
    Why should I let all this go to win that?
    My mind would not be traitor if it's wise;
    I am no treason lover, of my nature,
    nor would I ever dare to join a plot.
    Prove what I say. Go to the oracle
    at Pytho and inquire about the answers,
    if they are as I told you. For the rest,
    if you discover I laid any plot
    together with the seer, kill me, I say,
    not only by your vote but by my own.
    But do not charge me on obscure opinion
    without some proof to back it. It's not just
    lightly to count your knaves as honest men,
    nor honest men as knaves. To throw away
    an honest friend is, as it were, to throw
    your life away, which a man loves the best.
    In time you will know all with certainty;
    time is the only test of honest men,

Creon has all the rewards of a king w/out the worries of a king

one day is space enough to know a rogue.

CHORUS   His words are wise, king, if one fears to fall.
Those who are quick of temper are not safe.

OEDIPUS   When he that plots against me secretly
moves quickly, I must quickly counterplot.
If I wait taking no decisive measure
his business will be done, and mine be spoiled.

CREON   What do you want to do then? Banish me?

OEDIPUS   No, certainly; kill you, not banish you.

CREON   I do not think that you've your wits about you.

OEDIPUS   For my own interests, yes.

CREON   But for mine, too,
you should think equally.

OEDIPUS   You are a rogue.

CREON   Suppose you do not understand?

OEDIPUS   But yet
I must be ruler.

CREON   Not if you rule badly.

OEDIPUS   O, city, city!

CREON   I too have some share
in the city; it is not yours alone.

CHORUS   Stop, my lords! Here — and in the nick of time
I see Jocasta coming from the house;
with her help lay the quarrel that now stirs you.

(*Enter* JOCASTA.)

JOCASTA   For shame! Why have you raised this foolish squabbling
brawl? Are you not ashamed to air your private
griefs when the country's sick? Go in, you, Oedipus,
and you, too, Creon, into the house. Don't magnify
your nothing troubles.

CREON   Sister, Oedipus,
your husband, thinks he has the right to do
terrible wrongs — he has but to choose between
two terrors: banishing or killing me.

OEDIPUS   He's right, Jocasta; for I find him plotting
with knavish tricks against my person.

CREON   That God may never bless me! May I die
accursed, if I have been guilty of
one tittle of the charge you bring against me!

JOCASTA   I beg you, Oedipus, trust him in this,
spare him for the sake of this his oath to God,
for my sake, and the sake of those who stand here.

CHORUS   Be gracious, be merciful,
we beg of you.

OEDIPUS   In what would you have me yield?

CHORUS   He has been no silly child in the past.
He is strong in his oath now.
Spare him.

OEDIPUS   Do you know what you ask?

CHORUS   Yes.

OEDIPUS   Tell me then.

CHORUS   He has been your friend before all men's eyes; do not cast him
away dishonoured on an obscure conjecture.

OEDIPUS   I would have you know that this request of yours
really requests my death or banishment.

CHORUS   May the Sun God, king of Gods, forbid! May I die without God's
blessing, without friends' help, if I had any such thought. But my spirit is
broken by my unhappiness for my wasting country; and this would but add
troubles amongst ourselves to the other troubles.

OEDIPUS   Well, let him go then — if I must die ten times for it,
or be sent out dishonoured into exile.
It is your lips that prayed for him I pitied,
not his; wherever he is, I shall hate him.

CREON   I see you sulk in yielding and you're dangerous
when you are out of temper; natures like yours
are justly heaviest for themselves to bear.

OEDIPUS   Leave me alone! Take yourself off, I tell you.

CREON   I'll go, you have not known me, but they have,
and they have known my innocence.

(*Exit.*)

CHORUS   Won't you take him inside, lady?

JOCASTA   Yes, when I've found out what was the matter.

CHORUS   There was some misconceived suspicion of a story, and on the
other side the sting of injustice.

JOCASTA   So, on both sides?

CHORUS   Yes.

JOCASTA   What was the story?

CHORUS   I think it best, in the interests of the country, to leave it where
it ended.

OEDIPUS   You see where you have ended, straight of judgment
although you are, by softening my anger.

CHORUS   Sir, I have said before and I say again — be sure that I would have
been proved a madman, bankrupt in sane council, if I should put you away,
you who steered the country I love safely when she was crazed with troubles. God grant that now, too, you may prove a fortunate guide for us.

JOCASTA   Tell me, my lord, I beg of you, what was it
that roused your anger so?

OEDIPUS   Yes, I will tell you.
I honour you more than I honour them.
It was Creon and the plots he laid against me.

JOCASTA   Tell me — if you can clearly tell the quarrel —

OEDIPUS   Creon says
that I'm the murderer of Laius.

JOCASTA   Of his own knowledge or on information?

OEDIPUS   He sent this rascal prophet to me, since
he keeps his own mouth clean of any guilt.

JOCASTA   Do not concern yourself about this matter;
Irony   listen to me and learn that human beings
have no part in the craft of prophecy.
Of that I'll show you a short proof.
There was an oracle once that came to Laius, —
I will not say that it was Phoebus' own,
but it was from his servants — and it told him
that it was fate that he should die a victim
at the hands of his own son, a son to be born
of Laius and me. But, see now, he,
the king, was killed by foreign highway robbers
at a place where three roads meet — so goes the story;
and for the son — before three days were out
after his birth King Laius pierced his ankles
and by the hands of others cast him forth
upon a pathless hillside. So Apollo
failed to fulfill his oracle to the son,
that he should kill his father, and to Laius
also proved false in that the thing he feared,
death at his son's hands, never came to pass.
So clear in this case were the oracles,
so clear and false. Give them no heed, I say;
what God discovers need of, easily
he shows to us himself.

Jocasta acts ignorant, saying that the oracle didn't work

762   *Drama*

OEDIPUS   O dear Jocasta,
as I hear this from you, there comes upon me
a wandering of the soul — I could run mad.

JOCASTA   What trouble is it, that you turn again
and speak like this?

OEDIPUS   I thought I heard you say
that Laius was killed at a crossroads.

JOCASTA   Yes, that was how the story went and still
that word goes round.

OEDIPUS   Where is this place, Jocasta,
where he was murdered?

JOCASTA   Phocis is the country
and the road splits there, one of two roads from Delphi,
another comes from Daulia.

OEDIPUS   How long ago is this?

JOCASTA   The news came to the city just before
you became king and all men's eyes looked to you.
What is it, Oedipus, that's in your mind?

OEDIPUS   What have you designed, O Zeus, to do with me?

JOCASTA   What is the thought that troubles your heart?

OEDIPUS   Don't ask me yet — tell me of Laius —
How did he look? How old or young was he?

JOCASTA   He was a tall man and his hair was grizzled
already — nearly white — and in his form
not unlike you.

OEDIPUS   O God, I think I have
called curses on myself in ignorance.

JOCASTA   What do you mean? I am terrified
when I look at you.

OEDIPUS   I have a deadly fear
that the old seer had eyes. You'll show me more
if you can tell me one more thing.

JOCASTA   I will.
I'm frightened, — but if I can understand,
I'll tell you all you ask.

OEDIPUS   How was his company?
Had he few with him when he went this journey,
or many servants, as would suit a prince?

JOCASTA   In all there were but five, and among them
a herald; and one carriage for the king.

OEDIPUS   It's plain — it's plain — who was it told you this?

JOCASTA   The only servant that escaped safe home.

OEDIPUS   Is he at home now?

JOCASTA   No, when he came home again
   and saw you king and Laius was dead,
   he came to me and touched my hand and begged
   that I should send him to the fields to be
   my shepherd and so he might see the city
   as far off as he might. So I
   sent him away. He was an honest man,
   as slaves go, and was worthy of far more
   than what he asked of me.

OEDIPUS   O, how I wish that he could come back quickly!

JOCASTA   He can. Why is your heart so set on this?

OEDIPUS   O dear Jocasta, I am full of fears
   that I have spoken far too much; and therefore
   I wish to see this shepherd.

JOCASTA   He will come;
   but, Oedipus, I think I'm worthy too
   to know what it is that disquiets you.

OEDIPUS   It shall not be kept from you, since my mind
   has gone so far with its forebodings. Whom
   should I confide in rather than you, who is there
   of more importance to me who have passed
   through such a fortune?
   Polybus was my father, king of Corinth,
   and Merope, the Dorian, my mother.
   I was held greatest of the citizens
   in Corinth till a curious chance befell me
   as I shall tell you — curious, indeed,
   but hardly worth the store I set upon it.
   There was a dinner and at it a man,
   a drunken man, accused me in his drink
   of being bastard. I was furious
   but held my temper under for that day.
   Next day I went and taxed my parents with it;
   they took the insult very ill from him,
   the drunken fellow who had uttered it.
   So I was comforted for their part, but
   still this thing rankled always, for the story
   crept about widely. And I went at last
   to Pytho, though my parents did not know.
   But Phoebus sent me home again unhonoured
   in what I came to learn, but he foretold
   other and desperate horrors to befall me,
   that I was fated to lie with my mother,

and show to daylight an accursed breed
which men would not endure, and I was doomed
to be murderer of the father that begot me.
When I heard this I fled, and in the days
that followed I would measure from the stars
the whereabouts of Corinth — yes, I fled
to somewhere where I should not see fulfilled
the infamies told in that dreadful oracle.
And as I journeyed I came to the place
where, as you say, this king met with his death.
Jocasta, I will tell you the whole truth.
When I was near the branching of the crossroads,
going on foot, I was encountered by
a herald and a carriage with a man in it,
just as you tell me. He that led the way
and the old man himself wanted to thrust me
out of the road by force. I became angry
and struck the coachman who was pushing me.
When the old man saw this he watched his moment,
and as I passed he struck me from his carriage,
full on the head with his two pointed goad.
But he was paid in full and presently
my stick had struck him backwards from the car
and he rolled out of it. And then I killed them
all. If it happened there was any tie
of kinship twixt this man and Laius,
who is then now more miserable than I,
what man on earth so hated by the Gods,
since neither citizen nor foreigner
may welcome me at home or even greet me,
but drive me out of doors? And it is I,
I and no other have so cursed myself.
And I pollute the bed of him I killed
by the hands that killed him. Was I not born evil?
Am I not utterly unclean? I had to fly
and in my banishment not even see
my kindred nor set foot in my own country,
or otherwise my fate was to be yoked
in marriage with my mother and kill my father,
Polybus who begot me and had reared me.
Would not one rightly judge and say that on me
these things were sent by some malignant God?
O no, no, no — O holy majesty
of God on high, may I not see that day!
May I be gone out of men's sight before
I see the deadly taint of this disaster
come upon me.

CHORUS Sir, we too fear these things. But until you see this man face to face
and hear his story, hope.

OEDIPUS   Yes, I have just this much of hope — to wait until the herdsman comes.

JOCASTA   And when he comes, what do you want with him?

OEDIPUS   I'll tell you; if I find that his story is the same as yours, I at least will be clear of this guilt.

JOCASTA   Why what so particularly did you learn from my story?

OEDIPUS   You said that he spoke of highway *robbers* who killed Laius. Now if he uses the same number, it was not I who killed him. One man cannot be the same as many. But if he speaks of a man travelling alone, then clearly the burden of the guilt inclines towards me.

JOCASTA   Be sure, at least, that this was how he told the story. He cannot unsay it now, for every one in the city heard it — not I alone. But, Oedipus, even if he diverges from what he said then, he shall never prove that the murder of Laius squares rightly with the prophecy — for Loxias declared that the king should be killed by his own son. And that poor creature did not kill him surely, — for he died himself first. So as far as prophecy goes, henceforward I shall not look to the right hand or the left.

OEDIPUS   Right. But yet, send some one for the peasant to bring him here; do not neglect it.

JOCASTA   I will send quickly. Now let me go indoors. I will do nothing except what pleases you.

(*Exeunt.*)

Strophe

CHORUS   May destiny ever find me
pious in word and deed
prescribed by the laws that live on high:
laws begotten in the clear air of heaven,
whose only father is Olympus;
no mortal nature brought them to birth,
no forgetfulness shall lull them to sleep;
for God is great in them and grows not old.

Antistrophe

Insolence breeds the tyrant, insolence
if it is glutted with a surfeit, unseasonable, unprofitable,
climbs to the roof-top and plunges
sheer down to the ruin that must be,
and there its feet are no service.
But I pray that the God may never
abolish the eager ambition that profits the state.
For I shall never cease to hold the God as our protector.

Strophe

If a man walks with haughtiness
of hand or word and gives no heed

to Justice and the shrines of Gods
despises — may an evil doom
smite him for his ill-starred pride of heart! —
if he reaps gains without justice
and will not hold from impiety
and his fingers itch for untouchable things.
When such things are done, what man shall contrive
to shield his soul from the shafts of the God?
When such deeds are held in honour,
why should I honour the Gods in the dance?

Antistrophe

No longer to the holy place,
to the navel of earth I'll go
to worship, nor to Abae
nor to Olympia,
unless the oracles are proved to fit,
for all men's hands to point at.
O Zeus, if you are rightly called
the sovereign lord, all-mastering,
let this not escape you nor your ever-living power!
The oracles concerning Laius
are old and dim and men regard them not.
Apollo is nowhere clear in honour; God's service perishes.

(*Enter* JOCASTA, *carrying garlands.*)

JOCASTA   Princes of the land, I have had the thought to go
to the Gods' temples, bringing in my hand
garlands and gifts of incense, as you see.
For Oedipus excites himself too much
at every sort of trouble, not conjecturing,
like a man of sense, what will be from what was,
but he is always at the speaker's mercy,
when he speaks terrors. I can do no good
by my advice, and so I came as suppliant
to you, Lycaean Apollo, who are nearest.
These are the symbols of my prayer and this
my prayer: grant us escape free of the curse.
Now when we look to him we are all afraid;
he's pilot of our ship and he is frightened.

(*Enter* MESSENGER.)

MESSENGER   Might I learn from you, sirs, where is the house of Oedipus? Or best of all, if you know, where is the king himself?

CHORUS   This is his house and he is within doors. This lady is his wife and mother of his children.

MESSENGER   God bless you, lady, and God bless your household! God bless Oedipus' noble wife!

JOCASTA   God bless you, sir, for your kind greeting! What do you want of us that you have come here? What have you to tell us?

MESSENGER   Good news, lady. Good for your house and for your husband.

JOCASTA   What is your news? Who sent you to us?

MESSENGER   I come from Corinth and the news I bring will give you pleasure. Perhaps a little pain too.

JOCASTA   What is this news of double meaning?

MESSENGER   The people of the Isthmus will choose Oedipus to be their king. That is the rumour there.

JOCASTA   But isn't their king still old Polybus?

MESSENGER   No. He is in his grave. Death has got him.

JOCASTA   Is that the truth? Is Oedipus' father dead?

MESSENGER   May I die myself if it be otherwise!

JOCASTA (*to a servant*)   Be quick and run to the King with the news! O oracles of the Gods, where are you now? It was from this man Oedipus fled, lest he should be his murderer! And now he is dead, in the course of nature, and not killed by Oedipus.

(*Enter* OEDIPUS.)

OEDIPUS   Dearest Jocasta, why have you sent for me?

JOCASTA   Listen to this man and when you hear reflect what is the outcome of the holy oracles of the Gods.

OEDIPUS   Who is he? What is his message for me?

JOCASTA   He is from Corinth and he tells us that your father Polybus is dead and gone.

OEDIPUS   What's this you say, sir? Tell me yourself.

MESSENGER   Since this is the first matter you want clearly told: Polybus has gone down to death. You may be sure of it.

OEDIPUS   By treachery or sickness?

MESSENGER   A small thing will put old bodies asleep.

OEDIPUS   So he died of sickness, it seems, — poor old man!

MESSENGER   Yes, and of age — the long years he had measured.

OEDIPUS   Ha! Ha! O dear Jocasta, why should one
look to the Pythian hearth? Why should one look
to the birds screaming overhead? They prophesied
that I should kill my father! But he's dead,
and hidden deep in earth, and I stand here
who never laid a hand on spear against him, —

unless perhaps he died of longing for me,
and thus I am his murderer. But they,
the oracles, as they stand — he's taken them
away with him, they're dead as he himself is,
and worthless.

JOCASTA   That I told you before now.

OEDIPUS   You did, but I was misled by my fear.

JOCASTA   Then lay no more of them to heart, not one.

OEDIPUS   But surely I must fear my mother's bed?

JOCASTA   Why should man fear since chance is all in all
for him, and he can clearly foreknow nothing?
Best to live lightly, as one can, unthinkingly.
As to your mother's marriage bed, — don't fear it.
Before this, in dreams too, as well as oracles,
many a man has lain with his own mother.
But he to whom such things are nothing bears
his life most easily.

OEDIPUS   All that you say would be said perfectly
if she were dead; but since she lives I must
still fear, although you talk so well, Jocasta.

JOCASTA   Still in your father's death there's light of comfort?

OEDIPUS   Great light of comfort; but I fear the living.

MESSENGER   Who is the woman that makes you afraid?

OEDIPUS   Merope, old man, Polybus' wife.

MESSENGER   What about her frightens the queen and you?

OEDIPUS   A terrible oracle, stranger, from the Gods.

MESSENGER   Can it be told? Or does the sacred law
forbid another to have knowledge of it?

OEDIPUS   O no! Once on a time Loxias said
that I should lie with my own mother and
take on my hands the blood of my own father.
And so for these long years I've lived away
from Corinth; it has been to my great happiness;
but yet it's sweet to see the face of parents.

MESSENGER   This was the fear which drove you out of Corinth?

OEDIPUS   Old man, I did not wish to kill my father.

MESSENGER   Why should I not free you from this fear, sir,
since I have come to you in all goodwill?

OEDIPUS   You would not find me thankless if you did.

MESSENGER   Why, it was just for this I brought the news, —
  to earn your thanks when you had come safe home.

OEDIPUS   No, I will never come near my parents.

MESSENGER   Son,
  it's very plain you don't know what you're doing.

OEDIPUS   What do you mean, old man? For God's sake, tell me.

MESSENGER   If your homecoming is checked by fears like these.

OEDIPUS   Yes, I'm afraid that Phoebus may prove right.

MESSENGER   The murder and the incest?

OEDIPUS   Yes, old man;
  that is my constant terror.

MESSENGER   Do you know
  that all your fears are empty?

OEDIPUS   How is that,
  if they are father and mother and I their son?

MESSENGER   Because Polybus was no kin to you in blood.

OEDIPUS   What, was not Polybus my father?

MESSENGER   No more than I but just so much.

OEDIPUS   How can
  my father be my father as much as one
  that's nothing to me?

MESSENGER   Neither he nor I
  begat you.

OEDIPUS   Why then did he call me son?

MESSENGER   A gift he took you from these hands of mine.

OEDIPUS   Did he love so much what he took from another's hand?

MESSENGER   His childlessness before persuaded him.

OEDIPUS   Was I a child you bought or found when I
  was given to him?

MESSENGER   On Cithaeron's slopes
  in the twisting thickets you were found.

OEDIPUS   And why
  were you a traveller in those parts?

MESSENGER   I was
  in charge of mountain flocks.

OEDIPUS   You were a shepherd?
  A hireling vagrant?

MESSENGER   Yes, but at least at that time
    the man that saved your life, son.

OEDIPUS   What ailed me when you took me in your arms?

MESSENGER   In that your ankles should be witnesses.

OEDIPUS   Why do you speak of that old pain?

MESSENGER   I loosed you;
    the tendons of your feet were pierced and fettered, —

OEDIPUS   My swaddling clothes brought me a rare disgrace.

MESSENGER   So that from this you're called your present name.

OEDIPUS   Was this my father's doing or my mother's?
    For God's sake, tell me.

MESSENGER   I don't know, but he
    who gave you to me has more knowledge than I.

OEDIPUS   You yourself did not find me then? You took me
    from someone else?

MESSENGER   Yes, from another shepherd.

OEDIPUS   Who was he? Do you know him well enough
    to tell?

MESSENGER   He was called Laius' man.

OEDIPUS   You mean the king who reigned here in the old days?

MESSENGER   Yes, he was that man's shepherd.

OEDIPUS   Is he alive
    still, so that I could see him?

MESSENGER   You who live here
    would know that best.

OEDIPUS   Do any of you here
    know of this shepherd whom he speaks about
    in town or in the fields? Tell me. It's time
    that this was found out once for all.

CHORUS   I think he is none other than the peasant
    whom you have sought to see already; but
    Jocasta here can tell us best of that.

OEDIPUS   Jocasta, do you know about this man
    whom we have sent for? Is he the man he mentions?

JOCASTA   Why ask of whom he spoke? Don't give it heed;
    nor try to keep in mind what has been said.
    It will be wasted labour.

OEDIPUS   With such clues
    I could not fail to bring my birth to light.

JOCASTA   I beg you — do not hunt this out — I beg you,
    if you have any care for your own life.
    What I am suffering is enough.

OEDIPUS   Keep up
    your heart, Jocasta. Though I'm proved a slave,
    thrice slave, and though my mother is thrice slave,
    you'll not be shown to be of lowly lineage.

JOCASTA   O be persuaded by me, I entreat you;
    do not do this.

OEDIPUS   I will not be persuaded to let be
    the chance of finding out the whole thing clearly.

JOCASTA   It is because I wish you well that I
    give you this counsel — and it's the best counsel.

OEDIPUS   Then the best counsel vexes me, and has
    for some while since.

JOCASTA   O Oedipus, God help you!
    God keep you from the knowledge of who you are!

OEDIPUS   Here, some one, go and fetch the shepherd for me;
    and let her find her joy in her rich family!

JOCASTA   O Oedipus, unhappy Oedipus!
    that is all I can call you, and the last thing
    that I shall ever call you.

    (*Exit.*)

CHORUS   Why has the queen gone, Oedipus, in wild
    grief rushing from us? I am afraid that trouble
    will break out of this silence.

OEDIPUS   Break out what will! I at least shall be
    willing to see my ancestry, though humble.
    Perhaps she is ashamed of my low birth,
    for she has all a woman's high-flown pride.
    But I account myself a child of Fortune,
    beneficent Fortune, and I shall not be
    dishonoured. She's the mother from whom I spring;
    the months, my brothers, marked me, now as small,
    and now again as mighty. Such is my breeding,
    and I shall never prove so false to it,
    as not to find the secret of my birth.

    Strophe

CHORUS   If I am a prophet and wise of heart
    you shall not fail, Cithaeron,
    by the limitless sky, you shall not! —
    to know at tomorrow's full moon
    that Oedipus honours you,

as native to him and mother and nurse at once;
and that you are honoured in dancing by us, as finding favour in sight of our
  king.
Apollo, to whom we cry, find these things pleasing!

Antistrophe

Who was it bore you, child? One of
the long-lived nymphs who lay with Pan —
the father who treads the hills?
Or was she a bride of Loxias, your mother? The grassy slopes
are all of them dear to him. Or perhaps Cyllene's king
or the Bacchants' God that lives on the tops
of the hills received you a gift from some
one of the Helicon Nymphs, with whom he mostly plays?

(Enter an old man, led by Oedipus' servants.)

OEDIPUS If some one like myself who never met him
  may make a guess, — I think this is the herdsman,
  whom we were seeking. His old age is consonant
  with the other. And besides, the men who bring him
  I recognize as my own servants. You
  perhaps may better me in knowledge since
  you've seen the man before.

CHORUS   You can be sure
  I recognize him. For if Laius
  had ever an honest shepherd, this was he.

OEDIPUS You, sir, from Corinth, I must ask you first,
  is this the man you spoke of?

MESSENGER   This is he
  before your eyes.

OEDIPUS   Old man, look here at me
  and tell me what I ask you. Were you ever
  a servant of King Laius?

HERDSMAN   I was, —
  no slave he bought but reared in his own house.

OEDIPUS What did you do as work? How did you live?

HERDSMAN Most of my life was spent among the flocks.

OEDIPUS In what part of the country did you live?

HERDSMAN Cithaeron and the places near to it.

OEDIPUS And somewhere there perhaps you knew this man?

HERDSMAN What was his occupation? Who?

OEDIPUS   This man here,
  have you had any dealings with him?

HERDSMAN   No —
   not such that I can quickly call to mind.

MESSENGER   That is no wonder, master. But I'll make him remember what he
   does not know. For I know, that he well knows the country of Cithaeron,
   how he with two flocks, I with one kept company for three years — each
   year half a year — from spring till autumn time and then when winter came
   I drove my flocks to our fold home again and he to Laius' steadings. Well
   — am I right or not in what I said we did?

HERDSMAN   You're right — although it's a long time ago.

MESSENGER   Do you remember giving me a child
   to bring up as my foster child?

HERDSMAN   What's this?
   Why do you ask this question?

MESSENGER   Look old man,
   here he is — here's the man who was that child!

HERDSMAN   Death take you! Won't you hold your tongue?

OEDIPUS   No, no,
   do not find fault with him, old man. Your words
   are more at fault than his.

HERDSMAN   O best of masters,
   how do I give offense?

OEDIPUS   When you refuse
   to speak about the child of whom he asks you.

HERDSMAN   He speaks out of his ignorance, without meaning.

OEDIPUS   If you'll not talk to gratify me, you
   will talk with pain to urge you.

HERDSMAN   O please, sir,
   don't hurt an old man, sir.

OEDIPUS (*to the servants*)   Here, one of you,
   twist his hands behind him.

HERDSMAN   Why, God help me, why?
   What do you want to know?

OEDIPUS   You gave a child
   to him, — the child he asked you of?

HERDSMAN   I did.
   I wish I'd died the day I did.

OEDIPUS   You will
   unless you tell me truly.

HERDSMAN   And I'll die
   far worse if I should tell you.

OEDIPUS   This fellow
    is bent on more delays, as it would seem.

HERDSMAN   O no, no! I have told you that I gave it.

OEDIPUS   Where did you get this child from? Was it your own or did you get
    it from another?

HERDSMAN   Not
    my own at all; I had it from some one.

OEDIPUS   One of these citizens? or from what house?

HERDSMAN   O master, please — I beg you, master, please
    don't ask me more.

OEDIPUS   You're a dead man if I
    ask you again.

HERDSMAN   It was one of the children
    of Laius.

OEDIPUS   A slave? Or born in wedlock?

HERDSMAN   O God, I am on the brink of frightful speech.

OEDIPUS   And I of frightful hearing. But I must hear.

HERDSMAN   The child was called his child; but she within,
    your wife would tell you best how all this was.

OEDIPUS   *She* gave it to you?

HERDSMAN   Yes, she did, my lord.

OEDIPUS   To do what with it?

HERDSMAN   Make away with it.

OEDIPUS   She was so hard — its mother?

HERDSMAN   Aye, through fear
    of evil oracles.

OEDIPUS   Which?

HERDSMAN   They said that he
    should kill his parents.

OEDIPUS   How was it that you
    gave it away to this old man?

HERDSMAN   O master,
    I pitied it, and thought that I could send it
    off to another country and this man
    was from another country. But he saved it
    for the most terrible troubles. If you are
    the man he says you are, you're bred to misery.

OEDIPUS   O, O, O, they will all come,
        all come out clearly! Light of the sun, let me
        look upon you no more after today!
        I who first saw the light bred of a match
        accursed, and accursed in my living
        with them I lived with, cursed in my killing.

(*Exeunt all but the* CHORUS.)

Strophe

CHORUS   O generations of men, how I
        count you as equal with those who live
        not at all!
        What man, what man on earth wins more
        of happiness than a seeming
        and after that turning away?
        Oedipus, you are my pattern of this,
        Oedipus, you and your fate!
        Luckless Oedipus, whom of all men
        I envy not at all.

Antistrophe

    In as much as he shot his bolt
    beyond the others and won the prize
    of happiness complete —
    O Zeus — and killed and reduced to nought
    the hooked taloned maid of the riddling speech,
    standing a tower against death for my land:
    hence he was called my king and hence
    was honoured the highest of all
    honours; and hence he ruled
    in the great city of Thebes.

Strophe

    But now whose tale is more miserable?
    Who is there lives with a savager fate?
    Whose troubles so reverse his life as his?

    O Oedipus, the famous prince
    for whom a great haven
    the same both as father and son
    sufficed for generation,
    how, O how, have the furrows ploughed
    by your father endured to bear you, poor wretch,
    and hold their peace so long?

Antistrophe

    Time who sees all has found you out
    against your will; judges your marriage accursed,
    begetter and begot at one in it.

    O child of Laius,

would I had never seen you.
I weep for you and cry
a dirge of lamentation.

To speak directly, I drew my breath
from you at the first and so now I lull
my mouth to sleep with your name.

(*Enter a* SECOND MESSENGER.)

SECOND MESSENGER   O Princes always honoured by our country,
what deeds you'll hear of and what horrors see,
what grief you'll feel, if you as true born Thebans
care for the house of Labdacus's sons.
Phasis nor Ister cannot purge this house,
I think, with all their streams, such things
it hides, such evils shortly will bring forth
into the light, whether they will or not;
and troubles hurt the most
when they prove self-inflicted.

CHORUS   What we had known before did not fall short
of bitter groaning's worth; what's more to tell?

SECOND MESSENGER   Shortest to hear and tell — our glorious queen
Jocasta's dead.

CHORUS   Unhappy woman! How?

SECOND MESSENGER   By her own hand. The worst of what was done
you cannot know. You did not see the sight.
Yet in so far as I remember it
you'll hear the end of our unlucky queen.
When she came raging into the house she went
straight to her marriage bed, tearing her hair
with both her hands, and crying upon Laius
long dead — Do you remember, Laius,
that night long past which bred a child for us
to send you to your death and leave
a mother making children with her son?
And then she groaned and cursed the bed in which
she brought forth husband by her husband, children
by her own child, an infamous double bond.
How after that she died I do not know, —
for Oedipus distracted us from seeing.
He burst upon us shouting and we looked
to him as he paced frantically around,
begging us always: Give me a sword, I say,
to find this wife no wife, this mother's womb,
this field of double sowing whence I sprang
and where I sowed my children! As he raved
some god showed him the way — none of us there.
Bellowing terribly and led by some

invisible guide he rushed on the two doors, —
wrenching the hollow bolts out of their sockets,
he charged inside. There, there, we saw his wife
hanging, the twisted rope around her neck.
When he saw her, he cried out fearfully
and cut the dangling noose. Then, as she lay,
poor woman, on the ground, what happened after,
was terrible to see. He tore the brooches —
the gold chased brooches fastening her robe —
away from her and lifting them up high
dashed them on his own eyeballs, shrieking out
such things as: they will never see the crime
I have committed or had done upon me!
Dark eyes, now in the days to come look on
forbidden faces, do not recognize
those whom you long for — with such imprecations
he struck his eyes again and yet again
with the brooches. And the bleeding eyeballs gushed
and stained his beard — no sluggish oozing drops
but a black rain and bloody hail poured down.

So it has broken — and not on one head
but troubles mixed for husband and for wife.
The fortune of the days gone by was true
good fortune — but today groans and destruction
and death and shame — of all ills can be named
not one is missing.

CHORUS Is he now in any ease from pain?

SECOND MESSENGER   He shouts
for some one to unbar the doors and show him
to all the men of Thebes, his father's killer,
his mother's — no I cannot say the word,
it is unholy — for he'll cast himself,
out of the land, he says, and not remain
to bring a curse upon his house, the curse
he called upon it in his proclamation. But
he wants for strength, aye, and some one to guide him;
his sickness is too great to bear. You, too,
will be shown that. The bolts are opening.
Soon you will see a sight to waken pity
even in the horror of it.

(*Enter the blinded* OEDIPUS.)

CHORUS This is a terrible sight for men to see!
I never found a worse!
Poor wretch, what madness came upon you!
What evil spirit leaped upon your life
to your ill-luck — a leap beyond man's strength!
Indeed I pity you, but I cannot

look at you, though there's much I want to ask
and much to learn and much to see.
I shudder at the sight of you.

OEDIPUS   O, O,
where am I going? Where is my voice
borne on the wind to and fro?
Spirit, how far have you sprung?

CHORUS   To a terrible place whereof men's ears
may not hear, nor their eyes behold it.

OEDIPUS   Darkness!
Horror of darkness enfolding, resistless, unspeakable visitant sped by an ill
wind in haste!
madness and stabbing pain and memory
of evil deeds I have done!

CHORUS   In such misfortunes it's no wonder
if double weighs the burden of your grief.

OEDIPUS   My friend,
you are the only one steadfast, the only one that attends on me;
you still stay nursing the blind man.
Your care is not unnoticed. I can know
your voice, although this darkness is my world.

CHORUS   Doer of dreadful deeds, how did you dare
so far to do despite to your own eyes?
what spirit urged you to it?

OEDIPUS   It was Apollo, friends, Apollo,
that brought this bitter bitterness, my sorrows to completion.
But the hand that struck me
was none but my own.
Why should I see
whose vision showed me nothing sweet to see?

CHORUS   These things are as you say.

OEDIPUS   What can I see to love?
What greeting can touch my ears with joy?
Take me away, and haste — to a place out of the way!
Take me away, my friends, the greatly miserable,
the most accursed, whom God too hates
above all men on earth!

CHORUS   Unhappy in your mind and your misfortune,
would I had never known you!

OEDIPUS   Curse on the man who took
the cruel bonds from off my legs, as I lay in the field.
He stole me from death and saved me,
no kindly service.

Had I died then
I would not be so burdensome to friends.

CHORUS   I, too, could have wished it had been so.

OEDIPUS   Then I would not have come
to kill my father and marry my mother infamously.
Now I am godless and child of impurity,
begetter in the same seed that created my wretched self.
If there is any ill worse than ill,
that is the lot of Oedipus.

CHORUS   I cannot say your remedy was good;
you would be better dead than blind and living.

OEDIPUS   What I have done here was best done — don't tell me
otherwise, do not give me further counsel.
I do not know with what eyes I could look
upon my father when I die and go
under the earth, nor yet my wretched mother —
those two to whom I have done things deserving
worse punishment than hanging. Would the sight
of children, bred as mine are, gladden me?
No, not these eyes, never. And my city,
its towers and sacred places of the Gods,
of these I robbed my miserable self
when I commanded all to drive *him* out,
the criminal since proved by God impure
and of the race of Laius.
To this guilt I bore witness against myself —
with what eyes shall I look upon my people?
No. If there were a means to choke the fountain
of hearing I would not have stayed my hand
from locking up my miserable carcase,
seeing and hearing nothing; it is sweet
to keep our thoughts out of the range of hurt.

Cithaeron, why did you receive me? why
having received me did you not kill me straight?
And so I had not shown to men my birth.

O Polybus and Corinth and the house,
the old house that I used to call my father's —
what fairness you were nurse to, and what foulness
festered beneath! Now I am found to be
a sinner and a son of sinners. Crossroads,
and hidden glade, oak and the narrow way
at the crossroads, that drank my father's blood
offered you by my hands, do you remember
still what I did as you looked on, and what
I did when I came here? O marriage, marriage!
you bred me and again when you had bred

bred children of your child and showed to men
brides, wives and mothers and the foulest deeds
that can be in this world of ours.

Come — it's unfit to say what is unfit
to do. I beg of you in God's name hide me
somewhere outside your country, yes, or kill me,
or throw me into the sea, to be forever
out of your sight. Approach and deign to touch me
for all my wretchedness, and do not fear.
No man but I can bear my evil doom.

CHORUS   Here Creon comes in fit time to perform
or give advice in what you ask of us.
Creon is left sole ruler in your stead.

OEDIPUS   Creon! Creon! What shall I say to him?
How can I justly hope that he will trust me?
In what is past I have been proved towards him
an utter liar.

(*Enter* CREON.)

CREON   Oedipus, I've come
not so that I might laugh at you nor taunt you
with evil of the past. But if you still
are without shame before the face of men
reverence at least the flame that gives all life,
our Lord the Sun, and do not show unveiled
to him pollution such that neither land
nor holy rain nor light of day can welcome.

(*To a servant.*)

Be quick and take him in. It is most decent
that only kin should see and hear the troubles
of kin.

OEDIPUS   I beg you, since you've torn me from
my dreadful expectations and have come
in a most noble spirit to a man
that has used you vilely — do a thing for me.
I shall speak for your own good, not for my own.

CREON   What do you need that you would ask of me?

OEDIPUS   Drive me from here with all the speed you can
to where I may not hear a human voice.

CREON   Be sure, I would have done this had not I
wished first of all to learn from the God the course
of action I should follow.

OEDIPUS   But his word
has been quite clear to let the parricide,
the sinner, die.

CREON   Yes, that indeed was said.
But in the present need we had best discover
what we should do.

OEDIPUS   And will you ask about
a man so wretched?

CREON   Now even you will trust
the God.

OEDIPUS   So. I command you — and will beseech you —
to her that lies inside that house give burial
as you would have it; she is yours and rightly
you will perform the rites for her. For me —
never let this my father's city have me
living a dweller in it. Leave me live
in the mountains where Cithaeron is, that's called
my mountain, which my mother and my father
while they were living would have made my tomb.
So I may die by their decree who sought
indeed to kill me. Yet I know this much:
no sickness and no other thing will kill me.
I would not have been saved from death if not
for some strange evil fate. Well, let my fate
go where it will.
               Creon, you need not care
about my sons; they're men and so wherever
they are, they will not lack a livelihood.
But my two girls — so sad and pitiful —
whose table never stood apart from mine,
and everything I touched they always shared —
O Creon, have a thought for them! And most
I wish that you might suffer me to touch them
and sorrow with them.

(*Enter* ANTIGONE *and* ISMENE, OEDIPUS' *two daughters.*)

O my lord! O true noble Creon! Can I
really be touching them, as when I saw?
What shall I say?
Yes, I can hear them sobbing — my two darlings!
and Creon has had pity and has sent me
what I loved most?
Am I right?

CREON   You're right: it was I gave you this
because I knew from old days how you loved them
as I see now.

OEDIPUS   God bless you for it, Creon,
and may God guard you better on your road
than he did me!
               O Children,
where are you? Come here, come to my hands,

a brother's hands which turned your father's eyes,
those bright eyes you knew once, to what you see,
a father seeing nothing, knowing nothing,
begetting you from his own source of life.
I weep for you — I cannot see your faces —
I weep when I think of the bitterness
there will be in your lives, how you must live
before the world. At what assemblages
of citizens will you make one? to what
gay company will you go and not come home
in tears instead of sharing in the holiday?
And when you're ripe for marriage, who will he be,
the man who'll risk to take such infamy
as shall cling to my children, to bring hurt
on them and those that marry with them? What
curse is not there? "Your father killed his father
and sowed the seed where he had sprung himself
and begot you out of the womb that held him."
These insults you will hear. Then who will marry you?
No one, my children; clearly you are doomed
to waste away in barrenness unmarried.
Son of Menoeceus, since you are all the father
left these two girls, and we, their parents, both
are dead to them — do not allow them wander
like beggars, poor and husbandless.
They are of your own blood.
And do not make them equal with myself
in wretchedness; for you can see them now
so young, so utterly alone, save for you only.
Touch my hand, noble Creon, and say yes.
If you were older, children, and were wiser,
there's much advice I'd give you. But as it is,
let this be what you pray: give me a life
wherever there is opportunity
to live, and better life than was my father's.

CREON   Your tears have had enough of scope; now go within the house.

OEDIPUS   I must obey, though bitter of heart.

CREON   In season, all is good.

OEDIPUS   Do you know on what conditions I obey?

CREON   You tell me them,
and I shall know them when I hear.

OEDIPUS   That you shall send me out
to live away from Thebes.

CREON   That gift you must ask of the God.

OEDIPUS   But I'm now hated by the Gods.

CREON   So quickly you'll obtain your prayer.

OEDIPUS   You consent then?

CREON   What I do not mean, I do not use to say.

OEDIPUS   Now lead me away from here.

CREON   Let go the children, then, and come.

OEDIPUS   Do not take them from me.

CREON   Do not seek to be master in everything;
    for the things you mastered did not follow you throughout your life.

    (*As* CREON *and* OEDIPUS *go out.*)

CHORUS   You that live in my ancestral Thebes, behold this Oedipus, —
    him who knew the famous riddles and was a man most masterful;
    not a citizen who did not look with envy on his lot —
    see him now and see the breakers of misfortune swallow him!
    Look upon that last day always. Count no mortal happy till
    he has passed the final limit of his life secure from pain.

Exercises

1. The five choral odes divide the drama into six distinct parts. What does each contribute to the tight, well-knit structure of the plot?

2. In addition to connecting the present action with the past action, what purposes does the prologue serve?

3. Discuss the function of the chorus.

4. The play concentrates not on Oedipus' patricide, regicide, or incest, but on the most "dramatic" moment in his life. What is that moment?

5. In what ways is Oedipus noble, admirable, or good?

6. What flaws in Oedipus' character contribute to his fall?

7. How is Oedipus responsible for his misfortunes? How is Fate responsible?

8. The literal meaning of the name *Oedipus* is "swollen foot," and the more liberal meaning is "on the track of knowledge." How appropriate are these names to the character of Oedipus?

9. Explain the roles of Teiresias and Creon as contrasts to the character of Oedipus.

10. What possible themes does the drama suggest?

Topics for Writing

1. Discuss the crime of Laius and Jocasta, who knowingly attempted to kill their infant son by abandoning him.

2. The drama contains several clusters of images, all of them integrated with the theme. Show how the metaphors of vision and blindness bear on the theme.

3. Support the position of those critics who view *Oedipus the King* as one of the greatest tragedies in literature.

4. In his "Poetics," Aristotle defines the composition of the ideal tragedy. One of his requisites for the perfect plot is that an action be probable and, further, that it be the direct consequence of a preceding action. Demonstrate how this works in *Oedipus the King.*

5. Compare and contrast the injustices suffered by Oedipus and Jocasta. Consider these injustices as punishment — moderate or excessive.

Selected Bibliography   Sophocles

Adams, Sinclair M. *Sophocles the Playwright.* Toronto: University of Toronto Press, 1957.

Barstow, Marjorie. "Oedipus Rex: A Typical Greek Tragedy." *Classical Weekly,* October 5, 1912.

Bowra, C. M. *Sophoclean Tragedy.* Oxford: Oxford University Press, 1944.

Cameron, Alister. *The Identity of Oedipus the King: Five Essays on the Oedipus Tyrannus.* New York: New York University Press, 1968.

Carroll, J. P. "Some Remarks on the Questions in the *Oedipus Tyrannus.*" *Classical Journal,* 32 (April 1937), 406–416.

Cook, Albert. *Oedipus Rex: A Mirror for Greek Drama.* Belmont, Calif.: Wadsworth, 1963.

Cooper, Lane. *The Greek Genius and Its Influence.* Ithaca: Cornell University Press, 1952.

Earp, Frank R. *The Style of Sophocles.* New York: Russell & Russell, 1972.

Ehrenberg, V. *Sophocles and Pericles.* New York: Humanities Press, 1954.

Faber, M. D. "Self-Destruction in *Oedipus Rex.*" *American Imago,* 27 (Spring 1970), 41–51.

Fergusson, Francis. "*Oedipus Rex*: The Tragic Rhythm of Action." In *The Idea of a Theater.* Princeton, N.J.: Princeton University Press, 1949.

Harshbarger, Karl. "Who Killed Laïus?" *Tulane Drama Review,* 9 (1965), 120–131.

Hathorn, Richmond Y. "The Existential Oedipus." In *Tragedy, Myth, and Mystery.* Bloomington: Indiana University Press, 1962.

Hembold, W. C. "The Paradox of the Oedipus." *American Journal of Philology,* 72 (1951), 239 ff.

Kirkwood, Gordon M. *A Study of Sophoclean Drama.* Ithaca, N.Y.: Johnson Reprint, 1958.

Kitto, H. D. F. *Greek Tragedy: A Literary Study.* London: Methuen, 1950.

Knox, Bernard M. *The Heroic Temper: Studies in Sophoclean Tragedy*. Berkeley: University of California Press, 1965.

Mendell, Clarence W. "Oedipus: Sophocles and Seneca." In *Oedipus: Myth and Dramatic Form*. Eds. James L. Sanderson and Everett Zimmerman. Boston: Houghton Mifflin, 1968.

Musurillo, Herbert. "Sunken Imagery in Sophocles' Oedipus." *American Journal of Philology*, 77 (1957), 36–51.

Norwood, Gilbert. *Greek Tragedy*. New York: Hill & Wang, n.d.

Waldock, A. J. *Sophocles the Dramatist*. Cambridge: Cambridge University Press, 1951.

Whitman, Cedric H. *Sophocles: A Study in Heroic Humanism*. Cambridge, Mass.: Harvard University Press, 1951.

Woodward, Thomas, ed. *Sophocles: A Collection of Critical Essays*. Englewood Cliffs, N.J.: Prentice-Hall, 1966.

Bernard Shaw   *(1856–1950)*

Arms and the Man

Preface (1898)

Readers of the discourse with which the preceding volume commences will remember that I turned my hand to play-writing when a great deal of talk about "the New Drama," followed by the actual establishment of a "New Theatre" (the Independent), threatened to end in the humiliating discovery that the New Drama, in England at least, was a figment of the revolutionary imagination. This was not to be endured. I had rashly taken up the case; and rather than let it collapse I manufactured the evidence.

Man is a creature of habit. You cannot write three plays and then stop. Besides, the New movement did not stop. In 1894, Florence Farr, who had already produced Ibsen's Rosmersholm, was placed in command of the Avenue Theatre in London for a season on the new lines by Miss A. E. F. Horniman, who had family reasons for not yet appearing openly as a pioneer-manageress. There were, as available New Dramatists, myself, discovered by the Independent Theatre (at my own suggestion); Dr John Todhunter, who had been discovered before (his play The Black Cat had been one of the Independent's successes); and Mr W. B. Yeats, a genuine discovery. Dr Todhunter supplied A Comedy of Sighs: Mr Yeats, The Land of Heart's Desire. I, having nothing but unpleasant plays in my desk, hastily completed a first attempt at a pleasant one, and called it Arms and The Man, taking the title from the first line of Dryden's Virgil. It passed for a success, the applause on the first night being as promising as could be wished; and it ran from the 21st of April to the 7th of July. To witness it the public paid £1777:5:6, an average of £23:2:5 per representation (including nine matinées). A publisher receiving £1700 for a book would have made a satisfactory profit: experts in West End theatrical management will contemplate that figure with a grim smile.

In the autumn of 1894 I spent a few weeks in Florence, where I occupied myself with the religious art of the Middle Ages and its destruction by the Renascence. From a former visit to Italy on the same business I had hurried back to Birmingham to discharge my duties as musical critic at the Festival there. On that occasion a very remarkable collection of the works of our British "pre-Raphaelite" painters was on view. I looked at these, and then went into the Birmingham churches to see the windows of William Morris and Burne-Jones. On the whole, Birmingham was more hopeful than the Italian cities; for the art it had to shew me was the work of living men, whereas modern Italy had, as far as I could see, no more connection with Giotto than Port Said has with Ptolemy. Now I am no believer in the worth of any mere taste for art that cannot produce what it professes to appreciate. When my subsequent visit to Italy found me practising the playwright's craft, the time was ripe for a modern pre-Raphaelite play. Religion was alive again, coming back upon men, even upon clergymen, with such power that not the Church of England itself could keep it out. Here my activity as a Socialist had placed me on sure and familiar ground. To me the members of the Guild of St Matthew were no more "High Church clergymen," Dr Clifford no more "an eminent Nonconformist divine," than I was to them "an infidel." There is only one religion, though there are a hundred versions of it. We all had the same thing to say; and though some of us cleared our throats to say it by singing revolutionary lyrics and republican hymns, we thought nothing of singing them to the music of Sullivan's Onward Christian Soldiers or Haydn's God Preserve the Emperor.

Now unity, however desirable in political agitations, is fatal to drama; for every drama must present a conflict. The end may be reconciliation or destruction; or, as in life itself, there may be no end; but the conflict is indispensable: no conflict, no drama. Certainly it is easy to dramatize the prosaic conflict of Christian Socialism with vulgar Unsocialism: for instance, in Widowers' Houses, the clergyman, who does not appear on the stage at all, is the real antagonist of the slum landlord. But the obvious conflicts of unmistakeable good with unmistakable evil can only supply the crude drama of villain and hero, in which some absolute point of view is taken, and the dissentients are treated by the dramatist as enemies to be piously glorified or indignantly vilified. In such cheap wares I do not deal. Even in my unpleasant propagandist plays I have allowed every person his or her own point of view, and have, I hope, to the full extent of my understanding of him, been as sympathetic with Sir George Crofts as with any of the more genial and popular characters in the present volume. To distil the quintessential drama from pre-Raphaelitism, medieval or modern, it must be shewn at its best in conflict with the first broken, nervous, stumbling attempts to formulate its own revolt against itself as it develops into something higher. A coherent explanation of any such revolt, addressed intelligibly and prosaically to the intellect, can only come when the work is done, and indeed *done with*: that is to say, when the development, accomplished, admitted, and assimilated, is a story of yesterday. Long before any such understanding can be reached, the eyes of men begin to turn towards the distant light of the new age. Discernible at first only by the eyes of the man of genius, it must be focussed by him on the speculum of a work of art, and flashed back from that into the eyes of the common man. Nay, the artist himself has no other way of making himself conscious of the ray: it is by a blind instinct that he keeps on building up his masterpieces until their pinnacles catch the glint of the unrisen sun. Ask him to explain himself prosaically, and you find that he "writes like an angel and talks like poor Poll," and is himself the first to make that epigram at his own expense. John Ruskin has told us clearly enough what is in the pictures of Carpaccio and Bellini: let him explain, if he can, where we shall be when the sun that is caught by the summits of the work of his favorite Tintoretto, of his aversion Rembrandt, of Mozart, of Beethoven and Wagner, of Blake and of Shelley, shall have reached the valleys. Let Ibsen explain, if he can, why the building of churches and happy homes is not the ultimate destiny of Man, and why, to thrill the unsatisfied younger generations, he must mount beyond it to heights that now seem unspeakably giddy and dreadful to him, and from which the first climbers must fall and dash themselves to pieces. He cannot explain it: he can only shew it to you as a vision in the magic glass of his artwork; so that you may catch his presentiment and make what you can of it. And this is the function that raises dramatic art above imposture and pleasure hunting, and enables the playwright to be something more than a skilled liar and pandar.

Here, then, was the higher but vaguer and timider vision, the incoherent, mischievous, and even ridiculous unpracticalness, which offered me a dramatic antagonist for the clear, bold, sure, sensible, benevolent, salutarily shortsighted

Christian Socialist idealism. I availed myself of it in Candida, the drunken scene in which has been much appreciated, I am told, in Aberdeen. I purposely contrived the play in such a way as to make the expenses of representation insignificant; so that, without pretending that I could appeal to a very wide circle of playgoers, I could reasonably sound a few of our more enlightened managers as to an experiment with half a dozen afternoon performances. They admired the play generously: indeed I think that if any of them had been young enough to play the poet, my proposal might have been acceded to, in spite of many incidental difficulties. Nay, if only I had made the poet a cripple, or at least blind, so as to combine an easier disguise with a larger claim for sympathy, something might have been done. Richard Mansfield, who had, with apparent ease, made me quite famous in America by his productions of my plays, went so far as to put the play actually into rehearsal before he would confess himself beaten by the physical difficulties of the part. But they did beat him; and Candida did not see the footlights until my old ally the Independent Theatre, making a propagandist tour through the provinces with A Doll's House, added Candida to its repertory, to the great astonishment of its audiences.

In an idle moment in 1895 I began the little scene called The Man of Destiny, which is hardly more than a bravura piece to display the virtuosity of the two principal performers.

In the meantime I had devoted the spare moments of 1896 to the composition of two more plays, only the first of which appears in this volume. You Never Can Tell was an attempt to comply with many requests for a play in which the much paragraphed "brilliancy" of Arms and The Man should be tempered by some consideration for the requirements of managers in search of fashionable comedies for West End theatres. I had no difficulty in complying, as I have always cast my plays in the ordinary practical comedy form in use at all the theatres; and far from taking an unsympathetic view of the popular preference for fun, fashionable dresses, a little music, and even an exhibition of eating and drinking by people with an expensive air, attended by an if-possible-comic waiter, I was more than willing to shew that the drama can humanize these things as easily as they, in the wrong hands, can dehumanize the drama. But as often happens it was easier to do this than to persuade those who had asked for it that they had indeed got it. A chapter in Cyril Maude's history of the Haymarket Theatre records how the play was rehearsed there, and why I withdrew it. And so I reached the point at which, as narrated in the preface to the Unpleasant volume, I resolved to avail myself of my literary expertness to put my plays before the public in my own way.

It will be noticed that I have not been driven to this expedient by any hostility on the part of our managers. I will not pretend that the modern actor-manager's talent as player can in the nature of things be often associated with exceptional critical insight. As a rule, by the time a manager has experience enough to make him as safe a judge of plays as a Bond Street dealer is of pictures he begins to be thrown out in his calculations by the slow but constant change of public taste, and by his own growing conservatism. But his need for new plays is so great, and the few accredited authors are so little able to keep pace with their commissions, that he is always apt to overrate rather than to underrate his discoveries in the way of new pieces by new authors. An original work by a man of genius like Ibsen may, of course, baffle him as it baffles many professed critics; but in the beaten path of drama no unacted works of merit, suitable to his purposes, have been discovered; whereas the production, at great expense, of very faulty plays written by novices (not "backers") is by no means an unknown event. Indeed, to anyone who can estimate, even vaguely, the complicated trouble, the risk of heavy loss, and the initial expense and thought, involved by the production of a play, the ease with which dramatic authors, known and unknown, get their works performed must needs seem a wonder.

Only, authors must not expect managers to invest many thousands of pounds in plays, however fine (or the reverse), which will clearly not attract perfectly commonplace people. Playwriting and theatrical management, on the present commercial basis, are businesses like other businesses, depending on the patronage of great numbers of very ordinary customers. When the managers and authors study the wants of these customers, they succeed: when they do not, they fail. A public-spirited manager, or an author with a keen artistic conscience, may choose to pursue his business with the minimum of profit and the maximum of social usefulness by keeping as close as he can to the highest marketable limit of quality, and constantly feeling for an extension of that limit through the advance of popular culture. An unscrupulous manager or author may aim simply at the maximum of profit with the minimum of risk. These are the opposite poles of our system, represented in practice by our first rate managements at the one end, and the syndicates which exploit pornographic farces at the other. Between them there is plenty of room for most talents to breathe freely: at all events there is a career, no harder of access than any cognate career, for all qualified playwrights who bring the manager what his customers want and understand, or even enough of it to induce them to swallow at the same time a great deal that they neither want nor understand; for the public is touchingly humble in such matters.

For all that, the commercial limits are too narrow for our social welfare. The theatre is growing in importance as a social organ. Bad theatres are as mischievous as bad schools or bad churches; for modern civilization is rapidly multiplying the class to which the theatre is both school and church. Public and private life become daily more theatrical: the modern Kaiser, Dictator, President or Prime Minister is nothing if not an effective actor; all newspapers are now edited histrionically; and the records of our law courts shew that the stage is affecting personal conduct to an unprecedented extent, and affecting it by no means for the worse, except in so far as the theatrical education of the persons concerned has been romantic: that is, spurious, cheap, and vulgar. The truth is that dramatic invention is the first effort of man to become intellectually conscious. No frontier can be marked between drama and history or religion, or between acting and conduct, nor any distinction made between them that is not also the distinction between the masterpieces of the great dramatic poets and the commonplaces of our theatrical seasons. When this chapter of science is convincingly written, the national importance of the theatre will be as unquestioned as that of the army, the fleet, the Church, the law, and the schools.

For my part, I have no doubt that the commercial limits should be overstepped, and that the highest prestige, with a financial position of reasonable security and comfort, should be attainable in theatrical management by keeping the public in constant touch with the highest achievements of dramatic art. Our managers will not dissent to this: the best of them are so willing to get as near that position as they can without ruining themselves, that they can all point to honorable losses incurred through aiming "over the heads of the public," and will no doubt risk such loss again, for the sake of their reputation as artists, as soon as a few popular successes enable them to afford it. But even if it were possible for them to educate the nation at their own private cost, why should they be expected to do it? There are much stronger objections to the pauperization of the public by private doles than were ever entertained, even by the Poor Law Commissioners of 1834, to the pauperization of private individuals by public doles. If we want a theatre which shall be to the drama what the National Gallery and British Museum are to painting and literature, we can get it by endowing it in the same way. In the meantime there are many possibilities of local activity. Groups of amateurs can form permanent societies and persevere until they develop into professional companies in established repertory theatres. In big cities it should be feasible to form influential committees, preferably without any actors, critics, or playwrights on them, and with as many persons of title as possible, for the purpose of approaching one of the leading local managers with a proposal that they shall, under a guarantee against loss, undertake a certain number of afternoon performances of the class required by the committee, in addition to their ordinary business. If the committee is influential enough, the offer will be accepted. In that case, the first performance will be the beginning of a classic repertory for the manager and his company which every subsequent performance will extend. The formation of the repertory will go hand in hand with the discovery and habituation of a regular audience for it; and it will eventually become profitable for the manager to multiply the number of performances at his own risk. It might even become worth his while to take a second theatre and establish the repertory permanently in it. In the event of any of his classic productions proving a fashionable success, he could transfer it to his fashionable house and make the most of it there. Such managership would carry a knighthood with it; and such a theatre would be the needed nucleus for municipal or national endowment. I make the suggestion quite disinterestedly; for as I am not an academic person, I should not be welcomed as an unacted classic by such a committee; and cases like mine would still leave forlorn hopes like The Independent Theatre its reason for existing. The committee plan, I may remind its critics, has been in operation in London for two hundred years in support of Italian opera.

Returning now to the actual state of things, it is clear that I have no grievance against our theatres. Knowing quite well what I was doing, I have heaped difficulties in the way of the performance of my plays by ignoring the majority of the manager's customers: nay, by positively making war on them. To the actor I have been more considerate, using all my cunning to enable him to make the most of his technical methods; but I have not hesitated on occasion to tax his intelligence very severely, making the stage effect depend not only on *nuances* of execution quite beyond the average skill produced by the routine of the English stage in its present condition, but on a perfectly sincere and straightforward conception of states of mind which still seem cynically perverse to most people, and on a goodhumoredly contemptuous or profoundly pitiful attitude towards ethical conventions which seem to them validly heroic or venerable. It is inevitable that actors should suffer more than most of us from the sophistication of their consciousness by romance; and my view of romance as the great heresy to be swept off from art and life—as the food of modern pessimism and the bane of modern self-respect, is far more puzzling to the performers than it is to the pit. It is hard for an actor whose point of honor it is to be a perfect gentleman, to sympathize with an author who regards gentility as a dishonest folly, and gallantry and chivalry as treasonable to women and stultifying to men.

The misunderstanding is complicated by the fact that actors, in their demonstrations of emotion, have made a second nature of stage custom, which is often very much out of date as a representation of contemporary life. Sometimes the stage custom is not only obsolete, but fundamentally wrong: for instance, in the simple case of laughter and tears, in which it deals too liberally, it is certainly not based on the fact, easily enough discoverable in real life, that we only cry now in the effort to bear happiness, whilst we laugh and exult in destruction, confusion, and ruin. When a comedy is performed, it is nothing to me that the spectators laugh: any fool can make an audience laugh. I want to see how many of them, laughing or grave, are in the melting mood. And this result cannot be achieved, even by actors who thoroughly understand my purpose, except through an artistic beauty of execution unattainable without long and arduous practice, and an intellectual effort which my plays probably do not seem serious enough to call forth.

Beyond the difficulties thus raised by the nature and quality of my work, I have none to complain of. I have come upon no ill will, no inaccessibility, on the part of the very few managers with whom I have discussed it. As a rule I find that the actor-manager is over-sanguine, because he has the artist's habit of underrating the force of circumstances and exaggerating the power of the talented individual to prevail against them; whilst I have acquired the politician's habit of regarding the individual, however talented, as having no choice but to make the most of his circumstances. I half suspect that those managers who have had most to do with me, if asked to name the main obstacle to the performance of my plays, would unhesitatingly and unanimously reply "The author." And I confess that though as a matter of business I wish my plays to be performed, as a matter of instinct I fight against the inevitable misrepresentation of them with all the subtlety needed to conceal my ill will from myself as well as from the manager.

The main difficulty, of course, is the incapacity for serious drama of thousands of playgoers of all classes whose shillings and half guineas will buy as much in the market as if they delighted in the highest art. But with them I must frankly take the superior position. I know that many managers are wholly dependent on them, and that no manager is wholly independent of them; but I can no more write what they want than Joachim can put aside his fiddle and oblige a happy company of beanfeasters with a marching tune on the German concertina. They must keep away from my plays: that is all.

There is no reason, however, why I should take this haughty attitude towards those representative critics whose complaint is that my talent, though not unentertaining, lacks elevation of sentiment and seriousness of purpose. They can find, under the surface-brilliancy for which they give me credit, no coherent thought or sympathy, and accuse me, in various terms and degrees, of an inhuman and freakish wantonness; of preoccupation with "the seamy side of life"; of paradox, cynicism, and eccentricity, reducible, as some contend, to a trite formula of treating bad as good and good as bad, important as trivial and trivial as important, serious as laughable and laughable as serious, and so forth. As to this formula I can only say that if any gentleman is simple enough to think that even a good comic opera can be produced by it, I invite him to try his hand, and see whether anything resembling one of my plays will reward him.

I could explain the matter easily enough if I chose; but the result would be that the people who misunderstand the plays would misunderstand the explanation ten times more. The particular exceptions taken are seldom more than symptoms of the underlying fundamental disagreement between the romantic morality of the critics and the natural morality of the plays. For example, I am quite aware that the much criticized Swiss officer in Arms and The Man is not a conventional stage soldier. He suffers from want of food and sleep; his nerves go to pieces after three days under fire, ending in the horrors of a rout and pursuit; he has found by experience that it is more important to have a few bits of chocolate to eat in the field than cartridges for his revolver. When many of my critics rejected these circumstances as fantastically improbable and cynically unnatural, it was not necessary to argue them into common sense: all I had to do was to brain them, so to speak, with the first half dozen military authorities at hand, beginning with the present Commander in Chief. But when it proved that such unromantic (but all the more dramatic) facts implied to them a denial of the existence of courage, patriotism, faith, hope, and charity, I saw that it was not really mere matter of fact that was at issue between us. One strongly Liberal critic, the late Moy Thomas, who had, in the teeth of a chorus of dissent, received my first play with the most generous encouragement, declared, when Arms and The Man was produced, that I had struck a wanton blow at the cause of liberty in the Balkan Peninsula by mentioning that it was not a matter of course for a Bulgarian in 1885 to wash his hands every day. He no doubt saw soon afterwards the squabble, reported all through Europe, between Stambouloff and an eminent lady of the Bulgarian court who took exception to his neglect of his fingernails. After that came the news of his ferocious assassination, with a description of the room prepared for the reception of visitors by his widow, who draped it with black, and decorated it with photographs of the mutilated body of her husband. Here was a sufficiently sensational confirmation of the accuracy of my sketch of the theatrical nature of the first apings of western civilization by spirited races just emerging from slavery. But it had no bearing on the real issue between my critic and myself, which was, whether the political and religious idealism which had inspired Gladstone to call for the rescue of these Balkan principalities from the despotism of the Turk, and converted miserably enslaved provinces into hopeful and gallant little States, will survive the general onslaught on idealism which is implicit, and indeed explicit, in Arms and The Man and the naturalist plays of the modern school. For my part I hope not; for idealism, which is only a flattering name for romance in politics and morals, is as obnoxious to me as romance in ethics or religion. In spite of a Liberal Revolution or two, I can no longer be satisfied with fictitious morals and fictitious good conduct, shedding fictitious glory on robbery, starvation, disease, crime, drink, war, cruelty, cupidity, and all the other commonplaces of civilization which drive men to the theatre to make foolish pretences that such things are progress, science, morals, religion, patriotism, imperial supremacy, national greatness and all the other names the newspapers call them. On the other hand, I see plenty of good in the world working itself out as fast as the idealists will allow it; and if they would only let it alone and learn to respect reality, which would include the beneficial exercise of respecting themselves, and incidentally respecting me, we should all get along much better and faster. At all events, I do not see moral chaos and anarchy as the alternative to romantic convention; and I am not going to pretend I do merely to please the people who are convinced that the world is held together only by the force of unanimous, strenuous, eloquent, trumpet-tongued lying. To me the tragedy and comedy of life lie in the consequences, sometimes terrible, sometimes ludicrous, of our persistent attempts to found our institutions on the ideals suggested to our imaginations by our half-satisfied passions, instead of on a genuinely scientific natural history. And with that hint as to what I am driving at, I withdraw and ring up the curtain.

Characters

MAJOR PAUL PETKOFF	NICOLA
MAJOR SERGIUS SARANOFF	CATHERINE PETKOFF
CAPTAIN BLUNTSCHLI	RAÏNA PETKOFF
MAJOR PLECHANOFF	LOUKA

The action occurs at Major Petkoff's House in a small Bulgarian town, near the Dragoman Pass. 1885–86.

Act One

Night: A lady's bedchamber in Bulgaria, in a small town near the Dragoman Pass, late in November in the year 1885. Through an open window with a little balcony a peak of the Balkans, wonderfully white and beautiful in the starlit snow, seems quite close at hand, though it is really miles away. The interior of the room is not like anything to be seen in the west of Europe. It is half rich Bulgarian, half cheap Viennese. Above the head of the bed, which stands against a little wall cutting off the left hand corner of the room, is a painted wooden shrine, blue and gold, with an ivory image of Christ, and a light hanging before it in a pierced metal ball suspended by three chains. The principal seat, placed towards the other side of the room and opposite the window, is a Turkish ottoman. The counterpane and hangings of the bed, the window curtains, the little carpet, and all the ornamental textile fabrics in the room are oriental and gorgeous: the paper on the walls is occidental and paltry. The washstand, against the wall on the side nearest the ottoman and window, consists of an enamelled iron basin with a pail beneath it in a painted metal frame, and a single towel on the rail at the side. The dressing table, between the bed and the window, is a common pine table, covered with a cloth of many colors, with an expensive toilet mirror on it. The door is on the side nearest the bed; and there is a chest of drawers between. This chest of drawers is also covered by a variegated native cloth; and on it there is a pile of paper backed novels, a box of chocolate creams, and a miniature easel with a large photograph of an extremely handsome officer, whose lofty bearing and magnetic glance can be felt even from the portrait. The room is lighted by a candle on the chest of drawers, and another on the dressing table with a box of matches beside it.

The window is hinged doorwise and stands wide open. Outside, a pair of wooden shutters, opening outwards, also stand open. On the balcony a young lady, intensely conscious of the romantic beauty of the night, and of the fact that her own youth and beauty are part of it, is gazing at the snowy Balkans. She is in her nightgown, well covered by a long mantle of furs, worth, on a moderate estimate, about three times the furniture of her room.

Her reverie is interrupted by her mother, CATHERINE PETKOFF, *a woman over forty, imperiously energetic, with magnificent black hair and eyes, who might be a very splendid specimen of the wife of a mountain farmer, but is determined to be a Viennese lady, and to that end wears a fashionable tea gown on all occasions.*

CATHERINE (*entering hastily, full of good news*) Raina! (*She pronounces it Rah-eena, with the stress on the ee*). Raina! (*She goes to the bed, expecting to find* RAINA *there*). Why, where — ? (RAINA *looks into the room*). Heavens, child! are you out in the night air instead of in your bed? You'll catch your death. Louka told me you were asleep.

RAINA (*dreamily*) I sent her away. I wanted to be alone. The stars are so beautiful! What is the matter?

CATHERINE Such news! There has been a battle.

RAINA (*her eyes dilating*) Ah! (*She comes eagerly to* CATHERINE).

CATHERINE A great battle at Slivnitza! A victory! And it was won by Sergius.

RAINA (*with a cry of delight*) Ah! (*They embrace rapturously*) Oh, mother! (*Then, with sudden anxiety*) Is father safe?

CATHERINE Of course: he sends me the news. Sergius is the hero of the hour, the idol of the regiment.

RAINA Tell me, tell me. How was it? (*Ecstatically*) Oh, mother! mother! mother! (*She pulls her mother down on the ottoman; and they kiss one another frantically*).

CATHERINE (*with surging enthusiasm*) You cant guess how splendid it is. A cavalry charge! think of that! He defied our Russian commanders — acted without orders — led a charge on his own responsibility — headed it himself — was the first man to sweep through their guns. Cant you see it, Raina: our gallant splendid Bulgarians with their swords and eyes flashing, thundering down like an avalanche and scattering the wretched Serbs and their dandified Austrian officers like chaff. And you! you kept Sergius waiting a year before you would be betrothed to him. Oh, if you have a drop of Bulgarian blood in your veins, you will worship him when he comes back.

RAINA What will he care for my poor little worship after the acclamations of a whole army of heroes? But no matter: I am so happy! so proud! (*She rises and walks about excitedly*). It proves that all our ideas were real after all.

CATHERINE (*indignantly*) Our ideas real! What do you mean?

RAINA Our ideas of what Sergius would do. Our patriotism. Our heroic ideals. I sometimes used to doubt whether they were anything but dreams. Oh, what faithless little creatures girls are! When I buckled on Sergius's sword he looked so noble: it was treason to think of disillusion or humiliation or failure. And yet — and yet — (*She sits down again suddenly*) Promise me youll never tell him.

CATHERINE Dont ask me for promises until I know what I'm promising.

RAINA Well, it came into my head just as he was holding me in his arms and looking into my eyes, that perhaps we only had our heroic ideas because we are so fond of reading Byron and Pushkin, and because we were so delighted with the opera that season at Bucharest. Real life is so seldom like that!

indeed never, as far as I knew it then. (*Remorsefully*) Only think, mother: I doubted him: I wondered whether all his heroic qualities and his soldiership might not prove mere imagination when he went into a real battle. I had an uneasy fear that he might cut a poor figure there beside all those clever officers from the Tsar's court.

CATHERINE A poor figure! Shame on you! The Serbs have Austrian officers who are just as clever as the Russians; but we have beaten them in every battle for all that.

RAINA (*laughing and snuggling against her mother*) Yes: I was only a prosaic little coward. Oh, to think that it was all true! that Sergius is just as splendid and noble as he looks! that the world is really a glorious world for women who can see its glory and men who can act its romance! What happiness! what unspeakable fulfilment!

They are interrupted by the entry of LOUKA, *a handsome proud girl in a pretty Bulgarian peasant's dress with double apron, so defiant that her servility to* RAINA *is almost insolent. She is afraid of* CATHERINE, *but even with her goes as far as she dares.*

LOUKA If you please, madam, all the windows are to be closed and the shutters made fast. They say there may be shooting in the streets. (RAINA *and* CATHERINE *rise together, alarmed*). The Serbs are being chased right back through the pass; and they say they may run into the town. Our cavalry will be after them; and our people will be ready for them, you may be sure, now theyre running away. (*She goes out on the balcony, and pulls the outside shutters to; then steps back into the room*).

CATHERINE (*businesslike, her housekeeping instincts aroused*) I must see that everything is made safe downstairs.

RAINA I wish our people were not so cruel. What glory is there in killing wretched fugitives?

CATHERINE Cruel! Do you suppose they would hesitate to kill you — or worse?

RAINA (*to* LOUKA) Leave the shutters so that I can just close them if I hear any noise.

CATHERINE (*authoritatively, turning on her way to the door*) Oh no, dear: you must keep them fastened. You would be sure to drop off to sleep and leave them open. Make them fast, Louka.

LOUKA Yes, madam. (*She fastens them*).

RAINA Dont be anxious about me. The moment I hear a shot, I shall blow out the candles and roll myself up in bed with my ears well covered.

CATHERINE Quite the wisest thing you can do, my love. Goodnight.

RAINA Goodnight. (*Her emotion comes back for a moment*). Wish me joy. (*They kiss*). This is the happiest night of my life — if only there are no fugitives.

CATHERINE Go to bed, dear; and dont think of them. (*She goes out*).

LOUKA (*secretly, to* RAINA) If you would like the shutters open, just give them a push like this (*she pushes them: they open: she pulls them to again*). One of them ought to be bolted at the bottom; but the bolt's gone.

RAINA (*with dignity, reproving her*) Thanks, Louka; but we must do what we are told. (LOUKA *makes a grimace*). Goodnight.

LOUKA (*carelessly*) Goodnight. (*She goes out, swaggering*).

RAINA, *left alone, takes off her fur cloak and throws it on the ottoman. Then she goes to the chest of drawers, and adores the portrait there with feelings that are beyond all expression. She does not kiss it or press it to her breast, or shew it any mark of bodily affection; but she takes it in her hands and elevates it, like a priestess.*

RAINA (*looking up at the picture*) Oh, I shall never be unworthy of you any more, my soul's hero: never, never, never. (*She replaces it reverently. Then she selects a novel from the little pile of books. She turns over the leaves dreamily; finds her page; turns the book inside out at it; and, with a happy sigh, gets into bed and prepares to read herself to sleep. But before abandoning herself to fiction, she raises her eyes once more, thinking of the blessed reality, and murmurs*) My hero! my hero!

A distant shot breaks the quiet of the night. She starts, listening; and two more shots, much nearer, follow, startling her so that she scrambles out of bed, and hastily blows out the candle on the chest of drawers. Then, putting her fingers in her ears, she runs to the dressing table, blows out the light there, and hurries back to bed in the dark, nothing being visible but the glimmer of the light in the pierced ball before the image, and starlight seen through the slits at the top of the shutters. The firing breaks out again: there is a startling fusillade quite close at hand. Whilst it is still echoing, the shutters disappear, pulled open from without; and for an instant the rectangle of snowy starlight flashes out with the figure of a man silhouetted in black upon it. The shutters close immediately; and the room is dark again. But the silence is now broken by the sound of panting. Then there is a scratch and the flame of a match is seen in the middle of the room.

RAINA (*crouching on the bed*) Who's there? (*The match is out instantly*). Who's there? Who is that?

A MAN'S VOICE (*in the darkness, subduedly, but threateningly*) Sh — sh! Dont call out; or youll be shot. Be good; and no harm will happen to you. (*She is heard leaving her bed, and making for the door*). Take care: it's no use trying to run away.

RAINA But who —

THE VOICE (*warning*) Remember: if you raise your voice my revolver will go off. (*Commandingly*). Strike a light and let me see you. Do you hear. (*Another moment of silence and darkness as she retreats to the chest of drawers. Then she lights a candle; and the mystery is at an end. He is a man of about 35, in a deplorable plight, bespattered with mud and blood and snow, his belt and the strap of his revolver-case keeping together the torn ruins of the blue tunic of a Serbian artillery officer. All that the candlelight and his unwashed unkempt condition make it possible to discern is that he is of middling stature and undistinguished appearance, with strong neck and shoulders, roundish obstinate looking head covered with short crisp bronze curls, clear quick eyes and good brows and mouth, hopelessly prosaic nose like that of a strong minded baby, trim soldierlike carriage and energetic manner, and with all his wits about him in spite of his desperate predicament: even with a sense of the humor of it, without, however, the least intention of trifling with it or throwing away a chance. Reckoning up what he can guess about* RAINA: *her age, her social position, her character, and the extent to which she is frightened, he continues, more politely but still most determinedly*) Excuse my disturbing you; but you recognize my uniform? Serb! If I'm caught I shall be killed. (*Menacingly*) Do you understand that?

RAINA Yes.

THE MAN   Well I dont intend to get killed if I can help it. (*Still more formidably*) Do you understand that? (*He locks the door quickly but quietly*).

RAINA (*disdainfully*)   I suppose not. (*She draws herself up superbly, and looks him straight in the face, adding with cutting emphasis*) Some soldiers, I know, are afraid to die.

THE MAN (*with grim goodhumor*)   All of them, dear lady, all of them, believe me. It is our duty to live as long as we can. Now, if you raise an alarm —

RAINA (*cutting him short*)   You will shoot me. How do you know that *I* am afraid to die?

THE MAN (*cunningly*)   Ah; but suppose I dont shoot you, what will happen then? A lot of your cavalry will burst into this pretty room of yours and slaughter me here like a pig; for I'll fight like a demon: they shant get me into the street to amuse themselves with: I know what they are. Are you prepared to receive that sort of company in your present undress? (RAINA, *suddenly conscious of her nightgown, instinctively shrinks, and gathers it more closely about her neck. He watches her, and adds, pitilessly*) Hardly presentable, eh? (*She turns to the ottoman. He raises his pistol instantly, and cries*) Stop! (*She stops*). Where are you going?

RAINA (*with dignified patience*)   Only to get my cloak.

THE MAN (*passing swiftly to the ottoman and snatching the cloak*)   A good idea! I'll keep the cloak; and youll take care that nobody comes in and sees you without it. This is a better weapon than the revolver: eh? (*He throws the pistol down on the ottoman*).

RAINA (*revolted*)   It is not the weapon of a gentleman!

THE MAN   It's good enough for a man with only you to stand between him and death. (*As they look at one another for a moment,* RAINA *hardly able to believe that even a Serbian officer can be so cynically and selfishly unchivalrous, they are startled by a sharp fusillade in the street. The chill of imminent death hushes the man's voice as he adds*) Do you hear? If you are going to bring those blackguards in on me you shall receive them as you are.

Clamor and disturbance. The pursuers in the street batter at the house door, shouting Open the door! Open the door! Wake up, will you! *A man servant's voice calls to them angrily from within. This is Major Petkoff's house: you cant come in here; but a renewal of the clamor, and a torrent of blows on the door, end with his letting a chain down with a clank, followed by a rush of heavy footsteps and a din of triumphant yells, dominated at last by the voice of* CATHERINE, *indignantly addressing an officer with* What does this mean, sir? Do you know where you are? *The noise subsides suddenly.*

LOUKA (*outside, knocking at the bedroom door*)   My lady! my lady! get up quick and open the door. If you dont they will break it down.

The fugitive throws up his head with the gesture of a man who sees that it is all over with him, and drops the manner he has been assuming to intimidate RAINA.

THE MAN (*sincerely and kindly*)   No use, dear: I'm done for. (*Flinging the cloak to her*) Quick! wrap yourself up: theyre coming.

RAINA   Oh, thank you. (*She wraps herself up with intense relief*).

THE MAN (*between his teeth*)   Dont mention it.

RAINA (*anxiously*)   What will you do?

THE MAN (*grimly*) The first man in will find out. Keep out of the way; and dont look. It wont last long; but it will not be nice. (*He draws his sabre and faces the door, waiting*).

RAINA (*impulsively*) I'll help you. I'll save you.

THE MAN You cant.

RAINA I can. I'll hide you. (*She drags him towards the window*). Here! behind the curtains.

THE MAN (*yielding to her*) Theres just half a chance, if you keep your head.

RAINA (*drawing the curtain before him*) S-sh! (*She makes for the ottoman*).

THE MAN (*putting out his head*) Remember —

RAINA (*running back to him*) Yes?

THE MAN — nine soldiers out of ten are born fools.

RAINA Oh! (*She draws the curtain angrily before him*).

THE MAN (*looking out at the other side*) If they find me, I promise you a fight: a devil of a fight.

She stamps at him. He disappears hastily. She takes off her cloak, and throws it across the foot of the bed. Then, with a sleepy, disturbed air, she opens the door. LOUKA *enters excitedly.*

LOUKA One of those beasts of Serbs has been seen climbing up the waterpipe to your balcony. Our men want to search for him; and they are so wild and drunk and furious. (*She makes for the other side of the room to get as far from the door as possible*). My lady says you are to dress at once, and to — (*She sees the revolver lying on the ottoman, and stops, petrified*).

RAINA (*as if annoyed at being disturbed*) They shall not search here. Why have they been let in?

CATHERINE (*coming in hastily*) Raina, darling: are you safe? Have you seen anyone or heard anything?

RAINA I heard the shooting. Surely the soldiers will not dare come in here?

CATHERINE I have found a Russian officer, thank Heaven: he knows Sergius. (*Speaking through the door to someone outside*) Sir: will you come in now. My daughter will receive you.

A young Russian officer, in Bulgarian uniform, enters, sword in hand.

OFFICER (*with soft feline politeness and stiff military carriage*) Good evening, gracious lady. I am sorry to intrude; but there is a Serb hiding on the balcony. Will you and the gracious lady your mother please to withdraw whilst we search?

RAINA (*petulantly*) Nonsense, sir: you can see that there is no one on the balcony. (*She throws the shutters wide open and stands with her back to the curtain where the man is hidden, pointing to the moonlit balcony. A couple of shots are fired right under the window; and a bullet shatters the glass opposite* RAINA, *who winks and gasps, but stands her ground; whilst* CATHERINE *screams, and the officer, with a cry of* Take care! *rushes to the balcony*).

THE OFFICER (*on the balcony, shouting savagely down to the street*) Cease firing there, you fools: do you hear? Cease firing, damn you! (*He glares down for a moment; then turns to* RAINA, *trying to resume his polite manner*). Could anyone have got in without your knowledge? Were you asleep?

RAINA No: I have not been to bed.

THE OFFICER (*impatiently, coming back into the room*) Your neighbors have their heads so full of runaway Serbs that they see them everywhere. (*Politely*) Gracious lady: a thousand pardons. Goodnight. (*Military bow,*

which RAINA *returns coldly. Another to* CATHERINE, *who follows him out).*
RAINA *closes the shutters. She turns and sees* LOUKA, *who has been watching the scene curiously.*

RAINA   Dont leave my mother, Louka, until the soldiers go away.

LOUKA *glances at* RAINA, *at the ottoman, at the curtain; then purses her lips secretively, laughs insolently, and goes out.* RAINA, *highly offended by this demonstration, follows her to the door, and shuts it behind her with a slam, locking it violently. The man immediately steps out from behind the curtain, sheathing his sabre. Then, dismissing the danger from his mind in a business-like way, he comes affably to* RAINA.

THE MAN   A narrow shave; but a miss is as good as a mile. Dear young lady: your servant to the death. I wish for your sake I had joined the Bulgarian army instead of the other one. I am not a native Serb.

RAINA (*haughtily*)   No: you are one of the Austrians who set the Serbs on to rob us of our national liberty, and who officer their army for them. We hate them!

THE MAN   Austrian! not I. Dont hate me, dear young lady. I am a Swiss, fighting merely as a professional soldier. I joined the Serbs because they came first on the road from Switzerland. Be generous: youve beaten us hollow.

RAINA   Have I not been generous?

THE MAN   Noble! Heroic! But I'm not saved yet. This particular rush will soon pass through; but the pursuit will go on all night by fits and starts. I must take my chance to get off in a quiet interval. (*Pleasantly*) You dont mind my waiting just a minute or two, do you?

RAINA (*putting on her most genteel society manner*)   Oh, not at all. Wont you sit down?

THE MAN   Thanks. (*He sits on the foot of the bed*).

RAINA *walks with studied elegance to the ottoman and sits down. Unfortunately she sits on the pistol, and jumps up with a shriek. The man, all nerves, shies like a frightened horse to the other side of the room.*

THE MAN (*irritably*)   Dont frighten me like that. What is it?

RAINA   Your revolver! It was staring that officer in the face all the time. What an escape!

THE MAN (*vexed at being unnecessarily terrified*)   Oh, is that all?

RAINA (*staring at him rather superciliously as she conceives a poorer and poorer opinion of him, and feels proportionately more and more at her ease*)   I am sorry I frightened you. (*She takes up the pistol and hands it to him*). Pray take it to protect yourself against me.

THE MAN (*grinning wearily at the sarcasm as he takes the pistol*)   No use, dear young lady: theres nothing in it. It's not loaded. (*He makes a grimace at it, and drops it disparagingly into his revolver case*).

RAINA   Load it by all means.

THE MAN   Ive no ammunition. What use are cartridges in battle? I always carry chocolate instead; and I finished the last cake of that hours ago.

RAINA (*outraged in her most cherished ideals of manhood*)   Chocolate! Do you stuff your pockets with sweets — like a schoolboy — even in the field?

THE MAN (*grinning*)   Yes: isnt it contemptible? (*Hungrily*) I wish I had some now.

RAINA   Allow me. (*She sails away scornfully to the chest of drawers, and re-*

turns with the box of confectionery in her hand). I am sorry I have eaten all except these. (*She offers him the box*).

THE MAN (*ravenously*) Youre an angel! (*He gobbles the contents*). Creams! Delicious! (*He looks anxiously to see whether there are any more. There are none: he can only scrape the box with his fingers and suck them. When that nourishment is exhausted he accepts the inevitable with pathetic goodhumor, and says, with grateful emotion*) Bless you, dear lady! You can always tell an old soldier by the inside of his holsters and cartridge boxes. The young ones carry pistols and cartridges: the old ones, grub. Thank you. (*He hands back the box. She snatches it contemptuously from him and throws it away. He shies again, as if she had meant to strike him*). Ugh! Dont do things so suddenly, gracious lady. It's mean to revenge yourself because I frightened you just now.

RAINA (*loftily*) Frighten me! Do you know, sir, that though I am only a woman, I think I am at heart as brave as you.

THE MAN I should think so. You havnt been under fire for three days as I have. I can stand two days without shewing it much; but no man can stand three days: I'm as nervous as a mouse. (*He sits down on the ottoman, and takes his head in his hands*). Would you like to see me cry?

RAINA (*alarmed*) No.

THE MAN If you would, all you have to do is to scold me just as if I were a little boy and you my nurse. If I were in camp now, theyd play all sorts of tricks on me.

RAINA (*a little moved*) I'm sorry. I wont scold you. (*Touched by the sympathy in her tone, he raises his head and looks gratefully at her: she immediately draws back and says stiffly*) You must excuse me: our soldiers are not like that. (*She moves away from the ottoman*).

THE MAN Oh yes they are. There are only two sorts of soldiers: old ones and young ones. Ive served fourteen years: half of your fellows never smelt powder before. Why, how is it that youve just beaten us? Sheer ignorance of the art of war, nothing else. (*Indignantly*) I never saw anything so unprofessional.

RAINA (*ironically*) Oh! was it unprofessional to beat you?

THE MAN Well, come! is it professional to throw a regiment of cavalry on a battery of machine guns, with the dead certainty that if the guns go off not a horse or man will ever get within fifty yards of the fire? I couldnt believe my eyes when I saw it.

RAINA (*eagerly turning to him, as all her enthusiasm and her dreams of glory rush back on her*) Did you see the great cavalry charge? Oh, tell me about it. Describe it to me.

THE MAN You never saw a cavalry charge, did you?

RAINA How could I?

THE MAN Ah, perhaps not. No: of course not! Well, it's a funny sight. It's like slinging a handful of peas against a window pane: first one comes; then two or three close behind him; and then all the rest in a lump.

RAINA (*her eyes dilating as she raises her clasped hands ecstatically*) Yes, first One! the bravest of the brave!

THE MAN (*prosaically*) Hm! you should see the poor devil pulling at his horse.

RAINA Why should he pull at his horse?

THE MAN (*impatient of so stupid a question*) It's running away with him, of course: do you suppose the fellow wants to get there before the others and be killed? Then they all come. You can tell the young ones by their wildness and their slashing. The old ones come bunched up under the number one guard: they know that theyre mere projectiles, and that it's no use trying to fight. The wounds are mostly broken knees, from the horses cannoning together.

RAINA Ugh! But I dont believe the first man is a coward. I know he is a hero!

THE MAN (*goodhumoredly*) Thats what youd have said if youd seen the first man in the charge today.

RAINA (*breathless, forgiving him everything*) Ah, I knew it! Tell me. Tell me about him.

THE MAN He did it like an operatic tenor. A regular handsome fellow, with flashing eyes and lovely moustache, shouting his war-cry and charging like Don Quixote at the windmills. We did laugh.

RAINA You dared to laugh!

THE MAN Yes; but when the sergeant ran up as white as a sheet, and told us theyd sent us the wrong ammunition, and that we couldnt fire a round for the next ten minutes, we laughed at the other side of our mouths. I never felt so sick in my life; though I've been in one or two very tight places. And I hadnt even a revolver cartridge: only chocolate. We'd no bayonets: nothing. Of course, they just cut us to bits. And there was Don Quixote flourishing like a drum major, thinking he'd done the cleverest thing ever known, whereas he ought to be courtmartialled for it. Of all the fools ever let loose on a field of battle, that man must be the very maddest. He and his regiment simply committed suicide; only the pistol missed fire: thats all.

RAINA (*deeply wounded, but steadfastly loyal to her ideals*) Indeed! Would you know him again if you ever saw him?

THE MAN Shall I ever forget him!

She again goes to the chest of drawers. He watches her with a vague hope that she may have something more for him to eat. She takes the portrait from its stand and brings it to him.

RAINA That is a photograph of the gentleman — the patriot and hero — to whom I am betrothed.

THE MAN (*recognizing it with a shock*) I'm really very sorry. (*Looking at her*) Was it fair to lead me on? (*He looks at the portrait again*) Yes: thats Don Quixote: not a doubt of it. (*He stifles a laugh*).

RAINA (*quickly*) Why do you laugh?

THE MAN (*apologetic, but still greatly tickled*) I didnt laugh, I assure you. At least I didnt mean to. But when I think of him charging the windmills and imagining he was doing the finest thing — (*He chokes with suppressed laughter*).

RAINA (*sternly*) Give me back the portrait, sir.

THE MAN (*with sincere remorse*) Of course. Certainly. I'm really very sorry. (*He hands her the picture. She deliberately kisses it and looks him straight in the face before returning to the chest of drawers to replace it. He follows her, apologizing*). Perhaps I'm quite wrong, you know: no doubt I am. Most likely he had got wind of the cartridge business somehow, and knew it was a safe job.

RAINA That is to say, he was a pretender and a coward! You did not dare say that before.

THE MAN (*with a comic gesture of despair*)   It's no use, dear lady: I cant make you see it from the professional point of view. (*As he turns away to get back to the ottoman, a couple of distant shots threaten renewed trouble*).

RAINA (*sternly, as she sees him listening to the shots*)   So much the better for you!

THE MAN (*turning*)   How?

RAINA   You are my enemy; and you are at my mercy. What would I do if I were a professional soldier?

THE MAN   Ah, true, dear young lady: youre always right. I know how good youve been to me: to my last hour I shall remember those three chocolate creams. It was unsoldierly; but it was angelic.

RAINA (*coldly*)   Thank you. And now I will do a soldierly thing. You cannot stay here after what you have just said about my future husband; but I will go out on the balcony and see whether it is safe for you to climb down into the street. (*She turns to the window*).

THE MAN (*changing countenance*)   Down that waterpipe! Stop! Wait! I cant! I darent! The very thought of it makes me giddy. I came up it fast enough with death behind me. But to face it now in cold blood — ! (*He sinks on the ottoman*). It's no use: I give up: I'm beaten. Give the alarm. (*He drops his head on his hands in the deepest dejection*).

RAINA (*disarmed by pity*)   Come: dont be disheartened. (*She stoops over him almost maternally: he shakes his head*). Oh, you are a very poor soldier: a chocolate cream soldier! Come, cheer up! it takes less courage to climb down than to face capture: remember that.

THE MAN (*dreamily, lulled by her voice*)   No: capture only means death; and death is sleep: oh, sleep, sleep, sleep, undisturbed sleep! Climbing down the pipe means doing something — exerting myself — thinking! Death ten times over first.

RAINA (*softly and wonderingly, catching the rhythm of his weariness*)   Are you as sleepy as that?

THE MAN   Ive not had two hours undisturbed sleep since I joined. I havnt closed my eyes for forty-eight hours.

RAINA (*at her wit's end*)   But what am I to do with you?

THE MAN (*staggering up, roused by her desperation*)   Of course. I must do something. (*He shakes himself; pulls himself together; and speaks with rallied vigor and courage*). You see, sleep or no sleep, hunger or no hunger, tired or not tired, you can always do a thing when you know it must be done. Well, that pipe must be got down: (*he hits himself on the chest*) do you hear that, you chocolate cream soldier? (*He turns to the window*).

RAINA (*anxiously*)   But if you fall?

THE MAN   I shall sleep as if the stones were a feather bed. Goodbye. (*He makes boldly for the window; and his hand is on the shutter when there is a terrible burst of firing in the street beneath*).

RAINA (*rushing to him*)   Stop! (*She seizes him recklessly, and pulls him quite round*). Theyll kill you.

THE MAN (*coolly, but attentively*)   Never mind: this sort of thing is all in my day's work. I'm bound to take my chance. (*Decisively*) Now do what I tell you. Put out the candle; so that they shant see the light when I open the shutters. And keep away from the window, whatever you do. If they see me theyre sure to have a shot at me.

RAINA (*clinging to him*) Theyre sure to see you: it's bright moonlight. I'll save you. Oh, how can you be so indifferent! You want me to save you, dont you?

THE MAN I really dont want to be troublesome. (*She shakes him in her impatience*). I am not indifferent, dear young lady, I assure you. But how is it to be done?

RAINA Come away from the window. (*She takes him firmly back to the middle of the room. The moment she releases him he turns mechanically towards the window again. She seizes him and turns him back, exclaiming*) Please! (*He becomes motionless, like a hypnotized rabbit, his fatigue gaining fast on him. She releases him, and addresses him patronizingly*). Now listen. You must trust to our hospitality. You do not yet know in whose house you are. I am a Petkoff.

THE MAN A pet what?

RAINA (*rather indignantly*) I mean that I belong to the family of the Petkoffs, the richest and best known in our country.

THE MAN Oh yes, of course. I beg your pardon. The Petkoffs, to be sure. How stupid of me!

RAINA You know you never heard of them until this moment. How can you stoop to pretend!

THE MAN Forgive me: I'm too tired to think; and the change of subject was too much for me. Dont scold me.

RAINA I forgot. It might make you cry. (*He nods, quite seriously. She pouts and then resumes her patronizing tone*). I must tell you that my father holds the highest command of any Bulgarian in our army. He is (*proudly*) a Major.

THE MAN (*pretending to be deeply impressed*) A Major! Bless me! Think of that!

RAINA You shewed great ignorance in thinking that it was necessary to climb up to the balcony because ours is the only private house that has two rows of windows. There is a flight of stairs inside to get up and down by.

THE MAN Stairs! How grand! You live in great luxury indeed, dear young lady.

RAINA Do you know what a library is?

THE MAN A library? A roomful of books?

RAINA Yes. We have one, the only one in Bulgaria.

THE MAN Actually a real library! I should like to see that.

RAINA (*affectedly*) I tell you these things to shew you that you are not in the house of ignorant country folk who would kill you the moment they saw your Serbian uniform, but among civilized people. We go to Bucharest every year for the opera season; and I have spent a whole month in Vienna.

THE MAN I saw that, dear young lady. I saw at once that you knew the world.

RAINA Have you ever seen the opera of Ernani?

THE MAN Is that the one with the devil in it in red velvet, and a soldiers' chorus?

RAINA (*contemptuously*) No!

THE MAN (*stifling a heavy sigh of weariness*) Then I dont know it.

RAINA I thought you might have remembered the great scene where Ernani, flying from his foes just as you are tonight, takes refuge in the castle of his bitterest enemy, an old Castilian noble. The noble refuses to give him up. His guest is sacred to him.

THE MAN (*quickly, waking up a little*) Have your people got that notion?

RAINA (*with dignity*) My mother and I can understand that notion, as you call it. And if instead of threatening me with your pistol as you did you had simply thrown yourself as a fugitive on our hospitality, you would have been as safe as in your father's house.

THE MAN Quite sure?

RAINA (*turning her back on him in disgust*) Oh, it is useless to try to make you understand.

THE MAN Dont be angry: you see how awkward it would be for me if there was any mistake. My father is a very hospitable man: he keeps six hotels; but I couldn't trust him as far as that. What about your father?

RAINA He is away at Slivnitza fighting for his country. I answer for your safety. There is my hand in pledge of it. Will that reassure you? (*She offers him her hand*).

THE MAN (*looking dubiously at his own hand*) Better not touch my hand, dear young lady. I must have a wash first.

RAINA (*touched*) That is very nice of you. I see that you are a gentleman.

THE MAN (*puzzled*) Eh?

RAINA You must not think I am surprised. Bulgarians of really good standing — people in our position — wash their hands nearly every day. So you see I can appreciate your delicacy. You may take my hand. (*She offers it again*).

THE MAN (*kissing it with his hands behind his back*) Thanks, gracious young lady: I feel safe at last. And now would you mind breaking the news to your mother? I had better not stay here secretly longer than is necessary.

RAINA If you will be so good as to keep perfectly still whilst I am away.

THE MAN Certainly. (*He sits down on the ottoman*).

RAINA *goes to the bed and wraps herself in the fur cloak. His eyes close. She goes to the door. Turning for a last look at him, she sees that he is dropping off to sleep.*

RAINA (*at the door*) You are not going asleep, are you? (*He murmurs inarticulately: she runs to him and shakes him*). Do you hear? Wake up: you are falling asleep.

THE MAN Eh? Falling aslee — ? Oh no: not the least in the world: I was only thinking. It's all right: I'm wide awake.

RAINA (*severely*) Will you please stand up while I am away. (*He rises reluctantly*) All the time, mind.

THE MAN (*standing unsteadily*) Certainly. Certainly: you may depend on me.

RAINA *looks doubtfully at him. He smiles weakly. She goes reluctantly, turning again at the door, and almost catching him in the act of yawning. She goes out.*

THE MAN (*drowsily*) Sleep, sleep, sleep, sleep, slee — (*The words trail off into a murmur. He wakes again with a shock on the point of falling*). Where am I? Thats what I want to know: where am I? Must keep awake. Nothing keeps me awake except danger: remember that: (*intently*) danger, danger, danger, dan — (*trailing off again: another shock*) Wheres danger? Mus' find it. (*He starts off vaguely round the room in search of it*). What am I looking for? Sleep — danger — dont know. (*He stumbles against the bed*). Ah yes: now I know. All right now. I'm to go to bed, but not to sleep. Be sure not to sleep, because of danger. Not to lie down either, only sit down.

(*He sits on the bed. A blissful expression comes into his face*). Ah! (*With a happy sigh he sinks back at full length; lifts his boots into the bed with a final effort; and falls fast asleep instantly*).

CATHERINE *comes in, followed by* RAINA.

RAINA (*looking at the ottoman*)   He's gone! I left him here.

CATHERINE   Here! Then he must have climbed down from the —

RAINA (*seeing him*)   Oh! (*She points*).

CATHERINE (*scandalized*)   Well! (*She strides to the bed,* RAINA *following until she is opposite her on the other side*). He's fast asleep. The brute!

RAINA (*anxiously*)   Sh!

CATHERINE (*shaking him*)   Sir! (*Shaking him again, harder*) Sir!! (*Vehemently, shaking very hard*) Sir!!!

RAINA (*catching her arm*)   Dont, mamma: the poor darling is worn out. Let him sleep.

CATHERINE (*letting him go, and turning amazed to* RAINA)   The poor darling! Raina!!! (*She looks sternly at her daughter*).

The man sleeps profoundly.

Act Two

The sixth of March, 1886. In the garden of Major Petkoff's house. It is a fine spring morning: the garden looks fresh and pretty. Beyond the paling the tops of a couple of minarets can be seen, shewing that there is a valley there, with the little town in it. A few miles further the Balkan mountains rise and shut in the landscape. Looking towards them from within the garden, the side of the house is seen on the left, with a garden door reached by a little flight of steps. On the right the stable yard, with its gateway, encroaches on the garden. There are fruit bushes along the paling and house, covered with washing spread out to dry. A path runs by the house, and rises by two steps at the corner, where it turns out of sight. In the middle, a small table, with two bent wood chairs at it, is laid for breakfast with Turkish coffee pot, cups, rolls, etc.; but the cups have been used and the bread broken. There is a wooden garden seat against the wall on the right.

LOUKA, *smoking a cigaret, is standing between the table and the house, turning her back with angry disdain on a man servant who is lecturing her. He is a middle-aged man of cool temperament and low but clear and keen intelligence, with the complacency of the servant who values himself on his rank in servitude, and the imperturbability of the accurate calculator who has no illusions. He wears a white Bulgarian costume: jacket with embroidered border, sash, wide knickerbockers, and decorated gaiters. His head is shaved up to the crown, giving him a high Japanese forehead. His name is* NICOLA.

NICOLA   Be warned in time, Louka: mend your manners. I know the mistress. She is so grand that she never dreams that any servant could dare be disrespectful to her; but if she once suspects that you are defying her, out you go.

LOUKA   I do defy her. I will defy her. What do I care for her?

NICOLA   If you quarrel with the family, I never can marry you. It's the same as if you quarrelled with me!

LOUKA   You take her part against me, do you?

NICOLA (*sedately*) I shall always be dependent on the good will of the family. When I leave their service and start a shop in Sofia, their custom will be half my capital: their bad word would ruin me.

LOUKA You have no spirit. I should like to catch them saying a word against me!

NICOLA (*pityingly*) I should have expected more sense from you, Louka. But youre young: youre young!

LOUKA Yes; and you like me the better for it, dont you? But I know some family secrets they wouldnt care to have told, young as I am. Let them quarrel with me if they dare!

NICOLA (*with compassionate superiority*) Do you know what they would do if they heard you talk like that?

LOUKA What could they do?

NICOLA Discharge you for untruthfulness. Who would believe any stories you told after that? Who would give you another situation? Who in this house would dare be seen speaking to you ever again? How long would your father be left on his little farm? (*She impatiently throws away the end of her cigaret, and stamps on it*). Child: you dont know the power such high people have over the like of you and me when we try to rise out of our poverty against them. (*He goes close to her and lowers his voice*). Look at me, ten years in their service. Do you think I know no secrets? I know things about the mistress that she wouldnt have the master know for a thousand levas. I know things about him that she wouldnt let him hear the last of for six months if I blabbed them to her. I know things about Raina that would break off her match with Sergius if —

LOUKA (*turning on him quickly*) How do you know? I never told you!

NICOLA (*opening his eyes cunningly*) So thats your little secret, is it? I thought it might be something like that. Well, you take my advice and be respectful; and make the mistress feel that no matter what you know or dont know, she can depend on you to hold your tongue and serve the family faithfully. Thats what they like; and thats how youll make most out of them.

LOUKA (*with searching scorn*) You have the soul of a servant, Nicola.

NICOLA (*complacently*) Yes: thats the secret of success in service.

A loud knocking with a whip handle on a wooden door is heard from the stable yard.

MALE VOICE OUTSIDE Hollo! Hollo there! Nicola!

LOUKA Master! back from the war!

NICOLA (*quickly*) My word for it, Louka, the war's over. Off with you and get some fresh coffee. (*He runs out into the stable yard*).

LOUKA (*as she collects the coffee pot and cups on the tray, and carries it into the house*) Youll never put the soul of a servant into me.

MAJOR PETKOFF *comes from the stable yard, followed by* NICOLA. *He is a cheerful, excitable, insignificant, unpolished man of about 50, naturally unambitious except as to his income and his importance in local society, but just now greatly pleased with the military rank which the war has thrust on him as a man of consequence in his town. The fever of plucky patriotism which the Serbian attack roused in all the Bulgarians has pulled him through the war; but he is obviously glad to be home again.*

PETKOFF (*pointing to the table with his whip*) Breakfast out here, eh?

NICOLA Yes, sir. The mistress and Miss Raina have just gone in.

PETKOFF (*sitting down and taking a roll*)   Go in and say Ive come; and get me some fresh coffee.

NICOLA   It's coming, sir. (*He goes to the house door.* LOUKA, *with fresh coffee, a clean cup, and a brandy bottle on her tray, meets him*). Have you told the mistress?

LOUKA   Yes: she's coming.

NICOLA *goes into the house.* LOUKA *brings the coffee to the table.*

PETKOFF   Well: the Serbs havnt run away with you, have they?

LOUKA   No, sir.

PETKOFF   Thats right. Have you brought me some cognac?

LOUKA (*putting the bottle on the table*)   Here, sir.

PETKOFF   Thats right. (*He pours some into his coffee*).

CATHERINE, *who, having at this early hour made only a very perfunctory toilet, wears a Bulgarian apron over a once brilliant but now half worn-out dressing gown, and a colored handkerchief tied over her thick black hair, comes from the house with Turkish slippers on her bare feet, looking astonishingly handsome and stately under all the circumstances.* LOUKA *goes into the house.*

CATHERINE   My dear Paul: what a surprise for us! (*She stoops over the back of his chair to kiss him*). Have they brought you fresh coffee?

PETKOFF   Yes: Louka's been looking after me. The war's over. The treaty was signed three days ago at Bucharest; and the decree for our army to demobilize was issued yesterday.

CATHERINE (*springing erect, with flashing eyes*)   Paul: have you let the Austrians force you to make peace?

PETKOFF (*submissively*)   My dear: they didnt consult me. What could *I* do? (*She sits down and turns away from him*). But of course we saw to it that the treaty was an honorable one. It declares peace —

CATHERINE (*outraged*)   Peace!

PETKOFF (*appeasing her*)   — but not friendly relations: remember that. They wanted to put that in; but I insisted on its being struck out. What more could I do?

CATHERINE   You could have annexed Serbia and made Prince Alexander Emperor of the Balkans. Thats what I would have done.

PETKOFF   I dont doubt it in the least, my dear. But I should have had to subdue the whole Austrian Empire first; and that would have kept me too long away from you. I missed you greatly.

CATHERINE (*relenting*)   Ah! (*She stretches her hand affectionately across the table to squeeze his*).

PETKOFF   And how have you been, my dear?

CATHERINE   Oh, my usual sore throats: thats all.

PETKOFF (*with conviction*)   That comes from washing your neck every day. Ive often told you so.

CATHERINE   Nonsense, Paul!

PETKOFF (*over his coffee and cigaret*)   I dont believe in going too far with these modern customs. All this washing cant be good for the health: it's not natural. There was an Englishman at Philippopolis who used to wet himself all over with cold water every morning when he got up. Disgusting! It all comes from the English: their climate makes them so dirty that they have to be perpetually washing themselves. Look at my father! he never had a bath in his life; and he lived to be ninety-eight, the healthiest man in Bulgaria. I dont mind a good wash once a week to keep up my position; but once a day is carrying the thing to a ridiculous extreme.

CATHERINE You are a barbarian at heart still, Paul. I hope you behaved yourself before all those Russian officers.

PETKOFF I did my best. I took care to let them know that we have a library.

CATHERINE Ah; but you didnt tell them that we have an electric bell in it? I have had one put up.

PETKOFF Whats an electric bell?

CATHERINE You touch a button; something tinkles in the kitchen; and then Nicola comes up.

PETKOFF Why not shout for him?

CATHERINE Civilized people never shout for their servants. Ive learnt that while you were away.

PETKOFF Well, I'll tell you something Ive learnt too. Civilized people dont hang out their washing to dry where visitors can see it; so youd better have all that (*indicating the clothes on the bushes*) put somewhere else.

CATHERINE Oh, thats absurd, Paul: I dont believe really refined people notice such things.

SERGIUS (*knocking at the stable gates*) Gate, Nicola!

PETKOFF Theres Sergius. (*Shouting*) Hollo, Nicola!

CATHERINE Oh, dont shout, Paul: it really isnt nice.

PETKOFF Bosh! (*He shouts louder than before*) Nicola!

NICOLA (*appearing at the house door*) Yes, sir.

PETKOFF Are you deaf? Dont you hear Major Saranoff knocking? Bring him round this way. (*He pronounces the name with the stress on the second syllable: Sarahnoff*).

NICOLA Yes, major. (*He goes into the stable yard*).

PETKOFF You must talk to him, my dear, until Raina takes him off our hands. He bores my life out about our not promoting him. Over my head, if you please.

CATHERINE He certainly ought to be promoted when he marries Raina. Besides, the country should insist on having at least one native general.

PETKOFF Yes; so that he could throw away whole brigades instead of regiments. It's no use, my dear: he hasnt the slightest chance of promotion until we're quite sure that the peace will be a lasting one.

NICOLA (*at the gate, announcing*) Major Sergius Saranoff! (*He goes into the house and returns presently with a third chair, which he places at the table. He then withdraws*).

MAJOR SERGIUS SARANOFF, *the original of the portrait in Raina's room, is a tall romantically handsome man, with the physical hardihood, the high spirit, and the susceptible imagination of an untamed mountaineer chieftain. But his remarkable personal distinction is of a characteristically civilized type. The ridges of his eyebrows, curving with an interrogative twist round the projections at the outer corners; his jealously observant eye; his nose, thin, keen, and apprehensive in spite of the pugnacious high bridge and large nostril; his assertive chin, would not be out of place in a Parisian salon, shewing that the clever imaginative barbarian has an acute critical faculty which has been thrown into intense activity by the arrival of western civilization in the Balkans. The result is precisely what the advent of nineteenth*

*century thought first produced in England: to wit, Byronism. By his brood-
ing on the perpetual failure, not only of others, but of himself, to live up to
his ideals; by his consequent cynical scorn for humanity; by his jejune
credulity as to the absolute validity of his concepts and the unworthiness of
the world in disregarding them; by his wincings and mockeries under the
sting of the petty disillusions which every hour spent among men brings to
his sensitive observation, he has acquired the half tragic, half ironic air, the
mysterious moodiness, the suggestion of a strange and terrible history that
has left nothing but undying remorse, by which Childe Harold fascinated
the grandmothers of his English contemporaries. It is clear that here or nowhere is Raina's ideal hero.* CATHERINE *is hardly less enthusiastic about him
than her daughter, and much less reserved in shewing her enthusiasm. As
he enters from the stable gate, she rises effusively to greet him.* PETKOFF *is
distinctly less disposed to make a fuss about him.*

PETKOFF   Here already, Sergius! Glad to see you.

CATHERINE   My dear Sergius! (*She holds out both her hands*).

SERGIUS (*kissing them with a scrupulous gallantry*)   My dear mother, if I may
call you so.

PETKOFF (*drily*)   Mother-in-law, Sergius: mother-in-law! Sit down; and have
some coffee.

SERGIUS   Thank you: none for me. (*He gets away from the table with a certain distaste for Petkoff's enjoyment of it, and posts himself with conscious
dignity against the rail of the steps leading to the house*).

CATHERINE   You look superb. The campaign has improved you, Sergius.
Everybody here is mad about you. We were all wild with enthusiasm about
that magnificent cavalry charge.

SERGIUS (*with grave irony*)   Madam: it was the cradle and the grave of my
military reputation.

CATHERINE   How so?

SERGIUS   I won the battle the wrong way when our worthy Russian generals
were losing it the right way. In short, I upset their plans, and wounded
their self-esteem. Two Cossack colonels had their regiments routed on the
most correct principles of scientific warfare. Two major-generals got killed
strictly according to military etiquette. The two colonels are now major-
generals; and I am still a simple major.

CATHERINE   You shall not remain so, Sergius. The women are on your side;
and they will see that justice is done you.

SERGIUS   It is too late. I have only waited for the peace to send in my resignation.

PETKOFF (*dropping his cup in his amazement*)   Your resignation!

CATHERINE   Oh, you must withdraw it!

SERGIUS (*with resolute measured emphasis, folding his arms*)   I never withdraw.

PETKOFF (*vexed*)   Now who could have supposed you were going to do such
a thing?

SERGIUS (*with fire*)   Everyone that knew me. But enough of myself and my
affairs. How is Raina; and where is Raina?

RAINA (*suddenly coming round the corner of the house and standing at the top
of the steps in the path*)   Raina is here.

She makes a charming picture as they turn to look at her. She wears an underdress of pale green silk, draped with an overdress of thin ecru canvas embroidered with gold. She is crowned with a dainty eastern cap of gold tinsel. SERGIUS *goes impulsively to meet her. Posing regally, she presents her hand: he drops chivalrously on one knee and kisses it.*

PETKOFF (*aside to Catherine, beaming with parental pride*) Pretty, isnt it? She always appears at the right moment.

CATHERINE (*impatiently*) Yes: she listens for it. It is an abominable habit.

SERGIUS *leads* RAINA *forward with splendid gallantry. When they arrive at the table, she turns to him with a bend of the head: he bows; and thus they separate, he coming to his place, and she going behind her father's chair.*

RAINA (*stooping and kissing her father*) Dear father! Welcome home!

PETKOFF (*patting her cheek*) My little pet girl. (*He kisses her. She goes to the chair left by* NICOLA *for* SERGIUS, *and sits down*).

CATHERINE And so youre no longer a soldier, Sergius.

SERGIUS I am no longer a soldier. Soldiering, my dear madam, is the coward's art of attacking mercilessly when you are strong, and keeping out of harm's way when you are weak. That is the whole secret of successful fighting. Get your enemy at a disadvantage; and never, on any account, fight him on equal terms.

PETKOFF They wouldnt let us make a fair stand-up fight of it. However, I suppose soldiering has to be a trade like any other trade.

SERGIUS Precisely. But I have no ambition to shine as a tradesman; so I have taken the advice of that bagman of a captain that settled the exchange of prisoners with us at Pirot, and given it up.

PETKOFF What! that Swiss fellow? Sergius: Ive often thought of that exchange since. He over-reached us about those horses.

SERGIUS Of course he over-reached us. His father was a hotel and livery stable keeper; and he owed his first step to his knowledge of horse-dealing. (*With mock enthusiasm*) Ah, he was a soldier: every inch a soldier! If only I had bought the horses for my regiment instead of foolishly leading it into danger, I should have been a field-marshal now!

CATHERINE A Swiss? What was he doing in the Serbian army?

PETKOFF A volunteer, of course: keen on picking up his profession. (*Chuckling*) We shouldnt have been able to begin fighting if these foreigners hadnt shewn us how to do it: we knew nothing about it; and neither did the Serbs. Egad, there'd have been no war without them!

RAINA Are there many Swiss officers in the Serbian Army?

PETKOFF No. All Austrians, just as our officers were all Russians. This was the only Swiss I came across. I'll never trust a Swiss again. He humbugged us into giving him fifty ablebodied men for two hundred worn out chargers. They werent even eatable!

SERGIUS We were two children in the hands of that consummate soldier, Major: simply two innocent little children.

RAINA What was he like?

CATHERINE Oh, Raina, what a silly question!

SERGIUS He was like a commercial traveller in uniform. Bourgeois to his boots!

PETKOFF (*grinning*)   Sergius: tell Catherine that queer story his friend told us about how he escaped after Slivnitza. You remember. About his being hid by two women.

SERGIUS (*with bitter irony*)   Oh yes: quite a romance! He was serving in the very battery I so unprofessionally charged. Being a thorough soldier, he ran away like the rest of them, with our cavalry at his heels. To escape their sabres he climbed a waterpipe and made his way into the bedroom of a young Bulgarian lady. The young lady was enchanted by his persuasive commercial traveller's manners. She very modestly entertained him for an hour or so, and then called in her mother lest her conduct should appear unmaidenly. The old lady was equally fascinated; and the fugitive was sent on his way in the morning, disguised in an old coat belonging to the master of the house, who was away at the war.

RAINA (*rising with marked stateliness*)   Your life in the camp has made you coarse, Sergius. I did not think you would have repeated such a story before me. (*She turns away coldly*).

CATHERINE (*also rising*)   She is right, Sergius. If such women exist, we should be spared the knowledge of them.

PETKOFF   Pooh! nonsense! what does it matter?

SERGIUS (*ashamed*)   No, Petkoff: I was wrong. (*To* RAINA, *with earnest humility*) I beg your pardon. I have behaved abominably. Forgive me, Raina. (*She bows reservedly*). And you too, madam. (CATHERINE *bows graciously and sits down. He proceeds solemnly, again addressing* RAINA) The glimpses I have had of the seamy side of life during the last few months have made me cynical; but I should not have brought my cynicism here: least of all into your presence, Raina. I — (*Here, turning to the others, he is evidently going to begin a long speech when the* MAJOR *interrupts him*).

PETKOFF   Stuff and nonsense, Sergius! Thats quite enough fuss about nothing: a soldier's daughter should be able to stand up without flinching to a little strong conversation. (*He rises*). Come: it's time for us to get to business. We have to make up our minds how those three regiments are to get back to Philippopolis: theres no forage for them on the Sofia route. (*He goes towards the house*). Come along. (SERGIUS *is about to follow him when* CATHERINE *rises and intervenes*).

CATHERINE   Oh, Paul, cant you spare Sergius for a few moments? Raina has hardly seen him yet. Perhaps I can help you to settle about the regiments.

SERGIUS (*protesting*)   My dear madam, impossible: you —

CATHERINE (*stopping him playfully*)   You stay here, my dear Sergius: theres no hurry. I have a word or two to say to Paul. (SERGIUS *instantly bows and steps back*). Now, dear (*taking Petkoff's arm*): come and see the electric bell.

PETKOFF   Oh, very well, very well.

They go into the house together affectionately. SERGIUS, *left alone with* RAINA, *looks anxiously at her, fearing that she is still offended. She smiles, and stretches out her arms to him.*

SERGIUS (*hastening to her*)   Am I forgiven?

RAINA (*placing her hands on his shoulders as she looks up at him with admiration and worship*)   My hero! My king!

SERGIUS   My queen! (*He kisses her on the forehead*).

RAINA   How I have envied you, Sergius! You have been out in the world, on the field of battle, able to prove yourself there worthy of any woman in the world; whilst I have had to sit at home inactive — dreaming — useless — doing nothing that could give me the right to call myself worthy of any man.

SERGIUS Dearest: all my deeds have been yours. You inspired me. I have gone through the war like a knight in a tournament with his lady looking down at him!

RAINA And you have never been absent from my thoughts for a moment. (*Very solemnly*) Sergius: I think we two have found the higher love. When I think of you, I feel that I could never do a base deed, or think an ignoble thought.

SERGIUS My lady and my saint! (*He clasps her reverently*).

RAINA (*returning his embrace*) My lord and my —

SERGIUS Sh — sh! Let me be the worshipper, dear. You little know how unworthy even the best man is of a girl's pure passion!

RAINA I trust you. I love you. You will never disappoint me, Sergius. (LOUKA *is heard singing within the house. They quickly release each other*). I cant pretend to talk indifferently before her: my heart is too full. (LOUKA *comes from the house with her tray. She goes to the table, and begins to clear it, with her back turned to them*). I will get my hat; and then we can go out until lunch time. Wouldnt you like that?

SERGIUS Be quick. If you are away five minutes, it will seem five hours. (RAINA *runs to the top of the steps, and turns there to exchange looks with him and wave him a kiss with both hands. He looks after her with emotion for a moment; then turns slowly away, his face radiant with the loftiest exaltation. The movement shifts his field of vision, into the corner of which there now comes the tail of Louka's double apron. His attention is arrested at once. He takes a stealthy look at her, and begins to twirl his moustache mischievously, with his left hand akimbo on his hip. Finally, striking the ground with his heels in something of a cavalry swagger, he strolls over to the other side of the table, opposite her, and says*) Louka: do you know what the higher love is?

LOUKA (*astonished*) No, sir.

SERGIUS Very fatiguing thing to keep up for any length of time, Louka. One feels the need of some relief after it.

LOUKA (*innocently*) Perhaps you would like some coffee, sir? (*She stretches her hand across the table for the coffee pot*).

SERGIUS (*taking her hand*) Thank you, Louka.

LOUKA (*pretending to pull*) Oh, sir, you know I didnt mean that. I'm surprised at you!

SERGIUS (*coming clear of the table and drawing her with him*) I am surprised at myself, Louka. What would Sergius, the hero of Slivnitza, say if he saw me now? What would Sergius, the apostle of the higher love, say if he saw me now? What would the half dozen Sergiuses who keep popping in and out of this handsome figure of mine say if they caught us here? (*Letting go her hand and slipping his arm dexterously round her waist*) Do you consider my figure handsome, Louka?

LOUKA Let me go, sir. I shall be disgraced. (*She struggles: he holds her inexorably*). Oh, will you let go?

SERGIUS (*looking straight into her eyes*) No.

LOUKA Then stand back where we cant be seen. Have you no common sense?

SERGIUS Ah! thats reasonable. (*He takes her into the stableyard gateway, where they are hidden from the house*).

LOUKA (*plaintively*) I may have been seen from the windows: Miss Raina is sure to be spying about after you.

SERGIUS (*stung: letting her go*) Take care, Louka. I may be worthless enough to betray the higher love; but do not you insult it.

LOUKA (*demurely*) Not for the world, sir, I'm sure. May I go on with my work, please, now?

SERGIUS (*again putting his arm round her*) You are a provoking little witch, Louka. If you were in love with me, would you spy out of windows on me?

LOUKA Well, you see, sir, since you say you are half a dozen different gentlemen all at once, I should have a great deal to look after.

SERGIUS (*charmed*) Witty as well as pretty. (*He tries to kiss her*).

LOUKA (*avoiding him*) No: I dont want your kisses. Gentlefolk are all alike: you making love to me behind Miss Raina's back; and she doing the same behind yours.

SERGIUS (*recoiling a step*) Louka!

LOUKA It shews how little you really care.

SERGIUS (*dropping his familiarity, and speaking with freezing politeness*) If our conversation is to continue, Louka, you will please remember that a gentleman does not discuss the conduct of the lady he is engaged to with her maid.

LOUKA It's so hard to know what a gentleman considers right. I thought from your trying to kiss me that you had given up being so particular.

SERGIUS (*turning from her and striking his forehead as he comes back into the garden from the gateway*) Devil! devil!

LOUKA Ha! ha! I expect one of the six of you is very like me, sir; though I am only Miss Raina's maid. (*She goes back to her work at the table, taking no further notice of him*).

SERGIUS (*speaking to himself*) Which of the six is the real man? thats the question that torments me. One of them is a hero, another a buffoon, another a humbug, another perhaps a bit of a blackguard. (*He pauses, and looks furtively at* LOUKA *as he adds, with deep bitterness*) And one, at least, is a coward: jealous, like all cowards. (*He goes to the table*). Louka.

LOUKA Yes?

SERGIUS Who is my rival?

LOUKA You shall never get that out of me, for love or money.

SERGIUS Why?

LOUKA Never mind why. Besides, you would tell that I told you; and I should lose my place.

SERGIUS (*holding out his right hand in affirmation*) No! on the honor of a — (*He checks himself; and his hand drops, nerveless, as he concludes sardonically*) — of a man capable of behaving as I have been behaving for the last five minutes. Who is he?

LOUKA I dont know. I never saw him. I only heard his voice through the door of her room.

SERGIUS Damnation! How dare you?

LOUKA (*retreating*) Oh, I mean no harm: youve no right to take up my words like that. The mistress knows all about it. And I tell you that if that gentleman ever comes here again, Miss Raina will marry him, whether he likes it or not. I know the difference between the sort of manner you and she put on before one another and the real manner.

SERGIUS *shivers as if she had stabbed him. Then, setting his face like iron, he strides grimly to her, and grips her above the elbows with both hands.*

SERGIUS Now listen you to me.

LOUKA (*wincing*) Not so tight: youre hurting me.

SERGIUS That doesnt matter. You have stained my honor by making me a party to your eavesdropping. And you have betrayed your mistress.

LOUKA (*writhing*) Please —

SERGIUS That shews that you are an abominable little clod of common clay, with the soul of a servant. (*He lets her go as if she were an unclean thing, and turns away, dusting his hands of her, to the bench by the wall, where he sits down with averted head, meditating gloomily*).

LOUKA (*whimpering angrily with her hands up her sleeves, feeling her bruised arms*) You know how to hurt with your tongue as well as with your hands. But I dont care, now Ive found out that whatever clay I'm made of, youre made of the same. As for her, she's a liar; and her fine airs are a cheat; and I'm worth six of her. (*She shakes the pain off hardily; tosses her head; and sets to work to put the things on the tray*).

He looks doubtfully at her. She finishes packing the tray, and laps the cloth over the edges, so as to carry all out together. As she stoops to lift it, he rises.

SERGIUS Louka! (*She stops and looks defiantly at him*). A gentleman has no right to hurt a woman under any circumstances. (*With profound humility, uncovering his head*) I beg your pardon.

LOUKA That sort of apology may satisfy a lady. Of what use is it to a servant?

SERGIUS (*rudely crossed in his chivalry, throws it off with a bitter laugh, and says slightingly*) Oh! you wish to be paid for the hurt? (*He puts on his shako, and takes some money from his pocket*).

LOUKA (*her eyes filling with tears in spite of herself*) No: I want my hurt made well.

SERGIUS (*sobered by her tone*) How?

She rolls up her left sleeve; clasps her arm with the thumb and fingers of her right hand; and looks down at the bruise. Then she raises her head and looks straight at him. Finally, with a superb gesture, she presents her arm to be kissed. Amazed, he looks at her; at the arm; at her again; hesitates; and then, with shuddering intensity, exclaims Never! *and gets away as far as possible from her.*

Her arm drops. Without a word, and with unaffected dignity, she takes her tray, and is approaching the house when RAINA *returns, wearing a hat and jacket in the height of the Vienna fashion of the previous year, 1885.* LOUKA *makes way proudly for her, and then goes into the house.*

RAINA I'm ready. Whats the matter? (*Gaily*) Have you been flirting with Louka?

SERGIUS (*hastily*) No, no. How can you think such a thing?

RAINA (*ashamed of herself*) Forgive me, dear: it was only a jest. I am so happy today.

He goes quickly to her, and kisses her hand remorsefully. CATHERINE *comes out and calls to them from the top of the steps.*

CATHERINE (*coming down to them*) I am sorry to disturb you, children; but

Paul is distracted over those three regiments. He doesnt know how to send them to Philippopolis; and he objects to every suggestion of mine. You must go and help him, Sergius. He is in the library.

RAINA (*disappointed*)   But we are just going out for a walk.

SERGIUS   I shall not be long. Wait for me just five minutes. (*He runs up the steps to the door*).

RAINA (*following him to the foot of the steps and looking up at him with timid coquetry*)   I shall go round and wait in full view of the library windows. Be sure you draw father's attention to me. If you are a moment longer than five minutes, I shall go in and fetch you, regiments or no regiments.

SERGIUS (*laughing*)   Very well. (*He goes in*).

RAINA *watches him until he is out of her sight. Then, with a perceptible relaxation of manner, she begins to pace up and down the garden in a brown study.*

CATHERINE   Imagine their meeting that Swiss and hearing the whole story! The very first thing your father asked for was the old coat we sent him off in. A nice mess you have got us into!

RAINA (*gazing thoughtfully at the gravel as she walks*)   The little beast!

CATHERINE   Little beast! What little beast?

RAINA   To go and tell! Oh, if I had him here, I'd cram him with chocolate creams til he couldnt ever speak again!

CATHERINE   Dont talk such stuff. Tell me the truth, Raina. How long was he in your room before you came to me?

RAINA (*whisking round and recommencing her march in the opposite direction*)   Oh, I forget.

CATHERINE   You cannot forget! Did he really climb up after the soldiers were gone; or was he there when that officer searched the room?

RAINA   No. Yes: I think he must have been there then.

CATHERINE   You think! Oh, Raina! Raina! Will anything ever make you straightforward? If Sergius finds out, it will be all over between you.

RAINA (*with cool impertinence*)   Oh, I know Sergius is your pet. I sometimes wish you could marry him instead of me. You would just suit him. You would pet him, and spoil him, and mother him to perfection.

CATHERINE (*opening her eyes very widely indeed*)   Well, upon my word!

RAINA (*capriciously: half to herself*)   I always feel a longing to do or say something dreadful to him — to shock his propriety — to scandalize the five senses out of him. (*To* CATHERINE, *perversely*)   I dont care whether he finds out about the chocolate cream soldier or not. I half hope he may. (*She again turns and strolls flippantly away up the path to the corner of the house*).

CATHERINE   And what should I be able to say to your father, pray?

RAINA (*over her shoulder, from the top of the two steps*)   Oh, poor father! As if he could help himself! (*She turns the corner and passes out of sight*).

CATHERINE (*looking after her, her fingers itching*)   Oh, if you were only ten years younger! (LOUKA *comes from the house with a salver, which she carries hanging down by her side*). Well?

LOUKA   Theres a gentleman just called, madam. A Serbian officer.

CATHERINE (*flaming*)   A Serb! And how dare he — (*checking herself bitterly*) Oh, I forgot. We are at peace now. I suppose we shall have them calling every day to pay their compliments. Well: if he is an officer why dont you tell your master? He is in the library with Major Saranoff. Why do you come to me?

LOUKA But he asks for you, madam. And I dont think he knows who you are: he said the lady of the house. He gave me this little ticket for you. (*She takes a card out of her bosom; puts it on the salver; and offers it to* CATHERINE).

CATHERINE (*reading*) "Captain Bluntschli"? Thats a German name.

LOUKA Swiss, madam, I think.

CATHERINE (*with a bound that makes* LOUKA *jump back*) Swiss! What is he like?

LOUKA (*timidly*) He has a big carpet bag, madam.

CATHERINE Oh Heavens! he's come to return the coat. Send him away: say we're not at home: ask him to leave his address and I'll write to him. Oh stop: that will never do. Wait! (*She throws herself into a chair to think it out.* LOUKA *waits*). The master and Major Saranoff are busy in the library, arnt they?

LOUKA Yes, madam.

CATHERINE (*decisively*) Bring the gentleman out here at once. (*Peremptorily*) And be very polite to him. Dont delay. Here (*impatiently snatching the salver from her*): leave that here; and go straight back to him.

LOUKA Yes, madam (*going*).

CATHERINE Louka!

LOUKA (*stopping*) Yes, madam.

CATHERINE Is the library door shut?

LOUKA I think so, madam.

CATHERINE If not, shut it as you pass through.

LOUKA Yes, madam (*going*).

CATHERINE Stop! (LOUKA *stops*). He will have to go that way (*indicating the gate of the stableyard*). Tell Nicola to bring his bag here after him. Dont forget.

LOUKA (*surprised*) His bag?

CATHERINE Yes: here: as soon as possible. (*Vehemently*) Be quick! (LOUKA *runs into the house.* CATHERINE *snatches her apron off and throws it behind a bush. She then takes up the salver and uses it as a mirror, with the result that the handkerchief tied round her head follows the apron. A touch to her hair and a shake to her dressing gown make her presentable*). Oh, how? how? how can a man be such a fool! Such a moment to select! (LOUKA *appears at the door of the house, announcing* CAPTAIN BLUNTSCHLI. *She stands aside at the top of the steps to let him pass before she goes in again. He is the man of the midnight adventure in Raina's room, clean, well brushed, smartly uniformed, and out of trouble, but still unmistakably the same man. The moment Louka's back is turned,* CATHERINE *swoops on him with impetuous, urgent, coaxing appeal*). Captain Bluntschli: I am very glad to see you; but you must leave this house at once. (*He raises his eyebrows*). My husband has just returned with my future son-in-law; and they know nothing. If they did, the consequences would be terrible. You are a foreigner: you do not feel our national animosities as we do. We still hate the Serbs: the effect of the peace on my husband has been to make him feel like a lion baulked of his prey. If he discovers our secret, he will never forgive me; and my daughter's life will hardly be safe. Will you, like the chivalrous gentleman and soldier you are, leave at once before he finds you here?

BLUNTSCHLI (*disappointed, but philosophical*) At once, gracious lady. I only came to thank you and return the coat you lent me. If you will allow me to take it out of my bag and leave it with your servant as I pass out, I need detain you no further. (*He turns to go into the house*).

CATHERINE (*catching him by the sleeve*) Oh, you must not think of going back that way. (*Coaxing him across to the stable gates*) This is the shortest way out. Many thanks. So glad to have been of service to you. Goodbye.

BLUNTSCHLI But my bag?

CATHERINE It shall be sent on. You will leave me your address.

BLUNTSCHLI True. Allow me. (*He takes out his card-case, and stops to write his address, keeping* CATHERINE *in an agony of impatience. As he hands her the card,* PETKOFF, *hatless, rushes from the house in a fluster of hospitality, followed by* SERGIUS).

PETKOFF (*as he hurries down the steps*) My dear Captain Bluntschli —

CATHERINE Oh Heavens! (*She sinks on the seat against the wall*).

PETKOFF (*too preoccupied to notice her as he shakes Bluntschli's hand heartily*) Those stupid people of mine thought I was out here, instead of in the — haw! — library (*he cannot mention the library without betraying how proud he is of it*). I saw you through the window. I was wondering why you didnt come in. Saranoff is with me: you remember him, dont you?

SERGIUS (*saluting humorously, and then offering his hand with great charm of manner*) Welcome, our friend the enemy!

PETKOFF No longer the enemy, happily. (*Rather anxiously*) I hope youve called as a friend, and not about horses or prisoners.

CATHERINE Oh, quite as a friend, Paul. I was just asking Captain Bluntschli to stay to lunch; but he declares he must go at once.

SERGIUS (*sardonically*) Impossible, Bluntschli. We want you here badly. We have to send on three cavalry regiments to Philippopolis; and we dont in the least know how to do it.

BLUNTSCHLI (*suddenly attentive and businesslike*) Philippopolis? The forage is the trouble, I suppose.

PETKOFF (*eagerly*) Yes: thats it. (*To* SERGIUS) He sees the whole thing at once.

BLUNTSCHLI I think I can shew you how to manage that.

SERGIUS Invaluable man! Come along! (*Towering over* BLUNTSCHLI, *he puts his hand on his shoulder and takes him to the steps,* PETKOFF *following*). RAINA *comes from the house as* BLUNTSCHLI *puts his foot on the first step.*

RAINA Oh! The chocolate cream soldier!

BLUNTSCHLI *stands rigid.* SERGIUS, *amazed, looks at* RAINA, *then at* PETKOFF, *who looks back at him and then at his wife.*

CATHERINE (*with commanding presence of mind*) My dear Raina, dont you see that we have a guest here? Captain Bluntschli: one of our new Serbian friends.

RAINA *bows:* BLUNTSCHLI *bows.*

RAINA How silly of me! (*She comes down into the centre of the group, between* BLUNTSCHLI *and* PETKOFF). I made a beautiful ornament this morning for the ice pudding; and that stupid Nicola has just put down a pile of plates on it and spoilt it. (*To* BLUNTSCHLI, *winningly*) I hope you didnt think that you were the chocolate cream soldier, Captain Bluntschli.

BLUNTSCHLI (*laughing*) I assure you I did. (*Stealing a whimsical glance at her*) Your explanation was a relief.

PETKOFF (*suspiciously, to* RAINA) And since when, pray, have you taken to cooking?

CATHERINE Oh, whilst you were away. It is her latest fancy.

PETKOFF (*testily*) And has Nicola taken to drinking? He used to be careful enough. First he shews Captain Bluntschli out here when he knew quite well I was in the library; and then he goes downstairs and breaks Raina's chocolate soldier. He must — (NICOLA *appears at the top of the steps with the bag. He descends; places it respectfully before* BLUNTSCHLI; *and waits for further orders. General amazement.* NICOLA, *unconscious of the effect he is producing, looks perfectly satisfied with himself. When* PETKOFF *recovers his power of speech, he breaks out at him with*) Are you mad, Nicola?

NICOLA (*taken aback*) Sir?

PETKOFF What have you brought that for?

NICOLA My lady's orders, major. Louka told me that —

CATHERINE (*interrupting him*) My orders! Why should I order you to bring Captain Bluntschli's luggage out here? What are you thinking of, Nicola?

NICOLA (*after a moment's bewilderment, picking up the bag as he addresses* BLUNTSCHLI *with the very perfection of servile discretion*) I beg your pardon, captain, I am sure. (*To* CATHERINE) My fault, madam: I hope youll overlook it. (*He bows, and is going to the steps with the bag, when* PETKOFF *addresses him angrily*).

PETKOFF Youd better go and slam that bag, too, down on Miss Raina's ice pudding! (*This is too much for* NICOLA. *The bag drops from his hand almost on his master's toes, eliciting a roar of*) Begone, you butterfingered donkey.

NICOLA (*snatching up the bag, and escaping into the house*) Yes, major.

CATHERINE Oh, never mind, Paul: dont be angry.

PETKOFF (*blustering*) Scoundrel! He's got out of hand while I was away. I'll teach him. Infernal blackguard! The sack next Saturday! I'll clear out the whole establishment — (*He is stifled by the caresses of his wife and daughter, who hang round his neck, petting him*).

CATHERINE 〕
                 ⎱ (*together*) ⎰
RAINA   〕

⎰ Now, now, now, it mustnt be angry. He meant no
⎱ Wow, wow, wow: not on your first day at home. I'll
⎰ harm. Be good to please me, dear. Sh-sh-sh-sh!
⎱ make another ice pudding. Tch-ch-ch!

PETKOFF (*yielding*) Oh well, never mind. Come, Bluntschli: lets have no more nonsense about going away. You know very well youre not going back to Switzerland yet. Until you do go back youll stay with us.

RAINA Oh, do, Captain Bluntschli.

PETKOFF (*to* CATHERINE) Now, Catherine: it's of you he's afraid. Press him; and he'll stay.

CATHERINE Of course I shall be only too delighted if (*appealingly*) Captain Bluntschli really wishes to stay. He knows my wishes.

BLUNTSCHLI (*in his driest military manner*) I am at madam's orders.

SERGIUS (*cordially*) That settles it!

PETKOFF (*heartily*) Of course!

RAINA You see you must stay.

BLUNTSCHLI (*smiling*) Well, if I must, I must.

Gesture of despair from CATHERINE.

Act Three

In the library after lunch. It is not much of a library. Its literary equipment consists of a single fixed shelf stocked with old paper covered novels, broken backed, coffee stained, torn and thumbed; and a couple of little hanging shelves with a few gift books on them: the rest of the wall space being occupied by trophies of war and the chase. But it is a most comfortable sitting room. A row of three large windows shews a mountain panorama, just now seen in one of its friendliest aspects in the mellowing afternoon light. In the corner next the right hand window a square earthenware stove, a perfect tower of glistening pottery, rises nearly to the ceiling and guarantees plenty of warmth. The ottoman is like that in Raina's room, and similarly placed; and the window seats are luxurious with decorated cushions. There is one object, however, hopelessly out of keeping with its surroundings. This is a small kitchen table, much the worse for wear, fitted as a writing table with an old canister full of pens, an eggcup filled with ink, and a deplorable scrap of heavily used pink blotting paper.

At the side of this table, which stands to the left of anyone facing the window, BLUNTSCHLI *is hard at work with a couple of maps before him, writing orders. At the head of it sits* SERGIUS, *who is supposed to be also at work, but is actually gnawing the feather of a pen, and contemplating Bluntschli's quick, sure, businesslike progress with a mixture of envious irritation at his own incapacity and awestruck wonder at an ability which seems to him almost miraculous, though its prosaic character forbids him to esteem it. The Major is comfortably established on the ottoman, with a newspaper in his hand and the tube of his hookah within easy reach.* CATHERINE *sits at the stove, with her back to them, embroidering.* RAINA, *reclining on the divan, is gazing in a daydream out at the Balkan landscape, with a neglected novel in her lap.*

The door is on the same side as the stove, farther from the window. The button of the electric bell is at the opposite side, behind BLUNTSCHLI.

PETKOFF (*looking up from his paper to watch how they are getting on at the table*) Are you sure I cant help you in any way, Bluntschli?

BLUNTSCHLI (*without interrupting his writing or looking up*) Quite sure, thank you. Saranoff and I will manage it.

SERGIUS (*grimly*) Yes: we'll manage it. He finds out what to do; draws up the orders; and I sign em. Division of labor! (BLUNTSCHLI *passes him a paper*). Another one? Thank you. (*He plants the paper squarely before him; sets his chair carefully parallel to it; and signs with his cheek on his elbow and his protruded tongue following the movements of his pen*). This hand is more accustomed to the sword than to the pen.

PETKOFF It's very good of you, Bluntschli: it is indeed, to let yourself be put upon in this way. Now are you quite sure I can do nothing?

CATHERINE (*in a low warning tone*)   You can stop interrupting, Paul.

PETKOFF (*starting and looking round at her*)   Eh? Oh! Quite right, my love: quite right. (*He takes his newspaper up again, but presently lets it drop*). Ah, you havnt been campaigning, Catherine: you dont know how pleasant it is for us to sit here, after a good lunch, with nothing to do but enjoy ourselves. Theres only one thing I want to make me thoroughly comfortable.

CATHERINE   What is that?

PETKOFF   My old coat. I'm not at home in this one: I feel as if I were on parade.

CATHERINE   My dear Paul, how absurd you are about that old coat! It must be hanging in the blue closet where you left it.

PETKOFF   My dear Catherine, I tell you Ive looked there. Am I to believe my own eyes or not? (CATHERINE *rises and crosses the room to press the button of the electric bell*). What are you shewing off that bell for? (*She looks at him majestically, and silently resumes her chair and her needlework*). My dear: if you think the obstinacy of your sex can make a coat out of two old dressing gowns of Raina's, your waterproof, and my mackintosh, youre mistaken. Thats exactly what the blue closet contains at present.

NICOLA *presents himself.*

CATHERINE   Nicola: go to the blue closet and bring your master's old coat here: the braided one he wears in the house.

NICOLA   Yes, madam. (*He goes out*).

PETKOFF   Catherine.

CATHERINE   Yes, Paul.

PETKOFF   I bet you any piece of jewellery you like to order from Sofia against a week's housekeeping money that the coat isnt there.

CATHERINE   Done, Paul!

PETKOFF (*excited by the prospect of a gamble*)   Come: heres an opportunity for some sport. Wholl bet on it? Bluntschli: I'll give you six to one.

BLUNTSCHLI (*imperturbably*)   It would be robbing you, major. Madam is sure to be right. (*Without looking up, he passes another batch of papers to* SERGIUS).

SERGIUS (*also excited*)   Bravo, Switzerland! Major: I bet my best charger against an Arab mare for Raina that Nicola finds the coat in the blue closet.

PETKOFF (*eagerly*)   Your best char —

CATHERINE (*hastily interrupting him*)   Dont be foolish, Paul. An Arabian mare will cost you 50,000 levas.

RAINA (*suddenly coming out of her picturesque revery*)   Really, mother, if you are going to take the jewellery, I dont see why you should grudge me my Arab.

NICOLA *comes back with the coat, and brings it to* PETKOFF, *who can hardly believe his eyes.*

CATHERINE   Where was it, Nicola?

NICOLA   Hanging in the blue closet, madam.

PETKOFF   Well, I am d —

CATHERINE (*stopping him*)   Paul!

PETKOFF   I could have sworn it wasnt there. Age is beginning to tell on me. I'm getting hallucinations. (*To* NICOLA) Here: help me to change. Excuse me, Bluntschli. (*He begins changing coats,* NICOLA *acting as valet*). Remember: I didnt take that bet of yours, Sergius. Youd better give Raina that Arab steed yourself, since youve roused her expectations. Eh, Raina? (*He looks round at her; but she is again rapt in the landscape. With a little gush of parental affection and pride, he points her out to them, and says*) She's dreaming, as usual.

SERGIUS   Assuredly she shall not be the loser.

PETKOFF   So much the better for her. *I* shant come off so cheaply, I expect. (*The change is now complete.* NICOLA *goes out with the discarded coat*). Ah, now I feel at home at last. (*He sits down and takes his newspaper with a grunt of relief*).

BLUNTSCHLI (*to* SERGIUS, *handing a paper*)   Thats the last order.

PETKOFF (*jumping up*)   What! Finished?

BLUNTSCHLI   Finished.

PETKOFF (*with childlike envy*)   Havnt you anything for me to sign?

BLUNTSCHLI   Not necessary. His signature will do.

PETKOFF (*inflating his chest and thumping it*)   Ah well, I think weve done a thundering good day's work. Can I do anything more?

BLUNTSCHLI   You had better both see the fellows that are to take these. (SERGIUS *rises*) Pack them off at once; and shew them that Ive marked on the orders the time they should hand them in by. Tell them that if they stop to drink or tell stories — if theyre five minutes late, theyll have the skin taken off their backs.

SERGIUS (*stiffening indignantly*)   I'll say so. (*He strides to the door*). And if one of them is man enough to spit in my face for insulting him, I'll buy his discharge and give him a pension. (*He goes out*).

BLUNTSCHLI (*confidentially*)   Just see that he talks to them properly, major, will you?

PETKOFF (*officiously*)   Quite right, Bluntschli, quite right. I'll see to it. (*He goes to the door importantly, but hesitates on the threshold*). By the bye, Catherine, you may as well come too. Theyll be far more frightened of you than of me.

CATHERINE (*putting down her embroidery*)   I daresay I had better. You would only splutter at them. (*She goes out,* PETKOFF *holding the door for her and following her*).

BLUNTSCHLI   What an army! They make cannons out of cherry trees; and the officers send for their wives to keep discipline! (*He begins to fold and docket the papers*).

RAINA, *who has risen from the divan, marches slowly down the room with her hands clasped behind her, and looks mischievously at him.*

RAINA   You look ever so much nicer than when we last met. (*He looks up, surprised*). What have you done to yourself?

BLUNTSCHLI   Washed; brushed; good night's sleep and breakfast. Thats all.

RAINA   Did you get back safely that morning?

BLUNTSCHLI   Quite, thanks.

RAINA   Were they angry with you for running away from Sergius's charge?

BLUNTSCHLI (*grinning*)   No: they were glad; because theyd all just run away themselves.

RAINA (*going to the table, and leaning over it towards him*)   It must have made a lovely story for them: all that about me and my room.

BLUNTSCHLI   Capital story. But I only told it to one of them: a particular friend.

RAINA   On whose discretion you could absolutely rely?

BLUNTSCHLI   Absolutely.

RAINA   Hm! He told it all to my father and Sergius the day you exchanged the prisoners. (*She turns away and strolls carelessly across to the other side of the room*).

BLUNTSCHLI (*deeply concerned, and half incredulous*)   No! You dont mean that, do you?

RAINA (*turning, with sudden earnestness*)   I do indeed. But they dont know that it was in this house you took refuge. If Sergius knew, he would challenge you and kill you in a duel.

BLUNTSCHLI   Bless me! then dont tell him.

RAINA   Please be serious, Captain Bluntschli. Can you not realize what it is to me to deceive him? I want to be quite perfect with Sergius: no meanness, no smallness, no deceit. My relation to him is the one really beautiful and noble part of my life. I hope you can understand that.

BLUNTSCHLI (*sceptically*)   You mean that you wouldnt like him to find out that the story about the ice pudding was a — a — a — You know.

RAINA (*wincing*)   Ah, dont talk of it in that flippant way. I lied: I know it. But I did it to save your life. He would have killed you. That was the second time I ever uttered a falsehood. (BLUNTSCHLI *rises quickly and looks doubtfully and somewhat severely at her*). Do you remember the first time?

BLUNTSCHLI   I! No. Was I present?

RAINA   Yes; and I told the officer who was searching for you that you were not present.

BLUNTSCHLI   True. I should have remembered it.

RAINA (*greatly encouraged*)   Ah, it is natural that you should forget it first. It cost you nothing: it cost me a lie! A lie!

She sits down on the ottoman, looking straight before her with her hands clasped round her knee. BLUNTSCHLI, *quite touched, goes to the ottoman with a particularly reassuring and considerate air, and sits down beside her.*

BLUNTSCHLI   My dear young lady, dont let this worry you. Remember: I'm a soldier. Now what are the two things that happen to a soldier so often that he comes to think nothing of them? One is hearing people tell lies (RAINA *recoils*): the other is getting his life saved in all sorts of ways by all sorts of people.

RAINA (*rising in indignant protest*)   And so he becomes a creature incapable of faith and of gratitude.

BLUNTSCHLI (*making a wry face*)   Do you like gratitude? I dont. If pity is akin to love, gratitude is akin to the other thing.

RAINA   Gratitude! (*Turning on him*) If you are incapable of gratitude you are incapable of any noble sentiment. Even animals are grateful. Oh, I see now exactly what you think of me! You were not surprised to hear me lie. To you it was something I probably did every day! every hour!! That is how men think of women. (*She paces the room tragically*).

BLUNTSCHLI (*dubiously*)   Theres reason in everything. You said youd told only two lies in your whole life. Dear young lady: isnt that rather a short allowance? I'm quite a straightforward man myself; but it wouldnt last me a whole morning.

RAINA (*staring haughtily at him*)   Do you know, sir, that you are insulting me?

BLUNTSCHLI   I cant help it. When you strike that noble attitude and speak in that thrilling voice, I admire you; but I find it impossible to believe a single word you say.

RAINA (*superbly*) Captain Bluntschli!

BLUNTSCHLI (*unmoved*) Yes?

RAINA (*standing over him, as if she could not believe her senses*) Do you mean what you said just now? Do you know what you said just now?

BLUNTSCHLI I do.

RAINA (*gasping*) I! I!!! (*She points to herself increduously, meaning "I, Raina Petkoff tell lies!" He meets her gaze unflinchingly. She suddenly sits down beside him, and adds, with a complete change of manner from the heroic to a babyish familiarity*). How did you find me out?

BLUNTSCHLI (*promptly*) Instinct, dear young lady. Instinct, and experience of the world.

RAINA (*wonderingly*) Do you know, you are the first man I ever met who did not take me seriously?

BLUNTSCHLI You mean, dont you, that I am the first man that has ever taken you quite seriously?

RAINA Yes: I suppose I do mean that. (*Cosily, quite at her ease with him*) How strange it is to be talked to in such a way! You know, Ive always gone on like that.

BLUNTSCHLI You mean the — ?

RAINA I mean the noble attitude and the thrilling voice. (*They laugh together*). I did it when I was a tiny child to my nurse. She believed in it. I do it before my parents. They believe in it. I do it before Sergius. He believes in it.

BLUNTSCHLI Yes: he's a little in that line himself, isnt he?

RAINA (*startled*) Oh! Do you think so?

BLUNTSCHLI You know him better than I do.

RAINA I wonder — I wonder is he? If I thought that — ! (*Discouraged*) Ah, well: what does it matter? I suppose now youve found me out, you despise me.

BLUNTSCHLI (*warmly, rising*) No, my dear young lady, no, no, no a thousand times. It's part of your youth: part of your charm. I'm like all the rest of them: the nurse, your parents, Sergius: I'm your infatuated admirer.

RAINA (*pleased*) Really?

BLUNTSCHLI (*slapping his breast smartly with his hand, German fashion*) Hand aufs Herz! Really and truly.

RAINA (*very happy*) But what did you think of me for giving you my portrait?

BLUNTSCHLI (*astonished*) Your portrait! You never gave me your portrait.

RAINA (*quickly*) Do you mean to say you never got it?

BLUNTSCHLI No. (*He sits down beside her, with renewed interest, and says, with some complacency*) When did you send it to me?

RAINA (*indignantly*) I did not send it to you. (*She turns her head away, and adds, reluctantly*) It was in the pocket of that coat.

BLUNTSCHLI (*pursing his lips and rounding his eyes*) Oh-o-oh! I never found it. It must be there still.

RAINA (*springing up*) There still! for my father to find the first time he puts his hand in his pocket! Oh, how could you be so stupid?

BLUNTSCHLI (*rising also*) It doesnt matter: I suppose it's only a photograph: how can he tell who it was intended for? Tell him he put it there himself.

RAINA (*bitterly*)   Yes: that is so clever! isnt it? (*Distractedly*) Oh! what shall I do?

BLUNTSCHLI   Ah, I see. You wrote something on it. That was rash.

RAINA (*vexed almost to tears*)   Oh, to have done such a thing for you, who care no more — except to laugh at me — oh! Are you sure nobody has touched it?

BLUNTSCHLI   Well. I cant be quite sure. You see, I couldnt carry it about with me all the time: one cant take much luggage on active service.

RAINA   What did you do with it?

BLUNTSCHLI   When I got through to Pirot I had to put it in safe keeping somehow. I thought of the railway cloak room; but thats the surest place to get looted in modern warfare. So I pawned it.

RAINA   Pawned it!!!

BLUNTSCHLI   I know it doesnt sound nice; but it was much the safest plan. I redeemed it the day before yesterday. Heaven only knows whether the pawnbroker cleared out the pockets or not.

RAINA (*furious: throwing the words right into his face*)   You have a low shopkeeping mind. You think of things that would never come into a gentleman's head.

BLUNTSCHLI (*phlegmatically*)   Thats the Swiss national character, dear lady. (*He returns to the table*).

RAINA   Oh, I wish I had never met you. (*She flounces away, and sits at the window fuming*).

LOUKA *comes in with a heap of letters and telegrams on her salver, and crosses, with her bold free gait, to the table. Her left sleeve is looped up to the shoulder with a brooch, shewing her naked arm, with a broad gilt bracelet covering the bruise.*

LOUKA (*to* BLUNTSCHLI)   For you. (*She empties the salver with a fling on to the table*). The messenger is waiting. (*She is determined not to be civil to an enemy, even if she must bring him his letters*).

BLUNTSCHLI (*to* RAINA)   Will you excuse me: the last postal delivery that reached me was three weeks ago. These are the subsequent accumulations. Four telegrams: a week old. (*He opens one*). Oho! Bad news!

RAINA (*rising and advancing a little remorsefully*)   Bad news?

BLUNTSCHLI   My father's dead. (*He looks at the telegram with his lips pursed, musing on the unexpected changes in his arrangements.* LOUKA *crosses herself hastily*).

RAINA   Oh, how very sad!

BLUNTSCHLI   Yes: I shall have to start for home in an hour. He has left a lot of big hotels behind him to be looked after. (*He takes up a fat letter in a long blue envelope*). Here's a whacking letter from the family solicitor. (*He pulls out the enclosures and glances over them*). Great Heavens! Seventy! Two hundred! (*In a crescendo of dismay*) Four hundred! Four thousand!! Nine thousand six hundred!!! What on earth am I to do with them all?

RAINA (*timidly*)   Nine thousand hotels?

BLUNTSCHLI   Hotels! nonsense. If you only knew! Oh, it's too ridiculous! Excuse me: I must give my fellow orders about starting. (*He leaves the room hastily, with the documents in his hand*).

LOUKA (*knowing instinctively that she cannot annoy* RAINA *by disparaging*

BLUNTSCHLI) He has not much heart that Swiss. He has not a word of grief for his poor father.

RAINA (*bitterly*) Grief! A man who has been doing nothing but killing people for years! What does he care? What does any soldier care? (*She goes to the door, restraining her tears with difficulty*).

LOUKA Major Saranoff has been fighting too; and he has plenty of heart left. (RAINA, *at the door, draws herself up haughtily and goes out*). Aha! I thought you wouldnt get much feeling out of your soldier. (*She is following* RAINA *when* NICOLA *enters with an armful of logs for the stove*).

NICOLA (*grinning amorously at her*) Ive been trying all the afternoon to get a minute alone with you, my girl. (*His countenance changes as he notices her arm*). Why, what fashion is that of wearing your sleeve, child?

LOUKA (*proudly*) My own fashion.

NICOLA Indeed! If the mistress catches you, she'll talk to you. (*He puts the logs down, and seats himself comfortably on the ottoman*).

LOUKA Is that any reason why you should take it on yourself to talk to me?

NICOLA Come! dont be so contrary with me. Ive some good news for you. (*She sits down beside him. He takes out some paper money.* LOUKA, *with an eager gleam in her eyes, tries to snatch it; but he shifts it quickly to his left hand, out of her reach*). See! a twenty leva bill! Sergius gave me that, out of pure swagger. A fool and his money are soon parted. Theres ten levas more. The Swiss gave me that for backing up the mistress's and Raina's lies about him. He's no fool, he isnt. You should have heard old Catherine downstairs as polite as you please to me, telling me not to mind the Major being a little impatient; for they knew what a good servant I was — after making a fool and liar of me before them all! The twenty will go to our savings; and you shall have the ten to spend if youll only talk to me so as to remind me I'm a human being. I get tired of being a servant occasionally.

LOUKA Yes: sell your manhood for 30 levas, and buy me for 10! (*Rising scornfully*) Keep your money. You were born to be a servant. I was not. When you set up your shop you will only be everybody's servant instead of somebody's servant. (*She goes moodily to the table and seats herself regally in Sergius's chair*).

NICOLA (*picking up his logs, and going to the stove*) Ah, wait til you see. We shall have our evenings to ourselves; and I shall be master in my own house, I promise you. (*He throws the logs down and kneels at the stove*).

LOUKA You shall never be master in mine.

NICOLA (*turning, still on his knees, and squatting down rather forlornly on his calves, daunted by her implacable disdain*) You have a great ambition in you, Louka. Remember: if any luck comes to you, it was I that made a woman of you.

LOUKA You!

NICOLA (*scrambling up and going at her*) Yes, me. Who was it made you give up wearing a couple of pounds of false black hair on your head and reddening your lips and cheeks like any other Bulgarian girl! I did. Who taught you to trim your nails, and keep your hands clean, and be dainty about yourself, like a fine Russian lady? Me: do you hear that? me! (*She tosses her head defiantly; and he turns away, adding, more coolly*) Ive often thought that if Raina were out of the way, and you just a little less of a fool and Sergius just a little more of one, you might come to be one of my grandest customers, instead of only being my wife and costing me money.

LOUKA   I believe you would rather be my servant than my husband. You would make more out of me. Oh, I know that soul of yours.

NICOLA (*going closer to her for greater emphasis*)   Never you mind my soul; but just listen to my advice. If you want to be a lady, your present behavior to me wont do at all, unless when we're alone. It's too sharp and impudent; and impudence is a sort of familiarity: it shews affection for me. And dont you try being high and mighty with me, either. Youre like all country girls: you think it's genteel to treat a servant the way I treat a stableboy. Thats only your ignorance; and dont you forget it. And dont be so ready to defy everybody. Act as if you expected to have your own way, not as if you expected to be ordered about. The way to get on as a lady is the same as the way to get on as a servant: youve got to know your place: thats the secret of it. And you may depend on me to know my place if you get promoted. Think over it, my girl. I'll stand by you: one servant should always stand by another.

LOUKA (*rising impatiently*)   Oh, I must behave in my own way. You take all the courage out of me with your cold-blooded wisdom. Go and put those logs on the fire: thats the sort of thing you understand.

Before NICOLA *can retort,* SERGIUS *comes in. He checks himself a moment on seeing* LOUKA; *then goes to the stove.*

SERGIUS (*to* NICOLA)   I am not in the way of your work, I hope.

NICOLA (*in a smooth, elderly manner*)   Oh no, sir: thank you kindly. I was only speaking to this foolish girl about her habit of running up here to the library whenever she gets a chance, to look at the books. Thats the worst of her education, sir: it gives her habits above her station. (*To* LOUKA) Make that table tidy, Louka, for the Major. (*He goes out sedately*).

LOUKA, *without looking at* SERGIUS, *pretends to arrange the papers on the table. He crosses slowly to her, and studies the arrangement of her sleeve reflectively.*

SERGIUS   Let me see: is there a mark there? (*He turns up the bracelet and sees the bruise made by his grasp. She stands motionless, not looking at him: fascinated, but on her guard*). Ffff! Does it hurt?

LOUKA   Yes.

SERGIUS   Shall I cure it?

LOUKA (*instantly withdrawing herself proudly, but still not looking at him*)   No. You cannot cure it now.

SERGIUS (*masterfully*)   Quite sure? (*He makes a movement as if to take her in his arms*).

LOUKA   Dont trifle with me, please. An officer should not trifle with a servant.

SERGIUS (*indicating the bruise with a merciless stroke of his forefinger*)   That was no trifle, Louka.

LOUKA (*flinching; then looking at him for the first time*)   Are you sorry?

SERGIUS (*with measured emphasis, folding his arms*)   I am never sorry.

LOUKA (*wistfully*)   I wish I could believe a man could be as unlike a woman as that. I wonder are you really a brave man?

SERGIUS (*unaffectedly, relaxing his attitude*)   Yes: I am a brave man. My heart jumped like a woman's at the first shot; but in the charge I found that I was brave. Yes: that at least is real about me.

LOUKA   Did you find in the charge that the men whose fathers are poor like mine were any less brave than the men who are rich like you.

SERGIUS (*with bitter levity*)   Not a bit. They all slashed and cursed and yelled like heroes. Psha! the courage to rage and kill is cheap. I have an English bull terrier who has as much of that sort of courage as the whole Bulgarian nation, and the whole Russian nation at its back. But he lets my groom thrash him, all the same. Thats your soldier all over! No, Louka: your poor men can cut throats; but they are afraid of their officers; they put up with insults and blows; they stand by and see one another punished like children: aye, and help to do it when they are ordered. And the officers!!! Well (*with a short harsh laugh*) I am an officer. Oh, (*fervently*) give me the man who will defy to the death any power on earth or in heaven that sets itself up against his own will and conscience: he alone is the brave man.

LOUKA   How easy it is to talk! Men never seem to me to grow up: they all have schoolboy's ideas. You dont know what true courage is.

SERGIUS (*ironically*)   Indeed! I am willing to be instructed. (*He sits on the ottoman, sprawling magnificently*).

LOUKA   Look at me! how much am I allowed to have my own will? I have to get your room ready for you: to sweep and dust, to fetch and carry. How could that degrade me if it did not degrade you to have it done for you? But (*with subdued passion*) if I were Empress of Russia, above everyone in the world, then!! Ah then, though according to you I could shew no courage at all, you should see, you should see.

SERGIUS   What would you do, most noble Empress?

LOUKA   I would marry the man I loved, which no other queen in Europe has the courage to do. If I loved you, though you would be as far beneath me as I am beneath you, I would dare to be the equal of my inferior. Would you dare as much if you loved me? No: if you felt the beginnings of love for me you would not let it grow. You would not dare: you would marry a rich man's daughter because you would be afraid of what other people would say of you.

SERGIUS (*bounding up*)   You lie: it is not so, by all the stars! If I loved you, and I were the Czar himself, I would set you on the throne by my side. You know that I love another woman, a woman as high above you as heaven is above earth. And you are jealous of her.

LOUKA   I have no reason to be. She will never marry you now. The man I told you of has come back. She will marry the Swiss.

SERGIUS (*recoiling*)   The Swiss!

LOUKA   A man worth ten of you. Then you can come to me; and I will refuse you. You are not good enough for me. (*She turns to the door*).

SERGIUS (*springing after her and catching her fiercely in his arms*)   I will kill the Swiss; and afterwards I will do as I please with you.

LOUKA (*in his arms, passive and steadfast*)   The Swiss will kill you, perhaps. He has beaten you in love. He may beat you in war.

SERGIUS (*tormentedly*)   Do you think I believe that she — she! whose worst thoughts are higher than your best ones, is capable of trifling with another man behind my back?

LOUKA   Do you think she would believe the Swiss if he told her now that I am in your arms?

SERGIUS (*releasing her in despair*)   Damnation! Oh, damnation! Mockery!

mockery everywhere! everything I think is mocked by everything I do. (*He strikes himself frantically on the breast*). Coward! liar! fool! Shall I kill myself like a man, or live and pretend to laugh at myself? (*She again turns to go*). Louka! (*She stops near the door*). Remember: you belong to me.

LOUKA (*turning*) What does that mean? An insult?

SERGIUS (*commandingly*) It means that you love me, and that I have had you here in my arms, and will perhaps have you there again. Whether that is an insult I neither know nor care: take it as you please. But (*vehemently*) I will not be a coward and a trifler. If I choose to love you, I dare marry you, in spite of all Bulgaria. If these hands ever touch you again, they shall touch my affianced bride.

LOUKA We shall see whether you dare keep your word. And take care. I will not wait long.

SERGIUS (*again folding his arms and standing motionless in the middle of the room*) Yes: we shall see. And you shall wait my pleasure.

BLUNTSCHLI, *much preoccupied, with his papers still in his hand, enters, leaving the door open for* LOUKA *to go out. He goes across to the table, glancing at her as he passes.* SERGIUS, *without altering his resolute attitude, watches him steadily.* LOUKA *goes out, leaving the door open.*

BLUNTSCHLI (*absently, sitting at the table as before, and putting down his papers*) Thats a remarkable looking young woman.

SERGIUS (*gravely, without moving*) Captain Bluntschli.

BLUNTSCHLI Eh?

SERGIUS You have deceived me. You are my rival. I brook no rivals. At six oclock I shall be in the drilling-ground on the Klissoura road, alone, on horseback, with my sabre. Do you understand?

BLUNTSCHLI (*staring, but sitting quite at his ease*) Oh, thank you: thats a cavalry man's proposal. I'm in the artillery; and I have the choice of weapons. If I go, I shall take a machine gun. And there shall be no mistake about the cartridges this time.

SERGIUS (*flushing, but with deadly coldness*) Take care, sir. It is not our custom in Bulgaria to allow invitations of that kind to be trifled with.

BLUNTSCHLI (*warmly*) Pooh! don't talk to me about Bulgaria. You dont know what fighting is. But have it your own way. Bring your sabre along. I'll meet you.

SERGIUS (*fiercely delighted to find his opponent a man of spirit*) Well said. Switzer. Shall I lend you my best horse?

BLUNTSCHLI No: damn your horse! thank you all the same, my dear fellow. (RAINA *comes in, and hears the next sentence*). I shall fight you on foot. Horseback's too dangerous: I dont want to kill you if I can help it.

RAINA (*hurrying forward anxiously*) I have heard what Captain Bluntschli said, Sergius. You are going to fight. Why? (SERGIUS *turns away in silence, and goes to the stove, where he stands watching her as she continues, to* BLUNTSCHLI) What about?

BLUNTSCHLI I dont know: he hasnt told me. Better not interfere, dear young lady. No harm will be done: Ive often acted as sword instructor. He wont be able to touch me; and I'll not hurt him. It will save explanations. In the morning I shall be off home; and youll never see me or hear of me again. You and he will then make it up and live happily ever after.

RAINA (*turning away deeply hurt, almost with a sob in her voice*)   I never said I wanted to see you again.

SERGIUS (*striding forward*)   Ha! That is a confession.

RAINA (*haughtily*)   What do you mean?

SERGIUS   You love that man!

RAINA (*scandalized*)   Sergius!

SERGIUS   You allow him to make love to you behind my back, just as you treat me as your affianced husband behind his. Bluntschli: you knew our relations; you deceived me. It is for that I call you to account, not for having received favors *I* never enjoyed.

BLUNTSCHLI (*jumping up indignantly*)   Stuff! Rubbish! I have received no favors. Why, the young lady doesnt even know whether I'm married or not.

RAINA (*forgetting herself*)   Oh! (*Collapsing on the ottoman*) Are you?

SERGIUS   You see the young lady's concern, Captain Bluntschli. Denial is useless. You have enjoyed the privilege of being received in her own room, late at night —

BLUNTSCHLI (*interrupting him pepperily*)   Yes, you blockhead! she received me with a pistol at her head. Your cavalry were at my heels. I'd have blown out her brains if she'd uttered a cry.

SERGIUS (*taken aback*)   Bluntschli! Raina: is this true?

RAINA (*rising in wrathful majesty*)   Oh, how dare you, how dare you?

BLUNTSCHLI   Apologize, man: apologize. (*He resumes his seat at the table*).

SERGIUS (*with the old measured emphasis, folding his arms*)   I never apologize!

RAINA (*passionately*)   This is the doing of that friend of yours, Captain Bluntschli. It is he who is spreading this horrible story about me. (*She walks about excitedly*).

BLUNTSCHLI   No: he's dead. Burnt alive.

RAINA (*Stopping, shocked*)   Burnt alive!

BLUNTSCHLI   Shot in the hip in a woodyard. Couldnt drag himself out. Your fellows' shells set the timber on fire and burnt him, with half a dozen other poor devils in the same predicament.

RAINA   How horrible!

SERGIUS   And how ridiculous! Oh, war! war! the dream of patriots and heroes! A fraud, Bluntschli. A hollow sham, like love.

RAINA (*outraged*)   Like love! You say that before me!

BLUNTSCHLI   Come, Saranoff: that matter is explained.

SERGIUS   A hollow sham, I say. Would you have come back here if nothing had passed between you except at the muzzle of your pistol? Raina is mistaken about your friend who was burnt. He was not my informant.

RAINA   Who then? (*Suddenly guessing the truth*) Ah, Louka! my maid! my servant! You were with her this morning all that time after — after — Oh, what sort of god is this I have been worshipping! (*He meets her gaze with sardonic enjoyment of her disenchantment. Angered all the more, she goes closer to him, and says, in a lower, intenser tone*) Do you know that I looked out of the window as I went upstairs, to have another sight of my hero; and I saw something I did not understand then. I know now that you were making love to her.

SERGIUS (*with grim humor*)   You saw that?

RAINA   Only too well. (*She turns away, and throws herself on the divan under the centre window, quite overcome*).

SERGIUS (*cynically*) Raina: our romance is shattered. Life's a farce.

BLUNTSCHLI (*to Raina, whimsically*) You see: he's found himself out now.

SERGIUS (*going to him*) Bluntschli: I have allowed you to call me a blockhead. You may now call me a coward as well. I refuse to fight you. Do you know why?

BLUNTSCHLI No; but it doesnt matter. I didnt ask the reason when you cried on; and I dont ask the reason now that you cry off. I'm a professional soldier: I fight when I have to, and am very glad to get out of it when I havnt to. Youre only an amateur: you think fighting's an amusement.

SERGIUS (*sitting down at the table, nose to nose with him*) You shall hear the reason all the same, my professional. The reason is that it takes two men — real men — men of heart, blood and honor — to make a genuine combat. I could no more fight with you than I could make love to an ugly woman. Youve no magnetism: youre not a man: youre a machine.

BLUNTSCHLI (*apologetically*) Quite true, quite true. I always was that sort of chap. I'm very sorry.

SERGIUS Psha!

BLUNTSCHLI But now that youve found that life isnt a farce, but something quite sensible and serious, what further obstacle is there to your happiness?

RAINA (*rising*) You are very solicitous about my happiness and his. Do you forget his new love — Louka? It is not you that he must fight now, but his rival, Nicola.

SERGIUS Rival!! (*bounding half across the room*).

RAINA Dont you know that theyre engaged?

SERGIUS Nicola! Are fresh abysses opening? Nicola!!

RAINA (*sarcastically*) A shocking sacrifice, isnt it? Such beauty! such intellect! such modesty! wasted on a middle-aged servant man. Really, Sergius, you cannot stand by and allow such a thing. It would be unworthy of your chivalry.

SERGIUS (*losing all self-control*) Viper! Viper! (*He rushes to and fro, raging*).

BLUNTSCHLI Look here, Saranoff: youre getting the worst of this.

RAINA (*getting angrier*) Do you realize what he has done, Captain Bluntschli? He has set this girl as a spy on us; and her reward is that he makes love to her.

SERGIUS False! Monstrous!

RAINA Monstrous! (*Confronting him*) Do you deny that she told you about Captain Bluntschli being in my room?

SERGIUS No; but —

RAINA (*interrupting*) Do you deny that you were making love to her when she told you?

SERGIUS No; but I tell you —

RAINA (*cutting him short contemptuously*) It is unnecessary to tell us anything more. That is quite enough for us. (*She turns away from him and sweeps majestically back to the window*).

BLUNTSCHLI (*quietly, as* SERGIUS, *in an agony of mortification, sinks on the ottoman, clutching his averted head between his fists*) I told you you were getting the worst of it, Saranoff.

SERGIUS Tiger cat!

RAINA (*running excitedly to* BLUNTSCHLI) You hear this man calling me names, Captain Bluntschli?

BLUNTSCHLI   What else can he do, dear lady? He must defend himself somehow. Come (*very persuasively*): dont quarrel. What good does it do?

*RAINA, with a gasp, sits down on the ottoman, and after a vain effort to
look vexedly at* BLUNTSCHLI, *falls a victim to her sense of humor, and actually leans back babyishly against the writhing shoulder of* SERGIUS.

SERGIUS   Engaged to Nicola! Ha! ha! Ah well, Bluntschli, you are right to
take this huge imposture of a world coolly.

RAINA (*quaintly to* BLUNTSCHLI, *with an intuitive guess at his state of mind*)
I daresay you think us a couple of grown-up babies, dont you?

SERGIUS (*grinning savagely*)   He does: he does. Swiss civilization nursetending
Bulgarian barbarism? eh?

BLUNTSCHLI (*blushing*)   Not at all, I assure you. I'm only very glad to get you
two quieted. There! there! let's be pleasant and talk it over in a friendly way.
Where is this other young lady?

RAINA   Listening at the door, probably.

SERGIUS (*shivering as if a bullet had struck him, and speaking with quiet but
deep indignation*)   I will prove that that, at least, is a calumny. (*He goes
with dignity to the door and opens it. A yell of fury bursts from him as he
looks out. He darts into the passage, and returns dragging in* LOUKA, *whom
he flings violently against the table, exclaiming*) Judge her, Bluntschli. You,
the cool impartial man: judge the eavesdropper.

LOUKA stands her ground, proud and silent.

BLUNTSCHLI (*shaking his head*)   I mustnt judge her. I once listened myself
outside a tent when there was a mutiny brewing. It's all a question of the
degree of provocation. My life was at stake.

LOUKA   My love was at stake. I am not ashamed.

RAINA (*contemptuously*)   Your love! Your curiosity, you mean.

LOUKA (*facing her and retorting her contempt with interest*)   My love, stronger
than anything you can feel, even for your chocolate cream soldier.

SERGIUS (*with quick suspicion, to* LOUKA)   What does that mean?

LOUKA (*fiercely*)   It means —

SERGIUS (*interrupting her slightingly*)   Oh, I remember: the ice pudding. A
paltry taunt, girl!

MAJOR PETKOFF enters, in his shirtsleeves.

PETKOFF   Excuse my shirtsleeves, gentlemen. Raina: somebody has been wearing that coat of mine: I'll swear it. Somebody with a differently shaped back.
It's all burst open at the sleeve. Your mother is mending it. I wish she'd
make haste: I shall catch cold. (*He looks more attentively at them*). Is anything the matter?

RAINA   No. (*She sits down at the stove, with a tranquil air*).

SERGIUS   Oh no. (*He sits down at the end of the table, as at first*).

BLUNTSCHLI (*who is already seated*)   Nothing. Nothing.

PETKOFF (*sitting down on the ottoman in his old place*)   Thats all right. (*He
notices* LOUKA). Anything the matter, Louka?

LOUKA   No, sir.

PETKOFF (*genially*)   Thats all right. (*He sneezes*) Go and ask your mistress
for my coat, like a good girl, will you?

*NICOLA enters with the coat. LOUKA makes a pretence of having business
in the room by taking the little table with the hookah away to the wall near
the windows.*

RAINA (*rising quickly as she sees the coat on Nicola's arm*) Here it is, papa. Give it to me, Nicola; and do you put some more wood on the fire. (*She takes the coat, and brings it to the* MAJOR, *who stands up to put it on.* NICOLA *attends to the fire*).

PETKOFF (*to* RAINA, *teasing her affectionately*) Aha! Going to be very good to poor old papa just for one day after his return from the wars, eh?

RAINA (*with solemn reproach*) Ah, how can you say that to me, father?

PETKOFF Well, well, only a joke, little one. Come: give me a kiss. (*She kisses him*). Now give me the coat.

RAINA No: I am going to put it on for you. Turn your back. (*He turns his back and feels behind him with his arms for the sleeves. She dexterously takes the photograph from the pocket and throws it on the table before* BLUNTSCHLI, *who covers it with a sheet of paper under the very nose of* SERGIUS, *who looks on amazed, with his suspicions roused in the highest degree. She then helps* PETKOFF *on with his coat*). There, dear! Now are you comfortable?

PETKOFF Quite, little love. Thanks. (*He sits down; and* RAINA *returns to her seat near the stove*). Oh, by the bye, Ive found something funny. Whats the meaning of this? (*He puts his hand into the picked pocket*). Eh? Hallo! (*He tries the other pocket*). Well, I could have sworn — ! (*Much puzzled, he tries the breast pocket*). I wonder — (*trying the original pocket*). Where can it — ? (*He rises, exclaiming*) Your mother's taken it!

RAINA (*very red*) Taken what?

PETKOFF Your photograph, with the inscription: "Raina, to her Chocolate Cream Soldier: a Souvenir." Now you know theres something more in this than meets the eye; and I'm going to find it out. (*Shouting*) Nicola!

NICOLA (*coming to him*) Sir!

PETKOFF Did you spoil any pastry of Miss Raina's this morning?

NICOLA You heard Miss Raina say that I did, sir.

PETKOFF I know that, you idiot. Was it true?

NICOLA I am sure Miss Raina is incapable of saying anything that is not true, sir.

PETKOFF Are you? Then I'm not. (*Turning to the others*) Come: do you think I dont see it all? *He goes to* SERGIUS, *and slaps him on the shoulder*). Sergius: youre the chocolate cream soldier, arnt you?

SERGIUS (*starting up*) I! A chocolate cream soldier! Certainly not.

PETKOFF Not! (*He looks at them. They are all very serious and very conscious*). Do you mean to tell me that Raina sends things like that to other men?

SERGIUS (*enigmatically*) The world is not such an innocent place as we used to think, Petkoff.

BLUNTSCHLI (*rising*) It's all right, Major. I'm the chocolate cream soldier. (PETKOFF *and* SERGIUS *are equally astonished*). The gracious young lady saved my life by giving me chocolate creams when I was-starving: shall I ever forget their flavour! My late friend Stolz told you the story at Pirot. I was the fugitive.

PETKOFF You! (*He gasps*). Sergius: do you remember how those two women went on this morning when we mentioned it? (SERGIUS *smiles cynically*. PETKOFF *confronts* RAINA *severely*). Youre a nice young woman, arnt you?

RAINA (*bitterly*)   Major Saranoff has changed his mind. And when I wrote that on the photograph, I did not know that Captain Bluntschli was married.

BLUNTSCHLI (*startled into vehement protest*)   I'm not married.

RAINA (*with deep reproach*)   You said you were.

BLUNTSCHLI   I did not. I positively did not. I never was married in my life.

PETKOFF (*exasperated*)   Raina: will you kindly inform me, if I am not asking too much, which of these gentlemen you are engaged to?

RAINA   To neither of them. This young lady (*introducing* LOUKA, *who faces them all proudly*) is the object of Major Saranoff's affections at present.

PETKOFF   Louka! Are you mad, Sergius? Why, this girl's engaged to Nicola.

NICOLA   I beg your pardon, sir. There is a mistake. Louka is not engaged to me.

PETKOFF   Not engaged to you, you scoundrel! Why, you had twenty-five levas from me on the day of your betrothal; and she had that gilt bracelet from Miss Raina.

NICOLA (*with cool unction*)   We gave it out so, sir. But it was only to give Louka protection. She had a soul above her station; and I have been no more than her confidential servant. I intend, as you know, sir, to set up a shop later on in Sofia; and I look forward to her custom and recommendation should she marry into the nobility. (*He goes out with impressive discretion, leaving them all staring after him*).

PETKOFF (*breaking the silence*)   Well, I am — hm!

SERGIUS   This is either the finest heroism or the most crawling baseness. Which is it, Bluntschli?

BLUNTSCHLI   Never mind whether it's heroism or baseness. Nicola's the ablest man Ive met in Bulgaria. I'll make him manager of a hotel if he can speak French and German.

LOUKA (*suddenly breaking out at Sergius*)   I have been insulted by everyone here. You set them the example. You owe me an apology.

SERGIUS, *like a repeating clock of which the spring has been touched, immediately begins to fold his arms.*

BLUNTSCHLI (*before he can speak*)   It's no use. He never apologizes.

LOUKA   Not to you, his equal and his enemy. To me, his poor servant, he will not refuse to apologize.

SERGIUS (*approvingly*)   You are right. (*He bends his knee in his grandest manner*) Forgive me.

LOUKA   I forgive you. (*She timidly gives him her hand, which he kisses*) That touch makes me your affianced wife.

SERGIUS (*spring up*)   Ah! I forgot that.

LOUKA (*coldly*)   You can withdraw if you like.

SERGIUS   Withdraw! Never! You belong to me. (*He puts his arm about her*).

CATHERINE *comes in and finds* LOUKA *in Sergius's arms, with all the rest gazing at them in bewildered astonishment.*

CATHERINE   What does this mean?

SERGIUS *releases* LOUKA.

PETKOFF   Well, my dear, it appears that Sergius is going to marry Louka instead of Raina. (*She is about to break out indignantly at him: he stops her by exclaiming testily*) Dont blame me: Ive nothing to do with it. (*He retreats to the stove*).

CATHERINE   Marry Louka! Sergius: you are bound by your word to us!

SERGIUS (*folding his arms*)   Nothing binds me.

BLUNTSCHLI (*much pleased by this piece of common sense*)   Saranoff: your hand. My congratulations. These heroics of yours have their practical side after all. (*To* LOUKA) Gracious young lady: the best wishes of a good Republican! (*He kisses her hand, to Raina's great disgust, and returns to his seat*).

CATHERINE   Louka: you have been telling stories.

LOUKA   I have done Raina no harm.

CATHERINE (*haughtily*)   Raina!

RAINA, *equally indignant, almost snorts at the liberty*.

LOUKA   I have a right to call her Raina: she calls me Louka. I told Major Saranoff she would never marry him if the Swiss gentleman came back.

BLUNTSCHLI (*rising, much surprised*)   Hallo!

LOUKA (*turning to* RAINA)   I thought you were fonder of him than of Sergius. You know best whether I was right.

BLUNTSCHLI   What nonsense! I assure you, my dear Major, my dear Madam, the gracious young lady simply saved my life, nothing else. She never cared two straws for me. Why, bless my heart and soul, look at the young lady and look at me. She, rich, young, beautiful, with her imagination full of fairy princes and noble natures and cavalry charges and goodness knows what! And I, a commonplace Swiss soldier who hardly knows what a decent life is after fifteen years of barracks and battles: a vagabond, a man who has spoiled all his chances in life through an incurably romantic disposition, a man —

SERGIUS (*starting as if a needle had pricked him and interrupting* BLUNTSCHLI *in incredulous amazement*)   Excuse me, Bluntschli: what did you say had spoiled your chances in life?

BLUNTSCHLI (*promptly*)   An incurably romantic disposition. I ran away from home twice when I was a boy. I went into the army instead of into my father's business. I climbed the balcony of this house when a man of sense would have dived into the nearest cellar. I came sneaking back here to have another look at the young lady when any other man of my age would have sent the coat back —

PETKOFF   My coat!

BLUNTSCHLI   — yes: thats the coat I mean — would have sent it back and gone quietly home. Do you suppose I am the sort of fellow a young girl falls in love with? Why, look at our ages! I'm thirty-four: I dont suppose the young lady is much over seventeen. (*This estimate produces a marked sensation, all the rest turning and staring at one another. He proceeds innocently*) All that adventure which was life or death to me, was only a schoolgirl's game to her — chocolate creams and hide and seek. Heres the proof! (*He takes the photograph from the table*). Now, I ask you, would a woman who took the affair seriously have sent me this and written on it, "Raina, to her Chocolate Cream Soldier: a Souvenir"? (*He exhibits the photograph triumphantly, as if it settled the matter beyond all possibility of refutation*).

PETKOFF   Thats what I was looking for. How the deuce did it get there? (*He comes from the stove to look at it, and sits down at the ottoman*).

BLUNTSCHLI (*to* RAINA, *complacently*)   I have put everything right, I hope, gracious young lady.

RAINA (*going to the table to face him*)   I quite agree with your account of yourself. You are a romantic idiot. (BLUNTSCHLI *is unspeakably taken aback*). Next time, I hope you will know the difference between a school-girl of seventeen and a woman of twenty-three.

BLUNTSCHLI (*stupefied*) Twenty-three!

RAINA *snaps the photograph contemptuously from his hand; tears it up; throws the pieces in his face; and sweeps back to her former place.*

SERGIUS (*with grim enjoyment of his rival's discomfiture*) Bluntschli: my one last belief is gone. Your sagacity is a fraud, like everything else. You have less sense than even I!

BLUNTSCHLI (*overwhelmed*) Twenty-three! Twenty-three!! (*He considers*). Hm! (*Swiftly making up his mind and coming to his host*) In that case, Major Petkoff, I beg to propose formally to become a suitor for your daughter's hand, in place of Major Saranoff retired.

RAINA You dare!

BLUNTSCHLI If you were twenty-three when you said those things to me this afternoon, I shall take them seriously.

CATHERINE (*loftily polite*) I doubt, sir, whether you quite realize either my daughter's position or that of Major Sergius Saranoff, whose place you propose to take. The Petkoffs and the Saranoffs are known as the richest and most important families in the country. Our position is almost historical: we can go back for twenty years.

PETKOFF Oh never mind that, Catherine. (*To* BLUNTSCHLI) We should be most happy, Bluntschli, if it were only a question of your position; but hang it, you know, Raina is accustomed to a very comfortable establishment. Sergius keeps twenty horses.

BLUNTSCHLI But who wants twenty horses? We're not going to keep a circus.

CATHERINE (*severely*) My daughter, sir, is accustomed to a first-rate stable.

RAINA Hush, mother: youre making me ridiculous.

BLUNTSCHLI Oh well, if it comes to a question of an establishment, here goes! (*He darts impetuously to the table; seizes the papers in the blue envelope; and turns to* SERGIUS). How many horses did you say?

SERGIUS Twenty, noble Switzer.

BLUNTSCHLI I have two hundred horses. (*They are amazed*). How many carriages?

SERGIUS Three.

BLUNTSCHLI I have seventy. Twenty-four of them will hold twelve inside, besides two on the box, without counting the driver and conductor. How many tablecloths have you?

SERGIUS How the deuce do I know?

BLUNTSCHLI Have you four thousand?

SERGIUS No.

BLUNTSCHLI I have. I have nine thousand six hundred pairs of sheets and blankets, with two thousand four hundred eider-down quilts. I have ten thousand knives and forks, and the same quantity of dessert spoons. I have three hundred servants. I have six palatial establishments, besides two livery stables, a tea garden, and a private house. I have four medals for distinguished services; I have the rank of an officer and the standing of a gentleman; and I have three native languages. Shew me any man in Bulgaria that can offer as much!

PETKOFF (*with childish awe*) Are you Emperor of Switzerland?

BLUNTSCHLI My rank is the highest known in Switzerland: I am a free citizen.

CATHERINE Then, Captain Bluntschli, since you are my daughter's choice —

RAINA (*mutinously*) He's not.

CATHERINE (*ignoring her*) — I shall not stand in the way of her happiness. (PETKOFF *is about to speak*) That is Major Petkoff's feeling also.

PETKOFF Oh, I shall be only too glad. Two hundred horses! Whew!

SERGIUS What says the lady?

RAINA (*pretending to sulk*) The lady says that he can keep his tablecloths and his omnibuses. I am not here to be sold to the highest bidder. (*She turns her back on him*).

BLUNTSCHLI I wont take that answer. I appealed to you as a fugitive, a beggar, and a starving man. You accepted me. You gave me your hand to kiss, your bed to sleep in, and your roof to shelter me.

RAINA I did not give them to the Emperor of Switzerland.

BLUNTSCHLI Thats just what I say. (*He catches her by the shoulders and turns her face-to-face with him*). Now tell us whom you did give them to.

RAINA (*succumbing with a shy smile*) To my chocolate cream soldier.

BLUNTSCHLI (*with a boyish laugh of delight*) Thatll do. Thank you. (*He looks at his watch and suddenly becomes businesslike*). Time's up, Major. Youve managed those regiments so well that youre sure to be asked to get rid of some of the infantry of the Timok division. Send them home by way of Lom Palanka. Saranoff: dont get married until I come back: I shall be here punctually at five in the evening on Tuesday fortnight. Gracious ladies (*his heels click*) good evening. (*He makes them a military bow, and goes*).

SERGIUS What a man! Is he a man!

Exercises

1. Delineate the plot.

2. Outline the dramatic function of Act I.

3. Is Shaw primarily concerned with plot, character, or ideas? Explain.

4. Identify and describe the protagonist and that person's chief role in the play.

5. Does Raina change in the course of the play? Explain.

6. The play is a comedy. What means does Shaw employ to amuse us? Cite examples.

7. Shaw expresses strong views about the nature of war. Define these views and tell how they are conveyed.

8. Defend or refute charges by some critics that Shaw permits his characters to talk too much and act too little.

Topics for Writing

1. Describe Shaw's picture of middle-class society.

2. Explore how Shaw makes use of Bluntschli, Sergius, and Major Petkoff to transmit his views about the nature of war.

3. Examine the play as satire.

Selected Bibliography   George Bernard Shaw

Beerbohm, Max. *Around Theatres*. Elmsford, N.Y.: British Book Centre, 1953.

Bentley, Eric. *Bernard Shaw*. New York: New Directions, 1957.

Berst, Charles A. "Romance and Reality in 'Arms and the Man.'" *Modern Language Quarterly*, 27 (1966), 197–211.

Crompton, Louis. *Shaw the Dramatist*. Lincoln: University of Nebraska Press, 1969.

Ervine, St. John. *Bernard Shaw: His Life, Works, and Friends*. New York: Morrow, 1956.

Ganz, Arthur. "The Ascent to Heaven: A Shavian Pattern (Early Plays, 1894–1898)." *Modern Drama*, 14 (December 1971), 253–263.

Hummert, Paul A. *Bernard Shaw's Marxian Romance*. Lincoln: University of Nebraska Press, 1973.

Kaufmann, R. J., ed. *Shaw: A Collection of Critical Essays*. Englewood Cliffs, N.J.: Prentice-Hall, 1965.

Kaul, A. N. *The Action of English Comedy: Studies in the Encounter of Abstraction and Experience from Shakespeare to Shaw*. New Haven, Conn.: Yale University Press, 1970.

Kronenberger, Louis, ed. *George Bernard Shaw: A Critical Survey*. Cleveland: World, 1953.

Morgan, Margery M. *The Shavian Playground: An Exploration of the Art of Bernard Shaw*. London: Methuen, 1972.

Nethercot, Arthur. *Men and Supermen*. Cambridge, Mass.: Harvard University Press, 1954.

Novick, Julia. *Beyond Broadway: The Quest for Permanent Theatres*. New York: Hill & Wang, 1968.

Ohmann, Richard. *Shaw: The Style and the Man*. Middletown, Conn.: Wesleyan University Press, 1962.

Quinn, Michael. "Form and Intention: A Negative View of *Arms and the Man*." *Critical Quarterly*, 5 (1963), 148–154.

Shaw, George Bernard. *Shaw on Theatre,* ed. E. J. West. New York: Hill & Wang, 1958.

Smiley, Sam. *Playwriting: The Structure of Action*. Englewood Cliffs, N.J.: Prentice-Hall, 1971.

Valency, Maurice. *The Cart and the Trumpet: The Plays of George Bernard Shaw*. New York: New York University Press, 1973.

17. CHARACTER

Characters in drama, like their counterparts in fiction, divide into two broad categories. They are three-dimensional or one-dimensional.

Three-dimensional characters are developed fully, that is, as fully as is necessary to let us know them intimately. We know about their physical attributes, background, drives, frustrations, and perhaps even the cut of clothes they fancy. These round, or fully developed, characters are also known as **dynamic** or developing characters, which means that through the course of the action they grow and change. Something in the conflict has touched them deeply, so that at the final curtain they are different people from the ones we met at the opening.

Unlike three-dimensional characters, whose complex nature demands full treatment, **one-dimensional characters** (flat, stock, or stereotyped) are sketched simply, to give them one or two easily recognizable personality traits. They are **static** or flat characters who rarely change their essential nature or beliefs. Generally, we can identify the "type" quickly.

To be sure, each character is important; each serves a function, and all must be convincing. Among the many aspects of character, none is more important in our evaluation than **plausibility.** By plausibility we mean that what a character says or does is believable. And words and actions are believable if the character is *consistent*, not, as the common phrase reminds us, "out of character," and if the motivation is adequate — that is, if there are sufficient reasons within the characterization to account for words and actions.

Characters in plays resemble people in real life, and like their living counterparts manifest their personalities chiefly in what they do and say. In plays as in life, we get to know people by observing the way they look and the gestures they make, and by listening to the tone of voice they use and the remarks others make about them. Thus, the playwright reveals the personality of characters by means of action, dialogue, and (to a lesser degree) appearance and gesture.

Although the **methods of characterization** in fiction and drama are similar, the limitations of the dramatic form dictate two unmistakable differences.

First, the dramatic story, which imposes a time limitation on the playwright, forces him or her to compress delineations of characters and their actions. Unable to develop many of the characters completely, the dramatist makes use of any number of **stock** or type characters — the braggart, the dreamer, the fool, the liar, the do-gooder, the bumbler, the busybody, and so on.

Second, because drama permits us little or no direct access to the minds of characters, viewers or readers of drama must infer character. We must presuppose that in those selected moments of existence through which the characters pass, we are hearing and seeing significant aspects of their innermost natures.

In a well-crafted play, this is indeed true: every speech imparts something of the nature of the person speaking, the person spoken about, and sometimes the person spoken to; every action divulges something about the doer and the characters involved in or affected by that action. A **dramatic action** reveals character most prominently. In *Arms and the Man,* Sergius's amorous attentions to Louka while he is engaged to Raina reveal a false nature. In *Othello* (Chapter 19), masterful manipulations and schemes prove Iago to be a jealous, suspicious, lustful villain. Just as we learn something about people during the course of living, so we learn something about characters during the course of reading or seeing a play.

A **character's words** can generally tell us a lot about him or her. We form judgments about people based upon their opinions of others and their convictions about issues that concern them. The following speech by Marty, in Chayefsky's play (this chapter), clearly reveals his sensitive nature and his feelings of inferiority and failure with women.

Sooner or later, there comes a point in a man's life when he gotta face some facts, and one fact I gotta face is that whatever it is that women like, I ain't got it. I chased enough girls in my life. I went to enough dances. I got hurt enough. I don't wanna get hurt no more. I just called a girl this afternoon, and I got a real brush-off, boy. I figured I was past the point of being hurt, but that hurt. Some stupid woman who I didn't even wanna call up. She gave me the brush. That's the history of my life. I don't wanna go to the Waverly Ballroom because all that ever happened to me there was girls made me feel like I was a bug. I got feelings, you know. I had enough pain. No, thank you.

In the words below, Strindberg's Julie (Chapter 18) reveals herself to be utterly confused and helpless. She does not know who she is, what she wants, or how she should react to save her honor and her father's name.

Oh, I'm so tired! I can't do anything. Can't be sorry, can't run away, can't stay, can't live — can't die. Help me. Order me, and I'll obey like a dog. Do me this last service — save my honour, save his name. You know what I ought to do. . . . Use your strength and order me to do it.

A segment of dialogue from *The Sandbox* (Chapter 19) demonstrates the total domination of Mommy over Daddy.

MOMMY (*looking about*) This will do perfectly . . . don't you think so, Daddy? There's sand there . . . and the water beyond. What do you think, Daddy?
DADDY (*vaguely*) Whatever you say, Mommy.
MOMMY (*with the same little laugh*) Well, of course . . . whatever I say. Then, it's settled, is it?

In judging character, however, we may find that *how* something is said is just as valuable as *what* is said; the several occasions on which Oedipus reprimands Teiresias, Creon, Jocasta, and the shepherd for actions of which he disapproves show a king who loses his temper easily. What a character has to say about another character also tells us a great deal about the people that populate the stage. Biff's exchange of words with his father in *Death of a Salesman* (this chapter) reveals a young man with a new awareness of both himself and his father, as well as a determination to change his way of life.

> I am not a leader of men, Willy, and neither are you. You were never anything but a hard-working drummer who landed in the ash can like all the rest of them! I'm one dollar an hour, Willy! I tried seven states and couldn't raise it. A buck an hour! Do you gather my meaning? I'm not bringing home any prizes any more, and you're going to stop waiting for me to bring them home!

Physical appearance may also add significance to a characterization. Marty, who has difficulty getting dates with girls, sees himself as a fat, ugly, little man. Othello is a dark-skinned Moor. And Raina, as we see her at the very beginning of *Arms and the Man,* has wrapped herself in an expensive "mantle of furs" to look at the mountains from her balcony.

Everything that happens in a play is important. The way a character eats, laughs, opens doors, or hangs up a telephone may divulge a quirk, a motive, an attitude. In analyzing character, we need to ask *how* character is revealed. It is also important to determine *who* and *what* the characters are, *how* they act, and *why* they act as they do. To ask, and answer, these questions, we shall turn to two dramas from our own half-century, *Death of a Salesman* and *Marty*.

Death of a Salesman

Characters

WILLY LOMAN	HOWARD WAGNER
LINDA	JENNY
BIFF	STANLEY
HAPPY	MISS FORSYTHE
BERNARD	LETTA
THE WOMAN	CHARLEY
UNCLE BEN	

The place: Willy Loman's house and yard and various places he visits in the New York and Boston of today.

Throughout the play, in the stage directions, left and right mean stage left and stage right.

Act One

A melody is heard, played upon a flute. It is small and fine, telling of grass and trees and the horizon. The curtain rises.

Before us is the Salesman's house. We are aware of towering, angular shapes behind it, surrounding it on all sides. Only the blue light of the sky falls upon the house and forestage; the surrounding area shows an angry glow of orange. As more light appears, we see a solid vault of apartment houses around the small, fragile-seeming home. An air of the dream clings to the place, a dream rising out of reality. The kitchen at center seems actual enough, for there is a kitchen table with three chairs, and a refrigerator. But no other fixtures are seen. At the back of the kitchen there is a draped entrance, which leads to the living-room. To the right of the kitchen, on a level raised two feet, is a bedroom furnished only with a brass bedstead and a straight chair. On a shelf over the bed a silver athletic trophy stands. A window opens onto the apartment house at the side.

Behind the kitchen, on a level raised six and a half feet, is the boys' bedroom, at present barely visible. Two beds are dimly seen, and at the back of the room a dormer window. (This bedroom is above the unseen living-room.) At the left a stairway curves up to it from the kitchen.

The entire setting is wholly or, in some places, partially transparent. The roof-line of the house is one-dimensional; under and over it we see the apartment buildings. Before the house lies an apron, curving beyond the forestage into the orchestra. This forward area serves as the back yard as well as the locale of all WILLY'S imaginings and of his city scenes. Whenever the action is in the present the actors observe the imaginary wall-lines, entering the house only through its door at the left. But in the scenes of the past these boundaries are broken, and characters enter or leave a room by stepping "through" a wall onto the forestage.

From the right, WILLY LOMAN, *the Salesman, enters, carrying two large sample cases. The flute plays on. He hears but is not aware of it. He is past sixty years of age, dressed quietly. Even as he crosses the stage to the doorway of the house, his exhaustion is apparent. He unlocks the door, comes into the kitchen, and thankfully lets his burden down, feeling the soreness of his palms. A word-sigh escapes his lips — it might be "Oh, boy, oh, boy." He closes the door, then carries his cases out into the living-room, through the draped kitchen doorway.*

LINDA, *his wife, has stirred in her bed at the right. She gets out and puts on a robe, listening. Most often jovial, she has developed an iron repression of her exceptions to* WILLY'S *behavior — she more than loves him, she admires him, as though his mercurial nature, his temper, his massive dreams and little cruelties, served her only as sharp reminders of the turbulent longings within him, longings which she shares but lacks the temperament to utter and follow to their end.*

LINDA (*hearing* WILLY *outside the bedroom, calls with some trepidation*)   Willy!

WILLY   It's all right. I came back.

LINDA   Why? What happened? (*Slight pause*) Did something happen, Willy?

WILLY   No, nothing happened.

LINDA   You didn't smash the car, did you?

WILLY (*with casual irritation*)   I said nothing happened. Didn't you hear me?

LINDA   Don't you feel well?

WILLY   I'm tired to the death. (*The flute has faded away. He sits on the bed beside her, a little numb.*) I couldn't make it. I just couldn't make it, Linda.

LINDA (*very carefully, delicately*)   Where were you all day? You look terrible.

WILLY   I got as far as a little above Yonkers. I stopped for a cup of coffee. Maybe it was the coffee.

LINDA   What?

WILLY (*after a pause*)   I suddenly couldn't drive any more. The car kept going off onto the shoulder, y'know?

LINDA (*helpfully*)   Oh. Maybe it was the steering again. I don't think Angelo knows the Studebaker.

WILLY   No, it's me, it's me. Suddenly I realize I'm goin' sixty miles an hour and I don't remember the last five minutes. I'm — I can't seem to — keep my mind to it.

LINDA   Maybe it's your glasses. You never went for your new glasses.

WILLY   No, I see everything. I came back ten miles an hour. It took me nearly four hours from Yonkers.

LINDA (*resigned*)   Well, you'll just have to take a rest, Willy, you can't continue this way.

WILLY   I just got back from Florida.

LINDA   But you didn't rest your mind. Your mind is overactive, and the mind is what counts, dear.

WILLY   I'll start out in the morning. Maybe I'll feel better in the morning. (*She is taking off his shoes.*) These goddam arch supports are killing me.

LINDA   Take an aspirin. Should I get you an aspirin? It'll soothe you.

WILLY (*with wonder*)   I was driving along, you understand? And I was fine. I was even observing the scenery. You can imagine, me looking at scenery, on the road every week of my life. But it's so beautiful up there, Linda, the trees are so thick, and the sun is warm. I opened the windshield and just let the warm air bathe over me. And then all of a sudden I'm goin' off the road! I'm tellin' ya, I absolutely forgot I was driving. If I'd've gone the other way over the white line I might've killed somebody. So I went on again — and five minutes later I'm dreamin' again, and I nearly — (*He presses two fingers against his eyes.*) I have such thoughts, I have such strange thoughts.

LINDA   Willy, dear. Talk to them again. There's no reason why you can't work in New York.

WILLY   They don't need me in New York. I'm the New England man. I'm vital in New England.

LINDA   But you're sixty years old. They can't expect you to keep traveling every week.

WILLY   I'll have to send a wire to Portland. I'm supposed to see Brown and Morrison tomorrow morning at ten o'clock to show the line. Goddammit, I could sell them! (*He starts putting on his jacket.*)

LINDA   (*taking the jacket from him*)   Why don't you go down to the place tomorrow and tell Howard you've simply got to work in New York? You're too accommodating, dear.

WILLY   If old man Wagner was alive I'd a been in charge of New York now! That man was a prince, he was a masterful man. But that boy of his, that Howard, he don't appreciate. When I went north the first time, the Wagner Company didn't know where New England was!

LINDA   Why don't you tell those things to Howard, dear?

WILLY   (*encouraged*)   I will, I definitely will. Is there any cheese?

LINDA   I'll make you a sandwich.

WILLY   No, go to sleep. I'll take some milk. I'll be up right away. The boys in?

LINDA   They're sleeping. Happy took Biff on a date tonight.

WILLY   (*interested*)   That so?

LINDA   It was so nice to see them shaving together, one behind the other, in the bathroom. And going out together. You notice? The whole house smells of shaving lotion.

WILLY   Figure it out. Work a lifetime to pay off a house. You finally own it, and there's nobody to live in it.

LINDA   Well, dear, life is a casting off. It's always that way.

WILLY   No, no, some people — some people accomplish something. Did Biff say anything after I went this morning?

LINDA   You shouldn't have criticized him, Willy, especially after he just got off the train. You mustn't lose your temper with him.

WILLY   When the hell did I lose my temper? I simply asked him if he was making any money. Is that a criticism?

LINDA   But, dear, how could he make any money?

WILLY   (*worried and angered*)   There's such an undercurrent in him. He became a moody man. Did he apologize when I left this morning?

LINDA   He was crestfallen, Willy. You know how he admires you. I think if he finds himself, then you'll both be happier and not fight any more.

WILLY   How can he find himself on a farm? Is that a life? A farmhand? In the beginning, when he was young, I thought, well, a young man, it's good for him to tramp around, take a lot of different jobs. But it's more than ten years now and he has yet to make thirty-five dollars a week!

LINDA He's finding himself, Willy.

WILLY Not finding yourself at the age of thirty-four is a disgrace!

LINDA Shh!

WILLY The trouble is he's lazy, goddammit!

LINDA Willy, please!

WILLY Biff is a lazy bum!

LINDA They're sleeping. Get something to eat. Go on down.

WILLY Why did he come home? I would like to know what brought him home.

LINDA I don't know. I think he's still lost, Willy. I think he's very lost.

WILLY Biff Loman is lost. In the greatest country in the world a young man with such — personal attractiveness, gets lost. And such a hard worker. There's one thing about Biff — he's not lazy.

LINDA Never.

WILLY (*with pity and resolve*) I'll see him in the morning; I'll have a nice talk with him. I'll get him a job selling. He could be big in no time. My God! Remember how they used to follow him around in high school? When he smiled at one of them their faces lit up. When he walked down the street. . . . (*He loses himself in reminiscences.*)

LINDA (*trying to bring him out of it*) Willy, dear, I got a new kind of American-type cheese today. It's whipped.

WILLY Why do you get American when I like Swiss?

LINDA I just thought you'd like a change —

WILLY I don't want a change! I want Swiss cheese. Why am I always being contradicted?

LINDA (*with a covering laugh*) I thought it would be a surprise.

WILLY Why don't you open a window in here, for God's sake?

LINDA (*with infinite patience*) They're all open, dear.

WILLY The way they boxed us in here. Bricks and windows, windows and bricks.

LINDA We should've bought the land next door.

WILLY The street is lined with cars. There's not a breath of fresh air in the neighborhood. The grass don't grow any more, you can't raise a carrot in the back yard. They should've had a law against apartment houses. Remember those two beautiful elm trees out there? When I and Biff hung the swing between them?

LINDA Yeah, like being a million miles from the city.

WILLY They should've arrested the builder for cutting those down. They massacred the neighborhood. (*Lost*) More and more I think of those days, Linda. This time of year it was lilac and wisteria. And then the peonies would come out, and the daffodils. What fragrance in this room!

LINDA Well, after all, people had to move somewhere.

WILLY No, there's more people now.

LINDA I don't think there's more people. I think —

WILLY There's more people! That's what's ruining this country! Population is getting out of control. The competition is maddening! Smell the stink from that apartment house! And another one on the other side . . . How can they whip cheese?

(*On* WILLY'S *last line,* BIFF *and* HAPPY *raise themselves up in their beds, listening.*)

LINDA   Go down, try it. And be quiet.

WILLY   (*turning to* LINDA, *guiltily*)   You're not worried about me, are you, sweetheart?

BIFF   What's the matter?

HAPPY   Listen!

LINDA   You've got too much on the ball to worry about.

WILLY   You're my foundation and my support, Linda.

LINDA   Just try to relax, dear. You make mountains out of molehills.

WILLY   I won't fight with him any more. If he wants to go back to Texas, let him go.

LINDA   He'll find his way.

WILLY   Sure. Certain men just don't get started till later in life. Like Thomas Edison, I think. Or B. F. Goodrich.[1] One of them was deaf. (*He starts for the bedroom doorway.*) I'll put my money on Biff.

LINDA   And Willy — if it's warm Sunday we'll drive in the country. And we'll open the windshield, and take lunch.

WILLY   No, the windshields don't open on the new cars.

LINDA   But you opened it today.

WILLY   Me? I didn't. (*He stops.*) Now isn't that peculiar! Isn't that a remarkable — (*He breaks off in amazement and fright as the flute is heard distantly.*)

LINDA   What, darling?

WILLY   That is the most remarkable thing.

LINDA   What, dear?

WILLY   I was thinking of the Chevvy. (*Slight pause*) Nineteen twenty-eight . . . when I had that red Chevvy — (*Breaks off*) That funny? I coulda sworn I was driving that Chevvy today.

LINDA   Well, that's nothing. Something must've reminded you.

WILLY   Remarkable. Ts. Remember those days? The way Biff used to simonize that car? The dealer refused to believe there was eighty thousand miles on it. (*He shakes his head.*) Heh! (*To* LINDA) Close your eyes, I'll be right up. (*He walks out of the bedroom.*)

HAPPY   (*to* BIFF)   Jesus, maybe he smashed up the car again!

LINDA   (*calling after* WILLY)   Be careful on the stairs, dear! The cheese is on the middle shelf! (*She turns, goes over to the bed, takes his jacket, and goes out of the bedroom.*)

(*Light has risen on the boys' room. Unseen,* WILLY *is heard talking to himself, "Eighty thousand miles," and a little laugh.* BIFF *gets out of bed, comes downstage a bit, and stands attentively.* BIFF *is two years older than his brother* HAPPY, *well built, but in these days bears a worn air and seems less self-assured. He has succeeded less, and his dreams are stronger and less acceptable than* HAPPY'S. HAPPY *is tall, powerfully made. Sexuality is*

---

1. *Edison . . . Goodrich:* Thomas A. Edison (1847–1931), inventor in such fields as electric lighting, phonography, photography, and telegraphy; B. F. Goodrich (1841–1888), founder of one of the largest rubber manufacturing companies in the United States (1870); figures viewed by Willy as prime examples of the American success story.

like a visible color on him, or a scent that many women have discovered. He, like his brother, is lost, but in a different way, for he has never allowed himself to turn his face toward defeat and is thus more confused and hard-skinned, although seemingly more content.)

HAPPY (*getting out of bed*) He's going to get his license taken away if he keeps that up. I'm getting nervous about him, y'know, Biff?

BIFF His eyes are going.

HAPPY No, I've driven with him. He sees all right. He just doesn't keep his mind on it. I drove into the city with him last week. He stops at a green light and then it turns red and he goes. (*He laughs.*)

BIFF Maybe he's color-blind.

HAPPY Pop? Why he's got the finest eye for color in the business. You know that.

BIFF (*sitting down on his bed*) I'm going to sleep.

HAPPY You're not still sour on Dad, are you, Biff?

BIFF He's all right, I guess.

WILLY (*underneath them, in the living-room*) Yes, sir, eighty thousand miles — eighty-two thousand!

BIFF You smoking?

HAPPY (*holding out a pack of cigarettes*) Want one?

BIFF (*taking a cigarette*) I can never sleep when I smell it.

WILLY What a simonizing job, heh!

HAPPY (*with deep sentiment*) Funny, Biff, y'know? Us sleeping in here again? The old beds. (*He pats his bed affectionately.*) All the talk that went across those two beds, huh? Our whole lives.

BIFF Yeah. Lotta dreams and plans.

HAPPY (*with a deep and masculine laugh*) About five hundred women would like to know what was said in this room.
(*They share a soft laugh.*)

BIFF Remember that big Betsy something — what the hell was her name — over on Bushwick Avenue?

HAPPY (*combing his hair*) With the collie dog!

BIFF That's the one. I got you in there, remember?

HAPPY Yeah, that was my first time — I think. Boy, there was a pig! (*They laugh, almost crudely.*) You taught me everything I know about women. Don't forget that.

BIFF I bet you forgot how bashful you used to be. Especially with girls.

HAPPY Oh, I still am, Biff.

BIFF Oh, go on.

HAPPY I just control it, that's all. I think I got less bashful and you got more so. What happened, Biff? Where's the old humor, the old confidence? (*He shakes* BIFF's *knee.* BIFF *gets up and moves restlessly about the room.*) What's the matter?

BIFF Why does Dad mock me all the time?

HAPPY He's not mocking you, he —

BIFF Everything I say there's a twist of mockery on his face. I can't get near him.

HAPPY He just wants you to make good, that's all. I wanted to talk to you about Dad for a long time, Biff. Something's — happening to him. He — talks to himself.

BIFF   I noticed that this morning. But he always mumbled.

HAPPY   But not so noticeable. It got so embarrassing I sent him to Florida. And you know something? Most of the time he's talking to you.

BIFF   What's he say about me?

HAPPY   I can't make it out.

BIFF   What's he say about me?

HAPPY   I think the fact that you're not settled, that you're still kind of up in the air . . .

BIFF   There's one or two other things depressing him, Happy.

HAPPY   What do you mean?

BIFF   Never mind. Just don't lay it all to me.

HAPPY   But I think if you just got started — I mean — is there any future for you out there?

BIFF   I tell ya, Hap, I don't know what the future is. I don't know — what I'm supposed to want.

HAPPY   What do you mean?

BIFF   Well, I spent six or seven years after high school trying to work myself up. Shipping clerk, salesman, business of one kind or another. And it's a measly manner of existence. To get on that subway on the hot mornings in summer. To devote your whole life to keeping stock, or making phone calls, or selling or buying. To suffer fifty weeks of the year for the sake of a two-week vacation, when all you really desire is to be outdoors, with your shirt off. And always to have to get ahead of the next fella. And still — that's how you build a future.

HAPPY   Well, you really enjoy it on a farm? Are you content out there?

BIFF   (*with rising agitation*)   Hap, I've had twenty or thirty different kinds of jobs since I left home before the war, and it always turns out the same. I just realized it lately. In Nebraska when I herded cattle, and the Dakotas, and Arizona, and now in Texas. It's why I came home now, I guess, because I realized it. This farm I work on, it's spring there now, see? And they've got about fifteen new colts. There's nothing more inspiring or — beautiful than the sight of a mare and a new colt. And it's cool there now, see? Texas is cool now, and it's spring. And whenever spring comes to where I am, I suddenly get the feeling, my God, I'm not gettin' anywhere! What the hell am I doing, playing around with horses, twenty-eight dollars a week! I'm thirty-four years old, I oughta be makin' my future. That's when I come running home. And now, I get here, and I don't know what to do with myself. (*After a pause*) I've always made a point of not wasting my life, and everytime I come back here I know that all I've done is to waste my life.

HAPPY   You're a poet, you know that, Biff? You're a — you're an idealist!

BIFF   No, I'm mixed up very bad. Maybe I oughta get married. Maybe I oughta get stuck into something. Maybe that's my trouble. I'm like a boy. I'm not married, I'm not in business, I just — I'm like a boy. Are you content, Hap? You're a success, aren't you? Are you content?

HAPPY   Hell, no!

BIFF   Why? You're making money, aren't you?

HAPPY   (*moving about with energy, expressiveness*)   All I can do now is wait for the merchandise manager to die. And suppose I get to be merchandise manager? He's a good friend of mine, and he just built a terrific estate on

Long Island. And he lived there about two months and sold it, and now he's building another one. He can't enjoy it once it's finished. And I know that's just what I would do. I don't know what the hell I'm workin' for. Sometimes I sit in my apartment — all alone. And I think of the rent I'm paying. And it's crazy. But then, it's what I always wanted. My own apartment, a car, and plenty of women. And still, goddammit, I'm lonely.

BIFF (*with enthusiasm*) Listen, why don't you come out West with me?

HAPPY You and I, heh?

BIFF Sure, maybe we could buy a ranch. Raise cattle, use our muscles. Men built like we are should be working out in the open.

HAPPY (*avidly*) The Loman Brothers, heh?

BIFF (*with vast affection*) Sure, we'd be known all over the counties!

HAPPY (*enthralled*) That's what I dream about, Biff. Sometimes I want to just rip my clothes off in the middle of the store and outbox that goddam merchandise manager. I mean I can outbox, outrun, and outlift anybody in that store, and I have to take orders from those common, petty sons-of-bitches till I can't stand it any more.

BIFF I'm tellin' you, kid, if you were with me I'd be happy out there.

HAPPY (*enthused*) See, Biff, everybody around me is so false that I'm constantly lowering my ideals. . . .

BIFF Baby, together we'd stand up for one another, we'd have someone to trust.

HAPPY If I were around you —

BIFF Hap, the trouble is we weren't brought up to grub for money. I don't know how to do it.

HAPPY Neither can I!

BIFF Then let's go!

HAPPY The only thing is — what can you make out there?

BIFF But look at your friend. Builds an estate and then hasn't the peace of mind to live in it.

HAPPY Yeah, but when he walks into the store the waves part in front of him. That's fifty-two thousand dollars a year coming through the revolving door, and I got more in my pinky finger than he's got in his head.

BIFF Yeah, but you just said —

HAPPY I gotta show some of those pompous, self-important executives over there that Hap Loman can make the grade. I want to walk into the store the way he walks in. Then I'll go with you, Biff. We'll be together yet, I swear. But take those two we had tonight. Now weren't they gorgeous creatures?

BIFF Yeah, yeah, most gorgeous I've had in years.

HAPPY I get that any time I want, Biff. Whenever I feel disgusted. The only trouble is, it gets like bowling or something. I just keep knockin' them over and it doesn't mean anything. You still run around a lot?

BIFF Naa. I'd like to find a girl — steady, somebody with substance.

HAPPY That's what I long for.

BIFF Go on! You'd never come home.

HAPPY I would! Somebody with character, with resistance! Like Mom, y'know? You're gonna call me a bastard when I tell you this. That girl Charlotte I was with tonight is engaged to be married in five weeks. (*He tries on his new hat.*)

BIFF No kiddin'!

HAPPY Sure, the guy's in line for the vice-presidency of the store. I don't know what gets into me, maybe I just have an overdeveloped sense of competition or something, but I went and ruined her, and furthermore I can't get rid of her. And he's the third executive I've done that to. Isn't that a crummy characteristic? And to top it all, I go to their weddings! (*Indignantly, but laughing*) Like I'm not supposed to take bribes. Manufacturers offer me a hundred-dollar bill now and then to throw an order their way. You know how honest I am, but it's like this girl, see. I hate myself for it. Because I don't want the girl, and, still, I take it and — I love it!

BIFF   Let's go to sleep.

HAPPY   I guess we didn't settle anything, heh?

BIFF   I just got one idea that I think I'm going to try.

HAPPY   What's that?

BIFF   Remember Bill Oliver?

HAPPY   Sure, Oliver is very big now. You want to work for him again?

BIFF   No, but when I quit he said something to me. He put his arm on my shoulder, and he said, "Biff, if you ever need anything, come to me."

HAPPY   I remember that. That sounds good.

BIFF   I think I'll go to see him. If I could get ten thousand or even seven or eight thousand dollars I could buy a beautiful ranch.

HAPPY   I bet he'd back you. 'Cause he thought highly of you, Biff. I mean, they all do. You're well liked, Biff. That's why I say to come back here, and we both have the apartment. And I'm tellin' you, Biff, any babe you want. . . .

BIFF   No, with a ranch I could do the work I like and still be something. I just wonder though. I wonder if Oliver still thinks I stole that carton of basket-balls.

HAPPY   Oh, he probably forgot that long ago. It's almost ten years. You're too sensitive. Anyway, he didn't really fire you.

BIFF   Well, I think he was going to. I think that's why I quit. I was never sure whether he knew or not. I know he thought the world of me, though. I was the only one he'd let lock up the place.

WILLY (*below*)   You gonna wash the engine, Biff?

HAPPY   Shh!

(BIFF *looks at* HAPPY, *who is gazing down, listening.* WILLY *is mumbling in the parlor.*)

HAPPY   You hear that?

(*They listen.* WILLY *laughs warmly.*)

BIFF (*growing angry*)   Doesn't he know Mom can hear that?

WILLY   Don't get your sweater dirty, Biff!

(*A look of pain crosses* BIFF's *face.*)

HAPPY   Isn't that terrible? Don't leave again, will you? You'll find a job here. You gotta stick around. I don't know what to do about him, it's getting embarrassing.

WILLY   What a simonizing job!

BIFF   Mom's hearing that!

WILLY   No kiddin', Biff, you got a date? Wonderful!

HAPPY   Go on to sleep. But talk to him in the morning, will you?

BIFF (*reluctantly getting into bed*)   With her in the house. Brother!

HAPPY (*getting into bed*)   I wish you'd have a good talk with him.

(*The light on their room begins to fade.*)

BIFF (*to himself in bed*)   That selfish, stupid . . .

HAPPY   Sh . . . Sleep, Biff.

(*Their light is out. Well before they have finished speaking,* WILLY'S *form is dimly seen below in the darkened kitchen. He opens the refrigerator, searches in there, and takes out a bottle of milk. The apartment houses are fading out, and the entire house and surroundings become covered with leaves. Music insinuates itself as the leaves appear.*)

WILLY   Just wanna be careful with those girls, Biff, that's all. Don't make any promises. No promises of any kind. Because a girl, y'know, they always believe what you tell 'em, and you're very young, Biff, you're too young to be talking seriously to girls.

(*Light rises on the kitchen.* WILLY, *talking, shuts the refrigerator door and comes downstage to the kitchen table. He pours milk into a glass. He is totally immersed in himself, smiling faintly.*)

WILLY   Too young entirely, Biff. You want to watch your schooling first. Then when you're all set, there'll be plenty of girls for a boy like you. (*He smiles broadly at a kitchen chair.*) That so? The girls pay for you? (*He laughs.*) Boy, you must really be makin' a hit.

(WILLY *is gradually addressing — physically — a point offstage, speaking through the wall of the kitchen, and his voice has been rising in volume to that of a normal conversation.*)

WILLY   I been wondering why you polish the car so careful. Ha! Don't leave the hubcaps, boys. Get the chamois to the hubcaps. Happy, use newspaper on the windows, it's the easiest thing. Show him how to do it, Biff! You see, Happy? Pad it up, use it like a pad. That's it, that's it, good work. You're doin' all right, Hap. (*He pauses, then nods in approbation for a few seconds, then looks upward.*) Biff, first thing we gotta do when we get time is clip that big branch over the house. Afraid it's gonna fall in a storm and hit the roof. Tell you what. We get a rope and sling her around, and then we climb up there with a couple of saws and take her down. Soon as you finish the car, boys, I wanna see ya. I got a surprise for you, boys.

BIFF (*offstage*)   Whatta ya got, Dad?

WILLY   No, you finish first. Never leave a job till you're finished — remember that. (*Looking toward the "big trees"*) Biff, up in Albany I saw a beautiful hammock. I think I'll buy it next trip, and we'll hang it right between those two elms. Wouldn't that be something? Just swingin' there under those branches. Boy, that would be. . . .

(YOUNG BIFF *and* YOUNG HAPPY *appear from the direction* WILLY *was addressing.* HAPPY *carries rags and a pail of water.* BIFF, *wearing a sweater with a block "S," carries a football.*)

BIFF (*pointing in the direction of the car offstage*)   How's that, Pop, professional?

WILLY   Terrific. Terrific job, boys. Good work, Biff.

HAPPY   Where's the surprise, Pop?

WILLY   In the back seat of the car.

HAPPY   Boy! (*He runs off.*)

BIFF   What is it, Dad? Tell me, what'd you buy?

WILLY (*laughing, cuffs him*)   Never mind, something I want you to have.

BIFF (*turns and starts off*)   What is it, Hap?

HAPPY (*offstage*)   It's a punching bag!

BIFF   Oh, Pop!

WILLY   It's got Gene Tunney's[2] signature on it!

(HAPPY *runs onstage with a punching bag.*)

BIFF   Gee, how'd you know we wanted a punching bag?

WILLY   Well, it's the finest thing for the timing.

HAPPY (*lies down on his back and pedals with his feet*)   I'm losing weight, you notice, Pop?

WILLY (*to* HAPPY)   Jumping rope is good too.

BIFF   Did you see the new football I got?

WILLY (*examining the ball*)   Where'd you get a new ball?

BIFF   The coach told me to practice my passing.

WILLY   That so? And he gave you the ball, heh?

BIFF   Well, I borrowed it from the locker room. (*He laughs confidentially.*)

WILLY (*laughing with him at the theft*)   I want you to return that.

HAPPY   I told you he wouldn't like it!

BIFF (*angrily*)   Well, I'm bringing it back!

WILLY (*stopping the incipient argument, to* HAPPY)   Sure, he's gotta practice with a regulation ball, doesn't he? (*To* BIFF) Coach'll probably congratulate you on your initiative!

BIFF   Oh, he keeps congratulating my initiative all the time, Pop.

WILLY   That's because he likes you. If somebody else took that ball there'd be an uproar. So what's the report, boys, what's the report?

BIFF   Where'd you go this time, Dad? Gee we were lonesome for you.

WILLY (*pleased, puts an arm around each boy and they come down to the apron*)   Lonesome, heh?

BIFF   Missed you every minute.

WILLY   Don't say? Tell you a secret, boys. Don't breathe it to a soul. Someday I'll have my own business, and I'll never have to leave home any more.

HAPPY   Like Uncle Charley, heh?

WILLY   Bigger than Uncle Charley! Because Charley is not — liked. He's liked, but he's not — well liked.

BIFF   Where'd you go this time, Dad?

WILLY   Well, I got on the road, and I went north to Providence. Met the Mayor.

BIFF   The Mayor of Providence!

WILLY   He was sitting in the hotel lobby.

BIFF   What'd he say?

WILLY   He said, "Morning!" And I said, "You got a fine city here, Mayor." And then he had coffee with me. And then I went to Waterbury. Waterbury is a fine city. Big clock city, the famous Waterbury clock. Sold a nice bill there. And then Boston — Boston is the cradle of the Revolution. A fine city. And a couple of other towns in Mass., and on to Portland and Bangor and straight home!

BIFF   Gee, I'd love to go with you sometime, Dad.

WILLY   Soon as summer comes.

HAPPY   Promise?

WILLY   You and Hap and I, and I'll show you all the towns. America is full of beautiful towns and fine, upstanding people. And they know me, boys, they

2. *Gene Tunney:* Undefeated heavyweight boxing champion of the world between 1926 and 1928.

know me up and down New England. The finest people. And when I bring you fellas up, there'll be open sesame for all of us, 'cause one thing, boys: I have friends. I can park my car in any street in New England, and the cops protect it like their own. This summer, heh?

BIFF AND HAPPY (*together*)   Yeah! You bet!

WILLY   We'll take our bathing suits.

HAPPY   We'll carry your bags, Pop!

WILLY   Oh, won't that be something! Me comin' into the Boston stores with you boys carryin' my bags. What a sensation!

(BIFF *is prancing around, practicing passing the ball.*)

WILLY   You nervous, Biff, about the game?

BIFF   Not if you're gonna be there.

WILLY   What do they say about you in school, now that they made you captain?

HAPPY   There's a crowd of girls behind him everytime the classes change.

BIFF (*taking* WILLY'S *hand*)   This Saturday, Pop, this Saturday — just for you, I'm going to break through for a touchdown.

HAPPY   You're supposed to pass.

BIFF   I'm takin' one play for Pop. You watch me, Pop, and when I take off my helmet, that means I'm breakin' out. Then you watch me crash through that line!

WILLY (*kisses* BIFF)   Oh, wait'll I tell this in Boston!

(BERNARD *enters in knickers. He is younger than* BIFF, *earnest and loyal, a worried boy.*)

BERNARD   Biff, where are you? You're supposed to study with me today.

WILLY   Hey, looka Bernard. What're you lookin' so anemic about, Bernard?

BERNARD   He's gotta study, Uncle Willy. He's got Regents next week.

HAPPY (*tauntingly, spinning* BERNARD *around*)   Let's box, Bernard!

BERNARD   Biff! (*He gets away from* HAPPY.) Listen, Biff, I heard Mr. Birnbaum say that if you don't start studyin' math he's gonna flunk you, and you won't graduate. I heard him!

WILLY   You better study with him, Biff. Go ahead now.

BERNARD   I heard him!

BIFF   Oh, Pop, you didn't see my sneakers! (*He holds up a foot for* WILLY *to look at.*)

WILLY   Hey, that's a beautiful job of printing!

BERNARD (*wiping his glasses*)   Just because he printed University of Virginia on his sneakers doesn't mean they've got to graduate him, Uncle Willy!

WILLY (*angrily*)   What're you talking about? With scholarships to three universities they're gonna flunk him?

BERNARD   But I heard Mr. Birnbaum say —

WILLY   Don't be a pest, Bernard! (*To his boys*) What an anemic!

BERNARD   Okay, I'm waiting for you in my house, Biff.

(BERNARD *goes off.* THE LOMANS *laugh.*)

WILLY   Bernard is not well liked, is he?

BIFF   He's liked, but he's not well liked.

HAPPY   That's right, Pop.

WILLY   That's just what I mean. Bernard can get the best marks in school, y'understand, but when he gets out in the business world, y'understand, you are going to be five times ahead of him. That's why I thank Almighty God you're both built like Adonises. Because the man who makes an appearance in the business world, the man who creates personal interest, is the man who gets ahead. Be liked and you will never want. You take me, for instance. I never have to wait in line to see a buyer. "Willy Loman is here!" That's all they have to know, and I go right through.

BIFF   Did you knock them dead, Pop?

WILLY   Knocked 'em cold in Providence, slaughtered 'em in Boston.

HAPPY (*on his back, pedaling again*)   I'm losing weight, you notice, Pop?

(LINDA *enters, as of old, a ribbon in her hair, carrying a basket of washing.*)

LINDA (*with youthful energy*)   Hello, dear!

WILLY   Sweetheart!

LINDA   How'd the Chevvy run?

WILLY   Chevrolet, Linda, is the greatest car ever built. (*To the boys*) Since when do you let your mother carry wash up the stairs?

BIFF   Grab hold there, boy!

HAPPY   Where to, Mom?

LINDA   Hang them up on the line. And you better go down to your friends, Biff. The cellar is full of boys. They don't know what to do with themselves.

BIFF   Ah, when Pop comes home they can wait!

WILLY (*laughs appreciatively*)   You better go down and tell them what to do, Biff.

BIFF   I think I'll have them sweep out the furnace room.

WILLY   Good work, Biff.

BIFF (*goes through wall-line of kitchen to doorway at back and calls down*) Fellas! Everybody sweep out the furnace room! I'll be right down!

VOICES   All right! Okay, Biff.

BIFF   George and Sam and Frank, come out back! We're hangin' up the wash! Come on, Hap, on the double! (*He and* HAPPY *carry out the basket.*)

LINDA   The way they obey him!

WILLY   Well, that's training, the training. I'm tellin' you, I was sellin' thousands and thousands, but I had to come home.

LINDA   Oh, the whole block'll be at that game. Did you sell anything?

WILLY   I did five hundred gross in Providence and seven hundred gross in Boston.

LINDA   No! Wait a minute, I've got a pencil. (*She pulls pencil and paper out of her apron pocket.*) That makes your commission. . . . Two hundred — my God! Two hundred and twelve dollars!

WILLY   Well, I didn't figure it yet, but. . . .

LINDA   How much did you do?

WILLY   Well, I — I did — about a hundred and eighty gross in Providence. Well, no — it came to — roughly two hundred gross on the whole trip.

LINDA (*without hesitation*)   Two hundred gross. That's. . . . (*She figures.*)

WILLY   The trouble was that three of the stores were half closed for inventory in Boston. Otherwise I woulda broke records.

LINDA   Well, it makes seventy dollars and some pennies. That's very good.

WILLY   What do we owe?

LINDA   Well, on the first there's sixteen dollars on the refrigerator —

WILLY   Why sixteen?

LINDA   Well, the fan belt broke, so it was a dollar eighty.

WILLY   But it's brand new.

LINDA Well, the man said that's the way it is. Till they work themselves in, y'know.

(*They move through the wall-line into the kitchen.*)

WILLY I hope we didn't get stuck on that machine.

LINDA They got the biggest ads of any of them!

WILLY I know, it's a fine machine. What else?

LINDA Well, there's nine-sixty for the washing machine. And for the vacuum cleaner there's three and a half due on the fifteenth. Then the roof, you got twenty-one dollars remaining.

WILLY It don't leak, does it?

LINDA No, they did a wonderful job. Then you owe Frank for the carburetor.

WILLY I'm not going to pay that man! That goddam Chevrolet, they ought to prohibit the manufacture of that car!

LINDA Well, you owe him three and a half. And odds and ends, comes to around a hundred and twenty dollars by the fifteenth.

WILLY A hundred and twenty dollars! My God, if business don't pick up I don't know what I'm gonna do!

LINDA Well, next week you'll do better.

WILLY Oh, I'll knock 'em dead next week. I'll go to Hartford. I'm very well liked in Hartford. You know, the trouble is, Linda, people don't seem to take to me.

(*They move onto the forestage.*)

LINDA Oh, don't be foolish.

WILLY I know it when I walk in. They seem to laugh at me.

LINDA Why? Why would they laugh at you? Don't talk that way, Willy.

(WILLY *moves to the edge of the stage.* LINDA *goes into the kitchen and starts to darn stockings.*)

WILLY I don't know the reason for it, but they just pass me by. I'm not noticed.

LINDA But you're doing wonderful, dear. You're making seventy to a hundred dollars a week.

WILLY But I gotta be at it ten, twelve hours a day. Other men — I don't know — they do it easier. I don't know why — I can't stop myself — I talk too much. A man oughta come in with a few words. One thing about Charley. He's a man of few words, and they respect him.

LINDA You don't talk too much, you're just lively.

WILLY (*smiling*) Well, I figure, what the hell, life is short, a couple of jokes. (*To himself*) I joke too much! (*The smile goes.*)

LINDA Why? You're —

WILLY I'm fat. I'm very — foolish to look at, Linda. I didn't tell you, but Christmas time I happened to be calling on F. H. Stewarts, and a salesman I know, as I was going in to see the buyer I heard him say something about — walrus. And I — I cracked him right across the face. I won't take that. I simply will not take that. But they do laugh at me. I know that.

LINDA Darling. . . .

WILLY I gotta overcome it. I know I gotta overcome it. I'm not dressing to advantage, maybe.

LINDA Willy, darling, you're the handsomest man in the world —

WILLY Oh, no, Linda.

LINDA To me you are. (*Slight pause*) The handsomest.

(From the darkness is heard the laughter of a woman. WILLY *doesn't turn to it, but it continues through* LINDA'S *lines.)*

LINDA And the boys, Willy. Few men are idolized by their children the way you are.

(Music is heard as behind a scrim, to the left of the house, THE WOMAN, *dimly seen, is dressing.)*

WILLY *(with great feeling)* You're the best there is, Linda, you're a pal, you know that? On the road — on the road I want to grab you sometimes and just kiss the life outa you.

(The laughter is loud now, and he moves into a brightening area at the left, where THE WOMAN *has come from behind the scrim and is standing, putting on her hat, looking into a "mirror" and laughing.)*

WILLY 'Cause I get so lonely — especially when business is bad and there's nobody to talk to. I get the feeling that I'll never sell anything again, that I won't make a living for you, or a business, a business for the boys. *(He talks through* THE WOMAN'S *subsiding laughter;* THE WOMAN *primps at the "mirror.")* There's so much I want to make for —

THE WOMAN Me? You didn't make me, Willy. I picked you.

WILLY *(pleased)* You picked me?

THE WOMAN *(who is quite proper-looking,* WILLY'S *age).* I did. I've been sitting at that desk watching all the salesmen go by, day in, day out. But you've got such a sense of humor, and we do have such a good time together, don't we?

WILLY Sure, sure. *(He takes her in his arms.)* Why do you have to go now?

THE WOMAN It's two o'clock. . . .

WILLY No, come on in! *(He pulls her.)*

THE WOMAN . . . my sisters'll be scandalized. When'll you be back?

WILLY Oh, two weeks about. Will you come up again?

THE WOMAN Sure thing. You do make me laugh. It's good for me. *(She squeezes his arm, kisses him.)* And I think you're a wonderful man.

WILLY You picked me, heh?

THE WOMAN Sure. Because you're so sweet. And such a kidder.

WILLY Well, I'll see you next time I'm in Boston.

THE WOMAN I'll put you right through to the buyers.

WILLY *(slapping her bottom)* Right. Well, bottoms up!

THE WOMAN *(slaps him gently and laughs)* You just kill me, Willy. *(He suddenly grabs her and kisses her roughly.)* You kill me. And thanks for the stockings. I love a lot of stockings. Well, good night.

WILLY Good night. And keep your pores open!

THE WOMAN Oh, Willy!

*(*THE WOMAN *bursts out laughing, and* LINDA'S *laughter blends in.* THE WOMAN *disappears into the dark. Now the area at the kitchen table brightens.* LINDA *is sitting where she was at the kitchen table, but now is mending a pair of her silk stockings.)*

LINDA You are, Willy. The handsomest man. You've got no reason to feel that —

WILLY *(coming out of* THE WOMAN'S *dimming area and going over to* LINDA) I'll make it all up to you, Linda, I'll —

LINDA There's nothing to make up, dear. You're doing fine, better than —

WILLY *(noticing her mending)* What's that?

LINDA   Just mending my stockings. They're so expensive —

WILLY   (*angrily, taking them from her*)   I won't have you mending stockings in this house! Now throw them out!

(LINDA *puts the stockings in her pocket.*)

BERNARD   (*entering on the run*)   Where is he? If he doesn't study!

WILLY   (*moving to the forestage, with great agitation*)   You'll give him the answers!

BERNARD   I do, but I can't on a Regents! That's a state exam! They're liable to arrest me!

WILLY   Where is he? I'll whip him, I'll whip him!

LINDA   And he'd better give back that football, Willy, it's not nice.

WILLY   Biff! Where is he? Why is he taking everything?

LINDA   He's too rough with the girls, Willy. All the mothers are afraid of him!

WILLY   I'll whip him!

BERNARD   He's driving the car without a license!

(THE WOMAN's *laugh is heard.*)

WILLY   Shut up!

LINDA   All the mothers —

WILLY   Shut up!

BERNARD   (*backing quietly away and out*)   Mr. Birnbaum says he's stuck up.

WILLY   Get outa here!

BERNARD   If he doesn't buckle down he'll flunk math! (*He goes off.*)

LINDA   He's right, Willy, you've gotta —

WILLY   (*exploding at her*)   There's nothing the matter with him! You want him to be a worm like Bernard? He's got spirit, personality. . . .

(*As he speaks,* LINDA, *almost in tears, exits into the living-room.* WILLY *is alone in the kitchen, wilting and staring. The leaves are gone. It is night again, and the apartment houses look down from behind.*)

WILLY   Loaded with it. Loaded! What is he stealing? He's giving it back, isn't he? Why is he stealing? What did I tell him? I never in my life told him anything but decent things.

(HAPPY *in pajamas has come down the stairs;* WILLY *suddenly becomes aware of* HAPPY'S *presence.*)

HAPPY   Let's go now, come on.

WILLY   (*sitting down at the kitchen table*)   Huh! Why did she have to wax the floors herself? Everytime she waxes the floors she keels over. She knows that!

HAPPY   Shh! Take it easy. What brought you back tonight?

WILLY   I got an awful scare. Nearly hit a kid in Yonkers. God! Why didn't I go to Alaska with my brother Ben that time! Ben! That man was a genius, that man was success incarnate! What a mistake! He begged me to go.

HAPPY   Well, there's no use in —

WILLY   You guys! There was a man started with the clothes on his back and ended up with diamond mines!

HAPPY   Boy, someday I'd like to know how he did it.

WILLY   What's the mystery? The man knew what he wanted and went out and got it! Walked into a jungle, and comes out, the age of twenty-one, and he's rich! The world is an oyster, but you don't crack it open on a mattress!

HAPPY   Pop, I told you I'm gonna retire you for life.

WILLY   You'll retire me for life on seventy goddam dollars a week? And your women and your car and your apartment, and you'll retire me for life! Christ's sake, I couldn't get past Yonkers today! Where are you guys, where are you? The woods are burning! I can't drive a car!

(CHARLEY *has appeared in the doorway. He is a large man, slow of speech, laconic, immovable. In all he says, despite what he says, there is pity, and, now, trepidation. He has a robe over pajamas, slippers on his feet. He enters the kitchen.*)

CHARLEY   Everything all right?

HAPPY   Yeah, Charley, everything's . . .

WILLY   What's the matter?

CHARLEY   I heard some noise. I thought something happened. Can't we do something about the walls? You sneeze in here, and in my house hats blow off.

HAPPY   Let's go to bed, Dad. Come on.

(CHARLEY *signals to* HAPPY *to go.*)

WILLY   You go ahead, I'm not tired at the moment.

HAPPY (*to* WILLY)   Take it easy, huh? (*He exits.*)

WILLY   What're you doin' up?

CHARLEY (*sitting down at the kitchen table opposite* WILLY)   Couldn't sleep good. I had a heartburn.

WILLY   Well, you don't know how to eat.

CHARLEY   I eat with my mouth.

WILLY   No, you're ignorant. You gotta know about vitamins and things like that.

CHARLEY   Come on, let's shoot. Tire you out a little.

WILLY (*hesitantly*)   All right. You got cards?

CHARLEY (*taking a deck from his pocket*)   Yeah, I got them. Someplace. What is it with those vitamins?

WILLY (*dealing*)   They build up your bones. Chemistry.

CHARLEY   Yeah, but there's no bones in a heartburn.

WILLY   What are you talkin' about? Do you know the first thing about it?

CHARLEY   Don't get insulted.

WILLY   Don't talk about something you don't know anything about.

(*They are playing. Pause*)

CHARLEY   What're you doin' home?

WILLY   A little trouble with the car.

CHARLEY   Oh. (*Pause*) I'd like to take a trip to California.

WILLY   Don't say.

CHARLEY   You want a job?

WILLY   I got a job, I told you that. (*After a slight pause*) What the hell are you offering me a job for?

CHARLEY   Don't get insulted.

WILLY   Don't insult me.

CHARLEY   I don't see no sense in it. You don't have to go on this way.

WILLY   I got a good job. (*Slight pause*) What do you keep comin' in here for?

CHARLEY   You want me to go?

WILLY (*after a pause, withering*)   I can't understand it. He's going back to Texas again. What the hell is that?

CHARLEY   Let him go.

WILLY   I got nothin' to give him, Charley, I'm clean, I'm clean.

CHARLEY   He won't starve. None a them starve. Forget about him.

WILLY   Then what have I got to remember?

CHARLEY   You take it too hard. To hell with it. When a deposit bottle is broken you don't get your nickel back.

WILLY   That's easy enough for you to say.

CHARLEY   That ain't easy for me to say.

WILLY   Did you see the ceiling I put up in the living-room?

CHARLEY   Yeah, that's a piece of work. To put up a ceiling is a mystery to me. How do you do it?

WILLY   What's the difference?

CHARLEY   Well, talk about it.

WILLY   You gonna put up a ceiling?

CHARLEY   How could I put up a ceiling?

WILLY   Then what the hell are you bothering me for?

CHARLEY   You're insulted again.

WILLY   A man who can't handle tools is not a man. You're disgusting.

CHARLEY   Don't call me disgusting, Willy.

   (UNCLE BEN, *carrying a valise and an umbrella, enters the forestage from around the right corner of the house. He is a stolid man, in his sixties, with a mustache and an authoritative air. He is utterly certain of his destiny, and there is an aura of far places about him. He enters exactly as* WILLY *speaks.*)

WILLY   I'm getting awfully tired, Ben.

   (BEN'S *music is heard.* BEN *looks around at everything.*)

CHARLEY   Good, keep playing; you'll sleep better. Did you call me Ben?

   (BEN *looks at his watch.*)

WILLY   That's funny. For a second there you reminded me of my brother Ben.

BEN   I only have a few minutes. (*He strolls, inspecting the place.* WILLY *and* CHARLEY *continue playing.*)

CHARLEY   You never heard from him again, heh? Since that time?

WILLY   Didn't Linda tell you? Couple of weeks ago we got a letter from his wife in Africa. He died.

CHARLEY   That so.

BEN   (*chuckling*)   So this is Brooklyn, eh?

CHARLEY   Maybe you're in for some of his money.

WILLY   Naa, he had seven sons. There's just one opportunity I had with that man. . . .

BEN   I must make a train, William. There are several properties I'm looking at in Alaska.

WILLY   Sure, sure! If I'd gone with him to Alaska that time, everything would've been totally different.

CHARLEY   Go on, you'd froze to death up there.

WILLY   What're you talking about?

BEN   Opportunity is tremendous in Alaska, William. Surprised you're not up there.

WILLY   Sure, tremendous.

CHARLEY   Heh?

WILLY   There was the only man I ever met who knew the answers.

CHARLEY   Who?

BEN   How are you all?

WILLY   (*taking a pot, smiling*)   Fine, fine.

CHARLEY   Pretty sharp tonight.

BEN   Is Mother living with you?

WILLY   No, she died a long time ago.

CHARLEY   Who?

BEN   That's too bad. Fine specimen of a lady, Mother.

WILLY (*to* CHARLEY)   Heh?

BEN   I'd hoped to see the old girl.

CHARLEY   Who died?

BEN   Heard anything from Father, have you?

WILLY (*unnerved*)   What do you mean, who died?

CHARLEY (*taking a pot*)   What're you talkin' about?

BEN (*looking at his watch*)   William, it's half past eight!

WILLY (*as though to dispel his confusion he angrily stops* CHARLEY'S *hand*)
    That's my build!

CHARLEY   I put the ace —

WILLY   If you don't know how to play the game I'm not gonna throw my
    money away on you!

CHARLEY (*rising*)   It was my ace, for God's sake!

WILLY   I'm through, I'm through!

BEN   When did Mother die?

WILLY   Long ago. Since the beginning you never knew how to play cards.

CHARLEY (*picks up the cards and goes to the door*)   All right! Next time I'll
    bring a deck with five aces.

WILLY   I don't play that kind of game!

CHARLEY (*turning to him*)   You ought to be ashamed of yourself!

WILLY   Yeah?

CHARLEY   Yeah! (*He goes out.*)

WILLY (*slamming the door after him*)   Ignoramus!

BEN (*as* WILLY *comes toward him through the wall-line of the kitchen*)   So
    you're William.

WILLY (*shaking* BEN'S *hand*)   Ben! I've been waiting for you so long! What's
    the answer? How did you do it?

BEN   Oh, there's a story in that.

    (LINDA *enters the forestage, as of old, carrying the wash basket.*)

LINDA   Is this Ben?

BEN (*gallantly*)   How do you do, my dear.

LINDA   Where've you been all these years? Willy's always wondered why you —

WILLY (*pulling* BEN *away from her impatiently*)   Where is Dad? Didn't you
    follow him? How did you get started?

BEN   Well, I don't know how much you remember.

WILLY   Well, I was just a baby, of course, only three or four years old —

BEN   Three years and eleven months.

WILLY   What a memory, Ben!

BEN   I have many enterprises, William, and I have never kept books.

WILLY   I remember I was sitting under the wagon in — was it Nebraska?

BEN   It was South Dakota, and I gave you a bunch of wild flowers.

WILLY   I remember you walking away down some open road.

BEN (*laughing*)   I was going to find Father in Alaska.

WILLY   Where is he?

BEN   At that age I had a very faulty view of geography, William. I discovered after a few days that I was heading due south, so instead of Alaska, I ended up in Africa.

LINDA Africa!

WILLY The Gold Coast!

BEN Principally diamond mines.

LINDA Diamond mines!

BEN Yes, my dear. But I've only a few minutes —

WILLY No! Boys! Boys! (YOUNG BIFF and HAPPY appear.) Listen to this. This is your Uncle Ben, a great man! Tell my boys, Ben!

BEN Why, boys, when I was seventeen I walked into the jungle, and when I was twenty-one I walked out. (He laughs.) And by God I was rich.

WILLY (to the boys) You see what I been talking about? The greatest things can happen!

BEN (glancing at his watch) I have an appointment in Ketchikan Tuesday week.

WILLY No, Ben! Please tell about Dad. I want my boys to hear. I want them to know the kind of stock they spring from. All I remember is a man with a big beard, and I was in Mamma's lap, sitting around a fire, and some kind of high music.

BEN His flute. He played the flute.

WILLY Sure, the flute, that's right!

(New music is heard, a high, rollicking tune.)

BEN Father was a very great and a very wild-hearted man. We would start in Boston, and he'd toss the whole family into the wagon, and then he'd drive the team right across the country; through Ohio, and Indiana, Michigan, Illinois, and all the Western states. And we'd stop in the towns and sell the flutes that he'd made on the way. Great inventor, Father. With one gadget he made more in a week than a man like you could make in a lifetime.

WILLY That's just the way I'm bringing them up, Ben — rugged, well liked, all-around.

BEN Yeah? (To BIFF) Hit that, boy — hard as you can. (He pounds his stomach.)

BIFF Oh, no, sir!

BEN (taking boxing stance) Come on, get to me! (He laughs.)

WILLY Go to it, Biff! Go ahead, show him!

BIFF Okay! (He cocks his fists and starts in.)

LINDA (to WILLY) Why must he fight, dear?

BEN (sparring with BIFF) Good boy! Good boy!

WILLY How's that, Ben, heh?

HAPPY Give him the left, Biff!

LINDA Why are you fighting?

BEN Good boy! (Suddenly comes in, trips BIFF, and stands over him, the point of his umbrella poised over BIFF's eye)

LINDA Look out, Biff!

BIFF Gee!

BEN (patting BIFF's knee) Never fight fair with a stranger, boy. You'll never get out of the jungle that way. (Taking LINDA's hand and bowing) It was an honor and a pleasure to meet you, Linda.

LINDA (withdrawing her hand coldly, frightened) Have a nice — trip.

BEN (*to* WILLY)   And good luck with your — what do you do?

WILLY   Selling.

BEN   Yes. Well . . . (*He raises his hand in farewell to all.*)

WILLY   No, Ben, I don't want you to think . . . (*He takes* BEN's *arm to show him.*)   It's Brooklyn, I know, but we hunt too.

BEN   Really, now.

WILLY   Oh, sure, there's snakes and rabbits and — that's why I moved out here. Why, Biff can fell any one of these trees in no time! Boys! Go right over to where they're building the apartment house and get some sand. We're gonna rebuild the entire front stoop right now! Watch this, Ben!

BIFF   Yes, sir! On the double, Hap!

HAPPY (*as he and* BIFF *run off*)   I lost weight, Pop, you notice?

(CHARLEY *enters in knickers, even before the boys are gone.*)

CHARLEY   Listen, if they steal any more from that building the watchman'll put the cops on them!

LINDA (*to* WILLY)   Don't let Biff . . .

(BEN *laughs lustily.*)

WILLY   You shoulda seen the lumber they brought home last week. At least a dozen six-by-tens worth all kinds a money.

CHARLEY   Listen, if that watchman —

WILLY   I gave them hell, understand. But I got a couple of fearless characters there.

CHARLEY   Willy, the jails are full of fearless characters.

BEN (*clapping* WILLY *on the back, with a laugh at* CHARLEY)   And the stock exchange, friend!

WILLY (*joining in* BEN's *laughter*)   Where are the rest of your pants?

CHARLEY   My wife bought them.

WILLY   Now all you need is a golf club and you can go upstairs and go to sleep. (*To* BEN)   Great athlete! Between him and his son Bernard they can't hammer a nail!

BERNARD (*rushing in*)   The watchman's chasing Biff!

WILLY (*angrily*)   Shut up! He's not stealing anything!

LINDA (*alarmed, hurrying off left*)   Where is he? Biff, dear! (*She exits.*)

WILLY (*moving toward the left, away from* BEN)   There's nothing wrong. What's the matter with you?

BEN   Nervy boy. Good!

WILLY (*laughing*)   Oh, nerves of iron, that Biff!

CHARLEY   Don't know what it is. My New England man comes back and he's bleedin', they murdered him up there.

WILLY   It's contacts, Charley, I got important contacts!

CHARLEY (*sarcastically*)   Glad to hear it, Willy. Come in later, we'll shoot a little casino. I'll take some of your Portland money. (*He laughs at* WILLY *and exits.*)

WILLY (*turning to* BEN)   Business is bad, it's murderous. But not for me, of course.

BEN   I'll stop by on my way back to Africa.

WILLY (*longingly*)   Can't you stay a few days? You're just what I need, Ben, because I — I have a fine position here, but I — well, Dad left when I was such a baby and I never had a chance to talk to him and I still feel — kind of temporary about myself.

BEN   I'll be late for my train.

(*They are at opposite ends of the stage.*)

WILLY   Ben, my boys — can't we talk? They'd go into the jaws of hell for me, see, but I —

BEN   William, you're being first-rate with your boys. Outstanding, manly chaps!

WILLY (*hanging on to his words*)   Oh, Ben, that's good to hear! Because sometimes I'm afraid that I'm not teaching them the right kind of — Ben, how should I teach them?

BEN (*giving great weight to each word, and with a certain vicious audacity*) William, when I walked into the jungle, I was seventeen. When I walked out I was twenty-one. And, by God, I was rich! (*He goes off into darkness around the right corner of the house.*)

WILLY   . . . was rich! That's just the spirit I want to imbue them with! To walk into a jungle! I was right! I was right! I was right!

(BEN *is gone, but* WILLY *is still speaking to him as* LINDA, *in nightgown and robe, enters the kitchen, glances around for* WILLY, *then goes to the door of the house, looks out and sees him. Comes down to his left. He looks at her.*)

LINDA   Willy, dear? Willy?

WILLY   I was right!

LINDA   Did you have some cheese? (*He can't answer.*) It's very late, darling. Come to bed, heh?

WILLY (*looking straight up*)   Gotta break your neck to see a star in this yard.

LINDA   You coming in?

WILLY   Whatever happened to that diamond watch fob? Remember? When Ben came from Africa that time? Didn't he give me a watch fob with a diamond in it?

LINDA   You pawned it, dear. Twelve, thirteen years ago. For Biff's radio correspondence course.

WILLY   Gee, that was a beautiful thing. I'll take a walk.

LINDA   But you're in your slippers.

WILLY (*starting to go around the house at the left*)   I was right! I was! (*Half to* LINDA, *as he goes, shaking his head*) What a man! There was a man worth talking to. I was right!

LINDA (*calling after* WILLY)   But in your slippers, Willy!

(WILLY *is almost gone when* BIFF, *in his pajamas, comes down the stairs and enters the kitchen.*)

BIFF   What is he doing out there?

LINDA   Sh!

BIFF   God Almighty, Mom, how long has he been doing this?

LINDA   Don't, he'll hear you.

BIFF   What the hell is the matter with him?

LINDA   It'll pass by morning.

BIFF   Shouldn't we do anything?

LINDA   Oh, my dear, you should do a lot of things, but there's nothing to do, so go to sleep.

(HAPPY *comes down the stair and sits on the steps.*)

HAPPY   I never heard him so loud, Mom.

LINDA   Well, come around more often; you'll hear him. (*She sits down at the table and mends the lining of* WILLY'S *jacket.*)

BIFF   Why didn't you ever write me about this, Mom?

LINDA   How would I write to you? For over three months you had no address.

BIFF   I was on the move. But you know I thought of you all the time. You know that, don't you, pal?

LINDA   I know, dear, I know. But he likes to have a letter. Just to know that there's still a possibility for better things.

BIFF   He's not like this all the time, is he?

LINDA   It's when you come home he's always the worst.

BIFF   When I come home?

LINDA   When you write you're coming, he's all smiles, and talks about the future, and — he's just wonderful. And then the closer you seem to come, the more shaky he gets, and then, by the time you get here, he's arguing, and he seems angry at you. I think it's just that maybe he can't bring himself to — to open up to you. Why are you so hateful to each other? Why is that?

BIFF (*evasively*)   I'm not hateful, Mom.

LINDA   But you no sooner come in the door than you're fighting!

BIFF   I don't know why. I mean to change. I'm tryin', Mom, you understand?

LINDA   Are you home to stay now?

BIFF   I don't know. I want to look around, see what's doin'.

LINDA   Biff, you can't look around all your life, can you?

BIFF   I just can't take hold, Mom. I can't take hold of some kind of a life.

LINDA   Biff, a man is not a bird, to come and go with the springtime.

BIFF   Your hair.... (*He touches her hair.*) Your hair got so gray.

LINDA   Oh, it's been gray since you were in high school. I just stopped dyeing it, that's all.

BIFF   Dye it again, will ya? I don't want my pal looking old. (*He smiles.*)

LINDA   You're such a boy! You think you can go away for a year and . . . You've got to get it into your head now that one day you'll knock on this door and there'll be strange people here —

BIFF   What are you talking about? You're not even sixty, Mom.

LINDA   But what about your father?

BIFF (*lamely*)   Well, I meant him too.

HAPPY   He admires Pop.

LINDA   Biff, dear, if you don't have any feeling for him, then you can't have any feeling for me.

BIFF   Sure I can, Mom.

LINDA   No. You can't just come to see me, because I love him. (*With a threat, but only a threat, of tears*) He's the dearest man in the world to me, and I won't have anyone making him feel unwanted and low and blue. You've got to make up your mind now, darling, there's no leeway any more. Either he's your father and you pay him that respect, or else you're not to come here. I know he's not easy to get along with — nobody knows that better than me — but. . . .

WILLY (*from the left, with a laugh*)   Hey, hey, Biffo!

BIFF (*starting to go out after* WILLY)   What the hell is the matter with him? (HAPPY *stops him.*)

LINDA   Don't — don't go near him!

BIFF   Stop making excuses for him! He always, always wiped the floor with you. Never had an ounce of respect for you.

HAPPY   He's always had respect for —

BIFF   What the hell do you know about it?

HAPPY   (*surlily*)   Just don't call him crazy!

BIFF   He's got no character — Charley wouldn't do this. Not in his own house — spewing out that vomit from his mind.

HAPPY   Charley never had to cope with what he's got to.

BIFF   People are worse off than Willy Loman. Believe me, I've seen them.

LINDA   Then make Charley your father, Biff. You can't do that, can you? I don't say he's a great man. Willy Loman never made a lot of money. His name was never in the paper. He's not the finest character that ever lived. But he's a human being, and a terrible thing is happening to him. So attention must be paid. He's not to be allowed to fall into his grave like an old dog. Attention, attention must be finally paid to such a person. You called him crazy —

BIFF   I didn't mean —

LINDA   No, a lot of people think he's lost his — balance. But you don't have to be very smart to know what his trouble is. The man is exhausted.

HAPPY   Sure!

LINDA   A small man can be just as exhausted as a great man. He works for a company thirty-six years this March, opens up unheard-of territories to their trademark, and now in his old age they take his salary away.

HAPPY   (*indignantly*)   I didn't know that, Mom.

LINDA   You never asked, my dear! Now that you get your spending money someplace else you don't trouble your mind with him.

HAPPY   But I gave you money last —

LINDA   Christmas time, fifty dollars! To fix the hot water it cost ninety-seven fifty! For five weeks he's been on straight commission, like a beginner, an unknown!

BIFF   Those ungrateful bastards!

LINDA   Are they any worse than his sons? When he brought them business, when he was young, they were glad to see him. But now his old friends, the old buyers that loved him so and always found some order to hand him in a pinch — they're all dead, retired. He used to be able to make six, seven calls a day in Boston. Now he takes his valises out of the car and puts them back and takes them out again and he's exhausted. Instead of walking he talks now. He drives seven hundred miles, and when he gets there no one knows him any more, no one welcomes him. And what goes through a man's mind, driving seven hundred miles home without having earned a cent? Why shouldn't he talk to himself? Why? When he has to go to Charley and borrow fifty dollars a week and pretend to me that it's his pay? How long can that go on? How long? You see what I'm sitting here and waiting for? And you tell me he has no character? The man who never worked a day but for your benefit? When does he get the medal for that? Is this his reward — to turn around at the age of sixty-three and find his sons, who he loved better than his life, one a philandering bum —

HAPPY   Mom!

LINDA   That's all you are, my baby! (*To* BIFF) And you! What happened to the love you had for him? You were such pals! How you used to talk to him on the phone every night! How lonely he was till he could come home to you!

BIFF   All right, Mom. I'll live here in my room, and I'll get a job. I'll keep away from him, that's all.

LINDA   No, Biff. You can't stay here and fight all the time.

BIFF   He threw me out of this house, remember that.

LINDA   Why did he do that? I never knew why.

BIFF   Because I know he's a fake and he doesn't like anybody around who knows!

LINDA   Why a fake? In what way? What do you mean?

BIFF   Just don't lay it all at my feet. It's between me and him — that's all I have to say. I'll chip in from now on. He'll settle for half my pay check. He'll be all right. I'm going to bed. (*He starts for the stairs.*)

LINDA   He won't be all right.

BIFF   (*turning on the stairs, furiously*)   I hate this city and I'll stay here. Now what do you want?

LINDA   He's dying, Biff.

(HAPPY *turns quickly to her, shocked.*)

BIFF   (*after a pause*)   Why is he dying?

LINDA   He's been trying to kill himself.

BIFF   (*with great horror*)   How?

LINDA   I live from day to day.

BIFF   What're you talking about?

LINDA   Remember I wrote you that he smashed up the car again? In February?

BIFF   Well?

LINDA   The insurance inspector came. He said that they have evidence. That all these accidents in the last year — weren't — weren't — accidents.

HAPPY   How can they tell that? That's a lie.

LINDA   It seems there's a woman. . . . (*She takes a breath as*)

BIFF   (*sharply but contained*)   What woman?

LINDA   (*simultaneously*)   . . . and this woman . . .

LINDA   What?

BIFF   Nothing. Go ahead.

LINDA   What did you say?

BIFF   Nothing. I just said what woman?

HAPPY   What about her?

LINDA   Well, it seems she was walking down the road and saw his car. She says that he wasn't driving fast at all, and that he didn't skid. She says he came to that little bridge, and then deliberately smashed into the railing, and it was only the shallowness of the water that saved him.

BIFF   Oh, no, he probably just fell asleep again.

LINDA   I don't think he fell asleep.

BIFF   Why not?

LINDA   Last month. . . . (*With great difficulty*) Oh, boys, it's so hard to say a thing like this! He's just a big stupid man to you, but I tell you there's more good in him than in many other people. (*She chokes, wipes her eyes.*) I was looking for a fuse. The lights blew out, and I went down the cellar. And behind the fuse box — it happened to fall out — was a length of rubber pipe — just short.

HAPPY   No kidding?

LINDA   There's a little attachment on the end of it. I knew right away. And sure enough, on the bottom of the water heater there's a new little nipple on the gas pipe.

HAPPY   (*angrily*)   That — jerk.

BIFF   Did you have it taken off?

LINDA   I'm — I'm ashamed to. How can I mention it to him? Every day I go down and take away that little rubber pipe. But, when he comes home, I put it back where it was. How can I insult him that way? I don't know what to do. I live from day to day, boys. I tell you, I know every thought in his mind. It sounds so old-fashioned and silly, but I tell you he put his whole life into you and you've turned your backs on him. (*She is bent over in the chair, weeping, her face in her hands.*) Biff, I swear to God! Biff, his life is in your hands!

HAPPY   (*to* BIFF)   How do you like that damned fool!

BIFF   (*kissing her*)   All right, pal, all right. It's all settled now. I've been remiss. I know that, Mom. But now I'll stay, and I swear to you, I'll apply myself. (*Kneeling in front of her, in a fever of self-reproach*) It's just — you see, Mom, I don't fit in business. Not that I won't try. I'll try, and I'll make good.

HAPPY   Sure you will. The trouble with you in business was you never tried to please people.

BIFF   I know, I —

HAPPY   Like when you worked for Harrison's. Bob Harrison said you were tops, and then you go and do some damn fool thing like whistling whole songs in the elevator like a comedian.

BIFF   (*against* HAPPY)   So what? I like to whistle sometimes.

HAPPY   You don't raise a guy to a responsible job who whistles in the elevator!

LINDA   Well, don't argue about it now.

HAPPY   Like when you'd go off and swim in the middle of the day instead of taking the line around.

BIFF   (*his resentment rising*)   Well, don't you run off? You take off sometimes, don't you? On a nice summer day?

HAPPY   Yeah, but I cover myself!

LINDA   Boys!

HAPPY   If I'm going to take a fade the boss can call any number where I'm supposed to be and they'll swear to him that I just left. I'll tell you something that I hate to say, Biff, but in the business world some of them think you're crazy.

BIFF   (*angered*)   Screw the business world!

HAPPY   All right, screw it! Great, but cover yourself!

LINDA   Hap, Hap!

BIFF   I don't care what they think! They've laughed at Dad for years, and you know why? Because we don't belong in this nuthouse of a city! We should be mixing cement on some open plain, or — or carpenters. A carpenter is allowed to whistle!

(WILLY *walks in from the entrance of the house, at left.*)

WILLY   Even your grandfather was better than a carpenter. (*Pause. They watch him.*) You never grew up. Bernard does not whistle in the elevator, I assure you.

BIFF   (*as though to laugh* WILLY *out of it*)   Yeah, but you do, Pop.

WILLY I never in my life whistled in an elevator! And who in the business world thinks I'm crazy?

BIFF I didn't mean it like that, Pop. Now don't make a whole thing out of it, will ya?

WILLY Go back to the West! Be a carpenter, a cowboy, enjoy yourself!

LINDA Willy, he was just saying —

WILLY I heard what he said!

HAPPY (*trying to quiet* WILLY) Hey, Pop, come on now. . . .

WILLY (*continuing over* HAPPY's *line*) They laugh at me, heh? Go to Filene's, go to the Hub, go to Slattery's, Boston. Call out the name Willy Loman and see what happens! Big shot!

BIFF All right, Pop.

WILLY Big!

BIFF All right!

WILLY Why do you always insult me?

BIFF I didn't say a word. (*To* LINDA) Did I say a word?

LINDA He didn't say anything, Willy.

WILLY (*going to the doorway of the living-room*) All right, good night, good night.

LINDA Willy, dear, he just decided. . . .

WILLY (*to* BIFF) If you get tired hanging around tomorrow, paint the ceiling I put up in the living-room.

BIFF I'm leaving early tomorrow.

HAPPY He's going to see Bill Oliver, Pop.

WILLY (*interestedly*) Oliver? For what?

BIFF (*with reserve, but trying, trying*) He always said he'd stake me. I'd like to go into business, so maybe I can take him up on it.

LINDA Isn't that wonderful?

WILLY Don't interrupt. What's wonderful about it? There's fifty men in the City of New York who'd stake him. (*To* BIFF) Sporting goods?

BIFF I guess so. I know something about it and —

WILLY He knows something about it! You know sporting goods better than Spalding, for God's sake! How much is he giving you?

BIFF I don't know, I didn't even see him yet, but —

WILLY Then what're you talkin' about?

BIFF (*getting angry*) Well, all I said was I'm gonna see him, that's all!

WILLY (*turning away*) Ah, you're counting your chickens again.

BIFF (*starting left for the stairs*) Oh, Jesus, I'm going to sleep!

WILLY (*calling after him*) Don't curse in this house!

BIFF (*turning*) Since when did you get so clean?

HAPPY (*trying to stop them*) Wait a. . . .

WILLY Don't use that language to me! I won't have it!

HAPPY (*grabbing* BIFF, *shouts*) Wait a minute! I got an idea. I got a feasible idea. Come here, Biff, let's talk this over now, let's talk some sense here. When I was down in Florida last time, I thought of a great idea to sell sporting goods. It just came back to me. You and I, Biff — we have a line, the Loman Line. We train a couple of weeks, and put on a couple of exhibitions, see?

WILLY That's an idea!

HAPPY Wait! We form two basketball teams, see? Two water-polo teams. We play each other. It's a million dollars' worth of publicity. Two brothers, see? The Loman Brothers. Displays in the Royal Palms — all the hotels. And banners over the ring and the basketball court: "Loman Brothers." Baby, we could sell sporting goods!

WILLY   That is a one-million-dollar idea!

LINDA   Marvelous!

BIFF   I'm in great shape as far as that's concerned.

HAPPY   And the beauty of it is, Biff, it wouldn't be like a business. We'd be out playin' ball again. . . .

BIFF (*enthused*)   Yeah, that's. . . .

WILLY   Million-dollar. . . .

HAPPY   And you wouldn't get fed up with it, Biff. It'd be the family again. There'd be the old honor, and comradeship, and if you wanted to go off for a swim or somethin' — well, you'd do it! Without some smart cooky gettin' up ahead of you!

WILLY   Lick the world! You guys together could absolutely lick the civilized world.

BIFF   I'll see Oliver tomorrow. Hap, if we could work that out. . . .

LINDA   Maybe things are beginning to —

WILLY (*wildly enthused, to* LINDA)   Stop interrupting! (*To* BIFF) But don't wear sport jacket and slacks when you see Oliver.

BIFF   No, I'll —

WILLY   A business suit, and talk as little as possible, and don't crack any jokes.

BIFF   He did like me. Always liked me.

LINDA   He loved you!

WILLY (*to* LINDA)   Will you stop! (*To* BIFF) Walk in very serious. You are not applying for a boy's job. Money is to pass. Be quiet, fine, and serious. Everybody likes a kidder, but nobody lends him money.

HAPPY   I'll try to get some myself, Biff. I'm sure I can.

WILLY   I see great things for you kids, I think your troubles are over. But remember, start big and you'll end big. Ask for fifteen. How much you gonna ask for?

BIFF   Gee, I don't know —

WILLY   And don't say "Gee." "Gee" is a boy's word. A man walking in for fifteen thousand dollars does not say "Gee!"

BIFF   Ten, I think, would be top though.

WILLY   Don't be so modest. You always started too low. Walk in with a big laugh. Don't look worried. Start off with a couple of your good stories to lighten things up. It's not what you say, it's how you say it — because personality always wins the day.

LINDA   Oliver always thought the highest of him —

WILLY   Will you let me talk?

BIFF   Don't yell at her, Pop, will ya?

WILLY (*angrily*)   I was talking, wasn't I?

BIFF   I don't like you yelling at her all the time, and I'm tellin' you, that's all.

WILLY   What're you, takin' over this house?

LINDA   Willy —

WILLY (*turning on her*)   Don't take his side all the time, goddammit!

BIFF (*furiously*)   Stop yelling at her!

WILLY (*suddenly pulling on his cheek, beaten down, guilt ridden*)   Give my best to Bill Oliver — he may remember me. (*He exits through the living-room doorway.*)

LINDA (*her voice subdued*) What'd you have to start that for? (BIFF *turns away.*) You see how sweet he was as soon as you talked hopefully? (*She goes over to* BIFF.) Come up and say good night to him. Don't let him go to bed that way.

HAPPY Come on, Biff, let's buck him up.

LINDA Please, dear. Just say good night. It takes so little to make him happy. Come. (*She goes through the living-room doorway, calling upstairs from within the living-room.*) Your pajamas are hanging in the bathroom, Willy!

HAPPY (*looking toward where* LINDA *went out*) What a woman! They broke the mold when they made her. You know that, Biff?

BIFF He's off salary. My God, working on commission!

HAPPY Well, let's face it: he's no hot-shot selling man. Except that sometimes, you have to admit, he's a sweet personality.

BIFF (*deciding*) Lend me ten bucks, will ya? I want to buy some new ties.

HAPPY I'll take you to a place I know. Beautiful stuff. Wear one of my striped shirts tomorrow.

BIFF She got gray. Mom got awful old. Gee, I'm gonna go in to Oliver tomorrow and knock him for a —

HAPPY Come on up. Tell that to Dad. Let's give him a whirl. Come on.

BIFF (*steamed up*) You know, with ten thousand bucks, boy!

HAPPY (*as they go into the living-room*) That's the talk, Biff, that's the first time I've heard the old confidence out of you! (*From within the living-room, fading off*) You're gonna live with me, kid, and any babe you want just say the word. . . . (*The last lines are hardly heard. They are mounting the stairs to their parents' bedroom.*)

LINDA (*entering her bedroom and addressing* WILLY, *who is in the bathroom. She is straightening the bed for him*) Can you do anything about the shower? It drips.

WILLY (*from the bathroom*) All of a sudden everything falls to pieces! Goddam plumbing, oughta be sued, those people. I hardly finished putting it in and the thing. . . . (*His words rumble off.*)

LINDA I'm just wondering if Oliver will remember him. You think he might?

WILLY (*coming out of the bathroom in his pajamas*) Remember him? What's the matter with you, you crazy? If he'd've stayed with Oliver he'd be on top by now! Wait'll Oliver gets a look at him. You don't know the average caliber any more. The average young man today — (*he is getting into bed*) — is got a caliber of zero. Greatest thing in the world for him was to bum around.

(BIFF *and* HAPPY *enter the bedroom. Slight pause*)

WILLY (*stops short, looking at* BIFF) Glad to hear it, boy.

HAPPY He wanted to say good night to you, sport.

WILLY (*to* BIFF) Yeah. Knock him dead, boy. What'd you want to tell me?

BIFF Just take it easy, Pop. Good night. (*He turns to go.*)

WILLY (*unable to resist*) And if anything falls off the desk while you're talking to him — like a package or something — don't you pick it up. They have office boys for that.

LINDA I'll make a big breakfast —

WILLY   Will you let me finish? (*To* BIFF) Tell him you were in the business in the West. Not farm work.

BIFF   All right, Dad.

LINDA   I think everything —

WILLY (*going right through her speech*)   And don't undersell yourself. No less than fifteen thousand dollars.

BIFF (*unable to bear him*)   Okay. Good night, Mom. (*He starts moving.*)

WILLY   Because you got a greatness in you, Biff, remember that. You got all kinds a greatness. . . . (*He lies back, exhausted.* BIFF *walks out.*)

LINDA (*calling after* BIFF)   Sleep well, darling!

HAPPY   I'm gonna get married, Mom. I wanted to tell you.

LINDA   Go to sleep, dear.

HAPPY (*going*)   I just wanted to tell you.

WILLY   Keep-up the good work. (HAPPY *exits.*) God. . . . remember that Ebbets Field game? The championship of the city?

LINDA   Just rest. Should I sing to you?

WILLY   Yeah. Sing to me. (LINDA *hums a soft lullaby.*) When that team came out — he was the tallest, remember?

LINDA   Oh, yes. And in gold.

(BIFF *enters the darkened kitchen, takes a cigarette, and leaves the house. He comes downstage into a golden pool of light. He smokes, staring at the night.*)

WILLY   Like a young god. Hercules — something like that. And the sun, the sun all around him. Remember how he waved to me? Right up from the field, with the representatives of three colleges standing by? And the buyers I brought, and the cheers when he came out — Loman, Loman, Loman! God Almighty, he'll be great yet. A star like that, magnificent, can never really fade away!

(*The light on* WILLY *is fading. The gas heater begins to glow through the kitchen wall, near the stairs, a blue flame beneath red coils.*)

LINDA (*timidly*)   Willy dear, what has he got against you?

WILLY   I'm so tired. Don't talk any more.

(BIFF *slowly returns to the kitchen. He stops, stares toward the heater.*)

LINDA   Will you ask Howard to let you work in New York?

WILLY   First thing in the morning. Everything'll be all right.

(BIFF *reaches behind the heater and draws out a length of rubber tubing. He is horrified and turns his head toward* WILLY's *room, still dimly lit, from which the strains of* LINDA's *desperate but monotonous humming rise.*)

WILLY (*staring through the window into the moonlight*)   Gee, look at the moon moving between the buildings!

(BIFF *wraps the tubing around his hand and quickly goes up the stairs.*)

Curtain

Act Two

Music is heard, gay and bright. The curtain rises as the music fades away. WILLY, *in shirt sleeves, is sitting at the kitchen table, sipping coffee, his hat in his lap.* LINDA *is filling his cup when she can.*

WILLY   Wonderful coffee. Meal in itself.

LINDA Can I make you some eggs?

WILLY No. Take a breath.

LINDA You look so rested, dear.

WILLY I slept like a dead one. First time in months. Imagine, sleeping till ten on a Tuesday morning. Boys left nice and early, heh?

LINDA They were out of here by eight o'clock.

WILLY Good work!

LINDA It was so thrilling to see them leaving together. I can't get over the shaving lotion in this house!

WILLY (*smiling*) Mmm —

LINDA Biff was very changed this morning. His whole attitude seemed to be hopeful. He couldn't wait to get downtown to see Oliver.

WILLY He's heading for a change. There's no question, there simply are certain men that take longer to get — solidified. How did he dress?

LINDA His blue suit. He's so handsome in that suit. He could be a — anything in that suit!

(WILLY *gets up from the table.* LINDA *holds his jacket for him.*)

WILLY There's no question, no question at all. Gee, on the way home tonight I'd like to buy some seeds.

LINDA (*laughing*) That'd be wonderful. But not enough sun gets back there. Nothing'll grow any more.

WILLY You wait, kid, before it's all over we're gonna get a little place out in the country, and I'll raise some vegetables, a couple of chickens. . . .

LINDA You'll do it yet, dear.

(WILLY *walks out of his jacket.* LINDA *follows him.*)

WILLY And they'll get married, and come for a weekend. I'd build a little guest house. 'Cause I got so many fine tools, all I'd need would be a little lumber and some peace of mind.

LINDA (*joyfully*) I sewed the lining. . . .

WILLY I could build two guest houses, so they'd both come. Did he decide how much he's going to ask Oliver for?

LINDA (*getting him into the jacket*) He didn't mention it, but I imagine ten or fifteen thousand. You going to talk to Howard today?

WILLY Yeah. I'll put it to him straight and simple. He'll just have to take me off the road.

LINDA And Willy, don't forget to ask for a little advance, because we've got the insurance premium. It's the grace period now.

WILLY That's a hundred . . . ?

LINDA A hundred and eight, sixty-eight. Because we're a little short again.

WILLY Why are we short?

LINDA Well, you had the motor job on the car . . .

WILLY That goddam Studebaker!

LINDA And you got one more payment on the refrigerator . . .

WILLY But it just broke again!

LINDA Well, it's old, dear.

WILLY I told you we should've bought a well-advertised machine. Charley bought a General Electric and it's twenty years old and it's still good, that son-of-a-bitch.

LINDA But, Willy —

WILLY Whoever heard of a Hastings refrigerator? Once in my life I would like to own something outright before it's broken! I'm always in a race with the junkyard! I just finished paying for the car and it's on its last legs. The refrigerator consumes belts like a goddam maniac. They time those things. They time them so when you finally paid for them, they're used up.

LINDA (*buttoning up his jacket as he unbuttons it*) All told, about two hundred dollars would carry us, dear. But that includes the last payment on the mortgage. After this payment, Willy, the house belongs to us.

WILLY It's twenty-five years!

LINDA Biff was nine years old when we bought it.

WILLY Well, that's a great thing. To weather a twenty-five year mortgage is —

LINDA It's an accomplishment.

WILLY All the cement, the lumber, the reconstruction I put in this house! There ain't a crack to be found in it any more.

LINDA Well, it served its purpose.

WILLY What purpose? Some stranger'll come along, move in, and that's that. If only Biff would take this house, and raise a family.... (*He starts to go.*) Good-by, I'm late.

LINDA (*suddenly remembering*) Oh, I forgot! You're supposed to meet them for dinner.

WILLY Me?

LINDA At Frank's Chop House on Forty-eighth near Sixth Avenue.

WILLY Is that so! How about you?

LINDA No, just the three of you. They're gonna blow you to a big meal!

WILLY Don't say! Who thought of that?

LINDA Biff came to me this morning, Willy, and he said, "Tell Dad, we want to blow him to a big meal." Be there six o'clock. You and your two boys are going to have dinner.

WILLY Gee whiz! That's really somethin'. I'm gonna knock Howard for a loop, kid. I'll get an advance, and I'll come home with a New York job. Goddammit, now I'm gonna do it!

LINDA Oh, that's the spirit, Willy!

WILLY I will never get behind a wheel the rest of my life!

LINDA It's changing, Willy, I can feel it changing!

WILLY Beyond a question. G'by, I'm late. (*He starts to go again.*)

LINDA (*calling after him as she runs to the kitchen table for a handkerchief*) You got your glasses?

WILLY (*feels for them, then comes back in*) Yeah, yeah, got my glasses.

LINDA (*giving him the handkerchief*) And a handkerchief.

WILLY Yeah, handkerchief.

LINDA And your saccharine?

WILLY Yeah, my saccharine.

LINDA Be careful on the subway stairs.

(*She kisses him, and a silk stocking is seen hanging from her hand.* WILLY *notices it.*)

WILLY Will you stop mending stockings? At least while I'm in the house. It gets me nervous. I can't tell you. Please.

(LINDA *hides the stocking in her hand as she follows* WILLY *across the forestage in front of the house.*)

LINDA Remember, Frank's Chop House.

WILLY (*passing the apron*) Maybe beets would grow out there.

LINDA (*laughing*) But you tried so many times.

WILLY Yeah. Well, don't work hard today. (*He disappears around the right corner of the house.*)

LINDA Be careful!

(*As* WILLY *vanishes,* LINDA *waves to him. Suddenly the phone rings. She runs across the stage and into the kitchen and lifts it.*)

LINDA Hello? Oh, Biff! I'm so glad you called, I just.... Yes, sure, I just told him. Yes, he'll be there for dinner at six o'clock, I didn't forget. Listen, I was just dying to tell you. You know that little rubber pipe I told you about? That he connected to the gas heater? I finally decided to go down the cellar this morning and take it away and destroy it. But it's gone! Imagine? He took it away himself, it isn't there! (*She listens.*) When? Oh, then you took it. Oh — nothing, it's just that I'd hoped he'd taken it away himself. Oh, I'm not worried, darling, because this morning he left in such high spirits, it was like the old days! I'm not afraid any more. Did Mr. Oliver see you?... Well, you wait there then. And make a nice impression on him, darling. Just don't perspire too much before you see him. And have a nice time with Dad. He may have big news too!... That's right, a New York job. And be sweet to him tonight, dear. Be loving to him. Because he's only a little boat looking for a harbor. (*She is trembling with sorrow and joy.*) Oh, that's wonderful, Biff, you'll save his life. Thanks, darling. Just put your arm around him when he comes into the restaurant. Give him a smile. That's the boy.... Good-by, dear.... You got your comb?... That's fine. Good-by, Biff dear.

(*In the middle of her speech,* HOWARD WAGNER, *thirty-six, wheels on a small typewriter table on which is a wire-recording machine and proceeds to plug it in. This is on the left forestage. Light slowly fades on* LINDA *as it rises on* HOWARD. HOWARD *is intent on threading the machine and only glances over his shoulder as* WILLY *appears.*)

WILLY Pst! Pst!

HOWARD Hello, Willy, come in.

WILLY Like to have a little talk with you, Howard.

HOWARD Sorry to keep you waiting. I'll be with you in a minute.

WILLY What's that, Howard?

HOWARD Didn't you ever see one of these? Wire recorder.

WILLY Oh. Can we talk a minute?

HOWARD Records things. Just got delivery yesterday. Been driving me crazy, the most terrific machine I ever saw in my life. I was up all night with it.

WILLY What do you do with it?

HOWARD I bought it for dictation, but you can do anything with it. Listen to this. I had it home last night. Listen to what I picked up. The first one is my daughter. Get this. (*He flicks the switch and "Roll out the Barrel" is heard being whistled.*) Listen to that kid whistle.

WILLY That is lifelike, isn't it?

HOWARD Seven years old. Get that tone.

WILLY Ts, ts. Like to ask a little favor if you . . .

(*The whistling breaks off, and the voice of* HOWARD'S *daughter is heard.*)

HIS DAUGHTER "Now you, Daddy."

HOWARD She's crazy for me! (*Again the same song is whistled.*) That's me! Ha! (*He winks.*)

WILLY You're very good!

(*The whistling breaks off again. The machine runs slient for a moment.*)

HOWARD Sh! Get this now, this is my son.

HIS SON "The capital of Alabama is Montgomery; the capital of Arizona is Phoenix; the capital of Arkansas is Little Rock; the capital of California is Sacramento . . ." (*and on, and on.*)

HOWARD (*holding up five fingers*) Five years old, Willy!

WILLY He'll make an announcer some day!

HIS SON (*continuing*) "The capital . . ."

HOWARD Get that — alphabetical order! (*The machine breaks off suddenly.*) Wait a minute. The maid kicked the plug out.

WILLY It certainly is a —

HOWARD Sh, for God's sake!

HIS SON "It's nine o'clock, Bulova watch time. So I have to go to sleep."

WILLY That really is —

HOWARD Wait a minute! The next is my wife.

(*They wait.*)

HOWARD'S VOICE "Go on, say something." (*Pause*) "Well, you gonna talk?"

HIS WIFE "I can't think of anything."

HOWARD'S VOICE "Well, talk — it's turning."

HIS WIFE (*shyly, beaten*) "Hello." (*Silence*) "Oh, Howard, I can't talk into this . . ."

HOWARD (*snapping the machine off*) That was my wife.

WILLY That is a wonderful machine. Can we —

HOWARD I tell you, Willy, I'm gonna take my camera, and my bandsaw, and all my hobbies, and out they go. This is the most fascinating relaxation I ever found.

WILLY I think I'll get one myself.

HOWARD Sure, they're only a hundred and a half. You can't do without it. Supposing you wanna hear Jack Benny, see? But you can't be at home at that hour. So you tell the maid to turn the radio on when Jack Benny comes on, and this automatically goes on with the radio. . . .

WILLY And when you come home you. . . .

HOWARD You can come home twelve o'clock, one o'clock, any time you like, and you get yourself a Coke and sit yourself down, throw the switch, and there's Jack Benny's program in the middle of the night!

WILLY I'm definitely going to get one. Because lots of time I'm on the road, and I think to myself, what I must be missing on the radio!

HOWARD Don't you have a radio in the car?

WILLY Well, yeah, but who ever thinks of turning it on?

HOWARD Say, aren't you supposed to be in Boston?

WILLY That's what I want to talk to you about, Howard. You got a minute? (*He draws a chair in from the wing.*)

HOWARD What happened? What're you doing here?

WILLY Well. . . .

HOWARD You didn't crack up again, did you?

WILLY Oh, no. No. . . .

HOWARD Geez, you had me worried there for a minute. What's the trouble?

WILLY Well, tell you the truth, Howard. I've come to the decision that I'd rather not travel any more.

HOWARD Not travel! Well, what'll you do?

WILLY Remember, Christmas time, when you had the party here? You said you'd try to think of some spot for me here in town.

HOWARD With us?

WILLY Well, sure.

HOWARD Oh, yeah, yeah. I remember. Well, I couldn't think of anything for you, Willy.

WILLY I tell ya, Howard. The kids are all grown up, y'know. I don't need much any more. If I could take home — well, sixty-five dollars a week, I could swing it.

HOWARD Yeah, but Willy, see I —

WILLY I tell ya why, Howard. Speaking frankly and between the two of us, y'know — I'm just a little tired.

HOWARD Oh, I could understand that, Willy. But you're a road man, Willy, and we do a road business. We've only got a half-dozen salesmen on the floor here.

WILLY God knows, Howard, I never asked a favor of any man. But I was with the firm when your father used to carry you in here in his arms.

HOWARD I know that, Willy, but —

WILLY Your father came to me the day you were born and asked me what I thought of the name of Howard, may he rest in peace.

HOWARD I appreciate that, Willy, but there just is no spot here for you. If I had a spot I'd slam you right in, but I just don't have a single solitary spot. (*He looks for his lighter.* WILLY *has picked it up and gives it to him. Pause.*)

WILLY (*with increasing anger*) Howard, all I need to set my table is fifty dollars a week.

HOWARD But where am I going to put you, kid?

WILLY Look, it isn't a question of whether I can sell merchandise, is it?

HOWARD No, but it's a business, kid, and everybody's gotta pull his own weight.

WILLY (*desperately*) Just let me tell you a story, Howard —

HOWARD 'Cause you gotta admit, business is business.

WILLY (*angrily*) Business is definitely business, but just listen for a minute. You don't understand this. When I was a boy — eighteen, nineteen — I was already on the road. And there was a question in my mind as to whether selling had a future for me. Because in those days I had a yearning to go to Alaska. See, there were three gold strikes in one month in Alaska, and I felt like going out. Just for the ride, you might say.

HOWARD (*barely interested*) Don't say.

WILLY Oh, yeah, my father lived many years in Alaska. He was an adventurous man. We've got quite a little streak of self-reliance in our family. I thought I'd go out with my older brother and try to locate him, and maybe settle in the North with the old man. And I was almost decided to go, when I met a salesman in the Parker House. His name was Dave Singleman. And he was eighty-four years old, and he'd drummed merchandise in thirty-one states. And old Dave, he'd go up to his room, y'understand, put on his green velvet slippers — I'll never forget — and pick up his phone and call the buyers, and without ever leaving his room, at the age of eighty-four, he made his living. And when I saw that, I realized that selling was the greatest career a man could want. 'Cause what could be more satisfying than to be able to go, at the age of eighty-four, into twenty or thirty different cities, and pick up a phone, and be remembered and loved and helped by so many different people? Do you know? when he died — and by the way he died the death of a salesman, in his green velvet slippers in the smoker of the New York, New Haven and Hartford, going into Boston — when he died, hundreds of salesmen and buyers were at his funeral. Things were sad on a lotta trains for months after that. (*He stands up.* HOWARD *has not looked at him.*) In those days there was personality in it, Howard. There was respect, and comradeship, and gratitude in it. Today, it's all cut and dried, and there's no chance for bringing friendship to bear — or personality. You see what I mean? They don't know me any more.

HOWARD (*moving away, to the right*)   That's just the thing, Willy.

WILLY   If I had forty dollars a week — that's all I'd need. Forty dollars, Howard.

HOWARD   Kid, I can't take blood from a stone, I —

WILLY (*desperation is on him now*)   Howard, the year Al Smith was nominated, your father came to me and —

HOWARD (*starting to go off*)   I've got to see some people, kid.

WILLY (*stopping him*)   I'm talking about your father! There were promises made across this desk! You mustn't tell me you've got people to see — I put thirty-four years into this firm, Howard, and now I can't pay my insurance! You can't eat the orange and throw the peel away — a man is not a piece of fruit! (*After a pause*) Now pay attention. Your father — in 1928 I had a big year. I averaged a hundred and seventy dollars a week in commissions.

HOWARD (*impatiently*)   Now, Willy, you never averaged —

WILLY (*banging his hand on the desk*)   I averaged a hundred and seventy dollars a week in the year of 1928! And your father came to me — or rather, I was in the office here — it was right over this desk — and he put his hand on my shoulder —

HOWARD (*getting up*)   You'll have to excuse me, Willy, I gotta see some people. Pull yourself together. (*Going out*) I'll be back in a little while.

(*On* HOWARD'S *exit, the light on his chair grows very bright and strange.*)

WILLY   Pull myself together! What the hell did I say to him? My God, I was yelling at him! How could I! (WILLY *breaks off, staring at the light, which occupies the chair, animating it. He approaches this chair, standing across the desk from it.*) Frank, Frank, don't you remember what you told me that time? How you put your hand on my shoulder, and Frank . . . (*He leans on the desk and as he speaks the dead man's name he accidentally switches on the recorder, and instantly*)

HOWARD'S SON   ". . . of New York is Albany. The capital of Ohio is Cincinnati, the capital of Rhode Island is . . ." (*The recitation continues.*)

WILLY (*leaping away with fright, shouting*)   Ha! Howard! Howard! Howard!

HOWARD (*rushing in*)   What happened?

WILLY (*pointing at the machine, which continues nasally, childishly, with the capital cities*)   Shut it off! Shut it off!

HOWARD (*pulling the plug out*)   Look, Willy . . .

WILLY (*pressing his hands to his eyes*)   I gotta get myself some coffee. I'll get some coffee . . .

(WILLY *starts to walk out.* HOWARD *stops him.*)

HOWARD (*rolling up the cord*)   Willy, look . . .

WILLY   I'll go to Boston.

HOWARD   Willy, you can't go to Boston for us.

WILLY   Why can't I go?

HOWARD   I don't want you to represent us. I've been meaning to tell you for a
long time now.

WILLY   Howard, are you firing me?

HOWARD   I think you need a good long rest, Willy.

WILLY   Howard —

HOWARD   And when you feel better, come back, and we'll see if we can work
something out.

WILLY   But I gotta earn money, Howard. I'm in no position to —

HOWARD   Where are your sons? Why don't your sons give you a hand?

WILLY   They're working on a very big deal.

HOWARD   This is no time for false pride, Willy. You go to your sons and you
tell them that you're tired. You've got two great boys, haven't you?

WILLY   Oh, no question, no question, but in the meantime . . .

HOWARD   Then that's that, heh?

WILLY   All right, I'll go to Boston tomorrow.

HOWARD   No, no.

WILLY   I can't throw myself on my sons. I'm not a cripple!

HOWARD   Look, kid, I'm busy this morning.

WILLY (*grasping* HOWARD's *arm*)   Howard, you've got to let me go to Boston!

HOWARD (*hard, keeping himself under control*)   I've got a line of people to see
this morning. Sit down, take five minutes, and pull yourself together, and
then go home, will ya? I need the office, Willy. (*He starts to go, turns, remembering the recorder, starts to push off the table holding the recorder.*)
Oh, yeah. Whenever you can this week, stop by and drop off the samples.
You'll feel better, Willy, and then come back and we'll talk. Pull yourself
together, kid, there's people outside.

(HOWARD *exits, pushing the table off left.* WILLY *stares into space, exhausted.
Now the music is heard —* BEN's *music — first distantly, then closer,
closer. As* WILLY *speaks,* BEN *enters from the right. He carries valise and
umbrella.*)

WILLY   Oh, Ben, how did you do it? What is the answer? Did you wind up
the Alaska deal already?

BEN   Doesn't take much time if you know what you're doing. Just a short
business trip. Boarding ship in an hour. Wanted to say good-by.

WILLY   Ben, I've got to talk to you.

BEN (*glancing at his watch*)   Haven't the time, William.

WILLY (*crossing the apron to* BEN)   Ben, nothing's working out. I don't know
what to do.

BEN   Now, look here, William. I've bought timberland in Alaska and I need
a man to look after things for me.

WILLY   God, timberland! Me and my boys in those grand outdoors!

BEN   You've a new continent at your doorstep, William. Get out of these cities,
they're full of talk and time payments and courts of law. Screw on your
fists and you can fight for a fortune up there.

WILLY   Yes, yes! Linda, Linda!

(LINDA *enters as of old, with the wash.*)

LINDA   Oh, you're back?

BEN   I haven't much time.

WILLY   No, wait! Linda, he's got a proposition for me in Alaska.

LINDA   But you've got — (*To* BEN) He's got a beautiful job here.

WILLY   But in Alaska, kid, I could —

LINDA   You're doing well enough, Willy!

BEN (*to* LINDA)   Enough for what, my dear?

LINDA (*frightened of* BEN *and angry at him*)   Don't say those things to him! Enough to be happy right here, right now. (*To* WILLY, *while* BEN *laughs*) Why must everybody conquer the world? You're well liked, and the boys love you, and someday — (*to* BEN) — why, old man Wagner told him just the other day that if he keeps it up he'll be a member of the firm, didn't he, Willy?

WILLY   Sure, sure. I am building something with this firm, Ben, and if a man is building something he must be on the right track, mustn't he?

BEN   What are you building? Lay your hand on it. Where is it?

WILLY (*hesitantly*)   That's true, Linda, there's nothing.

LINDA   Why? (*To* BEN) There's a man eighty-four years old —

WILLY   That's right, Ben, that's right. When I look at that man I say, what is there to worry about?

BEN   Bah!

WILLY   It's true, Ben. All he has to do is go into any city, pick up the phone, and he's making his living and you know why?

BEN (*picking up his valise*)   I've got to go.

WILLY (*holding* BEN *back*)   Look at this boy!

(BIFF, *in his high school sweater, enters carrying suitcase.* HAPPY *carries* BIFF's *shoulder guards, gold helmet, and football pants.*)

WILLY   Without a penny to his name, three great universities are begging for him, and from there the sky's the limit, because it's not what you do, Ben. It's who you know and the smile on your face! It's contacts, Ben, contacts! The whole wealth of Alaska passes over the lunch table at the Commodore Hotel, and that's the wonder, the wonder of this country, that a man can end with diamonds here on the basis of being liked! (*He turns to* BIFF.) And that's why when you get out on that field today it's important. Because thousands of people will be rooting for you and loving you. (*To* BEN, *who has again begun to leave*) And Ben! when he walks into a business office his name will sound out like a bell and all the doors will open to him! I've seen it, Ben, I've seen it a thousand times! You can't feel it with your hand like timber, but it's there!

BEN   Good-by, William.

WILLY   Ben, am I right? Don't you think I'm right? I value your advice.

BEN   There's a new continent at your doorstep, William. You could walk out rich. Rich! (*He is gone.*)

WILLY   We'll do it here, Ben! You hear me? We're gonna do it here!

(*Young* BERNARD *rushes in. The gay music of* THE BOYS *is heard.*)

BERNARD   Oh, gee, I was afraid you left already!

WILLY   Why? What time is it?

BERNARD   It's half-past one!

WILLY Well, come on, everybody! Ebbets Field [3] next stop! Where's the pennants? (*He rushes through the wall-line of the kitchen and out into the living-room.*)

LINDA (*to* BIFF) Did you pack fresh underwear?

BIFF (*who has been limbering up*) I want to go!

BERNARD Biff, I'm carrying your helmet, ain't I?

HAPPY No, I'm carrying the helmet.

BERNARD Oh, Biff, you promised me.

HAPPY I'm carrying the helmet.

BERNARD How am I going to get in the locker room?

LINDA Let him carry the shoulder guards. (*She puts her coat and hat on in the kitchen.*)

BERNARD Can I, Biff? 'Cause I told everybody I'm going to be in the locker room.

HAPPY In Ebbets Field it's the clubhouse.

BERNARD I meant the clubhouse, Biff!

HAPPY Biff!

BIFF (*grandly, after a slight pause*) Let him carry the shoulder guards.

HAPPY (*as he gives* BERNARD *the shoulder guards*) Stay close to us now.
(WILLY *rushes in with the pennants.*)

WILLY (*handing them out*) Everybody wave when Biff comes out on the field.
(HAPPY *and* BERNARD *run off.*) You set now, boy?
(*The music has died away.*)

BIFF Ready to go, Pop. Every muscle is ready.

WILLY (*at the edge of the apron*) You realize what this means?

BIFF That's right, Pop.

WILLY (*feeling* BIFF's *muscles*) You're comin' home this afternoon captain of the All-Scholastic Championship Team of the City of New York.

BIFF I got it, Pop. And remember, pal, when I take off my helmet, that touch-down is for you.

WILLY Let's go! (*He is starting out, with his arm around* BIFF, *when* CHARLEY *enters, as of old, in knickers.*) I got no room for you, Charley.

CHARLEY Room? For what?

WILLY In the car.

CHARLEY You goin' for a ride? I wanted to shoot some casino.

WILLY (*furiously*) Casino! (*Incredulously*) Don't you realize what today is?

LINDA Oh, he knows, Willy. He's just kidding you.

WILLY That's nothing to kid about!

CHARLEY No, Linda, what's goin' on?

LINDA He's playing in Ebbets Field.

CHARLEY Baseball in this weather?

WILLY Don't talk to him. Come on, come on! (*He is pushing them out.*)

CHARLEY Wait a minute, didn't you hear the news?

WILLY What?

CHARLEY Don't you listen to the radio? Ebbets Field just blew up.

WILLY You go to hell! (CHARLEY *laughs. Pushing them out*) Come on, come on! We're late.

---

3. *Ebbets Field:* Baseball stadium of Brooklyn Dodgers prior to their move to Los Angeles in the late 1950s.

CHARLEY (*as they go*) Knock a homer, Biff, knock a homer!

WILLY (*the last to leave, turning to* CHARLEY) I don't think that was funny, Charley. This is the greatest day of his life.

CHARLEY Willy, when are you going to grow up?

WILLY Yeah, heh? When this game is over, Charley, you'll be laughing out of the other side of your face. They'll be calling him another Red Grange. Twenty-five thousand a year.

CHARLEY (*kidding*) Is that so?

WILLY Yeah, that's so.

CHARLEY Well, then, I'm sorry, Willy. But tell me something.

WILLY What?

CHARLEY Who is Red Grange?

WILLY Put up your hands. Goddam you, put up your hands!

(CHARLEY, *chuckling, shakes his head and walks away, around the left corner of the stage.* WILLY *follows him. The music rises to a mocking frenzy.*)

WILLY Who the hell do you think you are, better than everybody else? You don't know everything, you big, ignorant, stupid . . . Put up your hands!

(*Light rises, on the right side of the forestage, on a small table in the reception room of* CHARLEY'S *office. Traffic sounds are heard.* BERNARD, *now mature, sits whistling to himself. A pair of tennis rackets and an overnight bag are on the floor beside him.*)

WILLY (*offstage*) What are you walking away for? Don't walk away! If you're going to say something say it to my face! I know you laugh at me behind my back. You'll laugh out of the other side of your goddam face after this game. Touchdown! Touchdown! Eighty thousand people! Touchdown! Right between the goal posts.

(BERNARD *is a quiet, earnest, but self-assured young man.* WILLY'S *voice is coming from right upstage now.* BERNARD *lowers his feet off the table and listens.* JENNY, *his father's secretary, enters.*)

JENNY (*distressed*) Say, Bernard, will you go out in the hall?

BERNARD What is that noise? Who is it?

JENNY Mr. Loman. He just got off the elevator.

BERNARD (*getting up*) Who's he arguing with?

JENNY Nobody. There's nobody with him. I can't deal with him any more, and your father gets all upset everytime he comes. I've got a lot of typing to do, and your father's waiting to sign it. Will you see him?

WILLY (*entering*) Touchdown! Touch— (*He sees* JENNY.) Jenny, Jenny, good to see you. How're ya? Workin'? Or still honest?

JENNY Fine. How've you been feeling?

WILLY Not much any more, Jenny. Ha, Ha! (*He is surprised to see the rackets.*)

BERNARD Hello, Uncle Willy.

WILLY (*almost shocked*) Bernard! Well, look who's here! (*He comes quickly, guiltily, to* BERNARD *and warmly shakes his hand.*)

BERNARD How are you? Good to see you.

WILLY What are you doing here?

BERNARD Oh, just stopped by to see Pop. Get off my feet till my train leaves. I'm going to Washington in a few minutes.

WILLY Is he in?

BERNARD.   Yes, he's in his office with the accountant. Sit down.

WILLY (*sitting down*)   What're you going to do in Washington?

BERNARD   Oh, just a case I've got there, Willy.

WILLY   That so? (*Indicating the rackets*) You going to play tennis there?

BERNARD   I'm staying with a friend who's got a court.

WILLY   Don't say. His own tennis court. Must be fine people, I bet.

BERNARD   They are, very nice. Dad tells me Biff's in town.

WILLY (*with a big smile*)   Yeah, Biff's in. Working on a very big deal, Bernard.

BERNARD   What's Biff doing?

WILLY   Well, he's been doing very big things in the West. But he decided to establish himself here. Very big. We're having dinner. Did I hear your wife had a boy?

BERNARD   That's right. Our second.

WILLY   Two boys! What do you know!

BERNARD   What kind of a deal has Biff got?

WILLY   Well, Bill Oliver — very big sporting goods man — he wants Biff very badly. Called him in from the West. Long distance, carte blanche, special deliveries. Your friends have their own private tennis court?

BERNARD   You still with the old firm, Willy?

WILLY (*after a pause*)   I'm — I'm overjoyed to see how you made the grade, Bernard, overjoyed. It's an encouraging thing to see a young man really — really — Looks very good for Biff — very — (*He breaks off, then*) Bernard — (*He is so full of emotion, he breaks off again.*)

BERNARD   What is it, Willy?

WILLY (*small and alone*)   What — what's the secret?

BERNARD   What secret?

WILLY   How — how did you? Why didn't he ever catch on?

BERNARD   I wouldn't know that, Willy.

WILLY (*confidentially, desperately*)   You were his friend, his boyhood friend. There's something I don't understand about it. His life ended after that Ebbets Field game. From the age of seventeen nothing good ever happened to him.

BERNARD   He never trained himself for anything.

WILLY   But he did, he did. After high school he took so many correspondence courses. Radio mechanics; television; God knows what, and never made the slightest mark.

BERNARD (*taking off his glasses*)   Willy, do you want to talk candidly?

WILLY (*rising, faces* BERNARD)   I regard you as a very brilliant man, Bernard. I value your advice.

BERNARD   Oh, the hell with the advice, Willy. I couldn't advise you. There's just one thing I've always wanted to ask you. When he was supposed to graduate, and the math teacher flunked him —

WILLY   Oh, that son-of-a-bitch ruined his life.

BERNARD   Yeah, but, Willy, all he had to do was go to summer school and make up that subject.

WILLY   That's right, that's right.

BERNARD   Did you tell him not to go to summer school?

WILLY   Me? I begged him to go. I ordered him to go!

BERNARD   Then why wouldn't he go?

WILLY   Why? Why! Bernard, that question has been trailing me like a ghost for the last fifteen years. He flunked the subject, and laid down and died like a hammer hit him!

BERNARD   Take it easy, kid.

WILLY   Let me talk to you — I got nobody to talk to. Bernard, Bernard, was it my fault? Y'see? It keeps going around in my mind, maybe I did something to him. I got nothing to give him.

BERNARD   Don't take it so hard.

WILLY   Why did he lay down? What is the story there? You were his friend!

BERNARD   Willy, I remember, it was June, and our grades came out. And he'd flunked math.

WILLY   That son-of-a-bitch!

BERNARD   No, it wasn't right then. Biff just got very angry, I remember, and he was ready to enroll in summer school.

WILLY   (*surprised*)   He was?

BERNARD   He wasn't beaten by it at all. But then, Willy, he disappeared from the block for almost a month. And I got the idea that he'd gone up to New England to see you. Did he have a talk with you then?

(WILLY *stares in silence.*)

BERNARD   Willy?

WILLY   (*with a strong edge of resentment in his voice*)   Yeah, he came to Boston. What about it?

BERNARD   Well, just that when he came back — I'll never forget this, it always mystifies me. Because I thought so well of Biff, even though he'd always taken advantage of me. I loved him, Willy, y'know? And he came back after that month and took his sneakers — remember those sneakers with "University of Virginia" printed on them? He was so proud of those, wore them every day. And he took them down in the cellar, and burned them up in the furnace. We had a fist fight. It lasted at least half an hour. Just the two of us, punching each other down the cellar, and crying right through it. I've often thought of how strange it was that I knew he'd given up his life. What happened in Boston, Willy?

(WILLY *looks at him as at an intruder.*)

BERNARD   I just bring it up because you asked me.

WILLY   (*angrily*)   Nothing. What do you mean, "What happened?" What's that got to do with anything?

BERNARD   Well, don't get sore.

WILLY   What are you trying to do, blame it on me? If a boy lays down is that my fault?

BERNARD   Now, Willy, don't get —

WILLY   Well, don't — don't talk to me that way! What does that mean, "What happened?"

(CHARLEY *enters. He is in his vest, and he carries a bottle of bourbon.*)

CHARLEY   Hey, you're going to miss that train. (*He waves the bottle.*)

BERNARD   Yeah, I'm going. (*He takes the bottle.*) Thanks, Pop. (*He picks up his rackets and bag.*) Good-by, Willy, and don't worry about it. You know, "If at first you don't succeed . . ."

WILLY   Yes, I believe in that.

BERNARD   But sometimes, Willy, it's better for a man just to walk away.

WILLY   Walk away?

BERNARD   That's right.

WILLY   But if you can't walk away?

BERNARD   (*after a slight pause*)   I guess that's when it's tough. (*Extending his hand*) Good-by, Willy.

WILLY   (*shaking* BERNARD'S *hand*)   Good-by, boy.

CHARLEY   (*an arm on* BERNARD'S *shoulder*)   How do you like this kid? Gonna argue a case in front of the Supreme Court.

BERNARD   (*protesting*)   Pop!

WILLY   (*genuinely shocked, pained, and happy*)   No! The Supreme Court!

BERNARD   I gotta run. 'By, Dad!

CHARLEY   Knock 'em dead, Bernard!

(BERNARD *goes off.*)

WILLY   (*as* CHARLEY *takes out his wallet*)   The Supreme Court! And he didn't even mention it!

CHARLEY   (*counting out money on the desk*)   He don't have to — he's gonna do it.

WILLY   And you never told him what to do, did you? You never took any interest in him.

CHARLEY   My salvation is that I never took any interest in anything. There's some money — fifty dollars. I got an accountant inside.

WILLY   Charley, look . . . (*With difficulty*) I got my insurance to pay. If you can manage it — I need a hundred and ten dollars.

(CHARLEY *doesn't reply for a moment; merely stops moving.*)

WILLY   I'd draw it from my bank but Linda would know, and I. . . .

CHARLEY   Sit down, Willy.

WILLY   (*moving toward the chair*)   I'm keeping an account of everything, remember. I'll pay every penny back. (*He sits.*)

CHARLEY   Now listen to me, Willy.

WILLY   I want you to know I appreciate . . .

CHARLEY   (*sitting down on the table*)   Willy, what're you doin'? What the hell is goin' on in your head?

WILLY   Why? I'm simply. . . .

CHARLEY   I offered you a job. You can make fifty dollars a week. And I won't send you on the road.

WILLY   I've got a job.

CHARLEY   Without pay? What kind of job is a job without pay? (*He rises.*) Now, look, kid, enough is enough. I'm no genius but I know when I'm being insulted.

WILLY   Insulted?

CHARLEY   Why don't you want to work for me?

WILLY   What's the matter with you? I've got a job.

CHARLEY   Then what're you walkin' in here every week for?

WILLY   (*getting up*)   Well, if you don't want me to walk in here —

CHARLEY   I am offering you a job.

WILLY   I don't want your goddam job!

CHARLEY   When the hell are you going to grow up?

WILLY   (*furiously*)   You big ignoramus, if you say that to me again I'll rap you one! I don't care how big you are! (*He's ready to fight.*)

(*Pause*)

CHARLEY   (*kindly, going to him*)   How much do you need, Willy?

WILLY Charley, I'm strapped. I'm strapped. I don't know what to do. I was just fired.

CHARLEY Howard fired you?

WILLY That snotnose. Imagine that? I named him. I named him Howard.

CHARLEY Willy, when're you gonna realize that them things don't mean anything? You named him Howard, but you can't sell that. The only thing you got in this world is what you can sell. And the funny thing is that you're a salesman, and you don't know that.

WILLY I've always tried to think otherwise, I guess. I always felt that if a man was impressive, and well liked, that nothing —

CHARLEY Why must everybody like you? Who liked J. P. Morgan? Was he impressive? In a Turkish bath he'd look like a butcher. But with his pockets on he was very well liked. Now listen, Willy, I know you don't like me, and nobody can say I'm in love with you, but I'll give you a job because — just for the hell of it, put it that way. Now what do you say?

WILLY I — I just can't work for you, Charley.

CHARLEY What're you, jealous of me?

WILLY I can't work for you, that's all, don't ask me why.

CHARLEY (*angered, takes out more bills*) You been jealous of me all your life, you damned fool! Here, pay your insurance. (*He puts the money in* WILLY'S *hand.*)

WILLY I'm keeping strict accounts.

CHARLEY I've got some work to do. Take care of yourself. And pay your insurance.

WILLY (*moving to the right*) Funny, y'know? After all the highways, and the trains, and the appointments, and the years, you end up worth more dead than alive.

CHARLEY Willy, nobody's worth nothin' dead. (*After a slight pause*) Did you hear what I said?

(WILLY *stands still, dreaming.*)

CHARLEY Willy!

WILLY Apologize to Bernard for me when you see him. I didn't mean to argue with him. He's a fine boy. They're all fine boys, and they'll end up big — all of them. Someday they'll all play tennis together. Wish me luck, Charley. He saw Bill Oliver today.

CHARLEY Good luck.

WILLY (*on the verge of tears*) Charley, you're the only friend I got. Isn't that a remarkable thing? (*He goes out.*)

CHARLEY Jesus!

(CHARLEY *stares after him a moment and follows. All light blacks out. Suddenly raucous music is heard, and a red glow rises behind the screen at right.* STANLEY, *a young waiter, appears, carrying a table, followed by* HAPPY, *who is carrying two chairs.*)

STANLEY (*putting the table down*) That's all right, Mr. Loman, I can handle it myself. (*He turns and takes the chairs from* HAPPY *and places them at the table.*)

HAPPY (*glancing around*) Oh, this is better.

STANLEY Sure, in the front there you're in the middle of all kinds of noise. Whenever you got a party, Mr. Loman, you just tell me and I'll put you back here. Y'know, there's a lotta people they don't like it private, because when they go out they like to see a lotta action around them because they're sick and tired to stay in the house by theirself. But I know you, you ain't from Hackensack. You know what I mean?

HAPPY (*sitting down*) So how's it coming, Stanley?

STANLEY Ah, it's a dog's life. I only wish during the war they'd a took me in the Army. I coulda been dead by now.

HAPPY My brother's back, Stanley.

STANLEY Oh, he come back, heh? From the Far West.

HAPPY Yeah, big cattle man, my brother, so treat him right. And my father's coming too.

STANLEY Oh, your father too!

HAPPY You got a couple of nice lobsters?

STANLEY Hundred per cent, big.

HAPPY I want them with the claws.

STANLEY Don't worry, I don't give you no mice. (HAPPY *laughs.*) How about some wine? It'll put a head on the meal.

HAPPY No. You remember, Stanley, that recipe I brought you from overseas? With the champagne in it?

STANLEY Oh, yeah, sure. I still got it tacked up yet in the kitchen. But that'll have to cost a buck apiece anyways.

HAPPY That's all right.

STANLEY What'd you, hit a number or somethin'?

HAPPY No, it's a little celebration. My brother is — I think he pulled off a big deal today. I think we're going into business together.

STANLEY Great! That's the best for you. Because a family business, you know what I mean? — that's the best.

HAPPY That's what I think.

STANLEY 'Cause what's the difference? Somebody steals? It's in the family. Know what I mean? (*Sotto voce*) Like this bartender here. The boss is goin' crazy what kinda leak he's got in the cash register. You put it in but it don't come out.

HAPPY (*raising his head*) Sh!

STANLEY What?

HAPPY You notice I wasn't lookin' right or left, was I?

STANLEY No.

HAPPY And my eyes are closed.

STANLEY So what's the — ?

HAPPY Strudel's comin'.

STANLEY (*catching on, looks around*) Ah, no, there's no —
(*He breaks off as a furred, lavishly dressed girl enters and sits at the next table. Both follow her with their eyes.*)

STANLEY Geez, how'd ya know?

HAPPY I got radar or something. (*Staring directly at her profile*) Oooooooo . . . Stanley.

STANLEY I think that's for you, Mr. Loman.

HAPPY Look at that mouth. Oh, God. And the binoculars.

STANLEY Geez, you got a life, Mr. Loman.

HAPPY Wait on her.

STANLEY (*going to the girl's table*) Would you like a menu, ma'am?

GIRL   I'm expecting someone, but I'd like a —

HAPPY   Why don't you bring her — excuse me, miss, do you mind? I sell champagne, and I'd like you to try my brand. Bring her a champagne, Stanley.

GIRL   That's awfully nice of you.

HAPPY   Don't mention it. It's all company money. (*He laughs.*)

GIRL   That's a charming product to be selling, isn't it?

HAPPY   Oh, gets to be like everything else. Selling is selling, y'know.

GIRL   I suppose.

HAPPY   You don't happen to sell, do you?

GIRL   No, I don't sell.

HAPPY   Would you object to a compliment from a stranger? You ought to be
on a magazine cover.

GIRL   (*looking at him a little archly*)   I have been.

    (STANLEY *comes in with a glass of champagne.*)

HAPPY   What'd I say before, Stanley? You see? She's a cover girl.

STANLEY   Oh, I could see, I could see.

HAPPY   (*to the* GIRL)   What magazine?

GIRL   Oh, a lot of them. (*She takes the drink.*)   Thank you.

HAPPY   You know what they say in France, don't you? "Champagne is the
drink of the complexion" — Hya, Biff!

    (BIFF *has entered and sits with* HAPPY.)

BIFF   Hello, kid. Sorry I'm late.

HAPPY   I just got here. Uh, Miss — ?

GIRL   Forsythe.

HAPPY   Miss Forsythe, this is my brother.

BIFF   Is Dad here?

HAPPY   His name is Biff. You might've heard of him. Great football player.

GIRL   Really? What team?

HAPPY   Are you familiar with football?

GIRL   No, I'm afraid I'm not.

HAPPY   Biff is quarterback with the New York Giants.

GIRL   Well, that is nice, isn't it? (*She drinks.*)

HAPPY   Good health.

GIRL   I'm happy to meet you.

HAPPY   That's my name. Hap. It's really Harold, but at West Point they called
me Happy.

GIRL   (*now really impressed*)   Oh, I see. How do you do? (*She turns her
profile.*)

BIFF   Isn't Dad coming?

HAPPY   You want her?

BIFF   Oh, I could never make that.

HAPPY   I remember the time that idea would never come into your head.
Where's the old confidence, Biff?

BIFF   I just saw Oliver —

HAPPY   Wait a minute. I've got to see that old confidence again. Do you want
her? She's on call.

BIFF   Oh, no. (*He turns to look at the* GIRL.)

HAPPY   I'm telling you. Watch this. (*Turning to the* GIRL) Honey? (*She turns
to him.*)   Are you busy?

GIRL   Well, I am . . . but I could make a phone call.

HAPPY   Do that, will you, honey? And see if you can get a friend. We'll be here for a while. Biff is one of the greatest football players in the country.

GIRL (*standing up*)   Well, I'm certainly happy to meet you.

HAPPY   Come back soon.

GIRL   I'll try.

HAPPY   Don't try, honey, try hard.

(*The* GIRL *exits.* STANLEY *follows, shaking his head in bewildered admiration.*)

HAPPY   Isn't that a shame now? A beautiful girl like that? That's why I can't get married. There's not a good woman in a thousand. New York is loaded with them, kid!

BIFF   Hap, look —

HAPPY   I told you she was on call!

BIFF (*strangely unnerved*)   Cut it out, will ya? I want to say something to you.

HAPPY   Did you see Oliver?

BIFF   I saw him all right. Now look. I want to tell Dad a couple of things and I want you to help me.

HAPPY   What? Is he going to back you?

BIFF   Are you crazy? You're out of your goddam head, you know that?

HAPPY   Why? What happened?

BIFF (*breathlessly*)   I did a terrible thing today, Hap. It's been the strangest day I ever went through. I'm all numb, I swear.

HAPPY   You mean he wouldn't see you?

BIFF   Well, I waited six hours for him, see? All day. Kept sending my name in. Even tried to date his secretary so she'd get me to him, but no soap.

HAPPY   Because you're not showin' the old confidence, Biff. He remembered you, didn't he?

BIFF (*stopping* HAPPY *with a gesture*)   Finally, about five o'clock, he comes out. Didn't remember who I was or anything. I felt like such an idiot, Hap.

HAPPY   Did you tell him my Florida idea?

BIFF   He walked away. I saw him for one minute. I got so mad I could've torn the walls down! How the hell did I ever get the idea I was a salesman there? I even believed myself that I'd been a salesman for him! And then he gave me one look and — I realized what a ridiculous lie my whole life has been! We've been talking in a dream for fifteen years. I was a shipping clerk.

HAPPY   What'd you do?

BIFF (*with great tension and wonder*)   Well, he left, see. And the secretary went out. I was all alone in the waiting-room. I don't know what came over me, Hap. The next thing I know I'm in his office — paneled walls, everything. I can't explain it. I — Hap, I took his fountain pen.

HAPPY   Geez, did he catch you?

BIFF   I ran out. I ran down all eleven flights. I ran and ran and ran.

HAPPY   That was an awful dumb — what'd you do that for?

BIFF (*agonized*)   I don't know, I just — wanted to take something, I don't know. You gotta help me, Hap, I'm gonna tell Pop.

HAPPY   You crazy? What for?

BIFF   Hap, he's got to understand that I'm not the man somebody lends that kind of money to. He thinks I've been spiting him all these years and it's eating him up.

HAPPY   That's just it. You tell him something nice.

BIFF   I can't.

HAPPY   Say you got a lunch date with Oliver tomorrow.

BIFF   So what do I do tomorrow?

HAPPY   You leave the house tomorrow and come back at night and say Oliver is thinking it over. And he thinks it over for a couple of weeks, and gradually it fades away and nobody's the worse.

BIFF   But it'll go on forever!

HAPPY   Dad is never so happy as when he's looking forward to something!
        (WILLY *enters*.)

HAPPY   Hello, scout!

WILLY   Gee, I haven't been here in years!
        (STANLEY *has followed* WILLY *in and sets a chair for him.* STANLEY *starts off but* HAPPY *stops him*.)

HAPPY   Stanley!
        (STANLEY *stands by, waiting for an order*.)

BIFF   (*going to* WILLY *with guilt, as to an invalid*)   Sit down, Pop. You want a drink?

WILLY   Sure, I don't mind.

BIFF   Let's get a load on.

WILLY   You look worried.

BIFF   N-no. (*To* STANLEY) Scotch all around. Make it doubles.

STANLEY   Doubles, right. (*He goes*.)

WILLY   You had a couple already, didn't you?

BIFF   Just a couple, yeah.

WILLY   Well, what happened, boy? (*Nodding affirmatively, with a smile*) Everything go all right?

BIFF   (*takes a breath, then reaches out and grasps* WILLY'S *hand*)   Pal . . . (*He is smiling bravely, and* WILLY *is smiling too*.) I had an experience today.

HAPPY   Terrific, Pop.

WILLY   That so? What happened?

BIFF   (*high, slightly alcoholic, above the earth*)   I'm going to tell you everything from first to last. It's been a strange day. (*Silence. He looks around, composes himself as best he can, but his breath keeps breaking the rhythm of his voice*.) I had to wait quite a while for him, and —

WILLY   Oliver?

BIFF   Yeah, Oliver. All day, as a matter of cold fact. And a lot of — instances — facts, Pops, facts about my life came back to me. Who was it, Pop? Who ever said I was a salesman with Oliver?

WILLY   Well, you were.

BIFF   No, Dad, I was a shipping clerk.

WILLY   But you were practically —

BIFF   (*with determination*)   Dad, I don't know who said it first, but I was never a salesman for Bill Oliver.

WILLY   What're you talking about?

BIFF   Let's hold on to the facts tonight, Pop. We're not going to get anywhere bullin' around. I was a shipping clerk.

WILLY   (*angrily*)   All right, now listen to me —

BIFF   Why don't you let me finish?

WILLY   I'm not interested in stories about the past or any crap of that kind because the woods are burning, boys, you understand? There's a big blaze going on all around. I was fired today.

BIFF (*shocked*)   How could you be?

WILLY   I was fired, and I'm looking for a little good news to tell your mother, because the woman has waited and the woman has suffered. The gist of it is that I haven't got a story left in my head, Biff. So don't give me a lecture about facts and aspects. I am not interested. Now what've you got to say to me?

(STANLEY *enters with three drinks. They wait until he leaves.*)

WILLY   Did you see Oliver?

BIFF   Jesus, Dad!

WILLY   You mean you didn't go up there?

HAPPY   Sure he went up there.

BIFF   I did. I — saw him. How could they fire you?

WILLY (*on the edge of his chair*)   What kind of a welcome did he give you?

BIFF   He won't even let you work on commission?

WILLY   I'm out! (*Driving*) So tell me, he gave you a warm welcome?

HAPPY   Sure, Pop, sure!

BIFF (*driven*)   Well, it was kind of —

WILLY   I was wondering if he'd remember you. (*To* HAPPY) Imagine, man doesn't see him for ten, twelve years and gives him that kind of a welcome!

HAPPY   Damn right!

BIFF (*trying to return to the offensive*)   Pop, look —

WILLY   You know why he remembered you, don't you? Because you impressed him in those days.

BIFF   Let's talk quietly and get this down to the facts, huh?

WILLY (*as though* BIFF *had been interrupting*)   Well, what happened? It's great news, Biff. Did he take you into his office or'd you talk in the waiting-room?

BIFF   Well, he came in, see, and —

WILLY (*with a big smile*)   What'd he say? Betcha he threw his arm around you.

BIFF   Well, he kinda —

WILLY   He's a fine man. (*To* HAPPY) Very hard man to see, y'know.

HAPPY (*agreeing*)   Oh, I know.

WILLY (*to* BIFF)   Is that where you had the drinks?

BIFF   Yeah, he gave me a couple of — no, no!

HAPPY (*cutting in*)   He told him my Florida idea.

WILLY   Don't interrupt. (*To* BIFF) How'd he react to the Florida idea?

BIFF   Dad, will you give me a minute to explain?

WILLY   I've been waiting for you to explain since I sat down here! What happened? He took you into his office and what?

BIFF   Well — I talked. And — and he listened, see.

WILLY   Famous for the way he listens, y'know. What was his answer?

BIFF   His answer was — (*He breaks off, suddenly angry.*) Dad, you're not letting me tell you what I want to tell you!

WILLY (*accusing, angered*)   You didn't see him, did you?

BIFF   I did see him!

WILLY   What'd you insult him or something? You insulted him, didn't you?

BIFF   Listen, will you let me out of it, will you just let me out of it!

HAPPY   What the hell!

WILLY   Tell me what happened!

BIFF (*to* HAPPY)   I can't talk to him!
(*A single trumpet note jars the ear. The light of green leaves stains the house, which holds the air of night and a dream.* YOUNG BERNARD *enters and knocks on the door of the house.*)
YOUNG BERNARD (*frantically*)   Mrs. Loman, Mrs. Loman!
HAPPY   Tell him what happened!
BIFF (*to* HAPPY)   Shut up and leave me alone!
WILLY   No, No! You had to go and flunk math!
BIFF   What math? What're you talking about?
YOUNG BERNARD   Mrs. Loman, Mrs. Loman!
(LINDA *appears in the house, as of old.*)
WILLY (*wildly*)   Math, math, math!
BIFF   Take it easy, Pop!
YOUNG BERNARD   Mrs. Loman!
WILLY (*furiously*)   If you hadn't flunked you'd've been set by now!
BIFF   Now, look, I'm gonna tell you what happened, and you're going to listen to me.
YOUNG BERNARD   Mrs. Loman!
BIFF   I waited six hours —
HAPPY   What the hell are you saying?
BIFF   I kept sending in my name but he wouldn't see me. So finally he . . . (*He continues unheard as light fades below on the restaurant.*)
YOUNG BERNARD   Biff flunked math!
LINDA   No!
YOUNG BERNARD   Birnbaum flunked him! They won't graduate him!
LINDA   But they have to. He's gotta go to the university. Where is he? Biff! Biff!
YOUNG BERNARD   No, he left. He went to Grand Central.
LINDA   Grand — You mean he went to Boston!
YOUNG BERNARD   Is Uncle Willy in Boston?
LINDA   Oh, maybe Willy can talk to the teacher, Oh, the poor, poor boy!
(*Light on house area snaps out.*)
BIFF (*at the table, now audible, holding up a gold fountain pen*)   . . . so I'm washed up with Oliver, you understand? Are you listening to me?
WILLY (*at a loss*)   Yeah, sure. If you hadn't flunked —
BIFF   Flunked what? What're you talking about?
WILLY   Don't blame everything on me! I didn't flunk math — you did! What pen?
HAPPY   That was awful dumb, Biff, a pen like that is worth —
WILLY (*seeing the pen for the first time*)   You took Oliver's pen?
BIFF (*weakening*)   Dad, I just explained it to you.
WILLY   You stole Bill Oliver's fountain pen!
BIFF   I didn't exactly steal it! That's just what I've been explaining to you!
HAPPY   He had it in his hand and just then Oliver walked in, so he got nervous and stuck it in his pocket!
WILLY   My God, Biff!
BIFF   I never intended to do it, Dad!
OPERATOR'S VOICE   Standish Arms, good evening!
WILLY (*shouting*)   I'm not in my room!
BIFF (*frightened*)   Dad, what's the matter? (*He and* HAPPY *stand up.*)

OPERATOR   Ringing Mr. Loman for you!

WILLY   I'm not there, stop it!

BIFF (*horrified, gets down on one knee before* WILLY)   Dad, I'll make good, I'll make good. (WILLY *tries to get to his feet.* BIFF *holds him down.*) Sit down now.

WILLY   No, you're no good, you're no good for anything.

BIFF   I am, Dad, I'll find something else, you understand? Now don't worry about anything. (*He holds up* WILLY's *face.*) Talk to me, Dad.

OPERATOR   Mr. Loman does not answer. Shall I page him?

WILLY (*attempting to stand, as though to rush and silence the* OPERATOR)   No, no, no!

HAPPY   He'll strike something, Pop.

WILLY   No, no . . .

BIFF (*desperately, standing over* WILLY)   Pop, listen! Listen to me! I'm telling you something good. Oliver talked to his partner about the Florida idea. You listening? He — he talked to his partner, and he came to me . . . I'm going to be all right, you hear? Dad, listen to me, he said it was just a question of the amount!

WILLY   Then you . . . got it?

HAPPY   He's gonna be terrific, Pop!

WILLY (*trying to stand*)   Then you got it, haven't you? You got it! You got it!

BIFF (*agonized, holds* WILLY *down*)   No, no. Look, Pop. I'm supposed to have lunch with them tomorrow. I'm just telling you this so you'll know that I can still make an impression, Pop. And I'll make good somewhere, but I can't go tomorrow, see?

WILLY   Why not? You simply —

BIFF   But the pen, Pop!

WILLY   You give it to him and tell him it was an oversight!

HAPPY   Sure, have lunch tomorrow!

BIFF   I can't say that —

WILLY   You were doing a crossword puzzle and accidentally used his pen!

BIFF   Listen, kid, I took those balls years ago, now I walk in with his fountain pen? That clinches it, don't you see? I can't face him like that! I'll try elsewhere.

PAGE'S VOICE   Paging Mr. Loman!

WILLY   Don't you want to be anything?

BIFF   Pop, how can I go back?

WILLY   You don't want to be anything, is that what's behind it?

BIFF (*now angry at* WILLY *for not crediting his sympathy*)   Don't take it that way! You think it was easy walking into that office after what I'd done to him? A team of horses couldn't have dragged me back to Bill Oliver!

WILLY   Then why'd you go?

BIFF   Why did I go? Why did I go! Look at you! Look at what's become of you!

(*Off left,* THE WOMAN *laughs.*)

WILLY   Biff, you're going to go to that lunch tomorrow, or —

BIFF   I can't go. I've got no appointment!

HAPPY   Biff, for . . . !

WILLY   Are you spiting me?

BIFF   Don't take it that way! Goddammit!

WILLY (*strikes* BIFF *and falters away from the table*) You rotten little louse!
Are you spiting me?

THE WOMAN Someone's at the door, Willy!

BIFF I'm no good, can't you see what I am?

HAPPY (*separating them*) Hey, you're in a restaurant! Now cut it out, both of
you! (*The girls enter.*) Hello, girls, sit down.
(THE WOMAN *laughs, off left.*)

MISS FORSYTHE I guess we might as well. This is Letta.

THE WOMAN Willy, are you going to wake up?

BIFF (*ignoring* WILLY) How're ya, miss, sit down. What do you drink?

MISS FORSYTHE Letta might not be able to stay long.

LETTA I gotta get up very early tomorrow. I got jury duty. I'm so excited!
Were you fellows ever on a jury?

BIFF No, but I been in front of them! (*The girls laugh.*) This is my father.

LETTA Isn't he cute? Sit down with us, Pop.

HAPPY Sit him down, Biff!

BIFF (*going to him*) Come on, slugger, drink us under the table. To hell with
it! Come on, sit down, pal.
(*On* BIFF'S *last insistence,* WILLY *is about to sit.*)

THE WOMAN (*now urgently*) Willy, are you going to answer the door!
(THE WOMAN'S *call pulls* WILLY *back. He starts right, befuddled.*)

BIFF Hey, where are you going?

WILLY Open the door.

BIFF The door?

WILLY The washroom . . . the door . . . where's the door?

BIFF (*leading* WILLY *to the left*) Just go straight down.
(WILLY *moves left.*)

THE WOMAN Willy, Willy, are you going to get up, get up, get up, get up?
(WILLY *exits left.*)

LETTA I think it's sweet you bring your daddy along.

MISS FORSYTHE Oh, he isn't really your father!

BIFF (*at left, turning to her resentfully*) Miss Forsythe, you've just seen a
prince walk by. A fine, troubled prince. A hard-working, unappreciated
prince. A pal, you understand? A good companion. Always for his boys.

LETTA That's so sweet.

HAPPY Well, girls, what's the program? We're wasting time. Come on, Biff.
Gather round. Where would you like to go?

BIFF Why don't you do something for him?

HAPPY Me!

BIFF Don't you give a damn for him, Hap?

HAPPY What're you talking about? I'm the one who —

BIFF I sense it, you don't give a good goddam about him. (*He takes the
rolled-up hose from his pocket and puts it on the table in front of* HAPPY.)
Look what I found in the cellar, for Christ's sake. How can you bear to let
it go on?

HAPPY Me? Who goes away? Who runs off and —

BIFF Yeah, but he doesn't mean anything to you. You could help him — I
can't! Don't you understand what I'm talking about? He's going to kill himself, don't you know that?

HAPPY Don't I know it! Me!

BIFF Hap, help him! Jesus . . . help him . . . Help me, help me, I can't bear to look at his face! (*Ready to weep, he hurries out, up right.*)

HAPPY (*starting after him*) Where are you going?

MISS FORSYTHE What's he so mad about?

HAPPY Come on, girls, we'll catch up with him.

MISS FORSYTHE (*as* HAPPY *pushes her out*) Say, I don't like that temper of his!

HAPPY He's just a little overstrung, he'll be all right!

WILLY (*off left, as* THE WOMAN *laughs*) Don't answer! Don't answer!

LETTA Don't you want to tell your father —

HAPPY No, that's not my father. He's just a guy. Come on, we'll catch Biff, and, honey, we're going to paint this town! Stanley, where's the check! Hey, Stanley!

(*They exit.* STANLEY *looks toward left.*)

STANLEY (*calling to* HAPPY *indignantly*) Mr. Loman! Mr. Loman!

(STANLEY *picks up a chair and follows them off. Knocking is heard off left.* THE WOMAN *enters, laughing.* WILLY *follows her. She is in a black slip; he is buttoning his shirt. Raw, sensuous music accompanies their speech.*)

WILLY Will you stop laughing? Will you stop?

THE WOMAN Aren't you going to answer the door? He'll wake the whole hotel.

WILLY I'm not expecting anybody.

THE WOMAN Whyn't you have another drink, honey, and stop being so damn self-centered?

WILLY I'm so lonely.

THE WOMAN You know you ruined me, Willy? From now on, whenever you come to the office, I'll see that you go right through to the buyers. No waiting at my desk any more, Willy. You ruined me.

WILLY That's nice of you to say that.

THE WOMAN Gee, you are self-centered! Why so sad? You are the saddest, self-centeredest soul I ever did see-saw. (*She laughs. He kisses her.*) Come on inside, drummer boy. It's silly to be dressing in the middle of the night. (*As knocking is heard*) Aren't you going to answer the door?

WILLY They're knocking on the wrong door.

THE WOMAN But I felt the knocking. And he heard us talking in here. Maybe the hotel's on fire!

WILLY (*his terror rising*) It's a mistake.

THE WOMAN Then tell him to go away!

WILLY There's nobody there.

THE WOMAN It's getting on my nerves, Willy. There's somebody standing out there and it's getting on my nerves!

WILLY (*pushing her away from him*) All right, stay in the bathroom here, and don't come out. I think there's a law in Massachusetts about it, so don't come out. It may be that new room clerk. He looked very mean. So don't come out. It's a mistake, there's no fire.

(*The knocking is heard again. He takes a few steps away from her, and she vanishes into the wing. The light follows him, and now he is facing* YOUNG BIFF, *who carries a suitcase.* BIFF *steps toward him. The music is gone.*)

BIFF Why didn't you answer?

WILLY Biff! What are you doing in Boston?

BIFF Why didn't you answer? I've been knocking for five minutes, I called you on the phone —

WILLY   I just heard you. I was in the bathroom and had the door shut. Did
    anything happen home?
BIFF   Dad — I let you down.
WILLY   What do you mean?
BIFF   Dad . . .
WILLY   Biffo, what's this about? (*Putting his arm around* BIFF) Come on, let's
    go downstairs and get you a malted.
BIFF   Dad, I flunked math.
WILLY   Not for the term?
BIFF   The term. I haven't got enough credits to graduate.
WILLY   You mean to say Bernard wouldn't give you the answers?
BIFF   He did, he tried, but I only got a sixty-one.
WILLY   And they wouldn't give you four points?
BIFF   Birnbaum refused absolutely. I begged him, Pop, but he won't give me
    those points. You gotta talk to him before they close the school. Because
    if he saw the kind of man you are, and you just talked to him in your way,
    I'm sure he'd come through for me. The class came right before practice,
    see, and I didn't go enough. Would you talk to him? He'd like you, Pop.
    You know the way you could talk.
WILLY   You're on. We'll drive right back.
BIFF   Oh, Dad, good work! I'm sure he'll change it for you!
WILLY   Go downstairs and tell the clerk I'm checkin' out. Go right down.
BIFF   Yes, sir! See, the reason he hates me, Pop — one day he was late for
    class so I got up at the blackboard and imitated him. I crossed my eyes and
    talked with a lithp.
WILLY (*laughing*)   You did? The kids like it?
BIFF   They nearly died laughing!
WILLY   Yeah? What'd you do?
BIFF   The thquare root of thixthy twee is . . . (WILLY *bursts out laughing;* BIFF
    joins him.)   And in the middle of it he walked in!
    (WILLY *laughs and* THE WOMAN *joins in offstage.*)
WILLY (*without hesitation*)   Hurry downstairs and —
BIFF   Somebody in there?
WILLY   No, that was next door.
    (THE WOMAN *laughs offstage.*)
BIFF   Somebody got in your bathroom!
WILLY   No, it's the next room, there's a party —
THE WOMAN (*enters, laughing. She lisps this*)   Can I come in? There's some-
    thing in the bathtub, Willy, and it's moving!
    (WILLY *looks at* BIFF, *who is staring open-mouthed and horrified at* THE
    WOMAN.)
WILLY   Ah — you better go back to your room. They must be finished painting
    by now. They're painting her room so I let her take a shower here. Go back,
    go back . . . (*He pushes her.*)
THE WOMAN (*resisting*)   But I've got to get dressed, Willy, I can't —
WILLY   Get out of here! Go back, go back . . . (*Suddenly striving for the ordi-
    nary.*) This is Miss Francis, Biff, she's a buyer. They're painting her room.
    Go back, Miss Francis, go back . . .
THE WOMAN   But my clothes, I can't go out naked in the hall!

WILLY (*pushing her offstage*)   Get outa here! Go back, go back!

(BIFF *slowly sits down on his suitcase as the argument continues offstage.*)

THE WOMAN   Where's my stockings? You promised me stockings. Willy!

WILLY   I have no stockings here!

THE WOMAN   You had two boxes of size nine sheers for me, and I want them!

WILLY   Here, for God's sake, will you get outa here!

THE WOMAN (*enters holding a box of stockings*)   I just hope there's nobody in the hall. That's all I hope. (*To* BIFF) Are you football or baseball?

BIFF   Football.

THE WOMAN (*angry, humiliated*)   That's me too. G'night. (*She snatches her clothes from* WILLY *and walks out.*)

WILLY (*after a pause*)   Well, better get going. I want to get to the school first thing in the morning. Get my suits out of the closet. I'll get my valise. (BIFF *doesn't move.*) What's the matter? (BIFF *remains motionless, tears falling.*) She's a buyer. Buys for J. H. Simmons. She lives down the hall — they're painting. You don't imagine — (*He breaks off. After a pause*) Now listen, pal, she's just a buyer. She sees merchandise in her room and they have to keep it looking just so . . . (*Pause. Assuming command*) All right, get my suits. (BIFF *doesn't move.*) Now stop crying and do as I say. I gave you an order. Biff, I gave you an order! Is that what you do when I give you an order? How dare you cry? (*Putting his arm around* BIFF) Now look, Biff, when you grow up you'll understand about these things. You mustn't overemphasize a thing like this. I'll see Birnbaum first thing in the morning.

BIFF   Never mind.

WILLY (*getting down beside* BIFF)   Never mind! He's going to give you those points. I'll see to it.

BIFF   He wouldn't listen to you.

WILLY   He certainly will listen to me. You need those points for the U. of Virginia.

BIFF   I'm not going there.

WILLY   Heh? If I can't get him to change that mark you'll make it up in summer school. You've got all summer to —

BIFF (*his weeping breaking from him*)   Dad . . .

WILLY (*infected by it*)   Oh, my boy . . .

BIFF   Dad . . .

WILLY   She's nothing to me, Biff. I was lonely, I was terribly lonely.

BIFF   You — you gave her Mama's stockings! (*His tears break through and he rises to go.*)

WILLY (*grabbing for* BIFF)   I gave you an order!

BIFF   Don't touch me, you — liar!

WILLY   Apologize for that!

BIFF   You fake! You phony little fake! You fake! (*Overcome, he turns quickly and weeping fully goes out with his suitcase.* WILLY *is left on the floor on his knees.*)

WILLY   I gave you an order! Biff, come back here or I'll beat you! Come back here! I'll whip you!

(STANLEY *comes quickly in from the right and stands in front of* WILLY.)

WILLY (*shouts at* STANLEY)   I gave you an order . . .

STANLEY   Hey, let's pick it up, pick it up, Mr. Loman. (*He helps* WILLY *to his feet.*) Your boys left with the chippies. They said they'll see you home.
(*A second waiter watches some distance away.*)

WILLY   But we were supposed to have dinner together.
(*Music is heard,* WILLY'S *theme.*)

STANLEY   Can you make it?

WILLY   I'll — sure, I can make it. (*Suddenly concerned about his clothes*) Do I — look all right?

STANLEY   Sure, you look all right. (*He flicks a speck off* WILLY'S *lapel.*)

WILLY   Here — here's a dollar.

STANLEY   Oh, your son paid me. It's all right.

WILLY   (*putting it in* STANLEY'S *hand*)   No, take it. You're a good boy.

STANLEY   Oh, no, you don't have to . . .

WILLY   Here — here's some more, I don't need it any more. (*After a slight pause*) Tell me — is there a seed store in the neighborhood?

STANLEY   Seeds? You mean like to plant?
(*As* WILLY *turns,* STANLEY *slips the money back into his jacket pocket.*)

WILLY   Yes. Carrots, peas . . .

STANLEY   Well, there's hardware stores on Sixth Avenue, but it may be too late now.

WILLY   (*anxiously*)   Oh, I'd better hurry. I've got to get some seeds. (*He starts off to the right.*) I've got to get some seeds, right away. Nothing's planted. I don't have a thing in the ground.
(WILLY *hurries out as the light goes down.* STANLEY *moves over to the right after him, watches him off. The other waiter has been staring at* WILLY.)

STANLEY   (*to the waiter*)   Well, whatta you looking at?
(*The waiter picks up the chairs and moves off right.* STANLEY *takes the table and follows him. The light fades on this area. There is a long pause, the sound of the flute coming over. The light gradually rises on the kitchen, which is empty.* HAPPY *appears at the door of the house, followed by* BIFF. HAPPY *is carrying a large bunch of long-stemmed roses. He enters the kitchen, looks around for* LINDA. *Not seeing her, he turns to* BIFF, *who is just outside the house door, and makes a gesture with his hands, indicating "Not here, I guess." He looks into the living-room and freezes. Inside,* LINDA, *unseen, is seated,* WILLY'S *coat on her lap. She rises ominously and quietly and moves toward* HAPPY, *who backs up into the kitchen, afraid.*)

HAPPY   Hey, what're you doing up? (LINDA *says nothing but moves toward him implacably.*) Where's Pop? (*He keeps backing to the right, and now* LINDA *is in full view in the doorway to the living-room.*) Is he sleeping?

LINDA   Where were you?

HAPPY   (*trying to laugh it off*)   We met two girls, Mom, very fine types. Here, we brought you some flowers. (*Offering them to her*) Put them in your room, Ma.
(*She knocks them to the floor at* BIFF'S *feet. He has now come inside and closed the door behind him. She stares at* BIFF, *silent.*)

HAPPY   Now what'd you do that for? Mom, I want you to have some flowers —

LINDA   (*cutting* HAPPY *off, violently to* BIFF)   Don't you care whether he lives or dies?

HAPPY   (*going to the stairs*)   Come upstairs, Biff.

BIFF (*with a flare of disgust, to* HAPPY) Go away from me! (*To* LINDA) What do you mean, lives or dies? Nobody's dying around here, pal.

LINDA Get out of my sight! Get out of here!

BIFF I wanna see the boss.

LINDA You're not going near him!

BIFF Where is he? (*He moves into the living-room and* LINDA *follows.*)

LINDA (*shouting after* BIFF) You invite him for dinner. He looks forward to it all day — (BIFF *appears in his parents' bedroom, looks around, and exits*) — and then you desert him there. There's no stranger you'd do that to!

HAPPY Why? He had a swell time with us. Listen, when I — (LINDA *comes back into the kitchen*) — desert him I hope I don't outlive the day!

LINDA Get out of here!

HAPPY Now look, Mom . . .

LINDA Did you have to go to women tonight? You and your lousy rotten whores!

(BIFF *re-enters the kitchen.*)

HAPPY Mom, all we did was follow Biff around trying to cheer him up! (*To* BIFF) Boy, what a night you gave me!

LINDA Get out of here, both of you, and don't come back! I don't want you tormenting him any more. Go on now, get your things together! (*To* BIFF) You can sleep in his apartment. (*She starts to pick up the flowers and stops herself.*) Pick up this stuff, I'm not your maid any more. Pick it up, you bum, you!

(HAPPY *turns his back to her in refusal.* BIFF *slowly moves over and gets down on his knees, picking up the flowers.*)

LINDA You're a pair of animals! Not one, not another living soul would have had the cruelty to walk out on that man in a restaurant!

BIFF (*not looking at her*) Is that what he said?

LINDA He didn't have to say anything. He was so humiliated he nearly limped when he came in.

HAPPY But, Mom, he had a great time with us —

BIFF (*cutting him off violently*) Shut up!

(*Without another word,* HAPPY *goes upstairs.*)

LINDA You! You didn't even go in to see if he was all right!

BIFF (*still on the floor in front of* LINDA, *the flowers in his hand; with self-loathing*). No. Didn't. Didn't do a damned thing. How do you like that, heh? Left him babbling in a toilet.

LINDA You louse. You . . .

BIFF Now you hit it on the nose! (*He gets up, throws the flowers in the waste-basket.*) The scum of the earth, and you're looking at him!

LINDA Get out of here!

BIFF I gotta talk to the boss, Mom. Where is he?

LINDA You're not going near him. Get out of this house!

BIFF (*with absolute assurance, determination*) No. We're gonna have an abrupt conversation, him and me.

LINDA You're not talking to him!

(*Hammering is heard from outside the house, off right.* BIFF *turns toward the noise.*)

LINDA (*suddenly pleading*) Will you please leave him alone?

BIFF What's he doing out there?

LINDA He's planting the garden!

BIFF (*quietly*) Now? Oh, my God!

> (BIFF *moves outside*, LINDA *following. The light dies down on them and comes up on the center of the apron as* WILLY *walks into it. He is carrying a flashlight, a hoe, and a handful of seed packets. He raps the top of the hoe sharply to fix it firmly, and then moves to the left, measuring off the distance with his foot. He holds the flashlight to look at the seed packets, reading off the instructions. He is in the blue of night.*)

WILLY Carrots . . . quarter-inch apart. Rows . . . one-foot rows. (*He measures it off.*) One foot. (*He puts down a package and measures off.*) Beets. (*He puts down another package and measures again.*) Lettuce. (*He reads the package, puts it down.*) One foot — (*He breaks off as* BEN *appears at the right and moves slowly down to him.*) What a proposition, ts, ts. Terrific, terrific. 'Cause she's suffered, Ben, the woman has suffered. You understand me? A man can't go out the way he came in, Ben, a man has got to add up to something. You can't, you can't — (BEN *moves toward him as though to interrupt.*) You gotta consider, now. Don't answer so quick. Remember, it's a guaranteed twenty-thousand-dollar proposition. Now look, Ben, I want you to go through the ins and outs of this thing with me. I've got nobody to talk to, Ben, and the woman has suffered, you hear me?

BEN (*standing still, considering*) What's the proposition?

WILLY It's twenty thousand dollars on the barrelhead. Guaranteed, gilt-edged, you understand?

BEN You don't want to make a fool of yourself. They might not honor the policy.

WILLY How can they dare refuse? Didn't I work like a coolie to meet every premium on the nose? And now they don't pay off? Impossible!

BEN It's called a cowardly thing, William.

WILLY Why? Does it take more guts to stand here the rest of my life ringing up a zero?

BEN (*yielding*) That's a point, William. (*He moves, thinking, turns.*) And twenty thousand — that *is* something one can feel with the hand, it is there.

WILLY (*now assured, with rising power*) Oh, Ben, that's the whole beauty of it! I see it like a diamond, shining in the dark, hard and rough, that I can pick up and touch in my hand. Not like — like an appointment! This would not be another damned-fool appointment, Ben, and it changes all the aspects. Because he thinks I'm nothing, see, and so he spites me. But the funeral — (*Straightening up*) Ben, that funeral will be massive! They'll come from Maine, Massachusetts, Vermont, New Hampshire! All the old-timers with the strange license plates — that boy will be thunder-struck, Ben, because he never realized — I am known! Rhode Island, New York, New Jersey — I am known, Ben, and he'll see it with his eyes once and for all. He'll see what I am, Ben! He's in for a shock, that boy!

BEN (*coming down to the edge of the garden*) He'll call you a coward.

WILLY (*suddenly fearful*) No, that would be terrible.

BEN Yes. And a damned fool.

WILLY No, no, he mustn't, I won't have that! (*He is broken and desperate.*)

BEN He'll hate you, William.

> (*The gay music of* THE BOYS *is heard.*)

WILLY Oh, Ben, how do we get back to all the great times? Used to be so full of light, and comradeship, the sleigh-riding in winter and the ruddiness on his cheeks. And always some kind of good news coming up, always something nice coming up ahead. And never even let me carry the valises in the house, and simonizing, simonizing that little red car! Why, why can't I give him something and not have him hate me?

BEN Let me think about it. (*He glances at his watch.*) I still have a little time. Remarkable proposition, but you've got to be sure you're not making a fool of yourself.

(BEN *drifts off upstage and goes out of sight.* BIFF *comes down from the left.*)

WILLY (*suddenly conscious of* BIFF, *turns and looks up at him, then begins picking up the packages of seeds in confusion*) Where the hell is that seed? (*Indignantly*) You can't see nothing out here! They boxed in the whole goddam neighborhood!

BIFF There are people all around here. Don't you realize that?

WILLY I'm busy. Don't bother me.

BIFF (*taking the hoe from* WILLY) I'm saying good-by to you, Pop. (WILLY *looks at him, silent, unable to move.*) I'm not coming back any more.

WILLY You're not going to see Oliver tomorrow?

BIFF I've got no appointment, Dad.

WILLY He put his arm around you, and you've got no appointment?

BIFF Pop, get this now, will you? Everytime I've left it's been a fight that sent me out of here. Today I realized something about myself and I tried to explain it to you and I — I think I'm just not smart enough to make any sense out of it for you. To hell with whose fault it is or anything like that. (*He takes* WILLY'S *arm.*) Let's just wrap it up, heh? Come on in, we'll tell Mom. (*He gently tries to pull* WILLY *to left.*)

WILLY (*frozen, immobile, with guilt in his voice*) No, I don't want to see her.

BIFF Come on! (*He pulls again, and* WILLY *tries to pull away.*)

WILLY (*highly nervous*) No, no, I don't want to see her.

BIFF (*tries to look into* WILLY'S *face, as if to find the answer there.*) Why don't you want to see her?

WILLY (*more harshly now*) Don't bother me, will you?

BIFF What do you mean, you don't want to see her? You don't want them calling you yellow, do you? This isn't your fault; it's me, I'm a bum. Now come inside! (WILLY *strains to get away.*) Did you hear what I said to you? (WILLY *pulls away and quickly goes by himself into the house.* BIFF *follows.*)

LINDA (*to* WILLY) Did you plant, dear?

BIFF (*at the door, to* LINDA) All right, we had it out. I'm going and I'm not writing any more.

LINDA (*going to* WILLY *in the kitchen*) I think that's the best way, dear. 'Cause there's no use drawing it out, you'll just never get along.

(WILLY *doesn't respond.*)

BIFF People ask where I am and what I'm doing, you don't know, and you don't care. That way it'll be off your mind and you can start brightening up again. All right? That clears it, doesn't it? (WILLY *is silent, and* BIFF *goes to him.*) You gonna wish me luck, scout? (*He extends his hand.*) What do you say?

LINDA Shake his hand, Willy.

WILLY (*turning to her, seething with hurt*)   There's no necessity to mention the pen at all, y'know.

BIFF (*gently*)   I've got no appointment, Dad.

WILLY (*erupting fiercely*)   He put his arm around. . . ?

BIFF   Dad, you're never going to see what I am, so what's the use of arguing? If I strike oil I'll send you a check. Meantime forget I'm alive.

WILLY (*to* LINDA)   Spite, see?

BIFF   Shake hands, Dad.

WILLY   Not my hand.

BIFF   I was hoping not to go this way.

WILLY   Well, this is the way you're going. Good-by.

(BIFF *looks at him a moment, then turns sharply and goes to the stairs.*)

WILLY (*stops him with*)   May you rot in hell if you leave this house!

BIFF (*turning*)   Exactly what is it that you want from me?

WILLY   I want you to know, on the train, in the mountains, in the valleys, wherever you go, that you cut down your life for spite!

BIFF   No, no.

WILLY   Spite, spite, is the word of your undoing! And when you're down and out, remember what did it. When you're rotting some where beside the railroad tracks, remember, and don't you dare blame it on me!

BIFF   I'm not blaming it on you!

WILLY   I won't take the rap for this, you hear?

(HAPPY *comes down the stairs and stands on the bottom step, watching.*)

BIFF   That's just what I'm telling you!

WILLY (*sinking into a chair at the table, with full accusation*)   You're trying to put a knife in me — don't think I don't know what you're doing!

BIFF   All right, phony! Then let's lay it on the line. (*He whips the rubber tube out of his pocket and puts it on the table.*)

HAPPY   You crazy —

LINDA   Biff! (*She moves to grab the hose, but* BIFF *holds it down with his hand.*)

BIFF   Leave it there! Don't move it!

WILLY (*not looking at it*)   What is that?

BIFF   You know goddam well what that is.

WILLY (*caged, wanting to escape*)   I never saw that.

BIFF   You saw it. The mice didn't bring it into the cellar! What is this supposed to do, make a hero out of you? This supposed to make me sorry for you?

WILLY   Never heard of it.

BIFF   There'll be no pity for you, you hear it? No pity!

WILLY (*to* LINDA)   You hear the spite!

BIFF   No, you're going to hear the truth — what you are and what I am!

LINDA   Stop it!

WILLY   Spite!

HAPPY (*coming down toward* BIFF)   You cut it now!

BIFF (*to* HAPPY)   The man don't know who we are! The man is gonna know! (*To* WILLY) We never told the truth for ten minutes in this house!

HAPPY   We always told the truth!

BIFF (*turning on him*)   You big blow, are you the assistant buyer? You're one of the two assistants to the assistant, aren't you?

HAPPY   Well, I'm practically —

BIFF   You're practically full of it! We all are! And I'm through with it. (*To* WILLY.) Now hear this, Willy, this is me.

WILLY   I know you!

BIFF   You know why I had no address for three months! I stole a suit in Kansas City and I was in jail. (*To* LINDA, *who is sobbing*) Stop crying. I'm through with it.

(LINDA *turns away from them, her hands covering her face.*)

WILLY   I suppose that's my fault!

BIFF   I stole myself out of every good job since high school!

WILLY   And whose fault is that?

BIFF   And I never got anywhere because you blew me so full of hot air I could never stand taking orders from anybody! That's whose fault it is!

WILLY   I hear that!

LINDA   Don't, Biff!

BIFF   It's goddam time you heard that! I had to be boss big shot in two weeks, and I'm through with it!

WILLY   Then hang yourself! For spite, hang yourself!

BIFF   No! Nobody's hanging himself, Willy! I ran down eleven flights with a pen in my hand today. And suddenly I stopped, you hear me? And in the middle of that office building, do you hear this? I stopped in the middle of that building and I saw — the sky. I saw the things that I love in this world. The work and the food and time to sit and smoke. And I looked at the pen and said to myself, what the hell am I grabbing this for? Why am I trying to become what I don't want to be? What am I doing in an office, making a contemptuous, begging fool of myself, when all I want is out there, waiting for me the minute I say I know who I am! Why can't I say that, Willy? (*He tries to make* WILLY *face him, but* WILLY *pulls away and moves to the left.*)

WILLY (*with hatred, threateningly*)   The door of your life is wide open!

BIFF   Pop! I'm a dime a dozen, and so are you!

WILLY (*turning on him now in an uncontrolled outburst*)   I am not a dime a dozen! I am Willy Loman, and you are Biff Loman!

(BIFF *starts for* WILLY, *but is blocked by* HAPPY. *In his fury,* BIFF *seems on the verge of attacking his father.*)

BIFF   I am not a leader of men, Willy, and neither are you. You were never anything but a hard-working drummer who landed in the ash can like all the rest of them! I'm one dollar an hour, Willy! I tried seven states and couldn't raise it. A buck an hour! Do you gather my meaning? I'm not bringing home any prizes any more, and you're going to stop waiting for me to bring them home!

WILLY (*directly to* BIFF)   You vengeful, spiteful mutt!

(BIFF *breaks from* HAPPY. WILLY, *in fright, starts up the stairs.* BIFF *grabs him.*)

BIFF (*at the peak of his fury*)   Pop, I'm nothing! I'm nothing, Pop. Can't you understand that? There's no spite in it any more. I'm just what I am, that's all.

(BIFF'S *fury has spent itself, and he breaks down, sobbing, holding on to* WILLY, *who dumbly fumbles for* BIFF'S *face.*)

WILLY (*astonished*) What're you doing? What're you doing? (*To* LINDA) Why is he crying?

BIFF (*crying, broken*) Will you let me go, for Christ's sake? Will you take that phony dream and burn it before something happens? (*Struggling to contain himself, he pulls away and moves to the stairs.*) I'll go in the morning. Put him — put him to bed. (*Exhausted,* BIFF *moves up the stairs to his room.*)

WILLY (*after a long pause, astonished, elevated*) Isn't that — isn't that remarkable? Biff — he likes me!

LINDA He loves you, Willy!

HAPPY (*deeply moved*) Always did, Pop.

WILLY Oh, Biff! (*Staring wildly*) He cried! Cried to me. (*He is choking with his love, and now cries out his promise.*) That boy — that boy is going to be magnificent!

(BEN *appears in the light just outside the kitchen.*)

BEN Yes, outstanding, with twenty thousand behind him.

LINDA (*sensing the racing of his mind, fearfully, carefully*) Now come to bed, Willy. It's all settled now.

WILLY (*finding it difficult not to rush out of the house*) Yes, we'll sleep. Come on. Go to sleep, Hap.

BEN And it does take a great kind of a man to crack the jungle.

(*In accents of dread,* BEN's *idyllic music starts up.*)

HAPPY (*his arm around* LINDA) I'm getting married, Pop, don't forget it. I'm changing everything. I'm gonna run that department before the year is up. You'll see, Mom. (*He kisses her.*)

BEN The jungle is dark but full of diamonds, Willy.

(WILLY *turns, moves, listening to* BEN.)

LINDA Be good. You're both good boys, just act that way, that's all.

HAPPY 'Night, Pop. (*He goes upstairs.*)

LINDA (*to* WILLY) Come, dear.

BEN (*with greater force*) One must go in to fetch a diamond out.

WILLY (*to* LINDA, *as he moves slowly along the edge of the kitchen, toward the door*) I just want to get settled down, Linda. Let me sit alone for a little.

LINDA (*almost uttering her fear*) I want you upstairs.

WILLY (*taking her in his arms*) In a few minutes, Linda. I couldn't sleep right now. Go on, you look awful tired. (*He kisses her.*)

BEN Not like an appointment at all. A diamond is rough and hard to the touch.

WILLY Go on now. I'll be right up.

LINDA I think this is the only way, Willy.

WILLY Sure, it's the best thing.

BEN Best thing!

WILLY The only way. Everything is gonna be — go on, kid, get to bed. You look so tired.

LINDA Come right up.

WILLY Two minutes.

(LINDA *goes into the living-room, then reappears in her bedroom.* WILLY *moves just outside the kitchen door.*)

WILLY Loves me. (*Wonderingly*) Always loved me. Isn't that a remarkable thing? Ben, he'll worship me for it!

BEN (*with promise*) It's dark there, but full of diamonds.

WILLY Can you imagine that magnificence with twenty thousand dollars in his pocket?

LINDA (*calling from her room*) Willy! Come up!

WILLY (*calling into the kitchen*) Yes! Yes. Coming! It's very smart, you realize that, don't you, sweetheart? Even Ben sees it. I gotta go, baby. 'By! 'By! (*Going over to* BEN, *almost dancing*) Imagine? When the mail comes he'll be ahead of Bernard again!

BEN A perfect proposition all around.

WILLY Did you see how he cried to me? Oh, if I could kiss him, Ben!

BEN Time, William, time!

WILLY Oh, Ben, I always knew one way or another we were gonna make it, Biff and I!

BEN (*looking at his watch*) The boat. We'll be late. (*He moves slowly off into the darkness.*)

WILLY (*elegiacally, turning to the house*) Now when you kick off, boy, I want a seventy-yard boot, and get right down the field under the ball, and when you hit, hit low and hit hard, because it's important, boy. (*He swings around and faces the audience.*) There's all kinds of important people in the stands, and the first thing you know . . . (*Suddenly realizing he is alone*) Ben! Ben, where do I . . . ? (*He makes a sudden movement of search.*) Ben, how do I . . . ?

LINDA (*calling*) Willy, you coming up?

WILLY (*uttering a gasp of fear, whirling about as if to quiet her*) Sh! (*He turns around as if to find his way; sounds, faces, voices, seem to be swarming in upon him and he flicks at them, crying*) Sh! Sh! (*Suddenly music, faint and high, stops him. It rises in intensity, almost to an unbearable scream. He goes up and down on his toes, and rushes off around the house.*) Shhh!

LINDA Willy?

(*There is no answer.* LINDA *waits.* BIFF *gets up off his bed. He is still in his clothes.* HAPPY *sits up.* BIFF *stands listening.*)

LINDA (*with real fear*) Willy, answer me! Willy!

(*There is the sound of a car starting and moving away at full speed.*)

LINDA No!

BIFF (*rushing down the stairs*) Pop!

(*As the car speeds off, the music crashes down in a frenzy of sound, which becomes the soft pulsation of a single cello string.* BIFF *slowly returns to his bedroom. He and* HAPPY *gravely don their jackets.* LINDA *slowly walks out of her room. The music has developed into a dead march. The leaves of day are appearing over everything.* CHARLEY *and* BERNARD, *somberly dressed, appear and knock on the kitchen door.* BIFF *and* HAPPY *slowly descend the stairs to the kitchen as* CHARLEY *and* BERNARD *enter. All stop a moment when* LINDA, *in clothes of mourning, bearing a little bunch of roses, comes through the draped doorway into the kitchen. She goes to* CHARLEY *and takes his arm. Now all move toward the audience, through the wall-line of the kitchen. At the limit of the apron,* LINDA *lays down the flowers, kneels, and sits back on her heels. All stare down at the grave.*)

Requiem

CHARLEY It's getting dark, Linda.

(LINDA *doesn't react. She stares at the grave.*)

BIFF How about it, Mom? Better get some rest, heh? They'll be closing the gate soon.

(LINDA *makes no move. Pause*)

HAPPY (*deeply angered*) He had no right to do that. There was no necessity for it. We would've helped him.

CHARLEY (*grunting*) Hmmm.

BIFF Come along, Mom.

LINDA Why didn't anybody come?

CHARLEY It was a very nice funeral.

LINDA But where are all the people he knew? Maybe they blame him.

CHARLEY Naa. It's a rough world, Linda. They wouldn't blame him.

LINDA I can't understand it. At this time especially. First time in thirty-five years we were just about free and clear. He only needed a little salary. He was even finished with the dentist.

CHARLEY No man only needs a little salary.

LINDA I can't understand it.

BIFF There were a lot of nice days. When he'd come home from a trip; or on Sundays, making the stoop; finishing the cellar; putting on the new porch; when he built the extra bathroom; and put up the garage. You know something, Charley, there's more of him in that front stoop than in all the sales he ever made.

CHARLEY Yeah. He was a happy man with a batch of cement.

LINDA He was so wonderful with his hands.

BIFF He had the wrong dreams. All, all, wrong.

HAPPY (*almost ready to fight* BIFF) Don't say that!

BIFF He never knew who he was.

CHARLEY (*stopping* HAPPY'S *movement and reply. To* BIFF) Nobody dast blame this man. You don't understand: Willy was a salesman. And for a salesman, there is no rock bottom to the life. He don't put a bolt to a nut, he don't tell you the law or give you medicine. He's a man way out there in the blue, riding on a smile and a shoeshine. And when they start not smiling back — that's an earthquake. And then you get yourself a couple of spots on your hat, and you're finished. Nobody dast blame this man. A salesman is got to dream, boy. It comes with the territory.

BIFF Charley, the man didn't know who he was.

HAPPY (*infuriated*) Don't say that!

BIFF Why don't you come with me, Happy?

HAPPY I'm not licked that easily. I'm staying right in this city, and I'm gonna beat this racket! (*He looks at* BIFF, *his chin set.*) The Loman Brothers!

BIFF I know who I am, kid.

HAPPY All right, boy. I'm gonna show you and everybody else that Willy Loman did not die in vain. He had a good dream. It's the only dream you can have — to come out number-one man. He fought it out here, and this is where I'm gonna win it for him.

BIFF (*with a hopeless glance at* HAPPY, *bends toward his mother*) Let's go, Mom.

LINDA   I'll be with you in a minute. Go on, Charley. (*He hesitates.*) I want to, just for a minute. I never had a chance to say good-by.

(CHARLEY *moves away, followed by* HAPPY. BIFF *remains a slight distance up and left of* LINDA. *She sits there, summoning herself. The flute begins, not far away, playing behind her speech.*)

LINDA   Forgive me, dear. I can't cry. I don't know what it is, but I can't cry. I don't understand it. Why did you ever do that? Help me, Willy, I can't cry. It seems to me that you're just on another trip. I keep expecting you. Willy, dear, I can't cry. Why did you do it? I search and search and I search, and I can't understand it, Willy. I made the last payment on the house to-day. Today, dear. And there'll be nobody home. (*A sob rises in her throat.*) We're free and clear. (*Sobbing more fully, released*) We're free. (BIFF *comes slowly toward her.*) We're free . . . We're free . . .

(BIFF *lifts her to her feet and moves out up right with her in his arms.* LINDA *sobs quietly.* BERNARD *and* CHARLEY *come together and follow them, followed by* HAPPY. *Only the music of the flute is left on the darkening stage as over the house the hard towers of the apartment buildings rise into sharp focus, and*)

The curtain falls

Exercises

1. Prepare an eight-point analysis of the play. (See Chapter 16.)

2. Does Miller gain your attention immediately in this play? By what means?

3. Describe Willy Loman. What are his flaws? What human qualities does he show? Do they make him a sympathetic character?

4. Compare Willy Loman with his sons, Biff and Happy. Do you sympathize with both young men? Why?

5. How does Linda complicate Willy's problems?

6. Explain the role of the minor characters Ben, Charley, Howard, and Bernard.

7. Bernard, Howard, and even Biff call Willy Loman a kid. Why?

8. What significance do you attach to the title and Willy's surname as you consider the central meaning of the drama?

9. Discuss how Willy attains total or partial self-awareness before he performs his sacrifice.

10. Interpret Linda's final speech.

Topics for Writing

1. Consider the play as a social commentary on the "American dream."

2. Write an essay entitled "Willy Loman — Everyman."

Bates, B. W. "The Lost Past in *Death of a Salesman*." *Modern Drama,* 11 (September 1968), 164–172.

Bettina, Sister M. "Willy Loman's Brother Ben: Tragic Insight in *Death of a Salesman*." *Modern Drama,* 4 (1962), 409–412.

Bliquez, G. "Linda's Role in *Death of a Salesman*." *Modern Drama,* 10 (February 1968), 383–386.

Cook, L. W. "The Function of Ben and Dave Singleman in *Death of a Salesman*." *Notes on Contemporary Literature,* 5 (1975), i, 7–9.

De Schweinitz, G. "*Death of a Salesman*: A Note on Epic and Tragedy." *Western Humanities Review,* 14 (1960), 91–96.

Field, B. S., Jr. "Hamartia in *Death of a Salesman*." *Twentieth Century Literature,* 18 (January 1972), 19–24.

Gross, B. E. "Peddler and Pioneer in *Death of a Salesman*." *Modern Drama,* 7 (1965), 405–410.

Gupta, R. K. "*Death of a Salesman* and Miller's Concept of Tragedy." *Kyushu American Literature,* 15 (1974), 10–19.

Hagopian, J. V. "Arthur Miller: The Salesman's Two Cases." *Modern Drama,* 6 (1963), 117–125.

Jackson, E. M. "*Death of a Salesman*: Tragic Myth in the Modern Theater." *College Language Association Journal,* 7 (1963), 63–76.

Jacobson, I. "Family Dreams in *Death of a Salesman*." *American Literature,* 47 (May 1975), 247–258.

Lawrence, S. A. "The Right Dream in Miller's *Death of a Salesman*." *College English,* 25 (1964), 547–549.

McAnany, S. J. "The Tragic Commitment: Some Notes on Arthur Miller." *Modern Drama,* 5 (1962), 11–20.

Miller, Arthur. "Tragedy and the Common Man." *Theatre Arts,* 48 (March 1951), 35.

Moss, L. "Arthur Miller and the Common Man's Language." *Modern Drama,* 7 (May 1964), 52–59.

Oberg, A. K. "*Death of a Salesman* and Arthur Miller's Search for a Style." *Criticism,* 9 (1967), 303–311.

Otten, C. F. "Who Am I? A Re-Investigation of Arthur Miller's *Death of a Salesman*." *Cresset,* 26 (1963), 11–13.

Parker, B. "Point of View in Arthur Miller's *Death of a Salesman*." *University of Toronto Quarterly,* 35 (1966), 144–157.

Popkin, H. "Arthur Miller: The Strange Encounter." *Sewanee Review,* 66 (1960), 34–60.

Price, J. R. "Arthur Miller: Fall or Rise?" *Drama Quarterly Theatre Review,* 73 (Summer 1964), 39–40.

Ranald, M. K. "*Death of a Salesman*: Fifteen Years After." *Comment,* 6 (1965), 28–35.

Shatzky, J. "The 'Reactive Image' and Miller's *Death of a Salesman*." *Players,* 48 (1973), 104–110.

Paddy Chayefsky (1923–1981)

Marty

Cast

MARTY PILLETTI	BARTENDER
CLARA DAVIS	TWENTY-YEAR-OLD
ANGIE	ITALIAN WOMAN
MOTHER	SHORT GIRL
AUNT CATHERINE	GIRL
VIRGINIA	YOUNG MOTHER
THOMAS	STAG
YOUNG MAN	FORTY-YEAR-OLD
CRITIC	

Act One

FADE-IN: *A butcher shop in the Italian district of New York City. Actually, we fade in on a close-up of a butcher's saw being carefully worked through a side of beef, and we dolly back to show the butcher at work, and then the whole shop. The butcher is a mild-mannered, stout, short, balding young man of thirty-six. His charm lies in an almost indestructible good-natured amiability.*

The shop contains three women customers. One is a YOUNG MOTHER *with a baby carriage. She is chatting with a second woman of about forty at the door. The customer being waited on at the moment is a stout, elderly* ITALIAN WOMAN *who is standing on tiptoe, peering over the white display counter, checking the butcher as he saws away*

ITALIAN WOMAN   Your kid brother got married last Sunday, eh, Marty?

MARTY (*absorbed in his work*)   That's right, Missus Fusari. It was a very nice affair.

ITALIAN WOMAN   That's the big tall one, the fellow with the mustache.

MARTY (*sawing away*)   No, that's my other brother Freddie. My other brother Freddie, he's been married four years already. He lives down on Quincy Street. The one who got married Sunday, that was my little brother Nickie.

ITALIAN WOMAN   I thought he was a big, tall, fat fellow. Didn't I meet him here one time? Big, tall, fat fellow, he tried to sell me life insurance?

MARTY (*sets the cut of meat on the scale, watches its weight register*)   No, that's my sister Margaret's husband Frank. My sister Margaret, she's married to the insurance salesman. My sister Rose, she married a contractor. They moved to Detroit last year. And my other sister, Frances, she got married about two and a half years ago in Saint John's Church on Adams Boulevard. Oh, that was a big affair. Well, Missus Fusari, that'll be three dollars, ninety-four cents. How's that with you?

The ITALIAN WOMAN *produces an old leather change purse from her pocketbook and painfully extracts three single dollar bills and ninety-four cents to the penny and lays the money piece by piece on the counter*

YOUNG MOTHER (*calling from the door*)   Hey, Marty, I'm inna hurry.

MARTY (*wrapping the meat, calls amiably back*)   You're next right now, Missus Canduso.

The old ITALIAN WOMAN *has been regarding* MARTY *with a baleful scowl*

ITALIAN WOMAN   Well, Marty, when you gonna get married? You should be ashamed. All your brothers and sisters, they all younger than you, and they married, and they got children. I just saw your mother inna fruit shop, and she says to me: "Hey, you know a nice girl for my boy Marty?" Watsa matter with you? That's no way. Watsa matter with you? Now, you get married, you hear me what I say?

MARTY (*amiably*)   I hear you, Missus Fusari.

The old lady takes her parcel of meat, but apparently feels she still hasn't quite made her point

ITALIAN WOMAN   My son Frank, he was married when he was nineteen years old. Watsa matter with you?

MARTY   Missus Fusari, Missus Canduso over there, she's inna big hurry, and . . .

ITALIAN WOMAN   You be ashamed of yourself.

She takes her package of meat, turns, and shuffles to the door and exits. MARTY *gathers up the money on the counter, turns to the cash register behind him to ring up the sale*

YOUNG MOTHER   Marty, I want a nice big fat pullet, about four pounds. I hear your kid brother got married last Sunday.

MARTY   Yeah, it was a very nice affair, Missus Canduso.

YOUNG MOTHER   Marty, you oughtta be ashamed. All your kid brothers and sisters, married and have children. When you gonna get married?

CLOSE-UP: MARTY. *He sends a glance of weary exasperation up to the ceiling. With a gesture of mild irritation, he pushes the plunger of the cash register. It makes a sharp ping.*

DISSOLVE TO: *Close-up of television set. A baseball game is in progress. Camera pulls back to show we are in a typical neighborhood bar — red leatherette booths — a jukebox, some phone booths. About half the bar stools are occupied by neighborhood folk.* MARTY *enters, pads amiably to one of the booths where a young man of about thirty-odd already sits. This is* ANGIE. MARTY *slides into the booth across from* ANGIE. ANGIE *is a little wasp of a fellow. He has a newspaper spread out before him to the sports pages.* MARTY *reaches over and pulls one of the pages over for himself to read. For a moment the two friends sit across from each other, reading the sports pages. Then* ANGIE, *without looking up, speaks*

ANGIE   Well, what do you feel like doing tonight?

MARTY   I don't know, Angie. What do you feel like doing?

ANGIE   Well, we oughtta do something. It's Saturday night. I don't wanna go bowling like last Saturday. How about calling up that big girl we picked up inna movies about a month ago in the RKO Chester?

MARTY (*not very interested*)   Which one was that?

ANGIE   That big girl that was sitting in front of us with the skinny friend.

MARTY   Oh, yeah.

ANGIE   We took them home alla way out in Brooklyn. Her name was Mary Feeney. What do you say? You think I oughtta give her a ring? I'll take the skinny one.

MARTY   It's five o'clock already, Angie. She's probably got a date by now.

ANGIE   Well, let's call her up. What can we lose?

MARTY   I didn't like her, Angie. I don't feel like calling her up.

ANGIE   Well, what do you feel like doing tonight?

MARTY   I don't know. What do you feel like doing?

ANGIE   Well, we're back to that, huh? I say to you: "What do you feel like
doing tonight?" And you say to me: "I don't know, what do you feel like
doing?" And then we wind up sitting around your house with a couple of
cans of beer, watching Sid Caesar on television. Well, I tell you what I feel
like doing. I feel like calling up this Mary Feeney. She likes you.

MARTY *looks up quickly at this*

MARTY   What makes you say that?

ANGIE   I could see she likes you.

MARTY   Yeah, sure.

ANGIE   (*half rising in his seat*)   I'll call her up.

MARTY   You call her up for yourself, Angie. I don't feel like calling her up.

ANGIE *sits down again. They both return to reading the paper for a moment.*
Then ANGIE *looks up again*

ANGIE   Boy, you're getting to be a real drag, you know that?

MARTY   Angie, I'm thirty-six years old. I been looking for a girl every Saturday
night of my life. I'm a little, short, fat fellow, and girls don't go for me,
that's all. I'm not like you. I mean, you joke around, and they laugh at you,
and you get along fine. I just stand around like a bug. What's the sense of
kidding myself? Everybody's always telling me to get married. Get married.
Get married. Don't you think I wanna get married? I wanna get married.
They drive me crazy. Now, I don't wanna wreck your Saturday night for
you, Angie. You wanna go somewhere, you go ahead. I don't wanna go.

ANGIE   Boy, they drive me crazy too. My old lady, every word outta her mouth,
when you gonna get married?

MARTY   My mother, boy, she drives me crazy.

ANGIE *leans back in his seat, scowls at the paper-napkin container.* MARTY
returns to the sports page. For a moment a silence hangs between them.
Then . . .

ANGIE   So what do you feel like doing tonight?

MARTY   (*without looking up*)   I don't know. What do you feel like doing?

They both just sit, ANGIE *frowning at the napkin container,* MARTY *at the*
sports page.

The camera slowly moves away from the booth, looks down the length of
the bar, up the wall, past the clock — which reads ten to five — and over
to the television screen, where the baseball game is still going on.

DISSOLVE SLOWLY TO: *The television screen, now blank. The clock now*
reads a quarter to six.

Back in the booth, MARTY *now sits alone. In front of him are three*
empty beer bottles and a beer glass, half filled. He is sitting there, his face
expressionless, but his eyes troubled. Then he pushes himself slowly out of
the booth and shuffles to the phone booth; he goes inside, closing the booth
door carefully after him. For a moment MARTY *just sits squatly. Then with*
some exertion — due to the cramped quarters — he contrives to get a small
address book out of his rear pants pocket. He slowly flips through it, finds
the page he wants, and studies it, scowling; then he takes a dime from the
change he has just received, plunks it into the proper slot, waits for a dial

tone . . . then carefully dials a number. . . . He waits. He is beginning to
sweat a bit in the hot little booth, and his chest begins to rise and fall deeply

MARTY (*with a vague pretense at good diction*)   Hello, is this Mary Feeney? . . .
Could I please speak to Miss Mary Feeney? . . . Just tell her an old friend . . .
(*He waits again. With his free hand he wipes the gathering sweat from his
brow*) . . . Oh, hello there, is this Mary Feeney? Hello there, this is Marty
Pilletti. I wonder if you recall me . . . Well, I'm kind of a stocky guy. The
last time we met was inna movies, the RKO Chester. You was with another
girl, and I was with a friend of mine name Angie. This was about a month
ago . . .

The girl apparently doesn't remember him. A sort of panic begins to seize
MARTY. *His voice rises a little*

The RKO Chester on Payne Boulevard. You was sitting in front of us, and
we was annoying you, and you got mad, and . . . I'm the fellow who works
inna butcher shop . . . come on, you know who I am! . . . That's right, we
went to Howard Johnson's and we had hamburgers. You hadda milk
shake . . . Yeah, that's right. I'm the stocky one, the heavy-set fellow. . . .
Well, I'm glad you recall me, because I hadda swell time that night, and I
was just wondering how everything was with you. How's everything? . . .
That's swell . . . Yeah, well, I'll tell you why I called . . . I was figuring on
taking in a movie tonight, and I was wondering if you and your friend would
care to see a movie tonight with me and my friend . . . (*his eyes are closed
now*) Yeah, tonight. I know it's pretty late to call for a date, but I didn't
know myself till . . . Yeah, I know, well how about . . . Yeah, I know, well
maybe next Saturday night. You free next Saturday night? . . . Well, how
about the Saturday after that? . . . Yeah, I know . . . Yeah . . . Yeah . . .
Oh, I understand, I mean . . .

*He just sits now, his eyes closed, not really listening. After a moment he
returns the receiver to its cradle and sits, his shoulders slack, his hands resting listlessly in the lap of his spotted white apron. . . . Then he opens his
eyes, straightens himself, pushes the booth door open, and advances out into
the bar. He perches on a stool across the bar from the* BARTENDER, *who
looks up from his magazine*

BARTENDER   I hear your kid brother got married last week, Marty.

MARTY (*looking down at his hands on the bar*)   Yeah, it was a very nice affair.

BARTENDER   Well, Marty, when you gonna get married?

MARTY *tenders the bartender a quick scowl, gets off his perch, and starts for
the door — untying his apron as he goes*

MARTY   If my mother calls up, Lou, tell her I'm on my way home.

DISSOLVE TO: *Marty's* MOTHER *and a young couple sitting around the table
in the dining room of Marty's home. The young couple — we will soon find
out — are* THOMAS, *Marty's cousin, and his wife,* VIRGINIA. *They have apparently just been telling the mother some sad news, and the three are sitting
around frowning.*

*The dining room is a crowded room filled with chairs and lamps, pictures
and little statues, perhaps even a small grotto of little vigil lamps. To the
right of the dining room is the kitchen, old-fashioned, Italian, steaming, and
overcrowded. To the left of the dining room is the living room, furnished in
same fashion as the dining room. Just off the living room is a small bedroom, which is Marty's. This bedroom and the living room have windows*

looking out on front. The dining room has windows looking out to side alleyway. A stairway in the dining room leads to the second floor.

The MOTHER *is a round, dark, effusive little woman*

MOTHER (*after a pause*) Well, Thomas, I knew sooner or later this was gonna happen. I told Marty, I said: "Marty, you watch. There's gonna be real trouble over there in your cousin Thomas' house." Because your mother was here, Thomas, you know?

THOMAS When was this, Aunt Theresa?

MOTHER This was one, two, three days ago. Wednesday. Because I went to the fruit shop on Wednesday, and I came home. And I come arounna back, and there's your mother sitting onna steps onna porch. And I said: "Catherine, my sister, wadda you doing here?" And she look uppa me, and she beganna cry.

THOMAS (*to his wife*) Wednesday. That was the day you threw the milk bottle.

MOTHER That's right. Because I said to her: "Catherine, watsa matter?" And she said to me: "Theresa, my daughter-in-law, Virginia, she just threw the milk bottle at me."

VIRGINIA Well, you see what happen, Aunt Theresa . . .

MOTHER I know, I know . . .

VIRGINIA She comes inna kitchen, and she begins poking her head over my shoulder here and poking her head over my shoulder there . . .

MOTHER I know, I know . . .

VIRGINIA And she begins complaining about this, and she begins complaining about that. And she got me so nervous, I spilled some milk I was making for the baby. You see, I was making some food for the baby, and . . .

MOTHER So I said to her, "Catherine . . ."

VIRGINIA So, she got me so nervous I spilled some milk. So she said: "You're spilling the milk." She says: "Milk costs twenty-four cents a bottle. Wadda you, a banker?" So I said: "Mama, leave me alone, please. You're making me nervous. Go on in the other room and turn on the television set." So then she began telling me how I waste money, and how I can't cook, and how I'm raising my baby all wrong, and she kept talking about these couple of drops of milk I spilt, and I got so mad, I said: "Mama, you wanna see me really spill some milk?" So I took the bottle and threw it against the door. I didn't throw it at her. That's just something she made up. I didn't throw it anywheres near her. Well, of course, alla milk went all over the floor. The whole twenty-four cents. Well, I was sorry right away, you know, but she ran outta the house.

Pause

MOTHER Well, I don't know what you want me to do, Virginia. If you want me, I'll go talk to her tonight.

THOMAS *and* VIRGINIA *suddenly frown and look down at their hands as if of one mind*

THOMAS Well, I'll tell you, Aunt Theresa . . .

VIRGINIA Lemme tell it, Tommy.

THOMAS Okay.

VIRGINIA (*leaning forward to the* MOTHER) We want you to do a very big favor for us, Aunt Theresa.

MOTHER Sure.

VIRGINIA Aunt Theresa, you got this big house here. You got four bedrooms upstairs. I mean, you got this big house just for you and Marty. All your other kids are married and got their own homes. And I thought maybe Tommy's mother could come here and live with you and Marty.

MOTHER Well . . .

VIRGINIA She's miserable living with Tommy and me, and you're the only one that gets along with her. Because I called up Tommy's brother, Joe, and I said: "Joe, she's driving me crazy. Why don't you take her for a couple of years?" And he said: "Oh, no!" I know I sound like a terrible woman . . .

MOTHER No, Virginia, I know how you feel. My husband, may God bless his memory, his mother, she lived with us for a long time, and I know how you feel.

VIRGINIA (*practically on the verge of tears*) I just can't stand it no more! Every minute of the day! Do this! Do that! I don't have ten minutes alone with my husband! We can't even have a fight! We don't have no privacy! Everybody's miserable in our house!

THOMAS All right, Ginnie, don't get so excited.

MOTHER She's right. She's right. Young husband and wife, they should have their own home. And my sister, Catherine, she's my sister, but I gotta admit, she's an old goat. And plenny-a times in my life I feel like throwing the milk bottle at her myself. And I tell you now, as far as I'm concerned, if Catherine wantsa come live here with me and Marty, it's all right with me.

VIRGINIA *promptly bursts into tears*

THOMAS (*not far from tears himself, lowers his face*) That's very nice-a you, Aunt Theresa.

MOTHER We gotta ask Marty, of course, because this is his house too. But he's gonna come home any minute now.

VIRGINIA (*having mastered her tears*) That's very nice-a you, Aunt Theresa.

MOTHER (*rising*) Now, you just sit here. I'm just gonna turn onna small fire under the food. (*She exits into the kitchen*)

VIRGINIA (*calling after her*) We gotta go right away because I promised the baby sitter we'd be home by six, and it's after six now . . .

She kind of fades out. A moment of silence. THOMAS *takes out a cigarette and lights it*

THOMAS (*calling to his aunt in the kitchen*) How's Marty been lately, Aunt Theresa?

MOTHER (*off in kitchen*) Oh, he's fine. You know a nice girl he can marry? (*She comes back into the dining room, wiping her hands on a kitchen towel*) I'm worried about him, you know? He's thirty-six years old, gonna be thirty-seven in January.

THOMAS Oh, he'll get married, don't worry, Aunt Theresa.

MOTHER (*sitting down again*) Well, I don't know. You know a place where he can go where he can find a bride?

THOMAS The Waverly Ballroom. That's a good place to meet girls, Aunt Theresa. That's a kind of big dance hall, Aunt Theresa. Every Saturday night, it's just loaded with girls. It's a nice place to go. You pay seventy-seven cents. It used to be seventy-seven cents. It must be about a buck and a half now. And you go in and you ask some girl to dance. That's how I met Virginia. Nice, respectable place to meet girls. You tell Marty, Aunt Theresa, you tell him: "Go to the Waverly Ballroom. It's loaded with tomatoes."

MOTHER (*committing the line to memory*) The Waverly Ballroom. It's loaded with tomatoes.

THOMAS Right.

VIRGINIA You tell him, go to the Waverly Ballroom.

There is the sound of a door being unlatched off through the kitchen. The MOTHER *promptly rises*

MOTHER He's here.

She hurries into the kitchen. At the porch entrance to the kitchen, MARTY *has just come in. He is closing the door behind him. He carries his butcher's apron in a bundle under his arm*

MARTY Hello, Ma.

She comes up to him, lowers her voice to a whisper

MOTHER (*whispers*) Marty, Thomas and Virginia are here. They had another big fight with your Aunt Catherine. So they ask me, would it be all right if Catherine come to live with us. So I said, all right with me, but we have to ask you. Marty, she's a lonely old lady. Nobody wants her. Everybody's throwing her outta their house. . . .

MARTY Sure, Ma, it's okay with me.

The MOTHER's *face breaks into a fond smile. She reaches up and pats his cheek with genuine affection*

MOTHER You gotta good heart. (*Turning and leading the way back to the dining room.* THOMAS *has risen*) He says okay, it's all right Catherine comes here.

THOMAS Oh, Marty, thanks a lot. That really takes a load offa my mind.

MARTY Oh, we got plenny-a room here.

MOTHER Sure! Sure! It's gonna be nice! It's gonna be nice! I'll come over tonight to your house, and I talk to Catherine, and you see, everything is gonna work out all right.

THOMAS I just wanna thank you people again because the situation was just becoming impossible.

MOTHER Siddown, Thomas, siddown. All right, Marty, siddown. . . .

She exits into the kitchen.

MARTY *has taken his seat at the head of the table and is waiting to be served.* THOMAS *takes a seat around the corner of the table from him and leans across to him*

THOMAS You see, Marty, the kinda thing that's been happening in our house is Virginia was inna kitchen making some food for the baby. Well, my mother comes in, and she gets Virginia so nervous, she spills a couple-a drops . . .

VIRGINIA (*tugging at her husband*) Tommy, we gotta go. I promise the baby sitter six o'clock.

THOMAS (*rising without interrupting his narrative*) So she starts yelling at Virginia, waddaya spilling the milk for. So Virginia gets mad . . .

His wife is slowly pulling him to the kitchen door

She says, "You wanna really see me spill milk?" So Virginia takes the bottle and she throws it against the wall. She's got a real Italian temper, my wife, you know that . . .

He has been tugged to the kitchen door by now

VIRGINIA Marty, I don't have to tell you how much we appreciate what your mother and you are doing for us.

THOMAS   All right, Marty, I'll see you some other time . . . I'll tell you all about
it.

MARTY   I'll see you, Tommy.

THOMAS disappears into the kitchen after his wife

VIRGINIA (*off, calling*)   Good-by, Marty!

Close in on MARTY, *sitting at table*

MARTY   Good-by, Virginia! See you soon!

He folds his hands on the table before him and waits to be served.

The MOTHER *enters from the kitchen. She sets the meat plate down in
front of him and herself takes a chair around the corner of the table from
him.* MARTY *without a word takes up his knife and fork and attacks the
mountain of food in front of him. His mother sits quietly, her hands a little
nervous on the table before her, watching him eat. Then . . .*

MOTHER   So what are you gonna do tonight, Marty?

MARTY   I don't know, Ma. I'm all knocked out. I may just hang arounna house.

The MOTHER *nods a couple of times. There is a moment of silence. Then . . .*

MOTHER   Why don't you go to the Waverly Ballroom?

This gives MARTY *pause. He looks up*

MARTY   What?

MOTHER   I say, why don't you go to the Waverly Ballroom? It's loaded with
tomatoes.

MARTY *regards his mother for a moment*

MARTY   It's loaded with what?

MOTHER   Tomatoes.

MARTY (*snorts*)   Ha! Who told you about the Waverly Ballroom?

MOTHER   Thomas, he told me it was a very nice place.

MARTY   Oh, Thomas. Ma, it's just a big dance hall, and that's all it is. I been
there a hundred times. Loaded with tomatoes. Boy, you're funny, Ma.

MOTHER   Marty, I don't want you hang arounna house tonight. I want you to
go take a shave and go out and dance.

MARTY   Ma, when are you gonna give up? You gotta bachelor on your hands.
I ain't never gonna get married.

MOTHER   You gonna get married.

MARTY   Sooner or later, there comes a point in a man's life when he gotta face
some facts, and one fact I gotta face is that whatever it is that women like,
I ain't got it. I chased enough girls in my life. I went to enough dances. I
got hurt enough. I don't wanna get hurt no more. I just called a girl this
afternoon, and I got a real brush-off, boy. I figured I was past the point of
being hurt, but that hurt. Some stupid woman who I didn't even wanna call
up. She gave me the brush. That's the history of my life. I don't wanna go
to the Waverly Ballroom because all that ever happened to me there was
girls made me feel like I was a bug. I got feelings, you know. I had
enough pain. No, thank you.

MOTHER   Marty . . .

MARTY   Ma, I'm gonna stay home and watch Sid Caesar.

MOTHER   You gonna die without a son.

MARTY   So I'll die without a son.

MOTHER   Put on your blue suit . . .

MARTY   Blue suit, gray suit, I'm still a fat little man. A fat little ugly man.

MOTHER   You not ugly.

MARTY (*his voice rising*)   I'm ugly . . . I'm ugly! . . . I'm UGLY!
MOTHER   Marty . . .
MARTY (*crying aloud, more in anguish than in anger*)   Ma! Leave me alone!
. . . (*He stands abruptly, his face pained and drawn. He makes half-formed
gestures to his mother, but he can't find words at the moment. He turns and
marches a few paces away, turns to his mother again*) Ma, waddaya want
from me?! Waddaya want from me?! I'm miserable enough at it is! Leave
me alone! I'll go to the Waverly Ballroom! I'll put onna blue suit and I'll go!
And you know what I'm gonna get for my trouble? Heartache! A big night
of heartache! (*He sullenly marches back to his seat, sits down, picks up his
fork, plunges it into the lasagna, and stuffs a mouthful into his mouth; he
chews vigorously for a moment. It is impossible to remain angry for long.
After a while he is shaking his head and muttering*) Loaded with tomatoes
. . . boy, that's rich . . .
*He plunges his fork in again. Camera pulls slowly away from him and his
mother, who is seated — watching him*

Fade out

Act Two

FADE IN: *Exterior, three-story building. Pan up to second floor . . . bright
neon lights reading "Waverly Ballroom" . . . The large, dirty windows are
open; and the sound of a fair-to-middling swing band whooping it up comes
out.*

DISSOLVE TO: *Interior, Waverly Ballroom — large dance floor crowded
with jitterbugging couples, eight-piece combination hitting a loud kick. Ballroom is vaguely dark, made so by papier-mâché over the chandeliers to create alleged romantic effect. The walls are lined with stags and waiting girls,
singly and in small murmuring groups. Noise and mumble and drone.*

DISSOLVE TO: *Live shot — a row of stags along a wall. Camera is looking
lengthwise down the row. Camera dollies slowly past each face, each staring
out at the dance floor, watching in his own manner of hungry eagerness.
Short, fat, tall, thin stags. Some pretend diffidence. Some exhibit patent
hunger.*

Near the end of the line, we find MARTY *and* ANGIE, *freshly shaved and
groomed. They are leaning against the wall, smoking, watching their more
fortunate brethren out on the floor.*

ANGIE   Not a bad crowd tonight, you know?
MARTY   There was one nice-looking one there in a black dress and beads, but
she was a little tall for me.
ANGIE (*looking down past* MARTY *along the wall right into the camera*)   There's
a nice-looking little short one for you right now.
MARTY (*following his gaze*)   Where?
ANGIE   Down there. That little one there.
*The camera cuts about eight faces down, to where the girls are now standing.
Two are against the wall. One is facing them, with her back to the dance
floor. This last is the one* ANGIE *has in mind. She is a cute little kid, about*

twenty, and she has a bright smile on — as if the other two girls are just amusing her to death.

MARTY   Yeah, she looks all right from here.

ANGIE   Well, go on over and ask her. You don't hurry up, somebody else'll grab her.

MARTY *scowls, shrugs*

MARTY   Okay, let's go.

They slouch along past the eight stags, a picture of nonchalant unconcern. The three girls, aware of their approach, stiffen, and their chatter comes to a halt. ANGIE *advances to one of the girls along the wall*

ANGIE   Waddaya say, you wanna dance?

The girl looks surprised — as if this were an extraordinary invitation to receive in this place — looks confounded at her two friends, shrugs, detaches herself from the group, moves to the outer fringe of the pack of dancers, raises her hand languidly to dancing position, and awaits ANGIE *with ineffable boredom.* MARTY, *smiling shyly, addresses the short girl.*

MARTY   Excuse me, would you care for this dance?

The short girl gives MARTY *a quick glance of appraisal, then looks quickly at her remaining friend*

SHORT GIRL   (*not unpleasantly*)   Sorry. I just don't feel like dancing just yet.

MARTY   Sure.

He turns and moves back past the eight stags, all of whom have covertly watched his attempt. He finds his old niche by the wall, leans there. A moment later he looks guardedly down to where the short girl and her friend are. A young, dapper boy is approaching the short girl. He asks her to dance. The short girl smiles, excuses herself to her friend, and follows the boy out onto the floor. MARTY *turns back to watching the dancers bleakly. A moment later he is aware that someone on his right is talking to him. . . . He turns his head. It is a young man of about twenty-eight*

MARTY   You say something to me?

YOUNG MAN   Yeah. I was just asking you if you was here stag or with a girl.

MARTY   I'm stag.

YOUNG MAN   Well, I'll tell you. I got stuck onna blind date with a dog, and I just picked up a nice chick, and I was wondering how I'm gonna get ridda the dog. Somebody to take her home, you know what I mean? I be glad to pay you five bucks if you take the dog home for me.

MARTY   (*a little confused*)   What?

YOUNG MAN   I'll take you over, and I'll introduce you as an old army buddy of mine, and then I'll cut out. Because I got this chick waiting for me out by the hatcheck, and I'll pay you five bucks.

MARTY   (*stares at the* YOUNG MAN)   Are you kidding?

YOUNG MAN   No, I'm not kidding.

MARTY   You can't just walk off onna girl like that.

The YOUNG MAN *grimaces impatiently and moves down the line of stags. . . .* MARTY *watches him, still a little shocked at the proposition. About two stags down, the* YOUNG MAN *broaches his plan to another* STAG. *This* STAG, *frowning and pursing his lips, seems more receptive to the idea. . . . The* YOUNG MAN *takes out a wallet and gives the* STAG *a five-dollar bill. The* STAG *detaches himself from the wall and, a little ill at ease, follows the* YOUNG MAN *back past* MARTY *and into the lounge.* MARTY *pauses a moment and then, concerned, walks to the archway that separates the lounge from the ball-room and looks in.*

The lounge is a narrow room with a bar and booths. In contrast to the ballroom, it is brightly lighted — causing MARTY *to squint.*

In the second booth from the archway sits a GIRL, *about twenty-eight. Despite the careful grooming that she has put into her cosmetics, she is blatantly plain. The* YOUNG MAN *and the* STAG *are standing, talking to her. She is looking up at the* YOUNG MAN, *her hands nervously gripping her Coca-Cola glass. We cannot hear what the* YOUNG MAN *is saying, but it is apparent that he is introducing his new-found army buddy and is going through some cock-and-bull story about being called away on an emergency. The* STAG *is presented as her escort-to-be, who will see to it that she gets home safely. The* GIRL *apparently is not taken in at all by this, though she is trying hard not to seem affected.*

She politely rejects the STAG's *company and will get home by herself, thanks for asking anyway. The* YOUNG MAN *makes a few mild protestations, and then he and the* STAG *leave the booth and come back to the archway from where* MARTY *has been watching the scene. As they pass* MARTY, *we overhear a snatch of dialogue*

YOUNG MAN . . . In that case, as long as she's going home alone, give me the five bucks back . . .

STAG . . . Look, Mac, you paid me five bucks. I was willing. It's my five bucks. . . .

They pass on. MARTY *returns his attention to the* GIRL. *She is still sitting as she was, gripping and ungripping the glass of Coca-Cola in front of her. Her eyes are closed. Then, with a little nervous shake of her head, she gets out of the booth and stands — momentarily at a loss for what to do next. The open fire doors leading out onto the large fire escape catch her eye. She crosses to the fire escape, nervous, frowning, and disappears outside.*

MARTY *stares after her, then slowly shuffles to the open fire-escape door-way. It is a large fire escape, almost the size of a small balcony. The* GIRL *is standing by the railing, her back to the doorway, her head slunk on her bosom. For a moment* MARTY *is unaware that she is crying. Then he notices the shivering tremors running through her body and the quivering shoulders. He moves a step onto the fire escape. He tries to think of something to say*

MARTY Excuse me, Miss. Would you care to dance?

The GIRL *slowly turns to him, her face streaked with tears, her lip trembling. Then, in one of those peculiar moments of simultaneous impulse, she lurches to* MARTY *with a sob, and* MARTY *takes her to him. For a moment they stand in an awkward embrace,* MARTY *a little embarrassed, looking out through the doors to the lounge, wondering if anybody is seeing them. Reaching back with one hand, he closes the fire doors, and then, replacing the hand around her shoulder, he stands stiffly, allowing her to cry on his chest.*

DISSOLVE TO: *Exterior, apartment door. The* MOTHER *is standing, in a black coat and a hat with a little feather, waiting for her ring to be answered.*

The door opens, VIRGINIA *stands framed in the doorway*

VIRGINIA Hello, Aunt Theresa, come in.

The MOTHER *goes into the small foyer.* VIRGINIA *closes the door*

MOTHER (*in a low voice, as she pulls her coat off*) Is Catherine here?

VIRGINIA (*helps her off with coat, nods — also in a low voice*) We didn't tell her nothing yet. We thought we'd leave it to you. We thought you'd put it like how you were lonely, and why don't she come to live with you. Because that way it looks like she's doing you a favor, insteada we're throwing her out, and it won't be so cruel on her. Thomas is downstairs with the neighbors . . . I'll go call him.

MOTHER   You go downstairs to the neighbors and stay there with Thomas.

VIRGINIA   Wouldn't it be better if we were here?

MOTHER   You go downstairs. I talk to Catherine alone. Otherwise, she's gonna start a fight with you.

A shrill, imperious woman's voice from an offstage room suddenly breaks into the muttered conference in the foyer

AUNT (*off*)   Who's there?! Who's there?!

The MOTHER *heads up the foyer to the living room, followed by* VIRGINIA, *holding the* MOTHER'*s coat*

MOTHER (*calls back*)   It's me, Catherine! How you feel?

At the end of the foyer, the two sisters meet. The AUNT *is a spare, gaunt woman with a face carved out of granite. Tough, embittered, deeply hurt type of face*

AUNT   Hey! What are you doing here?

MOTHER   I came to see you. (*The two sisters quickly embrace and release each other*) How you feel?

AUNT   I gotta pain in my left side and my leg throbs like a drum.

MOTHER   I been getting pains in my shoulder.

AUNT   I got pains in my shoulder, too. I have a pain in my hip, and my right arm aches so much I can't sleep. It's a curse to be old. How you feel?

MOTHER   I feel fine.

AUNT   That's nice.

Now that the standard greetings are over, AUNT CATHERINE *abruptly turns and goes back to her chair. It is obviously her chair. It is an old, heavy oaken chair with thick armrests. The rest of the apartment is furnished in what is known as "modern" — a piece from* House Beautiful *here, a piece from* Better Homes and Gardens *there.* AUNT CATHERINE *sits, erect and forbidding, in her chair. The* MOTHER *seats herself with a sigh in a neighboring chair.* VIRGINIA, *having hung the* MOTHER'*s coat, now turns to the two older women. A pause*

VIRGINIA   I'm going downstairs to the Cappacini's. I'll be up inna little while.

AUNT CATHERINE *nods expressionlessly.* VIRGINIA *looks at her for a moment, then impulsively crosses to her mother-in-law*

VIRGINIA   You feel all right?

The old lady looks up warily, suspicious of this sudden solicitude

AUNT   I'm all right.

VIRGINIA *nods and goes off to the foyer. The two old sisters sit, unmoving, waiting for the door to close behind* VIRGINIA. *Then the* MOTHER *addresses herself to* AUNT CATHERINE

MOTHER   We gotta post card from my son, Nickie, and his bride this morning. They're in Florida inna big hotel. Everything is very nice.

AUNT   That's nice.

MOTHER   Catherine, I want you come live with me in my house with Marty and me. In my house, you have your own room. You don't have to sleep onna couch inna living room like here.

The AUNT *looks slowly and directly at the* MOTHER

Catherine, your son is married. He got his own home. Leave him in peace. He wants to be alone with his wife. They don't want no old lady sitting inna balcony. Come and live with me. We will cook in the kitchen and talk like when we were girls. You are dear to me, and you are dear to Marty. We are pleased for you to come.

AUNT   Did they come to see you?

MOTHER   Yes.

AUNT   Did my son Thomas come with her?

MOTHER   Your son Thomas was there.

AUNT   Did he also say he wishes to cast his mother from his house?

MOTHER   Catherine, don't make an opera outta this. The three-a you anna baby live in three skinny rooms. You are an old goat, and she has an Italian temper. She is a good girl, but you drive her crazy. Leave them alone. They have their own life.

The old AUNT *turns her head slowly and looks her sister square in the face. Then she rises slowly from her chair*

AUNT (*coldly*)   Get outta here. This is my son's house. This is where I live. I am not to be cast out inna street like a newspaper.

The MOTHER *likewise rises. The two old women face each other directly*

MOTHER   Catherine, you are very dear to me. We have cried many times together. When my husband died, I would have gone insane if it were not for you. I ask you to come to my house because I can make you happy. Please come to my house.

The two sisters regard each other. Then AUNT CATHERINE *sits again in her oaken chair, and the* MOTHER *returns to her seat. The hardened muscles in the old* AUNT*'s face suddenly slacken, and she turns to her sister*

AUNT   Theresa, what shall become of me?

MOTHER   Catherine . . .

AUNT   It's gonna happen to you. Mark it well. These terrible years. I'm afraida look inna mirror. I'm afraid I'm gonna see an old lady with white hair, like the old ladies inna park, little bundles inna black shawl, waiting for the coffin. I'm fifty-six years old. What am I to do with myself? I have strength in my hands. I wanna cook. I wanna clean. I wanna make dinner for my children. I wanna be of use to somebody. Am I an old dog to lie in fronta the fire till my eyes close? These are terrible years, Theresa! Terrible years!

MOTHER   Catherine, my sister . . .

The old AUNT *stares, distraught, at the* MOTHER

AUNT   It's gonna happen to you! It's gonna happen to you! What will you do if Marty gets married?! What will you cook?! What happen to alla children tumbling in alla rooms?! Where is the noise?! It is a curse to be a widow! A curse! What will you do if Marty gets married?! What will you do?!

She stares at the MOTHER — *her deep, gaunt eyes haggard and pained. The* MOTHER *stares back for a moment, then her own eyes close. The* AUNT *has hit home. The* AUNT *sinks back onto her chair, sitting stiffly, her arms on the thick armrests. The* MOTHER *sits hunched a little forward, her hands nervously folded in her lap*

(*Quietly*)   I will put my clothes inna bag and I will come to you tomorrow.

The camera slowly dollies back from the two somber sisters.

SLOW FADE-OUT.

CUT TO: *Close-up, intimate,* MARTY *and the* GIRL *dancing cheek to cheek. Occasionally the heads of other couples slowly waft across the camera view, temporarily blocking our view of* MARTY *and the* GIRL. *Camera stays with them as the slow dance carries them around the floor. Tender scene*

GIRL   . . . The last time I was here the same sort of thing happened.

MARTY   Yeah?

GIRL   Well, not exactly the same thing. The last time I was up here about four months ago. Do you see that girl in the gray dress sitting over there?

MARTY   Yeah.

GIRL   That's where I sat. I sat there for an hour and a half without moving a muscle. Now and then, some fellow would sort of walk up to me and then change his mind. I just sat there, my hands in my lap. Well, about ten o'clock, a bunch of kids came in swaggering. They weren't more than seventeen, eighteen years old. Well, they swaggered down along the wall, leering at all the girls. I thought they were kind of cute . . . and as they passed me, I smiled at them. One of the kids looked at me and said: "Forget it, ugly, you ain't gotta chance." I burst out crying. I'm a big crier, you know.

MARTY   So am I.

GIRL   And another time when I was in college . . .

MARTY   I cry alla time. Any little thing. I can recognize pain a mile away. My brothers, my brother-in-laws, they're always telling me what a goodhearted guy I am. Well, you don't get goodhearted by accident. You get kicked around long enough you get to be a real professor of pain. I know exactly how you feel. And I also want you to know I'm having a very good time with you now and really enjoying myself. So you see, you're not such a dog as you think you are.

GIRL   I'm having a very good time too.

MARTY   So there you are. So I guess I'm not such a dog as I think I am.

GIRL   You're a very nice guy, and I don't know why some girl hasn't grabbed you off long ago.

MARTY   I don't know either. I think I'm a very nice guy. I also think I'm a pretty smart guy in my own way.

GIRL   I think you are.

MARTY   I'll tell you some of my wisdom which I thunk up on those nights when I got stood up, and nights like that, and you walk home thinking: "Watsa matter with me? I can't be that ugly." Well, I figure, two people get married, and they gonna live together forty, fifty years. So it's just gotta be more than whether they're good-looking or not. My father was a real ugly man, but my mother adored him. She told me that she used to get so miserable sometimes, like everybody, you know? And she says my father always tried to understand. I used to see them sometimes when I was a kid, sitting in the living room, talking and talking, and I used to adore my old man because he was so kind. That's one of the most beautiful things I have in my life, the way my father and my mother were. And my father was a real ugly man. So it don't matter if you look like a gorilla. So you see, dogs like us, we ain't such dogs as we think we are.

They dance silently for a moment, cheeks pressed against each other. Close-ups of each face

GIRL   I'm twenty-nine years old. How old are you?

MARTY   Thirty-six.

They dance silently, closely. Occasionally the heads of other couples sway in front of the camera, blocking our view of MARTY *and the* GIRL. *Slow, sweet dissolve.*

DISSOLVE TO: *Interior, kitchen,* MARTY'S *home. Later that night. It is dark. Nobody is home. The rear porch door now opens, and the silhouettes of* MARTY *and the* GIRL *appear — blocking up the doorway*

MARTY   Wait a minute. Lemme find the light.

He finds the light. The kitchen is suddenly brightly lit. The two of them stand squinting to adjust to the sudden glare

I guess my mother ain't home yet. I figure my cousin Thomas and Virginia musta gone to the movies, so they won't get back till one o'clock, at least.

The GIRL *has advanced into the kitchen, a little ill at ease, and is looking around.* MARTY *closes the porch door*

This is the kitchen.

GIRL   Yes, I know.

MARTY *leads the way into the dining room*

MARTY   Come on inna dining room. (*He turns on the light in there as he goes. The* GIRL *follows him in*) Siddown, take off your coat. You want something to eat? We gotta whole halfa chicken left over from yesterday.

GIRL   (*perching tentatively on the edge of a chair*)   No, thank you. I don't think I should stay very long.

MARTY   Sure. Just take off your coat a minute.

He helps her off with her coat and stands for a moment behind her, looking down at her. Conscious of his scrutiny, she sits uncomfortably, her breasts rising and falling unevenly. MARTY *takes her coat into the dark living room. The* GIRL *sits patiently, nervously.* MARTY *comes back, sits down on another chair. Awkward silence*

So I was telling you, my kid brother Nickie got married last Sunday . . . That was a very nice affair. And they had this statue of some woman, and they had whisky spouting outta her mouth. I never saw anything so grand in my life. (*The silence falls between them again*) And watta meal. I'm a butcher, so I know a good hunka steak when I see one. That was choice filet, right off the toppa the chuck. A buck-eighty a pound. Of course, if you wanna cheaper cut, get rib steak. That gotta lotta waste on it, but it comes to about a buck and a quarter a pound, if it's trimmed. Listen, Clara, make yourself comfortable. You're all tense.

GIRL   Oh, I'm fine.

MARTY   You want me to take you home, I'll take you home.

GIRL   Maybe that would be a good idea.

She stands. He stands, frowning, a little angry — turns sullenly and goes back into the living room for her coat. She stands unhappily. He comes back and wordlessly starts to help her into her coat. He stands behind her, his hands on her shoulders. He suddenly seizes her, begins kissing her on the neck. Camera comes up quickly to intensely intimate close-up, nothing but the heads. The dialogue drops to quick, hushed whispers

No, Marty, please . . .

MARTY   I like you, I like you, I been telling you all night I like you . . .

GIRL   Marty . . .

MARTY   I just wanna kiss, that's all . . .

He tries to turn her face to him. She resists

GIRL   No . . .

MARTY   Please . . .

GIRL   No . . .

MARTY   Please . . .

GIRL   Marty . . .

He suddenly releases her, turns away violently

MARTY   (*crying out*)   All right! I'll take you home! All right! (*He marches a few angry paces away, deeply disturbed. Turns to her*) All I wanted was a lousy kiss! What am I, a leper or something?!

He turns and goes off into the living room to hide the flush of hot tears threatening to fill his eyes. The GIRL *stands, herself on the verge of tears*

GIRL   (*mutters, more to herself than to him*)   I just didn't feel like it, that's all. *She moves slowly to the archway leading to the living room.* MARTY *is sitting on the couch, hands in his lap, looking straight ahead. The room is dark except for the overcast of the dining-room light reaching in. The* GIRL *goes to the couch, perches on the edge beside him. He doesn't look at her.*

MARTY   Well, that's the history of my life. I'm a little, short, fat, ugly guy. Comes New Year's Eve, everybody starts arranging parties, I'm the guy they gotta dig up a date for. I'm old enough to know better. Let me get a packa cigarettes, and I'll take you home.

He starts to rise, but doesn't . . . sinks back onto the couch, looking straight ahead. The GIRL *looks at him, her face peculiarly soft and compassionate*

GIRL   I'd like to see you again, very much. The reason I didn't let you kiss me was because I just didn't know how to handle the situation. You're the kindest man I ever met. The reason I tell you this is because I want to see you again very much. Maybe, I'm just so desperate to fall in love that I'm trying too hard. But I know that when you take me home, I'm going to just lie on my bed and think about you. I want very much to see you again.

MARTY *stares down at his hands in his lap*

MARTY   (*without looking at her*)   Waddaya doing tomorrow night?

GIRL   Nothing.

MARTY   I'll call you up tomorrow morning. Maybe we'll go see a movie.

GIRL   I'd like that very much.

MARTY   The reason I can't be definite about it now is my Aunt Catherine is probably coming over tomorrow, and I may have to help out.

GIRL   I'll wait for your call.

MARTY   We better get started to your house because the buses only run about one an hour now.

GIRL   All right.

She stands

MARTY   I'll just get a packa cigarettes.

He goes into his bedroom. We can see him through the doorway, opening his bureau drawer and extracting a pack of cigarettes. He comes out again and looks at the girl for the first time. They start to walk to the dining room. In the archway, MARTY *pauses, turns to the* GIRL

Waddaya doing New Year's Eve?

GIRL   Nothing.

They quietly slip into each other's arms and kiss. Slowly their faces part, and MARTY's *head sinks down upon her shoulder. He is crying. His shoulders shake slightly. The* GIRL *presses her cheek against the back of his head. They stand . . . there is the sound of the rear porch door being unlatched. They both start from their embrace. A moment later the* MOTHER's *voice is heard off in the kitchen*

MOTHER Hallo! Hallo, Marty? (*She comes into the dining room, stops at the sight of the* GIRL) Hallo, Marty, when you come home?

MARTY We just got here about fifteen minutes ago, Ma. Ma, I want you to meet Miss Clara Davis. She's a graduate of New York University. She teaches history in Benjamin Franklin High School.

This seems to impress the MOTHER

MOTHER Siddown, siddown. You want some chicken? We got some chicken in the icebox.

GIRL No, Mrs. Pilletti, we were just going home. Thank you very much anyway.

MOTHER Well, siddown a minute. I just come inna house. I'll take off my coat. Siddown a minute. (*She pulls her coat off*)

MARTY How'd you come home, Ma? Thomas give you a ride?

The MOTHER *nods*

MOTHER Oh, it's a sad business, a sad business.

She sits down on a dining-room chair, holding her coat in her lap. She turns to the GIRL, *who likewise sits*

My sister Catherine, she don't get along with her daughter-in-law, so she's gonna come live with us.

MARTY Oh, she's coming, eh, Ma?

MOTHER Oh, sure. (*To the* GIRL) It's a very sad thing. A woman, fifty-six years old, all her life, she had her own home. Now, she's just an old lady, sleeping on her daughter-in-law's couch. It's a curse to be a mother, I tell you. Your children grow up and then what is left for you to do? What is a mother's life but her children? It is a very cruel thing when your son has no place for you in his home.

GIRL Couldn't she find some sort of hobby to fill out her time?

MOTHER Hobby! What can she do? She cooks and she cleans. You gotta have a house to clean. You gotta have children to cook for. These are the terrible years for a woman, the terrible years.

GIRL You mustn't feel too harshly against her daughter-in-law. She also wants to have a house to clean and a family to cook for.

The MOTHER *darts a quick, sharp look at the* GIRL — *then looks back to her hands which are beginning to twist nervously*

MOTHER You don't think my sister Catherine should live in her daughter-in-law's house?

GIRL Well, I don't know the people, of course, but, as a rule, I don't think a mother-in-law should live with a young couple.

MOTHER Where do you think a mother-in-law should go?

GIRL I don't think a mother should depend so much upon her children for her rewards in life.

MOTHER That's what it says in the book in New York University. You wait till you are a mother. It don't work out that way.

GIRL Well, it's silly for me to argue about it. I don't know the people involved.

MARTY   Ma, I'm gonna take her home now. It's getting late, and the buses only run about one an hour.

MOTHER (*standing*)   Sure.

The GIRL *stands*

GIRL   It was very nice meeting you, Mrs. Pilletti. I hope I'll see you again.

MOTHER   Sure.

MARTY *and the* GIRL *move to the kitchen*

MARTY   All right, Ma. I'll be back in about an hour.

MOTHER   Sure.

GIRL   Good night, Mrs. Pilletti.

MOTHER   Good night.

MARTY *and the* GIRL *exit into the kitchen. The* MOTHER *stands, expressionless, by her chair watching them go. She remains standing rigidly even after the porch door can be heard being opened and shut. The camera moves up to a close-up of the* MOTHER. *Her eyes are wide. She is staring straight ahead. There is fear in her eyes*

Fade out

of being
alone like her
sister
Catherine

Act Three

FADE-IN: *Film — close-up of church bells clanging away. Pan down church to see typical Sunday morning, people going up the steps of a church and entering. It is a beautiful June morning.*

DISSOLVE TO: *Interior, Marty's bedroom — sun fairly streaming through the curtains.* MARTY *is standing in front of his bureau, slipping his arms into a clean white shirt. He is freshly shaved and groomed. Through the doorway of his bedroom we can see the* MOTHER *in the dining room, in a coat and hat, all set to go to Mass, taking the last breakfast plates away and carrying them into the kitchen. The camera moves across the living room into the dining room. The* MOTHER *comes out of the kitchen with a paper napkin and begins crumbing the table.*

There is a knock on the rear porch door. The MOTHER *leaves her crumbing and goes into the kitchen. Camera goes with her. She opens the rear door to admit* AUNT CATHERINE, *holding a worn old European carpetbag. The* AUNT *starts to go deeper into the kitchen, but the* MOTHER *stays her with her hand.*

MOTHER (*in low, conspiratorial voice*)   Hey, I come home from your house last night, Marty was here with a girl.

AUNT   Who?

MOTHER   Marty.

AUNT   Your son Marty?

MOTHER   Well, what Marty you think is gonna be here in this house with a girl?

AUNT   Were the lights on?

MOTHER   Oh, sure. (*Frowns suddenly at her sister*) The girl is a college graduate.

AUNT   They're the worst. College girls are one step from the streets. They smoke like men inna saloon.

The AUNT *puts her carpetbag down and sits on one of the wooden kitchen chairs. The* MOTHER *sits on another*

MOTHER That's the first time Marty ever brought a girl to this house. She seems like a nice girl. I think he has a feeling for this girl.

At this moment a burst of spirited whistling emanates from MARTY's *bedroom.*

CUT TO: MARTY's *bedroom — * MARTY *standing in front of his mirror, buttoning his shirt or adjusting his tie, whistling a gay tune.*

CUT BACK TO: *The two sisters, both their faces turned in the direction of the whistling. The whistling abruptly stops. The two sisters look at each other. The* AUNT *shrugs*

He been whistling like that all morning.

The AUNT *nods bleakly*

AUNT He is bewitched. You will see. Today, tomorrow, inna week, he's gonna say to you: "Hey, Ma, it's no good being a single man. I'm tired running around." Then he's gonna say: "Hey, Ma, wadda we need this old house? Why don't we sell this old house, move into a nicer parta town? A nice little apartment?"

MOTHER I don't sell this house, I tell you that. This is my husband's house, and I had six children in this house.

AUNT You will see. A couple-a months, you gonna be an old lady, sleeping onna couch in your daughter-in-law's house.

MOTHER Catherine, you are a blanket of gloom. Wherever you go, the rain follows. Some day, you gonna smile, and we gonna declare a holiday.

Another burst of spirited whistling comes from MARTY, *off. It comes closer, and* MARTY *now enters in splendid spirits, whistling away. He is slipping into his jacket*

MARTY (*ebulliently*) Hello, Aunt Catherine! How are you? You going to Mass with us?

AUNT I was at Mass two hours ago.

MARTY Well, make yourself at home. The refrigerator is loaded with food. Go upstairs, take any room you want. It's beautiful outside, ain't it?

AUNT There's a chill. Watch out, you catch a good cold and pneumonia.

MOTHER My sister Catherine, she can't even admit it's a beautiful day.

MARTY — *now at the sink, getting himself a glass of water — is examining a piece of plaster that has fallen from the ceiling*

MARTY (*examining the chunk of plaster in his palm*) Boy, this place is really coming to pieces. (*Turns to* MOTHER) You know, Ma, I think, sometime we oughtta sell this place. The plumbing is rusty — everything. I'm gonna have to replaster that whole ceiling now. I think we oughtta get a little apartment somewheres in a nicer parta town. . . . You all set, Ma?

MOTHER I'm all set.

She starts for the porch door. She slowly turns and looks at MARTY, *and then at* AUNT CATHERINE — *who returns her look.* MOTHER *and* MARTY *exit.*

DISSOLVE TO: *Church. The* MOTHER *comes out of the doors and down a few steps to where* MARTY *is standing, enjoying the clearness of the June morning*

MOTHER In a couple-a minutes nine o'clock Mass is gonna start — in a couple-a minutes . . . (*To passers-by off*) hallo, hallo . . . (*To* MARTY) Well, that was a nice girl last night, Marty. That was a nice girl.

MARTY   Yeah.

MOTHER   She wasn't a very good-looking girl, but she look like a nice girl. I said, she wasn't a very good-looking girl, not very pretty.

MARTY   I heard you, Ma.

MOTHER   She look a little old for you, about thirty-five, forty years old?

MARTY   She's twenty-nine, Ma.

MOTHER   She's more than twenny-nine years old, Marty. That's what she tells you. She looks thirty-five, forty. She didn't look Italian to me. I said, is she an Italian girl?

MARTY   I don't know. I don't think so.

MOTHER   She don't look like Italian to me. What kinda family she come from? There was something about her I don't like. It seems funny, the first time you meet her she comes to your empty house alone. These college girls, they all one step from the streets.

MARTY *turns, frowning, to his* MOTHER

MARTY   What are you talkin' about? She's a nice girl.

MOTHER   I don't like her.

MARTY   You don't like her? You only met her for two minutes.

MOTHER   Don't bring her to the house no more.

MARTY   What didn't you like about her?

MOTHER   I don't know! She don't look like Italian to me, plenty nice Italian girls around.

MARTY   Well, let's not get into a fight about it, Ma. I just met the girl. I probably won't see her again.

MARTY *leaves frame*

MOTHER   Eh, I'm no better than my sister Catherine.

DISSOLVE TO: *Interior, the bar . . . about an hour later. The after-Mass crowd is there, about six men ranging from twenty to forty. A couple of women in the booths. One woman is holding a glass of beer in one hand and is gently rocking a baby carriage with the other.*

Sitting in the booth of Act One are ANGIE *and three other fellows, ages twenty, thirty-two, and forty. One of the fellows, aged thirty-two, is giving a critical resumé of a recent work of literature by Mickey Spillane*

CRITIC   . . . So the whole book winds up, Mike Hammer, he's inna room there with this doll. So he says: "You rat, you are the murderer." So she begins to con him, you know? She tells him she loves him. And then Bam! He shoots her in the stomach. So she's laying there, gasping for breath, and she says: "How could you do that?" And he says: "It was easy."

TWENTY-YEAR-OLD   Boy, that Mickey Spillane. Boy, he can write.

ANGIE (*leaning out of the booth and looking down the length of the bar, says with some irritation*)   What's keeping Marty?

CRITIC   What I like about Mickey Spillane is he knows how to handle women. In one book, he picks up a tomato who gets hit with a car, and she throws a pass at him. And then he meets two beautiful twins, and they throw passes at him. And then he meets some beautiful society leader, and she throws a pass at him, and . . .

TWENTY-YEAR-OLD   Boy, that Mickey Spillane, he sure can write . . .

ANGIE (*looking out, down the bar again*)   I don't know watsa matter with Marty.

FORTY-YEAR-OLD   Boy, Angie, what would you do if Marty ever died? You'd die right with him. A couple-a old bachelors hanging to each other like barnacles. There's Marty now.

ANGIE *leans out of the booth*

ANGIE (*calling out*)   Hello, Marty, where you been?

CUT TO: *Front end of the bar.* MARTY *has just come in. He waves back to* ANGIE, *acknowledges another hello from a man by the bar, goes over to the bar, and gets the bartender's attention*

MARTY   Hello, Lou, gimme change of a half and put a dime in it for a telephone call.

The BARTENDER *takes the half dollar, reaches into his apron pocket for the change*

BARTENDER   I hear you was at the Waverly Ballroom last night.

MARTY   Yeah. Angie tell you?

BARTENDER (*picking out change from palm full of silver*)   Yeah, I hear you really got stuck with a dog.

MARTY *looks at him*

MARTY   She wasn't so bad.

BARTENDER (*extending the change*)   Angie says she was a real scrawny-looking thing. Well, you can't have good luck alla time.

MARTY *takes the change slowly and frowns down at it. He moves down the bar and would make for the telephone booth, but* ANGIE *hails him from the booth*

ANGIE   Who you gonna call, Marty?

MARTY   I was gonna call that girl from last night, take her to a movie tonight.

ANGIE   Are you kidding?

MARTY   She was a nice girl. I kinda liked her.

ANGIE (*indicating the spot in the booth vacated by the* FORTY-YEAR-OLD)   Sid-down. You can call her later.

MARTY *pauses, frowning, and then shuffles to the booth where* ANGIE *and the other two sit. The* CRITIC *moves over for* MARTY. *There is an exchange of hellos*

TWENTY-YEAR-OLD   I gotta girl, she's always asking me to marry her. So I look at that face, and I say to myself: "Could I stand looking at that face for the resta my life?"

CRITIC   Hey, Marty, you ever read a book called *I, the Jury,* by Mickey Spillane?

MARTY   No.

ANGIE   Listen, Marty, I gotta good place for us to go tonight. The kid here, he says, he was downna bazaar at Our Lady of Angels last night and . . .

MARTY   I don't feel like going to the bazaar, Angie. I thought I'd take this girl to a movie.

ANGIE   Boy, you really musta made out good last night.

MARTY   We just talked.

ANGIE   Boy, she must be some talker. She musta been about fifty years old.

CRITIC   I always figger a guy oughtta marry a girl who's twenny years younger than he is, so that when he's forty, his wife is a real nice-looking doll.

TWENTY-YEAR-OLD   That means he'd have to marry the girl when she was one year old.

CRITIC   I never thoughta that.

MARTY   I didn't think she was so bad-looking.

ANGIE   She musta kept you inna shadows all night.

CRITIC   Marty, you don't wanna hang around with dogs. It gives you a bad reputation.

ANGIE   Marty, let's go downna bazaar.

MARTY   I told this dog I was gonna call her today.

ANGIE   Brush her.

MARTY *looks questioningly at* ANGIE

MARTY   You didn't like her at all?

ANGIE   A nothing. A real nothing.

MARTY *looks down at the dime he has been nervously turning between two fingers and then, frowning, he slips it into his jacket pocket. He lowers his face and looks down, scowling at his thoughts. Around him, the voices clip along*

CRITIC   What's playing on Fordham Road? I think there's a good picture in the Loew's Paradise.

ANGIE   Let's go down to Forty-second Street and walk around. We're sure to wind up with something.

Slowly MARTY *begins to look up again. He looks from face to face as each speaks*

CRITIC   I'll never forgive La Guardia for cutting burlesque outta New York City.

TWENTY-YEAR-OLD   There's burlesque over in Union City. Let's go to Union City. . . .

ANGIE   Ah, they're always crowded on Sunday night.

CRITIC   So wadda you figure on doing tonight, Angie?

ANGIE   I don't know. Wadda you figure on doing?

CRITIC   I don't know. (*Turns to the* TWENTY-YEAR-OLD) Wadda you figure on doing?

The TWENTY-YEAR-OLD *shrugs.*

Suddenly MARTY *brings his fist down on the booth table with a crash. The others turn, startled, toward him.* MARTY *rises in his seat*

MARTY   "What are you doing tonight?" "I don't know, what are you doing?" Burlesque! Loew's Paradise! Miserable and lonely! Miserable and lonely and stupid! What am I, crazy or something?! I got something good! What am I hanging around with you guys for?!

He has said this in tones so loud that it attracts the attention of everyone in the bar. A little embarrassed, MARTY *turns and moves quickly to the phone booth, pausing outside the door to find his dime again.* ANGIE *is out of his seat immediately and hurries after him*

ANGIE   (*a little shocked at* MARTY*'s outburst*)   Watsa matter with you?

MARTY   (*in a low, intense voice*)   You don't like her. My mother don't like her. She's a dog, and I'm a fat, ugly little man. All I know is I had a good time last night. I'm gonna have a good time tonight. If we have enough good times together, I'm going down on my knees and beg that girl to marry me. If we make a party again this New Year's, I gotta date for the party. You don't like her, that's too bad. (*He moves into the booth, sits, turns again to* ANGIE, *smiles*) When you gonna get married, Angie? You're thirty-four years old. All your kid brothers are married. You oughtta be ashamed of yourself.

Still smiling at his private joke, he puts the dime into the slot and then — with a determined finger — he begins to dial

Fade out

Exercises

1. What actions move the plot forward?

2. Identify the protagonist, the prize, and the obstacle. What incident brings together these three elements for the first time and thereby makes clear the conflict that is being introduced?

3. List several complications.

4. What purpose is served by the subplot that involves Aunt Catherine?

5. By what means are the bartender, the stag, and the critic characterized? Explain their roles in the play.

6. What is the dramatic function of Angie?

7. Are Virginia and Thomas necessary to the story? Explain.

8. What aspect of Marty's character is dramatized in Act I when he gives quick approval to Aunt Catherine's coming to live with him and his mother? Illustrate the consistency of this trait in Marty's later decisions or actions.

9. Identify speeches that help you infer the character of Clara Davis or of Marty's mother.

10. What significance can you ascribe to Marty's final speech?

Topics for Writing

1. Characterize Marty by the actions he takes and the speeches he makes. Is he innocent? Stupid? Ugly? Weak? Good?

2. Discuss the following student's statement of theme: "How a bug and a dog can find love and happiness in a room full of tomatoes." Or express and discuss your version of the major theme of the play.

3. Compare and contrast the physical attributes, background, and psychology that make up the characters of Clara and Marty. Are they well suited to each other? Support your conclusion with specific evidence from the text.

Selected Bibliography   Paddy Chayefsky

Goldstein, Malcolm. "Body and Soul on Broadway." *Modern Drama,* 7 (February 1965), 411–421.

Lewis, A. "Man's Relation to God — MacLeish, Chayefsky." *American Plays and Playwrights of the Contemporary Theatre.* New York: Crown Publishers, 1970, pp. 116–128.

Sayre, Nora, and Robert B. Silvers. "An Interview with Paddy Chayefsky." *Horizon,* 3 (September 1960), 50–56.

Weales, G. C. "The Video Boys." In *American Drama Since World War II.* New York: Harcourt, Brace & World, 1962, pp. 57–75.

18. THEME OR MEANING

The **theme** or meaning of a play — some truth about human life or experience — is mainly contained in and chiefly revealed by the actions and speeches of the characters. It exists in the dramatic story itself, not outside it.

Usually playwrights are avid readers and profound thinkers. Like most people, they possess attitudes that make up a philosophy of life. Intentionally or not, these attitudes invade the action and dialogue of the characters, and from those dialogues a reader or spectator derives meaning.

Concerned as playwrights are with people and problems, they present in their dramas the myriad issues of life's unchanging events. In most dramas that have endured the test of time, we discover the themes of universal truth, the relationships and interrelationships of men and women, their society, and the forces in control of the world. What the playwrights have to say about life may be far-reaching or piddling, true or false, and they may lead us to perceive these truths, half-truths, and lies by being glaringly obvious or deviously subtle.

Although drama seldom expresses a philosophy of life or suggests a *modus vivendi* with society in a wholly systematic way, we can usually depend upon some element of plot, characterization, or action, or on all the elements together (the complete story), to give us glimpses of meaning, if not total meaning. From many plays we do glean some code of psychological, moral, or ethical beliefs. Because the heart of drama beats with actions and words that exhibit human life, it must inevitably carry some conclusion about life. In searching for interpretation, then, we must endeavor to understand what that conclusion is.

Let us review several plays for the purpose of discovering theme through various **elements of plot.** Oedipus has vowed to appease the gods and end the pestilence in Thebes by bringing the unpunished murderer of Laius to justice. Once he discovers that he himself is the murderer, and learns of his marriage to his mother, who bore him two sons and two daughters, he blinds himself and asks to be exiled. In the course of the action, Oedipus defies the gods and what they have prophesied for him. Is Oedipus' arrogance a sin against the gods? Does one of the major themes focus on a struggle that pits humans against the gods?

Toward the end of *The Sandbox,* which you will find in the next chapter, Grandma buries herself in sand. With this action, Edward Albee is surely expressing an attitude toward life and death. We might also look at Willy Loman in *Death of a Salesman,* who has failed miserably as a businessman and a father to two sons. When Biff confronts him in the climactic scene and exposes him for what he is — "a very ordinary man" — Willy commits suicide. The incident, the resolution of the play, suggests several possible themes. Has Willy enjoyed a brief triumph? Has he achieved an inner dignity as a result of his sacrifice? Or has he simply admitted defeat?

In *Arms and the Man,* Shaw uses a set of characters in conflict with real and romantic notions of love and war, and cocks his satiric gun at aristocratic pretensions and political systems. What likely themes does the play suggest? Finally, in the play by Chayefsky, when Marty makes a telephone call to Clara Davis, he is rejecting the narrow-minded influences of his background; he is instead moving toward accepting the stranger he met in a dime-a-dance hall as his Cinderella. Why? Perhaps the playwright wishes to prove that it is possible for two lonely, physically unattractive people from two different worlds to find real romantic love.

Sometimes the very forces in conflict with one another will shed light on what the playwright intends to say to us. If, for example, *The Sandbox* presents a family incapable of communication with and love for one another, a theme central to the story must consequently express something about these matters. Similarly, if *Arms and the Man* treats idealized notions of love and war, then surely the comedy has something to say about love and war.

Frequently, the study of **main characters** will lead us to discover meaning. Under the pressures of conflict, a character speaks not only as a mouthpiece for the playwright but, more important, as a human being in the throes of new insights and attitudes which develop as a consequence of actions taken or refused. The character of Oedipus, for example, is central to an understanding of the Sophoclean drama in which he appears. Here is a strong human will arrogantly bent on challenging the will of the gods. Oedipus vows to bring to justice the murderer of Laius; he persists in searching for this person's identity; he refuses to believe the prophecy; he has in fact murdered his father and married his mother; he blinds himself and demands exile. What is the nature of such a man? What motivates him? Can we not extract a theme from our understanding of this character? In looking at Othello, in Shakespeare's tragedy, we may conclude that he has acted irrationally, out of jealousy, in murdering his wife, or that he has committed the deed to rid the state of an immoral soul. And we might view Miller's Loman as so caught up in the American dream of material success and so insensitive to human values that he feels he must lie, cheat, and steal. Therein lies one certain theme for *Death of a Salesman.*

Characters' **speeches** may also reveal feelings, opinions, decisions, and conclusions that enlighten us. Some speeches focus directly on thematic substance; in fact, occasionally they are explicit declarations of what the dramatist wishes to convey. When the blind Oedipus gropes his way through the multitude toward the end of the drama, the Theban citizens offer this comment: "No man ever really finds happiness until he dies." Would you select this statement as an appropriate theme? Or is the theme explicitly stated by the chorus: "O the generations of man!/ His life is vanity and nothingness"? Perhaps Sergius's final remark about Bluntschli — "What a man! Is he a man?" — conveys succinctly and precisely the real message of Shaw's comedy. And in Shakespeare's tragedy, a clue to meaning comes to us when Othello, at the beginning of Act V, Scene 2, says:

It is the cause, it is the cause, my soul;
Let me not name it to you, you chaste stars!
It is the cause. Yet I'll not shed her blood,
Nor scar that whiter skin of hers than snow,
And smooth as monumental alabaster.
Yet she must die, else she'll betray more men.

However, in taking a statement by a character in a play as an expression of a chosen theme, we must ascertain that it is consistent with the entire action and verify that it represents a reasonable assessment of the total emphasis in the play.

Another element worth considering as an avenue toward understanding is **setting.** For example, how effectively does Albee's bare and empty stage in *The Sandbox* lead us to an appropriate interpretation of the life he attempts to portray?

Many other details — titles of plays, names of characters, ironies, imagery, and symbols — may lead us to understand a playwright's purpose. The words in the **title** *Arms and the Man* may refer to arms in both love and war, someone in love or a soldier. The words used as this title are also borrowed from Virgil's *Aeneid,* which begins, "I sing of arms and the man"; Shaw's play pokes fun at the attitudes toward war and love exemplified by heroic poetry and sanctioned by long tradition. In entitling his play *Death of a Salesman,* Miller surely is offering a comment about the protagonist beyond the literal fact of his end. Similarly useful are the **names of characters:** as we have mentioned, *Oedipus* means "swollen foot" and also "on the track of knowledge," while *Willy Loman* hints at "low man," on the ladder of success and, possibly, in other ways, too.

As in fiction and poetry, in drama **ironies, imagery,** and **symbols** can point to a theme. We will look at these aspects more closely in the next chapter.

Finally, we may expand our understanding or even recognize some new aspect of theme by external means. That is, knowledge of literary conventions and of the social and historical backgrounds of the period in which a play was written may help us grasp its central idea.

Numerous details as well as plot, character, conflict, action, and speech, to mention only a few of the elements of the dramatic form, afford us various opportunities to discover a theme and then move toward total meaning, which, of course, comes to us only as the by-product of the total impression we experience from seeing or reading a play. Bertolt Brecht's *The Caucasian Chalk Circle* and August Strindberg's *Miss Julie* are both rich dramatic fields for a search for meaning, and it is to them that we now turn.

Bertolt Brecht (1898–1956)

The Caucasian Chalk Circle

Adapted by Eric Bentley

Characters

OLD MAN, *On the right*

PEASANT WOMAN, *On the right*

YOUNG PEASANT

A VERY YOUNG WORKER

OLD MAN, *On the left*

PEASANT WOMAN, *On the left*

AGRICULTURIST KATO

GIRL TRACTORIST

WOUNDED SOLDIER

THE DELEGATE *From the capital*

THE SINGER

GEORGI ABASHWILI, *The Governor*

NATELLA, *The Governor's wife*

MICHAEL, *Their son*

SHALVA, *An adjutant*

ARSEN KAZBEKI, *A fat prince*

MESSENGER, *From the capital*

NIKO MIKADZE and MIKA LOLADZE, *Doctors*

SIMON SHASHAVA, *A soldier*

GRUSHA VASHNADZE, *A kitchen maid*

OLD PEASANT, *With the milk*

CORPORAL and PRIVATE

PEASANT and HIS WIFE

LAVRENTI VASHNADZE, GRUSHA'S *brother*

ANIKO, *His wife*

PEASANT WOMAN, *For a while* GRUSHA'S *mother-in-law*

JUSSUP, *Her son*

MONK

AZDAK, *Village recorder*

SHAUWA, *A policeman*

GRAND DUKE

DOCTOR

INVALID

LIMPING MAN

BLACKMAILER

LUDOVICA

INNKEEPER, *Her father-in-law*

STABLEBOY

POOR OLD PEASANT WOMAN

IRAKLI, *Her brother-in-law, a bandit*

THREE WEALTHY FARMERS

ILLO SHUBOLADZE and SANDRO OBOLADZE, *Lawyers*

OLD MARRIED COUPLE

SOLDIERS, SERVANTS

PEASANTS, BEGGARS

MUSICIANS, MERCHANTS

NOBLES, ARCHITECTS

Prologue

Among the ruins of a war-ravaged Caucasian village the members of two Kolkhoz[1] villages, mostly women and older men, are sitting in a circle, smoking and drinking wine. With them is a delegate of the state reconstruction commission from Nuka, the capital.

PEASANT WOMAN (*Left*) (*Pointing*) In those hills over there we stopped three Nazi tanks, but the apple orchard was already destroyed.

1. *Kolkhoz:* A collective farm in the Soviet Union.

OLD MAN (*Right*)   Our beautiful dairy farm: a ruin.

GIRL TRACTORIST   I laid the fire, Comrade. (*Pause*)

THE DELEGATE   Now listen to the report. Delegates from the goat-breeding Kolkhoz "Rosa Luxemburg" have been to Nuka. When Hitler's armies approached, the Kolkhoz had moved its goat-herds further east on orders from the authorities. They are now thinking of returning. Their delegates have investigated the village and the land and found a lot of it destroyed.

> (DELEGATES *on right nod*)

> The neighboring fruit-culture Kolkhoz (*To the left*) "Galinsk" is proposing to use the former grazing land of Kolkhoz "Rosa Luxemburg," a valley with scanty growth of grass, for orchards and vineyards. As a delegate of the Reconstruction Commission, I request that the two Kolkhoz villages decide between themselves whether Kolkhoz "Rosa Luxemburg" shall return here or not.

OLD MAN (*Right*)   First of all, I want to protest against the restriction of time for discussion. We of Kolkhoz "Rosa Luxemburg" have spent three days and three nights getting here. And now discussion is limited to half a day.

WOUNDED SOLDIER (*Left*)   Comrade, we haven't as many villages as we used to have. We haven't as many hands. We haven't as much time.

GIRL TRACTORIST   All pleasures have to be rationed. Tobacco is rationed, and wine. Discussion should be rationed.

OLD MAN (*Right*) (*Sighing*)   Death to the fascists! But I will come to the point and explain why we want our valley back. There are a great many reasons, but I'll begin with one of the simplest. Makina Abakidze, unpack the goat cheese. (*A* PEASANT WOMAN *from right takes from a basket an enormous cheese wrapped in a cloth. Applause and laughter*) Help yourselves, Comrades, start in!

OLD MAN (*Left*) (*Suspiciously*)   Is this a way of influencing us?

OLD MAN (*Right*) (*Amid laughter*)   How could it be a way of influencing you, Surab, you valley-thief? Everyone knows you will take the cheese and the valley, too. (*Laughter*) All I expect from you is an honest answer. Do you like the cheese?

OLD MAN (*Left*)   The answer is: yes.

OLD MAN (*Right*)   Really. (*Bitterly*) I ought to have known you know nothing about cheese.

OLD MAN (*Left*)   Why not? When I tell you I like it?

OLD MAN (*Right*)   Because you can't like it. Because it's not what it was in the old days. And why not? Because our goats don't like the new grass as they did the old. Cheese is not cheese because grass is not grass, that's the thing. Please put that in your report.

OLD MAN (*Left*)   But your cheese is excellent.

OLD MAN (*Right*)   It isn't excellent. It's just passable. The new grazing land is no good, whatever the young people may say. One can't live there. It doesn't even smell of morning in the morning. (SEVERAL PEOPLE *laugh*)

THE DELEGATE   Don't mind their laughing: they understand you. Comrades, why does one love one's country? Because the bread tastes better there, the air smells better, voices sound stronger, the sky is higher, the ground is easier to walk on. Isn't that so?

OLD MAN (*Right*)   The valley has belonged to us from all eternity.

SOLDIER (*Left*)   What does *that* mean — from all eternity? Nothing belongs to anyone from all eternity. When you were young you didn't even belong to yourself. You belonged to the Kazbeki[2] princes.

OLD MAN (*Right*)   Doesn't it make a difference, though, what kind of trees stand next to the house you are born in? Or what kind of neighbors you have? Doesn't that make a difference? We want to go back just to have you as our neighbors, valley-thieves! Now you can all laugh again.

OLD MAN (*Left*) (*Laughing*)   Then why don't you listen to what your neighbor, Kato Wachtang, our agriculturist, has to say about the valley?

PEASANT WOMAN (*Right*)   We've not said all there is to be said about our valley. By no means. Not all the houses are destroyed. As for the dairy farm, at least the foundation wall is still standing.

DELEGATE   You can claim State support — here and there — you know that. I have suggestions here in my pocket.

PEASANT WOMAN (*Right*)   Comrade Specialist, we haven't come here to bargain. I can't take your cap and hand you another, and say "This one's better." The other one might *be* better; but you *like* yours better.

GIRL TRACTORIST   A piece of land is not a cap — not in our country, Comrade.

DELEGATE   Don't get angry. It's true we have to consider a piece of land as a tool to produce something useful, but it's also true that we must recognize love for a particular piece of land. As far as I'm concerned, I'd like to find out more exactly what you (*To those on the left*) want to do with the valley.

OTHERS   Yes, let Kato speak.

DELEGATE   Comrade Agriculturist!

KATO (*Rising,* SHE'S *in military uniform*)   Comrades, last winter, while we were fighting in these hills as Partisans, we discussed how, after the expulsion of the Germans, we could build up our fruit culture to ten times its original size. I've prepared a plan for an irrigation project. By means of a cofferdam on our mountain lake, 300 hectares of unfertile land can be irrigated. Our Kolkhoz could not only cultivate more fruit, but also have vineyards. The project, however, would pay only if the disputed valley of Kolkhoz "Galinsk" were also included. Here are the calculations. (SHE *hands the* DELEGATE *a briefcase*)

OLD MAN (*Right*)   Write into a report that our Kolkhoz plans to start a new stud farm.

GIRL TRACTORIST   Comrades, the project was conceived during days and nights when we had to take cover in the mountains. We were often without ammunition for our half-dozen rifles. Even getting a pencil was difficult. (*Applause from both sides*)

OLD MAN (*Right*)   Our thanks to the Comrades of Kolkhoz "Galinsk" and all who have defended our country! (THEY *shake hands and embrace*)

PEASANT WOMAN (*Left*)   In doing this our thought was that our soldiers — both your men and our men — should return to a still more productive homeland.

GIRL TRACTORIST   As the poet Mayakovsky[3] said: "The home of the Soviet people shall also be the home of Reason"!

(*The* DELEGATES *including the* OLD MAN *have got up, and with the* DELEGATE

---

2. *Kazbeki:* A Caucasian district.   3. *Vladimir Mayakovsky* (1894–1930): One of the greatest Russian poets of this century.

specified proceed to study the Agriculturist's drawings . . . exclamations such as: "Why is the altitude of all 22 meters?" — "This rock must be blown up" — "Actually, all they need is cement and dynamite" — "They force the water to come down here, that's clever!")

A VERY YOUNG WORKER (*Right*) (*To* OLD MAN, *right*) They're going to irrigate all the fields between the hills, look at that, Aleko!

OLD MAN (*Right*) I'm not going to look. I knew the project would be good. I won't have a revolver aimed at my chest.

DELEGATE But they only want to aim a pencil at your chest. (*Laughter*)

OLD MAN (*Right*) (*Gets up gloomily, and walks over to look at the drawings*) These valley-thieves know only too well that we can't resist machines and projects in this country.

PEASANT WOMAN (*Right*) Aleko Bereshwili, you have a weakness for new projects. That's well known.

DELEGATE What about my report? May I write that you will all support the cession of your old valley in the interests of this project when you get back to your Kolkhoz?

PEASANT WOMAN (*Right*) I will. What about you, Aleko?

OLD MAN (*Right*) (*Bent over drawings*) I suggest that you give us copies of the drawings to take along.

PEASANT WOMAN (*Right*) Then we can sit down and eat. Once he has the drawings and he's ready to discuss them, the matter is settled. I know him. And it will be the same with the rest of us. (DELEGATES *laughingly embrace again*)

OLD MAN (*Left*) Long live the Kolkhoz "Rosa Luxemburg" and much luck to your horsebreeding project!

PEASANT WOMAN (*Left*) In honor of the visit of the delegates from Kolkhoz "Rosa Luxemburg" and of the Specialist, the plan is that we all hear a presentation of the Singer Arkadi Tscheidse. (*Applause.* GIRL TRACTORIST *has gone off to bring the* SINGER)

PEASANT WOMAN (*Right*) Comrades, your entertainment had better be good. We're going to pay for it with a valley.

PEASANT WOMAN (*Left*) Arkadi Tscheidse knows about our discussion. He's promised to perform something that has a bearing on the problem.

KATO We wired to Tiflis[4] three times. The whole thing nearly fell through at the last minute because his driver had a cold.

PEASANT WOMAN (*Left*) Arkadi Tscheidse knows 21,000 lines of verse.

OLD MAN (*Left*) It's very difficult to get him. You and the Planning Commission should see to it that you get him to come North more often, Comrade.

DELEGATE We are more interested in economics, I'm afraid.

OLD MAN (*Left*) (*Smiling*) You arrange the redistribution of vines and tractors, why not of songs?

(*Enter the* SINGER ARKADI TSCHEIDSE, *led by* GIRL TRACTORIST. HE *is a well-built man of simple manners, accompanied by* FOUR MUSICIANS *with their instruments. The* ARTISTS *are greeted with applause*)

GIRL TRACTORIST This is the Comrade Specialist, Arkadi. (*The* SINGER *greets them all*)

4. *Tiflis:* Capital of the Georgian Republic of the U.S.S.R.

DELEGATE I'm honored to make your acquaintance. I heard about your songs when I was a boy at school. Will it be one of the old legends?

THE SINGER A very old one. It's called The Chalk Circle and comes from the Chinese. But we'll do it, of course, in a changed version. Comrades, it's an honor for me to entertain you after a difficult debate. We hope you will find that the voice of the old poet also sounds well in the shadow of Soviet tractors. It may be a mistake to mix different wines, but old and new wisdom mix admirably. Now I hope we'll get something to eat before the performance begins — it would certainly help.

VOICES Surely. Everyone into the Club House! (*While* EVERYONE *begins to move, the* DELEGATE *turns to the* GIRL TRACTORIST)

DELEGATE I hope it won't take long. I've got to get back tonight.

GIRL TRACTORIST How long will it last, Arkadi? The Comrade Specialist must get back to Tiflis tonight.

THE SINGER (*Casually*) It's actually two stories. An hour or two.

GIRL TRACTORIST (*Confidentially*) Couldn't you make it shorter?

THE SINGER No.

VOICE Arkadi Tscheidse's performance will take place here in the square after the meal. (*And* THEY ALL *go happily to eat*)

1. The Noble Child

As the lights go up, THE SINGER *is seen sitting on the floor, a black sheepskin cloak round his shoulders, and a little well-thumbed notebook in his hand. A small group of listeners — the* CHORUS — *sits with him. The manner of his recitation makes it clear that* HE *has told his story over and over again.* HE *mechanically fingers the pages, seldom looking at them. With appropriate gestures,* HE *gives the signal for each scene to begin.*

THE SINGER In olden times, in a bloody time,
There ruled in a Caucasian city —
Men called it City of the Damned —
A governor.
His name was Georgi Abashwili.
He was rich as Croesus
He had a beautiful wife
He had a healthy baby.
No other governor in Grusinia
Had so many horses in his stable
So many beggars on his doorstep
So many soldiers in his service
So many petitioners in his courtyard.
Georgi Abashwili — how shall I describe him to you?
He enjoyed his life.
On the morning of Easter Sunday
The governor and his family went to church.
(*At the left a large doorway, at the right an even larger gateway.* BEGGARS *and* PETITIONERS *pour from the gateway, holding up thin* CHILDREN, *crutches, and petitions.* THEY *are followed by* IRONSHIRTS, *and then, expensively dressed, the* GOVERNOR'S FAMILY)

BEGGARS AND PETITIONERS Mercy! Mercy, Your Grace! The taxes are too high.
— I lost my leg in the Persian War, where can I get . . .
— My brother is innocent, Your Grace, a misunderstanding . . .
— The child is starving in my arms!
— Our petition is for our son's discharge from the army, our last remaining son!
— Please, Your Grace, the water inspector takes bribes.
(ONE SERVANT *collects the petitions,* ANOTHER *distributes coins from a purse.* SOLDIERS *push the* CROWD *back, lashing at them with thick leather whips*)

THE SOLDIER Get back! Clear the church door! (*Behind the* GOVERNOR, HIS WIFE, *and the* ADJUTANT, *the* GOVERNOR'S CHILD *is brought through the gateway in an ornate carriage*)

THE CROWD — The baby!
— I can't see it, don't shove so hard!
— God bless the child, Your Grace!

THE SINGER (*While the* CROWD *is driven back with whips*) For the first time on that Easter Sunday, the people saw the Governor's heir.
Two doctors never moved from the noble child, apple of the Governor's eye. Even the mighty Prince Kazbeki bows before him at the church door. (*A* FAT PRINCE *steps forward and greets the family*)

THE FAT PRINCE Happy Easter, Natella Abashwili! What a day! When it was raining last night, I thought to myself, gloomy holidays! But this morning the sky was gay. I love a gay sky, a simple heart, Natella Abashwili. And little Michael is a governor from head to foot! Tititi! (HE *tickles the* CHILD)

THE GOVERNOR'S WIFE What do you think, Arsen, at last Georgi has decided to start building the wing on the east side. All those wretched slums are to be torn down to make room for the garden.

THE FAT PRINCE Good news after so much bad! What's the latest on the war, Brother Georgi? (*The* GOVERNOR *indicates a lack of interest*)

THE FAT PRINCE Strategical retreat, I hear. Well, minor reverses are to be expected. Sometimes things go well, sometimes not. Such is war. Doesn't mean a thing, does it?

THE GOVERNOR'S WIFE He's coughing. Georgi, did you hear? (SHE *speaks sharply to the* DOCTORS, *two dignified men standing close to the little carriage*) He's coughing!

THE FIRST DOCTOR (*To the* SECOND) May I remind you, Niko Mikadze, that I was against the lukewarm bath? (*To the* GOVERNOR'S WIFE) There's been a little error over warming the bath water, Your Grace.

THE SECOND DOCTOR (*Equally polite*) Mika Loladze, I'm afraid I can't agree with you. The temperature of the bath water was exactly what our great, beloved Mishiko Oboladze prescribed. More likely a slight draft during the night, Your Grace.

THE GOVERNOR'S WIFE But do pay more attention to him. He looks feverish, Georgi.

THE FIRST DOCTOR (*Bending over the* CHILD) No cause for alarm, Your Grace. The bath water will be warmer. It won't occur again.

THE SECOND DOCTOR (*With a venomous glance at the* FIRST) I won't forget that, my dear Mika Loladze. No cause for concern, Your Grace.

THE FAT PRINCE Well, well, well! I always say: "A pain in my liver? Then the doctor gets fifty strokes on the soles of his feet." We live in a decadent age. In the old days one said: "Off with his head!"

THE GOVERNOR'S WIFE   Let's go into church. Very likely it's the draft here. (*The procession of* FAMILY *and* SERVANTS *turns into the doorway. The* FAT PRINCE *follows, but the* GOVERNOR *is kept back by the* ADJUTANT, *a handsome young man. When the crowd of* PETITIONERS *has been driven off, a young dust-stained* RIDER, *his arm in a sling, remains behind*)

THE ADJUTANT   (*Pointing at the* RIDER, *who steps forward*)   Won't you hear the messenger from the capital, your Excellency? He arrived this morning. With confidential papers.

THE GOVERNOR   Not before Service, Shalva. But did you hear Brother Kazbeki wish me a happy Easter? Which is all very well, but I don't believe it did rain last night.

THE ADJUTANT   (*Nodding*)   We must investigate.

THE GOVERNOR   Yes, at once. Tomorrow.

(THEY *pass through the doorway. The* RIDER, *who has waited in vain for an audience, turns sharply round and, muttering a curse, goes off. Only one of the palace guards* — SIMON SHASHAVA — *remains at the door*)

THE SINGER   The city is still.
Pigeons strut in the church square.
A soldier of the Palace Guard
Is joking with a kitchen maid
As she comes up from the river with a bundle.

(*A girl* — GRUSHA VASHADZE — *comes through the gateway with a bundle made of large green leaves under her arm*)

SIMON   What, the young lady is not in church? Shirking?

GRUSHA   I was dressed to go. But they needed another goose for the banquet. And they asked me to get it. I know about geese.

SIMON   A goose? (HE *feigns suspicion*) I'd like to see that goose. (GRUSHA *does not understand*) One has to be on one's guard with women "I only went for a fish," they tell you, but it turns out to be something else.

GRUSHA   (*Walking resolutely toward him and showing him the goose*)   There! If it isn't a fifteen-pound goose stuffed full of corn, I'll eat the feathers.

SIMON   A queen of a goose! The Governor himself will eat it. So the young lady has been down to the river again?

GRUSHA   Yes, at the poultry farm.

SIMON   Really? At the poultry farm, down by the river . . . not higher up maybe? Near those willows?

GRUSHA   I only go to the willows to wash the linen.

SIMON   (*Insinuatingly*)   Exactly.

GRUSHA   Exactly what?

SIMON   (*Winking*)   Exactly that.

GRUSHA   Why shouldn't I wash the linen by the willows?

SIMON   (*With exaggerated laughter*)   "Why shouldn't I wash the linen by the willows!" That's good, really good!

GRUSHA   I don't understand the soldier. What's so good about it?

SIMON   (*Slyly*)   "If something I know someone learns, she'll grow hot and cold by turns!"

GRUSHA   I don't know what I could learn about those willows.

SIMON Not even if there was a bush opposite? That one could see everything from? Everything that goes on there when a certain person is — "washing linen"?

GRUSHA What does go on? Won't the soldier say what he means and have done?

SIMON Something goes on. And something can be seen.

GRUSHA Could the soldier mean I dip my toes in the water when it is hot? There is nothing else.

SIMON More. Your toes. And more.

GRUSHA More what? At most my foot?

SIMON Your foot. And a little more. (HE *laughs heartily*)

GRUSHA (*Angrily*) Simon Shashava, you ought to be ashamed of yourself! To sit in a bush on a hot day and wait till someone comes and dips her leg in the river! And I bet you bring a friend along too! (SHE *runs off*)

SIMON (*Shouting after her*) I didn't bring any friend along! (*As the* SINGER *resumes his tale, the* SOLDIER *steps into the doorway as though to listen to the service*)

THE SINGER The city lies still
But why are there armed men?
The Governor's palace is at peace
But why is it a fortress?
And the Governor returned to his palace
And the fortress was a trap
And the goose was plucked and roasted
But the goose was not eaten this time
And noon was no longer the hour to eat:
Noon was the hour to die.

(*From the doorway at the left the* FAT PRINCE *quickly appears, stands still, looks around. Before the gateway at the right* TWO IRONSHIRTS *are squatting and playing dice. The* FAT PRINCE *sees them, walks slowly past, making a sign to them.* THEY *rise:* ONE *goes through the gateway, the* OTHER *goes off at the right. Muffled voices are heard from various directions in the rear: "To your posts!" The palace is surrounded. The* FAT PRINCE *quickly goes off. Church bells in the distance. Enter, through the doorway, the* GOVERNOR'S FAMILY *and* PROCESSION, *returning from church*)

THE GOVERNOR'S WIFE (*Passing the* ADJUTANT) It's impossible to live in such a slum. But Georgi, of course, will only build for his little Michael. Never for me! Michael is all! All for Michael!

(*The* PROCESSION *turns into the gateway. Again the* ADJUTANT *lingers behind.* HE *waits. Enter the* WOUNDED RIDER *from the doorway.* TWO IRONSHIRTS *of the palace guard have taken up positions by the gateway*)

THE ADJUTANT (*To the* RIDER) The Governor does not wish to receive military reports before dinner — especially if they're depressing, as I assume. In the afternoon His Excellency will confer with prominent architects. They're coming to dinner too. And here they are! (*Enter* THREE GENTLEMEN *through the doorway*) Go in the kitchen and get yourself something to eat, my friend. (*As the* RIDER *goes, the* ADJUTANT *greets the* ARCHITECTS) Gentlemen, His Excellency expects you at dinner. He will devote all his time to you and your great new plans. Come!

ONE OF THE ARCHITECTS We marvel that His Excellency intends to build.

There are disquieting rumors that the war in Persia has taken a turn for the worse.

THE ADJUTANT All the more reason to build! There's nothing to those rumors anyway. Persia is a long way off, and the garrison here would let itself be hacked to bits for its Governor. (*Noise from the palace. The shrill scream of a woman. Someone is shouting orders. Dumbfounded, the* ADJUTANT *moves toward the gateway. An* IRONSHIRT *steps out, points his lance at him*) What's this? Put down that lance, you dog.

ONE OF THE ARCHITECTS It's the Princes! Don't you know the Princes met last night in the capital? And they're against the Grand Duke and his Governors? Gentlemen, we'd better make ourselves scarce. (THEY *rush off. The* ADJU-TANT *remains helplessly behind*)

THE ADJUTANT (*Furiously to the* PALACE GUARD) Down with those lances! Don't you see the Governor's life is threatened?

(*The* IRONSHIRTS *of the Palace Guard refuse to obey.* THEY *stare coldly and indifferently at the* ADJUTANT *and follow the next events without interest*)

THE SINGER O blindness of the great!
They go their way like gods,
Great over bent backs,
Sure of hired fists,
Trusting in the power
Which has lasted so long.
But long is not forever.
O change from age to age!
Thou hope of the people!
(*Enter the* GOVERNOR, *through the gateway, between* TWO SOLDIERS *armed to the teeth.* HE *is in chains. His face is gray*)
Up, great sir, deign to walk upright!
From your palace the eyes of many foes follow you!
And now you don't need an architect, a carpenter will do.
You won't be moving into a new palace
But into a little hole in the ground.
Look about you once more, blind man!
(*The arrested man looks round*)
Does all you had please you?
Between the Easter Mass and the Easter meal
You are walking to a place whence no one returns.
(*The* GOVERNOR *is led off. A horn sounds an alarm. Noise behind the gate-way*)
When the house of a great one collapses
Many little ones are slain.
Those who had no share in the *good* fortunes of the mighty
Often have a share in their *mis*fortunes.
The plunging wagon
Drags the sweating oxen down with it
Into the abyss.
(*The* SERVANTS *come rushing through the gateway in panic*)

THE SERVANTS (*Among themselves*) — The baskets!
— Take them all into the third courtyard! Food for five days!
— The mistress has fainted! Someone must carry her down.

— She must get away.

— What about us? We'll be slaughtered like chickens, as always.

— Goodness, what'll happen? There's bloodshed already in the city, they say.

— Nonsense, the Governor has just been asked to appear at a Princes' meeting. All very correct. Everything'll be ironed out. I heard this on the best authority . . .

(*The* TWO DOCTORS *rush into the courtyard*)

THE FIRST DOCTOR (*Trying to restrain the other*) Niko Mikadze, it is your duty as a doctor to attend Natella Abashwili.

THE SECOND DOCTOR My duty! It's yours!

THE FIRST DOCTOR Whose turn is it to look after the child today, Niko Mikadze, yours or mine?

THE SECOND DOCTOR Do you really think, Mika Loladze, I'm going to stay a minute longer in this accursed house on that little brat's account?

(THEY *start fighting. All one hears is: "You neglect your duty!" and "Duty, my foot!" Then the* SECOND DOCTOR *knocks the* FIRST *down*)

Go to hell!

(*Exit*)

(*Enter the* SOLDIER, SIMON SHASHAVA. HE *searches in the crowd for* GRUSHA)

SIMON Grusha! There you are at last! What are you going to do?

GRUSHA Nothing. If worst comes to worst, I've a brother in the mountains. How about you?

SIMON Forget about me. (*Formally again*) Grusha Vashnadze, your wish to know my plans fills me with satisfaction. I've been ordered to accompany Madam Natella Abashwili as her guard.

GRUSHA But hasn't the Palace Guard mutinied?

SIMON (*Seriously*) That's a fact.

GRUSHA Isn't it dangerous to go with her?

SIMON In Tiflis, they say: Isn't the stabbing dangerous for the knife?

GRUSHA You're not a knife, you're a man, Simon Shashava, what has that woman to do with you?

SIMON That woman has nothing to do with me. I have my orders, and I go.

GRUSHA The soldier is pigheaded: he is getting himself into danger for nothing — nothing at all. I must get into the third courtyard, I'm in a hurry.

SIMON Since we're both in a hurry we shouldn't quarrel. You need time for a good quarrel. May I ask if the young lady still has parents?

GRUSHA No, just a brother.

SIMON As time is short — my second question is this: Is the young lady as healthy as a fish in water?

GRUSHA I may have a pain in the right shoulder once in a while. Otherwise I'm strong enough for my job. No one has complained. So far.

SIMON That's well-known. When it's Easter Sunday, and the question arises who'll run for the goose all the same, she'll be the one. My third question is this: Is the young lady impatient? Does she want apples in winter?

GRUSHA Impatient? No. But if a man goes to war without any reason and then no message comes — that's bad.

SIMON A message will come. And now my final question . . .

GRUSHA Simon Shashava, I must get to the third courtyard at once. My answer is yes.

SIMON (*Very embarrassed*)   Haste, they say, is the wind that blows down the scaffolding. But they also say: The rich don't know what haste is. I'm from ...

GRUSHA   Kutsk ...

SIMON   So the young lady has been inquiring about me? I'm healthy, I have no dependants, I make ten piasters a month, as paymaster twenty piasters, and I'm asking — very sincerely — for your hand.

GRUSHA   Simon Shashava, it suits me well.

SIMON (*Taking from his neck a thin chain with a little cross on it*)   My mother gave me this cross, Grusha Vashnadze. The chain is silver. Please wear it.

GRUSHA   Many thanks, Simon.

SIMON (*Hangs it round her neck*)   It would be better for the young lady to go to the third courtyard now. Or there'll be difficulties. Anyway, I must harness the horses. The young lady will understand?

GRUSHA   Yes, Simon. (THEY *stand undecided*)

SIMON   I'll just take the mistress to the troops that have stayed loyal. When the war's over, I'll be back. In two weeks. Or three. I hope my intended won't get tired, awaiting my return.

GRUSHA   Simon Shashava, I shall wait for you.

Go calmly into battle, soldier
The bloody battle, the bitter battle
From which not everyone returns:
When you return I shall be there.
I shall be waiting for you under the green elm
I shall be waiting for you under the bare elm
I shall wait until the last soldier has returned
And longer.
When you come back from the battle
No boots will stand at my door
The pillow beside mine will be empty
And my mouth will be unkissed.
When you return, when you return
You will be able to say: It is just as it was.

SIMON   I thank you, Grusha Vashnadze. And goodbye! (HE *bows low before her.* SHE *does the same before him. Then* SHE *runs quickly off without looking round. Enter the* ADJUTANT *from the gateway*)

THE ADJUTANT (*Harshly*)   Harness the horses to the carriage! Don't stand there doing nothing, louse! (SIMON SHASHAVA *stands to attention and goes off*)

(TWO SERVANTS *crowd from the gateway, bent low under huge trunks. Behind them, supported by her* WOMEN, *stumbles* NATELLA ABASHWILI. SHE *is followed by a* WOMAN *carrying the* CHILD)

THE GOVERNOR'S WIFE   I hardly know if my head's still on. Where's Michael? Don't hold him so clumsily. Pile the trunks onto the carriage. Shalva, is there no news from the city?

THE ADJUTANT   None. All's quiet so far, but there's not a minute to lose. No room for all these trunks in the carriage. Pick out what you need.

(*Exit quickly*)

THE GOVERNOR'S WIFE   Only essentials! Quick, open the trunks! I'll tell you what I need. (*The trunks are lowered and opened.* SHE *points at some brocade dresses*) The green one! And, of course, the one with the fur trimming. Where are Niko Mikadze and Mika Loladze? I've suddenly got the most terrible migraine again. It always starts in the temples.

(*Enter* GRUSHA)

Taking your time, eh? Go at once and get the hot water bottles! (GRUSHA *runs off, returns later with hot water bottles; the* GOVERNOR'S WIFE *orders her about by signs*) Don't tear the sleeves.

A YOUNG WOMAN   Pardon, madam, no harm has come to the dress.

THE GOVERNOR'S WIFE   Because I stopped you. I've been watching you for a long time. Nothing in your head but making eyes at Shalva Tzereteli. I'll kill you, you bitch! (SHE *beats the woman*)

THE ADJUTANT (*Appearing in the gateway*)   Please make haste, Natella Abashwili. Firing has broken out in the city.

(*Exit*)

THE GOVERNOR'S WIFE (*Letting go of the* YOUNG WOMAN)   Oh dear, do you think they'll lay hands on us? Why should they? Why? (SHE *herself begins to rummage in the trunks*) How's Michael? Asleep?

THE WOMAN WITH THE CHILD   Yes, madam.

THE GOVERNOR'S WIFE   Then put him down a moment and get my little saffron-colored boots from the bedroom. I need them for the green dress. (*The* WOMAN *puts down the* CHILD *and goes off*) Just look how these things have been packed! No love! No understanding! If you don't give them every order yourself . . . At such moments you realize what kind of servants you have! They gorge themselves at your expense, and never a word of gratitude! I'll remember this.

THE ADJUTANT (*Entering, very excited*)   Natella, you must leave at once!

THE GOVERNOR'S WIFE   Why? I've got to take this silver dress — it cost a thousand piasters. And that one there, and where's the wine-colored one?

THE ADJUTANT (*Trying to pull her away*)   Riots have broken out! We must leave at once. Where's the baby?

THE GOVERNOR'S WIFE (*Calling to the* YOUNG WOMAN *who was holding the baby*) Maro, get the baby ready! Where on earth are you?

THE ADJUTANT (*Leaving*)   We'll probably have to leave the carriage behind and go ahead on horseback.

(*The* GOVERNOR'S WIFE *rummages again among her dresses, throws some onto the heap of chosen clothes, then takes them off again. Noises, drums are heard. The* YOUNG WOMAN *who was beaten creeps away. The sky begins to grow red*)

THE GOVERNOR'S WIFE (*Rummaging desperately*)   I simply cannot find the wine-colored dress. Take the whole pile to the carriage. Where's Asja? And why hasn't Maro come back? Have you all gone crazy?

THE ADJUTANT (*Returning*)   Quick! Quick!

THE GOVERNOR'S WIFE (*To the* FIRST WOMAN)   Run! Just throw them into the carriage!

THE ADJUTANT   We're not taking the carriage. And if you don't come now, I'll ride off on my own.

THE GOVERNOR'S WIFE (*As the* FIRST WOMAN *can't carry everything*)   Where's the bitch Asja? (*The* ADJUTANT *pulls her away*) Maro, bring the baby! (*To the* FIRST WOMAN) Go and look for Masha. No, first take the dresses to the carriage. Such nonsense! I wouldn't dream of going on horseback! (*Turning round,* SHE *sees the red sky, and starts back rigid. The fire burns.*

SHE *is pulled out by the* ADJUTANT. *Shaking, the* FIRST WOMAN *follows with the dresses*)

MARO (*From the doorway with the boots*) Madam! (SHE *sees the trunks and dresses and runs toward the* BABY, *picks it up, and holds it a moment*) They left it behind, the beasts. (SHE *hands it to* GRUSHA) Hold it a moment. (SHE *runs off, following the* GOVERNOR'S WIFE)

(*Enter* SERVANTS *from the gateway*)

THE COOK Well, so they've actually gone. Without the food wagons, and not a minute too early. It's time for us to clear out.

A GROOM This'll be an unhealthy neighborhood for quite a while. (*To one of the* WOMEN) Suliko, take a few blankets and wait for me in the foal stables.

GRUSHA What have they done with the governor?

THE GROOM (*Gesturing throat cutting*) Ffffft.

A FAT WOMAN (*Seeing the gesture and becoming hysterical*) Oh dear, oh dear, oh dear, oh dear! Our master Georgi Abashwili! A picture of health he was, at the Morning Mass — and now! Oh, take me away, we're all lost, we must die in sin like our master, Georgi Abashwili!

THE OTHER WOMAN (*Soothing her*) Calm down, Nina! You'll be taken to safety. You've never hurt a fly.

THE FAT WOMAN (*Being led out*) Oh dear, oh dear, oh dear! Quick! Let's all get out before they come, before they come!

A YOUNG WOMAN Nina takes it more to heart than the mistress, that's a fact. They even have to have their weeping done for them.

THE COOK We'd better get out, all of us.

ANOTHER WOMAN (*Glancing back*) That must be the East Gate burning.

THE YOUNG WOMAN (*Seeing the* CHILD *in* GRUSHA'S *arms*) The baby! What are you doing with it?

GRUSHA It got left behind.

THE YOUNG WOMAN She simply left it there. Michael, who was kept out of all the drafts!

(*The* SERVANTS *gather round the* CHILD)

GRUSHA He's waking up.

THE GROOM Better put him down, I tell you. I'd rather not think what'd happen to anybody who was found with that baby.

THE COOK That's right. Once they get started, they'll kill each other off, whole families at a time. Let's go.

(*Exeunt all but* GRUSHA, *with the* CHILD *on her arm, and* TWO WOMEN)

THE TWO WOMEN Didn't you hear? Better put him down.

GRUSHA The nurse asked me to hold him a moment.

THE OLDER WOMAN She's not coming back, you simpleton.

THE YOUNGER WOMAN Keep your hands off it.

THE OLDER WOMAN (*Amiably*) Grusha, you're a good soul, but you're not very bright, and you know it. I tell you, if he had the plague he couldn't be more dangerous.

GRUSHA (*Stubbornly*) He hasn't got the plague. He looks at me! He's human!

THE OLDER WOMAN Don't look at *him*. You're a fool — the kind that always gets put upon. A person need only say, "Run for the salad, you have the longest legs," and you run. My husband has an ox cart — you can come with us if you hurry! Lord, by now the whole neighborhood must be in flames.

(BOTH WOMEN *leave, sighing. After some hesitation,* GRUSHA *puts the sleeping*

CHILD *down, looks at it for a moment, then takes a brocade blanket from the heap of clothes and covers it. Then* BOTH WOMEN *return, dragging bundles.* GRUSHA *starts guiltily away from the* CHILD *and walks a few steps to one side*)

THE YOUNGER WOMAN Haven't you packed anything yet? There isn't much time, you know. The Ironshirts will be here from the barracks.

GRUSHA Coming. (SHE *runs through the doorway.* BOTH WOMEN *go to the gateway and wait. The sound of horses is heard.* THEY *flee, screaming*)

(*Enter the* FAT PRINCE *with drunken* IRONSHIRTS. *One of them carries the governor's head on a lance*)

THE FAT PRINCE Here! In the middle! (ONE SOLDIER *climbs onto the other's back, takes the head, holds it tentatively over the door*) That's not the middle. Farther to the right. That's it. What I do, my friends, I do well. (*While, with hammer and nail, the* SOLDIER *fastens the head to the wall by its hair*) This morning at the church door I said to Georgi Abashwili: "I love a clear sky." Actually, I prefer the lightning that comes out of a clear sky. Yes, indeed. It's a pity they took the brat along, though, I need him, urgently. (*Exit, with* IRONSHIRTS *through the gateway. Trampling of horses again. Enter* GRUSHA *through the doorway looking cautiously about her. Clearly* SHE *has waited for the* IRONSHIRTS *to go. Carrying a bundle,* SHE *walks toward the gateway. At the last moment,* SHE *turns to see if the* CHILD *is still there. Catching sight of the head over the doorway,* SHE *screams. Horrified,* SHE *picks up her bundle again, and is about to leave when the* SINGER *starts to speak.* SHE *stands rooted to the spot*)

THE SINGER   As she was standing between courtyard and gate,
She heard or she thought she heard a low voice calling.
The child called to her,
Not whining, but calling quite sensibly,
Or so it seemed to her.
"Woman," it said, "help me."
And it went on, not whining, but saying quite sensibly:
"Know, woman, he who hears not a cry for help
But passes by with troubled ears will never hear
The gentle call of a lover nor the blackbird at dawn
Nor the happy sigh of the tired grape-picker as the Angelus rings."
(SHE *walks a few steps toward the* CHILD *and bends over it*)
Hearing this she went back for one more look at the child:
Only to sit with him for a moment or two,
Only till someone should come,
His mother, or anyone.
(*Leaning on a trunk,* SHE *sits facing the* CHILD)
Only till she would have to leave, for the danger was too great,
The city was full of flame and crying.
(*The light grows dimmer, as though evening and night were coming on*)
Fearful is the seductive power of goodness!
(GRUSHA *now settles down to watch over the* CHILD *through the night. Once,* SHE *lights a small lamp to look at it. Once,* SHE *tucks it in with a coat. From time to time* SHE *listens and looks to see whether someone is coming*)
And she sat with the child a long time,
Till evening came, till night came, till dawn came.

She sat too long, too long she saw
The soft breathing, the small clenched fists,
Till toward morning the seduction was complete
And she rose, and bent down and, sighing, took the child
And carried it away.
(SHE *does what the* SINGER *says as* HE *describes it*)
As if it was stolen goods she picked it up.
As if she was a thief she crept away.

2. The Flight into the Northern Mountains

THE SINGER When Grusha Vashnadze left the city
    On the Grusinian highway
    On the way to the Northern Mountains
    She sang a song, she bought some milk.
THE CHORUS How will this human child escape
    The bloodhounds, the trap-setters?
    Into the deserted mountains she journeyed
    Along the Grusinian highway she journeyed
    She sang a song, she bought some milk.
    (GRUSHA VASHNADZE *walks on. On her back* SHE *carries the* CHILD *in a sack,
    in one hand is a large stick, in the other a bundle.* SHE *sings*)

The Song of the Four Generals

Four generals
Set out for Iran.
With the first one, war did not agree.
The second never won a victory.
For the third the weather never was right.
For the fourth the men would never fight.
Four generals
And not a single man!

Sosso Robakidse
Went marching to Iran
With him the war did so agree
He soon had won a victory.
For him the weather was always right.
For him the men would always fight.
Sosso Robakidse,
He is our man!

(*A peasant's cottage appears*)

GRUSHA (*To the* CHILD) Noontime is meal time. Now we'll sit hopefully in the
    grass, while the good Grusha goes and buys a little pitcher of milk. (SHE
    lays the CHILD *down and knocks at the cottage door. An* OLD MAN *opens it*)
    Grandfather, could I have a little pitcher of milk? And a corn cake, maybe?
THE OLD MAN Milk? We have no milk. The soldiers from the city have our
    goats. Go to the soldiers if you want milk.

GRUSHA   But grandfather, you must have a little pitcher of milk for a baby?

THE OLD MAN   And for a God-bless-you, eh?

GRUSHA   Who said anything about a God-bless-you? (SHE *shows her purse*) We'll pay like princes. "Head in the clouds, backside in the water." (*The* PEASANT *goes off, grumbling, for milk*) How much for the milk?

THE OLD MAN   Three piasters. Milk has gone up.

GRUSHA   Three piasters for this little drop? (*Without a word the* OLD MAN *shuts the door in her face*) Michael, did you hear that? Three piasters! We can't afford it! (SHE *goes back, sits down again and gives the* CHILD *her breast*) Suck. Think of the three piasters. There's nothing there, but you *think* you're drinking, and that's something. (*Shaking her head,* SHE *sees that the* CHILD *isn't sucking any more.* SHE *gets up, walks back to the door, and knocks again*) Open grandfather, we'll pay. (*Softly*) May lightning strike you! (*When the* OLD MAN *appears*) I thought it would be half a piaster. But the baby must be fed. How about one piaster for that little drop?

THE OLD MAN.   Two.

GRUSHA   Don't shut the door again. (SHE *fishes a long time in her bag*) Here are two piasters. The milk better be good. I still have two days' journey ahead of me. It's a murderous business you have here — and sinful, too!

THE OLD MAN   Kill the soldiers if you want milk.

GRUSHA (*Giving the* CHILD *some milk*)   This is an expensive joke. Take a sip, Michael, it's a week's pay. Around here they think we earned our money just sitting around. Oh, Michael, Michael, you're a nice little load for a girl to take on! (*Uneasy,* SHE *gets up, puts the* CHILD *on her back, and walks on. The* OLD MAN, *grumbling, picks up the pitcher and looks after her unmoved*)

THE SINGER   As Grusha Vashnadze went northward

The Princes' Ironshirts went after her.

THE CHORUS   How will the barefoot girl escape the Ironshirts,

The bloodhounds, the trap-setters?

They hunt even by night.

Pursuers never tire.

Butchers sleep little.

(TWO IRONSHIRTS *are trudging along the highway*)

THE CORPORAL   You'll never amount to anything, blockhead, your heart's not in it. Your senior officer sees this in little things. Yesterday, when I made the fat gal, yes, you grabbed her husband as I commanded, and you did kick him in the stomach, at my request, but did you *enjoy* it, like a loyal Private, or were you just doing your duty? I've kept an eye on you blockhead, you're a hollow reed and a tinkling cymbal, you won't get promoted. (THEY *walk a while in silence*) Don't think I've forgotten how insubordinate you are, either. Stop limping! I forbid you to limp! You limp because I sold the horses, and I sold the horses because I'd never have got that price again. You limp to show me you don't like marching. I know you. It won't help. You wait. Sing!

THE TWO IRONSHIRTS (*Singing*)   Sadly to war I went my way

Leaving my loved one at her door.

My friends will keep her honor safe

Till from the war I'm back once more.

THE CORPORAL   Louder!

THE TWO IRONSHIRTS (*Singing*)   When 'neath a headstone I shall be
My love a little earth will bring:
"Here rest the feet that oft would run to me
And here the arms that oft to me would cling."
(THEY *begin to walk again in silence*)

THE CORPORAL   A good soldier has his heart and soul in it. When he receives an order, he gets a hard on, and when he drives his lance into the enemy's guts, he comes. (HE *shouts for joy*) He lets himself be torn to bits for his superior officer, and as he lies dying he takes note that his corporal is nodding approval, and that is reward enough, it's his dearest wish. *You* won't get any nod of approval, but you'll croak all right. Christ, how'm I to get my hands on the Governor's bastard with the help of a fool like you! (THEY *stay on the stage behind*)

THE SINGER   When Grusha Vashnadze came to the River Sirra
Flight grew too much for her, the helpless child too heavy.
In the cornfields the rosy dawn
Is cold to the sleepless one, only cold.
The gay clatter of the milk cans in the farmyard where the smoke rises
Is only a threat to the fugitive.
She who carries the child feels its weight and little more.
(GRUSHA *stops in front of a farm. A* FAT PEASANT WOMAN *is carrying a milk can through the door.* GRUSHA *waits until* SHE *has gone in, then approaches the house cautiously*)

GRUSHA (*To the* CHILD)   Now you've wet yourself again, and you know I've no linen. Michael, this is where we part company. It's far enough from the city. They wouldn't want you *so* much that they'd follow you all *this* way, little good-for-nothing. The peasant woman is kind, and can't you just smell the milk? (SHE *bends down to lay the* CHILD *on the threshold*) So farewell. Michael, I'll forget how you kicked me in the back all night to make me walk faster. And you can forget the meager fare — it was meant well. I'd like to have kept you — your nose is so tiny — but it can't be. I'd have shown you your first rabbit, I'd have trained you to keep dry, but now I must turn around. My sweetheart the soldier might be back soon, and suppose he didn't find me? You can't ask that, can you?
(SHE *creeps up to the door and lays the* CHILD *on the threshold. Then, hiding behind a tree,* SHE *waits until the* PEASANT WOMAN *opens the door and sees the bundle*)

THE PEASANT WOMAN   Good heavens, what's this? Husband!

THE PEASANT   What is it? Let me finish my soup.

THE PEASANT WOMAN (*To the* CHILD)   Where's your mother then? Haven't you got one? It's a boy. Fine linen. He's from a good family, you can see that. And they just leave him on our doorstep. Oh, these are times!

THE PEASANT   If you think we're going to feed it, they're wrong. You can take it to the priest in the village. That's the best we can do.

THE PEASANT WOMAN   What'll the priest do with him? He needs a mother. There, he's waking up. Don't you think we could keep him, though?

THE PEASANT (*Shouting*)   No!

THE PEASANT WOMAN   I could lay him in the corner by the armchair. All I need is a crib. I can take him into the fields with me. See him laughing?

Husband, we have a roof over our heads. We can do it. Not another word out of you!

(SHE *carries the* CHILD *into the house. The* PEASANT *follows protesting.* GRUSHA *steps out from behind the tree, laughs, and hurries off in the opposite direction*)

THE SINGER   Why so cheerful, making for home?

THE CHORUS   Because the child has won new parents with a laugh,

Because I'm rid of the little one, I'm cheerful.

THE SINGER   And why so sad?

THE CHORUS   Because I'm single and free, I'm sad

Like someone who's been robbed

Someone who's newly poor.

(SHE WALKS *for a short while, then meets the* TWO IRONSHIRTS, *who point their lances at her*)

THE CORPORAL   Lady, you are running straight into the arms of the Armed Forces. Where are you coming from? And when? Are you having illicit relations with the enemy? Where is he hiding? What movements is he making in your rear? How about the hills? How about the valleys? How are your stockings fastened? (GRUSHA *stands there frightened*) Don't be scared, we always stage a retreat, if necessary . . . what, blockhead? I always stage retreats. In that respect at least, I can be relied on. Why are you staring like that at my lance? In the field no soldier drops his lance, that's a rule. Learn it by heart, blockhead. Now, lady, where are you headed?

GRUSHA   To meet my intended, one Simon Shashava, of the Palace Guard in Nuka.

THE CORPORAL   Simon Shashava? Sure, I know him. He gave me a key so I could look you up once in a while. Blockhead, we are getting to be unpopular. We must make her realize we have honorable intentions. Lady, behind apparent frivolity I conceal a serious nature, so let me tell you officially: I want a child from you. (GRUSHA *utters a little scream*) Blockhead, she understood me. Uh-huh, isn't it a sweet shock? "Then first I must take the noodles out of the oven, Officer. Then first I must change my torn shirt, Colonel." But away with jokes, away with my lance! We are looking for a baby. A baby from a good family. Have you heard of such a baby, from the city, dressed in fine linen, and suddenly turning up here?

GRUSHA   No, I haven't heard a thing.

(*Suddenly* SHE *turns round and runs back, panic-stricken. The* IRONSHIRTS *glance at each other, then follow her, cursing*)

THE SINGER   Run, kind girl! The killers are coming!

Help the helpless babe, helpless girl!

And so she runs!

THE CHORUS   In the bloodiest times

There are kind people.

(*As* GRUSHA *rushes into the cottage, the* PEASANT WOMAN *is bending over the* CHILD'S *crib*)

GRUSHA   Hide him. Quick! The Ironshirts are coming! I laid him on your doorstep. But he isn't mine. He's from a good family.

THE PEASANT WOMAN   Who's coming? What Ironshirts?

GRUSHA   Don't ask questions. The Ironshirts that are looking for it.

THE PEASANT WOMAN They've no business in my house. But I must have a little talk with you, it seems.

GRUSHA Take off the fine linen. It'll give us away.

THE PEASANT WOMAN Linen, my foot! In this house I make the decisions! "*You* can't vomit in *my* room!" Why did you abandon it? It's a sin.

GRUSHA (*Looking out of the window*) Look, they're coming out from behind those trees! I shouldn't have run away, it made them angry. Oh, what shall I do?

THE PEASANT WOMAN (*Looking out of the window and suddenly starting with fear*) Gracious! Ironshirts!

GRUSHA They're after the baby.

THE PEASANT WOMAN Suppose they come in!

GRUSHA You mustn't give him to them. Say he's yours.

THE PEASANT WOMAN Yes.

GRUSHA They'll run him through if you hand him over.

THE PEASANT WOMAN But suppose they ask for it? The silver for the harvest is in the house.

GRUSHA If you let them have him, they'll run him through, right here in this room! You've got to say he's yours!

THE PEASANT WOMAN Yes. But what if they don't believe me?

GRUSHA You must be firm.

THE PEASANT WOMAN They'll burn the roof over our heads.

GRUSHA That's why you must say he's yours. His name's Michael. But I shouldn't have told you. (*The* PEASANT WOMAN *nods*) Don't nod like that. And don't tremble — they'll notice.

THE PEASANT WOMAN Yes.

GRUSHA And stop saying yes, I can't stand it. (SHE *shakes the* WOMAN) Don't you have any children?

THE PEASANT WOMAN (*Muttering*) He's in the war.

GRUSHA Then maybe *he's* an Ironshirt? Do you want *him* to run children through with a lance? You'd bawl him out. "No fooling with lances in *my* house!" you'd shout, "is that what I've reared you for? Wash your neck before you speak to your mother!"

THE PEASANT WOMAN That's true, he couldn't get away with anything around here!

GRUSHA So you'll say he's yours?

THE PEASANT WOMAN Yes.

GRUSHA Look! They're coming!

(*There is a knocking at the door. The* WOMEN *don't answer. Enter* IRON-SHIRTS. *The* PEASANT WOMAN *bows low*)

THE CORPORAL Well, here she is. What did I tell you? What a nose I have! I *smelt* her. Lady, I have a question for you. Why did you run away? What did you think I would do to you? I'll bet it was something dirty. Confess!

GRUSHA (*While the* PEASANT WOMAN *bows again and again*) I'd left some milk on the stove, and I suddenly remembered it.

THE CORPORAL Or maybe you imagined I looked at you in a dirty way? Like there could be something between us? A lewd sort of look, know what I mean?

GRUSHA I didn't see it.

THE CORPORAL   But it's possible, huh? You admit that much. After all, I might be a pig. I'll be frank with you: I could think of all sorts of things if we were alone. (*To the* PEASANT WOMAN) Shouldn't you be busy in the yard? Feeding the hens?

THE PEASANT WOMAN (*falling suddenly to her knees*)   Soldier, I didn't know a thing about it. Please don't burn the roof over our heads.

THE CORPORAL   What are you talking about?

THE PEASANT WOMAN   I had nothing to do with it. She left it on my doorstep, I swear it!

THE CORPORAL (*Suddenly seeing the* CHILD *and whistling*)   Ah, so there's a little something in the crib! Blockhead, I smell a thousand piasters. Take the old girl outside and hold on to her. It looks like I have a little cross-examining to do.

(*The* PEASANT WOMAN *lets herself be led out by the* PRIVATE, *without a word*)
So, you've got the child I wanted from you! (HE *walks toward the crib*)

GRUSHA   Officer, he's mine. He's not the one you're after.

THE CORPORAL   I'll just take a look. (HE *bends over the crib.* GRUSHA *looks round in despair*)

GRUSHA   He's mine! He's mine!

THE CORPORAL   Fine linen!

(GRUSHA *dashes at him to pull him away.* HE *throws her off and again bends over the crib. Again looking round in despair,* SHE *sees a log of wood, seizes it, and hits the* CORPORAL *over the head from behind. The* CORPORAL *collapses.* SHE *quickly picks up the* CHILD *and rushes off*)

THE SINGER   And in her flight from the Ironshirts
After twenty-two days of journeying
At the foot of the Janga-Tu Glacier
Grusha Vashnadze decided to adopt the child.

THE CHORUS   The helpless girl adopted the helpless child.

(GRUSHA *squats over a half-frozen stream to get the* CHILD *water in the hollow of her hand*)

GRUSHA   Since no one else will take you, son,
I must take you.
Since no one else will take you, son,
You must take me.
O black day in a lean, lean year,
The trip was long, the milk was dear,
My legs are tired, my feet are sore:
But I wouldn't be without you any more.
I'll throw your silken shirt away
And dress you in rags and tatters.
I'll wash you, son, and christen you in glacier water.
We'll see it through together.

(SHE *has taken off the* CHILD's *fine linen and wrapped it in a rag*)

THE SINGER   When Grusha Vashnadze
Pursued by the Ironshirts
Came to the bridge on the glacier
Leading to the villages of the Eastern Slope
She sang the Song of the Rotten Bridge
And risked two lives.

(*A wind has risen. The bridge on the glacier is visible in the dark. One rope is broken and half the bridge is hanging down the abyss.* MERCHANTS, TWO MEN *and a* WOMAN, *stand undecided before the bridge as* GRUSHA *and the* CHILD *arrive.* ONE MAN *is trying to catch the hanging rope with a stick*)

THE FIRST MAN   Take your time, young woman. You won't get across here anyway.

GRUSHA   But I *have* to get the baby to the east side. To my brother's place.

THE MERCHANT WOMAN   Have to? How d'you mean, "have to"? I have to get there, too — because I have to buy carpets in Atum[5] — carpets a woman had to sell because her husband had to die. But can *I* do what I have to? Can she? Andrei's been fishing for that rope for hours. And I ask you, how are we going to fasten it, even if he gets it up?

THE FIRST MAN (*Listening*)   Hush, I think I hear something.

GRUSHA   The bridge isn't quite rotted through. I think I'll try it.

THE MERCHANT WOMAN   *I* wouldn't — if the devil himself were after me. It's suicide.

THE FIRST MAN (*Shouting*)   Hi!

GRUSHA   Don't shout! (*To the* MERCHANT WOMAN) Tell him not to shout.

THE FIRST MAN   But there's someone down there calling. Maybe they've lost their way.

THE MERCHANT WOMAN   Why shouldn't he shout? Is there something funny about you? Are they after you?

GRUSHA   All right, I'll tell. The Ironshirts are after me. I knocked one down.

THE SECOND MAN   Hide our merchandise!

(*The* WOMAN *hides a sack behind a rock*)

THE FIRST MAN   Why didn't you say so right away? (*To the* OTHERS) If they catch her they'll make mincemeat out of her!

GRUSHA   Get out of my way. I've got to cross that bridge.

THE SECOND MAN   You can't. The precipice is two thousand feet deep.

THE FIRST MAN   Even with the rope it'd be no use. We could hold it up with our hands. But then we'd have to do the same for the Ironshirts.

GRUSHA   Go away.

(*There are calls from the distance: "Hi, up there!"*)

THE MERCHANT WOMAN   They're getting near. But you can't take the child on that bridge. It's sure to break. And look!

(GRUSHA *looks down into the abyss. The* IRONSHIRTS *are heard calling again from below*)

THE SECOND MAN   Two thousand feet!

GRUSHA   But those men are worse.

THE FIRST MAN   You can't do it. Think of the baby. Risk your life but not a child's.

THE SECOND MAN   With the child she's that much heavier!

THE MERCHANT WOMAN   Maybe she's *really* got to get across. Give *me* the baby. I'll hide it. Cross the bridge alone!

GRUSHA   I won't. We belong together. (*To the* CHILD) "Live together, die together."

(SHE *sings*)

5. *Atum:* A trading center.

The Song of the Rotten Bridge

Deep is the abyss, son,
I see the weak bridge sway
But it's not for us, son,
To choose the way.

The way I know
Is the one you must tread,
And all you will eat
Is my bit of bread.

Of every four pieces
You shall have three.
Would that I knew
How big they will be!

Get out of my way, I'll try it without the rope.
THE MERCHANT WOMAN   You are tempting God!
   (*There are shouts from below*)
GRUSHA   Please, throw that stick away, or they'll get the rope and follow me.
   (*Pressing the* CHILD *to her,* SHE *steps onto the swaying bridge. The* MER-
   CHANT WOMAN *screams when it looks as though the bridge is about to col-
   lapse. But* GRUSHA *walks on and reaches the far side*)
THE FIRST MAN   She made it!
THE MERCHANT WOMAN (*Who has fallen on her knees and begun to pray, an-
   grily*)   I still think it was a sin.
   (*The* IRONSHIRTS *appear; the* CORPORAL'S *head is bandaged*)
THE CORPORAL   Seen a woman with a child?
THE FIRST MAN (*While the* SECOND MAN *throws the stick into the abyss*)   Yes,
   there! But the bridge won't carry you!
THE CORPORAL   You'll pay for this, blockhead!
   (GRUSHA, *from the far bank, laughs and shows the* CHILD *to the* IRONSHIRTS.
   SHE *walks on. The wind blows*)
GRUSHA (*Turning to the* CHILD)   You mustn't be afraid of the wind. He's a
   poor thing too. He has to push the clouds along and he gets quite cold do-
   ing it. (*Snow starts falling*) And the snow isn't so bad, either, Michael. It
   covers the little fir trees so they won't die in winter. Let me sing you a little
   song.
SHE *sings*)

The Song of the Child

Your father is a bandit
A harlot the mother who bore you.
Yet honorable men
Shall kneel down before you.

Food to the baby horses
The tiger's son will take.
The mothers will get milk
From the son of the snake.

3. In The Northern Mountains

THE SINGER   Seven days the sister, Grusha Vashnadze,
Journeyed across the glacier
And down the slopes she journeyed.
"When I enter my brother's house," she thought
"He will rise and embrace me."
"Is that you, sister?" he will say,
"I have long expected you.
This is my dear wife,
And this is my farm, come to me by marriage,
With eleven horses and thirty-one cows. Sit down.
Sit down with your child at our table and eat."
The brother's house was in a lovely valley.
When the sister came to the brother,
She was ill from walking.
The brother rose from the table.

(*A* FAT PEASANT COUPLE *rise from the table.* LAVRENTI VASHNADZE *still has a napkin round his neck, as* GRUSHA, *pale and supported by a* SERVANT, *enters with the* CHILD)

LAVRENTI   Where've *you* come from, Grusha?

GRUSHA (*Feebly*)   Across the Janga-Tu Pass, Lavrenti.

THE SERVANT   I found her in front of the hay barn. She has a baby with her.

THE SISTER-IN-LAW   Go and groom the mare.

(*Exit the* SERVANT)

LAVRENTI   This is my wife Aniko.

THE SISTER-IN-LAW   I thought you were in service in Nuka.

GRUSHA (*Barely able to stand*)   Yes, I was.

THE SISTER-IN-LAW   Wasn't it a good job? We were told it was.

GRUSHA   The Governor got killed.

LAVRENTI   Yes, we heard there were riots. Your aunt told us. Remember, Aniko?

THE SISTER-IN-LAW   Here with us, it's very quiet. City people always want something going on. (SHE *walks toward the door, calling*) Sosso, Sosso, don't take the cake out of the oven yet, d'you hear? Where on earth are you?

(*Exit, calling*)

LAVRENTI (*Quietly, quickly*)   Is there a father? (*As* SHE *shakes her head*) I thought not. We must think up something. She's religious.

THE SISTER-IN-LAW (*Returning*)   Those servants! (*To* GRUSHA) You have a child.

GRUSHA   It's mine.

(SHE *collapses.* LAVRENTI *rushes to her assistance*)

THE SISTER-IN-LAW   Heavens, she's ill — what are we going to do?

LAVRENTI (*Escorting her to a bench near the stove*)   Sit down, sit. I think it's just weakness, Aniko.

THE SISTER-IN-LAW   As long as it's not scarlet fever!

LAVRENTI   She'd have spots if it was. It's only weakness. Don't worry, Aniko. (*To* GRUSHA) Better, sitting down?

THE SISTER-IN-LAW   Is the child hers?

GRUSHA   Yes, mine.

LAVRENTI   She's on her way to her husband.

THE SISTER-IN-LAW   I see. Your meat's getting cold. (LAVRENTI *sits down and begins to eat*) Cold food's not good for you, the fat mustn't get cold, you know your stomach's your weak spot. (*To* GRUSHA) If your husband's not in the city, where is he?

LAVRENTI   She got married on the other side of the mountain, she says.

THE SISTER-IN-LAW   On the other side of the mountain. I see. (SHE *also sits down to eat*)

GRUSHA   I think I should lie down somewhere, Lavrenti.

THE SISTER-IN-LAW   If it's consumption we'll all get it. (SHE *goes on cross-examining her*) Has your husband got a farm?

GRUSHA   He's a soldier.

LAVRENTI   But he's coming into a farm — a small one — from his father.

THE SISTER-IN-LAW   Isn't he in the war? Why not?

GRUSHA (*With effort*)   Yes, he's in the war.

THE SISTER-IN-LAW   Then why d'you want to go to the farm?

LAVRENTI   When he comes back from the war, he'll return to his farm.

THE SISTER-IN-LAW   But you're going there now?

LAVRENTI   Yes, to wait for him.

THE SISTER-IN-LAW (*Calling shrilly*)   Sosso, the cake!

GRUSHA (*Murmuring feverishly*)   A farm — a soldier — waiting — sit down, eat.

THE SISTER-IN-LAW   It's scarlet fever.

GRUSHA (*Starting up*)   Yes, he's got a farm!

LAVRENTI   I think it's just weakness. Aniko. Would you look after the cake yourself, dear?

THE SISTER-IN-LAW   But when will he come back if war's broken out again as people say? (SHE *waddles off, shouting*) Sosso! Where on earth are you? Sosso!

LAVRENTI (*Getting up quickly and going to* GRUSHA)   You'll get a bed in a minute. She has a good heart. But wait till after supper.

GRUSHA (*Holding out the* CHILD *to him*)   Take him.

LAVRENTI (*Taking it and looking around*)   But you can't stay here long with the child. She's religious, you see.

(GRUSHA *collapses.* LAVRENTI *catches her*)

THE SINGER   The sister was so ill,

The cowardly brother had to give her shelter.

Summer departed, winter came.

The winter was long, the winter was short

People mustn't know anything,

Rats mustn't bite,

Spring mustn't come.

(GRUSHA *sits over the weaving loom in a workroom.* SHE *and the* CHILD, *who is squatting on the floor, are wrapped in blankets.*)

(SHE *sings*)

The Song of the Center

And the lover started to leave

And his betrothed ran pleading after him

Pleading and weeping, weeping and teaching:

"Dearest mine, dearest mine
When you go to war as now you do
When you fight the foe as soon you will
Don't lead with the front line
And don't push with the rear line
At the front is red fire
In the rear is red smoke
Stay in the war's center
Stay near the standard bearer
The first always die
The last are also hit
Those in the center come home."

Michael, we must be clever. If we make ourselves as small as cockroaches, the sister-in law will forget we're in the house, and then we can stay till the snow melts.

(*Enter* LAVRENTI. HE *sits down beside his* SISTER)

LAVRENTI   Why are you sitting there muffled up like coachmen, you two? Is it too cold in the room?

GRUSHA (*Hastily removing one shawl*)   It's not too cold, Lavrenti.

LAVRENTI   If it's too cold, you shouldn't be sitting here with the child. Aniko would never forgive herself! (*Pause*) I hope our priest didn't question you about the child?

GRUSHA   He did, but I didn't tell him anything.

LAVRENTI   That's good. I wanted to speak to you about Aniko. She has a good heart but she's very, very sensitive. People need only mention our farm and she's worried. She takes everything hard, you see. One time our milkmaid went to church with a hole in her stocking. Ever since, Aniko has worn two pairs of stockings in church. It's the old family in her. (HE *listens*) Are you sure there are no rats around? If there are rats, you couldn't live here.

(*There are sounds as of dripping from the roof*)

What's that, dripping?

GRUSHA   It must be a barrel leaking.

LAVRENTI   Yes, it must be a barrel. You've been here six months, haven't you? Was I talking about Aniko? (THEY *listen again to the snow melting*) You can't imagine how worried she gets about your soldier-husband. "Suppose he comes back and can't find her!" she says and lies awake. "He can't come before the spring," I tell her. The dear woman! (*The drops begin to fall faster*) When d'you think he'll come? What do *you* think? (GRUSHA *is silent*) Not before the spring, you agree? (GRUSHA *is silent*) You don't be-lieve he'll come at all? (GRUSHA *is silent*) But when the spring comes and the snow melts here and on the passes, you can't stay on. They may come and look for you. There's already talk of an illegitimate child. (*The "glock-enspiel" of the falling drops has grown faster and steadier*) Grusha, the snow is melting on the roof. Spring is here.

GRUSHA   Yes.

LAVRENTI (*Eagerly*)   I'll tell you what we'll do. You need a place to go, and, because of the child, (HE *sighs*) you have to have a husband, so people won't talk. Now I've made cautious inquiries to see if we can find you a husband. Grusha, I *have* one. I talked to a peasant woman who has a son. Just the other side of the mountain. A small farm. And she's willing.

GRUSHA But I *can't* marry! I must wait for Simon Shashava.

LAVRENTI Of course. That's all been taken care of. You don't need a man in bed — you need a man on paper. And I've found you one. The son of this peasant woman is going to die. Isn't that wonderful? He's at his last gasp. And all in line with our story — a husband from the other side of the mountain! And when you met him he was at the last gasp. So you're a widow. What do you say?

GRUSHA It's true I could use a document with stamps on it for Michael.

LAVRENTI Stamps make all the difference. Without something in writing the Shah couldn't prove he's a Shah. And you'll have a place to live.

GRUSHA How much does the peasant woman want?

LAVRENTI Four hundred piasters.

GRUSHA Where will you find it?

LAVRENTI (*Guiltily*) Aniko's milk money.

GRUSHA No one would know us there. I'll do it.

LAVRENTI (*Getting up*) I'll let the peasant woman know.

(*Quick exit*)

GRUSHA Michael, you cause a lot of fuss. I came to you as the pear tree comes to the sparrows. And because a Christian bends down and picks up a crust of bread so nothing will go to waste. Michael, it would have been better had I walked quickly away on that Easter Sunday in Nuka in the second courtyard. Now I *am* a fool.

THE SINGER The bridegroom was lying on his deathbed when the bride arrived. The bridegroom's mother was waiting at the door, telling her to hurry. The bride brought a child along. The witness hid it during the wedding.

(*On one side the bed. Under the mosquito net lies a very* SICK MAN. GRUSHA *is pulled in at a run by her future* MOTHER-IN-LAW. THEY *are followed by* LAVRENTI *and the* CHILD)

THE MOTHER-IN-LAW Quick! Quick! Or he'll die on us before the wedding. (*To* LAVRENTI) I was never told she had a child already.

LAVRENTI What difference does it make? (*Pointing toward the* DYING MAN) It can't matter to him — in his condition.

THE MOTHER-IN-LAW To him? But *I'll* never survive the shame! We are honest people. (SHE *begins to weep*) My Jussup doesn't have to marry a girl with a child!

LAVRENTI All right, make it another two hundred piasters. You'll have it in writing that the farm will go to you: but she'll have the right to live here for two years.

THE MOTHER-IN-LAW (*Drying her tears*) It'll hardly cover the funeral expenses. I hope she'll really lend a hand with the work. And what's happened to the monk? He must have slipped out through the kitchen window. We'll have the whole village round our necks when they hear Jussup's end is come! Oh dear! I'll run and get the monk. But he mustn't see the child!

LAVRENTI I'll take care he doesn't. But why only a monk? Why not a priest?

THE MOTHER-IN-LAW Oh, he's just as good. I only made one mistake: I paid half his fee in advance. Enough to send him to the tavern. I only hope . . . (SHE *runs off*)

LAVRENTI She saved on the priest, the wretch! Hired a cheap monk.

GRUSHA You *will* send Simon Shashava over to see me if he turns up after all?

LAVRENTI Yes. (*Pointing at the* SICK MAN) Won't you take a look at him?

(GRUSHA, *taking* MICHAEL *to her, shakes her head*)

He's not moving an eyelid. I hope we aren't too late.

(THEY *listen. On the opposite side enter* NEIGHBORS *who look around and take up positions against the walls, thus forming another wall near the bed, yet leaving an opening so that the bed can be seen.* THEY *start murmuring prayers. Enter the* MOTHER-IN-LAW *with a* MONK. *Showing some annoyance and surprise,* SHE *bows to the* GUESTS)

THE MOTHER-IN-LAW I hope you won't mind waiting a few moments? My son's bride has just arrived from the city. An emergency wedding is about to be celebrated. (*To the* MONK *in the bedroom*) I might have known you couldn't keep your trap shut. (*To* GRUSHA) The wedding can take place at once. Here's the license. I myself and the bride's brother (LAVRENTI *tries to hide in the background, after having quietly taken* MICHAEL *back from* GRUSHA. *The* MOTHER-IN-LAW *waves him away*), who will be here in a moment, are the witnesses.

(GRUSHA *has bowed to the* MONK. THEY *go to the bed. The* MOTHER-IN-LAW *lifts the mosquito net. The* MONK *starts reeling off the marriage ceremony in Latin. Meanwhile, the* MOTHER-IN-LAW *beckons to* LAVRENTI *to get rid of the* CHILD, *but fearing that it will cry* HE *draws its attention to the ceremony.* GRUSHA *glances once at the* CHILD, *and* LAVRENTI *waves the* CHILD's *hand in a greeting*)

THE MONK Are you prepared to be a faithful, obedient, and good wife to this man, and to cleave to him until death you do part?

GRUSHA (*Looking at the* CHILD) I am.

THE MONK (*To the* SICK PEASANT) And are you prepared to be a good and loving husband to your wife until death you do part?

(*As the sick* PEASANT *does not answer, the* MONK *looks inquiringly around*)

THE MOTHER-IN-LAW Of course he is! Didn't you hear him say yes?

THE MONK All right. We declare the marriage contracted! How about extreme unction?

THE MOTHER-IN-LAW Nothing doing! The wedding cost quite enough. Now I must take care of the mourners. (*To* LAVRENTI) Did we say seven hundred?

LAVRENTI Six hundred. (HE *pays*) Now I don't want to sit with the guests and get to know people. So farewell, Grusha, and if my widowed sister comes to visit me, she'll get a welcome from my wife, or I'll show my teeth. (*Nods, gives the* CHILD *to* GRUSHA, *and leaves*)

(*The* MOURNERS *glance after him without interest*)

THE MONK May one ask where this child comes from?

THE MOTHER-IN-LAW Is there a child? I don't see a child. And you don't see a child either — you understand? Or it may turn out I saw all sorts of things in the tavern! Now come on.

(*After* GRUSHA *has put the* CHILD *down and told him to be quiet,* THEY *move over left,* GRUSHA *is introduced to the* NEIGHBORS)

This is my daughter-in-law. She arrived just in time to find dear Jussup still alive.

ONE WOMAN He's been ill now a whole year, hasn't he? When our Vassili was drafted he was there to say goodbye.

ANOTHER WOMAN   Such things are terrible for a farm. The corn all ripe and the farmer in bed! It'll really be a blessing if he doesn't suffer too long, I say.

THE FIRST WOMAN (*Confidentially*)   You know why we thought he'd taken to his bed? Because of the draft! And now his end is come!

THE MOTHER-IN-LAW   Sit yourselves down, please! And have some cakes!

(SHE *beckons to* GRUSHA *and* BOTH WOMEN *go into the bedroom, where* THEY *pick up the cake pans off the floor. The* GUESTS, *among them the* MONK, *sit on the floor and begin conversing in subdued voices*)

ONE PEASANT (*To whom the* MONK *has handed the bottle which* HE *has taken from his soutane*)   There's a child, you say! How can that have happened to Jussup?

A WOMAN   She was certainly lucky to get herself hitched, with him so sick!

THE MOTHER-IN-LAW   They're gossiping already. And gorging themselves on the funeral cakes at the same time! If he doesn't die today, I'll have to bake some more tomorrow!

GRUSHA   I'll bake them for you.

THE MOTHER-IN-LAW   Yesterday some horsemen rode by, and I went out to see who it was. When I came in again he was lying there like a corpse! So I sent for you. I can't take much longer. (SHE *listens*)

THE MONK   Dear wedding and funeral guests! Deeply touched, we stand before a bed of death and marriage. The bride gets a veil; the groom, a shroud: how varied, my children, are the fates of men! Alas! One man dies and has a roof over his head, and the other is married and the flesh turns to dust from which it was made. Amen.

THE MOTHER-IN-LAW   He's getting his own back. I shouldn't have hired such a cheap one. It's what you'd expect. A more expensive monk would behave himself. In Sura there's one with a real air of sanctity about him, but of course he charges a fortune. A fifty-piaster monk like that has no dignity, and as for piety, just fifty piasters' worth and no more! When I came to get him in the tavern he'd just made a speech, and he was shouting: "The war is over, beware of the peace!" We must go in.

GRUSHA (*Giving* MICHAEL *a cake*)   Eat this cake, and keep nice and still, Michael.

(*The* TWO WOMEN *offer cakes to the* GUESTS. *The* DYING MAN *sits up in bed.* HE *puts his head out from under the mosquito net, stares at the* TWO WOMEN, *then sinks back again. The* MONK *takes two bottles from his soutane and offers them to the* PEASANT *beside him. Enter* THREE MUSICIANS *who are greeted with a sly wink by the* MONK)

THE MOTHER-IN-LAW (*To the* MUSICIANS)   What are you doing here? With instruments?

ONE MUSICIAN   Brother Anastasius here (*Points at the* MONK) told us there was a wedding on.

THE MOTHER-IN-LAW   What? You brought them? Three more on my neck! Don't you know there's a dying man in the next room?

THE MONK   A very tempting assignment for a musician: something that could be either a subdued Wedding March or a spirited Funeral Dance.

THE MOTHER-IN-LAW   Well, you might as well play. Nobody can stop you eating in any case.

(*The* MUSICIANS *play a potpouri. The* WOMEN *serve cakes*)

THE MONK The trumpet sounds like a whining baby. And you, little drum, what have you got to tell the world?

THE DRUNKEN PEASANT (*Beside the* MONK, *sings*) Miss Roundass took the old old man

And said that marriage was the thing

To everyone who met 'er.

She later withdrew from the contract because

Candles are better.

(*The* MOTHER-IN-LAW *throws the* DRUNKEN PEASANT *out. The music stops. The* GUESTS *are embarrassed*)

THE GUESTS (*Loudly*) — Have you heard? The Grand Duke is back! But the Princes are against him.

— They say the Shah of Persia has lent him a great army to restore order in Grusinia.

— But how is that possible? The Shah of Persia is the enemy . . .

— The enemy of Grusinia, you donkey, not the enemy of the Grand Duke!

— In any case, the war's over, so our soldiers are coming back.

(GRUSHA *drops a cake pan*, GUESTS *help her pick up the cake*)

AN OLD WOMAN (*To* GRUSHA) Are you feeling bad? It's just excitement about dear Jussup. Sit down and rest a while, my dear. (GRUSHA *staggers*)

THE GUESTS Now everything'll be the way it was. Only the taxes'll go up because now we'll have to pay for the war.

GRUSHA (*Weakly*) Did someone say the soldiers are back?

A MAN I did.

GRUSHA It can't be true.

THE FIRST MAN (*To a* WOMAN) Show her the shawl. We bought it from a soldier. It's from Persia.

GRUSHA (*Looking at the shawl*) They are here. (SHE *gets up, takes a step, kneels down in prayer, takes the silver cross and chain out of her blouse, and kisses it*)

THE MOTHER-IN-LAW (*While the* GUESTS *silently watch* GRUSHA) What's the matter with you? Aren't you going to look after our guests? What's all this city nonsense got to do with us?

THE GUESTS (*Resuming conversation while* GRUSHA *remains in prayer*)— You can buy Persian saddles from the soldiers too. Though many want crutches in exchange for them.

— The big shots on one side can win a war, the soldiers on both sides lose it.

— Anyway, the war's over. It's something they can't draft you any more.

(*The* DYING MAN *sits bolt upright in bed.* HE *listens*)

— What we need is two weeks of good weather.

— Our pear trees are hardly bearing a thing this year.

THE MOTHER-IN-LAW (*Offering cakes*) Have some more cakes and welcome! There are more!

(*The* MOTHER-IN-LAW *goes to the bedroom with the empty cake pans. Unaware of the* DYING MAN, SHE *is bending down to pick up another tray when* HE *begins to talk in a hoarse voice*)

THE PEASANT How many more cakes are you going to stuff down their throats? Think I'm a fucking goldmine?

(*The* MOTHER-IN-LAW *starts, stares at him aghast, while* HE *climbs out from behind the mosquito net*)

THE FIRST WOMAN (*Talking kindly to* GRUSHA *in the next room*)   Has the young wife got someone at the front?

A MAN   It's good news that they're on their way home, huh?

THE PEASANT   Don't stare at me like that! Where's this wife you've hung round my neck?

(*Receiving no answer,* HE *climbs out of bed and in his nightshirt staggers into the other room. Trembling,* SHE *follows him with the cake pan*)

THE GUESTS (*Seeing him and shrieking*)   Good God! Jussup!

(EVERYONE *leaps up in alarm. The* WOMEN *rush to the door.* GRUSHA, *still on her knees, turns round and stares at the* MAN)

THE PEASANT   A funeral supper! You'd enjoy that, wouldn't you? Get out before I throw you out! (*As the* GUESTS *stampede from the house, gloomily to* GRUSHA) I've upset the apple cart, huh? (*Receiving no answer,* HE *turns round and takes a cake from the pan which his* MOTHER *is holding*)

THE SINGER   O confusion! The wife discovers she has a husband.

By day there's the child, by night there's the husband.

The lover is on his way both day and night.

Husband and wife look at each other.

The bedroom is small.

(*Near the bed the* PEASANT *is sitting in a high wooden bathtub, naked, the* MOTHER-IN-LAW *is pouring water from a pitcher. Opposite* GRUSHA *cowers with* MICHAEL, *who is playing at mending straw mats*)

THE PEASANT (*To his* MOTHER)   That's her work, not yours. Where's she hiding out now?

THE MOTHER-IN-LAW (*Calling*)   Grusha! The peasant wants you!

GRUSHA (*To* MICHAEL)   There are still two holes to mend.

THE PEASANT (*When* GRUSHA *approaches*)   Scrub my back!

GRUSHA   Can't the peasant do it himself?

THE PEASANT   "Can't the peasant do it himself?" Get the brush! To hell with you! Are you the wife here? Or are you a visitor? (*To the* MOTHER-IN-LAW). It's too cold!

THE MOTHER-IN-LAW   I'll run for hot water.

GRUSHA   Let me go.

THE PEASANT   You stay here. (*The* MOTHER-IN-LAW *exits*) Rub harder. And no shirking. You've seen a naked fellow before. That child didn't come out of thin air.

GRUSHA   The child was not conceived in joy, if that's what the peasant means.

THE PEASANT (*Turning and grinning*)   You don't look the type. (GRUSHA *stops scrubbing him, starts back*)

(*Enter the* MOTHER-IN-LAW)

THE PEASANT   A nice thing you've hung around my neck! A simpleton for a wife!

THE MOTHER-IN-LAW   She just isn't co-operative.

THE PEASANT   Pour — but go easy! Ow! Go easy, I said. (*To* GRUSHA) Maybe you did something wrong in the city . . . I wouldn't be surprised. Why else should you be here? But I won't talk about that. I've not said a word about the illegitimate object you brought into my house either. But my patience has its limits! It's against nature. (*To the* MOTHER-IN-LAW) More! (*To* GRUSHA) And even if your soldier does come back, you're married.

GRUSHA   Yes.

THE PEASANT   But your soldier won't come back. Don't you believe it.

GRUSHA   No.

THE PEASANT   You're cheating me. You're my wife and you're not my wife. Where you lie, nothing lies, and yet no other woman can lie there. When I go to work in the morning I'm tired — when I lie down at night I'm awake as the devil. God has given you sex — and what d'you do? I don't have ten piasters to buy myself a woman in the city. Besides, it's a long way. Woman weeds the fields and opens up her legs, that's what our calendar says. D'you hear?

GRUSHA (*Quietly*)   Yes. I didn't mean to cheat you out of it.

THE PEASANT   She didn't mean to cheat me out of it! Pour some more water! (*The* MOTHER-IN-LAW *pours*) Ow!

THE SINGER   As she sat by the stream to wash the linen
She saw his image in the water
And his face grew dimmer with the passing moons.
As she raised herself to wring the linen
She heard his voice from the murmuring maple
And his voice grew fainter with the passing moons.
Evasions and sighs grew more numerous,
Tears and sweat flowed.
With the passing moons the child grew up.

(GRUSHA *sits by a stream, dipping linen into the water. In the rear, a few* CHILDREN *are standing*)

GRUSHA (*To* MICHAEL)   You can play with them, Michael, but don't let them boss you around just because you're the littlest.

(MICHAEL *nods and joins the* CHILDREN. THEY *start playing*)

THE BIGGEST BOY   Today it's the Heads-Off Game. (*To a* FAT BOY) You're the Prince and you laugh. (*To* MICHAEL) You're the Governor. (*To a* GIRL) You're the Governor's wife and you cry when his head's cut off. And I do the cutting. (HE *shows his wooden sword*) With this. First, they lead the Governor into the yard. The Prince walks in front. The Governor's wife comes last.

(THEY *form a procession. The* FAT BOY *is first and laughs. Then comes* MICHAEL, *then the* BIGGEST BOY, *and then the* GIRL, *who weeps*)

MICHAEL (*Standing still*)   Me cut off head!

THE BIGGEST BOY   That's my job. You're the littlest. The Governor's the easy part. All you do is kneel down and get your head cut off — simple.

MICHAEL   Me want sword!

THE BIGGEST BOY   It's mine! (HE *gives him a kick*)

THE GIRL (*Shouting to* GRUSHA)   He won't play his part!

GRUSHA (*Laughing*)   Even the little duck is a swimmer, they say.

THE BIGGEST BOY   You can be the Prince if you can laugh.

(MICHAEL *shakes his head*)

THE FAT BOY   I laugh best. Let him cut off the head just once. Then you do it, then me.

(*Reluctantly, the* BIGGEST BOY *hands* MICHAEL *the wooden sword and kneels down. The* FAT BOY *sits down, slaps his thigh, and laughs with all his might. The* GIRL *weeps loudly.* MICHAEL *swings the big sword and "cuts off" the head. In doing so,* HE *topples over*)

THE BIGGEST BOY   Hey! I'll show you how to cut heads off!

(MICHAEL *runs away. The* CHILDREN *run after him.* GRUSHA *laughs, following them with her eyes. On looking back,* SHE *sees* SIMON SHASHAVA *standing on the opposite bank.* HE *wears a shabby uniform*)

GRUSHA Simon!

SIMON Is that Grusha Vashnadze?

GRUSHA Simon!

SIMON (*Formally*) A good morning to the young lady. I hope she is well.

GRUSHA (*Getting up gaily and bowing low*) A good morning to the soldier.
God be thanked he has returned in good health.

SIMON They found better fish, so they didn't eat me, said the haddock.

GRUSHA Courage, said the kitchen boy. Good luck, said the hero.

SIMON How are things here? Was the winter bearable? The neighbor considerate?

GRUSHA The winter was a trifle rough, the neighbor as usual, Simon.

SIMON May one ask if a certain person still dips her foot in the water when
rinsing the linen?

GRUSHA The answer is no. Because of the eyes in the bushes.

SIMON The young lady is speaking of soldiers. Here stands a paymaster.

GRUSHA A job worth twenty piasters?

SIMON And lodgings.

GRUSHA (*With tears in her eyes*) Behind the barracks under the date trees.

SIMON Yes, there. A certain person has kept her eyes open.

GRUSHA She has, Simon.

SIMON And has not forgotten (GRUSHA *shakes her head*) So the door is still on
its hinges as they say? (GRUSHA *looks at him in silence and shakes her head
again*) What's this? Is something not as it should be?

GRUSHA Simon Shashava, I can never return to Nuka. Something has happened.

SIMON What can have happened?

GRUSHA For one thing, I knocked an Ironshirt down.

SIMON Grusha Vashnadze must have had her reasons for that.

GRUSHA Simon Shashava, I am no longer called what I used to be called.

SIMON (*After a pause*) I do not understand.

GRUSHA When do women change their names, Simon? Let me explain. Nothing stands between us. Everything is just as it was. You must believe that.

SIMON Nothing stands between us and yet there's something?

GRUSHA How can I explain it so fast and with the stream between us? Couldn't
you cross the bridge there?

SIMON Maybe it's no longer necessary.

GRUSHA It is very necessary. Come over on this side, Simon. Quick!

SIMON Does the young lady wish to say someone has come too late?

(GRUSHA *looks up at him in despair, her face streaming with tears.* SIMON
stares before him. HE *picks up a piece of wood and starts cutting it*)

THE SINGER So many words are said, so many left unsaid.

The soldier has come.

Where he comes from, he does not say.

Hear what he thought and did not say:

"The battle began, gray at dawn, grew bloody at noon.

The first man fell in front of me, the second behind me, the third at my side.

captain.

One of my brothers died by steel, the other by smoke.

My neck caught fire, my hands froze in my gloves, my toes in my socks.

I fed on aspen buds, I drank maple juice, I slept on stone, in water."

SIMON   I see a cap in the grass. Is there a little one already?

GRUSHA   There is, Simon. There's no keeping that from you. But please don't worry, it is not mine.

SIMON   When the wind once starts to blow, they say, it blows through every cranny. The wife need say no more.

(GRUSHA *looks into her lap and is silent*)

THE SINGER   There was yearning but there was no waiting.

The oath is broken. Neither could say why.

Hear what she thought but did not say:

"While you fought in the battle, soldier,

The bloody battle, the bitter battle

I found a helpless infant

I had not the heart to destroy him

I had to care for a creature that was lost

I had to stoop for breadcrumbs on the floor

I had to break myself for that which was not mine

That which was other people's.

Someone must help!

For the little tree needs water

The lamb loses its way when the shepherd is asleep

And its cry is unheard!"

SIMON   Give me back the cross I gave you. Better still, throw it in the stream.

(HE *turns to go*)

GRUSHA (*Getting up*)   Simon Shashava, don't go away! He isn't mine! He isn't mine! He isn't mine! (SHE *hears the* CHILDREN *calling*) What's the matter, children?

VOICES   Soldiers! And they're taking Michael away!

(GRUSHA *stands aghast as* TWO IRONSHIRTS, *with* MICHAEL *between them, come toward her*)

ONE OF THE IRONSHIRTS   Are you Grusha? (SHE *nods*) Is this your child?

GRUSHA   Yes.   (SIMON *goes*)

Simon!

THE IRONSHIRT   We have orders, in the name of the law, to take this child, found in your custody, back to the city. It is suspected that the child is Michael Abashwili, son and heir of the late Governor Georgi Abashwili, and his wife, Natella Abashwili. Here is the document and the seal. (THEY *lead the* CHILD *away*)

GRUSHA (*Running after them, shouting*)   Leave him here. Please! He's mine!

THE SINGER   The Ironshirts took the child, the beloved child.

The unhappy girl followed them to the city, the dreaded city.

She who had borne him demanded the child.

She who had raised him faced trial.

Who will decide the case?

To whom will the child be assigned?

Who will the judge be? A good judge? A bad?
The city was in flames.
In the judge's seat sat Azdak.[6]

4. The Story of the Judge

THE SINGER Hear the story of the judge
How he turned judge, how he passed judgment, what kind of judge he was.
On that Easter Sunday of the great revolt, when the Grand Duke was over-
thrown
And his Governor Abashwili, father of our child, lost his head
The Village Scrivener Azdak found a fugitive in the woods and hid him in
his hut. (AZDAK, *in rags and slightly drunk, is helping an* OLD BEGGAR *into
his cottage*)

AZDAK Stop snorting, you're not a horse. And it won't do you any good
with the police, to run like a snotty nose in April. Stand still, I say. (HE
catches the OLD MAN, *who has marched into the cottage as if* HE'd *like to go
through the walls*) Sit down. Feed. Here's a hunk of cheese. (*From under
some rags, in a chest,* HE *fishes out some cheese, and the* OLD MAN *greedily
begins to eat*) Haven't eaten in a long time, huh? (*The* OLD MAN *growls*)
Why were you running like that, asshole? The cop wouldn't even have seen
you.

THE OLD MAN Had to! Had to!

AZDAK Blue Funk? (*The* OLD MAN *stares, uncomprehending*) Cold feet? Panic?
Don't lick your chops like a Grand Duke. Or an old sow. I can't stand it.
We have to accept respectable stinkers as God made them, but not you! I
once heard of a senior judge who farted at a public dinner to show an independent spirit! Watching you eat like that gives me the most awful ideas.
Why don't you say something? (*Sharply*) Show me your hand. Can't you
hear? (*The* OLD MAN *slowly puts out his hand*) White! So you're not a
beggar at all! A fraud, a walking swindle! And I'm hiding you from the
cops as though you were an honest man! Why were you running like that if
you're a landowner? For that's what you are. Don't deny it! I see it in your
guilty face! (HE *gets up*) Get out! (*The* OLD MAN *looks at him uncertainly*)
What are you waiting for, peasant-flogger?

THE OLD MAN Pursued. Need undivided attention. Make proposition . . .

AZDAK Make what? A proposition? Well, if that isn't the height of insolence.
He's making me a proposition! The bitten man scratches his fingers bloody,
and the leech that's biting him makes him a proposition! Get out, I tell you!

THE OLD MAN Understand point of view! Persuasion! Pay hundred thousand
piasters one night! Yes?

AZDAK What, you think you can buy me? For a hundred thousand piasters?
Let's say a hundred and fifty thousand. Where are they?

THE OLD MAN Have not them here. Of course. Will be sent. Hope do not
doubt.

AZDAK Doubt very much. Get out!
(*The* OLD MAN *gets up, waddles to the door. A voice is heard off stage*)

6. The name *Azdak* should be accented on the second syllable.

A VOICE Azdak!

(*The* OLD MAN *turns, waddles to the opposite corner, stands still*)

AZDAK (*Calling out*) I'm not in! (HE *walks to door*) So you're sniffing around here again, Shauwa?

POLICEMAN SHAUWA (*Reproachfully*) You've caught another rabbit, Azdak. And you promised me it wouldn't happen again!

AZDAK (*Severely*) Shauwa, don't talk about things you don't understand. The rabbit is a dangerous and destructive beast. It feeds on plants, especially on the species of plants known as weeds. It must therefore be exterminated.

SHAUWA Azdak, don't be so hard on me. I'll lose my job if I don't arrest you. I know you have a good heart.

AZDAK I do not have a good heart! How often must I tell you I'm a man of intellect?

SHAUWA (*Slyly*) I know, Azdak. You're a superior person. You say so yourself. I'm just a Christian and an ignoramus. So I ask you: When one of the Prince's rabbits is stolen, and I'm a policeman, what should I do with the offending party?

AZDAK Shauwa, Shauwa, shame on you. You stand and ask me a question, than which nothing could be more seductive. It's like you were a woman — let's say that bad girl Nunowna, and you showed me your thigh — Nunowna's thigh, that would be — and asked me: "What shall I do with my thigh, it itches?" Is she as innocent as she pretends? Of course not. I catch a rabbit, but you catch a man. Man is made in God's image. Not so a rabbit, you know that. I'm a rabbit-eater, but you're a man-eater, Shauwa. And God will pass judgment on you. Shauwa, go home and repent. No, stop, there's something . . . (HE *looks at the* OLD MAN *who stands trembling in the corner*) No, it's nothing. Go home and repent. (HE *slams the door behind* SHAUWA) Now you're surprised, huh? Surprised I didn't hand you over? I couldn't hand over a bedbug to that animal. It goes against the grain. Now don't tremble because of a cop! So old and still so scared? Finish your cheese, but eat it like a poor man, or else they'll still catch you. Must I even explain how a poor man behaves? (HE *pushes him down, and then gives him back the cheese*) That box is the table. Lay your elbows on the table. Now, encircle the cheese on the plate like it might be snatched from you at any moment — what right have you to be safe, huh? — now, hold your knife like an undersized sickle, and give your cheese a troubled look because, like all beautiful things, it's already fading away. (AZDAK *watches him*) They're after you, which speaks in your favor, but how can we be sure they're not mistaken about you? In Tiflis one time they hanged a landowner, a Turk, who could prove he quartered his peasants instead of merely cutting them in half, as is the custom, and he squeezed twice the usual amount of taxes out of them, his zeal was above suspicion. And yet they hanged him like a common criminal — because he was a Turk — a thing he couldn't do much about. What injustice! He got onto the gallows by a sheer fluke. In short, I don't trust you.

THE SINGER Thus Azdak gave the old beggar a bed,
And learned that old beggar was the old butcher, the Grand Duke himself,
And was ashamed.
He denounced himself and ordered the policeman to take him to Nuka, to court, to be judged.

(*In the court of justice* THREE IRONSHIRTS *sit drinking. From a beam hangs a man in judge's robes. Enter* AZDAK, *in chains, dragging* SHAUWA *behind him*)

AZDAK (*Shouting*) I've helped the Grand Duke, the Grand Thief, the Grand Butcher, to escape! In the name of justice I ask to be severely judged in public trial!

THE FIRST IRONSHIRT Who's this queer bird?

SHAUWA That's our Village Scrivener, Azdak.

AZDAK I am contemptible! I am a traitor! A branded criminal! Tell them, flat-foot, how I insisted on being chained up and brought to the capital. Because I sheltered the Grand Duke, the Grand Swindler, by mistake. And how I found out afterwards. See the marked man denounce himself! Tell them how I forced you to walk with me half the night to clear the whole thing up.

SHAUWA And all by threats. That wasn't nice of you, Azdak.

AZDAK Shut your mouth, Shauwa. You don't understand. A new age is upon us! It'll go thundering over you. You're finished. The police will be wiped out — poof! Everything will be gone into, everything will be brought into the open. The guilty will give themselves up. Why? They couldn't escape the people in any case. (*To* SHAUWA) Tell them how I shouted all along Shoemaker Street: (*With big gestures, looking at the* IRONSHIRTS) "In my ignorance I let the Grand Swindler escape! So tear me to pieces, brothers!" I wanted to get it in first.

THE FIRST IRONSHIRT And what did your brothers answer?

SHAUWA They comforted him in Butcher Street, and they laughed themselves sick in Shoemaker Street. That's all.

AZDAK But with you it's different. I can see you're men of iron. Brothers, where's the judge? I must be tried.

THE FIRST IRONSHIRT (*Points at the hanged man*) There's the judge. And please stop "brothering" us. It's rather a sore spot this evening.

AZDAK "There's the judge." An answer never heard in Grusinia before. Towns-man, where's His Excellency the Governor? (*Pointing to the floor*) There's His Excellency, stranger. Where's the Chief Tax Collector? Where's the official Recruiting Officer? The Patriarch? The Chief of Police? There, there, there — all there. Brothers, I expected no less of you.

THE SECOND IRONSHIRT What? *What* was it you expected, funny man?

AZDAK What happened in Persia, brother, what happened in Persia?

THE SECOND IRONSHIRT What did happen in Persia?

AZDAK Everybody was hanged. Viziers, tax collectors. Everybody. Forty years ago now. My grandfather, a remarkable man by the way, saw it all. For three whole days. Everywhere.

THE SECOND IRONSHIRT And who ruled when the Vizier was hanged?

AZDAK A peasant ruled when the Vizier was hanged.

THE SECOND IRONSHIRT And who commanded the army?

AZDAK A soldier, a soldier.

THE SECOND IRONSHIRT And who paid the wages?

AZDAK A dyer. A dyer paid the wages.

THE SECOND IRONSHIRT Wasn't it a weaver, maybe?

THE FIRST IRONSHIRT And why did all this happen, Persian?

AZDAK Why did all this happen? Must there be a special reason? Why do you scratch yourself, brother? War! Too long a war! And no justice! My grandfather brought back a song that tells how it was. I will sing it for you. With my friend the policeman. (*To* SHAUWA) And hold the rope tight. It's very suitable.

(HE *sings, with* SHAUWA *holding the rope tight around him*)

The Song of Injustice in Persia

Why don't our sons bleed any more? Why don't our daughters weep?
Why do only the slaughter-house cattle have blood in their veins?
Why do only the willows shed tears on Lake Urmi?

The king must have a new province, the peasant must give up his savings.
That the roof of the world might be conquered, the roof of the cottage is torn down.
Our men are carried to the ends of the earth, so that great ones can eat at home.
The soldiers kill each other, the marshals salute each other.
They bite the widow's tax money to see if it's good, their swords break.
The battle was lost, the helmets were paid for.
(*Refrain*)
Is it so? Is it so?
(*Refrain*) (*By* SHAUWA)
Yes, yes, yes, yes, yes it's so.

AZDAK   Do you want to hear the rest of it? (*The* FIRST IRONSHIRT *nods*)
THE SECOND IRONSHIRT (*To* SHAUWA) Did he teach you that song?
SHAUWA   Yes, only my voice isn't very good.
THE SECOND IRONSHIRT   No. (*To* AZDAK) Go on singing.
AZDAK   The second verse is about the peace.
   (HE *sings*)
The offices are packed, the streets overflow with officials.
The rivers jump their banks and ravage the fields.
Those who cannot let down their own trousers rule countries.
They can't count up to four, but they devour eight courses.
The corn farmers, looking round for buyers, see only the starving.
The weavers go home from their looms in rags.
(*Refrain*)
Is it so? Is it so?
(*Refrain*) (*By* SHAUWA)
Yes, yes, yes, yes, yes it's so.

AZDAK   That's why our sons don't bleed any more, that's why our daughters don't weep.
That's why only the slaughter-house cattle have blood in their veins,
And only the willows shed tears by Lake Urmi toward morning.
THE FIRST IRONSHIRT   Are you going to sing that song here in town?
AZDAK   Sure. What's wrong with it?
THE FIRST IRONSHIRT   Have you noticed that the sky's getting red? (*Turning round,* AZDAK *sees the sky red with fire*) It's the people's quarters. On the outskirts of town. The carpet weavers have caught the "Persian Sickness," too. And they've been asking if Prince Kazbeki isn't eating too many courses. This morning they strung up the city judge. As for us we beat them to pulp. We were paid one hundred piasters per man, you understand?

AZDAK (*After a pause*)   I understand.

(HE *glances shyly round and, creeping away, sits down in a corner, his head in his hands*)

THE IRONSHIRTS (*To each other*)   — If there ever was a trouble-maker it's him.
— He must've come to the capital to fish in the troubled waters.

SHAUWA   Oh, I don't think he's a really bad character, gentlemen. Steals a few chickens here and there. And maybe a rabbit.

THE SECOND IRONSHIRT (*Approaching* AZDAK)   Came to fish in the troubled waters, huh?

AZDAK (*Looking up*)   I don't know why I came.

THE SECOND IRONSHIRT   Are you in with the carpet weavers maybe? (AZDAK *shakes his head*) How about that song?

AZDAK   From my grandfather. A silly and ignorant man.

THE SECOND IRONSHIRT   Right. And how about the dyer who paid the wages?

AZDAK (*Muttering*)   That was in Persia.

THE FIRST IRONSHIRT   And this denouncing of yourself? Because you didn't hang the Grand Duke with your own hands?

AZDAK   Didn't I tell you I let him run? (HE *creeps farther away and sits on the floor*)

SHAUWA   I can swear to that: he let him run.

(*The* IRONSHIRTS *burst out laughing and slap* SHAUWA *on the back.* AZDAK *laughs loudest.* THEY *slap* AZDAK *too, and unchain him.* THEY ALL *start drinking as the* FAT PRINCE *enters with a* YOUNG MAN)

THE FIRST IRONSHIRT (*To* AZDAK, *pointing at the* FAT PRINCE)   There's your "new age" for you! (*More laughter*)

THE FAT PRINCE   Well, my friends, what is there to laugh about? Permit me a serious word. Yesterday morning the Princes of Grusinia overthrew the war-mongering government of the Grand Duke and did away with his Governors. Unfortunately the Grand Duke himself escaped. In this fateful hour our carpet weavers, those eternal trouble-makers, had the effrontery to stir up a rebellion and hang the universally loved city judge, our dear Illo Orbeliani. Ts-ts-ts. My friends, we need peace, peace, peace in Grusinia! And Justice! So I've brought along my dear nephew Bizergan Kazbeki. He'll be the new judge, hm? A very gifted fellow. What do you say? I want your opinion. Let the people decide!

THE SECOND IRONSHIRT   Does this mean *we* elect the judge?

THE FAT PRINCE   Precisely. Let the people propose some very gifted fellow! Confer among yourselves, my friends. (*The* IRONSHIRTS *confer*) Don't worry, my little fox. The job's yours. And when we catch the Grand Duke we won't have to kiss this rabble's ass any longer.

THE IRONSHIRTS (*Between themselves*)   — Very funny: they're wetting their pants because they haven't caught the Grand Duke.
— When the outlook isn't so bright, they say: "My friends!" and "Let the people decide!"
— Now he even wants justice for Grusinia! But fun is fun as long as it lasts! (*Pointing at* AZDAK)
— *He* knows all about justice. Hey, rascal, would you like this nephew fellow to be the judge?

AZDAK   Are you asking me? You're not asking *me?!*

THE FIRST IRONSHIRT   Why not? Anything for a laugh!

AZDAK   You'd like to test him to the marrow, correct? Have you a criminal on hand? An experienced one? So the candidate can show what he knows?

THE SECOND IRONSHIRT   Let's see. We do have a couple of doctors downstairs. Let's use them.

AZDAK   Oh, no, that's no good, we can't take real criminals till we're sure the judge will be appointed. He may be dumb, but he must be appointed, or the Law is violated. And the Law is a sensitive organ. It's like the spleen, you mustn't hit it — that would be fatal. Of course you can hang those two without violating the Law, because there was no judge in the vicinity. But Judgment, when pronounced, must be pronounced with absolute gravity — it's all such nonsense. Suppose, for instance, a judge jails a woman — let's say she's stolen a corncake to feed her child — and this judge isn't wearing his robes — or maybe he's scratching himself while passing sentence and half his body is uncovered — a man's thigh *will* itch once in a while — the sentence this judge passes is a disgrace and the Law is violated. In short it would be easier for a judge's robe and a judge's hat to pass judgment than for a man with no robe and no hat. If you don't treat it with respect, the Law just disappears on you. Now you don't try out a bottle of wine by offering it to a dog; you'd only lose your wine.

THE FIRST IRONSHIRT   Then what do you suggest, hair-splitter?

AZDAK   I'll be the defendant.

THE FIRST IRONSHIRT   You? (HE *bursts out laughing*)

THE FAT PRINCE   What have you decided?

THE FIRST IRONSHIRT   We've decided to stage a rehearsal. Our friend here will be the defendant. Let the candidate be the judge and sit there.

THE FAT PRINCE   It isn't customary, but why not? (*To the* NEPHEW) A mere formality, my little fox. What have I taught you? Who got there first — the slow runner or the fast?

THE NEPHEW   The silent runner, Uncle Arsen.

(*The* NEPHEW *takes the chair. The* IRONSHIRTS *and the* FAT PRINCE *sit on the steps. Enter* AZDAK, *mimicking the gait of the Grand Duke*)

AZDAK (*In the Grand Duke's accent*)   Is any here knows me? Am Grand Duke.

THE IRONSHIRTS   — *What* is he?

— The Grand Duke. He knows him, too.

— Fine. So get on with the trial.

AZDAK   Listen! Am accused instigating war? Ridiculous! Am saying ridiculous! That enough? If not, have brought lawyers. Believe five hundred. (HE *points behind him, pretending to be surrounded by lawyers*) Requisition all available seats for lawyers!

(*The* IRONSHIRTS *laugh, the* FAT PRINCE *joins in*)

THE NEPHEW (*To the* IRONSHIRTS)   You really wish me to try this case? I find it rather unusual. From the taste angle, I mean.

THE FIRST IRONSHIRT   Let's go!

THE FAT PRINCE (*Smiling*)   Let him have it, my little fox!

THE NEPHEW   All right. People of Grusinia versus Grand Duke. Defendant, what have you got to say for yourself?

AZDAK   Plenty. Naturally, have read war lost. Only started on the advice of patriots. Like Uncle Arsen Kazbeki. Call Uncle Arsen as witness.

THE FAT PRINCE (*To the* IRONSHIRTS, *delightedly*)   What a screw-ball!

THE NEPHEW   Motion rejected. One cannot be arraigned for declaring a war, which every ruler has to do once in a while, but only for running a war badly.

AZDAK   Rubbish! Did not run it at all! Had it run! Had it run by Princes! Naturally, they messed it up.

THE NEPHEW   Do you by any chance deny having been commander-in-chief?

AZDAK   Not at all! Always *was* commander-in-chief. At birth shouted at wet nurse. Was trained drop turds in toilet, grew accustomed to command. Always commanded officials rob my cash box. Officers flog soldiers only on command. Landowners sleep with peasants' wives only on strictest command. Uncle Arsen here grew his belly at *my* command!

THE IRONSHIRTS (*Clapping*)   He's good! Long live the Grand Duke!

THE FAT PRINCE   Answer him, my little fox. I'm with you.

THE NEPHEW   I shall answer him according to the dignity of the law. Defendant, preserve the dignity of the law!

AZDAK   Agreed. Command you to proceed with the trial!

THE NEPHEW   It is not your place to command me. You claim that the Princes forced you to declare war. How can you claim, then, that they — er — "messed it up"?

AZDAK   Did not send enough people. Embezzled funds. Sent sick horses. During attack, drinking in whorehouse. Call Uncle Arsen as witness.

THE NEPHEW   Are you making the outrageous suggestion that the Princes of this country did not fight?

AZDAK   No. Princes fought. Fought for war contracts.

THE FAT PRINCE (*Jumping up*)   That's too much! This man talks like a carpet weaver!

AZDAK   Really? I told nothing but the truth.

THE FAT PRINCE   Hang him! Hang him!

THE FIRST IRONSHIRT (*Pulling the* PRINCE *down*)   Keep quiet! Go on, Excellency!

THE NEPHEW   Quiet! I now render a verdict: You must be hanged! By the neck! Having lost war!

AZDAK   Young man, seriously advise not fall publicly into jerky clipped manner of speech. Cannot be employed as watchdog if howl like wolf. Got it? If people realize Princes speak same language as Grand Duke, may hang Grand Duke *and Princes,* huh? By the way, must overrule verdict. Reason? War lost, but not for Princes. Princes won their war. Got 3,863,000 piasters for horses not delivered, 8,240,000 piasters for food supplies not produced. Are therefore victors. War lost only for Grusinia, which as such is not present in this court.

THE FAT PRINCE   I think that will do, my friends. (*To* AZDAK) You can withdraw, funny man. (*To the* IRONSHIRTS) you may now ratify the new judge's appointment, my friends.

THE FIRST IRONSHIRT   Yes, we can. Take down the judge's gown.

(ONE IRONSHIRT *climbs on the back of the* OTHER, *pulls the gown off the hanged man*)

THE FIRST IRONSHIRT (*To the* NEPHEW)   Now you run away so the right ass can get on the right chair. (*To* AZDAK) Step forward! Go to the judge's seat! Now sit in it!

(AZDAK *steps up, bows, and sits down*)

The judge was always a rascal! Now the rascal shall be a judge!

(*The judge's gown is placed round his shoulders, the hat on his head*)

And what a judge!

THE SINGER   And there was civil war in the land.

The mighty were not safe.

And Azdak was made a judge by the Ironshirts.

And Azdak remained a judge for two years.

THE SINGER AND CHORUS   When the towns were set afire.

And rivers of blood rose higher and higher,

Cockroaches crawled out of every crack.

And the court was full of schemers

And the church of foul blasphemers.

In the judge's cassock sat Azdak.

(AZDAK *sits in the judge's chair, peeling an apple.* SHAUWA *is sweeping out the hall. On one side an* INVALID *in a wheelchair. Opposite a* YOUNG MAN *accused of blackmail. An* IRONSHIRT *stands guard, holding the Ironshirt's banner*)

AZDAK   In consideration of the large number of cases, the Court today will hear two cases at a time. Before I open the proceedings, a short announcement — I accept.

(HE *stretches out his hand. The* BLACKMAILER *is the only one to produce any money.* HE *hands it to* AZDAK)

I reserve the right to punish one of the parties for contempt of court. (HE *glances at* THE INVALID) You (*To the* DOCTOR) are a doctor, and you (*To the* INVALID) are bringing a complaint against him. Is the doctor responsible for your condition?

THE INVALID   Yes. I had a stroke on his account.

AZDAK   That would be professional negligence.

THE INVALID   Worse than negligence. I gave this man money for his studies. So far, he hasn't paid me back a cent. It was when I heard he was treating a patient free that I had my stroke.

AZDAK   Rightly. (*To a* LIMPING MAN) And what are *you* doing here?

THE LIMPING MAN   I'm the patient, your honor.

AZDAK   He treated your leg for nothing?

THE LIMPING MAN   The wrong leg! My rheumatism was in the left leg, and he operated on the right. That's why I limp now.

AZDAK   And you were treated free?

THE INVALID   A five-hundred piaster operation free! For nothing! For a God-bless-you! And I paid for this man's studies! (*To the* DOCTOR) Did they teach you to operate free?

THE DOCTOR   Your Honor, it is actually the custom to demand the fee before the operation, as the patient is more willing to pay before an operation than after. Which is only human. In the case in question I was convinced, when I started the operation, that my servant had already received the fee. In this I was mistaken.

THE INVALID   He was mistaken! A good doctor doesn't make mistakes! He examines before he operates!

AZDAK   That's right. (*To* SHAUWA) Public Prosecutor, what's the other case about?

SHAUWA (*Busily sweeping*)   Blackmail.

THE BLACKMAILER High Court of Justice, I'm innocent. I only wanted to find out from the landowner concerned if he really *had* raped his niece. He informed me very politely that this was not the case, and gave me the money only so I could pay for my uncle's studies.

AZDAK Hm. (*To the* DOCTOR) You, on the other hand, can cite no extenuating circumstances for your offense, huh?

THE DOCTOR Except that to err is human.

AZDAK And you are aware that in money matters a good doctor is a highly responsible person? I once heard of a doctor who got a thousand piasters for a sprained finger by remarking that sprains have something to do with blood circulation, which after all a less good doctor might have overlooked, and who, on another occasion made a real gold mine out of a somewhat disordered gall bladder, he treated it with such loving care. You have no excuse, Doctor. The corn merchant, Uxu, had his son study medicine to get some knowledge of trade, our medical schools are so good. (*To the* BLACK-MAILER) What's the landowner's name?

SHAUWA He doesn't want it mentioned.

AZDAK In that case I will pass judgment. The Court considers the blackmail proved. And you (*To the* INVALID) are sentenced to a fine of one thousand piasters. If you have a second stroke, the doctor will have to treat you free. Even if he has to amputate. (*To the* LIMPING MAN) As compensation, you will receive a bottle of rubbing alcohol. (*To the* BLACKMAILER) You are sentenced to hand over half the proceeds of your deal to the Public Prosecutor to keep the landowner's name secret. You are advised, moreover, to study medicine — you seem well suited to that calling. (*To the* DOCTOR) You have perpetrated an unpardonable error in the practice of your profession: you are acquitted. Next cases!

THE SINGER AND CHORUS Men won't do much for a shilling.
For a pound they may be willing.
For 20 pounds the verdict's in the sack.
As for the many, all too many,
Those who've only got a penny —
They've one single, sole recourse: Azdak.

(*Enter* AZDAK *from the caravansary on the high-road, followed by an old bearded* INNKEEPER. *The judge's chair is carried by a* STABLEMAN *and* SHAUWA. *An* IRONSHIRT, *with a banner, takes up his position*)

AZDAK Put me down. Then we'll get some air, maybe even a good stiff breeze from the lemon grove there. It does justice good to be done in the open: the wind blows her skirts up and you can see what she's got. Shauwa, we've been eating too much. These official journeys are exhausting. (*To the* INN-KEEPER) It's a question of your daughter-in-law?

THE INNKEEPER Your Worship, it's a question of the family honor. I wish to bring an action on behalf of my son, who's on business on the other side of the mountain. This is the offending stableman, and here's my daughter-in-law.

(*Enter the* DAUGHTER-IN-LAW, *a voluptuous wench.* SHE *is veiled*)

AZDAK (*Sitting down*) I accept.

(*Sighing, the* INNKEEPER *hands him some money*)

Good. Now the formalities are disposed of. This is a case of rape?

THE INNKEEPER Your Honor, I caught the fellow in the act. Ludovica was in the straw on the stable floor.

AZDAK   Quite right, the stable. Lovely horses! I specially liked the little roan.

THE INNKEEPER   The first thing I did, of course, was to question Ludovica. On my son's behalf.

AZDAK (*Seriously*)   I said I specially liked the little roan.

THE INNKEEPER (*Coldly*)   Really? Ludovica confessed the stableman took her against her will.

AZDAK   Take your veil off, Ludovica. (SHE *does so*) Ludovica, you please the Court. Tell us how it happened.

LUDOVICA (*Well-schooled*)   When I entered the stable to see the new foal the stableman said to me on his own accord: "It's hot today!" and laid his hand on my left breast. I said to him: "Don't do that!" But he continued to handle me indecently, which provoked my anger. Before I realized his sinful intentions, he got much closer. It was all over when my father-in-law entered and accidentally trod on me.

THE INNKEEPER (*Explaining*)   On my son's behalf.

AZDAK (*To the* STABLEMAN)   You admit you started it?

THE STABLEMAN   Yes.

AZDAK   Ludovica, you like to eat sweet things?

LUDOVICA   Yes, sunflower seeds!

AZDAK   You like to lie a long time in the bathtub?

LUDOVICA   Half an hour or so.

AZDAK   Public Prosecutor, drop your knife — there — on the ground. (SHAUWA *does so*) Ludovica, pick up that knife. (LUDOVICA, *swaying her hips, does so*) See that? (HE *points at her*) The way it moves? The rape is now proven. By eating too much — sweet things, especially — by lying too long in warm water, by laziness and too soft a skin, you have raped that unfortunate man. Think you can run around with a behind like that and get away with it in court? This is a case of intentional assault with a dangerous weapon! You are sentenced to hand over to the Court the little roan which your father liked to ride "on his son's behalf." And now, come with me to the stables, so the Court may inspect the scene of the crime, Ludovica.

THE SINGER AND THE CHORUS   When the sharks the sharks devour
Little fishes have their hour.
For a while the load is off their back.
On Grusinia's highways faring
Fixed-up scales of justice bearing
Strode the poor man's magistrate: Azdak.

And he gave to the forsaken
All that from the rich he'd taken.
And a bodyguard of roughnecks was Azdak's.
And our good and evil man, he
Smiled upon Grusinia's Granny.
His emblem was a tear in sealing wax.

All mankind should love each other
But when visiting your brother
Take an ax along and hold it fast.
Not in theory but in practice
Miracles are wrought with axes
And the age of miracles is not past.

(AZDAK'S *judge's chair is in a tavern.* THREE RICH FARMERS *stand before* AZDAK. SHAUWA *brings him wine. In a corner stands an* OLD PEASANT WOMAN. *In the open doorway, and outside, stand* VILLAGERS *looking on. An* IRONSHIRT *stands guard with a banner*)

AZDAK   The Public Prosecutor has the floor.

SHAUWA   It concerns a cow. For five weeks the defendant has had a cow in her stable, the property of the farmer Suru. She was also found to be in possession of a stolen ham, and a number of cows belonging to Shutoff were killed after he asked the defendant to pay the rent on a piece of land.

THE FARMERS   — It's a matter of my ham, Your Honor.
— It's a matter of my cow, Your Honor.
— It's a matter of my land, Your Honor.

AZDAK   Well, Granny, what have *you* got to say to all this?

THE OLD WOMAN   Your Honor, one night toward morning, five weeks ago, there was a knock at my door, and outside stood a bearded man with a cow. "My dear woman," he said, "I am the miracle-working Saint Banditus and because your son has been killed in the war, I bring you this cow as a souvenir. Take good care of it."

THE FARMERS   — The robber, Irakli, Your Honor!
— Her brother-in-law, Your Honor!
— The cow-thief!
— The incendiary!
— He must be beheaded!

(*Outside, a* WOMAN *screams. The* CROWD *grows restless, retreats. Enter the* BANDIT IRAKLI *with a huge ax*)

THE BANDIT   A very good evening, dear friends! A glass of vodka!

THE FARMERS (*Crossing themselves*)   Irakli!

AZDAK   Public Prosecutor, a glass of vodka for our guest. And who are you?

THE BANDIT   I'm a wandering hermit, Your Honor. Thanks for the gracious gift.
(HE *empties the glass which* SHAUWA *has brought*)
Another!

AZDAK   I am Azdak. (HE *gets up and bows. The* BANDIT *also bows*) The Court welcomes the foreign hermit. Go on with your story, Granny.

THE OLD WOMAN   Your Honor, that first night I didn't yet know Saint Banditus could work miracles, it was only the cow. But one night, a few days later, the farmer's servants came to take the cow away again. Then they turned round in front of my door and went off without the cow. And bumps as big as a fist sprouted on their heads. So I knew that Saint Banditus had changed their hearts and turned them into friendly people. (*The* BANDIT *roars with laughter*)

THE FIRST FARMER   I know what changed them.

AZDAK   That's fine. You can tell us later. Continue.

THE OLD WOMAN   Your Honor, the next one to become a good man was the farmer Shutoff — a devil, as everyone knows. But Saint Banditus arranged it so he let me off the rent on the little piece of land.

THE SECOND FARMER   Because my cows were killed in the field. (*The* BANDIT *laughs*)

THE OLD WOMAN (*Answering* AZDAK'S *sign to continue*)   Then one morning the ham came flying in at my window. It hit me in the small of the back. I'm

still lame, Your Honor, look. (SHE *limps a few steps*) (*The* BANDIT *laughs*)
Your Honor, was there ever a time when a poor old woman could get a ham
without a miracle?
(*The* BANDIT *starts sobbing*)

AZDAK (*Rising from his chair*)   Granny, that's a question that strikes straight
at the Court's heart. Be so kind as to sit here.
(*The* OLD WOMAN, *hesitating, sits in the judge's chair*)

AZDAK (*Sits on the floor, glass in hand, reciting*)   Granny
We could almost call you Granny Grusinia
The Woebegone
The Bereaved Mother
Whose sons have gone to war
Receiving the present of a cow
She bursts out crying.
When she is beaten
She remains hopeful.
When she's not beaten
She's surprised.
On us
Who are already damned
May you render a merciful verdict
Granny Grusinia!
(*Bellowing at the* FARMERS)
Admit you don't believe in miracles, you atheists! Each of you is sentenced
to pay five hundred piasters! For godlessness! Get out!
(*The* FARMERS *slink out*)
And you Granny, and you (*To the* BANDIT) pious man, empty a pitcher of
wine with the Public Prosecutor and Azdak!

THE SINGER AND THE CHORUS   And he broke the rules to save them.
Broken law like bread he gave them,
Brought them to shore upon his crooked back.
At long last the poor and lowly
Had someone who was not too holy
To be bribed by empty hands: Azdak.

For two years it was his pleasure
To give the beasts of prey short measure:
He became a wolf to fight the pack.
From All Hallows to All Hallows
On his chair beside the gallows
Dispensing justice in his fashion sat Azdak.

THE SINGER   But the era of disorder came to an end.
The Grand Duke returned.
The Governor's wife returned.
A trial was held.
Many died.
The people's quarters burned anew.
And fear seized Azdak.
(AZDAK'S *judge's chair stands again in the court of justice.* AZDAK *sits on the*

floor, shaving and talking to SHAUWA. *Noises outside. In the rear the* FAT
PRINCE'S *head is carried by on a lance*)

AZDAK Shauwa, the days of your slavery are numbered, maybe even the minutes. For a long time now I have held you in the iron curb of reason, and
it has torn your mouth till it bleeds. I have lashed you with reasonable
arguments, I have manhandled you with logic. You are by nature a weak
man, and if one slyly throws an argument in your path, you *have* to snap it
up, you can't resist. It is your nature to lick the hand of some superior being. But superior beings can be of very different kinds. And now, with your
liberation, you will soon be able to follow your natural inclinations, which
are low. You will be able to follow your infallible instinct, which teaches you
to plant your fat heel on the faces of men. Gone is the era of confusion and
disorder, which I find described in the Song of Chaos. Let us now sing that
song together in memory of those terrible days. Sit down and don't do violence to the music. Don't be afraid. It sounds all right. And it has a fine
refrain. (HE *sings*)

The Song of the Chaos

Sister, hide your face! Brother, take your knife!
The times are out of joint!
Big men are full of complaint
And small men full of joy.
The city says:
"Let me drive the strong ones from our midst!"
Offices are raided. Lists of serfs are destroyed.
They have set Master's nose to the grindstone.
They who lived in the dark have seen the light.
The ebony poor box is broken.
Magnificent wood is sawed up for beds.
Who had no bread have barns full.
Who begged for alms of corn now mete it out.

SHAUWA (*Refrain*) Oh, oh, oh, oh.

AZDAK (*Refrain*) Where are you, General, where are you?
Please, please, please, restore order!
The nobleman's son can no longer be recognized;
The lady's child becomes the son of her slave.
The councilors meet in a shed.
Once, this man was barely allowed to sleep on the wall;
Now, he stretches his limbs in a bed.
Once, this man rowed a boat; now, he owns ships.
Their owner looks for them, but they're his no longer.
Five men are sent on a journey by their master.
"Go yourself," they say, "we have arrived."

SHAUWA (*Refrain*) Oh, oh, oh, oh.

AZDAK (*Refrain*) Where are you, General, where are you?
Please, please, please, restore order!

Yes, So it might have been, had order been neglected much longer. But now
the Grand Duke has returned to the capital, and the Persians have lent him
an army to restore order with. The suburbs are already aflame. Go and get

me the big book I always sit on. (SHAUWA *brings the big book from the judge's chair.* AZDAK *opens it*) This is the Statute Book and I've always used it, as you can testify. Now I'd better look in this book and see what they can do to me. I've let the down-and-outs get away with murder, and I'll have to pay for it. I helped poverty onto its skinny legs, so they'll hang me for drunkedness. I peeped into the rich man's pocket, which is bad taste. And I can't hide anywhere — everybody knows me because I've helped everybody.

SHAUWA   Someone's coming!

AZDAK (*In panic,* HE *walks trembling to the chair*)   It's the end. And now they'd enjoy seeing what a Great Man I am. I'll deprive them of that pleasure. I'll beg on my knees for mercy. Spittle will slobber down my chin. The fear of death is in me.

(*Enter* NATELLA ABASHWILI, *the* GOVERNOR'S WIFE, *followed by the* ADJUTANT *and an* IRONSHIRT)

THE GOVERNOR'S WIFE   What sort of a creature is that, Shalva?

AZDAK   A willing one, Your Highness, a man ready to oblige.

THE ADJUTANT   Natella Abashwili, wife of the late Governor, has just returned. She is looking for her two-year-old son, Michael. She has been informed that the child was carried off to the mountains by a former servant.

AZDAK   The child will be brought back, Your Highness, at your service.

THE ADJUTANT   They say that the person in question is passing it off as her own.

AZDAK   She will be beheaded, Your Highness, at your service.

THE ADJUTANT   That is all.

THE GOVERNOR'S WIFE (*Leaving*)   I don't like the man.

AZDAK (*Following her to door, bowing*)   At your service, Your Highness, it will all be arranged.

5. The Chalk Circle

THE SINGER   Hear now the story of the trial
Concerning Governor Abashwili's child
And the establishing of the true mother
By the famous test of the Chalk Circle.

(*The court of justice in Nuka.* IRONSHIRTS *lead* MICHAEL *across stage and out at the back.* IRONSHIRTS *hold* GRUSHA *back with their lances under the gateway until the* CHILD *has been led through. Then* SHE *is admitted.* SHE *is accompanied by the former governor's* COOK. *Distant noises and a fire-red sky*)

GRUSHA (*Trying to hide*)   He's brave, he can wash himself now.

THE COOK   You're lucky. It's not a real judge. It's Azdak, a drunk who doesn't know what he's doing. The biggest thieves have got by through him. Because he gets everything mixed up and the rich never offer him big enough bribes, the likes of us sometimes do pretty well.

GRUSHA   I *need* luck right now.

THE COOK   Touch wood. (SHE *crosses herself*)   I'd better offer up another prayer that the judge may be drunk.

(SHE *prays with motionless lips, while* GRUSHA *looks around, in vain, for the* CHILD)

Why must you hold on to it at any price if it isn't yours? In days like these?

GRUSHA He's mine. I brought him up.

THE COOK Have you never thought what'd happen when she came back?

GRUSHA At first I thought I'd give him to her. Then I thought she wouldn't come back.

THE COOK And even a borrowed coat keeps a man warm, hm? (GRUSHA *nods*) I'll swear to anything for you. You're a decent girl. (SHE *sees the soldier* SIMON SHASHAVA *approaching*) You've done wrong by Simon, though. I've been talking with him. He just can't understand.

GRUSHA (*Unaware of* SIMON's *presence*) Right now I can't be bothered whether he understands or not!

THE COOK He knows the child isn't yours, but you married and not free "til death you do part" — he can't understand *that*.

(GRUSHA *sees* SIMON *and greets him*)

SIMON (*Gloomily*) I wish the lady to know I will swear I am the father of the child.

GRUSHA (*Low*) Thank you, Simon.

SIMON At the same time I wish the lady to know my hands are not tied — nor are hers.

THE COOK You needn't have said that. You know she's married.

SIMON And it needs no rubbing in.

(*Enter an* IRONSHIRT)

THE IRONSHIRT Where's the judge? Has anyone seen the judge?

ANOTHER IRONSHIRT (*Stepping forward*) The judge isn't here yet. Nothing but a bed and a pitcher in the whole house!

(*Exeunt* IRONSHIRTS)

THE COOK I hope nothing has happened to him. With any other judge you'd have about as much chance as a chicken has teeth.

GRUSHA (*Who has turned away and covered her face*) Stand in front of me. I shouldn't have come to Nuka. If I run into the Ironshirt, the one I hit over the head . . .

(SHE *screams. An* IRONSHIRT *had stopped and, turning his back, had been listening to her.* HE *now wheels around. It is the* CORPORAL, *and* HE *has a huge scar across his face*)

THE IRONSHIRT (*In the gateway*) What's the matter, Shotta? Do you know her?

THE CORPORAL (*After staring for some time*) No.

THE IRONSHIRT She's the one who stole the Abashwili child, or so they say. If you know anything about it you can make some money, Shotta.

(*Exit the* CORPORAL, *cursing*)

THE COOK Was it him? (GRUSHA *nods*) I think he'll keep his mouth shut, or he'd be admitting he was after the child.

GRUSHA I'd almost forgotten him.

(*Enter* THE GOVERNOR'S WIFE, *followed by the* ADJUTANT *and* TWO LAWYERS)

THE GOVERNOR'S WIFE At least there are no common people here, thank God. I can't stand their smell. It always gives me migraine.

THE FIRST LAWYER Madam, I must ask you to be careful what you say until we have another judge.

THE GOVERNOR'S WIFE But I didn't say anything, Illo Shuboladze. I love the people with their simple straightforward minds. It's only that their smell brings on my migraine.

THE SECOND LAWYER   There won't be many spectators. The whole population is sitting at home behind locked doors because of the riots on the outskirts of town.

THE GOVERNOR'S WIFE (*Looking at* GRUSHA)   Is that the creature?

THE FIRST LAWYER   Please, most gracious Natella Abashwili, abstain from invective until it is certain the Grand Duke has appointed a new judge and we're rid of the present one, who's about the lowest fellow ever seen in judge's gown. Things are all set to move, you see.

(*Enter* IRONSHIRTS *from the courtyard*)

THE COOK   Her Grace would pull your hair out on the spot if she didn't know Azdak is for the poor. He goes by the face.

(IRONSHIRTS *begin fastening a rope to a beam.* AZDAK, *in chains, is led in, followed by* SHAUWA, *also in chains. The* THREE FARMERS *bring up the rear*)

AN IRONSHIRT   Trying to run away, were you? (HE *strikes* AZDAK)

ONE FARMER   Off with his judge's gown before we string him up!

(IRONSHIRTS *and* FARMERS *tear off* AZDAK'S *gown. His torn underwear is visible. Then someone kicks him*)

AN IRONSHIRT (*Pushing him into someone else*)   If you want a heap of justice, here it is!

(*Accompanied by shouts of "You take it!" and "Let me have him, Brother!"* THEY *throw* AZDAK *back and forth until* HE *collapses. Then* HE *is lifted up and dragged under the noose*)

THE GOVERNOR'S WIFE (*Who, during this "Ball-game," has clapped her hands hysterically*)   I disliked that man from the moment I first saw him.

AZDAK (*Covered with blood, panting*)   I can't see. Give me a rag.

AN IRONSHIRT   What is it you want to see?

AZDAK   You, you dogs! (HE *wipes the blood out of his eyes with his shirt*) Good morning, dogs! How goes it, dogs! How's the dog world! Does it smell good? Got another boot for me to lick? Are you back at each other's throats, dogs?

(*Accompanied by a* CORPORAL, *a dust-covered* RIDER *enters.* HE *takes some documents from a leather case, looks at them, then interrupts*)

THE RIDER   Stop! I bring a dispatch from the Grand Duke, containing the latest appointments.

THE CORPORAL (*Bellowing*)   Atten-shun!

THE RIDER   Of the new judge it says: "We appoint a man whom we have to thank for saving a life indispensable to the country's welfare — a certain Azdak of Nuka." Which is he?

SHAUWA (*Pointing*)   That's him, Your Excellency.

THE CORPORAL (*Bellowing*)   What's going on here?

AN IRONSHIRT   I beg to report that His Honor Azdak was already His Honor Azdak, but on these farmers' denunciation was pronounced the Grand Duke's enemy.

THE CORPORAL (*Pointing at the* FARMERS)   March them off! (THEY *are marched off.* THEY *bow all the time*) See to it that His Honor Azdak is exposed to no more violence.

(*Exeunt* RIDER *and* CORPORAL)

THE COOK (*To* SHAUWA)   She clapped her hands! I hope he saw it!

THE FIRST LAWYER   It's a catastrophe.

(AZDAK *has fainted. Coming to,* HE *is dressed again in judge's robes.* HE *walks, swaying, toward the* IRONSHIRTS)

AN IRONSHIRT   What does Your Honor desire?

AZDAK   Nothing, fellow dogs, or just an occasional boot to lick. (*To* SHAUWA) I pardon you. (HE *is unchained*) Get me some red wine, the sweet kind.

(SHAUWA *stumbles off*)

Get out of here, I've got to judge a case.

(*Exeunt* IRONSHIRTS. SHAUWA *returns with a pitcher of wine.* AZDAK *gulps it down*)

AZDAK   Something for my backside. (SHAUWA *brings the Statute Book, puts it on the judge's chair.* AZDAK *sits on it*) I accept.

(*The* PROSECUTORS, *among whom a worried council has been held, smile with relief.* THEY *whisper*)

THE COOK   Oh dear!

SIMON   A well can't be filled with dew, they say.

THE LAWYERS (*Approaching* AZDAK, *who stands up, expectantly*)   A quite ridiculous case, Your Honor. The accused has abducted a child and refuses to hand it over.

AZDAK (*Stretching out his hand, glancing at* GRUSHA)   A most attractive person. (HE *fingers the money, then sits down, satisfied*) I declare the proceedings open and demand the whole truth. (*To* GRUSHA) Especially from you.

THE FIRST LAWYER   High Court of Justice! Blood, as the popular saying goes, is thicker than water. This old adage . . .

AZDAK (*Interrupting*)   The Court wants to know the lawyers' fee.

THE FIRST LAWYER (*Surprised*)   I beg your pardon? (AZDAK, *smiling, rubs his thumb and index finger*) Oh, I see. Five hundred piasters, Your Honor, to answer the Court's somewhat unusual question.

AZDAK   Did you hear? The question is unusual. I ask it because I listen in quite a different way when I know you're good.

THE FIRST LAWYER (*Bowing*)   Thank you, Your Honor. High Court of Justice, of all ties the ties of blood are strongest. Mother and child — is there a more intimate relationship? Can one tear a child from its mother? High Court of Justice, she has conceived it in the holy ecstasies of love. She has carried it in her womb. She has fed it with her blood. She has borne it with pain. High Court of Justice, it has been observed that even the wild tigress, robbed of her young, roams restless through the mountains, shrunk to a shadow. Nature herself . . .

AZDAK (*Interrupting, to* GRUSHA)   What's your answer to all this and anything else that lawyer might have to say?

GRUSHA   He's mine.

AZDAK   Is that all? I hope you can prove it. Why should I assign the child to you in any case?

GRUSHA   I brought him up like the priest says "according to my best knowledge and conscience." I always found him something to eat. Most of the time he had a roof over his head. And I went to such trouble for him. I had expenses too. I didn't look out for my own comfort. I brought the child up to be friendly with everyone, and from the beginning taught him to work. As well as he could, that is. He's still very little.

THE FIRST LAWYER   Your Honor, it is significant that the girl herself doesn't claim any tie of blood between her and the child.

AZDAK   The Court takes note of that.

THE FIRST LAWYER   Thank you, Your Honor. And now permit a woman bowed in sorrow — who has already lost her husband and now has also to fear the loss of her child — to address a few words to you. The gracious Natella Abashwili is . . .

THE GOVERNOR'S WIFE (*Quietly*)   A most cruel fate, Sir, forces me to describe to you the tortures of a bereaved mother's soul, the anxiety, the sleepless nights, the . . .

THE SECOND LAWYER (*Bursting out*)   It's outrageous the way this woman is being treated! Her husband's palace is closed to her! The revenue of her estates is blocked, and she is cold-bloodedly told that it's tied to the heir. She can't do a thing without that child. She can't even pay her lawyers!! (*To the* FIRST LAWYER, *who desperate about this outburst, makes frantic gestures to keep him from speaking*) Dear Illo Shuboladze, surely it can be divulged now that the Abashwili estates are at stake?

THE FIRST LAWYER   Please, Honored Sandro Oboladze! We agreed . . . (*To* AZDAK) Of course it is correct that the trial will also decide if our noble client can dispose of the Abashwili estates, which are rather extensive. I say "also" advisedly, for in the foreground stands the human tragedy of a mother, as Natella Abashwili very properly explained in the first words of her moving statement. Even if Michael Abashwili were not heir to the estates, he would still be the dearly beloved child of my client.

AZDAK   Stop! The Court is touched by the mention of estates. It's a proof of human feeling.

THE SECOND LAWYER   Thanks, Your Honor. Dear Illo Shuboladze, we can prove in any case that the woman who took the child is not the child's mother. Permit me to lay before the Court the bare facts. High Court of Justice, by an unfortunate chain of circumstances, Michael Abashwili was left behind on that Easter Sunday while his mother was making her escape. Grusha, a palace kitchen maid, was seen with the baby . . .

THE COOK   All her mistress was thinking of was what dresses she'd take along!

THE SECOND LAWYER (*Unmoved*)   Nearly a year later Grusha turned up in a mountain village with a baby and there entered into the state of matrimony with . . .

AZDAK   How did you get to that mountain village?

GRUSHA   On foot, Your Honor. And it was mine.

SIMON   I am the father, Your Honor.

THE COOK   I used to look after it for them, Your Honor. For five piasters.

THE SECOND LAWYER   This man is engaged to Grusha, High Court of Justice: his testimony is not trustworthy.

AZDAK   Are you the man she married in the mountain village?

SIMON   No, Your Honor, she married a peasant.

AZDAK (*To* GRUSHA)   Why? (*Pointing at* SIMON) Is he no good in bed? Tell the truth.

GRUSHA   We didn't get that far. I married because of the baby. So it'd have a roof over his head. (*Pointing at* SIMON) He was in the war, Your Honor.

AZDAK   And now he wants you back again, huh?

SIMON   I wish to state in evidence . . .

GRUSHA (*Angrily*)   I am no longer free, Your Honor.

AZDAK   And the child, you claim, comes from whoring? (GRUSHA *doesn't answer*) I'm going to ask you a question: What kind of child is it? Is it a ragged little bastard or from a well-to-do family?

GRUSHA (*Angrily*)   He's just an ordinary child.

AZDAK   I mean — did he have refined features from the beginning?

GRUSHA   He had a nose on his face.

AZDAK   A very significant comment! It has been said of me that I went out one time and sniffed at a rosebush before rendering a verdict — tricks like that are needed nowadays. Well, I'll make it short, and not listen to any more lies. (*To* GRUSHA) Especially not yours. (*To* ALL *the accused*) I can imagine what you've cooked up to cheat me! I know you people. You're swindlers.

GRUSHA (*Suddenly*)   I can understand your wanting to cut it short, now I've seen what you accepted!

AZDAK   Shut up! Did I accept anything from you?

GRUSHA (*While the* COOK *tries to restrain her*)   I haven't got anything.

AZDAK   True. Quite true. From starvelings I never get a thing. I might just as well starve, myself. You want justice, but do you want to pay for it, hm? When you go to a butcher you know you have to pay, but you people go to a judge as if you were going to a funeral supper.

SIMON (*Loudly*)   When the horse was shod, the horse-fly held out its leg, as the saying is.

AZDAK (*Eagerly accepting the challenge*)   Better a treasure in manure than a stone in a mountain stream.

SIMON   A fine day. Let's go fishing, said the angler to the worm.

AZDAK   I'm my own master, said the servant, and cut off his foot.

SIMON   I love you as a father, said the Czar to the peasants, and had the Czarevitch's head chopped off.

AZDAK   A fool's worst enemy is himself.

SIMON   However, a fart has no nose.

AZDAK   Fined ten piasters for indecent language in court! That'll teach you what justice is.

GRUSHA (*Furiously*)   A fine kind of justice! You play fast and loose with us because we don't talk as refined as that crowd with their lawyers!

AZDAK   That's true. You people are too dumb. It's only right you should get it in the neck.

GRUSHA   You want to hand the child over to her, and she wouldn't even know how to keep it dry, she's so "refined"! You know about as much about justice as I do!

AZDAK   There's something in that. I'm an ignorant man. Haven't even a decent pair of pants on under this gown. Look! With me, everything goes for food and drink — I was educated at a convent. Incidentally, I'll fine you ten piasters for contempt of court. And you're a very silly girl, to turn me against you, instead of making eyes at me and wiggling your backside a little to keep me in a good temper. Twenty piasters!

GRUSHA   Even if it was thirty, I'd tell you what I think of your justice, you drunken onion! (*Incoherently*) How dare you talk to me like the cracked Isaiah on the church window? As if you were somebody? For you weren't born to this. You weren't born to rap your own mother on the knuckles if she swipes a little bowl of salt someplace. Aren't you ashamed of yourself when you see how I tremble before you? You've made yourself their servant so no one will take their houses from them — houses they had stolen! Since when have houses belonged to the bedbugs? But you're on the watch, or they couldn't drag our men into their wars! You bribe-taker! (AZDAK *half gets up, starts beaming. With his little hammer* HE *half-heartedly knocks on the table as if to get silence. As* GRUSHA'S *scolding continues,* HE *only beats time with his hammer*). I've no respect for you. No more than for a thief or a bandit with a knife! You can do what you want. You can take the child away from me, a hundred against one, but I tell you one thing: only extortioners should be chosen for a profession like yours, and men who rape children! As punishment! Yes, let *them* sit in judgment on their fellow creatures. It is worse than to hang from the gallows.

AZDAK (*Sitting down*) Now it'll be thirty! And I won't go on squabbling with you — we're not in a tavern. What'd happen to my dignity as a judge? Anyway, I've lost interest in your case. Where's the couple who wanted a divorce? (*To* SHAUWA) Bring 'em in. This case is adjourned for fifteen minutes.

THE FIRST LAWYER (*To the* GOVERNOR'S WIFE) Even without using the rest of the evidence, Madam, we have the verdict in the bag.

THE COOK (*To* GRUSHA) You've gone and spoiled your chances with him. You won't get the child now.

THE GOVERNOR'S WIFE Shalva, my smelling salts!

(*Enter a* VERY OLD COUPLE)

AZDAK *I accept.* (*The* OLD COUPLE *don't understand*) I hear you want to be divorced. How long have you been together?

THE OLD WOMAN Forty years, Your Honor.

AZDAK And why do you want a divorce?

THE OLD MAN We don't like each other, Your Honor.

AZDAK Since when?

THE OLD WOMAN Oh, from the very beginning, Your Honor.

AZDAK I'll think about your request and render my verdict when I'm through with the other case. (SHAUWA *leads them back*) I need the child. (HE *beckons* GRUSHA *to him and bends not unkindly toward her*) I've noticed you have a soft spot for justice. I don't believe he's your child, but if he *were* yours, woman, wouldn't you want him to be rich? You'd only have to say he wasn't yours, and he'd have a palace and many horses in his stable and many beggars on his doorstep and many soldiers in his service and many petitioners in his courtyard, wouldn't he? What do you say — don't you want him to be rich? (GRUSHA *is silent*)

THE SINGER Hear now what the angry girl thought but did not say:

Had he golden shoes to wear
He'd be cruel as a bear.
Evil would his life disgrace.
He'd laugh in my face.
Carrying a heart of flint
Is too troublesome a stint.
Being powerful and bad
Is hard on a lad.
Then let hunger be his foe!
Hungry men and women, no.
Let him fear the darksome night
But not daylight!

AZDAK I think I understand you, woman.

GRUSHA (*Suddenly and loudly*) I won't give him up. I've raised him, and he knows me.

(*Enter* SHAUWA *with the* CHILD)

THE GOVERNOR'S WIFE It's in rags!

GRUSHA That's not true. But I wasn't given time to put his good shirt on.

THE GOVERNOR'S WIFE It must have been in a pigsty.

GRUSHA (*Furiously*) I'm not a pig, but there are some who are! Where did you leave your baby?

THE GOVERNOR'S WIFE I'll show you, you vulgar creature! (SHE *is about to throw herself on* GRUSHA, *but is restrained by her* LAWYERS) She's a criminal, she must be whipped. Immediately!

THE SECOND LAWYER (*Holding his hand over her mouth*) Natella Abashwili. you promised . . . Your Honor, the plaintiff's nerves . . .

AZDAK Plaintiff and defendant! The Court has listened to your case, and has come to no decision as to who the real mother is, therefore, I, the judge, am obliged to *choose* a mother for the child. I'll make a test. Shauwa, get a piece of chalk and draw a circle on the floor.

(SHAUWA *does so*)

AZDAK Now place the child in the center. (SHAUWA *puts* MICHAEL, *who smiles at* GRUSHA, *in the center of the circle*) Stand near the circle, both of you. (THE GOVERNOR'S WIFE *and* GRUSHA *step up to the circle*) Now each of you take the child by one hand. (THEY *do so*) The true mother is she who can pull the child out of the circle.

THE SECOND LAWYER (*Quickly*) High Court of Justice, I object! The fate of the great Abashwili estates, which are tied to the child, as the heir, should not be made dependent on such a doubtful duel. In addition, my client does not command the strength of this person, who is accustomed to physical work.

AZDAK She looks pretty well fed to me. Pull! (GOVERNOR'S WIFE *pulls the* CHILD *out of the circle on her side;* GRUSHA *has let go and stands aghast*) What's the matter with you? You didn't pull!

GRUSHA I didn't hold on to him.

THE FIRST LAWYER (*Congratulating the* GOVERNOR'S WIFE) What did I say! The ties of blood!

GRUSHA (*Running to* AZDAK) Your Honor, I take back everything I said against you. I ask your forgiveness. But could I keep him till he can speak all the words? He knows a few.

AZDAK Don't influence the Court. I bet you only know about twenty words yourself. All right, I'll make the test once more, just to be certain. (*The* TWO WOMEN *take up their positions again*) Pull! (*Again* GRUSHA *lets go of the* CHILD)

GRUSHA (*In despair*) I brought him up! Shall I also tear him to pieces? I can't!

AZDAK (*Rising*) And in this manner the Court has established the true mother. (*To* GRUSHA) Take your child and be off. I advise you not to stay in the city with him. (*To the* GOVERNOR'S WIFE) And you disappear before I fine you for fraud. Your estates fall to the city. They'll be converted into a playground for the children. They need one, and I've decided it shall be called after me: Azdak's Garden. (THE GOVERNOR'S WIFE *has fainted and is carried out by the* LAWYERS *and the* ADJUTANT. GRUSHA *stands motionless.*

SHAUWA *leads the* CHILD *toward her*) Now I'll take off this judge's gown —
it's grown too hot for me. I'm not cut out for a hero. In token of farewell
I invite you all to a little dance outside on the meadow. Oh, I'd almost forgotten something in my excitement . . . to sign the divorce decree.
(*Using the judge's chair as a table,* HE *writes something on a piece of paper,
and prepares to leave. Dance music has started*)

SHAUWA (*Having read what is on the paper*)   But that's not right. You've not
divorced the old people. You've divorced Grusha!

AZDAK   Have I divorced the wrong couple? What a pity! And I never retract!
If I did, how could we keep order in the land? (*To the* OLD COUPLE) I'll invite you to my party instead. You don't mind dancing with each other, do
you? (*To* GRUSHA *and* SIMON) I've got forty piasters coming from you.

SIMON (*Pulling out his purse*)   Cheap at the price, Your Honor. And many
thanks.

AZDAK (*Pocketing the cash*)   I'll be needing this.

GRUSHA (*To* MICHAEL)   So we'd better leave the city tonight, Michael. (*To*
SIMON) You like him?

SIMON   With my respects, I like him.

GRUSHA   Now I can tell you: I took him because on that Easter Sunday I got
engaged to you. So he's a child of love. Michael, let's dance.
(SHE *dances with* MICHAEL, SIMON *dances with the* COOK, *the* OLD COUPLE
with each other. AZDAK *stands lost in thought. The* DANCERS *soon hide him
from view. Occasionally* HE *is seen, but less and less as* MORE COUPLES *join
the dance*)

THE SINGER   And after that evening Azdak vanished and was never seen again.
The people of Grusinia did not forget him but long remembered
The period of his judging as a brief golden age,
Almost an age of justice.
(ALL THE COUPLES *dance off.* AZDAK *has disappeared*)

THE SINGER   But you, you who have listened to the Story of the Chalk Circle,
Take note what men of old concluded:
That what there is shall go to those who are good for it,
Children to the motherly, that they prosper,
Carts to good drivers, that they be driven well,
The valley to the waterers, that it yield fruit.

Exercises

1. How does the playwright characterize the peasant class? The ruling class?

2. What function do the proverbs (spoken mostly by Simon) serve?

3. Why would anyone accept the absurdities in the action of the play? Consider
Grusha's journey into the northern mountains with the Governor's baby.

4. What parallels do you discover in the two main actions involving Grusha and
Azdak?

5. What do you think is Brecht's simple definition of good and bad people?

Topics for Writing

1. The play explores, among many topics, the value of work. Show what attitudes toward work it expresses and how this motif is developed.

2. Brecht's drama treats extremely serious matters such as hunger, war, violence, and child abandonment, and yet the playwright manages to evoke laughter as well as pity. What means does he use to elicit these contradictory responses? For what purpose?

Selected Bibliography Bertolt Brecht

Bentley, E. "An Un-American Chalk Circle?" *Tulane Drama Review,* 10 (Summer 1966), 64–77.

————. "What is Epic Theater?" *Accent,* 6 (Winter 1946), 120–123.

Brecht, B. "Notes on the 'Caucasian Chalk Circle.' " *Tulane Drama Review,* 12 (Fall 1967), 88–100.

————. "Prologue to the 'Caucasian Chalk Circle.' " *Tulane Drama Review,* 4 (December 1959), 45–59.

Bunge, H. "The Dispute Over the Valley." *Tulane Drama Review,* 4 (December 1959), 50–66.

Gaskell, R. "The Form of the 'Caucasian Chalk Circle.' " *Modern Drama,* 10 (1967/68), 195–201.

Gaskill, W. "And the Time of the Great Taking Over (An Interview)." *Encore,* 9 (July/August 1962), 10–24.

Goodman, H. "Bertolt Brecht as 'Traditional' Dramatist." *Educational Theatre Journal,* 4 (1952), 111–113.

Ludowyk, E. "The Chalk Circle: A Legend in Four Centuries." *Comparative Literature,* I (1960), 249–256.

Marinello, L. "The Christian Side of Brecht? An Examination of the 'Caucasian Chalk Circle.' " *Drama Critique,* 4 (May 1961), 77–86.

Milne, T. " 'The Caucasian Chalk Circle.' " *Encore,* 9 (May/June 1962), 45–46.

Milnes, H. "The Concept of Man in Bertolt Brecht." *University of Toronto Quarterly,* 32 (April 1963), 224–225.

Politzer, H. "How Epic Is Brecht's Epic Theater." *Modern Language Quarterly,* 23 (1962), 104–110.

Sagar, K. "Brecht in Nevereverland." *Modern Drama,* 9 (1966/67), 11–17.

Solem, D. "Brecht's Theatre." *Hopkins Review* (Summer 1949).

Steer, W. "Brecht's Epic Theater." *Modern Language Review,* 63 (1968), 636–647.

————. "The Thematic Unity of Der Kaukasische Kreiderkreis." *German Life and Letters,* 21 (October 1967), 1–10.

Williams, R. "The Achievement of Brecht." *Critical Quarterly,* 3 (Summer 1961), 157–158.

August Strindberg (1849–1912)

Miss Julie

Translated by Elizabeth Sprigge

Characters

MISS JULIE, *Aged 25*
JEAN, *The valet, aged 30*
KRISTIN, *The cook, aged 35*

Scene: The large kitchen of a Swedish manor house in a country district in the eighties.

Midsummer eve.

The kitchen has three doors, two small ones into JEAN's *and* KRISTIN's *bedrooms, and a large, glass fronted double one, opening on to a courtyard. This is the only way to the rest of the house.*

Through these glass doors can be seen part of a fountain with a cupid, lilac bushes in flower and the tops of some Lombardy poplars. On one wall are shelves edged with scalloped paper on which are kitchen utensils of copper, iron and tin.

To the left is the corner of a large tiled range and part of its chimney-hood, to the right the end of the servants' dinner table with chairs beside it.

The stove is decorated with birch boughs, the floor strewn with twigs of juniper. On the end of the table is a large Japanese spice jar full of lilac.

There are also an ice-box, a scullery table and a sink. Above the double door hangs a big old-fashioned bell; near it is a speaking-tube.

A fiddle can be heard from the dance in the barn near-by. KRISTIN *is standing at the stove, frying something in a pan. She wears a light-coloured cotton dress and a big apron.*

JEAN *enters, wearing livery and carrying a pair of large riding-boots with spurs, which he puts in a conspicuous place.*

JEAN   Miss Julie's crazy again to-night, absolutely crazy.

KRISTIN   Oh, so you're back, are you?

JEAN   When I'd taken the Count to the station, I came back and dropped in at the Barn for a dance. And who did I see there but our young lady leading off with the gamekeeper. But the moment she sets eyes on me, up she rushes and invites me to waltz with her. And how she waltzed — I've never seen anything like it! She's crazy.

KRISTIN   Always has been, but never so bad as this last fortnight since the engagement was broken off.

JEAN   Yes, that was a pretty business, to be sure. He's a decent enough chap, too, even if he isn't rich. Oh, but they're choosy! (*Sits down at the end of the table.*)   In any case, it's a bit odd that our young — er — lady would rather stay at home with the yokels than go with her father to visit her relations.

KRISTIN   Perhaps she feels a bit awkward, after that bust-up with her fiancé.

JEAN   Maybe. That chap had some guts, though. Do you know the sort of thing that was going on, Kristin? I saw it with my own eyes, though I didn't let on I had.

KRISTIN   You saw them . . . ?

JEAN   Didn't I just! Came across the pair of them one evening in the stable-yard. Miss Julie was doing what she called "training" him. Know what that was? Making him jump over her riding-whip — the way you teach a dog. He did it twice and got a cut each time for his pains, but when it came to the third go, he snatched the whip out of her hand and broke it into smithereens. And then he cleared off.

KRISTIN   What goings on! I never did!

JEAN   Well, that's how it was with that little affair . . . Now, what have you got for me, Kristin? Something tasty?

KRISTIN   (*serving from the pan to his plate*)   Well, it's just a little bit of kidney I cut off their joint.

JEAN   (*smelling it*)   Fine! That's my special delice. (*Feels the plate.*) But you might have warmed the plate.

KRISTIN   When you choose to be finicky you're worse than the Count himself. (*Pulls his hair affectionately.*)

JEAN   (*crossly*)   Stop pulling my hair. You know how sensitive I am.

KRISTIN   There, there! It's only love, you know.

(JEAN *eats.* KRISTIN *brings a bottle of beer.*)

JEAN   Beer on Midsummer Eve? No thanks! I've got something better than that. (*From a drawer in the table brings out a bottle of red wine with a yellow seal.*) Yellow seal, see! Now get me a glass. You use a glass with a stem, of course, when you're drinking it straight.

KRISTIN   (*giving him a wine-glass*)   Lord help the woman who gets you for a husband, you old fusser! (*She puts the beer in the ice-box and sets a small saucepan on the stove.*)

JEAN   Nonsense! You'll be glad enough to get a fellow as smart as me. And I don't think it's done you any harm people calling me your fiancé. (*Tastes the wine.*) Good. Very good indeed. But not quite warmed enough. (*Warms the glass in his hand.*) We bought this in Dijon. Four francs the litre without the bottle, and duty on top of that. What are you cooking now? It stinks.

KRISTIN   Some bloody muck Miss Julie wants for Diana.

JEAN   You should be more refined in your speech, Kristin. But why should you spend a holiday cooking for that bitch? Is she sick or what?

KRISTIN   Yes, she's sick. She sneaked out with the pug at the lodge and got in the usual mess. And that, you know, Miss Julie won't have.

JEAN   Miss Julie's too high-and-mighty in some respects, and not enough in others, just like her mother before her. The Countess was more at home in the kitchen and cowsheds than anywhere else, but would she ever go driving with only one horse? She went round with her cuffs filthy, but she had to have the coronet on the cuff-links. Our young lady — to come back to her — hasn't any proper respect for herself or her position. I mean she isn't refined. In the Barn just now she dragged the gamekeeper away from Anna and made him dance with her — no waiting to be asked. We wouldn't do a thing like that. But that's what happens when the gentry try to behave like the common people — they become common . . . Still, she's a fine girl. Smashing! What shoulders! And what — er etcetera!

KRISTIN Oh come off it! I know what Clara says, and she dresses her.

JEAN Clara? Pooh, you're all jealous! But I've been out riding with her . . . and as for her dancing!

KRISTIN Listen, Jean. You will dance with me, won't you, as soon as I'm through?

JEAN Of course I will.

KRISTIN Promise?

JEAN Promise? When I say I'll do a thing I do it. Well, thanks for the supper. It was a real treat. (*Corks the bottle.*)

(JULIE *appears in the doorway, speaking to someone outside.*)

JULIE I'll be back in a moment. Don't wait.

(JEAN *slips the bottle into the drawer and rises respectfully.* JULIE *enters and joins* KRISTIN *at the stove.*)

Well, have you made it? (KRISTIN *signs that* JEAN *is near them.*)

JEAN (*gallantly*) Have you ladies got some secret?

JULIE (*flipping his face with her handkerchief*) You're very inquisitive.

JEAN What a delicious smell! Violets.

JULIE (*coquettishly*) Impertinence! Are you an expert of scent too? I must say you know how to dance. Now don't look. Go away. (*The music of a schottische begins.*)

JEAN (*with impudent politeness*) Is it some witches' brew you're cooking on Midsummer Eve? Something to tell your stars by, so you can see your future?

JULIE (*sharply*) If you could see that you'd have good eyes. (*To* KRISTIN.) Put it in a bottle and cork it tight. Come and dance this schottische with me, Jean.

JEAN (*hesitating*) I don't want to be rude, but I've promised to dance this one with Kristin.

JULIE Well, she can have another, can't you, Kristin? You'll lend me Jean, won't you?

KRISTIN (*bottling*) It's nothing to do with me. When you're so condescending, Miss, it's not his place to say no. Go on, Jean, and thank Miss Julie for the honour.

JEAN Frankly speaking, Miss, and no offence meant, I wonder if it's wise for you to dance twice running with the same partner, specially as those people are so ready to jump to conclusions.

JULIE (*flaring up*) What did you say? What sort of conclusions? What do you mean?

JEAN (*meekly*) As you choose not to understand, Miss Julie, I'll have to speak more plainly. It looks bad to show a preference for one of your retainers when they're all hoping for the same unusual favour.

JULIE Show a preference! The very idea! I'm surprised at you. I'm doing the people an honour by attending their ball when I'm mistress of the house, but if I'm really going to dance, I mean to have a partner who can lead and doesn't make me look ridiculous.

JEAN If those are your orders, Miss, I'm at your service.

JULIE (*gently*) Don't take it as an order. To-night we're all just people enjoying a party. There's no question of class. So now give me your arm. Don't worry, Kristin. I shan't steal your sweetheart.

(JEAN *gives* JULIE *his arm and leads her out.*)

Left alone, KRISTIN *plays her scene in an unhurried, natural way, humming to the tune of the schottische, played on a distant violin. She clears* JEAN's *place, washes up and puts things away, then takes off her apron, brings out a small mirror from a drawer, props it against the jar of lilac, lights a candle, warms a small pair of tongs and curls her fringe. She goes to the door and listens, then turning back to the table finds* MISS JULIE's *forgotten handkerchief. She smells it, then meditatively smooths it out and folds it. Enter* JEAN.)

JEAN   She really *is* crazy. What a way to dance! With people standing grinning at her too from behind the doors. What's got into her, Kristin?

KRISTIN   Oh, it's just her time coming on. She's always queer then. Are you going to dance with me now?

JEAN   Then you're not wild with me for cutting that one?

KRISTIN   You know I'm not — for a little thing like that. Besides, I know my place.

JEAN (*putting his arm around her waist*)   You're a sensible girl, Kristin, and you'll make a very good wife . . .

(*Enter* JULIE, *unpleasantly surprised.*)

JULIE (*with forced gaiety*)   You're a fine beau — running away from your partner.

JEAN   Not away, Miss Julie, but as you see, back to the one I deserted.

JULIE (*changing her tone*)   You really can dance, you know. But why are you wearing your livery on a holiday? Take it off at once.

JEAN   Then I must ask you to go away for a moment, Miss. My black coat's here. (*Indicates it hanging on the door to his room.*)

JULIE   Are you so shy of me — just over changing a coat? Go into your room then — or stay here and I'll turn my back.

JEAN   Excuse me then, Miss. (*He goes to his room and is partly visible as he changes his coat.*)

JULIE   Tell me, Kristin, is Jean your fiancé You seem very intimate.

KRISTIN   My fiancé? Yes, if you like. We call it that.

JULIE   Call it?

KRISTIN   Well, you've had a fiancé yourself, Miss, and . . .

JULIE   But we really were engaged.

KRISTIN   All the same it didn't come to anything.

(JEAN *returns in his black coat.*)

JULIE   Très gentil, Monsieur Jean. Très gentil.

JEAN   Vous voulez plaisanter, Madame.

JULIE   Et vous voulez parler français.[1] Where did you learn it?

JEAN   In Switzerland, when I was sommelier at one of the biggest hotels in Lucerne.

JULIE   You look quite the gentleman in that get-up. Charming. (*Sits at the table.*)

JEAN   Oh, you're just flattering me!

JULIE (*annoyed*)   Flattering you?

JEAN   I'm too modest to believe you would pay real compliments to a man like

---

1. *Très gentil . . . parler français:* Julie: Very nice, Mr. Jean. Very nice; Jean: "You wish to jest, my lady; Julie: And you wish to speak French.

me, so I must take it you are exaggerating — that this is what's known as flattery.

JULIE   Where on earth did you learn to make speeches like that? Perhaps you've been to the theatre a lot.

JEAN   That's right. And travelled a lot too.

JULIE   But you come from this neighbourhood, don't you?

JEAN   Yes, my father was a labourer on the next estate — the District Attorney's place. I often used to see you, Miss Julie, when you were little, though you never noticed me.

JULIE   Did you really?

JEAN   Yes. One time specially I remember . . . but I can't tell you about that.

JULIE   Oh do! Why not? This is just the time.

JEAN   No, I really can't now. Another time, perhaps.

JULIE   Another time means never. What harm in now?

JEAN   No harm, but I'd rather not. (*Points to* KRISTIN, *now fast asleep.*) Look at her.

JULIE   She'll make a charming wife, won't she? I wonder if she snores.

JEAN   No, she doesn't, but she talks in her sleep.

JULIE (*cynically*)   How do you know she talks in her sleep?

JEAN (*brazenly*)   I've heard her. (*Pause. They look at one another.*)

JULIE   Why don't you sit down?

JEAN   I can't take such a liberty in your presence.

JULIE   Supposing I order you to.

JEAN   I'll obey.

JULIE   Then sit down. No, wait a minute. Will you get me a drink first?

JEAN   I don't know what's in the icebox. Only beer, I expect.

JULIE   There's no only about it. My taste is so simple I prefer it to wine.
(JEAN *takes a bottle from the ice-box, fetches a glass and plate and serves the beer.*)

JEAN   At your service.

JULIE   Thank you. Won't you have some yourself?

JEAN   I'm not really a beer-drinker, but if it's an order . . .

JULIE   Order? I should have thought it was ordinary manners to keep your partner company.

JEAN   That's a good way of putting it. (*He opens another bottle and fetches a glass.*)

JULIE   Now, drink my health. (*He hesitates.*) I believe the man really is shy.
(JEAN *kneels and raises his glass with mock ceremony.*)

JEAN   To the health of my lady!

JULIE   Bravo! Now kiss my shoe and everything will be perfect. (*He hesitates, then boldly takes hold of her foot and lightly kisses it.*) Splendid. You ought to have been an actor.

JEAN (*rising*)   We can't go on like this, Miss Julie. Someone might come in and see us.

JULIE   Why would that matter?

JEAN   For the simple reason that they'd talk. And if you knew the way their tongues were wagging out there just now, you . . .

JULIE   What were they saying? Tell me. Sit down.

JEAN (*sitting*)   No offence meant, Miss, but . . . well, their language wasn't nice, and they were hinting . . . oh, you know quite well what. You're not a child, and if a lady's seen drinking alone at night with a man — and a servant at that then . . .

JULIE Then what? Besides, we're not alone. Kristin's here.

JEAN Yes, asleep.

JULIE I'll wake her up. (*Rises.*) Kristin, are you asleep? (KRISTIN *mumbles in her sleep.*) Kristin! Goodness, how she sleeps!

KRISTIN (*in her sleep*) The Count's boots are cleaned — put the coffee on — yes, yes, at once . . . (*Mumbles incoherently.*)

JULIE (*tweaking her nose*) Wake up, can't you!

JEAN (*sharply*) Let her sleep.

JULIE What?

JEAN When you've been standing at the stove all day you're likely to be tired at night. And sleep should be respected.

JULIE (*changing her tone*) What a nice idea. It does you credit. Thank you for it. (*Holds out her hand to him.*) Now come out and pick some lilac for me.

(*During the following,* KRISTIN *goes sleepily into her bedroom.*)

JEAN Out with you, Miss Julie?

JULIE Yes.

JEAN It wouldn't do. It really wouldn't.

JULIE I don't know what you mean. You can't possibly imagine that . . .

JEAN I don't, but others do.

JULIE What? That I'm in love with the valet?

JEAN I'm not a conceited man, but such a thing's been known to happen, and to these rustics nothing's sacred.

JULIE You, I take it, are an aristocrat.

JEAN Yes, I am.

JULIE And I'm coming down in the world.

JEAN Don't come down, Miss Julie. Take my advice. No one will believe you came down of your own accord. They'll all say you fell.

JULIE I have a higher opinion of our people than you. Come and put it to the test. Come on. (*Gazes into his eyes.*)

JEAN You're very strange, you know.

JULIE Perhaps I am, but so are you. For that matter everything is strange. Life, human beings, everything, just scum drifting about on the water until it sinks — down and down. That reminds me of a dream I sometimes have, in which I'm on top of a pillar and can't see any way of getting down. When I look down I'm dizzy; I have to get down but I haven't the courage to jump. I can't stay there and I long to fall, but I don't fall. There's no respite. There can't be any peace at all for me until I'm down, right down on the ground. And if I did get to the ground I'd want to be under the ground . . . Have you ever felt like that?

JEAN No. In my dream I'm lying under a great tree in a dark wood. I want to get up, up to the top of it, and look out over the bright landscape where the sun is shining and rob that high nest of its golden eggs. And I climb and climb, but the trunk is so thick and smooth and it's so far to the first branch. But I know if I can once reach that first branch I'll go to the top just as if I'm on a ladder. I haven't reached it yet, but I shall get there, even if only in my dreams.

JULIE Here I am chattering about dreams with you. Come on. Only into the park. (*She takes his arm and they go towards the door.*)

JEAN We must sleep on nine midsummer flowers tonight; then our dreams will come true, Miss Julie. (*They turn at the door. He has a hand to his eye.*)

JULIE Have you got something in your eye? Let me see.

JEAN Oh, it's nothing. Just a speck of dust. It'll be gone in a minute.

JULIE My sleeve must have rubbed against you. Sit down and let me see to it. (*Takes him by the arm and makes him sit down, bends his head back and tries to get the speck out with the corner of her handkerchief.*) Keep still now, quite still. (*Slaps his hand.*) Do as I tell you. Why, I believe you're trembling, big, strong man though you are! (*Feels his biceps.*) What muscles!

JEAN (*warning*) Miss Julie!

JULIE Yes, Monsieur Jean?

JEAN Attention. Je ne suis qu'un homme.[2]

JULIE Will you stay still! There now. It's out. Kiss my hand and say thank you.

JEAN (*rising*) Miss Julie, listen. Kristin's gone to bed now. Will you listen?

JULIE Kiss my hand first.

JEAN Very well, but you'll have only yourself to blame.

JULIE, For what?

JEAN For what! Are you still a child at twenty-five? Don't you know it's dangerous to play with fire?

JULIE Not for me. I'm insured.

JEAN (*bluntly*) No, you're not. And even if you are, there's still stuff here to kindle a flame.

JULIE Meaning yourself?

JEAN Yes. Not because I'm me, but because I'm a man and young and . . .

JULIE And good-looking? What incredible conceit! A Don Juan perhaps? Or a Joseph? Good Lord, I do believe you are a Joseph!

JEAN Do you?

JULIE I'm rather afraid so.
(JEAN *goes boldly up and tries to put his arms round her and kiss her. She boxes his ears.*)
How dare you!

JEAN Was that in earnest or a joke?

JULIE In earnest.

JEAN Then what went before was in earnest too. You take your games too seriously and that's dangerous. Anyhow, I'm tired of playing now and beg leave to return to my work. The Count will want his boots first thing and it's past midnight now.

JULIE Put those boots down.

JEAN No. This is my work, which it's my duty to do. But I never undertook to be your playfellow and I never will be. I consider myself too good for that.

JULIE You're proud.

JEAN In some ways — not all.

---

2. *Attention . . . homme:* Be careful. I am only a man.

JULIE   Have you ever been in love?

JEAN   We don't put it that way, but I've been gone on quite a few girls. And once I went sick because I couldn't have the one I wanted. Sick, I mean, like those princes in the Arabian Nights who couldn't eat or drink for love.

JULIE   Who was she? (*No answer.*) Who was she?

JEAN   You can't force me to tell you that.

JULIE   If I ask as an equal, ask as a — friend? Who was she?

JEAN   You.

JULIE (*sitting*)   How absurd!

JEAN   Yes, ludicrous, if you like. That's the story I wouldn't tell you before, see, but now I will . . . Do you know what the world looks like from below? No, you don't, No more than the hawks and falcons do whose backs one hardly ever sees because they're always soaring up aloft. I lived in a labourer's hovel with seven other children and a pig, out in the grey fields where there isn't a single tree. But from the window I could see the wall round the Count's park with apple-trees above it. That was the Garden of Eden, guarded by many terrible angels with flaming swords. All the same I and the other boys managed to get to the tree of life. Does all this make you despise me?

JULIE   Goodness all boys steal apples!

JEAN   You say that now, but all the same you do despise me. However, one time I went into the Garden of Eden with my mother to weed the onion beds. Close to the kitchen garden there was a Turkish pavilion hung all over with jasmine and honeysuckle. I hadn't any idea what it was used for, but I'd never seen such a beautiful building. People used to go in and then come out again, and one day the door was left open. I crept up and saw the walls covered with pictures and kings and emperors, and the windows had red curtains with fringes — you know now what the place was, don't you? I . . . (*Breaks off a piece of lilac and holds it for* JULIE *to smell. As he talks, she takes it from him.*)   I had never been inside the manor, never seen anything but the church, and this was more beautiful. No matter where my thoughts went, they always came back — to that place. The longing went on growing in me to enjoy it fully, just once. Enfin,[3] I sneaked in, gazed and admired. Then I heard someone coming. There was only one way out for the gentry, but for me there was another and I had no choice but to take it. (JULIE *drops the lilac on the table.*)   Then I took to my heels, plunged through the raspberry canes, dashed across the strawberry beds and found myself on the rose terrace. There I saw a pink dress and a pair of white stockings — it was you. I crawled into a weed pile and lay there right under it among prickly thistles and damp rank earth. I watched you walking among the roses and said to myself: "If it's true that a thief can get to heaven and be with the angels, it's pretty strange that a labourer's child here on God's earth mayn't come in the park and play with the Count's daughter."

JULIE (*sentimentally*)   Do you think all poor children feel the way you did?

JEAN (*taken aback, then rallying*)   *All* poor children? . . . Yes, of course they do. Of course.

JULIE   It must be terrible to be poor.

3. *Enfin:* Finally.

JEAN (*with exaggerated distress*) Oh yes, Miss Julie, yes. A dog may lie on the Countess's sofa, a horse may have his nose stroked by a young lady, but a servant . . . (*change of tone*) well, yes, now and then you meet one with guts enough to rise in the world, but how often? Anyhow, do you know what I did? Jumped in the millstream with my clothes on, was pulled out and got a hiding. But the next Sunday, when Father and all the rest went to Granny's, I managed to get left behind. Then I washed with soap and hot water, put my best clothes on and went to church so as to see you. I did see you and went home determined to die. But I wanted to die beautifully and peacefully, without any pain. Then I remembered it was dangerous to sleep under an elder bush. We had a big one in full bloom, so I stripped it and climbed into the oatsbin with the flowers. Have you ever noticed how smooth oats are? Soft to touch as human skin . . . Well, I closed the lid and shut my eyes, fell asleep, and when they woke me I was very ill. But I didn't die, as you see. What I meant by all that, I don't know. There was no hope of winning you — you were simply a symbol of the hopelessness of ever getting out of the class I was born in.

JULIE   You put things very well, you know. Did you go to school?

JEAN   For a while. But I've read a lot of novels and been to the theatre. Besides, I've heard educated folk talking — that's what's taught me the most.

JULIE   Do you stand round listening to what we're saying?

JEAN   Yes, of course. And I've heard quite a bit too! On the carriage box or rowing the boat. Once I heard you, Miss Julie, and one of your young lady friends . . .

JULIE   Oh! Whatever did you hear?

JEAN   Well, it wouldn't be nice to repeat it. And I must say I was pretty startled. I couldn't think where you had learnt such words. Perhaps, at bottom, there isn't as much difference between people as one's led to believe.

JULIE   How dare you! We don't behave as you do when we're engaged.

JEAN (*looking hard at her*)   Are you sure? It's no use making out so innocent to me.

JULIE   The man I gave my love to was a rotter.

JEAN   That's what you always say — afterwards.

JULIE   Always?

JEAN   I think it must be always. I've heard the expression several times in similar circumstances.

JULIE   What circumstances?

JEAN   Like those in question. The last time . . .

JULIE (*rising*)   Stop. I don't want to hear any more.

JEAN   Nor did *she* — curiously enough. May I go to bed now, please?

JULIE (*gently*)   Go to bed on Midsummer Eve? [4]

JEAN   Yes. Dancing with that crowd doesn't really amuse me.

JULIE   Get the key of the boathouse and row me out on the lake. I want to see the sun rise.

JEAN   Would that be wise?

JULIE   You sound as though you're frightened for your reputation.

JEAN   Why not? I don't want to be made a fool of, nor to be sent packing

---

4. *Midsummer Eve:* A festive occasion, of pagan origin, celebrated especially in Norway, Sweden, and Finland.

without a character when I'm trying to better myself. Besides, I have Kristin to consider.

JULIE   So now it's Kristin.

JEAN   Yes, but it's you I'm thinking about too. Take my advice and go to bed.

JULIE   Am I to take orders from you?

JEAN   Just this once, for your own sake. Please. It's very late and sleepiness goes to one's head and makes one rash. Go to bed. What's more, if my ears don't deceive me, I hear people coming this way. They'll be looking for me, and if they find us here, you're done for.

(*The* CHORUS *approaches, singing. During the following dialogue the song is heard in snatches, and in full when the peasants enter.*)

> Out of the wood two women came,
> Tridiri-ralla, tridiri-ra.
> The feet of one were bare and cold,
> Tridiri-ralla-la
>
> The other talked of bags of gold,
> Tridiri-ralla, tridiri-ra.
> But neither had a sou to her name,
> Tridiri-ralla-la.
>
> The bridal wreath I give to you,
> Tridiri-ralla, tridiri-ra.
> But to another I'll be true,
> Tridiri-ralla-la.

JULIE   I know our people and I love them, just as they do me. Let them come. You'll see.

JEAN   No, Miss Julie, they don't love you. They take your food, then spit at it. You must believe me. Listen to them, just listen to what they're singing . . . No, don't listen.

JULIE (*listening*)   What are they singing?

JEAN   They're mocking — you and me.

JULIE   Oh no! How horrible! What cowards!

JEAN   A pack like that's always cowardly. But against such odds there's nothing we can do but run away.

JULIE   Run away? Where to? We can't get out and we can't go into Kristin's room.

JEAN   Into mine, then. Necessity knows no rules. And you can trust me. I really am your true and devoted friend.

JULIE   But supposing . . . supposing they were to look for you in there?

JEAN   I'll bolt the door, and if they try to break in I'll shoot. Come on. (*Pleading.*) Please come.

JULIE (*tensely*)   Do you promise . . . ?

JEAN   I swear!

(JULIE *goes quickly into his room and he excitedly follows her. Led by the fiddler, the peasants enter in festive attire with flowers in their hats. They put a barrel of beer and a keg of spirits, garlanded with leaves, on the table, fetch glasses and begin to carouse. The scene becomes a ballet. They form a ring and dance and sing and mime: "Out of the wood two women came," Finally they go out, still singing.*)

JULIE *comes in alone. She looks at the havoc in the kitchen, wrings her hands, then takes out her powder puff and powders her face.*

JEAN *enters in high spirits.*)

JEAN Now you see! And you heard, didn't you? Do you still think it's possible for us to stay here?

JULIE No, I don't. But what can we do?

JEAN Run away. Far away. Take a journey.

JULIE Journey? But where to?

JEAN Switzerland. The Italian lakes. Ever been there?

JULIE No. Is it nice?

JEAN Ah! Eternal summer, oranges, evergreens . . . ah!

JULIE But what would we do there?

JEAN I'll start a hotel. First-class accommodation and first-class customers.

JULIE Hotel?

JEAN There's life for you. New faces all the time, new languages — no time for nerves or worries, no need to look for something to do — work rolling up of its own accord. Bells ringing night and day, trains whistling, buses coming and going, and all the time gold pieces rolling on to the counter. There's life for you!

JULIE For *you*. And I?

JEAN Mistress of the house, ornament of the firm. With your looks, and your style . . . oh, it's bound to be a success! Terrific! You'll sit like a queen in the office and set your slaves in motion by pressing an electric button. The guests will file past your throne and nervously lay their treasure on your table. You've no idea the way people tremble when they get their bills. I'll salt the bills and you'll sugar them with your sweetest smiles. Ah, let's get away from here! (*Produces a time-table.*) At once, by the next train. We shall be at Malmö at six-thirty, Hamburg eight-forty next morning, Frankfurt-Basle the following day, and Como[5] by the St. Gothard pass in — let's see — three days. Three days!

JULIE That's all very well. But Jean, you must give me courage. Tell me you love me. Come and take me in your arms.

JEAN (*reluctantly*) I'd like to, but I daren't. Not again in this house. I love you — that goes without saying. You can't doubt that, Miss Julie, can you?

JULIE (*shyly, very feminine*) Miss? Call me Julie. There aren't any barriers between us now. Call me Julie.

JEAN (*uneasily*) I can't. As long as we're in this house, there *are* barriers between us. There's the past and there's the Count. I've never been so servile to anyone as I am to him. I've only got to see his gloves on a chair to feel small. I've only to hear his bell and I shy like a horse. Even now, when I look at his boots, standing there so proud and stiff, I feel my back beginning to bend. (*Kicks the boots.*) It's those old, narrow-minded notions drummed into us as children . . . but they can soon be forgotten. You've only got to get to another country, a republic, and people will bend themselves double before my porter's livery. Yes, double they'll bend themselves, but I shan't. I wasn't

---

5. *Malmö:* City in southern tip of Sweden across from Copenhagen; *Hamburg:* Large city in northern West Germany; *Frankfurt:* Large city in central West Germany; *Como:* Small city in northern Italy, north of Milan.

born to bend. I've got guts, I've got character, and once I reach that first branch, you'll watch me climb. Today I'm valet, next year I'll be proprietor, in ten years I'll have made a fortune, and then I'll go to Roumania, get myself decorated and I may, I only say *may,* mind you, end up as a Count.

JULIE (*sadly*)   That would be very nice.

JEAN   You see in Roumania one can buy a title, and then you'll be a Countess after all. My Countess.

JULIE   What do I care about all that? I'm putting those things behind me. Tell me you love me, because if you don't . . . if you don't, what am I?

JEAN   I'll tell you a thousand times over — later. But not here. No sentimentality now or everything will be lost. We must consider this thing calmly like reasonable people. (*Takes a cigar, cuts and lights it.*) You sit down there and I'll sit here and we'll talk as if nothing has happened.

JULIE   My God, have you no feelings at all?

JEAN   Nobody has more. But I know how to control them.

JULIE   A short time ago you were kissing my shoe. And now . . .

JEAN (*harshly*)   Yes, that was then. Now, we have something else to think about.

JULIE   Don't speak to me so brutally.

JEAN   I'm not. Just sensibly. One folly's been committed, don't let's have more. The Count will be back at any moment and we've got to settle our future before that. Now, what do you think of my plans? Do you approve?

JULIE   It seems a very good idea — but just one thing. Such a big undertaking would need a lot of capital. Have you got any?

JEAN (*chewing his cigar*)   I certainly have. I've got my professional skill, my wide experience and my knowledge of foreign languages. That's capital worth having, it seems to me.

JULIE   But it won't buy even one railway ticket.

JEAN   Quite true. That's why I need a backer to advance some ready cash.

JULIE   How could you get that at a moment's notice?

JEAN   You must get it, if you want to be my partner.

JULIE   I can't. I haven't any money of my own. (*Pause.*)

JEAN   Then the whole thing's off.

JULIE   And . . . ?

JEAN   We go on as we are.

JULIE   Do you think I'm going to stay under this roof as your mistress? With everyone pointing at me? Do you think I can face my father after this? No. Take me away from here, away from this shame, this humiliation. Oh my God, what have I done? My God, my God! (*Weeps.*)

JEAN   So that's the tune now, is it? What have you done? Same as many before you.

JULIE (*hysterically*)   And now you despise me. I'm falling, I'm falling.

JEAN   Fall as far as me and I'll lift you up again.

JULIE   Why was I so terribly attracted to you? The weak to the strong, the falling to the rising? Or was it love? Is that love? Do you know what love is?

JEAN   Do I? You bet I do. Do you think I never had a girl before?

JULIE   The things you say, the things you think!

JEAN   That's what life's taught me, and that's what I am. It's no good getting hysterical or giving yourself airs. We're both in the same boat now. Here, my dear girl, let me give you a glass of something special. (*Opens the drawer, takes out the bottle of wine and fills two used glasses.*)

JULIE   Where did you get that wine?

JEAN   From the cellar.

JULIE   My father's burgundy.

JEAN   Why not, for his son-in-law?

JULIE   And I drink beer.

JEAN   That only shows your taste's not so good as mine.

JULIE   Thief!

JEAN   Are you going to tell on me?

JULIE   Oh God! The accomplice of a petty thief! Was I blind drunk? Have I dreamt this whole night? Midsummer Eve, the night for innocent merry-making.

JEAN   Innocent, eh?

JULIE   Is anyone on earth as wretched as I am now?

JEAN   Why should *you* be? After such a conquest. What about Kristin in there? Don't you think she has any feelings?

JULIE   I did think so, but I don't any longer. No. A menial is a menial . . .

JEAN   And a whore is a whore.

JULIE   (*falling to her knees, her hands clasped*)   O God in heaven, put an end to my miserable life! Lift me out of this filth in which I'm sinking. Save me! Save me!

JEAN   I must admit I'm sorry for you. When I was in the onion bed and saw you up there among the roses, I . . . yes, I'll tell you now . . . I had the same dirty thoughts as all boys.

JULIE   You, who wanted to die because of me?

JEAN   In the oats-bin? That was just talk.

JULIE   Lies, you mean.

JEAN   (*getting sleepy*)   More or less. I think I read a story in some paper about a chimney-sweep who shut himself up in a chest full of lilac because he'd been summonsed for not supporting some brat . . .

JULIE   So this is what you're like.

JEAN   I had to think up something. It's always the fancy stuff that catches the women.

JULIE   Beast!

JEAN   Merde!

JULIE   Now you have seen the falcon's back.

JEAN   Not exactly its *back*.

JULIE   I was to be the first branch.

JEAN   But the branch was rotten.

JULIE   I was to be a hotel sign.

JEAN   And I the hotel.

JULIE   Sit at your counter, attract your clients and cook their accounts.

JEAN   I'd have done that myself.

JULIE   That any human being can be so steeped in filth!

JEAN   Clean it up, then.

JULIE   Menial! Lackey! Stand up when I speak to you.

JEAN   Menial's whore, lackey's harlot, shut your mouth and get out of here! Are you the one to lecture me for being coarse? Nobody of my kind would ever be as coarse as you were tonight. Do you think any servant girl would throw herself at a man that way? Have you ever seen a girl of my class asking for it like that? I haven't. Only animals and prostitutes.

JULIE (*broken*) Go on. Hit me, trample on me — it's all I deserve. I'm rotten. But help me! If there's any way out at all, help me.

JEAN (*more gently*) I'm not denying myself a share in the honour of seducing you, but do you think anybody in my place would have dared look in your direction if you yourself hadn't asked for it? I'm still amazed . . .

JULIE And proud.

JEAN Why not? Though I must admit the victory was too easy to make me lose my head.

JULIE Go on hitting me.

JEAN (*rising*) No. On the contrary, I apologise for what I've said. I don't hit a person who's down — least of all a woman. I can't deny there's a certain satisfaction in finding that what dazzled one below was just moonshine, that that falcon's back is grey after all, that there's powder on the lovely cheek, that polished nails can have black tips, that the handkerchief is dirty although it smells of scent. On the other hand, it hurts to find that what I was struggling to reach wasn't high and isn't real. It hurts to see you fallen so low you're far lower than your own cook. Hurts like when you see the last flowers of summer lashed to pieces by rain and turned to mud.

JULIE You're talking as if you're already my superior.

JEAN I am. I might make you a Countess, but you could never make me a Count, you know.

JULIE But I am the child of a Count, and you could never be that.

JEAN True, but I might be the father of Counts if . . .

JULIE You're a thief. I'm not.

JEAN There are worse things than being a thief — much lower. Besides, when I'm in a place I regard myself as a member of the family to some extent, as one of the children. You don't call it stealing when children pinch a berry from overladen bushes. (*His passion is roused again.*) Miss Julie, you're a glorious woman, far too good for a man like me. You were carried away by some kind of madness, and now you're trying to cover up your mistake by persuading yourself you're in love with me. You're not, although you may find me physically attractive, which means your love's no better than mine. But I wouldn't be satisfied with being nothing but an animal for you, and I could never make you love me.

JULIE Are you sure?

JEAN You think there's a chance? Of my loving you, yes, of course. You're beautiful, refined (*takes her hand*), educated, and you can be nice when you want to be. The fire you kindle in a man isn't likely to go out. (*Puts his arm round her.*) You're like mulled wine, full of spices, and your kisses . . . (*He tries to pull her to him, but she breaks away.*)

JULIE Let go of me! You won't win me that way.

JEAN Not that way, how then? Not by kisses and fine speeches, not by planning the future and saving you from shame? How then?

JULIE How? How? I don't know. There isn't any way. I loathe you — loathe you as I loathe rats, but I can't escape from you.

JEAN Escape with me.

JULIE (*pulling herself together*) Escape? Yes, we must escape. But I'm so tired. Give me a glass of wine. (*He pours it out. She looks at her watch.*) First we must talk. We still have a little time. (*Empties the glass and holds it out for more.*)

JEAN   Don't drink like that. You'll get tipsy.

JULIE   What's the matter?

JEAN   What's it matter? It's vulgar to get drunk. Well, what have you got to say?

JULIE   We've got to run away, but we must talk first — or rather, I must, for so far you've done all the talking. You've told me about your life, now I want to tell you about mine, so that we really know each other before we begin this journey together.

JEAN   Wait. Excuse my saying so, but don't you think you may be sorry afterwards if you give away your secrets to me?

JULIE   Aren't you my friend?

JEAN   On the whole. But don't rely on me.

JULIE   You can't mean that. But anyway, everyone knows my secrets. Listen. My mother wasn't well-born; she came of quite humble people, and was brought up with all those new ideas of sex-equality and women's rights and so on. She thought marriage was quite wrong. So when my father proposed to her, she said she would never become his *wife* . . . but in the end she did. I came into the world, as far as I can make out, against my mother's will, and I was left to run wild, but I had to do all the things a boy does — to prove women are as good as men. I had to wear boys' clothes; I was taught to handle horses — and I wasn't allowed in the dairy. She made me groom and harness and go out hunting; I even had to try to plough. All the men on the estate were given the women's jobs, and the women the men's, until the whole place went to rack and ruin and we were the laughing-stock of the neighbourhood. At last my father seems to have come to his senses and rebelled. He changed everything and ran the place his own way. My mother got ill — I don't know what was the matter with her, but she used to have strange attacks and hide herself in the attic or the garden. Sometimes she stayed out all night. Then came the great fire which you have heard people talking about. The house and the stables and the barns — the whole place burnt to the ground. In very suspicious circumstances. Because the accident happened the very day the insurance had to be renewed, and my father had sent the new premium, but through some carelessness of the messenger it arrived too late. (*Refills her glass and drinks.*)

JEAN   Don't drink any more.

JULIE   Oh, what does it matter? We were destitute and had to sleep in the carriages. My father didn't know how to get money to rebuild, and then my mother suggested he should borrow from an old friend of hers, a local brick manufacturer. My father got the loan and, to his surprise, without having to pay interest. So the place was rebuilt. (*Drinks.*) Do you know who set fire to it?

JEAN   Your lady mother.

JULIE   Do you know who the brick manufacturer was?

JEAN   Your mother's lover?

JULIE   Do you know whose the money was?

JEAN   Wait . . . no, I don't know that.

JULIE   It was my mother's.

JEAN   In other words, the Count's, unless there was a settlement.

JULIE   There wasn't any settlement. My mother had a little money of her own which she didn't want my father to control, so she invested it with her — friend.

JEAN   Who grabbed it.

JULIE   Exactly. He appropriated it. My father came to know all this. He couldn't bring an action, couldn't pay his wife's lover, nor prove it was his wife's money. That was my mother's revenge because he made himself master in his own house. He nearly shot himself then — at least there's a rumour he tried and didn't bring it off. So he went on living, and my mother had to pay dearly for what she'd done. Imagine what those five years were like for me. My natural sympathies were with my father, yet I took my mother's side, because I didn't know the facts. I'd learnt from her to hate and distrust men — you know how she loathed the whole male sex. And I swore to her I'd never become the slave of any man.

JEAN   And so you got engaged to that attorney.

JULIE   So that he should be my slave.

JEAN   But he wouldn't be.

JULIE   Oh yes, he wanted to be, but he didn't have the chance. I got bored with him.

JEAN   Is that what I saw — in the stable-yard?

JULIE   What did you see?

JEAN   What I saw was him breaking off the engagement.

JULIE   That's a lie. It was I who broke it off. Did he say it was him? The cad.

JEAN   He's not a cad. Do you hate men, Miss Julie?

JULIE   Yes . . . most of the time. But when that weakness comes, oh . . . the shame!

JEAN   Then, do you hate me?

JULIE   Beyond words. I'd gladly have you killed like an animal.

JEAN   Quick as you'd shoot a mad dog, eh?

JULIE   Yes.

JEAN   But there's nothing here to shoot with — and there isn't a dog. So what do we do now?

JULIE   Go abroad.

JEAN   To make each other miserable for the rest of our lives?

JULIE   No, to enjoy ourselves for a day or two, for a week, for as long as enjoyment lasts, and then — to die . . .

JEAN   Die? How silly! I think it would be far better to start a hotel.

JULIE   (*without listening*)   . . . die on the shores of Lake Como, where the sun always shines and at Christmas time there are green trees and glowing oranges.

JEAN   Lake Como's a rainy hole and I didn't see any oranges outside the shops. But it's a good place for tourists. Plenty of villas to be rented by — er — honeymoon couples. Profitable business, that. Know why? Because they all sign a lease for six months and all leave after three weeks.

JULIE   (*naïvely*)   After three weeks? Why?

JEAN   They quarrel, of course. But the rent has to be paid just the same. And then it's let again. So it goes on and on, for there's plenty of love although it doesn't last long.

JULIE   You don't want to die with me?

JEAN   I don't want to die at all. For one thing I like living and for another I consider suicide's a sin against the Creator who gave us life.

JULIE   You believe in God — *you?*

JEAN   Yes, of course. And I go to church every Sunday. Look here. I'm tired of all this. I'm going to bed.

JULIE   Indeed! And do you think I'm going to leave things like this? Don't you know what you owe the woman you've ruined?

JEAN   (*taking out his purse and throwing a silver coin on the table*)   There you are. I don't want to be in anybody's debt.

JULIE   (*pretending not to notice the insult*)   Don't you know what the law is?

JEAN   There's no law unfortunately that punishes a woman for seducing a man.

JULIE   But can you see anything for it but to go abroad, get married and then divorce?

JEAN   What if I refuse this mésalliance? [6]

JULIE   Mésalliance?

JEAN   Yes, for me. I'm better bred than you, see! Nobody in my family committed arson.

JULIE   How do you know?

JEAN   Well, you can't prove otherwise, because we haven't any family records outside the Registrar's office. But I've seen your family tree in that book on the drawing-room table. Do you know who the founder of your family was? A miller who let his wife sleep with the King one night during the Danish war. I haven't any ancestors like that. I haven't any ancestors at all, but I might become one.

JULIE   This is what I get for confiding in someone so low, for sacrificing my family honour . . .

JEAN   Dishonour! Well, I told you so. One shouldn't drink, because then one talks. And one shouldn't talk.

JULIE   Oh, how ashamed I am, how bitterly ashamed! If at least you loved me!

JEAN   Look here — for the last time — what do you want? Am I to burst into tears? Am I to jump over your riding whip? Shall I kiss you and carry you off to Lake Como for three weeks, after which . . . What am I to do? What do you want? This is getting unbearable, but that's what comes of playing around with women. Miss Julie, I can see how miserable you are; I know you're going through hell, but I don't understand you. We don't have scenes like this; we don't go in for hating each other. We make love for fun in our spare time, but we haven't all day and all night for it like you. I think you must be ill. I'm sure you're ill.

JULIE   Then you must be kind to me. You sound almost human now.

JEAN   Well, be human yourself. You spit at me, then won't let me wipe it off — on you.

JULIE   Help me, help me! Tell me what to do, where to go.

JEAN   Jesus, as if I knew!

JULIE   I've been mad, raving mad, but there must be a way out.

JEAN   Stay here and keep quiet. Nobody knows anything.

JULIE   I can't. People do know. Kristin knows.

JEAN   They don't know and they wouldn't believe such a thing.

6. *mésalliance:* Marriage with a person of inferior social position.

JULIE (*hesitating*) But — it might happen again.

JEAN That's true.

JULIE And there might be — consequences.

JEAN (*in panic*) Consequences! Fool that I am I never thought of that. Yes, there's nothing for it but to go. At once. I can't come with you. That would be a complete giveaway. You must go alone — abroad — anywhere.

JULIE Alone? Where to? I can't.

JEAN You must. And before the Count gets back. If you stay, we know what will happen. Once you've sinned you feel you might as well go on, as the harm's done. Then you get more and more reckless and in the end you're found out. No. You must go abroad. Then write to the Count and tell him everything, except that it was me. He'll never guess that — and I don't think he'll want to.

JULIE I'll go if you come with me.

JEAN Are you crazy, woman? "Miss Julie elopes with valet." Next day it would be in the headlines, and the Count would never live it down.

JULIE I can't go. I can't stay. I'm so tired, so completely worn out. Give me orders. Set me going. I can't think any more, can't act . . .

JEAN You see what weaklings you are. Why do you give yourselves airs and turn up your noses as if you're the lords of creation? Very well, I'll give you your orders. Go upstairs and dress. Get money for the journey and come down here again.

JULIE (*softly*) Come up with me.

JEAN To your room? Now you've gone crazy again. (*Hesitates a moment.*) No! Go along at once. (*Takes her hand and pulls her to the door.*)

JULIE (*as she goes*) Speak kindly to me, Jean.

JEAN Orders always sound unkind. Now you know. Now you know.
(*Left alone,* JEAN *sighs with relief, sits down at the table, takes out a notebook and pencil and adds up figures, now and then aloud. Dawn begins to break.* KRISTIN *enters dressed for church, carrying his white dickey and tie.*)

KRISTIN Lord Jesus, look at the state the place is in! What have you been up to? (*Turns out the lamp.*)

JEAN Oh, Miss Julie invited the crowd in. Did you sleep through it? Didn't you hear anything?

KRISTIN I slept like a log.

JEAN And dressed for church already.

KRISTIN Yes, you promised to come to Communion with me today.

JEAN Why, so I did. And you've got my bib and tucker, I see. Come on then. (*Sits.* KRISTIN *begins to put his things on. Pause. Sleepily.*) What's the lesson today?

KRISTIN It's about the beheading of John the Baptist, I think.

JEAN That's sure to be horribly long. Hi, you're choking me! O Lord, I'm so sleepy, so sleepy!

KRISTIN Yes, what have you been doing up all night? You look absolutely green.

JEAN Just sitting here talking with Miss Julie.

KRISTIN She doesn't know what's proper, that one. (*Pause.*)

JEAN I say, Kristin.

KRISTIN What?

JEAN It's queer really, isn't it, when you come to think of it? Her.

KRISTIN What's queer?

JEAN The whole thing. (*Pause.*)

KRISTIN (*looking at the half-filled glasses on the table*) Have you been drinking together too?

JEAN Yes.

KRISTIN More shame you. Look me straight in the face.

JEAN Yes.

KRISTIN Is it possible? Is it possible?

JEAN (*after a moment*) Yes, it is.

KRISTIN Oh! This I would never have believed. How low!

JEAN You're not jealous of her, surely?

KRISTIN No, I'm not. If it had been Clara or Sophie I'd have scratched your eyes out. But not of her. I don't know why; that's how it is, though. But it's disgusting.

JEAN You're angry with her, then.

KRISTIN No. With you. It was wicked of you, very very wicked. Poor girl. And, mark my words, I won't stay here any longer now — in a place where one can't respect one's employers.

JEAN Why should one respect them?

KRISTIN You should know since you're so smart. But you don't want to stay in the service of people who aren't respectable, do you? I wouldn't demean myself.

JEAN But it's rather a comfort to find out they're no better than us.

KRISTIN I don't think so. If they're no better there's nothing for us to live up to. Oh and think of the Count! Think of him. He's been through so much already. No, I won't stay in the place any longer. A fellow like you too! If it had been that attorney, now, or somebody of her own class . . .

JEAN Why, what's wrong with . . .

KRISTIN Oh, you're all right in your own way, but when all's said and done there is a difference between one class and another. No, this is something I'll never be able to stomach. That our young lady who was so proud and so down on men you'd never believe she'd let one come near her should go and give herself to one like you. She who wanted to have poor Diana shot for running after the lodge-keeper's pug. No, I must say . . . ! Well, I won't stay here any longer. On the twenty-fourth of October I quit.

JEAN And then?

KRISTIN Well, since you mention it, it's about time you began to look around, if we're ever going to get married.

JEAN But what am I to look for? I shan't get a place like this when I'm married.

KRISTIN I know you won't. But you might get a job as porter or caretaker in some public institution. Government rations are small but sure, and there's a pension for the widow and children.

JEAN That's all very fine, but it's not in my line to start thinking at once about dying for my wife and children. I must say I had rather bigger ideas.

KRISTIN You and your ideas! You've got obligations too, and you'd better start thinking about them.

JEAN Don't *you* start pestering me about obligations. I've had enough of that. (*Listens to a sound upstairs.*) Anyway, we've plenty of time to work things out. Go and get ready, now, and we'll be off to church.

KRISTIN   Who's that walking about upstairs?

JEAN   Don't know — unless it's Clara.

KRISTIN   (*going*)   You don't think the Count could have come back without our hearing him?

JEAN   (*scared*)   The Count? No, he can't have. He'd have rung for me.

KRISTIN   God help us! I've never known such goings on.

(*Exit.*)

(*The sun has now risen and is shining on the treetops. The light gradually changes until it slants in through the windows.* JEAN *goes to the door and beckons.* JULIE *enters in travelling clothes, carrying a small bird-cage covered with a cloth which she puts on a chair.*)

JULIE   I'm ready.

JEAN   Hush! Kristin's up.

JULIE   (*in a very nervous state*)   Does she suspect anything?

JEAN   Not a thing. But, my God, what a sight you are!

JULIE   Sight? What do you mean?

JEAN   You're white as a corpse and — pardon me — your face is dirty.

JULIE   Let me wash, then. (*Goes to the sink and washes her face and hands.*) There. Give me a towel. Oh! The sun is rising!

JEAN   And that breaks the spell.

JULIE   Yes. The spell of Midsummer Eve . . . But listen, Jean. Come with me. I've got the money.

JEAN   (*skeptically*)   Enough?

JULIE   Enough to start with. Come with me. I can't travel alone today. It's Midsummer Day, remember. I'd be packed into a suffocating train among crowds of people who'd all stare at me. And it would stop at every station while I yearned for wings. No, I can't do that, I simply can't. There will be memories too; memories of Midsummer Days when I was little. The leafy church — birch and lilac — the gaily spread dinner table, relatives, friends — evening in the park — dancing and music and flowers and fun. Oh, however far you run away — there'll always be memories in the baggage car — and remorse and guilt.

JEAN   I will come with you, but quickly now then, before it's too late. At once.

JULIE   Put on your things. (*Picks up the cage.*)

JEAN   No luggage, mind. That would give us away.

JULIE   No, only what we can take with us in the carriage.

JEAN   (*fetching his hat*)   What on earth have you got there? What is it?

JULIE   Only my greenfinch. I don't want to leave it behind.

JEAN   Well, I'll be damned! We're to take a bird-cage along, are we? You're crazy. Put that cage down.

JULIE   It's the only thing I'm taking from my home. The only living creature who cares for me since Diana went off like that. Don't be cruel. Let me take it.

JEAN   Put that cage down, I tell you — and don't talk so loud. Kristin will hear.

JULIE   No, I won't leave it in strange hands. I'd rather you killed it.

JEAN   Give the little beast here, then, and I'll wring its neck.

JULIE   But don't hurt it, don't . . . no, I can't.

JEAN   Give it here. I *can*.

JULIE   (*taking the bird out of the cage and kissing it*)   Dear little Serena, must you die and leave your mistress?

JEAN Please don't make a scene. It's *your* life and future we're worrying about. Come on, quick now!

(*He snatches the bird from her, puts it on a board and picks up a chopper.* JULIE *turns away.*)

You should have learnt how to kill chickens instead of target-shooting. Then you wouldn't faint at a drop of blood.

JULIE (*screaming*) Kill me too! Kill me! You who can butcher an innocent creature without a quiver. Oh, how I hate you, how I loathe you! There is blood between us now. I curse the hour I first saw you. I curse the hour I was conceived in my mother's womb.

JEAN What's the use of cursing? Let's go.

JULIE (*going to the chopping-block as if drawn against her will*) No, I won't go yet. I can't . . . I must look. Listen! There's a carriage. (*Listens without taking her eyes off the board and chopper.*) You don't think I can bear the sight of blood. You think I'm so weak. Oh, how I should like to see your blood and your brains on a chopping-block! I'd like to see the whole of your sex swimming like that in a sea of blood. I think I could drink out of your skull, bathe my feet in your broken breast and eat your heart roasted whole. You think I'm weak. You think I love you, that my womb yearned for your seed and I want to carry your offspring under my heart and nourish it with my blood. You think I want to bear your child and take your name. By the way, what is your name? I've never heard your surname. I don't suppose you've got one. I should be "Mrs. Hovel" or "Madam Dunghill." You dog wearing my collar, you lackey with my crest on your buttons! I share you with my cook; I'm my own servant's rival! Oh! Oh! Oh! . . . You think I'm a coward and will run away. No, now I'm going to stay — and let the storm break. My father will come back . . . find his desk broken open . . . his money gone. Then he'll ring that bell — twice for the valet — and then he'll send for the police . . . and I shall tell everything. Everything. Oh how wonderful to make an end of it all — a real end! He has a stroke and dies and that's the end of all of us. Just peace and quietness . . . eternal rest. The coat of arms broken on the coffin and the Count's line extinct . . . But the valet's line goes on in an orphanage, wins laurels in the gutter and ends in jail.

JEAN There speaks the noble blood! Bravo, Miss Julie. But now, don't let the cat out of the bag.

(KRISTIN *enters dressed for church, carrying a prayer-book.* JULIE *rushes to her and flings herself into her arms for protection.*)

JULIE Help me, Kristin! Protect me from this man!

KRISTIN (*unmoved and cold*) What goings-on for a feast day morning! (*Sees the board.*) And what a filthy mess. What's it all about? Why are you screaming and carrying on so?

JULIE Kristin, you're a woman and my friend. Beware of that scoundrel!

JEAN (*embarrassed*) While you ladies are talking things over, I'll go and shave. (*Slips into his room.*)

JULIE You must understand. You must listen to me.

KRISTIN I certainly don't understand such loose ways. Where are you off to in those travelling clothes? And he had his hat on, didn't he, eh?

JULIE Listen, Kristin. Listen, I'll tell you everything.

KRISTIN I don't want to know anything.

JULIE You must listen.

Theme or Meaning 1011

KRISTIN   What to? Your nonsense with Jean? I don't care a rap about that; it's nothing to do with me. But if you're thinking of getting him to run off with you, we'll soon put a stop to that.

JULIE (*very nervously*)   Please try to be calm, Kristin, and listen. I can't stay here, nor can Jean — so we must go abroad.

KRISTIN   Hm, hm!

JULIE (*brightening*)   But you see, I've had an idea. Supposing we all three go — abroad — to Switzerland and start a hotel together . . . I've got some money, you see . . . and Jean and I could run the whole thing — and I thought you would take charge of the kitchen. Wouldn't that be splendid? Say yes, do. If you come with us everything will be fine. Oh do say yes! (*Puts her arms round* KRISTIN.)

KRISTIN (*coolly thinking*)   Hm, hm.

JULIE (*presto tempo*)   You've never travelled, Kristin. You should go abroad and see the world. You've no idea how nice it is travelling by train — new faces all the time and new countries. On our way through Hamburg we'll go to the zoo — you'll love that — and we'll go to the theatre and the opera too . . . and when we get to Munich there'll be the museums, dear, and pictures by Rubens and Raphael — the great painters, you know . . . You've heard of Munich, haven't you? Where King Ludwig lived — you know, the king who went mad. . . . We'll see his castles — some of his castles are still just like in fairy-tales . . . and from there it's not far to Switzerland — and the Alps. Think of the Alps, Kristin dear, covered with snow in the middle of summer . . . and there are oranges there and trees that are green the whole year round . . .

(JEAN *is seen in the door of his room, sharpening his razor on a strop which he holds with his teeth and his left hand. He listens to the talk with satisfaction and now and then nods approval.* JULIE *continues, tempo prestissimo.*) And then we'll get a hotel . . . and I'll sit at the desk, while Jean receives the guests and goes out marketing and writes letters . . . There's life for you! Trains whistling, buses driving up, bells ringing upstairs and downstairs . . . and I shall make out the bills — and I shall cook them too . . . you've no idea how nervous travellers are when it comes to paying their bills. And you — you'll sit like a queen in the kitchen . . . of course there won't be any standing at the stove for you. You'll always have to be nicely dressed and ready to be seen, and with your looks — no, I'm not flattering you — one fine day you'll catch yourself a husband . . . some rich Englishman, I shouldn't wonder — they're the ones who are easy (*slowing down*) to catch . . . and then we'll get rich and build ourselves a villa on Lake Como . . . of course it rains there a little now and then — but — (*dully*) — the sun must shine there too sometimes — even though it seems gloomy — and if not — then we can come home again — come back — (*pause*) — here or somewhere else . . . .

KRISTIN   Look here, Miss Julie, do you believe all that yourself?

JULIE (*exhausted*)   Do I believe it?

KRISTIN   Yes.

JULIE (*wearily*)   I don't know. I don't believe anything any more. (*Sinks down on the bench; her head in her arms on the table.*) Nothing. Nothing at all.

KRISTIN (*turning to* JEAN)   So you meant to beat it, did you?

JEAN (*disconcerted, putting the razor on the table*) Beat it? What are you talking about? You've heard Miss Julie's plan, and though she's tired now with being up all night, it's a perfectly sound plan.

KRISTIN Oh, is it? If you thought I'd work for that . . .

JEAN (*interrupting*) Kindly use decent language in front of your mistress. Do you hear?

KRISTIN Mistress?

JEAN Yes.

KRISTIN Well, well, just listen to that!

JEAN Yes, it would be a good thing if you did listen and talked less. Miss Julie is your mistress and what's made you lose your respect for her now ought to make you feel the same about yourself.

KRISTIN I've always had enough self-respect ——

JEAN To despise other people.

KRISTIN — not to go below my own station. Has the Count's cook ever gone with the groom or the swineherd? Tell me that.

JEAN No, you were lucky enough to have a high-class chap for your beau.

KRISTIN High-class all right — selling the oats out of the Count's stable. *Stealing*

JEAN You're a fine one to talk — taking a commission on the groceries and bribes from the butcher.

KRISTIN What the devil . . . ?

JEAN And now you can't feel any respect for your employers. You, you!

KRISTIN Are you coming to church with me? I should think you need a good sermon after your fine deeds.

JEAN No, I'm not going to church today. You can go alone and confess your own sins.

KRISTIN Yes, I'll do that and bring back enough forgiveness to cover yours too. The Saviour suffered and died on the cross for all our sins, and if we go to Him with faith and a penitent heart, He takes all our sins upon Himself.

JEAN Even grocery thefts?

JULIE Do you believe that, Kristin?

KRISTIN That is my living faith, as sure as I stand here. The faith I learnt as a child and have kept ever since, Miss Julie. "But where sin abounded, grace did much more abound."

JULIE Oh, if I had your faith! Oh, if . . .

KRISTIN But you see you can't have it without God's special grace, and it's not given to all to have that.

JULIE Who is it given to then?

KRISTIN That's the great secret of the workings of grace, Miss Julie. God is no respecter of persons, and with Him the last shall be first . . .

JULIE Then I suppose He does respect the last.

KRISTIN (*continuing*) . . . and it is easier for a camel to go through the eye of a needle than for a rich man to enter into the kingdom of God. That's how it is, Miss Julie. Now I'm going — alone, and on my way I shall tell the groom not to let any of the horses out, in case anyone should want to leave before the Count gets back. Goodbye. (*Exit.*)

JEAN What a devil! And all on account of a greenfinch.

JULIE (*wearily*) Never mind the greenfinch. Do you see any way out of this, any end to it?

JEAN (*pondering*) No.

JULIE   If you were in my place, what would you do?

JEAN   In your place? Wait a bit. If I was a woman — a lady of rank who had — fallen. I don't know. Yes, I do know now.

JULIE (*picking up the razor and making a gesture*)   This?

JEAN   Yes. But *I* wouldn't do it, you know. There's a difference between us.

JULIE   Because you're a man and I'm a woman? What is the difference?

JEAN   The usual difference — between man and woman.

JULIE (*holding the razor*)   I'd like to. But I can't. My father couldn't either, that time he wanted to.

JEAN   No, he didn't want to. He had to be revenged first.

JULIE   And now my mother is revenged again, through me.

JEAN   Didn't you ever love your father, Miss Julie?

JULIE   Deeply, but I must have hated him too — unconsciously. And he let me be brought up to despise my own sex, to be half woman, half man. Whose fault is what's happened? My father's, my mother's or my own? My own? I haven't anything that's my own. I haven't one single thought that I didn't get from my father, one emotion that didn't come from my mother, and as for this last idea — about all people being equal — I got that from him, my fiancé — that's why I call him a cad. How can it be my fault? Push the responsibility on to Jesus, like Kristin does? No, I'm too proud and — thanks to my father's teaching — too intelligent. As for all that about a rich person not being able to get into heaven, it's just a lie, but Kristin, who has money in the savings-bank, will certainly not get in. Whose fault is it? What does it matter whose fault it is? In any case I must take the blame and bear the consequences.

JEAN   Yes, but ... (*There are two sharp rings on the bell.* JULIE *jumps to her feet.* JEAN *changes into his livery.*) The Count is back. Supposing Kristin ... (*Goes to the speaking-tube, presses it and listens.*)

JULIE   Has he been to his desk yet?

JEAN   This is Jean, sir. (*Listens.*) Yes, sir. (*Listens.*) Yes, sir, very good, sir. (*Listens.*) At once, sir? (*Listens.*) Very good, sir. In half an hour.

JULIE (*in panic*)   What did he say? My God, what did he say?

JEAN   He ordered his boots and his coffee in half an hour.

JULIE   Then there's half an hour ... Oh, I'm so tired! I can't do anything. Can't be sorry, can't run away, can't stay, can't live — can't die. Help me. Order me, and I'll obey like a dog. Do me this last service — save my honour, save his name. You know what I ought to do, but haven't the strength to do. Use your strength and order me to do it.

JEAN   I don't know why — I can't now — I don't understand ... It's just as if this coat made me — I can't give you orders — and now that the Count has spoken to me — I can't quite explain, but ... well, that devil of a lackey is bending my back again. I believe if the Count came down now and ordered me to cut my throat, I'd do it on the spot.

JULIE   Then pretend you're him and I'm you. You did some fine acting before, when you knelt to me and played the aristocrat. Or ... Have you ever seen a hypnotist at the theatre? (*He nods.*) He says to the person "Take the broom," and he takes it. He says "Sweep," and he sweeps ...

JEAN   But the person has to be asleep.

JULIE (*as if in a trance*)   I am asleep already ... the whole room has turned to smoke — and you look like a stove — a stove like a man in black with a tall hat — your eyes are glowing like coals when the fire is low — and your face is a white patch like ashes. (*The sunlight has now reached the floor and lights up* JEAN.) How nice and warm it is! (*She holds out her hands as though warming them at a fire.*) And so light — and so peaceful.

JEAN (*putting the razor in her hand*) Here is the broom. Go now while it's light — out to the barn — and . . . (*Whispers in her ear.*)

JULIE (*waking*) Thank you. I am going now — to rest. But just tell me that even the first can receive the gift of grace.

JEAN The first? No, I can't tell you that. But wait . . . Miss Julie, I've got it! You aren't one of the first any longer. You're one of the last.

JULIE That's true. I'm one of the very last. I *am* the last. Oh! . . . But now I can't go. Tell me again to go.

JEAN No, I can't now, either. I can't.

JULIE And the first shall be last.

JEAN Don't think, don't think. You're taking my strength away too and making me a coward. What's that? I thought I saw the bell move . . . To be so frightened of a bell! Yes, but it's not just a bell. There's somebody behind it — a hand moving it — and something else moving the hand — and if you stop your ears — if you stop your ears — yes, then it rings louder than ever. Rings and rings until you answer — and then it's too late. Then the police come and . . . and . . . (*The bell rings twice loudly.* JEAN *flinches, then straightens himself up.*) It's horrible. But there's no other way to end it . . . Go!

(JULIE *walks firmly out through the door.*)

Curtain

Exercises

1. Describe Julie's character in terms of her conflicts.

2. What does Julie want? What must she do to triumph?

3. Identify two or three complications and explain why they are stumbling blocks in the path of the protagonist's goal.

4. Discuss the many circumstances that contrbute to Julie's tragic fate.

5. What kind of person is Jean? Is he a coward, a liar, and an opportunist? Explain.

6. Shed light on the character of Kristin. What function does she have?

7. Although the Father (the Master) never appears on stage, consider the significance of his role. What important decision follows his ringing of the bell?

8. Agree or disagree with Strindberg's belief that Julie's suicide is inevitable.

9. Suggest the significance in the play of (a) the seduction; (b) the peasants' dance; and (c) the greenfinch.

10. How does the play address the question of inequality?

Topics for Writing

1. In his foreword to *Miss Julie,* Strindberg says, "My plot is not simple, nor its point single." Defend or refute this assertion.

2. Explore the development of the following theme, which Strindberg has identified in the play: "A love relationship in the 'higher sense' cannot exist between people of such different quality."

Selected Bibliography   August Strindberg

Arestad, Sverre. "Ibsen, Strindberg and Naturalistic Tragedy." *Theatre Annual,* 24 (1968), 6–13.

Benston, Alice N. "From Naturalism to the Dream Play: A Study of the Evolution of Strindberg's Unique Theatrical Form." *Modern Drama,* 7 (1964/ 65), 382–404.

Brustein, Robert Sanford. *The Theatre of Revolt: An Approach to the Modern Drama.* Boston: Little, Brown, 1964.

Cole, Toby, ed. *Playwrights on Playwriting: The Meaning and Making of Modern Drama from Ibsen to Ionesco.* New York: Hill & Wang, 1960.

Corrigan, Robert W., and James L. Rosenberg, eds. *The Art of the Theatre: A Critical Anthology of Drama.* San Francisco: Chandler, 1964.

Freedman, Morris. *The Moral Impulse: Modern Drama from Ibsen to the Present.* Carbondale: Southern Illinois University Press, 1967.

Gassner, John, and Ralph G. Allen, eds. *Theatre and Drama in the Making.* Boston: Houghton Mifflin, 1964.

Harrison, A. Cleveland. "*Miss Julie*: Essence and Anomaly of Naturalism." *Central States Speech Journal,* 21 (1970), 87–92.

Hayes, Stephen G. "Strindberg's *Miss Julie*: Lilacs and Beer." *Scandinavian Studies,* 45 (1973), 59–64.

Offenbacher, Emil. "A Contribution to the Origin of Strindberg's *Miss Julie.*" *Psychoanalytical Review,* 31 (1944), 81–87.

Reinert, Otto, ed. *Strindberg: A Collection of Critical Essays.* Englewood Cliffs, N.J.: Prentice-Hall, 1971.

Sprinchorn, Evert. "Strindberg and the Greater Naturalism." *The Drama Review,* 13 (Winter 1968), 119–129.

Steene, Birgitta. *The Greatest Fire: A Study of August Strindberg.* Carbondale: Southern Illinois University Press, 1973.

Valency, Maurice. *The Flower and the Castle: Introduction to Modern Drama.* New York: Macmillan, 1963.

Williams, Raymond. *Drama from Ibsen to Brecht.* London: Chatto & Windus, 1968.

———. *Modern Tragedy.* Stanford: Stanford University Press, 1966.

Young, Vernon. "The History of *Miss Julie.*" *Hudson Review,* 8 (Spring 1955), 123–130.

19. DRAMATIC LANGUAGE

The study of language in drama deals almost exclusively with dramatic dialogue. Although dialogue is used sparingly in poetry and more freely in fiction, it is *all* the language in drama — it is the play. Only in stage directions does the playwright use other language.

Unlike the speeches of characters, written to be spoken and aimed primarily at presenting the play's argument, **stage directions** are written to be read and intended chiefly to inform. Older drama eschews stage directions, which are rarely used except to indicate entrances and exits. But modern drama makes ample use of stage directions to serve many diverse functions especially valuable to the director, the actor, and the reader. In the main, they establish mood, atmosphere, and setting, describe character, interpret motivation, and editorialize. Shaw is particularly detailed in his directions. In *Arms and the Man,* he even states that the "long mantle of furs" Raina has wrapped herself in is "worth, on a moderate estimate, about three times the furniture" of her room.

Successful **dramatic dialogue** is concentrated, not desultory. It employs a pattern of affirmation and denial. The speech between characters proceeds by assents and dissents, as one speaker echoes or differs with another, with all the harmony or discord between these extremes. Dialogue often involves a collision of opposed forces. It is the playwright's chief means of breathing life into a dramatic story, and perhaps one of the sacrosanct elements of the play. Seldom will characters on stage remain stationary or speechless. They are continually on the move — opening and closing doors, sitting down and getting up, eating, drinking, dancing, swaggering, brandishing swords, swinging fists and hatchets — and talking all the while. Nearly everything that we know about the characters, their backgrounds, their feelings, and their beliefs, we learn through dialogue.

Dramatic dialogue entails special obligations as well as certain restrictions. As in fiction, dialogue must be characteristic of the speakers and appropriate to the situation in which they are involved.

Furthermore, to be effective, dialogue must fulfill one of three **principal functions:** delineate character, advance the plot, or explain motive. Mainly because of the limitations of time, playwrights have to try to accomplish all that they can with a few well-chosen words and well-turned phrases. If the dialogue is good, everything within it is vital and serves a purpose. After all, a speech during a performance of a play will be heard only once. Moreover, dialogue should sound natural, even though it is compounded of artifice and differs from actual speech. Paradoxically, few people in the real world speak as easily and eloquently — never at a loss to utter the right words at the right moment — as the characters who populate the make-believe world of the stage.

In *Arms and the Man,* the Petkoffs talk volubly, but their words often prick the bubble of vanity in which they live. Thus Major Petkoff's speech on the bad habit of frequent bathing contrasts comically with the family's self-importance and pretensions to culture.

> I dont believe in going too far with these modern customs. All this washing cant be good for the health: it's not natural. There was an Englishman at Philippopolis who used to wet himself all over with cold water every morning when he got up. Disgusting! It all comes from the English: their climate makes them so dirty that they have to be perpetually washing themselves. Look at my father! he never had a bath in his life; and he lived to be ninety-eight, the healthiest man in Bulgaria. I dont mind a good wash once a week to keep up my position; but once a day is carrying the thing to a ridiculous extreme.

Jean, the footman in *Miss Julie,* at first expresses his sexual yearning for Julie in lyrical terms, remembering the "pink dress and a pair of white stockings" he saw her in when they were youngsters, and recalling his subsequent attempt to kill himself for love of her.

> I crawled into a weed pile and lay there right under it among prickly thistles and damp rank earth. I watched you walking among the roses. . . . the next Sunday. . . . I washed with soap and hot water, put my best clothes on and went to church so as to see you. I did see you and went home determined to die. But I wanted to die beautifully and peacefully, without any pain. Then I remembered it was dangerous to sleep under an elder bush. We had a big one in full bloom, so I stripped it and climbed into the oatsbin with the flowers. Have you ever noticed how smooth oats are? Soft to touch as human skin. . . .

But after satisfying his desire, Jean spews vulgarities at Julie and tells her that the oatsbin story was "just talk" based on something he had read "in some paper," since "it's always the fancy stuff that catches the women." Eventually, he gives her a razor to kill herself with. The change in his tone and language not only indicates a change of feelings and a growing uneasiness about any entanglements with Julie, but also reveals his selfishness and hypocrisy.

The dialogue between Willy Loman and his boss, Howard Wagner, in *Death of a Salesman,* when Willy asks for a job that would not involve traveling, shows that Willy is still living in a world of illusion, despite the harsh reality that has begun to close in on him. But it also moves the plot in a new direction, for Willy's request provokes Howard to fire him.

Since **imagery, allusions,** and **symbols** have been discussed at length in Chapters 8, 9, and 12, in the poetry section, and in Chapter 5, in the section on fiction, we do not need to go over the groundwork here. But you may want to review those chapters, for the stylistic devices discussed in them are the playwright's tools of trade as much as the poet's or the short-story writer's.

Shakespeare, of course, was a poet as well as a dramatist, and wrote most of his dialogues in blank verse. In the following speech from *Othello,* the protagonist, newly reunited with his wife, expresses his joy in terms of the storm he has just experienced.

It gives me wonder great as my content
To see you here before me. O my soul's joy!
If after every tempest come such calms,
May the winds blow till they have waken'd death!
And let the labouring bark climb hills of seas
Olympus-high, and duck again as low
All hell's from heaven! If it were now to die,
'Twere now to be most happy, for I fear
My soul hath her content so absolute
That not another comfort like to this
Succeeds in unknown fate.

Flower and bird imagery recurs in *Miss Julie,* where Jean also alludes to the Garden of Eden. As we have noted earlier, Shaw alludes in the title *Arms and the Man* to Virgil and the heroic view of war and love. In Albee's play *The Sandbox,* which is part of this chapter, the title surely refers to something besides a literal sandbox; we need to ponder the other level, or levels, of meaning — the symbolic value that not only the sandbox but other "literal facts" in the play, such as the sand itself, light and darkness, and even the young man's kiss, assume in the context of the action.

Another rhetorical device that we have considered in relation to both poetry and fiction, **irony,** is particularly effective in drama, and especially in tragedy. Sophocles is the master of tragic irony. All three types of irony abound in *Oedipus the King.*

Examples of verbal irony: Oedipus curses the murderer of Laius when in effect he is cursing himself; he vows to avenge the dead king "just as though I were his son," which in fact he is.

Examples of irony of situation: Oedipus castigates Teiresias for his arrogance, a trait Oedipus himself possesses; he berates the seer who is blind but knows the truth, when he himself has eyes to see but is blind to the truth; he is ingenious enough to solve the riddle of the Sphinx but not sufficiently clever to know his true identity; once again he saves Thebes by cleansing it of pollution (by bringing the murderer to justice), but in the process he discovers pollution in himself, and it destroys him.

Example of dramatic irony: Oedipus curses the murderer of Laius, whom we know to be Oedipus himself; he rejects the truth that the blind Teiresias imparts when he himself is blind and ignorant of the facts; he falsely charges Creon of treachery when he himself has been traitorous; he bitterly accuses Jocasta of arrogance when she begs him not to pursue the matter of his parentage, and it is his own hubris that causes his downfall; he shifts from his search for the identity of the killer of Laius to a search for his own identity, when in fact his purpose has not changed; and, finally, he compels the old shepherd to reveal his parentage, a fact we have known all along.

These tragic ironies give *Oedipus the King* its power. The effects of the drama would be lost if we were ignorant of the truth about Laius murderer.

Later playwrights, too, have made use of irony; indeed, you will find it in all the plays you have read so far in this book. Though the two plays that follow, Shakespeare's *Othello* and Albee's *The Sandbox,* differ greatly from each other, we need to watch for irony in both of them and to consider whether it underscores meaning, reveals character, or heightens the emotional tension.

William Shakespeare (1564–1616)

Othello, The Moor of Venice

[*Dramatis Personæ*]

DUKE OF VENICE
BRABANTIO, [*a senator,*] *father to*
  Desdemona
[Other] Senators
GRATIANO, [*brother to Brabantio,*] ⎫
LODOVICO, [*kinsman to Brabantio,*] ⎬
  two noble Venetians ⎭
OTHELLO, *the Moor* [*in the military*
  service of Venice]
CASSIO, *an honourable lieutenant*
IAGO, [*an ensign,*] *a villain*

RODERIGO, *a gulled gentleman*
MONTANO, *governor of Cyprus* [*before*
  Othello]
CLOWN [*servant to Othello*]
DESDEMONA, [*daughter to Brabantio*
  and] *wife to Othello*
EMILIA, *wife to Iago*
BIANCA, *a courtezan*
Gentlemen of Cyprus, Sailors [Officers,
  Messenger, Herald, Musicians, and
  Attendants]

[*Scene: Venice; a sea-port in Cyprus.*]

Act One   *Scene I.* [*Venice. A street.*]†
Enter RODERIGO *and* IAGO.

RODERIGO   [Tush]! never tell me! I take it much unkindly
  That thou, Iago, who hast had my purse
  As if the strings were thine, shouldst know of this.†
IAGO   ['Sblood], but you'll not hear me.
  If ever I did dream of such a matter,   5
  Abhor me.
RODERIGO   Thou told'st me thou didst hold him in thy hate.
IAGO   Despise me if I do not. Three great ones of the city,
  In personal suit to make me his lieutenant,
  Off-capp'd to him; and, by the faith of man,   10
  I know my price; I am worth no worse a place.
  But he, as loving his own pride and purposes,
  Evades them with a bombast circumstance†
  Horribly stuff'd with epithets of war,
  [And, in conclusion,]   15
  Nonsuits my mediators; for, "Certes," says he,
  "I have already chose my officer."
  And what was he?
  Forsooth, a great arithmetician,
  One Michael Cassio, a Florentine,   20
  (A fellow almost damn'd in a fair wife)
  That never set a squadron in the field,

Words and passages enclosed in
square brackets throughout the text
are either emendations of the copy
text or additions to it.

3. *this:* Desdemona's elopement.
13. *circumstance:* discourse.

Nor the division† of a battle knows
More than a spinster, unless the bookish theoric,
Wherein the [toged] consuls can propose   25
As masterly as he. Mere prattle without practice
Is all his soldiership. But he, sir, had th' election;
And I, of whom his eyes had seen the proof
At Rhodes, at Cyprus, and on other grounds
Christen'd and heathen, must be be-lee'd and calm'd   30
By debitor and creditor; this counter-caster,†
He, in good time, must his lieutenant be,
And I — [God] bless the mark! — his Moorship's ancient.
RODERIGO   By heaven, I rather would have been his hangman.
IAGO   Why, there's no remedy. 'Tis the curse of service,   35
Preferment goes by letter† and affection,
And not by old gradation,† where each second
Stood heir to th' first. Now, sir, be judge yourself
Whether I in any just term am affin'd†
To love the Moor.
RODERIGO   I would not follow him then.   40
IAGO   O, sir, content you;
I follow him to serve my turn upon him.
We cannot all be masters, nor all masters
Cannot be truly follow'd. You shall mark
Many a duteous and knee-crooking knave   45
That, doting on his own obsequious bondage,
Wears out his time, much like his master's ass,
For nought but provender, and when he's old, cashier'd.†
Whip me such honest knaves. Others there are
Who, trimm'd in forms and visages† of duty,   50
Keep yet their hearts attending on themselves,
And, throwing but shows of service on their lords,
Do well thrive by them and, when they have lin'd their coats,
Do themselves homage. These fellows have some soul;
And such a one do I profess myself. For, sir,   55
It is as sure as you are Roderigo,
Were I the Moor, I would not be Iago.
In following him, I follow but myself;
Heaven is my judge, not I for love and duty,
But seeming so, for my peculiar† end;   60
For when my outward action doth demonstrate
The native act and figure of my heart
In compliment extern,† 'tis not long after
But I will wear my heart upon my sleeve
For daws to peck at. I am not what I am.   65

23. *division:* array.   48. *cashier'd:* dismissed.
31. *counter-caster:* accountant.   50. *visages:* semblances.
36. *letter:* i.e., of recommendation.   60. *peculiar:* private.
37. *old gradation:* seniority.   63. *compliment extern:* external
39. *affin'd:* bound.   show.

RODERIGO   What a full fortune does the thick-lips† owe,†
    If he can carry 't thus!
IAGO   Call up her father,
    Rouse him. Make after him, poison his delight,
    Proclaim him in the streets. Incense her kinsmen,
    And, though he in a fertile climate dwell,   *70*
    Plague him with flies. Though that his joy be joy,
    Yet throw such [changes] of vexation on't,
    As it may lose some colour.
RODERIGO   Here is her father's house; I'll call aloud.
IAGO   Do, with like timorous† accent and dire yell   *75*
    As when, by night and negligence, the fire
    Is spied in populous cities.
RODERIGO   What, ho, Brabantio! Signior Brabantio, ho!
IAGO   Awake! what, ho, Brabantio! thieves! thieves!
    Look to your house, your daughter, and your bags!   *80*
    Thieves! thieves!

    BRABANTIO [*appears*] *above, at a window.*

BRABANTIO   What is the reason of this terrible summons?
    What is the matter there?
RODERIGO   Signior, is all your family within?
IAGO   Are your doors lock'd?
BRABANTIO   Why, wherefore ask you this?   *85*
IAGO   ['Zounds], sir, you're robb'd! For shame, put on your gown.
    Your heart is burst, you have lost half your soul;
    Even now, now, very now, an old black ram
    Is tupping your white ewe. Arise, arise!
    Awake the snorting† citizens with the bell,   *90*
    Or else the devil will make a grandsire of you.
    Arise, I say!
BRABANTIO   What, have you lost your wits?
RODERIGO   Most reverend signior, do you know my voice?
BRABANTIO   Not I. What are you?
RODERIGO   My name is Roderigo.
BRABANTIO   The worser welcome;   *95*
    I have charg'd thee not to haunt about my doors.
    In honest plainness thou hast heard me say
    My daughter is not for thee; and now, in madness,
    Being full of supper and distemp'ring† draughts,
    Upon malicious [bravery]† dost thou come   *100*
    To start† my quiet.
RODERIGO   Sir, sir, sir, —
BRABANTIO   But thou must needs be sure
    My spirits and my place have in their power
    To make this bitter to thee.
RODERIGO   Patience, good sir.

---

66. *thick-lips:* i.e., the Moor. *owe:*   99. *distemp'ring:* intoxicating.
own.   100. [*bravery*]: swaggering.
75. *timorous:* terrifying.   101. *start:* startle.
90. *snorting:* snoring.

BRABANTIO   What tell'st thou me of robbing? This is Venice;   105
     My house is not a grange.†
RODERIGO   Most grave Brabantio,
     In simple and pure soul I come to you.
IAGO   ['Zounds], sir, you are one of those that will not serve God, if the
     devil bid you. Because we come to do you service and you think we
     are ruffians, you'll have your daughter cover'd with a Barbary horse;   110
     you'll have your nephews† neigh to you; you'll have coursers for cous-
     ins, and gennets† for germans.†
BRABANTIO   What profane wretch art thou?
IAGO   I am one, sir, that comes to tell you your daughter and the Moor are
     [now] making the beast with two backs.   115
BRABANTIO   Thou art a villain.
IAGO   You are — a senator.
BRABANTIO   This thou shalt answer; I know thee, Roderigo.
RODERIGO   Sir, I will answer anything. But, I beseech you,
     If 't be your pleasure and most wise consent,
     As partly I find it is, that your fair daughter,   120
     At this odd-even† and dull† watch o' th' night,
     Transported, with no worse nor better guard
     But with a knave of common hire, a gondolier,
     To the gross clasps of a lascivious Moor, —
     If this be known to you and your allowance,†   125
     We then have done you bold and saucy wrongs;
     But if you know not this, my manners tell me
     We have your wrong rebuke. Do not believe
     That, from† the sense of all civility,
     I thus would play and trifle with your reverence.   130
     Your daughter, if you have not given her leave,
     I say again, hath made a gross revolt,
     Tying her duty, beauty, wit, and fortunes
     In an extravagant† and wheeling† stranger
     Of here and everywhere. Straight satisfy yourself.   135
     If she be in her chamber or your house,
     Let loose on me the justice of the state
     For thus deluding you.
BRABANTIO   Strike on the tinder, ho!
     Give me a taper! Call up all my people!
     This accident is not unlike my dream;   140
     Belief of it oppresses me already.
     Light, I say! light!   [Exit [above].
IAGO   Farewell; for I must leave you.
     It seems not meet, nor wholesome to my place,
     To be produc'd — as, if I stay, I shall —

---

106. *grange:* isolated farm.
111. *nephews:* grandsons.
112. *gennets:* Spanish horses. *ger-mans:* relatives.
121. *odd-even:* midnight. *dull:* dead.

125. *your allowance:* has your approval.
129. *from:* contrary to.
134. *extravagant:* vagabond. *wheeling:* roving.

Against the Moor; for, I do know, the state,   *145*
However this may gall him with some check,†
Cannot with safety cast† him, for he's embark'd
With such loud reason to the Cyprus wars,
Which even now [stand] in act, that, for their souls,
Another of his fathom† they have none   *150*
To lead their business; in which regard,
Though I do hate him as I do hell-pains,
Yet, for necessity of present life,
I must show out a flag and sign of love,
Which is indeed but sign. That you shall surely find him,   *155*
Lead to the Sagittary† the raised search;
And there will I be with him. So, farewell.   [*Exit.*
    Enter [below,] BRABANTIO *in his night-gown,† and Servants with torches.*
BRABANTIO   It is too true an evil; gone she is;
   And what's to come of my despised time
   Is nought but bitterness. Now, Roderigo,   *160*
   Where didst thou see her? O unhappy girl!
   With the Moor, say'st thou? Who would be a father!
   How didst thou know 'twas she? O, she deceives me
   Past thought! What said she to you? Get moe tapers;
   Raise all my kindred. Are they married, think you?   *165*
RODERIGO   Truly, I think they are.
BRABANTIO   O heaven! How got she out? O treason of the blood!
   Fathers, from hence trust not your daughters' minds
   By what you see them act. Is there not charms
   By which the property† of youth and maidhood   *170*
   May be abus'd?† Have you not read, Roderigo,
   Of some such thing?
RODERIGO   Yes, sir, I have indeed.
BRABANTIO   Call up my brother. — O, would you had had her! —
   Some one way, some another. — Do you know
   Where we may apprehend her and the Moor?   *175*
RODERIGO   I think I can discover him, if you please
   To get good guard and go along with me.
BRABANTIO   Pray you, lead on. At every house I'll call;
   I may command at most. Get weapons, ho!
   And raise some special officers of [night].   *180*
   On, good Roderigo; I'll deserve† your pains.   [*Exeunt.*

Scene II. [*Another street.*]
    Enter OTHELLO, IAGO, *and Attendants with torches.*

IAGO   Though in the trade of war I have slain men,
   Yet do I hold it very stuff o' th' conscience

---

146. *check:* rebuke.
147. *cast:* dismiss.
150. *fathom:* capacity.
156. *Sagittary:* an inn (with a Cen-
taur on its sign). It has also been
proposed that the word is a translation of *Frezzaria,* the Street of

the Arrow-makers in Venice.
158. S.D. *night-gown:* dressing
gown.
170. *property:* nature.
171. *abus'd:* deceived.
181. *deserve:* reward.

To do no contriv'd murder. I lack iniquity
Sometimes to do me service. Nine or ten times
I'd thought to have yerk'd† him here under the ribs.

OTHELLO   'Tis better as it is.

IAGO   Nay, but he prated,
And spoke such scurvy and provoking terms
Against your honour
That, with the little godliness I have,
I did full hard forbear him. But, I pray you, sir,
Are you fast married? Be assur'd of this,
That the magnifico is much belov'd,
And hath in his effect a voice potential
As double† as the Duke's. He will divorce you,
Or put upon you what restraint or grievance
The law, with all his might to enforce it on,
Will give him cable.

OTHELLO   Let him do his spite;
My services which I have done the signiory
Shall out-tongue his complaints. 'Tis yet to know, —
Which, when I know that boasting is an honour,
I shall promulgate — I fetch my life and being
From men of royal siege,† and my demerits†
May speak unbonneted† to as proud a fortune
As this that I have reach'd; for know, Iago,
But that I love the gentle Desdemona,
I would not my unhoused† free condition
Put into circumscription and confine
For the sea's worth. But, look! what lights come yond?

Enter CASSIO, *with lights,* Officers, *and torches.*

IAGO   Those are the raised father and his friends.
You were best go in.

OTHELLO   Not I; I must be found.
My parts, my title, and my perfect soul†
Shall manifest me rightly. Is it they?

IAGO   By Janus, I think no.

OTHELLO   The servants of the Duke, and my lieutenant.
The goodness of the night upon you, friends!
What is the news?

CASSIO   The Duke does greet you, general,
And he requires your haste-post-haste appearance,
Even on the instant.

OTHELLO   What is the matter, think you?

CASSIO   Something from Cyprus, as I may divine;
It is a business of some heat. The galleys†
Have sent a dozen sequent messengers
This very night at one another's heels,

5

10

15

20

25

30

35

40

---

5. *yerk'd:* stabbed.
14. *double:* strong.
22. *siege:* rank. *demerits:* deserts.
23. *unbonneted:* without taking my
hat off, on equal terms.

26. *unhoused:* unconfined.
31. *perfect soul:* clear conscience.
40. *galleys:* i.e., officers of the
galleys.

And many of the consuls, rais'd and met,
Are at the Duke's already. You have been hotly call'd for;
When, being not at your lodging to be found,   45
The Senate hath sent about three several quests
To search you out.
OTHELLO   'Tis well I am found by you.
I will but spend a word here in the house.
And go with you.   [*Exit.*
CASSIO   Ancient, what makes he here?
IAGO   Faith, he to-night hath boarded a land carack.†   50
If it prove lawful prize, he's made for ever.
CASSIO   I do not understand.
IAGO   He's married.
CASSIO   To who?
    [*Re-enter* OTHELLO.]
IAGO   Marry, to — Come, captain, will you go?
OTHELLO   Have with you.
CASSIO   Here comes another troop to seek for you.
    Enter BRABANTIO, RODERIGO, *and* OFFICERS *with torches and weapons.*
IAGO   It is Brabantio. General, be advis'd;   55
He comes to bad intent.
OTHELLO   Holla! stand there!
RODERIGO   Signior, it is the Moor.
BRABANTIO   Down with him, thief!
                            [*They draw on both sides.*]
IAGO   You, Roderigo! come, sir, I am for you.
OTHELLO   Keep up your bright swords, for the dew will rust them.
Good signior, you shall more command with years   60
Than with your weapons.
BRABANTIO   O thou foul thief, where hast thou stow'd my daughter?
Damn'd as thou art, thou hast enchanted her;
For I'll refer me to all things of sense,
If she in chains of magic were not bound,   65
Whether a maid so tender, fair, and happy,
So opposite to marriage that she shunn'd
The wealthy curled darlings of our nation,
Would ever have, t' incur a general mock,
Run from her guardage to the sooty bosom   70
Of such a thing as thou — to fear, not to delight.
Judge me the world, if 'tis not gross in sense†
That thou hast practis'd on her with foul charms,
Abus'd her delicate youth with drugs or minerals
That weakens motion.† I'll have 't disputed on;†   75
'Tis probable, and palpable to thinking.
I therefore apprehend and do attach† thee
For an abuser of the world, a practiser
Of arts inhibited† and out of warrant.†

---

50. *carack:* large trading ship.   77. *attach:* arrest.
72. *gross in sense:* perfectly clear. 79. *inhibited:* prohibited. *out of*
75. *motion:* will power. *disputed*   *warrant:* unjustifiable.
on: argued legally.

Lay hold upon him; if he do resist,   80
Subdue him at his peril.

OTHELLO   Hold your hands,
Both you of my inclining,† and the rest.
Were it my cue to fight, I should have known it
Without a prompter. [Where] will you that I go
To answer this your charge?

BRABANTIO   To prison, till fit time   85
Of law and course of direct session†
Call thee to answer.

OTHELLO   What if [I] do obey?
How may the Duke be therewith satisfi'd,
Whose messengers are here about my side
Upon some present business of the state   90
To bring me to him?

OFFICER   'Tis true, most worthy signior.
The Duke 's in council; and your noble self,
I am sure, is sent for.

BRABANTIO   How! the Duke in council!
In this time of the night! Bring him away;
Mine's not an idle cause. The Duke himself,   95
Or any of my brothers of the state,
Cannot but feel this wrong as 'twere their own;
For if such actions may have passage free,
Bond-slaves and pagans shall our statesmen be.   [*Exeunt.*

Scene III. [*A council-chamber.*]
The DUKE *and* SENATORS *set at a table, with lights;* OFFICERS *attending.*

DUKE   There is no composition† in [these] news
That gives them credit.

1. SENATOR   Indeed, they are disproportion'd;
My letters say a hundred and seven galleys.

DUKE   And mine, a hundred forty.

2. SENATOR   And mine, two hundred!
But though they jump† not on a just† account, —   5
As in these cases, where the aim reports,†
'Tis oft with difference — yet do they all confirm
A Turkish fleet, and bearing up to Cyprus.

DUKE   Nay, it is possible enough to judgement.
I do not so secure me in the error†   10
But the main article I do approve†
In fearful sense.

SAILOR (*Within.*)   What, ho! what, ho! what, ho!
Enter a SAILOR.

82. *inclining:* party.
85. *course ... session:* due course
of law.
Sc. iii, 1. *composition:* consistency.
5. *jump:* agree. *just:* exact.

6. *the ... reports:* the reports are
conjectural.
10. *so ... error:* take such assurance from the disagreement.
11. *approve:* assent to.

OFFICER   A messenger from the galleys.

DUKE   Now, what's the business?

SAILOR   The Turkish preparation makes for Rhodes;
   So was I bid report here to the state   15
   By SigniorAngelo.

DUKE   How say you by this change?

1. SENATOR   This cannot be,
   By no assay of reason; 'tis a pageant,†
   To keep us in false gaze. When we consider
   Th' importancy of Cyprus to the Turk,   20
   And let ourselves again but understand
   That, as it more concerns the Turk than Rhodes,
   So may he with more facile question bear it,†
   For that it stands not in such warlike brace,†
   But altogether lacks th' abilities   25
   That Rhodes is dress'd in; if we make thought of this,
   We must not think the Turk is so unskilful
   To leave that latest which concerns him first,
   Neglecting an attempt of ease and gain
   To wake and wage a danger profitless.   30

DUKE   Nay, in all confidence, he's not for Rhodes.

OFFICER   Here is more news.

   Enter a MESSENGER.

MESSENGER   The Ottomites, reverend and gracious,
   Steering with due course towards the isle of Rhodes,
   Have there injointed them with an after† fleet.   35

1. SENATOR   Ay, so I thought. How many, as you guess?

MESSENGER   Of thirty sail; and now they do restem
   Their backward course, bearing with frank appearance
   Their purposes toward Cyprus. Signior Montano,
   Your trusty and most valiant servitor,   40
   With his free duty recommends you thus,
   And prays you to believe him.

DUKE   'Tis certain, then, for Cyprus.
   Marcus Luccicos, is not he in town?

1. SENATOR   He's now in Florence.   45

DUKE   Write from us to him; post-post-haste dispatch.

1. SENATOR   Here comes Brabantio and the valiant Moor.

   Enter BRABANTIO, OTHELLO, CASSIO, IAGO, RODERIGO, *and* Officers.

DUKE   Valiant Othello, we must straight employ you
   Against the general enemy Ottoman.
   [*To* BRABANTIO.] I did not see you; welcome, gentle signior;   50
   We lack'd your counsel and your help to-night.

BRABANTIO   So did I yours. Good your Grace, pardon me;
   Neither my place nor aught I heard of business
   Hath rais'd me from my bed, nor doth the general care
   Take hold on me; for my particular† grief   55

---

18. *pageant:* pretence.   24. *brace:* defense.
23. *with . . . it:* capture it more   35. *after:* i.e., sent after.
easily.   55. *particular:* personal.

Is of so flood-gate and o'erbearing nature
That it engluts and swallows other sorrows
And it is still itself.

DUKE   Why, what's the matter?

BRABANTIO   My daughter! O, my daughter!

SENATOR   Dead?

BRABANTIO   Ay, to me;
She is abus'd, stol'n from me, and corrupted   60
By spells and medicines bought of mountebanks;
For nature so prepost'rously to err,
Being not deficient, blind, or lame of sense,
Sans witchcraft could not.

DUKE   Whoe'er he be that in this foul proceeding   65
Hath thus beguil'd your daughter of herself
And you of her, the bloody book of law
You shall yourself read in the bitter letter
After your own sense, yea, though our proper son
Stood in your action.

BRABANTIO   Humbly I thank your Grace.   70
Here is the man, — this Moor, whom now, it seems,
Your special mandate for the state affairs
Hath hither brought.

ALL   We are very sorry for 't.

DUKE [*To* OTHELLO.]   What, in your own part, can you say to this?

BRABANTIO   Nothing, but this is so.   75

OTHELLO   Most potent, grave, and reverend signiors,
My very noble and approv'd good masters,
That I have ta'en away this old man's daughter,
It is most true; true, I have married her:
The very head and front of my offending   80
Hath this extent, no more. Rude am I in my speech,
And little bless'd with the soft phrase of peace;
For since these arms of mine had seven years' pith
Till now, some nine moons wasted, they have us'd
Their dearest action in the tented field,   85
And little of this great world can I speak
More than pertains to feats of broils and battle,
And therefore little shall I grace my cause
In speaking for myself. Yet, by your gracious patience,
I will a round† unvarnish'd tale deliver   90
Of my whole course of love — what drugs, what charms,
What conjuration, and what mighty magic,
(For such proceeding I am charg'd withal,)
I won his daughter.

BRABANTIO   A maiden never bold;
Of spirit so still and quiet that her motion†   95
Blush'd at herself; and she, in spite of nature,
Of years, of country, credit, everything,

90. *round:* plain.   95. *motion:* impulses.

To fall in love with what she fear'd to look on!
It is a judgement maim'd and most imperfect
That will confess perfection so could err   100
Against all rules of nature, and must be driven
To find out practices of cunning hell,
Why this should be. I therefore vouch again
That with some mixtures powerful o'er the blood,
Or with some dram conjur'd to this effect,   105
He wrought upon her.
[DUKE.]   To vouch this is no proof,
Without more wider and more overt test
Than these thin habits† and poor likelihoods
Of modern† seeming do prefer against him.
[1.] SENATOR   But, Othello, speak.   110
Did you by indirect and forced courses
Subdue and poison this young maid's affections?
Or came it by request and such fair question
As soul to soul affordeth?
OTHELLO   I do beseech you,
Send for the lady to the Sagittary,   115
And let her speak of me before her father.
If you do find me foul in her report,
The trust, the office I do hold of you,
Not only take away, but let your sentence
Even fall upon my life.
DUKE   Fetch Desdemona hither.   120

                                        [*Exeunt two or three.*
OTHELLO   Ancient, conduct them; you best know the place.   [*Exit* IAGO.]
And, till she come, as truly as to heaven
I do confess the vices of my blood,
So justly to your grave ears I'll present
How I did thrive in this fair lady's love,   125
And she in mine.
DUKE   Say it, Othello.
OTHELLO   Her father lov'd me; oft invited me;
Still question'd me the story of my life
From year to year, the battles, sieges, fortunes,   130
That I have pass'd.
I ran it through, even from my boyish days
To the very moment that he bade me tell it;
Wherein I spoke of most disastrous chances,
Of moving accidents by flood and field,   135
Of hair-breadth scapes i' th' imminent deadly breach,
Of being taken by the insolent foe
And sold to slavery, of my redemption thence
And portance† in my travel's history;
Wherein of antres† vast and deserts idle,†   140

        108. *thin habits:* slight semblances.   139. *portance:* behavior.
        109. *modern:* ordinary, trivial.   140. *antres:* caves. *idle:* barren.

Rough quarries, rocks, [and] hills whose heads touch heaven,
It was my hint† to speak, — such was my process, —
And of the Cannibals that each other eat,
The Anthropophagi, and men whose heads
[Do grow] beneath their shoulders. These to hear   *145*
Would Desdemona seriously incline;
But still the house-affairs would draw her thence,
Which ever as she could with haste dispatch,
She'd come again, and with a greedy ear
Devour up my discourse: which I observing,   *150*
Took once a pliant† hour, and found good means
To draw from her a prayer of earnest heart
That I would all my pilgrimage dilate,
Whereof by parcels she had something heard,
But not [intentively.]† I did consent,   *155*
And often did beguile her of her tears
When I did speak of some distressful stroke
That my youth suffer'd. My story being done,
She gave me for my pains a world of [sighs].
She swore, in faith, 'twas strange, 'twas passing strange,   *160*
'Twas pitiful, 'twas wondrous pitiful.
She wish'd she had not heard it; yet she wish'd
That Heaven had made her such a man. She thank'd me,
And bade me, if I had a friend that lov'd her,
I should but teach him how to tell my story,   *165*
And that would woo her. Upon this hint† I spake:
She love'd me for the dangers I had pass'd,
And I lov'd her that she did pity them.
This only is the witchcraft I have us'd.
Here comes the lady; let her witness it.   *170*
    Enter DESDEMONA, IAGO, *and Attendants.*
DUKE   I think this tale would win my daughter too.
    Good Brabantio,
    Take up this mangled matter at the best;
    Men do their broken weapons rather use
    Than their bare hands.
BRABANTIO   I pray you, hear her speak.   *175*
    If she confess that she was half the wooer,
    Destruction on my head if my bad blame
    Light on the man! Come hither, gentle mistress.
    Do you perceive in all this noble company
    Where most you owe obedience?
DESDEMONA   My noble father,   *180*
    I do perceive here a divided duty.
    To you I am bound for life and education;
    My life and education both do learn me

142. *hint:* occasion.   166. *hint:* opportunity (not consci-
151. *pliant:* convenient.   ously given).
155. [*intentively*]: attentively.

How to respect you; you are the lord of duty;
I am hitherto your daughter. But here's my husband; 185
And so much duty as my mother show'd
To you, preferring you before her father,
So much I challenge that I may profess
Due to the Moor, my lord.

BRABANTIO   God be with you! I have done.
Please it your Grace, on to the state-affairs. 190
I had rather to adopt a child than get it.
Come hither, Moor.
I here do give thee that with all my heart
Which, but thou hast already, with all my heart
I would keep from thee. For your sake, jewel, 195
I am glad at soul I have no other child;
For thy escape would teach me tyranny,
To hang clogs on them. I have done, my lord.

DUKE   Let me speak like yourself,† and lay a sentence,
Which, as a grise† or step, may help these lovers 200
[Into your favour].
When remedies are past, the griefs are ended
By seeing the worst, which late on hopes depended.
To mourn a mischief that is past and gone
Is the next way to draw new mischief on. 205
What cannot be preserv'd when fortune takes,
Patience her injury a mock'ry makes.
The robb'd that smiles steals something from the thief;
He robs himself that spends a bootless grief.

BRABANTIO   So let the Turk of Cyprus us beguile; 210
We lose it not, so long as we can smile.
He bears the sentence well that nothing bears
But the free comfort which from thence he hears,
But he bears both the sentence and the sorrow
That, to pay grief, must of poor patience borrow. 215
These sentences,† to sugar or to gall
Being strong on both sides, are equivocal.†
But words are words; I never yet did hear
That the bruis'd heart was pierced through the ear.
I humbly beseech you, proceed to the affairs of state. 220

DUKE   The Turk with a most mighty preparation makes for Cyprus.
Othello, the fortitude† of the place is best known to you; and though
we have there a substitute of most allowed† sufficiency, yet opinion, a
sovereign mistress of effects, throws a more safer voice on you. You
must therefore be content to slubber† the gloss of your new fortunes 225
with this more stubborn and boist'rous expedition.

OTHELLO   The tyrant custom, most grave senators,
Hath made the flinty and steel couch of war

---

199. *like yourself:* as you should.
200. *grise:* degree.
216. *sentences:* maxims.
217. *equivocal:* equal.

222. *fortitude:* strength, fortification.
223. *allowed:* admitted.
225. *slubber:* sully.

My thrice-driven† bed of down. I do agnize†
A natural and prompt alacrity   230
I find in hardness, and do undertake
These present wars against the Ottomites.
Most humbly therefore bending to your state,
I crave fit disposition for my wife,
Due reference† of place and exhibition,†   235
With such accommodation and besort†
As levels with† her breeding.

DUKE   [If you please,
   Be 't at her father's.]

BRABANTIO   I'll not have it so.

OTHELLO   Nor I.

DESDEMONA   Nor I; [I would not] there reside,
   To put my father in impatient thoughts   240
   By being in his eye. Most gracious Duke,
   To my unfolding lend your prosperous† ear;
   And let me find a charter† in your voice
   T' assist my simpleness.

DUKE   What would you, Desdemona?   245

DESDEMONA   That I [did] love the Moor to live with him,
   My downright violence and storm of fortunes†
   May trumpet to the world. My heart's subdu'd
   Even to the very quality of my lord.
   I saw Othello's visage in his mind,   250
   And to his honours and his valiant parts
   Did I my soul and fortunes consecrate.
   So that, dear lords, if I were left behind,
   A moth of peace, and he go to the war,
   The rites for [which] I love him are bereft me,   255
   And I a heavy interim shall support
   By his dear absence. Let me go with him.

OTHELLO   Let her have your voice.
   Vouch with me, Heaven, I therefore beg it not
   To please the palate of my appetite,   260
   Nor to comply with heat, the young affects
   In my defunct† and proper satisfaction,
   But to be free and bounteous to her mind;
   And Heaven defend† your good souls, that you think
   I will your serious and great business scant   265
   When she is with me. No, when light-wing'd toys
   Of feather'd Cupid seel† with wanton dullness

229. *thrice-driven:* thoroughly sift-
ed. *agnize:* acknowledge.
235. *reference:* assignment. *exhibition:* provision.
236. *besort:* company.
237. *levels with:* befits.
242. *prosperous:* propitious.
243. *charter:* privilege.

247. *My . . . fortunes:* my precipi-
tate assault upon my fortunes.
262. *defunct:* The modern meaning is here excluded, and no convincing explanation has been found.
264. *defend:* forbid.
267. *seel:* blind (from falconry).

My speculative and offic'd instruments†
That my disports corrupt and taint my business,
Let housewives make a skillet of my helm,   270
And all indign† and base adversities
Make head against my estimation!†
DUKE   Be it as you shall privately determine,
Either for her stay or going. Th' affair cries haste,
And speed must answer it.
1. SENATOR   You must away to-night.   275
[DESDEMONA   To-night, my lord?
DUKE   This night.]
OTHELLO   With all my heart.
DUKE   At nine i' th' morning here we'll meet again.
Othello, leave some officer behind,
And he shall our commission bring to you,
And such things else of quality and respect   280
As doth import† you.
OTHELLO   So please your Grace, my ancient;
A man he is of honesty and trust.
To his conveyance I assign my wife,
With what else needful your good Grace shall think
To be sent after me.
DUKE   Let it be so.   285
Good-night to every one. [To BRABANTIO.] And, noble signior,
If virtue no delighted† beauty lack,
Your son-in-law is far more fair than black.
1. SENATOR   Adieu, brave Moor; use Desdemona well.
BRABANTIO   Look to her, Moor, if thou hast eyes to see;   290
She has deceiv'd her father, and may thee.

                                    [Exeunt [DUKE, SENATORS, OFFICERS, etc.].
OTHELLO   My life upon her faith! Honest Iago,
My Desdemona must I leave to thee.
I prithee, let thy wife attend on her;
And bring them after in the best advantage.†   295
Come, Desdemona; I have but an hour
Of love, of worldly matters and direction,
To spend with thee. We must obey the time.

                                    [Exeunt OTHELLO and DESDEMONA.

RODERIGO   Iago, —
IAGO   What say'st thou, noble heart?   300
RODERIGO   What will I do, think'st thou?
IAGO   Why, go to bed and sleep.
RODERIGO   I will incontinently† drown myself.
IAGO   If thou dost, I shall never love thee after. Why, thou silly gentle-
man!   305

268. *My . . . instruments:* my fac-   281. *import:* concern.
ulties whose office is to perceive.   287. *delighted:* delightful.
271. *indign:* unworthy.   295. *advantage:* opportunity.
272. *estimation:* reputation.   303. *incontinently:* straightway.

Good line

RODERIGO   It is silliness to live when to live is torment; and then have we
a prescription to die when Death is our physician.

IAGO   O villanous! I have look'd upon the world for four times seven
years; and since I could distinguish betwixt a benefit and an injury, I
never found man that knew how to love himself. Ere I would say I   _310_
would drown myself for the love of a guinea-hen, I would change my
humanity with a baboon.

RODERIGO   What should I do? I confess it is my shame to be so fond, but
it is not in my virtue to amend it.

IAGO   Virtue! a fig! 'tis in ourselves that we are thus or thus. Our bodies   _315_
are our gardens, to the which our wills are gardeners; so that if we will
plant nettles or sow lettuce, set hyssop† and weed up thyme, supply it
with one gender† of herbs or distract it with many, either to have it
sterile with idleness or manured with industry, why, the power and
corrigible authority† of this lies in our wills. If the [balance] of our   _320_
lives had not one scale of reason to poise another of sensuality, the
blood and baseness of our natures would conduct us to most preposterous conclusions; but we have reason to cool our raging motions,†
our carnal stings, our unbitted lusts, whereof I take this that you call
love to be a sect or scion.†   _325_

RODERIGO   It cannot be.

IAGO   It is merely a lust of the blood and a permission of the will. Come,
be a man! Drown thyself? drown cats and blind puppies! I have profess'd me thy friend, and I confess me knit to thy deserving with cables
of perdurable† toughness; I could never better stead thee than now. Put   _330_
money in thy purse; follow thou the wars; defeat thy favour† with an
usurp'd beard. I say, put money in thy purse. It cannot be long that
Desdemona should continue her love to the Moor, — put money in thy
purse, — nor he his to her. It was a violent commencement in her, and
thou shalt see an answerable sequestration.† Put but money in thy   _335_
purse. These Moors are changeable in their wills — fill thy purse with
money; — the food that to him now is as luscious as locusts,† shall be
to him shortly as bitter as coloquintida.† She must change for youth;
when she is sated with his body, she will find the error of her choice;
[she must have change, she must:] therefore put money in thy purse. If   _340_
thou wilt needs damn thyself, do it a more delicate way than drowning.
Make all the money thou canst. If sanctimony and a frail vow betwixt
an erring barbarian and a super-subtle Venetian be not too hard for
my wits and all the tribe of hell, thou shalt enjoy her; therefore make
money. A pox of drowning thyself! it is clean out of the way. Seek   _345_
thou rather to be hang'd in compassing thy joy than to be drown'd and
go without her.

RODERIGO   Wilt thou be fast to my hopes, if I depend on the issue?†

317. _hyssop:_ fragrant herb.
318. _gender:_ kind.
320. _corrigible authority:_ correc-
tive power.
323. _motions:_ appetites.
325. _sect or scion:_ cutting or off-
shoot.
330. _perdurable:_ eternal.

331. _defeat thy favour:_ disguise
thy face.
335. _sequestration:_ separation.
337. _locusts:_ the fruit of the carob
tree.
338. _coloquintida:_ a bitter fruit.
348. _depend . . . issue:_ rely on the
outcome.

IAGO Thou art sure of me. Go, make money. I had told thee often, and I
re-tell thee again and again, I hate the Moor. My cause is hearted†; *350*
thine hath no less reason. Let us be conjunctive† in our revenge against
him. If thou canst cuckold him, thou dost thyself a pleasure, me a
sport. There are many events in the womb of time which will be delivered. Traverse†! go, provide thy money. We will have more of this
to-morrow. Adieu. *355*

RODERIGO Where shall we meet i' th' morning?

IAGO At my lodging.

RODERIGO I'll be with thee betimes.

IAGO Go to; farewell. Do you hear, Roderigo?

[RODERIGO What say you? *360*

IAGO No more of drowning, do you hear?

RODERIGO I am chang'd;] I'll sell all my land. [*Exit.*

IAGO Thus do I ever make my fool my purse;
For I mine own gain'd knowledge should profane
If I would time expend with such a snipe† *365*
But for my sport and profit. I hate the Moor;
And it is thought abroad that 'twixt my sheets
He has done my office. I know not if 't be true;
But I, for mere suspicion in that kind,
Will do as if for surety. He holds me well; *370*
The better shall my purpose work on him.
Cassio's a proper† man: let me see now:
To get his place and to plume up my will
In† double knavery — How, how? — Let's see: —
After some time, to abuse Othello's ear *375*
That he is too familiar with his wife.
He hath a person and a smooth dispose†
To be suspected, fram'd to make women false.
The Moor is of a free and open nature,
That thinks men honest that but seem to be so, *380*
And will as tenderly be led by th' nose
As asses are.
I have't. It is engend'red. Hell and night
Must bring this monstrous birth to the world's light. [*Exit.*

Act Two *Scene I. [A sea-port in Cyprus. An open place near the
quay.]*

Enter MONTANO *and two* GENTLEMEN.

MONTANO What from the cape can you discern at sea?

1. GENTLEMAN Nothing at all; it is a high-wrought flood.
I cannot, 'twixt the heaven and the main,
Descry a sail.

---

350. *hearted:* heart-felt.   372. *proper:* handsome.
351. *conjunctive:* united.   373–374. *plume . . . In:* brace my-
354. *Traverse:* forward.   self to.
365. *snipe:* woodcock, a silly bird.   377. *dispose:* disposition.

MONTANO   Methinks the wind hath spoke aloud at land;   5
    A fuller blast ne'er shook our battlements.
    If it hath ruffian'd so upon the sea,
    What ribs of oak, when mountains melt on them,
    Can hold the mortise†? What shall we hear of this?
2. GENTLEMAN   A segregation† of the Turkish fleet.   10
    For do but stand upon the foaming shore,
    The chidden billow seems to pelt the clouds;
    The wind-shak'd surge, with high and monstrous mane,
    Seems to cast water on the burning Bear
    And quench the guards† of th' ever-fixed Pole.   15
    I never did like molestation view
    On the enchafed flood.
MONTANO   If that the Turkish fleet
    Be not enshelter'd and embay'd, they are drown'd;
    It is impossible to bear it out.
    Enter a third GENTLEMAN.
3. GENTLEMAN   News, lads! our wars are done.   20
    The desperate tempest hath so bang'd the Turks,
    That their designment halts. A noble ship of Venice
    Hath seen a grievous wreck and sufferance†
    On most part of their fleet.
MONTANO   How! is this true?
3. GENTLEMAN   The ship is here put in.   25
    A Veronese,† Michael Cassio,
    Lieutenant to the warlike Moor Othello,
    Is come on shore; the Moor himself at sea,
    And is in full commission here for Cyprus.
MONTANO   I am glad on't; 'tis a worthy governor.   30
3. GENTLEMAN   But this same Cassio, though he speak of comfort
    Touching the Turkish loss, yet he looks sadly
    And prays the Moor be safe, for they were parted
    With foul and violent tempest.
MONTANO   Pray heavens he be;
    For I have serv'd him, and the man commands   35
    Like a full soldier. Let's to the seaside, ho!
    As well to see the vessel that's come in
    As to throw out our eyes for brave Othello,
    Even till we make the main and th' aerial blue
    An indistinct regard.
3. GENTLEMAN   Come, let's do so;   40
    For every minute is expectancy
    Of more arrivance.
    Enter CASSIO.
CASSIO   Thanks, you the valiant of this warlike isle,
    That so approve the Moor! O, let the heavens

9. *hold the mortise:* hold their
joints together.
10. *segregation:* dispersion.
15. *guards:* stars in the Little Bear
in line with the pole star.

23. *sufferance:* disaster.
26. *A Veronese:* In I.i.20 Cassio
is called a Florentine.

Give him defence against the elements,
For I have lost him on a dangerous sea.
MONTANO   Is he well shipp'd?
CASSIO   His bark is stoutly timber'd, and his pilot
Of very expert and approv'd allowance;†   50
Therefore my hopes, not surfeited to death,
Stand in bold cure.† [*Within,* "A sail, a sail, a sail!"
Enter a [*fourth* GENTLEMAN].
CASSIO   What noise?
[4.] GENTLEMAN   The town is empty; on the brow o' th' sea
Stand ranks of people, and they cry, "A sail!"
CASSIO   My hopes do shape him for the governor.   55
                                                          [*A shot.*

2. GENTLEMAN   They do discharge their shot of courtesy.
Our friends at least.
CASSIO   I pray you, sir, go forth,
And give us truth who 'tis that is arriv'd.
2. GENTLEMAN   I shall.   [*Exit.*
MONTANO   But, good Lieutenant, is your General wiv'd?   60
CASSIO   Most fortunately. He hath achiev'd a maid
That paragons† description and wild fame;
One that excels the quirks† of blazoning† pens,
And in th' essential vesture of creation†
Does tire the [ingener].†
Re-enter second GENTLEMAN.
                        How now! who has put in?   65
2. GENTLEMAN   'Tis one Iago, ancient to the general.
CASSIO   He has had most favourable and happy speed.
Tempests themselves, high seas, and howling winds,
The gutter'd† rocks and congregated sands,
Traitors ensteep'd† to enclog the guiltless keel,   70
As having sense of beauty, do omit
Their mortal† natures, letting go safely by
The divine Desdemona.
MONTANO   What is she?
CASSIO   She that I spake of, our great captain's captain,
Left in the conduct of the bold Iago,   75
Whose footing here anticipates our thoughts
A se'nnight's speed. Great Jove, Othello guard,
And swell his sail with thine own powerful breath,

---

49. *approv'd allowance:* tested re-pute.
50–51. *my hopes . . . cure.* The sense seems to be: "My hopes, though far from being nourished to excess, yet stand a good chance of being fulfilled."
62. *paragons:* excels.

63. *quirks:* flourishes. *blazoning:* praising.
64. *essential . . . creation:* i.e., just as she is, in her essential quality.
65. [*ingener*] (Steevens conj.): inventor (of praise).
69. *gutter'd:* furrowed, jagged.
70. *ensteep'd:* submerged.
72. *mortal:* deadly.

That he may bless this bay with his tall ship,
Make love's quick pants in Desdemona's arms,   80
Give renew'd fire to our extincted spirits,
[And bring all Cyprus comfort!]
Enter DESDEMONA, EMILIA, IAGO, RODERIGO [*and Attendants*].
                              O, behold,
The riches of the ship is come on shore!
You men of Cyprus, let her have your knees.
Hail to thee, lady! and the grace of heaven,   85
Before, behind thee, and on every hand,
Enwheel thee round!

DESDEMONA   I thank you, valiant Cassio.
What tidings can you tell [me] of my lord?

CASSIO   He is not yet arriv'd; nor know I aught
But that he's well and will be shortly here.   90

DESDEMONA   O, but I fear — How lost you company?

CASSIO   The great contention of sea and skies
Parted our fellowship. — But, hark! a sail.
                    [*Within*, "A sail, a sail!" [*Guns heard*.]

2. GENTLEMAN   They give [their] greeting to the citadel.   95
This likewise is a friend.

CASSIO   See for the news.   [*Exit* GENTLEMAN.]
Good ancient, you are welcome. [*To Emilia*.] Welcome, mistress.
Let it not gall your patience, good Iago,
That I extend my manners; 'tis my breeding
That gives me this bold show of courtesy.   100
                                        [*Kissing her*.]

IAGO   Sir, would she give you so much of her lips
As of her tongue she oft bestows on me,
You'd have enough.

DESDEMONA   Alas, she has no speech.

IAGO   In faith, too much;
I find it still, when I have [list]† to sleep.   105
Marry, before your ladyship, I grant,
She puts her tongue a little in her heart,
And chides with thinking.†

EMILIA   You have little cause to say so.

IAGO   Come on, come on; you are pictures out of door,   110
Bells† in your parlours, wild-cats in your kitchens,
Saints in your injuries,† devils being offended,
Players† in your housewifery, and housewives† in your beds.

DESDEMONA   O, fie upon thee, slanderer!

IAGO   Nay, it is true, or else I am a Turk.   115
You rise to play and go to bed to work.

EMILIA   You shall not write my praise.

---

105. [*list*]: inclination.   112. *Saints . . . injuries:* i.e., you of-
108. *with thinking:* i.e., without   fend sanctimoniously.
words.   113. *Players:* triflers. *housewives:*
111. *Bells:* i.e., clanging tongues.   hussies.

IAGO   No, let me not.

DESDEMONA   What wouldst thou write of me, if thou shouldst praise me?

IAGO   O gentle lady, do not put me to't;
    For I am nothing if not critical.   120

DESDEMONA   Come on, assay. — There's one gone to the harbour?

IAGO   Ay, madam.

DESDEMONA   I am not merry; but I do beguile
    The thing I am by seeming otherwise. —
    Come, how wouldst thou praise me?   125

IAGO   I am about it; but indeed my invention
    Comes from my pate as birdlime does from frieze;
    It plucks out brains and all. But my Muse labours,
    And thus she is deliver'd:
    If she be fair and wise, fairness and wit,   130
    The one 's for use, the other useth it.

DESDEMONA   Well prais'd! How if she be black† and witty?

IAGO   If she be black, and thereto have a wit,
    She'll find a white† that shall her blackness fit.

DESDEMONA   Worse and worse.   135

EMILIA   How if fair and foolish?

IAGO   She never yet was foolish that was fair;
    For even her folly help'd her to an heir.

DESDEMONA   These are old fond paradoxes to make fools laugh i' th' ale-
    house. What miserable praise hast thou for her that's foul and foolish?   140

IAGO   There's none so foul and foolish thereunto, But does foul pranks
    which fair and wise ones do.

DESDEMONA   O heavy ignorance! thou praisest the worst best. But what
    praise couldst thou bestow on a deserving woman indeed, one that, in
    the authority of her merit, did justly put on the vouch† of very malice   145
    itself?

IAGO   She that was ever fair and never proud,
    Had tongue at will and yet was never loud,
    Never lack'd gold and yet went never gay,
    Fled from her wish and yet said, "Now I may;"   150
    She that being ang'red, her revenge being nigh,
    Bade her wrong stay and her displeasure fly;
    She that in wisdom never was so frail
    To change the cod's head for the salmon's tail;†
    She that could think and ne'er disclose her mind,   155
    See suitors following and not look behind,
    She was a wight, if ever such wights were, —

DESDEMONA   To do what?

IAGO   To suckle fools and chronicle small beer.†

DESDEMONA   O most lame and impotent conclusion! Do not learn of him,   160

132. *black:* brunette.
134. *white:* with a pun on *wight*
(person).
145. *put . . . vouch:* compel the
testimony.

154. *To . . . tail:* to take the worthless in exchange for the worthy.
159. *chronicle small beer:* i.e., to
keep petty accounts.

Emilia, though he be thy husband. How say you, Cassio? Is he not a most profane and liberal† counsellor?

CASSIO   He speaks home, madam. You may relish him more in the soldier than in the scholar.

IAGO [*Aside.*]   He takes her by palm; ay, well said,† whisper. With as little   165
a web as this will I ensnare as great a fly as Cassio. Ay, smile upon her, do; I will gyve† thee in thine own courtship.† — You say true; 'tis so, indeed. — If such tricks as these strip you out of your lieutenantry, it had been better you had not kiss'd your three fingers so oft, which now again you are most apt to play the sir† in. Very good; well kiss'd! an   170
excellent curtsy! 'Tis so, indeed. Yet again your fingers to your lips? Would they were clyster-pipes† for your sake! (*Trumpet within.*) — The Moor! I know his trumpet.

CASSIO   'Tis truly so.

DESDEMONA   Let's meet him and receive him.   175

CASSIO   Lo, where he comes!

Enter OTHELLO *and Attendants.*

OTHELLO   O my fair warrior!

DESDEMONA   My dear Othello!

OTHELLO   It gives me wonder great as my content
To see you here before me. O my soul's joy!
If after every tempest come such calms,   180
May the winds blow till they have waken'd death!
And let the labouring bark climb hills of seas
Olympus-high, and duck again as low
As hell's from heaven! If it were now to die,
'Twere now to be most happy; for, I fear,   185
My soul hath her content so absolute
That not another comfort like to this
Succeeds in unknown fate.

DESDEMONA   The heavens forbid
But that our loves and comforts should increase,
Even as our days do grow!

OTHELLO   Amen to that, sweet powers!   190
I cannot speak enough of this content;
It stops me here; it is too much of joy.
And this, and this, the greatest discords be   [*Kissing her.*
That e'er our hearts shall make!

IAGO [*Aside.*]   O, you are well tun'd now!   195
But I'll set down the pegs that make this music,
As honest as I am.

OTHELLO   Come, let us to the castle.
News, friends: our wars are done, the Turks are drown'd.
How does my old acquaintance of this isle?
Honey, you shall be well desir'd† in Cyprus;   200

162. *liberal:* free-spoken.
165. *well said:* well done.
167. *gyve:* fetter, entangle. *court-*
ship: courtesy.
170. *sir:* gentleman.
172. *clyster-pipes:* syringes.
200. *desir'd:* beloved.

I have found great love amongst them. O my sweet,
I prattle out of fashion, and I dote
In mine own comforts. I prithee, good Iago,
Go to the bay and disembark my coffers.
Bring thou the master† to the citadel;   205
He is a good one, and his worthiness
Does challenge much respect. Come, Desdemona,
Once more, well met at Cyprus.

                         [*Exeunt* OTHELLO, DESDEMONA [*and Attendants*].

IAGO   Do thou meet me presently at the harbour. — Come [hither]. If
thou be'st valiant, — as, they say, base men being in love have then a   210
nobility in their natures more than is native to them, — list me. The
lieutenant to-night watches on the court of guard; — first, I must tell
thee this: Desdemona is directly in love with him.

RODERIGO   With him! why, 'tis not possible.

IAGO   Lay thy finger thus, and let thy soul be instructed. Mark me with   215
what violence she first lov'd the Moor, but for bragging and telling her
fantastical lies. To love him still for prating — let not thy discreet
heart think it. Her eye must be fed; and what delight shall she have to
look on the devil? When the blood is made dull with the act of sport,
there should be, [again] to inflame it and to give satiety a fresh appetite,   220
loveliness in favour, sympathy in years, manners, and beauties; all
which the Moor is defective in. Now, for want of these requir'd con-
veniences, her delicate tenderness will find itself abus'd, begin to heave
the gorge,† disrelish and abhor the Moor. Very nature will instruct her
in it and compel her to some second choice. Now, sir, this granted, —   225
as it is a most pregnant† and unforc'd position — who stands so eminent in the degree of this fortune as Cassio does? a knave very voluble;
no further conscionable† than in putting on the mere form of civil and
humane seeming, for the better compassing of his salt† and most hidden loose affection? Why, none; why, none; a slipper† and subtle   230
knave, a finder of occasion, that has an eye can stamp and counterfeit
advantages, though true advantage never present itself; a devilish
knave. Besides, the knave is handsome, young, and hath all those
requisites in him that folly and green minds look after; a pestilent complete knave, and the woman hath found him already.   235

RODERIGO   I cannot believe that in her; she's full of most bless'd condition.†

IAGO   Bless'd fig's-end! The wine she drinks is made of grapes. If she
had been bless'd, she would never have lov'd the Moor. Bless'd pudding! Didst thou not see her paddle with the palm of his hand? Didst   240
not mark that?

RODERIGO   Yes, that I did; but that was but courtesy.

IAGO   Lechery, by this hand; an index and obscure prologue to the history
of lust and foul thoughts. They met so near with their lips that their

---

205. *master:* ship's master.   228. *conscionable:* conscientious.
223–224. *heave the gorge:* be nau-   229. *salt:* lewd.
seated.   230. *slipper:* slippery.
226. *pregnant:* evident.   236. *condition:* character.

breaths embrac'd together. Villanous thoughts, Roderigo! When these 245
[mutualities] so marshal the way, hard at hand comes the master and
main exercise, th' incorporate conclusion. Pish! But, sir, be you rul'd
by me; I have brought you from Venice. Watch you to-night; for the
command, I'll lay 't upon you. Cassio knows you not. I'll not be far
from you. Do you find some occasion to anger Cassio, either by speak- 250
ing too loud, or tainting his discipline; or from what other course you
please, which the time shall more favourably minister.

RODERIGO   Well?

IAGO   Sir, he's rash and very sudden in choler, and haply may strike at
you. Provoke him, that he may; for even out of that will I cause these 255
of Cyprus to mutiny, whose qualification† shall come into no true taste
again but by the displanting of Cassio. So shall you have a shorter
journey to your desires by the means I shall then have to prefer them;
and the impediment most profitably removed, without the which there
were no expectation of our prosperity. 260

RODERIGO   I will do this, if you can bring it to any opportunity.

IAGO   I warrant thee. Meet me by and by at the citadel; I must fetch his
necessaries ashore. Farewell.

RODERIGO   Adieu.   [*Exit.*
265

IAGO   That Cassio loves her, I do well believe 't;
That she loves him, 'tis apt† and of great credit;†
The Moor, howbeit that I endure him not,
Is of a constant, loving, noble nature,
And I dare think he'll prove to Desdemona
A most dear husband. Now, I do love her too; 270
Not out of absolute lust, though peradventure
I stand accountant for as great a sin,
But partly led to diet my revenge,
For that I do suspect the lusty Moor
Hath leap'd into my seat; the thought whereof 275
Doth, like a poisonous mineral, gnaw my inwards;
And nothing can or shall content my soul
Till I am even'd with him, wife for [wife];
Or failing so, yet that I put the Moor
At least into a jealousy so strong 280
That judgement cannot cure. Which thing to do,
If this poor trash† of Venice, whom I [trash]
For his quick hunting, stand the putting on,†
I'll have our Michael Cassio on the hip,
Abuse him to the Moor in the [rank]† garb† — 285
For I fear Cassio with my night-cap too —
Make the Moor thank me, love me, and reward me
For making him egregiously an ass
And practising upon† his peace and quiet

---

256. *qualification:* appeasement.
266. *apt:* natural. *of . . . credit:*
most credible.
282. *trash:* worthless fellow.

283. *putting on:* inciting.
285. [*rank*]: gross. *garb:* manner.
289. *practising upon:* plotting
against.

Even to madness. 'Tis here, but yet confus'd;   *290*
Knavery's plain face is never seen till us'd.   [*Exit.*

Scene II. [*A street.*]
Enter Othello's HERALD, *with a proclamation* [People *following*].

HERALD   It is Othello's pleasure, our noble and valiant general, that, upon
certain tidings now arriv'd importing the mere† perdition of the Turkish fleet, every man put himself into triumph; some to dance, some to
make bonfires, each man to what sport and revels his [addiction]† leads
him; for, beside these beneficial news, it is the celebration of his nuptial.   *5*
So much was his pleasure should be proclaimed. All offices† are open,
and there is full liberty of feasting from this present hour of five till the
bell have told eleven. [Heaven] bless the isle of Cyprus and our noble
general Othello!   [*Exeunt.*

Scene III. [*A hall in the castle.*]
Enter OTHELLO, DESDEMONA, CASSIO, *and Attendants.*

OTHELLO   Good Michael, look you to the guard to-night.
Let's teach ourselves that honourable stop,
Not to outsport discretion.
CASSIO   Iago hath direction what to do;
But, notwithstanding, with my personal eye   *5*
Will I look to't.
OTHELLO   Iago is most honest.
Michael, good-night; to-morrow with your earliest
Let me have speech with you. [*To* DESDEMONA.]
Come, my dear love,
The purchase made, the fruits are to ensue;   *10*
That profit's yet to come 'tween me and you.
Good-night.   [*Exeunt* [OTHELLO, DESDEMONA, *and Attendants*].
Enter IAGO.
CASSIO   Welcome, Iago; we must to the watch.
IAGO   Not this hour, Lieutenant; 'tis not yet ten o' th' clock. Our general
cast† us thus early for the love of his Desdemona; who let us not there-   *15*
fore blame. He hath not yet made wanton the night with her; and she
is sport for Jove.
CASSIO   She's a most exquisite lady.
IAGO   And, I'll warrant her, full of game.
CASSIO   Indeed, she's a most fresh and delicate creature.   *20*
IAGO   What an eye she has! Methinks it sounds a parley to provocation.
CASSIO   An inviting eye; and yet methinks right modest.
IAGO   And when she speaks, is it not an alarum to love?

2. *mere:* utter.   6. *offices:* kitchens, etc.
4. [*addiction*]: inclination.   **Sc. iii,** 15. *cast:* dismissed.

CASSIO She is indeed perfection.

IAGO Well, happiness to their sheets! Come, Lieutenant, I have a stoup of   25
wine; and here without are a brace of Cyprus gallants that would fain
have a measure to the health of black Othello.

CASSIO Not to-night, good Iago. I have very poor and unhappy brains for
drinking; I could well wish courtesy would invent some other custom
of entertainment.   30

IAGO O, they are our friends. But one cup; I'll drink for you.

CASSIO I have drunk but one cup to-night, and that was craftily qualified†
too, and, behold, what innovation it makes here. I am unfortunate in
the infirmity, and dare not task my weakness with any more.

IAGO What, man! 'tis a night of revels. The gallants desire it.   35

CASSIO Where are they?

IAGO Here at the door; I pray you, call them in.

CASSIO I'll do't; but it dislikes me.†   [Exit.

IAGO If I can fasten but one cup upon him,
With that which he hath drunk to-night already,   40
He'll be as full of quarrel and offence
As my young mistress' dog. Now, my sick fool Roderigo,
Whom love hath turn'd almost the wrong side out,
To Desdemona hath to-night carous'd
Potations pottle-deep;† and he's to watch.   45
Three [lads] of Cyprus, noble swelling spirits
That hold their honours in a wary distance,†
The very elements† of this warlike isle,
Have I to-night fluster'd with flowing cups,
And they watch too. Now, 'mongst this flock of drunkards   50
Am I to put our Cassio in some action
That may offend the isle. But here they come.
Re-enter CASSIO; *with him* MONTANO *and* GENTLEMEN *[Servants follow
with wine].*
If consequence do but approve my dream,
My boat sails freely, both with wind and stream.

CASSIO 'Fore [God], they have given me a rouse† already.   55

MONTANO Good faith, a little one; not past a pint, as I am a soldier.

IAGO Some wine, ho!
[*Sings.*] "And let me the canakin clink, clink;
And let the canakin clink.
A soldier's a man;   60
O, man's life's but a span;
Why, then, let a soldier drink."
Some wine, boys!

CASSIO 'Fore [God], an excellent song.

IAGO I learn'd it in England, where, indeed, they are most potent in   65

32. *craftily qualified:* slyly diluted.   48. *very elements:* true represen-
38. *it dislikes me:* I don't want to.   tatives.
45. *pottle-deep:* to the bottom of   55. *rouse:* bumper.
the tankard.
47. *hold ... distance:* i.e., are
quick to quarrel.

potting; your Dane, your German, and your swag-belli'd Hollander —
Drink, ho! — are nothing to your English.

CASSIO Is your Englishman so exquisite in his drinking?

IAGO Why, he drinks you, with facility, your Dane dead drunk; he sweats
not to overthrow your Almain;† he gives your Hollander a vomit ere   70
the next pottle can be fill'd.

CASSIO To the health of our general!

MONTANO I am for it, Lieutenant; and I'll do you justice.

IAGO O sweet England!

"King Stephen was and-a worthy peer,   75
    His breeches cost him but a crown;
He held them sixpence all too dear,
    With that he call'd the tailor lown.†

"He was a wight of high renown,
    And thou art but of low degree.   80
'Tis pride that pulls the country down;
    And take thy auld cloak about thee."
Some wine, ho!

CASSIO Why, this is a more exquisite song than the other.

IAGO Will you hear 't again?   85

CASSIO No; for I hold him to be unworthy of his place that does those
things. Well, [God's] above all; and there be souls must be saved, and
there be souls must not be saved.

IAGO It's true, good Lieutenant.

CASSIO For mine own part — no offence to the general, nor any man of   90
quality — I hope to be saved.

IAGO And so do I too, Lieutenant.

CASSIO Ay, but, by your leave, not before me; the lieutenant is to be saved
before the ancient. Let's have no more of this; let's to our affairs. —
[God] forgive us our sins! — Gentlemen, let's look to our business. Do   95
not think, gentlemen, I am drunk. This is my ancient; this is my right
hand, and this is my left. I am not drunk now; I can stand well enough,
and I speak well enough.

GENTLEMEN Excellent well.

CASSIO Why, very well then; you must not think then that I am drunk.   100
                                                                    [Exit.

MONTANO To the platform, masters; come, let's set the watch.

IAGO You see this fellow that is gone before:
He is a soldier fit to stand by Cæsar
And give direction; and do but see his vice.
'Tis to his virtue a just equinox,†   105
The one as long as th' other; 'tis pity of him.
I fear the trust Othello puts him in,
On some odd time of his infirmity,
Will shake this island.

MONTANO   But is he often thus?

---

70. *Almain:* German.   105. *equinox:* counterpart, equiv-
78. *lown:* fellow, rascal.   alent.

IAGO   'Tis evermore his prologue to his sleep.   110
    He'll watch the horologe a double set†
    If drink rock not his cradle.
MONTANO   It were well
    The general were put in mind of it.
    Perhaps he sees it not; or his good nature
    Prizes the virtue that appears in Cassio,   115
    And looks not on his evils. Is not this true?
    Enter RODERIGO.
IAGO [*Aside to him.*]   How now, Roderigo!
    I pray you, after the lieutenant; go.   [*Exit* RODERIGO.
MONTANO   And 'tis great pity that the noble Moor
    Should hazard such a place as his own second   120
    With one of an ingraft infirmity.
    It were an honest action to say
    So to the Moor.
IAGO   Not I, for this fair island.
    I do love Cassio well; and would do much
    To cure him of this evil. — But, hark! what noise?   125
                                        [*Cry within:* "Help! help!"]

    Re-enter CASSIO, *pursuing* RODERIGO.
CASSIO   'Zounds, you rogue! you rascal!
MONTANO   What's the matter, Lieutenant?
CASSIO   A knave teach me my duty!
    I'll beat the knave into a twiggen† bottle.
RODERIGO   Beat me!
CASSIO   Dost thou prate, rogue?   [*Striking* RODERIGO.]
MONTANO   Nay, good Lieutenant;
                                                [*Staying him.*]

    I pray you, sir, hold your hand.
CASSIO   Let me go, sir,   130
    Or I'll knock you o'er the mazzard.†
MONTANO   Come, come, you're drunk.
CASSIO   Drunk!   [*They fight.*
IAGO [*Aside to Roderigo.*]   Away, I say; go out, and cry a mutiny.
                                                [*Exit* RODERIGO.

    Nay, good Lieutenant, — [God's will], gentlemen; —
    Help, ho! — Lieutenant, — sir, — Montano, — [sir]; —   135
    Help, masters! — Here's a goodly watch indeed!   [*Bell rings.*
    Who's that which rings the bell? — Diablo, ho!
    The town will rise. Fie, fie, Lieutenant, [hold]!
    You will be sham'd for ever.
    Re-enter OTHELLO *and Attendants.*
OTHELLO   What is the matter here?
MONTANO   ['Zounds], I bleed still; I am hurt to the death. He dies!   140
OTHELLO   Hold, for your lives!
IAGO   Hold, ho! Lieutenant, — sir, — Montano, — gentlemen, —

---

111. *horologe ... set:* clock twice   128. *twiggen:* wicker-covered.
around.   131. *mazzard:* head.

Have you forgot all [sense of place] and duty?
Hold! the general speaks to you; hold, for shame!
OTHELLO   Why, how now, ho! from whence ariseth this?   *145*
Are we turn'd Turks, and to ourselves do that
Which Heaven hath forbid the Ottomites?
For Christian shame, put by this barbarous brawl.
He that stirs next to carve for his own rage†
Holds his soul light; he dies upon his motion.   *150*
Silence that dreadful bell; it frights the isle
From her propriety. What is the matter, masters?
Honest Iago, that looks dead with grieving,
Speak, who began this? On thy love, I charge thee.
IAGO   I do not know. Friends all but now, even now,   *155*
In quarter,† and in terms like bride and groom
Devesting them for bed; and then, but now —
As if some planet had unwitted men —
Swords out, and tilting one at other's breast,
In opposition bloody. I cannot speak   *160*
Any beginning to this peevish odds;†
And would in action glorious I had lost
Those legs that brought me to a part of it!
OTHELLO   How comes it, Michael, you are thus forgot?
CASSIO   I pray you, pardon me; I cannot speak.   *165*
OTHELLO   Worthy Montano, you were wont to be civil;
The gravity and stillness of your youth
The world hath noted, and your name is great
In mouths of wisest censure.† What's the matter
That you unlace your reputation thus,   *170*
And spend your rich opinion† for the name
Of a night-brawler? Give me answer to it.
MONTANO   Worthy Othello, I am hurt to danger.
Your officer, Iago, can inform you —
While I spare speech, which something now offends† me —   *175*
Of all that I do know; nor know I aught
By me that's said or done amiss this night,
Unless self-charity be sometimes a vice,
And to defend ourselves it be a sin
When violence assails us.
OTHELLO   Now, by heaven,   *180*
My blood begins my safer guides to rule;
And passion, having my best judgement collied,†
Assays to lead the way. If I once stir
Or do but lift this arm, the best of you
Shall sink in my rebuke. Give me to know   *185*
How this foul rout began, who set it on;

149. *carve . . . rage:* act on his own
impulse.
156. *quarter:* peace.
161. *peevish odds:* stupid quarrel.

169. *censure:* judgment.
171. *opinion:* reputation.
175. *offends:* pains.
182. *collied:* darkened.

And he that is approv'd† in this offence,
Though he had twinn'd with me, both at a birth,
Shall lose me. What! in a town of war,
Yet wild, the people's hearts brimful of fear,   *190*
To manage† private and domestic quarrel,
In night, and on the court and guard of safety!
'Tis monstrous. Iago, who began 't?

MONTANO If partially affin'd,† or leagu'd in office,
Thou dost deliver more or less than truth,   *195*
Thou art no soldier.

IAGO   Touch me not so near.
I had rather have this tongue cut from my mouth
Than it should do offence to Michael Cassio;
Yet, I persuade myself, to speak the truth
Shall nothing wrong him. [Thus] it is, General: *200*
Montano and myself being in speech,
There comes a fellow crying out for help;
And Cassio following him with determin'd sword
To execute upon him. Sir, this gentleman
Steps in to Cassio and entreats his pause;   *205*
Myself the crying fellow did pursue,
Lest by his clamour — as it so fell out —
The town might fall in fright. He, swift of foot,
Outran my purpose; and I return'd the rather
For that I heard the clink and fall of swords,   *210*
And Cassio high in oath; which till to-night
I ne'er might say before. When I came back —
For this was brief — I found them close together,
At blow and thrust; even as again they were
When you yourself did part them.   *215*
More of this matter cannot I report.
But men are men; the best sometimes forget.
Though Cassio did some little wrong to him,
As men in rage strike those that wish them best,
Yet surely Cassio, I believe, receiv'd   *220*
From him that fled some strange indignity
Which patience could not pass.

OTHELLO   I know, Iago,
Thy honesty and love doth mince this matter,
Making it light to Cassio. Cassio, I love thee;
But never more be officer of mine.   *225*

Re-enter DESDEMONA, *attended.*

Look, if my gentle love be not rais'd up!
I'll make thee an example.

DESDEMONA   What's the matter, dear?

OTHELLO All's well [now], sweeting; come away to bed.

187. *approv'd:* found guilty.   194. *partially affin'd:* biased be-
191. *manage:* carry on.   cause of ties.

Sir, for your hurts, myself will be your surgeon. —
Lead him off.   230

                          [*To* MONTANO, *who is led off.*]

Iago, look with care about the town,
And silence those whom this vile brawl distracted.
Come, Desdemona; 'tis the soldiers' life
To have their balmy slumbers wak'd with strife.

                        [*Exeunt all but* IAGO *and* CASSIO.

IAGO   What, are you hurt, Lieutenant?   235

CASSIO   Ay, past all surgery.

IAGO   Marry, God forbid!

CASSIO   Reputation, reputation, reputation! O, I have lost my reputation!
I have lost the immortal part of myself, and what remains is bestial.
My reputation, Iago, my reputation!   240

IAGO   As I am an honest man, I thought you had received some bodily
wound; there is more sense in that than in reputation. Reputation is an
idle and most false imposition; oft got without merit, and lost without
deserving. You have lost no reputation at all, unless you repute yourself such a loser. What, man! there are more ways to recover† the gen-   245
eral again. You are but now cast in his mood, a punishment more in
policy than in malice; even so as one would beat his offenceless dog to
affright an imperious lion. Sue to him again, and he's yours.

CASSIO   I will rather sue to be despis'd than to deceive so good a commander with so slight, so drunken, and so indiscreet an officer. Drunk?   250
and speak parrot?† and squabble? swagger? swear? and discourse
fustian† with one's own shadow? O thou invisible spirit of wine, if
thou hast no name to be known by, let us call thee devil!

IAGO   What was he that you follow'd with your sword? What had he
done to you?   255

CASSIO   I know not.

IAGO   Is't possible?

CASSIO   I remember a mass of things, but nothing distinctly; a quarrel, but
nothing wherefore. O [God], that men should put an enemy in their
mouths to steal away their brains! That we should, with joy, pleasance,   260
revel, and applause, transform ourselves into beasts!

IAGO   Why, but you are now well enough. How came you thus recovered?

CASSIO   It hath pleas'd the devil drunkenness to give place to the devil
wrath. One unperfectness shows me another, to make me frankly despise myself.   265

IAGO   Come, you are too severe a moraler. As the time, the place, and the
condition of this country stands, I could heartily wish this had not befallen; but since it is as it is, mend it for your own good.

CASSIO   I will ask him for my place again; he shall tell me I am a drunkard! Had I as many mouths as Hydra, such an answer would stop   270
them all. To be now a sensible man, by and by a fool, and presently a
beast! O strange! Every inordinate cup is unbless'd and the ingredient
is a devil.

     245. *recover:* regain favor with.   252. *fustian:* nonsense.
    251. *parrot:* nonsense.

IAGO Come, come, good wine is a good familiar creature, if it be well   275
us'd; exclaim no more against it. And, good Lieutenant, I think you
think I love you.

CASSIO I have well approved it, sir. I drunk!

IAGO You or any man living may be drunk at a time, man. [I'll] tell you
what you shall do. Our general's wife is now the general; — I may say
so in this respect, for that he hath devoted and given up himself to the   280
contemplation, mark, and [denotement] of her parts and graces; —
confess yourself freely to her; importune her help to put you in your
place again. She is of so free, so kind, so apt, so blessed a disposition,
she holds it a vice in her goodness not to do more than she is requested.
This broken joint between you and her husband entreat her to splinter;†   285
and, my fortunes against any lay† worth naming, this crack of your
love shall grow stronger than it was before.

CASSIO You advise me well.

IAGO I protest, in the sincerity of love and honest kindness.

CASSIO I think it freely; and betimes in the morning I will beseech the vir-   290
tuous Desdemona to undertake for me. I am desperate of my fortunes
if they check me [here].

IAGO You are in the right. Good-night, Lieutenant; I must to the watch.

CASSIO Good-night, honest Iago.   [Exit.
                                                                     295
IAGO And what's he then that says I play the villain?
When this advice is free I give and honest,
Probal† to thinking and indeed the course
To win the Moor again? For 'tis most easy
Th' inclining Desdemona to subdue
In any honest suit; she's fram'd as fruitful†   300
As the free elements. And then for her
To win the Moor, [were't] to renounce his baptism,
All seals and symbols of redeemed sin,
His soul is so enfetter'd to her love,
That she may make, unmake, do what she list,   305
Even as her appetite shall play the god
With his weak function.† How am I then a villain
To counsel Cassio to this parallel course,
Directly to his good? Divinity of hell!
When devils will the blackest sins put on,†   310
They do suggest at first with heavenly shows,
As I do now; for whiles this honest fool
Plies Desdemona to repair his fortune
And she for him pleads strongly to the Moor,
I'll pour this pestilence into his ear,   315
That she repeals him for her body's lust;
And by how much she strives to do him good,
She shall undo her credit with the Moor.
So will I turn her virtue into pitch,

285. *splinter:* bind with splints.   300. *fruitful:* generous.
286. *lay:* wager.   307. *function:* mental faculties.
297. *Probal:* probable.   310. *put on:* incite.

And out of her own goodness make the net   *320*
That shall enmesh them all.
Re-enter RODERIGO.
                              How now, Roderigo!
RODERIGO   I do follow here in the chase, not like a hound that hunts, but
   one that fills up the cry.† My money is almost spent; I have been to-
   night exceedingly well cudgell'd; and I think the issue will be, I shall
   have so much experience for my pains; and so, with no money at all   *325*
   and a little more wit, return again to Venice.
IAGO   How poor are they that have not patience!
   What wound did ever heal but by degrees?
   Thou know'st we work by wit, and not by witchcraft;
   And wit depends on dilatory time.   *330*
   Does't not go well? Cassio hath beaten thee,
   And thou, by that small hurt, hast cashier'd Cassio.
   Though other things grow fair against the sun,
   Yet fruits that blossom first will first be ripe.
   Content thyself a while. In troth, 'tis morning;   *335*
   Pleasure and action make the hours seem short.
   Retire thee; go where thou art billeted.
   Away, I say; thou shalt know more hereafter.
   Nay, get thee gone. [*Exit* RODERIGO.] Two things are to be done:
   My wife must move for Cassio to her mistress;   *340*
   I'll set her on;
   Myself a while to draw the Moor apart,
   And bring him jump† when he may Cassio find
   Soliciting his wife. Ay, that's the way;
   Dull not device by coldness and delay.   *345*
                                                                       [*Exit.*

Act Three   *Scene I.* [*Cyprus before the castle.*]
Enter CASSIO, *with* MUSICIANS.

CASSIO   Masters, play here; I will content† your pains;
   Something that's brief; and bid "Good morrow, General."   [*They play.*
   Enter CLOWN.
CLOWN   Why, masters, have your instruments been in Naples, that they
   speak i' th' nose thus ?
1. MUSICIAN   How, sir, how?   *5*
CLOWN   Are these, I pray you, wind-instruments?
1. MUSICIAN   Ay, marry, are they, sir.
CLOWN   O, thereby hangs a tail.
1. MUSICIAN   Whereby hangs a tale, sir?
CLOWN   Marry, sir, by many a wind-instrument that I know. But, mas-   *10*
   ters, here's money for you; and the General so likes your music, that
   he desires you, for love's sake, to make no more noise with it.

323. *cry:* pack.   **Act Three, Sc. i,** 1. *content:* requite.
343. *jump:* at the precise moment.

1. MUSICIAN   Well, sir, we will not.

CLOWN   If you have any music that may not be heard, to't again; but, as
   they say, to hear music the general does not greatly care.   15

1. MUSICIAN   We have none such, sir.

CLOWN   Then put up your pipes in your bag, for I'll away. Go, vanish
   into air, away!   [*Exeunt* MUSICIANS.

CASSIO   Dost thou hear mine honest friend?

CLOWN   No, I hear not your honest friend; I hear you.   20

CASSIO   Prithee, keep up thy quillets.† There's a poor piece of gold for
   thee. If the gentlewoman that attends the [General's wife] be stirring,
   tell her there's one Cassio entreats her a little favour of speech. Wilt
   thou do this?

CLOWN   She is stirring, sir. If she will stir hither, I shall seem to notify   25
   unto her.

CASSIO   [Do, good my friend.]   [*Exit* CLOWN.
   Enter IAGO.
                              In happy time, Iago.

IAGO   You have not been a-bed, then?

CASSIO   Why, no; the day had broke
   Before we parted. I have made bold, Iago,   30
   To send in to your wife. My suit to her
   Is that she will to virtuous Desdemona
   Procure me some access.

IAGO   I'll send her to you presently;
   And I'll devise a mean to draw the Moor
   Out of the way, that your converse and business   35
   May be more free.

CASSIO   I humbly thank you for't. I never knew   [*Exit* IAGO.
   A Florentine more kind and honest.
   Enter EMILIA.

EMILIA   Good morrow, good Lieutenant. I am sorry
   For your displeasure;† but all will sure be well.   40
   The General and his wife are talking of it,
   And she speaks for you stoutly. The Moor replies
   That he you hurt is of great fame in Cyprus
   And great affinity,† and that in wholesome wisdom
   He might not but refuse you; but he protests he loves you,   45
   And needs no other suitor but his likings
   [To take the safest occasion by the front]
   To bring you in again.

CASSIO   Yet, I beseech you,
   If you think fit, or that it may be done,
   Give me advantage of some brief discourse   50
   With Desdemon alone.

EMILIA   Pray you, come in.
   I will bestow you where you shall have time
   To speak your bosom freely.

CASSIO   I am much bound to you.   [*Exeunt.*

---

21. *quillets:* quibbles.   44. *affinity:* connections.
40. *displeasure:* disgrace.

Scene II. [*A room in the castle.*]
Enter OTHELLO, IAGO, *and* GENTLEMEN.

OTHELLO   These letters give, Iago, to the pilot;
And by him do my duties to the Senate.
That done, I will be walking on the works;†
Repair there to me.
IAGO   Well, my good lord, I'll do't.
OTHELLO   This fortification, gentlemen, shall we see't?   5
GENTLEMEN   We'll wait upon your lordship.   [*Exeunt.*

Scene III. [*The garden of the castle.*]
Enter DESDEMONA, CASSIO, *and* EMILIA.

DESDEMONA   Be thou assur'd, good Cassio, I will do
All my abilities in thy behalf.
EMILIA   Good madam, do. I warrant it grieves my husband
As if the cause were his.
DESDEMONA   O, that's an honest fellow. Do not doubt, Cassio,   5
But I will have my lord and you again
As friendly as you were.
CASSIO   Bounteous madam,
Whatever shall become of Michael Cassio,
He's never anything but your true servant.
DESDEMONA   I know 't; I thank you. You do love my lord;   10
You have known him long; and be you well assur'd
He shall in strangeness† stand no farther off
Than in a politic distance.
CASSIO   Ay, but, lady,
That policy may either last so long,
Or feed upon such nice and waterish diet,   15
Or breed itself so out of circumstances,
That, I being absent and my place supplied,
My general will forget my love and service.
DESDEMONA   Do not doubt† that; before Emilia here
I give thee warrant of thy place. Assure thee,   20
If I do vow a friendship, I'll perform it
To the last article. My lord shall never rest;
I'll watch him tame,† and talk him out of patience;
His bed shall seem a school, his board a shrift;†
I'll intermingle everything he does   25
With Cassio's suit. Therefore be merry, Cassio;
For thy solicitor shall rather die
Than give thy cause away.
ENTER OTHELLO *and* IAGO.

3. *works:* fortifications.
Sc. iii, 12. *strangeness:* aloofness.
19. *doubt:* fear.

23. *watch him tame:* keep him
awake till he gives in.
24 *shrift:* confessional.

EMILIA   Madam, here comes my lord.

CASSIO   Madam, I'll take my leave.   30

DESDEMONA   Why, stay, and hear me speak.

CASSIO   Madam, not now; I am very ill at ease,
   Unfit for mine own purposes.

DESDEMONA   Well, do your discretion.   [*Exit* CASSIO.

IAGO   Ha! I like not that.

OTHELLO   What dost thou say?   35

IAGO   Nothing, my lord; or if — I know not what.

OTHELLO   Was not that Cassio parted from my wife?

IAGO   Cassio, my lord! No, sure, I cannot think it,
   That he would steal away so guilty-like,
   Seeing your coming.

OTHELLO   I do believe 'twas he.   40

DESDEMONA   How now, my lord!
   I have been talking with a suitor here,
   A man that languishes in your displeasure.

OTHELLO   Who is't you mean?

DESDEMONA   Why, your lieutenant, Cassio. Good my lord,   45
   If I have any grace or power to move you,
   His present reconciliation take;
   For if he be not one that truly loves you,
   That errs in ignorance and not in cunning,
   I have no judgement in an honest face.   50
   I prithee, call him back.

OTHELLO   Went he hence now?

DESDEMONA   Yes, faith; so humbled
   That he hath left part of his grief with me
   To suffer with him. Good love, call him back.

OTHELLO   Not now, sweet Desdemon; some other time.   55

DESDEMONA   But shall't be shortly?

OTHELLO   The sooner, sweet, for you.

DESDEMONA   Shall't be to-night at supper?

OTHELLO   No, not to-night.

DESDEMONA   To-morrow dinner then?

OTHELLO   I shall not dine at home;
   I meet the captains at the citadel.

DESDEMONA   Why, then, to-morrow night; on Tuesday morn;   60
   On Tuesday noon, or night; on Wednesday morn.
   I prithee, name the time, but let it not
   Exceed three days. In faith, he's penitent;
   And yet his trespass, in our common reason —
   Save that, they say, the wars must make example   65
   Out of [their] best — is not almost† a fault
   T' incur a private check. When shall he come?
   Tell me, Othello. I wonder in my soul
   What you would ask me that I should deny,
   Or stand so mamm'ring† on. What! Michael Cassio,   70

      66. *not almost:* hardly.   70. *mamm'ring:* hesitating.

That came a-wooing with you, and so many a time,
When I have spoke of you dispraisingly,
Hath ta'en your part, — to have so much to do
To bring him in!† Trust me, I could do much, —

OTHELLO   Prithee, no more; let him come when he will,   *75*
I will deny thee nothing.

DESDEMONA   Why, this is not a boon.
'Tis as I should entreat you wear your gloves,
Or feed on nourishing dishes, or keep you warm,
Or sue to you to do a peculiar profit
To your own person. Nay, when I have a suit   *80*
Wherein I mean to touch your love indeed,
It shall be full of poise† and difficult weight
And fearful to be granted.

OTHELLO   I will deny thee nothing;
Whereon, I do beseech thee, grant me this,
To leave me but a little to myself.   *85*

DESDEMONA   Shall I deny you? No. Farewell, my lord.

OTHELLO   Farewell, my Desdemona; I'll come to thee straight.

DESDEMONA   Emilia, come. — Be as your fancies teach you;
Whate'er you be, I am obedient.   [*Exeunt* DESDEMONA *and* EMILIA.

OTHELLO   Excellent wretch! Perdition catch my soul,   *90*
But I do love thee! and when I love thee not,
Chaos is come again.

IAGO   My noble lord, —

OTHELLO   What dost thou say, Iago?

IAGO   Did Michael Cassio, when [you] woo'd my lady,
Know of your love?   *95*

OTHELLO   He did, from first to last. Why dost thou ask?

IAGO   But for a satisfaction of my thought;
No further harm.

OTHELLO   Why of thy thought, Iago?

IAGO   I did not think he had been acquainted with her.

OTHELLO   O, yes; and went between us very oft.   *100*

IAGO   Indeed!

OTHELLO   Indeed! ay, indeed. Discern'st thou aught in that?
Is he not honest?

IAGO   Honest, my lord?

OTHELLO   Honest! ay, honest.

IAGO   My lord, for aught I know.

OTHELLO   What dost thou think?

IAGO   Think, my lord?

OTHELLO   Think, my lord!   *105*
[By heaven, he echoes] me,
As if there were some monster in [his] thought
Too hideous to be shown. — Thou dost mean something.
I heard thee say even now, thou lik'st not that,

74. *bring . . . in:* i.e., into your   82. *poise:* weight.
favor.

When Cassio left my wife. What didst not like?   *110*
And when I told thee he was of my counsel
[In] my whole course of wooing, thou criedst, "Indeed!"
And didst contract and purse thy brow together,
As if thou then hadst shut up in thy brain
Some horrible conceit. If thou dost love me,   *115*
Show me thy thought.

IAGO   My lord, you know I love you.

OTHELLO   I think thou dost;
And, for I know thou'rt full of love and honesty,
And weigh'st thy words before thou giv'st them breath,
Therefore these stops of thine fright me the more;   *120*
For such things in a false disloyal knave
Are tricks of custom; but in a man that's just
They're close dilations,† working from the heart
That passion cannot rule.

IAGO   For Michael Cassio,
I dare be sworn I think that he is honest.   *125*

OTHELLO   I think so too.

IAGO   Men should be what they seem;
Or those that be not, would they might seem none!

OTHELLO   Certain, men should be what they seem.

IAGO   Why, then, I think Cassio's an honest man.

OTHELLO   Nay, yet there's more in this.   *130*
I prithee, speak to me as to thy thinkings,
As thou dost ruminate, and give thy worst of thoughts
The worst of words.

IAGO   Good my lord, pardon me.
Though I am bound to every act of duty,
I am not bound to that all slaves are free to.   *135*
Utter my thoughts? Why, say they are vile and false;
As where's that palace whereinto foul things
Sometimes intrude not? Who has that breast so pure
[But some] uncleanly apprehensions
Keep leets† and law-days and in sessions sit   *140*
With meditations lawful?

OTHELLO   Thou dost conspire against thy friend, Iago,
If thou but think'st him wrong'd and mak'st his ear
A stranger to thy thoughts.

IAGO   I do beseech you —
Though I perchance am vicious in my guess,   *145*
As, I confess, it is my nature's plague
To spy into abuses, and [oft] my jealousy†
Shapes faults that are not — that your wisdom yet,
From one that so imperfectly conceits,
Would take no notice, nor build yourself a trouble   *150*

---

123. *close dilations:* secret (i.e.,   140. *leets:* court-days.
unconscious) expressions.   147. *jealousy:* suspicion.

Out of his scattering† and unsure observance.
It were not for your quiet nor your good,
Nor for my manhood, honesty, and wisdom,
To let you know my thoughts.

OTHELLO   What dost thou mean?

IAGO   Good name in man and woman, dear my lord,   *155*
Is the immediate jewel of their souls.
Who steals my purse steals trash; 'tis something, nothing;
'Twas mine, 'tis his, and has been slave to thousands;
But he that filches from me my good name
Robs me of that which not enriches him,   *160*
And makes me poor indeed.

OTHELLO   [By heaven,] I'll know thy thoughts.

IAGO   You cannot, if my heart were in your hand;
Nor shall not, whilst 'tis in my custody.

OTHELLO   Ha!

IAGO   O, beware, my lord, of jealousy!   *165*
It is the green-ey'd monster which doth mock
The meat it feeds on. That cuckold lives in bliss
Who, certain of his fate, loves not his wronger;
But, O, what damned minutes tells he o'er
Who dotes, yet doubts, suspects, yet soundly loves!   *170*

OTHELLO   O misery!

IAGO   Poor and content is rich, and rich enough;
But riches fineless† is as poor as winter
To him that ever fears he shall be poor.
Good heaven, the souls of all my tribe defend   *175*
From jealousy!

OTHELLO   Why, why is this?
Think'st thou I'd make a life of jealousy,
To follow still the changes of the moon
With fresh suspicions? No! to be once in doubt
Is [once] to be resolv'd. Exchange me for a goat   *180*
When I shall turn the business of my soul
To such exsufflicate† and [blown] surmises,
Matching thy inference. 'Tis not to make me jealous
To say my wife is fair, feeds well, loves company,
Is free of speech, sings, plays, and dances [well];   *185*
Where virtue is, these are more virtuous.
Nor from mine own weak merits will I draw
The smallest fear or doubt of her revolt;
For she had eyes, and chose me. No, Iago;
I'll see before I doubt; when I doubt, prove;   *190*
And on the proof, there is no more but this,—
Away at once with love or jealousy!

IAGO   I am glad of this, for now I shall have reason
To show the love and duty that I bear you

151. *scattering:* random.   182. *exsufflicate:* inflated.
173. *fineless:* unlimited.

With franker spirit; therefore, as I am bound,   *195*
Receive it from me. I speak not yet of proof.
Look to your wife; observe her well with Cassio,
Wear your eyes thus, not jealous nor secure.†
I would not have your free and noble nature,
Out of self-bounty,† be abus'd; look to't.   *200*
I know our country disposition well;
In Venice they do let Heaven see the pranks
They dare not show their husbands. Their best conscience
Is not to leave 't undone, but keep 't unknown.

OTHELLO   Dost thou say so?   *205*

IAGO   She did deceive her father, marrying you;
And when she seem'd to shake and fear your looks,
She lov'd them most.

OTHELLO   And so she did.

IAGO   Why, go to then.
She that, so young, could give out such a seeming,
To seel her father's eyes up close as oak —   *210*
He thought 'twas witchcraft — but I am much to blame.
I humbly do beseech you of your pardon
For too much loving you.

OTHELLO   I am bound to thee for ever.

IAGO   I see this hath a little dash'd your spirits.

OTHELLO   Not a jot, not a jot.

IAGO   Trust me! I fear it has.   *215*
I hope you will consider what is spoke
Comes from [my] love. But I do see you're mov'd.
I am to pray you not to strain my speech
To grosser issues nor to larger reach
Than to suspicion.   *220*

OTHELLO   I will not.

IAGO   Should you do so, my lord,
My speech should fall into such vile success†
Which my thoughts aim'd not at. Cassio's my worthy friend, —
My lord, I see you're mov'd.

OTHELLO   No, not much mov'd.
I do not think but Desdemona's honest.†   *225*

IAGO   Long live she so! and long live you to think so!

OTHELLO   And yet, how nature erring from itself, —

IAGO   Ay, there's the point; as — to be bold with you —
Not to affect many proposed matches
Of her own clime, complexion, and degree,   *230*
Whereto we see in all things nature tends —
Foh! one may smell in such, a will† most rank,†
Foul disproportions, thoughts unnatural.

198. *secure:* careless.   225. *honest:* chaste.
200. *self-bounty:* inherent gener-   232, 236. *will:* desire, appetite.
osity.   232. *rank:* foul.
222. *success:* consequence.

But pardon me; I do not in position†
Distinctly speak of her; though I may fear   235
Her will,† recoiling to her better judgement,
May fall to match you with her country forms,
And happily repent.

OTHELLO   Farewell, farewell!
If more thou dost perceive, let me know more;
Set on thy wife to observe. Leave me, Iago.   240

IAGO [*Going.*]   My lord, I take my leave.

OTHELLO   Why did I marry? This honest creature doubtless
Sees and knows more, much more, than he unfolds.

IAGO [*Returning.*]   My lord, I would I might entreat your honour
To scan this thing no farther; leave it to time.   245
Although 'tis fit that Cassio have his place,
For, sure, he fills it up with great ability,
Yet, if you please to [hold] him off a while,
You shall by that perceive him and his means.
Note if your lady strain his entertainment†   250
With any strong or vehement importunity;
Much will be seen in that. In the mean time,
Let me be thought too busy in my fears —
As worthy cause I have to fear I am —
And hold her free,† I do beseech your honour.   255

OTHELLO   Fear not my government.†

IAGO   I once more take my leave.   [*Exit.*

OTHELLO   This fellow 's of exceeding honesty,
And knows all [qualities], with a learn'd spirit,
Of human dealings. If I do prove her haggard,†   260
Though that her jesses† were my dear heartstrings,
I'd whistle her off and let her down the wind
To prey at fortune. Haply, for I am black
And have not those soft parts of conversation†
That chamberers† have, or for I am declin'd   265
Into the vale of years, — yet that's not much —
She's gone. I am abus'd; and my relief
Must be to loathe her. O curse of marriage,
That we can call these delicate creatures ours.
And not their appetites! I had rather be a toad   270
And live upon the vapour of a dungeon
Than keep a corner in the thing I love
For others' uses. Yet, 'tis the plague [of] great ones;
Prerogativ'd are they less than the base.
'Tis destiny unshunnable, like death.   275

---

234. *position:* i.e., conviction.
250. *strain   his   entertainment:*
press his reappointment.
255. *free:* guiltless.
256. *government:* management.
260. *haggard:* wild.

261. *jesses:* strings by which hawks
were held.
264. *parts of conversation:* social
graces.
265. *chamberers:* gallants.

Even then this forked plague† is fated to us
When we do quicken.† Look where she comes,
Re-enter DESDEMONA *and* EMILIA.
If she be false, [O, then heaven mocks] itself!
I'll not believe 't.
DESDEMONA　　　　How now, my dear Othello!
Your dinner, and the generous† islanders　　　　　　　　*280*
By you invited, do attend your presence.
OTHELLO　I am to blame.
DESDEMONA　　　　Why do you speak so faintly?
Are you not well?
OTHELLO　I have a pain upon my forehead here.
DESDEMONA　Why, that's with watching; 'twill away again.　　*285*
Let me but bind it hard, within this hour
It will be well.
OTHELLO　　　　Your napkin† is too little;
[*He puts the handkerchief from him; and it drops.*]
Let it† alone. Come, I'll go in with you.
DESDEMONA　I am very sorry that you are not well.
　　　　　　　　　　　　　[*Exeunt* [OTHELLO *and* DESDEMONA].
EMILIA　I am glad I have found this napkin;　　　　　　　*290*
This was her first remembrance from the Moor.
My wayward husband hath a hundred times
Woo'd me to steal it; but she so loves the token,
For he conjur'd her she should ever keep it,
That she reserves it evermore about her　　　　　　　　*295*
To kiss and talk to. I'll have the work ta'en out†
And give 't Iago. What he will do with it
Heaven knows, not I;
I nothing but to please his fantasy.
Re-enter IAGO.
IAGO　How now! what do you here alone?　　　　　　　*300*
EMILIA　Do not you chide; I have a thing for you.
IAGO　A thing for me? It is a common thing —
EMILIA　Ha!
IAGO　To have a foolish wife.
EMILIA　O, is that all? What will you give me now　　　　*305*
For that same handkerchief?
IAGO　　　　　　　　　What handkerchief?
EMILIA　What handkerchief!
Why, that the Moor first gave to Desdemona;
That which so often you did bid me steal.
IAGO　Hast stol'n it from her?　　　　　　　　　　　*310*
EMILIA　No, [faith;] she let it drop by negligence,
And, to th' advantage,† I, being here, took 't up.
Look, here it is.

---

276. *forked plague:* curse of cuckold's horns.
277. *quicken:* begin to live.
280. *generous:* noble.

287. *napkin:* handkerchief.
288. *it:* i.e., his forehead.
296. *work . . . out:* pattern copied.
312. *to th' advantage:* opportunely.

IAGO   A good wench; give it me.

EMILIA   What will you do with 't, that you have been so earnest   315
    To have me filch it?

IAGO [*Snatching it.*]   Why, what is that to you?

EMILIA   If it be not for some purpose of import,
    Give 't me again. Poor lady, she'll run mad
    When she shall lack it.

IAGO   Be not acknown† on't; I have use for it.   320
    Go, leave me.   [*Exit* EMILIA.
    I will in Cassio's lodging lose this napkin,
    And let him find it. Trifles light as air
    Are to the jealous confirmations strong
    As proofs of holy writ; this may do something.   325
    The Moor already changes with my poison.
    Dangerous conceits are, in their natures poisons,
    Which at the first are scarce found to distaste,
    But with a little act† upon the blood
    Burn like the mines of sulphur. I did say so.   330
    Re-enter OTHELLO.
    Look, where he comes! Not poppy, nor mandragora,†
    Nor all the drowsy syrups of the world
    Shall ever medicine thee to that sweet sleep
    Which thou ow'dst† yesterday.

OTHELLO   Ha! ha! false to me?

IAGO   Why, how now, General! no more of that.   335

OTHELLO   Avaunt! be gone! thou hast set me on the rack.
    I swear 'tis better to be much abus'd
    Than but to know 't a little.

IAGO   How now, my lord!

OTHELLO   What sense had I [of] her stol'n hours of lust?
    I saw 't not, thought it not, it harm'd not me.   340
    I slept the next night well, fed well, was free and merry;
    I found not Cassio's kisses on her lips.
    He that is robb'd, not wanting what is stolen,
    Let him not know 't, and he's not robb'd at all.

IAGO   I am sorry to hear this.   345

OTHELLO   I had been happy, if the general camp,
    Pioners† and all, had tasted her sweet body,
    So I had nothing known. O, now, for ever
    Farewell the tranquil mind! farewell content!
    Farewell the plumed troops and the big wars   350
    That make ambition virtue! O, farewell!
    Farewell the neighing steed and the shrill trump,
    The spirit-stirring drum, th' ear-piercing fife,
    The royal banner, and all quality,
    Pride, pomp, and circumstance of glorious war!   355

---

320. *acknown:* aware.   334. *ow'dst:* hadst.
329. *act:* action.   347. *Pioners:* the lowest rank of
331. *mandragora:* a soporific.   soldiers.

And, O you mortal engines, whose rude throats
 Th' immortal Jove's dread clamours counterfeit,
 Farewell! Othello's occupation 's gone!

IAGO. Is 't possible, my lord?

OTHELLO Villain, be sure thou prove my love a whore;   *360*
 Be sure of it. Give me the ocular proof;
 Or, by the worth of mine eternal soul,
 Thou hadst been better have been born a dog
 Than answer my wak'd wrath!

IAGO   Is 't come to this?

OTHELLO Make me to see 't; or, at the least, so prove it *365*
 That the probation bear no hinge nor loop
 To hang a doubt on; or woe upon thy life!

IAGO My noble lord, —

OTHELLO If thou dost slander her and torture me,
 Never pray more; abandon all remorse; *370*
 On horror's head horrors accumulate;
 Do deeds to make heaven weep, all earth amaz'd;
 For nothing canst thou to damnation add
 Greater than that.

IAGO   O grace! O Heaven forgive me!
 Are you a man? Have you a soul or sense? *375*
 God buy† you; take mine office. O wretched fool,
 That lov'st to make thine honesty a vice!
 O monstrous world! Take note, take note, O world,
 To be direct and honest is not safe.
 I thank you for this profit; and from hence *380*
 I'll love no friend, sith love breeds such offence.

OTHELLO Nay, stay. Thou shouldst be honest.

IAGO I should be wise, for honesty 's a fool
 And loses that it works for.

OTHELLO   By the world,
 I think my wife be honest and think she is not; *385*
 I think that thou art just and think thou art not.
 I'll have some proof. [Her] name, that was as fresh
 As Dian's visage, is now begrim'd and black
 As mine own face. If there be cords, or knives,
 Poison, or fire, or suffocating streams, *390*
 I'll not endure it. Would I were satisfied!

IAGO I see, [sir], you are eaten up with passion;
 I do repent me that I put it to you.
 You would be satisfied?

OTHELLO   Would! nay, I will.

IAGO And may; but, how? How satisfied, my lord? *395*
 Would you, the [supervisor], grossly gape on —
 Behold her topp'd?

OTHELLO   Death and damnation! O!

IAGO It were a tedious difficulty, I think,

---

376. *buy:* be with.

To bring them to that prospect; [damn] them then,
If ever mortal eyes do see them bolster†   *400*
More than their own! What then? How then?
What shall I say? Where's satisfaction?
It is impossible you should see this,
Were they as prime† as goats, as hot as monkeys,
As salt as wolves in pride,† and fools as gross   *405*
As ignorance made drunk. But yet, I say,
If imputation and strong circumstances
Which lead directly to the door of truth
Will give you satisfaction, you might have't.

OTHELLO   Give me a living reason she's disloyal.   *410*

IAGO   I do not like the office;
But, sith I am ent'red in this cause so far,
Prick'd to't by foolish honesty and love,
I will go on. I lay with Cassio lately;
And, being troubled with a raging tooth,   *415*
I could not sleep.
There are a kind of men so loose of soul,
That in their sleeps will mutter their affairs;
One of this kind is Cassio.
In sleep I heard him say, "Sweet Desdemona,   *420*
Let us be wary, let us hide our loves;"
And then, sir, would he gripe and wring my hand,
Cry, "O sweet creature!" then kiss me hard,
As if he pluck'd up kisses by the roots
That grew upon my lips; then lay his leg   *425*
Over my thigh, and sigh, and kiss; and then
Cry, "Cursed fate that gave thee to the Moor!"

OTHELLO   O monstrous! monstrous!

IAGO   Nay, this was but his dream.

OTHELLO   But this denoted a foregone conclusion.†
'Tis a shrewd doubt,† though it be but a dream.   *430*

IAGO   And this may help to thicken other proofs
That do demonstrate thinly.

OTHELLO   I'll tear her all to pieces.

IAGO   Nay, [but] be wise; yet we see nothing done.
She may be honest yet. Tell me but this,
Have you not sometimes seen a handkerchief   *435*
Spotted with strawberries in your wife's hand?

OTHELLO   I gave her such a one; 'twas my first gift.

IAGO   I know not that; but such a handkerchief —
I am sure it was your wife's — did I to-day
See Cassio wipe his beard with.

400. *bolster:* lie on a bolster (together).
404. *prime:* lecherous.
405. *pride:* heat.

429. *foregone conclusion:* earlier
act.
430. *shrewd doubt:* strong reason
for suspicion.

OTHELLO   If it be that, —   440
IAGO   If it be that, or any [that] was hers,
       It speaks against her with the other proofs.
OTHELLO   O, that the slave had forty thousand lives!
       One is too poor, too weak for my revenge.
       Now do I see 'tis true. Look here, Iago;   445
       All my fond love thus do I blow to heaven.
       'Tis gone.
       Arise, black vengeance, from the hollow hell!
       Yield up, O love, thy crown and hearted throne
       To tyrannous hate! Swell, bosom, with thy fraught,†   450
       For 'tis of aspics' † tongues!
IAGO   Yet be content.
OTHELLO   O, blood, blood, blood!
IAGO   Patience, I say; your mind [perhaps] may change.
OTHELLO   Never, Iago. Like to the Pontic Sea,†
       Whose icy current and compulsive course   455
       Ne'er [feels] retiring ebb, but keeps due on
       To the Propontic and the Hellespont,
       Even so my bloody thoughts, with violent pace,
       Shall ne'er look back, ne'er ebb to humble love,
       Till that a capable† and wide revenge   460
       Swallow them up. Now, by yond marble heaven,
       In the due reverence of a sacred vow   [Kneels.]
       I here engage my words.
IAGO   Do not rise yet.
       Witness, you ever-burning lights above,
       You elements that clip† us round about,   [Kneels.
       Witness that here Iago doth give up   466
       The execution† of his wit, hands, heart,
       To wrong'd Othello's service! Let him command,
       And to obey shall be in me remorse,†
       What bloody business ever.   [They rise.]
OTHELLO   I greet thy love,   470
       Not with vain thanks, but with acceptance bounteous,
       And will upon the instant put thee to't:
       Within these three days let me hear thee say
       That Cassio's not alive.
IAGO   My friend is dead; 'tis done at your request.   475
       But let her live.
OTHELLO   Damn her, lewd minx! O, damn her! damn her!
       Come, go with me apart; I will withdraw
       To furnish me with some swift means of death
       For the fair devil. Now art thou my lieutenant.   480
IAGO   I am your own for ever.   [Exeunt.

       450. *fraught:* burden.   465. *clip:* embrace.
       451. *aspics':* asps'.   467. *execution:* action.
       454. *Pontic Sea:* Black Sea.   469. *remorse:* obligation.
       460. *capable:* comprehensive.

Scene IV. [*Before the castle*.]
Enter DESDEMONA, EMILIA, *and* CLOWN.

DESDEMONA   Do you know, sirrah, where Lieutenant Cassio lies?†
CLOWN   I dare not say he lies anywhere.
DESDEMONA   Why, man?
CLOWN   He's a soldier, and for me to say a soldier lies, 'tis stabbing.
DESDEMONA   Go to! Where lodges he?   5
CLOWN   To tell you where he lodges, is to tell you where I lie.
DESDEMONA   Can anything be made of this?
CLOWN   I know not where he lodges, and for me to devise a lodging and
   say he lies here or he lies there, were to lie in mine own throat.
DESDEMONA   Can you inquire him out, and be edified by report?   10
CLOWN   I will catechize the world for him; that is, make questions, and
   by them answer.
DESDEMONA   Seek him, bid him come hither. Tell him I have mov'd my
   lord on his behalf, and hope all will be well.
CLOWN   To do this is within the compass of man's wit; and therefore I   15
   will attempt the doing it.   [*Exit.*
DESDEMONA   Where should I lose the handkerchief, Emilia?
EMILIA   I know not, madam.
DESDEMONA   Believe me, I had rather have lost my purse
   Full of crusadoes;† and, but my noble Moor   20
   Is true of mind and made of no such baseness
   As jealous creatures are, it were enough
   To put him to ill thinking.
EMILIA   Is he not jealous?
DESDEMONA   Who, he? I think the sun where he was born
   Drew all such humours from him.
EMILIA   Look, where he comes.   25
   Enter OTHELLO.
DESDEMONA   I will not leave him now till Cassio
   Be call'd to him. — How is't with you, my lord?
OTHELLO   Well, my good lady. [*Aside.*] O, hardness to dissemble! —
   How do you, Desdemona?
DESDEMONA   Well, my good lord.
OTHELLO   Give me your hand. This hand is moist, my lady.   30
DESDEMONA   It [yet] hath felt no age nor known no sorrow.
OTHELLO   This argues fruitfulness and liberal heart;
   Hot, hot, and moist. This hand of yours requires
   A sequester† from liberty, fasting and prayer,
   Much castigation, exercise devout;   35
   For here's a young and sweating devil here
   That commonly rebels. 'Tis a good hand,
   A frank one.

1. *lies:* lodges.   34. *sequester:* separation.
20. *crusadoes:* Portuguese coins
stamped with a cross.

DESDEMONA   You may, indeed, say so;
    For 'twas that hand that gave away my heart.

OTHELLO   A liberal hand. The hearts of old gave hands;   *40*
    But our new heraldry† is hands, not hearts.

DESDEMONA   I cannot speak of this. Come now, your promise.

OTHELLO   What promise, chuck?

DESDEMONA   I have sent to bid Cassio come speak with you.

OTHELLO   I have a salt and sorry† rheum offends me;   *45*
    Lend me thy handkerchief.

DESDEMONA   Here, my lord.

OTHELLO   That which I gave you.

DESDEMONA   I have it not about me.

OTHELLO   Not?

DESDEMONA   No, indeed, my lord.

OTHELLO   That's a fault. That handkerchief
    Did an Egyptian† to my mother give;   *50*
    She was a charmer,† and could almost read
    The thoughts of people. She told her, while she kept it
    'Twould make her amiable† and subdue my father
    Entirely to her love, but if she lost it,
    Or made a gift of it, my father's eye   *55*
    Should hold her loathed and his spirits should hunt
    After new fancies. She, dying, gave it me
    And bid me, when my fate would have me wiv'd,
    To give it her. I did so; and take heed on't;
    Make it a darling like your precious eye.   *60*
    To lose't or give't away were such perdition
    As nothing else could match.

DESDEMONA   Is't possible?

OTHELLO   'Tis true; there's magic in the web of it.
    A sibyl, that had numb'red in the world
    The sun to course two hundred compasses,   *65*
    In her prophetic fury sew'd the work;
    The worms were hallowed that did breed the silk;
    And it was dy'd in mummy† which the skilful
    Conserv'd† of maidens' hearts.

DESDEMONA   Indeed! is't true?

OTHELLO   Most veritable; therefore look to't well.   *70*

DESDEMONA   Then would to [God] that I had never seen 't!

OTHELLO   Ha! wherefore?

DESDEMONA   Why do you speak so startingly and rash?

OTHELLO   Is't lost? Is't gone? Speak, is't out o' th' way?

DESDEMONA   [Heaven] bless us!   *75*

OTHELLO   Say you?

DESDEMONA   It is not lost; but what an if it were?

---

41. *our new heraldry:* probably a topical allusion.
45. *sorry:* distressing.
50. *Egyptian:* gypsy.
51. *charmer:* sorcerer.
53. *amiable:* lovable.
68. *mummy:* embalming fluid.
69. *Conserv'd:* prepared.

OTHELLO   How?

DESDEMONA   I say, it is not lost.

OTHELLO   Fetch 't, let me see 't.

DESDEMONA   Why, so I can, [sir,] but I will not now.   80
   This is a trick to put me from my suit.
   Pray you, let Cassio be receiv'd again.

OTHELLO   Fetch me the handkerchief; my mind misgives.

DESDEMONA   Come, come;
   You'll never meet a more sufficient man.   85

OTHELLO   The handkerchief!

[DESDEMONA   I pray, talk me of Cassio.

OTHELLO   The handkerchief!]

DESDEMONA   A man that all his time
   Hath founded his good fortunes on your love,
   Shar'd dangers with you, —

OTHELLO   The handkerchief!   90

DESDEMONA   In sooth, you are to blame.

OTHELLO   ['Zounds!]   [Exit.

EMILIA   Is not this man jealous?

DESDEMONA   I ne'er saw this before.
   Sure, there's some wonder in this handkerchief;   95
   I am most unhappy in the loss of it.

EMILIA   'Tis not a year or two shows us a man.
   They are all but stomachs, and we all but food;
   They eat us hungerly, and when they are full
   They belch us.
      Enter CASSIO *and* IAGO.
                     Look you, Cassio and my husband!   100

IAGO   There is no other way, 'tis she must do't;
   And, lo, the happiness!† Go, and importune her.

DESDEMONA   How now, good Cassio! What's the news with you?

CASSIO   Madam, my former suit. I do beseech you
   That by your virtuous† means I may again   105
   Exist, and be a member of his love
   Whom I with all the office of my heart
   Entirely honour. I would not be delay'd.
   If my offence be of such mortal kind
   That nor my service past, nor present sorrows,   110
   Nor purpos'd merit in futurity
   Can ransom me into his love again,
   But to know so must be my benefit;
   So shall I clothe me in a forc'd content,
   And shut myself up in some other course,   115
   To fortune's alms.

DESDEMONA   Alas, thrice-gentle Cassio!
   My advocation is not now in tune.
   My lord is not my lord; nor should I know him

---

   102. *happiness:* luck.   105. *virtuous:* effective.

1068   *Drama*

Were he in favour† as in humour alter'd.
So help me every spirit sanctified   120
As I have spoken for you all my best
And stood within the blank† of his displeasure
For my free speech! You must a while be patient.
What I can do I will; and more I will
Than for myself I dare. Let that suffice you.   125

IAGO   Is my lord angry?

EMILIA   He went hence but now,
And certainly in strange unquietness.

IAGO   Can he be angry? I have seen the cannon
When it hath blown his ranks into the air,
And, like the devil, from his very arm   130
Puff'd his own brother: — and is he angry?
Something of moment then. I will go meet him.
There's matter in't indeed, if he be angry.   [Exit IAGO.

DESDEMONA   I prithee, do so. Something, sure, of state,
Either from Venice, or some unhatch'd practice†   135
Made demonstrable here in Cyprus to him,
Hath puddled his clear spirit; and in such cases *like a toothache*
Men's natures wrangle with inferior things,—
Though great ones are their object. 'Tis even so;
For let our finger ache, and it indues   140
Our other, healthful members even to a sense
Of pain. Nay, we must think men are not gods,
Nor of them look for such observancy
As fits the bridal. Beshrew me much, Emilia,
I was, unhandsome warrior as I am,   145
Arraigning his unkindness with my soul;
But now I find I had suborn'd the witness,
And he's indicted falsely.

EMILIA   Pray Heaven it be state-matters, as you think,
And no conception nor no jealous toy   150
Concerning you.

DESDEMONA   Alas the day! I never gave him cause.

EMILIA   But jealous souls will not be answer'd so;
They are not ever jealous for the cause,
But jealous for they're jealous. It is a monster   155
Begot upon itself, born on itself.

DESDEMONA   Heaven keep the monster from Othello's mind!

EMILIA   Lady, amen.

DESDEMONA   I will go seek him. Cassio, walk hereabout;
If I do find him fit, I'll move your suit   160
And seek to effect it to my uttermost.

CASSIO   I humbly thank your ladyship.   [Exeunt [DESDEMONA and EMILIA].
Enter BIANCA.

---

119. *favour:* appearance.   135. *practice:* plot.
122. *blank:* target; strictly, the
white spot in the center.

BIANCA   Save you, friend Cassio!

CASSIO   What make you from home?
    How is it with you, my most fair Bianca?
    Indeed, sweet love, I was coming to your house.   165

BIANCA   And I was going to your lodging, Cassio.
    What, keep a week away? seven days and nights?
    Eightscore eight hours? and lovers' absent hours,
    More tedious than the dial eightscore times?
    O weary reck'ning!

CASSIO   Pardon me, Bianca.   170
    I have this while with leaden thoughts been press'd;
    But I shall, in a more continuate† time,
    Strike off this score of absence. Sweet Bianca,
    [*Giving her Desdemona's handkerchief.*]
    Take me this work out.

BIANCA   O Cassio, whence came this?
    This is some token from a newer friend;   175
    To the felt absence now I feel a cause.
    Is't come to this? Well, well.

CASSIO   Go to, woman!
    Throw your vile guesses in the devils' teeth,
    From whence you have them. You are jealous now
    That this is from some mistress, some remembrance.   180
    No, in good troth, Bianca.

BIANCA   Why, whose is it?

CASSIO   I know not, [sweet]; I found it in my chamber.
    I like the work well; ere it be demanded —
    As like enough it will — I'd have it copied.
    Take it, and do't; and leave me for this time.   185

BIANCA   Leave you! Wherefore?

CASSIO   I do attend here on the General;
    And think it no addition,† nor my wish,
    To have him see me woman'd.

BIANCA   Why, I pray you?

CASSIO   Not that I love you not.

BIANCA   But that you do not love me.   190
    I pray you, bring me on the way a little,
    And say if I shall see you soon at night.

CASSIO   'Tis but a little way that I can bring you,
    For I attend here; but I'll see you soon.

BIANCA   'Tis very good; I must be circumstanc'd.†   195

                                                        [*Exeunt.*

Act Four   *Scene I.* [*Cyprus. Before the castle.*]
    Enter OTHELLO *and* IAGO.

IAGO   Will you think so?

OTHELLO   Think so, Iago!

        172. *continuate*: uninterrupted.   195. *circumstanc'd*: reconciled.
        188. *addition*: credit.

IAGO   What,
   To kiss in private?
OTHELLO   An unauthoriz'd kiss.
IAGO   Or to be naked with her friend in bed
   An hour or more, not meaning any harm?
OTHELLO   Naked in bed, Iago, and not mean harm!   5
   It is hypocrisy against the devil.
   They that mean virtuously, and yet do so,
   The devil their virtue tempts, and they tempt heaven.
IAGO   If they do nothing, 'tis a venial slip;
   But if I give my wife a handkerchief, —   10
OTHELLO   What then?
IAGO   Why, then, 'tis hers, my lord; and, being hers,
   She may, I think, bestow 't on any man.
OTHELLO   She is protectress of her honour too;
   May she give that?   15
IAGO   Her honour is an essence that's not seen;
   They have it very oft that have it not:
   But, for the handkerchief, —
OTHELLO   By heaven, I would most gladly have forgot it.
   Thou said'st — O, it comes o'er my memory,   20
   As doth the raven o'er the infectious house,
   Boding to all — he had my handkerchief.
IAGO   Ay, what of that?
OTHELLO   That's not so good now.
IAGO   What
   If I had said I had seen him do you wrong?
   Or heard him say, — as knaves be such abroad,   25
   Who having, by their own importunate suit,
   Or voluntary dotage of some mistress,
   Convinced or suppli'd them, cannot choose
   But they must blab —
OTHELLO   Hath he said anything?
IAGO   He hath, my lord; but be you well assur'd,   30
   No more than he'll unswear.
OTHELLO   What hath he said?
IAGO   Why, that he did — I know not what he did.
OTHELLO   What? what?
IAGO   Lie —
OTHELLO   With her?
IAGO   With her, on her; what you will.   35
OTHELLO   Lie with her! lie on her! We say lie on her, when they belie
   her. Lie with her! ['Zounds,] that's fulsome! — Handkerchief — con-
   fessions — handkerchief! — To confess, and be hang'd for his labour;
   — first to be hang'd, and then to confess. — I tremble at it. Nature
   would not invest herself in such shadowing passion without some in-   40
   struction.† It is not words that shakes me thus. Pish! Noses, ears, and

   40–41. *invest . . . instruction:* i.e.,
   create such imaginings unless to
   teach me.

lips. — Is't possible? — Confess — handkerchief! — O devil!

[*Falls in a trance.*

IAGO   Work on,
My medicine, work! Thus credulous fools are caught;
And many worthy and chaste dames even thus,   45
All guiltless, meet reproach. — What, ho! my lord!
My lord, I say! Othello!
Enter CASSIO.

                                   How now, Cassio!

CASSIO   What's the matter?

IAGO   My lord is fall'n into an epilepsy.
This is his second fit; he had one yesterday.   50

CASSIO   Rub him about the temples.

IAGO   [No, forbear;]
The lethargy must have his quiet course;
If not, he foams at mouth and by and by†
Breaks out to savage madness. Look, he stirs.
Do you withdraw yourself a little while;   55
He will recover straight. When he is gone,
I would on great occasion speak with you.   [*Exit* CASSIO.
How is it, General? Have you not hurt your head?

OTHELLO   Dost thou mock me?

IAGO   I mock you not, by heaven.
Would you would bear your fortune like a man!   60

OTHELLO   A horned man's a monster and a beast.

IAGO   There's many a beast then in a populous city,
And many a civil† monster.

OTHELLO   Did he confess it?

IAGO   Good sir, be a man;
Think every bearded fellow that's but yok'd   65
May draw with you. There's millions now alive
That nightly lie in those unproper† beds
Which they dare swear peculiar;† your case is better.
O, 'tis the spite of hell, the fiend's arch-mock,
To lip a wanton in a secure† couch,   70
And to suppose her chaste! No, let me know;
And knowing what I am, I know what she shall be.

OTHELLO   O, thou art wise; 'tis certain.

IAGO   Stand you a while apart;
Confine yourself but in a patient list.†
Whilst you were here o'erwhelmed with your grief —   75
A passion most [unsuiting] such a man —
Cassio came hither. I shifted him away,
And laid good 'scuse upon your ecstasy;†

---

53. *by and by:* straightway.
63. *civil:* civilized.
67. *unproper:* not exclusively their own.
68. *peculiar:* their own.

70. *secure:* supposed safe from others.
74. *a patient list:* the bounds of patience.
78. *ecstasy:* trance.

Bade him anon return and here speak with me,
The which he promis'd. Do but encave yourself, 80
And mark the fleers, the gibes, and notable scorns
That dwell in every region of his face;
For I will make him tell the tale anew,
Where, how, how oft, how long ago, and when
He hath, and is again to cope your wife. 85
I say, but mark his gesture. Marry, patience;
Or I shall say you're all in all in spleen,†
And nothing of a man.

OTHELLO   Dost thou hear, Iago?
I will be found most cunning in my patience;
But — dost thou hear? — most bloody.

IAGO   That's not amiss; 90
But yet keep time in all. Will you withdraw?   [OTHELLO *retires*.]
Now will I question Cassio of Bianca,
A housewife that by selling her desires
Buys herself bread and clothes. It is a creature
That dotes on Cassio, as 'tis the strumpet's plague 95
To beguile many and be beguil'd by one.
He, when he hears of her, cannot [refrain]
From the excess of laughter. Here he comes.
Re-enter CASSIO.
As he shall smile, Othello shall go mad;
And his unbookish jealousy must [conster] 100
Poor Cassio's smiles, gestures, and light behaviours
Quite in the wrong. How do you, Lieutenant?

CASSIO   The worser that you give me the addition
Whose want even kills me.

IAGO   Ply Desdemona well, and you are sure on't. 105
[*Speaking lower*.] Now, if this suit lay in Bianca's [power].
How quickly should you speed!

CASSIO   Alas, poor caitiff!

OTHELLO   Look how he laughs already!

IAGO   I never knew woman love man so.

CASSIO   Alas, poor rogue! I think, indeed, she loves me. 110

OTHELLO   Now he denies it faintly, and laughs it out.

IAGO   Do you hear, Cassio?

OTHELLO   Now he importunes him
To tell it o'er. Go to; well said, well said.

IAGO   She gives it out that you shall marry her. Do you intend it? 115

CASSIO   Ha, ha, ha!

OTHELLO   Do ye triumph, Roman? Do you triumph?

CASSIO   I marry [her]!! What? a customer!† Prithee, bear some charity
to my wit; do not think it so unwholesome. Ha, ha, ha!

OTHELLO   So, so so, so; they laugh that win. 120

IAGO   Why, the cry goes that you [shall] marry her.

CASSIO   Prithee, say true.

87. *spleen:* anger, passion.   118. *customer:* harlot.

IAGO   I am a very villain else.

OTHELLO   Have you scor'd† me? Well.

CASSIO   This is the monkey's own giving out. She is persuaded I will   *125*
marry her, out of her own love and flattery, not out of my promise.

OTHELLO   Iago [beckons] me; now he begins the story.

CASSIO   She was here even now; she haunts me in every place. I was the
other day talking on the sea-bank with certain Venetians; and thither
comes the bauble, and, falls me thus about my neck —   *130*

OTHELLO   Crying, "O dear Cassio!" as it were; his gesture imports it.

CASSIO   So hangs, and lolls, and weeps upon me; so shakes and pulls me.
Ha, ha, ha!

OTHELLO   Now he tells how she pluck'd him to my chamber. Oh, I see
that nose of yours, but not that dog I shall throw it to.   *135*

CASSIO   Well, I must leave her company.

IAGO   Before me! look, where she comes.

Enter BIANCA.

CASSIO   'Tis such another fitchew!† Marry, a perfum'd one. — What do
you mean by this haunting of me?

BIANCA   Let the devil and his dam haunt you! What did you mean by   *140*
that same handkerchief you gave me even now? I was a fine fool to
take it. I must take out the work? — A likely piece of work, that you
should find it in your chamber, and know not who left it there! This
is some minx's token, and I must take out the work? There; give it
your hobby-horse. Wheresoever you had it, I'll take out no work on't.   *145*

CASSIO   How now, my sweet Bianca! how now! how now!

OTHELLO   By heaven, that should be my handkerchief!

BIANCA   If you'll come to supper to-night, you may; if you will not, come
when you are next prepar'd for.   [*Exit.*

IAGO   After her, after her.   *150*

CASSIO   [Faith,] I must; she'll rail in the streets else.

IAGO   Will you sup there?

CASSIO   Yes, I intend so.

IAGO   Well, I may chance to see you; for I would very fain speak with
you.   *155*

CASSIO   Prithee, come; will you?

IAGO   Go to; say no more.   [*Exit* CASSIO.

OTHELLO [*Advancing.*]   How shall I murder him, Iago?

IAGO   Did you perceive how he laugh'd at his vice?

OTHELLO   O Iago!   *160*

IAGO   And did you see the handkerchief?

OTHELLO   Was that mine?

IAGO   Yours, by this hand. And to see how he prizes the foolish woman
your wife! She gave it him, and he hath given it his whore.

OTHELLO   I would have him nine years a-killing.   *165*
A fine woman! a fair woman! a sweet woman!

IAGO   Nay, you must forget that.

OTHELLO   Ay, let her rot, and perish, and be damn'd to-night; for she
shall not live. No, my heart is turn'd to stone; I strike it, and it hurts

---

124. *scor'd:* branded.   138. *fitchew:* polecat.

my hand. O, the world hath not a sweeter creature! She might lie by   170
an emperor's side and command him tasks.

IAGO   Nay, that's not your way.

OTHELLO   Hang her! I do but say what she is. So delicate with her
needle! an admirable musician! O! she will sing the savageness out of
a bear. Of so high and plenteous wit and invention!   175

IAGO   She's the worse for all this.

OTHELLO   O, a thousand thousand times. And then, of so gentle a condition!

IAGO   Ay, too gentle.

OTHELLO   Nay, that's certain. But yet the pity of it, Iago! O Iago, the   180
pity of it, Iago!

IAGO   If you are so fond over her iniquity, give her patent to offend; for
if it touch not you, it comes near nobody.

OTHELLO   I will chop her into messes.† Cuckold me!

IAGO   O, 'tis foul in her.   185

OTHELLO   With mine officer!

IAGO   That's fouler.

OTHELLO   Get me some poison, Iago; this night. I'll not expostulate with
her, lest her body and beauty unprovide my mind again. This night,
Iago.   190

IAGO   Do it not with poison; strangle her in her bed, even the bed she hath
contaminated.

OTHELLO   Good, good; the justice of it pleases; very good.

IAGO   And for Cassio, let me be his undertaker.† You shall hear more by
midnight.   195

[A trumpet.

Enter LODOVICO, DESDEMONA, and Attendants.

OTHELLO   Excellent good. What trumpet is that same?

IAGO   I warrant, something from Venice. 'Tis Lodovico, this, comes from
the Duke. See, your wife's with him.

LODOVICO   Save you, worthy General!

OTHELLO   With all my heart, sir.

LODOVICO   The Duke and Senators of Venice greet you. [Gives him a   200
letter.]

OTHELLO   I kiss the instrument of their pleasures. [Opens the letter, and
reads.]

DESDEMONA   And what's the news, good cousin Lodovico?

IAGO   I am very glad to see you, signior;   205
Welcome to Cyprus.

LODOVICO   I thank you. How does Lieutenant Cassio?

IAGO   Lives, sir.

DESDEMONA   Cousin, there 's fall'n between him and my lord
An unkind breach; but you shall make all well.   210

OTHELLO   Are you sure of that?

DESDEMONA   My lord?

OTHELLO [Reads.] "This fail you not to do, as you will." —

184. messes: portions of food.   194. undertaker: dispatcher.

LODOVICO   He did not call; he's busy in the paper.
 Is there division 'twixt my lord and Cassio?   *215*
DESDEMONA   A most unhappy one. I would do much
 T' atone† them, for the love I bear to Cassio.
OTHELLO   Fire and brimstone!
DESDEMONA   My lord?
OTHELLO   Are you wise?
DESDEMONA   What, is he angry?
LODOVICO   May be the letter mov'd him;
 For, as I think, they do command him home,   *220*
 Deputing Cassio in his government.
DESDEMONA   Trust me, I am glad on't.
OTHELLO   Indeed!
DESDEMONA   My lord?
OTHELLO   I am glad to see you mad.
DESDEMONA   Why, sweet Othello, —
OTHELLO [*Striking her.*] Devil!
DESDEMONA   I have not deserv'd this.   *225*
LODOVICO   My lord, this would not be believ'd in Venice
 Though I should swear I saw 't. 'Tis very much.
 Make her amends: she weeps.
OTHELLO   O devil, devil!
 If that the earth could teem† with woman's tears,
 Each drop she falls would prove a crocodile.   *230*
 Out of my sight!
DESDEMONA   I will not stay to offend you. [*Going.*]
LODOVICO   Truly, [an] obedient lady:
 I do beseech your lordship, call her back.
OTHELLO   Mistress!
DESDEMONA   My lord?
OTHELLO   What would you with her, sir?
LODOVICO   Who, I, my lord?   *235*
OTHELLO   Ay; you did wish that I would make her turn.
 Sir, she can turn, and turn, and yet go on,
 And turn again; and she can weep, sir, weep;
 And she's obedient, as you say, obedient,
 Very obedient. Proceed you in your tears.   *240*
 Concerning this, sir, — O well-painted passion! —
 I am commanded home. — Get you away;
 I'll send for you anon. — Sir, I obey the mandate,
 And will return to Venice. — Hence, avaunt! —
          [*Exit* DESDEMONA.]
 Cassio shall have my place. And, sir, to-night   *245*
 I do entreat that we may sup together.
 You are welcome, sir, to Cyprus. — Goats and monkeys! [*Exit.*
LODOVICO   Is this the noble Moor whom our full Senate
 Call all in all sufficient? Is this the nature

---

217. *atone:* reconcile.   229. *teem:* breed.

Whom passion could not shake? whose solid virtue   250
The shot of accident nor dart of chance
Could neither graze nor pierce?

IAGO   He is much chang'd.

LODOVICO   Are his wits safe? Is he not light of brain?

IAGO   He's that he is; I may not breathe my censure
What he might be. If what he might he is not,   255
I would to heaven he were!

LODOVICO   What, strike his wife!

IAGO   Faith, that was not so well; yet would I knew
That stroke would prove the worst!

LODOVICO   Is it his use?
Or did the letters work upon his blood
And new-create [this] fault?

IAGO   Alas, alas!   260
It is not honesty in me to speak
What I have seen and known. You shall observe him,
And his own courses will denote him so
That I may save my speech. Do but go after,
And mark how he continues.   265

LODOVICO   I am sorry that I am deceiv'd in him.   [*Exeunt.*

Scene II. [*A room in the castle.*]
Enter OTHELLO *and* EMILIA.

OTHELLO   You have seen nothing then?

EMILIA   Nor ever heard, nor ever did suspect.

OTHELLO   Yes, you have seen Cassio and she together.

EMILIA   But then I saw no harm, and then I heard
Each syllable that breath made up between them.   5

OTHELLO   What, did they never whisper?

EMILIA   Never, my lord.

OTHELLO   Nor send you out o' th' way?

EMILIA   Never.

OTHELLO   To fetch her fan, her gloves, her mask, nor nothing?

EMILIA   Never, my lord.   10

OTHELLO   That's strange.

EMILIA   I durst, my lord, to wager she is honest,
Lay down my soul at stake. If you think other,
Remove your thought; it doth abuse your bosom.
If any wretch have put this in your head,   15
Let Heaven requite it with the serpent's curse!
For, if she be not honest, chaste, and true,
There's no man happy; the purest of their wives
Is foul as slander.

OTHELLO   Bid her come hither; go.   [*Exit* EMILIA.
She says enough; yet she's a simple bawd   20
That cannot say as much. This is a subtle whore,
A closet lock and key of villanous secrets;

And yet she'll kneel and pray; I have seen her do't.
Enter DESDEMONA *with* EMILIA.
DESDEMONA My lord, what is your will?
OTHELLO   Pray, chuck, come hither.
DESDEMONA What is your pleasure?
OTHELLO   Let me see your eyes;   25
　Look in my face.
DESDEMONA   What horrible fancy's this?
OTHELLO [*To* EMILIA.] Some of your function, mistress;
　Leave procreants alone and shut the door;
　Cough, or cry "hem," if anybody come.
　Your mystery, your mystery;† nay, dispatch.   30
                                          [*Exit* EMILIA.

DESDEMONA Upon my knee, what doth your speech import?
　I understand a fury in your words,
　[But not the words.]
OTHELLO Why, what art thou?
DESDEMONA   Your wife, my lord; your true
　And loyal wife.
OTHELLO   Come, swear it, damn thyself,   35
　Lest, being like one of heaven, the devils themselves
　Should fear to seize thee; therefore be double damn'd,
　Swear thou art honest.
DESDEMONA   Heaven doth truly know it.
OTHELLO Heaven truly knows that thou art false as hell.
DESDEMONA To whom, my lord? With whom? How am I false?   40
OTHELLO Ah, Desdemon! Away! away! away!
DESDEMONA Alas the heavy day! Why do you weep?
　Am I the motive of these tears, my lord?
　If haply you my father do suspect
　An instrument of this your calling back,   45
　Lay not your blame on me. If you have lost him,
　[Why,] I have lost him too.
OTHELLO   Had it pleas'd Heaven
　To try me with affliction; had they rain'd
　All kind of sores and shames on my bare head,
　Steep'd me in poverty to the very lips,   50
　Given to captivity me and my utmost hopes,
　I should have found in some place of my soul
　A drop of patience; but, alas, to make me
　The fixed figure for the time of scorn†
　To point his slow and moving† finger at!   55
　Yet could I bear that too, well, very well;
　But there, where I have garner'd up my heart,
　Where either I must live or bear no life;
　The fountain from the which my current runs
　Or else dries up; to be discarded thence!   60

30. *mystery:* trade.   55. *slow and moving:* slowly mov-
54. *time of scorn:* scorn of the age.   ing.

Or keep it as a cistern for foul toads
To knot and gender in! Turn thy complexion† there,
Patience, thou young and rose-lipp'd cherubin,
[Ay, there] look grim as hell!

DESDEMONA   I hope my noble lord esteems me honest.   65

OTHELLO   O, ay; as summer flies are in the shambles,
That quicken even with blowing.† O thou weed,
Who art so lovely fair and smell'st so sweet
That the sense aches at thee, would thou hadst ne'er been born!

DESDEMONA   Alas, what ignorant sin have I committed?   70

OTHELLO   Was this fair paper, this most goodly book,
Made to write "whore" upon? What committed!
Committed! O thou public commoner!†
I should make very forges of my cheeks,
That would to cinders burn up modesty,   75
Did I but speak thy deeds. What committed!
Heaven stops the nose at it, and the moon winks;†
The bawdy wind, that kisses all it meets,
Is hush'd within the hollow mine of earth
And will not hear it. What committed!   80
[Impudent strumpet!]

DESDEMONA   By heaven, you do me wrong.

OTHELLO   Are not you a strumpet?

DESDEMONA   No, as I am a Christian.
If to preserve this vessel for my lord
From any other foul unlawful touch
Be not to be a strumpet, I am none.   85

OTHELLO   What, not a whore?

DESDEMONA   No, as I shall be sav'd.

OTHELLO   Is't possible?

DESDEMONA   O, Heaven forgive us!

OTHELLO   I cry you mercy, then.
I took you for that cunning whore of Venice
That married with Othello. [*Raising his voice.*] — You, mistress,   90
Re-enter EMILIA.
That have the office opposite to Saint Peter,
And keeps the gate of hell! You, you, ay, you!
We have done our course; there's money for your pains.
I pray you, turn the key and keep our counsel.   [*Exit.*
                                                                              95

EMILIA   Alas, what does this gentleman conceive?
How do you, madam? How do you, my good lady?

DESDEMONA   Faith, half asleep.

EMILIA   Good madam, what's the matter with my lord?

DESDEMONA   With who?

EMILIA   Why, with my lord, madam.   100

62. *Turn thy complexion:* change   73. *commoner:* harlot.
thy color.   77. *winks:* shuts her eyes.
67. *quicken...blowing:* come to
life as soon as impregnated.

DESDEMONA   Who is thy lord?

EMILIA   He that is yours, sweet lady.

DESDEMONA   I have none. Do not talk to me, Emilia;
I cannot weep, nor answers have I none
But what should go by water.† Prithee, tonight
Lay on my bed my wedding sheets, remember;   *105*
And call thy husband hither.

EMILIA   Here's a change indeed!   [*Exit.*

DESDEMONA   'Tis meet I should be us'd so, very meet.
How have I been behav'd, that he might stick
The small'st opinion† on my least misuse?†
Re-enter EMILIA *with* IAGO

IAGO   What is your pleasure, madam? How is't with you?   *110*

DESDEMONA   I cannot tell. Those that do teach young babes
Do it with gentle means and easy tasks.
He might have chid me so; for, in good faith,
I am a child to chiding.

IAGO   What's the matter, lady?

EMILIA   Alas, Iago, my lord hath so bewhor'd her,   *115*
Thrown such despite and heavy terms upon her,
That true hearts cannot bear it.

DESDEMONA   Am I that name, Iago?

IAGO   What name, fair lady?

DESDEMONA   Such as she said my lord did say I was.

EMILIA   He call'd her whore. A beggar in his drink   *120*
Could not have laid such terms upon his callet.†

IAGO   Why did he so?

DESDEMONA   I do not know; I am sure I am none such.

IAGO   Do not weep, do not weep. Alas the day!

EMILIA   Hath she forsook so many noble matches,   *125*
Her father and her country and her friends,
To be call'd whore? Would it not make one weep?

DESDEMONA   It is my wretched fortune.

IAGO   Beshrew him for't!
How comes this trick upon him?

DESDEMONA   Nay, Heaven doth know.

EMILIA   I will be hang'd if some eternal villain,   *130*
Some busy and insinuating rogue,
Some cogging,† cozening† slave, to get some office,
Have not devis'd this slander. I'll be hang'd else.

IAGO   Fie, there is no such man; it is impossible.

DESDEMONA   If any such there be, Heaven pardon him!   *135*

EMILIA   A halter pardon him! and hell gnaw his bones!
Why should he call her whore? Who keeps her company?
What place? what time? what form? what likelihood?

---

104. *go by water:* be rendered by
tears.
109. *opinion:* censure. *misuse:*
misconduct.

121. *callet:* whore.
132. *cogging:* lying. *cozening:*
cheating.

The Moor's abus'd by some most villanous knave,
Some base notorious knave, some scurvy fellow.   140
O heavens, that such companions thou'dst unfold,†
And put in every honest hand a whip
To lash the rascals naked through the world
Even from the east to th' west!

IAGO   Speak within door.
EMILIA   O, fie upon them! Some such squire he was   145
That turn'd your wit the seamy side without,
And made you to suspect me with the Moor.
IAGO   You are a fool; go to.
DESDEMONA   Alas, Iago,
What shall I do to win my lord again?
Good friend, go to him; for, by this light of heaven,   150
I know not how I lost him. Here I kneel:
If e'er my will did trespass 'gainst his love,
Either in discourse† of thought or actual deed,
Or that mine eyes, mine ears, or any sense
Delighted them [in] any other form;   155
Or that I do not yet, and ever did,
And ever will — though he do shake me off
To beggarly divorcement — love him dearly,
Comfort forswear me! Unkindness may do much;
And his unkindness may defeat† my life,   160
But never taint my love. I cannot say "whore."
It does abhor me now I speak the word;
To do the act that might the addition earn
Not the world's mass of vanity could make me.
IAGO   I pray you, be content; 'tis but his humour.   165
The business of the state does him offence,
[And he does chide with you.]
DESDEMONA   If 'twere no other, —
IAGO   It is but so, I warrant.   [*Trumpets within.*]
Hark, how these instruments summon to supper!
The messengers of Venice stay the meat.†   170
Go in, and weep not; all things shall be well.

                                    [*Exeunt* DESDEMONA *and* EMILIA.

Enter RODERIGO.
How now, Roderigo!
RODERIGO   I do not find that thou deal'st justly with me.
IAGO   What in the contrary?
RODERIGO   Every day thou daff'st me† with some device, Iago; and rather,   175
as it seems to me now, keep'st from me all conveniency than suppliest
me with the least advantage of hope. I will indeed no longer endure it,
nor am I yet persuaded to put up in peace what already I have foolishly
suff'red.

---

141. *unfold:* expose.   170. *stay the meat:* wait to dine.
153. *discourse:* course.   175. *daff'st me:* puttest me off.
160. *defeat:* destroy.

IAGO   Will you hear me, Roderigo?   *180*

RODERIGO   I have heard too much, and your words and performances are
no kin together.

IAGO   You charge me most unjustly.

RODERIGO   With nought but truth. I have wasted myself out of my means.
The jewels you have had from me to deliver Desdemona would half   *185*
have corrupted a votarist.† You have told me she hath receiv'd them
and return'd me expectations and comforts of sudden respect† and acquaintance, but I find none.

IAGO   Well; go to; very well.

RODERIGO   Very well! go to! I cannot go to, man; nor 'tis not very well.   *190*
Nay, I think it is scurvy, and begin to find myself fopp'd† in it.

IAGO   Very well.

RODERIGO   I tell you 'tis not very well. I will make myself known to
Desdemona. If she will return me my jewels, I will give over my suit
and repent my unlawful solicitation; if not, assure yourself I will seek   *195*
satisfaction of you.

IAGO   You have said now.

RODERIGO   Ay, and said nothing but what I protest intendment of doing.

IAGO   Why, now I see there's mettle in thee, and even from this instant
do build on thee a better opinion than ever before. Give me thy hand,   *200*
Roderigo. Thou hast taken against me a most just exception; but yet,
I protest, I have dealt most directly in thy affair.

RODERIGO   It hath not appear'd.

IAGO   I grant indeed it hath not appear'd, and your suspicion is not without wit and judgement. But, Roderigo, if thou hast that in thee indeed,   *205*
which I have greater reason to believe now than ever, I mean purpose,
courage, and valour, this night show it. If thou the next night following enjoy not Desdemona, take me from this world with treachery and
devise engines† for my life.

RODERIGO   Well, what is it? Is it within reason and compass?   *210*

IAGO   Sir, there is especial commission come from Venice to depute Cassio
in Othello's place.

RODERIGO   Is that true? Why, then Othello and Desdemona return again
to Venice.

IAGO   O, no; he goes into Mauritania and taketh away with him the fair   *215*
Desdemona, unless his abode be ling'red here by some accident;
wherein none can be so determinate as the removing of Cassio.

RODERIGO   How do you mean, removing him?

IAGO   Why, by making him uncapable of Othello's place; knocking out his
brains.   *220*

RODERIGO   And that you would have me to do?

IAGO   Ay, if you dare do yourself a profit and a right. He sups to-night
with a harlotry, and thither will I go to him; he knows not yet of his
honourable fortune. If you will watch his going thence, which I will
fashion to fall out between twelve and one, you may take him at your   *225*
pleasure. I will be near to second your attempt, and he shall fall

---

186. *votarist:* nun.   191. *fopp'd:* duped.
187. *sudden respect:* speedy notice.   209. *engines:* plots.

between us. Come, stand not amaz'd at it, but go along with me; I will
show you such a necessity in his death that you shall think yourself
bound to put it on him. It is now high suppertime, and the night grows
to waste. About it.   230

RODERIGO   I will hear further reason for this.

IAGO   And you shall be satisfi'd.   [*Exeunt.*

Scene III. [*Another room in the castle.*]

Enter OTHELLO, LODOVICO, DESDEMONA, EMILIA, *and Attendants.*

LODOVICO   I do beseech you, sir, trouble yourself no further.

OTHELLO   O, pardon me; 'twill do me good to walk.

LODOVICO   Madam, good-night; I humbly thank your ladyship.

DESDEMONA   Your honour is most welcome.

OTHELLO   Will you walk, sir?   5

O, — Desdemona, —

DESDEMONA   My lord?

OTHELLO   Get you to bed on th' instant; I will be return'd forthwith. Dismiss your attendant there. Look 't be done.

DESDEMONA   I will, my lord.   [*Exeunt* [OTHELLO, LODOVICO, *and Attendants*].

EMILIA   How goes it now? He looks gentler than he did.   10

DESDEMONA   He says he will return incontinent;
And hath commanded me to go to bed,
And bid me to dismiss you.

EMILIA   Dismiss me!

DESDEMONA   It was his bidding; therefore, good Emilia,
Give me my nightly wearing, and adieu.   15
We must not now displease him.

EMILIA   I would you had never seen him!

DESDEMONA   So would not I. My love doth so approve him,
That even his stubbornness,† his checks, his frowns, —
Prithee, unpin me, — have grace and favour [in them].   20

EMILIA   I have laid those sheets you bade me on the bed.

DESDEMONA   All's one. Good [faith], how foolish are our minds!
If I do die before, prithee, shroud me
In one of these same sheets.

EMILIA   Come, come, you talk.

DESDEMONA   My mother had a maid call'd Barbary;   25
She was in love, and he she lov'd prov'd mad
And did forsake her. She had a song of "Willow";
An old thing 'twas, but it express'd her fortune,
And she died singing it. That song to-night
Will not go from my mind; I have much to do   30
But to go hang my head all at one side
And sing it like poor Barbary. Prithee, dispatch.

EMILIA   Shall I go fetch your night-gown?

DESDEMONA   No, unpin me here.

19. *stubbornness:* roughness.

This Lodovico is a proper man.

EMILIA A very handsome man.   *35*

DESDEMONA He speaks well.

EMILIA I know a lady in Venice would have walk'd barefoot to Palestine
for a touch of his nether lip.

DESDEMONA [*Singing*.] "The poor soul sat [sighing] by a sycamore tree,
      Sing all a green willow;   *40*
Her hand on her bosom, her head on her knee,
      Sing willow, willow, willow.
The fresh streams ran by her, and murmur'd her moans;
      Sing willow, willow, willow;
Her salt tears fell from her, and soft'ned the stones;   *45*
      Sing willow, willow, willow;"
Lay by these; —
[*Singing*.] "Willow, willow;" —
Prithee, hie thee; he'll come anon; —
[*Singing*.]
"Sing all a green willow must be my garland.   *50*
      Let nobody blame him, his scorn I approve," —
Nay, that's not next. — Hark! who is't that knocks?

EMILIA It's the wind.

DESDEMONA [*Singing*.]
"I call'd my love false love; but what said he then?   *55*
      Sing willow, willow, willow.
If I court moe women, you'll couch with moe men." —
So, get thee gone; good-night. Mine eyes do itch;
Doth that bode weeping?

EMILIA   'Tis neither here nor there.

DESDEMONA I have heard it said so. O, these men, these men!   *60*
Dost thou in conscience think, — tell me, Emilia, —
That there be women do abuse their husbands
In such gross kind?

EMILIA   There be some such, no question.

DESDEMONA Wouldst thou do such a deed for all the world?

EMILIA Why, would not you?

DESDEMONA   No, by this heavenly light!   *65*

EMILIA Nor I neither by this heavenly light;
I might do't as well i' th' dark.

DESDEMONA Wouldst thou do such a deed for all the world?

EMILIA The world's a huge thing; it is a great price.
For a small vice.

DESDEMONA   In troth, I think thou wouldst not.

EMILIA In troth, I think I should; and undo't when I had done. Marry, *70*
I would not do such a thing for a joint-ring,† nor for measure of lawn,
nor for gowns, petticoats, nor caps, nor any petty exhibition;† but, for
all the whole world. — ['ud's pity], who would not make her husband a
cuckold to make him a monarch? I should venture purgatory for't.

---

71. *joint-ring:* ring made in sepa-   72. *exhibition:* allowance.
rable halves.

DESDEMONA Beshrew me, if I would do such a wrong   75
    For the whole world.
EMILIA Why, the wrong is but a wrong i' th' world; and having the world
    for your labour, 'tis a wrong in your own world, and you might
    quickly make it right.
DESDEMONA I do not think there is any such woman.   80
EMILIA Yes, a dozen; and as many to th' vantage† as would store the
    world they play'd for.
    But I do think it is their husbands' faults
    If wives do fall. Say that they slack their duties
    And pour our treasures into foreign laps,   85
    Or else break out in peevish† jealousies,
    Throwing restraint upon us; or say they strike us,
    Or scant our former having† in despite;
    Why, we have galls,† and though we have some grace,
    Yet have we some revenge. Let husbands know   90
    Their wives have sense like them; they see and smell
    And have their palates both for sweet and sour
    As husbands have. What is it that they do
    When they change us for others? Is it sport?
    I think it is. And doth affection breed it?   95
    I think it doth. Is't frailty that thus errs?
    It is so too. And have not we affections,
    Desires for sport, and frailty, as men have?
    Then let them use us well; else let them know,
    The ills we do, their ills instruct us so.   100
DESDEMONA Good-night, good-night. Heaven me such uses send,
    Not to pick bad from bad, but by bad mend.   [Exeunt.

she thinks that because other men go to other women, women can turn to get other men - to get back at their husbands...etc

Act Five Scene I. [_Cyprus. A street._]
    Enter IAGO _and_ RODERIGO.

IAGO Here, stand behind this [bulk];† straight will he come.
    Wear thy good rapier bare, and put it home.
    Quick, quick; fear nothing; I'll be at thy elbow.
    It makes us, or it mars us; think on that,
    And fix most firm thy resolution.   5
RODERIGO Be near at hand; I may miscarry in't.
IAGO Here, at thy hand; be bold, and take thy stand.   [_Retires._]
RODERIGO I have no great devotion to the deed,
    And yet he hath given me satisfying reasons.
    'Tis but a man gone. Forth, my sword: he dies.   10
IAGO I have rubb'd this young quat† almost to the sense,†
    And he grows angry. Now, whether he kill Cassio,
    Or Cassio him, or each do kill the other,

81. _to th' vantage:_ more, to boot.   **Act Five, Sc. i,** 1. [_bulk_]: jutting
86. _peevish:_ silly.   part of a building.
88. _having:_ allowance.   11. _quat:_ pimple. _the sense:_ the
89. _galls:_ spirits to resent injury.   quick.

Every way makes my gain. Live Roderigo,
He calls me to a restitution large   15
Of gold and jewels that I bobb'd† from him
As gifts to Desdemona;
It must not be. If Cassio do remain,
He hath a daily beauty in his life
That makes me ugly; and, besides, the Moor   20
May unfold me to him; there stand I in much peril.
No, he must die. But so; I heard him coming.
Enter CASSIO.

RODERIGO   I know his gait, 'tis he. — Villain, thou diest! [*Makes a pass at*
   CASSIO.]
CASSIO   That thrust had been mine enemy indeed,
   But that my coat† is better than thou know'st.   25
   I will make proof of thine. [*Draws, and wounds* RODERIGO.]
RODERIGO   O, I am slain.

                              [IAGO *from behind wounds* CASSIO *in the leg, and exit.*]
CASSIO   I am maim'd for ever. Help, ho! murder! murder! [*Falls.*]
   Enter OTHELLO.
OTHELLO   The voice of Cassio! Iago keeps his word.
RODERIGO   O, villain that I am!
OTHELLO   It is even so.   30
CASSIO   O, help, ho! light! a surgeon!
OTHELLO   'Tis he! — O brave Iago, honest and just,
   That hast such noble sense of thy friend's wrong!
   Thou teachest me. Minion,† your dear lies dead,
   And your unblest fate hies; strumpet, I come.   35
   [Forth] of my heart those charms, thine eyes, are blotted;
   Thy bed, lust-stain'd, shall with lust's blood be spotted.   [*Exit.*
   Enter LODOVICO *and* GRATIANO.
CASSIO   What, ho! no watch? no passage?† Murder! murder!
GRATIANO   'Tis some mischance; the voice is very direful.
CASSIO   O, help!   40
LODOVICO   Hark!
RODERIGO   O wretched villain!
LODOVICO   Two or three groan. 'Tis heavy† night,
   These may be counterfeits; let's think 't unsafe
   To come in to the cry without more help.   45
RODERIGO   Nobody come? Then shall I bleed to death.
   Re-enter IAGO, *with a light.*
LODOVICO   Hark!
GRATIANO   Here's one comes in his shirt, with light and weapons.
IAGO   Who's there? Whose noise is this that cries on murder?
LODOVICO   We do not know.
IAGO   Do not you hear a cry?   50
CASSIO   Here, here! for Heaven's sake, help me!

---

16. *bobb'd:* cheated, swindled.   34. *Minion:* hussy.
25. *coat:* i.e., of mail (worn under   38. *passage:* passers-by.
outer clothing).   43. *heavy:* dark.

IAGO   What's the matter?

GRATIANO   This is Othello's ancient, as I take it.

LODOVICO   The same indeed; a very valiant fellow.

IAGO   What are you here that cry so grievously?

CASSIO   Iago? O, I am spoil'd, undone by villains!   55
    Give me some help.

IAGO   O me, Lieutenant! what villains have done this?

CASSIO   I think that one of them is hereabout
    And cannot make away.

IAGO   O treacherous villains!
    What are you there? — Come in, and give some help. [*To* LODOVICO
    and GRATIANO.]   60

RODERIGO   O, help me there!

CASSIO   That's one of them.

IAGO   O murd'rous slave! O villain! [*Thrusts*
    [RODERIGO] *in.*

RODERIGO   O damn'd Iago! O inhuman dog!

IAGO   Kill men i' th' dark! — Where be these bloody thieves? —
    How silent is this town! — Ho! murder! murder! —   65
    What may you be? Are you of good or evil?

LODOVICO   As you shall prove us, praise us.

IAGO   Signior Lodovico?

LODOVICO   He, sir.

IAGO   I cry you mercy. Here's Cassio hurt by villains.   70

GRATIANO   Cassio!

IAGO   How is't, brother!

CASSIO   My leg is cut in two.

IAGO   Marry, heaven forbid!
    Light, gentlemen! I'll bind it with my shirt.
    Enter BIANCA.

BIANCA   What is the matter, ho? Who is't that cried?   75

IAGO   Who is't that cried!

BIANCA   O my dear Cassio! my sweet Cassio! O Cassio, Cassio, Cassio!

IAGO.   O notable strumpet! Cassio, may you suspect
    Who they should be that have thus mangled you?

CASSIO   No.   80

GRATIANO   I am sorry to find you thus; I have been to seek you.

IAGO   Lend me a garter. So. O, for a chair,†
    To bear him easily hence!

BIANCA   Alas, he faints! O Cassio, Cassio, Cassio!

IAGO   Gentlemen all, I do suspect this trash   85
    To be a party in this injury.
    Patience a while, good Cassio. Come, come;
    Lend me a light. Know we this face or no?
    Alas, my friend and my dear countryman
    Roderigo! No: — yes, sure: — yes, 'tis Roderigo.   90

GRATIANO   What, of Venice?

IAGO   Even he, sir; did you know him?

82. *chair:* sedan chair.

GRATIANO   Know him! ay.

IAGO   Signior Gratiano? I cry your gentle pardon;
    These bloody accidents must excuse my manners
    That so neglected you.

GRATIANO   I am glad to see you.   *95*

IAGO   How do you, Cassio? O, a chair, a chair!

GRATIANO   Roderigo!

IAGO   He, he, 'tis he. [*A chair brought in.*] O, that's well said; the chair.
    Some good man bear him carefully from hence;
    I'll fetch the General's surgeon. [*To* BIANCA.] For you, mistress,   *100*
    Save you your labour. He that lies slain here, Cassio,
    Was my dear friend. What malice was between you?

CASSIO   None in the world; nor do I know the man.

IAGO   [*To* BIANCA.] What, look you pale? O, bear him out o' th' air.

                      [CASSIO *and* RODERIGO *are borne off.*]
    Stay you, good gentlemen. Look you pale, mistress?   *105*
    Do you perceive the gastness† of her eye?
    Nay, if you stare, we shall hear more anon.
    Behold her well; I pray you, look upon her.
    Do you see, gentlemen? Nay, guiltiness will speak,
    Though tongues were out of use.   *110*
    Enter EMILIA.

EMILIA   Alas, what's the matter? What's the matter, husband?

IAGO   Cassio hath here been set on in the dark
    By Roderigo and fellows that are scap'd.
    He's almost slain, and Roderigo quite dead.

EMILIA   Alas, good gentleman! alas, good Cassio!   *115*

IAGO   This is the fruits of whoring. Prithee, Emilia,
    Go know of Cassio where he supp'd to-night.
    [*To* BIANCA.] What, do you shake at that?

BIANCA   He supp'd at my house; but I therefore shake not.

IAGO   O, did he so? I charge you, go with me.   *120*

EMILIA   Oh, fie upon thee, strumpet!

BIANCA   I am no strumpet, but of life as honest
    As you that thus abuse me.

EMILIA   As I? Fie upon thee!

IAGO   Kind gentlemen, let's go see poor Cassio dress'd.
    Come, mistress, you must tell's another tale.   *125*
    Emilia, run you to the citadel,
    And tell my lord and lady what hath happ'd.
    Will you go on afore? [*Aside.*] This is the night
    That either makes me or fordoes† me quite.   [*Exeunt.*

Scene II. [*A bedchamber in the castle:*] DESDEMONA *in bed* [*asleep*].
    Enter OTHELLO *with a light.*

OTHELLO   It is the cause, it is the cause, my soul, —
    Let me not name it to you, you chaste stars! —

---

    106. *gastness:* ghastliness.   129. *fordoes:* destroys.

It is the cause. Yet I'll not shed her blood,
Nor scar that whiter skin of hers than snow,
And smooth as monumental alabaster.   5
Yet she must die, else she'll betray more men.
Put out the light, and then put out the light.
If I quench thee, thou flaming minister,
I can again thy former light restore,
Should I repent me; but once put out thy light,   10
Thou cunning'st pattern of excelling nature,
I know not where is that Promethean heat†
That can thy light relume. When I have pluck'd the rose
I cannot give it vital growth again,
It needs must wither. I'll smell [it] on the tree.   15

[*Kisses her.*

Oh, balmy breath, that dost almost persuade
Justice to break her sword! One more, one more.
Be thus when thou art dead, and I will kill thee
And love thee after. One more, and that's the last;
So sweet was ne'er so fatal. I must weep,   20
But they are cruel tears. This sorrow's heavenly;
It strikes where it doth love. She wakes.
DESDEMONA   Who's there? Othello?
OTHELLO   Ay, Desdemona.
DESDEMONA   Will you come to bed, my lord?
OTHELLO   Have you pray'd to-night, Desdemon?
DESDEMONA   Ay, my lord.   25
OTHELLO   If you bethink yourself of any crime
    Unreconcil'd as yet to Heaven and grace,
    Solicit for it straight.
DESDEMONA   Alack, my lord, what may you mean by that?
OTHELLO   Well, do it, and be brief; I will walk by.   30
    I would not kill thy unprepared spirit;
    No; heavens forfend! I would not kill thy soul.
DESDEMONA   Talk you of killing?
OTHELLO   Ay, I do.
DESDEMONA   Then Heaven
    Have mercy on me!
OTHELLO   Amen, with all my heart!
DESDEMONA   If you say [so], I hope you will not kill me.   35
OTHELLO   Hum!
DESDEMONA   And yet I fear you; for you're fatal then
    When your eyes roll so. Why I should fear I know not,
    Since guiltiness I know not; but yet I feel I fear.
OTHELLO   Think on thy sins.
DESDEMONA   They are loves I bear to you.   40
OTHELLO   Ay, and for that thou diest.
DESDEMONA   That death's unnatural that kills for loving.
    Alas, why gnaw you so your nether lip?
    Some bloody passion shakes your very frame.

12. *Promethean heat:* divine fire.

These are portents; but yet I hope, I hope,　　　　　　　　　　*45*
They do not point on me.
OTHELLO　　　　　　　　　　Peace, and be still!
DESDEMONA　I will so. What's the matter?
OTHELLO　That handkerchief which I so lov'd and gave thee
Thou gav'st to Cassio.
DESDEMONA　　　　　　　No, by my life and soul!
Send for the man, and ask him.
OTHELLO　　　　　　　　　Sweet soul, take heed,　　　　　*50*
Take heed of perjury; thou art on thy deathbed.
DESDEMONA　Ay, but not yet to die.
OTHELLO　　　　　　　　　[Yes], presently:
Therefore confess thee freely of thy sin;
For to deny each article with oath
Cannot remove nor choke the strong conception†　　　　　　*55*
That I do groan withal. Thou art to die.
DESDEMONA　O, Heaven, have mercy on me!
OTHELLO　　　　　　　　　　　I say, amen.
DESDEMONA　And have you mercy too! I never did
Offend you in my life; never lov'd Cassio
But with such general warranty of heaven　　　　　　　　*60*
As I might love; I never gave him token.
OTHELLO　By heaven, I saw my handkerchief in 's hand.
O perjur'd woman! thou dost stone my heart,
And makes me call what I intend to do
A murder, which I thought a sacrifice.　　　　　　　　　*65*
I saw the handkerchief.
DESDEMONA　　　　　　　He found it then;
I never gave it him. Send for him hither;
Let him confess a truth.
OTHELLO　　　　　　　　He hath confess'd.
DESDEMONA　What, my lord?
OTHELLO　That he hath us'd thee.
DESDEMONA　　　　　　　How? unlawfully?
OTHELLO　　　　　　　　　　　　Ay.　　　　　　　　*70*
DESDEMONA　He will not say so.
OTHELLO　　　　　　　　　No, his mouth is stopp'd;
Honest Iago hath ta'en order for't.
DESDEMONA　O! my fear interprets. What, is he dead?
OTHELLO　Had all his hairs been lives, my great revenge
Had stomach for them all.　　　　　　　　　　　　　*75*
DESDEMONA　Alas! he is betray'd and I undone.
OTHELLO　Out, strumpet! weep'st thou for him to my face?
DESDEMONA　O, banish me, my lord, but kill me not!
OTHELLO　Down, strumpet!
DESDEMONA　Kill me to-morrow; let me live to-night!　　　*80*
OTHELLO　Nay, if you strive, —
DESDEMONA　But half an hour!

55. *conception:* purpose.

OTHELLO   Being done, there is no pause.
DESDEMONA   But while I say one prayer!
OTHELLO   It is too late.   [*He smothers her.*
EMILIA [*At the door.*]   My lord, my lord!
    What, ho! my lord, my lord!
OTHELLO   What noise is this? Not dead? not yet quite dead?   85
    I that am cruel am yet merciful;
    I would not have thee linger in pain.
    So, so.
EMILIA [*Within.*]   What, ho! my lord, my lord!
OTHELLO   Who's there?
EMILIA [*Within.*]   O, good my lord, I would speak a word with you!   90
OTHELLO   Yes: — 'tis Emilia. — By and by. — She's dead.
    'Tis like she comes to speak of Cassio's death.
    The noise was high. Ha! no more moving?
    Still as the grave. Shall she come in? Were't good? —
    I think she stirs again: — no. What's best to do?   95
    If she come in, she'll sure speak to my wife.
    My wife! my wife! what wife? I have no wife.
    O, insupportable! O heavy hour!
    Methinks it should be now a huge eclipse
    Of sun and moon, and that th' affrighted globe   100
    Did yawn at alteration.
EMILIA   [*Within.*] I do beseech you
    That I may speak with you, O, good my lord!
OTHELLO   I had forgot thee. O, come in, Emilia.
    Soft; by and by. — Let me the curtains draw.
    Where art thou? [*Unlocks the door.*]
    Enter EMILIA.
                What's the matter with thee now?   105
EMILIA   O, my good lord, yonder's foul murders done!
OTHELLO   What, now?
EMILIA   But now, my lord.
OTHELLO   It is the very error† of the moon;
    She comes more nearer earth than she was wont,   110
    And makes men mad.
EMILIA   Cassio, my lord, hath kill'd a young Venetian
    Call'd Roderigo.
OTHELLO   Roderigo kill'd!
    And Cassio kill'd!
EMILIA   No, Cassio is not kill'd.
OTHELLO   Not Cassio kill'd! Then murder's out of tune,   115
    And sweet revenge grows harsh.
DESDEMONA   O, falsely, falsely murder'd!
EMILIA   O Lord, what cry is that?
OTHELLO   That! what?
EMILIA   Out, and alas! that was my lady's voice.
    Help! help, ho! help! O lady, speak again!   120

109. *error:* aberration.

Sweet Desdemona! O sweet mistress, speak!

DESDEMONA   A guiltless death I die.

EMILIA   O, who hath done this deed?

DESDEMONA   Nobody; I myself. Farewell!
Commend me to my kind lord. O, farewell!   125

[*Dies.*

OTHELLO   Why, how should she be murd'red?

EMILIA   Alas, who knows?

OTHELLO   You hear her say herself, it was not I.

EMILIA   She said so; I must needs report the truth.

OTHELLO   She's, like a liar, gone to burning hell.
'Twas I that kill'd her.

EMILIA   O, the more angel she,   130
And you the blacker devil!

OTHELLO   She turn'd to folly, and she was a whore.

EMILIA   Thou dost belie her, and thou art a devil.

ORTHELLO   She was false as water.

EMILIA   Thou art rash as fire to say
That she was false: O, she was heavenly true!   135

OTHELLO   Cassio did top her; ask thy husband else.
O, I were damn'd beneath all depth in hell
But that I did proceed upon just grounds
To this extremity. Thy husband knew it all.

EMILIA   My husband!   140

OTHELLO   Thy husband.

EMILIA   That she was false to wedlock?

OTHELLO   Ay, with Cassio. Had she been true,
If Heaven would make me such another world
Of one entire and perfect chrysolite,†   145
I'd not have sold her for it.

EMILIA   My husband!

OTHELLO   Ay, 'twas he that told me on her first.
An honest man he is, and hates the slime
That sticks on filthy deeds.

EMILIA   My husband!

OTHELLO   What needs this iterance,† woman? I say thy husband.   150

EMILIA   O mistress, villainy hath made mocks with love!
My husband say [that] she was false!

OTHELLO   He, woman;
I say thy husband; dost understand the word?
My friend, thy husband, honest, honest Iago.

EMILIA   If he say so, may his pernicious soul   155
Rot half a grain a day! He lies to the heart.
She was too fond of her most filthy bargain.

OTHELLO   Ha!

EMILIA   Do thy worst!
This deed of thine is no more worthy heaven   160
Than thou wast worthy her.

---

145. *chrysolite:* a precious stone.   150. *iterance:* repetition.

OTHELLO   Peace, you were best.

EMILIA   Thou hast not half that power to do me harm
 As I have to be hurt. O gull! O dolt!
 As ignorant as dirt! Thou hast done a deed —
 I care not for thy sword; I'll make thee known   165
 Though I lost twenty lives. — Help! help, ho! help!
 The Moor hath kill'd my mistress! Murder! murder!
 Enter MONTANO, GRATIANO, IAGO, *and others.*

MONTANO   What is the matter? How now, general!

EMILIA   O, are you come, Iago? You have done well,
 That men must lay their murders on your neck.   170

GRATIANO   What is the matter?

EMILIA   Disprove this villain, if thou be'st a man.
 He says thou told'st him that his wife was false.
 I know thou didst not, thou'rt not such a villain.
 Speak, for my heart is full.   175

IAGO   I told him what I thought, and told no more
 Than what he found himself was apt and true.

EMILIA   But did you ever tell him she was false?

IAGO   I did.

EMILIA   You told a lie, an odious, damned lie;   180
 Upon my soul, a lie, a wicked lie.
 She false with Cassio! — did you say with Cassio?

IAGO   With Cassio, mistress. Go to, charm your tongue.

EMILIA   I will not charm my tongue; I am bound to speak
 My mistress here lies murdered in her bed, —   185

ALL   O heavens forfend!

EMILIA   And your reports have set the murderer on.

OTHELLO   Nay, stare not, masters; it is true, indeed.

GRATIANO   'Tis a strange truth.

MONTANO   O monstrous act!

EMILIA   Villany, villany, villany!   190
 I think upon't, — I think I smell 't, — O villany!
 I thought so then,† — I'll kill myself for grief —
 O villany, villany!

IAGO   What, are you mad? I charge you, get you home.

EMILIA   Good gentlemen, let me have leave to speak;   195
 'Tis proper I obey him, but not now.
 Perchance, Iago, I will ne'er go home.

OTHELLO   O! O! O! [*He falls on the bed.*

EMILIA   Nay, lay thee down and roar;
 For thou hast kill'd the sweetest innocent
 That e'er did lift up eye.

OTHELLO [*Rising.*] O, she was foul!   200
 I scarce did know you, uncle; there lies your niece,
 Whose breath, indeed, these hands have newly stopp'd.
 I know this act shows horrible and grim.

GRATIANO   Poor Desdemon! I am glad thy father's dead.

192. *I . . . then:* See IV.ii.130–33.

Thy match was mortal to him, and pure grief   *205*
Shore his old thread in twain. Did he live now,
This sight would make him do a desperate turn,
Yea, curse his better angel from his side,
And fall to reprobance.†

OTHELLO   'Tis pitiful; but yet Iago knows   *210*
That she with Cassio hath the act of shame
A thousand times committed. Cassio confess'd it;
And she did gratify his amorous works
With that recognizance and pledge of love
Which I first gave her. I saw it in his hand;   *215*
It was a handkerchief, an antique token
My father gave my mother.

EMILIA   O [God]! O heavenly [God]!

IAGO   ['Zounds,] hold your peace.

EMILIA   'Twill out, 'twill out! I peace!
No, I will speak as liberal† as the north.   *220*
Let Heaven and men and devils, let them all,
All, all, cry shame against me, yet I'll speak.

IAGO   Be wise, and get home.

EMILIA   I will not.   [IAGO *offers to stab* EMILIA.]

GRATIANO   Fie!
Your sword upon a woman?

EMILIA   O thou dull Moor! that handkerchief thou speak'st of   *225*
I found by fortune and did give my husband;
For often, with a solemn earnestness,
More than indeed belong'd to such a trifle,
He begg'd of me to steal 't.

IAGO   Villanous whore!

EMILIA   She give it Cassio! No, alas! I found it,   *230*
And I did give't my husband.

IAGO   Filth, thou liest!

EMILIA   By heaven, I do not, I do not, gentlemen.
O murd'rous coxcomb! what should such a fool
Do with so good a wife?

OTHELLO   Are there no stones† in heaven
But what serves for the thunder? — Precious villain!   *235*

                          [*He runs at* IAGO: IAGO *kills* EMILIA.

GRATIANO   The woman falls; sure, he hath kill'd his wife.

EMILIA   Ay, ay! O, lay me by my mistress' side.

                                                        [*Exit* IAGO.

GRATIANO   He's gone, but his wife's kill'd.

MONTANO   'Tis a notorious villain. Take you this weapon
Which I have [here] recover'd from the Moor.   *240*
Come, guard the door without; let him not pass,
But kill him rather. I'll after that same villain,
For it's a damned slave.   [*Exeunt* MONTANO *and* GRATIANO.

---

209. *reprobance:* damnation.   234. *stones:* bolts.
220. *liberal:* freely.

OTHELLO   I am not valiant neither,
But every puny whipster† gets my sword.
But why should honour outlive honesty?   *245*
Let it go all.

EMILIA   What did thy song bode, lady?
Hark, canst thou hear me? I will play the swan,
And die in music. [*Singing.*] "Willow, willow, willow!" —
Moor, she was chaste; she lov'd thee, cruel Moor;
So come my soul to bliss, as I speak true;   *250*
So speaking as I think, alas, I die.   [*Dies.*

OTHELLO   I have another weapon in this chamber;
It was a sword of Spain, the ice-brook's temper,† —
O, here it is. Uncle, I must come forth.

GRATIANO (*Within.*)   If thou attempt it, it will cost thee dear: *255*
Thou hast no weapon, and perforce must suffer.

OTHELLO   Look in upon me then and speak with me,
Or, naked† as I am, I will assault thee.
    [*Re-enter* GRATIANO.]

GRATIANO   What is the matter?

OTHELLO   Behold, I have a weapon;
A better never did itself sustain   *260*
Upon a soldier's thigh. I have seen the day
That, with this little arm and this good sword,
I have made my way through more impediments
Than twenty times your stop.† But, O vain boast!
Who can control his fate? 'tis not so now.   *265*
Be not afraid though you do see me weapon'd;
Here is my journey's end, here is my butt†
And very sea-mark of my utmost sail.
Do you go back dismay'd? 'Tis a lost fear;
Man but a rush against Othello's breast   *270*
And he retires. Where should Othello go?
Now, how dost thou look now? O ill-starr'd wench!
Pale as thy smock! when we shall meet at compt,†
This look of thine will hurl my soul from heaven,
And fiends will snatch at it. Cold, cold, my girl!   *275*
Even like thy chastity. O cursed, cursed slave!
Whip me, ye devils,
From the possession of this heavenly sight!
Blow me about in winds! roast me in sulphur!
Wash me in steep-down gulfs of liquid fire!   *280*
O Desdemon! dead, Desdemon! dead!
Oh! Oh!

Enter LODOVICO, MONTANO, CASSIO *carried in a chair, and* Officers, *with* IAGO
[*prisoner*].

LODOVICO   Where is this rash and most unfortunate man?

---

244. *whipster:* term of contempt.
253. *ice-brook's temper:* its steel
tempered in icy water.
258. *naked:* unarmed.

264. *stop:* power to stop.
267. *butt:* goal.
273. *compt:* accounting, i.e., Judgment Day.

OTHELLO   That's he that was Othello; here I am.

LODOVICO   Where is that viper? Bring the villain forth.   285

OTHELLO   I look down towards his feet;† but that's a fable.
  If that thou be'st a devil, I cannot kill thee.   [*Wounds* IAGO.]

LODOVICO   Wrench his sword from him.

IAGO   I bleed, sir; but not kill'd.

OTHELLO   I am not sorry neither. I'd have thee live;
  For in my sense, 'tis happiness to die.   290

LODOVICO   O thou Othello, that [wast] once so good,
  Fall'n in the practice† of a cursed slave,
  What shall be said to thee?

OTHELLO   Why, anything.
  An honourable murderer, if you will;
  For nought I did in hate, but all in honour.   295

LODOVICO   This wretch hath part confess'd his villainy.
  Did you and he consent in Cassio's death?

OTHELLO   Ay.

CASSIO   Dear General, I never gave you cause.

OTHELLO   I do believe it, and I ask your pardon.   300
  Will you, I pray, demand that demi-devil
  Why he hath thus ensnar'd my soul and body?

IAGO   Demand me nothing; what you know, you know.
  From this time forth I never will speak word.

LODOVICO   What, not to pray?

GRATIANO   Torments will ope your lips.   305

OTHELLO   Well, thou dost best.

LODOVICO   Sir, you shall understand what hath befall'n,
  Which, as I think, you know not. Here is a letter
  Found in the pocket of the slain Roderigo,
  And here another. The one of them imports   310
  The death of Cassio to be undertook
  By Roderigo.

OTHELLO   O villain!

CASSIO   Most heathenish and most gross!

LODOVICO   Now here's another discontented paper,
  Found in his pocket too; and this, it seems,   315
  Roderigo meant t' have sent this damned villain;
  But that, belike, Iago in the interim
  Came in and satisfi'd him.

OTHELLO   O thou pernicious caitiff! —
  How came you, Cassio, by that handkerchief
  That was my wife's?

CASSIO   I found it in my chamber,   320
  And he himself confess'd but even now
  That there he dropp'd it for a special purpose
  Which wrought to his desire.

OTHELLO   O fool! fool! fool!

---

286. *I . . . feet:* i.e., to see if they   292. *practice:* plot.
are cloven.

CASSIO   There is besides in Roderigo's letter,
        How he upbraids Iago, that he made him
        Brave me upon the watch, whereon it came
        That I was cast; and even but now he spake,
        After long seeming dead, Iago hurt him,
        Iago set him on.
LODOVICO   You must forsake this room and go with us.   *330*
        Your power and your command is taken off,
        And Cassio rules in Cyprus. For this slave,
        If there be any cunning cruelty
        That can torment him much and hold him long,
        It shall be his. You shall close prisoner rest,   *335*
        Till that the nature of your fault be known
        To the Venetian state. Come, bring away.
OTHELLO   Soft you; a word or two before you go.
        I have done the state some service, and they know 't.
        No more of that. I pray you, in your letters,   *340*
        When you shall these unlucky deeds relate,
        Speak of me as I am; nothing extenuate,
        Nor set down aught in malice. Then must you speak
        Of one that lov'd not wisely but too well;
        Of one not easily jealous, but, being wrought,   *345*
        Perplex'd † in the extreme; of one whose hand,
        Like the base [Indian], threw a pearl away
        Richer than all his tribe; of one whose subdu'd eyes,
        Albeit unused to the melting mood,
        Drops tears as fast as the Arabian trees   *350*
        Their medicinal gum. Set you down this;
        And say besides, that in Aleppo once,
        Where a malignant and a turban'd Turk
        Beat a Venetian and traduc'd the state,
        I took by th' throat the circumcised dog,   *355*
        And smote him — thus.   [*Stabs himself.*
LODOVICO   O bloody period!
GRATIANO   All that's spoke is marr'd.
OTHELLO   I kiss'd thee ere I kill'd thee: no way but this,
        Killing myself, to die upon a kiss.   [*Falls on the bed, and*] *dies.*
CASSIO   This did I fear, but thought he had no weapon;   *360*
        For he was great of heart.
LODOVICO   [*To* IAGO.]   O Spartan dog,†
        More fell than anguish, hunger, or the sea!
        Look on the tragic loading of this bed;
        This is thy work. The object poisons sight;
        Let it be hid. Gratiano, keep the house,   *365*
        And seize upon† the fortunes of the Moor,
        For they succeed on you. To you, Lord Governor,

---

346. *Perplex'd:* distraught.   366. *seize upon:* take legal pos-
361. *Spartan dog:* bloodhound.   session of.

Remains the censure† of this hellish villain;
The time, the place, the torture. O, enforce it!
Myself will straight aboard; and to the state   *370*
This heavy act with heavy heart relate.   [*Exeunt.*

Exercises

1. Prepare an eight-point analysis of the plot. (See Chapter 16.)

2. Characterize Othello. Describe both his strengths and his weaknesses. How are these traits revealed?

3. Trace how others perceive Iago at various stages in the drama. Describe the kind of person he is.

4. Iago schemes to destroy the Moor. How? Why?

5. Is Iago's professed hatred of Othello enough motivation for the reader or playgoer to accept his behavior? Why or why not?

6. Describe the characters of Cassio, Desdemona, Roderigo, and Emilia. Define their roles.

7. Discuss how Othello, Iago, Cassio, and Desdemona are not what they seem.

8. Describe the subplots and explain their dramatic effectiveness.

9. Questions of consistency and plausibility in motivation for Othello's actions abound in the drama. Cite evidence to support your answers to the following questions:
   a. How believable is it that someone heroic in war — intelligent, strong-willed, well-trained, self-disciplined, and innately good — can succumb so quickly to the machinations of Iago?
   b. Why does Othello trust only Iago?
   c. Is the one tangible piece of evidence, the handkerchief, sufficient to turn Othello into an insanely jealous person?
   d. Why does he murder his wife?

Topics for Writing

1. George Lyman Kittredge, a well-known Shakespearean scholar, once made the following statement: "*Othello* is, in plan and structure, that rare phenomenon in literature — a tragedy in which the hero is passive (or acted upon) and the force that opposes him (the villain of the piece) is the power that sways him until the turning point." Make a case for Iago as the protagonist in this play.

2. Take a major speech of Othello's or Iago's and discuss the relationship of imagery and figurative language to meaning.

> 368. *censure:* sentencing.

3. Truth, deception, and pride, properties of the human character, are given ample attention in both *Othello* and *Oedipus*. Compare the use of these elements.

4. Develop the theme that uncontrolled jealousy leads to self-destruction, or that malicious hatred cannot triumph.

5. Consider Iago as the devil incarnate.

6. Modernize this tragedy by giving it new scenes, a modern set of characters, and conflicts similar to Shakespeare's. Prepare your scenario and share with the class.

7. What stylistic devices are used to create a picture of Desdemona for us?

Selected Bibliography   William Shakespeare

Adler, Doris. "The Rhetoric of Black and White in *Othello.*" *Shakespeare Quarterly,* 25 (1973), 248–257.

Babcock, R. W. "A Preface to *Othello.*" *Shakespeare Association Bulletin,* 21 (1946), 108–115.

Berry, Ralph. "Pattern in *Othello.*" *Shakespeare Quarterly,* 23 (1971), 3–19.

Champion, Larry S. "Tragic Perspective in *Othello.*" *English Studies,* 54 (1972), 447–460.

Charlton, H. B. *Shakespearian Tragedy.* London: Cambridge University Press, 1948.

Coe, Charles Norton. *Demi-Devils: The Character of Shakespeare's Villains.* New York: Bookman, 1963.

Coghill, Nevill. *Shakespeare's Professional Skills.* London: Cambridge University Press, 1964.

Cohen, E. Z. "Mirror of Virtue: The Role of Cassio in *Othello.*" *English Studies,* 52 (1976), 115–127.

Dean, Leonard Fellows, ed. *A Casebook on Othello.* New York: Crowell, 1961.

Dickes, Robert. "Desdemona: An Innocent Victim?" *American Imago,* 27 (1970), 279–297.

Edelson, Paul J. "All Coherence Gone: A Perspective for *Othello.*" *Connecticut Review,* 4 (1970), 41–48.

Elliott, George Roy. *Flaming Minister: A Study of Othello as Tragedy of Love and Hate.* Durham, N.C.: Duke University Press, 1953.

———. "*Othello* as a Love-Tragedy." *American Review,* 8 (1937), 257–288.

Evans, K. W. "The Racial Factor in Othello." *Shakespeare Studies,* 5 (1969), 124–140.

Flatter, Richard. *The Moor of Venice.* London: Heinemann, 1950.

Gardner, Helen Louise. *The Noble Moor.* London: Oxford University Press, 1955.

Heilman, Robert Bechtold. *Magic in the Web: Action and Language in Othello.* Lexington: University of Kentucky Press, 1956.

Hisman, Stanley C. *Iago: Some Approaches to the Illusion of His Motivation.* New York: Atheneum, 1970.

McLauchlan, Juliet. *Shakespeare: Othello.* London: Edward Arnold, 1971.

Muir, Kenneth. *Shakespeare: The Great Tragedies: Hamlet, Othello, King Lear, Macbeth.* London: Longmans, 1961.

Muir, Kenneth, and Phillip Edwards, eds. *Aspects of Othello: Articles Reprinted from Shakespeare Survey.* Cambridge: Cambridge University Press, 1977.

Nicoll, Allardyce. *Studies in Shakespeare.* London: Hogarth Press, 1927.

Ranald, Margaret Loftus. "The Indiscretions of Desdemona." *Shakespeare Quarterly,* 14 (1963), 127–139.

Shaw, George Bernard. *Shaw on Shakespeare.* London: Dutton, 1961.

Sisson, Charles Jasper. *Shakespeare's Tragic Justice.* London: Methuen, 1962.

Spivack, B. "Iago Revisited." *Shakespeare: The Tragedies: A Collection of Critical Essays.* Ed. Alfred Harbage. Englewood Cliffs, N.J.: Prentice-Hall, 1964, pp. 85–92.

Stoll, E. E. "Source and Motive in Macbeth and Othello." *Shakespeare: Modern Essays in Criticism.* Ed. Leonard Fellows Dean. London: Oxford University Press, 1967, pp. 317–328.

Wakefield, G. P. *Shakespeare's Othello.* London: Blackwell, 1968.

Sproule, Albert Frederick, "A Time Scheme for Othello." *Shakespeare Quarterly,* 7 (1956), 217–226.

West, Robert H. "The Christianness of *Othello.*" *Shakespeare Quarterly,* 15 (1964), 333–343.

Edward Albee (1928–   )

The Sandbox

Characters

THE YOUNG MAN, *25, a good-looking, well-built boy in a bathing suit*
MOMMY, *55, a well-dressed, imposing woman*

DADDY, *60, a small man; gray, thin*
GRANDMA, *86, a tiny, wizened woman with bright eyes*
THE MUSICIAN, *no particular age, but young; would be nice*

Note: When, in the course of the play, MOMMY *and* DADDY *call each other by these names, there should be no suggestion of regionalism. These names are of empty affection and point up the presenility and vacuity of their characters.*

The Scene: A bare stage, with only the following: Near the footlights, far stage-right, two simple chairs set side by side, facing the audience; near the footlights, far stage-left, a chair facing stage-right with a music stand before it; farther back, and stage-center, slightly elevated and raked, a large child's sandbox with a toy pail and shovel; the background is the sky, which alters from brightest day to deepest night.

At the beginning, it is brightest day; the YOUNG MAN *is alone on stage, to the rear of the sandbox, and to one side. He is doing calisthenics; he does calisthenics until quite at the very end of the play. These calisthenics, employing the arms only, should suggest the beating and fluttering of wings. The* YOUNG MAN *is, after all, the Angel of Death.*

MOMMY *and* DADDY *enter from stage-left,* MOMMY *first.*

MOMMY (*motioning to* DADDY) Well, here we are; this is the beach.

DADDY (*whining*) I'm cold.

MOMMY (*dismissing him with a little laugh*) Don't be silly; it's as warm as toast. Look at that nice young man over there: *he* doesn't think it's cold. (*Waves to the* YOUNG MAN) Hello.

YOUNG MAN (*with an endearing smile*) Hi!

MOMMY (*looking about*) This will do perfectly . . . don't you think so, Daddy? There's sand there . . . and the water beyond. What do you think, Daddy?

DADDY (*vaguely*) Whatever you say, Mommy.

MOMMY (*with the same little laugh*) Well, of course . . . whatever I say. Then, it's settled, is it?

DADDY (*shrugs*) She's *your* mother, not mine.

MOMMY I know she's my mother. What do you take me for? (*A pause*) All right, now; let's get on with it. (*She shouts into the wings, stage-left*) You! Out there! You can come in now.

(*The* MUSICIAN *enters, seats himself in the chair, stage-left, places music on the music stand, is ready to play.* MOMMY *nods approvingly.*)

MOMMY Very nice; very nice. Are you ready, Daddy? Let's go get Grandma.

DADDY Whatever you say, Mommy.

MOMMY (*leading the way out, stage-left*)   Of course, whatever I say. (*To the* MUSICIAN) You can begin now.

(*The* MUSICIAN *begins playing;* MOMMY *and* DADDY *exit; the* MUSICIAN, *all the while playing, nods to the* YOUNG MAN.)

YOUNG MAN (*with the same endearing smile*)   Hi!

(*After a moment,* MOMMY *and* DADDY *re-enter, carrying* GRANDMA. *She is borne in by their hands under her armpits; she is quite rigid; her legs are drawn up; her feet do not touch the ground; the expression on her ancient face is that of puzzlement and fear.*)

DADDY   Where do we put her?

MOMMY (*the same little laugh*)   Wherever I say, of course. Let me see . . . well . . . all right, over there . . . in the sandbox. (*Pause*) Well, what are you waiting for, Daddy? . . . The sandbox!

(*Together they carry* GRANDMA *over to the sandbox and more or less dump her in.*)

GRANDMA (*righting herself to a sitting position; her voice a cross between a baby's laugh and cry*)   Ahhhhhh! Graaaaa!

DADDY (*dusting himself*)   What do we do now?

MOMMY (*to the* MUSICIAN)   You can stop now. (*The* MUSICIAN *stops. Back to* DADDY) What do you mean, what do we do now? We go over there and sit down, of course. (*To the* YOUNG MAN) Hello there.

YOUNG MAN (*again smiling*)   Hi!

(MOMMY *and* DADDY *move to the chairs, stage-right, and sit down. A pause.*)

GRANDMA (*same as before*)   Ahhhhhh! Ah-haaaaaa! Graaaaaa!

DADDY   Do you think . . . do you think she's . . . comfortable?

MOMMY (*impatiently*)   How would I know?

DADDY (*pause*)   What do we do now?

MOMMY (*as if remembering*)   We . . . wait. We . . . sit here . . . and we wait . . . that's what we do.

DADDY (*after a pause*)   Shall we talk to each other?

MOMMY (*with that little laugh; picking something off her dress*)   Well, *you* can talk, if you want to . . . if you can think of anything to *say* . . . if you can think of anything *new*.

DADDY (*thinks*)   No . . . I suppose not.

MOMMY (*with a triumphant laugh*)   Of course not!

GRANDMA (*banging the toy shovel against the pail*)   Haaaaaa! Ah-haaaaaa!

MOMMY (*out over the audience*)   Be quiet, Grandma . . . just be quiet, and wait.

(GRANDMA *throws a shovelful of sand at* MOMMY.)

MOMMY (*still out over the audience*)   She's throwing sand at me! You stop that, Grandma; you stop throwing sand at Mommy! (*To* DADDY) She's throwing sand at me.

(DADDY *looks around at* GRANDMA, *who screams at him.*)

GRANDMA   GRAAAAAA!

MOMMY   Don't look at her. Just . . . sit here . . . be very still . . . and wait. (*To the* MUSICIAN) You . . . uh . . . you go ahead and do whatever it is you do.

(*The* MUSICIAN *plays.* MOMMY *and* DADDY *are fixed, staring out beyond the audience.* GRANDMA *looks at them, looks at the* MUSICIAN, *looks at the sandbox, throws down the shovel.*)

GRANDMA   Ah-haaaaaa! Graaaaaa! (*Looks for reaction; gets none. Now . . . directly to the audience*) Honestly! What a way to treat an old woman! Drag her out of the house . . . stick her in a car . . . bring her out here from the city . . . dump her in a pile of sand . . . and leave her here to set. I'm eighty-six years old! I was married when I was seventeen. To a farmer. He died when I was thirty. (*To the* MUSICIAN) Will you stop that, please? (*The* MUSICIAN *stops playing*) I'm a feeble old woman . . . how do you expect anybody to hear me over that peep! peep! peep! (*To herself*) There's no respect around here. (*To the* YOUNG MAN) There's no respect around here!

YOUNG MAN (*same smile*)   Hi!

GRANDMA (*after a pause, a mild double-take, continues, to the audience*)   My husband died when I was thirty (*indicates* MOMMY), and I had to raise that big cow over there all by my lonesome. You can imagine what *that* was like. Lordy! (*To the* YOUNG MAN) Where'd they get *you*?

YOUNG MAN   Oh . . . I've been around for a while.

GRANDMA   I'll bet you have! Heh, heh, heh. Will you look at you!

YOUNG MAN (*flexing his muscles*)   Isn't that something? (*Continues his calisthenics.*)

GRANDMA   Boy, oh boy; I'll say. Pretty good.

YOUNG MAN (*sweetly*)   I'll say.

GRANDMA   Where ya from?

YOUNG MAN   Southern California.

GRANDMA (*nodding*)   Figgers; figgers. What's your name, honey?

YOUNG MAN   I don't know. . . .

GRANDMA (*to the audience*)   Bright, too!

YOUNG MAN   I mean . . . I mean, they haven't given me one yet . . . the studio . . .

GRANDMA (*giving him the once-over*)   You don't say . . . you don't say. Well . . . uh, I've got to talk some more . . . don't you go 'way.

YOUNG MAN   Oh, no.

GRANDMA (*turning her attention back to the audience*)   Fine; fine. (*Then, once more, back to the* YOUNG MAN) You're . . . you're an actor, hunh?

YOUNG MAN (*beaming*)   Yes. I am.

GRANDMA (*to the audience again; shrugs*)   I'm smart that way. *Anyhow,* I had to raise . . . *that* over there all by my lonesome; and what's next to her there . . . that's what she married. Rich? I tell you . . . money, money, money. They took me off the *farm* . . . which was real decent of them . . . and they moved me into the big town house with *them* . . . fixed a nice place for me under the stove . . . gave me an army blanket . . . and my own dish . . . my very own dish! So, what have I got to complain about? Nothing, of course. I'm not complaining. (*She looks up at the sky, shouts to someone off stage*) Shouldn't it be getting dark, now, dear?

(*The lights dim; night comes on. The* MUSICIAN *begins to play; it becomes deepest night. There are spots on all the players, including the* YOUNG MAN, *who is, of course, continuing his calisthenics.*)

DADDY (*stirring*)   It's nighttime.

MOMMY   Shhhh. Be still . . . wait.

DADDY (*whining*)   It's so hot.

MOMMY   Shhhhhh. Be still . . . wait.

GRANDMA (*to herself*)   That's better. Night. (*To the* MUSICIAN) Honey, do you play all through this part? (*The* MUSICIAN *nods*) Well, keep it nice and soft; that's a good boy. (*The* MUSICIAN *nods again; plays softly*) That's nice. (*There is an off-stage rumble.*)

DADDY (*starting*)   What was that?

MOMMY (*beginning to weep*)   It was nothing.

DADDY   It was . . . it was . . . thunder . . . or a wave breaking . . . or something.

MOMMY (*whispering, through her tears*)   It was an off-stage rumble . . . and you know what *that* means. . . .

DADDY   I forget. . . .

MOMMY (*barely able to talk*)   It means the time has come for poor Grandma . . . and I can't bear it!

DADDY (*vacantly*)   I . . . I suppose you've got to be brave.

GRANDMA (*mocking*)   That's right, kid; be brave. You'll bear up; you'll get over it.

(*Another off-stage rumble . . . louder.*)

MOMMY   Ohhhhhhhhhh . . . poor Grandma . . . poor Grandma. . . .

GRANDMA (*to* MOMMY)   I'm fine! I'm all right! It hasn't happened yet!

(*A violent off-stage rumble. All the lights go out, save the spot on the* YOUNG MAN; *the* MUSICIAN *stops playing.*)

MOMMY   Ohhhhhhhhhh. . . . Ohhhhhhhhhh. . . .

(*Silence.*)

GRANDMA   Don't put the lights up yet . . . I'm not ready; I'm not quite ready. (*Silence*) All right, dear . . . I'm about done.

(*The lights come up again, to brightest day; the* MUSICIAN *begins to play.* GRANDMA *is discovered, still in the sandbox, lying on her side, propped up on an elbow, half covered, busily shoveling sand over herself.*)

GRANDMA (*muttering*)   I don't know how I'm supposed to do anything with this goddam toy shovel. . . .

DADDY   Mommy! It's daylight!

MOMMY (*brightly*)   So it is! Well! Our long night is over. We must put away our tears, take off our mourning . . . and face the future. It's our duty.

GRANDMA (*still shoveling; mimicking*)   . . . take off our mourning . . . face the future. . . . Lordy!

(MOMMY *and* DADDY *rise, stretch.* MOMMY *waves to the* YOUNG MAN.)

YOUNG MAN (*with that smile*)   Hi!

(GRANDMA *plays dead.* (!) MOMMY *and* DADDY *go over to look at her; she is a little more than half buried in the sand; the toy shovel is in her hands, which are crossed on her breast.*)

MOMMY (*before the sandbox; shaking her head*)   Lovely! It's . . . it's hard to be sad . . . she looks . . . so happy. (*With pride and conviction*) It pays to do things well. (*To the* MUSICIAN) All right, you can stop now, if you want to. I mean, stay around for a swim, or something; it's all right with us. (*She sighs heavily*) Well, Daddy . . . off we go.

DADDY   Brave Mommy!

MOMMY   Brave Daddy! (*They exit, stage-left.*)

GRANDMA (*after they leave; lying quite still*)   It pays to do things well. . . . Boy, oh boy! (*She tries to sit up*) . . . well, kids . . . (*but she finds she can't*) . . . I . . . I can't get up. I . . . I can't move. . . .

(*The* YOUNG MAN *stops his calisthenics, nods to the* MUSICIAN, *walks over to* GRANDMA, *kneels down by the sandbox.*)

GRANDMA   I . . . can't move. . . .

YOUNG MAN   Shhhhh . . . be very still. . . .

GRANDMA   I . . . I can't move. . . .

YOUNG MAN   Uh . . . ma'am; I . . . I have a line here.

GRANDMA   Oh, I'm sorry, sweetie! you go right ahead.

YOUNG MAN   I am . . . uh . . .

GRANDMA   Take your time, dear.

YOUNG MAN   (*prepares; delivers the line like a real amateur*)   I am the Angel of Death. I am . . . uh . . . I am come for you.

GRANDMA   What . . . wha . . . (*Then, with resignation*) . . . ohhhh . . . ohhhh, I see.

(*The* YOUNG MAN *bends over, kisses* GRANDMA *gently on the forehead.*)

GRANDMA   (*her eyes closed, her hands folded on her breast again, the shovel between her hands, a sweet smile on her face*)   Well . . . that was very nice, dear. . . .

YOUNG MAN   (*still kneeling*)   Shhhhhh . . . be still. . . .

GRANDMA   What I meant was . . . you did that very well, dear. . . .

YOUNG MAN   (*blushing*)   . . . oh . . .

GRANDMA   No; I mean it. You've got that . . . you've got a quality.

YOUNG MAN   (*with his endearing smile*)   Oh . . . thank you; thank you very much . . . ma'am.

GRANDMA   (*slowly; softly — as the* YOUNG MAN *puts his hands on top of* GRANDMA'S)   You're . . . you're welcome . . . dear.

(*Tableau. The* MUSICIAN *continues to play as the curtain slowly comes down.*)

Exercises

Albee has become identified with the "Theater of the Absurd," a movement that developed after World War II; its dramatists presented absurdities on the stage to show that life is absurd.

1. What meaning, if any, do you find in *The Sandbox*? Explain.

2. What is the play about? Comment on what it says about life and death.

3. How do Mommy and Daddy show their "empty affection" and "the presenility and vacuity of their characters" — traits with which Albee endows them in his introductory note to the play?

4. Describe Grandma and the Young Man, and explain their roles.

5. Are any of the characters concerned with others, or are they all concerned only with themselves? How does their attitude serve Albee's purpose?

6. What significance does the setting have?

7. Describe the characteristics of Albee's dramatic language. How well do they serve the author's overall intention?

8. Interpret the symbolism of the sandbox.

Topics for Writing

1. Compare and contrast Albee's attitude toward life and love with Chayefsky's.

2. Explain how character, symbol, and dialogue express Albee's views about the world.

3. Describe the play as an observance of a ritual — for example, a wake and a funeral.

4. Compare and contrast the use of language in *Arms and the Man* and *The Sandbox*.

Selected Bibliography   Edward Albee

Cappaletti, J. "Are You Afraid of Edward Albee?" *Drama Critique,* 6 (1963), 84–88.
Stavrou, C. N. "Albee in Wonderland," *Southwest Review,* 60 (1975), 46–61.

20. OTHER PLAYS TO READ

Anton Chekhov *(1860–1904)*

The Cherry Orchard

Translated by Constance Garnett

Characters

MADAME RANEVSKY (LYUBOV ANDRE-
  YEVNA), *The owner of the Cherry
  Orchard*
ANYA, *Her daughter, aged 17*
VARYA, *Her adopted daughter, aged
  24*
GAEV (LEONID ANDREYEVITCH),
  Brother of Madame Ranevsky
LOPAHIN (YERMOLAY ALEXEYEVITCH),
  A merchant
TROFIMOV (PYOTR SERGEYEVITCH), *A
  student*

SEMYONOV-PISHTCHIK, *A landowner*
CHARLOTTA IVANOVNA, *A governess*
EPIHODOV (SEMYON PANTALEYEVITCH),
  A clerk
DUNYASHA, *A maid*
FIRS, *An old valet, aged 87*
YASHA, *A young valet*
A WAYFARER
THE STATION MASTER
A POST-OFFICE CLERK
VISITORS, SERVANTS

The action takes place on the estate of MADAME RANEVSKY.

Act One

A room, which has always been called the nursery. One of the doors leads into ANYA'S *room. Dawn, sun rises during the scene. May, the cherry trees in flower, but it is cold in the garden with the frost of early morning. Windows closed.*

  Enter DUNYASHA *with a candle and* LOPAHIN *with a book in his hand.*

LOPAHIN   The train's in, thank God. What time is it?
DUNYASHA   Nearly two o'clock. (*Puts out the candle*) It's daylight already.
LOPAHIN   The train's late! Two hours, at least. (*Yawns and stretches*) I'm a
  pretty one; what a fool I've been. Came here on purpose to meet them at
  the station and dropped asleep.... Dozed off as I sat in the chair. It's
  annoying.... You might have waked me.

DUNYASHA I thought you had gone. (*Listens*) There, I do believe they're coming!

LOPAHIN (*Listens*) No, what with the luggage and one thing and another. (*A pause*) Lyubov Andreyevna has been abroad five years; I don't know what she is like now. . . . She's a splendid woman. A good-natured, kind-hearted woman. I remember when I was a lad of fifteen, my poor father — he used to keep a little shop here in the village in those days — gave me a punch in the face with his fist and made my nose bleed. We were in the yard here, I forget what we'd come about — he had had a drop. Lyubov Andreyevna — I can see her now — she was a slim young girl then — took me to wash my face, and then brought me into this very room, into the nursery. "Don't cry, little peasant," says she, "it will be well in time for your wedding day." . . . (*A pause*) Little peasant. . . . My father was a peasant, it's true, but here am I in a white waistcoat and brown shoes, like a pig in a bun shop. Yes, I'm a rich man, but for all my money, come to think, a peasant I was, and a peasant I am. (*Turns over the pages of the book*) I've been reading this book and I can't make head or tail of it. I fell asleep over it. (*A pause*)

DUNYASHA The dogs have been awake all night, they feel that the mistress is coming.

LOPAHIN Why, what's the matter with you, Dunyasha?

DUNYASHA My hands are all of a tremble. I feel as though I should faint.

LOPAHIN You're a spoilt soft creature, Dunyasha. And dressed like a lady too, and your hair done up. That's not the thing. One must know one's place.

(*Enter* EPIHODOV *with a nosegay, he wears a pea-jacket and highly polished creaking topboots; he drops the nosegay as he comes in*)

EPIHODOV (*Picking up the nosegay*) Here! the gardener's sent this, says you're to put it in the dining-room. (*Gives* DUNYASHA *the nosegay*)

LOPAHIN And bring me some kvass.

DUNYASHA I will. (*Goes out*)

EPIHODOV It's chilly this morning, three degrees of frost, though the cherries are all in flower. I can't say much for our climate. (*Sighs*) I can't. Our climate is not often propitious to the occasion. Yermolay Alexeyevitch, permit me to call your attention to the fact that I purchased myself a pair of boots the day before yesterday, and they creak, I venture to assure you, so that there's no tolerating them. What ought I to grease them with?

LOPAHIN Oh, shut up! Don't bother me.

EPIHODOV Every day some misfortune befalls me. I don't complain, I'm used to it, and I wear a smiling face.

(DUNYASHA *comes in, hands* LOPAHIN *the kvass*)

EPIHODOV I am going. (*Stumbles against a chair, which falls over*) There! (*As though triumphant*) There you see now, excuse the expression, an accident like that among others. . . . It's positively remarkable. (*Goes out*)

DUNYASHA Do you know, Yermolay Alexeyevitch, I must confess, Epihodov has made me a proposal.

LOPAHIN Ah!

DUNYASHA I'm sure I don't know. . . . He's a harmless fellow, but sometimes when he begins talking, there's no making anything of it. It's all very fine and expressive, only there's no understanding it. I've a sort of liking for him too. He loves me to distraction. He's an unfortunate man; every day there's something. They tease him about it — two and twenty misfortunes they call him.

LOPAHIN (*Listening*) There! I do believe they're coming.

DUNYASHA They are coming! What's the matter with me? . . . I'm cold all over.

LOPAHIN They really are coming. Let's go and meet them. Will she know me? It's five years since I saw her.

DUNYASHA (*In a flutter*) I shall drop this very minute. . . . Ah, I shall drop. (*There is a sound of two carriages driving up to the house.* LOPAHIN *and* DUNYASHA *go out quickly. The stage is left empty. A noise is heard in the adjoining rooms.* FIRS, *who has driven to meet* MADAME RANEVSKY, *crosses the stage hurriedly leaning on a stick. He is wearing old-fashioned livery and a high hat. He says something to himself, but not a word can be distinguished. The noise behind the scenes goes on increasing. A voice: "Come, let's go in here." Enter* LYUBOV ANDREYEVNA, ANYA, *and* CHARLOTTA IVANOVNA *with a pet dog on a chain, all in traveling dresses.* VARYA *in an out-door coat with a kerchief over her head,* GAEV, SEMYONOV-PISHTCHIK, LOPAHIN, DUNYASHA *with bag and parasol, servants with other articles. All walk across the room*)

ANYA Let's come in here. Do you remember what room this is, mamma?

LYUBOV (*Joyfully, through her tears*) The nursery!

VARYA How cold it is, my hands are numb (*To* LYUBOV ANDREYEVNA) Your rooms, the white room and the lavender one, are just the same as ever, mamma.

LYUBOV My nursery, dear delightful room. . . . I used to sleep here when I was little. . . . (*Cries*) And here I am, like a little child. . . . (*Kisses her brother and* VARYA, *and then her brother again*) Varya's just the same as ever, like a nun. And I knew Dunyasha. (*Kisses* DUNYASHA)

GAEV The train was two hours late. What do you think of that? Is that the way to do things?

CHARLOTTA (*To* PISHTCHIK) My dog eats nuts, too.

PISHTCHIK (*Wonderingly*) Fancy that!

(*They all go out except* ANYA *and* DUNYASHA)

DUNYASHA We've been expecting you so long. (*Takes* ANYA'S *hat and coat*)

ANYA I haven't slept for four nights on the journey. I feel dreadfully cold.

DUNYASHA You set out in Lent, there was snow and frost, and now? My darling! (*Laughs and kisses her*) I *have* missed you, my precious, my joy. I must tell you . . . I can't put it off a minute. . . .

ANYA (*Wearily*) What now?

DUNYASHA Epihodov, the clerk, made me a proposal just after Easter.

ANYA It's always the same thing with you. . . . (*Straightening her hair*) I've lost all my hairpins. (*She is staggering from exhaustion*)

DUNYASHA I don't know what to think, really. He does love me, he does love me so!

ANYA (*Looking towards her door, tenderly*) My own room, my windows just as though I had never gone away. I'm home! Tomorrow morning I shall get up and run into the garden. . . . Oh, if I could get to sleep! I haven't slept all the journey, I was so anxious and worried.

DUNYASHA Pyotr Sergeyevitch came the day before yesterday.

ANYA (*Joyfully*) Petya!

DUNYASHA He's asleep in the bath house, he has settled in there. I'm afraid of being in their way, says he. (*Glancing at her watch*) I was to have waked him, but Varvara Mihalovna told me not to. Don't you wake him, says she.

(*Enter* VARYA *with a bunch of keys at her waist*)

VARYA Dunyasha, coffee and make haste.... Mamma's asking for coffee.

DUNYASHA This very minute. (*Goes out*)

VARYA Well, thank God, you've come. You're home again. (*Petting her*) My little darling has come back! My precious beauty has come back again!

ANYA I have had a time of it!

VARYA I can fancy.

ANYA We set off in Holy Week — it was so cold then, and all the way Charlotta would talk and show off her tricks. What did you want to burden me with Charlotta for?

VARYA You couldn't have traveled all alone, darling. At seventeen!

ANYA We got to Paris at last, it was cold there — snow. I speak French shockingly. Mamma lives on the fifth floor, I went up to her and there were a lot of French people, ladies, an old priest with a book. The place smelt of tobacco and so comfortless. I felt sorry, oh! so sorry for mamma all at once, I put my arms round her neck, and hugged her and wouldn't let her go. Mamma was as kind as she could be, and she cried....

VARYA (*Through her tears*) Don't speak of it, don't speak of it!

ANYA She had sold her villa at Mentone, she had nothing left, nothing. I hadn't a farthing left either, we only just had enough to get here. And mamma doesn't understand! When we had dinner at the stations, she always ordered the most expensive things and gave the waiters a whole rouble. Charlotta's just the same. Yasha too must have the same as we do; it's simply awful. You know Yasha is mamma's valet now, we brought him here with us.

VARYA Yes, I've seen the young rascal.

ANYA Well, tell me — have you paid the arrears on the mortgage?

VARYA How could we get the money?

ANYA Oh, dear! Oh, dear!

VARYA In August the place will be sold.

ANYA My goodness!

LOPAHIN (*Peeps in at the door and moos like a cow*) Moo! (*Disappears*)

VARYA (*Weeping*) There, that's what I could do to him. (*Shakes her fist*)

ANYA (*Embracing* VARYA, *softly*) Varya, has he made you an offer? (VARYA *shakes her head*) Why, but he loves you. Why is it you don't come to an understanding? What are you waiting for?

VARYA I believe that there never will be anything between us. He has a lot to do, he has no time for me ... and takes no notice of me. Bless the man, it makes me miserable to see him.... Everyone's talking of our being married, everyone's congratulating me, and all the while there's really nothing in it; it's all like a dream. (*In another tone*) You have a new brooch like a bee.

ANYA (*Mournfully*) Mamma bought it. (*Goes into her own room and in a light-hearted childish tone*) And you know, in Paris I went up in a balloon!

VARYA My darling's home again! My pretty is home again!

(DUNYASHA *returns with the coffee-pot and is making the coffee*)

VARYA (*Standing at the door*) All day long, darling, as I go about looking after the house, I keep dreaming all the time. If only we could marry you to a rich man, then I should feel more at rest. Then I would go off by myself on a pilgrimage to Kiev, to Moscow ... and so I would spend my life going from one holy place to another. . . . I would go on and on. . . . What bliss!

ANYA The birds are singing in the garden. What time is it?

VARYA It must be nearly three. It's time you were asleep, darling. (*Going into* ANYA'S *room*) What bliss!

(YASHA *enters with a rug and a traveling bag*)

YASHA (*Crosses the stage, mincingly*) May one come in here, pray?

DUNYASHA I shouldn't have known you, Yasha. How you have changed abroad.

YASHA H'm! . . . And who are you?

DUNYASHA When you went away, I was that high. (*Shows distance from floor*) Dunyasha, Fyodor's daughter. . . . You don't remember me!

YASHA H'm! . . . You're a peach! (*Looks round and embraces her: she shrieks and drops a saucer.* YASHA *goes out hastily*)

VARYA (*In the doorway, in a tone of vexation*) What now?

DUNYASHA (*Through her tears*) I have broken a saucer.

VARYA Well, that brings good luck.

ANYA (*Coming out of her room*) We ought to prepare mamma: Petya is here.

VARYA I told them not to wake him.

ANYA (*Dreamily*) It's six years since father died. Then only a month later little brother Grisha was drowned in the river, such a pretty boy he was, only seven. It was more than mamma could bear, so she went away, went away without looking back. (*Shuddering*) . . . How well I understand her, if only she knew! (*A pause*) And Petya Trofimov was Grisha's tutor, he may remind her.

(*Enter* FIRS: *he is wearing a pea-jacket and a white waistcoat*)

FIRS (*Goes up to the coffee-pot, anxiously*) The mistress will be served here. (*Puts on white gloves*) Is the coffee ready? (*Sternly to Dunyasha*) Girl! Where's the cream?

DUNYASHA Ah, mercy on us! (*Goes out quickly*)

FIRS (*Fussing round the coffee-pot*) Ech! you good-for-nothing! (*Muttering to himself*) Come back from Paris. And the old master used to go to Paris too ... horses all the way. (*Laughs*)

VARYA What is it, Firs?

FIRS What is your pleasure? (*Gleefully*) My lady has come home! I have lived to see her again! Now I can die. (*Weeps with joy*)

(*Enter* LYUBOV ANDREYEVNA, GAEV *and* SEMYONOV-PISHTCHIK; *the latter is in a short-waisted full coat of fine cloth, and full trousers.* GAEV, *as he comes in, makes a gesture with his arms and his whole body, as though he were playing billiards*)

LYUBOV How does it go? Let me remember. Cannon off the red!

GAEV That's it — in off the white! Why, once, sister, we used to sleep together in this very room, and now I'm fifty-one, strange as it seems.

LOPAHIN   Yes, time flies.

GAEV   What do you say?

LOPAHIN   Time, I say, flies.

GAEV   What a smell of patchouli!

ANYA   I'm going to bed. Good-night, mamma. (*Kisses her mother*)

LYUBOV   My precious darling. (*Kisses her hands*) Are you glad to be home? I can't believe it.

ANYA   Good-night, uncle.

GAEV (*Kissing her face and hands*)   God bless you! How like you are to your mother! (*To his sister*) At her age you were just the same, Lyuba.

(ANYA *shakes hands with* LOPAHIN *and* PISHTCHIK, *then goes out, shutting the door after her*)

LYUBOV   She's quite worn out.

PISHTCHIK   Aye, it's a long journey, to be sure.

VARYA (*To* LOPAHIN *and* PISHTCHIK)   Well, gentlemen? It's three o'clock and time to say good-bye.

LYUBOV (*Laughs*)   You're just the same as ever, Varya. (*Draws her to her and kisses her*) I'll just drink my coffee and then we will all go and rest. (FIRS *puts a cushion under her feet*) Thanks, friend. I am so fond of coffee, I drink it day and night. Thanks, dear old man. (*Kisses* FIRS)

VARYA   I'll just see whether all the things have been brought in. (*Goes out*)

LYUBOV   Can it really be me sitting here? (*Laughs*) I want to dance about and clap my hands. (*Covers her face with her hands*) And I could drop asleep in a moment! God knows I love my country, I love it tenderly; I couldn't look out of the window in the train, I kept crying so. (*Through her tears*) But I must drink my coffee, though. Thank you, Firs, thanks, dear old man. I'm so glad to find you still alive.

FIRS   The day before yesterday.

GAEV   He's rather deaf.

LOPAHIN   I have to set off for Harkov directly, at five o'clock.... It is annoying! I wanted to have a look at you, and a little talk.... You are just as splendid as ever.

PISHTCHIK (*Breathing heavily*)   Handsomer, indeed.... Dressed in Parisian style ... completely bowled me over.

LOPAHIN   Your brother, Leonid Andreyevitch here, is always saying that I'm a low-born knave, that I'm a money-grubber, but I don't care one straw for that. Let him talk. Only I do want you to believe in me as you used to. I do want your wonderful tender eyes to look at me as they used to in the old days. Merciful God! My father was a serf of your father and of your grandfather, but you — you — did so much for me once, that I've forgotten all that; I love you as though you were my kin ... more than my kin.

LYUBOV   I can't sit still, I simply can't....

(*Jumps up and walks about in violent agitation*)

This happiness is too much for me.... You may laugh at me, I know I'm silly.... My own bookcase. (*Kisses the bookcase*) My little table.

GAEV   Nurse died while you were away.

LYUBOV (*Sits down and drinks coffee*)   Yes, the Kingdom of Heaven be hers! You wrote me of her death.

GAEV   And Anastasy is dead. Squinting Petruchka has left me and is in service now with the police captain in the town.

(*Takes a box of caramels out of his pocket and sucks one*)

PISHTCHIK   My daughter, Dashenka, wishes to be remembered to you.

LOPAHIN   I want to tell you something very pleasant and cheering. (*Glancing at his watch*) I'm going directly . . . there's no time to say much . . . well, I can say it in a couple of words. I needn't tell you your cherry orchard is to be sold to pay your debts; the 22nd of August is the date fixed for the sale; but don't you worry, dearest lady, you may sleep in peace, there is a way of saving it. . . . This is what I propose. I beg your attention! Your estate is not twenty miles from the town, the railway runs close by it, and if the cherry orchard and the land along the river bank were cut up into building plots and then let on lease for summer villas, you would make an income of at least 25,000 roubles a year out of it.

GAEV   That's all rot, if you'll excuse me.

LYUBOV   I don't quite understand you, Yermolay Alexeyevitch.

LOPAHIN   You will get a rent of at least 25 roubles a year for a three-acre plot from summer visitors, and if you say the word now, I'll bet you what you like there won't be one square foot of ground vacant by the autumn, all the plots will be taken up. I congratulate you; in fact, you are saved. It's a perfect situation with that deep river. Only, of course, it must be cleared — all the old buildings, for example, must be removed, this house too, which is really good for nothing and the old cherry orchard must be cut down.

LYUBOV   Cut down? My dear fellow, forgive me, but you don't know what you are talking about. If there is one thing interesting — remarkable indeed — in the whole province, it's just our cherry orchard.

LOPAHIN   The only thing remarkable about the orchard is that it's a very large one. There's a crop of cherries every alternate year, and then there's nothing to be done with them, no one buys them.

GAEV   This orchard is mentioned in the *Encyclopædia*.

LOPAHIN (*Glancing at his watch*)   If we don't decide on something and don't take some steps, on the 22nd of August the cherry orchard and the whole estate too will be sold by auction. Make up your minds! There is no other way of saving it, I'll take my oath on that. No, No!

FIRS   In old days, forty or fifty years ago, they used to dry the cherries, soak them, pickle them, make jam too, and they used ——

GAEV   Be quiet, Firs.

FIRS   And they used to send the preserved cherries to Moscow and to Harkov by the wagon-load. That brought the money in! And the preserved cherries in those days were soft and juicy, sweet and fragrant. . . . They knew the way to do them then. . . .

LYUBOV   And where is the recipe now?

FIRS   It's forgotten. Nobody remembers it.

PISHTCHIK (*To* LYUBOV ANDREYEVNA)   What's it like in Paris? Did you eat frogs there?

LYUBOV   Oh, I ate crocodiles.

PISHTCHIK   Fancy that now!

LOPAHIN   There used to be only the gentlefolks and the peasants in the country, but now there are these summer visitors. All the towns, even the small ones, are surrounded nowadays by these summer villas. And one may say for sure, that in another twenty years there'll be many more of these people and that they'll be everywhere. At present the summer visitor only drinks tea in his verandah, but maybe he'll take to working his bit of land too, and then your cherry orchard would become happy, rich and prosperous. . . .

GAEV (*Indignant*) What rot!

(*Enter* VARYA *and* YASHA)

VARYA There are two telegrams for you, mamma (*Takes out keys and opens an old-fashioned bookcase with a loud crack*) Here they are.

LYUBOV From Paris (*Tears the telegrams, without reading them*) I have done with Paris.

GAEV Do you know, Lyuba, how old that bookcase is? Last week I pulled out the bottom drawer and there I found the date branded on it. The bookcase was made just a hundred years ago. What do you say to that? We might have celebrated its jubilee. Though it's an inanimate object, still it is a *book* case.

PISHTCHIK (*Amazed*) A hundred years! Fancy that now.

GAEV Yes. . . . It is a thing. . . . (*Feeling the bookcase*) Dear, honored, bookcase! Hail to thee who for more than a hundred years hast served the pure ideals of good and justice; thy silent call to fruitful labor has never flagged in those hundred years, maintaining (*in tears*) in the generations of man, courage and faith in a brighter future and fostering in us ideals of good and social consciousness. (*A pause*)

LOPAHIN Yes. . . .

LYUBOV You are just the same as ever, Leonid.

GAEV (*A little embarrassed*) Cannon off the right into the pocket!

LOPAHIN (*Looking at his watch*) Well, it's time I was off.

YASHA (*Handing* LYUBOV ANDREYEVNA *medicine*) Perhaps you will take your pills now.

PISHTCHIK You shouldn't take medicines, my dear madam . . . they do no harm and no good. Give them here . . . honored lady (*Takes the pillbox, pours the pills into the hollow of his hand, blows on them, puts them in his mouth and drinks off some kvass*) There!

LYUBOV (*In alarm*) Why, you must be out of your mind!

PISHTCHIK I have taken all the pills.

LOPAHIN What a glutton! (*All laugh*)

FIRS His honor stayed with us in Easter week, ate a gallon and a half of cucumbers. . . . (*Mutters*)

LYUBOV What is he saying?

VARYA He has taken to muttering like that for the last three years. We are used to it.

YASHA His declining years!

(CHARLOTTA IVANOVNA, *a very thin, lanky figure in a white dress with a lorgnette in her belt, walks across the stage*)

LOPAHIN I beg your pardon, Charlotta Ivanovna, I have not had time to greet you. (*Tries to kiss her hand*)

CHARLOTTA (*Pulling away her hand*) If I let you kiss my hand, you'll be wanting to kiss my elbow, and then my shoulder.

LOPAHIN I've no luck to-day! (*All laugh*) Charlotta Ivanovna, show us some tricks!

LYUBOV Charlotta, do show us some tricks!

CHARLOTTA   I don't want to. I'm sleepy. (*Goes out*)

LOPAHIN   In three weeks' time we shall meet again. (*Kisses* LYUBOV ANDREY-EVNA's *hand*) Good-bye till then — I must go. (*To* GAEV) Good-bye. (*Kisses* PISHTCHIK) Good-bye. (*Gives his hand to* VARYA, *then to* FIRS *and* YASHA) I don't want to go. (*To* LYUBOV ANDREYEVNA) If you think over my plan for the villas and make up your mind, then let me know; I will lend you 50,000 roubles. Think of it seriously.

VARYA (*Angrily*)   Well, do go, for goodness sake.

LOPAHIN   I'm going, I'm going. (*Goes out*)

GAEV   Low-born knave! I beg pardon, though ... Varya is going to marry him, he's Varya's fiancé.

VARYA   Don't talk nonsense, uncle.

LYUBOV   Well, Varya, I shall be delighted. He's a good man.

PISHTCHIK   He is, one must acknowledge, a most worthy man. And my Dashenka ... says too that ... she says ... various things. (*Snores, but at once wakes up*) But all the same, honored lady, could you oblige me ... with a loan of 240 roubles ... to pay the interest on my mortgage to-morrow?

VARYA (*Dismayed*)   No, no.

LYUBOV   I really haven't any money.

PISHTCHIK   It will turn up. (*Laughs*) I never lose hope. I thought everything was over, I was a ruined man, and lo and behold — the railway passed through my land and ... they paid me for it. And something else will turn up again, if not to-day, then to-morrow ... Dashenka'll win two hundred thousand ... she's got a lottery ticket.

LYUBOV   Well, we've finished our coffee, we can go to bed.

FIRS (*Brushes* GAEV, *reprovingly*)   You have got on the wrong trousers again! What am I to do with you?

VARYA (*Softly*)   Anya's asleep. (*Softly opens the window*) Now the sun's risen, it's not a bit cold. Look, mamma, what exquisite trees! My goodness! And the air! The starlings are singing!

GAEV (*Opens another window*)   The orchard is all white. You've not forgotten it, Lyuba? That long avenue that runs straight, straight as an arrow, how it shines on a moonlight night. You remember? You've not forgotten?

LYUBOV (*Looking out of the window into the garden*)   Oh, my childhood, my innocence! It was in this nursery I used to sleep, from here I looked out into the orchard, happiness waked with me every morning and in those days the orchard was just the same, nothing has changed. (*Laughs with delight*) All, all white! Oh, my orchard! After the dark gloomy autumn, and the cold winter; you are young again, and full of happiness, the heavenly angels have never left you. ... If I could cast off the burden that weighs on my heart, if I could forget the past!

GAEV   H'm! and the orchard will be sold to pay our debts; it seems strange. ...

LYUBOV   See, our mother walking ... all in white, down the avenue! (*Laughs with delight*) It is she!

GAEV   Where?

VARYA   Oh, don't, mamma!

LYUBOV   There is no one. It was my fancy. On the right there, by the path to the arbor, there is a white tree bending like a woman. ...

(*Enter* TROFIMOV *wearing a shabby student's uniform and spectacles*)

LYUBOV   What a ravishing orchard! White masses of blossom, blue sky. . . .

TROFIMOV   Lyubov Andreyevna! (*She looks round at him*) I will just pay my respects to you and then leave you at once. (*Kisses her hand warmly*) I was told to wait until morning, but I hadn't the patience to wait any longer. . . .

(LYUBOV ANDREYEVNA *looks at him in perplexity*)

VARYA (*Through her tears*)   This is Petya Trofimov.

TROFIMOV   Petya Trofimov, who was your Grisha's tutor. . . . Can I have changed so much?

(LYUBOV ANDREYEVNA *embraces him and weeps quietly*)

GAEV (*In confusion*)   There, there, Lyuba.

VARYA (*Crying*)   I told you, Petya, to wait till to-morrow.

LYUBOV   My Grisha . . . my boy . . . Grisha . . . my son!

VARYA   We can't help it, mamma, it is God's will.

TROFIMOV (*Softly through his tears*)   There . . . there.

LYUBOV (*Weeping quietly*)   My boy was lost . . . drowned. Why? Oh, why, dear Petya? (*More quietly*) Anya is asleep in there, and I'm talking loudly . . . making this noise. . . . But, Petya? Why have you grown so ugly? Why do you look so old?

TROFIMOV   A peasant-woman in the train called me a mangy-looking gentleman.

LYUBOV   You were quite a boy then, a pretty little student, and now your hair's thin — and spectacles. Are you really a student still? (*Goes towards the door*)

TROFIMOV   I seem likely to be a perpetual student.

LYUBOV (*Kisses her brother, then* VARYA)   Well, go to bed. . . . You are older too, Leonid.

PISHTCHIK (*Follows her*)   I suppose it's time we were asleep. . . . Ugh! my gout. I'm staying the night! Lyubov Andreyevna, my dear soul, if you could . . . to-morrow morning . . . 240 roubles.

GAEV   That's always his story.

PISHTCHIK   240 roubles . . . to pay the interest on my mortgage.

LYUBOV   My dear man, I have no money.

PISHTCHIK   I'll pay it back, my dear . . . a trifling sum.

LYUBOV   Oh, well, Leonid will give it you. . . . You give him the money, Leonid.

GAEV   Me give it him! Let him wait till he gets it!

LYUBOV   It can't be helped, give it him. He needs it. He'll pay it back.

(LYUBOV ANDREYEVNA, TROFIMOV, PISHTCHIK *and* FIRS *go out.* GAEV, VARYA *and* YASHA *remain*)

GAEV   Sister hasn't got out of the habit of flinging away her money. (*To* YASHA) Get away, my good fellow, you smell of the hen-house.

YASHA (*With a grin*)   And you, Leonid Andreyevitch, are just the same as ever.

GAEV   What's that? (*To* VARYA) What did he say?

VARYA (*To* YASHA)   Your mother has come from the village; she has been sitting in the servants' room since yesterday, waiting to see you.

YASHA   Oh, bother her!

VARYA   For shame!

YASHA   What's the hurry? She might just as well have come to-morrow. (*Goes out*)

VARYA Mamma's just the same as ever, she hasn't changed a bit. If she had her own way, she'd give away everything.

GAEV Yes. (*A pause*) If a great many remedies are suggested for some disease, it means that the disease is incurable. I keep thinking and racking my brains; I have many schemes, a great many, and that really means none. If we could only come in for a legacy from somebody, or marry our Anya to a very rich man, or we might go to Yaroslavl and try our luck with our old aunt, the Countess. She's very, very rich, you know.

VARYA (*Weeps*) If God would help us.

GAEV Don't blubber. Aunt's very rich, but she doesn't like us. First, sister married a lawyer instead of a nobleman. . . .

(ANYA *appears in the doorway*)

GAEV And then her conduct, one can't call it virtuous. She is good, and kind, and nice, and I love her, but, however one allows for extenuating circumstances, there's no denying that she's an immoral woman. One feels it in her slightest gesture.

VARYA (*In a whisper*) Anya's in the doorway.

GAEV What do you say? (*A pause*) It's queer, there seems to be something wrong with my right eye. I don't see as well as I did. And on Thursday when I was in the district Court . . .

(*Enter* ANYA)

VARYA Why aren't you asleep, Anya?

ANYA I can't get to sleep.

GAEV My pet. (*Kisses* ANYA's *face and hands*) My child. (*Weeps*) You are not my niece, you are my angel, you are everything to me. Believe me, believe. . . .

ANYA I believe you, uncle. Everyone loves you and respects you . . . but, uncle dear, you must be silent . . . simply be silent. What were you saying just now about my mother, about your own sister? What made you say that?

GAEV Yes, yes. . . . (*Puts his hand over his face*) Really, that was awful! My God, save me! And to-day I made a speech to the bookcase . . . so stupid! And only when I had finished, I saw how stupid it was.

VARYA It's true, uncle, you ought to keep quiet. Don't talk, that's all.

ANYA If you could keep from talking, it would make things easier for you, too.

GAEV I won't speak. (*Kisses* ANYA's *and* VARYA's *hands*) I'll be silent. Only this is about business. On Thursday I was in the district Court; well, there was a large party of us there and we began talking of one thing and another, and this and that, and do you know, I believe that it will be possible to raise a loan on an I.O.U. to pay the arrears on the mortgage.

VARYA If the Lord would help us!

GAEV I'm going on Tuesday; I'll talk of it again. (*To* VARYA) Don't blubber. (*To* ANYA) Your mamma will talk to Lopahin; of course, he won't refuse her. And as soon as you're rested you shall go to Yaroslavl to the Countess, your great-aunt. So we shall all set to work in three directions at once, and the business is done. We shall pay off arrears, I'm convinced of it. (*Puts a caramel in his mouth*) I swear on my honor, I swear by anything you like, the estate shan't be sold. (*Excitedly*) By my own happiness, I swear it! Here's my hand on it, call me the basest, vilest of men, if I let it come to an auction! Upon my soul I swear it!

ANYA (*Her equanimity has returned, she is quite happy*) How good you are, uncle, and how clever! (*Embraces her uncle*) I'm at peace now! Quite at peace! I'm happy!

(*Enter* FIRS)

FIRS (*Reproachfully*) Leonid Andreyevitch, have you no fear of God? When are you going to bed?

GAEV Directly, directly. You can go, Firs. I'll . . . yes, I will undress myself. Come, children, bye-bye. We'll go into details to-morrow, but now go to bed. (*Kisses* ANYA *and* VARYA) I'm a man of the eighties. They run down that period, but still I can say I have had to suffer not a little for my convictions in my life, it's not for nothing that the peasant loves me. One must know the peasant! One must know how. . . .

ANYA At it again, uncle!

VARYA Uncle dear, you'd better be quiet!

FIRS (*Angrily*) Leonid Andreyevitch!

GAEV I'm coming. I'm coming. Go to bed. Potted the shot — there's a shot for you! A beauty! (*Goes out,* FIRS *hobbling after him*)

ANYA My mind's at rest now. I don't want to go to Yaroslavl, I don't like my great-aunt, but still my mind's at rest. Thanks to uncle. (*Sits down*)

VARYA We must go to bed. I'm going. Something unpleasant happened while you were away. In the old servants' quarters there are only the old servants, as you know — Efimyushka, Polya and Yevstigney — and Karp too. They began letting stray people in to spend the night — I said nothing. But all at once I heard they had been spreading a report that I gave them nothing but pease pudding to eat. Out of stinginess, you know. . . . And it was all Yevstigney's doing. . . . Very well, I said to myself. . . . If that's how it is, I thought, wait a bit. I sent for Yevstigney. . . . (*Yawns*) He comes. . . . "How's this, Yevstigney," I said, "you could be such a fool as to? . . ." (*Looking at* ANYA) Anitchka! (*A pause*) She's asleep. (*Puts her arm around* ANYA) Come to bed . . . come along! (*Leads her*) My darling has fallen asleep! Come . . . (*They go*)

(*Far away beyond the orchard a shepherd plays on a pipe.* TROFIMOV *crosses the stage and, seeing* VARYA *and* ANYA, *stands still*)

VARYA 'Sh! asleep, asleep. Come, my own.

ANYA (*Softly, half asleep*) I'm so tired. Still those bells. Uncle . . . dear . . . mamma and uncle. . . .

VARYA Come, my own, come along.

(*They go into* ANYA'S *room*)

TROFIMOV (*Tenderly*) My sunshine! My spring.

Curtain

Act Two

The open country. An old shrine, long abandoned and fallen out of the perpendicular; near it a well, large stones that have apparently once been tombstones, and an old garden seat. The road to GAEV'S *house is seen. On one side rise dark poplars; and there the cherry orchard begins. In the distance a row of telegraph poles and far, far away on the horizon there is faintly outlined a great town, only visible in very fine clear weather. It is near sunset.* CHARLOTTA, YASHA *and* DUNYASHA *are sitting on the seat.* EPIHODOV *is standing near, playing something mournful on a guitar. All sit plunged in thought.* CHARLOTTA *wears an old forage cap; she has taken a gun from her shoulder and is tightening the buckle on the strap.*

CHARLOTTA (*Musingly*) I haven't a real passport of my own, and I don't know how old I am, and I always feel that I'm a young thing. When I was a little girl, my father and mother used to travel about to fairs and give performances — very good ones. And I used to dance *salto mortale* and all sorts of things. And when papa and mamma died, a German lady took me and had me educated. And so I grew up and became a governess. But where I came from, and who I am, I don't know.... Who my parents were, very likely they weren't married.... I don't know. (*Takes a cucumber out of her pocket and eats*) I know nothing at all. (*A pause*) One wants to talk and has no one to talk to.... I have nobody.

EPIHODOV (*Plays on the guitar and sings*) "What care I for the noisy world! What care I for friends or foes!" How agreeable it is to play on the mandoline!

DUNYASHA That's a guitar, not a mandoline. (*Looks in a hand-mirror and powders herself*)

EPIHODOV To a man mad with love, it's a mandoline. (*Sings*) "Were her heart but aglow with love's mutual flame."
(YASHA *joins in*)

CHARLOTTA How shockingly these people sing! Foo! Like jackals!

DUNYASHA (*To* YASHA) What happiness, though, to visit foreign lands.

YASHA Ah, yes! I rather agree with you there. (*Yawns, then lights a cigar*)

EPIHODOV That's comprehensible. In foreign lands everything has long since reached full complexion.

YASHA That's so, of course.

EPIHODOV I'm a cultivated man, I read remarkable books of all sorts, but I can never make out the tendency I am myself precisely inclined for, whether to live or to shoot myself, speaking precisely, but nevertheless I always carry a revolver. Here it is.... (*Shows revolver*)

CHARLOTTA I've had enough, and now I'm going. (*Puts on the gun*) Epihodov, you're a very clever fellow, and a very terrible one too, all the women must be wild about you. Br-r-r! (*Goes*) These clever fellows are all so stupid; there's not a creature for me to speak to.... Always alone, alone, nobody belonging to me ... and who I am, and why I'm on earth, I don't know. (*Walks away slowly*)

EPIHODOV Speaking precisely, not touching upon other subjects, I'm bound to admit about myself, that destiny behaves mercilessly to me, as a storm to a little boat. If, let us suppose, I am mistaken, then why did I wake up this morning, to quote an example, and look round, and there on my chest was a spider of fearful magnitude ... like this. (*Shows with both hands*) And then I take up a jug of kvass, to quench my thirst, and in it there is something in the highest degree unseemly of the nature of a cockroach. (*A pause*) Have you read Buckle? (*A pause*) I am desirous of troubling you, Dunyasha, with a couple of words.

DUNYASHA Well, speak.

EPIHODOV I should be desirous to speak with you alone. (*Sighs*)

DUNYASHA (*Embarrassed*) Well — only bring me my mantle first. It's by the cupboard. It's rather damp here.

EPIHODOV   Certainly. I will fetch it. Now I know what I must do with my revolver. (*Takes guitar and goes off playing on it*)

YASHA   Two and twenty misfortunes! Between ourselves, he's a fool. (*Yawns*)

DUNYASHA   God grant he doesn't shoot himself! (*A pause*) I am so nervous, I'm always in a flutter. I was a little girl when I was taken into our lady's house, and now I have quite grown out of peasant ways, and my hands are white, as white as a lady's. I'm such a delicate, sensitive creature, I'm afraid of everything. I'm so frightened. And if you deceive me, Yasha, I don't know what will become of my nerves.

YASHA   (*Kisses her*) You're a peach! Of course a girl must never forget herself; what I dislike more than anything is a girl being flighty in her behavior.

DUNYASHA   I'm passionately in love with you, Yasha; you are a man of culture — you can give your opinion about anything. (*A pause*)

YASHA   (*Yawns*) Yes, that's so. My opinion is this: if a girl loves anyone, that means that she has no principles. (*A pause*) It's pleasant smoking a cigar in the open air. (*Listens*) Someone's coming this way . . . it's the gentlefolk. (DUNYASHA *embraces him impulsively*) Go home, as though you had been to the river to bathe; go by that path, or else they'll meet you and suppose I have made an appointment with you here. That I can't endure.

DUNYASHA   (*Coughing softly*) The cigar has made my head ache. . . . (*Goes off*)

(YASHA *remains sitting near the shrine. Enter* LYUBOV ANDREYEVNA, GAEV *and* LOPAHIN)

LOPAHIN   You must make up your mind once for all — there's no time to lose. It's quite a simple question, you know. Will you consent to letting the land for building or not? One word in answer: Yes or no? Only one word!

LYUBOV   Who is smoking such horrible cigars here? (*Sits down*)

GAEV   Now the railway line has been brought near, it's made things very convenient. (*Sits down*) Here we have been over and lunched in town. Cannon off the white! I should like to go home and have a game.

LYUBOV   You have plenty of time.

LOPAHIN   Only one word! (*Beseechingly*) Give me an answer!

GAEV   (*Yawning*) What do you say?

LYUBOV   (*Looks in her purse*) I had quite a lot of money here yesterday, and there's scarcely any left to-day. My poor Varya feeds us all on milk soup for the sake of economy; the old folks in the kitchen get nothing but pease pudding, while I waste my money in a senseless way. (*Drops purse, scattering gold pieces*) There, they have all fallen out! (*Annoyed*)

YASHA   Allow me, I'll soon pick them up. (*Collects the coins*)

LYUBOV   Pray do, Yasha. And what did I go off to the town to lunch for? Your restaurant's a wretched place with its music and the tablecloth smelling of soap. . . . Why drink so much, Leonid? And eat so much? And talk so much? To-day you talked a great deal again in the restaurant, and all so inappropriately. About the era of the seventies, about the decadents. And to whom? Talking to waiters about decadents!

LOPAHIN   Yes.

GAEV   (*Waving his hand*) I'm incorrigible; that's evident. (*Irritably to* YASHA) Why is it you keep fidgeting about in front of us!

YASHA   (*Laughs*) I can't help laughing when I hear your voice.

GAEV (*To his sister*) Either I or he. . . .

LYUBOV Get along! Go away, Yasha.

YASHA (*Gives* LYUBOV ANDREYEVNA *her purse*) Directly. (*Hardly able to suppress his laughter*) This minute. . . . (*Goes off*)

LOPAHIN Deriganov, the millionaire, means to buy your estate. They say he is coming to the sale himself.

LYUBOV Where did you hear that?

LOPAHIN That's what they say in town.

GAEV Our aunt in Yaroslavl has promised to send help; but when, and how much she will send, we don't know.

LOPAHIN How much will she send? A hundred thousand? Two hundred?

LYUBOV Oh, well! . . . Ten or fifteen thousand, and we must be thankful to get that.

LOPAHIN Forgive me, but such reckless people as you are — such queer, unbusiness-like people — I never met in my life. One tells you in plain Russian your estate is going to be sold, and you seem not to understand it.

LYUBOV What are we to do? Tell us what to do.

LOPAHIN I do tell you every day. Every day I say the same thing. You absolutely must let the cherry orchard and the land on building leases; and do it at once, as quick as may be — the auction's close upon us! Do understand! Once make up your mind to build villas, and you can raise as much money as you like, and then you are saved.

LYUBOV Villas and summer visitors — forgive me saying so — it's so vulgar.

GAEV There I perfectly agree with you.

LOPAHIN I shall sob, or scream, or fall into a fit. I can't stand it! You drive me mad! (*To* GAEV) You're an old woman!

GAEV What do you say?

LOPAHIN An old woman! (*Gets up to go*)

LYUBOV (*In dismay*) No, don't go! Do stay, my dear friend! Perhaps we shall think of something.

LOPAHIN What is there to think of?

LYUBOV Don't go, I entreat you! With you here it's more cheerful, anyway. (*A pause*) I keep expecting something, as though the house were going to fall about our ears.

GAEV (*In profound dejection*) Potted the white! It fails — a kiss.

LYUBOV We have been great sinners. . . .

LOPAHIN You have no sins to repent of.

GAEV (*Puts a caramel in his mouth*) They say I've eaten up my property in caramels. (*Laughs*)

LYUBOV Oh, my sins! I've always thrown my money away recklessly like a lunatic. I married a man who made nothing but debts. My husband died of champagne — he drank dreadfully. To my misery I loved another man, and immediately — it was my first punishment — the blow fell upon me, here, in the river . . . my boy was drowned and I went abroad — went away for ever, never to return, not to see that river again . . . I shut my eyes, and fled, distracted, and *he* after me . . . pitilessly, brutally. I bought a villa at Mentone, for *he* fell ill there, and for three years I had no rest day or night. His illness wore me out, my soul was dried up. And last year, when my villa was sold to pay my debts, I went to Paris and there he robbed me of everything and abandoned me for another woman; and I tried to poison myself.... So stupid, so shameful!... And suddenly I felt a yearning for Russia, for my country, for my little girl.... (*Dries her tears*) Lord, Lord, be merciful! Forgive my sins! Do not chastise me more! (*Takes a telegram out of her pocket*) I got this today from Paris. He implores forgiveness, entreats me to return. (*Tears up the telegram*) I fancy there is music somewhere. (*Listens*)

GAEV That's our famous Jewish orchestra. You remember, four violins, a flute and a double bass.

LYUBOV That still in existence? We ought to send for them one evening, and give a dance.

LOPAHIN (*Listens*) I can't hear.... (*Hums softly*) "For money the Germans will turn a Russian into a Frenchman." (*Laughs*) I did see such a piece at the theater yesterday! It was funny!

LYUBOV And most likely there was nothing funny in it. You shouldn't look at plays, you should look at yourselves a little oftener. How gray your lives are! How much nonsense you talk.

LOPAHIN That's true. One may say honestly, we live a fool's life. (*Pause*) My father was a peasant, an idiot; he knew nothing and taught me nothing, only beat me when he was drunk, and always with his stick. In reality I am just another blockhead and idiot. I've learnt nothing properly. I write a wretched hand. I write so that I feel ashamed before folks, like a pig.

LYUBOV You ought to get married, my dear fellow.

LOPAHIN Yes ... that's true.

LYUBOV You should marry our Varya, she's a good girl.

LOPAHIN Yes.

LYUBOV She's a good-natured girl, she's busy all day long, and what's more, she loves you. And you have liked her for ever so long.

LOPAHIN Well? I'm not against it.... She's a good girl. (*Pause*)

GAEV I've been offered a place in the bank: 6,000 roubles a year. Did you know?

LYUBOV You would never do for that! You must stay as you are.

(*Enter* FIRS *with overcoat*)

FIRS Put it on, sir, it's damp.

GAEV (*Putting it on*) You bother me, old fellow.

FIRS You can't go on like this. You went away in the morning without leaving word. (*Looks him over*)

LYUBOV You look older, Firs!

FIRS What is your pleasure?

LOPAHIN You look older, she said.

FIRS I've had a long life. They were arranging my wedding before your papa was born.... (*Laughs*) I was the head footman before the emancipation came. I wouldn't consent to be set free then; I stayed on with the old master.... (*A pause*) I remember what rejoicings they made and didn't know themselves what they were rejoicing over.

LOPAHIN Those were fine old times. There was flogging anyway.

FIRS (*Not hearing*) To be sure! The peasants knew their place, and the masters knew theirs; but now they're all at sixes and sevens, there's no making it out.

GAEV Hold your tongue, Firs. I must go to town to-morrow. I have been promised an introduction to a general, who might let us have a loan.

LOPAHIN   You won't bring that off. And you won't pay your arrears, you may rest assured of that.

LYUBOV   That's all his nonsense. There is no such general.

(*Enter* TROFIMOV, ANYA *and* VARYA)

GAEV   Here come our girls.

ANYA   There's mamma on the seat.

LYUBOV (*Tenderly*)   Come here, come along. My darlings! (*Embraces* ANYA *and* VARYA) If you only knew how I love you both. Sit beside me, there, like that. (*All sit down*)

LOPAHIN   Our perpetual student is always with the young ladies.

TROFIMOV   That's not your business.

LOPAHIN   He'll soon be fifty, and he's still a student.

TROFIMOV   Drop your idiotic jokes.

LOPAHIN   Why are you so cross, you queer fish?

TROFIMOV   Oh, don't persist!

LOPAHIN (*Laughs*)   Allow me to ask you what's your idea of me?

TROFIMOV   I'll tell you my idea of you. Yermolay Alexeyevitch: you are a rich man, you'll soon be a millionaire. Well, just as in the economy of nature a wild beast is of use, who devours everything that comes in his way, so you too have your use.

(*All laugh*)

VARYA   Better tell us something about the planets, Petya.

LYUBOV   No, let us go on with the conversation we had yesterday.

TROFIMOV   What was it about?

GAEV   About pride.

TROFIMOV   We had a long conversation yesterday, but we came to no conclusion. In pride, in your sense of it, there is something mystical. Perhaps you are right from your point of view; but if one looks at it simply, without subtlety, what sort of pride can there be, what sense is there in it, if man in his physiological formation is very imperfect, if in the immense majority of cases he is coarse, dull-witted, profoundly unhappy? One must give up glorification of self. One should work, and nothing else.

GAEV   One must die in any case.

TROFIMOV   Who knows? And what does it mean — dying? Perhaps man has a hundred senses, and only the five we know are lost at death, while the other ninety-five remain alive.

LYUBOV   How clever you are, Petya!

LOPAHIN (*Ironically*)   Fearfully clever!

TROFIMOV   Humanity progresses, perfecting its powers. Everything that is beyond its ken now will one day become familiar and comprehensible; only we must work, we must with all our powers aid the seeker after truth. Here among us in Russia the workers are few in number as yet. The vast majority of the intellectual people I know, seek nothing, do nothing, are not fit as yet for work of any kind. They call themselves intellectual, but they treat their servants as inferiors, behave to the peasants as though they were animals, learn little, read nothing seriously, do practically nothing, only talk about science and know very little about art. They are all serious people, they all have severe faces, they all talk of weighty matters and air their theories, and yet the vast majority of us — ninety-nine per cent — live like savages, at the least thing fly to blows and abuse, eat piggishly, sleep in filth and stuffiness, bugs everywhere, stench and damp and moral impurity. And it's clear all our fine talk is only to divert our attention and other people's. Show me where to find the *crèches* there's so much talk about, and the reading-rooms? They only exist in novels: in real life there are none of them. There is nothing but filth and vulgarity and Asiatic apathy. I fear and dislike very serious faces. I'm afraid of serious conversation. We should do better to be silent.

LOPAHIN   You know, I get up at five o'clock in the morning, and I work from morning to night; and I've money, my own and other people's, always passing through my hands, and I see what people are made of all round me. One has only to begin to do anything to see how few honest decent people there are. Sometimes when I lie awake at night, I think: "Oh! Lord, thou hast given us immense forests, boundless plains, the widest horizons, and living here we ourselves ought really to be giants."

LYUBOV   You ask for giants! They are no good except in story-books; in real life they frighten us.

(EPIHODOV *advances in the background, playing on the guitar*)

LYUBOV (*Dreamily*)   There goes Epihodov.

ANYA (*Dreamily*)   There goes Epihodov.

GAEV   The sun has set, my friends.

TROFIMOV   Yes.

GAEV (*Not loudly, but, as it were, declaiming*)   O nature, divine nature, thou art bright with eternal luster, beautiful and indifferent! Thou, whom we call mother, thou dost unite within thee life and death! Thou dost give life and dost destroy!

VARYA (*In a tone of supplication*)   Uncle!

ANYA   Uncle, you are at it again!

TROFIMOV   You'd much better be cannoning off the red!

GAEV   I'll hold my tongue, I will.

(*All sit plunged in thought. Perfect stillness. The only thing audible is the muttering of* FIRS. *Suddenly there is a sound in the distance, as it were from the sky — the sound of a breaking harp-string, mournfully dying away*)

LYUBOV   What is that?

LOPAHIN   I don't know. Somewhere far away a bucket fallen and broken in the pits. But somewhere very far away.

GAEV   It might be a bird of some sort — such as a heron.

TROFIMOV   Or an owl.

LYUBOV (*Shudders*)   I don't know why, but it's horrid. (*A pause*)

FIRS   It was the same before the calamity — the owl hooted and the samovar hissed all the time.

GAEV   Before what calamity?

FIRS   Before the emancipation. (*A pause*)

LYUBOV   Come, my friends, let us be going; evening is falling. (*To* ANYA) There are tears in your eyes. What is it, darling? (*Embraces her*)

ANYA   Nothing, mamma; it's nothing.

TROFIMOV   There is somebody coming.

(*The* WAYFARER *appears in a shabby white forage cap and an overcoat; he is slightly drunk*)

WAYFARER   Allow me to inquire, can I get to the station this way?

GAEV   Yes. Go along that road.

WAYFARER I thank you most feelingly. (*Coughing*) The weather is superb. (*Declaims*) My brother, my suffering brother!... Come out to the Volga! Whose groan do you hear?... (*To* VARYA) Mademoiselle, vouchsafe a hungry Russian thirty kopecks.

(VARYA *utters a shriek of alarm*)

LOPAHIN (*Angrily*) There's a right and a wrong way of doing everything!

LYUBOV (*Hurriedly*) Here, take this. (*Looks in her purse*) I've no silver. No matter — here's gold for you.

WAYFARER I thank you most feelingly! (*Goes off*)

(LAUGHTER)

VARYA (*Frightened*) I'm going home — I'm going.... Oh, mamma, the servants have nothing to eat, and you gave him gold!

LYUBOV There's no doing anything with me. I'm so silly! When we get home, I'll give you all I possess. Yermolay Alexeyevitch, you will lend me some more!...

LOPAHIN I will.

LYUBOV Come, friends, it's time to be going. And Varya, we have made a match of it for you. I congratulate you.

VARYA (*Through her tears*) Mamma, that's not a joking matter.

LOPAHIN "Ophelia, get thee to a nunnery!"

GAEV My hands are trembling; it's a long while since I had a game of billiards.

LOPAHIN "Ophelia! Nymph, in thy orisons be all my sins remember'd."

LYUBOV Come, it will soon be supper-time.

VARYA How he frightened me! My heart's simply throbbing.

LOPAHIN Let me remind you, ladies and gentlemen: on the 22nd of August the cherry orchard will be sold. Think about that! Think about it!

(*All go off, except* TROFIMOV *and* ANYA)

ANYA (*Laughing*) I'm grateful to the wayfarer! He frightened Varya and we are left alone.

TROFIMOV Varya's afraid we shall fall in love with each other, and for days together she won't leave us. With her narrow brain she can't grasp that we are above love. To eliminate the petty and transitory which hinder us from being free and happy — that is the aim and meaning of our life. Forward! We go forward irresistibly towards the bright star that shines yonder in the distance. Forward! Do not lag behind, friends.

ANYA (*Claps her hands*) How well you speak! (*A pause*) It is divine here to-day.

TROFIMOV Yes, it's glorious weather.

ANYA Somehow, Petya, you've made me so that I don't love the cherry orchard as I used to. I used to love it so dearly. I used to think that there was no spot on earth like our garden.

TROFIMOV All Russia is our garden. The earth is great and beautiful — there are many beautiful places in it. (*A pause*) Think only, Anya, your grandfather, and great-grandfather, and all your ancestors were slave-owners — the owners of living souls — and from every cherry in the orchard, from every leaf, from every trunk there are human creatures looking at you. Cannot you hear their voices? Oh, it is awful! Your orchard is a fearful thing, and when in the evening or at night one walks about the orchard, the old bark on the trees glimmers dimly in the dusk, and the old cherry trees seem to be dreaming of centuries gone by and tortured by fearful visions. Yes!

We are at least two hundred years behind, we have really gained nothing yet, we have no definite attitude to the past, we do nothing but theorize or complain of depression or drink vodka. It is clear that to begin to live in the present, we must first expiate our past; we must break with it; and we can expiate it only by suffering, by extraordinary unceasing labor. Understand that, Anya.

ANYA The house we live in has long ceased to be our own, and I shall leave it, I give you my word.

TROFIMOV If you have the house keys, fling them into the well and go away. Be free as the wind.

ANYA (*In ecstasy*) How beautifully you said that!

TROFIMOV Believe me, Anya, believe me! I am not thirty yet, I am young, I am still a student, but I have gone through so much already! As soon as winter comes I am hungry, sick, careworn, poor as a beggar, and what ups and downs of fortune have I not known! And my soul was always, every minute, day and night, full of inexplicable forebodings. I have a foreboding of happiness, Anya. I see glimpses of it already.

ANYA (*Pensively*) The moon is rising.

(EPIHODOV *is heard playing still the same mournful song on the guitar. The moon rises. Somewhere near the poplars* VARYA *is looking for* ANYA *and calling* "ANYA! where are you?")

TROFIMOV Yes, the moon is rising. (*A pause*) Here is happiness — here it comes! It is coming nearer and nearer; already I can hear its footsteps. And if we never see it — if we may never know it — what does it matter? Others will see it after us.

VARYA'S VOICE Anya! Where are you?

TROFIMOV That Varya again! (*Angrily*) It's revolting!

ANYA Well, let's go down to the river. It's lovely there.

TROFIMOV Yes, let's go. (*They go*)

VARYA'S VOICE Anya! Anya!

Curtain

Act Three

A drawing-room divided by an arch from a larger drawing-room. A chandelier burning. The Jewish orchestra, the same that was mentioned in Act II, is heard playing in the ante-room. It is evening. In the larger drawing-room they are dancing the grand chain. The voice of SEMYONOV-PISHTCHIK: "Promenade à une paire!" *Then enter the drawing-room in couples first* PISHTCHIK *and* CHARLOTTA IVANOVA, *then* TROFIMOV *and* LYUBOV ANDRE-YEVNA, *thirdly* ANYA *with the* POST-OFFICE CLERK, *fourthly* VARYA *with the* STATION MASTER, *and other guests.* VARYA *is quietly weeping and wiping away her tears as she dances. In the last couple is* DUNYASHA. *They move across the drawing-room.* PISHTCHIK *shouts:* "Grand rond, balancez!" *and* "Les Cavaliers à genou et remerciez vos dames."

FIRS *in a swallow-tail coat brings in seltzer water on a tray.* PISHTCHIK *and* TROFIMOV *enter the drawing-room.*

PISHTCHIK I am a full-blooded man; I have already had two strokes. Dancing's hard work for me, but as they say, if you're in the pack, you must bark with the rest. I'm as strong, I may say, as a horse. My parent, who would have his joke — may the Kingdom of Heaven be his! — used to say about our origin that the ancient stock of the Semyonov-Pishtchiks was derived from the very horse that Caligula made a member of the senate. (*Sits down*) But I've no money, that's where the mischief is. A hungry dog believes in nothing but meat. (*Snores, but at once wakes up*) That's like me . . . . I can think of nothing but money.

TROFIMOV There really is something horsy about your appearance.

PISHTCHIK Well . . . a horse is a fine beast . . . a horse can be sold.

(*There is the sound of billiards being played in an adjoining room.* VARYA *appears in the arch leading to the larger drawing-room*)

TROFIMOV (*Teasing*) Madame Lopahin! Madame Lopahin!

VARYA (*Angrily*) Mangy-looking gentleman!

TROFIMOV Yes, I am a mangy-looking gentleman, and I'm proud of it!

VARYA (*Pondering bitterly*) Here we have hired musicians and nothing to pay them! (*Goes out*)

TROFIMOV (*To* PISHTCHIK) If the energy you have wasted during your lifetime in trying to find the money to pay your interest had gone to something else, you might in the end have turned the world upside down.

PISHTCHIK Nietzsche, the philosopher, a very great and celebrated man . . . of enormous intellect . . . says in his works, that one can make forged banknotes.

TROFIMOV Why, have you read Nietzsche?

PISHTCHIK What next . . . Dashenka told me. . . . And now I am in such a position, I might just as well forge banknotes. The day after to-morrow I must pay 310 roubles — 130 I have procured. (*Feels in his pockets, in alarm*) The money's gone! I have lost my money! (*Through his tears*) Where's the money? (*Gleefully*) Why, here it is behind the lining. . . . It has made me hot all over.

(*Enter* LYUBOV ANDREYEVNA *and* CHARLOTTA IVANOVNA)

LYUBOV (*Hums the* Lezginka) Why is Leonid so long? What can he be doing in town? (*To* DUNYASHA) Offer the musicians some tea.

TROFIMOV The sale hasn't taken place, most likely.

LYUBOV It's the wrong time to have the orchestra, and the wrong time to give a dance. Well, never mind. (*Sits down and hums softly*)

CHARLOTTA (*Gives* PISHTCHIK *a pack of cards*) Here's a pack of cards. Think of any card you like.

PISHTCHIK I've thought of one.

CHARLOTTA Shuffle the pack now. That's right. Give it here, my dear Mr. Pishtchik. *Ein, zwei, drei* — now look, it's in your breast pocket.

PISHTCHIK (*Taking a card out of his breast pocket*) The eight of spades! Perfectly right! (*Wonderingly*) Fancy that now!

CHARLOTTA (*Holding pack of cards in her hands, to* TROFIMOV) Tell me quickly which is the top card.

TROFIMOV Well, the queen of spades.

CHARLOTTA It is! (*To* PISHTCHIK) Well, which card is uppermost?

PISHTCHIK The ace of hearts.

CHARLOTTA It is! (*Claps her hands, pack of cards disappears*) Ah! what lovely weather it is to-day!

(*A mysterious feminine voice which seems coming out of the floor answers her. "Oh, yes, it's magnificent weather, madam."*)

CHARLOTTA You are my perfect ideal.

VOICE And I greatly admire you too, madam.

STATION MASTER (*Applauding*) The lady ventriloquist — bravo!

PISHTCHIK (*Wonderingly*) Fancy that now! Most enchanting Charlotta Ivanovna. I'm simply in love with you.

CHARLOTTA In love? (*Shrugging shoulders*) What do you know of love, *guter Mensch, aber schlechter Musikant.*

TROFIMOV (*Pats* PISHTCHIK *on the shoulder*) You dear old horse. . . .

CHARLOTTA Attention, please! Another trick! (*Takes a traveling rug from a chair*) Here's a very good rug; I want to sell it. (*Shaking it out*) Doesn't anyone want to buy it?

PISHTCHIK (*Wonderingly*) Fancy that!

CHARLOTTA *Ein, zwei, drei!* (*Quickly picks up rug she has dropped; behind the rug stands* ANYA; *she makes a curtsey, runs to her mother, embraces her and runs back into the larger drawing-room amidst general enthusiasm*)

LYUBOV (*Applauds*) Bravo! Bravo!

CHARLOTTA Now again; *Ein, zwei, drei!* (*Lifts up the rug; behind the rug stands* VARYA, *bowing*)

PISHTCHIK (*Wonderingly*) Fancy that now!

CHARLOTTA That's the end. (*Throws the rug at* PISHTCHIK, *makes a curtsey, runs into the larger drawing-room*)

PISHTCHIK (*Hurries after her*) Mischievous creature! Fancy! (*Goes out*)

LYUBOV And still Leonid doesn't come. I can't understand what he's doing in the town so long! Why, everything must be over by now. The estate is sold, or the sale has not taken place. Why keep us so long in suspense?

VARYA (*Trying to console her*) Uncle's bought it. I feel sure of that.

TROFIMOV (*Ironically*) Oh, yes!

VARYA Great-aunt sent him an authorization to buy it in her name, and transfer the debt. She's doing it for Anya's sake, and I'm sure God will be merciful. Uncle will buy it.

LYUBOV My aunt in Yaroslavl sent fifteen thousand to buy the estate in her name, she doesn't trust us — but that's not enough even to pay the arrears. (*Hides her face in her hands*) My fate is being sealed today, my fate. . . .

TROFIMOV (*Teasing* VARYA) Madame Lopahin.

VARYA (*Angrily*) Perpetual student! Twice already you've been sent down from the University.

LYUBOV Why are you angry, Varya? He's teasing you about Lopahin. Well, what of that? Marry Lopahin if you like, he's a good man, and interesting; if you don't want to, don't! Nobody compels you, darling.

VARYA I must tell you plainly, mamma, I look at the matter seriously; he's a good man, I like him.

LYUBOV Well, marry him. I can't see what you're waiting for.

VARYA Mama. I can't make him an offer myself. For the last two years, everyone's been talking to me about him. Everyone talks; but he says nothing or else makes a joke. I see what it means. He's growing rich, he's absorbed in business, he has no thoughts for me. If I had money, were it ever so little, if I had only a hundred roubles, I'd throw everything up and go far away. I would go into a nunnery.

TROFIMOV What bliss!

VARYA (*To* TROFIMOV) A student ought to have sense! (*In a soft tone with tears*) How ugly you've grown, Petya! How old you look! (*To* LYUBOV ANDREYEVNA, *no longer crying*) But I can't do without work, mamma; I must have something to do every minute.

(*Enter* YASHA)

YASHA (*Hardly restraining his laughter*) Epihodov has broken a billiard cue! (*Goes out*)

VARYA What is Epihodov doing here? Who gave him leave to play billiards? I can't make these people out. (*Goes out*)

LYUBOV Don't tease her, Petya. You see she has grief enough without that.

TROFIMOV She is so very officious, meddling in what's not her business. All the summer she's given Anya and me no peace. She's afraid of a love affair between us. What's it to do with her? Besides, I have given no grounds for it. Such triviality is not in my line. We are above love!

LYUBOV And I suppose I am beneath love. (*Very uneasily*) Why is it Leonid's not here? If only I could know whether the estate is sold or not! It seems such an incredible calamity that I really don't know what to think. I am distracted . . . I shall scream in a minute . . . I shall do something stupid. Save me, Petya, tell me something, talk to me!

TROFIMOV What does it matter whether the estate is sold to-day or not? That's all done with long ago. There's no turning back, the path is overgrown. Don't worry yourself, dear Lyubov Andreyevna. You mustn't deceive yourself; for once in your life you must face the truth!

LYUBOV What truth? You see where the truth lies, but I seem to have lost my sight, I see nothing. You settle every great problem so boldly, but tell me, my dear boy, isn't it because you're young — because you haven't yet understood one of your problems through suffering? You look forward boldly, and isn't it that you don't see and don't expect anything dreadful because life is still hidden from your young eyes? You're bolder, more honest, deeper than we are, but think, be just a little magnanimous, have pity on me. I was born here, you know, my father and mother lived here, my grandfather lived here, I love this house. I can't conceive of life without the cherry orchard, and if it really must be sold, then sell me with the orchard. (*Embraces* TROFIMOV, *kisses him on the forehead*) My boy was drowned here. (*Weeps*) Pity me, my dear kind fellow.

TROFIMOV You know I feel for you with all my heart.

LYUBOV But that should have been said differently, so differently. (*Takes out her handkerchief, telegram falls on the floor*) My heart is so heavy to-day. It's so noisy here, my soul is quivering at every sound, I'm shuddering all over, but I can't go away; I'm afraid to be quiet and alone. Don't be hard on me, Petya . . . I love you as though you were one of ourselves. I would gladly let you marry Anya — I swear I would — only, my dear boy, you must take your degree, you do nothing — you're simply tossed by fate from place to place. That's so strange. It is, isn't it? And you must do something with your beard to make it grow somehow. (*Laughs*) You look so funny!

TROFIMOV (*Picks up the telegram*) I've no wish to be a beauty.

LYUBOV That's a telegram from Paris. I get one every day. One yesterday and one to-day. That savage creature is ill again, he's in trouble again. He begs forgiveness, beseeches me to go, and really I ought to go to Paris to see him. You look shocked, Petya. What am I to do, my dear boy, what am I to do?

He is ill, he is alone and unhappy, and who'll look after him, who'll keep him from doing the wrong thing, who'll give him his medicine at the right time? And why hide it or be silent? I love him, that's clear. I love him! I love him! He's a millstone about my neck, I'm going to the bottom with him, but I love that stone and can't live without it. (*Presses* TROFIMOV'S *hand*) Don't think ill of me, Petya, don't tell me anything, don't tell me. . . .

TROFIMOV (*Through his tears*)   For God's sake forgive my frankness: why, he robbed you!

LYUBOV   No! No! No! You mustn't speak like that. (*Covers her ears*)

TROFIMOV   He is a wretch! You're the only person that doesn't know it! He's a worthless creature! A despicable wretch!

LYUBOV (*Getting angry, but speaking with restraint*)   You're twenty-six or twenty-seven years old, but you're still a schoolboy.

TROFIMOV   Possibly.

LYUBOV   You should be a man at your age! You should understand what love means! And you ought to be in love yourself. You ought to fall in love! (*Angrily*) Yes, yes, and it's not purity in you, you're simply a prude, a comic fool, a freak.

TROFIMOV (*In horror*)   The things she's saying!

LYUBOV   I am above love! You're not above love, but simply as our Firs here says, "You are a good-for-nothing." At your age not to have a mistress!

TROFIMOV (*In horror*)   This is awful! The things she is saying! (*Goes rapidly into the larger drawing-room clutching his head*) This is awful! I can't stand it! I'm going. (*Goes off, but at once returns*) All is over between us! (*Goes off into the ante-room*)

LYUBOV (*Shouts after him*)   Petya! Wait a minute! You funny creature! I was joking! Petya! (*There is a sound of somebody running quickly downstairs and suddenly falling with a crash.* ANYA *and* VARYA *scream, but there is a sound of laughter at once*)

LYUBOV   What has happened?

ANYA (*Laughing*)   Petya's fallen downstairs! (*Runs out*)

LYUBOV   What a queer fellow that Petya is!

(*The* STATION MASTER *stands in the middle of the larger room and reads* The Magdalene, *by Alexey Tolstoy. They listen to him, but before he has recited many lines strains of a waltz are heard from the ante-room and the reading is broken off. All dance.* TROFIMOV, ANYA, VARYA *and* LYUBOV AN-DREYEVNA *come in from the ante-room*)

LYUBOV   Come, Petya — come, pure heart! I beg your pardon. Let's have a dance! (*Dances with Petya*)

(ANYA *and* VARYA *dance.* FIRS *comes in, puts his stick down near the side door.* YASHA *also comes into the drawing-room and looks on at the dancing*)

YASHA   What is it, old man?

FIRS   I don't feel well. In old days we used to have generals, barons and admirals dancing at our balls, and now we send for the post-office clerk and the station master and even they're not overanxious to come. I am getting feeble. The old master, the grandfather, used to give sealing-wax for all complaints. I have been taking sealing-wax for twenty years or more. Perhaps that's what's kept me alive.

YASHA   You bore me, old man! (*Yawns*) It's time you were done with.

FIRS   Ach, you're a good-for-nothing! (*Mutters*)

(TROFIMOV *and* LYUBOV ANDREYEVNA *dance in larger room and then on to the stage*)

LYUBOV *Merci*. I'll sit down a little. (*Sits down*) I'm tired.

(*Enter* ANYA)

ANYA (*Excitedly*) There's a man in the kitchen has been saying that the cherry orchard's been sold to-day.

LYUBOV Sold to whom?

ANYA He didn't say to whom. He's gone away.

(*She dances with* TROFIMOV, *and they go off into the larger room*)

YASHA There was an old man gossiping there, a stranger.

FIRS Leonid Andreyevitch isn't here yet, he hasn't come back. He has his light overcoat on, *demisaison,* he'll catch cold for sure. *Ach!* Foolish young things!

LYUBOV I feel as though I should die. Go, Yasha, find out to whom it has been sold.

YASHA But he went away long ago, the old chap. (*Laughs*)

LYUBOV (*With slight vexation*) What are you laughing at? What are you pleased at?

YASHA Epihodov is so funny. He's a silly fellow, two and twenty misfortunes.

LYUBOV Firs, if the estate is sold, where will you go?

FIRS Where you bid me, there I'll go.

LYUBOV Why do you look like that? Are you ill? You ought to be in bed.

FIRS Yes. (*Ironically*) Me go to bed and who's to wait here? Who's to see to things without me? I'm the only one in all the house.

YASHA (*To* LYUBOV ANDREYEVNA) Lyubov Andreyevna, permit me to make a request of you; if you go back to Paris again, be so kind as to take me with you. It's positively impossible for me to stay here. (*Looking about him; in an undertone*) There's no need to say it, you see for yourself — an uncivilized country, the people have no morals, and then the dullness! The food in the kitchen's abominable, and then Firs runs after one muttering all sorts of unsuitable words. Take me with you, please do!

(*Enter* PISHTCHIK)

PISHTCHIK Allow me to ask you for a waltz, my dear lady. (LYUBOV ANDREYEVNA *goes with him*) Enchanting lady, I really must borrow of you just 180 roubles, (*dances*) only 180 roubles. (*They pass into the larger room*) (*In the larger drawing-room, a figure in a gray top hat and in check trousers is gesticulating and jumping about. Shouts of* "Bravo, CHARLOTTA IVAN-OVNA")

DUNYASHA (*She has stopped to powder herself*) My young lady tells me to dance. There are plenty of gentlemen, and too few ladies, but dancing makes me giddy and makes my heart beat. Firs, the post-office clerk said something to me just now that quite took my breath away.

(*Music becomes more subdued*)

FIRS What did he say to you?

DUNYASHA He said I was like a flower.

YASHA (*Yawns*) What ignorance! (*Goes out*)

DUNYASHA Like a flower. I am a girl of such delicate feelings, I am awfully fond of soft speeches.

FIRS Your head's being turned.

(*Enter* EPIHODOV)

EPIHODOV   You have no desire to see me. Dunyasha. I might be an insect. (*Sighs*) Ah! life!

DUNYASHA   What do you want?

EPIHODOV   Undoubtedly you may be right. (*Sighs*) But, of course, if one looks at it from that point of view, if I may so express myself, you have, excuse my plain speaking, reduced me to a complete state of mind. I know my destiny. Every day some misfortune befalls me and I have long ago grown accustomed to it, so that I look upon my fate with a smile. You gave me your word, and though I —

DUNYASHA   Let us have a talk later, I entreat you, but now leave me in peace, for I am lost in reverie. (*Plays with her fan*)

EPIHODOV   I have a misfortune every day, and if I may venture to express myself, I merely smile at it, I even laugh.

(VARYA *enters from the larger drawing-room*)

VARYA   You still have not gone, Epihodov. What a disrespectful creature you are, really! (*To* DUNYASHA) Go along, Dunyasha! (*To* EPIHODOV) First you play billiards and break the cue, then you go wandering about the drawing-room like a visitor!

EPIHODOV   You really cannot, if I may so express myself, call me to account like this.

VARYA   I'm not calling you to account, I'm speaking to you. You do nothing but wander from place to place and don't do your work. We keep you as a counting-house clerk, but what use you are I can't say.

EPIHODOV   (*Offended*)   Whether I work or whether I walk, whether I eat or whether I play billiards, is a matter to be judged by persons of understanding and my elders.

VARYA   You dare to tell me that! (*Firing up*) You dare! You mean to say I've no understanding. Begone from here! This minute!

EPIHODOV   (*Intimidated*)   I beg you to express yourself with delicacy.

VARYA   (*Beside herself with anger*)   This moment! get out! away! (*He goes towards the door, she following him*) Two and twenty misfortunes! Take yourself off! Don't let me set eyes on you! (EPIHODOV *has gone out, behind the door his voice,* "I shall lodge a complaint against you") What! You're coming back? (*Snatches up the stick* FIRS *has put down near the door*) Come! Come! Come! I'll show you! What! you're coming? Then take that! (*She swings the stick, at the very moment that* LOPAHIN *comes in*)

LOPAHIN   Very much obliged to you!

VARYA   (*Angrily and ironically*)   I beg your pardon!

LOPAHIN   Not at all! I humbly thank you for your kind reception!

VARYA   No need of thanks for it. (*Moves away, then looks round and asks softly*) I haven't hurt you?

LOPAHIN   Oh, no! Not at all! There's an immense bump coming up, though!

VOICES FROM LARGER ROOM   Lopahin has come! Yermolay Alexeyevitch!

PISHTCHIK   What do I see and hear? (*Kisses* LOPAHIN) There's a whiff of cognac about you, my dear soul, and we're making merry here too!

(*Enter* LYUBOV ANDREYEVNA)

LYUBOV   Is it you, Yermolay Alexeyevitch? Why have you been so long? Where's Leonid?

LOPAHIN   Leonid Andreyevitch arrived with me. He is coming.

LYUBOV   (*In agitation*)   Well! Well! Was there a sale? Speak!

LOPAHIN (*Embarrassed, afraid of betraying his joy*) The sale was over at four o'clock. We missed our train — had to wait till half-past nine. (*Sighing heavily*) Ugh! I feel a little giddy.

(*Enter* GAEV. *In his right hand he has purchases, with his left hand he is wiping away his tears*)

LYUBOV Well, Leonid? What news? (*Impatiently, with tears*) Make haste, for God's sake!

GAEV (*Makes her no answer, simply waves his hand. To* FIRS, *weeping*) Here, take them; there's anchovies, Kertch herrings. I have eaten nothing all day. What I have been through! (*Door into the billiard room is open. There is heard a knocking of balls and the voice of* YASHA *saying* "Eighty-seven." GAEV'S *expression changes, he leaves off weeping*) I am fearfully tired. Firs, come and help me change my things. (*Goes to his own room across the larger drawing-room*)

PISHTCHIK How about the sale? Tell us, Do!

LYUBOV Is the cherry orchard sold?

LOPAHIN It is sold.

LYUBOV Who has bought it?

LOPAHIN I have bought it. (*A pause,* LYUBOV *is crushed; she would fall down if she were not standing near a chair and table*)

(VARYA *takes keys from her waistband, flings them on the floor in middle of drawing-room and goes out*)

LOPAHIN I have bought it! Wait a bit, ladies and gentlemen, pray. My head's a bit muddled, I can't speak. (*Laughs*) We came to the auction. Deriganov was there already. Leonid Andreyevitch only had 15,000 and Deriganov bid 30,000, besides the arrears, straight off. I saw how the land lay. I bid against him. I bid 40,000, he bid 45,000, I said 55, and so he went on, adding 5 thousands and I adding 10. Well . . . So it ended. I bid 90, and it was knocked down to me. Now the cherry orchard's mine! Mine! (*Chuckles*) My God, the cherry orchard's mine! Tell me that I'm drunk, that I'm out of my mind, that it's all a dream. (*Stamps with his feet*) Don't laugh at me! If my father and my grandfather could rise from their graves and see all that has happened! How their Yermolay, ignorant, beaten Yermolay, who used to run about barefoot in winter, how that very Yermolay has bought the finest estate in the world! I have bought the estate where my father and grandfather were slaves, where they weren't even admitted into the kitchen. I am asleep, I am dreaming! It is all fancy, it is the work of your imagination plunged in the darkness of ignorance. (*Picks up keys, smiling fondly*) She threw away the keys; she means to show she's not the housewife now. (*Jingles the keys*) Well, no matter. (*The orchestra is heard tuning up*) Hey, musicians! Play! I want to hear you. Come, all of you, and look how Yermolay Lopahin will take the ax to the cherry orchard, how the trees will fall to the ground! We will build houses on it and our grandsons and great-grandsons will see a new life springing up there. Music! Play up!

(*Music begins to play.* LYUBOV ANDREYEVNA *has sunk into a chair and is weeping bitterly*)

LOPAHIN (*Reproachfully*) Why, why didn't you listen to me? My poor friend! Dear lady, there's no turning back now. (*With tears*) Oh, if all this could be over, oh, if our miserable disjointed life could somehow soon be changed!

PISHTCHIK (*Takes him by the arm, in an undertone*) She's weeping, let us go and leave her alone. Come. (*Takes him by the arm and leads him into the larger drawing-room*)

LOPAHIN   What's that? Musicians, play up! All must be as I wish it. (*With irony*) Here comes the new master, the owner of the cherry orchard! (*Accidentally tips over a little table, almost upsetting the candelabra*) I can pay for everything! (*Goes out with* PISHTCHIK. *No one remains on the stage or in the larger drawing-room except* LYUBOV, *who sits huddled up, weeping bitterly. The music plays softly.* ANYA *and* TROFIMOV *come in quickly.* ANYA *goes up to her mother and falls on her knees before her.* TROFIMOV *stands at the entrance to the larger drawing-room*)

ANYA   Mamma! Mamma, you're crying, dear, kind, good mamma! My precious! I love you! I bless you! The cherry orchard is sold, it is gone, that's true, that's true! But don't weep, mamma! Life is still before you, you have still your good, pure heart! Let us go, let us go, darling, away from here! We will make a new garden, more splendid than this one; you will see it, you will understand. And joy, quiet, deep joy, will sink into your soul like the sun at evening! And you will smile, mamma! Come, darling, let us go!

Curtain

Act Four

Scene: Same as in First Act. There are neither curtains on the windows nor pictures on the walls: only a little furniture remains piled up in a corner as if for sale. There is a sense of desolation; near the outer door and in the background of the scene are packed trunks, traveling bags, etc. On the left the door is open, and from here the voices of VARYA *and* ANYA *are audible.* LOPAHIN *is standing waiting.* YASHA *is holding a tray with glasses full of champagne. In front of the stage* EPIHODOV *is tying up a box. In the background behind the scene a hum of talk from the peasants who have come to say good-bye. The voice of* GAEV: *"Thanks, brothers, thanks!"*

YASHA   The peasants have come to say good-bye. In my opinion, Yermolay Alexeyevitch, the peasants are good-natured, but they don't know much about things.

(*The hum of talk dies away. Enter across front of stage* LYUBOV ANDREYEVNA *and* GAEV. *She is not weeping, but is pale; her face is quivering — she cannot speak*)

GAEV   You gave them your purse, Lyuba. That won't do — that won't do!

LYUBOV   I couldn't help it! I couldn't help it!

(*Both go out*)

LOPAHIN   (*In the doorway, calls after them*)   You will take a glass at parting? Please do. I didn't think to bring any from the town, and at the station I could only get one bottle. Please take a glass. (*A pause*) What? You don't care for any? (*Comes away from the door*) If I'd known, I wouldn't have bought it. Well, and I'm not going to drink it. (YASHA *carefully sets the tray down on a chair*) You have a glass, Yasha, anyway.

YASHA   Good luck to the travelers, and luck to those that stay behind! (*Drinks*) This champagne isn't the real thing, I can assure you.

LOPAHIN   It cost eight roubles the bottle. (*A pause*) It's devilish cold here.

YASHA They haven't heated the stove to-day — it's all the same since we're going. (*Laughs*)

LOPAHIN What are you laughing for?

YASHA For pleasure.

LOPAHIN Though it's October, it's as still and sunny as though it were summer. It's just right for building! (*Looks at his watch; says in doorway*) Take note, ladies and gentlemen, the train goes in forty-seven minutes; so you ought to start for the station in twenty minutes. You must hurry up!

(TROFIMOV *comes in from out of doors wearing a great-coat*)

TROFIMOV I think it must be time to start, the horses are ready. The devil only knows what's become of my goloshes; they're lost. (*In the doorway*) Anya! My goloshes aren't here. I can't find them.

LOPAHIN And I'm getting off to Harkov. I am going in the same train with you. I'm spending all the winter at Harkov. I've been wasting all my time gossiping with you and fretting with no work to do. I can't get on without work. I don't know what to do with my hands, they flap about so queerly, as if they didn't belong to me.

TROFIMOV Well, we're just going away, and you will take up your profitable labors again.

LOPAHIN Do take a glass.

TROFIMOV No, thanks.

LOPAHIN Then you're going to Moscow now?

TROFIMOV Yes. I shall see them as far as the town, and to-morrow I shall go on to Moscow.

LOPAHIN Yes, I daresay, the professors aren't giving any lectures, they're waiting for your arrival.

TROFIMOV That's not your business.

LOPAHIN How many years have you been at the University?

TROFIMOV Do think of something newer than that — that's stale and flat. (*Hunts for goloshes*) You know we shall most likely never see each other again, so let me give you one piece of advice at parting: don't wave your arms about — get out of the habit. And another thing, building villas, reckoning up that the summer visitors will in time become independent farmers — reckoning like that, that's not the thing to do either. After all, I am fond of you: you have fine delicate fingers like an artist, you've a fine delicate soul.

LOPAHIN (*Embraces him*) Good-bye, my dear fellow. Thanks for everything. Let me give you money for the journey, if you need it.

TROFIMOV What for? I don't need it.

LOPAHIN Why, you haven't got a half-penny.

TROFIMOV Yes, I have, thank you. I got some money for a translation. Here it is in my pocket, (*anxiously*) but where can my goloshes be!

VARYA (*From the next room*) Take the nasty things! (*Flings a pair of goloshes on to the stage*)

TROFIMOV Why are you so cross, Varya? h'm! . . . but those aren't my goloshes.

LOPAHIN I sowed three thousand acres with poppies in the spring, and now I have cleared forty thousand profit. And when my poppies were in flower, wasn't it a picture! So here, as I say, I made forty thousand, and I'm offering you a loan because I can afford to. Why turn up your nose? I am a peasant — I speak bluntly.

TROFIMOV   Your father was a peasant, mine was a chemist — and that proves absolutely nothing whatever. (LOPAHIN *takes out his pocketbook*) Stop that — stop that. If you were to offer me two hundred thousand I wouldn't take it. I am an independent man, and everything that all of you, rich and poor alike, prize so highly and hold so dear, hasn't the slightest power over me — it's like so much fluff fluttering in the air. I can get on without you. I can pass by you. I am strong and proud. Humanity is advancing towards the highest truth, the highest happiness, which is possible on earth, and I am in the front ranks.

LOPAHIN   Will you get there?

TROFIMOV   I shall get there. (*A pause*) I shall get there, or I shall show others the way to get there.

(*In the distance is heard the stroke of an ax on a tree*)

LOPAHIN   Good-bye, my dear fellow; it's time to be off. We turn up our noses at one another, but life is passing all the while. When I am working hard without resting, then my mind is more at ease, and it seems to me as though I too know what I exist for; but how many people are in Russia, my dear boy, who exist, one doesn't know what for. Well, it doesn't matter. That's not what keeps things spinning. They tell me Leonid Andreyevitch has taken a situation. He is going to be a clerk at the bank — 6,000 roubles a year. Only, of course, he won't stick to it — he's too lazy.

ANYA   (*In the doorway*)   Mamma begs you not to let them chop down the orchard until she's gone.

TROFIMOV   Yes, really, you might have the tact. (*Walks out across the front of the stage*)

LOPAHIN   I'll see to it! I'll see to it! Stupid fellows! (*Goes out after him*)

ANYA   Has Firs been taken to the hospital?

YASHA   I told them this morning. No doubt they have taken him.

ANYA   (*To* EPIHODOV, *who passes across the drawing-room*)   Semyon Pantaleye-vitch, inquire, please, if Firs has been taken to the hospital.

YASHA   (*In a tone of offence*)   I told Yegor this morning — why ask a dozen times?

EPIHODOV   Firs is advanced in years. It's my conclusive opinion no treatment would do him good; it's time he was gathered to his fathers. And I can only envy him. (*Puts a trunk down on a cardboard hat-box and crushes it*) There, now, of course — I knew it would be so.

YASHA   (*Jeeringly*)   Two and twenty misfortunes!

VARYA   (*Through the door*)   Has Firs been taken to the hospital?

ANYA   Yes.

VARYA   Why wasn't the note for the doctor taken too?

ANYA   Oh, then, we must send it after them. (*Goes out*)

VARYA   (*From the adjoining room*)   Where's Yasha? Tell him his mother's come to say good-bye to him.

YASHA   (*Waves his hand*)   They put me out of all patience! (DUNYASHA *has all this time been busy about the luggage. Now, when* YASHA *is left alone, she goes up to him*)

DUNYASHA   You might just give me one look, Yasha. You're going away. You're leaving me. (*Weeps and throws herself on his neck*)

YASHA   What are you crying for? (*Drinks the champagne*) In six days I shall be in Paris again. To-morrow we shall get into the express train and roll away in a flash. I can scarcely believe it! *Vive la France!* It doesn't suit me here — it's not the life for me; there's no doing anything. I have seen enough of the ignorance here. I have had enough of it. (*Drinks champagne*) What are you crying for? Behave yourself properly, and then you won't cry.

DUNYASHA (*Powders her face, looking in a pocket-mirror*) Do send me a letter from Paris. You know how I loved you, Yasha — how I loved you! I am a tender creature, Yasha.

YASHA Here they are coming!

(*Busies himself about the trunks, humming softly. Enter* LYUBOV ANDREYEVNA, GAEV, ANYA *and* CHARLOTTA IVANOVNA)

GAEV We ought to be off. There's not much time now. (*Looking at* YASHA) What a smell of herrings!

LYUBOV In ten minutes we must get into the carriage. (*Casts a look about the room*) Farewell, dear house, dear old home of our fathers! Winter will pass and spring will come, and then you will be no more; they will tear you down! How much those walls have seen! (*Kisses her daughter passionately*) My treasure, how bright you look! Your eyes are sparkling like diamonds! Are you glad? Very glad?

ANYA Very glad! A new life is beginning, mamma.

GAEV Yes, really, everything is all right now. Before the cherry orchard was sold, we were all worried and wretched, but afterwards, when once the question was settled conclusively, irrevocably, we all felt calm and even cheerful. I am a bank clerk now — I am a financier — cannon off the red. And you, Lyuba, after all, you are looking better; there's no question of that.

LYUBOV Yes. My nerves are better, that's true. (*Her hat and coat are handed to her*) I'm sleeping well. Carry out my things, Yasha. It's time. (*To* ANYA) My darling, we shall soon see each other again. I am going to Paris. I can live there on the money your Yaroslavl auntie sent us to buy the estate with — hurrah for auntie! — but that money won't last long.

ANYA You'll come back soon, mamma, won't you? I'll be working up for my examination in the high school, and when I have passed that, I shall set to work and be a help to you. We will read all sorts of things together, mamma, won't we? (*Kisses her mother's hands*) We will read in the autumn evenings. We'll read lots of books, and a new wonderful world will open out before us. (*Dreamily*) Mamma, come soon.

LYUBOV I shall come, my precious treasure. (*Embraces her*)

(*Enter* LOPAHIN. CHARLOTTA *softly hums a song*)

GAEV Charlotta's happy; she's singing!

CHARLOTTA (*Picks up a bundle like a swaddled baby*) Bye, bye, my baby. (*A baby is heard crying: "Ooah! ooah!"*) Hush, hush, my pretty boy! (*Ooah! ooah!*) Poor little thing! (*Throws the bundle back*) You must please find me a situation. I can't go on like this.

LOPAHIN We'll find you one, Charlotta Ivanovna. Don't you worry yourself.

GAEV Everyone's leaving us. Varya's going away. We have become of no use all at once.

CHARLOTTA There's nowhere for me to be in the town. I must go away. (*Hums*) What care I . . .

(*Enter* PISHTCHIK)

LOPAHIN   The freak of nature.

PISHTCHIK (*Gasping*) Oh . . . let me get my breath. . . . I'm worn out . . . my most honored . . . Give me some water.

GAEV   Want some money, I suppose? Your humble servant! I'll go out of the way of temptation (*Goes out*)

PISHTCHIK It's a long while since I have been to see you . . . dearest lady. (*To* LOPAHIN) You are here . . . glad to see you . . . a man of immense intellect . . . take . . . here (*gives* LOPAHIN) 400 roubles. That leaves me owing 840.

LOPAHIN (*Shrugging his shoulders in amazement*) It's like a dream. Where did you get it?

PISHTCHIK Wait a bit . . . I'm hot . . . a most extraordinary occurrence. Some Englishmen came along and found in my land some sort of white clay. (*To* LYUBOV ANDREYEVNA) And 400 for you . . . most lovely . . . wonderful. (*Gives money*) The rest later. (*Sips water*) A young man in the train was telling me just now that a great philosopher advises jumping off a house-top. "Jump!" says he; "the whole gist of the problem lies in that." (*Wonderingly*) Fancy that, now! Water, please!

LOPAHIN   What Englishmen?

PISHTCHIK I have made over to them the rights to dig the clay for twenty-four years . . . and now, excuse me . . . I can't stay . . . I must be trotting on. I'm going to Znoikovo . . . to Kardamanovo. . . . I'm in debt all round. (*Sips*) . . . To your very good health! . . . I'll come in on Thursday.

LYUBOV   We are just off to the town, and tomorrow I start for abroad.

PISHTCHIK What! (*In agitation*) Why to the town? Oh, I see the furniture . . . the boxes. No matter . . . (*Through his tears*) . . . no matter . . . men of enormous intellect . . . these Englishmen. . . . Never mind . . . be happy. God will succor you . . . no matter . . . everything in this world must have an end. (*Kisses* LYUBOV ANDREYEVNA'S *hand*) If the rumor reaches you that my end has come, think of this . . . old horse, and say: "There once was such a man in the world . . . Semyonov-Pishtchik . . . the Kingdom of Heaven be his!" . . . most extraordinary weather . . . yes. (*Goes out in violent agitation, but at once returns and says in the doorway*) Dashenka wishes to be remembered to you. (*Goes out*)

LYUBOV   Now we can start. I leave with two cares in my heart. The first is leaving Firs ill. (*Looking at her watch*) We have still five minutes.

ANYA   Mamma, Firs has been taken to the hospital. Yasha sent him off this morning.

LYUBOV   My other anxiety is Varya. She is used to getting up early and working; and now, without work, she's like a fish out of water. She is thin and pale, and she's crying, poor dear! (*A pause*) You are well aware, Yermolay Alexeyevitch, I dreamed of marrying her to you, and everything seemed to show that you would get married. (*Whispers to* ANYA *and motions to* CHARLOTTA *and both go out*) She loves you — she suits you. And I don't know — I don't know why it is you seem, as it were, to avoid each other. I can't understand it!

LOPAHIN   I don't understand it myself, I confess. It's queer somehow, altogether. If there's still time, I'm ready now at once. Let's settle it straight off, and go ahead; but without you, I feel I shan't make her an offer.

LYUBOV   That's excellent. Why, a single moment's all that's necessary. I'll call her at once.

LOPAHIN   And there's champagne all ready too. (*Looking into the glasses*) Empty! Someone's emptied them already. (YASHA *coughs*) I call that greedy.

LYUBOV (*Eagerly*)   Capital! We will go out. Yasha, *allez!* I'll call her in. (*At the door*) Varya, leave all that; come here. Come along! (*Goes out with* YASHA)

LOPAHIN (*Looking at his watch*)   Yes.

(*A pause. Behind the door, smothered laughter and whispering, and, at last, enter* VARYA)

VARYA (*Looking a long while over the things*)   It is strange, I can't find it anywhere.

LOPAHIN   What are you looking for?

VARYA   I packed it myself, and I can't remember. (*A pause*)

LOPAHIN   Where are you going now, Varvara Mihailova?

VARYA   I? To the Ragulins. I have arranged to go to them to look after the house — as a housekeeper.

LOPAHIN   That's in Yashnovo? It'll be seventy miles away. (*A pause*) So this is the end of life in this house!

VARYA (*Looking among the things*)   Where is it? Perhaps I put it in the trunk. Yes, life in this house is over — there will be no more of it.

LOPAHIN   And I'm just off to Harkov — by this next train. I've a lot of business there. I'm leaving Epihodov here, and I've taken him on.

VARYA   Really!

LOPAHIN   This time last year we had snow already, if you remember; but now it's so fine and sunny. Though it's cold, to be sure — three degrees of frost.

VARYA   I haven't looked. (*A pause*) And besides, our thermometer's broken.
(*A pause*)

(*Voice at the door from the yard:* "YERMOLAY ALEXEYEVITCH!")

LOPAHIN (*As though he had long been expecting this summons*)   This minute!
(LOPAHIN *goes out quickly.* VARYA *sitting on the floor and laying her head on a bag full of clothes, sobs quietly. The door opens.* LYUBOV ANDREYEVNA *comes in cautiously*)

LYUBOV   Well? (*A pause*) We must be going.

VARYA (*Has wiped her eyes and is no longer crying*)   Yes, mamma, it's time to start. I shall have time to get to the Ragulins to-day, if only you're not late for the train.

LYUBOV (*In the doorway*)   Anya, put your things on.
(*Enter* ANYA, *then* GAEV *and* CHARLOTTA IVANOVNA. GAEV *has on a warm coat with a hood. Servants and cabmen come in.* EPIHODOV *bustles about the luggage*)

LYUBOV   Now we can start on our travels.

ANYA (*Joyfully*)   On our travels!

GAEV   My friends — my dear, my precious friends! Leaving this house for ever, can I be silent? Can I refrain from giving utterance at leave-taking to those emotions which now flood all my being?

ANYA (*Supplicatingly*)   Uncle!

VARYA   Uncle, you mustn't!

GAEV (*Dejectedly*)   Cannon and into the pocket . . . I'll be quiet. . . .
(*Enter* TROFIMOV *and afterwards* LOPAHIN)

TROFIMOV   Well, ladies and gentlemen, we must start.

LOPAHIN Epihodov, my coat!

LYUBOV I'll stay just one minute. It seems as though I have never seen before what the walls, what the ceilings in this house were like, and now I look at them with greediness, with such tender love.

GAEV I remember when I was six years old sitting in that window on Trinity Day watching my father going to church.

LYUBOV Have all the things been taken?

LOPAHIN I think all. (*Putting on overcoat, to* EPIHODOV) You, Epihodov, mind you see everything is right.

EPIHODOV (*In a husky voice*) Don't you trouble, Yermolay Alexeyevitch.

LOPAHIN Why, what's wrong with your voice?

EPIHODOV I've just had a drink of water, and I choked over something.

YASHA (*Contemptuously*) The ignorance!

LYUBOV We are going — and not a soul will be left here.

LOPAHIN Not till the spring.

VARYA (*Pulls a parasol out of a bundle, as though about to hit someone with it.* LOPAHIN *makes a gesture as though alarmed*) What is it? I didn't mean anything.

TROFIMOV Ladies and gentlemen, let us go into the carriage. It's time. The train will be in directly.

VARYA Petya, here they are, your goloshes, by that box. (*With tears*) And what dirty old things they are!

TROFIMOV (*Putting on his goloshes*) Let us go, friends!

GAEV (*Greatly agitated, afraid of weeping*) The train — the station! Double baulk, ah!

LYUBOV Let us go!

LOPAHIN Are we all here? (*Locks the sidedoor on left*) The things are all here. We must lock up. Let us go!

ANYA Good-bye, home! Good-bye to the old life!

TROFIMOV Welcome to the new life!

(TROFIMOV *goes out with* ANYA. VARYA *looks round the room and goes out slowly.* YASHA *and* CHARLOTTA IVANOVNA, *with her dog, go out*)

LOPAHIN Till the spring, then! Come, friends, till we meet! (*Goes out*)

(LYUBOV ANDREYEVNA *and* GAEV *remain alone. As though they had been waiting for this, they throw themselves on each other's necks, and break into subdued smothered sobbing, afraid of being overheard*)

GAEV (*In despair*) Sister, my sister!

LYUBOV Oh, my orchard! — my sweet, beautiful orchard! My life, my youth, my happiness, good-bye! good-bye!

VOICE OF ANYA (*Calling gaily*) Mamma!

VOICE OF TROFIMOV (*Gaily, excitedly*) Aa — oo!

LYUBOV One last look at the walls, at the windows. My dear mother loved to walk about this room.

GAEV Sister, sister!

VOICE OF ANYA Mamma!

VOICE OF TROFIMOV Aa — oo!

LYUBOV We are coming. (*They go out*)

(*The stage is empty. There is the sound of the doors being locked up, then of the carriages driving away. There is silence. In the stillness there is the dull stroke of an ax in a tree, clanging with a mournful lonely sound.*

Footsteps are heard. FIRS *appears in the doorway on the right. He is dressed as always — in a pea-jacket and white waistcoat, with slippers on his feet. He is ill)*

FIRS (*Goes up to the doors, and tries the handles*) Locked! They have gone ... (*Sits down on sofa*) They have forgotten me.... Never mind ... I'll sit here a bit.... I'll be bound Leonid Andreyevitch hasn't put his fur coat on and has gone off in his thin overcoat. (*Sighs anxiously*) I didn't see after him.... These young people ... (*Mutters something that can't be distinguished*) Life has slipped by as though I hadn't lived. (*Lies down*) I'll lie down a bit.... There's no strength in you, nothing left you — all gone! Ech! I'm good for nothing. (*Lies motionless*)

(*A sound is heard that seems to come from the sky, like a breaking harpstring, dying away mournfully. All is still again, and there is heard nothing but the strokes of the ax far away in the orchard*)

Curtain

Exercises

1. What makes the play a comedy?

2. What does the cherry orchard symbolize?

3. Describe the characteristics of Chekhov's dialogue.

Topics for Writing

1. Discuss the major themes of the play.

2. Analyze the character of Madame Ranevsky.

3. Discuss the roles of Varya and Firs.

Lillian Hellman (1905–)

The Little Foxes

Characters

ADDIE	REGINA GIDDENS
CAL	WILLIAM MARSHALL
BIRDIE HUBBARD	BENJAMIN HUBBARD
OSCAR HUBBARD	ALEXANDRA GIDDENS
LEO HUBBARD	HORACE GIDDENS

Act One

Scene: The living room of the Giddens house, in a small town in the deep South, the Spring of 1900. Upstage is a staircase leading to the second story. Upstage, right, are double doors to the dining room. When these doors are open we see a section of the dining room and the furniture. Upstage, left, is an entrance hall with a coat-rack and umbrella stand. There are large lace-curtained windows on the left wall. The room is lit by a center gas chandelier and painted china oil lamps on the tables. Against the wall is a large piano. Downstage, right, are a high couch, a large table, several chairs. Against the left back wall are a table and several chairs. Near the window there are a smaller couch and tables. The room is good-looking, the furniture expensive; but it reflects no particular taste. Everything is of the best and that is all.

At Rise: ADDIE, *a tall, nice-looking Negro woman of about fifty-five, is closing the windows. From behind the closed dining-room doors there is the sound of voices. After a second,* CAL, *a middle-aged Negro, comes in from the entrace hall carrying a tray with glasses and a bottle of port.* ADDIE *crosses, takes the tray from him, puts it on table, begins to arrange it.*

ADDIE (*pointing to the bottle*) You gone stark out of your head?

CAL No, smart lady, I ain't. Miss Regina told me to get out that bottle. (*Points to bottle.*) That very bottle for the mighty honored guest. When Miss Regina changes orders like that you can bet your dime she got her reason.

ADDIE (*points to dining room*) Go on. You'll be needed.

CAL Miss Zan she had two helpings frozen fruit cream and she tell that honored guest, she tell him that you make the best frozen fruit cream in all the South.

ADDIE (*smiles, pleased*) Did she? Well, see that Belle saves a little for her. She like it right before she go to bed. Save a few little cakes, too, she like — (*The dining-room doors are opened and quickly closed again by* BIRDIE HUBBARD. BIRDIE *is a woman of about forty, with a pretty, well-bred, faded face. Her movements are usually nervous and timid, but now, as she comes running into the room, she is gay and excited.* CAL *turns to* BIRDIE.)

BIRDIE Oh, Cal. (*Closes door.*) I want you to get one of the kitchen boys to run home for me. He's to look in my desk drawer and — (*To* ADDIE) My, Addie. What a good supper! Just as good as good can be.

ADDIE   You look pretty this evening, Miss Birdie, and young.

BIRDIE   (*laughing*)   Me, young? (*Turns back to* CAL.) Maybe you better find Simon and tell him to do it himself. He's to look in my desk, the left drawer, and bring my music album right away. Mr. Marshall is very anxious to see it because of his father and the opera in Chicago. (*To* ADDIE) Mr. Marshall is such a polite man with his manners and very educated and cultured and I've told him all about how my mama and papa used to go to Europe for the music — (*Laughs. To* ADDIE) Imagine going all the way to Europe just to listen to music. Wouldn't that be nice, Addie? Just to sit there and listen and — (*Turns and steps to* CAL.) *Left* drawer, Cal. Tell him that twice because he forgets. And tell him not to let any of the things drop out of the album and to bring it right in here when he comes back.

(*The dining-room doors are opened and quickly closed by* OSCAR HUBBARD. *He is a man in his late forties.*)

CAL   Yes'm. But Simon he won't get it right. But I'll tell him.

BIRDIE   Left drawer, Cal, and tell him to bring the blue book and —

OSCAR   (*sharply*)   Birdie.

BIRDIE   (*turning nervously*)   Oh, Oscar. I was just sending Simon for my music album.

OSCAR   (*to* CAL)   Never mind about the album. Miss Birdie has changed her mind.

BIRDIE   But, really, Oscar. Really I promised Mr. Marshall. I —

(CAL *looks at them, exits.*)

OSCAR   Why do you leave the dinner table and go running about like a child?

BIRDIE   (*trying to be gay*)   But, Oscar, Mr. Marshall said most specially he *wanted* to see my album. I told him about the time Mama met Wagner, and Mrs. Wagner gave her the signed program and the big picture. Mr. Marshall wants to see that. Very, very much. We had such a nice talk and —

OSCAR   (*taking a step to her*)   You have been chattering to him like a magpie. You haven't let him be for a second. I can't think he came South to be bored with you.

BIRDIE   (*quickly, hurt*)   He wasn't bored. I don't believe he was bored. He's a very educated, cultured gentleman. (*Her voice rises.*) I just don't believe it. You always talk like that when I'm having a nice time.

OSCAR   (*turning to her, sharply*)   You have had too much wine. Get yourself in hand now.

BIRDIE   (*drawing back, about to cry, shrilly*)   What am I doing? I am not doing anything. What am I doing?

OSCAR   (*taking a step to her, tensely*)   I said get yourself in hand. Stop acting like a fool.

BIRDIE   (*turns to him, quietly*)   I don't believe he was bored. I just don't believe it. Some people like music and like to talk about it. That's all I was doing.

(LEO HUBBARD *comes hurrying through the dining-room door. He is a young man of twenty, with a weak kind of good looks.*)

LEO   Mama! Papa! They are coming in now.

OSCAR   (*softly*)   Sit down, Birdie. Sit down now. (BIRDIE *sits down, bows her head as if to hide her face.*)

(*The dining-room doors are opened by* CAL. *We see people beginning to rise from the table.* REGINA GIDDENS *comes in with* WILLIAM MARSHALL. REGINA *is a handsome woman of forty.* MARSHALL *is forty-five, pleasant-looking, self-possessed. Behind them comes* ALEXANDRA GIDDENS, *a very pretty, rather delicate-looking girl of seventeen. She is followed by* BENJAMIN HUBBARD, *fifty-five, with a large jovial face and the light graceful movements that one often finds in large men.*)

REGINA   Mr. Marshall, I think you're trying to console me. Chicago may be the noisiest, dirtiest city in the world but I should still prefer it to the sound of our horses and the smell of our azaleas. I should like crowds of people, and theatres, and lovely women — *Very* lovely women, Mr. Marshall?

MARSHALL   (*crossing to sofa*)   In Chicago? Oh, I suppose so. But I can tell you this: I've never dined there with three *such* lovely ladies.

(ADDIE *begins to pass the port.*)

BEN   Our Southern women are well favored.

LEO   (*laughs*)   But one must go to Mobile for the ladies, sir. Very elegant worldly ladies, too.

BEN (*looks at him very deliberately*)   Worldly, eh? *Worldly,* did you say?

OSCAR (*hastily, to* LEO)   Your uncle Ben means that worldliness is not a mark of beauty in any woman.

LEO (*quickly*)   Of course, Uncle Ben. I didn't mean —

MARSHALL   Your port is excellent, Mrs. Giddens.

REGINA   Thank you, Mr. Marshall. We had been saving that bottle, hoping we could open it just for you.

ALEXANDRA (*as* ADDIE *comes to her with the tray*)   Oh. May I *really,* Addie?

ADDIE   Better ask Mama.

ALEXANDRA   May I, Mama?

REGINA (*nods, smiles*)   In Mr. Marshall's honor.

ALEXANDRA (*smiles*)   Mr. Marshall, this will be the first taste of port I've ever had.

(ADDIE *serves* LEO.)

MARSHALL   No one ever had their first taste of a better port. (*He lifts his glass in a toast; she lifts hers; they both drink.*) Well, I suppose it is all true, Mrs. Giddens.

REGINA   What is true?

MARSHALL   That you Southerners occupy a unique position in America. You live better than the rest of us, you eat better, you drink better. I wonder you find time, or want to find time, to do business.

BEN   A great many Southerners don't.

MARSHALL   Do all of you live here together?

REGINA   Here with me? (*Laughs.*) Oh, no. My brother Ben lives next door. My brother Oscar and his family live in the next square.

BEN   But we are a very close family. We've always *wanted* it that way.

MARSHALL   That is very pleasant. Keeping your family together to share each other's lives. My family moves around too much. My children seem never to come home. Away at school in the winter; in the summer, Europe with their mother —

REGINA (*eagerly*)   Oh, yes. Even down here we read about Mrs. Marshall in the society pages.

MARSHALL   I dare say. She moves about a great deal. And all of you are part of the same business? Hubbard Sons?

BEN (*motions to* OSCAR) Oscar and me. (*Motions to* REGINA.) My sister's good husband is a banker.

MARSHALL (*looks at* REGINA, *surprised*) Oh.

REGINA I am so sorry that my husband isn't here to meet you. He's been very ill. He is at Johns Hopkins. But he will be home soon. We think he is getting better now.

LEO I work for Uncle Horace. (REGINA *looks at him.*) I mean I work for Uncle Horace at his bank. I keep an eye on things while he's away.

REGINA (*smiles*) Really, Leo?

BEN (*looks at* LEO, *then to* MARSHALL) Modesty in the young is as excellent as it is rare. (*Looks at* LEO *again.*)

OSCAR (*to* LEO) Your uncle means that a young man should speak more modestly.

LEO (*hastily, taking a step to* BEN) Oh, I didn't mean, sir —

MARSHALL Oh, Mrs. Hubbard. Where's that Wagner autograph you promised to let me see? My train will be leaving soon and —

BIRDIE The autograph? Oh. Well. Really, Mr. Marshall, I didn't mean to chatter so about it. Really I — (*Nervously, looking at* OSCAR) You must excuse me. I didn't get it because, well, because I had — I — I had a little headache and —

OSCAR My wife is a miserable victim of headaches.

REGINA (*quickly*) Mr. Marshall said at supper that he would like you to play for him, Alexandra.

ALEXANDRA (*who has been looking at* BIRDIE) It's not I who play well, sir. It's my aunt. She plays just wonderfully. She's my teacher. (*Rises. Eagerly*) May we play a duet? May we, Mama?

BIRDIE (*taking* ALEXANDRA'S *hand*) Thank you, dear. But I have my headache now. I —

OSCAR (*sharply*) Don't be stubborn, Birdie. Mr. Marshall wants you to play.

MARSHALL Indeed I do. If your headache isn't —

BIRDIE (*hesitates, then gets up, pleased*) But I'd like to, sir. Very much. (*She and* ALEXANDRA *go to the piano.*)

MARSHALL It's very remarkable how you Southern aristocrats have kept together. Kept together and kept what belonged to you.

BEN You misunderstand, sir. Southern aristocrats have *not* kept together and have *not* kept what belonged to them.

MARSHALL (*laughs, indicates room*) You don't call this keeping what belongs to you?

BEN But we are not aristocrats. (*Points to* BIRDIE *at the piano*) Our brother's wife is the only one of us who belongs to the Southern aristocracy.

(BIRDIE *looks towards* BEN.)

MARSHALL (*smiles*) My information is that you people have been here, and solidly here, for a long time.

OSCAR And so we have. Since our great-grandfather.

BEN (*smiles*) Who was *not* an aristocrat, like Birdie's.

MARSHALL (*a little sharply*) You make great distinctions.

BEN Oh, they have been made for us. And maybe they are important distinctions. (*Leans forward, intimately.*) Now you take Birdie's family. When my great-grandfather came here they were the highest-tone plantation owners in this state.

LEO (*steps to* MARSHALL. *Proudly*)   My mother's grandfather was *governor* of the state before the war.

OSCAR   They owned the plantation, Lionnet. You may have heard of it, sir?

MARSHALL (*laughs*)   No, I've never heard of anything but brick houses on a lake, and cotton mills.

BEN   Lionnet in its day was the best cotton land in the South. It still brings us in a fair crop. (*Sits back.*) Ah, they were great days for those people — even when I can remember. They had the best of everything. (BIRDIE *turns to them.*) Cloth from Paris, trips to Europe, horses you can't raise any more, niggers to lift their fingers —

BIRDIE (*suddenly*)   We were good to our people. Everybody knew that. We were better to them than —

(MARSHALL *looks up at* BIRDIE.)

REGINA   Why, Birdie. You aren't playing.

BEN   But when the war comes these fine gentlemen ride off and leave the cotton, *and* the women, to rot.

BIRDIE   My father was killed in the war. He was a fine soldier, Mr. Marshall. A fine man.

REGINA   Oh, certainly, Birdie. A famous soldier.

BEN (*to* BIRDIE)   But that isn't the tale I am telling Mr. Marshall. (*To* MARSHALL) Well, sir, the war ends. (BIRDIE *goes back to piano.*) Lionnet is almost ruined, and the sons finish ruining it. And there were thousands like them. Why? (*Leans forward.*) Because the Southern aristocrat can adapt himself to nothing. Too high-tone to try.

MARSHALL   Sometimes it is difficult to learn new ways. (BIRDIE *and* ALEXANDRA *begin to play.* MARSHALL *leans forward, listening.*)

BEN   Perhaps, perhaps. (*He sees that* MARSHALL *is listening to the music. Irritated, he turns to* BIRDIE *and* ALEXANDRA *at the piano, then back to* MARSHALL.) You're right, Mr. Marshall. It is difficult to learn new ways. But maybe that's why it's profitable. *Our* grandfather and *our* father learned the new ways and learned how to make them pay. They work. (*Smiles nastily.*) *They* are in trade. Hubbard Sons, Merchandise. Others, Birdie's family, for example, look down on them. (*Settles back in chair.*) To make a long story short, Lionnet now belongs to *us*. (BIRDIE *stops playing.*) Twenty years ago we took over their land, their cotton, and their daughter. (BIRDIE *rises and stands stiffly by the piano.* MARSHALL, *who has been watching her, rises.*)

MARSHALL   May I bring you a glass of port, Mrs. Hubbard?

BIRDIE (*softly*)   No, thank you, sir. You are most polite.

REGINA (*sharply, to* BEN)   You are boring Mr. Marshall with these ancient family tales.

BEN   I hope not. I hope not. I am trying to make an important point — (*bows to* MARSHALL) for our future business partner.

OSCAR (*to* MARSHALL)   My brother always says that it's folks like us who have struggled and fought to bring to our land some of the prosperity of your land.

BEN   Some people call that patriotism.

REGINA (*laughs gaily*)   I hope you don't find my brothers too obvious, Mr. Marshall. I'm afraid they mean that this is the time for the ladies to leave the gentlemen to talk business.

MARSHALL (*hastily*)   Not at all. We settled everything this afternoon. (MAR-

SHALL *looks at his watch*.) I have only a few minutes before I must leave for the train. (*Smiles at her*.) And I insist they be spent with you.

REGINA *And* with another glass of port.

MARSHALL Thank you.

BEN (*to* REGINA) My sister is right. (*To* MARSHALL) I am a plain man and I am trying to say a plain thing. A man ain't only in business for what he can get out of it. It's got to give him something here. (*Puts hand to his breast*.) That's every bit as true for the nigger picking cotton for a silver quarter, as it is for you and me. (REGINA *gives* MARSHALL *a glass of port*.) If it don't give him something here, then he don't pick the cotton right. Money isn't all. Not by three shots.

MARSHALL Really? Well, I always thought it was a great deal.

REGINA And so did I, Mr. Marshall.

MARSHALL (*leans forward. Pleasantly, but with meaning*) Now you don't have to convince me that you are the right people for the deal. I wouldn't be here if you hadn't convinced me six months ago. You want the mill here, and I want it here. It isn't my business to find out *why* you want it.

BEN To bring the machine to the cotton, and not the cotton to the machine.

MARSHALL (*amused*) You have a turn for neat phrases, Hubbard. Well, however grand your reasons are, mine are simple: I want to make money and I believe I'll make it on you. (*As* BEN *starts to speak, he smiles*.) Mind you, I have no objections to more high-minded reasons. They are mighty valuable in business. It's fine to have partners who so closely follow the teachings of Christ. (*Gets up*.) And now I must leave for my train.

REGINA I'm sorry you won't stay over with us, Mr. Marshall, but you'll come again. Any time you like.

BEN (*motions to* LEO, *indicating the bottle*) Fill them up, boy, fill them up. (LEO *moves around filling the glasses as* BEN *speaks*.) Down here, sir, we have a strange custom. We drink the *last* drink for a toast. That's to prove that the Southerner is always still on his feet for the last drink. (*Picks up his glass*.) It was Henry Frick, your Mr. Henry Frick, who said, "Railroads are the Rembrandts of investments." Well, *I* say, "Southern cotton mills *will be* the Rembrandts of investments." So I give you the firm of Hubbard Sons and Marshall, Cotton Mills, and to it a long and prosperous life.

(*They all pick up their glasses.* MARSHALL *looks at them, amused. Then he, too, lifts his glass, smiles.*)

OSCAR The children will drive you to the depot. Leo! Alexandra! You will drive Mr. Marshall down.

LEO (*eagerly, looks at* BEN *who nods*) Yes, sir. (*To* MARSHALL) Not often Uncle Ben lets *me* drive the horses. And a beautiful pair they are. (*Starts for hall*.) Come on, Zan.

ALEXANDRA May I drive tonight, Uncle Ben, please? I'd like to and —

BEN (*shakes his head, laughs*) In your evening clothes? Oh, no, my dear.

ALEXANDRA But Leo always — (*stops, exits quickly*.)

REGINA I don't like to say good-bye to you, Mr. Marshall.

MARSHALL Then we won't say good-bye. You have promised that you would come and let me show you Chicago. Do I have to make you promise again?

REGINA (*looks at him as he presses her hand*) I promise again.

MARSHALL (*touches her hand again, then moves to* BIRDIE) Good-bye, Mrs. Hubbard.

BIRDIE (*shyly, with sweetness and dignity*) Good-bye, sir.

MARSHALL (*as he passes* REGINA) Remember.

REGINA I will.

OSCAR We'll see you to the carriage.

MARSHALL *exits, followed by* BEN *and* OSCAR. *For a second* REGINA *and* BIRDIE *stand looking after them. Then* REGINA *throws up her arms, laughs happily.*)

REGINA And there, Birdie, goes the man who has opened the door to our future.

BIRDIE (*surprised at the unaccustomed friendliness*) What?

REGINA (*turning to her*) Our future. Yours and mine, Ben's and Oscar's, the children — (*Looks at* BIRDIE'S *puzzled face, laughs.*) Our future! (*Gaily*) You were charming at supper, Birdie. Mr. Marshall certainly thought so.

BIRDIE (*pleased*) Why, Regina! Do you think he did?

REGINA Can't you tell when you're being admired?

BIRDIE Oscar said I bored Mr. Marshall. (*Then quietly.*) But he admired *you*. He told me so.

REGINA What did he say?

BIRDIE He said to me, "I hope your sister-in-law will come to Chicago. Chicago will be at her feet." He said the ladies would bow to your manners and the gentlemen to your looks.

REGINA Did he? He seems a lonely man. Imagine being lonely with all that money. I don't think he likes his wife.

BIRDIE Not like his wife? What a thing to say.

REGINA She's away a great deal. He said that several times. And once he made fun of her being so social and high-tone. But that fits in all right. (*Sits back, arms on back of sofa, stretches.*) Her being social, I mean. She can introduce me. It won't take long with an introduction from her.

BIRDIE (*bewildered*) Introduce you? In Chicago? You mean you really might go? Oh, Regina, you can't leave here. What about Horace?

REGINA Don't look so scared about everything, Birdie. I'm going to live in Chicago. I've always wanted to. And now there'll be plenty of money to go with.

BIRDIE But Horace won't be able to move around. You know what the doctor wrote.

REGINA There'll be millions, Birdie, millions. You know what I've always said when people told me we were rich? I said I think you should either be a nigger or a millionaire. In between, like us, what for? (*Laughs. Looks at* BIRDIE.) But I'm not going away tomorrow, Birdie. There's plenty of time to worry about Horace when he comes home. If he ever decides to come home.

BIRDIE Will we be going to Chicago? I mean, Oscar and Leo and me?

REGINA You? I shouldn't think so. (*Laughs.*) Well, we must remember tonight. It's a very important night and we mustn't forget it. We shall plan all the things we'd like to have and then we'll really have them. Make a wish, Birdie, any wish. It's bound to come true now.

(BEN *and* OSCAR *enter.*)

BIRDIE (*laughs*) Well. Well, I don't know. Maybe. (REGINA *turns to look at* BEN.) Well, I guess I'd know right off what I wanted.

(OSCAR *stands by the upper window, waves to the departing carriage.*)

REGINA (*looks up at* BEN, *smiles. He smiles back at her*) Well, you did it.

BEN Looks like it might be we did.

REGINA (*springs up, laughs*)   Looks like it! Don't pretend. You're like a cat who's been licking the cream. (*Crosses to wine bottle.*) Now we must all have a drink to celebrate.

OSCAR   The children, Alexandra and Leo, make a very handsome couple, Regina. Marshall remarked himself what fine young folks they were. How well they looked together!

REGINA (*sharply*)   Yes. You said that before, Oscar.

BEN   Yes, sir. It's beginning to look as if the deal's all set. I may not be a subtle man — but — (*Turns to them. After a second.*) Now somebody ask me how I know the deal is set.

OSCAR   What do you mean, Ben?

BEN   You remember I told him that down here we drink the *last* drink for a toast?

OSCAR (*thoughtfully*)   Yes. I never heard that before.

BEN   Nobody's ever heard it before. God forgives those who invent what they need. I already had his signature. But we've all done business with men whose word over a glass is better than a bond. Anyway it don't hurt to have both.

OSCAR (*turns to* REGINA)   You understand what Ben means?

REGINA (*smiles*)   Yes, Oscar. I understand. I understood immediately.

BEN (*looks at her admiringly*)   Did you, Regina? Well, when he lifted his glass to drink, I closed my eyes and saw the bricks going into place.

REGINA   And *I* saw a lot more than that.

BEN   Slowly, slowly. As yet we have only our hopes.

REGINA   Birdie and I have just been planning what we want. I know what I want. What will you want, Ben?

BEN   Caution. Don't count the chickens. (*Leans back, laughs.*) Well, God would allow us a little daydreaming. Good for the soul when you've worked hard enough to deserve it. (*Pauses.*) I think I'll have a stable. For a long time I've had my good eyes on Carter's in Savannah. A rich man's pleasure, the sport of kings, why not the sport of Hubbards? Why not?

REGINA (*smiles*)   Why not? What will you have, Oscar?

OSCAR   I don't know. (*Thoughtfully*) The pleasure of seeing the bricks grow will be enough for me.

BEN   Oh, of course. Our *greatest* pleasure will be to see the bricks grow. But we are all entitled to a little side indulgence.

OSCAR   Yes, I suppose so. Well, then, I think we might take a few trips here and there, eh, Birdie?

BIRDIE (*surprised at being consulted*)   Yes, Oscar. I'd like that.

OSCAR   We might even make a regular trip to Jekyll Island. I've heard the Cornelly place is for sale. We might think about buying it. Make a nice change. Do you good, Birdie, a change of climate. Fine shooting on Jekyll, the best.

BIRDIE   I'd like —

OSCAR (*indulgently*)   What would you like?

BIRDIE   *Two* things. Two things I'd like most.

REGINA   Two! I should like a thousand. You are modest, Birdie.

BIRDIE (*warmly delighted with the unexpected interest*)   I should like to have Lionnet back. I know you own it now, but I'd like to see it fixed up again, the way Mama and Papa had it. Every year it used to get a nice coat of paint — Papa was very particular about the paint — and the lawn was so smooth all the way down to the river, with the trims of zinnias and red-feather plush. And the figs and blue little plums and the scuppernongs — (*Smiles. Turns to* REGINA.) The organ is still there and it wouldn't cost much to fix. We could have parties for Zan, the way Mama used to have for me.

BEN That's a pretty picture, Birdie. Might be a most pleasant way to live. (*Dismissing* BIRDIE.) What do you want, Regina?

BIRDIE (*very happily, not noticing that they are no longer listening to her*) I could have a cutting garden. Just where Mama's used to be. Oh, I do think we could be happier there. Papa used to say that *nobody* had ever lost their temper at Lionnet, and *nobody* ever would. Papa would never let anybody be nasty-spoken or mean. No, sir. He just didn't like it.

BEN What do you want, Regina?

REGINA I'm going to Chicago. And when I'm settled there and know the right people and the right things to buy — because I certainly don't now — I shall go to Paris and buy them. (*Laughs.*) I'm going to leave you and Oscar to count the bricks.

BIRDIE Oscar. Please let me have Lionnet back.

OSCAR (*to* REGINA) You are serious about moving to Chicago?

BEN She is going to see the great world and leave us in the little one. Well, we'll come and visit you and meet all the great and be proud to think you are our sister.

REGINA (*gaily*) Certainly. And you won't even have to learn to be subtle, Ben. Stay as you are. You will be rich and the rich don't have to be subtle.

OSCAR But what about Alexandra? She's seventeen. Old enough to be thinking about marrying.

BIRDIE And, Oscar, I have one more wish. Just one more wish.

OSCAR (*turns*) What is it, Birdie? What are you saying?

BIRDIE I want you to stop shooting. I mean, so much. I don't like to see animals and birds killed just for the killing. You only throw them away —

BEN (*to* REGINA) It'll take a great deal of money to live as you're planning, Regina.

REGINA Certainly. But there'll be plenty of money. You have estimated the profits very high.

BEN I have —

BIRDIE (OSCAR *is looking at her furiously*) And you never let anybody else shoot, and the niggers need it so much to keep from starving. It's wicked to shoot food just because you like to shoot, when poor people need it so —

BEN (*laughs*) I have estimated the profits very high — for myself.

REGINA What did you say?

BIRDIE I've always wanted to speak about it, Oscar.

OSCAR (*slowly, carefully*) What are you chattering about?

BIRDIE (*nervously*) I was talking about Lionnet and — and about your shooting —

OSCAR You are exciting yourself.

REGINA (*to* BEN) I didn't hear you. There was so much talking.

OSCAR (*to* BIRDIE) You have been acting very childish, very excited, all evening.

BIRDIE Regina asked me what I'd like.

REGINA What did you say, Ben?

BIRDIE Now that we'll be so rich everybody was saying what they would like, so *I* said what *I* would like, too.

BEN I said — (*He is interrupted by* OSCAR.)

OSCAR (*to* BIRDIE) Very well. We've all heard you. That's enough now.

BEN I am waiting. (*They stop.*) I am waiting for you to finish. You and Birdie. Four conversations are three too many. (BIRDIE *slowly sits down.* BEN *smiles, to* REGINA.) I said that I had, and I do, estimate the profits very high — for myself, and Oscar, of course.

REGINA (*slowly*) And what does that mean?

(BEN *shrugs, looks towards* OSCAR.)

OSCAR (*looks at* BEN, *clears throat*) Well, Regina, it's like this. For forty-nine per cent Marshall will put up four hundred thousand dollars. For fifty-one per cent — (*smiles archly*) a controlling interest, mind you, we will put up two hundred and twenty-five thousand dollars besides offering him certain benefits that our (*looks at* BEN) local position allows us to manage. Ben means that two hundred and twenty-five thousand dollars is a lot of money.

REGINA I know the terms and I know it's a lot of money.

BEN (*nodding*) It is.

OSCAR Ben means that we are ready with our two-thirds of the money. Your third, Horace's I mean, doesn't seem to be ready. (*Raises his hand as* REGINA *starts to speak.*) Ben has written to Horace, I have written, and you have written. He answers. But he never mentions this business. Yet we have explained it to him in great detail, and told him the urgency. Still he never mentions it. Ben has been very patient, Regina. Naturally, you are our sister and we want you to benefit from anything we do.

REGINA And in addition to your concern for me, you do not want control to go out of the family. (*To* BEN) That right, Ben?

BEN That's cynical. (*Smiles.*) Cynicism is an unpleasant way of saying the truth.

OSCAR No need to be cynical. We'd have no trouble raising the third share, the share that you want to take.

REGINA I am sure you could get the third share, the share you were saving for me. But that would give you a strange partner. And strange partners sometimes want a great deal. (*Smiles unpleasantly.*) But perhaps it would be wise for you to find him.

OSCAR Now, now. Nobody says we *want* to do that. We would like to have you in and you would like to come in.

REGINA Yes. I certainly would.

BEN (*laughs, puts up his hand*) But we haven't heard from Horace.

REGINA I've given my word that Horace will put up the money. That should be enough.

BEN Oh, it was enough. I took your word. But I've got to have more than your word now. The contracts will be signed this week, and Marshall will want to see our money soon after. Regina, Horace has been in Baltimore for five months. I know that you've written him to come home, and that he hasn't come.

OSCAR It's beginning to look as if he doesn't want to come home.

REGINA   Of course he wants to come home. You can't move around with heart trouble at any moment you choose. You know what doctors are like once they get their hands on a case like this —

OSCAR   They can't very well keep him from answering letters, can they? (REGINA *turns to* BEN.) They couldn't keep him from arranging for the money if he wanted to —

REGINA   Has it occurred to you that Horace is also a good business man?

BEN   Certainly. He is a shrewd trader. Always has been. The bank is proof of that.

REGINA   Then, possibly, he may be keeping silent because he doesn't think he is getting enough for his money. (*Looks at* OSCAR.) Seventy-five thousand he has to put up. That's a lot of money, too.

OSCAR   Nonsense. He knows a good thing when he hears it. He knows that we can make *twice* the profit on cotton goods manufactured *here* than can be made in the North.

BEN   That isn't what Regina means. (*Smiles.*) May I interpret you, Regina? (*To* OSCAR) Regina is saying that Horace wants *more* than a third of our share.

OSCAR   But he's only putting up a third of the money. You put up a third and you get a third. What else *could* he expect?

REGINA   Well, *I* don't know. I don't know about these things. It would seem that if you put up a third you should only get a third. But then again, there's no law about it, is there? I should think that if you knew your money was very badly needed, well, you just might say, I want more, I want a bigger share. You boys have done that. I've heard you say so.

BEN   (*after a pause, laughs*)   So you believe he has deliberately held out? For a larger share? (*Leaning forward.*) Well, I *don't* believe it. But I *do* believe that's what *you* want. Am I right, Regina?

REGINA   Oh, I shouldn't like to be too definite. But I *could* say that I wouldn't like to persuade Horace unless he did get a larger share. I must look after his interests. It seems only natural —

OSCAR   And where would the larger share come from?

REGINA   I don't know. That's not my business. (*Giggles.*) But perhaps it could come off your share, Oscar.

(REGINA *and* BEN *laugh.*)

OSCAR   (*rises and wheels furiously on both of them as they laugh*)   What kind of talk is this?

BEN   I haven't said a thing.

OSCAR   (*to* REGINA)   *You* are talking very big tonight.

REGINA   (*stops laughing*)   Am I? Well, you should know me well enough to know that I wouldn't be asking for things I didn't think I could get.

OSCAR   Listen. I don't believe you can even get Horace to come home, much less get money from him or talk quite so big about what you want.

REGINA   Oh, I can get him home.

OSCAR   Then why haven't you?

REGINA   I thought I should fight his battles for him, before he came home. Horace is a very sick man. And even if *you* don't care how sick he is, I do.

BEN   Stop this foolish squabbling. How can you get him home?

REGINA   I will send Alexandra to Baltimore. She will ask him to come home.

She will say that she *wants* him to come home, and that *I* want him to come home.

BIRDIE (*suddenly*) Well, of course she wants him here, but he's sick and maybe he's happy where he is.

REGINA (*ignores* BIRDIE, *to* BEN) You agree that he will come home if she asks him to, if she says that I miss him and want him —

BEN (*looks at her, smiles*) I admire you, Regina. And I agree. That's settled now and — (*Starts to rise.*)

REGINA (*quickly*) But before she brings him home, I want to know what he's going to get.

BEN What do you want?

REGINA Twice what you offered.

BEN Well, you won't get it.

OSCAR (*to* REGINA) I think you've gone crazy.

REGINA I don't want to fight, Ben —

BEN I don't either. You won't get it. There isn't any chance of that. (*Roguishly*) You're holding us up, and that's not pretty, Regina, not pretty. (*Holds up his hand as he sees she is about to speak.*) But we need you, and I don't want to fight. Here's what I'll do: I'll give Horace forty per cent, instead of the thirty-three and a third he really should get. I'll do that, provided he is home and his money is up within two weeks. How's that?

REGINA All right.

OSCAR I've asked before: where is this extra share coming from?

BEN (*pleasantly*) From you. From your share.

OSCAR (*furiously*) From me, is it? That's just fine and dandy. That's my reward. For thirty-five years I've worked my hands to the bone for you. For thirty-five years I've done all the things you didn't want to do. And this is what I —

BEN (*turns slowly to look at* OSCAR. OSCAR *breaks off*) My, my. I am being attacked tonight on all sides. First by my sister, then by my brother. And I ain't a man who likes being attacked. I can't believe that God wants the strong to parade their strength, but I don't mind doing it if it's got to be done. (*Leans back in his chair.*) You ought to take these things better, Oscar. I've made you money in the past. I'm going to make you more money now. You'll be a very rich man. What's the difference to any of us if a little more goes here, a little less goes there — it's all in the family. And it will stay in the family. I'll never marry. (ADDIE *enters, begins to gather the glasses from the table.* OSCAR *turns to* BEN.) So my money will go to Alexandra and Leo. They may even marry some day and — (ADDIE *looks at* BEN.)

BIRDIE (*rising*) Marry — Zan and Leo —

OSCAR (*carefully*) That would make a great difference in my feelings. If they married.

BEN Yes, that's what I mean. Of course it would make a difference.

OSCAR (*carefully*) Is that what *you* mean, Regina?

REGINA Oh, it's too far away. We'll talk about it in a few years.

OSCAR I want to talk about it now.

BEN (*nods*) Naturally.

REGINA There's a lot of things to consider. They are first cousins, and —

OSCAR That isn't unusual. Our grandmother and grandfather were first cousins.

REGINA (*giggles*) And look at us.

(BEN *giggles*.)

OSCAR (*angrily*) You're both being very gay with my money.

BEN (*sighs*) These quarrels. I dislike them so. (*Leans forward to* REGINA.) A marriage might be a very wise arrangement, for several reasons. And then, Oscar has given up something for you. You should try to manage something for him.

REGINA I haven't said I was opposed to it. But Leo is a wild boy. There were those times when he took a little money from the bank and —

OSCAR That's all past history —

REGINA Oh, I know. And I know all young men are wild. I'm only mentioning it to show you that there are considerations —

BEN (*irritated because she does not understand that he is trying to keep* OSCAR *quiet*) All right, so there are. But please assure Oscar that you will think about it very seriously.

REGINA (*smiles, nods*) Very well. I assure Oscar that I will think about it seriously.

OSCAR (*sharply*) That is not an answer.

REGINA (*rises*) My, you're in a bad humor and you shall put me in one. I have said all that I am willing to say now. After all, Horace has to give his consent, too.

OSCAR Horace will do what you tell him to.

REGINA Yes, I think he will.

OSCAR And I have your word that you will try to —

REGINA (*patiently*) Yes, Oscar. You have my word that I will think about it. Now do leave me alone.

(*There is the sound of the front door being closed.*)

BIRDIE I — Alexandra is only seventeen. She —

REGINA (*calling*) Alexandra? Are you back?

ALEXANDRA Yes, Mama.

LEO (*comes into the room*) Mr. Marshall got off safe and sound. Weren't those fine clothes he had? You can always spot clothes made in a good place. Looks like maybe they were done in England. Lots of men in the North send all the way to England for their stuff.

BEN (*to* LEO) Were you careful driving the horses?

LEO Oh, yes, sir. I was.

(ALEXANDRA *has come in on* BEN'S *question, hears the answer, looks angrily at* LEO.)

ALEXANDRA It's a lovely night. You should have come, Aunt Birdie.

REGINA Were you gracious to Mr. Marshall?

ALEXANDRA I think so, Mama. I liked him.

REGINA Good. And now I have great news for you. You are going to Baltimore in the morning to bring your father home.

ALEXANDRA (*gasps, then delighted*) Me? Papa said I should come? That must mean — (*Turns to* ADDIE.) Addie, he must be well. Think of it, he'll be back home again. We'll bring him home.

REGINA You are going alone, Alexandra.

ADDIE (ALEXANDRA *has turned in surprise*) Going alone? Going by herself?

A child that age! Mr. Horace ain't going to like Zan traipsing up there by herself.

REGINA (*sharply*) Go upstairs and lay out Alexandra's things.

ADDIE He'd expect me to be along —

REGINA I'll be up in a few minutes to tell you what to pack. (ADDIE *slowly begins to climb the steps. To* ALEXANDRA) I should think you'd like going alone. At your age it certainly would have delighted me. You're a strange girl, Alexandra. Addie has babied you so much.

ALEXANDRA I only thought it would be more fun if Addie and I went together.

BIRDIE (*timidly*) Maybe I could go with her, Regina. I'd really like to.

REGINA She is going alone. She is getting old enough to take some responsibilities.

OSCAR She'd better learn now. She's almost old enough to get married. (*Jovially, to* LEO, *slapping him on shoulder*) Eh, son?

LEO Huh?

OSCAR (*annoyed with* LEO *for not understanding*) Old enough to get married, you're thinking, eh?

LEO Oh, yes, sir. (*Feebly*) Lots of girls get married at Zan's age. Look at Mary Prester and Johanna and —

REGINA Well, she's not getting married tomorrow. But she is going to Baltimore tomorrow, so let's talk about that. (*To* ALEXANDRA) You'll be glad to have Papa home again.

ALEXANDRA I wanted to go before, Mama. You remember that. But you said *you* couldn't go, and that *I* couldn't go alone.

REGINA I've changed my mind. (*Too casually*) You're to tell Papa how much you missed him, and that he must come home now — for your sake. Tell him that you *need* him home.

ALEXANDRA Need him home? I don't understand.

REGINA There is nothing for you to understand. You are simply to say what I have told you.

BIRDIE (*rises*) He may be too sick. She couldn't do that —

ALEXANDRA Yes. He may be too sick to travel. I couldn't make him think he had to come home for me, if he is too sick to —

REGINA (*looks at her, sharply, challengingly*) You *couldn't* do what I tell you to do, Alexandra?

ALEXANDRA (*quietly*) No. I couldn't. If I thought it would hurt him.

REGINA (*after a second's silence, smiles pleasantly*) But you are doing this for Papa's own good. (*Takes* ALEXANDRA'S *hand.*) You must let me be the judge of his condition. It's the best possible cure for him to come home and be taken care of here. He mustn't stay there any longer and listen to those alarmist doctors. You are doing this entirely for his sake. Tell your papa that I want him to come home, that I miss him very much.

ALEXANDRA (*slowly*) Yes, Mama.

REGINA (*to the others. Rises*) I must go and start getting Alexandra ready now. Why don't you all go home?

BEN (*rises*) I'll attend to the railroad ticket. One of the boys will bring it over. Good night, everybody. Have a nice trip, Alexandra. The food on the train is very good. The celery is so crisp. Have a good time and act like a little lady. (*Exits.*)

REGINA   Good night, Ben. Good night, Oscar — (*Playfully*) Don't be so glum, Oscar. It makes you look as if you had chronic indigestion.

BIRDIE   Good night, Regina.

REGINA   Good night, Birdie. (*Exits upstairs.*)

OSCAR (*starts for hall*)   Come along.

LEO (*to* ALEXANDRA)   Imagine your not wanting to go! What a little fool you are. Wish it were me. What I could do in a place like Baltimore!

ALEXANDRA (*angrily, looking away from him*)   Mind your business. I can guess the kind of things *you* could do.

LEO (*laughs*)   Oh, no, you couldn't. (*He exits.*)

REGINA (*calling from the top of the stairs*)   Come on, Alexandra.

BIRDIE (*quickly, softly*)   Zan.

ALEXANDRA   I don't understand about my going, Aunt Birdie. (*Shrugs.*) But anyway, Papa will be home again. (*Pats* BIRDIE's *arm.*) Don't worry about me. I can take care of myself. Really I can.

BIRDIE (*shakes her head, softly*)   That's not what I'm worried about. Zan —

ALEXANDRA (*comes close to her*)   What's the matter?

BIRDIE   It's about Leo —

ALEXANDRA (*whispering*)   He beat the horses. That's why we were late getting back. We had to wait until they cooled off. He always beats the horses as if —

BIRDIE (*whispering frantically, holding* ALEXANDRA's *hands*)   He's my son. My own son. But you are more to me — more to me than my own child. I love you more than anybody else —

ALEXANDRA   Don't worry about the horses. I'm sorry I told you.

BIRDIE (*her voice rising*)   *I am not worrying about the horses.* I am worrying about *you*. You are *not* going to marry Leo. I am not going to let them do that to you —

ALEXANDRA   Marry? To Leo? (*Laughs.*) I wouldn't marry, Aunt Birdie. I've never even thought about it —

BIRDIE   But they have thought about it. (*Wildly*) Zan, I couldn't stand to think about such a thing. You and —
(OSCAR *has come into the doorway on* ALEXANDRA's *speech. He is standing quietly, listening.*)

ALEXANDRA (*laughs*)   But I'm not going to marry. And I'm certainly not going to marry Leo.

BIRDIE   Don't you understand? They'll make you. They'll make you —

ALEXANDRA (*takes* BIRDIE's *hands, quietly, firmly*)   That's foolish, Aunt Birdie. I'm grown now. Nobody can make me do anything.

BIRDIE   I just couldn't stand —

OSCAR (*sharply*)   Birdie. (BIRDIE *looks up, draws quickly away from* ALEXANDRA. *She stands rigid, frightened. Quietly*) Birdie, get your hat and coat.

ADDIE (*calls from upstairs*)   Come on, baby. Your mama's waiting for you, and she ain't nobody to keep waiting.

ALEXANDRA   All right. (*Then softly, embracing* BIRDIE) Good night, Aunt Birdie. (*As she passes* OSCAR) Good night, Uncle Oscar. (BIRDIE *begins to move slowly towards the door as* ALEXANDRA *climbs the stairs.* ALEXANDRA *is almost out of view when* BIRDIE *reaches* OSCAR *in the doorway. As* BIRDIE *quickly attempts to pass him, he slaps her hard, across the face.* BIRDIE *cries out, puts her hand to her face. On the cry,* ALEXANDRA *turns, begins to run down the stairs.*) Aunt Birdie! What happened? What happened? I —

BIRDIE (*softly, without turning*) Nothing, darling. Nothing happened. (*Quickly, as if anxious to keep* ALEXANDRA *from coming close*) Now go to bed. (OSCAR *exits.*) Nothing happened. (*Turns to* ALEXANDRA, *who is holding her hand.*) I only — I only twisted my ankle. (*She goes out.* ALEXANDRA *stands on the stairs looking after her as if she were puzzled and frightened.*)

Act Two

Scene: Same as Act One. A week later, morning.

At Rise: The light comes from the open shutter of the right window; the other shutters are tightly closed. ADDIE *is standing at the window, looking out. Near the dining-room doors are brooms, mops, rags, etc. After a second,* OSCAR *comes into the entrance hall, looks in the room, shivers, decides not to take his hat and coat off, comes into the room. At the sound of the door,* ADDIE *turns to see who has come in.*

ADDIE (*without interest*) Oh, it's you, Mr. Oscar.

OSCAR What is this? It's not night. What's the matter here? (*Shivers.*) Fine thing at this time of the morning. Blinds all closed. (ADDIE *begins to open shutters.*) Where's Miss Regina? It's cold in here.

ADDIE Miss Regina ain't down yet.

OSCAR She had any word?

ADDIE (*wearily*) No, sir.

OSCAR Wouldn't you think a girl that age could get on a train at one place and have sense enough to get off at another?

ADDIE Something must have happened. If Zan say she was coming last night, she's coming last night. Unless something happened. Sure fire disgrace to let a baby like that go all that way alone to bring home a sick man without —

OSCAR You do a lot of judging around here, Addie, eh? Judging of your white folks, I mean.

ADDIE (*looks at him, sighs*) I'm tired. I been up all night watching for them.

REGINA (*speaking from the upstairs hall*) Who's downstairs, Addie? (*She appears in a dressing gown, peers down from the landing.* ADDIE *picks up broom, dustpan and brush and exits.*) Oh, it's you, Oscar. What are you doing here so early? I haven't been down yet. I'm not finished dressing.

OSCAR (*speaking up to her*) You had any word from them?

REGINA No.

OSCAR Then something certainly has happened. People don't just say they are arriving on Thursday night, and they haven't come by Friday morning.

REGINA Oh, nothing has happened. Alexandra just hasn't got sense enough to send a message.

OSCAR If nothing's happened, then why aren't they here?

REGINA You asked me that ten times last night. My, you do fret so, Oscar. Anything might have happened. They may have missed connections in Atlanta, the train may have been delayed — oh, a hundred things could have kept them.

OSCAR   Where's Ben?

REGINA   (*as she disappears upstairs*)   Where should he be? At home, probably. Really, Oscar, I don't tuck him in his bed and I don't take him out of it. Have some coffee and don't worry so much.

OSCAR   Have some coffee? There isn't any coffee. (*Looks at his watch, shakes his head. After a second* CAL *enters with a large silver tray, coffee urn, small cups, newspaper.*)   Oh, there you are. Is everything in this fancy house always late?

CAL   (*looks at him surprised*)   You ain't out shooting this morning, Mr. Oscar?

OSCAR   First day I missed since I had my head cold. First day I missed in eight years.

CAL   Yes, sir. I bet you. Simon he say you had a mighty good day yesterday morning. That's what Simon say. (*Brings* OSCAR *coffee and newspaper.*)

OSCAR   Pretty good, pretty good.

CAL   (*laughs, slyly*)   Bet you got enough bobwhite and squirrel to give every nigger in town a Jesus-party. Most of 'em ain't had no meat since the cotton picking was over. Bet they'd give anything for a little piece of that meat —

OSCAR   (*turns his head to look at* CAL)   Cal, if I catch a nigger in this town going shooting, you know what's going to happen.
(LEO *enters.*)

CAL   (*hastily*)   Yes, sir, Mr. Oscar. I didn't say nothing about nothing. It was Simon who told me and — Morning, Mr. Leo. You gentlemen having your breakfast with us here?

LEO   The boys in the bank don't know a thing. They haven't had any message.
(CAL *waits for an answer, gets none, shrugs, moves to door, exits.*)

OSCAR   (*peers at* LEO)   What you doing here, son?

LEO   You told me to find out if the boys at the bank had any message from Uncle Horace or Zan —

OSCAR   I told you if they had a message to bring it here. I told you that if they didn't have a message to stay at the bank and do your work.

LEO   Oh, I guess I misunderstood.

OSCAR   You didn't misunderstand. You just were looking for any excuse to take an hour off. (LEO *pours a cup of coffee.*) You got to stop that kind of thing. You got to start settling down. You going to be a married man one of these days.

LEO   Yes, sir.

OSCAR   You also got to stop with that woman in Mobile. (*As* LEO *is about to speak*) You're young and I haven't got no objections to outside women. That is, I haven't got no objections as long as they don't interfere with serious things. Outside women are all right in their place, but *now* isn't their place. You got to realize that.

LEO   (*nods*)   Yes, sir. I'll tell her. She'll act all right about it.

OSCAR   Also, you got to start working harder at the bank. You got to convince your Uncle Horace you going to make a fit husband for Alexandra.

LEO   What do you think has happened to them? Supposed to be here last night — (*Laughs.*) Bet you Uncle Ben's mighty worried. Seventy-five thousand dollars worried.

OSCAR   (*smiles happily*)   Ought to be worried. Damn well ought to be. First he don't answer the letters, then he don't come home — (*Giggles.*)

LEO   What will happen if Uncle Horace don't come home or don't —

OSCAR   Or don't put up the money? Oh, we'll get it from outside. Easy enough.

LEO   (*surprised*)   But *you* don't want outsiders.

OSCAR   What do I care who gets my share? I been shaved already. Serve Ben right if he had to give away some of his.

LEO   Damn shame what they did to you.

OSCAR   (*looking up the stairs*)   Don't talk so loud. Don't you worry. When I die, you'll have as much as the rest. You might have yours *and* Alexandra's. I'm not so easily licked.

LEO   I wasn't thinking of myself, Papa —

OSCAR   Well, you should be, you should be. It's every man's duty to think of himself.

LEO   You think Uncle Horace don't want to go in on this?

OSCAR   (*giggles*)   That's my hunch. He hasn't showed any signs of loving it yet.

LEO   (*laughs*)   But he hasn't listened to Aunt Regina yet, either. Oh, he'll go along. It's too good a thing. Why wouldn't he want to? He's got plenty and plenty to invest with. He don't even have to sell anything. Eighty-eight thousand worth of Union Pacific bonds sitting right in his safe-deposit box. All he's got to do is open the box.

OSCAR   (*after a pause. Looks at his watch*)   Mighty late breakfast in this fancy house. Yes, he's had those bonds for fifteen years. Bought them when they were low and just locked them up.

LEO   Yea. Just has to open the box and take them out. That's all. Easy as easy can be. (*Laughs.*) The things in that box! There's all those bonds, looking mighty fine. (OSCAR *slowly puts down his newspaper and turns to* LEO.) Then right next to them is a baby shoe of Zan's and a cheap old cameo on a string, and, *and* — nobody'd believe this — a piece of an old violin. Not even a whole violin. Just a piece of an old thing, a piece of a violin.

OSCAR   (*very softly, as if he were trying to control his voice*)   A piece of a violin! What do you think of that!

LEO   Yes sirree. A lot of other crazy things, too. A poem, I guess it is, signed with his mother's name, and two old schoolbooks with notes and — (LEO *catches* OSCAR'S *look. His voice trails off. He turns his head away.*)

OSCAR   (*very softly*)   How do you know what's in the box, son?

LEO   (*stops, draws back, frightened, realizing what he has said*)   Oh, well. Well, er. Well, one of the boys, sir. It was one of the boys at the bank. He took old Manders' keys. It was Joe Horns. He just up and took Manders' keys and, and — well, took the box out. (*Quickly.*) Then they all asked me if I wanted to see, too. So I looked a little, I guess, but then I made them close up the box quick and I told them never —

OSCAR   (*looks at him*)   Joe Horns, you say? He opened it?

LEO   Yes, sir, yes, he did. My word of honor. (*Very nervously looking away*) I suppose that don't excuse *me* for looking — (*Looking at* OSCAR) but I did make him close it up and put the keys back in Manders' drawer —

OSCAR   (*leans forward, very softly*)   Tell me the truth, Leo. I am not going to be angry with you. Did you open the box yourself?

LEO   *No, sir, I didn't.* I told you I didn't. No, I —

OSCAR (*irritated, patient*)   I am *not* going to be angry with you. (*Watching* LEO *carefully*) Sometimes a young fellow deserves credit for looking round him to see what's going on. Sometimes that's a good sign in a fellow your age. (OSCAR *rises*.) Many great men have made their fortune with their eyes. Did you open the box?

LEO (*very puzzled*)   No. I —

OSCAR (*moves to* LEO)   Did you open the box? It may have been — well, it may have been a good thing if you had.

LEO (*after a long pause*)   I opened it.

OSCAR (*quickly*)   Is that the truth? (LEO *nods*.) Does anybody else know that you opened it? Come, Leo, don't be afraid of speaking the truth to me.

LEO   No. Nobody knew. Nobody was in the bank when I did it. But —

OSCAR   Did your Uncle Horace ever know you opened it?

LEO (*shakes his head*)   He only looks in it once every six months when he cuts the coupons, and sometimes Manders even does that for him. Uncle Horace don't even have the keys. Manders keeps them for him. Imagine not looking at all that. You can bet if I had the bonds, I'd watch 'em like —

OSCAR   If you had them. (LEO *watches him*.) *If* you had them. Then you could have a share in the mill, you and me. A fine, big share, too. (*Pauses, shrugs*.) Well, a man can't be shot for wanting to see his son get on in the world, can he, boy?

LEO (*looks up, begins to understand*)   No, he can't. Natural enough. (*Laughs*.) But I haven't got the bonds and Uncle Horace has. And now he can just sit back and wait to be a millionaire.

OSCAR (*innocently*)   You think your Uncle Horace likes you well enough to lend you the bonds if he decides not to use them himself?

LEO   Papa, it must be that you haven't had your breakfast! (*Laughs loudly*.) Lend me the bonds! My God —

OSCAR (*disappointed*)   No, I suppose not. Just a fancy of mine. A loan for three months, maybe four, easy enough for us to pay it back then. Anyway, this is only April — (*Slowly counting the months on his fingers*) and if he doesn't look at them until Fall, he wouldn't even miss them out of the box.

LEO   That's it. He wouldn't even miss them. Ah, well —

OSCAR   No, sir. Wouldn't even miss them. How could he miss them if he never looks at them? (*Sighs as* LEO *stares at him*.) Well, here we are sitting around waiting for him to come home and invest his money in something he hasn't lifted his hand to get. But I can't help thinking he's acting strange. You laugh when I say he could lend you the bonds if he's not going to use them himself. But would it hurt him?

LEO (*slowly looking at* OSCAR)   No. No, it wouldn't.

OSCAR   People ought to help other people. But that's not always the way it happens. (BEN *enters, hangs his coat and hat in hall. Very carefully*) And so sometimes you got to think of yourself. (*As* LEO *stares at him,* BEN *appears in the doorway*.) Morning, Ben.

BEN (*coming in, carrying his newspaper*)   Fine sunny morning. Any news from the runaways?

REGINA (*on the staircase*)   There's no news or you would have heard it. Quite a convention so early in the morning, aren't you all? (*Goes to coffee urn*.)

OSCAR You rising mighty late these days. Is that the way they do things in Chicago society?

BEN (*looking at his paper*) Old Carter died up in Senateville. Eighty-one is a good time for us all, eh? What do you think has really happened to Horace, Regina?

REGINA Nothing.

BEN (*too casually*) You don't think maybe he never started from Baltimore and never intends to start?

REGINA (*irritated*) Of course they've started. Didn't I have a letter from Alexandra? What is so strange about people arriving late? He has that cousin in Savannah he's so fond of. He may have stopped to see him. They'll be along today some time, very flattered that you and Oscar are so worried about them. ı

BEN I'm a natural worrier. Especially when I am getting ready to close a business deal and one of my partners remains silent *and* invisible.

REGINA (*laughs*) Oh, is that it? I thought you were worried about Horace's health.

OSCAR Oh, that too. Who could help but worry? I'm worried. This is the first day I haven't shot since my head cold.

REGINA (*starts towards dining room*) Then you haven't had your breakfast. Come along. (OSCAR *and* LEO *follow her.*)

BEN Regina. (*She turns at dining-room door.*) That cousin of Horace's has been dead for years and, in any case, the train does not go through Savannah.

REGINA (*laughs, continues into dining room, seats herself*) Did he die? You're always remembering about people dying. (BEN *rises.*) Now I intend to eat my breakfast in peace, and read my newspaper.

BEN (*goes towards dining room as he talks*) This is second breakfast for me. My first was bad. Celia ain't the cook she used to be. Too old to have taste any more. If she hadn't belonged to Mama, I'd send her off to the country. (OSCAR *and* LEO *start to eat.* BEN *seats himself.*)

LEO Uncle Horace will have some tales to tell, I bet. Baltimore is a lively town.

REGINA (*to* CAL) The grits isn't hot enough. Take it back.

CAL Oh, yes'm. (*Calling into kitchen as he exits*) Grits didn't hold the heat. Grits didn't hold the heat.

LEO When I was at school three of the boys and myself took a train once and went over to Baltimore. It was so big we thought we were in Europe. I was just a kid then —

REGINA I find it very pleasant (ADDIE *enters*) to have breakfast alone. I hate chattering before I've had something hot. (CAL *closes the dining-room doors.*) Do be still, Leo.

(ADDIE *comes into the room, begins gathering up the cups, carries them to the large tray. Outside there are the sounds of voices. Quickly* ADDIE *runs into the hall. A few seconds later she appears again in the doorway, her arm around the shoulders of* HORACE GIDDENS, *supporting him.* HORACE *is a tall man of about forty-five. He has been good looking, but now his face is tired and ill. He walks stiffly, as if it were an enormous effort, and carefully, as if he were unsure of his balance.* ADDIE *takes off his overcoat and hangs it on the hall tree. She then helps him to a chair.*)

HORACE   How are you, Addie? How have you been?

ADDIE   I'm all right, Mr. Horace. I've just been worried about you.

(ALEXANDRA *enters. She is flushed and excited, her hat awry, her face dirty. Her arms are full of packages, but she comes quickly to* ADDIE.)

ALEXANDRA   Now don't tell me how worried you were. We couldn't help it and there was no way to send a message.

ADDIE   (*begins to take packages from* ALEXANDRA)   Yes sir, I was mighty worried.

ALEXANDRA   We had to stop in Mobile over night. Papa — (*looks at him*) Papa didn't feel well. The trip was too much for him, and I made him stop and rest — (*As* ADDIE *takes the last package*) No, don't take that. That's father's medicine. I'll hold it. It mustn't break. Now, about the stuff outside. Papa must have his wheel chair. I'll get that and the valises —

ADDIE   (*very happy, holding* ALEXANDRA'S *arms*)   Since when you got to carry your own valises? Since when I ain't old enough to hold a bottle of medicine? (HORACE *coughs*.) You feel all right, Mr. Horace?

HORACE   (*nods*)   Glad to be sitting down.

ALEXANDRA   (*opening package of medicine*)   He doesn't feel all right. (ADDIE *looks at her, then at* HORACE.) He just says that. The trip was very hard on him, and now he must go right to bed.

ADDIE   (*looking at him carefully*)   Them fancy doctors, they give you help?

HORACE   They did their best.

ALEXANDRA   (*has become conscious of the voices in the dining room*)   I bet Mama was worried. I better tell her we're here now. (*She starts for door*.)

HORACE   Zan. (*She stops*.) Not for a minute, dear.

ALEXANDRA   Oh, Papa, you feel bad again. I knew you did. Do you want your medicine?

HORACE   No, I don't feel that way. I'm just tired, darling. Let me rest a little.

ALEXANDRA   Yes, but Mama will be mad if I don't tell her we're here.

ADDIE   They're all in there eating breakfast.

ALEXANDRA   Oh, are they all here? Why do they *always* have to be here? I was hoping Papa wouldn't have to see anybody, that it would be nice for him and quiet.

ADDIE   Then let your papa rest for a minute.

HORACE   Addie, I bet your coffee's as good as ever. They don't have such good coffee up North. (*Looks at the urn*.) Is it as good, Addie? (ADDIE *starts for coffee urn*.)

ALEXANDRA   No. Dr. Reeves said not much coffee. Just now and then. I'm the nurse now, Addie.

ADDIE   You'd be a better one if you didn't look so dirty. Now go and take a bath, Miss Grown-up. Change your linens, get out a fresh dress and give your hair a good brushing — go on —

ALEXANDRA   Will you be all right, Papa?

ADDIE   Go on.

ALEXANDRA   (*on stairs, talks as she goes up*)   The pills Papa must take once every four hours. And the bottle only when — only if he feels very bad. Now don't move until I come back and don't talk much and remember about his medicine, Addie —

ADDIE   Ring for Belle and have her help you and then I'll make you a fresh breakfast.

ALEXANDRA (*as she disappears*) How's Aunt Birdie? Is she here?

ADDIE It ain't right for you to have coffee? It will hurt you?

HORACE (*slowly*) Nothing can make much difference now. Get me a cup, Addie. (*She looks at him, crosses to urn, pours a cup.*) Funny. They can't make coffee up North. (ADDIE *brings him a cup.*) They don't like red pepper, either. (*He takes the cup and gulps it greedily.*) God, that's good. You remember how I used to drink it? Ten, twelve cups a day. So strong it had to stain the cup. (*Then slowly*) Addie, before I see anybody else, I want to know why Zan came to fetch me home. She's tried to tell me, but she doesn't seem to know herself.

ADDIE (*turns away*) I don't know. All I know is big things are going on. Everybody going to be high-tone rich. Big rich. You too. All because smoke's going to start out of a building that ain't even up yet.

HORACE I've heard about it.

ADDIE And, er — (*Hesitates — steps to him.*) And — well, Zan, she going to marry Mr. Leo in a little while.

HORACE (*looks at her, then very slowly*) What are you talking about?

ADDIE That's right. That's the talk, God help us.

HORACE (*angrily*) *What's* the talk?

ADDIE I'm telling you. There's going to be a wedding — (*Angrily turns away.*) Over my dead body there is.

HORACE (*after a second, quietly*) Go and tell them I'm home.

ADDIE (*hesitates*) Now you ain't to get excited. You're to be in your bed —

HORACE Go on, Addie. Go and say I'm back. (ADDIE *opens dining-room doors. He rises with difficulty, stands stiff, as if he were in pain, facing the dining room.*)

ADDIE Miss Regina. They're home. They got here —

REGINA Horace! (REGINA *quickly rises, runs into the room. Warmly*) Horace! you've finally arrived. (*As she kisses him, the others come forward, all talking together.*)

BEN (*in doorway, carrying a napkin*) Well, sir, you had us all mighty worried. (*He steps forward. They shake hands.* ADDIE *exits.*)

OSCAR You're a sight for sore eyes.

HORACE Hello, Ben.

(LEO *enters, eating a biscuit.*)

OSCAR And how you feel? Tip-top, I bet, because that's the way you're looking.

HORACE (*coldly, irritated with* OSCAR'S *lie*) Hello, Oscar. Hello, Leo, how are you?

LEO (*shaking hands*) I'm fine, sir. But a lot better now that you're back.

REGINA Now sit down. What did happen to you and where's Alexandra? I am so excited about seeing you that I almost forgot about her.

HORACE I didn't feel good, a little weak, I guess, and we stopped over night to rest. Zan's upstairs washing off the train dirt.

REGINA Oh, I am so sorry the trip was hard on you. I didn't think that —

HORACE Well, it's just as if I had never been away. All of you here —

BEN Waiting to welcome you home.

BIRDIE *bursts in. She is wearing a flannel kimono and her face is flushed and excited.*)

BIRDIE (*runs to him, kisses him*) Horace!

HORACE (*warmly pressing her arm*) I was just wondering where you were, Birdie.

BIRDIE (*excited*) Oh, I would have been here. I didn't know you were back until Simon said he saw the buggy. (*She draws back to look at him. Her face sobers.*) Oh, you don't look well, Horace. No, you don't.

REGINA (*laughs*) Birdie, what a thing to say —

HORACE (*looking at* OSCAR) Oscar thinks I look very well.

OSCAR (*annoyed. Turns on* LEO) Don't stand there holding that biscuit in your hand.

LEO Oh, well. I'll just finish my breakfast, Uncle Horace, and then I'll give you all the news about the bank — (*He exits into the dining room.*)

OSCAR And what is that costume you have on?

BIRDIE (*looking at* HORACE) Now that you're home, you'll feel better. Plenty of good rest and we'll take such fine care of you. (*Stops.*) But where is Zan? I missed her so much.

OSCAR I asked you what is that strange costume you're parading around in?

BIRDIE (*nervously, backing towards stairs*) Me? Oh! It's my wrapper. I was so excited about Horace I just rushed out of the house —

OSCAR Did you come across the square dressed that way? My dear Birdie, I —

HORACE (*to* REGINA, *wearily*) Yes, it's just like old times.

REGINA (*quickly to* OSCAR) Now, no fights. This is a holiday.

BIRDIE (*runs quickly up the stairs*) Zan! Zannie!

OSCAR Birdie! (*She stops.*)

BIRDIE Oh. Tell Zan I'll be back in a little while. (*Whispers.*) Sorry, Oscar. (*Exits.*)

REGINA (*to* OSCAR *and* BEN) Why don't you go finish your breakfast and let Horace rest for a minute?

BEN (*crossing to dining room with* OSCAR) Never leave a meal unfinished. There are too many poor people who need the food. Mighty glad to see you home, Horace. Fine to have you back. Fine to have you back.

OSCAR (*to* LEO *as* BEN *closes dining-room doors*) Your mother has gone crazy. Running around the streets like a woman —

(*The moment* REGINA *and* HORACE *are alone, they become awkward and self-conscious.*)

REGINA (*laughs awkwardly*) Well. Here we are. It's been a long time. (HOR-ACE *smiles.*) Five months. You know, Horace, I wanted to come and be with you in the hospital, but I didn't know where my duty was. Here, or with you. But you know how much I *wanted* to come.

HORACE That's kind of you, Regina. There was no need to come.

REGINA Oh, but there was. Five months lying there all by yourself, no kin-folks, no friends. Don't try to tell me you didn't have a bad time of it.

HORACE I didn't have a bad time. (*As she shakes her head, he becomes insistent.*) No, I didn't, Regina. Oh, at first when I — when I heard the news about myself — but after I got used to that, I liked it there.

REGINA You *liked* it? (*Coldly*) Isn't that strange. You liked it so well you didn't want to come home?

HORACE That's not the way to put it. (*Then, kindly, as he sees her turn her head away*) But there I was and I got kind of used to it, kind of to like ly-ing there and thinking. (*Smiles.*) I never had much time to think before. And time's become valuable to me.

REGINA It sounds almost like a holiday.

HORACE (*laughs*) It was, sort of. The first holiday I've had since I was a little kid.

REGINA And here I was thinking you were in pain and —

HORACE (*quietly*) I was in pain.

REGINA And instead you were having a holiday! A holiday of thinking. Couldn't you have done that here?

HORACE I wanted to do it before I came here. I was thinking about us.

REGINA About us? About you and me? Thinking about you and me after all these years. (*Unpleasantly*) You shall tell me everything you thought — some day.

HORACE (*there is silence for a minute*) Regina. (*She turns to him.*) Why did you send Zan to Baltimore?

REGINA Why? Because I wanted you home. You can't make anything suspicious out of that, can you?

HORACE I didn't mean to make anything suspicious about it. (*Hesitantly, taking her hand*) Zan said you wanted me to come home. I was so pleased at that and touched, it made me feel good.

REGINA (*taking away her hand, turns*) Touched that I should want you home?

HORACE (*sighs*) I'm saying all the wrong things as usual. Let's try to get along better. There isn't so much more time. Regina, what's all this crazy talk I've been hearing about Zan and Leo? Zan and Leo marrying?

REGINA (*turning to him, sharply*) Who gossips so much around here?

HORACE (*shocked*) Regina!

REGINA (*annoyed, anxious to quiet him*) It's some foolishness that Oscar thought up. I'll explain later. I have no intention of allowing any such arrangement. It was simply a way of keeping Oscar quiet in all this business I've been writing you about —

HORACE (*carefully*) What has Zan to do with any business of Oscar's? Whatever it is, you had better put it out of Oscar's head immediately. You know what I think of Leo.

REGINA But there's no need to talk about it now.

HORACE There is no need to talk about it ever. Not as long as I live. (HORACE *stops, slowly turns to look at her.*) As long as I live. I've been in a hospital for five months. Yet since I've been here you have not once asked me about — about my health. (*Then gently*) Well, I suppose they've written you. I can't live very long.

REGINA (*coldly*) I've never understood why people have to talk about this kind of thing.

HORACE (*there is a silence. Then he looks up at her, his face cold*) You misunderstand. I don't intend to gossip about my sickness. I thought it was only fair to tell you. I was not asking for your sympathy.

REGINA (*sharply, turns to him*) What do the doctors think caused your bad heart?

HORACE What do you mean?

REGINA They didn't think it possible, did they, that your fancy women may have —

HORACE (*smiles unpleasantly*) Caused my heart to be bad? I don't think that's the best scientific theory. You don't catch heart trouble in bed.

REGINA (*angrily*) I didn't think you did. I only thought you might catch a bad conscience — in bed, as you say.

HORACE I didn't tell them about my bad conscience. Or about my fancy women. Nor did I tell them that my wife has not wanted me in bed with her for — (*sharply*) how long is it, Regina? (REGINA *turns to him.*) Ten years? Did you bring me home for this, to make me feel guilty again? That means you want something. But you'll not make me feel guilty any more. My "thinking" has made a difference.

REGINA   I see that it has. (*She looks towards dining-room door. Then comes to him, her manner warm and friendly.*) It's foolish for us to fight this way. I didn't mean to be unpleasant. I was stupid.

HORACE (*wearily*)   God knows I didn't either. I came home wanting so much not to fight, and then all of a sudden there we were. I got hurt and —

REGINA (*hastily*)   It's all my fault. I didn't ask about — about your illness because I didn't want to remind you of it. Anyway I never believe doctors when they talk about — (*brightly*) when they talk like that.

HORACE (*not looking at her*)   Well, we'll try our best with each other. (*He rises.*)

REGINA (*quickly*)   I'll try. Honestly, I will. Horace, Horace, I know you're tired but, but — couldn't you stay down here a few minutes longer? I want Ben to tell you something.

HORACE   Tomorrow.

REGINA   I'd like to now. It's very important to me. It's very important to all of us. (*Gaily, as she moves toward dining room*) Important to your beloved daughter. She'll be a very great heiress —

HORACE   Will she? That's nice.

REGINA (*opens doors*)   Ben, are you finished breakfast?

HORACE   Is this the mill business I've had so many letters about?

REGINA (*to BEN*)   Horace would like to talk to you now.

HORACE   Horace would not like to talk to you now. I am very tired, Regina —

REGINA (*comes to him*)   Please. You've said we'll try our best with each other. I'll try. Really, I will. Please do this for me now. You will see what I've done while you've been away. How I watched your interests. (*Laughs gaily.*) And I've done very well too. But things can't be delayed any longer. Everything must be settled this week — (HORACE *sits down.* BEN *enters.* OSCAR *has stayed in the dining room, his head turned to watch them.* LEO *is pretending to read the newspaper.*) Now you must tell Horace all about it. Only be quick because he is very tired and must go to bed. (HORACE *is looking up at her. His face hardens as she speaks.*) But I think your news will be better for him than all the medicine in the world.

BEN (*looking at HORACE*)   It could wait. Horace may not feel like talking today.

REGINA   What an old faker you are! You know it can't wait. You know it must be finished this week. You've been just as anxious for Horace to get here as I've been.

BEN (*very jovial*)   I suppose I have been. And why not? Horace has done Hubbard Sons many a good turn. Why shouldn't I be anxious to help him now?

REGINA (*laughs*)   Help him! Help him when you need him, that's what you mean.

BEN   What a woman you married, Horace. (*Laughs awkwardly when HORACE does not answer.*) Well, then I'll make it quick. You know what I've been telling you for years. How I've always said that every one of us little

Southern business men had great things — (*extends his arm*) — right beyond our finger tips. It's been my dream: my dream to make those fingers grow longer. I'm a lucky man, Horace, a lucky man. To dream and to live to get what you've dreamed of. That's *my* idea of a lucky man. (*Looks at his fingers as his arm drops slowly.*) For thirty years I've cried bring the cotton mills to the cotton. (HORACE *opens medicine bottle*) Well, finally I got up nerve to go to Marshall Company in Chicago.

HORACE   I know all this. (*He takes the medicine.* REGINA *rises, steps to him.*)

BEN   Can I get you something?

HORACE   Some water, please.

REGINA (*turns quickly*)   Oh, I'm sorry. Let me. (*Brings him a glass of water. He drinks as they wait in silence.*) You feel all right now?

HORACE   Yes. You wrote me. I know all that.

(OSCAR *enters from dining room.*)

REGINA (*triumphantly*)   But you don't know that in the last few days Ben has agreed to give us — you, I mean — a much larger share.

HORACE   Really? That's very generous of him.

BEN (*laughs*)   It wasn't so generous of me. It was smart of Regina.

REGINA (*as if she were signaling* HORACE)   I explained to Ben that perhaps you hadn't answered his letters because you didn't think he was offering you enough, and that the time was getting short and you could guess how much he needed you —

HORACE (*smiles at her, nods*)   And I could guess that he wants to keep control in the family?

REGINA (*to* BEN, *triumphantly*)   Exactly. (*To* HORACE) So I did a little bargaining for you and convinced my brothers they weren't the only Hubbards who had a business sense.

HORACE   Did you have to convince them of that? How little people know about each other! (*Laughs.*) But you'll know better about Regina next time, eh, Ben? (BEN, REGINA, HORACE *laugh together.* OSCAR's *face is angry.*) Now let's see. We're getting a bigger share. (*Looking at* OSCAR) Who's getting less?

BEN   Oscar.

HORACE   Well, Oscar, you've grown very unselfish. What's happened to you? (LEO *enters from dining room.*)

BEN (*quickly, before* OSCAR *can answer*)   Oscar doesn't mind. Not worth fighting about now, eh, Oscar?

OSCAR (*angrily*)   I'll get mine in the end. You can be sure of that. I've got my son's future to think about.

HORACE (*sharply*)   Leo? Oh, I see. (*Puts his head back, laughs.* REGINA *looks at him nervously.*) I am beginning to see. Everybody will get theirs.

BEN   I knew you'd see it. Seventy-five thousand, and that seventy-five thousand will make you a million.

REGINA (*steps to table, leaning forward*)   It will, Horace, it will.

HORACE   I believe you. (*After a second*) Now I can understand Oscar's self-sacrifice, but what did you have to promise Marshall Company besides the money you're putting up?

BEN   They wouldn't take promises. They wanted guarantees.

HORACE   Of what?

BEN (*nods*)   Water power. Free and plenty of it.

HORACE   You got them that, of course.

BEN   Cheap. You'd think the Governor of a great state would make his price a little higher. From pride, you know. (HORACE *smiles.* BEN *smiles.*) Cheap wages. "What do you mean by cheap wages?" I say to Marshall. "Less than Massachusetts," he says to me, "and that averages eight a week." "Eight a week! By God," I tell him, "*I'd* work for eight a week myself." Why, there ain't a mountain white or a town nigger but wouldn't give his right arm for three silver dollars every week, eh, Horace?

HORACE   Sure. And they'll take less than that when you get around to playing them off against each other. You can save a little money that way, Ben. (*Angrily*) And make them hate each other just a little more than they do now.

REGINA   What's all this about?

BEN   (*laughs*)   There'll be no trouble from anybody, white or black. Marshall said that to me. "What about strikes? That's all we've had in Massachusetts for the last three years." I say to him, "What's a strike? I never heard of one. Come South, Marshall. We got good folks and we don't stand for any fancy fooling."

HORACE   You're right. (*Slowly*) Well, it looks like you made a good deal for yourselves, and for Marshall, too. (*To* BEN) Your father used to say he made the thousands and you boys would make the millions. I think he was right. (*Rises.*)

REGINA   (*They are all looking at* HORACE. *She laughs nervously*)   Millions for *us,* too.

HORACE   Us? You and me? I don't think so. We've got enough money, Regina. We'll just sit by and watch the boys grow rich. (*They watch* HORACE *tensely as he begins to move towards the staircase. He passes* LEO, *looks at him for a second.*) How's everything at the bank, Leo?

LEO   Fine, sir. Everything is fine.

HORACE   How are all the ladies in Mobile? (HORACE *turns to* REGINA, *sharply*) Whatever made you think I'd let Zan marry —

REGINA   Do you mean that you are turning this down? Is it possible that's what you mean?

BEN   No, that's not what he means. Turning down a fortune. Horace is tired. He'd rather talk about it tomorrow —

REGINA   We can't keep putting it off this way. Oscar must be in Chicago by the end of the week with the money and contracts.

OSCAR   (*giggles, pleased*)   Yes, sir. Got to be there end of the week. No sense going without the money.

REGINA   (*tensely*)   I've waited long enough for your answer. I'm not going to wait any longer.

HORACE   (*very deliberately*)   I'm very tired now, Regina.

BEN   (*hastily*)   Now, Horace probably has his reasons. Things he'd like explained. Tomorrow will do. I can —

REGINA   (*turns to* BEN, *sharply*)   I want to know his reasons now! (*Turns back to* HORACE.)

HORACE   (*as he climbs the steps*)   I don't know them all myself. Let's leave it at that.

REGINA   We shall not leave it at that! We have waited for you here like children. Waited for you to come home.

HORACE   So that you could invest my money. So this is why you wanted me home? Well, I had hoped — (*Quietly*) If you are disappointed, Regina, I'm sorry. But I must do what I think best. We'll talk about it another day.

REGINA   We'll talk about it now. Just you and me.

HORACE   (*looks down at her. His voice is tense*)   Please, Regina. It's been a hard trip. I don't feel well. Please leave me alone now.

REGINA   (*quietly*)   I want to talk to you, Horace. I'm coming up. (*He looks at her for a minute, then moves on again out of sight. She begins to climb the stairs.*)

BEN   (*softly.* REGINA *turns to him as he speaks*)   Sometimes it is better to wait for the sun to rise again. (*She does not answer.*)   And sometimes, as our mother used to tell you, (REGINA *starts up stairs.*) it's unwise for a good-looking woman to frown. (BEN *rises, moves towards stairs.*)   Softness and a smile do more to the heart of men — (*She disappears.* BEN *stands looking up the stairs. There is a long silence. Then, suddenly,* OSCAR *giggles.*)

OSCAR   Let us hope she'll change his mind. Let us hope. (*After a second* BEN *crosses to table, picks up his newspaper.* OSCAR *looks at* BEN. *The silence makes* LEO *uncomfortable.*)

LEO   The paper says twenty-seven cases of yellow fever in New Orleans. Guess the flood-waters caused it. (*Nobody pays attention.*)   Thought they were building the levees high enough. Like the niggers always say: a man born of woman can't build nothing high enough for the Mississippi. (*Gets no answer. Gives an embarrassed laugh.*)
(*Upstairs there is the sound of voices. The voices are not loud, but* BEN, OSCAR, LEO *become conscious of them.* LEO *crosses to landing, looks up, listens.*)

OSCAR   (*pointing up*)   Now just suppose she don't change his mind? Just suppose he keeps on refusing?

BEN   (*without conviction*)   He's tired. It was a mistake to talk to him today. He's a sick man, but he isn't a crazy one.

OSCAR   (*giggles*)   But just suppose he is crazy. What then?

BEN   (*puts down his paper, peers at* OSCAR)   Then we'll go outside for the money. There's plenty who would give it.

OSCAR   And plenty who will want a lot for what they give. The ones who are rich enough to give will be smart enough to want. That means we'd be working for them, don't it, Ben?

BEN   You don't have to tell me the things I told you six months ago.

OSCAR   Oh, you're right not to worry. She'll change his mind. She always has. (*There is a silence. Suddenly* REGINA'S *voice becomes louder and sharper. All of them begin to listen now. Slowly* BEN *rises, goes to listen by the staircase.* OSCAR, *watching him, smiles. As they listen* REGINA'S *voice becomes very loud.* HORACE'S *voice is no longer heard.*)   Maybe. But I don't believe it. I never did believe he was going in with us.

BEN   (*turning on him*)   What the hell do you expect me to do?

OSCAR   (*mildly*)   Nothing. You done your almighty best. Nobody could blame you if the whole thing just dripped away right through our fingers. You can't do a thing. But there may be something I could do for us. (OSCAR *rises.*)   Or, I might better say, Leo could do for us. (BEN *stops, turns, looks at* OSCAR. LEO *is staring at* OSCAR.)   Ain't that true, son? Ain't it true, you might be able to help your own kinfolks?

LEO (*nervously taking a step to him*)   Papa, I —

BEN (*slowly*)   How would he help us, Oscar?

OSCAR   Leo's got a friend. Leo's friend owns eighty-eight thousand dollars in Union Pacific bonds. (BEN *turns to look at* LEO.) Leo's friend don't look at the bonds much — not for five or six months at a time.

BEN (*after a pause*)   Union Pacific. Uh, huh. Let me understand. Leo's friend would — would lend him these bonds and he —

OSCAR (*nods*)   Would be kind enough to lend them to us.

BEN   Leo.

LEO (*excited, comes to him*)   Yes, sir?

BEN   When would your friend be wanting the bonds back?

LEO (*very nervous*)   I don't know. I — well, I —

OSCAR (*sharply. Steps to him*)   You told me he won't look at them until Fall —

LEO   Oh, that's right. But I — not till Fall. Uncle Horace never —

BEN (*sharply*)   Be still.

OSCAR (*smiles at* LEO)   Your uncle doesn't wish to know your friend's name.

LEO (*starts to laugh*)   That's a good one. Not know his name —

OSCAR   Shut up, Leo! (LEO *turns away slowly, moves to table.* BEN *turns to* OSCAR.) He won't look at them again until September. That gives us five months. Leo will return the bonds in three months. And we'll have no trouble raising the money once the mills are going up. Will Marshall accept bonds?

(BEN *stops to listen to sudden sharp voices from above. The voices are now very angry and very loud.*)

BEN (*smiling*)   Why not? Why not? (*Laughs.*) Good. We are lucky. We'll take the loan from Leo's friend — I think he will make a safer partner than our sister. (*Nods towards stairs. Turns to* LEO.) How soon can you get them?

LEO   Today. Right now. They're in the safe-deposit box and —

BEN (*sharply*)   I don't want to know where they are.

OSCAR (*laughs*)   We will keep it secret from you. (*Pats* BEN's *arm.*)

BEN (*smiles*)   Good. Draw a check for our part. You can take the night train for Chicago. Well, Oscar (*holds out his hand*), good luck to us.

OSCAR   Leo will be taken care of?

LEO   I'm entitled to Uncle Horace's share. I'd enjoy being a partner —

BEN (*turns to stare at him*)   You would? You can go to hell, you little — (*Starts towards* LEO.)

OSCAR (*nervously*)   Now, now. He didn't mean that. I only want to be sure he'll get something out of all this.

BEN   Of course. We'll take care of him. We won't have any trouble about that. I'll see you at the store.

OSCAR (*nods*)   That's settled then. Come on, son. (*Starts for door.*)

LEO (*puts out his hand*)   I didn't mean just that. I was only going to say what a great day this was for me and — (BEN *ignores his hand.*)

BEN   Go on.

(LEO *looks at him, turns, follows* OSCAR *out.* BEN *stands where he is, thinking. Again the voices upstairs can be heard.* REGINA's *voice is high and furious.* BEN *looks up, smiles, winces at the noise.*)

ALEXANDRA (*upstairs*)   Mama — Mama — don't . . . (*The noise of running footsteps is heard and* ALEXANDRA *comes running down the steps, speaking as she comes.*) Uncle Ben! Uncle Ben! Please go up. Please make Mama stop. Uncle Ben, he's sick, he's so sick. How can Mama talk to him like that — please, make her stop. She'll —

BEN   Alexandra, you have a tender heart.

ALEXANDRA (*crying*)   Go on up, Uncle Ben, please —
    (*Suddenly the voices stop. A second later there is the sound of a door being slammed.*)

BEN   Now you see. Everything is over. Don't worry. (*He starts for the door.*) Alexandra, I want you to tell your mother how sorry I am that I had to leave. And don't worry so, my dear. Married folk frequently raise their voices, unfortunately. (*He starts to put on his hat and coat as* REGINA *appears on the stairs.*)

ALEXANDRA (*furiously*)   How can you treat Papa like this? He's sick. He's very sick. Don't you know that? I won't let you.

REGINA   Mind your business, Alexandra. (*To* BEN — *her voice is cold and calm*) How much longer can you wait for the money?

BEN (*putting on his coat*)   He has refused? My, that's too bad.

REGINA   He will change his mind. I'll find a way to make him. What's the longest you can wait now?

BEN   I could wait until next week. But I can't wait until next week. (*He giggles, pleased at the joke.*) I could but I can't. Could and can't. Well, I must go now. I'm very late —

REGINA (*coming downstairs towards him*)   You're not going. I want to talk to you.

BEN   I was about to give Alexandra a message for you. I wanted to tell you that Oscar is going to Chicago tonight, so we can't be here for our usual Friday supper.

REGINA (*tensely*)   Oscar is going to Chi — (*Softly*) What do you mean?

BEN   Just that. Everything is settled. He's going on to deliver to Marshall —

REGINA (*taking a step to him*)   I demand to know what — You are lying. You are trying to scare me. *You haven't got the money.* How could you have it? You can't have — (BEN *laughs.*) You will wait until I —
    (HORACE *comes into view on the landing.*)

BEN   You are getting out of hand. Since when do I take orders from you?

REGINA   Wait, you — (BEN *stops.*) How *can* he go to Chicago? Did a ghost arrive with the money? (BEN *starts for the hall.*) I don't believe you. Come back here. (REGINA *starts after him.*) Come back here, you — (*The door slams. She stops in the doorway, staring, her fists clenched. After a pause she turns slowly.*)

HORACE (*very quietly*)   It's a great day when you and Ben cross swords. I've been waiting for it for years.

ALEXANDRA   Papa, Papa, please go back! You will —

HORACE   And so they don't need you, and so you will not have your millions, after all.

REGINA (*turns slowly*)   You hate to see anybody live now, don't you? You hate to think that I'm going to be alive and have what I want.

HORACE   I should have known you'd think that was the reason.

REGINA   Because you're going to die and you know you're going to die.

ALEXANDRA (*shrilly*)   Mama! Don't — Don't listen, Papa. Just don't listen. Go away —

HORACE Not to keep you from getting what you want. Not even partly that. (*Holding to the rail*) I'm sick of you, sick of this house, sick of my life here. I'm sick of your brothers and their dirty tricks to make a dime. There must be better ways of getting rich than cheating niggers on a pound of bacon. Why should I give you the money? (*Very angrily*) To pound the bones of this town to make dividends for you to spend? You wreck the town, you and your brothers, *you* wreck the town and live on it. Not me. Maybe it's easy for the dying to be honest. But it's not my fault I'm dying. (ADDIE *enters, stands at door quietly.*) I'll do no more harm now. I've done enough. I'll die my own way. And I'll do it without making the world any worse. I leave that to you.

REGINA (*looks up at him slowly, calmly*) I hope you die. I hope you die soon. (*Smiles*) I'll be waiting for you to die.

ALEXANDRA (*shrieking*) Papa! Don't — Don't listen — Don't —

ADDIE Come here, Zan. Come out of this room.

(ALEXANDRA *runs quickly to* ADDIE, *who holds her.* HORACE *turns slowly and starts upstairs.*)

Act Three

Scene: Same as Act One. Two weeks later. It is late afternoon and it is raining.

At Rise: HORACE *is sitting near the window in a wheel chair. On the table next to him is a safe-deposit box, and a small bottle of medicine.* BIRDIE *and* ALEXANDRA *are playing the piano. On a chair is a large sewing basket.*

BIRDIE (*counting for* ALEXANDRA) One and two and three and four. One and two and three and four. (*Nods — turns to* HORACE.) We once played together, Horace. Remember?

HORACE (*has been looking out of the window*) What, Birdie?

BIRDIE We played together. You and me.

ALEXANDRA *Papa* used to play?

BIRDIE Indeed he did. (ADDIE *appears at the door in a large kitchen apron. She is wiping her hands on a towel.*) He played the fiddle and very well, too.

ALEXANDRA (*turns to smile at* HORACE) I never knew —

ADDIE Where's your mama?

ALEXANDRA Gone to Miss Safronia's to fit her dresses.

(ADDIE *nods, starts to exit.*)

HORACE Addie.

ADDIE Yes, Mr. Horace.

HORACE (*speaks as if he had made a sudden decision*) Tell Cal to get on his things. I want him to go an errand.

(ADDIE *nods, exits.* HORACE *moves nervously in his chair, looks out of the window.*)

ALEXANDRA (*who has been watching him*) It's too bad it's been raining all day, Papa. But you can go out in the yard tomorrow. Don't be restless.

HORACE I'm not restless, darling.

BIRDIE I remember so well the time we played together, your papa and me. It was the first time Oscar brought me here to supper. I had never seen all the

Hubbards together before, and you know what a ninny I am and how shy. (*Turns to look at* HORACE.) You said you could play the fiddle and you'd be much obliged if I'd play with you. I was obliged to *you,* all right, all right. (*Laughs when he does not answer her.*) Horace, you haven't heard a word I've said.

HORACE Birdie, when did Oscar get back from Chicago?

BIRDIE Yesterday. Hasn't he been here yet?

ALEXANDRA (*stops playing*) No. Neither has Uncle Ben since — since that day.

BIRDIE Oh, I didn't know it was *that* bad. Oscar never tells me anything —

HORACE (*smiles, nods*) The Hubbards have had their great quarrel. I knew it would come some day. (*Laughs.*) It came.

ALEXANDRA It came. It certainly came all right.

BIRDIE (*amazed*) But Oscar was in such a good humor when he got home, I didn't —

HORACE Yes, I can understand that.

(ADDIE *enters carrying a large tray with glasses, a carafe of elderberry wine and a plate of cookies, which she puts on the table.*)

ALEXANDRA Addie! A party! What for?

ADDIE Nothing for. I had the fresh butter, so I made the cakes, and a little elderberry does the stomach good in the rain.

BIRDIE Isn't this nice! A party just for us. Let's play party music, Zan.

(ALEXANDRA *begins to play a gay piece.*)

ADDIE (*to* HORACE, *wheeling his chair to center*) Come over here, Mr. Horace, and don't be thinking so much. A glass of elderberry will do more good. (ALEXANDRA *reaches for a cake.* BIRDIE *pours herself a glass of wine.*)

ALEXANDRA Good cakes, Addie. It's nice here. Just us. Be nice if it could always be this way.

BIRDIE (*nods happily*) Quiet and restful.

ADDIE Well, it won't be that way long. Little while now, even sitting here, you'll hear the red bricks going into place. The next day the smoke'll be pushing out the chimneys and by church time that Sunday every human born of woman will be living on chicken. That's how Mr. Ben's been telling the story.

HORACE (*looks at her*) They believe it that way?

ADDIE Believe it? They use to believing what Mr. Ben orders. There ain't been so much talk around here since Sherman's army didn't come near.

HORACE (*softly*) They are fools.

ADDIE (*nods, sits down with the sewing basket*) You ain't born in the South unless you're a fool.

BIRDIE (*has drunk another glass of wine*) But we didn't play together after that night. Oscar said he didn't like me to play on the piano. (*Turns to* ALEXANDRA.) You know what he said that night?

ALEXANDRA Who?

BIRDIE Oscar. He said that music made him nervous. He said he just sat and waited for the next note. (ALEXANDRA *laughs.*) He wasn't poking fun. He meant it. Ah, well — (*She finishes her glass, shakes her head.* HORACE *looks at her, smiles.*) Your papa don't like to admit it, but he's been mighty kind to me all these years. (*Running the back of her hand along his sleeve.*) Often he'd step in when somebody said something and once — (*She stops, turns away, her face still.*) Once he stopped Oscar from — (*She stops, turns. Quickly*) I'm sorry I said that. Why, here I am so happy and yet I think about bad things. (*Laughs nervously.*) That's not right, now, is it? (*She pours a drink.* CAL *appears in the door. He has on an old coat and is carrying a torn umbrella.*)

ALEXANDRA   Have a cake, Cal.

CAL (*comes in, takes a cake*)   Yes'm. You want me, Mr. Horace?

HORACE   What time is it, Cal?

CAL   Bout ten minutes before it's five.

HORACE   All right. Now you walk yourself down to the bank.

CAL   It'll be closed. Nobody'll be there but Mr. Manders, Mr. Joe Horns, Mr. Leo —

HORACE   Go in the back way. They'll be at the table, going over the day's business. (*Points to the deposit box.*) See that box?

CAL (*nods*)   Yes, sir.

HORACE   You tell Mr. Manders that Mr. Horace says he's much obliged to him for bringing the box, it arrived all right.

CAL (*bewildered*)   He know you got the box. He bring it himself Wednesday. I opened the door to him and he say, "Hello, Cal, coming on to summer weather."

HORACE   You say just what I tell you. Understand?
(BIRDIE *pours another drink, stands at table.*)

CAL   No, sir. I ain't going to say I understand. I'm going down and tell a man he give you something he already know he give you, and you say "understand."

HORACE   Now, Cal.

CAL   Yes, sir. I just going to say you obliged for the box coming all right. I ain't going to understand it, but I'm going to say it.

HORACE   And tell him I want him to come over here after supper, and to bring Mr. Sol Fowler with him.

CAL (*nods*)   He's to come after supper and bring Mr. Sol Fowler, your attorney-*at*-law, with him.

HORACE (*smiles*)   That's right. Just walk right in the back room and say your piece. (*Slowly*) In front of everybody.

CAL   Yes, sir. (*Mumbles to himself as he exits.*)

ALEXANDRA (*who has been watching* HORACE)   Is anything the matter, Papa?

HORACE   Oh, no. Nothing.

ADDIE   Miss Birdie, that elderberry going to give you a headache spell.

BIRDIE (*beginning to be drunk. Gaily*)   Oh, I don't think so. I don't think it will.

ALEXANDRA (*as* HORACE *puts his hand to his throat*)   Do you want your medicine, Papa?

HORACE   No, no. I'm all right, darling.

BIRDIE   Mama used to give me elderberry wine when I was a little girl. For hiccoughs. (*Laughs.*) You know, I don't think people get hiccoughs any more. Isn't that funny? (BIRDIE *laughs.* HORACE *and* ALEXANDRA *laugh.*) I used to get hiccoughs just when I shouldn't have.

ADDIE (*nods*)   And nobody gets growing pains no more. That is funny. Just as if there was some style in what you get. One year an ailment's stylish and the next year it ain't.

BIRDIE (*turns*) I remember. It was my first big party, at Lionnet I mean, and I was so excited, and there I was with hiccoughs and Mama laughing. (*Softly — looking at carafe*) Mama always laughed. (*Picks up carafe.*) A big party, a lovely dress from Mr. Worth in Paris, France, and hiccoughs. (*Pours drink.*) My brother pounding me on the back and Mama with the elderberry bottle, laughing at me. Everybody was on their way to come, and I was such a ninny, hiccoughing away. (*Drinks.*) You know, that was the first day I ever saw Oscar Hubbard. The Ballongs were selling their horses and he was going there to buy. He passed and lifted his hat — we could see him from the window — and my brother, to tease Mama, said maybe we should have invited the Hubbards to the party. He said Mama didn't like them because they kept a store, and he said that was old-fashioned of her. (*Her face lights up.*) And then, and *then,* I saw Mama angry for the first time in my life. She said that wasn't the reason. She said she was old-fashioned, but not that way. She said she was old-fashioned enough not to like people who killed animals they couldn't use, and who made their money charging awful interest to poor, ignorant niggers and cheating them on what they bought. She was very angry, Mama was. I had never seen her face like that. And then suddenly she laughed and said, "Look, I've frightened Birdie out of the hiccoughs." (*Her head drops. Then softly*) And so she had. They were all gone. (*Moves to sofa, sits.*)

ADDIE Yeah, they got mighty well off cheating niggers. Well, there are people who eat the earth and eat all the people on it like in the Bible with the locusts. Then there are people who stand around and watch them eat it. (*Softly*) Sometimes I think it ain't right to stand and watch them do it.

BIRDIE (*thoughtfully*) Like I say, if we could only go back to Lionnet. Everybody'd be better there. They'd be good and kind. I like people to be kind. (*Pours drink.*) Don't you, Horace; don't you like people to be kind?

HORACE Yes, Birdie.

BIRDIE (*very drunk now*) Yes, that was the first day I ever saw Oscar. Who would have thought — (*Quickly*) You all want to know something? Well, I don't like Leo. My very own son, and I don't like him. (*Laughs, gaily.*) My, I guess I even like Oscar more.

ALEXANDRA Why did you marry Uncle Oscar?

ADDIE (*sharply*) That's no question for you to be asking.

HORACE (*sharply*) Why not? She's heard enough around here to ask anything.

ALEXANDRA Aunt Birdie, why did you marry Uncle Oscar?

BIRDIE I don't know. I thought I liked him. He was kind to me and I thought it was because he liked me too. But that wasn't the reason — (*Wheels on* ALEXANDRA.) Ask why *he* married *me.* I can tell you that: He's told it to me often enough.

ADDIE (*leaning forward*) Miss Birdie, don't —

BIRDIE (*speaking very rapidly, tensely*) My family was good and the cotton on Lionnet's fields was better. Ben Hubbard wanted the cotton and (*rises*) Oscar Hubbard married it for him. He was kind to me, then. He used to smile at me. He hasn't smiled at me since. Everybody knew that's what he married me for. (ADDIE *rises.*) Everybody but me. Stupid, stupid me.

ALEXANDRA (*to* HORACE, *holding his hand, softly*) I see. (*Hesitates.*) Papa, I mean — when you feel better couldn't we go away? I mean, by ourselves. Couldn't we find a way to go —

HORACE   Yes, I know what you mean. We'll try to find a way. I promise you, darling.

ADDIE (*moves to* BIRDIE)   Rest a bit, Miss Birdie. You get talking like this you'll get a headache and —

BIRDIE (*sharply, turning to her*)   I've never had a headache in my life. (*Begins to cry hysterically.*) You know it as well as I do. (*Turns to* ALEXANDRA.) I never had a headache, Zan. That's a lie they tell for me. I drink. All by myself, in my own room, by myself, I drink. Then, when they want to hide it, they say, "Birdie's got a headache again" —

ALEXANDRA (*comes to her quickly*)   Aunt Birdie.

BIRDIE (*turning away*)   Even you won't like me now. You won't like me any more.

ALEXANDRA   I love you. I'll always love you.

BIRDIE (*furiously*)   Well, don't. Don't love me. Because in twenty years you'll just be like me. They'll do all the same things to you. (*Begins to laugh hysterically.*) You know what? In twenty-two years I haven't had a whole day of happiness. Oh, a little, like today with you all. But never a single, whole day. I say to myself, if only I had one more *whole* day, then — (*The laugh stops.*) And that's the way you'll be. And you'll trail after them, just like me, hoping they won't be so mean that day or say something to make you feel so bad — only you'll be worse off because you haven't got my Mama to remember — (*Turns away, her head drops. She stands quietly, swaying a little, holding onto the sofa.* ALEXANDRA *leans down, puts her cheek on* BIRDIE'S *arm.*)

ALEXANDRA (*to* BIRDIE)   I guess we were all trying to make a happy day. You know, we sit around and try to pretend nothing's happened. We try to pretend we are not here. We make believe we are just by ourselves, some place else, and it doesn't seem to work. (*Kisses* BIRDIE'S *hand.*) Come now, Aunt Birdie, I'll walk you home. You and me. (*She takes* BIRDIE'S *arm. They move slowly out.*)

BIRDIE (*softly as they exit*)   You and me.

ADDIE (*after a minute*)   Well. First time I ever heard Miss Birdie say a word. (HORACE *looks at her.*) Maybe it's good for her. I'm just sorry Zan had to hear it. (HORACE *moves his head as if he were uncomfortable.*) You feel bad, don't you? (*He shrugs.*)

HORACE   So you didn't want Zan to hear? It would be nice to let her stay innocent, like Birdie at her age. Let her listen now. Let her see everything. How else is she going to know that she's got to get away? I'm trying to show her that. I'm trying, but I've only got a little time left. She can even hate me when I'm dead, if she'll only learn to hate and fear this.

ADDIE   Mr. Horace —

HORACE   Pretty soon there'll be nobody to help her but you.

ADDIE (*crossing to him*)   What can I do?

HORACE   Take her away.

ADDIE   How can I do that? Do you think they'd let me just go away with her?

HORACE   I'll fix it so they can't stop you when you're ready to go. You'll go, Addie?

ADDIE (*after a second, softly*)   Yes, sir. I promise. (*He touches her arm, nods.*)

HORACE (*quietly*)   I'm going to have Sol Fowler make me a new will. They'll make trouble, but you make Zan stand firm and Fowler'll do the rest. Addie, I'd like to leave you something for yourself. I always wanted to.

ADDIE (*laughs*) Don't you do that, Mr. Horace. A nigger woman in a white man's will! I'd never get it nohow.

HORACE I know. But upstairs in the armoire drawer there's seventeen hundred dollar bills. It's money left from my trip. It's in an envelope with your name. It's for you.

ADDIE Seventeen hundred dollar bills! My God, Mr. Horace, I won't know how to count up that high. (*Shyly*) It's mighty kind and good of you. I don't know what to say for thanks —

CAL (*appears in doorway*) I'm back. (*No answer.*) I'm back.

ADDIE So we see.

HORACE Well?

CAL Nothing. I just went down and spoke my piece. Just like you told me. I say, "Mr. Horace he thank you mightily for the safe box arriving in good shape and he say you come right after supper to his house and bring Mr. Attorney-at-law Sol Fowler with you." Then I wipe my hands on my coat. Every time I ever told a lie in my whole life, I wipe my hands right after. Can't help doing it. Well, while I'm wiping my hands, Mr. Leo jumps up and say to me, "What box? What you talking about?"

HORACE (*smiles*) Did he?

CAL And Mr. Leo say he got to leave a little early cause he got something to do. And then Mr. Manders say Mr. Leo should sit right down and finish up his work and stop acting like somebody made him Mr. President. So he sit down. Now, just like I told you, Mr. Manders was mighty surprised with the message because he knows right well he brought the box — (*Points to box, sighs.*) But he took it all right. Some men take everything easy and some do not.

HORACE (*puts his head back, laughs*) Mr. Leo was telling the truth; he *has* got something to do. I hope Manders don't keep him too long. (*Outside there is the sound of voices.* CAL *exits.* ADDIE *crosses quickly to* HORACE, *puts basket on table, begins to wheel his chair towards the stairs. Sharply*) No. Leave me where I am.

ADDIE But that's Miss Regina coming back.

HORACE (*nods, looking at door*) Go away, Addie.

ADDIE (*hesitates*) Mr. Horace. Don't talk no more today. You don't feel well and it won't do no good —

HORACE (*as he hears footsteps in the hall*) Go on. (*She looks at him for a second, then picks up her sewing from table and exits as* REGINA *comes in from hall.* HORACE'S *chair is now so placed that he is in front of the table with the medicine.* REGINA *stands in the hall, shakes umbrella, stands it in the corner, takes off her cloak and throws it over the banister. She stares at* HORACE.)

REGINA (*as she takes off her gloves*) We had agreed that you were to stay in your part of this house and I in mine. This room is *my* part of the house. Please don't come down here again.

HORACE I won't.

REGINA (*crosses towards bell-cord*) I'll get Cal to take you upstairs.

HORACE (*smiles*) Before you do I want to tell you that after all, we have invested our money in Hubbard Sons and Marshall, Cotton Manufacturers.

REGINA (*stops, turns, stares at him*) What are you talking about? You haven't seen Ben — When did you change your mind?

HORACE I didn't change my mind. *I* didn't invest the money. (*Smiles.*) It was invested for me.

REGINA (*angrily*) What — ?

HORACE I had eighty-eight thousand dollars' worth of Union Pacific bonds in that safe-deposit box. They are not there now. Go and look. (*As she stares at him, he points to the box.*) Go and look, Regina. (*She crosses quickly to the box, opens it.*) Those bonds are as negotiable as money.

REGINA (*turns back to him*) What kind of joke are you playing now? Is this for my benefit?

HORACE I don't look in that box very often, but three days ago, on Wednesday it was, because I had made a decision —

REGINA I want to know what you are talking about.

HORACE (*sharply*) Don't interrupt me again. Because I had made a decision, I sent for the box. The bonds were gone. Eighty-eight thousand dollars gone. (*He smiles at her.*)

REGINA (*after a moment's silence, quietly*) Do you think I'm crazy enough to believe what you're saying?

HORACE (*shrugs*) Believe anything you like.

REGINA (*stares at him, slowly*) Where did they go to?

HORACE They are in Chicago. With Mr. Marshall, I should guess.

REGINA What did they do? Walk to Chicago? Have you really gone crazy?

HORACE Leo took the bonds.

REGINA (*turns sharply then speaks softly, without conviction*) I don't believe it.

HORACE (*leans forward*) I wasn't there but I can guess what happened. This fine gentleman, to whom you were willing to marry your daughter, took the keys and opened the box. You remember that the day of the fight Oscar went to Chicago? Well, he went with my bonds that his son Leo had stolen for him. (*Pleasantly*) And for Ben, of course, too.

REGINA (*slowly, nods*) When did you find out the bonds were gone?

HORACE Wednesday night.

REGINA I thought that's what you said. Why have you waited three days to do anything? (*Suddenly laughs.*) This *will* make a fine story.

HORACE (*nods*) Couldn't it?

REGINA (*still laughing*) A fine story to hold over their heads. How could they be such fools? (*Turns to him.*)

HORACE But I'm not going to hold it over their heads.

REGINA (*the laugh stops*) What?

HORACE (*turns his chair to face her*) I'm going to let them keep the bonds — as a loan from you. An eighty-eight-thousand-dollar loan; they should be grateful to you. They will be, I think.

REGINA (*slowly, smiles*) I see. You are punishing me. But I won't let you punish me. If you won't do anything, I will. Now. (*She starts for door.*)

HORACE You won't do anything. Because you can't. (REGINA *stops.*) It won't do you any good to make trouble because I shall simply say that I lent them the bonds.

REGINA (*slowly*) You would do that?

HORACE   Yes. For once in your life I am tying your hands. There is nothing for you to do. (*There is silence. Then she sits down.*)

REGINA   I see. You are going to lend them the bonds and let them keep all the profit they make on them, and there is nothing I can do about it. Is that right?

HORACE   Yes.

REGINA (*softly*)   Why did you say that I was making this gift?

HORACE   I was coming to that. I am going to make a new will, Regina, leaving you eighty-eight thousand dollars in Union Pacific bonds. The rest will go to Zan. It's true that your brothers have borrowed your share for a little while. After my death I advise you to talk to Ben and Oscar. They won't admit anything and Ben, I think, will be smart enough to see that he's safe. Because I knew about the theft and said nothing. Nor will I say anything as long as I live. Is that clear to you?

REGINA (*nods, softly, without looking at him*)   You will not say anything as long as you live.

HORACE   That's right. And by that time they will probably have replaced your bonds, and then they'll belong to you and nobody but us will ever know what happened. (*Stops, smiles.*) They'll be around any minute to see what I am going to do. I took good care to see that word reached Leo. They'll be mighty relieved to know I'm going to do nothing and Ben will think it all a capital joke on you. And that will be the end of that. There's nothing you can do to them, nothing you can do to me.

REGINA   You hate me very much.

HORACE   No.

REGINA   Oh, I think you do. (*Puts her head back, sighs.*) Well, we haven't been very good together. Anyway, I don't hate you either. I have only contempt for you. I've always had.

HORACE   From the very first?

REGINA   I think so.

HORACE   I was in love with *you.* But why did *you* marry *me?*

REGINA   I was lonely when I was young.

HORACE   You were lonely?

REGINA   Not the way people usually mean. Lonely for all the things I wasn't going to get. Everybody in this house was so busy and there was so little place for what I wanted. I wanted the world. Then and then — (*Smiles.*) Papa died and left the money to Ben and Oscar.

HORACE   And you married me?

REGINA   Yes, I thought — But I was wrong. You were a small-town clerk then. You haven't changed.

HORACE (*nods, smiles*)   And that wasn't what you wanted.

REGINA   No. No, it wasn't what I wanted. (*Pauses, leans back; pleasantly*) It took me a little while to find out I had made a mistake. As for you — I don't know. It was almost as if I couldn't stand the kind of man you were — (*Smiles; softly*) I used to lie there at night, praying you wouldn't come near —

HORACE   Really? It was as bad as that?

REGINA (*nods*)   Remember when I went to Doctor Sloan and I told you he said there was something the matter with me and that you shouldn't touch me any more?

HORACE I remember.

REGINA But you believed it. I couldn't understand that. I couldn't understand that anybody could be such a soft fool. That was when I began to despise you.

HORACE (*puts his hand to his throat, looks at the bottle of medicine on table*) Why didn't you leave me?

REGINA I told you I married you for something. It turned out it was only for this. (*Carefully*) This wasn't what I wanted, but it was something. I never thought about it much but if I had (HORACE *puts his hand to his throat*) I'd have known that you would die before I would. But I couldn't have known that you would get heart trouble so early and so bad. I'm lucky, Horace. I've always been lucky. (HORACE *turns slowly to the medicine.*) I'll be lucky again. (HORACE *looks at her. Then he puts his hand to his throat. Because he cannot reach the bottle he moves the chair closer. He reaches for the medicine, takes out the cork, picks up the spoon. The bottle slips and smashes on the table. He draws in his breath, gasps.*)

HORACE Please. Tell Addie — The other bottle is upstairs. (REGINA *has not moved. She does not move now. He stares at her. Then, suddenly as if he understood, he raises his voice. It is a panic-stricken whisper, too small to be heard outside the room*) Addie! Addie! Come — (*Stops as he hears the softness of his voice. He makes a sudden, furious spring from the chair to the stairs, taking the first few steps as if he were a desperate runner. On the fourth step he slips, gasps, grasps the rail, makes a great effort to reach the landing. When he reaches the landing, he is on his knees. His knees give way, he falls on the landing, out of view.* REGINA *has not turned during his climb up the stairs. Now she waits a second. Then she goes below the landing, speaks up.*)

REGINA Horace. Horace. (*When there is no answer, she turns, calls*) Addie! Cal! Come in here. (*She starts up the steps.* ADDIE *and* CAL *appear. Both run towards the stairs.*) He's had an attack. Come up here. (*They run up the steps quickly.*)

CAL My God. Mr. Horace —
(*They cannot be seen now.*)

REGINA (*her voice comes from the head of the stairs*) Be still, Cal. Bring him in here.
(*Before the footsteps and the voices have completely died away,* ALEXANDRA *appears in the hall door, in her raincloak and hood. She comes into the room, begins to unfasten the cloak, suddenly looks around, sees the empty wheel chair, stares, begins to move swiftly as if to look in the dining room. At the same moment* ADDIE *runs down the stairs.* ALEXANDRA *turns and stares up at* ADDIE.)

ALEXANDRA Addie! What?

ADDIE (*takes* ALEXANDRA *by the shoulders*) I'm going for the doctor. Go upstairs. (ALEXANDRA *looks at her, then quickly breaks away and runs up the steps.* ADDIE *exits. The stage is empty for a minute. Then the front door bell begins to ring. When there is no answer, it rings again. A second later* LEO *appears in the hall, talking as he comes in.*)

LEO (*very nervous*) Hello. (*Irritably*) Never saw any use ringing a bell when a door was open. If you are going to ring a bell, then somebody should answer it. (*Gets in the room, looks around, puzzled, listens, hears no sound.*) Aunt Regina. (*He moves around restlessly.*) Addie. (*Waits.*) Where the hell — (*Crosses to the bell cord, rings it impatiently, waits, gets no answer, calls*) Cal! Cal! (CAL *appears on the stair landing.*)

CAL (*his voice is soft, shaken*) Mr. Leo. Miss Regina says you stop that screaming noise.

LEO (*angrily*) Where is everybody?

CAL Mr. Horace he got an attack. He's bad. Miss Regina says you stop that noise.

LEO Uncle Horace — What — What happened? (CAL *starts down the stairs, shakes his head, begins to move swiftly off.* LEO *looks around wildly.*) But when — You seen Mr. Oscar or Mr. Ben? (CAL *shakes his head. Moves on.* LEO *grabs him by the arm.*) Answer me, will you?

CAL No, I ain't seen 'em. I ain't got time to answer you. I got to get things. (CAL *runs off.*)

LEO But what's the matter with him? When did this happen — (*Calling after* CAL) You'd think Papa'd be some place where you could find him. I been chasing him all afternoon.

(OSCAR *and* BEN *come into the room, talking excitedly.*)

OSCAR I hope it's not a bad attack.

BEN It's the first one he's had since he came home.

LEO Papa, I've been looking all over town for you and Uncle Ben —

BEN Where is he?

OSCAR Addie said it was sudden.

BEN (*to* LEO) Where is he? When did it happen?

LEO Upstairs. Will you listen to me, please? I been looking for you for —

OSCAR (*to* BEN) You think we should go up? (BEN, *looking up the steps, shakes his head.*)

BEN I don't know. I don't know.

OSCAR (*shakes his head*) But he was all right —

LEO (*yelling*) Will you listen to me?

OSCAR (*sharply*) What is the matter with you?

LEO I been trying to tell you. I been trying to find you for an hour —

OSCAR Tell me what?

LEO Uncle Horace knows about the bonds. He knows about them. He's had the box since Wednesday —

BEN (*sharply*) Stop shouting! What the hell are you talking about?

LEO (*furiously*) I'm telling you he knows about the bonds. Ain't that clear enough —

OSCAR (*grabbing* LEO's *arm*) You God-damn fool! Stop screaming!

BEN Now what happened? Talk quietly.

LEO You heard me. Uncle Horace knows about the bonds. He's known since Wednesday.

BEN (*after a second*) How do you know that?

LEO Because Cal comes down to Manders and says the box came O.K. and —

OSCAR (*trembling*) That might not mean a thing —

LEO (*angrily*) No? It might not, huh? Then he says Manders should come here tonight and bring Sol Fowler with him. I guess that don't mean a thing either.

OSCAR (*to* BEN) Ben — What — Do you think he's seen the —

BEN (*motions to the box*) There's the box. (*Both* OSCAR *and* LEO *turn sharply.*

LEO *makes a leap to the box.* You ass. Put it down. What are you going to do with it, eat it?

LEO   I'm going to — (*Starts.*)

BEN (*furiously*)   Put it down. Don't touch it again. Now sit down and shut up for a minute.

OSCAR   Since Wednesday. (*To* LEO) You said he had it since Wednesday. Why didn't he say something — (*To* BEN) I don't understand —

LEO (*taking a step*)   I can put it back. I can put it back before anybody knows.

BEN (*who is standing at the table, softly*)   He's had it since Wednesday. Yet he hasn't said a word to us.

OSCAR   *Why? Why?*

LEO   What's the difference why? He was getting ready to say plenty. He was going to say it to Fowler tonight —

OSCAR (*angrily*)   Be still. (*Turns to* BEN, *looks at him, waits.*)

BEN (*after a minute*)   I don't believe that.

LEO (*wildly*)   *You* don't believe it? What do I care what *you* believe? I do the dirty work and then —

BEN (*turning his head sharply to* LEO)   I'm remembering that. I'm remembering that, Leo.

OSCAR   What do you mean?

LEO   You —

BEN (*to* OSCAR)   If you don't shut that little fool up, I'll show you what I mean. For some reason he knows, but he don't say a word.

OSCAR   Maybe he didn't know that *we* —

BEN (*quickly*)   That *Leo* — He's no fool. Does Manders know the bonds are missing?

LEO   How could I tell? I was half crazy. I don't think so. Because Manders seemed kind of puzzled and —

OSCAR   But we got to find out — (*He breaks off as* CAL *comes into the room carrying a kettle of hot water.*)

BEN   How is he, Cal?

CAL   I don't know, Mr. Ben. He was bad. (*Going towards stairs.*)

OSCAR   But when did it happen?

CAL (*shrugs*)   He wasn't feeling bad early. (ADDIE *comes in quickly from the hall.*) Then there he is next thing on the landing, fallen over, his eyes tight —

ADDIE (*to* CAL)   Dr. Sloan's over at the Ballongs. Hitch the buggy and go get him. (*She takes the kettle and cloths from him, pushes him, runs up the stairs.*) Go on. (*She disappears.* CAL *exits.*)

BEN   Never seen Sloan anywhere when you need him.

OSCAR (*softly*)   Sounds bad.

LEO   He would have told *her* about it. Aunt Regina. He would have told his own wife —

BEN (*turning to* LEO)   Yes, he might have told her. But they weren't on such pretty terms and maybe he didn't. Maybe he didn't. (*Goes quickly to* LEO.) Now, listen to me. If she doesn't know, it may work out all right. If she does know, you're to say he lent you the bonds.

LEO   Lent them to me! Who's going to believe that?

BEN   Nobody.

OSCAR (*to* LEO)   Don't you understand? It can't do no harm to say it —

LEO   Why should I say he lent them to me? Why not to you? (*Carefully*) Why not to Uncle Ben?

BEN   (*smiles*)   Just because he didn't lend them to me. Remember that.

LEO   But all he has to do is say he didn't lend them to me —

BEN   (*furiously*)   But for some reason, he doesn't seem to be talking, does he? (*There are footsteps above. They all stand looking at the stairs.* REGINA *begins to come slowly down.*)

BEN   What happened?

REGINA   He's had a bad attack.

OSCAR   Too bad. I'm so sorry we weren't here when — when Horace needed us.

BEN   When *you* needed us.

REGINA   (*looks at him*)   Yes.

BEN   How is he? Can we — can we go up?

REGINA   (*shakes her head*)   He's not conscious.

OSCAR   (*pacing around*)   It's that — it's that bad? Wouldn't you think Sloan could be found quickly, just once, just once?

REGINA   I don't think there is much for him to do.

BEN   Oh, don't talk like that. He's come through attacks before. He will now. (REGINA *sits down. After a second she speaks softly.*)

REGINA   Well. We haven't seen each other since the day of our fight.

BEN   (*tenderly*)   That was nothing. Why, you and Oscar and I used to fight when we were kids.

OSCAR   (*hurriedly*)   Don't you think we should go up? Is there anything we can do for Horace —

BEN   You don't feel well. Ah —

REGINA   (*without looking at them*)   No, I don't. (*Slight pause.*) Horace told me about the bonds this afternoon. (*There is an immediate shocked silence.*)

LEO   The bonds. What do you mean? What bonds? What —

BEN   (*looks at him furiously. Then to* REGINA)   The Union Pacific bonds? *Horace's* Union Pacific bonds?

REGINA   Yes.

OSCAR   (*steps to her, very nervously*)   Well. Well what — what about them? What — what could he say?

REGINA   He said that Leo had stolen the bonds and given them to you.

OSCAR   (*aghast, very loudly*)   That's ridiculous, Regina, absolutely —

LEO   I don't know what you're talking about. What would I — Why —

REGINA   (*wearily to* BEN)   Isn't it enough that he stole them from me? Do I have to listen to this in the bargain?

OSCAR   You are talking —

LEO   I didn't steal anything. I don't know why —

REGINA   (*to* BEN)   Would you ask them to stop that, please? (*There is silence for a minute.* BEN *glowers at* OSCAR *and* LEO.)

BEN   Aren't we starting at the wrong end, Regina? What did Horace tell you?

REGINA   (*smiles at him*)   He told me that Leo had stolen the bonds.

LEO   I didn't steal —

REGINA   Please. Let me finish. Then he told me that he was going to pretend that he had lent them to you (LEO *turns sharply to* REGINA, *then looks at* OSCAR, *then looks back at* REGINA) as a present from me — to my brothers.

He said there was nothing I could do about it. He said the rest of his money would go to Alexandra. That is all. (*There is a silence.* OSCAR *coughs,* LEO *smiles slyly.*)

LEO (*taking a step to her*) I told you he had lent them — I could have told you —

REGINA (*ignores him, smiles sadly at* BEN) So I'm very badly off, you see. (*Carefully*) But Horace said there was nothing I could do about it as long as he was alive to say he had lent you the bonds.

BEN You shouldn't feel that way. It can all be explained, all be adjusted. It isn't as bad —

REGINA So you, at least, are willing to admit that the bonds were stolen?

BEN (OSCAR *laughs nervously*) I admit no such thing. It's possible that Horace made up that part of the story to tease you — (*Looks at her.*) Or perhaps to punish you. Punish you.

REGINA (*sadly*) It's not a pleasant story. I feel bad, Ben, naturally. I hadn't thought —

BEN Now you shall have the bonds safely back. That was the understanding, wasn't it, Oscar?

OSCAR Yes.

REGINA I'm glad to know that. (*Smiles.*) Ah, I had greater hopes —

BEN Don't talk that way. That's foolish. (*Looks at his watch.*) I think we ought to drive out for Sloan ourselves. If we can't find him we'll go over to Senateville for Doctor Morris. And don't think I'm dismissing this other business. I'm not. We'll have it all out on a more appropriate day.

REGINA (*looks up, quietly*) I don't think you had better go yet. I think you had better stay and sit down.

BEN We'll be back with Sloan.

REGINA Cal has gone for him. I don't want you to go.

BEN Now don't worry and —

REGINA You will come back in this room and sit down. I have something more to say.

BEN (*turns, comes towards her*) Since when do I take orders from you?

REGINA (*smiles*) You don't — yet. (*Sharply*) Come back, Oscar. You too, Leo.

OSCAR (*sure of himself, laughs*) My dear Regina.

BEN (*softly, pats her hand*) Horace has already clipped your wings and very wittily. Do I have to clip them, too? (*Smiles at her.*) You'd get farther with a smile, Regina. I'm a soft man for a woman's smile.

REGINA I'm smiling, Ben. I'm smiling because you are quite safe while Horace lives. But I don't think Horace will live. And if he doesn't live I shall want seventy-five per cent in exchange for the bonds.

BEN (*steps back, whistles, laughs*) Greedy! What a greedy girl you are! You want so much of everything.

REGINA Yes. And if I don't get what I want I am going to put all three of you in jail.

OSCAR (*furiously*) You're mighty crazy. Having just admitted —

BEN And on what evidence would you put Oscar and Leo in jail?

REGINA (*laughs, gaily*) Oscar, listen to him. He's getting ready to swear that it was you and Leo! What do you say to that? (OSCAR *turns furiously towards* BEN.) Oh, don't be angry, Oscar. I'm going to see that he goes in with you.

BEN   Try anything you like, Regina. (*Sharply*) And now we can stop all this and say good-bye to you. (ALEXANDRA *comes slowly down the steps.*) It's his money and he's obviously willing to let us borrow it. (*More pleasantly*) Learn to make threats when you can carry them through. For how many years have I told you a good-looking woman gets more by being soft and appealing? Mama used to tell you that. (*Looks at his watch.*) Where the hell is Sloan? (*To* OSCAR) Take the buggy and — (*As* BEN *turns to* OSCAR, *he sees* ALEXANDRA. *She walks stiffly. She goes slowly to the lower window, her head bent. They all turn to look at her.*)

OSCAR   (*after a second, moving toward her*) What? Alexandra — (*She does not answer. After a second,* ADDIE *comes slowly down the stairs, moving as if she were very tired. At foot of steps, she looks at* ALEXANDRA, *then turns and slowly crosses to door and exits.* REGINA *rises.* BEN *looks nervously at* ALEXANDRA, *at* REGINA.)

OSCAR   (*as* ADDIE *passes him, irritably to* ALEXANDRA) Well, what is — (*turns into room — sees* ADDIE *at foot of steps*) — what's? (BEN *puts up a hand, shakes his head.*) My God, I didn't know — who *could* have known — I didn't know he was that sick. Well, well — I — (REGINA *stands quietly, her back to them.*)

BEN   (*softly, sincerely*) Seems like yesterday when he first came here.

OSCAR   (*sincerely, nervously*) Yes, that's true. (*Turns to* BEN.) The whole town loved him and respected him.

ALEXANDRA   (*turns*) Did you love him, Uncle Oscar?

OSCAR   Certainly, I — What a strange thing to ask! I —

ALEXANDRA   Did you love him, Uncle Ben?

BEN   (*simply*) He had —

ALEXANDRA   (*suddenly starts to laugh very loudly*) And you, Mama, did you love him, too?

REGINA   I know what you feel, Alexandra, but please try to control yourself.

ALEXANDRA   (*still laughing*) I'm trying, Mama. I'm trying very hard.

BEN   Grief makes some people laugh and some people cry. It's better to cry, Alexandra.

ALEXANDRA   (*the laugh has stopped; tensely moves toward* REGINA) What was Papa doing on the staircase?

(BEN *turns to look at* ALEXANDRA.)

REGINA   Please go and lie down, my dear. We all need time to get over shocks like this. (ALEXANDRA *does not move.* REGINA'S *voice becomes softer, more insistent.*) Please go, Alexandra.

ALEXANDRA   No, Mama. I'll wait. I've got to talk to you.

REGINA   Later. Go and rest now.

ALEXANDRA   (*quietly*) I'll wait, Mama. I've plenty of time.

REGINA   (*hesitates, stares, makes a half shrug, turns back to* BEN) As I was saying. Tomorrow morning I am going up to Judge Simmes. I shall tell him about Leo.

BEN   (*motioning toward* ALEXANDRA) Not in front of the child, Regina. I —

REGINA   (*turns to him. Sharply*) I didn't ask her to stay. Tomorrow morning I go to Judge Simmes —

OSCAR And what proof? What proof of all this —

REGINA (*turns sharply*) None. I won't need any. The bonds are missing and they are with Marshall. That will be enough. If it isn't, I'll add what's necessary.

BEN I'm sure of that.

REGINA (*turns to* BEN) You can be quite sure.

OSCAR We'll deny —

REGINA Deny your heads off. You couldn't find a jury that wouldn't weep for a woman whose brothers steal from her. And you couldn't find twelve men in this state you haven't cheated and hate you for it.

OSCAR What kind of talk is this? You couldn't do anything like that! We're your own brothers. (*Points upstairs.*) How can you talk that way when upstairs not five minutes ago —

REGINA (*slowly*) There are people who can never go back, who must finish what they start. I am one of those people, Oscar. (*After a slight pause*) Where was I? (*Smiles at* BEN) Well, they'll convict you. But I won't care much if they don't. (*Leans forward; pleasantly*) Because by that time you'll be ruined. I shall also tell my story to Mr. Marshall, who likes me, I think, and who will not want to be involved in your scandal. A respectable firm like Marshall and Company. The deal would be off in an hour. (*Turns to them angrily.*) And you know it. Now I don't want to hear any more from any of you. *You'll do no more bargaining in this house.* I'll take my seventy-five per cent and we'll forget the story forever. That's one way of doing it, and the way I prefer. You know me well enough to know that I don't mind taking the other way.

BEN (*after a second, slowly*) None of us have ever known you well enough, Regina.

REGINA You're getting old, Ben. Your tricks aren't as smart as they used to be. (*There is no answer. She waits, then smiles.*) All right. I take it that's settled and I get what I asked for.

OSCAR (*furiously to* BEN) Are you going to let her do this —

BEN (*turns to look at him, slowly*) You have a suggestion?

REGINA (*puts her arms above her head, stretches, laughs*) No, he hasn't. All right. Now, Leo, I have forgotten that you ever saw the bonds. (*Archly, to* BEN *and* OSCAR) And as long as you boys both behave yourselves, I've forgotten that we ever talked about them. You can draw up the necessary papers tomorrow. (BEN *laughs.* LEO *stares at him, starts for door. Exits.* OSCAR *moves towards door angrily.* REGINA *looks at* BEN, *nods, laughs with him. For a second,* OSCAR *stands in the door, looking back at them. Then he exits.*)

REGINA You're a good loser, Ben. I like that.

BEN (*he picks up his coat, then turns to her*) Well, I say to myself, what's the good? You and I aren't like Oscar. We're not sour people. I think that comes from a good digestion. Then, too, one loses today and wins tomorrow. I say to myself, years of planning and I get what I want. Then I don't get it. But I'm not discouraged. The century's turning, the world is open. Open for people like you and me. Ready for us, waiting for us. After all this is just the beginning. There are hundreds of Hubbards sitting in rooms like this throughout the country. All their names aren't Hubbard, but they are all Hubbards and they will own this country some day. We'll get along.

REGINA (*smiles*)   I think so.

BEN   Then, too, I say to myself, things may change. (*Looks at* ALEXANDRA.) I agree with Alexandra. What is a man in a wheel chair doing on a staircase? I ask myself that.

REGINA (*looks up at him*)   And what do you answer?

BEN   I have no answer. But maybe some day I will. Maybe never, but maybe some day. (*Smiles. Pats her arm.*) When I do, I'll let you know. (*Goes towards hall.*)

REGINA   When you do, write me. I will be in Chicago. (*Gaily*) Ah, Ben, if Papa had only left me his money.

BEN   I'll see you tomorrow.

REGINA   Oh, yes. Certainly. You'll be sort of working for me now.

BEN (*as he passes* ALEXANDRA, *smiles*)   Alexandra, you're turning out to be a right interesting girl. (*Looks at* REGINA.) Well, good night all. (*He exits.*)

REGINA (*Sits quietly for a second, stretches, turns to look at* ALEXANDRA)   What do you want to talk to me about, Alexandra?

ALEXANDRA (*slowly*)   I've changed my mind. I don't want to talk. There's nothing to talk about now.

REGINA   You're acting very strange. Not like yourself. You've had a bad shock today. I know that. And you loved Papa, but you must have expected this to come some day. You knew how sick he was.

ALEXANDRA   I knew. We all knew.

REGINA   It will be good for you to get away from here. Good for me, too. Time heals most wounds, Alexandra. You're young, you shall have all the things I wanted. I'll make the world for you the way I wanted it to be for me. (*Uncomfortably*) Don't sit there staring. You've been around Birdie so much you're getting just like her.

ALEXANDRA (*nods*)   Funny. That's what Aunt Birdie said today.

REGINA (*nods*)   Be good for you to get away from all this.

(ADDIE *enters.*)

ADDIE   Cal is back, Miss Regina. He says Dr. Sloan will be coming in a few minutes.

REGINA   We'll go in a few weeks. A few weeks! That means two or three Saturdays, two or three Sundays. (*Sighs.*) Well, I'm very tired. I shall go to bed. I don't want any supper. Put the lights out and lock up. (ADDIE *moves to the piano lamp, turns it out.*) You go to your room, Alexandra. Addie will bring you something hot. You look very tired. (*Rises. To* ADDIE) Call me when Dr. Sloan gets here. I don't want to see anybody else. I don't want any condolence calls tonight. The whole town will be over.

ALEXANDRA   Mama, I'm not coming with you. I'm not going to Chicago.

REGINA (*turns to her*)   You're very upset, Alexandra.

ALEXANDRA (*quietly*)   I mean what I say. With all my heart.

REGINA   We'll talk about it tomorrow. The morning will make a difference.

ALEXANDRA   It won't make any difference. And there isn't anything to talk about. I am going away from you. Because I want to. Because I know Papa would want me to.

REGINA (*puzzled, careful, polite*)   You *know* your papa wanted you to go away from me?

ALEXANDRA   Yes.

REGINA (*softly*)   And if I say no?

ALEXANDRA (*looks at her*) Say it, Mama, say it. And see what happens.

REGINA (*softly, after a pause*) And if I make you stay?

ALEXANDRA That would be foolish. It wouldn't work in the end.

REGINA You're very serious about it, aren't you? (*Crosses to stairs.*) Well, you'll change your mind in a few days.

ALEXANDRA You only change your mind when you want to. And I won't want to.

REGINA (*going up the steps*) Alexandra, I've come to the end of my rope. Somewhere there has to be what I want, too. Life goes too fast. Do what you want; think what you want; go where you want. I'd like to keep you with me, but I won't make you stay. Too many people used to make me do too many things. No, I won't make you stay.

ALEXANDRA You couldn't, Mama, because I want to leave here. As I've never wanted anything in my life before. Because now I understand what Papa was trying to tell me. (*Pause.*) All in one day: Addie said there were people who ate the earth and other people who stood around and watched them do it. And just now Uncle Ben said the same thing. Really, he said the same thing. (*Tensely*) Well, tell him for me, Mama, I'm not going to stand around and watch you do it. Tell him I'll be fighting as hard as he'll be fighting (*rises*) some place where people don't just stand around and watch.

REGINA Well, you have spirit, after all. I used to think you were all sugar water. We don't have to be bad friends. I don't want us to be bad friends, Alexandra. (*Starts, stops, turns to* ALEXANDRA.) Would you like to come and talk to me, Alexandra? Would you — would you like to sleep in my room tonight?

ALEXANDRA (*takes a step towards her*) Are you afraid, Mama? (REGINA *does not answer. She moves slowly out of sight.* ADDIE *comes to* ALEXANDRA, *presses her arm.*)

Henrik Ibsen *(1828–1906)*

An Enemy of the People

Characters

DR. THOMAS STOCKMANN, *Medical Officer of the Municipal Baths*
MRS. STOCKMANN, *His wife*
PETRA, *Their daughter, a teacher*
EJLIF ⎱ *Their sons, aged 13 and*
MORTEN ⎰ *10 respectively*
PETER STOCKMANN, *The Doctor's elder brother; Mayor of the Town and Chief Constable, Chairman of the Baths' Committee, etc., etc.*

MORTEN KIIL, *A tanner* (MRS. STOCKMANN'S *adoptive father*)
HOVSTAD, *Editor of the* People's Messenger
BILLING, *Subeditor*
CAPTAIN HORSTER
ASLAKSEN, *A printer*
MEN, *Of various conditions and occupations, some few women, and a troop of schoolboys — the audience at a public meeting.*

The action takes place in a coast town in southern Norway.

Act One

Scene: DR. STOCKMANN'S *sitting-room. It is evening. The room is plainly but neatly appointed and furnished. In the right-hand wall are two doors; the farther leads out to the hall, the nearer to the doctor's study. In the left-hand wall, opposite the door leading to the hall, is a door leading to the other rooms occupied by the family. In the middle of the same wall stands the stove, and, further forward, a couch with a looking-glass hanging over it and an oval table in front of it. On the table, a lighted lamp, with a lamp-shade. At the back of the room, an open door leads to the dining-room.* BILLING *is seen sitting at the dining table, on which a lamp is burning. He has a napkin tucked under his chin, and* MRS. STOCKMANN *is standing by the table handing him a large plate-full of roast beef. The other places at the table are empty, and the table somewhat in disorder, a meal having evidently recently been finished.*

MRS. STOCKMANN   You see, if you come an hour late, Mr. Billing, you have to put up with cold meat.

BILLING (*as he eats*)   It is uncommonly good, thank you — remarkably good.

MRS. STOCKMANN   My husband makes such a point of having his meals punctually, you know —

BILLING   That doesn't affect me a bit. Indeed, I almost think I enjoy a meal all the better when I can sit down and eat all by myself and undisturbed.

MRS. STOCKMANN   Oh well, as long as you are enjoying it — . (*Turns to the hall door, listening*) I expect that is Mr. Hovstad coming too.

BILLING   Very likely.

(PETER STOCKMANN *comes in. He wears an overcoat and his official hat, and carries a stick.*)

PETER STOCKMANN   Good evening, Katherine.

MRS. STOCKMANN (*coming forward into the sitting-room*) Ah, good evening —
is it you? How good of you to come up and see us!

PETER STOCKMANN I happened to be passing, and so — (*Looks into the
dining-room*) But you have company with you, I see.

MRS. STOCKMANN (*a little embarrassed*) Oh, no — it was quite by chance he
came in. (*Hurriedly*) Won't you come in and have something, too?

PETER STOCKMANN I! No, thank you. Good gracious — hot meat at night!
Not with my digestion.

MRS. STOCKMANN Oh, but just once in a way —

PETER STOCKMANN No, no, my dear lady; I stick to my tea and bread and
butter. It is much more wholesome in the long run — and a little more
economical, too.

MRS. STOCKMANN (*smiling*) Now you mustn't think that Thomas and I are
spendthrifts.

PETER STOCKMANN Not you, my dear; I would never think that of you.
(*Points to the Doctor's study*) Is he not at home?

MRS. STOCKMANN No, he went out for a little turn after supper — he and the
boys.

PETER STOCKMANN I doubt if that is a wise thing to do. (*Listens.*) I fancy I
hear him coming now.

MRS. STOCKMANN No, I don't think it is he. (*A knock is heard at the door.*)
Come in! (HOVSTAD *comes in from the hall.*) Oh, it is you, Mr. Hovstad!

HOVSTAD Yes, I hope you will forgive me, but I was delayed at the printer's.
Good evening, Mr. Mayor.

PETER STOCKMANN (*bowing a little distantly*) Good evening. You have come
on business, no doubt.

HOVSTAD Partly. It's about an article for the paper.

PETER STOCKMANN So I imagined. I hear my brother has become a prolific
contributor to the "People's Messenger."

HOVSTAD Yes, he is good enough to write in the "People's Messenger" when
he has any home truths to tell.

MRS. STOCKMANN (*to* HOVSTAD) But won't you — ? (*Points to the dining-
room.*)

PETER STOCKMANN Quite so, quite so. I don't blame him in the least, as a
writer, for addressing himself to the quarters where he will find the readiest
sympathy. And, besides that, I personally have no reason to bear any ill
will to your paper, Mr. Hovstad.

HOVSTAD I quite agree with you.

PETER STOCKMANN Taking one thing with another, there is an excellent spirit
of toleration in the town — an admirable municipal spirit. And it all springs
from the fact of our having a great common interest to unite us — an interest that is in an equally high degree the concern of every right-minded
citizen —

HOVSTAD The Baths, yes.

PETER STOCKMANN Exactly — our fine, new, handsome Baths. Mark my
words, Mr. Hovstad — the Baths will become the focus of our municipal
life! Not a doubt of it!

MRS. STOCKMANN That is just what Thomas says.

PETER STOCKMANN Think how extraordinarily the place has developed within
the last year or two! Money has been flowing in, and there is some life and

some business doing in the town. Houses and landed property are rising in value every day.

HOVSTAD   And unemployment is diminishing.

PETER STOCKMANN   Yes, that is another thing. The burden of the poor rates has been lightened, to the great relief of the propertied classes; and that relief will be even greater if only we get a really good summer this year, and lots of visitors — plenty of invalids, who will make the Baths talked about.

HOVSTAD   And there is a good prospect of that, I hear.

PETER STOCKMANN   It looks very promising. Enquiries about apartments and that sort of thing are reaching us every day.

HOVSTAD   Well, the doctor's article will come in very suitably.

PETER STOCKMANN   Has he been writing something just lately?

HOVSTAD   This is something he wrote in the winter; a recommendation of the Baths — an account of the excellent sanitary conditions here. But I held the article over, temporarily.

PETER STOCKMANN   Ah, — some little difficulty about it, I suppose?

HOVSTAD   No, not at all; I thought it would be better to wait till the spring, because it is just at this time that people begin to think seriously about their summer quarters.

PETER STOCKMANN   Quite right; you were perfectly right, Mr. Hovstad.

HOVSTAD   Yes, Thomas is really indefatigable when it is a question of the Baths.

PETER STOCKMANN   Well — remember, he is the Medical Officer to the Baths.

HOVSTAD   Yes, and what is more, they owe their existence to him.

PETER STOCKMANN   To him? Indeed! It is true I have heard from time to time that some people are of that opinion. At the same time I must say I imagined that I look a modest part in the enterprise.

MRS. STOCKMANN   Yes, that is what Thomas is always saying.

HOVSTAD   But who denies it, Mr. Stockmann? You set the thing going and made a practical concern of it; we all know that. I only meant that the idea of it came first from the doctor.

PETER STOCKMANN   Oh, ideas — yes! My brother has had plenty of them in his time — unfortunately. But when it is a question of putting an idea into practical shape, you have to apply to a man of different mettle, Mr. Hovstad. And I certainly should have thought that in this house at least —

MRS. STOCKMANN   My dear Peter —

HOVSTAD   How can you think that — ?

MRS. STOCKMANN   Won't you go in and have something, Mr. Hovstad? My husband is sure to be back directly.

HOVSTAD   Thank you, perhaps just a morsel. (*Goes into the dining-room.*)

PETER STOCKMANN (*lowering his voice a little*)   It is a curious thing that these farmers' sons never seem to lose their want of tact.

MRS. STOCKMANN   Surely it is not worth bothering about! Cannot you and Thomas share the credit as brothers?

PETER STOCKMANN   I should have thought so; but apparently some people are not satisfied with a share.

MRS. STOCKMANN   What nonsense! You and Thomas get on so capitally together. (*Listens*) There he is at last, I think. (*Goes out and opens the door leading to the hall.*)

DR. STOCKMANN (*laughing and talking outside*)   Look here — here is another guest for you, Katherine. Isn't that jolly! Come in, Captain Horster; hang your coat up on this peg. Ah, you don't wear an overcoat. Just think, Katherine; I met him in the street and could hardly persuade him to come up! (CAPTAIN HORSTER *comes into the room and greets* MRS. STOCKMANN. *He is followed by* DR. STOCKMANN.) Come along in, boys. They are ravenously hungry again, you know. Come along, Captain Horster; you must have a slice of beef. (*Pushes* HORSTER *into the dining-room.* EJLIF *and* MORTEN *go in after them.*)

MRS. STOCKMANN   But, Thomas, don't you see — ?

DR. STOCKMANN (*turning in the doorway*)   Oh, is it you, Peter? (*Shakes hands with him.*) Now that is very delightful.

PETER STOCKMANN   Unfortunately I must go in a moment —

DR. STOCKMANN   Rubbish! There is some toddy just coming in. You haven't forgotten the toddy, Katherine?

MRS. STOCKMANN   Of course not; the water is boiling now. (*Goes into the dining-room.*)

PETER STOCKMANN   Toddy too!

DR. STOCKMANN   Yes, sit down and we will have it comfortably.

PETER STOCKMANN   Thanks, I never care about an evening's drinking.

DR. STOCKMANN   But this isn't an evening's drinking.

PETER STOCKMANN   It seems to me — . (*Looks towards the dining-room*) It is extraordinary how they can put away all that food.

DR. STOCKMANN (*rubbing his hands*)   Yes, isn't it splendid to see young people eat? They have always got an appetite, you know! That's as it should be. Lots of food — to build up their strength! They are the people who are going to stir up the fermenting forces of the future, Peter.

PETER STOCKMANN   May I ask what they will find here to "stir up," as you put it?

DR. STOCKMANN   Ah, you must ask the young people that — when the time comes. We shan't be able to see it, of course. That stands to reason — two old fogies, like us —

PETER STOCKMANN   Really, really! I must say that is an extremely odd expression to —

DR. STOCKMANN   Oh, you mustn't take me too literally, Peter. I am so heartily happy and contented, you know. I think it is such an extraordinary piece of good fortune to be in the middle of all this growing, germinating life. It is a splendid time to live in! It is as if a whole new world were being created around one.

PETER STOCKMANN   Do you really think so?

DR. STOCKMANN   Ah, naturally you can't appreciate it as keenly as I. You have lived all your life in these surroundings, and your impressions have got blunted. But I, who have been buried all these years in my little corner up north, almost without ever seeing a stranger who might bring new ideas with him — well, in my case it has just the same effect as if I had been transported into the middle of a crowded city.

PETER STOCKMANN   Oh, a city — !

DR. STOCKMANN   I know, I know; it is all cramped enough here, compared with many other places. But there is life here — there is promise — there are innumerable things to work for and fight for; and that is the main thing. (*Calls*) Katherine, hasn't the postman been here?

MRS. STOCKMANN (*from the dining-room*)   No.

DR. STOCKMANN   And then to be comfortably off, Peter! That is something one learns to value, when one has been on the brink of starvation, as we have.

PETER STOCKMANN   Oh, surely —

DR. STOCKMANN   Indeed I can assure you we have often been very hard put to it, up there. And now to be able to live like a lord! To-day, for instance, we had roast beef for dinner — and, what is more, for supper too. Won't you come and have a little bit? Or let me show it you, at any rate? Come here —

PETER STOCKMANN   No, no — not for worlds!

DR. STOCKMANN   Well, but just come here then. Do you see, we have got a table-cover?

PETER STOCKMANN   Yes, I noticed it.

DR. STOCKMANN   And we have got a lamp-shade too. Do you see? All out of Katherine's savings! It makes the room so cosy. Don't you think so? Just stand here for a moment — no, no, not there — just here, that's it! Look now, when you get the light on it altogether — I really think it looks very nice, doesn't it?

PETER STOCKMANN   Oh, if you can afford luxuries of this kind —

DR. STOCKMANN   Yes, I can afford it now. Katherine tells me I earn almost as much as we spend.

PETER STOCKMANN   Almost — yes!

DR. STOCKMANN   But a scientific man must live in a little bit of style. I am quite sure an ordinary civil servant spends more in a year than I do.

PETER STOCKMANN   I daresay. A civil servant — a man in a well-paid position —

DR. STOCKMANN   Well, any ordinary merchant, then! A man in that position spends two or three times as much as —

PETER STOCKMANN   It just depends on circumstances.

DR. STOCKMANN   At all events I assure you I don't waste money unprofitably. But I can't find it in my heart to deny myself the pleasure of entertaining my friends. I need that sort of thing, you know. I have lived for so long shut out of it all, that it is a necessity of life to me to mix with young, eager, ambitious men, men of liberal and active minds; and that describes every one of those fellows who are enjoying their supper in there. I wish you knew more of Hovstad —

PETER STOCKMANN   By the way, Hovstad was telling me he was going to print another article of yours.

DR. STOCKMANN   An article of mine?

PETER STOCKMANN   Yes, about the Baths. An article you wrote in the winter.

DR. STOCKMANN   Oh, that one! No, I don't intend that to appear just for the present.

PETER STOCKMANN   Why not? It seems to me that this would be the most opportune moment.

DR. STOCKMANN   Yes, very likely — under normal conditions. (*Crosses the room.*)

PETER STOCKMANN (*following him with his eyes*)   Is there anything abnormal about the present conditions?

DR. STOCKMANN (*standing still*)   To tell you the truth, Peter, I can't say just at this moment — at all events not to-night. There may be much that is very abnormal about the present conditions — and it is possible there may be nothing abnormal about them at all. It is quite possible it may be merely my imagination.

PETER STOCKMANN   I must say it all sounds most mysterious. Is there something going on that I am to be kept in ignorance of? I should have imagined that I, as Chairman of the governing body of the Baths —

DR. STOCKMANN   And I should have imagined that I — . Oh, come, don't let us fly out at one another, Peter.

PETER STOCKMANN   Heaven forbid! I am not in the habit of flying out at people, as you call it. But I am entitled to request most emphatically that all arrangements shall be made in a business-like manner, through the proper channels, and shall be dealt with by the legally constituted authorities. I can allow no going behind our backs by any roundabout means.

DR. STOCKMANN   Have I ever at any time tried to go behind your backs!

PETER STOCKMANN   You have an ingrained tendency to take your own way, at all events; and that is almost equally inadmissible in a well-ordered community. The individual ought undoubtedly to acquiesce in subordinating himself to the community — or, to speak more accurately, to the authorities who have the care of the community's welfare.

DR. STOCKMANN   Very likely. But what the deuce has all this got to do with me?

PETER STOCKMANN   That is exactly what you never appear to be willing to learn, my dear Thomas. But, mark my words, some day you will have to suffer for it — sooner or later. Now I have told you. Good-bye.

DR. STOCKMANN   Have you taken leave of your senses? You are on the wrong scent altogether.

PETER STOCKMANN   I am not usually that. You must excuse me now if I — (*calls into the dining-room*) Good night, Katherine. Good night, gentlemen. (*Goes out.*)

MRS. STOCKMANN (*coming from the dining-room*)   Has he gone?

DR. STOCKMANN   Yes, and in such a bad temper.

MRS. STOCKMANN   But, dear Thomas, what have you been doing to him again?

DR. STOCKMANN   Nothing at all. And, anyhow, he can't oblige me to make my report before the proper time.

MRS. STOCKMANN   What have you got to make a report to him about?

DR. STOCKMANN   Hm! Leave that to me, Katherine. — It is an extraordinary thing that the postman doesn't come.

(HOVSTAD, BILLINGS *and* HORSTER *have got up from the table and come into the sitting-room.* EJLIF *and* MORTEN *come in after them.*)

BILLING (*stretching himself*)   Ah — one feels a new man after a meal like that.

HOVSTAD   The mayor wasn't in a very sweet temper tonight, then.

DR. STOCKMANN   It is his stomach; he has a wretched digestion.

HOVSTAD   I rather think it was us two of the "People's Messenger" that he couldn't digest.

MRS. STOCKMANN   I thought you came out of it pretty well with him.

HOVSTAD   Oh yes; but it isn't anything more than a sort of truce.

BILLING   That is just what it is! That word sums up the situation.

DR. STOCKMANN   We must remember that Peter is a lonely man, poor chap. He has no home comforts of any kind; nothing but everlasting business. And all that infernal weak tea wash that he pours into himself! Now then, my boys, bring chairs up to the table. Aren't we going to have that toddy, Katherine?

MRS. STOCKMANN (*going into the dining-room*)   I am just getting it.

DR. STOCKMANN   Sit down here on the couch beside me, Captain Horster. We so seldom see you — . Please sit down, my friends.

(*They sit down at the table.* MRS. STOCKMANN *brings a tray, with a spirit-lamp, glasses, bottles, etc., upon it.*)

MRS. STOCKMANN   There you are! This is arrack, and this is rum, and this one is the brandy. Now every one must help himself.

DR. STOCKMANN (*taking a glass*)   We will. (*They all mix themselves some toddy.*) And let us have the cigars. Ejlif, you know where the box is. And you, Morten, can fetch my pipe. (*The two boys go into the room on the right.*)   I have a suspicion that Ejlif pockets a cigar now and then! — but I take no notice of it. (*Calls out*) And my smoking-cap too, Morten. Katherine, you can tell him where I left it. Ah, he has got it. (*The boys bring the various things.*) Now, my friends. I stick to my pipe, you know. This one has seen plenty of bad weather with me up north. (*Touches glasses with them*) Your good health! Ah! it is good to be sitting snug and warm here.

MRS. STOCKMANN (*who sits knitting*)   Do you sail soon, Captain Horster?

HORSTER   I expect to be ready to sail next week.

MRS. STOCKMANN   I suppose you are going to America?

HORSTER   Yes, that is the plan.

MRS. STOCKMANN   Then you won't be able to take part in the coming election.

HORSTER   Is there going to be an election?

BILLING   Didn't you know?

HORSTER   No, I don't mix myself up with those things.

BILLING   But do you not take an interest in public affairs?

HORSTER   No, I don't know anything about politics.

BILLING   All the same, one ought to vote, at any rate.

HORSTER   Even if one doesn't know anything about what is going on?

BILLING   Doesn't know! What do you mean by that? A community is like a ship; every one ought to be prepared to take the helm.

HORSTER   Maybe that is all very well on shore; but on board ship it wouldn't work.

HOVSTAD   It is astonishing how little most sailors care about what goes on on shore.

BILLING   Very extraordinary.

DR. STOCKMANN   Sailors are like birds of passage; they feel equally at home in any latitude. And that is only an additional reason for our being all the more keen, Hovstad. Is there to be anything of public interest in tomorrow's "Messenger"?

HOVSTAD   Nothing about municipal affairs. But the day after tomorrow I was thinking of printing your article —

DR. STOCKMANN   Ah, devil take it — my article! Look here, that must wait a bit.

HOVSTAD   Really? We had just got convenient space for it, and I thought it was just the opportune moment —

DR. STOCKMANN   Yes, yes, very likely you are right; but it must wait all the same. I will explain to you later.

(PETRA *comes in from the hall, in hat and cloak and with a bundle of exercise books under her arm.*)

PETRA   Good evening.

DR. STOCKMANN   Good evening, Petra; come along.

(*Mutual greetings;* PETRA *takes off her things and puts them down on a chair by the door.*)

PETRA   And you have all been sitting here enjoying yourselves, while I have been out slaving!

DR. STOCKMANN   Well, come and enjoy yourself too!

BILLING   May I mix a glass for you?

PETRA (*coming to the table*)   Thanks, I would rather do it; you always mix it too strong. But I forgot, father — I have a letter for you. (*Goes to the chair where she had laid her things.*)

DR. STOCKMANN   A letter? From whom?

PETRA (*looking in her coat pocket*)   The postman gave it to me just as I was going out —

DR. STOCKMANN (*getting up and going to her*)   And you only give to me now!

PETRA   I really had not time to run up again. There it is!

DR. STOCKMANN (*seizing the letter*)   Let's see, let's see, child! (*Looks at the address*) Yes, that's all right!

MRS. STOCKMANN   Is it the one you have been expecting so anxiously, Thomas?

DR. STOCKMANN   Yes, it is. I must go to my room now and — . Where shall I get a light, Katherine? Is there no lamp in my room again?

MRS. STOCKMANN   Yes, your lamp is all ready lit on your desk.

DR. STOCKMANN   Good, good. Excuse me for a moment — . (*Goes into his study.*)

PETRA   What do you suppose it is, mother?

MRS. STOCKMANN   I don't know; for the last day or two he has always been asking if the postman has not been.

BILLING   Probably some country patient.

PETRA   Poor old dad! — he will overwork himself soon. (*Mixes a glass for herself*) There, that will taste good!

HOVSTAD   Have you been teaching in the evening school again to-day?

PETRA (*sipping from her glass*)   Two hours.

BILLING   And four hours of school in the morning —

PETRA   Five hours.

MRS. STOCKMANN   And you have still got exercises to correct, I see.

PETRA   A whole heap, yes.

HORSTER   You are pretty full up with work too, it seems to me.

PETRA   Yes — but that is good. One is so delightfully tired after it.

BILLING   Do you like that?

PETRA   Yes, because one sleeps so well then.

MORTEN   You must be dreadfully wicked, Petra.

PETRA   Wicked?

MORTEN   Yes, because you work so much. Mr. Rörlund says work is a punishment for our sins.

EJLIF   Pooh, what a duffer you are, to believe a thing like that!

MRS. STOCKMANN   Come, come, Ejlif!

BILLING (*laughing*)   That's capital!

HOVSTAD   Don't you want to work as hard as that, Morten?

MORTEN   No, indeed I don't.

HOVSTAD   What do you want to be, then?

MORTEN   I should like best to be a Viking.

EJLIF   You would have to be a pagan then.

MORTEN   Well, I could become a pagan, couldn't I?

BILLING   I agree with you, Morten! My sentiments, exactly.

MRS. STOCKMANN (*signalling to him*)   I am sure that is not true, Mr. Billing.

BILLING   Yes, I swear it is! I am a pagan, and I am proud of it. Believe me, before long we shall all be pagans.

MORTEN   And then we shall be allowed to do anything we like?

BILLING   Well, you see, Morten — .

MRS. STOCKMANN   You must go to your room now, boys; I am sure you have some lessons to learn for to-morrow.

EJLIF   I should like so much to stay a little longer —

MRS. STOCKMANN   No, no; away you go, both of you.

(*The boys say good-night and go into the room on the left.*)

HOVSTAD   Do you really think it can do the boys any harm to hear such things?

MRS. STOCKMANN   I don't know; but I don't like it.

PETRA   But you know, mother, I think you really are wrong about it.

MRS. STOCKMANN   Maybe, but I don't like it — not in our own home.

PETRA   There is so much falsehood both at home and at school. At home one must not speak, and at school we have to stand and tell lies to the children.

HORSTER   Tell lies?

PETRA   Yes, don't you suppose we have to teach them all sorts of things that we don't believe?

BILLING   That is perfectly true.

PETRA   If only I had the means I would start a school of my own, and it would be conducted on very different lines.

BILLING   Oh, bother the means — !

HORSTER   Well if you are thinking of that, Miss Stockmann, I shall be delighted to provide you with a schoolroom. The great big old house my father left me is standing almost empty; there is an immense dining-room downstairs —

PETRA (*laughing*)   Thank you very much; but I am afraid nothing will come of it.

HOVSTAD   No, Miss Petra is much more likely to take to journalism, I expect. By the way, have you had time to do anything with that English story you promised to translate for us?

PETRA   No, not yet; but you shall have it in good time.

(DR. STOCKMANN *comes in from his room with an open letter in his hand.*)

DR. STOCKMANN (*waving the letter*)   Well, now the town will have something new to talk about, I can tell you!

BILLING   Something new?

MRS. STOCKMANN   What is this?

DR. STOCKMANN   A great discovery, Katherine.

HOVSTAD   Really?

MRS. STOCKMANN   A discovery of yours?

DR. STOCKMANN   A discovery of mine. (*Walks up and down.*) Just let them come saying, as usual, that it is all fancy and a crazy man's imagination! But they will be careful what they say this time, I can tell you!

PETRA   But, father, tell us what it is.

DR. STOCKMANN Yes, yes — only give me time, and you shall know all about it. If only I had Peter here now! It just shows how we men can go about forming our judgments, when in reality we are as blind as any moles —

HOVSTAD What are you driving at, Doctor?

DR. STOCKMANN (*standing still by the table*) Isn't it the universal opinion that our town is a healthy spot?

HOVSTAD Certainly.

DR. STOCKMANN Quite an unusually healthy spot, in fact — a place that deserves to be recommended in the warmest possible manner either for invalids or for people who are well —

MRS. STOCKMANN Yes, but my dear Thomas —

DR. STOCKMANN And we have been recommending it and praising it — I have written and written, both in the "Messenger" and in pamphlets —

HOVSTAD Well, what then?

DR. STOCKMANN And the Baths — we have called them the "main artery of the town's life-blood," the "nerve-centre of our town," and the devil knows what else —

BILLING "The town's pulsating heart" was the expression I once used on an important occasion —

DR. STOCKMANN Quite so. Well, do you know what they really are, these great, splendid, much praised Baths that have cost so much money — do you know what they are?

HOVSTAD No, what are they?

MRS. STOCKMANN Yes, what are they?

DR. STOCKMANN The whole place is a pesthouse!

PETRA The Baths, father?

MRS. STOCKMANN (*at the same time*) Our Baths!

HOVSTAD But, Doctor —

BILLING Absolutely incredible!

DR. STOCKMANN The whole Bath establishment is a whited, poisoned sepulchre, I tell you — the gravest possible danger to the public health! All the nastiness up at Mölledal, all that stinking filth, is infecting the water in the conduit-pipes leading to the reservoir; and the same cursed, filthy poison oozes out on the shore too —

HORSTER Where the bathing-place is?

DR. STOCKMANN Just there.

HOVSTAD How do you come to be so certain of all this, Doctor?

DR. STOCKMANN I have investigated the matter most conscientiously. For a long time past I have suspected something of the kind. Last year we had some very strange cases of illness among the visitors — typhoid cases, and cases of gastric fever —

MRS. STOCKMANN Yes, that is quite true.

DR. STOCKMANN At the time, we supposed the visitors had been infected before they came; but later on, in the winter, I began to have a different opinion; and so I set myself to examine the water, as well as I could.

MRS. STOCKMANN Then that is what you have been so busy with?

DR. STOCKMANN Indeed I have been busy, Katherine. But here I had none of the necessary scientific apparatus; so I sent samples, both of the drinking-water and of the sea-water, up to the University, to have an accurate analysis made by a chemist.

HOVSTAD   And have you got that?

DR. STOCKMANN (*showing him the letter*)   Here it is! It proves the presence of decomposing organic matter in the water — it is full of infusoria. The water is absolutely dangerous to use, either internally or externally.

MRS. STOCKMANN   What a mercy you discovered it in time.

DR. STOCKMANN   You may well say so.

HOVSTAD   And what do you propose to do now, Doctor?

DR. STOCKMANN   To see the matter put right — naturally.

HOVSTAD   Can that be done?

DR. STOCKMANN   It must be done. Otherwise the Baths will be absolutely useless and wasted. But we need not anticipate that; I have a very clear idea what we shall have to do.

MRS. STOCKMANN   But why have you kept this all so secret, dear?

DR. STOCKMANN   Do you suppose I was going to run about the town gossiping about it, before I had absolute proof? No, thank you. I am not such a fool.

PETRA   Still, you might have told us —

DR. STOCKMANN   Not a living soul. But to-morrow you may run round to the old Badger —

MRS. STOCKMANN   Oh, Thomas! Thomas!

DR. STOCKMANN   Well, to your grandfather, then. The old boy will have something to be astonished at! I know he thinks I am cracked — and there are lots of other people think so too, I have noticed. But now these good folks shall see — they shall just see — ! (*Walks about, rubbing his hands.*) There will be a nice upset in the town, Katherine; you can't imagine what it will be. All the conduit-pipes will have to be relaid.

HOVSTAD (*getting up*)   All the conduit-pipes — ?

DR. STOCKMANN   Yes, of course. The intake is too low down; it will have to be lifted to a position much higher up.

PETRA   Then you were right after all.

DR. STOCKMANN   Ah, you remember, Petra — I wrote opposing the plans before the work was begun. But at that time no one would listen to me. Well, I am going to let them have it, now! Of course I have prepared a report for the Baths Committee; I have had it ready for a week, and was only waiting for this to come. (*Shows the letter.*) Now it shall go off at once. (*Goes into his room and comes back with some papers.*) Look at that! Four closely written sheets! — and the letter shall go with them. Give me a bit of paper, Katherine — something to wrap them up in. That will do! Now give it to — to — (*stamps his foot*) — what the deuce is her name? — give it to the maid, and tell her to take it at once to the Mayor.

(MRS. STOCKMANN *takes the packet and goes out through the dining-room.*)

PETRA   What do you think Uncle Peter will say, father?

DR. STOCKMANN   What is there for him to say? I should think he would be very glad that such an important truth has been brought to light.

HOVSTAD   Will you let me print a short note about your discovery in the "Messenger"?

DR. STOCKMANN   I shall be very much obliged if you will.

HOVSTAD   It is very desirable that the public should be informed of it without delay.

DR. STOCKMANN   Certainly.

MRS. STOCKMANN (*coming back*)   She has just gone with it.

BILLING   Upon my soul, Doctor, you are going to be the foremost man in the town!

DR. STOCKMANN (*walking about happily*)   Nonsense! As a matter of fact I have done nothing more than my duty. I have only made a lucky find — that's all. Still, all the same —

BILLING   Hovstad, don't you think the town ought to give Dr. Stockmann some sort of testimonial?

HOVSTAD   I will suggest it, anyway.

BILLING   And I will speak to Aslaksen about it.

DR. STOCKMANN   No, my good friends, don't let us have any of that nonsense. I won't hear of anything of the kind. And if the Baths Committee should think of voting me an increase of salary, I will not accept it. Do you hear, Katherine — I won't accept it.

MRS. STOCKMANN   You are quite right, Thomas.

PETRA (*lifting her glass*)   Your health, father!

HOVSTAD *and* BILLING   Your health, Doctor! Good health!

HORSTER (*touches glasses with* DR. STOCKMANN)   I hope it will bring you nothing but good luck.

DR. STOCKMANN   Thank you, thank you, my dear fellows! I feel tremendously happy! It is a splendid thing for a man to be able to feel that he has done a service to his native town and to his fellow-citizens. Hurrah, Katherine! (*He puts his arms round her and whirls her round and round, while she protests with laughing cries. They all laugh, clap their hands and cheer the* DOCTOR. *The boys put their heads in at the door to see what is going on.*)

Act Two

Scene: The same. The door into the dining-room is shut. It is morning. MRS. STOCKMANN, *with a sealed letter in her hand, comes in from the dining-room, goes to the door of the* DOCTOR'S *study and peeps in.*

MRS. STOCKMANN   Are you in, Thomas?

DR. STOCKMANN (*from within his room*)   Yes, I have just come in. (*Comes into the room*) What is it?

MRS. STOCKMANN   A letter from your brother.

DR. STOCKMANN   Aha, let us see! (*Opens the letter and reads*) "I return herewith the manuscript you sent me" — (*reads on in a low murmur*) Hm! —

MRS. STOCKMANN   What does he say?

DR. STOCKMANN (*putting the papers in his pocket*)   Oh, he only writes that he will come up here himself about midday.

MRS. STOCKMANN   Well, try and remember to be at home this time.

DR. STOCKMANN   That will be all right; I have got through all my morning visits.

MRS. STOCKMANN   I am extremely curious to know how he takes it.

DR. STOCKMANN   You will see he won't like it's having been I, and not he, that made the discovery.

MRS. STOCKMANN   Aren't you a little nervous about that?

DR. STOCKMANN   Oh, he really will be pleased enough, you know. But, at the same time, Peter is so confoundedly afraid of anyone's doing any service to the town except himself.

MRS. STOCKMANN I will tell you what, Thomas — you should be good-natured, and share the credit of this with him. Couldn't you make out that it was he who set you on the scent of this discovery?

DR. STOCKMANN I am quite willing. If only I can get the thing set right. I — (MORTEN KIIL *puts his head in through the door leading from the hall, looks around in an inquiring manner and chuckles.*)

MORTEN KIIL (*slyly*) Is it — is it true?

MRS. STOCKMANN (*going to the door*) Father! — is it you?

DR. STOCKMANN Ah, Mr. Kiil — good morning, good morning!

MRS. STOCKMANN But come along in.

MORTEN KIIL If it is true, I will; if not, I am off.

DR. STOCKMANN If what is true?

MORTEN KIIL This tale about the water-supply. Is it true?

DR. STOCKMANN Certainly it is true. But how did you come to hear it?

MORTEN KIIL (*coming in*) Petra ran in on her way to the school —

DR. STOCKMANN Did she?

MORTEN KIIL Yes; and she declares that — . I thought she was only making a fool of me, but it isn't like Petra to do that.

DR. STOCKMANN Of course not. How could you imagine such a thing!

MORTEN KIIL Oh well, it is better never to trust anybody; you may find you have been made a fool of before you know where you are. But it is really true, all the same?

DR. STOCKMANN You can depend upon it that it is true. Won't you sit down? (*Settles him on the couch.*) Isn't it a real bit of luck for the town —

MORTEN KIIL (*suppressing his laughter*) A bit of luck for the town?

DR. STOCKMANN Yes, that I made the discovery in good time.

MORTEN KIIL (*as before*) Yes, yes, yes! — But I should never have thought you the sort of man to pull your own brother's leg like this!

DR. STOCKMANN Pull his leg!

MRS. STOCKMANN Really, father dear —

MORTEN KIIL (*resting his hands and his chin in the handle of his stick and winking slyly at the* DOCTOR). Let me see, what was the story? Some kind of beast that had got into the water-pipes, wasn't it?

DR. STOCKMANN Infusoria — yes.

MORTEN KIIL And a lot of these beasts had got in, according to Petra — a tremendous lot.

DR. STOCKMANN Certainly; hundreds of thousands of them, probably.

MORTEN KIIL But no one can see them — isn't that so?

DR. STOCKMANN Yes; you can't see them.

MORTEN KIIL (*with a quiet chuckle*) Damme — it's the finest story I have ever heard!

DR. STOCKMANN What do you mean?

MORTEN KIIL But you will never get the Mayor to believe a thing like that.

DR. STOCKMANN We shall see.

MORTEN KIIL Do you think he will be fool enough to — ?

DR. STOCKMANN I hope the whole town will be fools enough.

MORTEN KIIL The whole town! Well, it wouldn't be a bad thing. It would just serve them right and teach them a lesson. They think themselves so much cleverer than we old fellows. They hounded me out of the council; they did, I tell you — they hounded me out. Now they shall pay for it. You pull their legs too, Thomas!

DR. STOCKMANN   Really, I —

MORTEN KIIL   You pull their legs! (*Gets up.*) If you can work it so that the Mayor and his friends all swallow the same bait, I will give ten pounds to a charity — like a shot!

DR. STOCKMANN   That is very kind of you.

MORTEN KIIL   Yes, I haven't got much money to throw away, I can tell you; but if you can work this, I will give five pounds to a charity at Christmas. (HOVSTAD *comes in by the hall door.*)

HOVSTAD   Good morning! (*Stops.*) Oh, I beg your pardon —

DR. STOCKMANN   Not at all; come in.

MORTEN KIIL (*with another chuckle*)   Oho! — is he in this too?

HOVSTAD   What do you mean?

DR. STOCKMANN   Certainly he is.

MORTEN KIIL   I might have known it! It must get into the papers. You know how to do it, Thomas! Set your wits to work. Now I must go.

DR. STOCKMANN   Won't you stay a little while?

MORTEN KIIL   No, I must be off now. You keep up this game for all it is worth; you won't repent it, I'm damned if you will! (*He goes out;* MRS. STOCKMANN *follows him into the hall.*)

DR. STOCKMANN (*laughing*)   Just imagine — the old chap doesn't believe a word of all this about the water-supply.

HOVSTAD   Oh that was it, then?

DR. STOCKMANN   Yes, that was what we were talking about. Perhaps it is the same thing that brings you here?

HOVSTAD   Yes, it is. Can you spare me a few minutes, Doctor?

DR. STOCKMANN   As long as you like, my dear fellow.

HOVSTAD   Have you heard from the Mayor yet?

DR. STOCKMANN   Not yet. He is coming here later.

HOVSTAD   I have given the matter a great deal of thought since last night.

DR. STOCKMANN   Well?

HOVSTAD   From your point of view, as a doctor and a man of science, this affair of the water-supply is an isolated matter. I mean, you do not realise that it involves a great many other things.

DR. STOCKMANN   How, do you mean — let us sit down, my dear fellow. No, sit here on the couch. (HOVSTAD *sits down on the couch,* DR. STOCKMANN *on a chair on the other side of the table.*) Now then. You mean that — ?

HOVSTAD   You said yesterday that the pollution of the water was due to impurities in the soil.

DR. STOCKMANN   Yes, unquestionably it is due to that poisonous morass up at Mölledal.

HOVSTAD   Begging your pardon, doctor, I fancy it is due to quite another morass altogether.

DR. STOCKMANN   What morass?

HOVSTAD   The morass that the whole life of our town is built on and is rotting in.

DR. STOCKMANN   What the deuce are you driving at, Hovstad?

HOVSTAD   The whole of the town's interests have, little by little, got into the hands of a pack of officials.

DR. STOCKMANN   Oh, come! — they are not all officials.

HOVSTAD   No, but those that are not officials are at any rate the officials' friends and adherents; it is the wealthy folk, the old families in the town, that have got us entirely in their hands.

DR. STOCKMANN   Yes, but after all they are men of ability and knowledge.

HOVSTAD   Did they show any ability or knowledge when they laid the conduit-pipes where they are now?

DR. STOCKMANN   No, of course that was a great piece of stupidity on their part. But that is going to be set right now.

HOVSTAD   Do you think that will be all such plain sailing?

DR. STOCKMANN   Plain sailing or no, it has got to be done, anyway.

HOVSTAD   Yes, provided the press takes up the question.

DR. STOCKMANN   I don't think that will be necessary, my dear fellow, I am certain my brother —

HOVSTAD   Excuse me, Doctor; I feel bound to tell you I am inclined to take the matter up.

DR. STOCKMANN   In the paper?

HOVSTAD   Yes. When I took over the "People's Messenger" my idea was to break up this ring of self-opinionated old fossils who had got hold of all the influence.

DR. STOCKMANN   But you know you told me yourself what the result had been; you nearly ruined your paper.

HOVSTAD   Yes, at the time we were obliged to climb down a peg or two, it is quite true; because there was a danger of the whole project of the Baths coming to nothing if they failed us. But now the scheme has been carried through, and we can dispense with these grand gentlemen.

DR. STOCKMANN   Dispense with them, yes; but we owe them a great debt of gratitude.

HOVSTAD   That shall be recognised ungrudgingly. But a journalist of my democratic tendencies cannot let such an opportunity as this slip. The bubble of official infallibility must be pricked. This superstition must be destroyed, like any other.

DR. STOCKMANN   I am whole-heartedly with you in that, Mr. Hovstad; if it is a superstition, away with it!

HOVSTAD   I should be very reluctant to bring the Mayor into it, because he is your brother. But I am sure you will agree with me that truth should be the first consideration.

DR. STOCKMANN   That goes without saying. (*With sudden emphasis*) Yes, but — but —

HOVSTAD   You must not misjudge me. I am neither more self-interested nor more ambitious than most men.

DR. STOCKMANN   My dear fellow — who suggests anything of the kind?

HOVSTAD   I am of humble origin, as you know; and that has given me opportunities of knowing what is the most crying need in the humbler ranks of life. It is that they should be allowed some part in the direction of public affairs, Doctor. That is what will develop their faculties and intelligence and self-respect —

DR. STOCKMANN   I quite appreciate that.

HOVSTAD   Yes — and in my opinion a journalist incurs a heavy responsibility if he neglects a favourable opportunity of emancipating the masses — the humble and oppressed. I know well enough that in exalted circles I shall be called an agitator, and all that sort of thing; but they may call what they like. If only my conscience doesn't reproach me, then —

DR. STOCKMANN   Quite right! Quite right, Mr. Hovstad. But all the same — devil take it! (*A knock is heard at the door.*) Come in!

ASLAKSEN appears at the door. He is poorly but decently dressed, in black, with a slightly crumpled white neckcloth; he wears gloves and has a felt hat in his hand.)

ASLAKSEN (*bowing*)   Excuse my taking the liberty, Doctor —

DR. STOCKMANN (*getting up*)   Ah, it is you, Aslaksen!

ASLAKSEN   Yes, Doctor.

HOVSTAD (*standing up*)   Is it me you want, Aslaksen?

ASLAKSEN   No; I didn't know I should find you here. No, it was the Doctor I —

DR. STOCKMANN   I am quite at your service. What is it?

ASLAKSEN   Is what I heard from Mr. Billing true, sir — that you mean to improve our water-supply?

DR. STOCKMANN   Yes, for the Baths.

ASLAKSEN   Quite so, I understand. Well, I have come to say that I will back that up by every means in my power.

HOVSTAD (*to the Doctor*)   You see!

DR. STOCKMANN   I shall be very grateful to you, but —

ASLAKSEN   Because it may be no bad thing to have us small tradesmen at your back. We form, as it were, a compact majority in the town — if we choose. And it is always a good thing to have the majority with you, Doctor.

DR. STOCKMANN   That is undeniably true; but I confess I don't see why such unusual precautions should be necessary in this case. It seems to me that such a plain, straight-forward thing —

ASLAKSEN   Oh, it may be very desirable, all the same. I know our local authorities so well; officials are not generally very ready to act on proposals that come from other people. That is why I think it would not be at all amiss if we made a little demonstration.

HOVSTAD   That's right.

DR. STOCKMANN   Demonstration, did you say? What on earth are you going to make a demonstration about?

ASLAKSEN   We shall proceed with the greatest moderation, Doctor. Moderation is always my aim; it is the greatest virtue in a citizen — at least, I think so.

DR. STOCKMANN   It is well known to be a characteristic of yours, Mr. Aslaksen.

ASLAKSEN   Yes, I think I may pride myself on that. And this matter of the water-supply is of the greatest importance to us small tradesmen. The Baths promise to be a regular gold-mine for the town. We shall all make our living out of them, especially those of us who are householders. That is why we will back up the project as strongly as possible. And as I am at present Chairman of the Householders' Association —

DR. STOCKMANN   Yes — ?

ASLAKSEN   And, what is more, local secretary of the Temperance Society — you know sir, I suppose, that I am a worker in the temperance cause?

DR. STOCKMANN   Of course, of course.

ASLAKSEN Well, you can understand that I come into contact with a great many people. And as I have the reputation of a temperate and law-abiding citizen — like yourself, Doctor — I have a certain influence in the town, a little bit of power, if I may be allowed to say so.

DR. STOCKMANN I know that quite well, Mr. Aslaksen.

ASLAKSEN So you see it would be an easy matter for me to set on foot some testimonial, if necessary.

DR. STOCKMANN A testimonial?

ASLAKSEN Yes, some kind of an address of thanks from the townsmen for your share in a matter of such importance to the community. I need scarcely say that it would have to be drawn up with the greatest regard to moderation, so as not to offend the authorities — who, after all, have the reins in their hands. If we pay strict attention to that, no one can take it amiss, I should think!

HOVSTAD Well, and even supposing they didn't like it —

ASLAKSEN No, no, no; there must be no discourtesy to the authorities, Mr. Hovstad. It is no use falling foul of those upon whom our welfare so closely depends. I have done that in my time, and no good ever comes of it. But no one can take exception to a reasonable and frank expression of a citizen's views.

DR. STOCKMANN (shaking him by the hand) I can't tell you, dear Mr. Aslaksen, how extremely pleased I am to find such hearty support among my fellow-citizens. I am delighted — delighted! Now, you will take a small glass of sherry, eh?

ASLAKSEN No, thank you; I never drink alcohol of that kind.

DR. STOCKMANN Well, what do you say to a glass of beer, then?

ASLAKSEN Nor that either, thank you, Doctor. I never drink anything as early as this. I am going into town now to talk this over with one or two house-holders, and prepare the ground.

DR. STOCKMANN It is tremendously kind of you, Mr. Aslaksen; but I really cannot understand the necessity for all these precautions. It seems to me that the thing should go of itself.

ASLAKSEN The authorities are somewhat slow to move, Doctor. Far be it from me to seem to blame them —

HOVSTAD We are going to stir them up in the paper tomorrow, Aslaksen.

ASLAKSEN But not violently, I trust, Mr. Hovstad. Proceed with moderation, or you will do nothing with them. You may take my advice; I have gathered my experience in the school of life. Well, I must say good-bye, Doctor. You know now that we small tradesmen are at your back at all events, like a solid wall. You have the compact majority on your side, Doctor.

DR. STOCKMANN I am very much obliged, dear Mr. Aslaksen. (Shakes hands with him) Good-bye, good-bye.

ASLAKSEN Are you going my way, towards the printing-office, Mr. Hovstad?

HOVSTAD I will come later; I have something to settle up first.

ASLAKSEN Very well.

(Bows and goes out; STOCKMANN follows him into the hall.)

HOVSTAD (as STOCKMANN comes in again) Well, what do you think of that, Doctor? Don't you think it is high time we stirred a little life into all this slackness and vacillation and cowardice?

DR. STOCKMANN Are you referring to Aslaksen?

HOVSTAD Yes, I am. He is one of those who are floundering in a bog — decent enough fellow though he may be, otherwise. And most of the people here are in just the same case — see-sawing and edging first to one side and then to the other, so overcome with caution and scruple that they never dare to take any decided step.

DR. STOCKMANN Yes, but Aslaksen seemed to me so thoroughly well-intentioned.

HOVSTAD There is one thing I esteem higher than that; and that is for a man to be self-reliant and sure of himself.

DR. STOCKMANN I think you are perfectly right there.

HOVSTAD That is why I want to seize this opportunity, and try if I cannot manage to put a little virility into these well-intentioned people for once. The idol of Authority must be shattered in this town. This gross and inexcusable blunder about the water-supply must be brought home to the mind of every municipal voter.

DR. STOCKMANN Very well; if you are of opinion that it is for the good of the community, so be it. But not until I have had a talk with my brother.

HOVSTAD Anyway, I will get a leading article ready; and if the Mayor refuses to take the matter up —

DR. STOCKMANN How can you suppose such a thing possible?

HOVSTAD It is conceivable. And in that case —

DR. STOCKMANN In that case I promise you —. Look here, in that case you may print my report — every word of it.

HOVSTAD May I? Have I your word for it?

DR. STOCKMANN (giving him the MS.) Here it is; take it with you. It can do no harm for you to read it through, and you can give it me back later on.

HOVSTAD Good, good! That is what I will do. And now good-bye, Doctor.

DR. STOCKMANN Good-bye, good-bye. You will see everything will run quite smoothly, Mr. Hovstad — quite smoothly.

HOVSTAD Hm! — we shall see. (Bows and goes out.)

DR. STOCKMANN (opens the dining-room door and looks in) Katherine! Oh, you are back, Petra?

PETRA (coming in) Yes, I have just come from the school.

MRS. STOCKMANN (coming in) Has he not been here yet?

DR. STOCKMANN Peter? No. But I have had a long talk with Hovstad. He is quite excited about my discovery. I find it has a much wider bearing than I at first imagined. And he has put his paper at my disposal if necessity should arise.

MRS. STOCKMANN Do you think it will?

DR. STOCKMANN Not for a moment. But at all events it makes me feel proud to know that I have the liberal-minded independent press on my side. Yes, and — just imagine — I have had a visit from the Chairman of the Householders' Association!

MRS. STOCKMANN Oh! What did he want?

DR. STOCKMANN To offer me his support too. They will support me in a body if it should be necessary. Katherine — do you know what I have got behind me?

MRS. STOCKMANN Behind you? No, what have you got behind you?

DR. STOCKMANN The compact majority.

MRS. STOCKMANN Really? Is that a good thing for you, Thomas?

DR. STOCKMANN   I should think it was a good thing. (*Walks up and down rubbing his hands.*) By Jove, it's a fine thing to feel this bond of brotherhood between oneself and one's fellow-citizens!

PETRA   And to be able to do so much that is good and useful, father!

DR. STOCKMANN   And for one's own native town into the bargain, my child!

MRS. STOCKMANN   That was a ring at the bell.

DR. STOCKMANN   It must be he, then. (*A knock is heard at the door.*) Come in!

PETER STOCKMANN (*comes in from the hall*)   Good morning.

DR. STOCKMANN   Glad to see you, Peter!

MRS. STOCKMANN   Good morning, Peter. How are you?

PETER STOCKMANN   So so, thank you. (*To* DR. STOCKMANN) I received from you yesterday, after office-hours, a report dealing with the condition of the water at the Baths.

DR. STOCKMANN   Yes. Have you read it?

PETER STOCKMANN   Yes, I have.

DR. STOCKMANN   And what have you to say to it?

PETER STOCKMANN (*with a sidelong glance*)   Hm! —

MRS. STOCKMANN   Come along, Petra.

(*She and* PETRA *go into the room on the left.*)

PETER STOCKMANN (*after a pause*)   Was it necessary to make all these investigations behind my back?

DR. STOCKMANN   Yes, because until I was absolutely certain about it —

PETER STOCKMANN   Then you mean that you are absolutely certain now?

DR. STOCKMANN   Surely you are convinced of that.

PETER STOCKMANN   Is it your intention to bring this document before the Baths Committee as a sort of official communication?

DR. STOCKMANN   Certainly. Something must be done in the matter — and that quickly.

PETER STOCKMANN   As usual, you employ violent expressions in your report. You say, amongst other things, that what we offer visitors in our Baths is a permanent supply of poison.

DR. STOCKMANN   Well, can you describe it any other way, Peter? Just think — water that is poisonous, whether you drink it or bathe in it! And this we offer to the poor sick folk who come to us trustfully and pay us at an exorbitant rate to be made well again!

PETER STOCKMANN   And your reasoning leads you to this conclusion, that we must build a sewer to draw off the alleged impurities from Mölledal and must relay the water-conduits.

DR. STOCKMANN   Yes. Do you see any other way out of it? I don't.

PETER STOCKMANN   I made a pretext this morning to go and see the town engineer, and, as if only half seriously, broached the subject of these proposals as a thing we might perhaps have to take under consideration some time later on.

DR. STOCKMANN   Some time later on!

PETER STOCKMANN   He smiled at what he considered to be my extravagance, naturally. Have you taken the trouble to consider what your proposed alterations would cost? According to the information I obtained, the expenses would probably mount up to fifteen or twenty thousand pounds.

DR. STOCKMANN   Would it cost so much?

PETER STOCKMANN Yes; and the worst part of it would be that the work would take at least two years.

DR. STOCKMANN Two years? Two whole years?

PETER STOCKMANN At least. And what are we to do with the Baths in the meantime? Close them? Indeed we should be obliged to. And do you suppose any one would come near the place after it had got about that the water was dangerous?

DR. STOCKMANN Yes, but, Peter, that is what it is.

PETER STOCKMANN And all this at this juncture — just as the Baths are beginning to be known. There are other towns in the neighbourhood with qualifications to attract visitors for bathing purposes. Don't you suppose they would immediately strain every nerve to divert the entire stream of strangers to themselves? Unquestionably they would; and then where should we be? We should probably have to abandon the whole thing, which has cost us so much money — and then you would have ruined your native town.

DR. STOCKMANN I — should have ruined —!

PETER STOCKMANN It is simply and solely through the Baths that the town has before it any future worth mentioning. You know that just as well as I.

DR. STOCKMANN But what do you think ought to be done, then?

PETER STOCKMANN Your report has not convinced me that the condition of the water at the Baths is as bad as you represent it to be.

DR. STOCKMANN I tell you it is even worse! — or at all events it will be in summer, when the warm weather comes.

PETER STOCKMANN As I said, I believe you exaggerate the matter considerably. A capable physician ought to know what measures to take — he ought to be capable of preventing injurious influences or of remedying them if they become obviously persistent.

DR. STOCKMANN Well? What more?

PETER STOCKMANN The water-supply for the Baths is now an established fact, and in consequence must be treated as such. But probably the Committee, at its discretion, will not be disinclined to consider the question of how far it might be possible to introduce certain improvements consistently with a reasonable expenditure.

DR. STOCKMANN And do you suppose that I will have anything to do with such a piece of trickery as that?

PETER STOCKMANN Trickery!!

DR. STOCKMANN Yes, it would be a trick — a fraud, a lie, a downright crime towards the public, towards the whole community!

PETER STOCKMANN I have not, as I remarked before, been able to convince myself that there is actually any imminent danger.

DR. STOCKMANN You have! It is impossible that you should not be convinced. I know I have represented the facts absolutely truthfully and fairly. And you know it very well, Peter, only you won't acknowledge it. It was owing to your action that both the Baths and the water-conduits were built where they are; and that is what you won't acknowledge — that damnable blunder of yours. Pooh! — do you suppose I don't see through you?

PETER STOCKMANN And even if that were true? If I perhaps guard my reputation somewhat anxiously, it is in the interests of the town. Without moral authority I am powerless to direct public affairs as seems, to my judgment, to be best for the common good. And on that account — and for various other reasons, too — it appears to me to be a matter of importance that your report should not be delivered to the Committee. In the interests of the public, you must withhold it. Then, later on, I will raise the question and we will do our best, privately; but nothing of this unfortunate affair — not a single word of it — must come to the ears of the public.

DR. STOCKMANN I am afraid you will not be able to prevent that now, my dear Peter.

PETER STOCKMANN It must and shall be prevented.

DR. STOCKMANN It is no use, I tell you. There are too many people that know about it.

PETER STOCKMANN That know about it? Who? Surely you don't mean those fellows on the "People's Messenger"?

DR. STOCKMANN Yes, they know. The liberal-minded independent press is going to see that you do your duty.

PETER STOCKMANN (*after a short pause*) You are an extraordinarily independent man, Thomas. Have you given no thought to the consequences this may have for yourself?

DR. STOCKMANN Consequences? — for me?

PETER STOCKMANN For you and yours, yes.

DR. STOCKMANN What the deuce do you mean?

PETER STOCKMANN I believe I have always behaved in a brotherly way to you — have always been ready to oblige or to help you?

DR. STOCKMANN Yes, you have, and I am grateful to you for it.

PETER STOCKMANN There is no need. Indeed, to some extent I was forced to do so — for my own sake. I always hoped that, if I helped to improve your financial position, I should be able to keep some check on you.

DR. STOCKMANN What!! Then it was only for your own sake —!

PETER STOCKMANN Up to a certain point, yes. It is painful for a man in an official position to have his nearest relative compromising himself time after time.

DR. STOCKMANN And do you consider that I do that?

PETER STOCKMANN Yes, unfortunately, you do, without even being aware of it. You have a restless, pugnacious, rebellious disposition. And then there is that disastrous propensity of yours to want to write about every sort of possible and impossible thing. The moment an idea comes into your head, you must needs go and write a newspaper article or a whole pamphlet about it.

DR. STOCKMANN Well, but is it not the duty of a citizen to let the public share in any new ideas he may have?

PETER STOCKMANN Oh, the public doesn't require any new ideas. The public is best served by the good, old-established ideas it already has.

DR. STOCKMANN And that is your honest opinion?

PETER STOCKMANN Yes, and for once I must talk frankly to you. Hitherto I have tried to avoid doing so, because I know how irritable you are; but now I must tell you the truth, Thomas. You have no conception what an amount of harm you do yourself by your impetuosity. You complain of the authorities, you even complain of the government — you are always pulling them to pieces; you insist that you have been neglected and persecuted. But what else can such a cantankerous man as you expect?

DR. STOCKMANN   What next! Cantankerous, am I?

PETER STOCKMANN   Yes, Thomas, you are an extremely cantankerous man to work with — I know that to my cost. You disregard everything that you ought to have consideration for. You seem completely to forget that it is me you have to thank for your appointment here as medical officer to the Baths —

DR. STOCKMANN   I was entitled to it as a matter of course! — I and nobody else! I was the first person to see that the town could be made into a flourishing watering-place, and I was the only one who saw it at that time. I had to fight single-handed in support of the idea for many years; and I wrote and wrote —

PETER STOCKMANN   Undoubtedly. But things were not ripe for the scheme then — though, of course, you could not judge of that in your out-of-the-way corner up north. But as soon as the opportune moment came I — and the others — took the matter into our hands —

DR. STOCKMANN   Yes, and made this mess of all my beautiful plan. It is pretty obvious now what clever fellows you were!

PETER STOCKMANN   To my mind the whole thing only seems to mean that you are seeking another outlet for your combativeness. You want to pick a quarrel with your superiors — an old habit of yours. You cannot put up with any authority over you. You look askance at anyone who occupies a superior official position; you regard him as a personal enemy, and then any stick is good enough to beat him with. But now I have called your attention to the fact that the town's interests are at stake — and, incidentally, my own too. And therefore I must tell you, Thomas, that you will find me inexorable with regard to what I am about to require you to do.

DR. STOCKMANN   And what is that?

PETER STOCKMANN   As you have been so indiscreet as to speak of this delicate matter to outsiders, despite the fact that you ought to have treated it as entirely official and confidential, it is obviously impossible to hush it up now. All sorts of rumours will get about directly, and everybody who has a grudge against us will take care to embellish these rumours. So it will be necessary for you to refute them publicly.

DR. STOCKMANN   I! How? I don't understand.

PETER STOCKMANN   What we shall expect is that, after making further investigations, you will come to the conclusion that the matter is not by any means as dangerous or as critical as you imagined in the first instance.

DR. STOCKMANN   Oho! — so that is what you expect!

PETER STOCKMANN   And, what is more, we shall expect you to make public profession of your confidence in the Committee and in their readiness to consider fully and conscientiously what steps may be necessary to remedy any possible defects.

DR. STOCKMANN   But you will never be able to do that by patching and tinkering at it — never! Take my word for it, Peter; I mean what I say, as deliberately and emphatically as possible.

PETER STOCKMANN   As an officer under the Committee, you have no right to any individual opinion.

DR. STOCKMANN (*amazed*)   No right?

PETER STOCKMANN   In your official capacity, no. As a private person, it is quite another matter. But as a subordinate member of the staff of the Baths, you have no right to express any opinion which runs contrary to that of your superiors.

DR. STOCKMANN This is too much! I, a doctor, a man of science, have no right to —!

PETER STOCKMANN The matter in hand is not simply a scientific one. It is a complicated matter, and has its economic as well as its technical side.

DR. STOCKMANN I don't care what it is! I intend to be free to express my opinion on any subject under the sun.

PETER STOCKMANN As you please — but not on any subject concerning the Baths. That we forbid.

DR. STOCKMANN (shouting) You forbid —! You! A pack of —

PETER STOCKMANN I forbid it — I, your chief; and if I forbid it, you have to obey.

DR. STOCKMANN (controlling himself) Peter — if you were not my brother —

PETRA (throwing open the door) Father, you shan't stand this!

MRS. STOCKMANN (coming in after her) Petra, Petra!

PETER STOCKMANN Oh, so you have been eavesdropping.

MRS. STOCKMANN You were talking so loud, we couldn't help —

PETRA Yes, I was listening.

PETER STOCKMANN Well, after all, I am very glad —

DR. STOCKMANN (going up to him) You were saying something about forbidding and obeying?

PETER STOCKMANN You obliged me to take that tone with you.

DR. STOCKMANN And so I am to give myself the lie, publicly?

PETER STOCKMANN We consider it absolutely necessary that you should make some such public statement as I have asked for.

DR. STOCKMANN And if I do not — obey?

PETER STOCKMANN Then we shall publish a statement ourselves to reassure the public.

DR. STOCKMANN Very well; but in that case I shall use my pen against you. I stick to what I have said; I will show that I am right and that you are wrong. And what will you do then?

PETER STOCKMANN Then I shall not be able to prevent your being dismissed.

DR. STOCKMANN What —?

PETRA Father — dismissed!

MRS. STOCKMANN Dismissed!

PETER STOCKMANN Dismissed from the staff of the Baths. I shall be obliged to propose that you shall immediately be given notice, and shall not be allowed any further participation in the Baths' affairs.

DR. STOCKMANN You would dare to do that!

PETER STOCKMANN It is you that are playing the daring game.

PETRA Uncle, that is a shameful way to treat a man like father!

MRS. STOCKMANN Do hold your tongue, Petra!

PETER STOCKMANN (looking at PETRA) Oh, so we volunteer our opinions already, do we? Of course. (To MRS. STOCKMANN) Katherine, I imagine you are the most sensible person in this house. Use any influence you may have over your husband, and make him see what this will entail for his family as well as —

DR. STOCKMANN   My family is my own concern and nobody else's!

PETER STOCKMANN   — for his own family, as I was saying, as well as for the town he lives in.

DR. STOCKMANN   It is I who have the real good of the town at heart! I want to lay bare the defects that sooner or later must come to the light of day. I will show whether I love my native town.

PETER STOCKMANN   You, who in your blind obstinacy want to cut off the most important source of the town's welfare?

DR. STOCKMANN   The source is poisoned, man! Are you mad? We are making our living by retailing filth and corruption! The whole of our flourishing municipal life derives its sustenance from a lie!

PETER STOCKMANN   All imagination — or something even worse. The man who can throw out such offensive insinuations about his native town must be an enemy of our community.

DR. STOCKMANN (*going up to him*)   Do you dare to —!

MRS. STOCKMANN (*throwing herself between them*)   Thomas!

PETRA (*catching her father by the arm*)   Don't lose your temper, father!

PETER STOCKMANN   I will not expose myself to violence. Now you have had a warning; so reflect on what you owe to yourself and your family. Good-bye. (*Goes out.*)

DR. STOCKMANN (*walking up and down*)   Am I to put up with such treatment as this? In my own house, Katherine! What do you think of that!

MRS. STOCKMANN   Indeed it is both shameful and absurd, Thomas —

PETRA   If only I could give uncle a piece of my mind —

DR. STOCKMANN   It is my own fault. I ought to have flown out at him long ago! — shown my teeth! — bitten! To hear him call me an enemy to our community! Me! I shall not take that lying down, upon my soul!

MRS. STOCKMANN   But, dear Thomas, your brother has power on his side —

DR. STOCKMANN   Yes, but I have right on mine, I tell you.

MRS. STOCKMANN   Oh yes, right — right. What is the use of having right on your side if you have not got might?

PETRA   Oh, mother — how can you say such a thing!

DR. STOCKMANN   Do you imagine that in a free country it is no use having right on your side? You are absurd, Katherine. Besides, haven't I got the liberal-minded, independent press to lead the way, and the compact majority behind me? That is might enough, I should think!

MRS. STOCKMANN   But, good heavens, Thomas, you don't mean to —?

DR. STOCKMANN   Don't mean to what?

MRS. STOCKMANN   To set yourself up in opposition to your brother.

DR. STOCKMANN   In God's name, what else do you suppose I should do but take my stand on right and truth?

PETRA   Yes, I was just going to say that.

MRS. STOCKMANN   But it won't do you any earthly good. If they won't do it, they won't.

DR. STOCKMANN   Oho, Katherine! Just give me time, and you will see how I will carry the war into their camp.

MRS. STOCKMANN   Yes, you carry the war into their camp, and you get your dismissal — that is what you will do.

DR. STOCKMANN   In any case I shall have done my duty towards the public — towards the community. I, who am called its enemy!

MRS. STOCKMANN But towards your family, Thomas? Towards your own home! Do you think that is doing your duty towards those you have to provide for?

PETRA Ah, don't think always first of us, mother.

MRS. STOCKMANN Oh, it is easy for you to talk; you are able to shift for yourself, if need be. But remember the boys, Thomas; and think a little, too, of yourself, and of me —

DR. STOCKMANN I think you are out of your senses, Katherine! If I were to be such a miserable coward as to go on my knees to Peter and his damned crew, do you suppose I should ever know an hour's peace of mind all my life afterwards?

MRS. STOCKMANN I don't know anything about that; but God preserve us from the peace of mind we shall have, all the same, if you go on defying him! You will find yourself again without the means of subsistence, with no income to count upon. I should think we had had enough of that in the old days. Remember that, Thomas; think what that means.

DR. STOCKMANN (collecting himself with a struggle and clenching his fist). And this is what this slavery can bring upon a free, honorable man! Isn't it horrible, Katherine?

MRS. STOCKMANN Yes, it is sinful to treat you so, it is perfectly true. But, good heavens, one has to put up with so much injustice in this world. — There are the boys, Thomas! Look at them! What is to become of them? Oh no, no, you can never have the heart —.

EJLIF and MORTEN have come in while she was speaking, with their school books in their hands.)

DR. STOCKMANN The boys —! (Recovers himself suddenly.) No, even if the whole world goes to pieces, I will never bow my neck to this yoke! (Goes towards his room.)

MRS. STOCKMANN (following him) Thomas — what are you going to do!

DR. STOCKMANN (at his door) I mean to have the right to look my sons in the face when they are grown men. (Goes into his room.)

MRS. STOCKMANN (bursting into tears) God help us all!

PETRA Father is splendid! He will not give in.

(The boys look on in amazement; PETRA signs to them not to speak.)

Act Three

Scene: The editorial office of the People's Messenger. The entrance door is on the left-hand side of the back wall; on the right-hand side is another door with glass panels through which the printing-room can be seen. Another door in the right-hand wall. In the middle of the room is a large table covered with papers, newspapers and books. In the foreground on the left a window, before which stand a desk and a high stool. There are a couple of easy chairs by the table, and other chairs standing along the wall. The room is dingy and uncomfortable; the furniture is old, the chairs stained and torn. In the printing-room the compositors are seen at work, and a printer is working a hand-press. HOVSTAD is sitting at the desk, writing. BILLING comes in from the right with DR. STOCKMANN'S manuscript in his hand.

BILLING   Well, I must say!

HOVSTAD (*still writing*)   Have you read it through?

BILLING (*laying the MS. on the desk*)   Yes, indeed I have.

HOVSTAD   Don't you think the Doctor hits them pretty hard?

BILLING   Hard? Bless my soul, he's crushing! Every word falls like — how shall I put it? — like the blow of a sledgehammer.

HOVSTAD   Yes, but they are not the people to throw up the sponge at the first blow.

BILLING   That is true; and for that reason we must strike blow upon blow until the whole of this aristocracy tumbles to pieces. As I sat in there reading this, I almost seemed to see a revolution in being.

HOVSTAD (*turning around*)   Hush! — Speak so that Aslaksen cannot hear you.

BILLING (*lowering his voice*)   Aslaksen is a chicken-hearted chap, a coward: there is nothing of the man in him. But this time you will insist on your own way, won't you? You will put the Doctor's article in?

HOVSTAD   Yes, and if the Mayor doesn't like it —

BILLING   That will be the devil of a nuisance.

HOVSTAD   Well, fortunately we can turn the situation to good account, whatever happens. If the Mayor will not fall in with the Doctor's project, he will have all the small tradesmen down on him — the whole of the Householders' Association and the rest of them. And if he does fall in with it, he will fall out with the whole crowd of large shareholders in the Baths, who up to now have been his most valuable supporters —

BILLING   Yes, because they will certainly have to fork out a pretty penny —

HOVSTAD   Yes, you may be sure they will. And in this way the ring will be broken up, you see, and then in every issue of the paper we will enlighten the public on the Mayor's incapability on one point and another, and make it clear that all the positions of trust in the town, the whole control of municipal affairs, ought to be put in the hands of the Liberals.

BILLING   That is perfectly true! I see it coming — I see it coming; we are on the threshold of a revolution!

(*A knock is heard at the door.*)

HOVSTAD   Hush! (*Calls out*) Come in! (DR. STOCKMANN *comes in by the street door.* HOVSTAD *goes to meet him.*) Ah, it is you, Doctor! Well?

DR. STOCKMANN   You may set to work and print it, Mr. Hovstad!

HOVSTAD   Has it come to that, then?

BILLING   Hurrah!

DR. STOCKMANN   Yes, print away. Undoubtedly it has come to that. Now they must take what they get. There is going to be a fight in the town, Mr. Billing!

BILLING   War to the knife, I hope! We will get our knives to their throats, Doctor!

DR. STOCKMANN   This article is only a beginning. I have already got four or five more sketched out in my head. Where is Aslaksen?

BILLING (*calls into the printing-room*)   Aslaksen, just come here for a minute!

HOVSTAD   Four or five more articles, did you say? On the same subject?

DR. STOCKMANN   No — far from it, my dear fellow. No, they are about quite another matter. But they all spring from the question of the water-supply and the drainage. One thing leads to another, you know. It is like beginning to pull down an old house, exactly.

BILLING Upon my soul, it's true; you find you are not done till you have pulled all the old rubbish down.

ASLAKSEN (*coming in*) Pulled down? You are not thinking of pulling down the Baths surely, Doctor?

HOVSTAD Far from it, don't be afraid.

DR. STOCKMANN No, we meant something quite different. Well, what do you think of my article, Mr. Hovstad?

HOVSTAD I think it is simply a masterpiece —

DR. STOCKMANN Do you really think so? Well, I am very pleased, very pleased.

HOVSTAD It is so clear and intelligible. One need have no special knowledge to understand the bearing of it. You will have every enlightened man on your side.

ASLAKSEN And every prudent man too, I hope?

BILLING The prudent and the imprudent — almost the whole town.

ASLAKSEN In that case we may venture to print it.

DR. STOCKMANN I should think so!

HOVSTAD We will put it in to-morrow morning.

DR. STOCKMANN Of course — you must not lose a single day. What I wanted to ask you, Mr. Aslaksen, was if you would supervise the printing of it yourself.

ASLAKSEN With pleasure.

DR. STOCKMANN Take care of it as if it were a treasure! No misprints — every word is important. I will look in again a little later; perhaps you will be able to let me see a proof. I can't tell you how eager I am to see it in print, and see it burst upon the public —

BILLING Burst upon them — yes, like a flash of lightning!

DR. STOCKMANN — and to have it submitted to the judgment of my intelligent fellow-townsmen. You cannot imagine what I have gone through to-day. I have been threatened first with one thing and then with another; they have tried to rob me of my most elementary rights as a man —

BILLING What! Your rights as a man!

DR. STOCKMANN — they have tried to degrade me, to make a coward of me, to force me to put personal interests before my most sacred convictions —

BILLING That is too much — I'm damned if it isn't.

HOVSTAD Oh, you mustn't be surprised at anything from that quarter.

DR. STOCKMANN Well, they will get the worst of it with me; they may assure themselves of that. I shall consider the "People's Messenger" my sheet-anchor now, and every single day I will bombard them with one article after another, like bomb-shells —

ASLAKSEN Yes, but —

BILLING Hurrah! — it is war, it is war!

DR. STOCKMANN I shall smite them to the ground — I shall crush them — I shall break down all their defences, before the eyes of the honest public! That is what I shall do!

ASLAKSEN Yes, but in moderation, Doctor — proceed with moderation —

BILLING Not a bit of it, not a bit of it! Don't spare the dynamite!

DR. STOCKMANN Because it is not merely a question of water-supply and drains now, you know. No — it is the whole of our social life that we have got to purify and disinfect —

BILLING Spoken like a deliverer!

DR. STOCKMANN   All the incapables must be turned out, you understand — and that in every walk of life! Endless vistas have opened themselves to my mind's eye to-day. I cannot see it all quite clearly yet, but I shall in time. Young and vigorous standard-bearers — those are what we need and must seek, my friends; we must have new men in command at all our outposts.

BILLING   Hear, hear!

DR. STOCKMANN   We only need to stand by one another, and it will all be perfectly easy. The revolution will be launched like a ship that runs smoothly off the stocks. Don't you think so?

HOVSTAD   For my part I think we have now a prospect of getting the municipal authority into the hands where it should lie.

ASLAKSEN   And if only we proceed with moderation, I cannot imagine that there will be any risk.

DR. STOCKMANN   Who the devil cares whether there is any risk or not! What I am doing, I am doing in the name of truth and for the sake of my conscience.

HOVSTAD   You are a man who deserves to be supported, Doctor.

ASLAKSEN   Yes, there is no denying that the Doctor is a true friend to the town — a real friend to the community, that he is.

BILLING   Take my word for it, Aslaksen, Dr. Stockmann is a friend of the people.

ASLAKSEN   I fancy the Householders' Association will make use of that expression before long.

DR. STOCKMANN   (*affected, grasps their hands*)   Thank you, thank you, my dear staunch friends. It is very refreshing to me to hear you say that; my brother called me something quite different. By Jove, he shall have it back, with interest! But now I must be off to see a poor devil —. I will come back, as I said. Keep a very careful eye on the manuscript, Aslaksen, and don't for worlds leave out any of my notes of exclamation! Rather put one or two more in! Capital, capital! Well, good-bye for the present — good-bye, good-bye!

(*They show him to the door, and bow him out.*)

HOVSTAD   He may prove an invaluably useful man to us.

ASLAKSEN   Yes, so long as he confines himself to this matter of the Baths. But if he goes farther afield, I don't think it would be advisable to follow him.

HOVSTAD   Hm! — that all depends —

BILLING   You are so infernally timid, Aslaksen!

ASLAKSEN   Timid? Yes, when it is a question of the local authorities. I am timid, Mr. Billing; it is a lesson I have learnt in the school of experience, let me tell you. But try me in higher politics, in matters that concern the government itself, and then see if I am timid.

BILLING   No, you aren't, I admit. But this is simply contradicting yourself.

ASLAKSEN   I am a man with a conscience, and that is the whole matter. If you attack the government, you don't do the community any harm, anyway; those fellows pay no attention to attacks, you see — they go on just as they are, in spite of them. But *local* authorities are different, they *can* be turned out, and then perhaps you may get an ignorant lot into office who may do irreparable harm to the householders and everybody else.

HOVSTAD   But what of the education of citizens by self-government — don't you attach any importance to that?

ASLAKSEN   When a man has interests of his own to protect, he cannot think of everything, Mr. Hovstad.

HOVSTAD   Then I hope I shall never have interests of my own to protect!

BILLING   Hear, hear!

ASLAKSEN (*with a smile*)   Hm! (*Points to the desk*) Mr. Sheriff Stensgaard was your predecessor at that editorial desk.

BILLING (*spitting*)   Bah! That turncoat.

HOVSTAD   I am not a weathercock — and never will be.

ASLAKSEN   A politician should never be too certain of anything, Mr. Hovstad. And as for you, Mr. Billing, I should think it is time for you to be taking in a reef or two in your sails, seeing that you are applying for the post of secretary to the Bench.

BILLING   I — !

HOVSTAD   Are you, Billing?

BILLING   Well, yes — but you must clearly understand I am doing it only to annoy the bigwigs.

ASLAKSEN   Anyhow, it is no business of mine. But if I am to be accused of timidity and of inconsistency in my principles, this is what I want to point out: my political past is an open book. I have never changed, except perhaps to become a little more moderate, you see. My heart is still with the people; but I don't deny that my reason has a certain bias towards the authorities — the local ones, I mean. (*Goes into the printing-room.*)

BILLING   Oughtn't we to try and get rid of him, Hovstad?

HOVSTAD   Do you know anyone else who will advance the money for our paper and printing bill?

BILLING   It is an infernal nuisance that we don't possess some capital to trade on.

HOVSTAD (*sitting down at his desk*)   Yes, if we only had that, then —

BILLING   Suppose you were to apply to Dr. Stockmann?

HOVSTAD (*turning over some papers*)   What is the use? He has got nothing.

BILLING   No, but he has got a warm man in the background, old Morten Kiil — "the Badger," as they call him.

HOVSTAD (*writing*)   Are you so sure *he* has got anything?

BILLING   Good Lord, of course he has! And some of it must come to the Stockmanns. Most probably he will do something for the children, at all events.

HOVSTAD (*turning half round*)   Are you counting on that?

BILLING   Counting on it? Of course I am not counting on anything.

HOVSTAD   That is right. And I should not count on the secretaryship to the Bench either, if I were you; for I can assure you — you won't get it.

BILLING   Do you think I am not quite aware of that? My object is precisely *not* to get it. A slight of that kind stimulates a man's fighting power — it is like getting a supply of fresh bile — and I am sure one needs that badly enough in a hole-and-corner place like this, where it is so seldom anything happens to stir one up.

HOVSTAD (*writing*)   Quite so, quite so.

BILLING   Ah, I shall be heard of yet! — Now I shall go and write the appeal to the Householders' Association. (*Goes into the room on the right.*)

HOVSTAD (*sitting at his desk, biting his penholder, says slowly*)   Hm! — that's it, is it? (*A knock is heard*) Come in! (PETRA *comes in by the outer door.* HOVSTAD *gets up.*) What, you! — here?

PETRA Yes, you must forgive me —

HOVSTAD (*pulling a chair forward*) Won't you sit down?

PETRA No, thank you; I must go again in a moment.

HOVSTAD Have you come with a message from your father, by any chance?

PETRA No, I have come on my own account. (*Takes a book out of her coat pocket*) Here is the English story.

HOVSTAD Why have you brought it back?

PETRA Because I am not going to translate it.

HOVSTAD But you promised me faithfully —

PETRA Yes, but then I had not read it. I don't suppose you have read it either?

HOVSTAD No, you know quite well I don't understand English; but —

PETRA Quite so. That is why I wanted to tell you that you must find something else. (*Lays the book on the table*) You can't use this for the "People's Messenger."

HOVSTAD Why not?

PETRA Because it conflicts with all your opinions.

HOVSTAD Oh, for that matter —

PETRA You don't understand me. The burden of this story is that there is a supernatural power that looks after the so-called good people in this world and makes everything happen for the best in their case — while all the so-called bad people are punished.

HOVSTAD Well, but that is all right. That is just what our readers want.

PETRA And are you going to be the one to give it to them? For myself, I do not believe a word of it. You know quite well that things do not happen so in reality.

HOVSTAD You are perfectly right; but an editor cannot always act as he would prefer. He is often obliged to bow to the wishes of the public in unimportant matters. Politics are the most important thing in life — for a newspaper, anyway; and if I want to carry my public with me on the path that leads to liberty and progress, I must not frighten them away. If they find a moral tale of this sort in the serial at the bottom of the page, they will be all the more ready to read what is printed above it; they feel more secure, as it were.

PETRA For shame! You would never go and set a snare like that for your readers; you are not a spider!

HOVSTAD (*smiling*) Thank you for having such a good opinion of me. No; as a matter of fact that is Billing's idea and not mine.

PETRA Billing's!

HOVSTAD Yes; anyway he propounded that theory here one day. And it is Billing who is so anxious to have that story in the paper; I don't know anything about the book.

PETRA But how can Billing, with his emancipated views —

HOVSTAD Oh, Billing is a many-sided man. He is applying for the post of secretary to the Bench, too, I hear.

PETRA I don't believe it, Mr. Hovstad. How could he possibly bring himself to do such a thing?

HOVSTAD Ah, you must ask him that.

PETRA I should never have thought it of him.

HOVSTAD (*looking more closely at her*)   No? Does it really surprise you so much?

PETRA   Yes. Or perhaps not altogether. Really, I don't quite know —

HOVSTAD   We journalists are not much worth, Miss Stockmann.

PETRA   Do you really mean that?

HOVSTAD   I think so sometimes.

PETRA   Yes, in the ordinary affairs of everyday life, perhaps; I can understand that. But now, when you have taken a weighty matter in hand —

HOVSTAD   This matter of your father's, you mean?

PETRA   Exactly. It seems to me that now you must feel you are a man worth more than most.

HOVSTAD   Yes, to-day I do feel something of that sort.

PETRA   Of course you do, don't you? It is a splendid vocation you have chosen — to smooth the way for the march of unappreciated truths, and new and courageous lines of thought. If it were nothing more than because you stand fearlessly in the open and take up the cause of an injured man —

HOVSTAD   Especially when that injured man is — ahem! — I don't rightly know how to —

PETRA   When that man is so upright and so honest, you mean?

HOVSTAD (*more gently*)   Especially when he is your father, I meant.

PETRA (*suddenly checked*)   *That?*

HOVSTAD   Yes, Petra — Miss Petra.

PETRA   Is it *that,* that is first and foremost with you? Not the matter itself? Not the truth? — not my father's big generous heart?

HOVSTAD   Certainly — of course — that too.

PETRA   No, thank you; you have betrayed yourself, Mr. Hovstad, and now I shall never trust you again in anything.

HOVSTAD   Can you really take it so amiss in me that it is mostly for your sake — ?

PETRA   What I am angry with you for, is for not having been honest with my father. You talked to him as if the truth and the good of the community were what lay nearest to your heart. You have made fools of both my father and me. You are not the man you made yourself out to be. And that I shall never forgive you — never!

HOVSTAD   You ought not to speak so bitterly, Miss Petra — least of all now.

PETRA   Why not now, especially?

HOVSTAD   Because your father cannot do without my help.

PETRA (*looking him up and down*)   Are you that sort of man too? For shame!

HOVSTAD   No, no, I am not. This came upon me so unexpectedly — you must believe that.

PETRA   I know what to believe. Good-bye.

ASLAKSEN (*coming from the printing-room, hurriedly and with an air of mystery*)   Damnation, Hovstad! — (*Sees* PETRA) Oh, this is awkward —

PETRA   There is the book; you must give it to some one else. (*Goes towards the door.*)

HOVSTAD (*following her*)   But, Miss Stockmann —

PETRA   Good-bye. (*Goes out.*)

ASLAKSEN   I say — Mr. Hovstad —

HOVSTAD   Well, well! — what is it?

ASLAKSEN   The Mayor is outside in the printing-room.

HOVSTAD   The Mayor, did you say?

ASLAKSEN   Yes, he wants to speak to you. He came in by the back door — didn't want to be seen, you understand.

HOVSTAD   What can he want? Wait a bit — I will go myself. (*Goes to the door of the printing-room, opens it, bows and invites* PETER STOCKMANN *in*) Just see, Aslaksen, that no one —

ASLAKSEN   Quite so. (*Goes into the printing-room.*)

PETER STOCKMANN   You did not expect to see me here, Mr. Hovstad.

HOVSTAD   No, I confess I did not.

PETER STOCKMANN   (*looking round*)   You are very snug in here — very nice indeed.

HOVSTAD   Oh —

PETER STOCKMANN   And here I come, without any notice, to take up your time!

HOVSTAD   By all means, Mr. Mayor. I am at your service. But let me relieve you of your — (*Takes* STOCKMANN'S *hat and stick and puts them on a chair.*) Won't you sit down?

PETER STOCKMANN   (*sitting down by the table*)   Thank you. (HOVSTAD *sits down.*) I have had an extremely annoying experience to-day, Mr. Hovstad.

HOVSTAD   Really? Ah well, I expect with all the various business you have to attend to —

PETER STOCKMANN   The Medical Officer of the Baths is responsible for what happened to-day.

HOVSTAD   Indeed? The Doctor?

PETER STOCKMANN   He has addressed a kind of report to the Baths Committee on the subject of certain supposed defects in the Baths.

HOVSTAD   Has he indeed?

PETER STOCKMANN   Yes — has he not told you? I thought he said —

HOVSTAD   Ah, yes — it is true he did mention something about —

ASLAKSEN   (*coming from the printing-room*)   I ought to have that copy —

HOVSTAD   (*angrily*)   Ahem! — there it is on the desk.

ASLAKSEN   (*taking it*)   Right.

PETER STOCKMANN   But look there — that is the thing I was speaking of!

ASLAKSEN   Yes, that is the Doctor's article, Mr. Mayor.

HOVSTAD   Oh, is *that* what you were speaking about?

PETER STOCKMANN   Yes, that is it. What do you think of it?

HOVSTAD   Oh, I am only a layman — and I have only taken a very cursory glance at it.

PETER STOCKMANN   But you are going to print it?

HOVSTAD   I cannot very well refuse a distinguished man —

ASLAKSEN   I have nothing to do with editing the paper, Mr. Mayor —

PETER STOCKMANN   I understand.

ASLAKSEN   I merely print what is put into my hands.

PETER STOCKMANN   Quite so.

ASLAKSEN   And so I must — (*Moves off towards the printing-room.*)

PETER STOCKMANN   No, but wait a moment, Mr. Aslaksen. You will allow me, Mr. Hovstad?

HOVSTAD   If you please, Mr. Mayor.

PETER STOCKMANN   You are a discreet and thoughtful man, Mr. Aslaksen.

ASLAKSEN   I am delighted to hear you think so, sir.

PETER STOCKMANN   And a man of very considerable influence.

ASLAKSEN   Chiefly among the small tradesmen, sir.

PETER STOCKMANN   The small tax-payers are the majority — here as every-where else.

ASLAKSEN   That is true.

PETER STOCKMANN   And I have no doubt you know the general trend of opin-ion among them, don't you?

ASLAKSEN   Yes, I think I may say I do, Mr. Mayor.

PETER STOCKMANN   Yes. Well, since there is such a praiseworthy spirit of self-sacrifice among the less wealthy citizens of our town —

ASLAKSEN   What?

HOVSTAD   Self-sacrifice?

PETER STOCKMANN   It is pleasing evidence of a public-spirited feeling, ex-tremely pleasing evidence. I might almost say I hardly expected it. But you have a closer knowledge of public opinion than I.

ASLAKSEN   But, Mr. Mayor —

PETER STOCKMANN   And indeed it is no small sacrifice that the town is going to make.

HOVSTAD   The town?

ASLAKSEN   But I don't understand. Is it the Baths — ?

PETER STOCKMANN   At a provisional estimate, the alterations that the Medical Officer asserts to be desirable will cost somewhere about twenty thousand pounds.

ASLAKSEN   That is a lot of money, but —

PETER STOCKMANN   Of course it will be necessary to raise a municipal loan.

HOVSTAD (getting up)   Surely you never mean that the town must pay — ?

ASLAKSEN   Do you mean that it must come out of the municipal funds? — out of the ill-filled pockets of the small tradesmen?

PETER STOCKMANN   Well, my dear Mr. Aslaksen, where else is the money to come from?

ASLAKSEN   The gentlemen who own the Baths ought to provide that.

PETER STOCKMANN   The proprietors of the Baths are not in a position to incur any further expense.

ASLAKSEN   Is that absolutely certain, Mr. Mayor?

PETER STOCKMANN   I have satisfied myself that it is so. If the town wants these very extensive alterations, it will have to pay for them.

ASLAKSEN   But, damn it all — I beg your pardon — this is quite another matter, Mr. Hovstad!

HOVSTAD   It is, indeed.

PETER STOCKMANN   The most fatal part of it is that we shall be obliged to shut the Baths for a couple of years.

HOVSTAD   Shut them? Shut them altogether?

ASLAKSEN   For two years?

PETER STOCKMANN   Yes, the work will take as long as that — at least.

ASLAKSEN   I'm damned if we will stand that, Mr. Mayor! What are we house-holders to live upon in the meantime?

PETER STOCKMANN   Unfortunately, that is an extremely difficult question to answer, Mr. Aslaksen. But what would you have us do? Do you suppose we shall have a single visitor in the town, if we go about proclaiming that our water is polluted, that we are living over a plague spot, that the entire town —

ASLAKSEN   And the whole thing is merely imagination?

PETER STOCKMANN   With the best will in the world, I have not been able to come to any other conclusion.

ASLAKSEN   Well then I must say it is absolutely unjustifiable of Dr. Stockmann — I beg your pardon, Mr. Mayor —

PETER STOCKMANN   What you say is lamentably true, Mr. Aslaksen. My brother has, unfortunately, always been a headstrong man.

ASLAKSEN   After this, do you mean to give him your support, Mr. Hovstad?

HOVSTAD   Can you suppose for a moment that I — ?

PETER STOCKMANN   I have drawn up a short *resumé* of the situation as it appears from a reasonable man's point of view. In it I have indicated how certain possible defects might suitably be remedied without outrunning the resources of the Baths Committee.

HOVSTAD   Have you got it with you, Mr. Mayor?

PETER STOCKMANN (*fumbling in his pocket*)   Yes, I brought it with me in case you should —

ASLAKSEN   Good Lord, there he is!

PETER STOCKMANN   Who? My brother?

HOVSTAD   Where? Where?

ASLAKSEN   He has just gone through the printing-room.

PETER STOCKMANN   How unlucky! I don't want to meet him here, and I had still several things to speak to you about.

HOVSTAD (*pointing to the door on the right*)   Go in there for the present.

PETER STOCKMANN   But — ?

HOVSTAD   You will only find Billing in there.

ASLAKSEN   Quick, quick, Mr. Mayor — he is just coming.

PETER STOCKMANN   Yes, very well; but see that you get rid of him quickly. (*Goes out through the door on the right, which* ASLAKSEN *opens for him and shuts after him.*)

HOVSTAD   Pretend to be doing something, Aslaksen. (*Sits down and writes.* ASLAKSEN *begins foraging among a heap of newspapers that are lying on a chair.*)

DR. STOCKMANN (*coming in from the printing-room*)   Here I am again. (*Puts down his hat and stick.*)

HOVSTAD (*writing*)   Already, Doctor? Hurry up with what we were speaking about, Aslaksen. We are very pressed for time to-day.

DR. STOCKMANN (*to* ASLAKSEN)   No proof for me to see yet, I hear.

ASLAKSEN (*without turning round*)   You couldn't expect it yet, Doctor.

DR. STOCKMANN   No, no; but I am impatient, as you can understand. I shall not know a moment's peace of mind till I see it in print.

HOVSTAD   Hm! — it will take a good while yet, won't it, Aslaksen?

ASLAKSEN   Yes, I am almost afraid it will.

DR. STOCKMANN   All right, my dear friends; I will come back. I do not mind coming back twice if necessary. A matter of such great importance — the welfare of the town at stake — it is no time to shirk trouble. (*Is just going, but stops and comes back.*)   Look here — there is one thing more I want to speak to you about.

HOVSTAD   Excuse me, but could it not wait till some other time?

DR. STOCKMANN   I can tell you in half a dozen words. It is only this. When my article is read to-morrow and it is realised that I have been quietly working the whole winter for the welfare of the town —

HOVSTAD Yes, but, Doctor —

DR. STOCKMANN I know what you are going to say. You don't see how on earth it was any more than my duty — my obvious duty as a citizen. Of course it wasn't; I know that as well as you. But my fellow-citizens, you know — ! Good Lord, think of all the good souls who think so highly of me — !

ASLAKSEN Yes, our townsfolk have had a very high opinion of you so far, Doctor.

DR. STOCKMANN Yes, and that is just why I am afraid they — . Well, this is the point; when this reaches them, especially the poorer classes, and sounds in their ears like a summons to take the town's affairs into their own hands for the future —

HOVSTAD (*getting up*) Ahem! Doctor, I won't conceal from you the fact —

DR. STOCKMANN Ah! — I knew there was something in the wind! But I won't hear a word of it. If anything of that sort is being set on foot —

HOVSTAD Of what sort?

DR. STOCKMANN Well, whatever it is — whether it is a demonstration in my honour, or a banquet, or a subscription list for some presentation to me — whatever it is, you must promise me solemnly and faithfully to put a stop to it. You too, Mr. Aslaksen; do you understand?

HOVSTAD You must forgive me, Doctor, but sooner or later we must tell you the plain truth —

(*He is interrupted by the entrance of* MRS. STOCKMANN, *who comes in from the street door.*)

MRS. STOCKMANN (*seeing her husband*) Just as I thought!

HOVSTAD (*going towards her*) You too, Mrs. Stockmann?

DR. STOCKMANN What on earth do *you* want here, Katherine?

MRS. STOCKMANN I should think you know very well what I want.

HOVSTAD Won't you sit down? Or perhaps —

MRS. STOCKMANN No, thank you; don't trouble. And you must not be offended at my coming to fetch my husband; I am the mother of three children, you know.

DR. STOCKMANN Nonsense! — we know all about that.

MRS. STOCKMANN Well, one would not give you credit for much thought for your wife and children to-day; if you had had that, you would not have gone and dragged us all into misfortune.

DR. STOCKMANN Are you out of your senses, Katherine! Because a man has a wife and children, is he not to be allowed to proclaim the truth — is he not to be allowed to be an actively useful citizen — is he not to be allowed to do a service to his native town!

MRS. STOCKMANN Yes, Thomas — in reason.

ASLAKSEN Just what I say. Moderation is everything.

MRS. STOCKMANN And that is why you wrong us, Mr. Hovstad, in enticing my husband away from his home and making a dupe of him in all this.

HOVSTAD I certainly am making a dupe of no one —

DR. STOCKMANN Making a dupe of me! Do you suppose I should allow myself to be duped!

MRS. STOCKMANN It is just what you do. I know quite well you have more brains than anyone in the town, but you are extremely easily duped, Thomas. (*To* HOVSTAD) Please to realise that he loses his post at the Baths if you print what he has written —

ASLAKSEN   What!

HOVSTAD   Look here, Doctor —

DR. STOCKMANN (*laughing*)   Ha — ha! — just let them try! No, no — they will take good care not to. I have got the compact majority behind me, let me tell you!

MRS. STOCKMANN   Yes, that is just the worst of it — your having any such horrid thing behind you.

DR. STOCKMANN   Rubbish, Katherine! — Go home and look after your house and leave me to look after the community. How can you be so afraid, when I am so confident and happy? (*Walks up and down, rubbing his hands.*) Truth and the People will win the fight, you may be certain! I see the whole of the broad-minded middle class marching like a victorious army — ! (*Stops beside a chair*) What the deuce is that lying there?

ASLAKSEN   Good Lord!

HOVSTAD   Ahem!

DR. STOCKMANN   Here we have the topmost pinnacle of authority! (*Takes the Mayor's official hat carefully between his finger-tips and holds it up in the air.*)

MRS. STOCKMANN   The Mayor's hat!

DR. STOCKMANN   And here is the staff of office too. How in the name of all that's wonderful — ?

HOVSTAD   Well, you see —

DR. STOCKMANN   Oh, I understand. He has been here trying to talk you over. Ha — ha! — he made rather a mistake there! And as soon as he caught sight of me in the printing-room — . (*Bursts out laughing.*) Did he run away, Mr. Aslaksen?

ASLAKSEN (*hurriedly*)   Yes, he ran away, Doctor.

DR. STOCKMANN   Ran away without his stick or his — . Fiddlesticks! Peter doesn't run away and leave his belongings behind him. But what the deuce have you done with him? Ah! — in there, of course. Now you shall see, Katherine.

MRS. STOCKMANN   Thomas — please don't — !

ASLAKSEN   Don't be rash, Doctor.

   (DR. STOCKMANN *has put on the Mayor's hat and taken his stick in his hand. He goes up to the door, opens it and stands with his hand to his hat at the salute.* PETER STOCKMANN *comes in, red with anger.* BILLING *follows him.*)

PETER STOCKMANN   What does this tomfoolery mean?

DR. STOCKMANN   Be respectful, my good Peter. I am the chief authority in the town now. (*Walks up and down.*)

MRS. STOCKMANN (*almost in tears*)   Really, Thomas!

PETER STOCKMANN (*following him about*)   Give me my hat and stick.

DR. STOCKMANN (*in the same tone as before*)   If you are chief constable, let me tell you that I am the Mayor — I am the master of the whole town, please understand!

PETER STOCKMANN   Take off my hat, I tell you. Remember it is part of an official uniform.

DR. STOCKMANN   Pooh! Do you think the newly awakened lion-hearted people are going to be frightened by an official hat? There is going to be a revolution in the town to-morrow, let me tell you. You thought you could turn me out; but now I shall turn you out — turn you out of all your various offices. Do you think I cannot? Listen to me. I have triumphant social forces behind me. Hovstad and Billing will thunder in the "People's Messenger," and Aslaksen will take the field at the head of the whole Householders' Association —

ASLAKSEN   That I won't, Doctor.

DR. STOCKMANN   Of course you will —

PETER STOCKMANN   Ah! — may I ask then if Mr. Hovstad intends to join this agitation?

HOVSTAD   No, Mr. Mayor.

ASLAKSEN   No, Mr. Hovstad is not such a fool as to go and ruin his paper and himself for the sake of an imaginary grievance.

DR. STOCKMANN (*looking round him*)   What does this mean?

HOVSTAD   You have represented your case in a false light, Doctor, and therefore I am unable to give you my support.

BILLING   And after what the Mayor was so kind as to tell me just now, I —

DR. STOCKMANN   A false light! Leave that part of it to me. Only print my article; I am quite capable of defending it.

HOVSTAD   I am not going to print it. I cannot and will not and dare not print it.

DR. STOCKMANN   You dare not? What nonsense! — you are the editor; and an editor controls his paper, I suppose!

ASLAKSEN   No, it is the subscribers, Doctor.

PETER STOCKMANN   Fortunately, yes.

ASLAKSEN   It is public opinion — the enlightened public — householders and people of that kind; they control the newspapers.

DR. STOCKMANN (*composedly*)   And I have all these influences against me?

ASLAKSEN   Yes, you have. It would mean the absolute ruin of the community if your article were to appear.

DR. STOCKMANN   Indeed.

PETER STOCKMANN   My hat and stick, if you please. (DR. STOCKMANN *takes off the hat and lays it on the table with the stick.* PETER STOCKMANN *takes them up.*) Your authority as mayor has come to an untimely end.

DR. STOCKMANN   We have not got to the end yet. (*To* HOVSTAD) Then it is quite impossible for you to print my article in the "People's Messenger"?

HOVSTAD   Quite impossible — out of regard for your family as well.

MRS. STOCKMANN   You need not concern yourself about his family, thank you, Mr. Hovstad.

PETER STOCKMANN (*taking a paper from his pocket*)   It will be sufficient, for the guidance of the public, if this appears. It is an official statement. May I trouble you?

HOVSTAD (*taking the paper*)   Certainly; I will see that it is printed.

DR. STOCKMANN   But not mine. Do you imagine that you can silence me and stifle the truth! You will not find it so easy as you suppose. Mr. Aslaksen, kindly take my manuscript at once and print it as a pamphlet — at my expense. I will have four hundred copies — no, five — six hundred.

ASLAKSEN   If you offered me its weight in gold, I could not lend my press for any such purpose, Doctor. It would be flying in the face of public opinion. You will not get it printed anywhere in the town.

DR. STOCKMANN   Then give it me back.

HOVSTAD (*giving him the MS.*)   Here it is.

DR. STOCKMANN (*taking his hat and stick*)   It shall be made public all the same. I will read it out at a mass meeting of the townspeople. All my fellow-citizens shall hear the voice of truth!

PETER STOCKMANN   You will not find any public body in the town that will give you the use of their hall for such a purpose.

ASLAKSEN   Not a single one, I am certain.

BILLING   No, I'm damned if you will find one.

MRS. STOCKMANN   But this is too shameful! Why should every one turn against you like that?

DR. STOCKMANN (*angrily*)   I will tell you why. It is because all the men in this town are old women — like you; they all think of nothing but their families, and never of the community.

MRS. STOCKMANN (*putting her arm into his*)   Then I will show them that an — an old woman can be a man for once. I am going to stand by you, Thomas!

DR. STOCKMANN   Bravely said, Katherine! It shall be made public — as I am a living soul! If I can't hire a hall, I shall hire a drum, and parade the town with it and read it at every street-corner.

PETER STOCKMANN   You are surely not such an arrant fool as that!

DR. STOCKMANN   Yes, I am.

ASLAKSEN   You won't find a single man in the whole town to go with you.

BILLING   No, I'm damned if you will.

MRS. STOCKMANN   Don't give in, Thomas. I will tell the boys to go with you.

DR. STOCKMANN   That is a splendid idea!

MRS. STOCKMANN   Morten will be delighted; and Ejlif will do whatever he does.

DR. STOCKMANN   Yes, and Petra! — and you too, Katherine!

MRS. STOCKMANN   No, I won't do that; but I will stand at the window and watch you, that's what I will do.

DR. STOCKMANN (*puts his arms round her and kisses her*)   Thank you, my dear! Now you and I are going to try a fall, my fine gentlemen! I am going to see whether a pack of cowards can succeed in gagging a patriot who wants to purify society!

(*He and his wife go out by the street door.*)

PETER STOCKMANN (*shaking his head seriously*)   Now he has sent *her* out of her senses, too.

Act Four

Scene: A big old-fashioned room in CAPTAIN HORSTER'S *house. At the back folding-doors, which are standing open, lead to an ante-room. Three windows in the left-hand wall. In the middle of the opposite wall a platform has been erected. On this is a small table with two candles, a water-bottle and glass, and a bell. The room is lit by lamps placed between the windows. In the foreground on the left there is a table with candles and a chair. To the right is a door and some chairs standing near it. The room is nearly filled with a crowd of townspeople of all sorts, a few women and schoolboys being amongst them. People are still streaming in from the back, and the room is soon filled.*

1ST CITIZEN (*meeting another*)   Hullo, Lamstad! You here too?

2ND CITIZEN   I go to every public meeting, I do.

3RD CITIZEN   Brought your whistle too, I expect!

2ND CITIZEN   I should think so. Haven't you?

3RD CITIZEN   Rather! And old Evensen said he was going to bring a cow-horn, he did.

2ND CITIZEN   Good old Evensen!

(*Laughter among the crowd.*)

4TH CITIZEN (*coming up to them*)   I say, tell me what is going on here to-night.

2ND CITIZEN   Dr. Stockmann is going to deliver an address attacking the Mayor.

4TH CITIZEN   But the Mayor is his brother.

1ST CITIZEN   That doesn't matter; Dr. Stockmann's not the chap to be afraid.

3RD CITIZEN   But he is in the wrong; it said so in the "People's Messenger."

2ND CITIZEN   Yes, I expect he must be in the wrong this time, because neither the Householders' Association nor the Citizens' Club would lend him their hall for his meeting.

1ST CITIZEN   He couldn't even get the loan of the hall at the Baths.

2ND CITIZEN   No, I should think not.

A MAN (*in another part of the crowd*)   I say — who are we to back up in this?

ANOTHER MAN (*beside him*)   Watch Aslaksen, and do as he does.

BILLING (*pushing his way through the crowd, with a writing-case under his arm*)   Excuse me, gentlemen — do you mind letting me through? I am reporting for the "People's Messenger." Thank you very much! (*He sits down at the table on the left.*)

A WORKMAN   Who was that?

2ND WORKMAN   Don't you know him? It's Billing, who writes for Aslaksen's paper.

(CAPTAIN HORSTER *brings in* MRS. STOCKMANN *and* PETRA *through the door on the right.* EJLIF *and* MORTEN *follow them in.*)

HORSTER   I thought you might all sit here; you can slip out easily from here, if things get too lively.

MRS. STOCKMANN   Do you think there will be a disturbance?

HORSTER   One can never tell — with such a crowd. But sit down, and don't be uneasy.

MRS. STOCKMANN (*sitting down*)   It was extremely kind of you to offer my husband the room.

HORSTER   Well, if nobody else would —

PETRA (*who has sat down beside her mother*)   And it was a plucky thing to do, Captain Horster.

HORSTER   Oh, it is not such a great matter as all that.

(HOVSTAD *and* ASLAKSEN *make their way through the crowd.*)

ASLAKSEN (*going up to* HORSTER)   Has the Doctor not come yet?

HORSTER   He is waiting in the next room.

(*Movement in the crowd by the door at the back.*)

HOVSTAD   Look — here comes the Mayor!

BILLING   Yes, I'm damned if he hasn't come after all!

(PETER STOCKMANN *makes his way gradually through the crowd, bows courteously and takes up a position by the wall on the left. Shortly afterwards* DR. STOCKMANN *comes in by the right-hand door. He is dressed in a black frock-coat, with a white tie. There is a little feeble applause, which is hushed down. Silence is obtained.*)

DR. STOCKMANN (*in an undertone*) How do you feel, Katherine?

MRS. STOCKMANN All right, thank you. (*Lowering her voice*) Be sure not to lose your temper, Thomas.

DR. STOCKMANN Oh, I know how to control myself. (*Looks at his watch, steps on to the platform and bows.*) It is a quarter past — so I will begin. (*Takes his MS. out of his pocket.*)

ASLAKSEN I think we ought to elect a chairman first.

DR. STOCKMANN No, it is quite unnecessary.

SOME OF THE CROWD Yes — yes!

PETER STOCKMANN I certainly think, too, that we ought to have a chairman.

DR. STOCKMANN But I have called this meeting to deliver a lecture, Peter.

PETER STOCKMANN Dr. Stockmann's lecture may possibly lead to a considerable conflict of opinion.

VOICES IN THE CROWD A chairman! A chairman!

HOVSTAD The general wish of the meeting seems to be that a chairman should be elected.

DR. STOCKMANN (*restraining himself*) Very well — let the meeting have its way.

ASLAKSEN Will the Mayor be good enough to undertake the task?

THREE MEN (*clapping their hands*) Bravo! Bravo!

PETER STOCKMANN For various reasons, which you will easily understand, I must beg to be excused. But fortunately we have amongst us a man who I think will be acceptable to you all. I refer to the President of the Householders' Association, Mr. Aslaksen.

SEVERAL VOICES Yes — Aslaksen! Bravo Aslaksen!

(DR. STOCKMANN *takes up his MS. and walks up and down the platform.*)

ASLAKSEN Since my fellow-citizens choose to entrust me with this duty, I cannot refuse. (*Loud applause.* ASLAKSEN *mounts the platform.*)

BILLING (*writing*) "Mr. Aslaksen was elected with enthusiasm."

ASLAKSEN And now, as I am in this position, I should like to say a few brief words. I am a quiet and peaceable man, who believes in discreet moderation, and — and — in moderate discretion. All my friends can bear witness to that.

SEVERAL VOICES That's right! That's right, Aslaksen!

ASLAKSEN I have learnt in the school of life and experience that moderation is the most valuable virtue a citizen can possess —

PETER STOCKMANN Hear, hear!

ASLAKSEN — And moreover that discretion and moderation are what enable a man to be of most service to the community. I would therefore suggest to our esteemed fellow-citizen, who has called this meeting, that he should strive to keep strictly within the bounds of moderation.

A MAN (*by the door*) Three cheers for the Moderation Society!

A VOICE Shame!

SEVERAL VOICES Sh! — Sh!

ASLAKSEN No interruptions, gentlemen, please! Does anyone wish to make any remarks?

PETER STOCKMANN Mr. Chairman.

ASLAKSEN The Mayor will address the meeting.

PETER STOCKMANN   In consideration of the close relationship in which, as you all know, I stand to the present Medical Officer of the Baths, I should have preferred not to speak this evening. But my official position with regard to the Baths and my solicitude for the vital interests of the town compel me to bring forward a motion. I venture to presume that there is not a single one of our citizens present who considers it desirable that unreliable and exaggerated accounts of the sanitary condition of the Baths and the town should be spread abroad.

SEVERAL VOICES   No, no! Certainly not! We protest against it!

PETER STOCKMANN   Therefore I should like to propose that the meeting should not permit the Medical Officer either to read or to comment on his proposed lecture.

DR. STOCKMANN (*impatiently*)   Not permit — ! What the devil — !

MRS. STOCKMANN (*coughing*)   Ahem! — ahem!

DR. STOCKMANN (*collecting himself*)   Very well. Go ahead!

PETER STOCKMANN   In my communication to the "People's Messenger," I have put the essential facts before the public in such a way that every fair-minded citizen can easily form his own opinion. From it you will see that the main result of the Medical Officer's proposals — apart from their constituting a vote of censure on the leading men of the town — would be to saddle the ratepayers with an unnecessary expenditure of at least some thousands of pounds.

(*Sounds of disapproval among the audience, and some cat-calls.*)

ASLAKSEN (*ringing his bell*)   Silence, please, gentlemen! I beg to support the Mayor's motion. I quite agree with him that there is something behind this agitation started by the Doctor. He talks about the Baths; but it is a revolution he is aiming at — he wants to get the administration of the town put into new hands. No one doubts the honesty of the Doctor's intentions — no one will suggest that there can be any two opinions as to that. I myself am a believer in self-government for the people, provided it does not fall too heavily on the ratepayers. But that would be the case here; and that is why I will see Dr. Stockmann damned — I beg your pardon — before I go with him in the matter. You can pay too dearly for a thing sometimes; that is my opinion.

(*Loud applause on all sides.*)

HOVSTAD   I, too, feel called upon to explain my position. Dr. Stockmann's agitation appeared to be gaining a certain amount of sympathy at first, so I supported it as impartially as I could. But presently we had reason to suspect that we had allowed ourselves to be misled by misrepresentation of the state of affairs —

DR. STOCKMANN   Misrepresentation — !

HOVSTAD   Well, let us say a not entirely trustworthy representation. The Mayor's statement has proved that. I hope no one here has any doubt as to my liberal principles; the attitude of the "People's Messenger" towards important political questions is well known to every one. But the advice of experienced and thoughtful men has convinced me that in purely local matters a newspaper ought to proceed with a certain caution.

ASLAKSEN   I entirely agree with the speaker.

HOVSTAD   And, in the matter before us, it is now an undoubted fact that Dr. Stockmann has public opinion against him. Now, what is an editor's first and most obvious duty, gentlemen? Is it not to work in harmony with his readers? Has he not received a sort of tacit mandate to work persistently and assiduously for the welfare of those whose opinions he represents? Or is it possible I am mistaken in that?

VOICES (*from the crowd*) No, no! You are quite right!

HOVSTAD It has cost me a severe struggle to break with a man in whose house I have been lately a frequent guest — a man who till to-day has been able to pride himself on the undivided goodwill of his fellow-citizens — a man whose only, or at all events whose essential, failing is that he is swayed by his heart rather than his head.

A FEW SCATTERED VOICES That is true! Bravo, Stockmann!

HOVSTAD But my duty to the community obliged me to break with him. And there is another consideration that impels me to oppose him, and, as far as possible, to arrest him on the perilous course he has adopted; that is, consideration for his family —

DR. STOCKMANN Please stick to the water-supply and drainage!

HOVSTAD — consideration, I repeat, for his wife and his children for whom he has made no provision.

MORTEN Is that us, mother?

MRS. STOCKMANN Hush!

ASLAKSEN I will now put the Mayor's proposition to the vote.

DR. STOCKMANN There is no necessity! To-night I have no intention of dealing with all that filth down at the Baths. No; I have something quite different to say to you.

PETER STOCKMANN (*aside*) What is coming now?

A DRUNKEN MAN (*by the entrance door*) I am a ratepayer! And therefore I have a right to speak too! And my entire — firm — inconceivable opinion is —

A NUMBER OF VOICES Be quiet, at the back there!

OTHERS He is drunk! Turn him out! (*They turn him out.*)

DR. STOCKMANN Am I allowed to speak?

ASLAKSEN (*ringing his bell*) Dr. Stockmann will address the meeting.

DR. STOCKMANN I should like to have seen anyone, a few days ago, dare to attempt to silence me as has been done to-night! I would have defended my sacred rights as a man, like a lion! But now it is all one to me; I have something of even weightier importance to say to you.

(*The crowd presses nearer to him,* MORTEN KIIL *conspicuous among them.*)

DR. STOCKMANN (*continuing*) I have thought and pondered a great deal, these last few days — pondered over such a variety of things that in the end my head seemed too full to hold them —

PETER STOCKMANN (*with a cough*) Ahem!

DR. STOCKMANN — but I got them clear in my mind at last, and then I saw the whole situation lucidly. And that is why I am standing here to-night. I have a great revelation to make to you, my fellow-citizens! I will impart to you a discovery of a far wider scope than the trifling matter that our water-supply is poisoned and our medicinal Baths are standing on pestiferous soil.

A NUMBER OF VOICES (*shouting*) Don't talk about the Baths! We won't hear you! None of that!

DR. STOCKMANN I have already told you that what I want to speak about is the great discovery I have made lately — the discovery that all the sources of our *moral* life are poisoned and that the whole fabric of our civic community is founded on the pestiferous soil of falsehood.

VOICES OF DISCONCERTED CITIZENS What is that he says?

PETER STOCKMANN Such an insinuation —

ASLAKSEN (*with his hand on his bell*) I call upon the speaker to moderate his language.

DR. STOCKMANN I have always loved my native town as a man only can love the home of his youthful days. I was not old when I went away from here; and exile, longing and memories cast, as it were, an additional halo over both the town and its inhabitants. (*Some clapping and applause.*) And there I stayed, for many years, in a horrible hole far away up north. When I came into contact with some of the people that lived scattered about among the rocks, I often thought it would have been more service to the poor half-starved creatures if a veterinary doctor had been sent up there, instead of a man like me. (*Murmurs among the crowd.*)

BILLING (*laying down his pen*) I'm damned if I have ever heard — !

HOVSTAD It is an insult to a respectable population!

DR. STOCKMANN Wait a bit! I do not think anyone will charge me with having forgotten my native town up there. I was like one of the eider-ducks brooding on its nest, and what I hatched was — the plans for these Baths. (*Applause and protests.*) And then when fate at last decreed for me the great happiness of coming home again — I assure you, gentlemen, I thought I had nothing more in the world to wish for. Or rather, there was one thing I wished for — eagerly, untiringly, ardently — and that was to be able to be of service to my native town and the good of the community.

PETER STOCKMANN (*looking at the ceiling*) You chose a strange way of doing it — ahem!

DR. STOCKMANN And so, with my eyes blinded to the real facts, I revelled in happiness. But yesterday morning — no, to be precise, it was yesterday afternoon — the eyes of my mind were opened wide, and the first thing I realised was the colossal stupidity of the authorities — .

(*Uproar, shouts and laughter.* MRS. STOCKMANN *coughs persistently.*)

PETER STOCKMANN Mr. Chairman!

ASLAKSEN (*ringing his bell*) By virtue of my authority — !

DR. STOCKMANN It is a petty thing to catch me up on a word, Mr. Aslaksen. What I mean is only that I got scent of the unbelievable piggishness our leading men had been responsible for down at the Baths. I can't stand leading men at any price! — I have had enough of such people in my time. They are like billy-goats in a young plantation; they do mischief everywhere. They stand in a free man's way, whichever way he turns, and what I should like best would be to see them exterminated like any other vermin — . (*Uproar.*)

PETER STOCKMANN Mr. Chairman, can we allow such expressions to pass?

ASLAKSEN (*with his hand on his bell*) Doctor — !

DR. STOCKMANN I cannot understand how it is that I have only now acquired a clear conception of what these gentry are, when I had almost daily before my eyes in this town such an excellent specimen of them — my brother Peter — slow-witted and hide-bound in prejudice — .

(*Laughter, uproar and hisses.* MRS. STOCKMANN *sits coughing assiduously.* ASLAKSEN *rings his bell violently.*)

THE DRUNKEN MAN (*who has got in again*) Is it me he is talking about? My name's Petersen, all right — but devil take me if I —

ANGRY VOICES Turn out that drunken man! Turn him out. (*He is turned out again.*)

PETER STOCKMANN Who was that person?

1ST CITIZEN I don't know who he is, Mr. Mayor.

2ND CITIZEN He doesn't belong here.

3RD CITIZEN I expect he is a navvy from over at (*the rest is inaudible*).

ASLAKSEN He had obviously had too much beer. — Proceed, Doctor; but please strive to be moderate in your language.

DR. STOCKMANN Very well, gentlemen, I will say no more about our leading men. And if anyone imagines, from what I have just said, that my object is to attack these people this evening, he is wrong — absolutely wide of the mark. For I cherish the comforting conviction that these parasites — all these venerable relics of a dying school of thought — are most admirably paving the way for their own extinction; they need no doctor's help to hasten their end. Nor is it folk of that kind who constitute the most pressing danger to the community. It is not they who are most instrumental in poisoning the sources of our moral life and infecting the ground on which we stand. It is not they who are the most dangerous enemies of truth and freedom amongst us.

SHOUTS (*from all sides*) Who then? Who is it? Name! Name!

DR. STOCKMANN You may depend upon it I shall name them! That is precisely the great discovery I made yesterday. (*Raises his voice.*) The most dangerous enemy of truth and freedom amongst us is the compact majority — yes, the damned compact Liberal majority — that is it! Now you know!

(*Tremendous uproar. Most of the crowd are shouting, stamping and hissing. Some of the older men among them exchange stolen glances and seem to be enjoying themselves.* MRS. STOCKMANN *gets up, looking anxious.* EJLIF *and* MORTEN *advance threateningly upon some schoolboys who are playing pranks.* ASLAKSEN *rings his bell and begs for silence.* HOVSTAD *and* BILLING *both talk at once, but are inaudible. At last quiet is restored.*)

ASLAKSEN As chairman, I call upon the speaker to withdraw the ill-considered expressions he has just used.

DR. STOCKMANN Never, Mr. Aslaksen! It is the majority in our community that denies me my freedom and seeks to prevent my speaking the truth.

HOVSTAD The majority always has right on its side.

BILLING And truth too, by God!

DR. STOCKMANN The majority *never* has right on its side. Never, I say! That is one of these social lies against which an independent, intelligent man must wage war. Who is it that constitute the majority of the population in a country? Is it the clever folk or the stupid? I don't imagine you will dispute the fact that at present the stupid people are in an absolutely overwhelming majority all the world over. But, good Lord! — you can never pretend that it is right that the stupid folk should govern the clever ones! (*Uproar and cries.*) Oh, yes — you can shout me down, I know! but you cannot answer me. The majority has *might* on its side — unfortunately; but *right* it has *not*. I am in the right — I and a few other scattered individuals. The minority is always in the right. (*Renewed uproar.*)

HOVSTAD Aha! — so Dr. Stockmann has become an aristocrat since the day before yesterday!

DR. STOCKMANN I have already said that I don't intend to waste a word on the puny, narrow-chested, short-winded crew whom we are leaving astern. Pulsating life no longer concerns itself with them. I am thinking of the few, the scattered few amongst us, who have absorbed new and vigorous truths. Such men stand, as it were, at the outposts, so far ahead that the compact majority has not yet been able to come up with them; and there they are fighting for truths that are too newly-born into the world of consciousness to have any considerable number of people on their side as yet.

HOVSTAD   So the Doctor is a revolutionary now!

DR. STOCKMANN   Good heavens — of course I am, Mr. Hovstad! I propose to raise a revolution against the lie that the majority has the monopoly of the truth. What sort of truths are they that the majority usually supports? They are truths that are of such advanced age that they are beginning to break up. And if a truth is as old as that, it is also in a fair way to become a lie, gentlemen. (*Laughter and mocking cries.*) Yes, believe me or not, as you like; but truths are by no means as long-lived as Methuselah — as some folk imagine. A normally constituted truth lives, let us say, as a rule seventeen or eighteen, or at most twenty years; seldom longer. But truths as aged as that are always worn frightfully thin, and nevertheless it is only then that the majority recognises them and recommends them to the community as wholesome moral nourishment. There is no great nutritive value in that sort of fare, I can assure you; and, as a doctor, I ought to know. These "majority truths" are like last year's cured meat — like rancid, tainted ham; and they are the origin of the moral scurvy that is rampant in our communities.

ASLAKSEN   It appears to me that the speaker is wandering a long way from his subject.

PETER STOCKMANN   I quite agree with the Chairman.

DR. STOCKMANN   Have you gone clean out of your senses, Peter? I am sticking as closely to my subject as I can; for my subject is precisely this, that it is the masses, the majority — this infernal compact majority — that poisons the sources of our moral life and infects the ground we stand on.

HOVSTAD   And all this because the great, broad-minded majority of the people is prudent enough to show deference only to well-ascertained and well-approved truths?

DR. STOCKMANN   Ah, my good Mr. Hovstad, don't talk nonsense about well-ascertained truths! The truths of which the masses now approve are the very truths that the fighters at the outposts held to in the days of our grandfathers. We fighters at the outposts nowadays no longer approve of them; and I do not believe there is any other well-ascertained truth except this, that no community can live a healthy life if it is nourished only on such old marrowless truths.

HOVSTAD   But instead of standing there using vague generalities, it would be interesting if you would tell us what these old marrowless truths are, that we are nourished on. (*Applause from many quarters.*)

DR. STOCKMANN   Oh, I could give you a whole string of such abominations; but to begin with I will confine myself to one well-approved truth, which at bottom is a foul lie, but upon which nevertheless Mr. Hovstad and the "People's Messenger" and all the "Messenger's" supporters are nourished.

HOVSTAD   And that is — ?

DR. STOCKMANN   That is, the doctrine you have inherited from your forefathers and proclaim thoughtlessly far and wide — the doctrine that the public, the crowd, the masses are the essential part of the population — that they constitute the People — that the common folk, the ignorant and incomplete element in the community, have the same right to pronounce judgment and to approve, to direct and to govern, as the isolated, intellectually superior personalities in it.

BILLING Well, damn me if ever I —

HOVSTAD (*at the same time, shouting out*) Fellow-citizens, take good note of that!

A NUMBER OF VOICES (*angrily*) Oho! — we are not the People! Only the superior folks are to govern, are they!

A WORKMAN Turn the fellow out, for talking such rubbish!

ANOTHER Out with him!

ANOTHER (*calling out*) Blow your horn, Evensen! (*A horn is blown loudly, amidst hisses and an angry uproar.*)

DR. STOCKMANN (*when the noise has somewhat abated*) Be reasonable! Can't you stand hearing the voice of truth for once? I don't in the least expect you to agree with me all at once; but I must say I did expect Mr. Hovstad to admit I was right, when he had recovered his composure a little. He claims to be a freethinker —

VOICES (*in murmurs of astonishment*) Freethinker, did he say? Is Hovstad a freethinker?

HOVSTAD (*shouting*) Prove it, Dr. Stockmann! When have I said so in print?

DR. STOCKMANN (*reflecting*) No, confound it, you are right! — you have never had the courage to. Well, I won't put you in a hole, Mr. Hovstad. Let us say it is I that am the freethinker, then. I am going to prove to you, scientifically, that the "People's Messenger" leads you by the nose in a shameful manner when it tells you that you — that the common people, the crowd, the masses are the real essence of the People. That is only a newspaper lie, I tell you! The common people are nothing more than the raw material of which a People is made. (*Groans, laughter and uproar.*) Well, isn't that the case? Isn't there an enormous difference between a well-bred and an ill-bred strain of animals? Take, for instance, a common barn-door hen. What sort of eating do you get from a shrivelled-up old scrag of a fowl like that? Not much, do you! And what sort of eggs does it lay? A fairly good crow or a raven can lay pretty nearly as good an egg. But take a well-bred Spanish or Japanese hen, or a good pheasant or a turkey — then you will see the difference. Or take the case of dogs, with whom we humans are on such intimate terms. Think first of an ordinary common cur — I mean one of the horrible, coarse-haired, low-bred curs that do nothing but run about the streets and befoul the walls of the houses. Compare one of these curs with a poodle whose sires for many generations have been bred in a gentleman's house, where they have had the best of food and had the opportunity of hearing soft voices and music. Do you not think that the poodle's brain is developed to quite a different degree from that of the cur? Of course it is. It is puppies of well-bred poodles like that, that showmen train to do incredibly clever tricks — things that a common cur could never learn to do even if it stood on its head. (*Uproar and mocking cries.*)

A CITIZEN (*calls out*) Are you going to make out we are dogs, now?

ANOTHER CITIZEN We are not animals, Doctor!

DR. STOCKMANN Yes, but bless my soul, we *are*, my friend! It is true we are the finest animals anyone could wish for; but, even amongst us, exceptionally fine animals are rare. There is a tremendous difference between poodle-men and cur-men. And the amusing part of it is, that Mr. Hovstad quite agrees with me as long as it is a question of four-footed animals —

HOVSTAD Yes, it is true enough as far as they are concerned.

DR. STOCKMANN Very well. But as soon as I extend the principle and apply it to two-legged animals, Mr. Hovstad stops short. He no longer dares to think independently, or to pursue his ideas to their logical conclusion; so he turns the whole theory upside down and proclaims in the "People's Messenger" that it is the barn-door hens and street curs that are the finest specimens in the menagerie. But that is always the way, as long as a man retains the traces of common origin and has not worked his way up to intellectual distinction.

HOVSTAD I lay no claim to any sort of distinction. I am the son of humble countryfolk, and I am proud that the stock I come from is rooted deep among the common people he insults.

VOICES Bravo, Hovstad! Bravo! Bravo!

DR. STOCKMANN The kind of common people I mean are not only to be found low down in the social scale; they crawl and swarm all around us — even in the highest social positions. You have only to look at your own fine, distinguished Mayor! My brother Peter is every bit as plebeian as anyone that walks in two shoes — (Laughter and hisses.)

PETER STOCKMANN I protest against personal allusions of this kind.

DR. STOCKMANN (imperturbably) — and that, not because he is, like myself, descended from some old rascal of a pirate from Pomerania or thereabouts — because that is who we are descended from —

PETER STOCKMANN An absurd legend. I deny it!

DR. STOCKMANN — but because he thinks what his superiors think and holds the same opinions as they. People who do that are, intellectually speaking, common people; and that is why my magnificent brother Peter is in reality so very far from any distinction — and consequently also so far from being liberal-minded.

PETER STOCKMANN Mr. Chairman — !

HOVSTAD So it is only the distinguished men that are liberal-minded in this country? We are learning something quite new! (Laughter.)

DR. STOCKMANN Yes, that is part of my new discovery too. And another part of it is that broad-mindedness is almost precisely the same thing as morality. That is why I maintain that it is absolutely inexcusable in the "People's Messenger" to proclaim, day in and day out, the false doctrine that it is the masses, the crowd, the compact majority that have the monopoly of broad-mindedness and morality — and that vice and corruption and every kind of intellectual depravity are the result of culture, just as all the filth that is draining into our Baths is the result of the tanneries up at Mölledal! (Uproar and interruptions. DR. STOCKMANN is undisturbed, and goes on, carried away by his ardour, with a smile.) And yet this same "People's Messenger" can go on preaching that the masses ought to be elevated to higher conditions of life! But, bless my soul, if the "Messenger's" teaching is to be depended upon, this very raising up the masses would mean nothing more or less than setting them straightway upon the paths of depravity! Happily the theory that culture demoralises is only an old falsehood that our forefathers believed in and we have inherited. No, it is ignorance, poverty, ugly conditions of life that do the devil's work! In a house which does not get aired and swept every day — my wife Katherine maintains that the floor ought to be scrubbed as well, but that is a debatable question — in such a house, let me tell you, people will lose within two or three years the power of thinking or acting in a moral manner. Lack of oxygen weakens the conscience. And there must be a plentiful lack of oxygen in very many houses in this town, I should think, judging from the fact that the whole compact majority can be unconscientious enough to wish to build the town's prosperity on a quagmire of falsehood and deceit.

ASLAKSEN We cannot allow such a grave accusation to be flung at a citizen community.

A CITIZEN I move that the Chairman direct the speaker to sit down.

VOICES (*angrily*) Hear, hear! Quite right! Make him sit down!

DR. STOCKMANN (*losing his self-control*) Then I will go and shout the truth at every street corner! I will write it in other towns' newspapers! The whole country shall know what is going on here!

HOVSTAD It almost seems as if Dr. Stockmann's intention were to ruin the town.

DR. STOCKMANN Yes, my native town is so dear to me that I would rather ruin it than see it flourishing upon a lie.

ASLAKSEN This is really serious.

(*Uproar and cat-calls.* MRS. STOCKMANN *coughs, but to no purpose; her husband does not listen to her any longer.*)

HOVSTAD (*shouting above the din*) A man must be a public enemy to wish to ruin a whole community!

DR. STOCKMANN (*with growing fervour*) What does the destruction of a community matter, if it lives on lies! It ought to be razed to the ground, I tell you! All who live by lies ought to be exterminated like vermin! You will end by infecting the whole country; you will bring about such a state of things that the whole country will deserve to be ruined. And if things come to that pass, I shall say from the bottom of my heart: Let the whole country perish, let all these people be exterminated!

VOICES (*from the crowd*) That is talking like an out-and-out enemy of the people!

BILLING There sounded the voice of the people, by all that's holy!

THE WHOLE CROWD (*shouting*) Yes, yes! He is an enemy of the people! He hates his country! He hates his own people!

ASLAKSEN Both as a citizen and as an individual, I am profoundly disturbed by what we have had to listen to. Dr. Stockmann has shown himself in a light I should never have dreamed of. I am unhappily obliged to subscribe to the opinion which I have just heard my estimable fellow-citizens utter; and I propose that we should give expression to that opinion in a resolution. I propose a resolution as follows: "This meeting declares that it considers Dr. Thomas Stockmann, Medical Officer of the Baths, to be an enemy of the people."

(*A storm of cheers and applause. A number of men surround the* DOCTOR *and hiss him.* MRS. STOCKMANN *and* PETRA *have got up from their seats.* MORTEN *and* EJLIF *are fighting the other schoolboys for hissing; some of their elders separate them.*)

DR. STOCKMANN (*to the men who are hissing him*) Oh, you fools! I tell you that —

ASLAKSEN (*ringing his bell*) We cannot hear you now, Doctor. A formal vote is about to be taken; but, out of regard for personal feelings, it shall be by ballot and not verbal. Have you any clean paper, Mr. Billing?

BILLING   I have both blue and white here.

ASLAKSEN (*going to him*)   That will do nicely; we shall get on more quickly that way. Cut it up into small strips — yes, that's it. (*To the meeting.*) Blue means no; white means yes. I will come round myself and collect votes. (PETER STOCKMANN *leaves the hall.* ASLAKSEN *and one or two others go round the room with the slips of paper in their hats.*)

1ST CITIZEN (*to* HOVSTAD)   I say, what has come to the Doctor? What are we to think of it?

HOVSTAD   Oh, you know how headstrong he is.

2ND CITIZEN (*to* BILLING)   Billing, you go to their house — have you ever noticed if the fellow drinks?

BILLING   Well I'm hanged if I know what to say. There are always spirits on the table when you go.

3RD CITIZEN   I rather think he goes quite off his head sometimes.

1ST CITIZEN   I wonder if there is any madness in his family?

BILLING   I shouldn't wonder if there were.

4TH CITIZEN   No, it is nothing more than sheer malice; he wants to get even with somebody for something or other.

BILLING   Well certainly he suggested a rise in his salary on one occasion lately, and did not get it.

THE CITIZENS (*together*)   Ah! — then it is easy to understand how it is!

THE DRUNKEN MAN (*who has got amongst the audience again*)   I want a blue one, I do! And I want a white one too!

VOICES   It's that drunken chap again! Turn him out!

MORTEN KIIL (*going up to* DR. STOCKMANN)   Well, Stockmann, do you see what these monkey tricks of yours lead to?

DR. STOCKMANN   I have done my duty.

MORTEN KIIL   What was that you said about the tanneries at Mölledal?

DR. STOCKMANN   You heard well enough. I said they were the source of all the filth.

MORTEN KIIL   My tannery too?

DR. STOCKMANN   Unfortunately your tannery is by far the worst.

MORTEN KIIL   Are you going to put that in the papers?

DR. STOCKMANN   I shall conceal nothing.

MORTEN KIIL   That may cost you dear, Stockmann. (*Goes out.*)

A STOUT MAN (*going up to* CAPTAIN HORSTER, *without taking any notice of the ladies*)   Well, Captain, so you lend your house to enemies of the people?

HORSTER   I imagine I can do what I like with my own possessions, Mr. Vik.

THE STOUT MAN   Then you can have no objection to my doing the same with mine.

HORSTER   What do you mean, sir?

THE STOUT MAN   You shall hear from me in the morning. (*Turns his back on him and moves off.*)

PETRA   Was that not your owner, Captain Horster?

HORSTER   Yes, that was Mr. Vik the ship-owner.

ASLAKSEN (*with the voting-papers in his hands, gets up on to the platform and rings his bell*)   Gentlemen, allow me to announce the result. By the votes of every one here except one person —

A YOUNG MAN   That is the drunk chap!

ASLAKSEN By the votes of every one here except a tipsy man, this meeting of citizens declares Dr. Thomas Stockmann to be an enemy of the people. (*Shouts and applause.*) Three cheers for our ancient and honourable citizen community! (*Renewed applause.*) Three cheers for our able and energetic Mayor, who has so loyally suppressed the promptings of family feeling! (*Cheers.*) The meeting is dissolved. (*Gets down.*)

BILLING Three cheers for the Chairman!

THE WHOLE CROWD Three cheers for Aslaksen! Hurrah!

DR. STOCKMANN My hat and coat, Petra! Captain, have you room on your ship for passengers to the New World?

HORSTER For you and yours we will make room, Doctor.

DR. STOCKMANN (*as* PETRA *helps him into his coat*) Good. Come, Katherine! Come, boys!

MRS. STOCKMANN (*in an undertone*) Thomas, dear, let us go out by the back way.

DR. STOCKMANN No back ways for me, Katherine. (*Raising his voice.*) You will hear more of this enemy of the people, before he shakes the dust off his shoes upon you! I am not so forgiving as a certain Person; I do not say: "I forgive you, for ye know not what ye do."

ASLAKSEN (*shouting*) That is a blasphemous comparison, Dr. Stockmann!

BILLING It is, by God! It's dreadful for an earnest man to listen to.

A COARSE VOICE Threatens us now, does he!

OTHER VOICES (*excitedly*) Let's go and break his windows! Duck him in the fjord!

ANOTHER VOICE Blow your horn, Evensen! Pip, pip!

(*Horn-blowing, hisses and wild cries.* DR. STOCKMANN *goes out through the hall with his family,* HORSTER *elbowing a way for them.*)

THE WHOLE CROWD (*howling after them as they go*) Enemy of the People! Enemy of the People!

BILLING (*as he puts his papers together*) Well, I'm damned if I go and drink toddy with the Stockmanns to-night!

(*The crowd presses towards the exit. The uproar continues outside; shouts of "Enemy of the People!" are heard from without.*)

Act Five

Scene: DR. STOCKMANN'S *study. Bookcases, and cabinets containing specimens, line the walls. At the back is a door leading to the hall; in the foreground on the left, a door leading to the sitting-room. In the right-hand wall are two windows, of which all the panes are broken. The* DOCTOR'S *desk, littered with books and papers, stands in the middle of the room, which is in disorder. It is morning.* DR. STOCKMANN *in dressing-gown, slippers and a smoking-cap, is bending down and raking with an umbrella under one of the cabinets. After a little while he rakes out a stone.*

DR. STOCKMANN (*calling through the open sitting-room door*) Katherine, I have found another one.

MRS. STOCKMANN (*from the sitting-room*) Oh, you will find a lot more yet, I expect.

DR. STOCKMANN (*adding the stone to a heap of others on the table*)   I shall treasure these stones as relics. Ejlif and Morten shall look at them every day, and when they are grown up they shall inherit them as heirlooms. (*Rakes about under a bookcase.*) Hasn't — what the deuce is her name — the girl, you know — hasn't she been to fetch the glazier yet?

MRS. STOCKMANN (*coming in*)   Yes, but he said he didn't know if he would be able to come to-day.

DR. STOCKMANN   You will see he won't dare to come.

MRS. STOCKMANN   Well, that is just what Randine thought — that he didn't dare to, on account of the neighbours. (*Calls into the sitting-room.*) What is it you want, Randine? Give it to me. (*Goes in, and comes out again directly.*) Here is a letter for you, Thomas.

DR. STOCKMANN   Let me see it. (*Opens and reads it.*) Ah! — of course.

MRS. STOCKMANN   Who is it from?

DR. STOCKMANN   From the landlord. Notice to quit.

MRS. STOCKMANN   Is it possible? Such a nice man —

DR. STOCKMANN (*looking at the letter*)   Does not dare do otherwise, he says. Doesn't like doing it, but dares not do otherwise — on account of his fellow-citizens — out of regard for public opinion. Is in a dependent position — dares not offend certain influential men —

MRS. STOCKMANN   There, you see, Thomas!

DR. STOCKMANN   Yes, yes, I see well enough; the whole lot of them in the town are cowards; not a man among them dares do anything for fear of the others. (*Throws the letter on to the table.*) But it doesn't matter to us, Katherine. We are going to sail away to the New World, and —

MRS. STOCKMANN   But, Thomas, are you sure we are well advised to take this step?

DR. STOCKMANN   Are you suggesting that I should stay here, where they have pilloried me as an enemy of the people — branded me — broken my windows! And just look here, Katherine — they have torn a great rent in my black trousers too!

MRS. STOCKMANN   Oh, dear — and they are the best pair you have got!

DR. STOCKMANN   You should never wear your best trousers when you go out to fight for freedom and truth. It is not that I care so much about the trousers, you know; you can always sew them up again for me. But that the common herd should dare to make this attack on me, as if they were my equals — that is what I cannot, for the life of me, swallow!

MRS. STOCKMANN   There is no doubt they have behaved very ill to you, Thomas; but is that sufficient reason for our leaving our native country for good and all?

DR. STOCKMANN   If we went to another town, do you suppose we should not find the common people just as insolent as they are here? Depend upon it, there is not much to choose between them. Oh, well, let the curs snap — that is not the worst part of it. The worst is that, from one end of this country to the other, every man is the slave of his Party. Although, as far as that goes, I daresay it is not much better in the free West either; the compact majority, and liberal public opinion, and all that infernal old bag of tricks are probably rampant there too. But there things are done on a larger scale, you see. They may kill you, but they won't put you to death by slow torture. They don't squeeze a free man's soul in a vice, as they do here.

And, if need be, one can live in solitude. (*Walks up and down.*) If only I knew where there was a virgin forest or a small South Sea island for sale, cheap —

MRS. STOCKMANN But think of the boys, Thomas.

DR. STOCKMANN (*standing still*) What a strange woman you are, Katherine! Would you prefer to have the boys grow up in a society like this? You saw for yourself last night that half the population are out of their minds; and if the other half have not lost their senses, it is because they are mere brutes, with no sense to lose.

MRS. STOCKMANN But, Thomas dear, the imprudent things you said had something to do with it, you know.

DR. STOCKMANN Well, isn't what I said perfectly true? Don't they turn every idea topsy-turvy? Don't they make a regular hotch-potch of right and wrong? Don't they say that the things I know are true, are lies? The craziest part of it all is the fact of these "liberals," men of full age, going about in crowds imagining that they are the broad-minded party! Did you ever hear anything like it, Katherine!

MRS. STOCKMANN Yes, yes, it's mad enough of them, certainly; but — (PETRA *comes in from the sitting-room*). Back from school already?

PETRA Yes. I have been given notice of dismissal.

MRS. STOCKMANN Dismissal?

DR. STOCKMANN You too?

PETRA Mrs. Busk gave me my notice; so I thought it was best to go at once.

DR. STOCKMANN You were perfectly right, too!

MRS. STOCKMANN Who would have thought Mrs. Busk was a woman like that!

PETRA Mrs. Busk isn't a bit like that, mother; I saw quite plainly how it hurt her to do it. But she didn't dare do otherwise, she said; and so I got my notice.

DR. STOCKMANN (*laughing and rubbing his hands*) She didn't dare do otherwise, either! It's delicious!

MRS. STOCKMANN Well, after the dreadful scenes last night —

PETRA It was not only that. Just listen to this, father!

DR. STOCKMANN Well?

PETRA Mrs. Busk showed me no less than three letters she received this morning —

DR. STOCKMANN Anonymous, I suppose?

PETRA Yes.

DR. STOCKMANN Yes, because they didn't dare to risk signing their names, Katherine!

PETRA And two of them were to the effect that a man who has been our guest here, was declaring last night at the Club that my views on various subjects are extremely emancipated —

DR. STOCKMANN You did not deny that, I hope?

PETRA No, you know I wouldn't. Mrs. Busk's own views are tolerably emancipated, when we are alone together; but now that this report about me is being spread, she dare not keep me on any longer.

MRS. STOCKMANN And some one who had been a guest of ours! That shows you the return you get for your hospitality, Thomas!

DR. STOCKMANN We won't live in such a disgusting hole any longer. Pack up as quickly as you can, Katherine; the sooner we can get away, the better.

MRS. STOCKMANN   Be quiet — I think I hear some one in the hall. See who it is, Petra.

PETRA (*opening the door*)   Oh, it's you, Captain Horster! Do come in.

HORSTER (*coming in*)   Good morning. I thought I would just come in and see how you were.

DR. STOCKMANN (*shaking his hand*)   Thanks — that is really kind of you.

MRS. STOCKMANN   And thank you, too, for helping us through the crowd, Captain Horster.

PETRA   How did you manage to get home again?

HORSTER   Oh, somehow or other. I am fairly strong, and there is more sound than fury about these folk.

DR. STOCKMANN   Yes, isn't their swinish cowardice astonishing? Look here, I will show you something! There are all the stones they have thrown through my windows. Just look at them! I'm hanged if there are more than two decently large bits of hardstone in the whole heap; the rest are nothing but gravel — wretched little things. And yet they stood out there bawling and swearing that they would do me some violence; but as for *doing* anything — you don't see much of that in this town.

HORSTER   Just as well for you this time, Doctor!

DR. STOCKMANN   True enough. But it makes one angry all the same; because if some day it should be a question of a national fight in real earnest, you will see that public opinion will be in favour of taking to one's heels, and the compact majority will turn tail like a flock of sheep, Captain Horster. That is what is so mournful to think of; it gives me so much concern, that —. No, devil take it, it is ridiculous to care about it! They have called me an enemy of the people, so an enemy of the people let me be!

MRS. STOCKMANN   You will never be that, Thomas.

DR. STOCKMANN   Don't swear to that, Katherine. To be called an ugly name may have the same effect as a pin-scratch in the lung. And that hateful name — I can't get quit of it. It is sticking here in the pit of my stomach, eating into me like a corrosive acid. And no magnesia will remove it.

PETRA   Bah — you should only laugh at them, father.

HORSTER   They will change their minds some day, Doctor.

MRS. STOCKMANN   Yes, Thomas, as sure as you are standing here.

DR. STOCKMANN   Perhaps, when it is too late. Much good may it do them! They may wallow in their filth then and rue the day when they drove a patriot into exile. When do you sail, Captain Horster?

HORSTER   Hm! — that was just what I had come to speak about —

DR. STOCKMANN   Why, has anything gone wrong with the ship?

HORSTER   No; but what has happened is that I am not to sail in it.

PETRA   Do you mean that you have been dismissed from your command?

HORSTER (*smiling*)   Yes, that's just it.

PETRA   You too.

MRS. STOCKMANN   There, you see, Thomas!

DR. STOCKMANN   And that for the truth's sake! Oh, if I had thought such a thing possible —

HORSTER   You mustn't take it to heart; I shall be sure to find a job with some ship-owner or other, elsewhere.

DR. STOCKMANN   And that is this man Vik — a wealthy man, independent of every one and everything —! Shame on him!

HORSTER   He is quite an excellent fellow otherwise; he told me himself he would willingly have kept me on, if only he had dared —

DR. STOCKMANN   But he didn't dare? No, of course not.

HORSTER   It is not such an easy matter, he said, for a party man —

DR. STOCKMANN   The worthy man spoke the truth. A party is like a sausage machine; it mashes up all sorts of heads together into the same mincemeat — fatheads and blockheads, all in one mash!

MRS. STOCKMANN   Come, come, Thomas dear!

PETRA (*to* HORSTER)   If only you had not come home with us, things might not have come to this pass.

HORSTER   I do not regret it.

PETRA (*holding out her hand to him*)   Thank you for that!

HORSTER (*to* DR. STOCKMANN)   And so what I came to say was that if you are determined to go away, I have thought of another plan —

DR. STOCKMANN   That's splendid! — if only we can get away at once.

MRS. STOCKMANN   Hush — wasn't that some one knocking?

PETRA   That is uncle, surely.

DR. STOCKMANN   Aha! (*Calls out.*) Come in!

MRS. STOCKMANN   Dear Thomas, promise me definitely —

(PETER STOCKMANN *comes in from the hall.*)

PETER STOCKMANN   Oh, you are engaged. In that case, I will —

DR. STOCKMANN   No, no, come in.

PETER STOCKMANN   But I wanted to speak to you alone.

MRS. STOCKMANN   We will go into the sitting-room in the meanwhile.

HORSTER   And I will look in again later.

DR. STOCKMANN   No, go in there with them, Captain Horster; I want to hear more about —

HORSTER   Very well, I will wait, then. (*He follows* MRS. STOCKMANN *and* PETRA *into the sitting-room.*)

DR. STOCKMANN   I daresay you find it rather draughty here to-day. Put your hat on.

PETER STOCKMANN   Thank you, if I may. (*Does so.*) I think I caught cold last night; I stood and shivered —

DR. STOCKMANN   Really? I found it warm enough.

PETER STOCKMANN   I regret that it was not in my power to prevent those excesses last night.

DR. STOCKMANN   Have you anything particular to say to me besides that?

PETER STOCKMANN (*taking a big letter from his pocket*)   I have this document for you, from the Baths Committee.

DR. STOCKMANN   My dismissal?

PETER STOCKMANN   Yes, dating from to-day. (*Lays the letter on the table.*) It gives us pain to do it; but, to speak frankly, we dared not do otherwise on account of public opinion.

DR. STOCKMANN (*smiling*)   Dared not? I seem to have heard that word before, to-day.

PETER STOCKMANN   I must beg you to understand your position clearly. For the future you must not count on any practice whatever in the town.

DR. STOCKMANN   Devil take the practice! But why are you so sure of that?

PETER STOCKMANN   The Householders' Association is circulating a list from house to house. All right-minded citizens are being called upon to give up employing you; and I can assure you that not a single head of a family will risk refusing his signature. They simply dare not.

DR. STOCKMANN   No, no; I don't doubt it. But what then?

PETER STOCKMANN   If I might advise you, it would be best to leave the place for a little while —

DR. STOCKMANN   Yes, the propriety of leaving the place *has* occurred to me.

PETER STOCKMANN   Good. And then, when you have had six months to think things over, if, after mature consideration, you can persuade yourself to write a few words of regret, acknowledging your error —

DR. STOCKMANN   I might have my appointment restored to me, do you mean?

PETER STOCKMANN   Perhaps. It is not at all impossible.

DR. STOCKMANN   But what about public opinion, then? Surely you would not dare to do it on account of public feeling.

PETER STOCKMANN   Public opinion is an extremely mutable thing. And, to be quite candid with you, it is a matter of great importance to us to have some admission of that sort from you in writing.

DR. STOCKMANN   Oh, that's what you are after, is it! I will just trouble you to remember what I said to you lately about foxy tricks of that sort!

PETER STOCKMANN   Your position was quite different then. At that time you had reason to suppose you had the whole town at your back —

DR. STOCKMANN   Yes, and now I feel I have the whole town *on* my back — (*flaring up*) I would not do it if I had the devil and his dam on my back — ! Never — never, I tell you!

PETER STOCKMANN   A man with a family has no right to behave as you do. You have no right to do it, Thomas.

DR. STOCKMANN   I have no right! There is only one single thing in the world a free man has no right to do. Do you know what that is?

PETER STOCKMANN   No.

DR. STOCKMANN   Of course you don't, but I will tell you. A free man has no right to soil himself with filth; he has no right to behave in a way that would justify his spitting in his own face.

PETER STOCKMANN   This sort of thing sounds extremely plausible, of course; and if there were no other explanation for your obstinacy — . But as it happens that there is.

DR. STOCKMANN   What do you mean?

PETER STOCKMANN   You understand very well what I mean. But, as your brother and as a man of discretion, I advise you not to build too much upon expectations and prospects that may so very easily fail you.

DR. STOCKMANN   What in the world is all this about?

PETER STOCKMANN   Do you really ask me to believe that you are ignorant of the terms of Mr. Kiil's will?

DR. STOCKMANN   I know that the small amount he possesses is to go to an institution for indigent old work-people. How does that concern me?

PETER STOCKMANN   In the first place, it is by no means a small amount that is in question. Mr. Kiil is a fairly wealthy man.

DR. STOCKMANN   I had no notion of that!

PETER STOCKMANN   Hm! — hadn't you really? Then I suppose you had no notion, either, that a considerable portion of his wealth will come to your children, you and your wife having a life-rent of the capital. Has he never told you so?

DR. STOCKMANN Never, on my honour! Quite the reverse; he has consistently done nothing but fume at being so unconscionably heavily taxed. But are you perfectly certain of this, Peter?

PETER STOCKMANN I have it from an absolutely reliable source.

DR. STOCKMANN Then, thank God, Katherine is provided for — and the children too! I must tell her this at once — (*Calls out.*) Katherine, Katherine!

PETER STOCKMANN (*restraining him*) Hush, don't say a word yet!

MRS. STOCKMANN (*opening the door*) What is the matter?

DR. STOCKMANN Oh, nothing, nothing; you can go back. (*She shuts the door. DR. STOCKMANN walks up and down in his excitement.*) Provided for! — Just think of it, we are all provided for! And for life! What a blessed feeling it is to know one is provided for!

PETER STOCKMANN Yes, but that is just exactly what you are not. Mr. Kiil can alter his will any day he likes.

DR. STOCKMANN But he won't do that, my dear Peter. The "Badger" is much too delighted at my attack on you and your wise friends.

PETER STOCKMANN (*starts and looks intently at him*) Ah, that throws a light on various things.

DR. STOCKMANN What things?

PETER STOCKMANN I see that the whole thing was a combined manoeuvre on your part and his. These violent, reckless attacks that you have made against the leading men of the town, under the pretence that it was in the name of truth —

DR. STOCKMANN What about them?

PETER STOCKMANN I see that they were nothing else than the stipulated price for that vindictive old man's will.

DR. STOCKMANN (*almost speechless*) Peter — you are the most disgusting plebeian I have ever met in all my life.

PETER STOCKMANN All is over between us. Your dismissal is irrevocable — we have a weapon against you now. (*Goes out.*)

DR. STOCKMANN For shame! For shame! (*Calls out.*) Katherine, you must have the floor scrubbed after him! Let — what's her name — devil take it, the girl who has always got soot on her nose —

MRS. STOCKMANN (*in the sitting-room*) Hush, Thomas, be quiet!

PETRA (*coming to the door*) Father, grandfather is here, asking if he may speak to you alone.

DR. STOCKMANN Certainly he may. (*Going to the door.*) Come in, Mr. Kiil. (MORTEN KIIL *comes in.* DR. STOCKMANN *shuts the door after him.*) What can I do for you? Won't you sit down?

MORTEN KIIL I won't sit. (*Looks around.*) You look very comfortable here to-day, Thomas.

DR. STOCKMANN Yes, don't we!

MORTEN KIIL Very comfortable — plenty of fresh air. I should think you have got enough to-day of that oxygen you were talking about yesterday. Your conscience must be in splendid order to-day, I should think.

DR. STOCKMANN It is.

MORTEN KIIL So I should think. (*Taps his chest.*) Do you know what I have got here?

DR. STOCKMANN A good conscience, too, I hope.

MORTEN KIIL Bah! — No, it is something better than that. (*He takes a thick* pocket-book *from his breast-pocket, opens it, and displays a packet of papers.*)

DR. STOCKMANN (*looking at him in astonishment*) Shares in the Baths?

MORTEN KIIL They were not difficult to get to-day.

DR. STOCKMANN And you have been buying —?

MORTEN KIIL As many as I could pay for.

DR. STOCKMANN But, my dear Mr. Kiil — consider the state of the Baths' affairs!

MORTEN KIIL If you behave like a reasonable man, you can soon set the Baths on their feet again.

DR. STOCKMANN Well, you can see for yourself that I have done all I can, but —. They are all mad in this town!

MORTEN KIIL You said yesterday that the worst of this pollution came from my tannery. If that is true, then my grandfather and my father before me, and I myself, for many years past, have been poisoning the town like three destroying angels. Do you think I am going to sit quiet under that reproach?

DR. STOCKMANN Unfortunately, I am afraid you will have to.

MORTEN KIIL No, thank you. I am jealous of my name and reputation. They call me "the Badger," I am told. A badger is a kind of pig, I believe; but I am not going to give them the right to call me that. I mean to live and die a clean man.

DR. STOCKMANN And how are you going to set about it?

MORTEN KIIL You shall cleanse me, Thomas.

DR. STOCKMANN I!

MORTEN KIIL Do you know what money I have bought these shares with? No, of course you can't know — but I will tell you. It is the money that Katherine and Petra and the boys will have when I am gone. Because I have been able to save a little bit after all, you know.

DR. STOCKMANN (*flaring up*) And you have gone and taken Katherine's money for *this!*

MORTEN KIIL Yes, the whole of the money is invested in the Baths now. And now I just want to see whether you are quite stark, staring mad, Thomas! If you still make out that these animals and other nasty things of that sort come from my tannery, it will be exactly as if you were to flay broad strips of skin from Katherine's body, and Petra's, and the boys'; and no decent man would do that — unless he were mad.

DR. STOCKMANN (*walking up and down*) Yes, but I *am* mad; I *am* mad!

MORTEN KIIL You cannot be so absurdly mad as all that, when it is a question of your wife and children.

DR. STOCKMANN (*standing still in front of him*) Why couldn't you consult me about it, before you went and bought all that trash?

MORTEN KIIL What is done cannot be undone.

DR. STOCKMANN (*walks about uneasily*) If only I were not so certain about it —! But I am absolutely convinced that I am right.

MORTEN KIIL (*weighing the pocket-book in his hand*) If you stick to your mad idea, this won't be worth much, you know. (*Puts the pocket-book in his pocket.*)

DR. STOCKMANN But, hang it all! it might be possible for science to discover some prophylactic, I should think — or some antidote of some kind —

MORTEN KIIL To kill these animals, do you mean?

DR. STOCKMANN   Yes, or to make them innocuous.

MORTEN KIIL   Couldn't you try some rat's-bane?

DR. STOCKMANN   Don't talk nonsense! They all say it is only imagination, you know. Well, let it go at that! Let them have their own way about it! Haven't the ignorant, narrow-minded curs reviled me as an enemy of the people? — and haven't they been ready to tear the clothes off my back too?

MORTEN KIIL   And broken all your windows to pieces!

DR. STOCKMANN   And then there is my duty to my family. I must talk it over with Katherine; she is great on those things.

MORTEN KIIL   That is right; be guided by a reasonable woman's advice.

DR. STOCKMANN   (*advancing towards him*)   To think you could do such a preposterous thing! Risking Katherine's money in this way, and putting me in such a horribly painful dilemma! When I look at you, I think I see the devil himself — .

MORTEN KIIL   Then I had better go. But I must have an answer from you before two o'clock — yes or no. If it is no, the shares go to a charity, and that this very day.

DR. STOCKMANN   And what does Katherine get?

MORTEN KIIL   Not a halfpenny. (*The door leading to the hall opens, and* HOVSTAD *and* ASLAKSEN *make their appearance.*)   Look at those two!

DR. STOCKMANN   (*staring at them*)   What the devil! — have *you* actually the face to come into my house?

HOVSTAD   Certainly.

ASLAKSEN   We have something to say to you, you see.

MORTEN KIIL   (*in a whisper*)   Yes or no — before two o'clock.

ASLAKSEN   (*glancing at* HOVSTAD)   Aha!

(MORTEN KIIL *goes out.*)

DR. STOCKMANN   Well, what do you want with me? Be brief.

HOVSTAD   I can quite understand that you are annoyed with us for our attitude at the meeting yesterday —

DR. STOCKMANN   Attitude, do you call it? Yes, it was a charming attitude! I call it weak, womanish — damnably shameful!

HOVSTAD   Call it what you like, we could not do otherwise.

DR. STOCKMANN   You *dared* not do otherwise — isn't that it?

HOVSTAD   Well, if you like to put it that way.

ASLAKSEN   But why did you not let us have word of it beforehand? — just a hint to Mr. Hovstad or to me?

DR. STOCKMANN   A hint? Of what?

ASLAKSEN   Of what was behind it all.

DR. STOCKMANN   I don't understand you in the least.

ASLAKSEN   (*with a confidential nod*)   Oh, yes, you do, Dr. Stockmann.

HOVSTAD   It is no good making a mystery of it any longer.

DR. STOCKMANN   (*looking first at one of them and then at the other*)   What the devil do you both mean?

ASLAKSEN   May I ask if your father in-law is not going round the town buying up all the shares in the Baths?

DR. STOCKMANN   Yes, he has been buying Baths' shares to-day; but —

ASLAKSEN   It would have been more prudent to get some one else to do it — some one less nearly related to you.

HOVSTAD   And you should not have let your name appear in the affair. There was no need for anyone to know that the attack on the Baths came from you. You ought to have consulted me, Dr. Stockmann.

DR. STOCKMANN (*looks in front of him; then a light seems to dawn on him and he says in amazement*) Are such things conceivable? Are such things possible?

ASLAKSEN (*with a smile*) Evidently they are. But it is better to use a little finesse, you know.

HOVSTAD And it is much better to have several persons in a thing of that sort; because the responsibility of each individual is lessened, when there are others with him.

DR. STOCKMANN (*composedly*) Come to the point, gentlemen. What do you want?

ASLAKSEN Perhaps Mr. Hovstad had better —

HOVSTAD No, you tell him, Aslaksen.

ASLAKSEN Well, the fact is that, now we know the bearings of the whole affair, we think we might venture to put the "People's Messenger" at your disposal.

DR. STOCKMANN Do you dare do that now? What about public opinion? Are you not afraid of a storm breaking upon our heads?

HOVSTAD We will try to weather it.

ASLAKSEN And you must be ready to go off quickly on a new tack, Doctor. As soon as your invective has done its work —

DR. STOCKMANN Do you mean, as soon as my father-in-law and I have got hold of the shares at a low figure?

HOVSTAD Your reasons for wishing to get the control of the Baths are mainly scientific, I take it.

DR. STOCKMANN Of course; it was for scientific reasons that I persuaded the old "Badger" to stand in with me in the matter. So we will tinker at the conduit-pipes a little, and dig up a little bit of the shore, and it shan't cost the town a sixpence. That will be all right — eh?

HOVSTAD I think so — if you have the "People's Messenger" behind you.

ASLAKSEN The Press is a power in a free community, Doctor.

DR. STOCKMANN Quite so. And so is public opinion. And you, Mr. Aslaksen — I suppose you will be answerable for the Householders' Association?

ASLAKSEN Yes, and for the Temperance Society. You may rely on that.

DR. STOCKMANN But, gentlemen — I really am ashamed to ask the question — but, what return do you — ?

HOVSTAD We should prefer to help you without any return whatever, believe me. But the "People's Messenger" is in rather a shaky condition; it doesn't go really well; and I should be very unwilling to suspend the paper now, when there is so much work to do here in the political way.

DR. STOCKMANN Quite so; that would be a great trial to such a friend of the people as you are. (*Flares up.*) But I am an enemy of the people, remember! (*Walks about the room.*) Where have I put my stick? Where the devil is my stick?

HOVSTAD What's that?

ASLAKSEN Surely you never mean — ?

DR. STOCKMANN (*standing still*) And suppose I don't give you a single penny of all I get out of it? Money is not very easy to get out of us rich folk, please to remember!

HOVSTAD   And you please to remember that this affair of the shares can be represented in two ways!

DR. STOCKMANN   Yes, and you are just the man to do it. If I don't come to the rescue of the "People's Messenger," you will certainly take an evil view of the affair; you will hunt me down, I can well imagine — pursue me — try to throttle me as a dog does a hare.

HOVSTAD   It is a natural law; every animal must fight for its own livelihood.

ASLAKSEN   And get its food where it can, you know.

DR. STOCKMANN   (*walking about the room*)   Then you go and look for yours in the gutter; because I am going to show you which is the strongest animal of us three! (*Finds an umbrella and brandishes it above his head.*) Ah, now — !

HOVSTAD   You are surely not going to use violence!

ASLAKSEN   Take care what you are doing with that umbrella.

DR. STOCKMANN   Out of the window with you, Mr. Hovstad!

HOVSTAD   (*edging to the door*)   Are you quite mad!

DR. STOCKMANN   Out of the window, Mr. Aslaksen! Jump, I tell you! You will have to do it, sooner or later.

ASLAKSEN   (*running round the writing-table*)   Moderation, Doctor — I am a delicate man — I can stand so little — (*Calls out.*) Help, help!

(MRS. STOCKMANN, PETRA *and* HORSTER *come in from the sitting-room.*)

MRS. STOCKMANN   Good gracious, Thomas! What is happening?

DR. STOCKMANN   (*brandishing the umbrella*)   Jump out, I tell you! Out into the gutter!

HOVSTAD   An assault on an unoffending man! I call you to witness, Captain Horster. (*Hurries out through the hall.*)

ASLAKSEN   (*irresolutely*)   If only I knew the way about here — . (*Steals out through the sitting-room.*)

MRS. STOCKMANN   (*holding her husband back*)   Control yourself, Thomas!

DR. STOCKMANN   (*throwing down the umbrella*)   Upon my soul, they have escaped after all.

MRS. STOCKMANN   What did they want you to do?

DR. STOCKMANN   I will tell you later on; I have something else to think about now. (*Goes to the table and writes something on a calling-card.*) Look there, Katherine; what is written there?

MRS. STOCKMANN   Three big No's; what does that mean?

DR. STOCKMANN   I will tell you that too, later on. (*Holds out the card to* PETRA.) There, Petra; tell sooty-face to run over to the "Badger's" with that, as quickly as she can. Hurry up!

(PETRA *takes the card and goes out to the hall.*)

DR. STOCKMANN   Well, I think I have had a visit from every one of the devil's messengers to-day! But now I am going to sharpen my pen till they can feel its point; I shall dip it in venom and gall; I shall hurl my ink-pot at their heads!

MRS. STOCKMANN   Yes, but we are going away, you know, Thomas.

(PETRA *comes back.*)

DR. STOCKMANN   Well?

PETRA   She has gone with it.

DR. STOCKMANN   Good. — Going away, did you say? No, I'll be hanged if we are going away! We are going to stay where we are, Katherine!

PETRA Stay here?

MRS. STOCKMANN Here, in the town?

DR. STOCKMANN Yes, here. This is the field of battle — this is where the fight will be. This is where I shall triumph! As soon as I have had my trousers sewn up I shall go out and look for another house. We must have a roof over our heads for the winter.

HORSTER That you shall have in my house.

DR. STOCKMANN Can I?

HORSTER Yes, quite well. I have plenty of room, and I am almost never at home.

MRS. STOCKMANN How good of you, Captain Horster!

PETRA Thank you!

DR. STOCKMANN (*grasping his hand*) Thank you, thank you! That is one trouble over! Now I can set to work in earnest at once. There is an endless amount of things to look through here, Katherine! Luckily I shall have all my time at my disposal; because I have been dismissed from the Baths, you know.

MRS. STOCKMANN (*with a sigh*) Oh, yes, I expected that.

DR. STOCKMANN And they want to take my practice away from me, too. Let them! I have got the poor people to fall back upon, anyway — those that don't pay anything; and, after all, they need me most, too. But, by Jove, they will have to listen to me; I shall preach to them in season and out of season, as it says somewhere.

MRS. STOCKMANN But, dear Thomas, I should have thought events had showed you what use it is to preach.

DR. STOCKMANN You are really ridiculous, Katherine. Do you want me to let myself be beaten off the field by public opinion and the compact majority and all that devilry? No, thank you! And what I want to do is so simple and clear and straightforward. I only want to drum into the heads of these curs the fact that the liberals are the most insidious enemies of freedom — that party programmes strangle every young and vigorous truth — that considerations of expediency turn morality and justice upside down — and that they will end by making life here unbearable. Don't you think, Captain Horster, that I ought to be able to make people understand that?

HORSTER Very likely; I don't know much about such things myself.

DR. STOCKMANN Well, look here — I will explain! It is the party leaders that must be exterminated. A party leader is like a wolf, you see — like a voracious wolf. He requires a certain number of smaller victims to prey upon every year, if he is to live. Just look at Hovstad and Aslaksen! How many smaller victims have they not put an end to — or at any rate maimed and mangled until they are fit for nothing except to be householders or subscribers to the "People's Messenger"! (*Sits down on the edge of the table.*) Come here, Katherine — look how beautifully the sun shines to-day! And this lovely spring air I am drinking in!

MRS. STOCKMANN Yes, if only we could live on sunshine and spring air, Thomas.

DR. STOCKMANN Oh, you will have to pinch and save a bit — then we shall get along. That gives me very little concern. What is much worse is that I know of no one who is liberal-minded and high-minded enough to venture to take up my work after me.

PETRA   Don't think about that, father; you have plenty of time before you. —
Hullo, here are the boys already!

(EJLIF *and* MORTEN *come in from the sitting-room.*)

MRS. STOCKMANN   Have you got a holiday?

MORTEN   No; but we were fighting with the other boys between lessons —

EJLIF   That isn't true; it was the other boys were fighting with us.

MORTEN   Well, and then Mr. Rörlund said we had better stay at home for a
day or two.

DR. STOCKMANN (*snapping his fingers and getting up from the table*)   I have it!
I have it, by Jove! You shall never set foot in the school again!

THE BOYS   No more school!

MRS. STOCKMANN   But, Thomas —

DR. STOCKMANN   Never, I say. I will educate you myself; that is to say, you
shan't learn a blessed thing —

MORTEN   Hooray!

DR. STOCKMANN   — but I will make liberal-minded and high-minded men of
you. You must help me with that, Petra.

PETRA   Yes, father, you may be sure I will.

DR. STOCKMANN   And my school shall be in the room where they insulted me
and called me an enemy of the people. But we are too few as we are; I
must have at least twelve boys to begin with.

MRS. STOCKMANN   You will certainly never get them in this town.

DR. STOCKMANN   We shall. (*To the boys.*) Don't you know any street urchins
— regular ragamuffins — ?

MORTEN   Yes, father, I know lots!

DR. STOCKMANN   That's capital! Bring me some specimens of them. I am going to experiment with curs, just for once; there may be some exceptional
heads amongst them.

MORTEN   And what are we going to do, when you have made liberal-minded
and high-minded men of us?

DR. STOCKMANN   Then you shall drive all the wolves out of the country, my
boys!

(EJLIF *looks rather doubtful about it;* MORTEN *jumps about crying* "Hurrah!")

MRS. STOCKMANN   Let us hope it won't be the wolves that will drive you out
of the country, Thomas.

DR. STOCKMANN   Are you out of your mind, Katherine? Drive me out! Now
— when I am the strongest man in the town!

MRS. STOCKMANN   The strongest — now?

DR. STOCKMANN   Yes, and I will go so far as to say that now I am the strongest
man in the whole world.

MORTEN   I say!

DR. STOCKMANN (*lowering his voice*)   Hush! You mustn't say anything about
it yet; but I have made a great discovery.

MRS. STOCKMANN   Another one?

DR. STOCKMANN   Yes. (*Gathers them round him, and says confidentially*) It
is this, let me tell you — that the strongest man in the world is he who stands
most alone.

MRS. STOCKMANN (*smiling and shaking her head*)   Oh, Thomas, Thomas!

PETRA (*encouragingly, as she grasps her father's hands*)   Father!

Exercises

1. Identify the protagonist, the antagonist, and the conflict.

2. Comment on the major theme of the play. How is it expressed?

3. Ibsen is a realist and exposes people as they are. Cite the qualities and faults of the two major characters.

Topic for Writing

Attack or defend Dr. Stockmann's indictment of the townspeople.

A Midsummer Night's Dream

[*Dramatis Personæ*

THESEUS, *Duke of Athens*	HIPPOLYTA, *Queen of the Amazons, betrothed to Theseus*
EGEUS, *Father to Hermia*	
LYSANDER, *Betrothed to Hermia*	HERMIA, *Daughter to Egeus, betrothed to Lysander*
DEMETRIUS, *In love with Hermia*	
PHILOSTRATE, *Master of the revels to Theseus*	HELENA, *In love with Demetrius*

QUINCE, *A carpenter,*
BOTTOM, *A weaver,*
FLUTE, *A bellows-mender,*
SNOUT, *A tinker,*
SNUG, *A joiner,*
STARVELING, *A tailor,*
⎫ *presenting* ⎧
PROLOGUE
PYRAMUS
THISBE
WALL
LION
MOONSHINE

OBERON, *King of the fairies*
TITANIA, *Queen of the fairies*
ROBIN GOODFELLOW, *A Puck*
PEASEBLOSSOM,
COBWEB,
MOTH,
MUSTARDSEED, ⎬ *Fairies*
Other fairies attending their King and Queen
Attendants on Theseus and Hippolyta

Scene: Athens, and a wood near it.]

Act One   *Scene I. Athens. The palace of* THESEUS.†
Enter THESEUS, HIPPOLYTA, [PHILOSTRATE,] *with others.*

THESEUS   Now, fair Hippolyta, our nuptial hour
  Draws on apace. Four happy days bring in
  Another moon; but, O, methinks, how slow
  This old moon wanes! She lingers my desires,
  Like to a step-dame or a dowager†   5
  Long withering out a young man's revenue.
HIPPOLYTA   Four days will quickly steep themselves in night;
  Four nights will quickly dream away the time;
  And then the moon, like to a silver bow
  New-bent in heaven, shall behold the night   10
  Of our solemnities.
THESEUS   Go, Philostrate,
  Stir up the Athenian youth to merriments;
  Awake the pert† and nimble spirit of mirth;

Words and passages enclosed in square brackets throughout the text are either emendations of the copy text or additions to it.

5. *dowager:* widow with a dowry from an estate.
13. *pert:* lively.

Turn melancholy forth to funerals:
The pale companion† is not for our pomp.   *15*

[*Exit* PHILOSTRATE.]

Hippolyta, I woo'd thee with my sword,
And won thy love doing thee injuries;
But I will wed thee in another key,
With pomp, with triumph,† and with revelling.
    Enter EGEUS, HERMIA, LYSANDER, *and* DEMETRIUS.
EGEUS Happy be Theseus, our renowned Duke!   *20*
THESEUS Thanks, good Egeus; what's the news with thee?
EGEUS Full of vexation come I, with complaint
  Against my child, my daughter Hermia.
  Stand forth, Demetrius. My noble lord,
  This man hath my consent to marry her.   *25*
  Stand forth, Lysander: and, my gracious Duke,
  This man hath bewitch'd the bosom of my child.
  Thou, thou, Lysander, thou hast given her rhymes
  And interchang'd love-tokens with my child.
  Thou hast by moonlight at her window sung   *30*
  With faining† voice verses of faining love,
  And stol'n the impression of her fantasy†
  With bracelets of thy hair, rings, gawds,† conceits,†
  Knacks,† trifles, nosegays, sweetmeats, — messengers
  Of strong prevailment in unhard'ned youth.   *35*
  With cunning hast thou filch'd my daughter's heart,
  Turn'd her obedience, which is due to me,
  To stubborn harshness; and, my gracious Duke,
  Be it so† she will not here before your Grace
  Consent to marry with Demetrius,   *40*
  I beg the ancient privilege of Athens,
  As she is mine, I may dispose of her;
  Which shall be either to this gentleman
  Or to her death, according to our law
  Immediately† provided in that case.   *45*
THESEUS What say you, Hermia? Be advis'd, fair maid.
  To you your father should be as a god,
  One that compos'd your beauties, yea, and one
  To whom you are but as a form in wax
  By him imprinted, and within his power   *50*
  To leave the figure or disfigure† it.
  Demetrius is a worthy gentleman.
HERMIA So is Lysander.
THESEUS   In himself he is;

---

15. *companion:* fellow, referring to
melancholy.
19. *triumph:* public festivity.
31. *faining:* longing.
32. *stol'n . . . fantasy:* captured her
fancy (by impressing it with gifts).

33. *gawds:* trinkets. *conceits:* devices.
34. *knacks:* knickknacks.
39. *Be it so:* if.
45. *Immediately:* expressly.
51. *disfigure:* obliterate.

But in this kind,† wanting your father's voice,†
The other must be held the worthier.   55
HERMIA   I would my father look'd but with my eyes.
THESEUS   Rather your eyes must with his judgement look.
HERMIA   I do entreat your Grace to pardon me.
I know not by what power I am made bold,
Nor how it may concern† my modesty,   60
In such a presence here to plead my thoughts;
But I beseech your Grace that I may know
The worst that may befall me in this case,
If I refuse to wed Demetrius.
THESEUS   Either to die the death or to abjure   65
For ever the society of men.
Therefore, fair Hermia, question your desires,
Know of your youth, examine well your blood,†
Whether,† if you yield not to your father's choice,
You can endure the livery of a nun,   70
For aye to be in shady cloister mew'd,†
To live a barren sister all your life,
Chanting faint hymns to the cold fruitless moon.
Thrice-blessed they that master so their blood
To undergo such maiden pilgrimage;   75
But earthlier happy is the rose distill'd
Than that which withering on the virgin thorn
Grows, lives, and dies in single blessedness.
HERMIA   So will I grow, so live, so die, my lord,
Ere I will yield my virgin patent† up   80
Unto his lordship, whose unwished yoke
My soul consents not to give sovereignty.
THESEUS   Take time to pause; and, by the next new moon —
The sealing-day betwixt my love and me
For everlasting bond of fellowship —   85
Upon that day either prepare to die
For disobedience to your father's will,
Or else to wed Demetrius, as he would,
Or on Diana's altar to protest†
For aye austerity and single life.   90
DEMETRIUS   Relent, sweet Hermia; and, Lysander, yield
Thy crazed† title to my certain right.
LYSANDER   You have her father's love, Demetrius,
Let me have Hermia's; do you marry him.
EGEUS   Scornful Lysander! true, he hath my love,   95
And what is mine my love shall render him.

54. *in ... kind:* i.e., as a husband.   71. *mew'd:* shut up (a term from
voice: approval.   falconry).
60. *concern:* beseem.   80. *patent:* privilege, liberty.
68. *blood:* passion.   89. *protest:* vow.
69. *Whether:* One syllable in pro-   92. *crazed:* unsound.
nunciation.

And she is mine, and all my right of her
I do estate unto† Demetrius.
LYSANDER   I am, my lord, as well deriv'd as he,
As well possess'd; my love is more than his;   100
My fortunes every way as fairly rank'd,
If not with vantage, as Demetrius';
And, which is more than all these boasts can be,
I am belov'd of beauteous Hermia.
Why should not I then prosecute my right?   105
Demetrius, I'll avouch it to his head,†
Made love to Nedar's daughter, Helena,
And won her soul; and she, sweet lady, dotes,
Devoutly dotes, dotes in idolatry,
Upon this spotted and inconstant man.   110
THESEUS   I must confess that I have heard so much,
And with Demetrius thought to have spoke thereof;
But, being over-full of self-affairs,
My mind did lose it. But, Demetrius, come;
And come, Egeus; you shall go with me;   115
I have some private schooling for you both.
For you, fair Hermia, look you arm yourself
To fit your fancies to your father's will;
Or else the law of Athens yields you up —
Which by no means we may extenuate† —   120
To death, or to a vow of single life.
Come, my Hippolyta; what cheer, my love?
Demetrius and Egeus, go along.
I must employ you in some business
Against† our nuptial, and confer with you   125
Of something nearly that concerns yourselves.
EGEUS   With duty and desire we follow you.
                              [*Exeunt all but* LYSANDER *and* HERMIA.
LYSANDER   How now, my love! why is your cheek so pale?
How chance the roses there do fade so fast?
HERMIA   Belike for want of rain, which I could well   130
Beteem† them from the tempest of my eyes.
LYSANDER   Ay me! for aught that I could ever read,
Could ever hear by tale or history,
The course of true love never did run smooth;
But, either it was different in blood, —   135
HERMIA   O cross! too high to be enthrall'd to [low].
LYSANDER   Or else misgraffed† in respect of years, —
HERMIA   O spite! too old to be engag'd to young.
LYSANDER   Or else it stood upon the choice of friends, —
HERMIA   O hell! to choose love by another's eyes.   140

        98. *estate unto:* settle upon.   125. *Against:* in anticipation of.
        106. *head:* face.   131. *Beteem:* allow.
        120. *extenuate:* weaken.   137. *misgraffed:* mismatched.

LYSANDER   Or, if there were a sympathy in choice,
        War, death, or sickness did lay siege to it,
        Making it momentany† as a sound,
        Swift as a shadow, short as any dream,
        Brief as the lightning in the collied† night,   145
        That, in a spleen,† unfolds both heaven and earth,
        And ere a man hath power to say "Behold!"
        The jaws of darkness do devour it up:
        So quick bright things come to confusion.
HERMIA   If then true lovers have been ever† cross'd,   150
        It stands as an edict in destiny.
        Then let us teach our trial patience,
        Because it is a customary cross,
        As due to love as thoughts and dreams and sighs,
        Wishes and tears, poor Fancy's† followers.   155
LYSANDER   A good persuasion; therefore, hear me, Hermia.
        I have a widow aunt, a dowager
        Of great revenue, and she hath no child.
        From Athens is her house remote seven leagues;
        And she respects† me as her only son.   160
        There, gentle Hermia, may I marry thee;
        And to that place the sharp Athenian law
        Cannot pursue us. If thou lov'st me then,
        Steal forth thy father's house to-morrow night;
        And in the wood, a league without the town,   165
        Where I did meet thee once with Helena
        To do observance to a morn of May,
        There will I stay for thee.
HERMIA   My good Lysander!
        I swear to thee, by Cupid's strongest bow,
        By his best arrow with the golden head,   170
        By the simplicity† of Venus' doves,
        By that which knitteth souls and prospers loves,
        And by that fire which burn'd the Carthage queen†
        When the false Troyan under sail was seen,
        By all the vows that ever men have broke,   175
        In number more than ever women spoke,
        In that same place thou hast appointed me
        To-morrow truly will I meet with thee.
LYSANDER   Keep promise, love. Look, here comes Helena.
        Enter HELENA.
HERMIA   God speed fair Helena! Whither away?   180
HELENA   Call you me fair? That fair again unsay.
        Demetrius loves your fair,† O happy fair!

143. *momentany:* momentary.   171. *simplicity:* innocence.
145. *collied:* blackened.   173. *Carthage queen:* Dido, who
146. *spleen:* burst of passion.   killed herself after the Trojan
150. *ever:* always.   Aeneas had deserted her.
155. *Fancy's:* love's.   182. *fair:* beauty.
160. *respects:* regards.

Your eyes are lode-stars, and your tongue's sweet air
More tuneable than lark to shepherd's ear
When wheat is green, when hawthorn buds appear.   *185*
Sickness is catching; O, were favour† so,
[Yours would] I catch, fair Hermia, ere I go;
My ear should catch your voice, my eye your eye,
My tongue should catch your tongue's sweet melody.
Were the world mine, Demetrius being bated,†   *190*
The rest I'll give to be to you translated.†
O, teach me how you look, and with what art
You sway the motion of Demetrius' heart.

HERMIA   I frown upon him, yet he loves me still.

HELENA   O that your frowns would teach my smiles such skill!   *195*

HERMIA   I give him curses, yet he gives me love.

HELENA   O that my prayers could such affection move!

HERMIA   The more I hate, the more he follows me.

HELENA   The more I love, the more he hateth me.

HERMIA   His folly, Helena, is no fault of mine.   *200*

HELENA   None, but your beauty. Would that fault were mine!

HERMIA   Take comfort; he no more shall see my face;
Lysander and myself will fly this place.
Before the time I did Lysander see,
Seem'd Athens as a paradise to me;   *205*
O, then, what graces in my love do dwell,
That he hath turn'd a heaven unto a hell!

LYSANDER   Helen, to you our minds we will unfold.
To-morrow night, when Phœbe† doth behold
Her silver visage in the wat'ry glass,   *210*
Decking with liquid pearl the bladed grass,
A time that lovers' flights doth still conceal,
Through Athens' gates have we devis'd to steal.

HERMIA   And in the wood, where often you and I
Upon faint† primrose-beds were wont to lie,   *215*
Emptying our bosoms of their counsel [sweet].
There my Lysander and myself shall meet;
And thence from Athens turn away our eyes,
To seek new friends and [stranger companies].
Farewell, sweet playfellow! Pray thou for us;   *220*
And good luck grant thee thy Demetrius!
Keep word, Lysander; we must starve our sight
From lovers' food till morrow deep midnight.

LYSANDER   I will, my Hermia.   [*Exit* HERMIA.
                        Helena, adieu:
As you on him, Demetrius dote on you!   *225*
                                                       [*Exit.*

HELENA   How happy some o'er other some can be!
Through Athens I am thought as fair as she.

---

186. *favour:* beauty.   209. *Phœbe:* Diana, the moon.
190. *bated:* excepted.   215. *faint:* pale.
191. *translated:* transformed.

But what of that? Demetrius thinks not so;
He will not know what all but he do know;
And as he errs, doting on Hermia's eyes, 230
So I, admiring of his qualities.
Things base and vile, holding no quantity,
Love can transpose to form and dignity.
Love looks not with the eyes but with the mind,
And therefore is wing'd Cupid painted blind. 235
Nor hath Love's mind of any judgement taste;
Wings and no eyes figure† unheedy haste;
And therefore is Love said to be a child,
Because in choice he is so oft beguil'd.
As waggish boys in game themselves forswear, 240
So the boy Love is perjur'd every where:
For ere Demetrius look'd on Hermia's eyne,†
He hail'd down oaths that he was only mine;
And when this hail some heat from Hermia felt,
So he dissolv'd, and show'rs of oaths did melt. 245
I will go tell him of fair Hermia's flight;
Then to the wood will he to-morrow night
Pursue her; and for this intelligence†
If I have thanks, it is a dear expense.†
But herein mean I to enrich my pain, 250
To have his sight† thither and back again. [*Exit.*

[*Scene II. Athens.* QUINCE's *house.*]
Enter QUINCE, SNUG, BOTTOM, FLUTE, SNOUT, *and* STARVELING.

QUINCE Is all our company here?

BOTTOM You were best to call them generally,† man by man, according
to the scrip.†

QUINCE Here is the scroll of every man's name, which is thought fit,
through all Athens, to play in our interlude before the Duke and the 5
Duchess, on his wedding-day at night.

BOTTOM First, good Peter Quince, say what the play treats on, then read
the names of the actors, and so grow to a point.†

QUINCE Marry, our play is *The most lamentable comedy, and most cruel
death of Pyramus and Thisby.* 10

BOTTOM A very good piece of work, I assure you, and a merry. Now,
good Peter Quince, call forth your actors by the scroll. Masters, spread
yourselves.

QUINCE Answer as I call you. Nick Bottom, the weaver.

BOTTOM Ready. Name what part I am for, and proceed. 15

QUINCE You, Nick Bottom, are set down for Pyramus.

237. *figure:* symbolize.
242. *eyne:* eyes.
248. *intelligence:* news.
249. *dear expense:* costly gain.
251. *his sight:* sight of him.

Sc. ii, 2. *generally:* Bottom's error
for *severally.*
3. *scrip:* written list.
8. *grow ... point:* come to the
point.

BOTTOM   What is Pyramus? A lover, or a tyrant?

QUINCE   A lover, that kills himself most gallant for love.

BOTTOM   That will ask some tears in the true performing of it. If I do
it, let the audience look to their eyes. I will move storms, I will con-   20
dole† in some measure. To the rest. Yet my chief humour is for a
tyrant. I could play Ercles† rarely, or a part to tear a cat in, to make
all split.†

> "The raging rocks
> And shivering shocks   25
> Shall break the locks
> Of prison gates;
> And Phibbus'† car
> Shall shine from far
> And make and mar   30
> The foolish Fates."

This was lofty! Now name the rest of the players. This is Ercles'
vein, a tyrant's vein; a lover is more condoling.

QUINCE   Francis Flute, the bellows-mender.

FLUTE   Here, Peter Quince.   35

QUINCE   Flute, you must take Thisby on you.

FLUTE   What is Thisby? A wand'ring knight?

QUINCE   It is the lady that Pyramus must love.

FLUTE   Nay, faith, let not me play a woman; I have a beard coming.

QUINCE   That's all one; you shall play it in a mask, and you may speak as   40
small as you will.

BOTTOM   An† I may hide my face, let me play Thisby too. I'll speak in a
monstrous little voice, "Thisne! Thisne! Ah Pyramus, my lover dear!
thy Thisby dear, and lady dear!"

QUINCE   No, no; you must play Pyramus; and, Flute, you Thisby.   45

BOTTOM   Well, proceed.

QUINCE   Robin Starveling, the tailor.

STARVELING   Here, Peter Quince.

QUINCE   Robin Starveling, you must play Thisby's mother. Tom Snout,
the tinker.   50

SNOUT   Here, Peter Quince.

QUINCE   You, Pyramus' father; myself, Thisby's father; Snug, the joiner,
you, the lion's part; and, I hope, here is a play fitted.

SNUG   Have you the lion's part written? Pray you, if it be, give it me, for
I am slow of study.   55

QUINCE   You may do it extempore, for it is nothing but roaring.

BOTTOM   Let me play the lion too. I will roar, that I will do any man's
heart good to hear me. I will roar, that I will make the Duke say, "Let
him roar again, let him roar again."

---

21. *condole:* grieve.
22. *Ercles:* Hercules, a common
ranting part in early drama.

22–23. *make all split:* i.e., with
passion.
28. *Phibbus':* Phoebus'.
42. *An:* if.

QUINCE   An you should do it too terribly, you would fright the Duchess   *60*
and the ladies, that they would shriek; and that were enough to hang
us all.

ALL   That would hang us, every mother's son.

BOTTOM   I grant you, friends, if you should fright the ladies out of their
wits, they would have no more discretion but to hang us; but I will   *65*
aggravate† my voice so that I will roar you as gently as any sucking
dove; I will roar you an 'twere any nightingale.

QUINCE   You can play no part but Pyramus; for Pyramus is a sweet-fac'd
man; a proper† man, as one shall see in a summer's day; a most lovely
gentleman-like man: therefore you must needs play Pyramus.   *70*

BOTTOM   Well, I will undertake it. What beard were I best to play it in?

QUINCE   Why, what you will.

BOTTOM   I will discharge it in either your strawcolour beard, your orange-
tawny beard, your purple-in-grain beard, or your French-crown-colour
beard, your perfect yellow.†   *75*

QUINCE   Some of your French crowns have no hair at all, and then you
will play barefac'd. But, masters, here are your parts; and I am to
entreat you, request you, and desire you, to con them by to-morrow
night; and meet me in the palace wood, a mile without the town, by
moonlight. There will we rehearse, for if we meet in the city, we shall   *80*
be dogg'd with company, and our devices known. In the meantime I
will draw a bill of properties, such as our play wants. I pray you, fail
me not.

BOTTOM   We will meet; and there we may rehearse most obscenely† and
courageously. Take pains; be perfect; adieu.   *85*

QUINCE   At the Duke's oak we meet.

BOTTOM   Enough; hold or cut bow-strings.†   *[Exeunt.*

Act Two   [*Scene I. A wood near Athens.*]
Enter a FAIRY *at one door and* ROBIN GOODFELLOW† *at another.*

ROBIN   How now, spirit! whither wander you?

FAIRY   Over hill, over dale,
    Thorough bush, thorough brier,
Over park, over pale,
    Thorough flood, thorough fire,   *5*
I do wander every where,

---

66. *aggravate:* Bottom's mistake
for *moderate.*
69. *proper:* handsome.
73–75. Bottom, the Weaver, refers
glibly to several familiar dyes.
84. *obscenely:* Bottom's mistake
for *obscurely.*
87. *hold . . . bow-strings:* Apparently an archer's expression. Bot-

tom probably means, "Keep your
appointments or everything is off."
Act Two, Sc. i, *Robin Goodfellow:*
This character is described as a
Puck, a name previously applied
in English folklore to a minor order of evil spirits. Shakespeare re-
creates him as he does the fairies.

Swifter than the moon's sphere;
And I serve the fairy Queen,
To dew her orbs† upon the green.
The cowslips tall her pensioners† be;　　　　　　　　10
In their gold coats spots you see;
Those be rubies, fairy favours,
In those freckles live their savours.†

I must go seek some dewdrops here
And hang a pearl in every cowslip's ear.　　　　　15
Farewell, thou lob† of spirits; I'll be gone.
Our Queen and all her elves come here anon.
ROBIN　The King doth keep his revels here tonight;
Take heed the Queen come not within his sight;
For Oberon is passing fell and wrath,†　　　　　　20
Because that she as her attendant hath
A lovely boy stolen from an Indian king.
She never had so sweet a changeling;†
And jealous Oberon would have the child
Knight of his train, to trace the forests wild;　　25
But she perforce withholds the loved boy,
Crowns him with flowers, and makes him all her joy;
And now they never meet in grove or green,
By fountain clear, or spangled starlight sheen,
But they do square,† that† all their elves for fear　30
Creep into acorn-cups and hide them there.
FAIRY　Either I mistake your shape and making quite,
Or else you are that shrewd† and knavish sprite
Call'd Robin Goodfellow. Are not you he
That frights the maidens of the villagery,　　　　35
Skim milk, and sometimes labour in the quern,†
And bootless make the breathless housewife churn,
And sometime make the drink to bear no barm,†
Mislead night-wanderers, laughing at their harm?
Those that Hobgoblin call you, and sweet Puck,　40
You do their work, and they shall have good luck.
Are not you he?
ROBIN　　　　　　Thou speakest aright;
I am that merry wanderer of the night.
I jest to Oberon and make him smile
When I a fat and bean-fed horse beguile,　　　　45

9. *orbs:* fairy rings.
10. *pensioners:* Elizabeth's body-guards were called gentlemen pensioners.
13. *savours:* perfumes.
16. *lob:* lout.
20. *passing ... wrath:* exceedingly angry and wrathful.

23. *changeling:* a child exchanged by fairies.
30. *square:* quarrel. *that:* so that.
33. *shrewd:* mischievous.
36. *quern:* handmill.
38. *barm:* yeast.

Neighing in likeness of a filly foal;
And sometime lurk I in a gossip's bowl,†
In very likeness of a roasted crab,†
And when she drinks, against her lips I bob
And on her withered dewlap† pour the ale.   50
The wisest aunt,† telling the saddest† tale,
Sometime for three-foot stool mistaketh me.
Then slip I from her bum, down topples she,
And "tailor" cries,† and falls into a cough;
And then the whole quire hold their hips and laugh,   55
And waxen† in their mirth, and neeze,† and swear
A merrier hour was never wasted there.
But, room, fairy! here comes Oberon.
FAIRY   And here my mistress. Would that he were gone!
Enter the King of Fairies [OBERON] *at one door with his train; and the Queen*
[TITANIA] *at another with hers.*
OBERON   Ill met by moonlight, proud Titania.   60
TITANIA   What, jealous Oberon! Fairies, skip hence:
I have forsworn his bed and company.
OBERON   Tarry, rash wanton! Am not I thy lord?
TITANIA   Then I must be thy lady; but I know
When thou hast stolen away from fairy land,   65
And in the shape of Corin† sat all day,
Playing on pipes of corn and versing love
To amorous Phillida.† Why art thou here,
Come from the farthest steep of India?
But that, forsooth, the bouncing Amazon,   70
Your buskin'd† mistress and your warrior love,
To Theseus must be wedded, and you come
To give their bed joy and prosperity.
OBERON   How canst thou thus for shame, Titania,
Glance at† my credit with Hippolyta,   75
Knowing I know thy love to Theseus?
Didst thou not lead him through the glimmering night
From Perigenia, whom he ravished?
And make him with fair Ægle break his faith,
With Ariadne, and Antiopa?†   80
TITANIA   These are the forgeries of jealousy;
And never, since the middle summer's spring,†

47. *gossip's bowl:* christening-cup.
Gossip is used here in the original
sense of godmother.
48. *crab:* crab apple.
50. *dewlap:* loose skin on the neck.
51. *aunt:* old woman. *saddest:* so-
berest.
54. *"tailor" cries:* Meaning obscure.
56. *waxen:* increase. *neeze:* sneeze.
66–68. *Corin . . . Phillida:* names
traditional in pastoral poetry.

71. *buskin'd:* wearing high boots.
75. *glance at:* cast reflections on.
79–80. *Ægle . . . Ariadne . . . Antiopa:* These names of women whom
Theseus had loved Shakespeare
found in North's *Plutarch.* Anti-
ope is sometimes identified with
Hippolyta, but in this speech they
are treated as two.
82. *middle summer's spring:* beginning of midsummer.

Met we on hill, in dale, forest or mead,
By paved fountain or by rushy brook,
Or in† the beached margent† of the sea,   85
To dance our ringlets† to the whistling wind,
But with thy brawls thou hast disturb'd our sport.
Therefore the winds, piping to us in vain,
As in revenge, have suck'd up from the sea
Contagious fogs; which, falling in the land,   90
Hath every pelting† river made so proud
That they have overborne their continents.†
The ox hath therefore stretch'd his yoke in vain,
The ploughman lost his sweat, and the green corn
Hath rotted ere his youth attain'd a beard.   95
The fold stands empty in the drowned field,
And crows are fatted with the murrain† flock,
The nine men's morris† is fill'd up with mud,
And the quaint mazes† in the wanton† green
For lack of tread are undistinguishable.   100
The human mortals want their winter [cheer];
No night is now with hymn or carol blest.
Therefore the moon, the governess of floods,
Pale in her anger, washes all the air,
That rheumatic diseases do abound.   105
And thorough this distemperature† we see
The seasons alter: hoary-headed frosts
Fall in the fresh lap of the crimson rose,
And on old Hiems'† thin and icy crown
An odorous chaplet of sweet summer buds   110
Is, as in mockery, set; the spring, the summer,
The childing† autumn, angry winter, change
Their wonted liveries; and the mazed† world,
By their increase, now knows not which is which.
And this same progeny of evils comes   115
From our debate, from our dissension;
We are their parents and original.†
OBERON   Do you amend it then; it lies in you.
Why should Titania cross her Oberon?
I do but beg a little changeling boy   120
To be my henchman.†
TITANIA   Set your heart at rest;
The fairy land buys not the child of me.
His mother was a vot'ress of my order,

85. *in:* on. *margent:* margin.
86. *ringlets:* circular dances.
91. *pelting:* paltry. Ff read *petty.*
92. *continents:* banks.
97. *murrain:* diseased.
98. *nine men's morris:* a game played in squares marked out on the turf of the village green; something like hopscotch.
99. *mazes:* figures. *wanton:* luxuriant.
106. *distemperature:* disturbance.
109. *Hiems:* the god of winter.
112. *childing:* fruitful.
113. *mazed:* amazed.
117. *original:* origin.
121. *henchman:* page.

And, in the spiced Indian air, by night,
Full often hath she gossip'd by my side,   125
And sat with me on Neptune's yellow sands,
Marking th' embarked traders on the flood,
When we have laugh'd to see the sails conceive
And grow big-bellied with the wanton wind;
Which she with pretty and with swimming gait   130
Following, her womb then rich with my young squire,
Would imitate, and sail upon the land
To fetch me trifles, and return again,
As from a voyage, rich with merchandise.
But she, being mortal, of that boy did die;   135
And for her sake do I rear up her boy,
And for her sake I will not part with him.

OBERON   How long within this wood intend you stay?

TITANIA   Perchance till after Theseus' wedding-day.
If you will patiently dance in our round   140
And see our moonlight revels, go with us;
If not, shun me, and I will spare your haunts.

OBERON   Give me that boy, and I will go with thee.

TITANIA   Not for thy fairy kingdom. Fairies, away!
We shall chide downright, if I longer stay.   145

[*Exit* [TITANIA *with her train*].

OBERON   Well, go thy way; thou shalt not from this grove
Till I torment thee for this injury.
My gentle Puck, come hither. Thou rememb'rest
Since† once I sat upon a promontory,
And heard a mermaid on a dolphin's back   150
Uttering such dulcet and harmonious breath
That the rude sea grew civil at her song,
And certain stars shot madly from their spheres,
To hear the sea-maid's music?

ROBIN   I remember.

OBERON   That very time I saw, but thou couldst not,   155
Flying between the cold moon and the earth,
Cupid all arm'd. A certain aim he took
At a fair vestal† throned by the west,
And loos'd his love-shaft smartly from his bow,
As it should pierce a hundred thousand hearts;   160
But I might see young Cupid's fiery shaft
Quench'd in the chaste beams of the wat'ry moon,
And the imperial vot'ress passed on,
In maiden meditation, fancy-free.
Yet mark'd I where the bolt of Cupid fell.   165
It fell upon a little western flower,
Before milk-white, now purple with love's wound,
And maidens call it love-in-idleness.†

149. *Since:* when.   168. *love-in-idleness:* pansy.
158. *vestal:* virgin.

Fetch me that flower, the herb I shew'd thee once.
The juice of it on sleeping eye-lids laid   *170*
Will make or man or woman madly dote
Upon the next live creature that it sees.
Fetch me this herb; and be thou here again
Ere the leviathan can swim a league.
ROBIN   I'll put a girdle round about the earth   *175*
    In forty minutes.   [*Exit.*]
OBERON   Having once this juice,
    I'll watch Titania when she is asleep,
    And drop the liquor of it in her eyes.
    The next thing then she waking looks upon,
    Be it on lion, bear, or wolf, or bull,   *180*
    On meddling monkey, or on busy ape,
    She shall pursue it with the soul of love;
    And ere I take this charm from off her sight,
    As I can take it with another herb,
    I'll make her render up her page to me.   *185*
    But who comes here? I am invisible;
    And I will overhear their conference.
    Enter DEMETRIUS, HELENA *following him.*
DEMETRIUS   I love thee not, therefore pursue me not.
    Where is Lysander and fair Hermia?
    The one I'll stay, the other stayeth† me.   *190*
    Thou told'st me they were stol'n unto this wood;
    And here am I, and wood† within this wood
    Because I cannot meet my Hermia.
    Hence, get thee gone, and follow me no more.
HELENA   You draw me, you hard-hearted adamant;†   *195*
    But yet you draw not iron, for my heart
    Is true as steel. Leave† you your power to draw,
    And I shall have no power to follow you.
DEMETRIUS   Do I entice you? Do I speak you fair?
    Or, rather, do I not in plainest truth   *200*
    Tell you, I do not nor I cannot love you?
HELENA   And even for that do I love you the more.
    I am your spaniel, and, Demetrius,
    The more you beat me, I will fawn on you.
    Use me but as your spaniel, spurn me, strike me,   *205*
    Neglect me, lose me; only give me leave,
    Unworthy as I am, to follow you.
    What worser place can I beg in your love, —
    And yet a place of high respect with me, —
    Than to be used as you use your dog?   *210*
DEMETRIUS   Tempt not too much the hatred of my spirit,

190. *stay . . . stayeth:* Thirlby's   195. *adamant:* probably with both
conjecture "slay...slayeth" has   senses of "lode-stone" (magnet)
been followed by many editors.   and "hardest metal."
192. *wood:* mad.   197. *Leave:* give up.

For I am sick when I do look on thee.

HELENA   And I am sick when I look not on you.

DEMETRIUS   You do impeach your modesty too much,
To leave the city and commit yourself   215
Into the hands of one that loves you not;
To trust the opportunity of night
And the ill counsel of a desert place
With the rich worth of your virginity.

HELENA   Your virtue is my privilege.† For that†   220
It is not night when I do see your face,
Therefore I think I am not in the night;
Nor doth this wood lack worlds of company,
For you in my respect† are all the world.
Then how can it be said I am alone,   225
When all the world is here to look on me?

DEMETRIUS   I'll run from thee and hide me in the brakes,
And leave thee to the mercy of wild beasts.

HELENA   The wildest hath not such a heart as you.
Run when you will, the story shall be chang'd: 230
Apollo flies, and Daphne holds the chase;†
The dove pursues the griffin;† the mild hind†
Makes speed to catch the tiger: bootless speed,
When cowardice pursues and valour flies.

DEMETRIUS   I will not stay thy questions;† let me go;   235
Or, if thou follow me, do not believe
But I shall do thee mischief in the wood.

HELENA   Ay, in the temple, in the town, the field,
You do me mischief. Fie, Demetrius!
Your wrongs do set a scandal on my sex.   240
We cannot fight for love, as men may do.
We should be woo'd and were not made to woo.   [*Exit* DEMETRIUS.]
I'll follow thee and make a heaven of hell,
To die upon† the hand I love so well.   [*Exit.*]

OBERON   Fare thee well, nymph. Ere he do leave this grove, 245
Thou shalt fly him and he shall seek thy love.
Re-enter [ROBIN GOODFELLOW].
Hast thou the flower there? Welcome, wanderer.

ROBIN   Ay, there it is.

OBERON   I pray thee, give it me.
I know a bank where the wild thyme blows,
Where oxlips and the nodding violet grows,   250
Quite over-canopi'd with luscious woodbine,
With sweet musk-roses and with eglantine.

220. *privilege:* safeguard. *For that:* because.
224. *in my respect:* to me.
231. *Apollo . . . chase:* According to the myth, Apollo pursued Daphne, but here the situation is reversed.
232. *griffin:* a monster having a lion's body and an eagle's head. *hind:* female of the red deer.
235. *questions:* arguments.
244. *upon:* by.

There sleeps Titania sometime of the night,
Lull'd in these flowers with dances and delight;†
And there the snake throws her enamell'd skin,   255
Weed† wide enough to wrap a fairy in;
And with the juice of this I'll streak† her eyes,
And make her full of hateful fantasies.
Take thou some of it, and seek through this grove.
A sweet Athenian lady is in love   260
With a disdainful youth. Anoint his eyes,
But do it when the next thing he espies
May be the lady. Thou shalt know the man
By the Athenian garments he hath on.
Effect it with some care, that he may prove   265
More fond on her than she upon her love;
And look thou meet me ere the first cock crow.
ROBIN   Fear not, my lord, your servant shall do so.   [*Exeunt.*

[*Scene II. Another part of the wood.*]
Enter TITANIA, *with her train.*

TITANIA   Come, now a roundel† and a fairy song;
Then, for the third part of a minute, hence,
Some to kill cankers† in the musk-rose buds,
Some war with rere-mice† for their leathern wings
To make my small elves coats, and some keep back   5
The clamorous owl that nightly hoots and wonders
At our quaint† spirits. Sing me now asleep;
Then to your offices and let me rest.
THE FAIRIES *sing.*
[1. FAIRY]   "You spotted snakes with double tongue,
                Thorny hedgehogs, be not seen;   10
            Newts† and blind-worms, do no wrong,
                Come not near our fairy queen."
[CHORUS]   "Philomel,† with melody
                Sing in our sweet lullaby;
            Lulla, lulla, lullaby; lulla, lulla, lullaby.   15
                Never harm
                Nor spell nor charm
            Come our lovely lady nigh.
            So, good night, with lullaby."
1. FAIRY   "Weaving spiders, come not here;   20
                Hence, you long-legg'd spinners, hence!
            Beetles black, approach not near;
                Worm nor snail, do no offence."

254. *dances and delight:* delightful dances.
256. *Weed:* garment.
257. *streak:* stroke.
Sc. ii, 1. *roundel:* circular dance.
3. *cankers:* cankerworms.
4. *rere-mice:* bats.
7. *quaint:* dainty.
11. *Newts:* water lizards.
13. *Philomel:* the nightingale.

[CHORUS] "Philomel, with melody," etc.
2. FAIRY Hence, away! now all is well.   25
              One aloof stand sentinel.   [*Exeunt* FAIRIES.] TITANIA *sleeps.*
      Enter OBERON [*and squeezes the flower on* TITANIA'S *eyelids*].
OBERON   What thou seest when thou dost wake,
              Do it for thy true-love take,
              Love and languish for his sake.
              Be it ounce,† or cat,† or bear,   30
              Pard,† or boar with bristled hair,
              In thy eye that shall appear
              When thou wak'st, it is thy dear.
              Wake when some vile thing is near.   [*Exit.*]
      Enter LYSANDER *and* HERMIA.
LYSANDER   Fair love, you faint with wand'ring in the wood;   35
              And to speak troth, I have forgot our way.
              We'll rest us, Hermia, if you think it good,
              And tarry for the comfort of the day.
HERMIA   Be it so, Lysander. Find you out a bed;
              For I upon this bank will rest my head.   40
LYSANDER   One turf shall serve as pillow for us both;
              One heart, one bed, two bosoms and one troth.
HERMIA   Nay, good Lysander; for my sake, my dear,
              Lie further off yet; do not lie so near.
LYSANDER   O, take the sense, sweet, of my innocence!   45
              Love takes the meaning in love's conference.†
              I mean, that my heart unto yours is knit
              So that but one heart we can make of it;
              Two bosoms interchained with an oath,
              So then two bosoms and a single troth.   50
              Then by your side no bed-room me deny;
              For lying so, Hermia, I do not lie.
HERMIA   Lysander riddles very prettily.
              Now much beshrew my manners and my pride,
              If Hermia meant to say Lysander lied.   55
              But, gentle friend, for love and courtesy
              Lie further off; in humane modesty,
              Such separation as may well be said
              Becomes a virtuous bachelor and a maid,
              So far be distant; and, good night, sweet friend.   60
              Thy love ne'er alter till thy sweet life end!
LYSANDER   Amen, amen, to that fair prayer, say I;
              And then end life when I end loyalty!
              Here is my bed; sleep give thee all his rest!
HERMIA   With half that wish the wisher's eyes be press'd!   65
                                                          [*They sleep.*

      Enter [ROBIN GOODFELLOW].
ROBIN   Through the forest have I gone,

      30. *ounce:* lynx. *cat:* wildcat.   46. *Love ... conference:* Love
      31. *Pard:* leopard.   gives lovers true understanding.

But Athenian found I none,
On whose eyes I might approve†
This flower's force in stirring love.
Night and silence — Who is here?   70
Weeds of Athens he doth wear!
This is he, my master said,
Despised the Athenian maid;
And here the maiden, sleeping sound,
On the dank and dirty ground.   75
Pretty soul! she durst not lie
Near this lack-love, this kill-courtesy.
Churl, upon thy eyes I throw
All the power this charm doth owe.†
When thou wak'st, let love forbid   80
Sleep his seat on thy eyelid;
So awake when I am gone,
For I must now to Oberon.   [*Exit.*

Enter DEMETRIUS *and* HELENA, *running.*

HELENA   Stay, though thou kill me, sweet Demetrius.
DEMETRIUS   I charge thee, hence, and do not haunt me thus.   85
HELENA   O, wilt thou darkling† leave me? Do not so.
DEMETRIUS   Stay, on thy peril; I alone will go.   [*Exit.*
HELENA   O, I am out of breath in this fond† chase!
The more my prayer, the lesser is my grace.†
Happy is Hermia, wheresoe'er she lies,   90
For she hath blessed and attractive eyes.
How came her eyes so bright? Not with salt tears;
If so, my eyes are oft'ner wash'd than hers.
No, no, I am as ugly as a bear,
For beasts that meet me run away for fear;   95
Therefore no marvel though Demetrius
Do, as a monster, fly my presence thus.
What wicked and dissembling glass of mine
Made me compare with Hermia's sphery eyne?†
But who is here? Lysander! on the ground!   100
Dead? or asleep? I see no blood, no wound.
Lysander, if you live, good sir, awake.
LYSANDER [*Awakening.*]   And run through fire I will for thy sweet sake.
Transparent Helena! Nature shows art,
That through thy bosom makes me see thy heart.   105
Where is Demetrius? O, how fit a word
Is that vile name to perish on my sword!
HELENA   Do not say so, Lysander; say not so.
What though he love your Hermia? Lord, what though?
Yet Hermia still loves you; then be content.   110

68. *approve:* test.   88. *fond:* foolish.
79. *owe:* own.   89. *my grace:* the favor I receive.
86. *darkling:* in the dark.   99. *sphery eyne:* starry eyes.

LYSANDER   Content with Hermia! No; I do repent
        The tedious minutes I with her have spent.
        Not Hermia but Helena I love.
        Who will not change a raven for a dove?
        The will of man is by his reason sway'd;   *115*
        And reason says you are the worthier maid.
        Things growing are not ripe until their season,
        So I, being young, till now ripe not to reason;
        And touching now the point of human skill,†
        Reason becomes the marshal to my will   *120*
        And leads me to your eyes, where I o'erlook
        Love's stories written in Love's richest book.
HELENA   Wherefore was I to this keen mockery born?
        When at your hands did I deserve this scorn?
        Is't not enough, is't not enough, young man,   *125*
        That I did never, no, nor never can,
        Deserve a sweet look from Demetrius' eye,
        But you must flout my insufficiency?
        Good troth, you do me wrong, good sooth you do,
        In such disdainful manner me to woo.   *130*
        But fare you well; perforce I must confess
        I thought you lord of more true gentleness.
        O, that a lady, of one man refus'd,
        Should of another therefore be abus'd!   [*Exit.*
LYSANDER   She sees not Hermia. Hermia, sleep thou there;   *135*
        And never mayst thou come Lysander near!
        For as a surfeit of the sweetest things
        The deepest loathing to the stomach brings,
        Or as the heresies that men do leave
        Are hated most of those they did deceive,   *140*
        So thou, my surfeit and my heresy,
        Of all be hated, but the most of me!
        And, all my powers, address your love and might
        To honour Helen and to be her knight.   [*Exit.*
HERMIA [*Awakening.*]   Help me, Lysander, help me! do thy best   *145*
        To pluck this crawling serpent from my breast!
        Ay me, for pity! what a dream was here!
        Lysander, look how I do quake with fear.
        Methought a serpent eat my heart away,
        And you sat smiling at his cruel prey.†   *150*
        Lysander! what, remov'd? Lysander! lord!
        What, out of hearing? Gone? No sound, no word?
        Alack, where are you? Speak, an if you hear;
        Speak, of all loves!† I swoon almost with fear.
        No? then I well perceive you are not nigh.   *155*
        Either death or you I'll find immediately.   [*Exit.*

119. *point . . . skill:* summit of hu-   150. *prey:* preying.
man discernment.   154. *of all loves:* for love's sake.

Act Three   [*The wood.* TITANIA *lying asleep.*]

Enter the Clowns [QUINCE, SNUG, BOTTOM, FLUTE, SNOUT, *and* STARVELING].

BOTTOM   Are we all met?

QUINCE   Pat, pat; and here's a marvellous convenient place for our rehearsal. This green plot shall be our stage, this hawthorn-brake our
tiring-house;† and we will do it in action as we will do it before the
Duke.   5

BOTTOM   Peter Quince!

QUINCE   What say'st thou, bully† Bottom?

BOTTOM   There are things in this comedy of Pyramus and Thisby that
will never please. First, Pyramus must draw a sword to kill himself,
which the ladies cannot abide. How answer you that?   10

SNOUT   By'r lakin,† a parlous† fear.

STARVELING   I believe we must leave the killing out, when all is done.

BOTTOM   Not a whit! I have a device to make all well. Write me a prologue; and let the prologue seem to say, we will do no harm with our
swords and that Pyramus is not kill'd indeed; and, for the more better   15
assurance, tell them that I Pyramus am not Pyramus, but Bottom the
weaver. This will put them out of fear.

QUINCE   Well, we will have such a prologue; and it shall be written in
eight and six.†

BOTTOM   No, make it two more; let it be written in eight and eight.   20

SNOUT   Will not the ladies be afeard of the lion?

STARVELING   I fear it, I promise you.

BOTTOM   Masters, you ought to consider with yourselves. To bring in —
God shield us! — a lion among ladies, is a most dreadful thing; for
there is not a more fearful wild-fowl than your lion living; and we   25
ought to look to't.

SNOUT   Therefore another prologue must tell he is not a lion.

BOTTOM   Nay, you must name his name, and half his face must be seen
through the lion's neck; and he himself must speak through, saying
thus, or to the same defect,† "Ladies," or "Fair ladies, I would wish   30
you," or "I would request you," or "I would entreat you, not to fear,
not to tremble: my life for yours. If you think I come hither as a lion,
it were pity of my life. No, I am no such thing; I am a man as other
men are;" and there indeed let him name his name, and tell them
plainly he is Snug the joiner.   35

QUINCE   Well, it shall be so. But there is two hard things; that is, to
bring the moonlight into a chamber; for, you know, Pyramus and
Thisby meet by moonlight.

SNOUT   Doth the moon shine that night we play our play?

BOTTOM   A calendar, a calendar! Look in the almanac! Find out moon-   40
shine, find out moonshine.

---

4. *tiring-house:* dressing room.
7. *bully:* "good old"; a term of
friendship.
11. *By'r lakin:* by our ladykin, i.e.,
the Virgin Mary. *parlous:* perilous.

19. *eight and six:* alternate lines of
eight and six syllables, ballad meter.
30. *defect:* error for *effect.*

QUINCE Yes, it doth shine that night.

BOTTOM Why, then may you leave a casement of the great chamber window, where we play, open, and the moon may shine in at the casement. 45

QUINCE Ay; or else one must come in with a bush of thorns and a lantern, and say he comes to disfigure,† or to present, the person of Moonshine. Then, there is another thing: we must have a wall in the great chamber; for Pyramus and Thisby, says the story, did talk through the chink of a wall. 50

SNOUT You can never bring in a wall. What say you, Bottom?

BOTTOM Some man or other must present Wall; and let him have some plaster, or some loam, or some rough-cast† about him, to signify wall; or let him hold his fingers thus, and through that cranny shall Pyramus and Thisby whisper. 55

QUINCE If that may be, then all is well. Come, sit down, every mother's son, and rehearse your parts. Pyramus, you begin. When you have spoken your speech, enter into that brake. And so every one according to his cue.

Enter ROBIN GOODFELLOW [*behind*].

ROBIN What hempen home-spuns have we swagg'ring here, 60
So near the cradle of the fairy queen?
What, a play toward!† I'll be an auditor;
An actor too perhaps, if I see cause.

QUINCE Speak, Pyramus. Thisby, stand forth.

BOTTOM "Thisby, the flowers of odious savours sweet," — 65

QUINCE Odorous, odorous.

BOTTOM —— "odours savours sweet;
So hath thy breath, my dearest Thisby dear.
But hark, a voice! Stay thou but here awhile, 69
And by and by I will to thee appear." [*Exit.*

ROBIN A stranger Pyramus than e'er play'd here. [*Exit.*]

FLUTE Must I speak now?

QUINCE Ay, marry, must you; for you must understand he goes but to see a noise that he heard, and is to come again.

FLUTE "Most radiant Pyramus, most lily-white of hue, 75
Of colour like the red rose on triumphant brier,
Most brisky juvenal† and eke most lovely Jew,†
As true as truest horse that yet would never tire,
I'll meet thee, Pyramus, at Ninny's tomb."

QUINCE "Ninus'† tomb," man. Why, you must not speak that yet; that 80
you answer to Pyramus. You speak all your part at once, cues and all. Pyramus enter. Your cue is past; it is, "never tire."

FLUTE O, — "As true as truest horse, that yet would never tire."

[*Re-enter* ROBIN GOODFELLOW, *and* BOTTOM *with an ass's head.*]

47. *disfigure:* blunder for *prefigure.*
53. *rough-cast:* plaster mixed with pebbles.
62. *toward:* afoot.
77. *brisky juvenal:* lively youth. *Jew:* Probably a nonsensical repetition of the first syllable of *juvenal.*
80. *Ninus:* mythical founder of Babylon, the setting of the tale of Pyramus and Thisbe.

BOTTOM   "If I were fair, Thisby, I were only thine."

QUINCE   O monstrous! O strange! we are haunted. Pray, masters, fly,   *85*
   masters! Help!   [*Exeunt* [QUINCE, SNUG, FLUTE, SNOUT, *and* STARVELING].

ROBIN   I'll follow you, I'll lead you about, around,
      Through bog, through bush, through brake, through brier.
   Sometime a horse I'll be, sometime a hound,
      A hog, a headless bear, sometime a fire;   *90*
   And neigh, and bark, and grunt, and roar, and burn,
      Like horse, hound, hog, bear, fire, at every turn.   [*Exit.*

BOTTOM   Why do they run away? This is a knavery of them to make me
   afeard.

Re-enter SNOUT.

SNOUT   O Bottom, thou art chang'd! What do I see on thee?   *95*

BOTTOM   What do you see? You see an ass-head of your own, do you?
                                        [*Exit* SNOUT.]

Re-enter QUINCE.

QUINCE   Bless thee, Bottom! bless thee! thou art translated.†   [*Exit.*

BOTTOM   I see their knavery; this is to make an ass of me, to fright me,
   if they could. But I will not stir from this place, do what they can. I
   will walk up and down here, and I will sing, that they shall hear I am   *100*
   not afraid.   [*Sings.*]
          "The ousel† cock so black of hue,
             With orange-tawny bill,
          The throstle with his note so true,
             The wren with little quill,"† —   *105*

TITANIA [*Awaking.*]   What angel wakes me from my flowery bed?

BOTTOM [*Sings.*]
          "The finch, the sparrow, and the lark,
             The plain-song† cuckoo gray,
          Whose note full many a man doth mark,
             And dares not answer nay;"† —   *110*
   for, indeed, who would set his wit to so foolish a bird? Who would
   give a bird the lie, though he cry "cuckoo" never so?

TITANIA   I pray thee, gentle mortal, sing again.
   Mine ear is much enamour'd of thy note;
   So is mine eye enthralled to thy shape;   *115*
   And thy fair virtue's force perforce doth move me
   On the first view to say, to swear, I love thee.

BOTTOM   Methinks, mistress, you should have little reason for that; and
   yet, to say the truth, reason and love keep little company together now-
   a-days; the more the pity that some honest neighbours will not make   *120*
   them friends. Nay, I can gleek† upon occasion.

TITANIA   Thou art as wise as thou art beautiful.

BOTTOM   Not so, neither; but if I had wit enough to get out of this wood,
   I have enough to serve mine own turn.

---

97. *translated:* transformed.
102. *ousel:* blackbird.
105. *quill:* pipe.
108. *plain-song:* melody without variations.

109–110. *Whose . . . nay:* The note of the cuckoo sounded not unlike "cuckold," an unwelcome word to husbands.
121. *gleek:* jest satirically.

TITANIA   Out of this wood do not desire to go;   *125*
          Thou shalt remain here, whether thou wilt or no.
          I am a spirit of no common rate;
          The summer still† doth tend upon my state;
          And I do love thee; therefore, go with me.
          I'll give thee fairies to attend on thee,   *130*
          And they shall fetch thee jewels from the deep,
          And sing while thou on pressed flowers dost sleep.
          And I will purge thy mortal grossness so
          That thou shalt like an airy spirit go.
          Peaseblossom! Cobweb! Moth! and Mustardseed!   *135*

Enter four FAIRIES [PEASEBLOSSOM, COBWEB, MOTH, *and* MUSTARDSEED].

PEASEBLOSSOM   Ready.
COBWEB   And I.
MOTH   And I.
MUSTARDSEED   And I.
ALL   Where shall we go?
TITANIA   Be kind and courteous to this gentleman.
          Hop in his walks and gambol in his eyes;
          Feed him with apricocks and dewberries,
          With purple grapes, green figs, and mulberries;   *140*
          The honey-bags steal from the humble-bees,
          And for night-tapers crop their waxen thighs
          And light them at the fiery glow-worm's eyes,
          To have my love to bed and to arise;
          And pluck the wings from painted butterflies   *145*
          To fan the moonbeams from his sleeping eyes.
          Nod to him, elves, and do him courtesies.
PEASEBLOSSOM   Hail, mortal!
COBWEB   Hail!
MOTH   Hail!   *150*
MUSTARDSEED   Hail!
BOTTOM   I cry your worships mercy, heartily. I beseech your worship's
         name.
COBWEB   Cobweb.
BOTTOM   I shall desire you of more acquaintance, good Master Cobweb.   *155*
         If I cut my finger, I shall make bold with you. Your name, honest
         gentleman?
PEASEBLOSSOM   Peaseblossom.
BOTTOM   I pray you commend me to Mistress Squash,† your mother, and
         to Master Peascod, your father. Good Master Peaseblossom, I shall   *160*
         desire you of more acquaintance too. Your name, I beseech you, sir?
MUSTARDSEED   Mustardseed.
BOTTOM   Good Master Mustardseed, I know your patience† well. That
         same cowardly, giant-like ox-beef hath devoured many a gentleman of
         your house. I promise you your kindred hath made my eyes water ere   *165*
         now. I desire you more acquaintance, good Master Mustardseed.

---

128. *still:* always.   163. *patience:* suffering.
159. *Squash:* unripe pea pod.

TITANIA   Come, wait upon him; lead him to my bower.
        The moon methinks looks with a wat'ry eye;
        And when she weeps, weeps every little flower,
        Lamenting some enforced† chastity.   *170*
        Tie up my [love's] tongue, bring him silently.   *[Exeunt.*

     [*Scene II. Another part of the wood.*]
     Enter OBERON.

OBERON   I wonder if Titania be awak'd;
     Then, what it was that next† came in her eye,
     Which she must dote on in extremity.†
     Enter ROBIN GOODFELLOW.
     Here comes my messenger.
                How now, mad spirit!
     What night-rule† now about this haunted grove?   *5*
ROBIN   My mistress with a monster is in love.
     Near to her close and consecrated bower,
     While she was in her dull and sleeping hour,
     A crew of patches,† rude mechanicals,†
     That work for bread upon Athenian stalls,   *10*
     Were met together to rehearse a play
     Intended for great Theseus' nuptial-day.
     The shallowest thickskin of that barren sort,†
     Who Pyramus presented in their sport,
     Forsook his scene and ent'red in a brake.   *15*
     When I did him at this advantage take,
     An ass's nole† I fixed on his head.
     Anon his Thisby must be answered,
     And forth my mimic† comes. When they him spy,
     As wild geese that the creeping fowler eye,   *20*
     Or russet-pated choughs,† many in sort,†
     Rising and cawing at the gun's report,
     Sever themselves and madly sweep the sky,
     So, at his sight,† away his fellows fly;
     And, at our stamp, here o'er and o'er one fails;   *25*
     He murder cries, and help from Athens calls.
     Their sense thus weak, lost with their fears thus strong,
     Made senseless things begin to do them wrong;
     For briers and thorns at their apparel snatch;
     Some sleeves, some hats, from yielders all things catch.   *30*
     I led them on in this distracted fear,

---

170. *enforced:* violated.
Sc. ii, 2. *next:* first.
3. *in extremity:* extremely.
5. *night-rule:* diversion planned for
the night.
9. *patches:* yokels. *mechanicals:*
artisans.

13. *barren sort:* dull crew.
17. *nole:* head.
19. *mimic:* buffoon, burlesque actor.
21. *choughs:* jackdaws. *in sort:*
together.
24. *his sight:* sight of him.

And left sweet Pyramus translated there;
When in that moment, so it came to pass,
Titania wak'd and straightway lov'd an ass.

OBERON   This falls out better than I could devise.   35
But hast thou yet latch'd† the Athenian's eyes
With the love-juice, as I did bid thee do?

ROBIN   I took him sleeping, — that is finish'd, too, —
And the Athenian woman by his side;
That, when he wak'd, of force† she must be ey'd.   40

Enter DEMETRIUS and HERMIA.

OBERON   Stand close; this is the same Athenian.

ROBIN   This is the woman, but not this the man.

DEMETRIUS   O, why rebuke you him that loves you so?
Lay breath so bitter on your bitter foe.

HERMIA   Now I but chide; but I should use thee worse,   45
For thou, I fear, hast given me cause to curse.
If thou hast slain Lysander in his sleep,
Being o'er shoes in blood, plunge in knee-deep,
And kill me too.
The sun was not so true unto the day   50
As he to me: would he have stolen away
From sleeping Hermia? I'll believe as soon
This whole earth may be bor'd and that the moon
May through the centre creep and so displease
Her brother's noontide with the Antipodes.   55
It cannot be but thou hast murd'red him;
So should a murderer look, so dread, so grim.

DEMETRIUS   So should the murd'red look, and so should I,
Pierc'd through the heart with your stern cruelty;
Yet you, the murderer, look as bright, as clear,   60
As yonder Venus in her glimmering sphere.

HERMIA   What's this to my Lysander? Where is he?
Ah, good Demetrius, wilt thou give him me?

DEMETRIUS   I had rather give his carcass to my hounds.

HERMIA   Out, dog! out, cur! thou driv'st me past the bounds   65
Of maiden's patience. Hast thou slain him, then?
Henceforth be never numb'red among men!
O, once tell true, tell true, even for my sake!
Durst thou have look'd upon him being awake,
And hast thou kill'd him sleeping? O brave touch!†   70
Could not a worm,† an adder, do so much?
An adder did it; for with doubler tongue
Than thine, thou serpent, never adder stung.

DEMETRIUS   You spend your passion on a mispris'd mood.†
I am not guilty of Lysander's blood;   75
Nor is he dead, for aught that I can tell.

36. *latch'd:* anointed.
40. *of force:* perforce.
70. *touch:* exploit.

71. *worm:* serpent.
74. *on . . . mood:* in mistaken anger.

HERMIA   I pray thee, tell me then that he is well.

DEMETRIUS   An if I could, what should I get therefore?

HERMIA   A privilege never to see me more.
  And from thy hated presence part I so: *80*
  See me no more, whether he be dead or no.   [*Exit.*

DEMETRIUS   There is no following her in this fierce vein;
  Here therefore for a while I will remain.
  So sorrow's heaviness doth heavier grow
  For debt that bankrupt sleep doth sorrow owe;   *85*
  Which now in some slight measure it will pay,
  If for his tender† here I make some stay.

            [*Lies down [and sleeps*].

OBERON   What hast thou done? Thou hast mistaken quite
  And laid the love-juice on some true-love's sight.
  Of thy misprision† must perforce ensue   *90*
  Some true love turn'd and not a false turn'd true.

ROBIN   Then fate o'er-rules, that, one man holding troth,
  A million fail, confounding oath on oath.

OBERON   About the wood go swifter than the wind,
  And Helena of Athens look thou find.   *95*
  All fancy-sick† she is and pale of cheer†
  With sighs of love, that costs the fresh blood† dear.
  By some illusion see thou bring her here.
  I'll charm his eyes against she do appear.†

ROBIN   I go, I go; look how I go,   *100*
  Swifter than arrow from the Tartar's bow.   [*Exit.*

OBERON   Flower of this purple dye,
  Hit with Cupid's archery,
  Sink in apple of his eye.
  When his love he doth espy,   *105*
  Let her shine as gloriously
  As the Venus of the sky.
  When thou wak'st, if she be by,
  Beg of her for remedy.

  Re-enter ROBIN GOODFELLOW.

ROBIN   Captain of our fairy band,   *110*
  Helena is here at hand;
  And the youth, mistook by me,
  Pleading for a lover's fee.
  Shall we their fond pageant† see?
  Lord, what fools these mortals be!   *115*

OBERON   Stand aside. The noise they make
  Will cause Demetrius to awake.

87. *for his tender:* i.e., until sleep tenders itself.
90. *misprision:* mistake.
96. *fancy-sick:* love-sick. *cheer:* face.
97. *sighs...blood:* It was commonly thought that each sigh took a drop of blood from the heart.
99. *against...appear:* in anticipation of her appearance.
114. *fond pageant:* foolish exhibition.

ROBIN   Then will two at once woo one;
              That must needs be sport alone.†
              And those things do best please me   120
              That befall preposterously.
         Enter LYSANDER *and* HELENA.
LYSANDER   Why should you think that I should woo in scorn?
              Scorn and derision never come in tears.
         Look, when I vow, I weep; and vows so born,
              In their nativity all truth appears.†   125
         How can these things in me seem scorn to you,
         Bearing the badge of faith, to prove them true?
HELENA   You do advance your cunning more and more.
              When truth kills truth, O devilish-holy fray!
         These vows are Hermia's; will you give her o'er?   130
              Weigh oath with oath, and you will nothing weigh.
         Your vows to her and me, put in two scales,
              Will even weigh, and both as light as tales.
LYSANDER   I had no judgement when to her I swore.
HELENA   Nor none, in my mind, now you give her o'er.   135
LYSANDER   Demetrius loves her, and he loves not you.
DEMETRIUS [*Awaking.*]   O Helen, goddess, nymph, perfect, divine!
         To what, my love, shall I compare thine eyne?
         Crystal is muddy. O, how ripe in show
         Thy lips, those kissing cherries, tempting grow!   140
         That pure congealed white, high Taurus'† snow,
         Fann'd with the eastern wind, turns to a crow
         When thou hold'st up thy hand. O, let me kiss
         This princess of pure white, this seal† of bliss!
HELENA   O spite! O hell! I see you all are bent   145
         To set against me for your merriment.
         If you were civil and knew courtesy,
         You would not do me thus much injury.
         Can you not hate me, as I know you do,
         But you must join in souls to mock me too?   150
         If you were men, as men you are in show,
         You would not use a gentle lady so;
         To vow, and swear, and superpraise my parts,†
         When I am sure you hate me with your hearts.
         You both are rivals, and love Hermia;   155
         And now both rivals, to mock Helena.
         A trim exploit, a manly enterprise,
         To conjure tears up in a poor maid's eyes
         With your derision! None of noble sort
         Would so offend a virgin and extort†   160
         A poor soul's patience, all to make you sport.

119. *alone:* unique.   144. *seal:* pledge.
124–125. *vows . . . appears:* vows so   153. *parts:* qualities.
born show wholly true.   160. *extort:* wrest, torture.
141. *Taurus:* a mountain range in
Asia Minor.

LYSANDER   You are unkind, Demetrius; be not so;
    For you love Hermia; this you know I know.
    And here, with all good will, with all my heart,
    In Hermia's love I yield you up my part;   165
    And yours of Helena to me bequeath,
    Whom I do love and will do till my death.
HELENA   Never did mockers waste more idle breath.
DEMETRIUS   Lysander, keep thy Hermia; I will none.†
    If e'er I lov'd her, all that love is gone.   170
    My heart to her but as guest-wise sojourn'd,
    And now to Helen is it home return'd,
    There to remain.
LYSANDER   Helen, it is not so.
DEMETRIUS   Disparage not the faith thou dost not know,
    Lest, to thy peril, thou aby† it dear.   175
    Look, where thy love comes; yonder is thy dear.
    Re-enter HERMIA.
HERMIA   Dark night, that from the eye his† function takes,
    The ear more quick of apprehension makes;
    Wherein it doth impair the seeing sense,
    It pays the hearing double recompense.   180
    Thou art not by mine eye, Lysander, found;
    Mine ear, I thank it, brought me to thy sound.
    But why unkindly didst thou leave me so?
LYSANDER   Why should he stay, whom love doth press to go?
HERMIA   What love could press Lysander from my side?   185
LYSANDER   Lysander's love, that would not let him bide,
    Fair Helena, who more engilds the night
    Than all yon fiery oes† and eyes of light.
    Why seek'st thou me? Could not this make thee know,
    The hate I bare thee made me leave thee so?   190
HERMIA   You speak not as you think. It cannot be.
HELENA   Lo, she is one of this confederacy!
    Now I perceive they have conjoin'd all three
    To fashion this false sport, in spite of me.
    Injurious† Hermia! most ungrateful maid!   195
    Have you conspir'd, have you with these contriv'd
    To bait me with this foul derision?
    Is all the counsel that we two have shar'd,
    The sisters' vows, the hours that we have spent,
    When we have chid the hasty-footed time   200
    For parting us, — O, is all forgot?
    All school-days' friendship, childhood innocence?
    We, Hermia, like two artificial† gods,
    Have with our needles created both one flower,
    Both on one sampler, sitting on one cushion,   205

169. *will none:* i.e., of her.
175. *aby:* pay for.
177. *his:* its.

188. *oes:* orbs, circles.
195. *Injurious:* insulting.
203. *artificial:* skilled in art.

Both warbling of one song, both in one key,
As if our hands, our sides, voices and minds
Had been incorporate.† So we grew together,
Like to a double cherry, seeming parted,
But yet an union in partition;   210
Two lovely berries moulded on one stem;
So, with two seeming bodies but one heart;
Two of the first,† [like] coats in heraldry,
Due but to one and crowned with one crest.
And will you rend our ancient love asunder,   215
To join with men in scorning your poor friend?
It is not friendly, 'tis not maidenly.
Our sex, as well as I, may chide you for it,
Though I alone do feel the injury.

HERMIA   I am amazed at your passionate words.   220
I scorn you not; it seems that you scorn me.

HELENA   Have you not set Lysander, as in scorn,
To follow me and praise my eyes and face?
And made your other love, Demetrius,
Who even but now did spurn me with his foot,   225
To call me goddess, nymph, divine and rare,
Precious, celestial? Wherefore speaks he this
To her he hates? And wherefore doth Lysander
Deny your love, so rich within his soul,
And tender me, forsooth, affection,   230
But by your setting on, by your consent?
What though I be not so in grace as you,
So hung upon with love, so fortunate,
But miserable most, to love unlov'd?
This you should pity rather than despise.   235

HERMIA   I understand not what you mean by this.

HELENA   Ay, do, persever, counterfeit sad† looks,
Make mouths upon me when I turn my back,
Wink each at other, hold the sweet jest up;
This sport, well carried, shall be chronicled.   240
If you have any pity, grace, or manners,
You would not make me such an argument.†
But fare ye well; 'tis partly my own fault,
Which death or absence soon shall remedy.

LYSANDER   Stay, gentle Helena; hear my excuse,   245
My love, my life, my soul, fair Helena!

HELENA   O excellent!

HERMIA   Sweet, do not scorn her so.

DEMETRIUS   If she cannot entreat, I can compel.

208. *incorporate:* joined in one body.
213. *Two of the first:* Apparently a heraldic phrase used of two coats of arms (such as those of husband and wife) arranged on either side of a vertical division of the shield, such division being known as "the first" of several possible divisions.
237. *sad:* grave.
242. *argument:* subject for scorn.

LYSANDER   Thou canst compel no more than she entreat.
  Thy threats have no more strength than her weak [prayers].   *250*
  Helen, I love thee; by my life, I do!
  I swear by that which I will lose for thee,
  To prove him false that says I love thee not.
DEMETRIUS   I say I love thee more than he can do.
LYSANDER   If thou say so, withdraw, and prove it too.   *255*
DEMETRIUS   Quick, come!
HERMIA   Lysander, whereto tends all this?
LYSANDER   Away, you Ethiope!
DEMETRIUS   No, no; he'll [but]
  Seem to break loose. Take on as you would follow,
  But yet come not. You are a tame man, go!
LYSANDER   Hang off, thou cat, thou burr! Vile thing, let loose.   *260*
  Or I will shake thee from me like a serpent!
HERMIA   Why are you grown so rude? What change is this?
  Sweet love, —
LYSANDER   Thy love! Out, tawny Tartar, out!
  Out, loathed medicine! O hated potion, hence!
HERMIA   Do you not jest?
HELENA   Yes, sooth; and so do you.   *265*
LYSANDER   Demetrius, I will keep my word with thee.
DEMETRIUS   I would I had your bond, for I perceive
  A weak bond holds you. I'll not trust your word.
LYSANDER   What, should I hurt her, strike her, kill her dead?
  Although I hate her, I'll not harm her so.   *270*
HERMIA   What, can you do me greater harm than hate?
  Hate me! wherefore? O me! what news,† my love!
  Am not I Hermia? Are not you Lysander?
  I am as fair now as I was erewhile.
  Since night you lov'd me; yet since night you left me: *275*
  Why, then you left me — O, the gods forbid! —
  In earnest, shall I say?
LYSANDER   Ay, by my life;
  And never did desire to see thee more.
  Therefore be out of hope, of question, doubt;
  Be certain, nothing truer; 'tis no jest   *280*
  That I do hate thee and love Helena.
HERMIA   O me! you juggler! you canker-blossom!†
  You thief of love! What, have you come by night
  And stolen my love's heart from him?
HELENA   Fine, i' faith!
  Have you no modesty, no maiden shame,   *285*
  No touch of bashfulness? What, will you tear
  Impatient answers from my gentle tongue?
  Fie, fie! you counterfeit, you puppet, you!
HERMIA   "Puppet?" Why so? Ay, that way goes the game.

---

272. *what news:* what is the matter?

282. *canker-blossom:* worm that
destroys a blossom.

Now I perceive that she hath made compare   *290*
  Between our statures; she hath urg'd her height;
  And with her personage, her tall personage,
  Her height, forsooth, she hath prevail'd with him.
  And are you grown so high in his esteem,
  Because I am so dwarfish and so low?   *295*
  How low am I, thou painted maypole? Speak,
  How low am I? I am not yet so low
  But that my nails can reach unto thine eyes.
HELENA   I pray you, though you mock me, gentlemen,
  Let her not hurt me. I was never curst;†   *300*
  I have no gift at all in shrewishness;
  I am a right† maid for my cowardice.
  Let her not strike me. You perhaps may think,
  Because she is something lower than myself,
  That I can match her.
HERMIA   "Lower!" hark, again.   *305*
HELENA   Good Hermia, do not be so bitter with me.
  I evermore did love you, Hermia,
  Did ever keep your counsels, never wrong'd you;
  Save that, in love unto Demetrius,
  I told him of your stealth† unto this wood.   *310*
  He followed you; for love I followed him;
  But he hath chid me hence and threat'ned me
  To strike me, spurn me, nay, to kill me too.
  And now, so you will let me quiet go,
  To Athens will I bear my folly back   *315*
  And follow you no further. Let me go.
  You see how simple and how fond I am.
HERMIA   Why, get you gone; who is't that hinders you?
HELENA   A foolish heart, that I leave here behind.
HERMIA   What, with Lysander?
HELENA   With Demetrius.   *320*
LYSANDER   Be not afraid; she shall not harm thee, Helena.
DEMETRIUS   No, sir, she shall not, though you take her part.
HELENA   O, when she's angry, she is keen and shrewd!†
  She was a vixen when she went to school;
  And though she be but little, she is fierce.   *325*
HERMIA   "Little" again! Nothing but "low" and "little"!
  Why will you suffer her to flout me thus?
  Let me come to her.
LYSANDER   Get you gone, you dwarf,
  You minimus,† of hind'ring knot-grass† made;
  You bead, you acorn.
DEMETRIUS   You are too officious   *330*

300. *curst:* shrewish.   329. *minimus:* dwarf. *knot-grass:*
302. *right:* true.   a weed supposed capable of stunt-
310. *stealth:* stealing away.   ing the growth.
323. *shrewd:* sharp-tongued.

In her behalf that scorns your services.
Let her alone; speak not of Helena;
Take not her part; for, if thou dost intend†
Never so little show of love to her,
Thou shalt aby it.

LYSANDER   Now she holds me not.   335
Now follow, if thou dar'st, to try whose right,
Of thine or mine, is most in Helena.

DEMETRIUS   Follow! Nay, I'll go with thee, cheek by jowl.

[*Exeunt* LYSANDER *and* DEMETRIUS.

HERMIA   You, mistress, all this coil† is 'long† of you.
Nay, go not back.

HELENA   I will not trust you, I,   340
Nor longer stay in your curst company.
Your hands than mine are quicker for a fray;
My legs are longer though, to run away.   [*Exit.*]

HERMIA   I am amaz'd, and know not what to say.   [*Exit.*

OBERON   This is thy negligence. Still thou mistak'st,   345
Or else committ'st thy knaveries wilfully.

ROBIN   Believe me, king of shadows, I mistook.
Did not you tell me I should know the man
By the Athenian garments he had on?
And so far blameless proves my enterprise,   350
That I have 'nointed an Athenian's eyes;
And so far am I glad it so did sort,†
As this their jangling I esteem a sport.

OBERON   Thou see'st these lovers seek a place to fight;
Hie therefore, Robin, overcast the night.   355
The starry welkin cover thou anon
With drooping fog as black as Acheron,†
And lead these testy rivals so astray
As one come not within another's way.
Like to Lysander sometime frame thy tongue,   360
Then stir Demetrius up with bitter wrong;†
And sometime rail thou like Demetrius;
And from each other look thou lead them thus,
Till o'er their brows death-counterfeiting sleep
With leaden legs and batty wings doth creep.   365
Then crush this herb into Lysander's eye;
Whose liquor hath this virtuous† property,
To take from thence all error with his might,†
And make his eyeballs roll with wonted sight.
When they next wake, all this derision   370
Shall seem a dream and fruitless vision;
And back to Athens shall the lovers wend

---

333. *intend:* proffer.   361. *wrong:* taunts.
339. *coil:* turmoil. *'long:* because.   367. *virtuous:* powerful.
352. *sort:* turn out.   368. *his might:* its power.
357. *Acheron:* river of Hades.

With league whose date till death shall never end.
Whiles I in this affair do thee employ,
I'll to my queen and beg her Indian boy;   375
And then I will her charmed eye release
From monster's view, and all things shall be peace.
ROBIN   My fairy lord, this must be done with haste,
For Night's swift dragons† cut the clouds full fast,
And yonder shines Aurora's harbinger,†   380
At whose approach, ghosts, wand'ring here and there,
Troop home to churchyards. Damned spirits all,
That in crossways and floods have burial,†
Already to their wormy beds are gone.
For fear lest day should look their shames upon,   385
They wilfully themselves exile from light
And must for aye consort with black-brow'd night.
OBERON   But we are spirits of another sort.
I with the Morning's love† have oft made sport,
And, like a forester, the groves may tread,   390
Even till the eastern gate, all fiery-red,
Opening on Neptune with fair blessed beams
Turns into yellow gold his salt green streams.
But, notwithstanding, haste, make no delay;
We may effect this business yet ere day.   [*Exit.*]
ROBIN   Up and down, up and down,   396
    I will lead them up and down.
    I am fear'd in field and town.
    Goblin, lead them up and down.
Here comes one.   400

Re-enter LYSANDER.

LYSANDER   Where art thou, proud Demetrius? Speak thou now.
ROBIN   Here, villain; drawn and ready. Where art thou?
LYSANDER   I will be with thee straight.
ROBIN   Follow me, then,
    To plainer ground.

              [*Exit* LYSANDER, *as following the voice.*]

Re-enter DEMETRIUS.

DEMETRIUS   Lysander, speak again!
Thou runaway, thou coward, art thou fled?   405
Speak! In some bush? Where dost thou hide thy head?
ROBIN   Thou coward, art thou bragging to the stars,
Telling the bushes that thou look'st for wars,
And wilt not come? Come, recreant; come, thou child,

---

379. *night's . . . dragons:* the dragons drawing the car of Night.
380. *Aurora's harbinger:* star announcing the dawn.
383. *crossways . . . burial:* Suicides were buried at crossroads, and like the ghosts of those who had drowned, having thus no proper burial, were believed condemned to cheerless wandering.
389. *Morning's love:* Cephalus, the youth loved by Aurora, or possibly Aurora herself.

I'll whip thee with a rod. He is defil'd   410
That draws a sword on thee.
DEMETRIUS   Yea, art thou there?
ROBIN   Follow my voice. We'll try no manhood here.   [Exeunt.
   [Re-enter LYSANDER.]
LYSANDER   He goes before me and still dares me on.
When I come where he calls, then he is gone.
The villain is much lighter-heel'd than I;   415
I followed fast, but faster he did fly,
That fallen am I in dark uneven way,
And here will rest me. Come, thou gentle day!   [Lies down.
For if but once thou show me thy grey light,
I'll find Demetrius and revenge this spite.   420
                                                                   [Sleeps.]

   Re-enter ROBIN GOODFELLOW and DEMETRIUS.
ROBIN   Ho, ho, ho! Coward, why com'st thou not?
DEMETRIUS   Abide me, if thou dar'st; for well I wot
Thou runn'st before me, shifting every place,
And dar'st not stand, nor look me in the face.
Where art thou now?
ROBIN   Come hither; I am here.   425
DEMETRIUS   Nay, then, thou mock'st me. Thou shalt buy this dear,
If ever I thy face by daylight see.
Now, go thy way. Faintness constraineth me
To measure out my length on this cold bed.
By day's approach look to be visited.   430
                                              [Lies down and sleeps.

   Re-enter HELENA.
HELENA   O weary night, O long and tedious night,
   Abate thy hours! Shine, comforts, from the east,
   That I may back to Athens by daylight,
      From these that my poor company detest.
   And sleep, that sometimes shuts up sorrow's eye,   435
   Steal me awhile from mine own company.
                                          [Lies down and] sleeps.

ROBIN   Yet but three? Come one more;
   Two of both kinds makes up four.
   Re-enter HERMIA.
      Here she comes, curst and sad.
      Cupid is a knavish lad,   440
      Thus to make poor females mad.
HERMIA   Never so weary, never so in woe,
   Bedabbled with the dew and torn with briers,
I can no further crawl, no further go;
   My legs can keep no pace with my desires.   445
Here will I rest me till the break of day.
Heavens shield Lysander, if they mean a fray!

                                          [Lies down and sleeps.]

ROBIN   On the ground
   Sleep sound.

I'll apply   *450*
To your eye,
Gentle lover, remedy.   [*Squeezing the juice on* LYSANDER'S *eyes.*]
  When thou wak'st,
  Thou tak'st
  True delight   *455*
  In the sight
Of thy former lady's eye;
And the country proverb known,
That every man should take his own,
In your waking shall be shown.   460
  Jack shall have Jill;
  Nought shall go ill;
The man shall have his mare again, and all shall be well.   [*Exit.*]

Act Four   [*Scene I. The same.*]

[LYSANDER, DEMETRIUS, HELENA, *and* HERMIA, *lying asleep.*]
Enter TITANIA *and Clown* [BOTTOM; PEASEBLOSSOM, COBWEB, MOTH, MUS-
TARDSEED,] *and* [*other*] *Fairies* [*attending*]; OBERON *behind* [*unseen*].

TITANIA   Come, sit thee down upon this flow'ry bed,
         While I thy amiable cheeks do coy†;
         And stick musk-roses in thy sleek smooth head,
         And kiss thy fair large ears, my gentle joy.
BOTTOM   Where's Peaseblossom?   5
PEASEBLOSSOM   Ready.
BOTTOM   Scratch my head, Peaseblossom. Where's Mounsieur Cobweb?
COBWEB   Ready.
BOTTOM   Mounsieur Cobweb, good mounsieur, get you your weapons in
         your hand, and kill me a red-hipp'd humble-bee on the top of a thistle;   *10*
         and, good mounsieur, bring me the honey-bag. Do not fret yourself
         too much in the action, mounsieur, and, good mounsieur, have a care
         the honey-bag break not; I would be loath to have you overflown with
         a honey-bag, signior. Where's Mounsieur Mustardseed?
MUSTARDSEED   Ready.   *15*
BOTTOM   Give me your neaf,† Mounsieur Mustardseed. Pray you, leave
         your courtesy,† good mounsieur.
MUSTARDSEED   What's your will?
BOTTOM   Nothing, good mounsieur, but to help, Cavalery† Cobweb to
         scratch. I must to the barber's, mounsieur; for methinks I am mar-   *20*
         vellous hairy about the face; and I am such a tender ass, if my hair do
         but tickle me, I must scratch.
TITANIA   What, wilt thou hear some music, my sweet love?

2. *coy:* caress.   16–17. *leave your courtesy:* put on
16. *neaf:* fist.   your hat.
                                     19. *Cavalery:* cavaliero, gentleman.

BOTTOM   I have a reasonable good ear in music.
Let's have the tongs and the bones.† 25

[*Music. Tongs. Rural music*

TITANIA   Or say, sweet love, what thou desir'st to eat.
BOTTOM   Truly, a peck of provender; I could munch your good dry
oats. Methinks I have a great desire to a bottle† of hay. Good hay,
sweet hay, hath no fellow.†
TITANIA   I have a venturous fairy that shall seek 30
The squirrel's hoard, and fetch [for] thee new nuts.
BOTTOM   I had rather have a handful or two of dried peas. But, I pray
you, let none of your people stir me; I have an exposition of† sleep
come upon me.
TITANIA   Sleep thou, and I will wind thee in my arms. 35
Fairies, be gone, and be always away.   [*Exeunt fairies.*]
So doth the woodbine the sweet honeysuckle
Gently entwist; the female ivy so
Enrings the barky fingers of the elm.
Oh, how I love thee! how I dote on thee! 40

[*They sleep.*]

Enter ROBIN GOODFELLOW.

OBERON [*Advancing.*]   Welcome, good Robin. See'st thou this sweet sight?
Her dotage now I do begin to pity;
For, meeting her of late behind the wood,
Seeking sweet favours† for this hateful fool,
I did upbraid her and fall out with her. 45
For she his hairy temples then had rounded
With coronet of fresh and fragrant flowers;
And that same dew, which sometime on the buds
Was wont to swell like round and orient† pearls,
Stood now within the pretty flowerets' eyes 50
Like tears that did their own disgrace bewail.
When I had at my pleasure taunted her
And she in mild terms begg'd my patience,
I then did ask of her her changeling child;
Which straight she gave me, and her fairy sent 55
To bear him to my bower in fairy land.
And, now I have the boy, I will undo
This hateful imperfection of her eyes;
And, gentle Puck, take this transformed scalp
From off the head of this Athenian swain, 60
That, he awaking when the other† do,
May all to Athens back again repair,
And think no more of this night's accidents

25. *tongs...bones:* rustic instruments of music.
28. *bottle:* bundle.
29. *fellow:* equal.
33. *exposition of:* He means *disposition to.*

44. *favours:* i.e., flowers for love-
tokens.
49. *orient:* eastern.
61. *other:* others.

But as the fierce vexation of a dream. 64
But first I will release the fairy queen.   *[Touching her eyes.]*
>Be as thou wast wont to be;
>See as thou wast wont to see:
>Dian's bud† o'er Cupid's flower
>Hath such force and blessed power.

Now, my Titania; wake you, my sweet queen. 70

TITANIA   My Oberon! what visions have I seen!
Methought I was enamour'd of an ass.

OBERON   There lies your love.

TITANIA   How came these things to pass?
O, how mine eyes do loathe his visage now! 75

OBERON   Silence awhile. Robin, take off this head.
Titania, music call; and strike more dead
Than common sleep of all these five the sense.

TITANIA   Music, ho! music, such as charmeth sleep!   *[Music, still.*

ROBIN   Now, when thou wak'st, with thine own fool's eyes peep. 80

OBERON   Sound, music! Come, my queen, take hands with me,
And rock the ground whereon these sleepers be.
Now thou and I are new in amity
And will to-morrow midnight solemnly
Dance in Duke Theseus' house triumphantly 85
And bless it to all fair prosperity.
There shall the pairs of faithful lovers be
Wedded, with Theseus, all in jollity.

ROBIN   Fairy king, attend and mark;
I do hear the morning lark. 90

OBERON   Then, my queen, in silence sad
Trip we after the night's shade.
We the globe can compass soon,
Swifter than the wand'ring moon.

TITANIA   Come, my lord, and in our flight 95
Tell me how it came this night
That I sleeping here was found
With these mortals on the ground.   *[Exeunt. Horns winded [within]*
Enter THESEUS, HIPPOLYTA, EGEUS, *and all his train.*

THESEUS   Go, one of you, find out the forester, 100
For now our observation† is perform'd,
And since we have the vaward† of the day,
My love shall hear the music of my hounds.
Uncouple in the western valley, let them go. 104
Despatch, I say, and find the forester.   *[Exit an attendant.]*
We will, fair queen, up to the mountain's top
And mark the musical confusion
Of hounds and echo in conjunction.

---

68. *Dian's bud:* The flower of the *agnus castus* or chaste tree was believed to preserve chastity.

101. *observation:* observance, May-day rites.
102. *vaward:* vanguard.

HIPPOLYTA   I was with Hercules and Cadmus once,
      When in a wood of Crete they bay'd the bear   *110*
      With hounds of Sparta. Never did I hear
      Such gallant chiding;† for, besides the groves,
      The skies, the fountains, every region near
      Seem'd all one mutual cry. I never heard
      So musical a discord, such sweet thunder.   *115*
THESEUS   My hounds are bred out of the Spartan kind,
      So flew'd,† so sanded,† and their heads are hung
      With ears that sweep away the morning dew;
      Crook-knee'd, and dew-lapp'd like Thessalian bulls;
      Slow in pursuit, but match'd in mouth like bells,   *120*
      Each under each.† A cry† more tuneable
      Was never holla'd to, nor cheer'd with horn,
      In Crete, in Sparta, nor in Thessaly.
      Judge when you hear. But, soft! what nymphs are these?
EGEUS   My lord, this is my daughter here asleep;   *125*
      And this, Lysander; this Demetrius is;
      This Helena, old Nedar's Helena.
      I wonder of their being here together.
THESEUS   No doubt they rose up early to observe
      The rite of May, and, hearing our intent,   *130*
      Came here in grace of our solemnity.†
      But speak, Egeus; is not this the day
      That Hermia should give answer of her choice?
EGEUS   It is, my lord.
THESEUS   Go, bid the huntsmen wake them with their horns.   *135*
      [*Horns and shout within.* LYSANDER, DEMETRIUS, HELENA, *and* HERMIA
      wake and start up.
      Good morrow, friends. Saint Valentine† is past;
      Begin these wood-birds but to couple now?
LYSANDER   Pardon, my lord.
THESEUS   I pray you all, stand up.
      I know you two are rival enemies;
      How comes this gentle concord in the world,   *140*
      That hatred is so far from jealousy
      To sleep by hate and fear no enmity?
LYSANDER   My lord, I shall reply amazedly,
      Half sleep, half waking; but as yet, I swear,
      I cannot truly say how I came here.   *145*
      But, as I think, — for truly would I speak,
      And now I do bethink me, so it is, —
      I came with Hermia hither. Our intent

112. *chiding:* baying.
117. *flew'd:* with large chaps.
sanded: of sandy color.
121. *Each . . . each:* with varied
pitch. Elizabethan huntsmen cov-
eted packs of hounds whose cries
would blend. *cry:* pack.

131. *solemnity:* marriage ceremony.
136. *Saint Valentine:* Birds were
popularly supposed to choose their
mates on Valentine's day.

Was to be gone from Athens, where† we might,
    Without† the peril of the Athenian law —   *150*
EGEUS   Enough, enough, my lord; you have enough.
    I beg the law, the law, upon his head.
    They would have stol'n away; they would, Demetrius,
    Thereby to have defeated you and me,
    You of your wife, and me of my consent,   *155*
    Of my consent that she should be your wife.
DEMETRIUS   My lord, fair Helen told me of their stealth,
    Of this their purpose hither to this wood;
    And I in fury hither follow'd them,
    Fair Helena in fancy following me.   *160*
    But, my good lord, I wot not by what power, —
    But by some power it is, — my love to Hermia,
    Melted as [is] the snow, seems to me now
    As the remembrance of an idle gaud
    Which in my childhood I did dote upon;   *165*
    And all the faith, the virtue of my heart,
    The object and the pleasure of mine eye,
    Is only Helena. To her, my lord,
    Was I betroth'd ere I saw Hermia;
    But like a sickness did I loathe this food;   *170*
    But, as in health, come to my natural taste,
    Now I do wish it, love it, long for it,
    And will for evermore be true to it.
THESEUS   Fair lovers, you are fortunately met;
    Of this discourse we more will hear anon.   *175*
    Egeus, I will overbear your will;
    For in the temple, by and by, with us
    These couples shall eternally be knit.
    And, for the morning now is something worn,
    Our purpos'd hunting shall be set aside.   *180*
    Away with us to Athens; three and three,
    We'll hold a feast in great solemnity.
    Come, Hippolyta.   [*Exeunt* THESEUS, HIPPOLYTA, EGEUS, *and train.*
DEMETRIUS   These things seem small and undistinguishable,
    Like far-off mountains turned into clouds.   *185*
HERMIA   Methinks I see these things with parted† eye,
    When every thing seems double.
HELENA   So methinks;
    And I have found Demetrius like a jewel,
    Mine own, and not mine own.
DEMETRIUS   [But] are you sure
    That we are [now] awake? It seems to me   *190*
    That yet we sleep, we dream. Do not you think
    The Duke was here, and bid us follow him?
HERMIA   Yea; and my father.

      149. *where:* to a place where.   186. *parted:* out of focus.
      150. *Without:* beyond.

HELENA   And Hippolyta.
LYSANDER   And he did bid us follow to the temple.
DEMETRIUS   Why, then, we are awake. Let's follow him;   *195*
   And by the way let us recount our dreams.   [*Exeunt lovers.*
BOTTOM (*Awaking.*)   When my cue comes, call me, and I will answer.
   My next is, "Most fair Pyramus." Heigh-ho! Peter Quince! Flute,
   the bellowsmender! Snout, the tinker! Starveling! God's my life,
   stolen hence, and left me asleep! I have had a most rare vision. I   *200*
   have had a dream, past the wit of man to say what dream it was. Man
   is but an ass, if he go about† to expound this dream. Methought I was
   — there is no man can tell what. Methought I was, — and methought
   I had, — but man is but a patch'd† fool, if he will offer to say what
   methought I had. The eye of man hath not heard, the ear of man   *205*
   hath not seen, man's hand is not able to taste, his tongue to conceive,
   nor his heart to report, what my dream was. I will get Peter Quince
   to write a ballad of this dream. It shall be called "Bottom's Dream,"
   because it hath no bottom; and I will sing it in the latter end of a play,
   before the Duke; peradventure, to make it the more gracious, I shall   *210*
   sing it at her death.†   [*Exit.*

[*Scene II. Athens.* QUINCE'*s house.*]
Enter QUINCE, FLUTE, SNOUT, *and* STARVELING.

QUINCE   Have you sent to Bottom's house? Is he come home yet?
STARVELING   He cannot be heard of. Out of doubt he is transported.
FLUTE   If he come not, then the play is marr'd. It goes not forward,
   doth it?
QUINCE   It is not possible. You have not a man in all Athens able to   *5*
   discharge Pyramus but he.
FLUTE   No, he hath simply the best wit of any handicraft man in Athens.
SNOUT   Yea, and the best person too; and he is a very paramour for a
   sweet voice.
FLUTE   You must say "paragon"; a paramour is, God bless us, a thing   *10*
   of naught.†
   Enter SNUG.
SNUG   Masters, the Duke is coming from the temple, and there is two or
   three lords and ladies more married. If our sport had gone forward,
   we had all been made men.
FLUTE   O sweet bully Bottom! Thus hath he lost sixpence a day† dur-   *15*
   ing his life; he could not have 'scaped sixpence a day. An the Duke
   had not given him sixpence a day for playing Pyramus, I'll be hang'd.
   He would have deserved it. Sixpence a day in Pyramus, or nothing.
   Enter BOTTOM.
BOTTOM   Where are these lads? Where are these hearts?

        202. *go about:* attempt.   **Sc. ii,** 10–11. *thing of naught:*
        204. *patch'd:* wearing motley.   naughty thing.
        211. *at her death:* i.e., Thisbe's.   15. *sixpence a day:* i.e., as royal
                                           pension.

QUINCE   Bottom! O most courageous day! O most happy hour!   *20*

BOTTOM   Masters, I am to discourse wonders, but ask me not what; for
if I tell you, I am no true Athenian. I will tell you everything, right
as it fell out.

QUINCE   Let us hear, sweet Bottom.

BOTTOM   Not a word of me. All that I will tell you is, that the Duke hath   *25*
dined. Get your apparel together, good strings to your beards, new
ribbons to your pumps; meet presently at the palace; every man look
o'er his part; for the short and the long is, our play is preferr'd.† In
any case, let Thisby have clean linen; and let not him that plays the
lion pare his nails, for they shall hang out for the lion's claws. And,   *30*
most dear actors, eat no onions nor garlic, for we are to utter sweet
breath; and I do not doubt but to hear them say, it is a sweet comedy.
No more words; away! go away!   [*Exeunt.*

Act Five   [*Scene I. The palace of* THESEUS.]

Enter THESEUS, HIPPOLYTA, PHILOSTRATE, Lords [*and* Attendants].

HIPPOLYTA   'Tis strange, my Theseus, that these lovers speak of.

THESEUS   More strange than true; I never may believe
These antique fables, nor these fairy toys.
Lovers and madmen have such seething brains,
Such shaping fantasies, that apprehend   *5*
More than cool reason ever comprehends.
The lunatic, the lover, and the poet
Are of imagination all compact.†
One sees more devils than vast hell can hold;
That is, the madman. The lover, all as frantic,   *10*
Sees Helen's† beauty in a brow of Egypt.†
The poet's eye, in a fine frenzy rolling,
Doth glance from heaven to earth, from earth to heaven;
And as imagination bodies forth
The forms of things unknown, the poet's pen   *15*
Turns them to shapes and gives to airy nothing
A local habitation and a name.
Such tricks hath strong imagination,
That, if it would but apprehend some joy,
It comprehends some bringer of that joy;   *20*
Or in the night, imagining some fear,
How easy is a bush suppos'd a bear!

HIPPOLYTA   But all the story of the night told over,
And all their minds transfigur'd so together,
More witnesseth than fancy's images,   *25*
And grows to something of great constancy;†

28. *preferr'd:* chosen.   11. *Helen:* Helen of Troy. *brow*
Act Five, Sc. i, 8. *compact:* com-   *of Egypt:* gypsy's face.
posed.   26. *constancy:* certainty.

But, howsoever, strange and admirable.

Enter lovers, LYSANDER, DEMETRIUS, HERMIA, *and* HELENA.

THESEUS   Here come the lovers, full of joy and mirth.
Joy, gentle friends! joy and fresh days of love
Accompany your hearts!

LYSANDER   More than to us   30
Wait in your royal walks, your board, your bed!

THESEUS   Come now; what masques, what dances shall we have,
To wear away this long age of three hours
Between our after-supper and bed-time?
Where is our usual manager of mirth?   35
What revels are in hand? Is there no play
To ease the anguish of a torturing hour?
Call Philostrate.

PHILOSTRATE   Here, mighty Theseus.

THESEUS   Say, what abridgement† have you for this evening?
What masque? what music? How shall we beguile   40
The lazy time, if not with some delight?

PHILOSTRATE   There is a brief† how many sports are ripe.
Make choice of which your Highness will see first.   [*Giving a paper.*]

THESEUS [*Reads.*]   "The battle with the Centaurs,† to be sung
By an Athenian eunuch to the harp."   45
We'll none of that: that have I told my love,
In glory of my kinsman Hercules.
"The riot of the tipsy Bacchanals,
Tearing the Thracian singer in their rage."†
That is an old device; and it was play'd   50
When I from Thebes came last a conqueror.
"The thrice three Muses† mourning for the death
Of Learning, late deceas'd in beggary."
That is some satire, keen and critical,
Not sorting with† a nuptial ceremony.   55
"A tedious brief scene of young Pyramus
And his love Thisbe; very tragical mirth."
Merry and tragical! Tedious and brief!
That is, hot ice and wondrous strange snow.
How shall we find the concord of this discord?   60

PHILOSTRATE   A play there is, my lord, some ten words long,
Which is as brief as I have known a play;
But by ten words, my lord, it is too long,
Which makes it tedious; for in all the play
There is not one word apt, one player fitted.   65

---

39. *abridgement:* pastime.
42. *brief:* list, schedule.
44. *Centaurs:* The Centaurs and the Lapithae fought at a wedding which Theseus would remember, since he had taken part on the side of the latter.
48–49. *The riot . . . rage:* Orpheus, the poet-musician, was killed by the frenzied women followers of Bacchus.
52. *The thrice three Muses:* A topical reference has been seen in these lines, but no explanation is satisfactory.
55. *sorting with:* befitting.

And tragical, my noble lord, it is;
For Pyramus therein doth kill himself.
Which, when I saw rehears'd, I must confess,
Made mine eyes water; but more merry tears
The passion of loud laughter never shed.   70

THESEUS   What are they that do play it?

PHILOSTRATE   Hard-handed men that work in Athens here,
Which never labour'd in their minds till now,
And now have toil'd their unbreath'd† memories
With this same play, against your nuptial.   75

THESEUS   And we will hear it.

PHILOSTRATE   No, my noble lord;
It is not for you. I have heard it over,
And it is nothing, nothing in the world;
Unless you can find sport in their intents,
Extremely stretch'd† and conn'd with cruel pain,   80
To do you service.

THESEUS   I will hear that play;
For never anything can be amiss,
When simpleness and duty tender it.
Go, bring them in; and take your places, ladies.   [*Exit* PHILOSTRATE.]

HIPPOLYTA   I love not to see wretchedness o'er-charged,†   85
And duty in his service perishing.

THESEUS   Why, gentle sweet, you shall see no such thing.

HIPPOLYTA   He says they can do nothing in this kind.

THESEUS   The kinder we, to give them thanks for nothing.
Our sport shall be to take what they mistake;   90
And what poor duty cannot do, noble respect
Takes it in might, not merit.†
Where I have come, great clerks† have purposed
To greet me with premeditated welcomes;
Where I have seen them shiver and look pale,   95
Make periods in the midst of sentences,
Throttle their practis'd accent in their fears,
And in conclusion dumbly have broke off,
Not paying me a welcome. Trust me, sweet,
Out of this silence yet I pick'd a welcome;   100
And in the modesty of fearful duty
I read as much as from the rattling tongue
Of saucy and audacious eloquence.
Love, therefore, and tongue-ti'd simplicity
In least speak most, to my capacity.†   105

[*Re-enter* PHILOSTRATE.]

74. *unbreath'd:* unpractised.
80. *stretch'd:* strained.
85. *wretchedness o'er-charged:*
weakness overburdened.
92. *takes...merit:* takes the will
for the deed.
93. *clerks:* scholars.

105. *to my capacity:* in my opinion. In the sympathetic speech of
Theseus a tribute was very likely
intended to the graciousness of
Queen Elizabeth, who may on
some occasion have witnessed
this play.

PHILOSTRATE   So please your Grace, the Prologue is address'd.†
THESEUS   Let him approach.   [*Flourish of trumpets.*
   Enter [QUINCE *for*] *the* Prologue.
PROLOGUE   If we offend, it is with our good will.†
      That you should think, we come not to offend,
    But with good will. To show our simple skill,   *110*
      That is the true beginning of our end.
    Consider then we come but in despite.
      We do not come as minding to content you,
    Our true intent is. All for your delight
      We are not here. That you should here repent you,   *115*
    The actors are at hand, and by their show
    You shall know all that you are like to know.
THESEUS   This fellow doth not stand upon points.†
LYSANDER   He hath rid his prologue like a rough colt; he knows not the
stop. A good moral, my lord: it is not enough to speak, but to speak   *120*
true.
HIPPOLYTA   Indeed he hath play'd on this prologue like a child on a
recorder;† a sound, but not in government.†
THESEUS   His speech was like a tangled chain; nothing impaired, but all
disordered. Who is next?   *125*
   Enter with a trumpet before them, PYRAMUS *and* THISBE, WALL, MOON-
SHINE, *and* LION.
PROLOGUE   Gentles, perchance you wonder at this show;
      But wonder on till truth make all things plain.
    This man is Pyramus, if you would know;
      This beauteous lady Thisby is certain.
    This man, with lime and rough-cast, doth present   *130*
      Wall, that vile Wall which did these lovers sunder;
    And through Wall's chink, poor souls, they are content
      To whisper. At the which let no man wonder.
    This man, with lantern, dog, and bush of thorn,
      Presenteth Moonshine; for, if you will know,   *135*
    By moonshine did these lovers think no scorn
      To meet at Ninus' tomb, there, there to woo.
    This grisly beast, which Lion hight† by name,
      The trusty Thisby, coming first by night,
    Did scare away, or rather did affright;   *140*
    And, as she fled, her mantle she did fall,
      Which Lion vile with bloody mouth did stain.
    Anon comes Pyramus, sweet youth and tall,
      And finds his trusty Thisby's mantle slain;
    Whereat, with blade, with bloody blameful blade,   *145*

---

106. *address'd:* ready.
108 ff. The comic device of mis-
construing punctuation had been
used some sixty years before in
Ralph Roister Doister.

118. *stand . . . points:* A quibble
upon (1) "to be scrupulous" and
(2) "heed punctuation."
123. *recorder:* an instrument like a
flageolet. *government:* control.
138. *hight:* is called.

He bravely broach'd† his boiling bloody breast;
And Thisby, tarrying in mulberry shade,
   His dagger drew, and died. For all the rest,
Let Lion, Moonshine, Wall, and lovers twain
At large discourse, while here they do remain.   *150*

              [*Exeunt* PROLOGUE, THISBE, LION, *and* MOONSHINE.

THESEUS   I wonder if the lion be to speak.

DEMETRIUS   No wonder, my lord; one lion may, when many asses do.

WALL   In this same interlude it doth befall
That I, one Snout by name, present a wall;
And such a wall, as I would have you think,   *155*
That had in it a crannied hole or chink,
Through which the lovers, Pyramus and Thisby,
Did whisper often very secretly.
This loam, this rough-cast, and this stone doth show
That I am that same wall; the truth is so;   *160*
And this the cranny is, right and sinister,
Through which the fearful lovers are to whisper.

THESEUS   Would you desire lime and hair to speak better?

DEMETRIUS   It is the wittiest partition that ever I heard discourse, my
lord.   *165*

Enter PYRAMUS.

THESEUS   Pyramus draws near the wall. Silence!

PYRAMUS   O grim-look'd night! O night with hue so black!
   O night, which ever art when day is not!
   O night, O night! alack, alack, alack,
      I fear my Thisby's promise is forgot!   *170*
   And thou, O wall, O sweet, O lovely wall,
      That stand'st between her father's ground and mine!
   Thou wall, O wall, O sweet and lovely wall,
      Show me thy chink, to blink through with mine eyne!

              [WALL *holds up his fingers.*]

   Thanks, courteous wall; Jove shield thee well for this!   *175*
      But what see I? No Thisby do I see.
   O wicked wall, through whom I see no bliss!
   Curs'd be thy stones for thus deceiving me!

THESEUS   The wall, methinks, being sensible,† should curse again.

PYRAMUS   No, in truth, sir, he should not. "Deceiving me" is Thisby's   *180*
cue. She is to enter now, and I am to spy her through the wall. You
shall see it will fall pat as I told you. Yonder she comes.

Enter THISBE.

THISBE   O wall, full often hast thou heard my moans,
      For parting my fair Pyramus and me!
   My cherry lips have often kiss'd thy stones,   *185*
      Thy stones with lime and hair knit up in thee.

PYRAMUS   I see a voice! Now will I to the chink,
To spy an I can hear my Thisby's face.
Thisby!

---

146. *broach'd:* stabbed.   179. *sensible:* capable of feeling.

THISBE   My love, thou art my love, I think.   190

PYRAMUS   Think what thou wilt, I am thy lover's grace;
   And, like Limander, am I trusty still.

THISBE   And I like Helen,† till the Fates me kill.

PYRAMUS   Not Shafalus to Procrus† was so true.

THISBE   As Shafalus to Procrus, I to you.   195

PYRAMUS   O, kiss me through the hole of this vile wall!

THISBE   I kiss the wall's hole, not your lips at all.

PYRAMUS   Wilt thou at Ninny's tomb meet me straightway?

THISBE   'Tide† life, 'tide death, I come without delay.

                              [*Exeunt* PYRAMUS *and* THISBE.]

WALL   Thus have I, Wall, my part discharged so;   200
   And, being done, thus Wall away doth go.   [*Exit.*

THESEUS   Now is the moon used between the two neighbours.

DEMETRIUS   No remedy, my lord, when walls are so wilful to hear without warning.

HIPPOLYTA   This is the silliest stuff that ever I heard.   205

THESEUS   The best in this kind are but shadows; and the worst are no
worse, if imagination amend them.

HIPPOLYTA   It must be your imagination then, and not theirs.

THESEUS   If we imagine no worse of them than they of themselves, they
may pass for excellent men. Here come two noble beasts in, a man   210
and a lion.

   Enter LION *and* MOONSHINE.

LION   You, ladies, you, whose gentle hearts do fear
     The smallest monstrous mouse that creeps on floor,
   May now perchance both quake and tremble here,
     When lion rough in wildest rage doth roar.   215
   Then know that I, as Snug the joiner, am
   A lion fell, nor else no lion's dam;
   For, if I should as lion come in strife
   Into this place, 'twere pity on my life.

THESEUS   A very gentle beast, and of a good conscience.   220

DEMETRIUS   The very best at a beast, my lord, that e'er I saw.

LYSANDER   This lion is a very fox for his valour.

THESEUS   True; and a goose for his discretion.

DEMETRIUS   Not so, my lord; for his valour cannot carry his discretion,
and the fox carries the goose.   225

THESEUS   His discretion, I am sure, cannot carry his valour; for the goose
carries not the fox. It is well; leave it to his discretion, and let us
hearken to the moon.

MOON   This lantern doth the horned moon present; —

DEMETRIUS   He should have worn the horns on his head.†   230

THESEUS   He is no crescent, and his horns are invisible within the circum-
ference.

192–193. *Limander . . . Helen:*
blunders for *Hero* and *Leander*.
194. *Shafalus to Procrus:* blunder
for *Cephalus to Procris,* also famous lovers.

199. *'Tide:* betide.
230. *horns . . . head:* The inescapable jest about the "horns" of the
"cuckold."

MOON   This lantern doth the horned moon present;
　　　Myself the man i' th' moon do seem to be.
THESEUS   This is the greatest error of all the rest. The man should be put   *235*
　　　into the lantern. How is it else the man i' th' moon?
DEMETRIUS   He dares not come there for the candle; for, you see, it is
　　　already in snuff.†
HIPPOLYTA   I am aweary of this moon. Would he would change!
THESEUS   It appears, by his small light of discretion, that he is in the   *240*
　　　wane; but yet, in courtesy, in all reason, we must stay the time.
LYSANDER   Proceed, Moon.
MOON   All that I have to say, is, to tell you that the lantern is the moon;
　　　I, the man i' th' moon; this thorn-bush, my thorn-bush; and this dog,
　　　my dog.   *245*
DEMETRIUS   Why, all these should be in the lantern; for all these are in
　　　the moon. But, silence! here comes Thisbe.
　　　Re-enter THISBE.
THISBE   This is old Ninny's tomb. Where is my love?
LION (*Roaring.*)   Oh——   [THISBE *runs off.*
DEMETRIUS   Well roar'd, Lion.   *250*
THESEUS   Well run, Thisbe.
HIPPOLYTA   Well shone, Moon. Truly, the moon shines with a good
　　　grace.   [*The* LION *shakes* THISBE'S *mantle and exit.*]
THESEUS   Well mous'd, Lion.
　　　Re-enter PYRAMUS.
DEMETRIUS   And then came Pyramus.   *255*
LYSANDER   And so the lion vanish'd.
PYRAMUS   Sweet Moon, I thank thee for thy sunny beams;
　　　　I thank thee, Moon, for shining now so bright;
　　　　For, by thy gracious, golden, glittering [gleams],
　　　　I trust to take of truest Thisby sight.   *260*
　　　　　But stay, O spite!
　　　　　But mark, poor knight,
　　　　What dreadful dole† is here!
　　　　Eyes, do you see?
　　　　How can it be?   *265*
　　　　O dainty duck! O dear!
　　　　Thy mantle good,
　　　　What, stain'd with blood!
　　　　Approach, ye Furies fell!
　　　　　O Fates, come, come,   *270*
　　　　　Cut thread and thrum;†
　　　　Quail,† crush, conclude, and quell!†
THESEUS   This passion, and the death of a dear friend, would go near to
　　　make a man look sad.
HIPPOLYTA   Beshrew my heart, but I pity the man.   *275*

238. *in snuff:* quibble on (1) "of-　271. *thrum:* the loose threads at
fended" and (2) "in need of snuf-　the end of the web.
fing."　272. *quail:* overpower.   *quell:* kill.
263. *dole:* grief.

PYRAMUS O wherefore, Nature, didst thou lions frame?
Since lion vile hath here deflow'r'd my dear;
Which is — no, no — which was the fairest dame
That liv'd, that lov'd, that lik'd, that look'd with cheer.
   Come, tears, confound;   *280*
   Out, sword, and wound
  The pap of Pyramus;
   Ay, that left pap,
   Where heart doth hop.   [*Stabs himself.*]
  Thus die I, thus, thus, thus.   *285*
   Now am I dead,
   Now am I fled;
  My soul is in the sky.
   Tongue, lose thy light;   *289*
   Moon, take thy flight.   [*Exit* MOONSHINE.]
  Now die, die, die, die, die.   [*Dies.*]

DEMETRIUS No die, but an ace,† for him; for he is but one.

LYSANDER Less than an ace, man, for he is dead; he is nothing.

THESEUS With the help of a surgeon he might yet recover, and yet prove
an ass.   *295*

HIPPOLYTA How chance Moonshine is gone before Thisbe comes back
and finds her lover?

Re-enter THISBE.

THESEUS She will find him by starlight. Here she comes; and her passion
ends the play.

HIPPOLYTA Methinks she should not use a long one for such a Pyramus. *300*
I hope she will be brief.

DEMETRIUS A mote will turn the balance, which Pyramus, which Thisbe,
is the better; he for a man, God warrant us; she for a woman, God
bless us.

LYSANDER She hath spied him already with those sweet eyes.   *305*

DEMETRIUS And thus she moans, *videlicet:*† —

THISBE Asleep, my love?
  What, dead, my dove?
 O Pyramus, arise!
  Speak, speak! Quite dumb?   *310*
  Dead, dead? A tomb
Must cover thy sweet eyes.
  These lily lips,
  This cherry nose,
These yellow cowslip cheeks,   *315*
  Are gone, are gone!
  Lovers, make moan.
His eyes were green as leeks.
  O Sisters Three,†
  Come, come to me,   *320*
With hands as pale as milk;

---

292. *ace:* the lowest cast of the 306. *videlicet:* as follows.
dice.   319. *Sisters Three:* the Fates.

                    Lay them in gore,
                    Since you have shore
              With shears his thread of silk.
                    Tongue, not a word!   *325*
                    Come, trusty sword;
              Come, blade, my breast imbrue!†   [*Stabs herself.*]
                    And, farewell, friends;
                    Thus, Thisby ends.
                Adieu, adieu, adieu.   [*Dies.*]
THESEUS Moonshine and Lion are left to bury the dead.   *331*
DEMETRIUS Ay, and Wall too.
BOTTOM [*Starting up.*] No, I assure you; the wall is down that parted
    their fathers. Will it please you to see the epilogue, or to hear a
    Bergomask dance† between two of our company?   *335*
THESEUS No epilogue, I pray you; for your play needs no excuse. Never
    excuse; for when the players are all dead, there need none to be
    blamed. Marry, if he that writ it had played Pyramus and hang'd himself
    in Thisbe's garter, it would have been a fine tragedy; and so it is, truly;
    and very notably discharg'd. But, come, your Bergomask; let your epi- *340*
    logue alone.   [*A dance.*]
The iron tongue of midnight hath told twelve.
Lovers, to bed; 'tis almost fairy time.
I fear we shall out-sleep the coming morn
As much as we this night have overwatch'd.   *345*
This palpable-gross† play hath well beguil'd
The heavy gait of night. Sweet friends, to bed.
A fortnight hold we this solemnity
In nightly revels and new jollity.   [*Exeunt.*
    Enter ROBIN GOODFELLOW.
ROBIN Now the hungry lion roars,   *350*
                And the wolf [behowls] the moon;
            Whilst the heavy ploughman snores,
                All with weary task fordone.†
            Now the wasted brands do glow,
                Whilst the screech-owl, screeching loud,   *355*
            Puts the wretch that lies in woe
                In remembrance of a shroud.
                Now it is the time of night
                That the graves, all gaping wide,
            Every one lets forth his sprite,   *360*
                In the church-way paths to glide.
            And we fairies, that do run
                By the triple Hecate's† team
            From the presence of the sun,

---

327. *imbrue:* stain with blood.   353. *fordone:* worn out.
335. *Bergomask dance:* a rustic   363. *triple Hecate's:* Hecate ruled
dance named from Bergamo in   in three capacities: as Diana on
Italy.   earth, as Cynthia in heaven, and as
346. *palpable-gross:* palpably   Proserpine in hell.
crude.

Following darkness like a dream,   365
Now are frolic.† Not a mouse
Shall disturb this hallowed house.
I am sent with broom before,
To sweep the dust behind† the door.

Enter OBERON *and* TITANIA *with their train.*

OBERON   Through the house give glimmering light   370
      By the dead and drowsy fire,
   Every elf and fairy sprite
      Hop as light as bird from brier;
   And this ditty, after me,
   Sing, and dance it trippingly.   375

TITANIA   First, rehearse your song by rote,
   To each word a warbling note.
   Hand in hand, with fairy grace,
   Will we sing, and bless this place.   *[Song [and dance].*

OBERON   Now, until the break of day,   380
   Through this house each fairy stray.
   To the best bride-bed will we,
   Which by us shall blessed be;
   And the issue there create
   Ever shall be fortunate.   385
   So shall all the couples three
   Ever true in loving be;
   And the blots of Nature's hand
   Shall not in their issue stand;
   Never mole, harelip, nor scar,   390
   Nor mark prodigious,† such as are
   Despised in nativity,
   Shall upon their children be.
   With this field-dew consecrate,
   Every fairy take his gait,   395
   And each several chamber bless,
   Through this palace, with sweet peace;
   And the owner of it blest
   Ever shall in safety rest.
   Trip away; make no stay;   400
   Meet me all by break of day.

            *[Exeunt [*OBERON, TITANIA, *and train].*

ROBIN If we shadows have offended,
   Think but this, and all is mended,
   That you have but slumb'red here
   While these visions did appear.   405
   And this weak and idle theme,
   No more yielding but a dream,
   Gentles, do not reprehend.
   If you pardon, we will mend.

366. *frolic:* merry.   391. *prodigious:* unnatural.
369. *behind:* from behind.

And, as I am an honest Puck,   *410*
If we have unearned luck
Now to 'scape the serpent's tongue,†
We will make amends ere long;
Else the Puck a liar call.
So, good night unto you all.   *415*
Give me your hands,† if we be friends,
And Robin shall restore amends.   [*Exit.*]

412. *serpent's tongue:* hissing.   416. *Give . . . hands:* applaud.

EVALUATING LITERATURE

MAKING JUDGMENTS ABOUT LITERATURE

Although the initial basis on which we judge literature is usually a personal reaction, if we are seriously interested in evaluation, we must go beyond such a response. While nothing can compel us to say more about a work of literature than "It's a good short story," or "The play left me cold," or "I think it's the best poem ever written," we are not exercising any critical faculty in voicing such opinions. Criticism, which is the art or skill of making discriminating judgments, is an art of definition, a logical act that goes beyond a merely emotional response into the realm of carefully considered and well-supported statements of opinion. To be convincing, criticism must be as objective as possible. Moreover, it must focus on the work and present an evaluation of it, not a sketch of the author's life or personality.

In any assessment of a work — whether our own or someone else's — we ought to be aware of the criteria, or standards of judgment, on which that evaluation is based. Generally speaking, critical criteria can be divided into two categories, the objective and the subjective. Because here we are using the terms *objective* and *subjective* in a specialized sense, we will define them. One simple way of differentiating the two may be to suggest that when we consider objective criteria, we mean any rational appeal to external authority, something beyond personal feelings. On the other hand, when we consider subjective criteria, we pay more attention to personal tastes and preferences than to standards set up by the experts. Naturally, each approach has its limitations. Perhaps the best approach is to use both.

In an order of descending validity — the logical strength of an argument — here are some objective criteria for arguing the relative worth of a work of literature.

The test of time. We can justifiably assume that a literary work deserves our respect and attention if each generation has kept it in circulation long enough to pass it on to a succeeding generation, all the way down to our own. Obviously, a limit to this measure of quality is the passage of time itself. The test of time does indeed work with the writings of Sophocles, Shakespeare, Shelley, and Keats. But what do we do with this particular criterion if we wish to assess the relative worth of the poetry of Sylvia Plath, the fiction of John Barth, and the plays of Edward Albee?

Other critics. If a large number of critics present convincing arguments on the merit of a particular author and his or her work, we at least ought to listen. For example, if we dislike a poem that a great many critics say we ought to admire, and if we cannot logically refute their positions, we ought to exercise care in offering our analysis. Although we do not need to change our opinion, we had better estimate how much it owes to personal taste and bias. We also need to examine a critic's evaluation for bias. Just because a review of a play or film has been published does not mean that we need to accept it unquestioningly. Of course, we cannot readily judge the opinions of others until we develop our own critical abilities; we might not recognize a fallacious line of reasoning if we ourselves are given to fallacy.

The opinions of others. We must distinguish between statements of opinion and statements of taste, even when these opinions come from our teachers or friends. If one is hard put to support one's "opinion" logically, it is probably just a matter of taste. We should not be fooled or browbeaten into accepting an unsupported opinion. Nor should we hesitate to ask the person expressing a view to explain and justify it. Too often we play the game of the emperor's new clothes with aesthetic questions. Until we ourselves can see clearly, or critically, we too often see things with another's eyes when we do not really see at all.

As to subjective criteria, these are subjective only in the sense that we arrive at an evaluation based largely on our own carefully considered private feelings. Here are some basic subjective criteria, also presented in a descending order of validity.

Comparison and contrast. We argue that a play is "good" by holding up the example of other plays written in the same style or genre, or on the same theme, or during the same period. This method contains two possibilities for error. Since we control the argument, we can always successfully argue that X is a better play than Y by purposely selecting a bad play as Y, or by ignoring the fact that Y was written two centuries before X (after all, styles in literary genres change as often as styles in clothing do). We must also have read enough drama by enough other dramatists from enough other periods to be aware of what has been and thus can be done with a particular genre or theme. Ignorance of tradition can skew our judgment.

Close technical analysis. Let us consider poetry. The poem is regarded as being in and of itself. Some essential questions need to be asked: On its own terms, how well does the poem work? How well does form fit content, and content form? How striking are the images, and how well do they interact? How effective is the use of language? Rhythm? Sound devices? If there is rhyme, does it fit into the pattern of the poem, or is it hammered into the lines at the expense of meaning and good sense? Always cite examples from the poem to illustrate each point. Always be aware that you as a reader are in the realm of interpretation — that for any interpretation you may offer, there may be others that are equally valid. The question ought to be not who is right, but who has argued and supported his or her case more effectively.

The writer's intentions vs. our interpretation. It is virtually impossible to know with any assurance what the writer's intentions are, but if we accept the central meaning, or significance, of a work as an author's overall purpose, then we can certainly offer sound, intelligent literary judgment. If we conclude that one of Crane's purposes in "The Open Boat" is to show nature's indifference to man, or that one of Fitzgerald's intentions in "Babylon Revisited" is to show the influence of the past on the present and future, then we may ask what elements or techniques each author uses to achieve his purpose and how well he succeeds.

Some authors' purposes can be identified by the techniques they use or the effects they achieve. For instance, knowing that the purpose of satire is to expose or discredit human vice or folly, we can proceed to questions that will lead to further insight. What is being satirized? Why? What does this contribute to the whole picture? We must, however, be careful not to postulate an entire argument on an unfair or overly generous assumption about what the writer is trying to do. We should remember, too, that a writer is intelligent and human, and that his or her condition is a life of words. If we encounter ambiguities, troublesome connotations, or difficult passages, we should assume that the writer probably meant them to be there. We should also ascertain that the problem we may be having is in the selection and not in our ignorance of the meaning or usage of a term. If a poem, short story, or play is worth our time, it should also be worth an effort on our part to understand and appreciate its author's skills.

We must first try to determine the nature of these skills. Some technically perfect plays are tremendously boring; some tremendously interesting poems are not well crafted. We should consider such disparity in our evaluation. At the same time, we should avoid viewing a story, novel, play, or poem as autobiography. Even that experience has probably been transmuted in the process of making it art. As you might remember from the various selections in this book, a writer may use a first-person pronoun yet not be speaking of himself or herself, the author. And if a writer uses details from personal life, he or she may well alter or rearrange them to suit the artistic purpose.

The poem vs. our reading. The most crucial critical task, yet the most difficult one to perform, is determining the distinction between a literary effect that is intended and one that has been read into the selection. Essentially, criticism requires that we divide the critic in ourselves (a publicly identifiable posture) from the unique individual in each of us (a private confluence of experience). As an example, let us say that a young woman has read a poem on death and feels that it is the most moving, the finest, the greatest poem she has ever read on that subject. She feels that way because the poem expresses precisely what she experienced when her grandmother, whom she loved dearly, died. We hope the point is obvious. Poetry — all art, for that matter — presupposes a common human experience. To identify closely with a poem because of an experience we have had is fine and beautiful. But criticism is another matter. Critically considered, the poem has to be regarded and presented as its own experience. Perhaps the poem that the student read is indeed a great poem; but she will be challenged to the utmost in trying to prove this to others simply by identifying the poem's greatness with a specific experience unique to herself. Even with subjective critical criteria, we must find some way of objectifying (making external to ourselves) our assessment of the poem. This does not preclude our talking about a poem strictly as it affects us; we should be aware, however, that that is what we are doing. Calling a poem great because it reminds us of a grandmother we loved cannot be considered objective criticism or be passed off as such. At best, it is a beginning.

In sum, our taste, the singularly private result of our own special reactions and preferences, is fine and precious, and always valuable as a starting point in any test of experience, aesthetic or otherwise. But taste is a poor substitute for that species of logical discourse which constitutes criticism. We may begin with taste, but it is a long road from taste to clear, concise, critical evaluation and statement. Nor should we forget the value of developing a finely honed critical faculty, for in the process of learning to articulate our thoughts and feelings so that others can understand our views and, if they wish, argue with them on logical grounds, we learn to weigh and evaluate our opinions. If Socrates can say that the unexamined life is not worth living, we can at least entertain the notion that the unexamined aesthetic response is not worth sharing with anyone except our diary and dearest friends.

WRITING ABOUT LITERATURE

The writing of an effective paper about literature must begin with precise reading. A close reading should reveal the kinds of significant details about the structure and the overall effects of a story, a poem, or a play that ultimately lead to a better understanding, deeper appreciation, and greater enjoyment of the author's work.

The combined exercises of reading literature and writing about it can be viewed as an inseparable process, a continuum; one activity merges into the other. Understanding one process, we understand the other. The intelligent reader who comprehends the structure of a literary piece, understands its meaning, and grasps the way in which its theme is manifested can also render an effective interpretation, whether oral or written. In either situation he or she advances a thesis and gives it support with relevant explanatory details.

Let us review some of the guidelines that are helpful in composing a paper.

Selecting a topic. This initial exercise, sometimes a chore for students, has been eliminated here, at least for the nonresearch paper. A variety of topics suitable for essays based solely on students' observations are available throughout the book. You may, of course, want to modify a topic, consider the instructor's suggestions, or develop your own line of thought.

Limiting a topic. Given a writing assignment that requires five hundred words, a writer cannot summarize the main action, analyze the chief characters, discuss point of view, interpret symbols, and explicate the significant themes in "The Open Boat," for example, and still produce a satisfactory paper. Obviously, the writer who attempts to cover so much material faces an impossible task. But why not limit the subject to one aspect of a story? A paper on "Everything That Rises Must Converge" could discuss Julian's mother as an aging, innocent, ignorant woman. Or it could deal with the issue of justice in race relations as it is depicted in that story, or in "King of the Bingo Game."

Gathering evidence. All the available evidence pertaining to a hypothesis or a thesis should be noted and examined carefully. Omitting pertinent information can undermine the truth or lead to misinterpretation. Such partial use of evidence might even destroy the credibility of a thesis. For instance, in an onrush of sympathy for Charlie Wales as he tries to get his daughter back in F. Scott Fitzgerald's "Babylon Revisited," we should not forget his past — the past that still devalues him in the eyes of his sister-in law, who is his daughter's guardian.

Even Charlie himself recognizes that he must pay for his past, and he has been trying to do so. Consequently, a paper on any topic relating to Charlie — his character, the conflict with his sister-in-law, her role in the story, the function of some minor characters who reappear in Charlie's life to haunt him — cannot leave out of account his previous irresponsibility and drinking problem.

Forming a thesis. Perhaps the simplest way to produce a thesis is to pose a specific question about a specific character or idea. For example, why is Mrs. Slade so nasty to Mrs. Ansley in Edith Wharton's "Roman Fever"? What are the two fathers in Kurt Vonnegut's "Manned Missiles" trying to accomplish by their exchange of letters? Why is the speaker of Frost's poem "stopping by woods on a snowy evening"? What is the function of setting in Steinbeck's "The Chrysanthemums"? Answers to these questions will inevitably yield one or more conclusions that you can then translate into a thesis. A response to the question about "The Chrysanthemums" might well lead to this determination: setting creates mood, foreshadows events, influences character, and symbolizes conflict. Such inferences will steer us to an affirmation of purpose as well as guide us to the kind of organic structure and emphasis the paper should have. If setting functions in these four ways in the Steinbeck story, the body of the paper will consist of and develop from these four characteristics. Thus, we might state briefly and plainly in the introduction what we propose to do: "The setting in 'The Chrysanthemums' helps to create mood and shape character, foreshadows events, and symbolizes conflict."

Preparing an outline. Having stated our purposes, we need to expand our generalizations and ask questions that relate to the *specific* kind of mood created, the *specific* events foreshadowed, the *specific* influences on character, and the *specific* elements symbolizing conflict. Once we have completed this task, we can enter the collected information under its appropriate main heading, and we will have the blueprint from which we can build our paper.

Writing the paper.

a. Employ standard diction and grammar. (Usually colloquialisms, slang expressions, and contractions are not allowed.)

b. Assume that your reader is reasonably familiar with the work you intend to discuss.

c. Use the present tense consistently. Say "Frost *uses* vivid imagery," not "Frost *used* vivid imagery."

d. Maintain proportion. Focus on the important points and choose your supporting evidence according to its value. Do not get bogged down in trivial matters.

e. Maintain balance. If you are dealing with two or three major points, give them an equal share of the discussion, and weigh the pros and cons of your argument carefully so that it does not become lopsided.

f. Support your statements with specific details from the text you are discussing.

g. Organize and develop your paper logically.

WRITING ABOUT PLOT

The ability to analyze a plot competently is essential to the process of writing about literature because plot analysis forms the base of a critical essay. How can we write a cogent essay about any facet of literature without first having comprehended what we have read — that is, without having recognized the essence of the story, uncovered its underlying logic, discerned its unity, perceived its vital details, and understood the nature, function, and interrelationship of the various parts?

A straightforward summary, which merely sets down the dominant action of a story from beginning to end, fails as a critique. Analyzing means separating the whole into components. Consequently, a plot analysis should not so much recapitulate the main sequence of events as show how they work together to achieve certain ends. Such an analysis should lead to a sound evaluation of the story's significance.

A good way for a reader to approach plot is to trace its pattern with the help of the eight-point analysis discussed in Chapters 1 and 16.

When writing a paper about plot, we need to remember one thing: that we should make clear not only *what* happens but also *how* and *why* it happens. And we need to keep this in mind even when we are writing about only one feature of a plot, such as setting.

We should never be satisfied with mere description when dealing with setting. There is more to the sea in "The Open Boat" than the vividness with which it is portrayed. Setting often has a significance larger than itself and relates to the central meaning of the story. An author chooses its details judiciously, not only to prove its reality or create interest but frequently also to unmask character, mirror conflict, or promote the theme.

Of course, there is no single topic or specific formula for writing a paper about setting. The possibilities abound. We might, for example, describe the general atmosphere of the racetrack at Saratoga in "I Want to Know Why" and explain the influence of that atmosphere on the emotions of the protagonist, a boy. Or we might investigate the psychological effects of setting on the character of Miss Emily as revealed by her actions in "A Rose for Emily." Or we might interpret the symbolic meaning of setting in another story.

A good example of a student paper that clearly avoids mere plot summary follows in the next section, "Writing About Character." The student considers the important events that bring us to an understanding of a significant aspect of the story — in this case, the development of a central character. Though the student does not recapitulate the chronological sequence of events, we do learn enough. We are told about the main characters and their world, the forces in conflict, and the principal actions, so that we can relate to the larger focus on character and at the same time come to an understanding of theme.

WRITING ABOUT CHARACTER

The analysis of principal characters can be one of the most interesting writing exercises. The aim of a paper examining character should be to discover *who* the given character is, *what* that character's significance is, and *why* he or she behaves in a particular fashion. To achieve this end we must consider what the character does, says, and thinks, how other characters see him or her, and what we can infer from all the perceptible evidence in the story.

The kind of questions we need to ask before we can start writing may be illustrated as follows: Is this character one-dimensional or three-dimensional? Is he or she a liar, a dreamer, a cynic, a romantic, an eccentric? What motivates her or his behavior? What aspect of human nature does the character exemplify? Answers to these questions should cover an ample range of interest and emphasis readily adaptable to nearly any kind of paper.

A paper, then, might trace the development or growth of a character, describe an author's attitude toward a central character, explain a character's behavior, indicate the influences that shape a character, or declare the flaw in character that causes a protagonist's downfall.

Further investigations might lead to other analyses. For instance, the relationship of several characters to one another may be more significant than what each character individually represents (the four men typifying humankind in "The Open Boat"). And a minor character may prove very important in leading us to a fuller understanding of plot, some other character, or theme. Here are two examples.

Fallen Monument

In a characterization of Emily Grierson, from William Faulkner's "A Rose for Emily," a woman of inherited and enforced grandeur is banished by time and circumstance from her position. Unable to cope with this turn of fate, she is forced to lose touch with reality in order to maintain her dignity.

The social position of the Grierson family was of long standing; they held themselves to be a cut above others in the town. The two female cousins who came to counsel Emily on the error of her ways were, in the words of the author, "more Grierson than Miss Emily had ever been." Public opinion, with its candid play-by-play commentary, held her to her *noblesse oblige* by expecting a socially advantageous marriage. Even Miss Emily's father demanded compliance with heritage — in life, with a horse whip, and in death, with his gaze from a crayon portrait.

As the years fell away, Emily's chances for marriage faded; the gentry wondered if indeed there had been chances or only wishful thoughts. Then the father, who had thwarted all aspirations, died leaving her only the house and faded splendor. Miss Emily was now a person to be pitied; she was alone, unchampioned, compelled to the same harsh lot as the rest.

During a prolonged sickness, Emily regained a shadow of that which she had lost in the form of a tragic and angelic-looking serenity.

The first brush with loss of reality occurred when Emily refused to give her father up to death in the finality of burial. This loss of reality was countered by a last desperate attempt at marriage in the form of an affair with Homer Barron. Miss Emily's choice of a suitor was in itself a necessary loss of reality in that Homer was a day laborer and not a part of her world; but any suitor would enable her to hold up her head in public.

With public opinion brought to bear and culminating in the visit of her relatives, Emily is once again forced out of touch with reality. She buys men's clothing, toiletries, and poison.

Miss Emily completely loses touch with the real world when Homer Barron is seen no more. She remains shut up in the house for the next few years and only touches reality on rare occasions. The night men sprinkled lime around her house, in an attempt to dispel the mysterious odor, she caught a fleeting glimpse of the real world.

Emily made a last feeble attempt at reality by giving china-painting lessons. As her clientele left her, not to be replaced, the lessons themselves proved to be a farewell to reality.

Events from this point on only serve to illustrate the total and complete loss of reality: the postal service and the taxes which had been remitted out of a sense of obligation by the older generation. These forgotten burdens were imposed again by a younger generation and subsequently ignored by Emily until the end.

Death for Emily revealed a certain victory for her that had been hidden from public view. In the faded bridal chamber — in the fleshless bones of her lover — there was dignity. Even though Homer Barron was dead, Emily still had a lover; the only thing that mattered was his being there.

The past splendor and the great lengths to which Emily went to preserve the things of value in her way of life are not by any means the only approach to a study of character in this short story. An equally interesting view is a parallel to the history of the South: great defeat in the Civil War, the destruction of a way of life, and the tenacious preservation of dignity and honor.

Comment

The student did a fine job of preparing the reader for the treatment to come by getting directly to the point in the first paragraph. With an excellent economy of words and clarity of thought, the student states the paper's thesis, making it clear in the process that the paper's topic will be an analysis of the development of Emily Grierson's character. The body of the paper continues to work along the lines of economy and clarity; nothing that is not relevant to Emily's character is introduced, and the development of Emily's character is treated in a neat chronological fashion. Finally, the student does not allow us to lose sight of the central thesis; it is picked up often, as in the penultimate paragraph by the use of the key word dignity. When we read this word, we are reminded that the thesis is that Emily "is forced to lose touch with reality in order to maintain her dignity."

Repetition of a key term does not necessarily make a successful argument. In this paper, however, the student convinces us that her thesis is an accurate assessment of a crucial aspect of Emily's actions and motives. That the student adds one last paragraph, in which the story is given an even broader point of reference, that is, its parallel to the history of the South, contributes more to a paper that has already fulfilled its expressed purpose.

The Human Being Inside Marty

What makes Marty Piletti a sympathetic character? What makes us cry in pity and joy? Well, Marty is a "human being" without someone to be close to. Were Marty not so kind, were he cruel, sarcastic, or temperamental, his lack of companionship would not move a reader to tears. It is the average reader — with a matchmaker's heart and mother's desire to see everyone paired off — that first sparks an interest in Marty. It is this observer who would say "Why 'The Human Being Inside Marty'? It is evident in everything he says and does; he is outwardly human." Perhaps this is true, considering the connotation of the words "human being" — a person capable of great joy and sorrow but with kindness for all. Yes, to the reader this is clear, but apparently by some of the other characters the point was missed. Some of Marty's deepest emotions are overlooked by his "friends and relations," and it is because of these insensitive fools that we give our hearts to Marty — we who see deeper.

It is not the average person, but rather the one who is less than attractive or the one who has often been left clinging to the wall watching couples dance by who identifies with Marty and thereby feels his hurt the most. To the young the future seems bright and full of opportunity; everything promising abounds. But, as the years pass one by one and acquaintances pass two by two, fear overtakes the early optimism, anxiety shadows the bright promises, and empty hearts yield to lost opportunity. Before long all that is left is quiet toleration of sorrow. This is Marty.

If one is reminded too often of his situation, very many times, as in Marty's case, it becomes a source of irritation and boredom. Marty is forced into embarrassment constantly with reminders of his nil marital prospects. His mother and all the curious friends may mean well, but apparently they overlook the fact that love or, especially the lack of it, is a most sensitive area. As a child the teasing one receives about boyfriends or girlfriends is a little embarrassing or painful if there is no such friend, but as this condition is prolonged it is the worst kind of hurt one can endure.

Marty has had thirty-six years of rejection. His troubles are rooted in his appearance. Were his problem personality, a change could be the road to a new life, but there is very little hope for the correction of "fat ugliness." At least this is how Marty views the situation each year as the dateless New Year's Eve rolls around. There comes a time when one can sink no farther into his problems, and he sees that there is no turning around or getting out by repeating the same motions he has been going through before. Marty realizes this when he calls Mary Feeney and is rejected. At this time, Marty faces the truth. He is prepared for Clara's arrival on the scene.

Clara may be a "dog" by all standard conceptions of beauty, but those who criticize first and loudest are usually those with problems of their own and with no real feeling and understanding for others. Angie would not be sitting in a bar with the guys on Saturday night asking what everyone feels like doing if he did not have some sort of problem himself.

It is the person inside the physical shell that is given a title like "human being." Marty has a self-realization of just what he is. He accepts it with Clara. More importantly, he accepts what she is — a dog — a dog that could possibly love the mutt he is.

It is his acceptance of life as it is, the ability he has for disguising hurt with toleration, and his determination to seize an opportunity both for himself and another, ignoring harmful influence that show us Marty's inner heart and pulls the tears from all the Martys who recognize themselves and wish for a Clara of their own.

Comment

Asked to write an original essay about the character of Marty which would reveal who he is, what he is, and why, this drama student has satisfactorily handled the assignment, but just barely. The student chose to focus on an aspect of character that particularly fascinated her — the human being inside Marty.

She presents her thesis quickly and succinctly in the first sentence. "What makes Marty Piletti a sympathetic character?" There follows an analysis that sees Marty as a first-rate human being, one with whom we can easily sympathize. But the student has allowed herself to be carried away with sentimentalizing and editorializing, which detract from and weaken her position.

Although this student establishes a valid controlling idea and draws sufficient evidence from the play to prove her thesis, the paper appears to suffer from lack of specificity. Too often she makes a point that begs for support from the text. Few specific details develop the controlling idea. For example, in the first paragraph the student states: "It is evident in everything he says and does; he is outwardly human." Then, instead of supporting her statement by references to the text, she offers a definition of "human being." Again, in paragraph three, she loses the opportunity to cite evidence to prove her thesis. She writes: "Marty is forced into embarrassment constantly with reminders of his nil marital prospects." Relevant, specific examples to illustrate this important point and hammer home the evidence that makes for a convincing argument are glaringly missing.

WRITING ABOUT POINT OF VIEW

Bare definition of point of view and mere identification of the narrator in a story hardly fulfill the requirements of a paper on this subject. A good analysis of point of view conveys a keen perception of the total emotional and intellectual effects a distinct narrative style produces. It informs us about the advantages and disadvantages of one method of narration over another; it reveals what the author expects to accomplish with the narrator; it furnishes reasons for the author's choice; it illustrates the effectiveness of the narration; and it discloses more specifically how a particular point of view contributes explicitly to an understanding of tone, character, and the meaning of a story.

Besides defining point of view and characterizing the narrator, through whose consciousness we experience the action, we might also consider the following points:

1. the reliability of the narrator

2. the impression a special point of view makes on the reader

3. the contribution of the narrator's attitude (his or her objectivity or lack of it) to an appreciation of a story

4. the degree of success with which an author's narrative technique suggests reality or authenticity.

Why "I Want to Know Why" Works

A boy of fifteen decides to fulfill his lifelong dream of going to a big horse race. Along with three of his friends he jumps a freight to Saratoga. While there, he observes a man whom he admires very much acting in a most disgraceful fashion in a "house of bad women." Through this and other experiences, he learns that people are not always what they should be or what we would like them to be. This realization is the beginning of his maturation.

* * *

The examination of point of view in a piece of literature must always be a two-part project. It is important to know why the particular point of view was chosen, as well as how it is used to enhance the story. Therefore, the most logical point to launch such a study from would be a general discussion of the advantages and the disadvantages of the point of view chosen.

The first person is the most intimate point of view an author can use. It allows the reader access to all the feelings, thoughts, opinions, and reactions of the character chosen to be the narrator. By having the story related first-hand, the feeling of being within the situation and living it with the characters becomes much more vivid. The reader can much more readily identify with an "I that *is seeing*" than a "he or she that *has seen.*" The illusion of the story happening in the present, as it is being read, promotes sympathy as well as suspense in the mind of the reader.

The disadvantages of the first person stem from the limited source of information. The reader learns everything from the narrator. If he should have an incorrect opinion or be deceived, then the reader has the same distorted view of the situation that the narrator does. One can only see what the narrator sees as he sees it. In addition, the reader is unaware of what is going on in the minds of other characters.

I feel, however, that in spite of the disadvantages, the first person is the ideal choice for this story. The only significance of the other characters in the story is in how the boy relates and reacts to them. Therefore, what they are thinking is of no importance. We are left, then, with the problem of imperfect knowledge — which is what the story is all about. No one person can ever possibly know why other people behave as they do.

In turning to a discussion of how the author uses the point of view within the story, I find that it operates on two levels. The most obvious, of course, is that it serves as a vehicle for telling the story. One might say that the boyish dialect and the meandering plot-line are merely tools for the author to establish the credibility of the narrator — to make the reader believe that a fifteen-year-old boy is really telling the story. However, I feel that these tools have other, more important functions.

The dialect sets the tone of the story. The reader reaches greater insights through its presence in the story. It serves to develop the character much more than a third-person narrative ever could. The boy is fresh and honest, but has a haunting concern over something that happened to him on his trip to Saratoga. His enthusiasm and trusting nature must be established so that the reader can understand how an incident that might have been a small moment in the life of someone else was to him traumatic. The author, then, through the use of the first person, builds up the reader's sympathy for the boy and sensitivity to his plight.

The wandering plot line also has an additional meaning, other than the fact that boys are always getting sidetracked when they tell stories. It serves as a means of mixing the narrative with the exposition in a very interesting fashion. It also gives the reader important information he needs to know about the boy. The information about his father reveals that these two have a trusting relationship, which, I feel, gave the boy the self-confidence necessary to face this step in his development. To those readers who have no knowledge of horseracing or horse tracks, the information the boy provides on the paddocks, the "niggers," and how he feels about horses is crucial to their understanding of what is going on. Certain things need to be felt and discovered before the actual incident is told. So the author keeps alluding to the incident to keep the reader's interest mounting, while letting the boy wander off to give us some necessary information.

The most important function of this point of view relates to the theme of the story. The boy is at that stage where he is beginning to recognize the inconsistency of human nature. He does not understand it. He wants to understand why people are the way they are and behave as they do. Throughout the story the reader is constantly being made aware of the boy's new awareness through cleverly placed asides. Quite often he says: "That's the way I feel about it" or "I don't know why." So the author brilliantly uses his first-person narrator again and again to bring his theme back to the reader.

Obviously no other character in the story and no third person outside this cast of characters could tell this story without damaging its total effect. Anderson has taken a simple element and made it into the foundation of the story itself. In short, the first-person narrative in this story is the pivotal point around which the style, plot development, characterization, and theme are neatly balanced.

Comment

This paper presents a mature, perceptive discussion and shows that the student has grasped the essential functions of the first-person point of view and their significance in the story. After establishing the central purpose of her essay, the student proceeds without hesitation to set forth her case logically and effectively. She enumerates the advantages and disadvantages of the author's chosen method of narration, comments on its effectiveness, and illustrates how the first-person point of view contributes to character, tone, and the interpretation of the story.

The one serious flaw in this paper is the very beginning of it. However interesting the initial paragraph, which relates the boy's conflict, may be, it is inappropriate as an introduction because it fails to signal the purpose of the paper. The student introduces the controlling idea in the next paragraph, ably develops each point she intends to make, and concludes the essay most effectively with her most powerful statements.

WRITING ABOUT THEME

A popular writing assignment often calls for discussing the central idea or one of the major themes of a literary work. The initial step in the process of writing such a paper involves a search for the meaning that will logically form the basis of the topic. Having discovered and isolated the central idea, we can proceed to define our thesis and state our intentions in the opening paragraph or paragraphs. Then we are ready to organize and develop the body of the paper with what supporting evidence the title, setting, characters, conflict, thought revelations, direct statements by the author, prominent actions, and other data may suggest to us.

As always, what we claim to be a valid summing-up of any meaning that a story, poem, or play communicates must be strengthened by textual proof, manifest or implied. We can be certain that the more thoughtfully we scrutinize the emotional and intellectual content of a selection, the more explicit our thesis statement is likely to become, and the more convincing our interpretation of any portion of the piece is likely to be.

A paper discussing theme may have a variety of purposes: it may divulge how setting points to theme, how character, action, or specific episodes disclose certain truths about the human experience, or how an author's style ministers to the expression of meaning in a story.

A Critique of Crane's "The Open Boat"

This paper intends to discuss the main theme of the short story "The Open Boat" which is "the indifference of nature toward the existence of man."

Throughout this story one sees four ship-wrecked men struggling against the forces of nature for their own survival. The reader can easily sense the terrible state that these men are in from the opening sentence: "None of them knew the color of the sky." These men, a captain, an oiler, a cook, and a correspondent (thought to be Crane himself), had been dazed by the storm.

Quite frequently one of the four would ask: "If I am going to be drowned, why, in the name of the seven mad gods who rule the sea, was I allowed to come thus far and contemplate sand and trees?" Here, it is shown that nature is indifferent to man. Man must face nature. He must show his power to struggle; however, in the end, nature will prevail. The characters then question Fate, the old "ninny-woman." "Just you drown me, now, and then hear what I call you!" Seemingly, man has enough intellect to one day conquer Fate, which is death. This same quotation shows the absurdity of man and the ridiculousness of life. Perhaps, the human race will one day overcome death. But to do this man may have to achieve a tragic death.

As one continues to read, he can feel man being tossed about on the sea of life: 'The billows that came at this time were more formidable. They seem always just about to break and roll over the little boat in a turmoil of foam." In everyday life there is nothing that can possibly be done to combat the forces of nature. Man has always had to change to fit the law of nature. As man travels through life, he is always tempted. Certain temptations may endanger his life and the life of his fellow comrades. Notice the symbolism exhibited in the story when sea gulls fly around the dinghy in which the men are sailing. One bird attempts to light on the top of the captain's head. If he had yielded to his temptation of knocking the bird away with the oar, he would have capsized the boat. Instead, he gently waved it away.

The reader can see the four men as united for one cause, which is survival for each one. All men are dependent on others for a while; however, when death enters the scene, it is every man for himself. There it can be seen how impersonal death is. When nature strikes and the boat is capsized by a wave, each man is forced to protect himself. Instead of worrying about his survival, the correspondent is troubled about the coldness of the water which surrounded him. As the correspondent reaches shore, he sees the oiler lying face down upon the sand. Here we come to learn that man needs others if he is to survive. One might also question the absurdity of life. The oiler was intellectual and powerful. This meant nothing to the forces of nature. His death, consequently, points to the ironic situation of the fittest man not surviving but dying.

In conclusion, nature has been shown to be indifferent toward the existence of man. When nature, fate, and death combine forces, man is doomed no matter how hard he might struggle. Thus, we know that man will continue to combat the forces of nature to no avail. These forces have remained the same throughout history and will probably remain indifferent to the end of time.

Comment

Note the student's simple, clear expression of thesis. In the body of the essay the writer may prove his point that nature is indifferent to man, but he is not very convincing. The thoughts he presents as supportive evidence are not unified, coherent, or adequately developed. The result is confusion. First, the student makes rambling statements that are only vaguely related to his central purpose. When he writes, "We know that man will continue to combat the forces of nature to no avail," he goes off on a tangent, for the statement serves no purpose at all. Second, he forgets about nature's indifference to the men in the dinghy. Instead, he cites examples of nature's hostility to the men, quite a different matter. Third, he needs not only additional specific examples but more appropriate examples of nature's indifference to the men to produce a strong, well-developed, convincing paper.

The Penultimate Line of John Keats's "Ode on a Grecian Urn"

John Keats's "Ode on a Grecian Urn" is perhaps the most famous of his poems, and certainly the best known of his odes. The poem presents a contrast between the permanence of art and the transiency of life. The penultimate line of the poem, however, presents a definite problem in relation to the ultimate meaning of the ode. It is the relationship of the final lines and the importance placed upon the Beauty-Truth concept of the poem that I wish to deal with in my paper. Before beginning, an explanation of the poem should be given and its theme incorporated into the final lines.

Keats knew the classics well and was acquainted with Grecian works of art. Speculation that he had a specific urn in mind when writing his ode is certainly far-fetched since no amount of research has revealed an urn with the same three scenes. He had also studied Homer's *Iliad, Odyssey,* and *Hymns,* and a translation of Ovid's *Metamorphoses.*

In Arthur Swanson's essay on "Form and Content," he states that "Keats, a Romantic poet, contemplates a Classical Greek urn; his Romantic reaction to Classical balance results in a poem whose form is Classical and whose content is Romantic."[1] Because Keats is a Romantic poet and artist, he is able to allow his reader to complete the art work by using his creative imagination. This type of vague, allusive poetry enables the reader to recognize and apply the "unheard" part to which the allusion is made.[2]

> Keats' "Ode" is an art work about an art work. The significance of the poem, its ultimate meaning, lies in the specific relationship between the art work Keats was creating and the already created art work of the urn.
>
> We can say with assurance that "the poem's the thing"; paradoxically the urn becomes less important as an art work than the poem, despite the imaginative rendering of the urn, the tale it has to tell. Paradoxically the beauty of the urn enhances the poem rather than the urn until in the closing stanza the beauty of the urn is secondary to the more significant and meaningful beauty of the poem. What becomes more important than the urn and its message, an integral part of its beauty, is what the poem has made of the urn — something more than a beautiful piece of pottery.[3]

The poem is about a Grecian urn, any urn, with bas reliefs superimposed on the surface. There are three main impressions on the urn: One of lovers chasing each other, a piper playing his instrument, and a priest leading a heifer to the sacrifice.

Verse one is an introduction to the three images on the urn. Keats has personified the urn and calls it an "unravish'd bride of quietness" as if it were virginal in essence. Although the urn does not speak directly to the viewer and is considered a "foster-child of silence," it conveys its ideas through visual images. The final six lines make up a series of questions, each beginning with the interrogative word "what." Each question is related to events occurring on the urn.

In each one of the above instances Keats is trying — and succeeding — to show the reader or give him an aesthetic experience toward art by relating it to an immortal, momentary experience with the eternal. He reveals to us that art is transitory. His words "Heard melodies are sweet, but those unheard are sweeter" reflect a harmony from the work of art that plays to the spirit.

The final six lines of stanza two show us a picture of love exemplified in youth and nature. Even though the piper can never stop playing, he will not tire of his song. Just as the leaves can never fall from the trees so will the lovers be forever pursuing one another. He will never be able to obtain a kiss "though winning near the goal." This is an idealized love with no change in it; it is almost as if it were immortal. Their beauty cannot fade because it has been wrought on the urn which (in my estimation) is also a symbol of immortality. This brings to mind Hopkins's poem "The Leaden Echo and the Golden Echo," in which he assures the reader that by giving over one's soul and spiritual being to God early in life, despairing is, or should be, erased from the heart and mind of the believer.

In stanza three Keats repeats the state of the piper, spring, and the lovers, but adds to it the adjective "happy." His repetition of the word is not meant to be sentimental or sickening to the reader's ears. He uses it as a linking word, or feeling, to tie together three different images, all of which should be happy events.

> All breathing human passion far above,
> That leaves a heart high-sorrowful and cloy'd,
> A burning forehead, and a parching tongue.

These last three lines would seem to indicate that art is above life and our sources.

Stanza four begins in the same manner that stanza one ends — questioning. A description of the city and sacrifice is given in the midst of all the questioning. The altar is described as green and the heifer as having silken flanks, indicating fertility and plenty. The town is by a river or sea shore or mountain. Why then is there no one in the town? Why are the streets silent and empty? Why is everything so desolate? Pictured on the urn is the priest leading a heifer to the sacrifice. The town is not even pictured on the urn at all; it is to be imagined. Everyone is attending the sacrifice. Here again we have the blending or combining of human and divine. And here again we are asked to use our imaginations to create the art work.

The final stanza again gives a brief description of the urn and its impressions. In line forty-four it is a "silent form" that "dost tease us out of thought/ As doth eternity: Cold Pastoral." This could possibly mean that we are brought into a world of imagination that is only momentary and we get only a small glimpse of the eternal.

We are now, finally, brought to the last few lines of the poem. Naturally, some critics will feel that these lines were added to give an aesthetic viewpoint to the poem or to make a highly moral statement about beauty and truth. Several articles relating to the concept will now be discussed and analyzed and my own interpretation rendered.

In his article "Keats' 'Ode on a Grecian Urn,' " Wayne Warncke states:

> In demanding that we be always aware, agonizingly aware, of the large discrepancy between an imaginatively perceived beauty and the reality of which it is a part, the poem actually relates itself to reality and thus identifies art with reality. In fact the poem constantly asks us to think, as well as to feel — to be teased "out of thought" but, at the same time, to be aware of the conflict between the ideal and the real.
>
> The poem's truth is that art is not simply ideal beauty, but more important, art *is* a reality in the world, a friend to man in the midst of his woe to which man can come generation upon generation for sustenance, for the human experience of beauty that gives life meaning and makes life worthwhile here and now.[4]

In reading poetry it is not necessary to be able to perceive what the poet has intended. The reader should use his imagination, and glean everything he can out of a line of verse or one word. Hopkins's poetry is a supreme example of this very idea. Why then should the poem have to relate itself to reality and identify art with reality? Anyone but a fool, idealist, or Romantic is aware of the conflicts between the ideal and the real. And by the way, what is the definition of real and ideal? Real: Having no imaginary part; not artificial, fraudulent, illusory, or apparent; of or relating to fixed, permanent, or immovable things. Ideal: Existing as a mere mental image or in fancy or imagination only; lacking practicality. Now, of course we know that art is a reality in the world. Why then, did Keats title his poem "Ode *on* a Grecian Urn" instead of substituting the word *to* in its place? Because the urn is relating a message to us through our imaginations and Keats is not seen through the poem.

Virgil Hutton has this to say of the Beauty-Truth concept:

> For the urn and its "overwrought" figures, "Beauty is truth, truth beauty," and that is all they know or need to know in their static world of beauty. But, the last line implies, man, because of his own and his world's mutability, knows that beauty is only a part of his truth. The urn befriends man by incarnating what he himself can attain so rarely: the enigma of beauty.
>
> Thus, the urn, where beauty and truth become one, offers its beauty-truth jingle to man not as a cryptic philosophical insight but as a feeble, slightly mocking consolation. And thus, as usual, an explication of the Ode's beginning has merely served as an excuse for discussing its close, which, when recognized as the culminating tragic contrast of the poem, attains a power similar to Swift's "serene peaceful state, of being a fool among knaves."[5]

The last lines of this statement ring true for most critics. There is no need to ruin a beautiful poem (up to this point) for the sake of a last "touch-up." Possibly the reader could *imagine* someone holding a gun to Keats's head and forcing him to write the last two lines — "Don't be a nerd. Your lines or your life!" Who would be so bold as to assault Keats?

Again, let me refer back to Swanson's essay for another encounter with the Classical and Romantic. When an aesthetically pleasing object stimulates a type of pure contemplation and a creation that is independent of the senses and, as Plato suggests in the *Symposium,* "the love of beauty, i.e., in a beautiful object, gives rise to the love of birth in beauty — then the derived pleasure is sweeter insofar as it is more abstract and less bound to sense."[6] Perhaps instead of "real" and "imaginary" we should use such concrete terms as "symmetry" and "asymmetry." In great art works, form and content coalesce, as one thing and another thing become the same thing: sound becomes silence, thought becomes experience, symmetry becomes asymmetry, the tangible becomes intangible, sculpture becomes literature, humanity becomes art, Classicism becomes Romanticism.[7] This is a truly great concept of the poem. Although art is reality, it can come alive in the mind of the artist and viewer.

We must, in studying the final lines of the poem, take into consideration its ultimate meaning. The intention of the poem should be to view art as the highest form of wisdom. A wisdom of the mortal and eternal. Earl Wasserman states that all man needs to know is: "The sum of earthly wisdom is that in this world of pain and decay, where love cannot be forever warm and where even the highest pleasures necessarily leave a burning forehead and a parching tongue, art remains, immutable in its essence because that essence is captured in a "Cold Pastoral," a form which has not been created for the destiny of progressing to a heaven-alter, as warm and passonate man is."[8]

Keats was a true artist. An artist in the sense of creating for us a tangible reality: poetry that we can comprehend, and the ability to imagine what we cannot. Keats wrote to Bailey on November 22, 1817, "I am certain of nothing but of the holiness of the Heart's affections, and the truth of Imagination — What the imagination seizes as Beauty must be truth — whether it existed before or not — for I have the same Idea of all our Passions as of Love they are all in their sublime, creative of essential Beauty."[9] As an artist, Keats has created for us a "thing of beauty."

Notes

1. Roy Arthur Swanson, "Form and Content in Keats' 'Ode on a Grecian Urn,'" *College English,* 23 (1962), 302.

2. Ibid., p. 304.

3. Wayne Warncke, "Keats' 'Ode on a Grecian Urn,'" *The Explicator,* 24, (1966), item 40.

4. Ibid., p. 38.

5. Virgil Hutton, "Keats' 'Ode on A Grecian Urn,'" *The Explicator,* 19 (1961), item 40.

6. Roy Arthur Swanson, "Form and Content in Keats' 'Ode on a Grecian Urn,'" *College English,* 23 (1962), 304.

7. Ibid., p. 304.

8. Walter Jackson Bate, *Keats: A Collection of Critical Essays,* Englewood Cliffs, N.J.: Prentice-Hall (1964), p. 140.

Bibliography

Bate, Walter Jackson. *Keats: A Collection of Critical Essays.* Englewood Cliffs, N.J.: Prentice-Hall, 1964.

Hutton, Virgil. "Keats' 'Ode on a Grecian Urn.'" *The Explicator,* 19 (1961), item 40.

Swanson, Roy Arthur. "Form and Content in Keats' 'Ode on a Grecian Urn.'" *College English,* 23 (1962).

Warncke, Wayne. "Keats' 'Ode on A Grecian Urn.'" *The Explicator,* 24 (1966), item 40.

Comment

This is a good example of a research-oriented student paper. A problem is set up early in the study, and the rest of the paper is devoted to solving this problem. The student is careful to include appropriate comments from outside sources and to give full credit for these comments in her notes and bibliography.

The basic fault in this paper is a nebulous quality, a tendency to drift away from the original problem. This weakens the argument.

The following critical essay, the work of Professor Robert Warnock of Yale University, is presented in its entirety. The student might find it most useful to read this analysis after a careful reading of Miller's play. Observe especially the manner in which this scholar and teacher of literature has developed his evalua-ation and how persuasive it is.

On *Death of a Salesman*

The great success of *Death of a Salesman* on the stage raised a critical con-troversy about the nature of its power. To have attracted vast audiences with a theme as somber and harrowing as suicide was in itself a remarkable achieve-ment, but some questioned whether the grimness of the hero's defeat was in any sense redeemed by the worth of his character or of the objective for which he died. Some suggested that this play is not so much a tragedy as a powerful social document.

Certainly Miller intended to imply more than a personal defeat in the col-lapse of Willy Loman. A highly American attitude toward life is dying with him, an outlook as false as the habitual lying that has become an accepted bol-ster for his ego. It is a by-product of our economic system, which has compli-cated the natural distribution of goods from producer to consumer with an artificial intermediary, and has manufactured a national philosophy from this code. The pressure of competition has exalted the role of the salesman to the point where he sells not so much his wares as himself. At least this is the basic fiction within the code by which he lives, and his self-respect comes to depend upon his continued ability to sell himself. The time-honored avenues to spiritual fulfillment have been replaced by a specious and vulgar goal which interprets success in purely economic terms and the worth of the individual in terms of his ability to acquire wealth. In pursuing this national dream an essentially de-cent little man has worn himself out for scant return and now finds himself fac-ing failure, with the affectionate pity of his faithful wife and the contempt of his two sons, whose lives his teachings have ruined.

Yet however false its premise, the salesman's aspiration partakes of the yearning of every man to be not only liked but "well-liked," and to be recog-nized as worthy and important. It is the loss of that recognition, not the eco-nomic plight of Willy, that is his tragedy. He had always dreamed that his prestige and its return were greater than they were, and now the lies grow wearier and more hollow as middle age finds him discredited and unable to maintain the pace. Pride makes it impossible for him to accept a humdrum job from his friend Charley, which would represent a double failure for him. Though we sense the foolishness of such an attitude toward economic necessity, we sympathize with his loyalty to himself and to what he has stood for, how-ever ill-founded it may have been. It is a tribute to the art of Miller that he has composed so devastating a comment on the American economic system and yet read understanding and a kind of heroism into the common middle-class man who embodies it. There is further relief from bleak pessimism in the awakening of Biff from the falsehood of his father's life and teachings, which at the same time revives in a way his devotion to the older man as a human being. So we sense a queer sort of triumph in Willy's suicide, as he dies for his family and to justify his son's respect, rather than simply to confirm his own defeat.

The old question of the fitness of the middle class for tragic treatment in drama, a question at least as old as Lillo's *The London Merchant* (1731), is revived by *Death of a Salesman*. By now it is not a snobbish question of social class, but of the extent to which the materialistic ideals of the bourgeoisie are capable of poetic interpretation. Is heroic stature a question of inner dignity alone or does it depend also upon the worth and universality of the things for which one sacrifices himself? Admitting objectively the worthlessness of Willy's dream of success, can we still find value in his devotion to it? Or is it his final release from the service of a false god that ennobles his death? Traditional critics armed with Aristotle's conception of tragic flaw and tragic mistake found this play particularly disturbing. All of Willy's life is in a sense at fault, because it is founded upon falsehood, however sincere and intense his delusion.

Comment

Note the introduction of the controlling idea in the first paragraph. As Professor Warnock clearly expresses, he intends to view the drama not only as a tragedy but also as a social documentary.

In the early stages he looks first at the American attitude, which he contends is bent on measuring success in purely economic terms. His examination takes into account the pressure of competition and the "exalted" role of the salesman in our society. In this system he places Willy Loman, whom he sees as representative of every person. Willy needs to belong, to be well-liked, and to be recognized as someone worthy and important. In this sense Willy Loman becomes a larger-than-life figure, and the theme has universal application. Willy's suicide the writer explains as a "queer sort of triumph." This point he again brings to our attention in the conclusion, as he contemplates Willy's death as a sacrificial, noble act.

The last third of the analysis is devoted to the question of how Death of a Salesman, *more particularly Willy Loman, fits the mold of Aristotle's concept of tragedy as defined in his* Poetics. *Perhaps in his conclusion Professor Warnock suggests exoneration for Willy. He seems to say that Willy is at fault, as are his life and teachings, because the system in which he operates is false. Consider your own estimate of the effectiveness of this argument.*

WRITING ABOUT STYLE

A critical paper that analyzes an author's style may well prove to be the most intellectually demanding and the most rewarding of all writing assignments in literature.

A paper on style may focus on a great variety of literary matters. We might consider the complexity, simplicity, or subtlety of an author's way of telling a story; assess a writer's powers of description or use of dialogue; test the atmosphere or mood of a poem; examine the pattern of allusions; or explore the symbolic meaning of an individual character, action, or setting.

from "The Othello Music"

Othello is dominated by its protagonist. Its supremely beautiful effects of style are all expressions of Othello's personal passion. Thus, in first analyzing Othello's poetry, we shall lay the basis for an understanding of the play's symbolism: this matter of style is, indeed, crucial, and I shall now indicate those qualities which clearly distinguish it from other Shakespearean poetry. It holds a rich music all its own, and possesses a unique solidity and precision of picturesque phrase or image, a peculiar chastity and serenity of thought. It is, as a rule, barren of direct metaphysical content. Its thought does not mesh with the reader's: rather it is always outside us, aloof. This aloofness is the resultant of an inward aloofness of image from image, word from word. The dominant quality is separation, not, as is more usual in Shakespeare, cohesion. Consider these exquisite poetic movements:

> O heavy hour!
> Methinks it should be now a huge eclipse
> Of sun and moon, and that the affrighted globe
> Should yawn at alteration.   (v.ii.97)

Or,

> It is the very error of the moon;
> She comes more near the earth than she was wont,
> And makes men mad.   (v.ii.107)

These are solid gems of poetry which lose little by divorce from their context: wherein they differ from the finest passages of *King Lear* or *Macbeth,* which are as wildflowers not to be uptorn from their rooted soil if they are to live. In these two quotations we should note how the human drama is thrown into sudden contrast and vivid, unexpected relation with the tremendous concrete machinery of the universe, which is thought of in terms of individual heavenly bodies: 'sun' and 'moon.' The same effect is apparent in:

> Nay, had she been true,
> If Heaven would make me such another world
> Of one entire and perfect chrysolite,
> I'd not have sold her for it.   (v.ii.141)

Notice the single word 'chrysolite' with its outstanding and remote beauty: this is typical of *Othello.*

The effect in such passages is primarily one of contrast. The vastness of the night sky, and its moving planets, or the earth itself — here conceived objectively as a solid, round, visualized object — these things, though thrown momentarily into sensible relation with the passions of man, yet remain vast, distant, separate, seen but not apprehended; something against which the dramatic movement may be silhouetted, but with which it cannot be merged. This poetic use of heavenly bodies serves to elevate the theme, to raise issues infinite and unknowable.

Comment

The author of this paper about Othello *clearly demonstrates one of the most important requirements of writing about style: to be specific. By quoting several lines from the play and pointing out Shakespeare's use of a particular kind of diction* (chrysolite), *the writer attempts to show the ways in which the dramatist's use of words is unique and influences our perception of the play's characters and events. Consider your own estimate of the effectiveness of his argument.*

GLOSSARY

Allegory   A narrative in which the characters, action, and sometimes the setting are symbolic abstractions of something other than their obvious representation. For instance, the characters may embody such concepts as truth,
beauty, or justice; a dark wood may represent the condition of being morally
lost.

Alliteration   The repetition of identical consonants, especially at the beginning
of words, or of stressed syllables; "O wild West Wind" in Shelley's "Ode to
the West Wind" is an example.

Allusion   An explicit or implied reference to a person, object, or event, usually biblical, classical, literary, or historical in nature.

Ambiguity   A poetic device that enables one statement to express more than
one meaning. Unintentional ambiguity that leaves meaning unclear is to be
avoided, but the conscious use of *multiple meaning* — an alternative term
for ambiguity — can enrich poetic language. A simple, intended ambiguity
is apparent in Surrey's use of "disease" to mean not only physical and mental illness (caused by unrequited love), but disease or lack of ease as well:

> For my sweet thoughts sometime do pleasure bring:
> But by and by the cause of my *disease*
> Gives me a pang that inwardly doth sting,
> When that I think what grief it is again
> To live and lack the thing should rid my pain.

Analogy   A correspondence between two different things, often involving a
similarity of certain properties or functions — for instance, the resemblance
between an automated meat-cutting machine and the modern military machine. (See John Lehmann's poem "This Excellent Machine" in Chapter 9.)

Anapest   A metrical foot comprised of two unstressed syllables followed by a
stressed one.

Antagonist   The character or group of characters against whom the protagonist struggles.

Antithesis   A figure of speech embodying a marked contrast in meanings of
words, or word groups, presented within a balanced grammatical structure.
Alexander Pope's "Man proposes, God disposes" is an example.

Apostrophe   A figure of speech in which an absent person, a thing, or an abstraction is addressed. In his "Ode on a Grecian Urn," Keats apostrophizes the urn: "Thou still unravished bride of quietness."

Artistic unity   The quality attained by a literary work in which all the parts are essential to the whole, develop logically, and function effectively together to achieve the central purpose.

Aside   A stage device in which a character addresses another character or the audience, but the other characters on stage supposedly do not hear.

Assonance   The repetition of similar vowel sounds, usually in stressed syllables that end with different consonant sounds. *Bat* and *map* show assonance, *bat* and *scat* rhyme.

Ballad stanza   A quatrain, rhyming *abcb,* with the first and third lines in iambic tetrameter and the second and fourth in iambic trimeter.

Blank verse   Unrhymed iambic pentameter, used most often in long serious poems. It is also the standard verse form of Elizabethan drama. Milton's *Paradise Lost* is written in blank verse, as is most of Shakespeare's *Othello.*

Caesura   A rest or pause in the metrical progression of a line.

Chorus   In Greek drama, a group of people speaking in unison and providing commentaries on past, present, and future action. In later drama, a single actor performs a similar function.

Climax   The point in the plot of a story or play at which the opposing forces reach the apex of their struggle; the highest emotional peak; the moment of truth.

Comedy   A humorous literary work, usually a play, often with a happy ending.

Complication   A moment of crisis; an occurrence that makes the conflict more difficult to resolve.

Conceit   An extended figure of speech that makes use of similes and metaphors to express a surprising and striking parallel — for instance, Donne's comparison of two lovers to a pair of drawing compasses in "A Valediction Forbidding Mourning." The lines from T. S. Eliot's "The Love Song of J. Alfred Prufrock,"

When the evening is spread out against the sky
Like a patient etherized upon a table;

offer a rare example of a conceit used effectively in modern poetry.

Conflict   In narrative fiction or in drama, a clash between opposing forces resulting in opposition to the desires of the protagonist.

Connotation   The implications and suggestions, and especially the emotional associations, that accrue to words in addition to their literal meanings (see *Denotation*).

Consistency A quality of behavior that corresponds to the dictates of a character's established nature; also, the internal coherence of a work of art in terms of tone and the relation of all parts.

Consonance The repetition of consonant sounds without corresponding repetition of vowel sounds, such as "ye*ll*ow, and b*l*ack, and pa*l*e" in the second stanza of Shelley's "Ode to the West Wind."

Context The passages surrounding a word, phrase, or section that illuminate its meaning.

Couplet A pair of rhymed lines.

Dactyl A metrical foot consisting of a stressed syllable followed by two unstressed ones.

Denotation A primary meaning, or dictionary definition, of a word (see also *Connotation*).

Dénouement See *Resolution*.

Dialogue The speeches of characters, particularly in a play.

Diction The author's choice of words.

Dimeter A poetic meter containing two feet to a line.

Dynamic character A developing character whose conflict brings about a lasting change in his or her personality, basic values, or concept of human nature.

Epic A long narrative poem dealing with a serious subject in a lofty, ceremonial style; also called *heroic poem.* Homer's *Iliad* and *Odyssey,* Virgil's *Aeneid,* and Milton's *Paradise Lost* are epics.

Epiphany A moment of awareness, revelation, or insight for the reader, and sometimes for the characters, which usually occurs near the end of a story.

Exposition The technique of furnishing background information necessary to an understanding of a story or play.

Fable A short tale, in verse or prose, that contains a moral.

Farce A type of comedy that grossly exaggerates the action with physical activity and slapstick.

Figurative language Language that involves an alteration of the normal, literal meaning or use of words and employs devices called *figures of speech,* which include simile, metaphor, personification, metonymy, synecdoche, and others. See these entries, as well as *Imagery.*

Flashback A literary device that interrupts the narrative to relate events that occurred in the past.

Flat character   A character drawn with only surface facts and details.

Foot   A group of two, three, or more syllables; the basic metrical unit in poetry.

Foreshadowing   The device of suggesting or presaging an event by a particular speech, action, or symbol.

Free verse   Poetry that does not conform to any predetermined configurations based on accents of syllables.

Heroic couplet   A rhymed pair of iambic pentameter lines that are end-stopped — that is, closed with a strong punctuation mark such as a period or colon. Each line is usually balanced with a caesura, or rest, somewhere in the middle.

Hexameter   A six-foot poetic line.

Hyperbole   A figure of speech employing exaggeration for comic or serious effect. Marvell's "To His Coy Mistress" offers several examples, including this one: "An hundred years should go to praise/Thine eyes. . . ."

Iamb   A metrical foot consisting of one unstressed syllable followed by a stressed one.

Imagery   As used in discussions of literature, *imagery* generally means the representation in sensory terms of an experience of the senses, a perception, or an idea. An *image* (*imagery* is simply a collective term for a group or pattern of images) need not be visual; it can involve any of the senses, as well as the sensations of temperature, pressure, distance, movement, and so forth. Thus, in "Dover Beach," Matthew Arnold evokes the sound of the sea:

> Listen! you hear the grating roar
> Of pebbles which the waves draw back, and fling
> At their return. . . .

In "Araby," James Joyce uses an image that is both tactile and thermal: "The cold air stung us." And in "The World," Henry Vaughan renders the concept of eternity as "a ring of pure and endless light." As these examples indicate, imagery is often created through *figures of speech*. However, images can also be *literal* without any change in meaning. In the quotation from Arnold, "the grating roar/Of pebbles" is a figurative image (pebbles do not roar), whereas *pebbles* and *waves* in themselves are literal images.

Internal rhyme   The repetition of terminal sounds in words, such as *cat* and *rat*, when they occur within a line of poetry rather than at the end.

Irony   A device that involves an incongruity or the opposite of what one expects. Three main types of irony are referred to in this book: *verbal irony*, or saying one thing but meaning another (usually the opposite); *dramatic irony*, or a discrepancy between what the reader knows to be true about the events and characters of a story and what a character believes to be true;

and *irony of situation,* or a discrepancy or incongruity between what one expects or considers appropriate and what actually happens.

Literal meaning   The standard, dictionary meaning, or denotation, of a word.

Melodrama   Pseudo-serious sentimental drama in which stereotyped characters abound and good always triumphs over evil.

Metaphor   A figure of speech implying a comparison between two unlike subjects. The major subject is the *tenor,* and the secondary subject which is identified with it is the *vehicle.* Thus, in Henry Thoreau's poem "Haze," haze (the tenor) is identified with "woof of the sun, ethereal gauze" (the vehicles). An *extended metaphor* develops the implied comparison and may incorporate multiple similarities. Thoreau's "Haze" becomes such a metaphor as the poem progresses:

> Woof of the sun, ethereal gauze,
> Woven of Nature's richest stuffs
>
>   *   *   *
>
> Bird of the sun, transparent-winged
> Owlet of noon, soft-pinioned,
> From heath or stubble rising without song,
> Establish thy serenity o'er the fields.

Metonymy   A figure of speech in which something closely associated with a subject is used in its stead — for example, "crown" for "king," or "womb to tomb" for "birth to death."

Mock epic   A poem that treats a trivial subject in the serious and ceremonial manner of the epic, with humorous results. Alexander Pope's "The Rape of the Lock" is probably the best-known mock epic in English literature.

Mock heroic   A term describing a mock epic but also applied to other types of literary works that treat an insignificant or frivolous subject in a grandiose fashion. For instance, Thomas Gray's "Ode on the Death of a Favorite Cat" in Chapter 14 is a mock-heroic poem, depicting a trivial event in lofty tones and inflated language.

Monometer   A line of poetry consisting of one foot.

Mood   See *Voice.*

Motivation   The reasons, grounded in a character's nature, that determine how he or she behaves.

Narrator   One who recounts the events or experiences of a story, poem, novel, or play.

Obstacle   The force opposing the protagonist — other human beings, society, environment, fate, or some aspect of the self.

Octave   An eight-line stanza.

One-dimensional character   A person whom the author sketches simply as a flat, stock, stereotyped, static, or unchanging character.

Onomatopoeia   The use of words whose sound seems to approximate the sound they denote, such as *buzz, hiss, patter.* The following lines from Tennyson's *The Princess* are a much-quoted example of literary onomatopoeia:

> The moan of doves in immemorial elms
> And murmuring of innumerable bees.

Ottava rima   A stanza consisting of eight lines of iambic pentameter with a rhyme scheme of *abababcc.*

Paradox   A statement that seems inherently contradictory or contrary to fact or experience but that makes sense if we consider it from another angle of experience. For example, a statement that is a contradiction according to physical law may be true according to religious metaphor: "Adam fell so that he might rise." Even when a paradoxical statement insists on logical nonsense, it may nevertheless resolve into emotional sense. The last line of Milton's sonnet "When I consider how my light is spent" contains a paradox: "They also serve who only stand and wait."

Pathetic fallacy   A variation of personification, ascribing human emotions to any nonhuman subject. George Herbert employs the pathetic fallacy in the following lines from "Virtue":

> Sweet day, so cool, so calm, so bright
>   The bridal of the earth and sky;
> The dew shall weep thy fall tonight,
>   For thou must die.

Pentameter   A line of poetry containing five feet.

Persona   See *Voice.*

Personification   A figure of speech that endows an inanimate object, an abstraction, or a natural phenomenon with the attributes of a living being, and particularly with human qualities or human form. In these lines from Milton's *Paradise Regained,* morning is personified by means of the words *pilgrim* and *steps* as well as the hood or cape (*amice*) associated with religious orders:

> Thus pass'd the night so foul till morning fair
> Came forth with Pilgrim steps in amice gray.

Plausibility   The quality in a literary work that makes action or speech seem believable to the reader.

Plot   The sequence of interrelated actions and events that make up a story or drama.

Point of attack   The incident or initial complication that introduces the conflict.

Point of view   The perspective from which a story is presented to the reader. There are four basic points of view: the *omniscient* point of view, which relies on a narrator, who tells the story in the third person and knows virtually everything about each character and event; the *limited omniscient* point of view, which also depends on a narrator, who speaks in the third person but allows full knowledge of only one character, so that the reader's perception of what happens in the story is limited by the consciousness of that character; the *first-person* point of view, which requires that the story be told in the first person; and the *dramatic,* or *objective,* point of view, which provides no access to the consciousness of any character but instead restricts the **third-person** narrator to reporting what the characters say or do without commentary or interpretation.

Prize   The goal of the protagonist; what the protagonist wants or strives to achieve.

Prologue   The introductory part of a poem, play, or novel which gives background information.

Protagonist   The chief character, who generally controls or forces most of the important action.

Quatrain   Any stanza or poem of four lines.

Resolution   The settlement or the outcome of the conflict.

Retrospection   A flashback, in which the action shifts to something that happened earlier.

Rhyme   The correspondence of terminal sounds in words, e.g., the repetition of the *ong* sound in *strong* and *along.*

Rhythm   Patterns of intonation and stress which are found in all language forms.

Round character   A fully developed character, as opposed to a flat or stock character.

Scanning   Analyzing a line of poetry in order to determine its meter.

Scene   Part of an action occurring in a single place; a subdivision within an act in drama.

Sestet   A six-line stanza.

Setting   The elements of time and place.

Shaped verse   A poem in which the printed version is shaped to suggest the topic. The technique, not common in English poetry, is represented in this book by Herrick's "The Pillar of Fame" and Herbert's "Easter-Wings."

Simile   A figure of speech employing an explicit comparison between two unlike subjects; the tenor and vehicle are clearly stated and are usually connected by such indicators as *like* or *as*. Cherokee poet Norman H. Russell uses a simile in this passage describing white teachers at an Indian school:

> . . . dumb and blind
> as the staggering old bear
> filled with many arrows.

Similes are *simple* if a single similarity is intended, *extended* if multiple (relevant) similarities are apparent.

Soliloquy   A speech by a character who is alone on the stage. This theatrical convention lets the audience know the character's thoughts and motives, for a character speaking a soliloquy is generally deemed to be thinking out loud.

Sonnet   A fourteen-line poem written in iambic pentameter with a specific rhyme scheme. The Italian, or Petrarchan, sonnet is divided into two parts, an octave usually rhymed *abbaabba* and a sestet rhyming much as the poet chooses. The English, or Shakespearean, sonnet is divided into three quatrains and ends with a rhymed couplet; its rhyme scheme is *abab cdcd efef gg*.

Spenserian stanza   A nine-line stanza with eight lines of iambic pentameter and a last line of iambic hexameter, called an *alexandrine*. The rhyme scheme is *ababbcbcc*.

Sprung rhythm   A theory of prosody developed by Gerard Manley Hopkins. According to Hopkins, the basis for the organization of the poetic lines is a fixed number of stressed syllables in the line, with no regard for the unstressed syllables.

Stanza   A group of lines organized into a regular pattern, usually involving both meter and rhyme.

Static character   A minor character who does not develop or change.

Stereotyped or stock character   A character sketched lightly with one or two easily recognizable traits.

Style   An author's distinct manner of writing a story, a poem, or a play.

Suspense   The quality of a literary work that keeps the reader uncertain yet eagerly expectant concerning the outcome of the plot.

Symbol   A person, place, action, or object which holds a multitude of possible meanings. Symbols are artificial referents that the mind makes on the basis of associations and resemblances, either drawn from common personal experiences or based on established literary conventions. A river is like time; a lion acts like a king; a flower is fragile and beautiful like youth and love. Every symbolic statement employs a metaphor and relies heavily upon the connotative quality of words.

Synecdoche   A figure of speech in which a part (usually an important part) is used for the whole, as in Blake's "Holy Thursday [II]":

> Babes reduced to misery,
> Fed with cold and usurious hand. . . .

It is, of course, not the hand that is "cold and usurious," but the person.

Syntax   The arrangement and interrelationship of words in phrases and sentences.

Tenor   One of the two essential elements of a metaphor or simile. The tenor constitutes the major subject and is compared with the vehicle or secondary subject. See *Metaphor*.

Tercet   A three-line stanza.

Terza rima   Three-line stanzas rhyming *aba, bcb, cdc, ded*, etc., to provide an interlocking rhyme scheme.

Tetrameter   A line of poetry containing four feet.

Theme   The central meaning, thesis, premise, or significance of a literary work.

Three-dimensional character   A character whom the author delineates fully; a round, dynamic, or developing character.

Tone   See *Voice*.

Tragedy   A serious drama in which the protagonist experiences a reversal of fortune at the end.

Tragic flaw   The fault, weakness, or vice of the protagonist that brings about his or her downfall.

Trimeter   A line of poetry consisting of three feet.

Troche   A metrical foot in which a stressed syllable is followed by an unstressed one.

Vehicle   The secondary subject in a metaphor or simile. See *Metaphor*.

Vers libre   French for *free verse*.

Villanelle   A poetic form made up of five tercets using only two rhymes, patterned *aba*, with a quatrain at the end rhyming *abaa*. In addition, the first line is repeated in lines 6, 12, and 18, while the third line is repeated in lines 9, 15, and 19.

Voice   The total effect of the writer's words. *Mood* constitutes the speaker's attitude toward the subject. *Tone* is the attitude toward the material and the reader that the writer's style suggests. *Persona* is the combination of those two attitudes, constituting the speaker's mask. The poet-as-speaker can assume the expressive "I" persona, or mask, of lyric poetry, or can play a character, as in dramatic poetry ("The Passionate Shepherd to His Love," "My Last Duchess"), or can tell us a story without being personally involved in the action, as in narrative poetry. Whatever role the speaker assumes, voice gives us a sense of the writer's attitude toward subject and reader and allows him or her to indicate how literally and on what level the statements in the work are to be taken.

BIBLIOGRAPHY

Fiction

History and Criticism

Bader, A. L. "The Structure of the Modern Short Story." *College English,* 7 (November 1945), 86–92.

Baker, Howard. "The Contemporary Short Story." *The Southern Review,* vol. 3, no. 3 (1937–1938), 576–596.

Bates, H. E. *The Modern Short Story: A Critical Survey.* Boston: The Writer, 1961. (This volume was originally published in 1941.)

Brooks, Cleanth, and Robert P. Warren. *Understanding Fiction.* New York: Crofts, 1943; 2nd ed., 1955.

Canby, Henry Seidel. *The Short Story in English.* New York: Holt, Rinehart and Winston, 1909.

Daiches, David. *The Present Age in British Literature.* Bloomington: University of Indiana, 1958.

Gold, Herbert, ed. *Fiction of the Fifties: A Decade of American Writing.* New York: Doubleday, 1959, pp. 7–15.

Hoffman, Frederick J. *The Twenties: American Writing in the Postwar Decade.* New York: Viking, 1955; New York: Macmillan, 1965.

Maugham, W. Somerset. "The Short Story." *Points of View: Five Essays.* Garden City, N.Y.: Doubleday, 1959, pp. 163–212.

O'Connor, Frank. *The Lonely Voice: A Study of the Short Story.* Cleveland and New York: World, 1963.

O'Faolain, Sean. *The Short Story.* New York: Devin-Adair, 1951.

Peden, William. *The American Short Story: Front Line in the National Defense of Literature.* Boston: Houghton Mifflin, 1964.

Rehder, Jessie, ed. *The Story at Work.* New York: Odyssey, 1963.

Ross, Danforth. *The American Short Story.* Minneapolis: University of Minnesota Press, 1961.

Trilling, Lionel. *The Experience of Literature.* New York: Holt, Rinehart and Winston, 1968.

Welty, Eudora. *Short Stories.* New York: Harcourt, Brace and World, 1949.

West, Ray B., Jr. *The Short Story in America: 1900–1950.* Chicago: Regnery, 1952.

Wright, Austin McGiffert. *The American Short Story in the Twenties.* Chicago: University of Chicago Press, 1961.

Other References

Altick, Richard D., and Andrew Wright. *Selective Bibliography for the Study of English and American Literature.*

Bateson, F. W., et al. *The Cambridge Bibliography of English Literature.*
————. *A Guide to English Literature.*
Herzberg, Max J., et al. *The Reader's Encyclopedia of American Literature.*
Jones, Howard Mumford. *Guide to American Literature and Its Backgrounds since 1890.*
Leary, Lewis. *Articles on American Literature, 1900–1950.*
Millett, Fred B. *Contemporary American Authors: A Critical Survey and 219 Bio-Bibliographies.*
Smith, Frank R. "Periodical Articles on the American Short Story: A Selected, Annotated Bibliography."
Spiller, Robert E., et al. *Literary History of the United States.*
Walker, Warren S. *Twentieth-Century Short Story Explication: Interpretations, 1900–1966.*
Wellek, Rene, and Austin Warren. *Theory of Literature.*
Woodress, James, ed. *American Literary Scholarship: An Annual.*
Wright, Andrew. *A Reader's Guide to English and American Literature.*

Periodicals

Abstracts of English Studies
American Literature
College English
College Language Association Journal
Contemporary Literature
English Journal
The Explicator
Journal of English and Germanic Philosophy
Kenyon Review
Literature and Psychology
Modern Fiction Studies
Modern Language Notes
Modern Language Quarterly
Modern Language Review
Modern Philology
Nineteenth Century Fiction
Notes and Queries
Philological Quarterly
PMLA: Publications of the Modern Language Association of America
Sewanee Review
South Atlantic Quarterly
Southern Review
Southwest Review
Studies in English Literature
Studies in Philology
Studies in Short Fiction
Twentieth Century Literature

Poetry

History and Theory

Allan, Donald M., and Warren Tallman, ed. *The Poetics of the New American Poetry.* New York: Grove, 1973.

Bodkin, Maud. *Archetypal Patterns in Poetry*. London, 1934, 1965. Oxford Paperbacks, No. 66.

Brooks, Cleanth. *Modern Poetry and the Tradition*. Chapel Hill, N.C., 1939; New York, 1965. Galaxy Books, GB–150.

———. *The Well-Wrought Urn: Studies in the Structure of Poetry*. New York, 1947, 1964. Harvest Books, HB–11.

Burke, Kenneth. *A Grammar of Motives*. Englewood Cliffs, N.J.: Prentice-Hall, 1945.

Bush, Douglas. *Mythology and the Renaissance Tradition in English Poetry*. London, 1932; New York, 1963. Norton Library, N–187.

———. *Mythology and the Romantic Tradition in English Poetry*. Cambridge, Mass., 1937, 1969. Norton Library, N–186.

Ciardi, John, and Miller Williams. *How Does a Poem Mean?* Boston: Houghton Mifflin, 1976.

Collingwood, R. G. *Essays in the Philosophy of Art*. Bloomington: University of Indiana Press, 1964.

Daiches, David. *Poetry and the Modern World: A Study of Poetry in England between 1900 and 1939*. New York: Biblo and Tannen, 1969.

Deutsch, Babette. *Poetry in Our Time*. 2d ed. Garden City, N.Y.: Doubleday (Anchor), 1963.

Dubos, René. *So Human an Animal*. New York: Scribners, 1969.

Empson, William. *Seven Types of Ambiguity*. New York: New Directions, 1949.

Frye, Northrop. *Anatomy of Criticism*. Princeton: Princeton University Press, 1971.

Gibbons, Reginald. *The Poet's Work*. Boston: Houghton Mifflin, 1979.

Housman, A. E. *The Name and Nature of Poetry*. New York: Macmillan, 1933.

Hulme, T. E. *Speculations*. New York: Harcourt, Brace, 1924.

Langbaum, Robert W. *The Poetry of Experience*. New York: Norton, 1957.

MacNeice, Louis. *Modern Poetry*. Oxford: Oxford University Press, 1938.

Miles, Josephine. *Eras and Modes in English Poetry*. Berkeley: University of California Press, 1957.

Pearce, Roy Harvey. *The Continuity of American Poetry*. Princeton: Princeton University Press, 1961.

Poulin, A., Jr., ed. *Contemporary American Poetry*. 3rd ed. Boston: Houghton Mifflin, 1980.

Ransom, John Crowe. *The New Criticism*. Norfolk, Conn.: New Directions, 1941.

———. *The World's Body*. New York: Scribners, 1938, 1968.

Richards, I. A. *Practical Criticism: A Study of Literary Judgement*. London and New York, 1929, 1962. Harvest Books, HB–16.

———. *Science and Poetry*. New York: Norton, 1926.

Scully, James, ed. *Modern Poetics*. New York: McGraw-Hill, 1965.

Shapiro, Karl, and Robert Beum. *A Prosody Handbook*. New York: 1965.

Waggoner, Hyatt H. *American Poets: From the Puritans to the Present*. Boston: Houghton Mifflin, 1968.

Individual Figures

Blackmur, R. P. *Form and Value in Modern Poetry*. Garden City, N.Y.: Doubleday (Anchor), 1957.

Eliot, T. S. *On Poetry and Poets*. New York: Farrar, Straus, 1957.

———. *Selected Essays*. New York: Harcourt Brace Jovanovich, 1950.

Jarrell, Randall. *Poetry and the Age*. New York, 1953, 1955. Vintage Books, K-12.

Leavis, F. R. *New Bearings in English Poetry.* London, 1932; New York, 1950. Ann Arbor Paperbacks, AA–36.
Miller, J. Hillis. *Poets of Reality: Six 20th-Century Writers.* New York: Atheneum, 1965.
Rosenthal, M. L. *The Modern Poets.* New York: Oxford University Press, 1960.
Wilson, Edmund. *Axel's Castle.* New York: Scribners, 1950.
Winters, Yvor. *In Defense of Reason.* Denver: Swallow, 1943.

Other References

Halle, Morris, and Samuel Jay Keyser. *English Stress: Its Form, Its Growth and Its Role in Verse.*
Kuntz, Joseph M. *Poetry Explication: A Checklist of Interpretation Since 1925 of British and American Poems Past and Present.*
Preminger, Alex, ed. *Princeton Encyclopedia of Poetry and Poetics.*
Shapiro, Karl. *Prose Keys to Modern Poetry.*

Periodicals

American Poetry Review
The Atlantic
Berkeley Poets Cooperative
Concerning Poetry
Essays in Criticism
Hudson Review
Kenyon Review
The Massachusetts Review
New York Quarterly
New York Review of Books
Paris Review
Poetry
Sewanee Review
Times Literary Supplement
Victorian Poetry
Yale Review

Drama

Theory

Altshuler, Thelma, and Richard Paul Janaro. *Responses to Drama: An Introduction to Plays and Movies.* Boston: Houghton Mifflin, 1967.
Bentley, Eric. *The Life of the Drama.* New York: Atheneum, 1964.
Brooks, Cleanth, and Robert B. Heilman. *Understanding Drama: Twelve Plays.* New York: Holt, 1948.
Butcher, S. H. *Aristotle's Theory of Poetry and Fine Art.* New York: Dover, 1951.
Cole, Toby, ed. *Playwrights on Playwriting: The Meaning and Making of Modern Drama from Ibsen to Ionesco.* New York: Hill and Wang (Dramabook), 1960.

Corrigan, Robert W., ed. *Comedy: Meaning and Form*. San Francisco: Chandler, 1965.

————, ed. *Tragedy: Vision and Form*. San Francisco: Chandler, 1965.

Corrigan, Robert W., and James L. Rosenberg, eds. *The Context and Craft of Drama*. San Francisco: Chandler, 1964.

Downer, Alan S. *The Art of the Play: An Anthology of Nine Plays*. New York: Holt, 1955.

Drew, Elizabeth. *Discovering Drama*. New York: Norton, 1937.

Fergusson, Francis. *The Human Image in Dramatic Literature*. Garden City, N.Y.: Doubleday (Anchor), 1957.

————. *The Idea of a Theater*. Garden City, N.Y.: Doubleday (Anchor), 1949.

Kerr, Walter. *Tragedy and Comedy*. New York: Simon and Schuster, 1967.

Kitto, H. D. F. *Greek Tragedy*. Garden City, N.Y.: Doubleday, 1955.

Marx, Milton. *The Enjoyment of Drama*. New York: Appleton-Century-Crofts, 1961.

McCallom, William C. *Tragedy*. New York: Macmillan, 1957.

Nicoll, Allardyce. *An Introduction to Dramatic Theory*. 4th ed. London: Harrap, 1958.

————. *The Theatre and Dramatic Theory*. New York: Barnes and Noble, 1962.

————. *The Theory of Drama*. London: Harrap, 1937.

Thompson, Alan Reynolds. *The Anatomy of Drama*. 2nd ed. Berkeley: University of California Press, 1948.

History and Criticism

Altenbernd, Lynn, and Leslie L. Lewis. *A Handbook for the Study of Drama*. New York: Macmillan, 1966.

Bentley, Eric. *In Search of Theater*. New York: Knopf, 1953.

————. *The Playwright as Thinker*. New York: Meridian, 1957.

Bogard, Travis, and William I. Oliver, eds. *Modern Drama: Essays in Criticism*. New York: Oxford University Press, 1965.

Brustein, Robert. *Seasons of Discontent: Dramatic Opinions 1959–1965*. New York: Simon and Schuster, 1965.

Clark, Barrett H., and George Freedley, eds. *A History of Modern Drama*. New York: Appleton-Century, 1947.

Corrigan, Robert W., ed. *Theatre in the Twentieth Century*. New York: Grove, 1963.

Downer, Alan S. *Fifty Years of American Drama*. Chicago: Regnery, 1951.

Esslin, Martin. *The Theatre of the Absurd*. Garden City, N.Y.: Doubleday (Anchor), 1961.

Freedman, Morris, ed. *Essays in the Modern Drama*. Boston: Heath, 1964.

————. *The Moral Impulse: Modern Drama from Ibsen to the Present*. Carbondale: Southern Illinois University Press, 1967.

Gassner, John. *Form and Idea in Modern Theatre*. New York: Dryden, 1956.

————. *Masters of the Drama*. 3d rev. ed. New York: Dover, 1954.

————. *The Theatre in Our Times*. New York: Crown, 1954.

Krutch, Joseph Wood. *"Modernism" in Modern Drama*. Ithaca, N.Y.: Cornell University Press, 1953.

Lumley, Frederick. *Trends in Twentieth Century Drama*. New York: Oxford University Press (Essential Books), 1960.

Michel, Laurence, and Richard B. Sewall. *Tragedy: Modern Essays in Criticism*. Englewood Cliffs, N.J.: Prentice-Hall, 1963.

Nicoll, Allardyce. *World Drama from Aeschylus to Anouilh*. London: Harrap, 1949.

Spencer, Theodore. *Shakespeare and the Nature of Man.* New York: Macmillan, 1961.

Williams, Raymond. *Drama from Ibsen to Eliot.* London: Chatto & Windus, 1952.

Periodicals

The American Theater Today
College English
The Drama Review
Drama Survey
Educational Theatre Journal
Modern Drama
Plays and Players
Shakespeare Quarterly
Theatre Arts
Tulane Drama Review
World Theatre

United States, the British Empire including the Dominion of Canada, and all other countries of the Copyright Union, is subject to royalty. All rights, including professional, amateur, motion-picture, recitation, lecturing, public reading, radio and television broadcasting, and the rights of translation into foreign languages, are strictly reserved. Particular emphasis is laid on the question of readings, permission for which must be obtained in writing from the author's agent, Harold Matson Co., Inc., 276 Fifth Avenue, New York, N.Y. 10001.   Hemingway, Ernest. Ernest Hemingway, "Hills Like White Elephants," in *Men Without Women.* Copyright 1927 Charles Scribner's Sons; copyright renewed 1955 Ernest Hemingway. (New York: Charles Scribner's Sons, 1927.) Reprinted with the permission of Charles Scribner's Sons.   Hershon, Robert. "The Cooper & Bailey Great London Circus" reprinted from *The Public Hug: New and Selected Poems,* Louisiana State University Press, copyright © 1980 by Robert Hershon. Reprinted by permission of the author.   Hobson, Geary. "Deer Hunting" © *Scree* (Fallon, Nevada), 1977, for "Deer Hunting." Reprinted by permission of the author.   Holden, Molly. "Giant Decorative Dahlia" copyright © 1969 by Molly Holden. Reprinted from *To Make Me Grieve* by permission of Chatto and Windus with The Hogarth Press and Wesleyan University Press.   Hopkins, Gerard Manley. "Felix Randal," "Pied Beauty," and "The Windhover" from *Poems of Gerard Manley Hopkins,* 4th ed., W. H. Gardner and N. H. MacKenzie, eds., New York, Oxford University Press, 1970.   Housman, A. E. "Terence, this is stupid stuff" and "To an Athlete Dying Young" from "A Shropshire Lad" — Authorised Edition and "R. L. S." from *The Collected Poems of A. E. Housman.* Copyright 1939, 1940, © 1965 by Holt, Rinehart and Winston. Copyright © 1967, 1968 by Robert E. Symons. Reprinted by permission of Holt, Rinehart and Winston, Publishers; The Society of Authors as the literary representative of the Estate of A. E. Housman; and Jonathan Cape Ltd., publishers of A. E. Housman's *Collected Poems.*   Hughes, Langston. "Dream Deferred" copyright 1951 by Langston Hughes. Reprinted from *The Panther and the Lash,* by Langston Hughes, by permission of Alfred A. Knopf, Inc. "I, Too" and "The Weary Blues" copyright 1926 by Alfred A. Knopf, Inc. and renewed 1954 by Langston Hughes. Reprinted from *Selected Poems of Langston Hughes,* by Langston Hughes, by permission of Alfred A. Knopf, Inc.   Hughes, Ted. "A Disaster" (page 641) from *Crow* by Ted Hughes. Copyright © 1971 by Ted Hughes. Reprinted by permission of Harper & Row, Publishers, Inc., and Faber and Faber Ltd.   Hugo, Richard. "2433 Agnes, First Home, Last House in Missoula" is reprinted from *The Lady in Kicking Horse Reservoir,* Poems by Richard Hugo, with the permission of W. W. Norton & Company, Inc. Copyright © 1973 by Richard Hugo.   Ibsen, Henrik. *An Enemy of the People,* tr. Michael Meyer, reprinted by permission of Harold Ober Associates Incorporated. Copyright © 1965 by Michael Meyer.   Iwasaki, Laura Tokunaga. Grateful acknowledgment is made to: Asian American Studies Center, UCLA, for permission to reprint "Tiger Years" by Laura Tokunaga in *Counterpoint: Perspectives on Asian America* © 1976.   Jackson, Shirley. "The Lottery" from *The Lottery* by Shirley Jackson. Copyright 1948, 1949 by Shirley Jackson. Copyright renewed © 1976, 1977 by Laurence Hyman, Barry Hyman, Mrs. Sarah Webster, and Mrs. Joanne Schnurer. "The Lottery" first appeared in *The New Yorker.* Reprinted by permission of Farrar, Straus & Giroux, Inc.   Jarrell, Randall. "The Orient Express" from *Randall Jarrell: The Complete Poems.* Copyright © 1950, 1969 by Mrs. Randall Jarrell. Copyright renewed © 1977 by Mrs. Randall Jarrell. "The Mockingbird" reprinted with permission of Macmillan Publishing Co., Inc. from *The Bat-Poet* by Randall Jarrell. Copyright © Macmillan Publishing Co., Inc. 1963, 1964. Originally appeared in *The New Yorker.*   Jennings, Elizabeth. "Answers" from *Collected Poems* and "In memory of anyone unknown to me" from *Relationships* reprinted by permission of David Higham Associates Limited.   Joyce, James. "Araby" from *Dubliners* by James Joyce. Copyright © 1967 by the Estate of James Joyce. Used by permission of Viking Penguin Inc.   Keyes, Sidney. "William Wordsworth" from *Collected Poems of Sidney Keyes,* London, Routledge & Kegan Paul Ltd. reprinted by permission of the publishers.   Knight, E. Wilson. Extract from *The Wheel of Fire,* Methuen, London, reprinted by permission of the publishers.   Lawrence, D. H. "Baby Running Barefoot" from *The Complete Poems of D. H. Lawrence,* Collected and Edited with an Introduction and Notes by Vivian de Sola Pinto and Warren Roberts. Copyright © 1964, 1971 by Angelo Ravagli and C. M. Weekley, Executors of the Estate of Frieda Lawrence Ravagli. © The Estate of Frieda Lawrence Ravagli 1972. "The Horse Dealer's Daughter" from *The Complete Short Stories* by D. H. Lawrence, Volume II. Copyright 1922 by Thomas Seltzer, Inc.; renewal copyright 1950 by Frieda Lawrence, and *The Collected Short Stories of D. H. Lawrence,* © The Estate of Frieda Lawrence Ravagli 1974. Reprinted by permission of Viking Penguin Inc., William Heinemann Ltd., Laurence Pollinger Ltd., and The Estate of Frieda Lawrence Ravagli.   Lazard, Naomi. "Missing Father Report" reprinted from *The Moonlit Upper Deckerina,* Sheep Meadow Press. Copyright © 1977 by Naomi Lazard. Used by permission of the author.   Lehmann, John. "This Excellent Machine" from *Collected Poems* reprinted by permission of David Higham Associates Limited.   Lennon, John, and Paul McCartney. "She's Leaving Home" copyright © 1967 Northern Songs Limited. All rights for the USA, Mexico, and the Philippines controlled by Maclen Music, Inc., c/o ATV Music Group. Used by permission. All rights reserved.   Levertov, Denise. "Scenes from the Life of the Peppertrees," Denise Levertov, *The Jacob's Ladder.* Copyright © 1958 by Denise Levertov Goodman. "The Secret" Denise Levertov, *O Taste & See.* Copyright © 1964 by Denise Levertov Goodman. Both reprinted by permission of New Directions Publishing Corporation.   Lim,

Shirley Geok-Lin. "Modern Secrets" from *Crossing the Peninsula and Other Poems* (Singapore: Heinemann Educational Books, 1980), © 1980 by Shirley Lim. Lindsay, Vachel. "General William Booth Enters into Heaven" from *Collected Poems*, New York, Macmillan, 1925. Looney, Jon. "Only the Garbage Collector" from *Headwaters* reprinted by permission of the author. Logue, Christopher. Excerpt from "Foreword" from *New Numbers* by Christopher Logue. Copyright © 1970 by Christopher Logue. Reprinted by permission of Alfred A. Knopf, Inc., copyright © 1969 by Christopher Logue, by permission of Tessa Sayle. Lowell, Amy. "Patterns" from *The Complete Poetical Works of Amy Lowell*. Copyright © 1955 by Houghton Mifflin Company. Reprinted by permission of the publisher. Lowell, Robert. "Bringing a Turtle Home" from *For Lizzie and Harriet* by Robert Lowell. Copyright © 1967, 1968, 1969, 1970, 1973 by Robert Lowell. Reprinted by permission of Farrar, Straus & Giroux, Inc. Lucero, Marcela Christine. "Roseville, Minn., U.S.A." reprinted by permission of the author. Mac-Leish, Archibald. "Ars Poetica" and "You, Andrew Marvell" from *New and Collected Poems 1917–1976* by Archibald MacLeish. Copyright © 1976 by Archibald MacLeish. Reprinted by permission of Houghton Mifflin Company. MacNeice, Louis. "Sunday Morning" reprinted by permission of Faber and Faber Ltd. from *The Collected Poems of Louis MacNeice*. Malamud, Bernard. "The Magic Barrel" from *The Magic Barrel* by Bernard Malamud. Copyright © 1954, 1958 by Bernard Malamud. Reprinted by permission of Farrar, Straus & Giroux, Inc. Mar, Laureen. "Chinatown 2" reprinted by permission of the author. Masters, Edgar Lee. "Margaret Fuller Slack" from *Spoon River Anthology* reprinted by permission of Ellen C. Masters. Maugham, W. Somerset. "The Colonel's Lady" copyright 1946 by Hearst Magazines, Inc. from the book *Creatures of Circumstance* by W. Somerset Maugham. Reprinted by permission of Doubleday & Company, Inc., the Estate of the late W. Somerset Maugham, William Heinemann Limited, and A. P. Watt Ltd. McCullers, Carson. "A Tree, A Rock, A Cloud" from *The Ballad of the Sad Cafe and Collected Short Stories* by Carson McCullers. Copyright 1936, 1941, 1942, 1950, 1951, 1955 by Carson McCullers. Reprinted by permission of Houghton Mifflin Company. McGinley, Phyllis. "Intimations of Mortality" from *Times Three* by Phyllis McGinley. Copyright 1950; © renewed 1978 by Phyllis McGinley. Used by permission of Viking Penguin Inc. McGraw, Patricia. "BluesBlack" reprinted by permission of the author. McKay, Claude. "The White House" from *Selected Poems of Claude McKay* copyright 1981 by Twayne Publishers, Inc., and reprinted with permission of Twayne Publishers, a division of G. K. Hall & Co., Boston. Miles, Josephine. "Belief" from *Poems 1930–1960* by Josephine Miles reprinted by permission of the publisher, Indiana University Press. Millay, Edna St. Vincent. "Never May the Fruit Be Plucked" and "The Concert" from *Collected Poems*, Harper & Row. Copyright 1923, 1951 by Edna St. Vincent Millay and Norma Millay Ellis. Reprinted by permission of Norma Millay (Ellis). Miller, Arthur. *Death of A Salesman* by Arthur Miller. Copyright 1949 by Arthur Miller. Copyright © renewed 1967 by Arthur Miller. Reprinted by permission of Viking Penguin Inc. CAUTION: This play in its printed form is designed for the reading public only. All dramatic rights in it are fully protected by copyrights and no public or private performance — professional or amateur — and no public readings for profit may be given without the written permission of the author and the payment of royalty. Anyone disregarding the author's rights renders himself liable to prosecution. Communications should be addressed to the author's representatives, International Creative Management, 40 West 57th Street, New York, N.Y. 10019. Moffett, Judith. "Biology Lesson" reprinted by permission of Louisiana State University Press from *Keeping Time* by Judith Moffett, copyright © 1976. Moore, Marianne. "Poetry" reprinted with permission of Macmillan Publishing Co., Inc. from *Collected Poems* by Marianne Moore. Copyright 1935 by Marianne Moore, renewed 1963 by Marianne Moore and T. S. Eliot. Nash, Ogden. "Inter-Office Memorandum" from *Verses from 1929* by Ogden Nash. Copyright 1935 by Ogden Nash. By permission of Little, Brown and Company. O'Connor, Flannery. "Everything that Rises Must Converge" from *Everything that Rises Must Converge* by Flannery O'Connor. Copyright © 1961, 1965 by the Estate of Mary Flannery O'Connor. Reprinted by permission of Farrar, Straus & Giroux, Inc. O'Connor, Frank. "Guests of the Nation" from *Collected Stories*, by Frank O'Connor. Copyright © 1981 by Harriet O'Donovan Sheehy, Executrix of the Estate of Frank O'Connor. Reprinted by permission of Alfred A. Knopf, Inc., and Joan Daves. Owen, Wilfred. "Anthem for Doomed Youth" and "Arms and the Boy," Wilfred Owen, *Collected Poems*. Copyright Chatto & Windus, Ltd., © 1946, 1963. Reprinted by permission of New Directions Publishing Corporation, the Owen Estate, and Chatto & Windus Ltd. Pearson, Carol Lynn. "Millie's Mother's Red Dress" and "Optical Illusion" from *The Growing Season* by Carol Lynn Pearson. Copyright © 1976 by Bookcraft, Inc. Reprinted by permission of the publisher. "Of Places Far" from *Beginnings* by Carol Lynn Pearson. Copyright © 1967 by Carol Lynn Pearson. Reprinted by permission of Doubleday & Company, Inc. Petry, Ann. "Doby's Gone" from *Phylon*, Volume 5, No. 4, pp. 361–366, reprinted by permission. Piercy, Marge. "The Crippling" reprinted by permission of Wallace & Sheil Agency, Inc. Copyright © 1973, 1982 by Marge Piercy. (From *Circles on the Water*, Alfred A. Knopf, Inc., 1982.) Plath, Sylvia. From *Ariel* by Sylvia Plath: "Lady Lazarus" and "Daddy" copyright © 1963 by Ted Hughes. Reprinted by permission of Harper & Row, Publishers, Inc., copyright Ted Hughes 1965, Faber and Faber, by permission of Olwyn Hughes. Porter, Peter. "A Consumer's Report" from *The Last of England* by Peter Porter, © Oxford University Press

1970. Reprinted by permission of Oxford University Press.　　Pound, Ezra. "Ballad of the Goodly Fere," Ezra Pound, *Personae*. Copyright 1926 by Ezra Pound. Reprinted by permission of New Directions Publishing Corporation.　　Ransom, John Crowe. "Bells for John Whiteside's Daughter," "Here Lies a Lady," and "Piazza Piece" copyright 1924, 1927 by Alfred A. Knopf, Inc., and renewed 1952, 1955 by John Crowe Ransom. Reprinted from *Selected Poems*, Third Edition, Revised and Enlarged, by John Crowe Ransom, by permission of the publisher.　　Reed, Ishmael. "Beware: Do Not Read this Poem" copyright © 1972, Ishmael Reed. Reprinted by permission.　　Rich, Adrienne. "Orion" is reprinted from *Poems*, Selected and New, 1950–1974, by Adrienne Rich, by permission of W. W. Norton & Company, Inc. Copyright © 1975, 1973, 1971, 1969, 1966 by W. W. Norton & Company, Inc.　　Robinson, Edwin Arlington. "Karma" and "Richard Cory" from *The Children of the Night* by Edwin Arlington Robinson. Copyright under the Berne Convention (New York: Charles Scribner's Sons, 1897). Reprinted with the permission of Charles Scribner's Sons.　　Roethke, Theodore. "The Waking" copyright 1953 by Theodore Roethke; "The Meadow Mouse" copyright © 1963 by Beatrice Roethke as Administratrix to the Estate of Theodore Roethke; "I Knew a Woman" copyright 1954 by Theodore Roethke; "Snake" copyright © 1955 by Theodore Roethke. From the book *The Collected Poems of Theodore Roethke*. Reprinted by permission of Doubleday & Company, Inc.　　Rose, Wendy. "For the White Poets Who Would Be Indian" from *Lost Copper* by Wendy Rose, Malki Museum Press, Banning, CA 1981. Copyright 1981, Malki Museum, Inc.　　Roth, Philip. "Defender of the Faith" from *Goodbye Columbus* by Philip Roth. Copyright © 1959 by Philip Roth. Reprinted by permission of Houghton Mifflin Company.　　Rukeyser, Muriel. "Boy with His Hair Cut Short" from *Collected Poems* reprinted by permission of International Creative Management, Inc. Copyright © 1938, 1978 by Muriel Rukeyser.　　Russell, Norman H. "indian school" copyright 1968 by Norman H. Russell. Reprinted by permission of the author.　　Sayers, Dorothy. Extract from Dante, *The Divine Comedy*, Penguin, 1955, reprinted by permission of David Higham Associates, Limited.　　Schwartz, Delmore. "Calmly We Walk through this April's Day" Delmore Schwartz, *Selected Poems: Summer Knowledge*. Copyright 1930 by New Directions Publishing Corporation. Reprinted by permission of New Directions Publishing Corporation.　　Sexton, Anne. "Lament" and "The Abortion" from *All My Pretty Ones* by Anne Sexton. Copyright © 1961, 1962 by Anne Sexton. Reprinted by permission of Houghton Mifflin Company.　　Shakespeare, William. All material from W. A. Neilson & C. J. Hill, *The Complete Plays and Poems of William Shakespeare*, Boston, Houghton Mifflin, 1942. Copyright, 1942. Copyright renewed, 1970 William Allan Neilson and Charles Jarvis Hill. Reprinted by permission of the publisher.　　Shapiro, Karl. "Drug Store" copyright 1941 and renewed 1969 by Karl Shapiro. Reprinted from *Collected Poems: 1940–1978*, by Karl Shapiro, by permission of Random House, Inc.　　Shaw, George Bernard. *Arms and the Man* by Bernard Shaw. Copyright 1898, 1913, 1926, 1931, 1933, 1941, by George Bernard Shaw. Copyright 1905, Brentano's. Copyright 1958, The Public Trustee as Executor of the Estate of George Bernard Shaw. Copyright © 1970, The Trustees of the British Museum, The Governors and Guardians of the National Gallery of Ireland and Royal Academy of Dramatic Art. Reprinted by permission of Dodd, Mead & Company, Inc., and The Society of Authors for the Estate of George Bernard Shaw.　　Silkin, Jon. "Creatures" copyright © 1966 by Jon Silkin. Reprinted from *Amana Grass* by permission of Wesleyan University Press. This poem first appeared in *Stand*. "Death of a Son" copyright © 1966 by John Silkin. Reprinted from *Poems New and Selected* by permission of Wesleyan University Press.　　Silko, Leslie Marmon. "Storyteller" reprinted by permission of the author.　　Sophocles. *Oedipus the King* reprinted from *The Complete Greek Tragedies, Sophocles*, Vol. II, pp. 10–76, David Grene and Richard Lattimore, eds, by permission of The University of Chicago Press. © 1942, 1954, 1957, 1960 by The University of Chicago.　　Steinbeck, John. "The Chrysanthemums" from *The Long Valley* by John Steinbeck. Copyright 1938 by John Steinbeck. Copyright renewed 1966 by John Steinbeck. Reprinted by permission of Viking Penguin Inc.　　Stevens, Wallace. "Disillusionment of Ten O'Clock" and "Thirteen Ways of Looking at a Blackbird" copyright 1923 and renewed 1951 by Wallace Stevens. Reprinted from *The Collected Poems of Wallace Stevens*, by Wallace Stevens, by permission of Alfred A. Knopf, Inc.　　Strindberg, August. *Miss Julie* from *Pre-Inferno Plays*, tr., Walter Johnson, reprinted by permission of the University of Washington Press. Copyright © 1971 by the University of Washington Press.　　Tafolla, Carmen. "San Antonio" a part of "La Isabela de Guadalupe y Otras Chucas" to be published in *Five Poets of Aztlan*, reprinted by permission of the Bilingual Review/Press.　　Taylor, Edward. "Housewifery" from *The Poetical Works of Edward Taylor*, ed. with an Introduction and Notes by Thomas H. Johnson. Copyright 1939 by Rockland, 1943 by Princeton University Press. Reprinted by permission of Princeton University Press.　　Taylor, Henry. "Speech," from *Cafe Solo*, 1971, reprinted by permission of Solo Press.　　Thomas, Dylan. "The hand that signed the paper" Dylan Thomas, *The Poems of Dylan Thomas*. Copyright 1933 by New Directions Publishing Corporation. "The Hunchback in the Park" and "Do not go gentle into that good night" Dylan Thomas, *The Poems of Dylan Thomas*. Copyright 1952 by Dylan Thomas. All reprinted by permission of New Directions Publishing Corporation, David Higham Associates Limited, and J. M. Dent.　　Thurber, James. "The Catbird Seat" copyright © 1945 James Thurber. Copyright © 1973 Helen W. Thurber and Rosemary T. Sauers. From *The Thurber Carnival*, published by Harper & Row.　　Viereck, Peter. "Game Called on Account of Darkness" copyright held by

Mr. Viereck. Poem excerpted from his book *Terror & Decorum,* Pulitzer prize-winning book, Greenwood Press, Westport, CT, and from his book *New and Selected Poems,* University Microfilms, P.O. Box 1467, Ann Arbor, MI 48106.   Vonnegut, Kurt, Jr. "The Manned Missiles" excerpted from the book *Welcome to the Monkey House* by Kurt Vonnegut Jr. Copyright © 1958 by Kurt Vonnegut Jr. Originally published in *Cosmopolitan.* Reprinted by permission of Delacorte Press/Seymour Lawrence.   Wakoski, Diane. "Thanking My Mother for Piano Lessons," from *Mediterranean Review,* Vol. I, No. 2, Winter 1971, 72–76, reprinted by permission of the *Mediterranean Review.*   Walsh, Marnie. "The Red Fox" from the Ahsahta Press, Boise State University, Boise, Idaho, Editor, Thomas Trusky. Reprinted by permission of the author.   Warnock, Robert. Excerpts from *Representative Modern Plays* by Robert Warnock. Copyright © 1952 by Scott, Foresman and Company. Reprinted by permission.   Welch, James. "The Man from Washington" reprinted by permission of the author.   Welty, Eudora. "A Worn Path" copyright 1941, 1969 by Eudora Welty. Reprinted from her volume *A Curtain of Green and Other Stories* by permission of Harcourt Brace Jovanovich, Inc.   Wharton, Edith. "Roman Fever" from *The World Over* copyright 1934 Liberty Magazine. Renewed © 1962 William R. Tyler. Reprinted by permission of A. Watkins, Inc.   Wilbur, Richard. "Juggler" copyright 1949, 1977 by Richard Wilbur. Reprinted from his volume *Ceremony and Other Poems* by permission of Harcourt Brace Jovanovich, Inc.   Williams, Miller. "Believing in Symbols" from *Distractions,* Baton Rouge, Louisiana State University Press, copyright Miller Williams, 1979. Reprinted by permission.   Williams, William Carlos. "Queen-Ann's-Lace," "The Rose," and "Young Woman at a Window" William Carlos Williams, *Collected Earlier Poems.* Copyright 1938 by New Directions Publishing Corporation. Reprinted by permission of New Directions Publishing Corporation.   Wilson, Ramona. "Keeping Hair" copyright © 1975 by Ramona Wilson. Reprinted from *Voices of the Rainbow* edited by Kenneth Rosen, published by Seaver Books, New York, 1980.   Wylie, Elinor. "The Eagle and the Mole" and "Velvet Shoes" copyright 1921 by Alfred A. Knopf, Inc. and renewed 1949 by William Rose Benet. Reprinted from *Collected Poems of Elinor Wylie,* by Elinor Wylie, by permission of the publisher.   Yamauchi, Wakako. "The Boatmen on the Toneh River" reprinted by permission of the author. The story has appeared in *Ameriasia Journal* and *Counterpoint: Perspectives on Asian America,* Asian American Studies Center, UCLA.   Yeats, William Butler. "Long-Legged Fly," "The Lake Isle of Innisfree," and "The Song of Wandering Aengus" reprinted with permission of Macmillan Publishing Co., Inc., Macmillan London Limited, and A. P. Watt Ltd. Copyright 1940 by Georgie Yeats, renewed 1968 by Bertha Georgie Yeats, Michael Butler Yeats and Anne Yeats. By permission of M. B. Yeats and Anne Yeats.   Young, Ian. "Poem Found in a Dime-Store Diary" reprinted by permission of the author.   Warncke, Wayne. Excerpt from "Keats' 'Ode on a Grecian Urn'," *The Explicator,* 24 (1966) reprinted by permission of the author.

INDEX OF TOPICS

INDEX OF AUTHORS, TITLES, AND
FIRST LINES OF POEMS

Names of authors appear in capitals, titles in italics, and first lines of poems in roman. Numbers in roman type indicate pages where authors and their selections appear; numbers in italics indicate discussion of story, poem, or play.